COLORADO
REAL ESTATE MANUAL

DEPARTMENT OF REGULATORY AGENCIES

Patty Salazar, Executive Director

THE COLORADO DIVISION OF REAL ESTATE

Marcia Waters, Director

Eric Turner, Deputy Director

REAL ESTATE COMMISSION

Michelle Espinoza, Henderson – Chair

Vacant Position
Vice Chair
Joe Chang, Denver
Graham Kaltenbach, Denver
Kim Rediker, Vail

BOARD OF REAL ESTATE APPRAISERS

Kristy Ann McFarland, Crested Butte – Chair

Patrice Campbell, Grand Junction - Vice Chair
Mickey Sanders, Denver
Tony Pistilli, Lone Tree
Chris Brownlee, Grand Junction
Larry Stark, Centennial
Christopher Chippendale, Littleton

BOARD OF MORTGAGE LOAN ORIGINATORS

Cindy Emerine, Evergreen – Chair

Dena Falbo, Westminster - Vice Chair
Charles "Buzz" Moore, Grand Junction
Fred Joseph, Denver
Jennifer Heinrich, Erie

PREFACE

The Colorado Division of Real Estate and LexisNexis have prepared this manual with assistance from members of the Real Estate Commission, the Board of Real Estate Appraisers, and the Board of Mortgage Loan Originators. We gratefully acknowledge the help of the many who have contributed their time and experience, especially Marcia Waters and the dedicated staff at the Division of Real Estate for their commitment to making this publication available to the industry.

We hope this manual will be helpful to new applicants for licensure and a benefit to practicing real estate brokers, appraisers, and mortgage professionals as a ready reference.

The information contained in this manual is fundamental to a sound introduction to the real estate industry. It is not intended as an all-inclusive real estate text; nor should it be relied upon as a source of legal advice.

For those who desire to increase their educational and professional competency, there are many classes and courses of instruction available throughout the State of Colorado and several colleges and universities that offer four-year programs leading to a degree in real estate and related fields. Suggestions, corrections, and criticisms for and of this publication are solicited and will receive careful consideration.

Disclaimer: The portions of the Colorado Revised Statutes, reprinted in this Manual with permission of the Committee on Legal Services in accordance with section 2-5-118, C.R.S., are unofficial publications of the Colorado Revised Statutes. They are included as: a reference for real estate practitioners, an aid to those preparing for licensure, and others with an interest in a digest of real estate related laws and information. The Division of Real Estate makes every effort to maintain accurate information; however, the State makes no warranties whatsoever in relation to the contents of this manual, and users rely upon the information contained herein at their own risk. Official statutes are maintained on the Colorado General Assembly website at: https://leg.colorado.gov.

Official rules of the Real Estate Commission, Board of Real Estate Appraisers, Board of Mortgage Loan Originators, and the Conservation Easement Oversight Commission are compiled and published by the Secretary of State in the Code of Colorado Regulations at: https://www.coloradosos.gov.

More information and portions of this Manual are available on the Colorado Division of Real Estate website at: https://dre.colorado.gov.

Matthew Bender & Company, Inc.
Editorial Offices
9443 Springboro Pike
Miamisburg, OH 45342
800-833-9844
www.lexisnexis.com
Printers and Distributors

Print Edition ISBN: 978-1-66333-232-5
Electronic Edition ISBN: 978-1-66333-233-2

TABLE OF CONTENTS

Chapter-Page

Chapter-Page

Chapter-Page

Chapter-Page

Chapter 1:
Real Estate Broker License Law

An * in the left margin indicates a change in the statute, rule, or text since the last publication of the manual.

I. Reason for Its Enactment

The Colorado Real Estate Broker License Law was passed to protect the people of the State of Colorado. Through licensing, the law seeks competency and integrity on the part of those engaged in the real estate business. The law has had the effect of raising the general standing of the real estate business and has helped to safeguard the interests of both the public and those engaged in the business.

II. What the Law Does Not Cover

The law does not dictate the ethical standards that should be observed in the real estate industry, or generally of any trade, business, or profession.

Codes of ethics have been voluntarily adopted by various real estate organizations as guiding standards of high moral and ethical practice. Adherence to such codes is recommended to all who are licensed to engage in real estate business, but is not regulated or enforced by the Colorado Real Estate Commission or the Division of Real Estate.

III. The Commission Office

The Division of Real Estate has a five-member Commission that meets bi-monthly to conduct rulemaking hearings, make policy decisions, consider licensing matters, review complaints, and take disciplinary action against real estate brokers. Rules are promulgated after notice and public hearings at which all interested parties may participate. The five Commission members consist of three real estate brokers who have had not less than five years' experience in the real estate business in Colorado, one of whom has substantial experience in property management, and two representatives of the public at large. Members of the Commission hold office for a period of three years.

The Division of Real Estate is part of the Department of Regulatory Agencies and is responsible for budgeting, purchasing, and related management functions. The director of the Division is an administrative officer who executes the directives of the Commission and is given statutory authority in all matters delegated by the Commission.

The Division of Real Estate is the licensing, regulation, and enforcement agency for real estate brokers, appraisers, mortgage loan originators, and subdivision developers. Additionally, the Division registers Homeowner's Associations (HOAs) and compiles regulatory statistics related to those HOAs. To become licensed, individuals must comply with education and/or experience requirements, qualify for reciprocity, and/or pass a general and/or state portion of the licensing exam.

The Division's objectives are to:

- Provide protection to consumers and other stakeholders.
- Promote consumer awareness throughout the State of Colorado.
- Enforce state and federal laws, rules, regulations, and standards and impose disciplinary action when recommended.
- License real estate brokers.
- License real estate appraisers.
- License mortgage loan originators.
- Register timeshares, raw land subdivisions developers and homeowners' associations.
- Investigate complaints.
- Enforce compliance with state and federal laws.
- Impose recommended disciplinary actions against licensees.
- Register HOAs and track and categorize complaints against those HOAs.

The Commission exercises its duties and authorities independently through the following programs or activities.

A. The Master File

The Division staff records the historical and day-to-day information concerning the licensing status of employers, employees, corporations, limited liability companies and partnership entities, trade names, office locations, and disciplinary actions.

* B. Licensing

The Licensing section's major responsibility is the data entry and upkeep of nearly 70,000 real estate broker, appraiser, and mortgage loan originator licensing records, as well as registration of subdivision/timeshare developers and homeowners' associations. The Licensing staff reviews and processes all incoming applications, which are screened for required qualifications, including education, experience, examinations, errors & omission (E&O) insurance, and criminal history background checks. The Licensing section also issues license histories to licensees who need to prove their credentials to other jurisdictions.

Colorado recognizes real estate licenses issued by many other jurisdictions if the licensee in the other jurisdiction has held that license for 2 years or more. Licensing currently administers this program and offers a limited recognition program to these licensees. The Division also reciprocates with most other appraisal jurisdictions.

Applicants with a past civil judgment or criminal conviction may request a "preliminary advisory opinion" regarding the likelihood of receiving a license before completing the requirements to apply for a license (Commission Rule 3.8). The Commission/Board may issue either a favorable or unfavorable opinion.

Both "preliminary advisory" applicants and license applicants are subject to pre-licensing investigations and fingerprinting to safeguard the statutory mandate for truthfulness, honesty, good moral character, and general fitness. (See §§ 12-10-202, -203(3), -606(6), and -711(1),

C.R.S.) All applications that disclose civil or criminal violations or any form of previous license discipline in any jurisdiction are reviewed and investigated thoroughly.

Licenses issued by the section include:

- Real estate broker
- Corporate/LLC real estate brokerage
- Partnership real estate brokerage
- Temporary real estate broker
- Ad Valorem appraiser
- Licensed appraiser
- Certified residential appraiser
- Certified general appraiser
- Temporary appraiser
- Mortgage loan originator

The Division also reviews and registers:

- Raw ground subdivision developers
- Timeshare and vacation club developers
- Condominium conversion developers
- Cooperative housing corporation developers
- Homeowners' associations

Information on licensing is located on the Division of Real Estate website at: https://dre.colorado.gov

C. Enforcement Section

The Real Estate Commission has the power upon its own motion to investigate any licensee's real estate activities. If a written complaint alleging a potential license law violation is filed, the office is compelled to investigate.

If the complaint against the licensee is of such a serious nature that it may result in disciplinary action against a licensee, a hearing may be held before an administrative law judge. The judge is appointed by the Department of Personnel and Administration. The administrative law judge will make an initial decision of revocation, suspension, censure, or dismissal. Education courses, probation, and fines can also be mandated. If written objections are not filed with the Commission within 30 days, the initial decision becomes final. If written objections are filed, the Commission may adopt the findings and initial decision of the administrative law judge, modify the disciplinary action, or refer the matter back for rehearing. The Commission can also issue letters of admonishment in instances where conduct does not warrant formal disciplinary proceedings.

This program also includes:

- Investigation of applicants.
- Evaluation of complaints.
- Investigation of complaints.
- Routine and investigative audits.

- Recommendations for dismissal or disciplinary action.
- Preparation and execution of subpoenas, and other legal documents.
- Preparation of cases for formal hearing, restraining orders, injunctions, or complaints for filing with district attorneys and local law enforcement agencies.
- Working with federal agencies, *e.g.*, the Securities and Exchange Commission or Housing and Urban Development, the Federal Bureau of Investigation, or the Internal Revenue Service.

The Real Estate Commission should *not* be confused with the Colorado Association of REALTORS®, which is a private trade organization affiliated with the National Association of REALTORS® whose members are the only licensees authorized to use the registered trademark "REALTOR"®.

IV. License Law

A. Part 1 – Common Definitions

§ 12-10-101, C.R.S. Definitions.

Editor's note: *Subsection (1) is similar to former §§12-61-702 (7) and 12-61-902 (3); subsection (2) is similar to former §§12-61-702 (8) and 12-61-902 (4); and subsection (3) is similar to former §§12-61-101 (1.2) and 12-61-401 (2.5), as those sections existed prior to 2019, and the former §12-10-101 was relocated to §12-110-101.*

As used in this article 10, unless the context otherwise requires:

(1) "Director" means the director of the division of real estate.

(2) "Division" means the division of real estate.

(3) "HOA" or "homeowners' association" means an association or unit owners' association formed before, on, or after July 1, 1992, as part of a common interest community as defined in section 38-33.3-103.

B. Part 2 – Brokers and Salespersons

§ 12-10-201, C.R.S. Definitions.

Editor's note: *This section is similar to former §12-61-101 as it existed prior to 2019; except that §12-61-101 (1.2) was relocated to §12-10-101 (3).*

As used in this part 2, unless the context otherwise requires:

(1) "Commission" means the real estate commission created in section 12-10-206.

(2) "Employing real estate broker" or "employing broker" means a broker who is shown in commission records as employing or engaging another broker.

(3) "Limited liability company" shall have the same meaning as it is given in section 7-80-102 (7).

(4) "Option dealer" means any person, firm, partnership, limited liability company, association, or corporation that, directly or indirectly, takes, obtains, or uses an option to purchase, exchange, rent, or lease real property or any interest therein with the intent or for the purpose of buying, selling, exchanging, renting, or leasing the real property or interest therein to another or others, whether or not the option is in that person's or its name and whether or not title to said property passes through the name of the person, firm, partnership, limited liability company, association, or corporation in connection with the purchase, sale, exchange, rental, or lease of the real property or interest therein.

(5) "Partnership" includes, but is not limited to, a registered limited liability partnership.

(6) (a) "Real estate broker" or "broker" means any person, firm, partnership, limited liability company, association, or corporation that, in consideration of compensation by fee, commission, salary, or anything of value or with the intention of receiving or collecting such compensation, engages in or offers or attempts to engage in, either directly or indirectly, by a continuing course of conduct or by any single act or transaction, any of the following acts:

(I) Selling, exchanging, buying, renting, or leasing real estate, or interest therein, or improvements affixed thereon;

(II) Offering to sell, exchange, buy, rent, or lease real estate, or interest therein, or improvements affixed thereon;

(III) Selling or offering to sell or exchange an existing lease of real estate, or interest therein, or improvements affixed thereon;

(IV) Negotiating the purchase, sale, or exchange of real estate, or interest therein, or improvements affixed thereon;

(V) Listing, offering, attempting, or agreeing to list real estate, or interest therein, or improvements affixed thereon for sale, exchange, rent, or lease;

(VI) Auctioning or offering, attempting, or agreeing to auction real estate, or interest therein, or improvements affixed thereon;

(VII) Buying, selling, offering to buy or sell, or otherwise dealing in options on real estate, or interest therein, or improvements affixed thereon, or acting as an "option dealer";

(VIII) Performing any of the foregoing acts as an employee of, or on behalf of, the owner of real estate, or interest therein, or improvements affixed thereon at a salary or for a fee, commission, or other consideration;

(IX) Negotiating or attempting or offering to negotiate the listing, sale, purchase, exchange, or lease of a business or business opportunity or the goodwill thereof or any interest therein when the act or transaction involves, directly or indirectly, any change in the ownership or interest in real estate, or in a leasehold interest or estate, or in a business or business opportunity that owns an interest in real estate or in a leasehold unless the act is performed by any broker-dealer licensed under the provisions of article 51 of title 11 who is actually engaged generally in the business of offering, selling, purchasing, or trading in securities or any officer, partner, salesperson, employee, or other authorized representative or agent thereof; or

(X) Soliciting a fee or valuable consideration from a prospective tenant for furnishing information concerning the availability of real property, including apartment housing that may be leased or rented as a private dwelling, abode, or place of residence. Any person, firm, partnership, limited liability company, association, or corporation or any employee or authorized agent thereof engaged in the act of soliciting a fee or valuable consideration from any person other than a prospective tenant for furnishing information concerning the availability of real property, including apartment housing that may be leased or rented as a private dwelling, abode, or place of residence, is exempt from this definition of "real estate broker" or "broker". This exemption applies only in respect to the furnishing of information concerning the availability of real property.

(b) "Real estate broker" or "broker" does not apply to any of the following:

(I) Any attorney-in-fact acting without compensation under a power of attorney, duly executed by an owner of real estate, authorizing the consummation of a real estate transaction;

(II) Any public official in the conduct of his or her official duties;

(III) Any receiver, trustee, administrator, conservator, executor, or guardian acting under proper authorization;

(IV) Any person, firm, partnership, limited liability company, or association acting personally or a corporation acting through its officers or regularly salaried employees, on behalf of that person or on its own behalf as principal in acquiring or in negotiating to acquire any interest in real estate;

(V) An attorney-at-law in connection with his or her representation of clients in the practice of law;

(VI) Any person, firm, partnership, limited liability company, association, or corporation, or any employee or authorized agent thereof, engaged in the act of negotiating, acquiring, purchasing, assigning, exchanging, selling, leasing, or dealing in oil and gas or other mineral leases or interests therein or other severed mineral or royalty interests in real property, including easements, rights-of-way, permits, licenses, and any other interests in real property for or on behalf of a third party, for the purpose of, or facilities related to, intrastate and interstate pipelines for oil, gas, and other petroleum products, flow lines, gas gathering systems, and natural gas storage and distribution;

(VII) A natural person acting personally with respect to property owned or leased by that person or a natural person who is a general partner of a partnership, a manager of a limited liability company, or an owner of twenty percent or more of such partnership or limited liability company, and authorized to sell or lease property owned by the partnership or limited liability company, except as provided in subsection (4) of this section;

(VIII) A corporation with respect to property owned or leased by it, acting through its officers or regularly salaried employees, when the acts are incidental and necessary in the ordinary course of the corporation's business activities of a non-real-estate nature (but only if the corporation is not engaged in the business of land transactions), except as provided in subsection (4) of this section. For the purposes of this subsection (6)(b)(VIII), the term "officers or regularly salaried employees" means persons regularly employed who derive not less than seventy-five percent of their compensation from the corporation in the form of salaries.

(IX) A principal officer of any corporation with respect to property owned by it when the property is located within the state of Colorado and when the principal officer is the owner of twenty percent or more of the outstanding stock of the corporation, except as provided in subsection (4) of this section, but this exemption does not include any corporation selling previously occupied one-family and two-family dwellings;

(X) A sole proprietor, corporation, partnership, or limited liability company, acting through its officers, partners, or regularly salaried employees, with respect to property owned or leased by the sole proprietor, corporation, partnership, or limited liability company on which has been or will be erected a commercial, industrial, or residential building that has not been previously occupied and where the consideration paid for the property includes the cost of the building, payable, less deposit or down payment, at the time of conveyance of the property and building;

(XI) (A) A corporation, partnership, or limited liability company acting through its officers, partners, managers, or regularly salaried employees receiving no additional compensation therefor, or its wholly owned subsidiary or officers, partners, managers, or regularly salaried employees thereof receiving no additional compensation, with respect to property located in Colorado that is owned or leased by the corporation, partnership, or limited liability company and on which has been or will be erected a shopping center, office building, or industrial park when such shopping center, office building, or industrial park is sold, leased, or otherwise offered for sale or lease in the ordinary course of the business of the corporation, partnership, limited liability company, or wholly owned subsidiary.

(B) For the purposes of this subsection (6)(b)(XI): "Shopping center" means land on which buildings are or will be constructed that are used for commercial and office purposes around or adjacent to which off-street parking is provided; "office building" means a building used primarily for office purposes; and "industrial park" means land on which buildings are or will be constructed for warehouse, research, manufacturing, processing, or fabrication purposes.

(XII) A regularly salaried employee of an owner of an apartment building or complex who acts as an on-site manager of such an apartment building or complex. This exemption applies only in respect to the customary duties of an on-site manager performed for his or her employer.

(XIII) A regularly salaried employee of an owner of condominium units who acts as an on-site manager of such units. For purposes of this subsection (6)(b)(XIII) only, the term "owner" includes a homeowners' association formed and acting pursuant to its recorded condominium declaration and bylaws. This exemption applies only in respect to the customary duties of an on-site manager performed for his or her employer.

(XIV) A real estate broker licensed in another state who receives a share of a commission or finder's fee on a cooperative transaction from a licensed Colorado real estate broker;

(XV) A sole proprietor, corporation, partnership, or limited liability company, acting through its officers, partners, or regularly salaried employees, with respect to property located in Colorado, where the purchaser of the property is in the business of developing land for residential, commercial, or industrial purposes;

(XVI) Any person, firm, partnership, limited liability company, association, or corporation, or any employee or authorized agent thereof, engaged in the act of negotiating, purchasing, assigning, exchanging, selling, leasing, or acquiring rights-of-way, permits, licenses, and any other interests in real property for, or on behalf, of a third party for the purpose of, or facilities related to:

(A) Telecommunication lines;

(B) Wireless communication facilities;

(C) CATV;

(D) Electric generation, transmission, and distribution lines;

(E) Water diversion, collection, distribution, treatment, and storage or use; and

(F) Transportation, so long as the person, firm, partnership, limited liability company, association, or corporation, including any employee or authorized agent thereof, does not represent any displaced person or entity as an agent thereof in the purchase, sale, or exchange of real estate, or an interest therein, resulting from residential or commercial relocations required under any transportation project, regardless of the source of public funding.

§ 12-10-202, C.R.S. License required.

Editor's note: *This section is similar to former §12-61-102 as it existed prior to 2019.*

It is unlawful for any person, firm, partnership, limited liability company, association, or corporation to engage in the business or capacity of real estate broker in this state without first having obtained a license from the commission. No person shall be granted a license until the person establishes compliance with the provisions of this part 2 concerning education, experience, and testing; truthfulness and honesty and otherwise good moral character; and, in addition to any other requirements of this section, competency to transact the business of a real estate broker in such manner as to safeguard the interest of the public and only after satisfactory proof of the qualifications, together with the application for the license, is filed in the office of the commission. In determining the person's character, the commission shall be governed by section 24-5-101.

§ 12-10-203, C.R.S. Application for license – rules – definition.

Editor's note: *(1) This section is similar to former §12-61-103 as it existed prior to 2019.*

(2) Before its relocation in 2019, this section was amended in HB 19-1166. Those amendments were superseded by the repeal and reenactment of this title 12, effective October 1, 2019. For those amendments to the former section in effect from April 18, 2019, to October 1, 2019, see HB 19-1166, chapter 125, Session Laws of Colorado 2019.

(3) Section 78 of chapter 125 (HB 19-1166), Session Laws of Colorado 2019, provides that the act changing this section takes effect October 1, 2019, only if HB 19-1172 becomes law. HB 19-1172 became law and took effect October 1, 2019.

(1) (a) All persons desiring to become real estate brokers shall apply to the commission for a license under the provisions of this part 2. Application for a license as a real estate broker shall be made to the commission upon forms or in a manner prescribed by the commission.

(b) (I) Prior to submitting an application for a license pursuant to subsection (1)(a) of this section, each applicant shall submit a set of fingerprints to the Colorado bureau of investigation for the purpose of conducting a state and national fingerprint-based criminal history record check utilizing records of the Colorado bureau of investigation and the federal bureau of investigation. The applicant shall pay the fee established by the Colorado bureau of investigation for conducting the fingerprint-based criminal history record check to the bureau. Upon completion of the criminal history record check, the bureau shall forward the results to the commission. The commission shall acquire a name-based criminal history record check, as defined in section 22-2-119.3 (6)(d), for an applicant who has twice submitted to a fingerprint-based criminal history record check and whose fingerprints are unclassifiable or when the results of a fingerprint-based criminal history record check of an applicant performed pursuant to this subsection (1)(b)(I) reveal a record of arrest without a disposition. The applicant shall pay the costs associated with a name-based criminal history record check.

(II) For purposes of this subsection (1)(b), "applicant" means an individual, or any person designated to act as broker for any partnership, limited liability company, or corporation pursuant to subsection (6) of this section.

(2) Every real estate broker licensed under this part 2 shall maintain a place of business within this state, except as provided in section 12-10-208. In case a real estate broker maintains more than one place of business within the state, the broker shall be responsible for supervising all licensed activities originating in the offices.

(3) The commission is authorized by this section to require and procure any such proof as is necessary in reference to the truthfulness, honesty, and good moral character of any applicant

for a real estate broker's license or, if the applicant is a partnership, limited liability company, or corporation, of any partner, manager, director, officer, member, or stockholder if the person has, either directly or indirectly, a substantial interest in the applicant prior to the issuance of the license.

(4) (a) An applicant for a broker's license shall be at least eighteen years of age. The applicant must furnish proof satisfactory to the commission that the applicant has either received a degree from an accredited degree-granting college or university with a major course of study in real estate or has successfully completed courses of study, approved by the commission, at any accredited college or university or any private occupational school that has a certificate of approval from the private occupational school division in accordance with the provisions of article 64 of title 23 or that has been approved by the commission or licensed by an official state agency of any other state as follows:

(I) Forty-eight hours of classroom instruction or equivalent correspondent hours in real estate law and real estate practice; and

(II) Forty-eight hours of classroom instruction or equivalent correspondent hours in understanding and preparation of Colorado real estate contracts; and

(III) A total of seventy-two hours of instruction or equivalent correspondence hours from the following areas of study:

(A) Trust accounts and record keeping;

(B) Real estate closings;

(C) Current legal issues; and

(D) Practical applications.

(b) An applicant for a broker's license who has been licensed as a real estate broker in another jurisdiction shall be required to complete only the course of study comprising the subject matter areas described in subsections (4)(a)(II) and (4)(a)(III)(B) of this section.

(c) An applicant for a broker's license who has been licensed as a real estate salesperson in another jurisdiction shall be required to complete only the course of study required in subsections (4)(a)(II) and (4)(a)(III) of this section.

(5) (a) The applicant for a broker's license shall submit to and pass an examination designated to determine the competency of the applicant and prepared by or under the supervision of the commission or its designated contractor. The commission may contract with an independent testing service to develop, administer, or grade examinations or to administer licensee records. The contract may allow the testing service to recover the costs of the examination and the costs of administering exam and license records from the applicant. The commission may contract separately for these functions and allow recovered costs to be collected and retained by a single contractor for distribution to other contractors. The commission shall have the authority to set the minimum passing score that an applicant must receive on the examination, and the score shall reflect the minimum level of competency required to be a broker. The examination shall be given at such times and places as the commission prescribes. The examination shall include, but not be limited to, ethics, reading, spelling, basic mathematics, principles of land economics, appraisal, financing, a knowledge of the statutes and law of this state relating to deeds, trust deeds, mortgages, listing contracts, contracts of sale, bills of sale, leases, agency, brokerage, trust accounts, closings, securities, the provisions of this part 2, and the rules of the commission. The examination for a broker's license shall also include the preparation of a real estate closing statement.

(b) An applicant for a broker's license who has held a real estate license in another jurisdiction that administers a real estate broker's examination and who has been licensed for two or more years prior to applying for a Colorado license may be issued a broker's license if the applicant establishes that he or she possesses credentials and qualifications that are substantively equivalent to the requirements in Colorado for licensure by examination.

(c) In addition to all other applicable requirements, the following provisions apply to brokers that did not hold a current and valid broker's license on December 31, 1996:

(I) No such broker shall engage in an independent brokerage practice without first having served actively as a real estate broker for at least two years. The commission shall adopt rules requiring an employing broker to ensure that a high level of supervision is exercised over such a broker during the two-year period.

(II) No such broker shall employ another broker without first having completed twenty-four clock hours of instruction, or the equivalent in correspondence hours, as approved by the commission, in brokerage administration.

(III) Effective January 1, 2019, a broker shall not act as an employing broker without first demonstrating, in accordance with rules of the commission, experience and knowledge sufficient to enable the broker to employ and adequately supervise other brokers, as appropriate to the broker's area of supervision. The commission's rules must set forth the method or methods by which the broker may demonstrate the experience and knowledge, either by documenting a specified number of transactions that the broker has completed or by other methods.

(6) (a) Real estate brokers' licenses may be granted to individuals, partnerships, limited liability companies, or corporations. A partnership, limited liability company, or corporation, in its application for a license, shall designate a qualified, active broker to be responsible for management and supervision of the licensed actions of the partnership, limited liability company, or corporation and all licensees shown in the commission's records as being in the employ of the entity. The application of the partnership, limited liability company, or corporation and the application of the broker designated by it shall be filed with the commission.

(b) No license shall be issued to any partnership, limited liability company, or corporation unless and until the broker so designated by the partnership, limited liability company, or corporation submits to and passes the examination required by this part 2 on behalf of the partnership, limited liability company, or corporation. Upon the broker successfully passing the examination and upon compliance with all other requirements of law by the partnership, limited liability company, or corporation, as well as by the designated broker, the commission shall issue a broker's license to the partnership, limited liability company, or corporation, which shall bear the name of the designated broker, and thereupon the broker so designated shall conduct business as a real estate broker only through the partnership, limited liability company, or corporation and not for the broker's own account.

(c) If the person so designated is refused a license by the commission or ceases to be the designated broker of the partnership, limited liability company, or corporation, the entity may designate another person to make application for a license. If the person ceases to be the designated broker of the partnership, limited liability company, or corporation, the director may issue a temporary license to prevent hardship for a period not to exceed ninety days to the licensed person so designated. The director may extend a temporary license for one additional period not to exceed ninety days upon proper application and a showing of good cause; if the director refuses, no further extension of a temporary license shall be granted except by the commission. If any broker or employee of any such partnership, limited liability company, or corporation, other than the one designated as provided in this section, desires to act as a real estate broker, the broker or employee shall first obtain a license as a real estate broker as provided in this section and shall pay the regular fee therefor.

(7) The broker designated to act as broker for any partnership, limited liability company, or corporation is personally responsible for the handling of any and all earnest money deposits or escrow or trust funds received or disbursed by the partnership, limited liability company, or corporation. In the event of any breach of duty by the partnership, limited liability company, or corporation as a fiduciary, any person aggrieved or damaged by the breach of fiduciary duty shall have a claim for relief against the partnership, limited liability company, or corporation, as well as against the designated broker, and may pursue the claim against the partnership, limited liability company, or corporation and the designated broker personally. The broker may be held responsible and liable for damages based upon the breach of fiduciary duty as may be recoverable against the partnership, limited liability company, or corporation, and any judgment so obtained may be enforced jointly or severally against the broker personally and the partnership, limited liability company, or corporation.

(8) No license for a broker registered as being in the employ of another broker shall be issued to a partnership, a limited liability company, or a corporation or under a fictitious name or trade name; except that a married woman may elect to use her birth name.

(9) No person shall be licensed as a real estate broker under more than one name, and no person shall conduct or promote a real estate brokerage business except under the name under which the person is licensed.

(10) A licensed attorney shall take and pass the examination referred to in this section after having completed twelve hours of classroom instruction or equivalent correspondent hours in trust accounts, record keeping, and real estate closings. *(Ed. Note: Attorney may be licensed at any bar)*

§ 12-10-204, C.R.S. Errors and omissions insurance required – rules.

Editor's note: *This section is similar to former §12-61-103.6 as it existed prior to 2019.*

(1) Every licensee under this part 2, except an inactive broker or an attorney licensee who maintains a policy of professional malpractice insurance that provides coverage for errors and omissions for their activities as a licensee under this part 2, shall maintain errors and omissions insurance to cover all activities contemplated under parts 2 to 6 of this article 10. The division shall make the errors and omissions insurance available to all licensees by contracting with an insurer for a group policy after a competitive bid process in accordance with article 103 of title 24. A group policy obtained by the division must be available to all licensees with no right on the part of the insurer to cancel a licensee. A licensee may obtain errors and omissions insurance independently if the coverage complies with the minimum requirements established by the division.

(2) (a) If the division is unable to obtain errors and omissions insurance coverage to insure all licensees who choose to participate in the group program at a reasonable annual premium, as determined by the division, a licensee shall independently obtain the errors and omissions insurance required by this section.

(b) The division shall solicit and consider information and comments from interested persons when determining the reasonableness of annual premiums.

(3) The division shall determine the terms and conditions of coverage required under this section based on rules promulgated by the commission. The commission shall notify each licensee of the required terms and conditions at least thirty days before the annual premium renewal date as determined by the commission. Each licensee shall file a certificate of coverage showing compliance with the required terms and conditions with the commission by the annual premium renewal date, as determined by the division.

(4) In addition to all other powers and duties conferred upon the commission by this article 10, the commission shall adopt such rules as it deems necessary or proper to carry out the provisions of this section.

§ 12-10-205, C.R.S. Licenses – issuance – contents – display.

Editor's note: *This section is similar to former §12-61-104 as it existed prior to 2019.*

The commission shall make available for each licensee a license in such form and size as the commission shall prescribe and adopt. The real estate license shall show the name of the licensee and shall have imprinted thereon the seal, or a facsimile, of the department and, in addition to the foregoing, shall contain such other matter as the commission shall prescribe.

§ 12-10-206, C.R.S. Real estate commission – created – compensation – immunity.

Editor's note: *This section is similar to former §12-61-105 as it existed prior to 2019.*

(1) There is hereby created a commission of five members, appointed by the governor, which shall administer parts 2 and 5 of this article 10. This commission is known as the real estate commission and consists of three real estate brokers who have had not less than five years' experience in the real estate business in Colorado, one of whom has substantial experience in property management, and two representatives of the public at large. Members of the commission hold office for a period of three years. Upon the death, resignation, removal, or otherwise of any member of the commission, the governor shall appoint a member to fill out the unexpired term. The governor may remove any member for misconduct, neglect of duty, or incompetence.

(2) Each member of the commission shall receive the same compensation and reimbursement of expenses as those provided for members of boards and commissions in the division of professions and occupations pursuant to section 12-20-103 (6). Payment for all such per diem compensation and expenses shall be made out of annual appropriations from the division of real estate cash fund provided for in section 12-10-215.

(3) Members of the commission, consultants, expert witnesses, and complainants shall be immune from suit in any civil action based upon any disciplinary proceedings or other official acts they performed in good faith.

(4) No real estate broker's license shall be denied, suspended, or revoked except as determined by a majority vote of the members of the commission.

§ 12-10-207, C.R.S. Division of real estate – creation – director, clerks, and assistants.

Editor's note: *This section is similar to former §12-61-106 as it existed prior to 2019.*

(1) There is hereby created within the department the division of real estate. The executive director is authorized by this section to employ, subject to the provisions of the state personnel system laws of the state, a director of the division, who in turn shall employ such attorneys, deputies, investigators, clerks, and assistants as are necessary to discharge the duties imposed by parts 2 and 5 of this article 10. The division and the director shall exercise their powers and perform their duties and functions under the department as if they were transferred to the department by a **type 2** transfer.

(2) It is the duty of the director, personally, or the director's designee to aid in the administration and enforcement of parts 2 and 5 of this article 10 and in the prosecution of all persons charged with violating any of their provisions, to conduct audits of business accounts of licensees, to perform such duties of the commission as the commission prescribes, and to act in behalf of the commission on such occasions and in such circumstances as the commission directs.

§ 12-10-208, C.R.S. Resident licensee – nonresident licensee – consent to service.

Editor's note: *This section is similar to former §12-61-107 as it existed prior to 2019.*

(1) A nonresident of the state may become a real estate broker in this state by conforming to all the conditions of this part 2; except that the nonresident broker shall not be required to maintain a place of business within this state if that broker maintains a definite place of business in another state.

(2) If a broker has no registered agent registered in this state, the registered agent is not located under its registered agent name at its registered agent address, or the registered agent cannot with reasonable diligence be served, the broker may be served by registered mail or by certified mail, return receipt requested, addressed to the entity at its principal address. Service is perfected under this subsection (2) at the earliest of:

(a) The date the broker receives the process, notice, or demand;

(b) The date shown on the return receipt, if signed by or on behalf of the broker; or

(c) Five days after mailing.

(3) All such applications shall contain a certification that the broker is authorized to act for the corporation.

§ 12-10-209, C.R.S. Record of licensees – publications.

Editor's note: *This section is similar to former §12-61-108 as it existed prior to 2019.*

The commission shall maintain a record of the names and addresses of all licensees licensed under the provisions of parts 2 and 5 of this article 10, together with such other information relative to the enforcement of the provisions as deemed by the commission to be necessary. Publication of the record and of any other information circulated in quantity outside the executive branch shall be in accordance with the provisions of section 24-1-136.

§ 12-10-210, C.R.S. Compilation and publication of passing rates per educational institution for real estate licensure examinations – definition – rules.

Editor's note: *This section is similar to former §12-61-108.5 as it existed prior to 2019.*

(1) The commission shall have the authority to obtain information from each educational institution authorized to offer courses in real estate for the purpose of compiling the number of applicants who pass the real estate licensure examination from each educational institution. The information shall include the name of each student who attended the institution and a statement of whether the student completed the necessary real estate courses required for licensure. The commission shall have access to such other information as necessary to accomplish the purpose of this section. For the purposes of this section, an "applicant" is a student who completed the required education requirements and who applied for and sat for the licensure examination.

(2) The commission shall compile the information obtained in subsection (1) of this section with applicant information retained by the commission. Specifically, the commission shall compile whether the student applied for the licensure examination and whether the applicant passed the licensure examination. The commission shall create statistical data setting forth:

(a) The name of the educational institution;

(b) The number of students who completed the necessary real estate course required for licensure;

(c) Whether the student registered and sat for the licensure examination; and

(d) The number of those applicants who passed the licensure examination.

(3) The commission shall publish this statistical data and make it available to the public quarterly.

(4) The commission shall retain the statistical data for three years.

(5) Specific examination scores for an applicant will be kept confidential by the commission unless the applicant authorizes release of the information.

(6) The commission may promulgate rules for the administration of this section.

§ 12-10-211, C.R.S. Change of license status – inactive – cancellation.

Editor's note: *This section is similar to former §12-61-109 as it existed prior to 2019.*

(1) Immediate notice shall be given in a manner acceptable to the commission by each licensee of any change of business location or employment. A change of business address or employment without notification to the commission shall automatically inactivate the licensee's license.

(2) A broker who transfers to the address of another broker or a broker applicant who desires to be employed by another broker shall inform the commission if the broker is to be in the employ of the other broker. The employing broker shall have the control and custody of the employed broker's license. The employed broker may not act on behalf of the broker or as broker for a partnership, limited liability company, or corporation during the term of the employment; but this shall not affect the employed broker's right to transfer to another employing broker or to a location where the employed broker may conduct business as an independent broker or as a broker acting for a partnership, limited liability company, or corporation.

(3) In the event that any licensee is discharged by or terminates employment with a broker, it shall be the **joint duty of both** such parties to immediately notify the commission. Either party may furnish the notice in a manner acceptable to the commission. The party giving notice shall notify the other party in person or in writing of the termination of employment.

(4) It is unlawful for any such licensee to perform any of the acts authorized under the license in pursuance of this part 2, either directly or indirectly, on or after the date that employment has been terminated. When any real estate broker whose employment has been terminated is employed by another real estate broker, the commission shall, upon proper notification, enter the change of employment in the records of the commission. Not more than one employer or place of employment shall be shown for any real estate broker for the same period of time.

§ 12-10-212, C.R.S. License fees – partnership, limited liability company, and corporation licenses – rules.

Editor's note: *This section is similar to former §12-61-110 as it existed prior to 2019.*

(1) Fees established pursuant to section 12-10-215 shall be charged by and paid to the commission or the agent for the commission for the following:

- (a) Each broker's examination;
- (b) Each broker's original application and license;
- (c) Each renewal of a broker's license;
- (d) Any change of name, address, or employing broker requiring a change in commission records;
- (e) A new application that shall be submitted when a licensed real estate broker wishes to become the broker acting for a partnership, a limited liability company, or a corporation.

(2) The proper fee shall accompany each application for licensure. The fee shall not be refundable. Failure by the person taking an examination to file the appropriate broker's application within one year of the date the person passed the examination will automatically cancel the examination, and all rights to a passing score will be terminated.

(3) Each real estate broker's license granted to an individual shall entitle the individual to perform all the acts contemplated by this part 2, without any further application on his or her part and without the payment of any fee other than the fees specified in this section.

(4) (a) (I) The commission shall require that any person licensed under this part 2, whether on an active or inactive basis, renew the license on or before December 31 of every third year after issuance; except that an initial license issued under this part 2 on or after April 23, 2018, expires at 12 midnight on December 31 of the year in which it was issued.

(II) Renewal is conditioned upon fulfillment of the continuing education requirements set forth in section 12-10-213. For persons renewing or reinstating an active license, written certification verifying completion for the previous licensing period of the continuing education requirements set forth in section 12-10-213 must accompany and be submitted to the commission with the application for renewal or reinstatement. For persons who did not submit certification verifying compliance with section 12-10-213 at the time a license was renewed or reinstated on an inactive status, written certification verifying completion for the previous licensing period of the continuing education requirements set forth in that section must accompany and be submitted with any future application to reactivate the license. The commission may, by rule, establish procedures to facilitate such a renewal. In the absence of any reason or condition that might warrant the refusal of the granting of a license or the revocation thereof, the commission shall issue a new license upon receipt by the commission of the written request of the applicant and the appropriate fees required by this section. Applications for renewal will be accepted thirty days prior to January 1.

(III) A person who fails to renew a license before January 1 of the year succeeding the year of the expiration of the license may reinstate the license as follows:

(A) If proper application is made within thirty-one days after the date of expiration, by payment of the regular renewal fee;

(B) If proper application is made more than thirty-one days but within one year after the date of expiration, by payment of the regular renewal fee and payment of a reinstatement fee equal to one-half the regular renewal fee;

(C) If proper application is made more than one year but within three years after the date of expiration, by payment of the regular renewal fee and payment of a reinstatement fee equal to the regular renewal fee.

(IV) The commission may, by rule, establish procedures to facilitate the transition of the reinstatement license periods described in subsections (4)(a)(III)(A) to (4)(a)(III)(C) of this section from an anniversary expiration date to a December 31 expiration date.

(b) Any reinstated license shall be effective only as of the date of reinstatement. Any person who fails to apply for reinstatement within three years after the expiration of a license shall, without exception, be treated as a new applicant for licensure.

(c) All reinstatement fees shall be transmitted to the state treasurer, who shall credit the fees to the division of real estate cash fund, as established by section 12-10-215.

(5) The suspension, expiration, or revocation of a real estate broker's license shall automatically inactivate every real estate broker's license where the holder of the license is shown in the commission records to be in the employ of the broker whose license has expired or has been suspended or revoked pending notification to the commission by the employed licensee of a change of employment.

§ 12-10-213, C.R.S. Renewal of license – continuing education requirement – rules.

Editor's note: *This section is similar to former §12-61-110.5 as it existed prior to 2019.*

(1) A broker applying for renewal of a license pursuant to section 12-10-212 (4) shall include with the application a certified statement verifying successful completion of real estate courses in accordance with the following schedule:

(a) For licensees applying for renewal of a three-year license, passage within the previous three years of the Colorado portion of the real estate exam or completion of a minimum of twenty-four hours of credit, twelve of which must be the credits developed by the commission pursuant to subsection (2) of this section;

(b) For licensees applying for renewal of a license that expires less than three years after it was issued, passage within the license period of the Colorado portion of the real estate exam or completion of a minimum of twenty-four hours of credit, at least eight of which must be the credits developed by the commission pursuant to subsection (2) of this section.

(2) The commission shall develop twelve hours of credit designed to assure reasonable currency of real estate knowledge by licensees, which credits shall include an update of the current statutes and the rules promulgated by the commission that affect the practice of real estate. If a licensee takes a course pursuant to rule 250 of the Colorado rules of civil procedure and the course concerns real property law, the licensee shall receive credit for the course toward the fulfillment of the licensee's continuing education requirements pursuant to this section. The credits shall be taken from an accredited Colorado college or university; a Colorado community college; a Colorado private occupational school holding a certificate of approval from the state board for community colleges and occupational education; or an educational institution or an educational service described in section 23-64-104. Successful completion of the credits shall require satisfactory passage of a written examination or written examinations of the materials covered. The examinations shall be audited by the commission to verify their accuracy and the validity of the grades given. The commission shall set the standards required for satisfactory passage of the examinations.

(3) All credits, other than the credits specified in subsection (2) of this section, shall be acquired from educational courses approved by the commission that contribute directly to the professional competence of a licensee. The credits may be acquired through successful completion of instruction in one or more of the following subjects:

(a) Real estate law;

(b) Property exchanges;

(c) Real estate contracts;

(d) Real estate finance;

(e) Real estate appraisal;

(f) Real estate closing;

(g) Real estate ethics;

(h) Condominiums and cooperatives;

(i) Real estate time-sharing;

(j) Real estate marketing principles;

(k) Real estate construction;

(*l*) Land development;

(m) Real estate energy concerns;

(n) Real estate geology;

(o) Water and waste management;
(p) Commercial real estate;
(q) Real estate securities and syndications;
(r) Property management;
(s) Real estate computer principles;
(t) Brokerage administration and management;
(u) Agency; and
(v) Any other subject matter as approved by the commission.

(4) A licensee applying for renewal of a license that expires on December 31 of the year in which it was issued is not subject to the education requirements set forth in subsection (1) of this section.

(5) The commission shall promulgate rules to implement this section.

§ 12-10-214, C.R.S. Disposition of fees.

Editor's note: *This section is similar to former §12-61-111 as it existed prior to 2019.*

All fees collected by the commission under parts 2 and 5 of this article 10, not including administrative fees that are in the nature of an administrative fine and fees retained by contractors pursuant to contracts entered into in accordance with section 12-10-203 or 24-34-101, shall be transmitted to the state treasurer, who shall credit the same to the division of real estate cash fund. Pursuant to section 12-10-215, the general assembly shall make annual appropriations from the fund for expenditures of the commission incurred in the performance of its duties under parts 2 and 5 of this article 10. The commission may request an appropriation specifically designated for educational and enforcement purposes. The expenditures incurred by the commission under parts 2 and 5 of this article 10 shall be made out of the appropriations upon vouchers and warrants drawn pursuant to law.

§ 12-10-215, C.R.S. Fee adjustments – cash fund created.

Editor's note: *This section is similar to former §12-61-111.5 as it existed prior to 2019.*

(1) This section applies to all activities of the division under parts 2, 5, 6, and 7 of this article 10.

(2) (a) (I) The division shall propose, as part of its annual budget request, an adjustment in the amount of each fee that it is authorized by law to collect under parts 2, 5, 6, and 7 of this article 10. The budget request and the adjusted fees for the division must reflect direct and indirect costs.

(II) The costs of the HOA information and resource center, created in section 12-10-801, shall be paid from the division of real estate cash fund created in this section. The division shall estimate the direct and indirect costs of operating the HOA information and resource center and shall establish the amount of the annual registration fee to be collected under section 38-33.3-401. The amount of the registration fee shall be sufficient to recover these costs, subject to a maximum limit of fifty dollars.

(b) Based upon the appropriation made and subject to the approval of the executive director, the division shall adjust its fees so that the revenue generated from the fees approximates its direct and indirect costs incurred in administering the programs and activities from which the fees are derived. The fees shall remain in effect for the fiscal year for which the budget request applies. All fees collected by the division, not including fees retained by contractors pursuant to contracts entered into in accordance with section 12-10-203 or 24-34-101, shall be transmitted to the state treasurer, who shall credit the same to the division of real estate cash fund, which fund is hereby created. All money credited to the division of real estate cash fund shall be used as provided in this section or in section 12-

10-214 and shall not be deposited in or transferred to the general fund of this state or any other fund.

(c) Beginning July 1, 1979, and each July 1 thereafter, whenever money appropriated to the division for its activities for the prior fiscal year is unexpended, the money shall be made a part of the appropriation to the division for the next fiscal year, and the amount shall not be raised from fees collected by the division. If a supplemental appropriation is made to the division for its activities, its fees, when adjusted for the fiscal year next following that in which the supplemental appropriation was made, shall be adjusted by an additional amount that is sufficient to compensate for the supplemental appropriation. Funds appropriated to the division in the annual long appropriations bill shall be designated as a cash fund and shall not exceed the amount anticipated to be raised from fees collected by the division.

§ 12-10-216, C.R.S. Records – evidence – inspection.

Editor's note: *This section is similar to former §12-61-112 as it existed prior to 2019.*

(1) The executive director shall adopt a seal by which all proceedings authorized under parts 2 and 5 of this article 10 shall be authenticated. Copies of records and papers in the office of the commission or department relating to the administration of parts 2 and 5 of this article 10, when duly certified and authenticated by the seal, shall be received as evidence in all courts equally and with like effect as the originals. All records kept in the office of the commission or department, under authority of parts 2 and 5 of this article 10, must be open to public inspection at such time and in such manner as may be prescribed by rules formulated by the commission.

(2) The commission shall not be required to maintain or preserve licensing history records of any person licensed under the provisions of this part 2 for any period of time longer than seven years.

§ 12-10-217, C.R.S. Investigation – revocation – actions against licensee or applicant – definition.

Editor's note: *This section is similar to former §12-61-113 as it existed prior to 2019.*

(1) The commission, upon its own motion, may, and, upon the complaint in writing of any person, shall, investigate the activities of any licensee or any person who assumes to act in the capacity of a licensee within the state, and the commission, after holding a hearing pursuant to section 12-10-219, has the power to impose an administrative fine not to exceed two thousand five hundred dollars for each separate offense and to censure a licensee, to place the licensee on probation and to set the terms of probation, or to temporarily suspend a license, or permanently revoke a license, when the licensee has performed, is performing, or is attempting to perform any of the following acts and is guilty of:

(a) Knowingly making any misrepresentation or knowingly making use of any false or misleading advertising;

(b) Making any promise of a character that influences, persuades, or induces another person when he or she could not or did not intend to keep the promise;

(c) Knowingly misrepresenting or making false promises through agents, advertising, or otherwise;

(d) Violating any provision of the "Colorado Consumer Protection Act", article 1 of title 6;

(e) Acting for more than one party in a transaction without the knowledge of all parties thereto;

(f) Representing or attempting to represent a real estate broker other than the licensee's employer without the express knowledge and consent of that employer;

(g) In the case of a broker registered as in the employ of another broker, failing to place, as soon after receipt as is practicably possible, in the custody of that licensed broker-employer any deposit money or other money or fund entrusted to the employee by any person dealing with the employee as the representative of that licensed broker-employer;

(h) Failing to account for or to remit, within a reasonable time, any money coming into the licensee's possession that belongs to others, whether acting as real estate brokers or otherwise, and failing to keep records relative to the money, which records shall contain such information as may be prescribed by the rules of the commission relative thereto and shall be subject to audit by the commission;

(i) Converting funds of others, diverting funds of others without proper authorization, commingling funds of others with the broker's own funds, or failing to keep the funds of others in an escrow or a trustee account with some bank or recognized depository in this state, which account may be any type of checking, demand, passbook, or statement account insured by an agency of the United States government, and to keep records relative to the deposit that contain such information as may be prescribed by the rules of the commission relative thereto, which records shall be subject to audit by the commission;

(j) Failing to provide the purchaser and seller of real estate with a closing statement of the transaction, containing such information as may be prescribed by the rules of the commission or failing to provide a signed duplicate copy of the listing contract and the contract of sale or the preliminary agreement to sell to the parties thereto;

(k) Failing to maintain possession, for future use or inspection by an authorized representative of the commission, for a period of four years, of the documents or records prescribed by the rules of the commission or to produce the documents or records upon reasonable request by the commission or by an authorized representative of the commission;

(*l*) Paying a commission or valuable consideration for performing any of the functions of a real estate broker, as described in this part 2, to any person not licensed under this part 2; except that a licensed broker may pay a finder's fee or a share of any commission on a cooperative sale when the payment is made to a real estate broker licensed in another state or country. If a country does not license real estate brokers, then the payee must be a citizen or resident of the country and represent that the payee is in the business of selling real estate in the country.

(m) Disregarding or violating any provision of this part 2 or part 4 of this article 10, violating any reasonable rule promulgated by the commission in the interests of the public and in conformance with the provisions of this part 2 or part 4 of this article 10; violating any lawful commission orders; or aiding and abetting a violation of any rule, commission order, or provision of this part 2 or part 4 of this article 10;

(n) (I) Conviction of, entering a plea of guilty to, or entering a plea of nolo contendere to any crime in article 3 of title 18; parts 1, 2, 3, and 4 of article 4 of title 18; part 1, 2, 3, 4, 5, 7, 8, or 9 of article 5 of title 18; article 5.5 of title 18; parts 3, 4, 6, 7, and 8 of article 6 of title 18; parts 1, 3, 4, 5, 6, 7, and 8 of article 7 of title 18; part 3 of article 8 of title 18; article 15 of title 18; article 17 of title 18; section 18-18-404, 18-18-405, 18-18-406, 18-18-411, 18-18-412.5, 18-18-412.7, 18-18-412.8, 18-18-415, 18-18-416, 18-18-422, or 18-18-423; or any other like crime under Colorado law, federal law, or the laws of other states. A certified copy of the judgment of a court of competent jurisdiction of the conviction or other official record indicating that the plea was entered shall be conclusive evidence of the conviction or plea in any hearing under this part 2.

(II) As used in this subsection (1)(n), "conviction" includes the imposition of a deferred judgment or deferred sentence.

(Editor's note: *The numbered articles in Title 18 of Colorado Revised Statute shown in this Part "n" refer to the following types of crimes:*

Article 3 is titled Offenses Against the Person and consists of six parts: homicide and related offenses, assaults, kidnapping, unlawful sexual behavior, human trafficking and slavery, and stalking.

Article 4 deals with ***offenses against property****, under which part 1 is arson, part 2 is burglary and related offenses, part 3 is robbery, and part 4 is theft.*

Article 5 consists of ***offenses involving fraud****, including part 1 – forgery, simulation, impersonation, and related offenses (obtaining a signature by deception, offering a false instrument for recording, et al.), part 2 – fraud in obtaining property or services (dual contracts), part 3 – fraudulent and deceptive sales and business practices (unlawful activity concerning the sale of land), part 4 – bribery and rigging of contests, part 5 – offenses relating to the uniform commercial code, part 7 – financial transaction device crime act (ATM's, et al), part 8 – equity skimming and related offenses, and part 9 – identity theft and related offenses.*

Article 5.5 consists of ***computer crime offenses****.*

Article 6 consists of ***offenses involving family relations****.*

Article 7 consists of ***offenses relating to morals****.*

Article 8 – part 3 refers to ***governmental operations****, specifically bribery and corrupt influences.*

Article 15 deals with making, financing, or collection of ***loans****.*

Article 17 is the Colorado ***Organized Crime*** *Control Act.*

Article 18 is the Uniform Controlled Substances Act, and part 4 deals with ***offenses*** *and* ***penalties****.)*

(o) Violating or aiding and abetting in the violation of the Colorado or federal fair housing laws;

(p) Failing to immediately notify the commission in writing of a conviction, plea, or violation pursuant to subsection (1)(n) or (1)(o) of this section;

(q) Having demonstrated unworthiness or incompetency to act as a real estate broker by conducting business in such a manner as to endanger the interest of the public;

(r) In the case of a broker licensee, failing to exercise reasonable supervision over the activities of licensed employees;

(s) Procuring, or attempting to procure, a real estate broker's license or renewing, reinstating, or reactivating, or attempting to renew, reinstate, or reactivate, a real estate broker's license by fraud, misrepresentation, or deceit or by making a material misstatement of fact in an application for the license;

(t) Claiming, arranging for, or taking any secret or undisclosed amount of compensation, commission, or profit or failing to reveal to the licensee's principal or employer the full amount of the licensee's compensation, commission, or profit in connection with any acts for which a license is required under this part 2;

(u) Using any provision allowing the licensee an option to purchase in any agreement authorizing or employing the licensee to sell, buy, or exchange real estate for compensation or commission, except when the licensee, prior to or coincident with election to exercise the option to purchase, reveals in writing to the licensee's principal or employer the full amount of the licensee's profit and obtains the written consent of the principal or employer approving the amount of the profit;

(v) Effective on and after August 26, 2013, fraud, misrepresentation, deceit, or conversion of trust funds that results in the entry of a civil judgment for damages;

(w) Any other conduct, whether of the same or a different character than specified in this subsection (1), that constitutes dishonest dealing;

(x) Having had a real estate broker's or a subdivision developer's license suspended or revoked in any jurisdiction, or having had any disciplinary action taken against the broker or subdivision developer in any other jurisdiction if the broker's or subdivision developer's action would constitute a violation of this subsection (1). A certified copy of the order of disciplinary action shall be prima facie evidence of the disciplinary action.

(y) Failing to keep records documenting proof of completion of the continuing education requirements in accordance with section 12-10-213 for a period of four years from the date of compliance with the section;

(z) (I) Violating any provision of section 12-10-218.

(II) In addition to any other remedies available to the commission pursuant to this article 10, after notice and a hearing pursuant to section 24-4-105, the commission may assess a penalty for a violation of section 12-10-218 or of any rule promulgated pursuant to section 12-10-218. The penalty shall be the amount of remuneration improperly paid and shall be transmitted to the state treasurer and credited to the general fund.

(aa) Within the last five years, having a license, registration, or certification issued by Colorado or another state revoked or suspended for fraud, deceit, material misrepresentation, theft, or the breach of a fiduciary duty, and such discipline denied the person authorization to practice as:

(I) A mortgage broker or mortgage loan originator;

(II) A real estate broker or salesperson;

(III) A real estate appraiser, as defined by section 12-10-602 (9);

(IV) An insurance producer, as defined by section 10-2-103 (6);

(V) An attorney;

(VI) A securities broker-dealer, as defined by section 11-51-201 (2);

(VII) A securities sales representative, as defined by section 11-51-201 (14);

(VIII) An investment advisor, as defined by section 11-51-201 (9.5); or

(IX) An investment advisor representative, as defined by section 11-51-201 (9.6).

(2) Every person licensed pursuant to section 12-10-201 (6)(a)(X) shall give a prospective tenant a contract or receipt; and the contract or receipt shall include the address and telephone number of the commission in prominent letters and shall state that the regulation of rental location agents is under the purview of the commission.

(3) In the event a firm, partnership, limited liability company, association, or corporation operating under the license of a broker designated and licensed as representative of the firm, partnership, limited liability company, association, or corporation is guilty of any of the foregoing acts, the commission may suspend or revoke the right of the firm, partnership, limited liability company, association, or corporation to conduct its business under the license of the broker, whether or not the designated broker had personal knowledge thereof and whether or not the commission suspends or revokes the individual license of the broker.

(4) Upon request of the commission, when any real estate broker is a party to any suit or proceeding, either civil or criminal, arising out of any transaction involving the sale or exchange of any interest in real property or out of any transaction involving a leasehold interest in the real property and when the broker is involved in the transaction in such capacity as a licensed broker, it shall be the duty of the broker to supply to the commission a copy of the

complaint, indictment, information, or other initiating pleading and the answer filed, if any, and to advise the commission of the disposition of the case and of the nature and amount of any judgment, verdict, finding, or sentence that may be made, entered, or imposed therein.

(5) This part 2 shall not be construed to relieve any person from civil liability or criminal prosecution under the laws of this state.

(6) Complaints of record in the office of the commission and commission investigations, including commission investigative files, are closed to public inspection. Stipulations and final agency orders are public records subject to sections 24-72-203 and 24-72-204.

(7) When a complaint or an investigation discloses an instance of misconduct that, in the opinion of the commission, does not warrant formal action by the commission but that should not be dismissed as being without merit, the commission may send a letter of admonition by certified mail, return receipt requested, to the licensee against whom a complaint was made and a copy thereof to the person making the complaint, but the letter shall advise the licensee that the licensee has the right to request in writing, within twenty days after proven receipt, that formal disciplinary proceedings be initiated to adjudicate the propriety of the conduct upon which the letter of admonition is based. If the request is timely made, the letter of admonition shall be deemed vacated, and the matter shall be processed by means of formal disciplinary proceedings.

(8) All administrative fines collected pursuant to this section shall be transmitted to the state treasurer, who shall credit the same to the division of real estate cash fund.

(9) Any application for licensure from a person whose license has been revoked shall not be considered until the passage of one year from the date of revocation.

(10) When the division becomes aware of facts or circumstances that fall within the jurisdiction of a criminal justice or other law enforcement authority upon investigation of the activities of a licensee, the division shall, in addition to the exercise of its authority under this part 2, refer and transmit the information, which may include originals or copies of documents and materials, to one or more criminal justice or other law enforcement authorities for investigation and prosecution as authorized by law.

§ 12-10-218, C.R.S. Affiliated business arrangements – definitions – disclosures – enforcement and penalties – reporting – rules – investigation information shared with the division of insurance.

Editor's note: *This section is similar to former §12-61-113.2 as it existed prior to 2019.*

(1) As used in this section, unless the context otherwise requires:

(a) "Affiliated business arrangement" means an arrangement in which:

(I) A provider of settlement services or an associate of a provider of settlement services has either an affiliate relationship with or a direct beneficial ownership interest of more than one percent in another provider of settlement services; and

(II) A provider of settlement services or the associate of a provider directly or indirectly refers settlement service business to another provider of settlement services or affirmatively influences the selection of another provider of settlement services.

(b) "Associate" means a person who has one or more of the following relationships with a person in a position to refer settlement service business:

(I) A spouse, parent, or child of the person;

(II) A corporation or business entity that controls, is controlled by, or is under common control with the person;

(III) An employer, officer, director, partner, franchiser, or franchisee of the person, including a broker acting as an independent contractor; or

(IV) Anyone who has an agreement, arrangement, or understanding with the person, the purpose or substantial effect of which is to enable the person in a position to refer settlement service business to benefit financially from referrals of the business.

(c) "Settlement service" means any service provided in connection with a real estate settlement including, but not limited to, the following:

(I) Title searches;

(II) Title examinations;

(III) The provision of title certificates;

(IV) Title insurance;

(V) Services rendered by an attorney;

(VI) The preparation of title documents;

(VII) Property surveys;

(VIII) The rendering of credit reports or appraisals;

(IX) Real estate appraisal services;

(X) Home inspection services;

(XI) Services rendered by a real estate broker;

(XII) Pest and fungus inspections;

(XIII) The origination of a loan;

(XIV) The taking of a loan application;

(XV) The processing of a loan;

(XVI) Underwriting and funding of a loan;

(XVII) Escrow handling services;

(XVIII) Thc handling of the processing; and

(XIX) Closing of settlement.

(2) (a) An affiliated business arrangement is permitted where the person referring business to the affiliated business arrangement receives payment only in the form of a return on an investment and where it does not violate the provisions of section 12-10-217.

(b) If a licensee or the employing broker of a licensee is part of an affiliated business arrangement when an offer to purchase real property is fully executed, the licensee shall disclose to all parties to the real estate transaction the existence of the arrangement. The disclosure shall be written, shall be signed by all parties to the real estate transaction, and shall comply with the federal "Real Estate Settlement Procedures Act of 1974", as amended, 12 U.S.C. sec. 2601 et seq.

(c) A licensee shall not require the use of an affiliated business arrangement or a particular provider of settlement services as a condition of obtaining services from that licensee for any settlement service. For the purposes of this subsection (2)(c), "require the use" shall have the same meaning as "required use" in 24 CFR 3500.2 (b).

(d) No licensee shall give or accept any fee, kickback, or other thing of value pursuant to any agreement or understanding, oral or otherwise, that business incident to or part of a settlement service involving an affiliated business arrangement shall be referred to any provider of settlement services.

(e) Nothing in this section shall be construed to prohibit payment of a fee to:

(I) An attorney for services actually rendered;

(II) A title insurance company to its duly appointed agent for services actually performed in the issuance of a policy of title insurance;

(III) A lender to its duly appointed agent for services actually performed in the making of a loan.

(f) Nothing in this section shall be construed to prohibit payment to any person of:

(I) A bona fide salary or compensation or other payment for goods or facilities actually furnished or for services actually performed;

(II) A fee pursuant to cooperative brokerage and referral arrangements or agreements between real estate brokers.

(g) It shall not be a violation of this section for an affiliated business arrangement:

(I) To require a buyer, borrower, or seller to pay for the services of any attorney, credit reporting agency, or real estate appraiser chosen by the lender to represent the lender's interest in a real estate transaction; or

(II) If an attorney or law firm represents a client in a real estate transaction and issues or arranges for the issuance of a policy of title insurance in the transaction directly as agent or through a separate corporate title insurance agency that may be established by that attorney or law firm and operated as an adjunct to his or her law practice.

(h) No person shall be liable for a violation of this section if the person proves by a preponderance of the evidence that the violation was not intentional and resulted from a bona fide error notwithstanding maintenance of procedures that are reasonably adopted to avoid the error.

(3) On and after July 1, 2006, a licensee shall disclose at the time the licensee enters into or changes an affiliated business arrangement, in a form and manner acceptable to the commission, the names of all affiliated business arrangements to which the licensee is a party. The disclosure shall include the physical locations of the affiliated businesses.

(4) On and after July 1, 2006, an employing broker, in a form and manner acceptable to the commission, shall at least annually disclose the names of all affiliated business arrangements to which the employing broker is a party. The disclosure shall include the physical locations of the affiliated businesses.

(5) The commission may promulgate rules concerning the creation and conduct of an affiliated business arrangement, including, but not limited to, rules defining what constitutes a sham affiliated business arrangement. The commission shall adopt the rules, policies, or guidelines issued by the United States department of housing and urban development concerning the federal "Real Estate Settlement Procedures Act of 1974", as amended, 12 U.S.C. sec. 2601 et seq. Rules adopted by the commission shall be at least as stringent as the federal rules and shall ensure that consumers are adequately informed about affiliated business arrangements. The commission shall consult with the insurance commissioner pursuant to section 10-11-124 (2), concerning rules, policies, or guidelines the insurance commissioner adopts concerning affiliated business arrangements. Neither the rules promulgated by the insurance commissioner nor the commission may create a conflicting regulatory burden on an affiliated business arrangement.

(6) The division of real estate may share information gathered during an investigation of an affiliated business arrangement with the division of insurance.

§ 12-10-219, C.R.S. Hearing – administrative law judge – review – rules.

Editor's note: *This section is similar to former §12-61-114 as it existed prior to 2019.*

(1) Except as otherwise provided in this section, all proceedings before the commission with respect to disciplinary actions and denial of licensure under this part 2 and part 4 of this article 10 and certifications issued under part 5 of this article 10 shall be conducted by an administrative law judge pursuant to the provisions of sections 24-4-104 and 24-4-105.

(2) The proceedings shall be held in the county where the commission has its office or in such other place as the commission may designate. If the licensee is an employed broker, the commission shall also notify the broker employing the licensee by mailing, by first-class mail, a copy of the written notice required under section 24-4-104 (3) to the employing broker's last-known business address.

(3) An administrative law judge shall conduct all hearings for denying, suspending, or revoking a license or certificate on behalf of the commission, subject to appropriations made to the department of personnel. Each administrative law judge shall be appointed pursuant to part 10 of article 30 of title 24. The administrative law judge shall conduct the hearing pursuant to the provisions of sections 24-4-104 and 24-4-105. No license shall be denied, suspended, or revoked until the commission has made its decision by a majority vote.

(4) The decision of the commission in any disciplinary action or denial of licensure under this section is subject to review by the court of appeals by appropriate proceedings under section 24-4-106 (11). In order to effectuate the purposes of parts 2, 4, and 5 of this article 10, the commission has the power to promulgate rules pursuant to article 4 of title 24. The commission may appear in court by its own attorney.

(5) Pursuant to the proceeding, the court has the right, in its discretion, to stay the execution or effect of any final order of the commission; but a hearing shall be held affording the parties an opportunity to be heard for the purpose of determining whether the public health, safety, and welfare would be endangered by staying the commission's order. If the court determines that the order should be stayed, it shall also determine at the hearing the amount of the bond and adequacy of the surety, which bond shall be conditioned upon the faithful performance by the petitioner of all obligations as a real estate broker and upon the prompt payment of all damages arising from or caused by the delay in the taking effect of or enforcement of the order complained of and for all costs that may be assessed or required to be paid in connection with the proceedings.

(6) In any hearing conducted by the commission in which there is a possibility of the denial, suspension, or revocation of a license because of the conviction of a felony or of a crime involving moral turpitude, the commission shall be governed by the provisions of section 24-5-101.

§ 12-10-220, C.R.S. Rules.

Editor's note: *This section is similar to former §12-61-114.5 as it existed prior to 2019.*

All rules adopted or amended by the commission are subject to sections 24-4-103 (8)(c) and (8)(d) and 24-34-104 (6)(b).

§ 12-10-221, C.R.S. Broker remuneration.

Editor's note: *This section is similar to former §12-61-117 as it existed prior to 2019.*

It is unlawful for a real estate broker registered in the commission office as in the employ of another broker to accept a commission or valuable consideration for the performance of any of the acts specified in this part 2 from any person except the broker's employer, who shall be a licensed real estate broker.

§ 12-10-222, C.R.S. Acts of third parties – broker's liability.

Editor's note: *This section is similar to former §12-61-118 as it existed prior to 2019.*

Any unlawful act or violation of any of the provisions of this part 2 upon the part of an employee, officer, or member of a licensed real estate broker shall not be cause for disciplinary action against a real estate broker, unless it appears to the satisfaction of the commission that the real estate broker had actual knowledge of the unlawful act or violation or had been negligent in the supervision of employees.

* ### *§ 12-10-223, C.R.S. Violations.*

Editor's note: *This section is similar to former §12-61-119 as it existed prior to 2019.*

[Editor's note: This version of this section is effective until March 1, 2022.] Any natural person, firm, partnership, limited liability company, association, or corporation violating the provisions of this part 2 by acting as real estate broker in this state without having obtained a license or by acting as real estate broker after the broker's license has been revoked or during any period for which the license may have been suspended is guilty of a misdemeanor and, upon conviction thereof, if a natural person, shall be punished by a fine of not more than five hundred dollars, or by imprisonment in the county jail for not more than six months, or by both such fine and imprisonment and, if an entity, shall be punished by a fine of not more than five thousand dollars. A second violation, if by a natural person, shall be punishable by a fine of not more than one thousand dollars, or by imprisonment in the county jail for not more than six months, or by both such fine and imprisonment.

[Editor's note: This version of this section is effective March 1, 2022.] Any natural person, firm, partnership, limited liability company, association, or corporation violating the provisions of this part 2 by acting as real estate broker in this state without having obtained a license or by acting as real estate broker after the broker's license has been revoked or during any period for which the license may have been suspended commits a class 2 misdemeanor.

§ 12-10-224, C.R.S. Subpoena compelling attendance of witnesses and production of records and documents.

Editor's note: *This section is similar to former §12-61-120 as it existed prior to 2019.*

The commission, the director, or the administrative law judge appointed for hearings may issue a subpoena compelling the attendance and testimony of witnesses and the production of books, papers, or records pursuant to an investigation or hearing of the commission. The subpoenas shall be served in the same manner as subpoenas issued by district courts and shall be issued without discrimination between public or private parties requiring the attendance of witnesses and the production of documents at hearings. If a person fails or refuses to obey a subpoena issued by the commission, the director, or the appointed administrative law judge, the commission may petition the district court having jurisdiction for issuance of a subpoena in the premises, and the court shall, in a proper case, issue its subpoena. Any person who refuses to obey a subpoena shall be punished as provided in section 12-10-225.

* ### *§ 12-10-225, C.R.S. Failure to obey subpoena – penalty.*

Editor's note: *This section is similar to former §12-61-121 as it existed prior to 2019.*

[Editor's note: This version of this section is effective until March 1, 2022.] Any person who willfully fails or neglects to appear and testify or to produce books, papers, or records required by subpoena, duly served upon him or her in any matter conducted under parts 2 and 5 of this article 10, is guilty of a misdemeanor and, upon conviction thereof, shall be punished by a fine of twenty-five dollars, or imprisonment in the county jail for not more than thirty days for each such offense, or by

both such fine and imprisonment. Each day a person so refuses or neglects constitutes a separate offense.

[Editor's note: This version of this section is effective March 1, 2022.] Any person who willfully fails or neglects to appear and testify or to produce books, papers, or records required by subpoena, duly served upon him or her in any matter conducted under parts 2 and 5 of this article 10 commits a petty offense. Each day a person so refuses or neglects constitutes a separate offense.

§ 12-10-226, C.R.S. Powers of commission – injunctions.

Editor's note: *This section is similar to former §12-61-122 as it existed prior to 2019.*

The commission may apply to a court of competent jurisdiction for an order enjoining any act or practice that constitutes a violation of parts 2 and 5 of this article 10, and, upon a showing that a person is engaging or intends to engage in any such act or practice, an injunction, restraining order, or other appropriate order shall be granted by the court regardless of the existence of another remedy therefor. Any notice, hearing, or duration of any injunction or restraining order shall be made in accordance with the provisions of the Colorado rules of civil procedure.

§ 12-10-227, C.R.S. Repeal of part – subject to review.

Editor's note: *This section is similar to former §12-61-123 as it existed prior to 2019.*

This part 2 is repealed, effective September 1, 2026. Before the repeal, the division, including the commission, is scheduled for review in accordance with section 24-34-104.

C. Part 3 – Brokers' Commissions

§ 12-10-301, C.R.S. When entitled to commission.

Editor's note: *This section is similar to former §12-61-201 as it existed prior to 2019.*

No real estate agent or broker is entitled to a commission for finding a purchaser who is ready, willing, and able to complete the purchase of real estate as proposed by the owner until the same is consummated or is defeated by the refusal or neglect of the owner to consummate the same as agreed upon.

§ 12-10-302, C.R.S. Objections on account of title.

Editor's note: *This section is similar to former §12-61-202 as it existed prior to 2019.*

No real estate agent or broker is entitled to a commission when a proposed purchaser fails or refuses to complete his or her contract of purchase because of defects in the title of the owner, unless the owner, within a reasonable time, has the defects corrected by legal proceedings or otherwise.

§ 12-10-303, C.R.S. When owner must perfect title.

Editor's note: *This section is similar to former §12-61-203 as it existed prior to 2019.*

The owner shall not be required to begin legal or other proceedings for the correction of a title until the agent or broker secures from the proposed purchaser an enforceable contract in writing, binding him or her to complete the purchase whenever the defects in the title are corrected.

§ 12-10-304, C.R.S. Referral fees – conformity with federal law required – remedies for violation – definitions.

Editor's note: *This section is similar to former §12-61-203.5 as it existed prior to 2019.*

(1) A person licensed under part 2, 3, or 5 of this article 10 shall not pay or receive a referral fee except in accordance with the federal "Real Estate Settlement Procedures Act of 1974", as

amended, 12 U.S.C. sec. 2601 et seq., and unless reasonable cause for payment of the referral fee exists. A reasonable cause for payment means:

(a) An actual introduction of business has been made;

(b) A contractual referral fee relationship exists; or

(c) A contractual cooperative brokerage relationship exists.

(2) (a) No person shall interfere with the brokerage relationship of a licensee.

(b) As used in this subsection (2):

(I) "Brokerage relationship" means a relationship entered into between a broker and a buyer, seller, landlord, or tenant under which the broker engages in any of the acts set forth in section 12-10-201 (6). A brokerage relationship is not established until a written brokerage agreement is entered into between the parties or is otherwise established by law.

(II) "Interfere with the brokerage relationship" means demanding a referral fee from a licensee without reasonable cause.

(III) "Referral fee" means any fee paid by a licensee to any person or entity, other than a cooperative commission offered by a listing broker to a selling broker or vice versa.

(3) Any person aggrieved by a violation of any provision of this section may bring a civil action in a court of competent jurisdiction. The prevailing party in any such action shall be entitled to actual damages and, in addition, the court may award an amount up to three times the amount of actual damages sustained as a result of any such violation plus reasonable attorney fees.

§ 12-10-305, C.R.S. Repeal of part – subject to review.

Editor's note: *This section is similar to former §12-61-204 as it existed prior to 2019.*

This part 3 is repealed, effective September 1, 2026. Before the repeal, this part 3 is scheduled for review in accordance with section 24-34-104.

D. Part 4 – Brokerage Relationships

§ 12-10-401, C.R.S. Legislative declaration.

Editor's note: *This section is similar to former §12-61-801 as it existed prior to 2019.*

(1) The general assembly finds, determines, and declares that the public will best be served through a better understanding of the public's legal and working relationships with real estate brokers and by being able to engage any such real estate broker on terms and under conditions that the public and the real estate broker find acceptable. This includes engaging a broker as a single agent or transaction-broker. Individual members of the public should not be exposed to liability for acts or omissions of real estate brokers that have not been approved, directed, or ratified by the individuals. Further, the public should be advised of the general duties, obligations, and responsibilities of the real estate broker they engage.

(2) This part 4 is enacted to govern the relationships between real estate brokers and sellers, landlords, buyers, and tenants in real estate transactions.

§ 12-10-402, C.R.S. Definitions.

Editor's note: *This section is similar to former §12-61-802 as it existed prior to 2019.*

As used in this part 4, unless the context otherwise requires:

(1) "Broker" shall have the same meaning as set forth in section 12-10-201 (6), except as otherwise specified in this part 4.

(2) "Customer" means a party to a real estate transaction with whom the broker has no brokerage relationship because the party has not engaged or employed a broker.

(3) (a) "Designated broker" means an employing broker or employed broker who is designated in writing by an employing broker to serve as a single agent or transaction-broker for a seller, landlord, buyer, or tenant in a real estate transaction.

(b) "Designated broker" does not include a real estate brokerage firm that consists of only one licensed natural person.

(4) "Dual agent" means a broker who, with the written informed consent of all parties to a contemplated real estate transaction, is engaged as a limited agent for both the seller and buyer or both the landlord and tenant.

(5) "Limited agent" means an agent whose duties and obligations to a principal are only those set forth in section 12-10-404 or 12-10-405, with any additional duties and obligations agreed to pursuant to section 12-10-403 (5).

(6) "Single agent" means a broker who is engaged by and represents only one party in a real estate transaction. A single agent includes the following:

(a) "Buyer's agent", which means a broker who is engaged by and represents the buyer in a real estate transaction;

(b) "Landlord's agent", which means a broker who is engaged by and represents the landlord in a leasing transaction;

(c) "Seller's agent", which means a broker who is engaged by and represents the seller in a real estate transaction; and

(d) "Tenant's agent", which means a broker who is engaged by and represents the tenant in a leasing transaction.

(7) "Subagent" means a broker engaged to act for another broker in performing brokerage tasks for a principal. The subagent owes the same obligations and responsibilities to the principal as does the principal's broker.

(8) "Transaction-broker" means a broker who assists one or more parties throughout a contemplated real estate transaction with communication, interposition, advisement, negotiation, contract terms, and the closing of the real estate transaction without being an agent or advocate for the interests of any party to the transaction. Upon agreement in writing pursuant to section 12-10-403 (2) or a written disclosure pursuant to section 12-10-408 (2)(c), a transaction-broker may become a single agent.

§ 12-10-403, C.R.S. Relationships between brokers and the public – definition – rules.

Editor's note: *This section is similar to former §12-61-803 as it existed prior to 2019.*

(1) When engaged in any of the activities enumerated in section 12-10-201 (6), a broker may act in any transaction as a single agent or transaction-broker. The broker's general duties and obligations arising from that relationship shall be disclosed to the seller and the buyer or to the landlord and the tenant pursuant to section 12-10-408.

(2) A broker shall be considered a transaction-broker unless a single agency relationship is established through a written agreement between the broker and the party or parties to be represented by the broker.

(3) A broker may work with a single party in separate transactions pursuant to different relationships including, but not limited to, selling one property as a seller's agent and working with that seller in buying another property as a transaction-broker or buyer's agent, but only if the broker complies with this part 4 in establishing the relationships for each transaction.

(4) (a) A broker licensed pursuant to part 2 of this article 10, whether acting as a single agent or transaction-broker, may complete standard forms for use in a real estate transaction, including standard forms intended to convey personal property as part of the real estate transaction, when a broker is performing the activities enumerated or referred to in section 12-10-201 (6) in the transaction.

(b) As used in this subsection (4), "standard form" means:

(I) A form promulgated by the real estate commission for current use by brokers, also referred to in this section as a "commission-approved form";

(II) A form drafted by a licensed Colorado attorney representing the broker, employing broker, or brokerage firm, so long as the name of the attorney or law firm and the name of the broker, employing broker, or brokerage firm for whom the form is prepared are included on the form itself;

(III) A form provided by a party to the transaction if the broker is acting in the transaction as either a transaction-broker or as a single agent for the party providing the form to the broker, so long as the broker retains written confirmation that the form was provided by a party to the transaction;

(IV) A form prescribed by a governmental agency, a quasi-governmental agency, or a lender regulated by state or federal law, if use of the form is mandated by the agency or lender;

(V) A form issued with the written approval of the Colorado Bar Association or its successor organization and specifically designated for use by brokers in Colorado, so long as the form is used within any guidelines or conditions specified by the Colorado Bar Association or successor organization in connection with the use of the form;

(VI) A form used for disclosure purposes only, if the disclosure does not purport to waive or create any legal rights or obligations affecting any party to the transaction and if the form provides only information concerning either:

(A) The real estate involved in the transaction specifically; or

(B) The geographic area in which the real estate is located generally;

(VII) A form prescribed by a title company that is providing closing services in a transaction for which the broker is acting either as a transaction-broker or as a single agent for a party to the transaction; or

(VIII) A letter of intent created or prepared by a broker, employing broker, or brokerage firm, so long as the letter of intent states on its face that it is nonbinding and creates no legal rights or obligations.

(c) A broker shall use a commission-approved form when such a form exists and is appropriate for the transaction. A broker's use of any standard form described in subsection (4)(b)(III) or (4)(b)(IV) of this section must be limited to inserting transaction-specific information within the form. In using standard forms described in subsection (4)(b)(II), (4)(b)(V), (4)(b)(VI), (4)(b)(VII), or (4)(b)(VIII) of this section, the broker may also advise the parties as to effects thereof, and the broker's use of those standard forms must be appropriate for the transaction and the circumstances in which they are used. In any transaction described in this subsection (4), the broker shall advise the parties that the forms have important legal consequences and that the parties should consult legal counsel before signing the forms.

(5) Nothing contained in this section shall prohibit the public from entering into written contracts with any broker that contain duties, obligations, or responsibilities that are in addition to those specified in this part 4.

(6) (a) If a real estate brokerage firm has more than one licensed natural person, the employing broker or an individual broker employed or engaged by that employing broker shall be designated to work with the seller, landlord, buyer, or tenant as a designated broker. The employing broker may designate more than one of its individual brokers to work with a seller, landlord, buyer, or tenant.

(b) The brokerage relationship established between the seller, landlord, buyer, or tenant and a designated broker, including the duties, obligations, and responsibilities of that relationship, shall not extend to the employing broker nor to any other broker employed or engaged by that employing broker who has not been so designated and shall not extend to the firm, partnership, limited liability company, association, corporation, or other entity that employs the broker.

(c) A real estate broker may have designated brokers working as single agents for a seller or landlord and a buyer or tenant in the same real estate transaction without creating dual agency for the employing real estate broker, or any broker employed or engaged by that employing real estate broker.

(d) An individual broker may be designated to work for both a seller or landlord and a buyer or tenant in the same transaction as a transaction-broker for both, as a single agent for the seller or landlord treating the buyer or tenant as a customer, or as a single agent for a buyer or tenant treating the seller or landlord as a customer, but not as a single agent for both. The applicable designated broker relationship shall be disclosed in writing to the seller or landlord and buyer or tenant in a timely manner pursuant to rules promulgated by the real estate commission.

(e) A designated broker may work with a seller or landlord in one transaction and work with a buyer or tenant in another transaction.

(f) When a designated broker serves as a single agent pursuant to section 12-10-404 or 12-10-405, there shall be no imputation of knowledge to the employing or employed broker who has not been so designated.

(g) The extent and limitations of the brokerage relationship with the designated broker shall be disclosed to the seller, landlord, buyer, or tenant working with that designated broker pursuant to section 12-10-408.

(7) No seller, buyer, landlord, or tenant shall be vicariously liable for a broker's acts or omissions that have not been approved, directed, or ratified by the seller, buyer, landlord, or tenant.

(8) Nothing in this section shall be construed to limit the employing broker's or firm's responsibility to supervise licensees employed by the broker or firm nor to shield the broker or firm from vicarious liability.

§ 12-10-404, C.R.S. Single agent engaged by seller or landlord.

Editor's note: *This section is similar to former §12-61-804 as it existed prior to 2019.*

(1) A broker engaged by a seller or landlord to act as a seller's agent or a landlord's agent is a limited agent with the following duties and obligations:

(a) To perform the terms of the written agreement made with the seller or landlord;

(b) To exercise reasonable skill and care for the seller or landlord;

(c) To promote the interests of the seller or landlord with the utmost good faith, loyalty, and fidelity, including, but not limited to:

(I) Seeking a price and terms that are acceptable to the seller or landlord; except that the broker shall not be obligated to seek additional offers to purchase the property while the property is subject to a contract for sale or to seek additional offers to lease the property while the property is subject to a lease or letter of intent to lease;

(II) Presenting all offers to and from the seller or landlord in a timely manner regardless of whether the property is subject to a contract for sale or a lease or letter of intent to lease;

(III) Disclosing to the seller or landlord adverse material facts actually known by the broker;

(IV) Counseling the seller or landlord as to any material benefits or risks of a transaction that are actually known by the broker;

(V) Advising the seller or landlord to obtain expert advice as to material matters about which the broker knows but the specifics of which are beyond the expertise of the broker;

(VI) Accounting in a timely manner for all money and property received; and

(VII) Informing the seller or landlord that the seller or landlord shall not be vicariously liable for the acts of the seller's or landlord's agent that are not approved, directed, or ratified by the seller or landlord;

(d) To comply with all requirements of this article 10 and any rules promulgated pursuant to this article 10; and

(e) To comply with any applicable federal, state, or local laws, rules, regulations, or ordinances including fair housing and civil rights statutes or regulations.

(2) The following information shall not be disclosed by a broker acting as a seller's or landlord's agent without the informed consent of the seller or landlord:

(a) That a seller or landlord is willing to accept less than the asking price or lease rate for the property;

(b) What the motivating factors are for the party selling or leasing the property;

(c) That the seller or landlord will agree to financing terms other than those offered;

(d) Any material information about the seller or landlord unless disclosure is required by law or failure to disclose the information would constitute fraud or dishonest dealing; or

(e) Any facts or suspicions regarding circumstances that may psychologically impact or stigmatize any real property pursuant to section 38-35.5-101.

(3) (a) A broker acting as a seller's or landlord's agent owes no duty or obligation to the buyer or tenant; except that a broker shall, subject to the limitations of section 38-35.5-101, concerning psychologically impacted property, disclose to any prospective buyer or tenant all adverse material facts actually known by the broker. The adverse material facts may include but shall not be limited to adverse material facts pertaining to the title and the physical condition of the property, any material defects in the property, and any environmental hazards affecting the property that are required by law to be disclosed.

(b) A seller's or landlord's agent owes no duty to conduct an independent inspection of the property for the benefit of the buyer or tenant and owes no duty to independently verify the accuracy or completeness of any statement made by the seller or landlord or any independent inspector.

(4) A seller's or landlord's agent may show alternative properties not owned by the seller or landlord to prospective buyers or tenants and may list competing properties for sale or lease and not be deemed to have breached any duty or obligation to the seller or landlord.

(5) A designated broker acting as a seller's or landlord's agent may cooperate with other brokers but may not engage or create any subagents.

§ 12-10-405, C.R.S. Single agent engaged by buyer or tenant.

Editor's note: *This section is similar to former §12-61-805 as it existed prior to 2019.*

(1) A broker engaged by a buyer or tenant to act as a buyer's or tenant's agent shall be a limited agent with the following duties and obligations:

(a) To perform the terms of the written agreement made with the buyer or tenant;

(b) To exercise reasonable skill and care for the buyer or tenant;

(c) To promote the interests of the buyer or tenant with the utmost good faith, loyalty, and fidelity, including, but not limited to:

(I) Seeking a price and terms that are acceptable to the buyer or tenant; except that the broker shall not be obligated to seek other properties while the buyer is a party to a contract to purchase property or while the tenant is a party to a lease or letter of intent to lease;

(II) Presenting all offers to and from the buyer or tenant in a timely manner regardless of whether the buyer is already a party to a contract to purchase property or the tenant is already a party to a contract or a letter of intent to lease;

(III) Disclosing to the buyer or tenant adverse material facts actually known by the broker;

(IV) Counseling the buyer or tenant as to any material benefits or risks of a transaction that are actually known by the broker;

(V) Advising the buyer or tenant to obtain expert advice as to material matters about which the broker knows but the specifics of which are beyond the expertise of the broker;

(VI) Accounting in a timely manner for all money and property received; and

(VII) Informing the buyer or tenant that the buyer or tenant shall not be vicariously liable for the acts of the buyer's or tenant's agent that are not approved, directed, or ratified by the buyer or tenant;

(d) To comply with all requirements of this article 10 and any rules promulgated pursuant to this article 10; and

(e) To comply with any applicable federal, state, or local laws, rules, regulations, or ordinances including fair housing and civil rights statutes or regulations.

(2) The following information shall not be disclosed by a broker acting as a buyer's or tenant's agent without the informed consent of the buyer or tenant:

(a) That a buyer or tenant is willing to pay more than the purchase price or lease rate for the property;

(b) What the motivating factors are for the party buying or leasing the property;

(c) That the buyer or tenant will agree to financing terms other than those offered;

(d) Any material information about the buyer or tenant unless disclosure is required by law or failure to disclose the information would constitute fraud or dishonest dealing; or

(e) Any facts or suspicions regarding circumstances that would psychologically impact or stigmatize any real property pursuant to section 38-35.5-101.

(3) (a) A broker acting as a buyer's or tenant's agent owes no duty or obligation to the seller or landlord; except that the broker shall disclose to any prospective seller or landlord all adverse material facts actually known by the broker including but not limited to adverse material facts concerning the buyer's or tenant's financial ability to perform the terms of the transaction and whether the buyer intends to occupy the property to be purchased as a principal residence.

(b) A buyer's or tenant's agent owes no duty to conduct an independent investigation of the buyer's or tenant's financial condition for the benefit of the seller or landlord and owes no duty to independently verify the accuracy or completeness of statements made by the buyer or tenant or any independent inspector.

(4) A buyer's or tenant's agent may show properties in which the buyer or tenant is interested to other prospective buyers or tenants without breaching any duty or obligation to the buyer or tenant. Nothing in this section shall be construed to prohibit a buyer's or tenant's agent from showing competing buyers or tenants the same property and from assisting competing buyers or tenants in attempting to purchase or lease a particular property.

(5) A broker acting as a buyer's or tenant's agent owes no duty to conduct an independent inspection of the property for the benefit of the buyer or tenant and owes no duty to independently verify the accuracy or completeness of statements made by the seller, landlord, or independent inspectors; except that nothing in this subsection (5) shall be construed to limit the broker's duties and obligations imposed pursuant to subsection (1) of this section.

(6) A broker acting as a buyer's or tenant's agent may cooperate with other brokers but may not engage or create any subagents.

§ 12-10-406, C.R.S. Dual agent.

Editor's note: *This section is similar to former §12-61-806 as it existed prior to 2019.*

A broker shall not establish dual agency with any seller, landlord, buyer, or tenant.

§ 12-10-407, C.R.S. Transaction-broker.

Editor's note: *This section is similar to former §12-61-807 as it existed prior to 2019.*

(1) A broker engaged as a transaction-broker is not an agent for either party.

(2) A transaction-broker shall have the following obligations and responsibilities:

(a) To perform the terms of any written or oral agreement made with any party to the transaction;

(b) To exercise reasonable skill and care as a transaction-broker, including, but not limited to:

(I) Presenting all offers and counteroffers in a timely manner regardless of whether the property is subject to a contract for sale or lease or letter of intent;

(II) Advising the parties regarding the transaction and suggesting that the parties obtain expert advice as to material matters about which the transaction-broker knows but the specifics of which are beyond the expertise of the broker;

(III) Accounting in a timely manner for all money and property received;

(IV) Keeping the parties fully informed regarding the transaction;

(V) Assisting the parties in complying with the terms and conditions of any contract including closing the transaction;

(VI) Disclosing to all prospective buyers or tenants any adverse material facts actually known by the broker including but not limited to adverse material facts pertaining to the title, the physical condition of the property, any defects in the property, and any environmental hazards affecting the property required by law to be disclosed;

(VII) Disclosing to any prospective seller or landlord all adverse material facts actually known by the broker including but not limited to adverse material facts pertaining to the buyer's or tenant's financial ability to perform the terms of the transaction and the buyer's intent to occupy the property as a principal residence; and

(VIII) Informing the parties that as seller and buyer or as landlord and tenant they shall not be vicariously liable for any acts of the transaction-broker;

(c) To comply with all requirements of this article 10 and any rules promulgated pursuant to this article 10; and

(d) To comply with any applicable federal, state, or local laws, rules, regulations, or ordinances including fair housing and civil rights statutes or regulations.

(3) The following information shall not be disclosed by a transaction-broker without the informed consent of all parties:

(a) That a buyer or tenant is willing to pay more than the purchase price or lease rate offered for the property;

(b) That a seller or landlord is willing to accept less than the asking price or lease rate for the property;

(c) What the motivating factors are for any party buying, selling, or leasing the property;

(d) That a seller, buyer, landlord, or tenant will agree to financing terms other than those offered;

(e) Any facts or suspicions regarding circumstances that may psychologically impact or stigmatize any real property pursuant to section 38-35.5-101; or

(f) Any material information about the other party unless disclosure is required by law or failure to disclose the information would constitute fraud or dishonest dealing.

(4) A transaction-broker has no duty to conduct an independent inspection of the property for the benefit of the buyer or tenant and has no duty to independently verify the accuracy or completeness of statements made by the seller, landlord, or independent inspectors.

(5) A transaction-broker has no duty to conduct an independent investigation of the buyer's or tenant's financial condition or to verify the accuracy or completeness of any statement made by the buyer or tenant.

(6) A transaction-broker may do the following without breaching any obligation or responsibility:

(a) Show alternative properties not owned by the seller or landlord to a prospective buyer or tenant;

(b) List competing properties for sale or lease;

(c) Show properties in which the buyer or tenant is interested to other prospective buyers or tenants; and

(d) Serve as a single agent or transaction-broker for the same or for different parties in other real estate transactions.

(7) There shall be no imputation of knowledge or information between any party and the transaction-broker or among persons within an entity engaged as a transaction-broker.

(8) A transaction-broker may cooperate with other brokers but shall not engage or create any subagents.

§ 12-10-408, C.R.S. Broker disclosures.

Editor's note: *This section is similar to former §12-61-808 as it existed prior to 2019.*

(1) (a) Any person, firm, partnership, limited liability company, association, or corporation acting as a broker shall adopt a written office policy that identifies and describes the relationships offered to the public by the broker.

(b) A broker shall not be required to offer or engage in any one or in all of the brokerage relationships enumerated in section 12-10-404, 12-10-405, or 12-10-407.

(c) Written disclosures and written agreements required by subsection (2) of this section shall contain a statement to the seller, landlord, buyer, or tenant that different brokerage relationships are available that include buyer agency, seller agency, or status as a transaction-broker. Should the seller, landlord, buyer, or tenant request information or ask questions concerning a brokerage relationship not offered by the broker pursuant to the broker's written office policy enumerated in subsection (1)(a) of this section, the broker shall provide to the party a written definition of that brokerage relationship that has been promulgated by the real estate commission.

(d) Disclosures made in accordance with this part 4 shall be sufficient to disclose brokerage relationships to the public.

(2) (a) (I) Prior to engaging in any of the activities enumerated in section 12-10-201 (6), a transaction-broker shall disclose in writing to the party to be assisted that the broker is not acting as agent for the party and that the broker is acting as a transaction-broker.

(II) As part of each relationship entered into by a broker pursuant to subsection (2)(a)(I) of this section, written disclosure shall be made that shall contain a signature block for the buyer, seller, landlord, or tenant to acknowledge receipt of the disclosure. The disclosure and acknowledgment, by itself, shall not constitute a contract with the broker. If the buyer, seller, landlord, or tenant chooses not to sign the acknowledgment, the broker shall note that fact on a copy of the disclosure and shall retain the copy.

(III) If the transaction-broker undertakes any obligations or responsibilities in addition to or different from those set forth in section 12-10-407, the obligations or responsibilities shall be disclosed in a writing that shall be signed by the involved parties.

(b) Prior to engaging in any of the activities enumerated in section 12-10-201 (6), a broker intending to establish a single agency relationship with a seller, landlord, buyer, or tenant shall enter into a written agency agreement with the party to be represented. The agreement shall disclose the duties and responsibilities specified in section 12-10-404 or 12-10-405, as applicable. Notice of the single agency relationship shall be furnished to any prospective party to the proposed transaction in a timely manner.

(c) (I) Prior to engaging in any of the activities enumerated in section 12-10-201 (6), a broker intending to work with a buyer or tenant as an agent of the seller or landlord shall provide a written disclosure to the buyer or tenant that shall contain the following:

(A) A statement that the broker is an agent for the seller or landlord and is not an agent for the buyer or tenant;

(B) A list of the tasks that the agent intends to perform for the seller or landlord with the buyer or tenant; and

(C) A statement that the buyer or tenant shall not be vicariously liable for the acts of the agent unless the buyer or tenant approves, directs, or ratifies the acts.

(II) The written disclosure required pursuant to subsection (2)(c)(I) of this section shall contain a signature block for the buyer or tenant to acknowledge receipt of the disclosure. The disclosure and acknowledgment, by itself, shall not constitute a contract with the broker. If the buyer or tenant does not sign the disclosure, the broker shall note that fact on a copy of the disclosure and retain the copy.

(d) A broker who has already established a relationship with one party to a proposed transaction shall advise at the earliest reasonable opportunity any other potential parties or their agents of the established relationship.

(e) (I) Prior to engaging in any of the activities enumerated in section 12-10-201 (6), the seller, buyer, landlord, or tenant shall be advised in any written agreement with a broker that the brokerage relationship exists only with the designated broker, does not extend to the employing broker or to any other brokers employed or engaged by the employing broker who are not so designated, and does not extend to the brokerage company.

(II) Nothing in this subsection (2)(e) shall be construed to limit the employing broker's or firm's responsibility to supervise licensees employed by the broker or firm nor to shield the broker or firm from vicarious liability.

§ 12-10-409, C.R.S. Duration of relationship.

Editor's note: *This section is similar to former §12-61-809 as it existed prior to 2019.*

(1) (a) The relationships set forth in this part 4 shall commence at the time that the broker is engaged by a party and shall continue until performance or completion of the agreement by which the broker was engaged.

(b) If the agreement by which the broker was engaged is not performed or completed for any reason, the relationship shall end at the earlier of the following:

(I) Any date of expiration agreed upon by the parties;

(II) Any termination or relinquishment of the relationship by the parties; or

(III) One year after the date of the engagement.

(2) (a) Except as otherwise agreed to in writing and pursuant to subsection (2)(b) of this section, a broker engaged as a seller's agent or buyer's agent owes no further duty or obligation after termination or expiration of the contract or completion of performance.

(b) Notwithstanding subsection (2)(a) of this section, a broker shall be responsible after termination or expiration of the contract or completion of performance for the following:

(I) Accounting for all money and property related to and received during the engagement; and

(II) Keeping confidential all information received during the course of the engagement that was made confidential by request or instructions from the engaging party unless:

(A) The engaging party grants written consent to disclose the information;

(B) Disclosure of the information is required by law; or

(C) The information is made public or becomes public by the words or conduct of the engaging party or from a source other than the broker.

(3) Except as otherwise agreed to in writing, a transaction-broker owes no further obligation or responsibility to the engaging party after termination or expiration of the contract for performance or completion of performance; except that the broker shall account for all money and property related to and received during the engagement.

§ 12-10-410, C.R.S. Compensation.

Editor's note: *This section is similar to former §12-61-810 as it existed prior to 2019.*

(1) In any real estate transaction, the broker's compensation may be paid by the seller, the buyer, the landlord, the tenant, a third party, or by the sharing or splitting of a commission or compensation between brokers.

(2) Payment of compensation shall not be construed to establish an agency relationship between the broker and the party who paid the compensation.

(3) A seller or landlord may agree that a transaction-broker or single agent may share the commission or other compensation paid by the seller or landlord with another broker.

(4) A buyer or tenant may agree that a single agent or transaction-broker may share the commission or other compensation paid by the buyer or tenant with another broker.

(5) A buyer's or tenant's agent shall obtain the written approval of the buyer or tenant before the agent may propose to the seller's or landlord's agent that the buyer's or tenant's agent be compensated by sharing compensation paid by the seller or landlord.

(6) Prior to entering into a brokerage or listing agreement or a contract to buy, sell, or lease, the identity of those parties, persons, or entities paying compensation or commissions to any broker shall be disclosed to the parties to the transaction.

(7) A broker may be compensated by more than one party for services in a transaction if those parties have consented in writing to such multiple payments prior to entering into a contract to buy, sell, or lease.

§ 12-10-411, C.R.S. Violations.

Editor's note: *This section is similar to former §12-61-811 as it existed prior to 2019.*

The violation of any provision of this part 4 by a broker constitutes an act pursuant to section 12-10-217 (1)(m) for which the real estate commission may investigate and take administrative action against any such broker pursuant to sections 12-10-217 and 12-10-219.

Chapter 2:
Real Estate Broker Rules and Regulations

An * in the left margin indicates a change in the statute, rule, or text since the last publication of the manual.

DEPARTMENT OF REGULATORY AGENCIES
DIVISION OF REAL ESTATE
COLORADO REAL ESTATE COMMISSION

4 CCR 725-1

RULES OF THE COLORADO REAL ESTATE COMMISSION

Chapter 1: Definitions

1.1. Active: A current, valid License that allows a person, firm, partnership, limited liability company, association, or corporation to engage in Real Estate Brokerage Services.

1.2. Advertise or Advertising: The promotion, solicitation, or representation of Real Estate Brokerage Services requiring a License. Advertising may include, but is not limited to, business cards, brochures, websites, signage, property flyers, mailings (paper or electronic), social media, letterhead, email signatures, and contract documents. A uniform resource locator (URL) and an email address are not considered Advertising for purposes of Rule 6.10 so long as they are not directly used to promote or solicit Real Estate Brokerage Services.

1.3. Affiliated Business Arrangement: Has the same meaning pursuant to section 12-10-218(1), C.R.S.

1.4. Anniversary Year Cycle: The three-year licensing period commencing on a Broker's initial date of licensure (anniversary date) and expiring three (3) years later on the same date. The anniversary date may be any day of the calendar year.

1.5. Applicant: A person or entity seeking a License from the Commission to perform the duties pursuant to section 12-10-201(6)(a), C.R.S.

1.6. Associate Broker: A Broker who holds an Associate Broker level license and works under the supervision of an Employing Broker. Associate Brokers may have an Independent Broker or Employing Broker level license even if they are still acting as an Associate Broker under the supervision of an Employing Broker.

1.7. Broker: Any person licensed by the Commission to perform Real Estate Brokerage Services regardless if the Broker is licensed as an Associate Broker, Independent Broker, or Employing Broker.

1.8. Brokerage Firm: Any sole proprietor, partnership, limited liability company, corporation, or any other authorized entity licensed by the Commission to employ or engage Brokers to perform Real Estate Brokerage Services. All Brokerage Firms that employ or engage Associate Brokers must have an Active Employing Broker.

1.9. Brokerage Relationship: Has the same meaning pursuant to section 12-10-304(2)(b)(I), C.R.S.

1.10. Calendar Year Cycle: This is the three-year licensing period commencing on January 1 of year one and expiring on December 31 of year three. All Brokers will eventually be on a Calendar Year Cycle for their License renewal.

1.11. Commercial Real Estate: Any real property other than real property containing one to four residential units, single-family or multi-family residential units including condominiums, townhouses, or homes in a subdivision when such real estate is sold, leased, or otherwise conveyed on a unit-by-unit basis even though the units may be part of a larger building or parcel of real property containing more than four residential units as defined pursuant to section 38-22.5-102(2), C.R.S.

1.12. Commission: The Colorado Real Estate Commission as defined pursuant to section 12-10-201(1), C.R.S.

1.13. Consumer: A member of the public that has sought or is seeking to engage Real Estate Brokerage Services provided by a Broker. A Consumer is a buyer, seller, tenant, or landlord, as applicable.

1.14. Customer: Has the same meaning pursuant to section 12-10-402(2), C.R.S.

1.15. Deemed Complete: An Applicant has submitted a complete and satisfactory application in compliance with sections 12-10-202 and 12-10-203, C.R.S. that includes the Fee and the accompanying required documentation as set forth in Chapters 2 and 3 of these Rules.

1.16. Designated Broker: Has the same meaning pursuant to section 12-10-402(3), C.R.S.

1.17. Director: The Director of the Division as defined pursuant to section 12-10-101(1), C.R.S.

1.18. Distance Learning: Education courses offered outside the traditional classroom setting in which the instructor and learner are separated by distance and/or time.

1.19. Division: The Division of Real Estate as defined pursuant to section 12-10-101(2), C.R.S.

1.20. Duplicate: A legible photocopy, carbon copy, facsimile, or electronic copies which contain a digital or electronic signature as defined pursuant to section 24-71-101(1), C.R.S.

1.21. Electronic Media: The method of communicating information that are in an electronic format rather than a paper format. Electronic Media may include, but is not limited to, websites, electronic mailings, social Media such as Twitter and Facebook, banner advertisements, and YouTube.

1.22. Electronic Record: A record generated, communicated, received, or stored by electronic means as defined to pursuant to section 24-71.3-102(7), C.R.S.

1.23. Employing Broker: Has the same meaning pursuant to section 12-10-201(2), C.R.S.

1.24. Expired: A License that was not renewed prior to the last day of the license cycle and is no longer valid for a person or entity to perform any Real Estate Brokerage Services. Such persons cannot hold themselves out to the public as Brokers and such entities cannot Advertise as Brokerage Firms.

1.25. Fee: The prescribed non-refundable fee as set by the Division.

1.26. Initial License or Initial Licensure: The first license granted by the Commission to an Applicant pursuant to sections 12-10-202 and 12-10-203, C.R.S.

1.27. Inactive: A Broker who holds a valid License shown in the Commission's records as being Inactive is not permitted to engage in Real Estate Brokerage Services. To maintain licensure on Inactive status, a Broker must still continue to renew their License as set forth in Chapter 3 of these Rules.

1.28. Independent Broker: A Broker either holding an Independent Broker level license or Employing Broker level license acting as their own Brokerage Firm or sole proprietor and not employing or supervising any Associate Brokers.

1.29. Invalid Payment: If the Fees accompanying any application including Fees for the recovery fund, renewals and transfers made to the Division are paid for by check and the check is not immediately paid upon presentment to the bank upon which the check was drawn, or if payment is submitted in any other manner, and payment is denied, rescinded or returned as invalid, the application will be immediately canceled. The application will only be reinstated if the Division has received valid payment of all application Fees together with any fees incurred by the Division including the fee required by state fiscal rules for clerical services necessary for reinstatement.

1.30. Jurisdiction: For purposes of Chapter 2 of these Rules, all 50 states, the District of Columbia, Guam, Puerto Rico, and the U.S. Virgin Islands.

1.31. License: A Broker's or Brokerage Firm's license issued by the Commission pursuant to section 12-10-203, C.R.S.

* 1.32. Listing Contract: An agreement between a Brokerage Firm and a Consumer in which a Broker licensed with the Brokerage Firm is designated to provide Real Estate Brokerage Services to the Consumer. Listing Agreements include: Exclusive Tenant Contract, Exclusive Right to Sell, Exclusive Right to Lease, Exclusive Right to Buy, and Management Agreements.

1.33. Management Agreement: An agreement between a Brokerage Firm and an owner of a property in which a Broker licensed with the Brokerage Firm is designated to provide Property Management Services on behalf of the owner.

1.34. Money Belonging to Others: Money Belonging to Others which is accepted by the Broker or Brokerage Firm for deposit in the Broker's or Brokerage Firm's Trust or Escrow Account that includes, but is not limited to, money received in connection with Management Agreements, partnerships, limited liability companies, syndications, lease agreements, advance fee contracts, guest deposits for short term rentals, rental receipts, security deposits, earnest money deposits, or Money Belonging to Others received for any other purpose.

1.35. New Associate Broker: An Associate Broker with less than two (2) years of accumulative Active experience.

1.36. Office Policy Manual: The Manual required for all Employing Brokers or the Employing Broker's Brokerage Firm, which contains certain policies and procedures.

1.37. Petitioner: For the purposes of implementing the provisions of Chapter 8 of these Rules, any person who has filed with the Commission a petition or has been granted leave to intervene by the Commission for a declaratory order pursuant to section 24-4-105(11), C.R.S. and as set forth in Chapter 8 of these Rules.

1.38. Property Management: An on-going relationship between a Brokerage Firm and an owner of a property in which the Brokerage Firm is designated to provide Property Management Services.

1.39. Property Management Services: The activities performed in leasing and subsequent management of a property on behalf of an owner that are pursuant to section 12-10-201(6), C.R.S. and further described in the Management Agreement.

1.40. Real Estate Brokerage Services: Any of the activities pursuant to section 12-10-201(6)(a), C.R.S. when performed on behalf of a Consumer.

1.41. Real Estate Licensing Examination: An examination that consists of two (2) parts; a national part and a Colorado part as set forth in Rule 2.2.

1.42. Real Estate School: Has the same meaning pursuant to section 23-64-103(20), C.R.S.

1.43. RESPA – The Real Estate Settlement Procedures Act of 1974, set forth in 12 U.S.C. 2601, et. seq. (Act), effective June 1, 2018, incorporated by reference in compliance with section 24-4-103(12.5), C.R.S. and does not include any later amendments or editions to the Act. A certified copy of the Act is readily available for public inspection at the Office of the Colorado Real Estate Commission at 1560 Broadway, Suite 925, Denver, Colorado. The Act may also be examined at the internet website of the Consumer Bureau of Financial Protection (CFPB) at *www.consumerfinance.gov*. The CFPB may also be contacted at 1700 G. Street, NW, Washington, D.C. 20552 or by telephone at (202) 435-7000.

1.44. Recognized Depository: Any bank, savings and loan association, or credit union that accepts deposits or shares insured by the Federal Deposit Insurance Corporation (FDIC) or the National Credit Union Administration (NCUA) respectively.

1.45. Reinstatement or Reinstating or Reinstate: Has the same meaning pursuant to section 12-10-212(4)(a)(III), C.R.S.

1.46. Single Agent: Has the same meaning pursuant to section 12-10-402(6), C.R.S.

1.47. Standard Form: Has the meaning pursuant to section 12-10-403(4), C.R.S. and also as set forth in Rule 7.1.

1.48. Supervisory Broker: A Broker, such as a managing broker, team lead, office manager, etc., who has been delegated in writing by an Employing Broker to assume some of the Employing Broker's duties and responsibilities as set forth in Rule 6.3.

1.49. Team: Two (2) or more Brokers within a Brokerage Firm that cooperate on an on-going basis to conduct a substantial portion of their Real Estate Brokerage Services together.

1.50. Temporary License: Has the same meaning pursuant to section 12-10-203(6)(c), C.R.S.

1.51. Things of Value: Monetary considerations as well as the exchange of tangible, non-monetary assets.

1.52. Trademark: Any logo, service mark, or other identifying mark used in conjunction with a Brokerage Firm's legal name or Trade Name. Trademarks may be registered with the Colorado Secretary of State pursuant to section 7-70-102, C.R.S. As an example, the brokerage "A Better Choice Real Estate" uses a logo bearing the initials "ABC". The logo is used to identify the Brokerage Firm and the Real Estate Brokerage Services that it provides to Consumers; therefore, it would be the trademark for the Brokerage Firm.

1.53. Trade Name: The name under which a Brokerage Firm does business other than the Brokerage Firm's legal name. Any Trade Name used by a Brokerage Firm must be on file with the Commission and must be filed with the Colorado Secretary of State pursuant to section 7-71-101, C.R.S. For example, a Brokerage Firm is licensed with the Commission under its legal name of "Colorado Real Estate Group LLC". However, the Brokerage is also a franchise of "International Realty" and does business under the Trade Name "International Realty of Colorado".

1.54. Transaction-Broker: Has the same meaning pursuant to section 12-10-402(8), C.R.S.

1.55. Transition Period: The two-year licensing period plus a partial year commencing on the anniversary date when a Broker's license expires in the years of 2018, 2019, or 2020 and expiring two (2) years plus the remaining days in the third year to reach December 31. The length of the Transition Period is dependent on the anniversary date and could be as long as three (3) years or as short as two (2) years and one day.

1.56. Trust or Escrow Account: Any checking, demand, passbook or statement account, which has, at a minimum, the following elements:

A. The account is separate and contains only Money Belonging to Others;

B. The account is custodial and fiduciary;

C. All funds are available on demand; and

D. The account is held with a Recognized Depository.

1.57. Trust or Escrow Accounting Equation: The reconciled trust or escrow bank account cash balance must equal the sum total of the individual ledger balance for each owner at any given point in time.

1.58. Unlicensed On-Site Manager: An unlicensed person who fills in blanks, as a scrivener, on lease forms, shows prospective tenants available units, quotes rental prices established by the owner or Broker, arranges for maintenance, and collects monies, including security deposits and rents. A Brokerage Firm which employs an Unlicensed On-Site Manager must do so either as a regularly salaried employee or as an independent contractor, and pay the Unlicensed On-Site Manager through the Brokerage Firm. The salary may include rent value or other non-commission income.

1.59. Viewable Page: A page that may or may not scroll beyond the border of the screen and includes the use of frame pages.

Chapter 2: Licensure Requirements

2.1. Educational Requirements

A. Associate Broker Level License

In order to obtain an Associate Broker level license, the Applicant must successfully complete the educational requirements pursuant to section 12-10-203(4)(a), C.R.S.:

1. A degree from an accredited college or university with a major course of study in real estate; or
2. Proof of completion of one hundred sixty-eight (168) hours of classroom instruction or equivalent Distance Learning hours from any accredited college or university, or any Real Estate School for the following courses:
   a. Real Estate Law and Real Estate Practice: 48 hours;
   b. Colorado Real Estate Contracts: 48 hours;
   c. Real Estate Closings: not less than 24 hours;
   d. Trust Accounts and Record Keeping: not less than 8 hours;
   e. Current Legal Issues: not less than 8 hours; and
   f. Practical Application: not less than 32 hours.

B. Employing Broker Level License

An Applicant desiring an Employing Broker level license must successfully complete the twenty-four (24) hours of classroom instruction or equivalent Distance Learning hours in Brokerage Administration pursuant to section 12-10-203(5)(c)(II), C.R.S.

C. Educational Principles

Completion of courses of study approved by the Commission as set forth in subsections A.2. and B. of this Rule, whether through classroom or Distance Learning, must be based upon educational principles acceptable to the Commission.

D. Course Audits

The Commission may audit courses set forth in subsection A.2. and B. of this Rule at any time and at no cost. The Commission may request all instructional materials and student attendance records from each accredited college or university, or Real Estate School for any approved course of study. The purpose of the audit is to ensure adherence to the approved course of study by verifying the course material and instruction are consistent with acceptable educational principles; and that instruction is provided in a manner that the desired learning objectives are met. Failure to comply with statutes and these Rules may result in the removal of the course provider, instructor, and/or the course from the approved provider list.

2.2. Examination Requirements

A. Real Estate Licensing Examination

The Real Estate Licensing Examination is administered and developed by a third party testing service and consists of two (2) parts, which include:

1. a national part; and
2. a Colorado part.

B. Test Administration Standards

Examinees must comply with the standards of test administration established by the Commission and the testing service provider.

C. Educational Requirements Completed Prior to Real Estate Licensing Examination

Educational requirements as set forth in Rule 2.1.A. must be completed and proof filed in a manner as prescribed by the Commission prior to taking the Real Estate Licensing Examination and applying for an Associate Broker level license.

D. Duly Qualified Applicants

The Real Estate Licensing Examination will be given to duly qualified Applicants; however, one (1) instructor from each accredited college or university or Real Estate School may take the examination one (1) time during any twelve (12) month period to conduct research for course content.

E. Retake Failed Parts of Real Estate Licensing Examination

If an Applicant fails one or both parts of the Real Estate Licensing Examination, the Applicant may retake the failed part(s) at a subsequent time.

F. Valid Testing Scores

A passing score for either part of the Real Estate Licensing Examination is valid for one (1) year. Failure to submit a complete application within one (1) year will result in the examination grade being invalid.

G. No Certification of Examination Results until Licensed

The Commission will not certify to any person, state, or agency any information concerning the results of any examination as it pertains to any person who has taken the Real Estate Licensing Examination unless such person is or has been licensed as a Broker.

2.3. Criminal Background Check Requirements

Pursuant to section 12-10-203(1)(b)(I), C.R.S., an Applicant must submit a set of fingerprints to the Colorado Bureau of Investigation for the purpose of conducting a state and national criminal history record check prior to submitting an application to the Division. Fingerprints must be submitted to the Colorado Bureau of Investigation for processing in a manner acceptable to the Colorado Bureau of Investigation. Fingerprints must be readable and all personal identification data completed in a manner satisfactory to the Colorado Bureau of Investigation. The Commission may, however, acquire a name-based criminal history record check for an Applicant who has twice submitted to a fingerprint-based criminal history record check and whose fingerprints are unclassifiable.

2.4. Certified License History Requirements

An Applicant who has held a real estate license (e.g. real estate salesperson or broker) in any other Jurisdiction must file a certification of licensing history issued by each Jurisdiction where the Applicant is currently or was previously licensed to practice real estate with their application. The certificate must bear a date of not more than ninety (90) days prior to the submission date of the application.

2.5. Experience Requirements

A. Associate Broker Level License

Pursuant to section 12-10-203, C.R.S., there are no prescribed experience requirements to apply for a Colorado Associate Broker level license.

B. Independent Broker Level License

Pursuant to section 12-10-203(5)(c)(I), C.R.S., each Applicant for a Colorado Independent Broker level license must have held an Associate Broker level license on Active status for at least two (2) years preceding the date of application.

C. Employing Broker Level License

1. Held a Real Estate Broker License on December 31, 1996

Pursuant to section 12-10-203(5)(c), C.R.S., a Broker that held a current and valid Colorado Real Estate Broker's license on December 31, 1996 does not need to demonstrate additional experience and knowledge to act as an Employing Broker.

2. Issued an Employing Broker Level License prior to January 1, 2018 but after December 31, 1996

   Pursuant to section 12-10-203(5)(c)(III), C.R.S., an Applicant that was issued an Employing Broker level license prior to January 1, 2018 but after December 31, 1996 must demonstrate additional experience and knowledge by satisfying one of the following requirements:

   a. The Applicant must have held an Active Employing Broker level license for at least two (2) years within the five (5) year period immediately preceding January 1, 2019;
   b. Proof of completion of classroom instruction or equivalent Distance Learning hours for the Employing Broker Refresher Course; or
   c. The Applicant meets the experience requirements as set forth in subsection C.3. of this Rule.

3. Applying for an Employing Broker Level License on or after January 1, 2018

   Pursuant to section 12-10-203(5)(c)(III), C.R.S., each Applicant for an Employing Broker level license who applies on or after January 1, 2018 must submit evidence satisfactory to the Commission that the Applicant has practiced as an Active Broker, as appropriate to the Broker's area of supervision, for at least two (2) years within the five (5) year period immediately preceding the date of application.

   a. The evidence must qualify the Applicant for a total of at least fifty (50) points having accumulated within the five (5) year period immediately preceding the date of application, based on the following point system:
      i. Each full year that the Applicant has practiced as an Employing Broker is worth ten (10) points.
      ii. Each full year that the Applicant was delegated supervisory authority from an Employing Broker that included responsibility for ensuring compliance with the Commission statutes and these Rules, and that ensured responsibility for the Brokerage Firm (excluding any mentorship) is worth five (5) points. A copy of the detailed executed delegation of authority must be included.
      iii. Each hour of an approved and designated continuing education course in the Broker's area of expertise completed after January 1, 2018, is worth one (1) point. This educational point category cannot exceed twenty (20) points.
      iv. Each completed or closed residential sales transaction is worth three (3) points.
      v. Each completed or closed commercial sales transaction is worth six (6) points.
      vi. Each completed or closed vacant land sales transaction is worth six (6) points.
      vii. Each administered commercial property management transaction is worth four (4) points.
      viii. Each administered residential property management transaction with two (2) points.
      ix. Each completed or closed commercial lease transaction is worth two (2) points.
      x. Each completed or closed residential lease transaction is worth one (1) point.

xi. Each completed or closed time share sales transaction is worth two (2) points.

b. Each Applicant must complete and submit the prescribed worksheet or form developed by the Commission and supporting documents with the application for an Employing Broker level license.

2.6. Associate Broker Level License Requirements

Applicants applying for an Associate Broker level license must satisfy the licensure requirements as set forth in one of the following:

A. New License

Pursuant to section 12-10-203(4)(a), C.R.S, an Applicant who has never held a real estate license in Colorado or any other Jurisdiction must complete the following requirements:

1. Proof of completion of the educational requirements as set forth in Rule 2.1.A.;
2. Successful completion of the Real Estate Licensing Examination as set forth in Rule 2.2.A.; and
3. Submission of fingerprints as set forth in Rule 2.3.

B. Licensed Attorney

Pursuant to section 12-10-203(10), C.R.S., an Applicant who is a licensed attorney in Colorado or any other Jurisdiction must complete the following requirements:

1. Proof of completion of twelve (12) hours of classroom instruction or equivalent Distance Learning hours for the following courses:
   a. Real Estate Closings as set forth in Rule 2.1.A.2.c.; and
   b. Trust Accounts and Record Keeping as set forth in Rule 2.1.A.2.d.
2. Successful completion of the Real Estate Licensing Examination as set forth in Rule 2.2.A.;
3. Submission of fingerprints as set forth in Rule 2.3.; and
4. Proof of law license.

C. Expired or Less than Two Years as a Real Estate Salesperson from Another Jurisdiction

Pursuant to section 12-10-203(4)(c), C.R.S., an Applicant holding a real estate salesperson license from another Jurisdiction that is either expired or held for less than two (2) years must complete the following requirements:

1. Proof of completion of classroom instruction or equivalent Distance Learning hours for the following courses:
   a. Colorado Real Estate Contracts as set forth in Rule 2.1.A.2.b.;
   b. Real Estate Closings as set forth in Rule 2.1.A.2.c.;
   c. Trust Accounts and Record Keeping as set forth in Rule 2.1.A.2.d.;
   d. Current Legal Issues as set forth in Rule 2.1.A.2.e.; and
   e. Practical Application as set forth in Rule 2.1.A.2.f.
2. Successful completion of the Real Estate Licensing Examination as set forth in Rule 2.2.A.;
3. Submission of fingerprints as required in Rule 2.3.; and
4. Submission of certified license history as set forth in Rule 2.4.

D. Expired or Less than Two Years as a Real Estate Broker from another Jurisdiction

Pursuant to section 12-10-203(4)(b), C.R.S., an Applicant holding a real estate broker license from another Jurisdiction that is either expired or held for less than two (2) years must complete the following requirements:

1. Proof of completion of classroom instruction or equivalent Distance Learning hours for the following courses:
   a. Colorado Real Estate Contracts as set forth in Rule 2.1.A.2.b.; and
   b. Real Estate Closings as set forth in Rule 2.1.A.2.c.
2. Successful completion of the Real Estate Licensing Examination as set forth in Rule 2.2.A.;
3. Submission of fingerprints as required in Rule 2.3.; and
4. Submission of certified license history as set forth in Rule 2.4.

E. Current Real Estate License from Another Jurisdiction Held for Two or More Years

Pursuant to section 12-10-203(5)(b), C.R.S., an Applicant holding a real estate license (e.g. real estate salesperson or broker), whether on Active or Inactive status, for two (2) or more years from another Jurisdiction must complete the following requirements:

1. There are no prescribed educational requirements;
2. Successful completion of the Real Estate Licensing Examination as set forth in Rule 2.2.A.2.;
3. Submission of fingerprints as set forth in Rule 2.3.; and
4. Submission of certified license history as set forth in Rule 2.4.

F. Expired Colorado Associate Broker Level License Issued After January 1, 1997

Pursuant to section 12-10-203, C.R.S., an Applicant who was issued a Colorado Associate Broker level license on or after January 1, 1997 that is expired beyond the three-year right to reinstate must complete the following requirements:

1. Verification by the Commission that the Associate Broker level license was issued by the Commission on or after January 1, 1997 to confirm prior completion of the educational requirements as set forth in Rule 2.1.A.;
2. Successful completion of the Real Estate Licensing Examination as set forth in Rule 2.2.A.; and
3. Submission of fingerprints as set forth in Rule 2.3.

G. Expired Colorado Salesperson License Issued on or before December 31, 1996

Pursuant to section 12-10-203, C.R.S., an Applicant who was issued a Colorado real estate salesperson license on or before December 31, 1996 that is expired beyond the three-year right to reinstate must complete the following requirements:

1. Proof of completion of classroom instruction or equivalent Distance Learning hours for the following courses:
   a. Colorado Real Estate Contracts as set forth in Rule 2.1.A.2.b.;
   b. Real Estate Closings as set forth in Rule 2.1.A.2.c.;
   c. Trust Accounts and Record Keeping as set forth in Rule 2.1.A.2.d.;
   d. Current Legal Issues as set forth in Rule 2.1.A.2.e.; and
   e. Practical Application as set forth in Rule 2.1.A.2.f.
2. Successful completion of the Real Estate Licensing Examination as set forth in Rule 2.2.A.; and
3. Submission of fingerprints as set forth in Rule 2.3.

H. Expired Colorado Real Estate Broker License Issued on or before December 31, 1996

Pursuant to section 12-10-203, C.R.S., an Applicant who was issued a Colorado real estate broker license on or before December 31, 1996 that is expired beyond the three-year right to reinstate must complete the following requirements:

1. Proof of completion of classroom instruction or equivalent Distance Learning hours for the following courses:
    a. Colorado Real Estate Contracts as set forth in Rule 2.1.A.2.b.; and
    b. Real Estate Closings as set forth in Rule 2.1.A.2.c.
2. Successful completion of the Real Estate Licensing Examination as set forth in Rule 2.2.A.; and
3. Submission of fingerprints as set forth in Rule 2.3.

2.7. Independent Broker Level License Requirements

A. Initial Licensure as an Independent Broker Level License

An Applicant with at least two (2) years of Active licensure as a Broker in either Colorado or another Jurisdiction preceding the date of application may apply for an Independent Broker level license by completing the applicable licensure requirements as set forth in Rule 2.6.

B. Upgrade to an Independent Broker Level License

Pursuant to section 12-10-203(5)(c)(I), C.R.S, an Applicant may apply to upgrade to an Independent Broker level license as set forth in Rule 2.5.B.

2.8. Employing Broker Level License Requirements on or after January 1, 2018

A. Initial Licensure as an Employing Broker Level License

An Applicant with at least two (2) years of Active licensure as a Broker in either Colorado or another Jurisdiction preceding the date of application may apply for an Employing Broker level license by completing the applicable licensure requirements as set forth in Rule 2.6. and subsection B. of this Rule.

B. Upgrade to an Employing Broker Level License

Pursuant to section 12-10-203(5)(c), C.R.S, an Applicant who applies to upgrade to an Employing Broker level license on or after January 1, 2018 must complete the following requirements:

1. Educational Requirement

   Proof of completion of classroom instruction or equivalent Distance Learning hours for Brokerage Administration as set forth in Rule 2.1.B.

2. Experience Requirement

   Submission of evidence as set forth in Rule 2.5.C. that the Applicant has practiced as an Active Broker, as appropriate to the Broker's area of supervision, for at least two (2) years within the five (5) year period immediately preceding the date of application.

3. Criminal Background Check Requirement

   Submission of fingerprints as set forth in Rule 2.3. for any Applicants who did not submit fingerprints with their Initial License.

4. Certified License History

   For Applicants licensed in another Jurisdiction, submission of certified license history as set forth in Rule 2.4.

2.9. Broker Qualifications for Sole Proprietors

A. The Broker must have either an Independent Broker or Employing Broker level license.

B. A Broker licensed as a sole proprietorship must not adopt a trade name, which includes the following words: corporation, partnership, limited liability company, limited, incorporated, or the abbreviations thereof.

C. A Broker licensed as a sole proprietorship or as a sole proprietorship doing business under a trade name must be the sole owner of the Brokerage Firm. Otherwise, the Brokerage Firm will be considered as a partnership and the partnership must apply for a Broker's License pursuant to section 12-10-203(6), C.R.S. and as set forth in Rule 2.10.

2.10. Broker Qualifications for Partnerships, Corporations, or Limited Liability Companies

A. When an Independent Broker or Employing Broker submits an application to qualify a partnership, corporation, or limited liability company as a Brokerage Firm, the Applicant must certify:

1. The partnership, corporation, or limited liability company has been properly registered with the Colorado Secretary of State and is in good standing, proof of which must be included with the application;
2. If an assumed or trade name is to be used, it has been properly filed with and accepted by the Colorado Secretary of State, proof of which must be included with the application; and
3. The Independent Broker or Employing Broker has been appointed as the Independent Broker or Employing Broker by the appropriate authority of the applicable Brokerage Firm.

B. Notice of Termination of the Employing Broker

The Employing Broker of a licensed corporation, partnership, or limited liability company must immediately notify the Commission in a manner acceptable to the Commission, of the Employing Broker's termination of employment with such licensed corporation, partnership, or limited liability company, or upon the Employing Broker's failure to continue to comply with section 12-10-203, C.R.S. and these Rules. Upon such notification, the Employing Broker and all Associate Brokers will be placed on Inactive status.

C. Temporary Employing Broker Level License

A Temporary License may be issued to a corporation, partnership or limited liability company to prevent hardship. No application for a Temporary License will be approved unless the designated person satisfies the licensure requirements of an Employing Broker. A Temporary License is valid for up to ninety (90) days. No more than two (2) Temporary Licenses may be issued to any corporation, partnership, or limited liability company, whether consecutive or not, during any eighteen (18) month period.

Chapter 3: Licensure, Renewal, License Status, and Insurance

3.1. Application Requirements

A. Applying for an Initial License

1. An Applicant must successfully complete the requisite educational requirements as set forth in Chapter 2 of these Rules;
2. An Applicant must take and successfully pass the appropriate part(s) of the Real Estate Licensing Examination as set forth in Chapter 2 of these Rules;
3. An Applicant must submit a set of fingerprints to the Colorado Bureau of Investigation as set forth in Rule 2.3.;
4. An Applicant must acquire errors and omissions insurance as set forth in Rule 3.9. prior to obtaining an Active License;
5. An Applicant must complete the appropriate Commission created application and submit the required documentation, such as course completion certificates or college transcripts, certified license history, and proof of errors and omissions insurance; and
6. An Applicant must pay the Fee.

B. Upgrading a License Level

1. An Applicant must successfully complete the educational and experience requirements as set forth in Chapter 2 of these Rules;
2. An Applicant must complete the appropriate Commission created application and submit any relevant required documentation, such as course completion certificates and experience requirements, as set forth in Chapter 2 of these Rules; and
3. An Applicant must pay the Fee.

3.2. Invalid Payment

If the Fees accompanying any application made to the Commission are paid for by check and the check is not immediately paid upon presentment to the bank upon which the check was drawn, or if payment is submitted in any other manner and payment is denied, rescinded, or returned as invalid, the application will not be deemed complete and will be canceled. The application, renewal, or transfer may be reinstated only at the discretion of the Commission and upon full payment of any Fees together with payment of the fee required by state fiscal rules for the clerical services necessary for reinstatement within thirty (30) days of the Division's notification of an incomplete application.

3.3. Review of Application Completeness

All applications will be reviewed by the Division for completeness of all required documentation and Fee. If the application is deemed incomplete by the Division, the Applicant will be notified in writing of the deficiencies identified within the application and will have thirty (30) days to provide the documentation; otherwise, the application will be canceled and the Fee will be forfeited.

3.4. Applicants with Prior or Pending Criminal Record

Pursuant to sections 12-10-203, and 24-5-101, C.R.S., Applicants who have at any time in the past been convicted of, entered a plea of guilty to, entered a plea of nolo contendere, received a deferred judgment and sentence to a misdemeanor (excluding misdemeanor traffic violations) or a felony or any like municipal code violation, or has such charges pending must submit with their application the required documentation as listed below. If the required documentation is no longer available, the Applicant must provide written confirmation by the appropriate authority that such documentation is no longer available. For any charges or convictions which have been dismissed, expunged, or sealed, the Applicant must include court document(s) evidencing the dismissal, expungement, or sealing of the criminal case(s). Failure to provide the required documentation within the time frame as set forth in Rule 3.3. will result in the cancellation of the application and forfeiture of the Fee. In addition to the required documentation, Applicants may submit supplemental documentation as listed below to demonstrate their rehabilitation, truthfulness, honesty, and good moral character for consideration by the Commission.

A. Required Documentation includes:

1. Court case disposition, registry of action, or a case action summary, which must include the following information:
   a. Offense(s) convicted of;
   b. Statute(s) or municipal code(s) violated;
   c. Classification(s) of offense(s) (i.e. felony or misdemeanor);
   d. Date of conviction;
   e. Date of sentencing;
   f. Sentencing terms; and
   g. Status of case.

i. If the sentencing and probation terms have been completed, the status of case should show as closed or dismissed.

ii. If the sentencing and probation terms have not been completed, documentation must be submitted that shows current compliance with the sentencing and probation terms. Proof of current compliance should include a letter from the parole or probation officer and, if applicable, a payment history from the court showing a current account balance of payment.

2. Police Officer's report(s), arrest report(s), or incident report(s);
3. A signed written explanation of the circumstances surrounding each violation and, including the statement attesting that "I have no other criminal violations either past or pending, other than those I have stated on the application";
4. If applying for an Active License, a signed written statement from the Employing Broker that indicates their understanding of the nature of the Applicant's violation(s) and willingness to supervise the Applicant if the License is granted by the Commission. The statement must also include the level of supervision, either a Reasonable or a High-Level of Supervision, that the Employing Broker feels is appropriate based upon the Applicant's violation(s). The Employing Broker may include additional comments relating to the Applicant's rehabilitation, truthfulness, honesty, and good moral character for the Commission's consideration; and
5. Any other information or documentation that the Commission deems necessary.

B. Supplemental Documentation includes:

1. Employment history for the preceding five (5) years;
2. Letter(s) of recommendation; and
3. A personal written statement that demonstrates and evidences the Applicant's rehabilitation, truthfulness, honesty, and good moral character.

3.5. Applicants with Past or Pending Professional Disciplinary Action(s)

Pursuant to sections 12-10-202 and 12-10-203(3), C.R.S., an Applicant who has any past or pending disciplinary actions of a real estate license or any other professional license from Colorado or any other jurisdiction must submit with their application any of the following information and documentation as listed below that is relevant and available to the Applicant. If the required documentation is no longer available or accessible, the Applicant must provide written confirmation by the appropriate authority that such documentation is no longer available or the reasons why the document is not accessible. Failure to provide the required documentation within the time frame as set forth in Rule 3.3. will result in the cancellation of the application and forfeiture of the Fee.

A. Any final agency order(s);

B. Any consent order(s);

C. Any stipulation(s);

D. Any investigative report(s); and

E. A signed written explanation of the circumstances surrounding each disciplinary action.

3.6. Issuance of a License

A. Submission of an application does not guarantee issuance of a License. Applicants must not represent themselves as a Broker until a License has been issued by the Commission.

B. Once an application is deemed complete and not subject to further review as set forth in Rules 3.4. and 3.5., the Commission will issue a License within ten (10) business days after review of satisfactory results from the fingerprint-based criminal history record check, if applicable.

C. Each Applicant who has successfully satisfied the licensure requirements as set forth in Chapter 2 of these Rules will be issued an Initial License expiring December 31 of the year of issuance.

D. A License may be issued on an Inactive status.

E. The License of a Broker whose application has been approved by the Commission subject to the receipt of errors and omission insurance and/or the identification of an Employing Broker for supervision will be issued on an Inactive status if such proof is not submitted within thirty (30) days after written notification by the Commission.

F. The Commission may refuse to issue a License to a partnership, limited liability company, or corporation if the name of said corporation, partnership, or limited liability company is the same as that of any person or entity whose License has been suspended or revoked or is so similar as to be easily confused with that of the suspended or revoked person or entity by members of the general public.

G. An Independent Broker or Employing Broker may adopt a Trade Name according to Colorado law and such Trade Name will respectively appear in the records of the Commission relating to the Independent Broker or Employing Broker. If an Employing Broker adopts a Trade Name, both the legal name and Trade Name will appear in the records of the Commission for the Associate Brokers.

H. No License will be issued to an Independent or Employing Broker under a Trade Name, corporate name, partnership name, or limited liability company name which is identical to another licensed Independent Broker's or Employing Broker's Trade Name, corporate, partnership, or limited liability company name.

3.7. Denial of a License

A. The Commission may deny an application for licensure pursuant to section 12-10-203(3), C.R.S.

B. If an Applicant for licensure is denied by the Commission for any reason, the Applicant will be informed of the denial and the reasons for the denial in writing.

3.8. Preliminary Advisory Opinions

Prior to an application for licensure, a person may request that the Commission issue a preliminary advisory opinion regarding the potential effect that previous professional conduct, criminal conviction(s), plea(s) of guilt or nolo contendere, deferred judgment(s) and sentence for criminal offense(s), or violation(s) of the real estate license law may have on a future formal application for licensure. A person requesting such an opinion is not an Applicant for licensure. The Commission may, at its sole discretion, issue an opinion which will not be binding on the Commission; is not appealable; and will not limit the authority of the Commission to investigate a future application for licensure. However, if the Commission issues a favorable advisory opinion, the Commission may elect to adopt such advisory opinion as the final decision of the Commission without further investigation or hearing. The issuance of a negative or unfavorable opinion will not prohibit a person from submitting an application for licensure. A person requesting an opinion must do so in a form prescribed by the Commission. Such form must be supported and documented by, without limitation, the following:

A. Pending or Past Criminal Record

The required and supplemental documentation as set forth in Rule 3.4. for any pending or past criminal record.

B. Pending or Past Professional Disciplinary Action(s)

The documentation as set forth in Rule 3.5. for any pending or past professional conduct.

3.9. Errors and Omissions Insurance

Pursuant to section 12-10-204, C.R.S., every Active Broker, including Brokerage Firms with more than one (1) Broker, must have in effect a policy of errors and omissions insurance to cover all acts requiring a License.

A. The Division must enter into a contract with a qualified insurance carrier to make available a group policy of insurance ("Commission Insurance Policy") under the following terms and conditions:

1. The insurance carrier is licensed or authorized by the Colorado Division of Insurance to write policies of errors and omissions insurance in this State.
2. The insurance carrier maintains an A.M. Best rating of "A-" or better.
3. The insurance carrier will collect premiums, maintain records and report names of those insured and a record of claims to the Commission on a timely basis and at no expense to the Division.
4. The insurance carrier has been selected through a competitive bidding process.
5. The contract and policy are in conformance with this Rule and all relevant Colorado statutory requirements.

B. The Commission Insurance Policy must provide, at a minimum, the following terms of coverage:

1. Coverage for all acts for which a License is required, except those illegal, fraudulent, or other acts which are normally excluded from such coverage.
2. That the coverage cannot be canceled by the insurance carrier except for nonpayment of the premium or in the event a Broker or Brokerage Firm becomes Inactive or is revoked or an Applicant is denied a License.
3. Pro-ration of premiums for coverage which is purchased during the course of a calendar year but with no provision for refunds of unused premiums.
4. Not less than one hundred thousand dollars ($100,000) coverage for each licensed person and entity per covered claim regardless of the number of Brokers or Brokerage Firms to which a settlement or claim may apply, not including costs of investigation and defense.
5. An annual aggregate limit of not less than three hundred thousand dollars ($300,000) per licensed Broker or Brokerage Firm, not including costs of investigation and defense.
6. Coverage for investigation and defense must be provided in addition to policy coverage limits.
7. A deductible amount for each occurrence of not more than one thousand dollars ($1,000) for claims and no deductible for legal expenses and defense.
8. The obligation of the insurance carrier to defend all covered claims and the ability of the insured Broker or Brokerage Firm to select counsel of choice subject to the written permission of the carrier, which must not be unreasonably withheld.
9. Coverage of a Broker's use of lock boxes, which coverage must not be less than twenty-five thousand dollars ($25,000) per occurrence.
10. The ability of a Broker or Brokerage Firm, upon payment of an additional premium, to obtain higher or excess coverage or to purchase additional coverage from the state carrier as may be determined by the carrier.
11. That coverage is individual and license specific and will cover the Broker or Brokerage Firm regardless of changes in Employing Broker.

12. The ability of a Broker or Brokerage Firm, upon payment of an additional premium to obtain an extended reporting period of not less than three hundred sixty-five (365) days.
13. A conformity endorsement allowing a Colorado resident Broker to meet the errors and omissions insurance requirement for a real estate license in another group mandated jurisdiction without the need to purchase separate coverage in that jurisdiction.
14. Prior acts coverage will be offered to Brokers or Brokerage Firms with continuous past coverage.

C. Brokers, Brokerage Firms, or Applicants may obtain errors and omissions coverage independent of the Commission Insurance Policy from any insurance carrier subject to the following terms and conditions:

1. For both individual and entity/group policies, the insurance carrier is in compliance with all applicable statutes and rules set forth by the Colorado Division of Insurance and is licensed or authorized to write policies of errors and omissions insurance in this State.
2. The insurance provider maintains an A.M. Best rating of "A-" or better.
3. Individual policies must, at a minimum, comply with the following conditions and the insurance carrier must certify compliance in an affidavit issued to the insured Broker, Brokerage Firm, or Applicant in a form specified by the Commission. Insurance carrier agrees to immediately notify the Commission of any cancellation or lapse in coverage. Independent individual coverage must provide, at a minimum, the following:
   a. The contract and policy are in conformance with all relevant Colorado statutory requirements.
   b. Coverage includes all acts for which a License is required, except those illegal, fraudulent, or other acts that are normally excluded from such coverage.
   c. Coverage cannot be canceled by the insurance carrier except for nonpayment of the premium or in the event a Broker or Brokerage Firm becomes Inactive or is revoked or an Applicant is denied a License. Cancellation notice must be provided in a manner that complies with section 10-4-109.7(1), C.R.S.
   d. Coverage is for not less than one hundred thousand dollars ($100,000) for each licensed Broker and Brokerage Firm per covered claim, with an annual aggregate limit of not less than three hundred thousand dollars ($300,000) per licensed person and entity, not including costs of investigation and defense. Coverage for investigation and defense must be provided in addition to policy coverage limits.
   e. A deductible amount for each occurrence of not more than one thousand dollars ($1,000) for claims and the insurance carrier must look to the insured for payment of any deductible.
   f. Payment of defense costs by the insurance carrier must be on a first dollar basis. That is, the insured is not required to pay anything towards the cost of defense of any claim or complaint.
   g. The ability of a Broker or Brokerage Firm, upon payment of an additional premium, to obtain an extended reporting period of not less than three hundred sixty-five (365) days within sixty (60) days of the initial coverage ending.
   h. Coverage of a Broker's use of lock boxes, which coverage must not be less than twenty-five thousand dollars ($25,000) per occurrence.

i. The obligation of the insurance carrier to defend all covered claims and the ability of the insured Broker or Brokerage Firm to select counsel of choice subject to the written permission of the carrier, which must not be unreasonably withheld.

j. Prior acts coverage must be offered to Brokers or Brokerage Firms with continuous past coverage.

k. Upon request, insurance carrier will execute an affidavit in a form and manner specified by the Commission attesting that the independent policy is in force and, at a minimum, complies with all relevant conditions set forth in this Rule and that the insurance carrier will immediately notify the Commission in writing of any cancellation or lapse in coverage of any independent policy.

4. For Brokerage Firms with independently carried firm coverage, all the requirements as set forth in subsection C.3. of this Rule will apply except subsections C.3.d. through e. and j. of this Rule, will be replaced with the following:

   a. The per claim limit must be not less than a million dollars ($1,000,000).

   b. The aggregate limit must be not less than a million dollars ($1,000,000).

   c. The maximum deductible amount for each occurrence must not exceed ten thousand dollars ($10,000) and the insurance carrier must look to the insured for payment of any deductible.

D. Applicants for licensure, activation, renewal, and Reinstatement must certify compliance with this Rule and section 12-10-204, C.R.S. in a manner prescribed by the Commission. Any Active Broker or Brokerage Firm who so certifies and fails to obtain errors and omissions coverage or to provide proof of continuous coverage, either through the state carrier or directly to the Commission, will be placed on Inactive status:

1. Immediately, if certification of current insurance coverage is not provided to the Commission; or

2. Immediately upon the expiration of any current insurance when certification of continued coverage is not provided.

3.10. Office

Every Independent Broker or Employing Broker residing in Colorado must maintain a place of business in this State, except for Associate Brokers or Brokers registered as Inactive.

3.11. Renewal

A. No Renewal Requirement for Brokerage Firms

Brokerage Firms are not required to renew their License; however, the Independent Broker or Employing Broker associated with the Brokerage Firm must renew as set forth in Rule 3.11.B.

B. Renewal Requirements for Brokers

1. Licensing Cycle for Renewal (Renewal Periods)

   Brokers will renew a License on a Calendar Year Cycle commencing on January 1 of year one and expiring on December 31 of year three.

2. Notification of Renewal

   Notification that a License will expire, unless renewed, will be sent to the electronic mail address on file with the Commission.

3. Renewal Application

   a. All Brokers, whether on Active or Inactive status, may renew their License beginning forty-five (45) days prior to the expiration date of their License by use of the renewal application form provided by the Commission.

b. Pay the renewal Fee.

c. Any Broker who has not submitted fingerprints to the Colorado Bureau of Investigation to be used to complete a one-time only criminal history record check must do so prior to renewal of an Active License. Fingerprints must be submitted to the Colorado Bureau of Investigation for processing in a manner acceptable to the Colorado Bureau of Investigation. Fingerprints must be readable and all personal identification data completed in a manner satisfactory to the Colorado Bureau of Investigation. The Commission may, however, acquire a name-based criminal history record check for an Applicant who has twice submitted to a fingerprint-based criminal history record check and whose fingerprints are unclassifiable. The renewed License will remain on Inactive status until the Commission has received and reviewed the results of a criminal record check.

3.12. Inactivation of License

A. A Broker may request that the Commission records show their License as Inactive until proper request for reactivation has been made.

B. It is the joint duty of both the Employing Broker and the Associate Broker to immediately notify the Commission when the employment of the Associate Broker terminates with the Brokerage Firm. Either party may give notice in a manner acceptable to the Commission. The party giving notice must notify the other party in person or in writing of the termination of employment.

C. A Broker whose License is on Inactive status must apply for renewal of such Inactive License and pay the renewal Fee.

D. A Broker whose License is on Inactive status may be compensated directly by a former Employing Broker for commissions earned during the term of employment when the Broker's License was on Active status.

3.13. Change in License Status

No changes in License status, whether Active or Inactive, will be made except in the manner acceptable to the Commission to affect such change and upon payment of the Fee for such change request.

3.14. Transfers

A. When an Associate Broker transfers to a different Brokerage Firm, the License must be transferred to the subsequent Employing Broker in the manner acceptable to the Commission to affect such transfer and upon payment of the Fee for such transfer request.

B. When a License has been transferred to a subsequent Employing Broker, an Associate Broker may be compensated directly by the former Employing Broker for commissions earned during that term of employment.

3.15. License Reinstatement

Brokers who failed to renew a License as set forth in Rule 3.11.B.3. may Reinstate the Expired License as follows :

A. If a proper application is made within thirty-one (31) days after the date of expiration of a License, by payment of the renewal Fee, the License will be issued as set forth in Rule 3.11.B.3.

B. If a proper application is made more than thirty-one (31) days but within one (1) year after the date of expiration of a License, by payment of the renewal Fee and payment of a reinstatement Fee equal to one-half (1/2) the renewal Fee, the reinstated License will be issued with an expiration date of three (3) years beginning from the expiration date of the prior expired License.

C. If a proper application is made more than one (1) year but within three (3) years after the date of expiration of a License, by payment of the renewal Fee and payment of a reinstatement Fee equal to the renewal Fee, the reinstated License will be issued with an expiration date of three (3) years beginning from the expiration date of the prior expired License.

Chapter 4: Continuing Education Requirement

4.1. Continuing Education Requirement

A. Brokers must satisfy the continuing education requirement for a licensing cycle prior to applying to renew an Active License, to activate an Inactive License, or to Reinstate an Expired License to Active status. The licensing cycles include: Anniversary Year, Calendar Year, and Transition Period.

B. Pursuant to section 12-10-213(4), C.R.S., Brokers applying for renewal of a License which expires on December 31 of the year in which it was first issued are not subject to the continuing education requirement pursuant to section 12-10-213(1)(a), C.R.S.

4.2. Methods for Satisfying Continuing Education

A. Brokers must satisfy the continuing education requirement for a licensing cycle through one (1) of the following options:

1. Brokers may complete the twelve (12) credit hours of continuing education pursuant to section 12-10-213(1)(a), C.R.S. and as set forth in subsection A.1. of this Rule in annual 4-hour increments developed by the Commission, the "Annual Commission Update". Brokers must also complete an additional twelve (12) credit hours of electives to meet the total 24-hour continuing education requirement during the licensing cycle in subject areas pursuant to section 12- 10-213(3), C.R.S. and as set forth in Rule 4.4.B.1. A Broker may not take the same version of the Annual Commission Update more than once.

2. During the Transition Period licensing cycle, Brokers may complete two (2) different versions of the Annual Commission Update for eight (8) credit hours of continuing education pursuant to section 12-10-213(1)(b), C.R.S. Brokers must also complete an additional sixteen (16) credit hours of electives to meet the total 24-hour continuing education requirement during the Transition Period in subject areas pursuant to section 12-10-213(3), C.R.S. and as set forth in Rule 4.4.B.1.

3. Brokers may complete the Commission approved 24-hour "Broker Reactivation Course". This option is only available to Brokers under one (1) of the following conditions:

   a. The Broker is currently Active and did not use the Broker Reactivation Course to satisfy the continuing education requirement in the previous licensing cycle; or

   b. The Broker is Inactive or Expired for an accumulative time period of up to thirty-six (36) months prior to activating an Inactive License or Reinstating an Expired License to Active status and unable to comply with the continuing education requirement as set forth in subsections A.1. or A.2. of this Rule.

4. Pass the Colorado portion of the Real Estate Licensing Examination as set forth in Rule 2.2.A.2.

5. Complete seventy-two (72) total hours of the educational requirements as set forth in Rules 2.1.A.2.b. and 2.1.A.2.c.

B. If a Broker cannot satisfy the continuing education requirement as set forth in subsections A.1. through A.3. of this Rule, the Broker must comply with the continuing education requirement as set forth in subsections A.4. or A.5. of this Rule prior to activating an Inactive License or Reinstating an Expired License to Active status.

4.3. Annual Commission Update Course Standards

A. Pursuant to section 12-10-213(2), C.R.S. and as set forth in Rule 4.2.A., the Annual Commission Update will be developed, presented by the Division, and furnished only to approved course providers. The course will be presented without any additional content by the course provider and/or instructor.

B. All course providers must apply annually for approval to offer the Annual Commission Update as set forth in Rule 4.6.B., except that the course outline as set forth in Rule 4.6.B.1. and course exam as set forth in Rule 4.6.B.2. will be furnished by the Commission.

C. Each Broker must complete the Annual Commission Update by achieving a passing score of seventy percent (70%) on a written or on-line course examination developed by the Commission. The Commission will provide an alternate examination for successive use by Brokers failing the end-of-course examination.

4.4. Standards for Continuing Education Courses

Courses approved for continuing education must meet the following standards:

A. Course Content

1. The course content must have been developed by persons qualified in the subject matter;
2. The content of the course must be current;
3. The course must maintain and improve a Broker's skill, knowledge, and competency in the real estate practice; and
4. The course must be at least one (1) hour increment in length, containing at least fifty (50) instructional minutes per one (1) hour increment.

B. Topics for Continuing Education Courses

1. Eligible Topics for Continuing Education Courses

Pursuant to section 12-10-213(3), C.R.S., courses approved for continuing education must include one (1) or more of the following topics:

a. Real Estate Law;
b. Property Exchanges;
c. Real Estate Contracts;
d. Real Estate Finance;
e. Real Estate Appraisal;
f. Real Estate Closing;
g. Real Estate Ethics;
h. Condominiums and Cooperatives;
i. Real Estate Time-Sharing;
j. Real Estate Marketing Principles;
k. Real Estate Construction;
l. Land Development;
m. Real Estate Energy Concerns;
n. Real Estate Geology;

o. Water and Waste Management;
p. Commercial Real Estate;
q. Real Estate Securities and Syndications;
r. Property Management;
s. Real Estate Computer Principles;
t. Brokerage Administration and Management;
u. Agency; and
v. Any other subject matter as approved by the Commission.

2. Ineligible Topics for Continuing Education Courses

The following types of courses will not qualify and be approved for continuing education:

a. Sales or marketing meetings conducted in the general course of a real estate brokerage practice;
b. Orientation, personal growth, self-improvement, self-promotion, or marketing sessions;
c. Motivational meetings or seminars; or
d. Examination preparation or exam technique courses.

C. Course Format

All continuing education courses may be offered and completed by classroom or Distance Learning.

4.5. Continuing Education Credit Requirements

A. A maximum of eight (8) hours of credit may be earned per day.

B. No course may be repeated for credit in the same calendar year.

C. Hours in excess of twenty-four (24) may not be carried forward to satisfy a subsequent licensing cycle.

D. Education stipulated to between a Broker and the Commission as part of a disciplinary action or alternative to disciplinary action will not be accepted to fulfill a Broker's continuing education requirement.

E. All continuing education must be taken from course providers either approved by the Commission or exempt as set forth in Rule 4.6.A.2.

F. Brokers must complete an entire course to receive any continuing education credit. Brokers will not be awarded partial credit for partial or incomplete attendance.

G. Instructors may receive continuing education credit for teaching an approved course; however, credit will be awarded for only one (1) course taught per calendar year.

H. The Commission will award two (2) hours of continuing education credit for Brokers who attend a Commission's public meeting in person under the following conditions:

1. The meeting must be open to the public and must be a minimum of two (2) hours in length;
2. The Broker must be present for at least a two (2) hour segment of the meeting to be eligible for elective credit; and
3. Elective credit will be awarded for a single Commission meeting per calendar year.

I. Each Broker is responsible for securing from the course provider proof of course completion in the form of an affidavit, certificate, or official transcript of the course as set forth in Rule 4.7.A.

J. Brokers must retain proof of continuing education completion certificates for four (4) years from the date of the Broker's most current renewal or, if newly licensed, from Initial Licensure.

K. The act of submitting an application for renewal, activation, or Reinstatement of a License means that the Broker attests to compliance with the continuing education requirement pursuant to section 12-10-213, C.R.S. However, if a Broker did not comply with the continuing education requirement, the Broker must provide written notification to the Division prior to submitting an application for renewal, activation, or Reinstatement of a License.

L. Upon written notification from the Commission, Brokers must provide proof of completion of the continuing education requirement in a manner that is acceptable to the Commission. Failure to provide said proof within the prescribed time set by the Commission in its notification will be grounds for disciplinary action unless the Commission has granted an extension.

4.6. Process for Course Approval

A. Course Providers

Continuing education must be taken from course providers either approved by the Commission or exempt as set forth in subsection A.2. of this Rule.

1. Approval of Course Providers

   All course providers must receive approval from the Commission prior to any course offering except for the course providers specifically exempted as set forth in subsection A.2. of this Rule.

2. Course Providers Exempt from Commission Approval

   The following course providers may provide course offerings for elective continuing education credit without Commission pre-approval only if the courses are within the topic areas pursuant to section 12-10-213(3), C.R.S. and as set forth in Rule 4.4.B.1. and comply with all other provisions of Chapter 4 of these Rules.

   a. Courses offered by accredited colleges, universities, community or junior colleges, public or parochial schools, or government agencies.

   b. Courses developed and offered by quasi-governmental agencies.

   c. Courses approved by and taken in satisfaction of another occupational licensing authority's education requirements.

   d. Courses in real property law by a provider approved by the Colorado Board of Continuing Legal and Judicial Education.

B. Course providers must, as set forth in Chapter 4 of these Rules, submit an application form prescribed by the Commission, along with the following information at least thirty (30) days prior to the initial proposed course date(s):

1. Detailed course outline or syllabus, including the intended learning outcomes, the course objectives, and the approximate time allocated for each topic.
2. A copy of the course exam(s) and instructor answer sheet, if applicable.
3. Copy of the instructor's teaching credential; if none, a resume showing education and experience which evidence a mastery of the material to be presented.
4. Upon Commission request, a copy of any advertising or promotional material used to announce the offering.
5. Upon Commission request, a copy of any textbook, manual, audio or videotapes, or other instructional material.

6. Course providers of continuing education offered through Distance Learning must submit evidence in a form prescribed by the Commission that the method of delivery and course structure is consistent with acceptable educational principles assuring that the desired learning objectives are met. The Commission will approve methods of delivery certified by the Association of Real Estate License Law Officials (ARELLO), or by a substantially equivalent authority and method.
7. Course approval certification will be for a period of three (3) years, except that an annual or one-time seminar or conference offering may be approved for a specific date or dates.

4.7. Course Provider Requirements

A. Course providers must provide to each student who successfully completes an approved course for continuing education credit with an affidavit, certificate, or official transcript, which must include the following information:

1. Name of the course provider;
2. Course title, which must describe the topical content;
3. Course number;
4. Number of continuing education hours/credits;
5. Course date(s);
6. Name of the student;
7. Authentication by the course provider; and
8. Course approval number as issued by the Division, if applicable.

B. A course provider may not waive, excuse completion of, or award partial credit for the full number of course hours.

C. Each course provider must retain copies of course outlines or syllabi and complete records of attendance for a period of four (4) years from the date of the course and provide the records to the Commission upon request.

D. By offering continuing education, each course provider agrees to comply with relevant Commission statutes and these Rules and to permit Commission audit of said courses at any time and at no cost. Failure to comply with the standards and requirements as set forth in Chapter 4 of these Rules may result in the invalidation of the course provider, instructor, and/or the course.

Chapter 5: Separate Accounts and Accounting

5.1. Establishment of Internal Accounting Controls

Any Brokerage Firm or Broker who receives Money Belonging to Others must establish written accounting control policies and procedures, which must include adequate checks and balances over the financial activities of the Broker, Brokerage Firm, and unlicensed persons, as well as manage the risk of fraud or illegal acts.

5.2. Trust or Escrow Accounts

All Money Belonging to Others accepted by a Broker or Brokerage Firm for deposit into the Broker's or Brokerage Firm's Trust or Escrow Account must be deposited in one or more accounts separate from other money belonging to the Broker or Brokerage Firm. The Broker or Brokerage Firm must identify the fiduciary nature of each separate Trust or Escrow Account in deposit agreements with a Recognized Depository by the use of the word "trust" or "escrow" and a label identifying the purpose of such account, such as "sales escrow", "rental escrow", "security deposit escrow", or other abbreviated form defined in the deposit agreement. The

Broker or Brokerage Firm must retain a copy of each executed Trust or Escrow Account deposit agreement for inspection by the Commission.

5.3. Accounts in the Name of the Brokerage Firm or Broker

A. Brokerage Firms acting in the name of the Employing Broker or Independent Broker as a sole- proprietor must maintain separate Trust or Escrow Accounts in the name of the Employing Broker or Independent Broker.

B. Brokerage Firms licensed as a partnership, corporation, or limited liability company must maintain separate Trust or Escrow Accounts in the name of the licensed partnership, corporation, or limited liability company.

C. The Employing Broker or Independent Broker are responsible for, must maintain and be able to withdraw money from each separate account, but may authorize other licensed or unlicensed cosigners. However, such authorization will not relieve the Employing Broker or Independent Broker of any responsibility under the Commission statutes and these Rules.

5.4. Number of Separate Trust or Escrow Accounts may vary from Zero to Unlimited

A Brokerage Firm is not limited as to the number of separate accounts, which may be maintained for Money Belonging to Others. If the Brokerage Firm is not in possession of Money Belonging to Others, there is no obligation to maintain a separate Trust or Escrow Account.

5.5. Separate Trust or Escrow Accounts Required for Rental Receipts and Security Deposits

A Brokerage Firm who engages in Property Management must deposit rental receipts and security deposits and disburse money collected for such purposes in separate Trust or Escrow Accounts, a minimum of one for rental receipts and a minimum of one for security deposits.

5.6. Trust or Escrow Funds must be Available Immediately without Penalty

Unless otherwise agreed to in writing by the parties, Money Belonging to Others must not be invested in any type of account, security, or certificate of deposit that has a fixed term for maturity or imposes any fee or penalty for withdrawal prior to maturity.

5.7. Time Limits for Deposit of Money Belonging to Others

A. All Money Belonging to Others received by a Brokerage Firm for Property Management must be deposited in the Brokerage Firm's appropriate Trust or Escrow Account no later than five (5) business days following receipt of funds or mutual execution of a lease, whichever is later.

B. All other Money Belonging to Others which is received by a Brokerage Firm must be deposited in the Brokerage Firm's Trust or Escrow Account no later than three (3) business days following receipt of funds or mutual execution of contract, whichever is later.

5.8. Transfer of Security Deposits

A. Owner-Held

A Brokerage Firm receipting for security deposits will not deliver such security deposits to an owner without the tenant's written authorization in a lease or unless written notice has been given to the tenant. Such notice must be given in a manner so the tenant will know who is holding the security deposit and the specific requirements for the procedure in which the tenant may request return of the security deposit. If a security deposit is delivered to the owner, the Management Agreement should place financial responsibility on the owner for its return, and in the event of a dispute over ownership of the security deposit, must authorize disclosure to the tenant of the owner's true name and current mailing address.

B. New Property Management Company

A Brokerage Firm which begins management of a property most recently managed by another Brokerage Firm must disclose to the owner and the current tenant, in writing, and within thirty (30) days after execution of a Management Agreement, the status of any security deposit held by the previous Brokerage Firm, including the amount of the security deposit and confirmation of receipt of the funds. The Brokerage Firm must verify that each security deposit transferred to them matches the amount listed in the current lease and disclose any discrepancy to the owner and current tenant. The Brokerage Firm must inform the tenant, in writing, if the owner is holding the security deposit.

5.9. Diversion and Conversion Prohibited

Money Belonging to Others belonging to one beneficiary must not be used for the benefit of another beneficiary. Money Belonging to Others must not be used for the benefit of the Brokerage Firm or Broker.

5.10. Commingling Prohibited

A Broker's or Brokerage Firm's personal or business operating funds must not be commingled with Money Belonging to Others. One or more separate Trust or Escrow Accounts may be maintained by a Brokerage Firm pursuant to the following duties and limitations:

A. Money held in a Trust or Escrow Account which becomes due and payable to the Brokerage Firm must be withdrawn monthly.

B. Money advanced by a Brokerage Firm for the benefit of another may be placed in the Trust or Escrow Account and identified as an advance but may be withdrawn by the Brokerage Firm only on behalf of such person. Any amount advanced to a Trust or Escrow Account must be identified and recorded in the journal and the ledger and disclosed in accounting to the beneficiary as set forth in Rule 5.15.

C. In the absence of a specific written agreement to the contrary, commissions, fees, and other charges collected by a Brokerage Firm for performing any service on behalf of another are considered "earned" and available for use by the Brokerage Firm only after all contracted services have been performed and there is no remaining right of recall by others for such money. The Brokerage Firm must identify and record all commissions, fees, or other charges withdrawn from a Trust or Escrow Account on the account journal and individual ledgers of those against whom the fees or commissions are charged. If a single disbursement of fees or commissions includes more than one (1) transaction, rental period or occupancy or includes withdrawals from the account of more than one (1) Trust or Escrow Account beneficiary, the Brokerage Firm, upon request, must produce for inspection by the Commission a schedule which details:

1. The individual components of all amounts included in the sum of such disbursement; and
2. Specifically identifies the affected beneficiary or property ledgers as set forth in Rule 5.14.B.

D. Rental proceeds received by a Broker for managing Broker's own properties through the Broker's Brokerage Firm, including any Broker's properties held in partnership with others, joint ventures, or syndications provided the Broker's ownership in the entity or property is more than the 20% threshold pursuant to section 12-10-201(6)(b)(VII), C.R.S. must be deposited in an account separate from any other Trust or Escrow Accounts maintained for Money Belonging to Others. Such funds are not subject to Trust or Escrow Accounts and record keeping requirements as set forth in Rules 5.2. and 5.14.

5.11. Money Belonging to Others for deposit by a Broker for Non-Real Estate Brokerage Services

A. Money Belonging to Others which is accepted for deposit in connection with activities not involving Real Estate Brokerage Services must be deposited into Broker's or

Brokerage Firm's Trust or Escrow Account(s). Such activities not involving Real Estate Brokerage Services include:

1. Guest deposits for short term rentals;
2. Security deposits for Broker's own rental properties including any Broker owned properties held in a partnership, or other entity with others, any join ventures, or syndications provided the Broker's ownership in the entity or property is more than the 20% threshold pursuant to section 12-10-201(6)(b)(VII), C.R.S. ;
3. Deposits from a buyer when the Broker is acting as a builder; or
4. Any other non-Real Estate Brokerage Service purposes.

B. If a Broker accepts Money Belonging to Others for deposit into Broker's or Brokerage Firm's Trust or Escrow Account as set forth in subsection A. of this Rule for activities not involving Real Estate Brokerage Services, the Broker must:

1. If required by the Broker's Brokerage Firm's Office Policy Manual, deposit the funds in the Broker's Brokerage Firm's Trust or Escrow Accounts as set forth in Chapter 5 of these Rules; or
2. Deposit the funds into Broker's own Trust or Escrow Accounts as set forth in Rule 5.2. and must also comply with the following Chapter 5 Rules:

   i. Rule 5.6. Trust or Escrow Funds must be Available Immediately without Penalty;

   ii. Rule 5.9. Diversion and Conversion Prohibited;

   iii. Rule 5.10. Commingling Prohibited;

   iv. Maintain a "journal" as set forth in Rule 5.14.A. and perform a two-way reconciliation monthly to show that on the date of reconciliation the cash balance shown in the journal and the reconciled bank balance are the same; and;

   v. Rule 5.21. Production of Documents and Records;

5.12. Earnest Money

A. Any Broker receiving earnest money must deliver such earnest money to the earnest money holder to be deposited in accordance with the contract. The Broker must obtain a dated and signed receipt from the person or entity to whom the Broker has been instructed to deliver the deposit.

B. If the Brokerage Firm will be holding the earnest money in a transaction, the earnest money must be deposited as set forth in Rule 5.7.B. The Brokerage Firm may transfer the earnest money from the Brokerage Firm's Trust or Escrow Account to a lawyer or a closing entity closing the transaction. The Brokerage Firm delivering the earnest money deposit to a lawyer or a closing entity providing settlement services must obtain a dated and signed receipt from the person or entity providing settlement services.

5.13. Promissory Note for Earnest Money

If a promissory note is received as earnest money pursuant to an executed contract, the seller must be informed of the date such promissory note becomes due. If payment is not made by the due date of the promissory note, the Broker must promptly notify the seller and deliver the original promissory note.

5.14. Recordkeeping Requirements

An Employing Broker or Independent Broker must maintain, at the Brokerage Firm's licensed place of business, a record keeping system as set forth in Rule 5.16., consisting of at least the following elements for each required Trust or Escrow Account:

A. A "journal" or an equivalent accounting system which records, in chronological order, all Money Belonging to Others which is received or disbursed by the Brokerage Firm.

1. For funds received, each journal record must include:
   a. The date of receipt and deposit;
   b. The name of the person who is giving the money;
   c. The name of the person and property for which the money was received;
   d. The purpose of the receipt;
   e. The amount; and
   f. A resulting cash balance for the account.
2. For funds disbursed, each journal record must include:
   a. The date of payment;
   b. The check number or electronic transfer record;
   c. The name of the payee;
   d. A reference to vendor documentation or other physical records verifying purpose for payment;
   e. The amount paid; and
   f. Resulting cash balance for the account.

B. A "ledger" or an equivalent component of an accounting system which records, in chronological order, all money which is received or disbursed by the Broker on behalf of each particular beneficiary of a Trust or Escrow Account. The ledger record must show the monetary transactions affecting each individual beneficiary and must segregate such transactions from those pertaining to other beneficiaries of the Trust or Escrow Account. The ledger record for each beneficiary must contain the same transactional information as set forth in subsection A of this Rule. No ledger may ever be allowed to have a negative cash balance. The sum of all ledger balances must agree at all times with the corresponding journal after each transaction has been posted.

C. Three-way reconciliation must be performed monthly to show that on the same date the cash balance shown in the journal, the sum of the cash balances for all ledgers, and the reconciled bank balance are the same. A three-way reconciliation report must be completed and maintained monthly to show such three-way reconciliation. The Broker is not required to maintain records or reconcile any Trust or Escrow Account when such account does not contain Money Belonging to Others.

D. A Brokerage Firm may deposit personal funds as may be required to pay any bank charges incurred in connection with maintaining a Trust or Escrow Account without violating Rule 5.10. An entry showing such money must be made in the journal and on the ledger as set forth in subsections A and B of this Rule.

E. The three-way reconciliation reports, ledgers, journals, and bank account statements may be kept electronically.

5.15. Maintenance and Production of Reports to Beneficiaries

A. Brokerage Firms holding Money Belonging to Others must provide detailed reports to each beneficiary. Any accounting report furnished to beneficiaries must be prepared and delivered according to the terms of the Management Agreement. In the absence of a provision in the Management Agreement to the contrary, Brokerage Firms must deliver these reports within thirty (30) days after the end of the month in which funds were either received or disbursed.

B. The Brokerage Firm must maintain supporting records, which accurately detail all cash received and disbursed under the terms of any Management Agreement.

1. All deposits of funds into a Trust or Escrow Account must identify each person tendering funds, the amount of funds tendered, types of funds received from each person, and the property address affected.
2. All disbursements of funds from a Trust or Escrow Account must be supported by documents such as bids, invoices, contracts, etc. Ledger and journal records must identify the payees, property addresses affected and amount of funds transferred for each property.

5.16. Method of Accounting

In the absence of a written agreement to the contrary, the "cash basis" of accounting must be used for maintaining all required Trust or Escrow Accounts and corresponding records. A Brokerage Firm may use another method of accounting if it is agreed upon in writing by the Brokerage Firm and the beneficiary. The Brokerage Firm must maintain separate Trust and Escrow Accounts and corresponding records for each beneficiary using a different accounting method.

5.17. Mark-Ups

Pursuant to sections 12-10-217(1)(d) and (t) and 6-1-105, C.R.S., the Broker and Brokerage Firm must obtain prior written consent from the owner to assess and receive mark-ups and/or other compensation for services performed, regardless if for the benefit of the Broker or another third party. The Broker and Brokerage Firm must retain accurate on-going records, which verify disclosure and consent and which fully account for the amounts or percentages of compensation assessed or received.

5.18. Items in Lieu of Cash

Any instrument, equity, or Thing of Value taken in lieu of cash must be held by the Brokerage Firm, except as otherwise agreed.

5.19. Branch Office Trust or Escrow Accounts Require Branch Office Recordkeeping

In the event a branch office of a Brokerage Firm maintains a Trust or Escrow Account separate from the Trust or Escrow Account(s) maintained by the Brokerage Firm's main office, a separate record keeping system must be maintained in the branch office. The responsibility of maintaining separate record keeping systems will be the responsibility of the Employing Broker.

5.20. Money Collected by Brokerage Firm

A. When money is collected by a Brokerage Firm for the performance of specific services or for the expenses of performing such services, or for any other expense, and such money is collected before the services have been performed, the Brokerage Firm must deposit such money in a Trust or Escrow Account pursuant to section 12-10-217(1)(i), C.R.S. No money may be withdrawn from the Trust or Escrow Account, except for authorized expenses for performing such services. A full and itemized accounting must be furnished as set forth in Rule 5.15.

B. Nothing in this Rule will prohibit a Brokerage Firm from taking a non-refundable retainer that need not be deposited into a Trust or Escrow Account provided this be specifically agreed to in writing between the Brokerage Firm and the person paying the retainer.

5.21. Production of Documents and Records

A Broker and Brokerage Firm must produce for inspection by the Commission any document or record as may be reasonably necessary for investigation or audit in the enforcement of the Commission statutes and these Rules. Failure to submit such documents or records within the time set by the Commission in its notification will be grounds for disciplinary action unless the Commission has granted an extension of time for such production.

5.22. Responsibility of the Employing Broker or Independent Broker for Brokerage Firm's Compliance

The Employing Broker or Independent Broker are held jointly responsible with the Brokerage Firm in complying with Chapter 5 of these Rules.

Chapter 6: Practice Standards

6.1. Real Estate License

A. A License is nontransferable.

B. Neither a Broker nor Brokerage Firm may lend their name or License for the benefit of another person, partnership, limited liability company, or corporation.

C. Associate Brokers must not present or hold themselves out to the public as an Employing Broker or Independent Broker.

D. An Employing Broker must not knowingly permit Associate Brokers to present or hold themselves out to the public as an Employing Broker or Independent Broker.

E. A Broker must not procure or attempt to procure a License by fraud, misrepresentation, deceit, or by making a material misstatement of fact in an application for such License pursuant to section 12-10-217(1)(s), C.R.S.

6.2. Competency

A. In order to conduct Real Estate Brokerage Services, a Broker must possess the necessary experience, training, and knowledge to provide Real Estate Brokerage Services and maintain compliance with the applicable federal, state and local laws, rules, regulations and ordinances.

B. If a Broker does not have the necessary experience, training, and knowledge, the Broker must:

1. Decline to provide Real Estate Brokerage Services;
2. Obtain the necessary experience, training, and knowledge;
3. Obtain the assistance of their Employing Broker, Supervisory Broker, a Broker who meets the requirements as set forth in subsection A. of this Rule, or legal counsel that is competent in the matter; or
4. Co-list with another Broker who meets the requirements as set forth in subsection A. of this Rule.

6.3. Employing Broker's Responsibilities and Supervision

A. Employing Broker Exercises Authority, Direction, and Supervision

1. Employing Brokers must exercise authority, direction, and supervision over any Associate Brokers shown in the records of the Commission as supervised by the Employing Broker to ensure conformance to the Commission statutes and these Rules in the performance of the Associate Broker's activities pursuant to sections 12-10-203(5)(c)(I), 12-10-217(1)(r), and 12-10-222, C.R.S., and these Rules. Whenever a complaint is filed with the Commission against an Associate Broker, the Commission may investigate whether there have been violations of section 12- 10-217(1)(r), C.R.S. by the Employing Broker.
2. Employing Brokers must also supervise, pursuant to section 12-10-222, C.R.S., all unlicensed employees, including, but not limited to, Unlicensed On-Site Managers, secretaries, bookkeepers, and personal assistants of Associate Brokers.

B. Employing Broker's Responsibilities Employing Brokers must:

1. Maintain all Trust and Escrow Accounts and records as set forth in Chapter 5 of these Rules;

2. Maintain all transaction records as set forth in Rule 6.20.;
3. Develop the Brokerage Firm's written policies as set forth in Rule 6.4.;
4. Provide for a "Reasonable-Level of Supervision" for all Associate Brokers as set forth in subsection C. of this Rule;
5. Provide for a "High-Level of Supervision" for New Associate Brokers as set forth in subsection D. of this Rule;
6. Take reasonable steps to ensure that violations of statutes, rules, and office policies do not occur or reoccur; and
7. Provide for adequate supervision of all branches or offices operated by the Employing Broker.

C. "Reasonable-Level of Supervision" by Employing Brokers

Pursuant to section 12-10-217(1)(r), C.R.S., Employing Brokers are required to provide all Associate Brokers with a "Reasonable-Level of Supervision," which includes:

1. Maintaining a written Office Policy Manual as set forth in Rule 6.4.B., which must:
   a. Be given to and signed by each Associate Broker; and
   b. Be available for inspection, upon request, by any authorized representative of the Commission.
2. Ensuring all executed contracts are reviewed to maintain assurance of competent preparation. If the Employing Broker has concerns about the preparation of a contract, Employing Broker should contact the Associate Broker.
3. Ensuring all transaction files are reviewed for the required documents. If required documents are not present, the Employing Broker should contact the Associate Broker.

D. "High-Level of Supervision" by Employing Brokers

In addition to the requirements of subsection C. of this Rule and pursuant to section 12-10- 203(5)(c)(I), C.R.S., an Employing Broker must provide a "High-Level of Supervision" for New Associate Brokers. "High-Level of Supervision" includes:

1. Providing specific training in office policies and procedures;
2. Being reasonably available for consultation;
3. Providing assistance in preparing contracts;
4. Monitoring transactions from contracting to closing;
5. Reviewing documents in preparation for closing; and
6. Ensuring that the Employing Broker or an experienced Associate Broker with more than two (2) years' Active licensure attends closings with a New Associate Broker or is available for assistance.

E. Supervision of Unlicensed On-Site Manager Employing Brokers must:

1. Actively and diligently supervise all activities of any Unlicensed On-Site Manager or delegate supervisory authority as set forth in subsection F. of this Rule;
2. Require the Unlicensed On-Site Manager to report directly to either the Employing Broker or a Supervisory Broker;
3. Require the Unlicensed On-Site Manager to account for and remit all monies, including rents and security deposits, collected on behalf of the Employing Broker or owner to the Employing Broker or Supervisory Broker;
4. Ensure that property maintenance scheduled by the Unlicensed On-Site Manager is performed in accordance with the Property Management Agreement; and

5. Instruct the Unlicensed On-Site Manager not to negotiate any of the material terms of a lease or rental agreement with a Consumer.

F. Delegation of Supervision

Employing Brokers may delegate supervisory authority to other experienced Associate Brokers for both "Reasonable-Level of Supervision" and "High-Level of Supervision" as follows:

1. Supervisory Brokers must bear responsibility along with the Employing Broker for ensuring compliance with the Commission statutes and these Rules for those persons the delegated Associate Broker is supervising.
2. Any delegation of authority must be in writing and signed by the Supervisory Broker. A copy of such delegation must be maintained by the Employing Broker for inspection, upon request, by any authorized Commission representative.
3. The Supervisory Broker must have competency as set forth in Rule 6.2. in the area of practice in which the Supervisory Broker is supervising.
4. An Employing Broker must not contract with any Associate Broker so as to circumvent the requirement that the Employing Broker supervise Associate Brokers. While an Employing Broker may delegate supervision duties, the Employing Broker is still ultimately responsible for the supervision provided.

G. Confidential Information Revealed to Employing Broker or Supervisory Broker

Associate Brokers may reveal to an Employing Broker or a Supervisory Broker confidential information about the Associate Broker's client. Associate Brokers' disclosure of such confidential information does not change or extend the Brokerage Relationship beyond the Associate Broker. Confidential information includes the information pursuant to sections 12-10-404(2), 12-10-405(2) and 12-10-407(3), C.R.S.

6.4. Brokerage Firm's Policies

A. Brokerage Firm's Brokerage Relationship Policy

1. An Employing Broker or Independent Broker must adopt a written office policy which identifies and describes the relationships in which such Employing Broker, Independent Broker, and any Associate Brokers may engage with any Consumers prior to providing any Real Estate Brokerage Services pursuant to sections 12- 10-403 and 12-10-408, C.R.S.
2. An Employing Broker or Associate Broker must be designated in writing by the Employing Broker to serve as a Single Agent or Transaction-Broker for a Consumer pursuant to section 12-10-402(3), C.R.S. and as set forth in Rule 6.6.

B. Office Policy Manual

Employing Brokers must also adopt any written policies suitable to the Brokerage Firm's business, subject to the following as applicable:

1. Applies to all Associate Brokers in the Brokerage Firm.
2. Be given to and signed by each Associate Broker.
3. Identifies the procedures for the designation of Brokers who are to work with Consumers pursuant to section 12-10-403(6), C.R.S. and as set forth in subsection A. of this Rule.
4. Identifies and provides adequate means and procedures for the maintenance and protection of confidential information that:
   a. The seller or landlord is willing to accept less;
   b. The buyer or tenant is willing to pay more;
   c. Information regarding motivating factors for the parties;

d. Information that a party will agree to other financing terms;

e. Material information about a party not required by law to be disclosed;

f. Facts or suspicions which may psychologically impact or stigmatize a property; and

g. All information required to be kept confidential pursuant to sections 12- 10-404(2), 12-10-405(2) and 12-10-407(3), C.R.S.

5. Permits an Employing Broker to supervise a transaction and to participate in the same transaction as a Designated Broker.

6.5. Brokerage Relationships Disclosures in Writing

A. Written disclosures pursuant to section 12-10-408, C.R.S. must be made to a Consumer prior to eliciting or discussing confidential information from a Consumer for Real Estate Brokerage Services.

B. Such activities do not include preliminary conversations or "small talk" concerning price range, location and property styles, or responding to general factual questions from a potential Consumer concerning properties which have been Advertised for sale or lease.

6.6. Brokerage Relationships

A. Listing Contract by Individual Associate Broker: An Associate Broker may enter into a Listing Contract as the Designated Broker for a particular Consumer in a particular transaction as either a Single Agent or Transaction-Broker.

B. Listing Contract by Members of a Team: The individual team member(s) must all be the Designated Broker for a particular Consumer in a particular transaction as either Single Agents or Transaction-Brokers. The names of all the members of the Team must be disclosed in the Listing Contract.

C. Transaction-Broker: A written disclosure that a Broker working with a Consumer as a Transaction-Broker is the Designated Broker for that Consumer.

D. Substitute or Additional Designated Brokers: The Employing Broker may substitute or add other Designated Brokers, as appropriate, which must be disclosed to the Consumer.

6.7. Brokers or Teams working with Consumers on Both Sides of the Same Transaction

Neither Brokers nor Teams may enter into a Brokerage Relationship with one Consumer as a Single Agent and the other Consumer as a Single Agent or Transaction-Broker in the same transaction. If properly disclosed, in writing (e.g. Listing Contracts), the Broker or Team that works with both Consumers in the same real estate transaction may do so as:

A. A Transaction-Broker for both Consumers to the transaction;

B. A Transaction-Broker for one Consumer in the transaction and treating the other Consumer as a Customer; or

C. A Single Agent for one Consumer and treating the other Consumer as a Customer.

6.8. Ministerial Tasks

When a Broker is engaged as a Single Agent or a Transaction-Broker for one party and treating the other party as a Customer, the Broker may assist the Customer by performing ministerial tasks following proper disclosure. Ministerial tasks include: showing a property, preparing as a scrivener, and conveying written offers and counteroffers, making known the different types of financing alternatives, and providing information related to professional, governmental, and community services which will contribute to completion of the transaction. Performing ministerial tasks will not of themselves violate the terms of any relationship between the Broker and the Consumer with which the Broker has a Brokerage Relationship and will not create an agency or Transaction-Broker relationship with the Customer being assisted.

6.9. Change of Status Disclosure in Writing

A Broker or Team who changes their Brokerage Relationship from a Single Agent for one Consumer to assisting both Consumers in the same real estate transaction as a Transaction-Broker must provide the written Commission-Approved "Change of Status" Form to the Consumer that has the changed relationship with the Broker, at the time the Broker begins to assist both Consumers as a Transaction-Broker, but not later than at the time the Consumer signs the contract.

* 6.10. Advertising

A. Names

1. Pursuant to section 12-10-203(9), C.R.S., no Broker will be licensed to conduct Real Estate Brokerage Services under more than one (1) Brokerage Firm.

* 2. Pursuant to section 12-10-203(9), C.R.S., no Broker or Brokerage Firm will conduct or promote Real Estate Brokerage Services except in the name under which that Broker or Brokerage Firm appears in the records of the Commission. A Brokerage Firm may also include the locations of its offices, to include branch offices in the Advertising.

3. Brokers will not Advertise so as to mislead the public concerning the identity of the Broker or the Broker's Brokerage Firm.

4. All Advertising must be done clearly and conspicuously in the name of the Broker's Brokerage Firm. However, a Broker who Advertises real property owned by the Broker which is not listed for sale or lease with the Broker's Brokerage Firm is exempt from Advertising the Broker's own property in the Broker's Brokerage Firm's name.

5. A Brokerage Firm may use a Trade Name in addition to or instead of the Brokerage Firm's legal name. The Trade Name must be filed with the Commission.

6. A Brokerage Firm may use a Trademark in conjunction with the Brokerage Firm's legal name or Trade Name with permission of the owner of such Trademark.

   a. A Brokerage Firm that uses a Trade Name or Trademark owned by a third party is required to use one (1) of the following statements, which must appear in a clear and conspicuous manner so as to attract the attention of the public:

      i. "Each (insert general Trade Name) brokerage business is independently owned and operated." or

      ii. "Each office independently owned and operated."

   b. Upon written request, the above statements may be modified with consent of the Commission.

7. No Brokerage Firm will use more than one (1) Trade Name; however, upon written request and with the consent of a representative of the Commission, a Brokerage Firm may use more than one (1) Trademark. Use of the Trademark(s) is only acceptable if the Brokerage Firm has obtained permission of the registrant of such Trademark.

8. No Broker may use a professional designation in Advertising unless the Broker is in good standing and the designation is easily verifiable by the public and the Commission. A Broker that Advertises an award, membership, or achievement must be able to provide verification of the validity of such claims upon request from any member of the public or Commission.

B. Teams

1. Brokers who form a Team must not Advertise in a manner that misleads the public as to the identity of the Team's Brokerage Firm. Teams are prohibited from using the following terms in the Team's name:

a. Realty,
b. Real estate,
c. Realtors,
d. Company,
e. Corporation,
f. Corp.,
g. Inc.,
h. LLC,
i. LP or LLP, or
j. Any other term that would imply a separate entity from the Brokerage Firm with which the Team Brokers are licensed.

2. All Team Advertising must clearly and conspicuously include and be in conjunction with the legal name or Trade Name of the Brokerage Firm.
3. If requested by a Consumer, the Commission, another Brokerage Firm or Broker, the Brokerage Firm will provide the names of the Brokers that belong to any Team licensed with the Brokerage Firm.
4. Brokers may not allow the use of the Team's name by other Brokers outside the Team's Brokerage Firm.

C. Brokerage Firms and Brokers are responsible for ensuring that all Advertising is accurate and complies with copyright laws and other applicable laws and regulations.

D. Electronic Media

* 1. When a Broker owns or controls Electronic Media, each Viewable Page must include the Broker's Brokerage Firm's name. Any expired listings must be removed from the Broker's Electronic Media within three (3) days of a Listing Contract expiring.

2. If a Broker authorizes a third party for the Broker's Electronic Media Advertising, the Broker is responsible for ensuring that the information provided to such third party is accurate. The Broker must submit a written request to any third party syndicators to have all expired listings removed from Electronic Media within three (3) days of a Listing Contract expiring.

* 3. A Broker who communicates through email, chat, instant messages, newsgroups, discussion lists, bulletin boards, blogs, or other similar means for purposes of Advertising the Broker's Real Estate Brokerage Services must use the Broker's Brokerage Firm's name. However, once a Broker has disclosed the Broker's Brokerage Firm to a specific Consumer, the Broker is not required to continue to make the same disclosure to the specific Consumer.

* 4. When it is not reasonable for a Broker to disclose the Broker's Brokerage Firm's name in an Electronic Media because space is limited, the Broker will disclose the Broker's Brokerage Firm's name clearly and conspicuously within the first click of the mouse.

* E. Past Sales Data Advertising

General sales data Advertising, regardless of the medium, which recaps sales activity over a period of time in a given subdivision or geographical area must include all of the following:

1. Cite the source of the data; and
2. Include a disclaimer, if accurate, that all reported sales:

a. Were not necessarily listed or sold by the Broker; and

b. Are intended only to show trends in the area or will separately identify the Broker's own sales activity.

* F. Authority to Advertise Available and Under Contract Properties

* Brokers may not Advertise the availability or price of a property whether for sale or lease without authority from the owner or the owner's Broker. If such authority is requested, an owner's Broker may not withhold the authority to advertise said property unless such authority is contradictory to instructions from the owner as memorialized in the Listing Contract or other writing. A Broker who has received written permission to disseminate another Broker's Advertising or an owner's Advertising who is not represented by a Brokerage Firm (For Sale by Owner) may do so as set forth in subsections F.1. and F.2. of this Rule.

* 1. A Broker may disseminate another Broker's Advertising in the following manner:

* a. A Broker must have the owner's Broker's written permission to disseminate the Advertising;

* b. The Broker discloses, in a conspicuous manner, the owner's Brokerage Firm;

* c. The Advertising is accurate and not misleading to Consumers; and

* d. The Advertising complies with subsection C. of this Rule.

* 2. A Broker may disseminate an owner's Advertising who is not represented by a Brokerage Firm in the following manner:

* a. The Broker must have the owner's written permission to disseminate the Advertising;

* b. The Broker discloses, in a conspicuous manner, that the owner is not represented by a Broker;

* c. The Advertising is accurate and not misleading to Consumers; and

* d. The dissemination of an owner's Advertising does not include submitting the information into a property exchange or multiple listing service.

G. Price Set by Owner

The price quoted in any Advertising will not be anything other than the price agreed upon between the Broker and the owner.

6.11. Square Footage Disclosure

When a Broker Advertises the square footage of a residential property, including for submission to a multiple listing service, the Broker must disclose the source of the square footage of the floor space of the living area of the residence to Consumers on the Commission-Approved Form.

A. Broker Measurement

A Broker is not required to measure the square footage of a property. If the Broker takes an actual measurement, it does not have to be exact; however, the Broker's objective must be to measure accurately and calculate competently in a manner that is not misleading and must:

1. Disclose to the Consumer the standard, methodology, or manner in which the measurement was taken;
2. Advise that the measurement is for purposes of marketing and is not a measurement for loan, valuation, or any other purpose; and
3. Advise that if exact square footage is a concern, then the property should be independently measured.

B. Other Sources of Square Footage

If a Consumer is provided information from a source other than the Broker's own measurement for square footage, that source (whether an actual measurement, building plans, prior appraisals, assessor's office, etc.) must include the date of issuance, if any, and must be disclosed to the Consumers in writing by the Broker in a timely manner. Such disclosure must be on the Commission-Approved Form. A Broker may not provide information to a person from a source known to be unreliable and is responsible for indicating obvious mismeasurement by others.

6.12. Notice Required on Competitive Market Analysis (CMA) or Broker's Price Opinion (BPO) for Purposes Other Than Marketing

When a Broker prepares a CMA or BPO for any reason other than the anticipated sale or purchase of the property, the Broker must include a notice stating: "This evaluation was prepared by a licensed real estate broker and is not an appraisal. This evaluation cannot be used for the purposes of obtaining financing." Pursuant to section 12-10-602(9)(b)(II), C.R.S, Brokers are prohibited from completing CMAs or BPOs that are used for the purpose of obtaining financing. Preparation of CMAs or BPOs for reasons other than anticipated sale, purchase, or lease is not considered Real Estate Brokerage Services. As such, any compensation received for such preparation is not required to be paid to the Broker's Brokerage Firm unless stated otherwise in Brokerage Firm's Office Policy Manual.

6.13. Offers must be Presented to Other Broker

A Broker must present all offers to the other Consumer's Broker if such other Consumer has an unexpired Listing Contract. If the Broker has made reasonable, but unsuccessful, attempts to present an offer to the other Consumer's Broker, the Broker must present the offer to the other Consumer's Broker's Employing Broker. If no Employing Broker exists, or if reasonable attempts to present the offer to the Employing Broker have failed, the Broker may present the offer directly to the other Consumer.

6.14. Contracts

A. Document Preparation and Duplicates

1. Contracting instruments prepared by a Broker performing Real Estate Brokerage Services for all real estate or business opportunity transactions must accurately reflect the financial terms of the transaction by itemizing Things of Value paid or received and identifying the party or parties conveying, receiving and/or ultimately benefitting from such Things of Value. All such terms made subsequent to the original contract must be disclosed in an amendment to the contract.
2. A Broker must deliver Duplicates of all documents prepared by the Broker to all Consumers or their representatives at the time such document was prepared by the Broker as set forth in Rule 6.19.

B. No Fees to Brokers for Legal Document Preparation

Brokers are not obligated to prepare any legal documents as part of a real estate transaction. If the Broker or the Broker's designee prepares any legal document, the Broker or the Broker's designee may not charge a separate fee for preparation of such legal documents. The Broker is not responsible for fees charged for the preparation of legal documents where they are prepared by an attorney representing the Consumer. Costs of closing not related to preparation of legal documents may be paid by the Broker or by any other person. A Broker who closes transactions and charges separately for costs of closing not related to the preparation of legal documents must specify the costs and obtain the written consent of the parties to be charged.

C. Listing must be in Writing

Regardless of the Brokerage Relationship, all seller Listing Contracts and landlord Listing Contracts must be in writing prior to performing any Real Estate Brokerage Services.

D. Listings must have Termination Date

All Listing Contracts or other written agreements between a Consumer and a Brokerage Firm or Broker to perform Real Estate Brokerage Services must have a definite date for termination pursuant to section 12-10-409(1)(b), C.R.S.

E. Holdover Agreement

When a Listing Contract or other written agreement contains a provision entitling a Brokerage Firm to a commission made after the expiration of the agreement, such provision must refer only to those persons or properties with whom or on which the Broker negotiated during the term of the agreement, and whose names or addresses were submitted in writing to the Consumer during the term of the agreement, including any extension thereof.

F. Brokers must recommend title exam and legal counsel

Brokers are not permitted to give advice on exceptions to title as such conduct would constitute the unauthorized practice of law. Brokers must recommend, before the applicable deadlines, that Consumers should examine all title exceptions and encourage Consumers to seek guidance from a licensed attorney.

G. Review of Deeds

Brokers should not give advice based on their review of deeds for conveyance of real property unless such deeds are drafted by the Broker.

6.15. Sign Crossing

A. Brokers will not negotiate a Listing Contract directly with a Consumer for compensation from said Consumer if such Broker knows the Consumer has an unexpired Listing Contract with another Brokerage Firm granting said Brokerage Firm an exclusive contract.

B. However, if a Broker is contacted by a Consumer who is currently subject to an exclusive Listing Contract, and the Broker has not initiated the discussion, the Broker may negotiate the terms upon which to take a future Listing Contract or, alternatively, may take a Listing Contract to become effective upon expiration or termination of any existing Exclusive Listing.

C. The burden of inquiry is on the Broker to determine the existence of the Listing Contract and to advise the Consumer to seek guidance from a licensed attorney.

6.16. Access Information for a Property

A Broker who is not the owner's Broker is prohibited from sharing access information to a property with any third party, such as an assistant, home inspector, contractor, or a Consumer without prior authorization from the owner's Broker.

6.17. Duty to Disclose Conflict of Interest and License Status

A. Brokerage Firms and Brokers have a continuing duty to disclose, in writing, any known conflict of interest that may arise in the course of any real estate transaction.

B. If a Broker sells, buys, or leases real property on the Broker's own account, such Broker must disclose in the contracting instrument, or in a separate concurrent writing, that they are a licensed Broker.

C. A Brokerage Firm or Broker engaged in Property Management Services has a duty to disclose, in writing, any known conflict of interest that may arise in the selection or use of a business or vendor that provides services applicable to lease transactions, including property maintenance. The Brokerage Firm or Broker is required to disclose any ownership, financial, or familial interest associated with the selection or use of a particular business or vendor.

6.18. Affiliated Business Arrangement Disclosures

Pursuant to section 12-10-218(2)(b), C.R.S., an Employing Broker and/or a Broker must make the following disclosures in writing:

A. The existence of an Affiliated Business Arrangement to the Consumer they are referring at or prior to the time the referral is made. The disclosure must comply with RESPA.

B. Prior to or at the time the Contract to Buy and Sell is executed by the Consumers, the existence of an Affiliated Business Arrangement with the Brokerage Firm or Broker must be disclosed in writing to all parties to the transaction.

C. A Broker is required to make the following disclosures to the Commission.

1. At the time a Broker enters into or changes an Affiliated Business Arrangement, the Broker must disclose the names of all Affiliated Business Arrangements to which the Broker is a party. The written disclosure must include the physical location of the affiliated businesses.
2. On an annual basis, each Employing Broker must disclose the names of all Affiliated Business Arrangements to which the Employing Broker or Brokerage Firm is a party. The written disclosure must include the physical location of the affiliated businesses.

D. Written disclosures to the Commission must be made through the Colorado Affiliated Business Online Services database, which is accessible through the Division's website.

6.19. Closing Responsibility

A. Pursuant to section 12-10-217(1)(j), C.R.S, at the time of closing, the Broker who has established a Brokerage Relationship with one or multiple Consumers in a transaction will be responsible for the proper closing of the transaction. The Broker must ensure such Consumer receives an accurate, complete and detailed closing statement that is signed by the Broker. If Broker is licensed with a Brokerage Firm, Broker must deliver closing statements to the Brokerage Firm along with any other closing documents, immediately following closing. Nothing in this Rule relieves an Employing Broker of the responsibility for fulfilling supervisory responsibilities pursuant to sections 12-10-203(5)(c)(I), 12-10- 217(1)(r), and 12-10-222, C.R.S and as set forth in subsections C. and D. of this Rule.

B. If closing documents and closing statements are prepared and closed by a Broker, the Broker is responsible for the accuracy and completeness of the closing statements and closing documents.

C. If a Broker has a Brokerage Relationship with a Consumer in a transaction, the Broker must review closing documents and attend closing or be reasonably available. If a Broker will not be available to attend closing and review closing documents, another Broker designated by the Brokerage Firm may review and attend closing on the Broker's behalf and will assume joint responsibility with the absent Broker for its accuracy, completeness, and delivery of the signed closing statement as set forth in subsection A. of this Rule.

D. Any Broker receiving earnest money must deliver earnest money as set forth in Rule 5.12.A.

E. Pursuant to section 38-35-125, C.R.S, a Broker or a Brokerage Firm must not disburse or authorize disbursement of funds until those funds have been received and are either:

1. Available for immediate withdrawal as a matter of right from the financial institution in which the funds have been deposited; or

2. Available for immediate withdrawal as a consequence of an agreement with a financial institution in which the funds are to be deposited or a financial institution upon which the funds are to be drawn. The agreement with a financial institution must be for the benefit of the Broker and Brokerage Firm providing the closing service. If the agreement contains contingencies or reservations, no disbursements can be made until these are satisfied.

6.20. Transaction File Requirements

Both a Broker and a Brokerage Firm must retain transactions files for all transactions for a period of four (4) years beginning from the consummation date of the transaction or the expiration date of any Listing Contracts that do not consummate. Required documents in a transaction file are designated in the Commission's Transaction File Checklist and may be found on the Division's website. A Broker is not required to obtain and retain copies of existing public records, title commitments, loan applications, lender required disclosures, or related affirmations from independent third party closing entities after the closing date.

6.21. Referral Fees and RESPA

A. Brokers and Brokerage Firms will not pay or receive a referral fee except in accordance with RESPA and unless a reasonable cause for payment of the referral fee exists pursuant to section 12-10-304(1), C.R.S.

B. RESPA prohibits settlement service providers from giving or receiving any Thing of Value to another settlement service provider for the referral of business when the transaction involves a federally related residential mortgage.

1. Transactions Involving a Federally related Residential Mortgage

   A Broker or Brokerage Firm, whether engaged in an Affiliated Business Arrangement pursuant to section 12-10-218, C.R.S. or not, will not accept or give any incentive, disincentive, remuneration, commission, fee, or other Thing of Value to or from a settlement service provider for the referral of business in a real estate transaction involving a federally related residential mortgage transaction. Nothing in subsection B. of this Rule prohibits a person or entity from receiving a bona fide salary, commission, or other compensation for services rendered or as a return on their ownership interest in an Affiliated Business Arrangement.

2. Transaction Not Involving a Federally related Residential Mortgage

   A Broker or Brokerage Firm will not accept, directly or indirectly, a placement fee, commission or other Thing of Value for referring a settlement service provider in any real estate transaction unless the Broker or Brokerage Firm first discloses in writing such compensation to whomever the Broker or Brokerage Firm is referring at the time of making such referral.

C. Only Brokerage Firms licensed in Colorado are permitted to receive a commission on transactions for real estate located in Colorado. Pursuant to section 12-10-217(1)(l), C.R.S., a Colorado Brokerage Firm may pay a brokerage firm or broker licensed in another Jurisdiction or country a referral fee under the following circumstances:

1. The brokerage firm or broker licensed in another Jurisdiction or country actually referred a client to the Broker or Brokerage Firm.
2. The brokerage firm or broker licensed in the other Jurisdiction or country must reside and maintain an office in the other Jurisdiction or country. Subsection C. of this Rule applies to payment made to citizens or residents of a country which does not license real estate brokers if the payee represents that they are in the business of selling real estate in that country.
3. All Advertising, negotiations, contracting, and conveyancing regarding the Colorado property must be performed by a Broker licensed in Colorado.

4. All money collected from the parties to the transaction prior to closing must be deposited in the name of the Brokerage Firm licensed in Colorado as set forth in Chapter 5 of these Rules.

6.22. Prohibited Remedies for Compensation

A. If for any reason the seller fails, refuses, neglects, or is unable to consummate the transaction as provided for in the contract, and through no fault or neglect of the buyer the real estate transaction cannot be completed, the Brokerage Firm has no right to any portion of the earnest money deposit which was deposited by the buyer.

B. In a residential transaction, unless Broker has adjudicated a claim and a judgment is entered, no Broker will file or threaten to file a lien, a lis pendens, record a Listing Contract to secure the payment of a commission or other fee associated with Real Estate Brokerage Services, cause the title to a property to become clouded or interfere with the transfer of title when the Broker is not a principal in the transaction.

C. A Brokerage Firm and Broker who has Commercial Real Estate listed for lease and has provided Real Estate Brokerage Services that resulted in procuring a tenant who has leased any interest in the Commercial Real Estate in accordance with the written agreement between the Brokerage Firm and the owner may file a lien pursuant to section 38-22.5-103, C.R.S. against the Commercial Real Estate in the amount of the compensation set forth in the written agreement. If the Commercial Real Estate has been conveyed to a bona fide buyer prior to the recording of the notice to lien pursuant to section 38-22.5-104, C.R.S., a Brokerage Firm or Broker may not file a lien for a commission that is due as the result of a lease renewal.

6.23. Immediate Notification of Conviction, Plea or Violation Required

A Broker must provide written notification to the Commission within thirty (30) calendar days for any of the following:

A. A plea of guilty, a plea of nolo contendere, or a conviction of any crime as pursuant to section 12-10-217(1)(n), C.R.S.;

B. A violation or aiding and abetting in the violation of the Colorado or federal fair housing laws;

C. Any disciplinary action taken against a Broker in any other Jurisdiction, if the Broker's action(s) would constitute a violation of Commission statutes and these Rules; and

D. A suspension or revocation of a license, registration, or certification by Colorado or another Jurisdiction, within the last five (5) years, for fraud, deceit, material misrepresentation, theft, or the breach of a fiduciary duty that denied the Broker the authorization to practice as a mortgage loan originator, a real estate broker or salesperson, a real estate appraiser, an insurance producer, an attorney, a securities broker-dealer, a securities sales representative, an investment advisor, or an investment advisor representative.

6.24. Electronic Records and Production of Records

All records required to be maintained by Brokers or Brokerage Firms may be maintained as Electronic Records. Electronic Records or printed records must be produced upon request by the Commission or any principal party to a transaction and must be in a format that has the continued capability to be retrieved and legibly printed.

* 6.25. Investigations or Audits by Commission

A. Notification of a Complaint that has been Assigned for Investigations or an Audit

1. A Broker or Brokerage Firm will receive written notification from the Commission regarding the following:

* a. A complaint has been filed and an investigation has been initiated. A copy of the complaint that has been filed against the Broker or Brokerage Firm will be provided; or

* b. A complaint has been initiated on the Commission's own motion. A summary of the complaint against the Broker or Brokerage Firm will be provided; or

* c. The Broker or Brokerage Firm has been selected for an audit.

2. Upon receipt of the Commission's notification, a Broker or Brokerage Firm must submit a written response to the Commission. Failure to submit a written response within the time set by the Commission in its notification will be grounds for disciplinary action regardless of the question of whether the underlying complaint or audit warrants further investigation or subsequent action by the Commission. The written response must contain the following:
   a. A complete and specific answer to the factual recitations, allegations, or averments made in the complaint filed against the Broker or Brokerage Firm, whether made by a member of the public, on the Commission's own motion, or by an authorized representative of the Commission.
   b. A complete and specific response to any additional questions, allegations, or averments presented in the notification letter.
   c. A complete transaction file and any documents or records requested in the notification letter.
   d. Any further information relative to the complaint or audit that the Broker or Brokerage Firm believes to be relevant or material to the matters addressed in the notification letter.

B. Extension to Respond

Upon request, the Commission will grant extensions of time for Brokers or Brokerage Firms to respond to any complaint or audit provided such request is reasonable.

C. Produce Records for Investigation or Audit

Brokers and Brokerage Firms must retain and produce for inspection by the Commission any document or record as may be reasonably necessary for investigation or audit in the enforcement of Commission statutes and these Rules. Failure to submit such documents or records within the time set by the Commission in its notification will be grounds for disciplinary action unless the Commission has granted an extension of time for such production.

6.26. Actions when License is Suspended, Revoked, Expired or Inactive

Upon suspension, revocation, expiration, or transfer to Inactive Status of a License, the Broker or Brokerage Firm is responsible for immediate compliance with the following:

A. If an Associate Broker:

1. Cease any activities requiring a License.
2. Inform the Employing Broker of the change in license status.
3. Cease all Advertising, including, but not limited to, use of office signs, yard signs, billboards, newspapers, magazines, the internet, direct mailings, and multiple listing services.
4. Inform all impacted Consumers within seven (7) days of the action taken and the impact that the change in license status will have on any pending transaction. It is the responsibility of the Employing Broker to ensure that another Associate Broker is designated to perform the duties requiring a License in all pending transactions, or to release the affected parties from any Listing Contract(s) with the Brokerage Firm.

B. If an Independent Broker:

1. Cease any activities requiring a License.
2. Cease all Advertising, including, but not limited to, use of office signs, yard signs, billboards, newspapers, magazines, the internet, direct mailings, and multiple listing services.
3. Notify all impacted Consumers within seven (7) days of the action taken and the impact that the change in license status will have on any pending transaction.
4. Release the affected parties from any active Listing Contract(s) with the Independent Broker.
5. Instruct the affected parties to seek guidance from a licensed attorney or retain a new Brokerage Firm regarding any pending transactions.
6. The Independent Broker is responsible for accounting for all funds, returning all Trust and Escrow Account records and making all final disbursements to the rightful beneficiaries within thirty (30) days of the change in license status. The Independent Broker is also responsible for providing the Commission with a full list of all impacted Consumers' contact information within seven (7) days and for maintaining all records for four (4) years.

C. If an Employing Broker:

1. Cease any activities requiring a License.
2. Cease all Advertising, including, but not limited to, use of office signs, yard signs, billboards, newspapers, magazines, the internet, direct mailings, and multiple listing services.
3. The Employing Broker is personally responsible for the handling of any and all earnest money deposits, Trust or Escrow Account funds received or disbursed by the Brokerage Firm. The Employing Broker is responsible for returning all Trust and Escrow Account records to the Brokerage Firm.
4. The Brokerage Firm must designate a new Employing Broker to be responsible for the management and supervision of the licensed actions of the Brokerage Firm and all Associate Brokers shown in the Commission's records as being in the employ of the Brokerage Firm. Pursuant to section 12-10-203(6)(c), C.R.S., the Brokerage Firm may also seek a Temporary License to prevent hardship if none of the Brokerage Firm's Associate Brokers hold an Employing Broker level license.
5. If the Brokerage Firm is unable to designate a new Employing Broker or is not granted a Temporary License, the Licenses of the Brokerage Firm and any Associate Brokers will be placed on Inactive status. The Employing Broker must also perform all duties as set forth in subsection C.6. of this Rule.
6. If a Brokerage Firm's License becomes Inactive, Expired or revoked, the Employing Broker will have seven (7) days to notify all Consumers impacted as to the effect of such license status change will have on the Associate Brokers and all pending transactions. The Employing Broker is responsible for accounting for all funds, returning all Trust and Escrow Account records and making all final disbursements to the rightful beneficiaries within thirty (30) days of the change in license status. The Employing Broker is also responsible for providing the Commission with a full list of all impacted Consumers' contact information within seven (7) days and for maintaining all records for four (4) years.

D. Commissions or fees may be received by a Broker or Brokerage Firm only for transactions where the commission or fee was earned prior to that Broker's or Brokerage Firm's suspension, revocation, expiration, or transfer to Inactive status.

Commission Approved Forms

Through the adoption and promulgation of the Chapter 7 Rules: Use of Standard Forms, it became compulsory for all real estate brokers licensed by the State of Colorado to use Commission approved forms in most of their contracting. §12-10-403(4), C.R.S., grants the Colorado Real Estate Commission statutory authority to promulgate standard forms for use by licensees.

One of the major purposes of the rule is to help to insure broker compliance with the Colorado Supreme Court Conway-Bogue decision. (See case summary in Chapter 10 – Landmark Case Law) A second purpose is to help promote uniformity in contracting to the end that the public is better protected. The privileges granted should not be abused by the real estate broker.

Chapter 7: Use of Standard Forms

7.1. Standard Forms

Pursuant to section 12-10-403(4), C.R.S., a Broker is authorized to complete Standard Forms for use in a real estate transaction, including Standard Forms intended to convey personal property as part of the real estate transaction, when a Broker is performing the activities for which a License is required and the Broker is acting as either a Single Agent or Transaction-Broker. The Broker's use of Standard Forms must be appropriate for the transaction and the circumstances in which they are used. The Broker must advise the parties that Standard Forms have important legal consequences and that the parties should consult legal counsel before signing such forms. A Standard Form is:

A. Commission-Approved Form

A "Commission-Approved Form" is a form promulgated by the Commission for current use by Brokers. A Broker must use a Commission-Approved Form when such form exists and is appropriate for the transaction. The Broker may advise the parties as to the effects thereof. To obtain the forms promulgated by the Commission, visit the Division's website.

B. Attorney Form

An "Attorney Form" is a form drafted by a licensed Colorado attorney representing the Broker, the Employing Broker, or the Brokerage Firm. A Broker may only use an Attorney Form if a Commission-Approved Form does not exist or is not appropriate for the transaction. The form must contain the language that says: "This form has not been approved by the Colorado Real Estate Commission". The form must also include: the name of the attorney or law firm that prepared the Attorney Form and the name of the Broker, Employing Broker, or the Brokerage Firm for whom the form was prepared. The form may not be altered by the Broker other than by completing any blank spaces in the form. The Broker may advise the parties as to the effects thereof.

C. Client Form

A "Client Form" is a form provided by a party to the transaction if the Broker is acting in the transaction as either a Single Agent or Transaction-Broker for the party providing the form. The Broker must retain written confirmation that the form was provided by said party to the transaction. A Broker's use of such form is limited to inserting transaction-specific information within the form.

D. Government/ Lender Form

A "Government/Lender Form" is a form prescribed by a governmental agency, a quasi-government agency, or a lender regulated by state or federal law and the use of the form is mandated by such agency or lender. A Broker's use of such form is limited to inserting transaction-specific information within the form.

E. Colorado Bar Association Form

A "Colorado Bar Association Form" is a form used with the written approval of the Colorado Bar Association, or its successor organization, and specifically designated for use by Brokers in Colorado. Brokers may only use the form when a Commission-Approved Form does not exist or is not appropriate for the transaction. A Broker must use the form within any guidelines or conditions specified by the Colorado Bar Association or its successor organization. The form may not be altered by the Broker other than by completing any blank spaces in the form. A Broker may not use any forms published or distributed by the Colorado Bar Association unless such form contains the following language that says: "This form has been approved by the Colorado Bar Association for use by Real Estate Brokers in Colorado in accordance with the guidelines provided with this form". The Broker may advise the parties as to the effects thereof.

F. Disclosure Form

A "Disclosure Form" is a form used for disclosure purposes only and the disclosure does not claim to waive or create any legal rights or obligations affecting any party to the transaction. The form must contain the language that says: "This form has not been approved by the Colorado Real Estate Commission". The Broker may advise the parties as to the effects thereof. The form may only provide information concerning:

1. The real estate involved in the transaction specifically; or
2. The geographic area in which the real estate is located generally.

G. Title Company Form

A "Title Company Form" is a form prescribed and completed by a title company that is providing closing services in a transaction. The Broker may advise the parties as to the effects thereof.

H. Letter of Intent

A "Letter of Intent" is created or prepared by a Broker, Employing Broker, or Brokerage Firm. The Letter of Intent must state on its face that it is nonbinding and creates no legal rights or obligations. The form must contain the language that says: "This form has not been approved by the Colorado Real Estate Commission". The Broker may advise the parties as to the effects thereof.

7.2. Permitted and Prohibited Modifications and Form Reproduction of Commission-Approved Forms as set forth in Rule 7.1.A.

A. A Broker or Brokerage Firm may add the Brokerage Firm's name, Trade Name, address, telephone, e-mail, Trademark or other identifying information on a Commission-Approved Form.

B. A Broker or Brokerage Firm may add initial lines at the bottom of a page of any Commission-Approved Form.

C. Any deletion or modification to the printed body of a Commission-Approved Form must result from negotiations or the instruction(s) of a party to the transaction. Any deletion must be made directly on the printed body of the form by striking through the deleted portion in a legible manner that does not obscure the deletion that has been made.

D. Blank spaces on a Commission-Approved Form may be lengthened or shortened to accommodate the relevant data or information.

E. Provisions that are inserted into blank spaces must be printed in a font style or type that clearly differentiates such insertions from the font style or type used for the Commission-Approved Form language.

F. A Broker may delete part or all of the following provisions of the Commission-Approved "Contract to Buy and Sell Real Estate" Forms (even if the provision has since been changed to a different section number) or corresponding provisions in other Commission-Approved Forms, if such provisions do not apply to the transaction. In the event any provision is deleted, the provision's caption or heading must remain unaltered on the form followed by the words "omitted-not applicable".

1. Section 2.5. Inclusions
2. Section 2.6. Exclusions
3. Section 2.7. Water Rights/Well Rights
4. Section 4.2. Seller Concession
5. Section 4.5. New Loan
6. Section 4.6. Assumption
7. Section 4.7. Seller or Private Financing
8. Section 5. Financing Conditions and Obligations
9. Section 6. Appraisal Provisions
10. Section 7. Owners' Association
11. Section 8.6. Right of First Refusal or Contract Approval
12. Section 9. New ILC, New Survey
13. Section 10.6. Due Diligence
14. Section 10.8. Source of Potable Water (CBS1, CBS2, CBS4, CBSF1)
15. Section 10.9. Existing Leases; Modification of Existing Leases; New Leases (CBS2, CBS3, CBS4)
16. Section 11. Estoppel Statements (CBS2, CBS3, CBS4)
17. Section 15.3. Status Letter and Record Change Fees
18. Section 15.4. Local Transfer Tax
19. Section 15.5. Private Transfer Fee
20. Section 15.7. Sales and Use Tax
21. Section 16.2. Rents
22. Section 16.3. Association Assessments

G. A Broker may delete part or all of the following provisions of the "Counterproposal" and the "Agreement to Amend/Extend Contract" if such provisions do not apply to the transaction. In the event any provision is deleted, the provision's caption or heading must remain unaltered on the form followed by the words "omitted-not applicable".

1. Section 3. Dates and Deadlines Table
2. Section 4. Purchase Price and Terms [in the Counterproposal only]

H. A Broker or Brokerage Firm may add signature lines and identifying labels for the parties' signatures on a Commission-Approved Form.

I. A Broker or Brokerage Firm may modify, strike, or delete such language on a Commission-Approved Form as the Commission may from time to time authorize the language to be modified, stricken, or deleted.

J. A Broker must explain all permitted modifications, deletions, omissions, insertions, additional provisions, and addenda to the principal party and must recommend that the parties obtain expert advice as to the material matters that are beyond the expertise of the Broker.

K. Commission-Approved Forms used by a Broker, including permitted modifications made by a Broker, must be legible.

L. Brokers or Brokerage Firms generating Commission-Approved Forms in an electronic format must ensure that the forms are protected so as to prevent inadvertent changes or prohibited modifications of Commission-Approved Forms by the Broker or recipient.

7.3. Additional Provisions

A. Any "Additional Provision" which by its terms serves to delete or modify portions of a Standard Form as set forth in Rule 7.1. must result from negotiations or the instruction(s) of a party to the transaction.

B. A Broker who uses a transaction-specific clause or clauses drafted by the Broker's, Employing Broker's, or Brokerage Firm's licensed Colorado attorney must ensure that the Broker understands the clause, and the clause is used and completed appropriately. The Broker must retain the clause(s) prepared by the Broker's, Employing Broker's, or Brokerage Firm's licensed Colorado attorney for four (4) years from the date that the clause was last used by the Broker. The Broker must provide those clause(s) and the name of the licensed Colorado attorney or law firm that prepared the clause(s) upon request by the Commission.

7.4. Prohibited Provisions

A. No contract provision, including modifications or additional provisions permitted as set forth in Rules 7.2. and 7.3., will relieve a Broker, Employing Broker, or Brokerage Firm from compliance with section 12-10-201, C.R.S., et seq., or these Rules.

B. A Broker who is not a principal party to the contract may not have personal provisions, personal disclaimers, or exculpatory language in favor of the Broker, Employing Broker, or Brokerage Firm inserted into a Standard Form. A Broker may, at the direction of a principal party, include language regarding the payment of the Broker's or Brokerage Firm's commission if this is a negotiated term between the principal parties of the Commission-Approved "Contract to Buy and Sell Real Estate" Form.

Ed. Note: The most current version of approved forms can be found on the Division of Real Estate website at: **www.dora.state.co.us/dre.**

Real estate brokers are required to use Commission-approved forms as appropriate to a transaction or circumstance to which a relevant form is applicable. Commission-approved forms are posted on the Division of Real Estate's website. Effective June 2009, the Commission will no longer post forms in the Code of Colorado Regulations. The Commission hereby withdraws all forms from the Code of Colorado Regulations. In instances when the Commission has not developed an approved form within the purview of this rule, and other forms are used, they are not governed by Chapter 7 of the Rules. Other forms used by a broker shall not be prepared by a broker, unless otherwise permitted by law.

To obtain the forms promulgated by the real estate commission that are within the purview of Chapter 7, visit the Division of Real Estate website at: *http://www.dora.state.co.us/dre* or the Division of Real Estate's offices at 1560 Broadway, Suite 925, Denver, Colorado 80202.

Chapter 8: Declaratory Orders

8.1. Petition for a Declaratory Order

Pursuant to section 24-4-105(11), C.R.S., a Petitioner may petition the Commission for a declaratory order to terminate controversies or to remove uncertainties as to the applicability of any statutory provision, rule, or order of the Commission as it would apply to the Petitioner.

8.2. Parties to the Proceedings

The parties to any proceeding as set forth in Chapter 8 of these Rules will be the Commission and the Petitioner. Any other person may seek leave of the Commission to intervene in such a proceeding. Permission to intervene will be granted at the sole discretion of the Commission. A petition to intervene will set forth the same matters as set forth in Rule 8.3.

8.3. Petition Contents

Any petition filed as set forth in Chapter 8 of these Rules will state the following:

A. The name and address of the Petitioner;

B. The statute, rule, or order to which the petition relates;

C. A concise statement of all the facts and law necessary to show the nature of the controversy or uncertainty and the manner in which the statute, rule, or order in question applies or potentially applies to the Petitioner; and

D. The Petitioner may submit a concise statement of the declaratory order sought.

8.4. Commission's Considerations Whether or Not to Rule

The Commission may determine, in its sole discretion and without prior notice to the Petitioner, whether or not to rule upon a petition. In determining whether or not to rule upon a petition filed as set forth in Chapter 8 of these Rules, the Commission may consider the following matters, among others:

A. Whether a ruling on the petition will terminate a controversy or remove uncertainties as to the applicability to the Petitioner of any statutory provision, rule, or order of the Commission.

B. Whether the petition involves any subject, question, or issue which is the subject of a formal or informal matter or investigation currently pending before the Commission or a court involving one or more of the Petitioners.

C. Whether the petition involves any subject, question, or issue which is the subject of a formal or informal matter or investigation currently pending before the Commission or a court not involving the Petitioner.

D. Whether the petition seeks a ruling on a hypothetical question.

E. Whether the Petitioner has some other adequate legal remedy, other than an action for declaratory order which will terminate the controversy or remove any uncertainty as to the applicability to the Petitioner of the statute, rule, or order in question.

8.5. Commission Determines Not to Rule

If the Commission determines it will not rule on a petition, the Commission will issue its written decision disposing of the petition, stating the reasons for declining to rule upon the petition. A copy of the decision will be provided to the Petitioner. A decision not to rule on a petition for a declaratory order is not final agency action subject to judicial review.

8.6. Commission Determines to Rule

If the Commission determines that it will rule on the petition:

A. The Commission may order the Petitioner to file an additional written brief, memorandum, statement of position, or request the Petitioner to submit additional facts or arguments in writing.

B. The Commission may take administrative notice of facts pursuant to the Administrative Procedure Act, section 24-4-105(8), C.R.S., and may utilize its experience, technical competence, and specialized knowledge when ruling on the petition.

C. The Commission may set the petition, upon due notice to the Petitioner, for a non-evidentiary hearing.

D. The Commission may, upon due notice to the Petitioner, set the petition for hearing for the purpose of obtaining additional facts or information, or to determine the truth of any facts set forth in the petition, or to hear oral arguments on the petition. Notice to the Petitioner setting such formal hearing will set forth, to the extent known, the factual or other matters into which the Commission intends to inquire. The Petitioner will have the burden of proving all of the facts stated in the petition, all of the facts necessary to show the nature of the controversy or uncertainty and the manner in which the statute, rule, or order in question applies or potentially applies to the Petitioner and any other facts the Petitioner desires the Commission to consider.

E. Any ruling by the Commission may be based solely on the matters set forth in the petition or may be based on any amendments to the petition, any information gathered by the Commission through a non-evidentiary hearing, formal hearing or otherwise, or any facts the Commission may take administrative notice of. Upon ruling on a petition, the Commission will issue its written order stating its basis for the order. A copy of the order will be provided to the Petitioner.

8.7. Declaratory Orders Subject to Judicial Review

Any declaratory order of a petition as set forth in Chapter 8 of these Rules will constitute agency action subject to judicial review pursuant to section 24-4-106, C.R.S.

Chapter 9: Commission Review of Initial Decisions and Exceptions

* 9.1. Written Form, Filing Requirements, and Service

A. All pleadings must be in written form, mailed with a certificate of service to the Commission.

* B. All pleadings must be filed with the Commission on the date the filing is due. Computation of time for the filing timelines for Chapter 9 of these Rules is pursuant to section 2-4-108, C.R.S. A pleading is considered filed upon receipt by the Commission. Chapter 9 of these Rules does not provide for any additional time for service by mail.

C. All pleadings must be filed with the Commission and not with the Office of Administrative Courts. Any pleadings filed in error with the Office of Administrative Courts will not be considered. The Commission's address is:

Colorado Real Estate Commission
1560 Broadway, Suite 925
Denver, CO 80202

D. All pleadings must be served on the opposing party on the date which the pleading is filed with the Commission. Electronic service between the parties is encouraged. The date and manner must be noted on the certificate of service.

9.2. Initial Decision

Upon receipt of the initial decision prepared and filed by the Administrative Law Judge from the Office of Administrative Courts, the Division will timely mail a copy of the initial decision to the parties at their respective addresses of record with the Commission pursuant to section 24-4-105(16)(a), C.R.S.

9.3. Commission's Authority to Review the Initial Decision

Pursuant to section 24-4-105(14)(a)(II), C.R.S., the Commission may initiate a review of an initial decision on its own motion within thirty (30) days of the date on which the Division mails the initial decision to the parties. A letter from the Division initiating the review of the initial decision constitutes a motion within the meaning of section 24-4-105(14)(a)(II), C.R.S.

9.4. Appeal of the Initial Decision by the Parties

A. Any party wishing to reverse or modify an initial decision of an Administrative Law Judge must file written exceptions with the Commission in accordance with the procedures and time frames as set forth in Rule 9.5.

B. If neither party appeals the initial decision by filing exceptions, the initial decision will become the final order of the Commission after thirty (30) days from the date on which the Division mails the initial decision pursuant to section 24-4-105(14)(b)(III), C.R.S. Failure to file exceptions will result in a waiver of the right to judicial review of the final order of the Commission unless the portion of the final order subject to review differs from the contents of the initial decision pursuant to section 24-4-105(14)(c), C.R.S.

9.5. Filing of Exceptions

A. Pursuant to section 24-4-105(15)(a), C.R.S., any party seeking to file exceptions must initially file with the Commission a designation of the relevant parts of the record and of parts of the transcript of the hearing within twenty (20) days of the date on which the Division mails the initial decision to the parties.

B. Transcripts:

Any party may designate the entire transcript, or may identify witness(es) whose testimony is to be transcribed, the legal ruling or argument to be transcribed, or other information necessary to identify a portion of the transcript. However, no transcript is required if the Commission's review is limited to pure questions of law. The deadline for filing exceptions depends on whether either of the parties designates a portion of the transcript.

1. If the parties do not designate parts of the transcript, exceptions are due within thirty (30) days from the date on which the Division mails the initial decision to the parties. Both parties' exceptions are due on the same day.
2. Any party wishing to designate all, or any part, of the transcript must adhere to the following procedures:
    a. Transcripts will not be deemed part of a designation unless specifically identified and ordered.
    b. If one party designates a portion of the transcript, the other party may file a supplemental designation in which that party may designate additional portions of the transcript. The supplemental designation must be filed with the Commission and served on the other party within ten (10) days after the date on which the original designation was filed.
    c. Any party who designates a transcript must order the transcript by the date on which they file their designation with the Commission whether they are filing an original or supplemental designation.
    d. The party ordering a transcript must direct the court reporter or transcribing service to complete and file with the Commission the original transcript and one (1) copy within thirty (30) days of their order.
    e. The party that designates a transcript must pay for such transcripts.
    f. Transcripts that are ordered and not filed with the Commission in a timely manner due to non-payment, insufficient payment, or failure to direct as set forth above may not be considered by the Commission.
    g. Upon receipt of transcripts identified in all designations and supplemental designations, the Commission will mail a notification to the parties stating that the transcripts have been received by the Commission.
    h. Exceptions are due within thirty (30) days from the date on which such notification is mailed. Both parties' exceptions are due on the same date.

C. A party's exceptions must include specific objections to the initial decision.

D. Either party may file a response to the other party's exceptions. All responses must be filed within ten (10) days of the date on which the exceptions were filed with the Commission. Subsequent replies will not be considered except for good cause shown.

E. The Commission may in its sole discretion grant an extension of time to file exceptions or responses, or may delegate the discretion to grant such an extension of time to the Commission's designee.

9.6. Request for Oral Arguments

A. All requests for oral argument must be in writing and included with a party's exceptions or response.

B. It is within the sole discretion of the Commission to grant or deny a request for oral argument. The Commission generally does not grant requests for oral argument. If an oral argument is granted, each party will have ten (10) minutes to present their argument. Questioning by members of the Commission will not count against the allocated ten (10) minutes.

C. The Commission or its designee may extend the time for oral arguments upon good cause shown.

9.7. Final Orders

A. The Commission may deliberate and vote on exceptions immediately following oral arguments or the Commission may take the matter under advisement.

B. When the Commission votes on exceptions, whether after oral arguments or at a subsequent Commission meeting, the ruling of the Commission will not be considered final until a written order is issued.

C. The date of the Commission's final order is the date on which the written order is signed, irrespective of any motions for reconsideration that are filed.

Chapter 3: Real Estate Commission Position Statements

An * in the left margin indicates a change in the statute, rule or text since the last publication of the manual.

CP-1 Commission Policy on Homebuilder's Exemption from Licensing

Corporations that build structures on land they own may sell the land and building together without licensing, provided that the sales are made by corporate officers or regularly salaried employees. The land and building must be sold as a unit and the building must not have been previously occupied. This exemption is usually referred to as the homebuilder's exemption. Since employees who sell must be regularly salaried employees, the question often arises as to what a regular salary is. This is the position of the Commission: 12-10-201(6)(b)(X), C.R.S., among other requirements, requires that a corporation use "regular salaried employees" to sell or negotiate the sale of real property.

It is the position of the Commission that the phrase, "regular salaried employees" means that:

1. The salary must be an actual and stated amount and must not be a draw or advance against future commissions.
2. The salary must be regularly paid (*i.e.*, weekly, monthly, etc.).
3. Although the amount of salary may vary, an employee must be paid at least the prevailing federal minimum wage.
4. The corporation should deduct amounts for state and federal withholding taxes, FICA taxes, and other commonly deductible expenses, which the corporation would employ with respect to other employees.

Payment of a commission, in addition to a regular salary, will not invalidate the exemption if the above guidelines are met.

CP-2 Commission Position on Earned Fees

(revised 10/03/2017)

<u>Commissions:</u>

Section 12-10-217(1)(l), C.R.S., of the license law forbids a broker from paying a commission or valuable consideration, for performing brokerage functions, to any person who is not licensed as a real estate broker. Brokerage functions include negotiating the purchase, sale or exchange of real estate. *See* section 12-10-201(6)(a), C.R.S. Pursuant to Colorado case law, "negotiating" means "the act of bringing two parties together for the purpose of consummating a real estate transaction." *Brakhage vs. Georgetown Associates, Inc.*, 523 P. 2d 145, 147 (1974). Therefore, any unlicensed person who directly or indirectly brings a buyer and seller together, is negotiating and would need a broker's license in order to be compensated. This includes, but is not limited to, such activities as referring potential time-share purchasers to a developer or referring potential purchasers to a homebuilder.

<u>Referral Fees:</u>

Section 12-10-304(1), C.R.S., permits a real estate broker to pay a referral fee if it is not prohibited by the federal "Real Estate Settlement and Procedures Act of 1974" ("RESPA") and reasonable cause for payment exists. Reasonable cause exists when:

1) An actual introduction of business has been made;
2) A contractual referral fee relationship exists; or
3) A contractual cooperative brokerage relationship exists.

Section 12-10-304(2)(b)(III), C.R.S., defines a referral fee as "any fee paid by a licensee to any person or entity, other than a cooperative commission offered by a listing broker to a selling broker or vice versa." Payment for providing a name to a licensed broker is not specifically addressed in Colorado statute. However, it would be illegal to pay such a fee to anyone performing acts that require a license (*e.g.*., negotiating, listing, and contracting). Care should be taken. At best, the unlicensed referrer can have no active involvement in the transaction beyond merely giving to a licensee the name of a prospective buyer, seller or tenant. If the payment is simply for the referral of a name to a licensee, with no further activity on the part of the referrer, and the referrer is not a provider of a settlement service, the Commission will not consider it to be a violation of the license law. Complaints and inquiries are dealt with on a case-by-case basis.

In real estate transactions involving federally related mortgage loans, Section 8 of RESPA, 12 U.S.C. §§ 2601 et seq., governs the payment of referral fees. Pursuant to 12 U.S.C. § 2602(1) of RESPA, the term "federally related mortgage loan" is defined to include:

(1) any loan (other than temporary financing such as a construction loan) which—

(A) is secured by a first or subordinate lien on residential real property (including individual units of condominiums and cooperatives) designed principally for the occupancy of from one to four families, including any such secured loan, the proceeds of which are used to prepay or pay off an existing loan secured by the same property; and

(B) (i) is made in whole or in part by any lender the deposits or accounts of which are insured by any agency of the Federal Government, or is made in whole or in part by any lender which is regulated by any agency of the Federal Government; or

(ii) is made in whole or in part, or insured, guaranteed, supplemented, or assisted in any way, by the Secretary or any other officer or agency of the Federal Government or under or in connection with a housing or urban development program administered by the Secretary or a housing or related program administered by any other such officer or agency; or

(iii) is intended to be sold by the originating lender to the Federal National Mortgage Association, the Government National Mortgage Association, the Federal Home Loan Mortgage Corporation, or a financial institution from which it is to be purchased by the Federal Home Loan Mortgage Corporation; or

(iv) is made in whole or in part by any "creditor", as defined in section 103(f) of the Consumer Credit Protection Act (15 U.S.C. § 1602(f)), who makes or invests in residential real estate loans aggregating more than $ 1,000,000 per year, except that for the purpose of this Act, the term "creditor" does not include any agency or instrumentality of any State.

RESPA and Commission Rule 6.21 prohibit the payment or receipt of referral fees and kickbacks which tend to increase unnecessarily the costs of settlement services. As part of this prohibition, any referral of a settlement service, including real estate brokerage services, is not compensable. Thus, an individual or company is not allowed to pay another individual or company for the referral of settlement business. Moreover, it is not appropriate for a settlement service provider to pay a broker, or offset a broker's expenses, for lead generation. The Commission views this as payment for the referral of business, which would be a violation of Rule 6.21. Additionally, Section 12-10-217(10), C.R.S., requires the Commission to refer such issues to the Consumer Financial Protection Bureau for investigation as a potential violation of RESPA.

RESPA, however, does permit:

1) A payment to an attorney at law for services actually rendered:
2) A payment by a title company to its duly appointed agent for services actually performed in the issuance of a policy of title insurance;
3) A payment by a lender to its duly appointed agent or contractor for services actually performed in the origination, processing, or funding of a loan;
4) A payment to any person of a bona fide salary or compensation for goods or facilities actually furnished or for services actually performed;

5) A payment pursuant to cooperative brokerage and referral arrangements or agreements between real estate brokers (all parties must be acting in a real estate brokerage capacity);
6) Normal promotional and educational activities that are not conditioned on the referral of business and that do not involve the defraying of expenses that otherwise would be incurred by persons in a position to refer settlement services or business incident thereto; or
7) An employer's payment to its own employees for any referral activities.

Administrative Fees:

As a result of the United States Supreme Court's decision in *Freeman v. Quicken Loans, Inc.*, 132 S. Ct. 2034, 2012 U.S. Lexis 3940 (2012), real estate brokers may charge administrative fees, either for services performed by the broker or the real estate brokerage, in addition to the broker's commission. In *Quicken* Loans, the Supreme Court held that while RESPA prohibits the splitting of fees if the charges are divided between two or more persons (i.e. settlement service providers) and the fee was paid for services not actually performed, dividing or splitting fees amongst a single settlement service provider is not prohibited. The Commission considers a real estate broker and his or her licensed broker-employer (or brokerage) to be a single provider of settlement services and fees may be split amongst them.

CP-3 Position Statement Concerning Commission Rule 6.15.

Commission Rule 6.15, commonly referred to as the "sign-crossing" rule, states as follows:

6.15.A. "Brokers will not negotiate a Listing Contract directly with a Consumer for compensation from said Consumer if such Broker knows the Consumer has an unexpired Listing Contract with another Brokerage Firm granting said Brokerage Firm an exclusive contract."

6,15.B. "However, if a Broker is contacted by a Consumer who is currently subject to an exclusive Listing Contract, and the Broker has not initiated the discussion, the Broker may negotiate the terms upon which to take a future Listing Contract or, alternatively, may take a Listing Contract to become effective upon expiration or termination of any existing Exclusive Listing."

6.15.C. "The burden of inquiry is on the Broker to determine the existence of the Listing Contract and to advise the Consumer to seek guidance from a licensed attorney."

The Commission's intent in promulgating Rule 6.15 was (1) to prevent brokers from interfering with existing listing contracts to the detriment of the owner and (2) to protect the owner from possible claims that two commissions are owed.

Many owners are extremely dependent on the expertise of the licensee. They may sincerely believe an existing listing contract is not in effect when, in fact, it is. The burden of inquiry is on the licensee.

Earlier versions of 6.15 had been criticized for being too restrictive. The current rule still provides that licensees shall not negotiate directly with an owner if they know that the owner has a written unexpired Exclusive Right to Sell or Lease. However, the licensee is now allowed to negotiate the terms for a future listing or take a listing effective upon expiration of a current listing so long as the licensee is first contacted by the owner.

This recognizes the fact that an owner with property currently listed may initiate the negotiations concerning a future listing. In addition, the current rule recognizes that in some instances owners become dissatisfied with the services of the broker with whom they have a listing and wish to cancel the listing. If a knowledgeable and informed seller wishes to cancel a listing and list with another company, this cannot be prevented. Of course, the seller runs the risk that improper cancellation of a listing contract can result in legal consequences. Brokers should never independently advise a seller in this area. Instead, an inquiring seller should be advised to seek legal counsel to explain the consequences of canceling an unexpired listing.

If the rule is followed closely it will provide greater opportunities for licensees to negotiate listings where a seller does not wish to re-list with the same broker while maintaining the integrity of the principal/agent brokerage relationship.

CP-4 Commission Position on Interest Bearing Trust Accounts

(Revised Position 8-04)

Section 12-10-217(1)(i), C.R.S., permits brokers to place entrusted money in an interest bearing account.

The Commission has taken the position that in the absence of a contract signed by the proper parties to the contrary, any interest accumulating on a trust account does not belong to the broker who is acting as escrow agent. (This position is based upon 12-10-217(1)(t) and upon the well-established tenet of agency that the agent may not profit personally from the agency relationship except for agreed upon compensation.)

Contracts calling for large earnest money deposits or other payments should contain a provision specifying which party is entitled to interest earned and under what conditions. In the absence of such a provision, accrued interest normally belongs to the seller if the contract is consummated or if the seller is successful in declaring a forfeiture. The entrusted money normally belongs to the purchaser if the contract fails.

In a property management trust account, the accrued interest on that portion of rental money received that belongs to the lessor beneficiary (landlord), would belong to the lessor beneficiary. The accrued interest on security deposits would belong to the respective tenants unless the lessor can establish a right to the security deposit (in the absence of a contract to the contrary).

However, in the case of the property management of mobile homes, by Colorado statute, the interest earned on security deposits may be retained by the landlord of a mobile home park as compensation for administering the trust account. (38-12-209(2)(b) C.R.S.)

Nothing in this position statement precludes a real estate broker from voluntarily transferring interest earned on a trust account to a fund established for the purpose of providing affordable housing to Colorado residents if such a fund is established.

CP-5 Commission Position on Advance Rentals and Security Deposits

Pursuant to C.R.S. 12-10-217(1)(i) and Commission Rules 5.2 and 5.8.A., all money belonging to others which is received by a broker must be placed in an escrow or trust account. This applies to tenant security deposits and advance rental deposits, including credit card receipts, held by a broker.

A broker may not deliver a security deposit to an owner unless notice is given to the tenant in the lease, rental agreement, or in a separate written notice that the security deposit will be held by the owner. Such notice must be given in a manner so that the tenant will know who is holding the security deposit, and shall include either the true' name and current mailing address of the owner or the true name and current mailing address of a person authorized to receive legal notices on behalf of such owner, along with specific requirements for how the tenant is to request return of the deposit.

If, after receipt by the broker, the security deposit is to be transferred to the owner or used for the owner's benefit, the broker, in addition to properly notifying the tenant, must secure the consent of the owner to assume full financial responsibility for the return of any deposit which may be refundable to the tenant. The broker shall not withhold the identity of the owner from the tenant if demand for the return of the deposit is properly made according to the lease, rental agreement, or separate notice, and the owner has refused to return the security deposit. The lease, rental agreement, or separate notice may also give notice that the security deposit will be transferred upon the happening of certain events, *e.g.*, sale of the property or the naming of a new property manager.

Delivery of the security deposit to the owner or to anyone (including a succeeding broker/manager of the property) without proper notice to the tenant, in addition to subjecting the broker to possible civil liability, will constitute a violation of the license law escrow statute cited above. The licensee must retain copies of such notices for inspection by the Commission.

Under a property management contract, the broker must transfer all escrowed money belonging to the owner of the property at reasonable and agreed upon intervals and with proper accounting pursuant to statutory requirements and Commission Rules in Chapter 5. If advance rental money is held by a broker but is subject to recall by the tenant or occupant, it must be escrowed until such time as it is earned and rightfully transferred or credited to the owner. A broker has no claim on or right to use advance deposits which are subject to recall by a tenant or prospective occupant. Deposits which are not subject to recall are the property of the owner and may not be transferred to the broker's account or used for the broker's benefit unless specifically authorized and agreed to by the owner in the management agreement.

If litigation concerning escrow money commences, the money may be placed with the court. The jurisdiction of the court will, of course, supersede the statutory requirement for escrowing money belonging to others.

CP-6 Commission Position on Release of Earnest Money Deposits

(Revised Position 8-6-2008)

Rule 6.22.A. states that: "If for any reason the seller fails, refuses, neglects or is unable to consummate the transaction as provided for in the contract, and through no fault or neglect of the buyer the real estate transaction cannot be completed, the Brokerage Firm has no right to any portion of the earnest money deposit which was deposited by the buyer."

The Commission will not pursue disciplinary action against a broker for refusal to disburse disputed funds when the broker is acting in accordance with the language of the appropriate Commission-approved contract to buy and sell. It is clear in the contract to buy and sell real estate that the broker holds the earnest money on behalf of <u>both</u> buyer and seller. If there is no dispute, the broker should disburse to the appropriate party immediately.

Some brokers unnecessarily require a signed release by both parties even when there is no disagreement. Audits have disclosed many instances where brokers have held deposits for extended periods just because one or both parties will not sign a release. While good judgment is always urged, releases are <u>not</u> a requirement of the Real Estate Commission. In addition, where one party has given written authorization for the release of a deposit to another, a written release by the other party is not required.

Exculpatory provisions holding the broker harmless do not belong in an agreement for the release of earnest money and should not be used to relieve the broker from liability unrelated to earnest money.

In the case of a dispute between the parties, the broker is authorized by the contract to buy and sell to obtain mutual written instructions (such as a release) before turning a deposit over to a party. The Commission has approved an optional use "Earnest Money Release" form when such a written release might help facilitate expeditious disbursement.

Unless otherwise indicated in the Commission-approved contract to buy and sell, a broker is not required to take any action regarding the release of the earnest money deposit when there is a controversy. If the following provisions are included in the contract, the broker may exercise three options in the event of an earnest money dispute, if the broker is the holder of the earnest money deposit. One option is that the broker may await any proceeding between the parties. Another option for the broker is to interplead all parties and deposit the earnest money into a court of competent jurisdiction. If included in the contract to buy and sell, the broker is entitled to recover court costs and reasonable attorney and legal fees. However, if this provision is struck from the contract to buy and sell, the broker may not be entitled to recover those costs. A third option available to the broker is to provide notice to the buyer and seller that unless the broker receives a copy of the Summons and Complaint or Claim (between the buyer and seller) containing a case number of the lawsuit within one hundred twenty (120) days of the broker's notice to the parties, the broker will be authorized to return the earnest money to the buyer.

If the broker is unable to locate the party due the refund, the broker may be required to transfer the deposit to the Colorado State Treasurer under the provisions of the Colorado "Unclaimed Property Act" C.R.S. 38-13-101. Notice of funds held is published in local newspapers under the "Great Colorado Payback Program" each year. Further information and reporting forms may be obtained from that office.

CP-7 Commission Position on Closing Costs

In the past, the Commission's position had been that real estate licensees were responsible for all costs of closing. This position has been modified after a re-examination of the Colorado Supreme Court case of Conway-Bogue vs. The Denver Bar Association and after the adoption of Rule 6.14.B.

Commission Rule 6.14.B. states:

> "Brokers are not obligated to prepare any legal documents as part of a real estate transaction. If the Broker or the Broker's designee prepares any legal document, the Broker or the Broker's designee may not charge a separate fee for preparation of such legal documents. The Broker is not responsible for fees charged for the preparation of legal documents where they are prepared by an attorney representing the Consumer. Costs of closing not related to preparation of legal documents may be paid by the Broker or by any other person. A Broker who closes transactions and charges separately for costs of closing not related to the preparation of legal documents must specify the costs and obtain the written consent of the parties to be charged."

Based on the new rule the position is as follows:

1. Licensees are still responsible for paying the costs of legal document preparation when they are preparing such documents for their clients. If the broker delegates this function to an agent (title company or closing service) the broker is still responsible for bearing the cost.
2. Other costs associated with closings can be paid for by the licensee or any other party. The Commission will no longer require that licensees bear these costs. Licensees are urged to use the Closing Instructions and Earnest Money Receipt form developed by the Commission.
3. It is now permissible for brokers to close their own transactions and make additional charges for providing closing services so long as the charges are not tied to legal document preparation. If a licensee does this it must be with the consent of the parties and all charges must be specified. This consent may be obtained through the Listing Contract, the Contract to Buy and Sell, the Closing Instructions and Earnest Money Receipt form, or otherwise.
4. Licensees are not responsible for bearing the cost of legal document preparation where the documents are prepared by an attorney representing the parties to the transaction. However, the broker should not designate the broker's own attorney to prepare legal documents for the parties and then charge as if the attorney had prepared the documents on behalf of a client.
5. The broker must still provide accurate closing statements.

Particular note should be paid to the first sentence of the rule. While there is no legal obligation for a broker to prepare the legal documents in a transaction the Commission strongly advises that licensees make this clear in the Listing Contract. Many persons, purchasers and sellers alike, normally look to the broker for the preparation of these documents. If the broker has not made it clear that the broker's company will not undertake the preparation of legal documents, the parties might well assume that the broker will do so at the broker's cost.

CP-8 Commission Position on Assignment of Contracts and Escrowed Funds

Assignments of contracts and escrowed funds usually occur when one real estate company is purchased or taken over by another real estate company.

The following reflects the general position of the Commission concerning the assignment of contracts and escrowed funds as it concerns the brokers.

1. All parties to a contract must be informed of assignments and all beneficiaries of escrowed funds must be informed of any transfer of escrowed funds.
2. Listing contracts may not be assigned by the listing broker to another broker (without the consent of the owner), because the listing contract is a personal contract of a type which would not be entered into except when the owner relies on the personal skills and expertise of the broker.
3. The broker concerned with an executory contract is not a party principal to the contract itself and, therefore, has no voice in its assignment. The broker signs the sales contract only as the receipting agent.
4. The right of entitlement of a broker to a commission, pursuant to a contract between the broker and a seller, is assignable. In the Commission approved form of executory contract, the agreement of the seller in regard to a commission is placed outside the body of the contract between the purchaser and seller.
5. The contract between the seller and the broker concerning commissions does not affect the contract between the principal parties in the sale.
6. Earnest money taken pursuant to an executory contract is money belonging to others and falls within the purview of 12-10-217(1)(h) and (i), C.R.S. Earnest money being held by the broker is not transferable to any party except to a closing agent as immediately prior to closing as is practicable.
7. The maintenance of earnest money held in escrow must be pursuant to the rules of the Commission. The broker may, for convenience, authorize other persons to withdraw money from this escrow account (see Commission Rule 5.3.C.), but the withdrawal must be pursuant to law and Commission rules.
8. Unless contracted to the contrary, the mechanical act of closing the transaction may be performed by any qualified person or persons with the agreement of the principal parties to the contract.
9. The absence of the closing broker or the Broker's agent will not relieve such broker from the broker's responsibilities of approving the Statement of Settlement. (See Commission Rule 6.19.). However, the absence of the broker cannot impede the closing of the transaction pursuant to the executory contract.
10. If a licensed broker receipts for earnest money pursuant to an executory contract and then transfers such earnest money to an unauthorized person, who is also a licensed broker, the licensed transferee, (as well as the transferor), is also subject to the law and rules of the Commission in regard to money belonging to others. Such licensed transferee is obligated to retain such money in a trust account until the transaction is consummated, defeated, or settlement has occurred, or unless directed otherwise by a court of law. If litigation concerning escrowed money commences, the money may be placed with the court. The jurisdiction of the court will supersede the statutory requirements and the Commission Rules.
11. If the seller and the buyer, who are the sole beneficiaries of the escrowed money, both agree that such escrowed money be transferred, then settlement has occurred and the broker must transfer the money according to the wishes of the beneficiaries. This does not defeat the broker's right to a commission whether by original contract with the seller or by assignment of such contract right.

CP-9 Commission Position on Record Keeping by Brokers

The Commission is often asked what documents must be kept in the broker's files which concern a particular transaction.

A duplicate means photocopy, carbon copy, or facsimile, or electronic copies which contain a digital or electronic signature as defined in 24-71-101(1) C.R.S. Pursuant to Rule 6.14.A. and 6.19.A., a broker shall maintain a duplicate of the original of any document (except deeds, notes and trust deeds or mortgages prepared for the benefit of third party lenders) which was prepared by or on behalf of the licensee and pertains to the consummation of the leasing, purchase, sale or exchange of real property in which the broker participates as a broker. The payoff statement and new loan statement monetarily affect the settlement statements and should be retained by the respective broker concerned. Cooperating brokers, including brokers acting as agents for buyers in a specific real estate transaction, shall have the same requirements for retention of duplicate records as is stated above, except that a cooperating broker who is not a party to the listing contract need not retain a copy of the listing contract or the seller's settlement statement. A broker is not required to obtain and retain copies of existing public records, title commitments, loan applications, lender required disclosures or related affirmations from independent third party closing entities after the settlement date. The broker shall retain documents bearing a duplicate signature for the disclosures required by Commission Rule7.1. The broker engaged by a party shall insure that the final sales agreement, settlement statement, or amendment of the settlement, delivered at closing for that party's tax reporting or future use, shall bear duplicate signatures as authorized by the parties concerned.

A complete listing of the documents normally required by the Commission for sales transactions and management activities can be found in the current edition of the Colorado Real Estate Manual, Chapter 20, and at the website address: http://www.dora.state.co.us/real-estate.

CP-10 Commission Position on Compensation Agreements Between Employing and Employed Brokers

In regard to an employed broker's claim for compensation from an employing broker, the Real Estate Commission has no legal authority to render a monetary judgment in a money dispute nor will it arbitrate such a matter. A broker's failure to pay an employee does not warrant disciplinary action.

The Commission's position is:

1. An employed broker is an employee of the employing broker.
2. That an employed broker may not accept a commission or valuable consideration for the sale of real property except from his or her employing broker. (12-10-221, C.R.S.)
3. That a commission or compensation paid to the employing or independent broker for real estate services is money belonging to such broker and is not money belonging to others as defined in 12-10-217(1)(h) and (i), C.R.S.
4. That a claim by an employed licensee for money allegedly owed by an employing broker must be decided by the civil courts on the basis of contract or "quantum merit."
5. That an employing broker pays their licensed or unlicensed employees pursuant to an oral or written employment contract.

Therefore, the contractual relationship between employing and employed brokers, as well as the office policy manual, should adequately cover the compensation of employed brokers.

CP-11 Commission Position on Assignments of Broker's Rights to a Commission

The Real Estate Commission recognizes and will enforce the statutory obligation of employed licensees as described in (12-10-217(1), C.R.S.), and more particularly:

> "12-10-217(1)(g), C.R.S. In the case of a broker registered as in the employ of another broker, failing to place, as soon after receipt as is practicably possible, in the custody of that licensed broker-employer any deposit money or other money or fund entrusted to the employee by any person dealing with the employee as the representative of that licensed broker-employer."

The Commission recognizes and will enforce the prohibition described in 12-10-221, C.R.S.:

> "12-10-221, C.R.S. It is unlawful for a real estate broker registered in the commission office as in the employ of another broker to accept a commission or valuable consideration for the performance of any of the acts specified in this part 2 from any person except the broker's employer, who shall be a licensed real estate broker."

However: If a broker is entitled to a commission pursuant to 12-10, Part 3, C.R.S., or, a broker is entitled to a commission in a transaction and title has passed from a seller to a buyer, the broker may assign any or all legal rights to such commission to any person including employed licensees and no disciplinary action will be invoked against such broker for having made such an assignment.

CP-12 Commission Position on the Broker's Payment or Rebating a Portion of an Earned Commission

The License Law forbids a broker from paying a commission or valuable consideration for performing brokerage functions to any person who is not licensed as a real estate broker. Thus, "referral fees" or "finder's fees" paid as the result of performing brokerage activities are prohibited.

The question of whether or not a broker may make payments from their earned commission to a buyer or a seller in a particular transaction will arise because usually neither the buyer nor the seller is licensed.

However, the License Law also permits any person to sell or acquire real property on such person's own account.

In a listing contract, the broker is principal party to the contract and the consideration offered is the brokerage services. The broker may add to this consideration the payment of money to the property owner in order to secure the listing. This is not a violation of the License Law.

Also, in a particular real estate transaction, the broker may pay a portion of commission to the unlicensed seller. This is merely a reduction in the amount of the earned commission and does not violate the License Law.

Payment to the unlicensed purchaser is often referred to as "rebating" and the intention to pay money to the purchaser is sometimes advertised and promoted as a sales inducement. The payment to the purchaser in itself is not a violation of the License Law because the broker is licensed to negotiate and the purchaser may negotiate on their own account. However, a broker representing the seller in a transaction should take care to insure that such payments do not conflict with fiduciary duties. For example, the "rebate" of a portion of a commission to a purchaser to be used by the purchaser as a down payment could distort the purchaser's financial qualifications and ultimately harm the seller. Additionally, a purchaser who does not receive a promised rebate of a partial commission may try to hold the seller liable for the wrongdoing of the broker on the theory of respondent superior. The Commission recommends that brokers disclose such payments to the seller and obtain the seller's consent prior to acceptance of any offer to purchase.

Gratuitous gifts to a purchaser subsequent to closing and not promised or offered as an inducement to buy would also be allowed (*i.e.*, a door knocker or dinner). Such gifts would not require disclosure and consent inasmuch as fiduciary duties would not be involved.

CP-13 Commission Policy on Single-Party Listings

Brokers often secure single-party listings because they have what they believe to be a good prospect for purchase. These listings are usually only for a few days, but occasionally the broker wishes to be protected for a longer period while the broker is negotiating with a particular prospective purchaser.

A single-party listing, when placed on a Commission approved form for an Exclusive Right to Sell or Exclusive Agency, results in greater protection to the broker than the broker needs to have and the owner is placed in a position which is unfair. The owner may not realize that if the owner signs a listing contract with another broker, the owner may become liable for the payment of two commissions even though the owner has excepted a sale to the person mentioned in a single-party listing contract.

In any and all contracting, the intent of the parties is paramount in its importance, in a listing contract, a broker is dealing with those less informed than the broker, and the broker has a duty to disclose the true meaning of the listing contract.

The Commission does not wish to limit any owner of the freedom to contract. However, the broker should fully disclose to the owner the effect of the exclusive right to sell listing contract or the exclusive agency contract.

Usually, when an owner signs an exclusive right to sell or exclusive agency agreement concerning a single party, the owner wishes to limit the rights of the broker under the listing contract. Therefore, in the space provided for additional provisions, one, two, or all of the following limitations should be inserted in this space:

1. The provisions of this listing contract shall apply only in the event a sale is made to __________________________________.
2. The termination date shall not be extended by the "Holdover Period" of this listing contract.
3. In the event a sale is made by the owner or their broker to any other party than the above names, this listing contract is void.

If an owner is misled to their disadvantage, the broker may be found guilty of endangering the public.

CP-14 Commission Position on Sale of Modular Homes by Licensees

The Commission is aware that many services rendered by licensees may or may not, in themselves, require licensing. Such services as collection of rents on real property, subdivision development services other than sales, or the general management of real property not involving renting or leasing may all be performed independently by an unlicensed person. When performed by a licensee, these services are all so integrated with real estate brokerage that all money received in connection therewith must be held or disbursed according to the law and rules of the Real Estate Commission.

Therefore, it is the position of the Commission that a licensee who sells land and a modular home to be affixed to the land, to the purchaser in concurrent or an arranged or pre-arranged or packaged transaction, is subject to the laws and rules of the Commission. Consequently, all money received concerning the integrated transaction, including the modular home, should be processed through the broker or the employing broker pursuant to 12-10-221, C.R.S., and 12-10-217(1)(g), C.R.S. and Commission Rules in Chapter 5 and Rule 6.19.

It is also the position of the Commission that if a licensee sells to an owner of land, a modular home to be affixed to the land, and there has been no brokerage relationship between the owners of the land and the licensee, such licensee in such a sale will not be required to comply with the requirements of 12-10-221, C.R.S., or 12-10-217(1)(g), C.R.S., or Commission Rules in Chapter 5 and 6.19.

CP-15 Commission Position on Sale of Items Other Than Real Estate

Inquiries have been made to the Commission as to the proper handling of sales, made by licensees, of items or services other than real estate. The following is the position of the Commission:

If the item, appliance, repair, remodeling or installation is performed in conjunction with a management contract or lease for a particular party or pursuant to an oral or written contingency in a specific executed contract of sale of the property, the employed licensee must process any fees or commissions received from the vendor or contractor through the employing broker. Also, disclosure must be made by the licensee to both the buyer and the seller of the property that the licensee is compensated by the vendor or contractor.

It is also the position of the Commission that if the sale of the item, appliance, repair, remodeling or installation is performed pursuant to a separate contract, and without reference to a specific contract of sale of the property, then the employed licensee may receive compensation directly from the vendor, or contractor and payment need not be made through the employing broker. However, if the sale of items or services is made to a buyer of real property during the term of the brokerage agreement with the seller of such property, then disclosure must be made by the licensee to both the buyer and the seller of the property that the licensee is compensated by the vendor or contractor.

The Commission takes no position when the licensee engages in selling items or services unconnected with real estate sales.

In any of the above situations the employed licensee may be subject to any requirements or prohibitions imposed by the employment agreement with the employing broker.

CP-16 Commission Position on Access to Properties Offered for Sale

(Revised November 1, 2005)

The Commission approved listing agreements (LC series) include a section titled OTHER BROKERAGE FIRMS ASSISTANCE – MULTIPLE LISTING SERVICE – MARKETING.

Provisions of this section allow the seller and listing broker to agree on whether or not to submit the property to a multiple listing service, information exchange, and whether there are limitations on the methods of marketing the property.

The provisions of the section also allow for discussion and the establishment of "Other Instructions" regarding access to the property by other brokerage firms such as through a lock box, for example.

It is the position of the Commission that the access information, and adherence to the Other Instructions, whether through lock box code or other means, is the responsibility of the listing broker. Listing brokers should take every effort to safeguard the access information on behalf of the seller. The listing agreements also include a section titled MAINTENANCE OF THE PROPERTY, which addresses the broker's liability for damage of any kind occurring to the property caused by the broker's negligence. Brokers are advised that failure to safeguard the access information and adhere to the instructions of the Seller related to access by other brokerage firms could result in a claim of negligence brought against the listing broker.

Selling brokers who obtain access information should safeguard that information at all times. At no time should a selling broker share the access information with a third party (inspector, appraiser, buyer, etc.) without the listing broker's authorization. Selling brokers are reminded that pursuant to the Contract to Buy and Sell, the Buyers indemnify the Seller against damage to the property in connection with the property inspection provision.

CP-18 Commission Position on Payments to a Wholly Owned Employee's Corporation

The Commission has received several inquiries concerning the payment of commissions or fees by an employing broker to a corporation that is wholly owned by an employed licensee.

C.R.S. 12-10-203(8), which prohibits the licensing of an employed broker as a corporation, partnership or limited liability company and the limitations on the payment or receipt of real estate fees, as described in 12-10-217(1)(i) and 12-10-221, are recognized by the Commission; however, it is the position of the Commission that:

An employing broker's payment of earned real estate fees to a corporation which is solely owned by an employed licensee of such employing broker shall not be considered by the Commission as a violation of 12-10-217(1)(i) or 12-10-221; however, a contract between the employing broker and such corporation or employed licensee shall not relieve the broker of any obligation to supervise such employed licensee or any other requirement of the licensing statute and Commission rules. It is not the intent of this position statement that the employed licensee be relieved from personal civil responsibility for any licensed activities by interposing the corporate form.

It must be stressed that the above position statement does not allow such corporations to be licensed under a broker and specifically refers only to corporations which are owned solely by the employed licensee.

CP-19 Commission Position on Short Term Occupancy Agreements

The Commission has been asked for its position concerning the need for a real estate broker to escrow funds coming into their possession involving short-term occupancies.

A short-term occupancy can be distinguished from a lease in that it is in the nature of a hotel reservation and a license to use. Short-term occupancy agreements, if properly treated, are not considered lease agreements. Activities relating to these agreements are exempt from the definition of real estate brokerage. Concerns arise when a licensed real estate broker wants to engage in short term occupancy activities either exclusively or as part of their separate brokerage practice. In some instances brokers have objected to holding money belonging to others in their trust accounts or accounting for these funds if the activity itself is exempt.

C.R.S. 12-10-217(1)(h) subjects a licensee to disciplinary action for "Failing to account for or to remit, within a reasonable time, any moneys coming into the licensee's possession that belong to others, whether acting as real estate brokers or otherwise, and failing to keep records relative to said moneys...." In addition, the case of Seibel vs. Colorado Real Estate Commission, 533 P.2nd 1290, gives the Commission jurisdiction over the acts of a licensed broker even where those acts would otherwise exempt the person from original licensure.

Based on the above, it is the position of the Commission that a licensed real estate broker engaging in short term occupancy agreements must escrow and account for funds coming into their possession which belong to others. To hold otherwise, would be to invite further confusion and mistrust on the part of the public in an already confusing real estate related practice. It has been the Commission's experience that most brokerage companies engaging in short term occupancy activities combine those activities with those requiring a license (*i.e.*, long term rental and lease agreements, sales). In addition, brokers continually hold themselves out to the public as being both licensed and professional. The public does not distinguish between an activity technically exempt from licensure and the overall business practices of a licensed real estate broker.

* CP-20 Commission Position Statement on Licensed and Unlicensed Real Estate Administrative Professionals ("REAPs")

(Revised April 6, 2021)

Real Estate Administrative Professionals ("REAPs") are generally thought of as employees or independent contractors that perform various functions, including clerical duties, on behalf of Brokers. For purposes of the Commission Position Statement, REAPs include, but are not limited to, Unlicensed On-Site Managers, secretaries, bookkeepers, assistants, transaction coordinators or short sale coordinators. REAPs can be grouped into two separate categories: unlicensed and licensed. The duties a licensed REAP can perform versus an unlicensed REAP vary depending on whether the licensed REAP has a Brokerage Relationship (named on the Listing Contracts) with the Broker's client. A Broker needs to be cognizant of these differences, along with the Broker's individual supervision responsibilities to the REAP. If a "licensed" REAP's Broker's license is currently on inactive or expired status, the REAP is considered to be unlicensed and may only perform those tasks that do not require a Broker's license.

§12-10-222, C.R.S. mandates that a Broker can be held liable for any unlawful act or violations of the license law committed by a REAP of a Broker, if the Broker had actual knowledge of the unlawful act or violation, or had been negligent in the supervision of such REAP. For purposes of the Real Estate Brokerage Practice Act, an employee includes an independent contractor. Commission Rule 6.3.A states that Employing Brokers are responsible for supervising all unlicensed employees, including those hired by Associate Brokers, and any licensed Brokers licensed with the Brokerage Firm.

The license law prohibits unlicensed persons from practicing real estate brokerage, which includes negotiating the sale, exchange or lease of real property on behalf of another person. An unlicensed REAP or a licensed REAP without a Brokerage Relationship should promptly disclose to Brokers representing the party on the other side of a transaction, other industry professionals (i.e. loan originators, lenders, appraisers, property inspectors, etc.) and consumers that he or she does not have a License or is not acting as a Broker in the transaction, and disclose the name of the Broker for whom the REAP works. An unlicensed REAP or a REAP without a Brokerage Relationship may complete the following tasks:

1. Complete forms prepared for, and as directed by a Broker. Unlicensed REAPs or REAPs without a Brokerage Relationship cannot independently draft legal documents such as listing or sales contracts, and they cannot offer opinions, advice or interpretations of these documents.
2. Distribute preprinted, objective information prepared by the Broker about a property listed for sale.
3. Perform clerical duties, including gathering information for a listing.
4. If authorized by the seller or listing broker, provide access to property, conduct showings or open houses.
5. Deliver paperwork to other Brokers, buyers or sellers or other professionals.
6. Completing administrative tasks necessary to help Brokers fulfill their uniform duties.
7. Send out disclosure documents to parties of the transaction.
8. Order title commitments and send contract copies to the lender, title company and others involved in the transaction.
9. Help collect due diligence documents to help Broker comply with the contract.
10. Review the entire transaction file to ensure that documents are not missing and the file itself complies with the Real Estate Commission's regulations and the Broker's Brokerage Firm's Office Policy Manual.
11. Deliver paperwork that requires signatures in regard to financing documents that are prepared by lending institutions.
12. Prepare market analyses on behalf of the Broker, if the analyses are approved and submitted by the Broker to the client with a disclosure that the market analyses were prepared by the REAP. The Broker must ensure that market analyses comply with Commission Rule 6.12.
13. Collect and receipt for earnest money deposits, security deposits or rents.
14. Schedule property repairs or schedule services on behalf of the Broker, if there is an existing agreement that authorizes the Broker to complete those tasks.

Individuals acting as REAPs may be licensed, but care must be taken to ensure that violations of the license law do not occur. If a licensed REAP is performing licensed duties (e.g. negotiating the resolution of inspection items, drafting contracts, etc.), the REAP will need to establish a Brokerage Relationship with the principal being represented. For example, if the seller's Broker hires a REAP, who is also a licensed Broker, and the licensed REAP begins performing licensed duties on the seller's behalf, the licensed REAP must establish a Brokerage Relationship with the seller. This would most likely result in the seller's Broker and the licensed REAP "co-listing" to represent the seller. The Brokerage Relationship established by the seller's Broker and the licensed REAP would have to be the same. The REAP does not have to be licensed with the same Brokerage Firm as the Broker, but the REAP must have an active license and comply with the license law requirements associated with the level of licensure the REAP possesses (e.g. a REAP that has an Associate Broker level license must have an Employing Broker). If the Broker, who established the Brokerage Relationship does not want to co-list with the licensed REAP or does not want the licensed REAP to perform Real Estate Brokerage Services, the licensed REAP cannot perform licensed brokerage duties. Licensed REAPs working on behalf of Brokers that fail to establish a Brokerage Relationship with a Client but still perform Real Estate Brokerage Services are likely violating the license law. Not only would the licensed REAP be subject to discipline, but so would the Broker that hired the licensed REAP and allowed them to do licensed activity without a Brokerage Relationship. Additionally, the Employing Brokers for the licensed REAP and/or the Broker Associate violating the license law could also potentially face discipline for failing to supervise.

Brokers seeking to engage the services of aREAP should perform their due diligence to evaluate the qualifications and services provided, along with any liability being assumed. The Broker hiring a REAP should inquire as to whether any of the REAP's activities are covered by the Broker's errors and omissions insurance policy. Furthermore, REAPs, whether licensed or not, may need their own separate errors and omissions insurance policy to cover the acts they perform on behalf of the Broker.

REAPs that are licensed and have a Brokerage Relationship with the Client must be paid by their Employing Broker as required by §12-10-221, C.R.S. However, if the Broker engages the services of an unlicensed REAP, any payments to such unliscensed REAP that are contingent on the closing of a transaction may result in a violation of the Real Estate Settlement and Procedures Act ("RESPA"), which precludes the splitting of commissions with unlicensed individuals. In addition, if a consumer is required to pay separately for the services performed by a REAP, which are done to assist the Broker with fulfilling the Broker's statutorily required duties, it may result in a separate violation of RESPA which precludes the charging of duplicate fees for one service rendered (e.g. a fee is paid to the REAP and the broker receives remuneration for providing the same services in the same transaction). If a REAP will be paid outside of closing, there may be tax implications affecting the individual remitting the payment. Brokers should seek advice from appropriate tax and/or legal counsel regarding if, when, and how payment may be made to a REAP for services rendered.

CP-21 Commission Position on Office Policy Manuals

(Revised and Adopted December 4, 2018)

12-10-Part 4 C.R.S., and Commission Rules 6.3. and 6.4. set out a broker's supervising responsibilities. In order to help brokers comply with the rules it is suggested that a policy manual contain procedures for at least the following:

1) typical real estate transactions
   a) review of contracts
   b) handling of earnest money deposits, including the release thereof
   c) back-up contracts
   d) closings
2) non-qualifying assumptions and owner financing
3) guaranteed buyouts
4) investor purchases
5) identifying brokerage relationships offered to public (required by 12-10-408, C.R.S.)
6) procedures for designation of brokers who are to work with a seller, landlord, buyer or tenant, individually or in teams (required by Rule 6.4.) (Does not apply to brokerage firms that consist of only one licensed natural person.)
7) identify and provide adequate means and procedures for the maintenance and protection of confidential information (required by Rule 6.4.B.4.)
8) procedures and practices for the reasonably secure maintenance and protection of personal identifying information (required by 6-1-713.5, C.R.S.)
9) procedures for the destruction or proper disposal of paper or electronic records by shredding, erasing, or otherwise modifying the following information to make it unreadable or indecipherable through any means:
   a) a social security number;
   b) a personal identification number;
   c) a password;
   d) a pass code;
   e) an official state or government-issued driver's license or identification card;
   f) a government passport number;
   g) biometric data, as defined in 6-1-716(1)(a), C.R.S.;
   h) an employer, student or military identification number; or
   i) a financial transaction device, as defined in 18-5-701, C.R.S.
10) procedures and practices for the identification and notification of a security breach of personal identifying information (required by 6-1-716, C.R.S.)
11) licensee's purchase and sale of property
12) monitoring of license renewals and transfers
13) delegation of authority
14) property management
15) property listing procedures, including release of listings
16) training
   a) dissemination of information
   b) staff meetings
17) use of personal assistants
18) fair housing/affirmative action marketing
19) listing syndication

   a) brokerage participation
   b) entry and maintenance of information

20) performance of and compensation for real estate related activities (i.e. broker price opinions, etc.)

Brokers are encouraged to add other policies as appropriate to their practice.

In the event that one or several of these suggested topics (e.g., guaranteed buyouts) are not applicable in a particular office, they should be addressed by stating that the office does not participate in that activity.

The Commission does not become involved in matters relating to independent contractor agreements, and disputes over earned commissions. Office policies in these areas do not fall within the purview of Commission rules.

CP-22 Commission Position Statement on Handling of Confidential Information in Real Estate Brokerage

(Adopted October 1, 2003)

Prior to designated brokerage, it was common for brokers to share the motivations of a buyer or seller during office sales meetings, for example. Under designated brokerage, the law specifically prohibits sharing of such information. Confidential information, and the broker responsibility thereto, are defined in C.R.S. 12-10-404(2), 12-10-405(2), 12-10-407(3), and Rules 6.3.D. and 6.4.B. Confidential information can include, but is not limited to, motivation of the parties.

Brokers are required to have a written office policy that identifies and provides adequate means and procedures for the maintenance and protection of confidential information. Situations where inadvertent disclosure of confidential information may occur, include, but are not limited to:

- sales meetings or marketing sessions,
- shared fax or copy machines,
- shared computer networks, printers and file directories,
- in-office mail boxes,
- hand written telephone messages,
- phone conversations or meetings with clients,
- relocation, divorce, pending foreclosure and other sensitive documents,
- conversations with affiliated business providers,
- production boards,
- social functions

Brokers must develop office policies and procedures to address the handling of confidential information. For example, some offices may have "locked" transaction files that include confidential information and other offices may elect not to include confidential information in transaction files.

A designated broker is permitted to share confidential information with a supervising broker without changing or extending the brokerage relationship beyond the designated broker. Brokers may want to consult legal counsel regarding the necessity of securing the authorization of the party to whom the information is confidential before the designated broker shares that confidential information with the supervising broker. Such advice could include modifications to the listing agreement or buyer agreement that create such authorization.

CP-23 Commission Position on Use of "Licensee Buyout Addendum"

(Revised January 17, 2006)

Rule 7.1.A. requires real estate licensees to use the Commission approved "Licensee Buyout Addendum to Contract to Buy and Sell Real Estate", when purchasing certain listed properties.

It is the Commission's position that Rule 7.1.A. requires use of the Buyout Addendum under the following circumstances:

1. When a licensee enters into a contract to purchase a property concurrent with the listing of such property.
2. When a licensee enters into a contract to purchase a property as an inducement or to facilitate the property owner's purchase of another property, the purchase or sale of which will generate a commission or fee to the licensee.
3. When a licensee enters into a contract to purchase a property from an owner but continues to market that property on behalf of the owner under an existing listing contract.

Unless one of the above situations exists, licensees are not required to use the Buyout Addendum.

The term "licensee", as used above, refers to the individual licensee who has personally taken a listing or to the listing broker or brokerage entity if the buyout is to be accomplished by that broker or brokerage entity. If the listing licensee or broker desires to acquire a listed property solely for personal use or future resale and not as an inducement to the owner, the licensee or broker is advised to (1) clearly sever their agency or listing relationship in writing; (2) renounce the right to any commission, fee or compensation in conjunction with acquisition of the listed property; and, (3) advise the owner to seek other assistance, representation or legal advice.

Future resale of a purchased property, as referred to above, means resale to a third party purchaser with whom the licensee has not negotiated during the listing period. Resale to a person with whom a licensee has conducted previous negotiations concerning the subject property during the listing period (often referred to as a "pocket buyer"), would constitute a violation of 12-10-217(1)(q) in the absence of full written disclosure and acknowledgment by the owner.

CP-24 Commission Position on Preparation of Market Analyses and Real Estate Evaluations Used for Loan Purposes

The Colorado Real Estate Appraiser Licensing Act contains special provisions which allow licensed real estate brokers to perform certain real estate valuation related activities without being registered, licensed or certified as real estate appraisers. These provisions are found in Sections 12-10-602 and 12-10-618, C.R.S.

The first of these allows a broker to prepare an "estimate of value" which is not represented as an appraisal and is not used to obtain financing. The position of the Commission is that this provision allows a broker to prepare a market analysis for use in the real estate brokerage process and to offer their estimate as to the value or market price of real estate for court testimony or tax purposes.

The second provision allows a broker to prepare what are termed "evaluations" in federal banking regulations. These evaluations may be used for lending purposes. This provision is very narrow in scope—a broker may prepare such an evaluation only for a federally regulated bank, savings and loan or credit union with whom they have a contract. The loan amount must be below the threshold which invokes the requirement for a true appraisal.

As the authority to prepare such estimates of value and evaluations is tied to the holding of a Colorado real estate broker license, the Colorado Real Estate Commission has jurisdiction over the activities of brokers engaged in such activities. The Commission will consider the conduct of licensees who prepare estimates of value and evaluations in light of Sections 12-10-217(1)(q) and (w), which speak to unworthiness, incompetency and dishonest dealing.

It is the position of the Commission that the mere holding of a broker license does not in itself assure the competency necessary to prepare more complex estimates of value or evaluations. Licensees preparing estimates of value and evaluations have a responsibility to possess training and experience commensurate with the complexity of the assignment undertaken.

Investigations undertaken by the Commission relating to unworthiness, incompetency and dishonest dealing will take into account the following:

- Brokers preparing estimates of value and evaluations must act independently at all times. The estimate or evaluation must be unbiased.
- The broker preparing an estimate or evaluation must not represent themselves as an appraiser, nor represent the work product as being an appraisal.
- The broker preparing an estimate or evaluation must at all times comply with the statutory requirement in Sections 12-10-602 and 12-10-618, Colorado Revised Statutes, for a written notice that they are not an appraiser. The wording and use of the written notice are specified in the Rules of the Board of Real Estate Appraisers. The required wording is:

  "NOTICE: The preparer of this appraisal is not registered, licensed or certified as a real estate appraiser by the State of Colorado".
- The broker must not prepare an estimate of value or evaluation of real property which requires a level of competency beyond the level of training and experience possessed by the licensee.

CP-25 Commission Position on Recording Contracts

Over the years the Commission has received many inquiries and complaints concerning the recording of listing contracts to protect claims for commissions. In addition, some licensees have attempted more "creative" ways of holding up a closing, such as filing mechanics liens or notices of lis pendens, as well as recording demand letters or purchase contracts. The end result is usually a cloud on the title and sometimes a slander of title action.

Some states have passed statutes authorizing the filing of such liens. Colorado has not. Filings and recordings such as these are inappropriate and will result in Commission action.

Here is a typical scenario: Broker lists a property at $125,000 for 120 days and actively markets it. No offers come in during the first 30 days. Broker advises her seller to lower the price by $5,000 to encourage some activity. The seller is adamant that the property is worth the list price and refuses. After another 15 days with no offers, the seller reluctantly lowers the price. He also tells the broker that he doesn't feel she is trying hard enough to sell the property and he's going to take it off the market if nothing happens.

A week later an offer for $100,000 comes in from another company, which is presented and rejected. The seller is quite upset at the low offer and demands to be released from the listing. There is no further communication between the parties, but the listing is never formally terminated. Three weeks later the broker learns that the seller has entered into a contract with the same buyer for $110,000 and closing is set. The broker is very upset and wants to protect her commission. What can she do?

1. File a mechanics lien?

   ANS: No. Real estate licensees are not a protected class of lien claimant under the statute except as provided in C.R.S. 38-22.5 (Commercial Real Estate Brokers Commission Security Act).

2. File a lis pendens (notice of pending lawsuit)?

   ANS: No. A lis pendens relates to a title or ownership dispute involving the land itself. The broker has no legal interest in the real estate.

3. Record the listing contract?

ANS: No. This will usually have the effect of clouding title to the property, which in turn affects the closing between buyer and seller. The broker should not interfere in the process of transferring title to property.

4. Escrow the disputed commission?

   ANS: Maybe. This is a touchy area. If the broker makes demand on the seller for the commission prior to closing and states her possible rights (mediation; arbitration; civil action) the parties may agree to an escrow pending settlement of the dispute. However, there is no legal requirement that the closing entity escrow funds absent an agreement.

5. Commence mediation, arbitration or civil action (as appropriate).

   ANS: Yes. Nothing prevents a licensee from asserting any legal claim against a principal.

A commission dispute is an emotional issue. Sometimes a licensee has put in considerable time on a listing only to be faced with a seller who refuses to pay, attempts to renegotiate or is outright deceitful. On the other side, the Commission has witnessed instances in which the licensee had no legitimate right to a commission and was using superior knowledge and scare tactics to force payment. Clearly this is a time to consult a good real estate attorney and avoid the risk of a complaint based on a hasty decision.

CP-26 Commission Position on Auctioning

(Adopted 5-1-97)

Real estate experts predict that the next decade will see a significant increase in the sale of real estate through auctions. For many years auctioning was associated with rural or distressed properties. However, forecasts are for a proliferation of sales activity in both residential and commercial real estate. Sales by auction are already occurring in the residential market in Colorado and other parts of the country.

The brokers act requires that real estate auctions be conducted by a licensed broker and defines the activity as ". . .offering, attempting or agreeing to auction real estate, or interest therein, or improvements affixed thereon. . ." (C.R.S. 12-10-201(6)(a)(VI)).

A long-standing Attorney General's opinion allows an unlicensed auctioneer to "cry" the bid at a real estate auction in the presence of a broker or seller. However, the control of the sale, including listing, advertising, showing the property and writing contracts must remain with the broker or the auctioneer will be violating the law.

Based on the statute and Attorney General's opinion, the following guidelines are established for unlicensed persons involved in the auction process:

1. Auctioneers should never hold themselves out as providing real estate brokerage services to the public (*e.g.*, listing, advertising, negotiating, contracting, legal document preparation);
2. Inquiries from sellers should be referred to a licensed broker or attorney;
3. Inquiries from buyers should be referred to the seller, listing broker or sellers attorney;
4. Only auctioning services should be advertised to buyers and sellers;
5. A potential buyer may be chauffeured to a property, so long as the property is shown by the seller or a licensed broker;
6. Information on listed properties may be distributed when such information has been prepared by a broker;
7. Auctioneers may "cry" the sale, but may not engage in subsequent negotiations, document drafting and the handling of earnest money;
8. Payment should be based on auctioning services performed regardless of the success of a sale.

CP-27 Commission Position on the Performance of Residential Leasing and Property Management Functions

(Adopted August 1998 – Revised August 2013)

Property management is one of the leading sources of complaints received by the Commission. This position statement is designed to identify common issues found during the course of a complaint investigation or an audit; however it does not encompass all of the potential issues associated with property management. Any licensed real estate broker ("Broker") interested in performing property management duties are strongly encouraged to complete educational offerings specific to property management, train with a Broker experienced in property management, and develop a strong familiarity with the Colorado Real Estate Manual chapters titled Escrow Records, and Property Management and Leases.

License Requirements

Pursuant to C.R.S. §12-10-201(6), the leasing and subsequent management of real estate for a fee or compensation, is included among the activities for which a license is required. As a result of the complaints received and issues identified in Commission investigations and audits, the Commission considers property management to be a complex area of practice. C.R.S. §12-10-217(1)(q) requires that a Broker be competent and worthy in the performance of their duties so as to not endanger the interest of the public. Furthermore, it is the Commission's position that prior to performing any acts that require a Broker's license, a Broker should determine whether he or she possesses the knowledge, experience and/or training necessary to perform the terms of the transaction and to maintain compliance with the applicable federal, state or local laws, rules, regulations, or ordinances. If the Broker does not have the requisite knowledge, experience and/or training necessary to fulfill the terms of the agreement, the Broker should either decline to provide brokerage services or seek the assistance of another Broker who does have the necessary experience, training and/or knowledge. A Broker who agrees to lease property, or perform ongoing property management duties, needs to ensure that he or she is competent to perform the duties he or she agrees to undertake and must have permission from the Broker's employing broker. Similarly, the employing broker has the responsibility to ensure that he or she is competent to supervise a broker that performs leasing or property management duties.

Leasing v. Property Management

While leasing and property management are similar, they are two distinctively different services. Leasing is a onetime activity in which the broker acts as a special agent, while property management is an ongoing relationship in which the broker is a general agent. If a Broker is performing leasing, the Broker may list a property for lease, advertise the property, help screen tenants and/or help negotiate a lease. Once the lease is signed by the landlord and tenant, the Broker's duty to the landlord or tenant is complete. With property management, a broker's obligations continue beyond the formation of the lease. A Broker performing property management duties may also perform leasing duties; where a Broker only performing leasing duties is not performing property management duties.

Generally, a Broker will function in one of three capacities with regards to rental properties. The Broker may provide leasing services only for a landlord, where the broker is involved in procuring a tenant and negotiating the lease terms. Alternatively, the broker may provide leasing services on behalf of the tenant in locating a suitable rental property and negotiating a lease. In the first two scenarios, the Broker's duties are fulfilled once the lease is executed and the broker is not involved in the transaction any further. In the third scenario, the Broker agrees not only to provide leasing services, but is also responsible for one or more of the following: maintaining the property's physical condition, communicating with tenants, collecting rent and/or collecting security deposits. In this scenario, the Broker's duties are ongoing; therefore the Broker is conducting property management services. Regardless of whether the Broker is working with the landlord or the tenant, the Broker must establish clear expectations regarding the services the Broker agrees to provide and communicate these expectations to the consumer.

Supervision

Before engaging in property management or leasing, the Broker should discuss with the employing broker whether the Broker is capable of and allowed to perform property management or leasing duties. The employing broker is responsible for maintaining all trust accounts and all transaction records, and the employing broker is responsible for exercising authority, direction and control over the Broker's conformance to statutes and Commission rules (Rules 6.3.A. and 6.3.B.). This includes reviewing all contracts to ensure competent preparation and reviewing all transaction files to ensure that required documents exist (Rule 6.3.C.). If the employing broker does not allow Brokers to perform leasing and/or property management duties, the Broker needs to refrain from leasing and/or property management activities or seek employment elsewhere. If the real estate brokerage firm does allow leasing and/or property management, regardless of how minor, the employing broker must ensure that the office policy manual addresses these activities, including management of the Broker's own property. Both the Broker and the employing broker need to be aware of state and local laws that impact the performance of property management duties, which include, but are not limited to, laws pertaining to security deposits, habitability, carbon monoxide alarms, asbestos, lead-based paint, handling of confidential information, zoning and agency.

Forms

C.R.S. §12-10-403(4)(a) indicates that a Broker may complete standard forms including those promulgated by the Commission. Forms that are not promulgated by the Commission must be drafted by an attorney. When the Broker provides leasing services for a tenant, the Broker should complete the Exclusive Tenant Listing Contract. When the Broker provides ONLY leasing services for the landlord, the Broker should complete the Commission-approved Exclusive Right to Lease Listing Contract. If the Broker also will be providing property management services in addition to leasing services for the landlord, a Broker should use the Brokerage Duties Addendum to Property Management Agreement with a property management agreement drafted by an attorney. Under Rule 6.14.A.2., the Broker must provide a copy of any executed contracts to the consumer. While not all property managers provide a physical copy of the lease to the landlord, because sometimes it is executed by the Broker on behalf of the landlord, the Broker should make the document available to the landlord upon request.

If the Broker is going to provide property management services, the Broker needs to provide a property management agreement. The property management agreement must be drafted by an attorney. The property management agreement should outline the duties and responsibilities of both parties. The property management agreement should, at the very minimum, address:

- Duration of the relationship;
- The parties;
- Identify the property to be managed;
- General duties performed by the Broker, including the signing of leases.
- Fees for the manager's services, including disclosure of any mark-ups (Commission Rule 5.17.). Before a mark-up can be charged, the Broker must obtain prior written consent to assess and receive mark-ups and/or other compensation for services performed by any third party or affiliated business entity;
- Tenant selection criteria. If the decision to lease will be based on criminal history or financial worthiness, the property management agreement should indicate who is responsible for collecting this data and what sources will be used. Additionally, the Broker must ensure compliance with the Fair Housing and Fair Credit Acts.
- Posting of eviction notices. If a Forcible Entry and Detainer (a/k/a eviction) is necessary, an attorney should represent the landlord in the filing of the Forcible Entry and Detainer.

A Broker that files a Forcible Entry and Detainer without the assistance of an attorney may be practicing law without a license;

- Ownership Interest. The Broker must disclose a Broker's direct or indirect ownership interest in any company which will be providing maintenance or other services to the landlord, and any other conflicts of interest (Rule 6.17.);
- Identity of the entity responsible for holding the security deposit, and if interest is earned on security deposit escrow accounts, who benefits from such interest and consent to transfer the interest to the beneficiary;
- Process to be followed for any subsequent transfer of the landlord's monies, security deposits, keys and documents (Rule 5.8.A.); and,
- Requirement that the landlord receive regular monthly accounting of all funds received and disbursed.

While these general duties should be addressed in the property management agreement, it is not an all-inclusive list of all the duties that may be performed by a property manager or that should be addressed within the property management agreement. Brokers are encouraged to pay close attention not only to Commission rules and regulations, but also the "Property Management and Leases" chapter in the Colorado Real Estate Manual.

Regardless of whether the Broker is acting as a leasing agent or a property manager, prior to engaging in any of the activities that require a real estate broker's license, the Broker is required to disclose in writing the different brokerage relationships that are available to the tenant (Rule 6.5.). The Commission-approved Brokerage Disclosure to Tenant form should be used to disclose the brokerage relationships available.

In Colorado there is not an approved lease form. Therefore, prior to a tenant being procured, the Broker must: 1) hire an attorney to draft a lease form for the Broker to use; or 2) the landlord will need to designate a lease. The terms of the lease need to be clear and in writing. A Broker may choose to limit which lease is used to only the lease form provided by their attorney so long as the landlord authorizes the Broker to use their attorney prepared lease form in the property management agreement.

Trust Accounts and Record Keeping

Any Broker performing property management duties in which the Broker is responsible for the collection and distribution of rent or security deposits needs to be especially cognizant of the Commission rules and regulations pertaining to the management of funds of others and records retention. Brokers should pay close attention to the chapters titled "Escrow Records" and "Property Management and Leases" in the Colorado Real Estate Manual. C.R.S §12-10-217(1)(h) requires that a Broker account for and remit, within a reasonable time, any moneys coming into the Broker's possession that belong to others. Rule 1.34. defines money belonging to others as including, but not limited to, funds received by a Broker in connection with property management agreements, rent or lease contracts, and money belonging to others that is collected for future investment or other purposes. All money belonging to others which is received by a Broker acting as a property manager must be deposited in the Broker's escrow or trust account within five (5) business days of receipt (Rule 5.7.A.).

If a Broker is going to deposit rent or security deposits into the employing broker's trust account(s), the Broker is required to keep records relative to these monies. Rule 5.10.requires that all money belonging to others that is accepted by the Broker be deposited in one or more accounts separate from money belonging to the Broker, employing broker or brokerage entity. Separate trust accounts must be maintained in the name of the employing broker, or the employing broker and the licensed business entity, and the maintenance of the separate accounts is the responsibility of the employing broker (Rule 5.3. and 5.6.). This includes rent checks. Rule 5.5. requires that "A Brokerage Firm who engages in Property Management must deposit rental receipts and security deposits and disburse money collected for such purposes in separate Trust or Escrow Accounts, a minimum of one for rental receipts and a minimum of one for security deposits." As an alternative to trust accounts, a Broker may deposit rent monies or security deposits directly into an account owned and controlled by the landlord.

Rule 5.8.A. prohibits a Broker who receipts for security deposits from delivering such deposits to a landlord, unless the tenant's written authorization is given in the lease or written notice is given to the tenant by first-class mail. The notice must identify who is holding the security deposit and the procedure the tenant must follow to request the return of the deposit. If the security deposit is held by or transferred to the landlord, the property management agreement must specify that the landlord is responsible for the security deposit's return and that, in the event of a dispute, the Broker is authorized to reveal the true name and current mailing address of the landlord. The Broker may not use any portion of the security deposit for the Broker's benefit.

Pursuant to Rule 5.14., a Broker is required to supervise and maintain a record keeping system, at the Broker's licensed place of business that consists of an "escrow or trust account journal", a "ledger" and a "bank reconciliation worksheet". The Broker must also maintain supporting records that detail all cash received and disbursed under the terms of the management and rental agreements. If a Broker has deposited personal funds into the trust account to open and maintain the trust account, the journal and "broker's ledger record" must contain entries documenting this money. The Broker's personal funds must also be included in the bank reconciliation worksheet. All deposits of funds into an escrow or trust account must be documented, as must all disbursements of funds from an escrow or trust account.

Absent a written agreement that indicates otherwise, the "cash basis" of accounting is required for maintaining all required escrow or trust accounts and records. Funds from one owner cannot be used to supplement operating capital, or to finance expenditures of other owners or the Broker (C.R.S. §§12-10-217(1)(h) and (i) and Rules 1.34. 5.9., 5.11., 5.18., 6.3.A. and 6.3.B.). The Broker is required to retain accurate, on-going records which verify disclosure of and consent to any mark-ups assessed or received, and fully account for the amounts or percentage of compensation assessed or received (Rule 5.17.). For Commission purposes, brokers may maintain their records in electronic format as long as the records are stored in a format that can be continually retrieved and legibly printed (Rule 6.24.). C.R.S. §12-10-217(1)(k) requires Brokers to maintain possession of their records for four (4) years.

Security Deposits

Brokers have to be very careful how they handle security deposits. The security deposit law is complicated and legal assistance is advisable. Wrongful withholding of a security deposit may result in the landlord, and the Broker as the landlord's agent, being liable for treble the amount wrongfully withheld, plus reasonable attorneys' fees and court costs. C.R.S. §38-12-103 requires that the security deposit be returned to the tenant within one month after a lease is terminated or the premises have been vacated and accepted, whichever occurs last. The lease may indicate a longer period of time to return the security deposit to the tenant; however state law does not allow this extension of time to exceed sixty days. Security deposits cannot be retained to cover normal wear and tear. C.R.S. §38-12-102 defines normal wear and tear as:

> "deterioration which occurs, based upon the use for which the rental unit is intended, without negligence, carelessness, accident, or abuse of the premises or equipment or chattels by the tenant or members of his household, or their invitees or guests."

Normal wear and tear is at the core of most security deposits lawsuits. Security deposits may be retained for nonpayment of rent, abandonment of the premises, or nonpayment of utility charges, repairs or cleaning contracted for by the tenant in the lease. If there is cause to retain any portion of the security deposit, the tenant must be provided with a written statement listing the exact reasons why all or a portion of the security deposit is being retained. The statement must be delivered with the difference between the amount of the security deposit and the amount retained. The Broker or the landlord is deemed to have complied with this requirement by mailing the statement and payment to the tenant's last known address. If the Broker or the landlord fails to provide the statement to the tenant within 30 days (or the alternative deadline specified in the lease) of the lease terminating or the surrender and acceptance of the premises, whichever occurs last, the landlord or the Broker may forfeit his right to retain any portion of the security deposit to offset amounts owed. The landlord does not lose the right to pursue amounts due, they just lose the right to utilize the security deposit to offset amounts owed. Furthermore, if the tenant pursues court action regarding any portion of the security deposit being retained, the landlord or the Broker bears the burden to prove that retention of any portion of the security deposit was not wrongful.

In the rare event that a lease is nullified and voided due to the landlord's failure to repair a hazardous condition attributed to a gas appliance, piping, or other gas equipment, the landlord or the Broker must deliver all, or the appropriate portion of, the security deposit plus any rent rebate owed to the tenant for the time period that the tenant vacated the premises. Payment must be made to the tenant within 72 hours of the tenant vacating the premises. If the 72nd hour falls on a Saturday, Sunday, or legal holiday, the security deposit, and any rent rebate due, must be delivered to the tenant by noon on the next day that is not a Saturday, Sunday, or legal holiday. If a portion of the security deposit is retained, the tenant must be provided with a written statement listing the exact reasons why all or a portion of the security deposit is being retained and payment of the remaining balance of the security deposit. If the tenant does not receive all or a portion of the security deposit with the statement within the required deadlines, the tenant may be entitled to three times the amount of the security deposit and reasonable attorney fees (C.R.S. §38-12-104).

Transfer of Services

If a Broker no longer will be managing a property, the Broker must transfer a copy of the entire file to the landlord or, upon written authorization from the landlord, to the new Broker engaged to perform the property management. At a minimum, the entire file should include:

(a) Copy of existing lease
(b) Copy of check-in condition report
(c) Keys
(d) Outstanding tenant balances
(e) Tenant(s) security deposit(s)
(f) Owner's funds (subject to outstanding obligations)

Although the Commission rules do not specifically address the transfer of management duties, there should be no delay in transferring the tenant's security deposit to either the landlord or the new Broker. The Broker must give written notice by first class mail to the tenant that the security deposit has been transferred to the landlord or new Broker along with the landlord's or new Broker's contact information. The notice must indicate who is holding the security deposit and the specific requirements for the procedure in which the tenant may request return of the deposit [reference Rule 5.8.A. and C.R.S. §38-12-103(4)]. Timely transfer of the deposit protects the Broker from getting caught between the landlord and the tenant regarding the accounting of the deposit. The Broker must also provide the landlord with a final accounting of all trust funds held by the Broker. Although the Broker may delay the transfer of the landlord's funds until all outstanding invoices or debts have been resolved, the transfer of the landlord's funds needs to occur within a reasonable amount of time. A Broker that fails to transfer funds in a reasonable amount of time may be subject to discipline by the Commission for unworthiness or incompetency, C.R.S. §12-10-217(1)(q).

Managing Broker's Own Property

Brokers are subject to the license law and Commission rules when they participate in real estate matters as principals, including managing the Broker's own property. See Seibel v. Colorado Real Estate Commission, 34 Colo. App. 415, 530 P.2d 1290 (1974). A Broker who manages his or her own rental property needs to disclose known conflicts of interest and that the Broker possesses a Colorado real estate broker's license (Rule 6.17.). The Broker also needs to use a lease drafted by an attorney for the transaction, along with disclosing in writing to the tenant the brokerage relationships under Colorado law (Rule 6.5.).

If the Broker has an employing broker, it is important for the Broker to consult with the employing broker regarding the brokerage firm's requirements or limitations regarding managing a Broker's own property. When a Broker personally receipts for a security deposit on his or her own property, the license law does not require that the security deposit be placed in an escrow account. Additionally, a Broker cannot deposit rental proceeds into the brokerage firm's escrow account(s) for properties owned by the Broker [Rule 1.34.].

CP-28 Commission Position on Showing Properties

(Adopted March 4th 1999)

The Real Estate Commission reminds licensees that the Brokerage Relationships Act imposes duties on agents to promote the interests of their buyers or sellers with the utmost good faith as well as to counsel their principals on material benefits or risks of a transaction. A transaction-broker must exercise reasonable skill and care, advise the parties and keep the parties fully informed regarding the transaction. Whether working as an agent or a transaction-broker, these duties include disclosing the accessibility of and actual access to a property or properties.

Working With a Seller: Pursuant to the section in the various listing contracts entitled, "OTHER BROKERS, ASSISTANCE", the licensee should advise the seller of the advantages and disadvantages of using multiple listing services and other methods of making the property accessible by other brokers (*e.g.*, using lock boxes, by appointment only showings, etc.). If applicable, it should be explained that some methods may limit the ability of a selling broker to access and show a particular property. The chosen methods of cooperating with other brokers should be included in the listing agreement.

Working With a Buyer: A licensee working with a buyer has an obligation to explain the possible methods used by a listing broker and seller to show a particular property. These methods may include limitations on the buyer and selling broker being able to access a property due to the type of lock box placed on the property, the seller's choice to have the property shown by appointment only, etc. The selling broker should include such showing limitations in the Exclusive Right to Buy Contract (agency or transaction-broker).

There should be no instances of a listing broker refusing to allow a property to be shown, unless the seller has given prior explicit, written authorization to do so.

CP-29 Commission Position on "Megan's Law"

(Adopted July 1, 1999)

The Commission has been asked for its position as to the disclosure requirements for real estate licensees with regard to "Megan's Law." In 1994, and primarily as a response to the murders of two young girls, a federal law was passed creating a registration and notification procedure to alert the public as to the presence of certain types of convicted sex offenders living in a neighborhood. This is commonly referred to as "Megan's Law." Identified sex offenders are required to register with local law enforcement officials. The federal law also required states to establish registries of convicted sex offenders. It contains no disclosure requirements for real estate licensees when working with the public.

In compliance with federal law, Colorado enacted legislation that sets procedures and timeframes for local registration. The office of chief of police is the designated place of registration for those offenders residing within any city, town or city and county. The office of the county sheriff is the designated place of registration for those living outside any city, town or city and county, in addition, the law enforcement agency is required to release information regarding registered persons. However, the duty to release information may differ depending on whether the inquiring party does or does not live within that jurisdiction.

While legislation in a few states has specifically imposed disclosure requirements on real estate licensees working with buyers and sellers, Colorado's legislation imposes no such requirements. Colorado's legislation clearly places the duty to release information on the local law enforcement agency, after considering a request.

It is the position of the Real Estate Commission that all real estate licensees should inform a potential buyer to contact local law enforcement officials for further information if the presence of a registered sex offender is a matter of concern to the buyer.

Editor's Note:

C.R.S. 18-3-412.5 requires the Colorado Bureau of Investigation to post on the Internet identifying information, including a picture, of each sex offender:

- *Sentenced as a sexually violent predator; or*
- *Convicted of a sexual offense involving children*

CP-30 State of Colorado Real Estate Commission and Board of Real Estate Appraisers Joint Position Statement

(Revised January 8, 2009)

The Colorado Real Estate Commission and the Colorado Board of Real Estate Appraisers have issued this Joint Position Statement to address mutual concerns pertaining to practices of real estate brokers and real estate appraisers with regard to residential sales transactions involving seller assisted down payments, seller concessions, personal property transferred with real property and other items of value included in the sale of residential real property.

A residential real estate transaction has a life well beyond closing and possession of the property. Accurate sales data is crucial for appraisals and comparative market analysis (CMA) work products. Both appraisers and real estate brokers can effectively work together to maintain the safeguards that accurate sold data affords.

A **real estate broker** can facilitate these safeguards by adherence to the following:

- Note the amount of any seller paid costs (including a seller assisted down payment or fee paid to a charitable organization on behalf of the buyer) or other seller concession in the proper transaction documents, including the Buy/Sell Contract, Closing Statements, and Real Property Transfer Declaration.
- Utilize all available fields in the multiple listing service to report sold information including all transaction terms and seller concessions. Sold information should be entered promptly following closing and be specific and detailed particularly when the sold price includes a seller assisted down payment or concessions.
- Advise buyers and sellers to consult legal and tax counsel for advice on tax consequences of seller contributions and inducements to purchase.
- Cooperate with appraisers as they perform their due diligence in asking questions about sales.

An **appraiser** can facilitate these safeguards by adherence to the following:

- Research and confirm subject property and comparable sales, including obtaining details of the contract and financing terms.
- Research and confirm all relevant information about a transaction, including determination of seller paid costs.
- Utilize all available data search tools, including the listing history and seller contributions features of multiple listing services.
- Make appropriate adjustments to comparables with seller contributions and inducements to purchase when developing work products.

- Comply with the applicable provisions of the Ethics Rule and Standards 1 & 2 of the Uniform Standards of Professional Appraisal Practice.
- Comply with any scope of work requirements required by agencies such as the Federal Housing Administration.

CP-31 Commission Position on Acting as a Transaction Broker or Agent in Particular Types of Transactions

(Adopted 9-8-04)

The public may enter into either a Transaction-Broker relationship or an Agency relationship with a Broker. Fundamental among the differences between Agency and Transaction-Brokerage is that an Agent is an advocate with fiduciary duties, while a Transaction-Broker should remain neutral, not advocate. However, in some situations the relationship of the Broker with a particular party or property may make a particular relationship inappropriate or problematic.

Before acting as a Transaction-Broker in transactions where neutrality is difficult, the Broker should consider whether the Transaction-Brokerage arrangement is suitable, consult with the Broker's supervising Broker and then make the necessary disclosures. Some examples of these situations include:

1. Selling or purchasing for one's own account (whether the property is solely or partially owned or to be acquired by the Broker), (See Rule 6.17. regarding proper disclosures);
2. Selling or purchasing for the account of a spouse or family member of the Broker;
3. Selling or purchasing for the account of a close personal friend, business associate, or other person where it would be difficult for the Broker to remain neutral; or
4. Selling or purchasing for the account of a repeat or regular client/party where it would be difficult for the Broker to remain neutral (*i.e.*, undertaking as a Transaction-Broker the listing of multiple units, lots or properties such as listing a real estate development or condominium complex for a single developer, listing multiple residential or commercial properties for the same seller that will be sold to different buyers, or listing for lease a multiple unit residential or commercial property that will be leased to different tenants).

An agency relationship between a Broker and a seller or landlord, buyer or tenant, requires a written agency agreement. The duties of an agent go beyond facilitation of the transaction as a neutral party and require representing the interests of the Broker's principal over the interests of the other party. In certain circumstances, fulfilling the duties of an Agent including acting as an advocate may be difficult. A Broker who enters into an agency relationship must fulfill the duties of advocacy, fidelity, loyalty and other fiduciary duties associated with a single agency relationship. In circumstances where the Broker may not be able to fulfill the duties imposed on an agent the Broker should consider whether the agency arrangement is appropriate, consult with the Broker's supervising Broker and act accordingly.

This Position Statement applies to relationships where Brokers are working with landlords or tenants, as well as sellers and buyers. It applies equally to residential and commercial transactions.

CP-32 Commission Position on Brokerage Disclosures

(Adopted 9-8-04)

The Commission believes that a broker who intends to act as a buyer's or tenant's agent in a transaction should attempt to secure a written agency agreement as early in the brokerage relationship as possible. However, the Commission also recognizes that in some instances, the buyer or tenant will not immediately execute such a written agency agreement.

In these situations, the broker should initially function as a transaction-broker by either entering into:

BC 60: Exclusive Right-to-Buy Contract (All Types of Properties); or
LC 57: Exclusive Right-to-Lease Listing Contract (All Types of Properties; or
ETC 59: Exclusive Tenant Contract (All Types of Properties)

With any of the three forms the broker should check the box "Transaction-Brokerage" whereby only the brokerage services and duties contained in Section 4 of the agreement would apply; or present a buyer or tenant with BD24 Brokerage Disclosure to Buyer.

The broker may then engage as a transaction-broker and may perform any of the activities enumerated in section 12-10-201(6), C.R.S., which are the acts of real estate brokerage.

However, **before** the broker begins to work as the buyer's or tenant's **agent** and advocate to secure the best possible price or lease rate and terms for the buyer or tenant, the parties must execute one of the above listed agreements with the "Agency" box checked. In an agency relationship the broker has the duties and responsibilities contained in Section 4 of the agreement, and the additional duties of an agent contained in Section 5 of the agreement.

CP-33 Joint Position Statement from the Division of Real Estate and Division of Insurance Concerning Application of the Good Funds Laws (Repealed)

CP-34 Commission Position on Settlement Service Provider Selection, Closing Instructions and Earnest Money Deposits (revised 08/07/2012)

The Commission issues this position statement to clarify how settlement service providers are selected, when closing instructions must be completed by a real estate broker ("broker") and how earnest money is to be handled.

Selection of settlement service providers

Regardless of whether a broker is acting as a single agent or transaction broker, all brokers acting in their licensed capacities are required to advise their clients to obtain expert advice as to material matters about which the broker knows but the specifics of which are beyond the expertise of the broker. See C.R.S. 12-10-404(1)(c)(V), 12-10-405(1)(c)(V), and 12-10-407(2)(b)(II). Expert advice includes, but is not limited to, the brokering of a mortgage, performing title searches and issuing insurance, appraising real property, surveying and issuing improvement location certificates, performing property inspections and other due diligence (including environmental) and practicing law (which also includes analyzing the legal implications of the foregoing). Brokers need to ensure that they perform the acts required by the real estate brokerage practice act, based on the capacity in which they have agreed to practice, i.e. as a single agent or transaction broker. A common standard of practice amongst brokers is to provide the names of three settlement services providers in a specific area of practice and allow the consumer to choose. The Commission understands that there are occasions when a broker cannot provide the names of three separate settlement service providers that practice in one specific area, but regardless of how many names may be provided, it is imperative that final selection of the settlement service provider be left to the consumer, not the broker.

Closing Instructions

The purpose of closing instructions is for the consumer to engage the company that will be responsible for ultimately closing the sales transaction. In most transactions, the company responsible for closing the transaction is a title company, although there are brokers that provide these services. As stated above, the consumer is responsible for the selection of settlement service providers, including the individual or company that performs the closing services. If the broker is performing the closing services, including the preparation, delivery and recording of closing documents and the disbursement of funds, the broker is the "Closing Company" and thereby is responsible for completing the Commission-approved Closing Instructions at the time that the Contract to Buy and Sell Real Estate is executed by the buyer and seller. As required by Commission Rule 5.21. and

C.R.S. 12-10-217(1)(k), the broker shall retain a copy of the Closing Instructions for future use or inspection by an authorized representative of the Real Estate Commission.

If a title company is engaged to perform the closing services, the Division of Insurance requires that a title entity provide closing and settlement services only when there are written instructions from all necessary parties. See Division of Insurance Rule 3-5-1. All amendments to existing written instructions with a title entity must also be in writing. If a title company is engaged to provide the closing services, it is the "Closing Company" and it is the responsibility of the title company to complete the closing instructions as required by the Division of Insurance. The broker should make a reasonable effort to obtain a copy of the closing instructions from the title entity for the broker's transaction file, to ensure compliance with Commission Rule 5.21. and C.R.S. 12-10-217(1)(k) as stated above.

Earnest Money Deposits

A listing broker who receives earnest money is required to deposit the money in the broker's escrow or trust account in a recognized depository no later than the third business day following the day on which the broker receives notice of contract acceptance. If the selling broker receipts for a promissory note, or thing of value, such note or thing of value must be delivered with the contract to the listing broker to be held by the listing broker. Any check or note must be payable, or assigned, to the listing broker. Upon receipt of the earnest money, the listing broker must complete the Earnest Money Receipt as the Earnest Money Holder. A copy of the receipt must be retained by the broker to ensure compliance with Commission Rule 5.21. and C.R.S. 12-10-217(1)(k).

If the buyer and seller have agreed in writing that a third party or entity will hold the earnest money, the listing broker must deliver the earnest money to the third party or entity. The listing broker must obtain a dated and signed Earnest Money Receipt from the third party or entity upon delivery of the earnest money. For record keeping purposes, the broker must retain a copy of the Earnest Money Receipt and a copy of the earnest money check, note or other thing of value as required by Commission Rule 5.21, and C.R.S. 12-10-217(1)(k).

CP-35 Commission Position on Brokers as Principals

The Commission regularly receives public complaints regarding real estate transactions involving a licensed real estate broker acting as a principal. Predominantly these complaints allege that the broker, who is a principal to the transaction, and may or may not also be serving as a broker in the transaction, has failed to disclose an adverse material fact; has failed to disclose brokerage relationships (when acting as more than a principal); has failed to ensure that the contract documents and/or settlement statements accurately reflect the terms of the transaction; has filed a document that unlawfully clouds the title to the property; has failed to disclose the broker's licensed status; has mismanaged funds belonging to others; and/or has falsified information used for the purpose of obtaining financing.

The Commission reminds licensees that the Commission may investigate and discipline a license if a licensee is acting in the capacity of a principal in a real estate transaction and violations of the license law occur. The Commission's authority to investigate and impose discipline in these transactions was determined by the Colorado Court of Appeals. See *Seibel v. Colorado Real Estate Commission*, 34 Colo.App. 415, 530 P.2d 1290 (1974). The court's decision affirmed that licensed real estate brokers are subject to the real estate brokers licensing act and rules adopted by the Commission when they participate in real estate matters as principals. In such cases, licensees need to be mindful of Rule 6.17. (regarding conflict of interest and license status disclosures) and position statement CP-31 (regarding acting as a transaction broker).

CP-36 Commission Position on Minimum Service Requirements

The Commission has received numerous inquiries regarding the minimum services that brokers must provide to buyers or sellers of real property. §12-10-403, C.R.S. requires that any broker performing the activities requiring a real estate broker's license as set forth in §12-10-201(6), C.R.S., act in the capacity of either a transaction broker or a single agent in the transaction. The minimum duties required to be performed by a real estate broker acting in the capacity of a single agent are set forth in §§12-10-404 and 12-10-405, C.R.S. §12-10-404, C.R.S. Single agent engaged by seller or landlord states, in part:

(1) A broker engaged by a seller or landlord to act as a seller's agent or a landlord's agent is a limited agent with the following duties and obligations:

(a) To perform the terms of the written agreement made with the seller or landlord;

(b) To exercise reasonable skill and care for the seller or landlord;

(c) To promote the interests of the seller or landlord with the utmost good faith, loyalty, and fidelity, including, but not limited to:

(I) Seeking a price and terms which are acceptable to the seller or landlord; except that the broker shall not be obligated to seek additional offers to purchase the property while the property is subject to a contract for sale or to seek additional offers to lease the property while the property is subject to a lease or letter of intent to lease:

(II) Presenting all offers to and from the seller or landlord in a timely manner regardless of whether the property is subject to a contract for sale or a lease or letter of intent to lease;

(III) Disclosing to the seller or landlord adverse material facts actually known by the broker;

(IV) Counseling the seller or landlord as to any material benefits or risks of a transaction which are actually known by the broker;

(V) Advising the seller or landlord to obtain expert advice as to material matters about which the broker knows but the specifics of which are beyond the expertise of such broker;

(VI) Accounting in a timely manner for all money and property received; and

(VII) Informing the seller or landlord that such seller or landlord shall not be vicariously liable for the acts of such seller's or landlord's agent that are not approved, directed or ratified by such seller or landlord.

(d) To comply with all requirements of this article and any rules promulgated pursuant to this article; and

(e) To comply with any applicable federal, state, or local laws, rules, regulations, or ordinances including fair housing and civil rights statutes or regulations.

§12-10-405, C.R.S. Single agent engaged by buyer or tenant states, in part:

(1) A broker engaged by a buyer or tenant to act as a buyer's or tenant's agent shall be a limited agent with the following duties and obligations:

(a) To perform the terms of the written agreement made with the buyer or tenant;

(b) To exercise reasonable skill and care for the buyer or tenant;

(c) To promote the interests of the buyer or tenant with the utmost good faith, loyalty, and fidelity, including but not limited to:

(I) Seeking a price and terms which are acceptable to the buyer or tenant; except that the broker shall not be obligated to seek other properties while the buyer is a party to a contract to purchase property or while the tenant is a party to a lease or letter of intent to lease;

(II) Presenting all offers to and from the buyer or tenant in a timely manner regardless of whether the buyer is already a party to a contract to purchase property or the tenant is already a party to a contract or a letter of intent to lease;

(III) Disclosing to the buyer or tenant adverse material facts actually known by the broker;

(IV) Counseling the buyer or tenant as to any material benefits or risks of a transaction which are actually known by the broker;

(V) Advising the buyer or tenant to obtain expert advice as to material matters about which the broker knows but the specifics of which are beyond the expertise of such broker;

(VI) Accounting in a timely manner for all money and property received; and

(VII) Informing the buyer or tenant that such buyer or tenant shall not be vicariously liable for the acts of such buyer's or tenant's agent that are not approved, directed, or ratified by such buyer or tenant;

(d) To comply with all requirements of this article and any rules promulgated pursuant to this article; and

(e) To comply with any applicable federal, state, or local laws, rules, regulations, or ordinances including fair housing and civil rights statutes or regulations.

The minimum duties required to be performed by a real estate broker acting in the capacity of a transaction broker are set forth in §12-10-407, C.R.S., which states, in part:

(1) A broker engaged as a transaction-broker is not an agent for either party;

(2) A transaction-broker shall have the following obligations and responsibilities:

(a) To perform the terms of any written or oral agreement made with any party to the transaction;

(b) To exercise reasonable skill and care as a transaction-broker, including, but not limited to:

(I) Presenting all offers and counteroffers in a timely manner regardless of whether the property is subject to a contract for sale or lease or letter of intent;

(II) Advising the parties regarding the transaction and suggesting that such parties obtain expert advice as to material matters about which the transaction-broker knows but the specifics of which are beyond the expertise of such broker;

(III) Accounting in a timely manner for all money and property received;

(IV) Keeping parties fully informed regarding the transaction;

(V) Assisting the parties in complying with the terms and conditions of any contract including closing the transaction;

(VI) Disclosing to prospective buyers or tenants any adverse material facts actually known by the broker including but not limited to adverse material facts pertaining to the title, the physical condition of the property, any defects in the property, and any environmental hazards affecting the property required by law to be disclosed;

(VII) Disclosing to any prospective seller or landlord all adverse material facts actually known by the broker including but not limited to adverse material facts pertaining to the buyer's or tenant's financial ability to perform the terms of the transaction and the buyer's intent to occupy the property as a principal residence; and

(VIII) Informing the parties that as a seller and buyer or as landlord and tenant they shall not be vicariously liable for any acts of the transaction-broker;

(c) To comply with all requirements of this article and any rules promulgated pursuant to this article; and

(d) To comply with any applicable federal, state, or local laws, rules, regulations, or ordinances including fair housing and civil rights statutes or regulations.

§12-10-403, C.R.S. allows real estate brokers to perform duties in addition to those established in §§12-10-404, 12-10-405 and 12-10-407, C.R.S. The additional duties may include, but are not limited to, holding open houses, property showings, providing a lockbox, use of multiple listing services or other information exchanges, etc. Additional services that brokers agree to provide their clients must be documented in writing. A broker is not allowed to solely perform "additional" services which require a real estate broker's license, i.e. offering the real property of another for sale through advertisements, without providing the minimum duties required by single agency or transaction brokerage. The Commission does not regulate the fees or commissions charged by brokers for minimum or additional services provided. Fees and commissions are negotiable between the broker and the principal.

CP-37 Commission Position on Survey and Lease Objections to the Contract to Buy and Sell Real Estate

The intention of the Commission in adopting the Contract to Buy and Sell Real Estate (CBS1-8-10 and the other versions of the Contract) is set forth below.

1. As background, under Section 8.1, Buyer has the right to object to title matters up to the **Title Objection Deadline**. Under Section 8.5, Seller has the obligation and right to use reasonable efforts to correct such objections and bear nominal expense prior to Closing. If any unsatisfactory title condition is not corrected prior to Closing, Buyer may either terminate the Contract or waive objection to any unsatisfactory title condition prior to Closing.
2. Under Section 8.2, if Buyer objects to any off-record matter on or before the **Off-Record Matters Objection Deadline**, the Contract will terminate. Seller has no right to cure such off-record matters. Seller does not have a right to cure any objection to existing surveys or leases under Section 8.2. Section 8.5 does not apply to objections under Section 8.2.
3. Under Section 7.3, Buyer may obtain a new, updated or recertified Survey (Current Survey) on or before the **Survey Deadline**. Current Surveys are different than existing surveys, surveys which are <u>not</u> current and which may be delivered to Buyer under Section 8.2 as an off-record matter; objections to existing surveys must be made on or before the **Off-Record Matters Objection Deadline**. Buyer may object to the Current Survey on or before the **Survey Objection Deadline**. If Buyer timely objects to the Current Survey, the Contract will terminate. Buyer's objection to the Current Survey is governed by Section 8.3.2, and Seller has no right to cure any objection to the Survey. Section 8.5 does not apply to objections under Section 8.3.2.
4. Under Sections 10.8.2 (Survey) and 10.8.3 (Leases) Buyer has a right to "terminate" the Contract. Seller has no right to cure any such objection. Section 8.5 does not apply to objections under Sections 10.8.2 and 10.8.3.

Conclusion: Buyer has a right terminate the Contract due to objections with any Survey (Existing or Current) or to any Lease. Seller has no right to cure any objection to the Survey or Lease (whether such objection is based on Section 7, 8 or 10 as Section 8.5 does not apply to Survey or Lease objections).

CP-38 Commission Position on Disclosure of Affiliated Business Arrangements and Conflicts of Interest (4-5-2011)

This statement supplements Rule 6.18. Affiliated Business Arrangements. §12-10-218, C.R.S. *Affiliated Business Arrangements* was enacted in Colorado to provide transparency, accountability, and consumer protection through disclosure and consistency concerning affiliated business arrangements. Affiliated business arrangements have also been regulated for many years by the Real Estate Settlement Procedures Act (RESPA). RESPA was precipitated by significant reforms identified by Congress as necessary to ensure that consumers did not pay disproportionately high settlement costs as the result of certain deleterious business practices by settlement service providers.

RESPA is applicable to any residential mortgage transaction involving a federally related mortgage loan. However, Colorado law requires disclosure of affiliated business arrangements to consumers even if the transaction does not involve a federally related residential mortgage loan.

Colorado law C.R.S. 12-10-218(1)(a) defines an "affiliated business arrangement" as an arrangement in which:

> *"A provider of settlement services or an associate of a provider of settlement services has either an affiliate relationship with or a direct beneficial ownership interest of more than one percent in another provider of settlement services;"*

and the provider directly or indirectly refers business to the other provider or affirmatively influences the selection of another provider of settlement services.

It is the Commission's position that real estate brokers must disclose affiliated business arrangements to consumers in all transactions intended to result in the transfer of title from one party to another. RESPA requires that affiliated business arrangements be disclosed before or at the time a referral is made to a provider of settlement services. Colorado law requires a licensee to disclose any affiliated business arrangement when an offer to purchase real property is fully executed. In Colorado, the disclosure is required to be in writing, must be given to both agents and transaction brokers, must comply with RESPA and Colorado law, and must be made using the Federal RESPA disclosure form. Colorado law requires real estate brokers to disclose their affiliated business arrangements to all parties to the real estate transaction and all parties are expected to sign the disclosure form. The Commission recommends that real estate brokers disclose their affiliated business arrangements to the party with whom they are working early in their relationship, i.e. at the time brokerage relationships are disclosed or when the listing contract or buyer broker agreement is negotiated. In those transactions where the broker does not deal with another party until the time of contracting written disclosure should be made to all parties at the time the purchase contract is fully executed.

Additionally, real estate brokers are required to make certain disclosures to the Division of Real Estate regarding their affiliated business arrangements. Colorado law requires every licensee to disclose to the Commission when they enter into or change an affiliated business arrangement. All affiliated business arrangements to which the licensee is a party must be disclosed. Disclosure is required at the time of a new application for licensure or at the time of activation of an inactive license. The disclosure must include the physical location of the affiliated business. Employing brokers are required to disclose the names of all affiliated business arrangements to which the employing broker is a party on an annual basis, at the least. The disclosure must include the physical location of the affiliated businesses. The Commission has determined that these disclosures shall be made electronically through the Division of Real Estate's website at www.dora.state.co.us/pls/real/AFB_Web.Logon?p_div=REC.

It is the Commission's position that Rule 6.17. *Continuing duty to disclose conflict of interest and license status*, applies to all licensees including real estate brokers who perform licensed property management services and are affiliated with businesses or vendors that provide services applicable to lease transactions. For example, a real estate broker acting on behalf of a landlord is required to disclose to the landlord that the real estate broker has partial ownership of the maintenance company that the real estate broker utilizes for the landlord's property repairs. The Commission strongly recommends that this type of information be disclosed to the principal early in the business relationship, i.e. at the time brokerage relationships are disclosed or when the listing contract is negotiated. Additionally, this disclosure should be made in writing.

CP-39 Commission Position on Lease Options, Lease Purchase Agreements and Installment Land Contracts (4-5-2011)

The Commission recognizes that in order to maintain the resilience of the real estate market during times when conventional lending requirements are rigorous, alternative funding practices are utilized to sustain the market conditions of supply and demand. The Commission has received and investigated numerous complaints pertaining to lease options, lease purchase agreements and installment land contracts. Although the Commission does not have the authority to prohibit the types of real estate transactions that real estate brokers participate in, the Commission strongly cautions real estate brokers to utilize the services of an attorney licensed to practice law within the State of Colorado. It has been the Commission's observation, based on complaints received, that lease option and lease purchase transactions are complex and generally contain provisions with significant financial risk posed to the prospective buyer and seller. Installment land contracts and the other transactions mentioned in this position statement afford buyers the opportunity to take possession of the real property and make installment payments to the seller. There is a significant potential for harm to the seller, buyer or assignee if the installment land contract is not properly drafted. In all of the above transactions, the seller retains legal title to the property while the buyer may acquire equitable title. The Commission does not have an approved contract form necessary to memorialize the terms and nuances related to these complex transactions, or any jurisdictional regulations that may be germane. Pursuant to Rule 7.1., et seq., the appropriate provisions of the license law and the brokerage relationship act (§§12-10-217, 12-10-404, 405 and 407, C.R.S.), real estate brokers are prohibited from drafting a contract document that would reflect the terms of such a transaction as it would exceed their level of competency and is a matter requiring the expertise and advice of an attorney. Additionally, such behavior may be construed as the unauthorized practice of law by the real estate broker and subject to civil penalties. The contracts for these transactions should not be prepared by a real estate broker; rather, the documents should be drafted by a licensed Colorado attorney-at-law engaged for each particular transaction.

CP-40 Commission Position on Teams (4-5-2011)

The Commission recognizes that there are benefits to both real estate brokers and consumers in the usage of real estate broker teams. Teams may be formed within a licensed brokerage firm with the approval of the employing broker. Real estate brokers operating as teams need to ensure that they are compliant with Commission rules regarding advertising, name usage and supervision.

Advertising and name usage:

While there is no prohibition of teams, real estate brokers need to ensure that they do not advertise in a manner that misleads the public as to the identity of the brokers' licensed brokerage. Real estate brokers that function as teams should not advertise teams using the terms "realty", "real estate", "company", "corporation", "corp.", "inc.", "LLC" or other similar language that would indicate a company other than the employing brokerage firm. Advertising includes, but is not limited to, websites, signage, property flyers, mailings, business cards, letterhead and contracts. The advertising of team names should never give the impression that the team is an entity separate from the licensed real estate brokerage. If the identity of the employing broker or the brokerage firm is difficult for the public or the Commission to ascertain, the team may be in violation of Rule 6.10. Advertising.

Supervision:

In addition to the supervision requirements set forth in Rules 6.3.C. and 6.3.D., Rule 6.3.B. Employing broker responsibilities requires that the broker designated to act as the broker for any partnership, limited liability company or corporation, i.e. the employing broker, fulfill the following duties:

1) Maintain all trust accounts and trust account records;
2) Maintain all transaction records;
3) Develop an office policy manual and periodically review office policies with all employees;
4) Provide for a high level of supervision for newly licensed persons pursuant to Rule- 6.3.D.;

5) Provide for a reasonable level of supervision for experienced licensees pursuant to Rule 6.3.C.;
6) Take reasonable steps to ensure that violations of statutes, rules and office policies do not occur or reoccur;
7) Provide for adequate supervision of all offices operated by the broker, whether managed by licensed or unlicensed persons.

Pursuant to §12-10-222, C.R.S., and Rule 6.3.A., employing brokers are also responsible for providing supervision over such activities with reference to the licensing statutes and Commission rules for all brokerage employees, including but not limited to administrative assistants, bookkeepers and personal assistants of licensed employees. Thus, employing brokers are responsible for the actions of unlicensed persons who perform functions within the real estate broker team. Employing brokers need to ensure that any unlicensed person acting within the team is not engaged in practices that require a real estate broker's license. Employing brokers also need to establish that the compensation paid to an unlicensed person for services provided is not in the form of a commission. Compensation paid to an unlicensed person is not required to be paid solely by the employing broker. However, §12-10-221, C.R.S., requires that all licensee compensation or valuable consideration for the performance of any acts requiring a broker's license is paid solely by the employing broker.

CP-41 Commission Position on Competency (December 6, 2011)

Pursuant to sections 12-10-404, 12-10-405 and 12-10-407, C.R.S., which are the laws that govern the duties of a real estate broker acting in the capacity of a single agent or transaction broker, real estate brokers are required to perform the terms of written or oral agreements they make with certain parties to a real estate transaction. Pursuant to sections 12-10-404 and 12-10-405, C.R.S., real estate brokers acting in the capacity of a single agent have a duty to promote the interests of their clients with the utmost good faith, loyalty, and fidelity. Pursuant to section 12-10-217(1)(q), C.R.S., it is a violation of the license law if a licensee demonstrates unworthiness or incompetency to act as a real estate broker by conducting business in such a manner as to endanger the interest of the public.

Prior to performing any acts that require a real estate broker's license, a broker should determine whether he or she possesses the knowledge, experience, and/or training necessary to perform the terms of the transaction and maintain compliance with the applicable federal, state or local laws, rules, regulations, or ordinances. If the broker does not have the requisite knowledge, experience and/or training necessary to consummate the terms of the agreement, the broker should either decline to provide brokerage services or seek the assistance of another real estate broker who does have the necessary experience, training, and/or knowledge. The Commission will have grounds to discipline a broker's license if a broker fails to take the measures necessary to gain competence and violations of the license law are substantiated.

CP-42 Commission Position on Apartment Building or Complex Management

The Commission recognizes that owners of apartment buildings or complexes will engage the services of real estate brokerages or unlicensed, on-site managers, or both. An "owner" includes either a person or an entity recognized under Colorado law. The owner must have a controlling interest in the entity formed by the owner to manage the apartment building or complex. In the instance of an entity, the "owner" may form a separate entity to manage the apartment building or complex. The ownership entity and the entity formed by the owner to manage the apartment building or complex must be under the control of the same person or persons.

Pursuant to §12-10-201(6)(b)(XII), C.R.S., a regularly salaried employee of the owner of an apartment building or complex is permitted to perform customary duties for his or her employer without a real estate broker's license. The unlicensed, on-site manager must either report directly to the owner or to the real estate broker, if a real estate broker is engaged to manage the property. The Commission views the following to be customary duties of an unlicensed, on-site manager:

1. Performance of clerical duties, including gathering information about competing projects.
2. Obtain information necessary to qualify perspective tenants for a lease. This includes obtaining and verifying information regarding employment history, credit information, references and personal information as necessary.
3. Provide access to a property available for lease and distribute preprinted, objective information prepared by a broker as long as no negotiating, offering or contracting is involved.
4. Distribute preprinted, objective information at an on-site leasing office that is prepared by an owner or broker, as long as no negotiating, offering or contracting is involved.
5. Quote the rental price established by the owner or the owner's licensed broker.
6. Act as a scrivener to the owner or the broker for purposes of completing predetermined lease terms on preprinted forms as negotiated by the owner or broker.
7. Deliver paperwork to other brokers.
8. Deliver paperwork to landlords and tenants, if such paperwork has already been reviewed by the owner, or a broker or has been prepared in accordance with the supervising broker's instructions.
9. Collect and deposit rents and security deposits in accordance with the owner's lease agreement or the brokerage firm's written office policy.
10. Schedule property maintenance in accordance with the brokerage firm's management agreement or the owner's lease agreement.

If the owner has executed a Power of Attorney form or a written delegation of authority that authorizes the unlicensed, on-site manager to sign and execute leases on behalf of the owner, the unlicensed, on-site manager may execute those without possessing a real estate broker's license. Brokers supervising unlicensed, on-site managers with this authority are expected to review the executed documents to ensure compliance with lease terms, management agreements, local, state and federal laws, including the real estate brokerage practice act and Commission rules.

Employing brokers need to be especially aware of their supervisory duties under the license law. Supervisory duties apply whether the on-site manager is an employee or independent contractor of the broker or brokerage firm, or if the on-site manager is a regularly salaried employee of the apartment building or complex owner. The employing broker should have a written office policy explaining the duties, responsibilities and limitation on the use of on-site managers. This policy should be periodically reviewed with all employees.

CP-43 Commission Position on Property Inspection Resolutions

The Commission has received inquiries and complaints claiming that real estate brokers ("Brokers") misrepresent property conditions and negotiate repairs in a manner that conceals issues from the buyer's lender, particularly when the property's condition would affect a lending decision. The Commission issues this position statement to clarify how Brokers can advise buyers regarding inspection objection issues and maintain compliance with Commission rules and regulations. Brokers must understand that in working with their clients to resolve inspection issues, Colorado law imposes upon Brokers the duty to avoid misrepresentations [C.R.S.§ 12-10-217(1)(a)] and dual contracts [C.R.S. § 18-5-208].

Other than terminating the contract based on inspection, there are generally five alternatives available to address property condition issues in a sales transaction: 1) the seller can repair the property prior to closing; 2) the seller can agree to pay a concession or contribution, for example, a portion of the buyer's closing costs; 3) after closing, the buyer can make the repair without assistance from the seller; 4) the buyer and the seller can negotiate a modification to the sales price; or 5) at closing, the seller can escrow funds or pay a contractor (if allowed by the lender).

If the buyer is obtaining a loan to fund the purchase of the property, any of these options can affect the mortgage financing. Prior to negotiating any of these alternatives, the broker should advise the buyer to ask their mortgage loan originator or lender whether the resolution may (1) have a detrimental impact on the Buyer's ability to get the loan; (2) cause delays in the lender's processing and funding of the loan by Closing; and (3) require further inspections and repairs.

Once items to negotiate have been identified, the buyer broker should use the Commission-approved Inspection Objection form to identify the inspection issues that the buyer seeks to have resolved (Note: the Inspection Objection form is a notice form and is not part of the contract). Then, once the buyer and seller have reached a resolution, the Brokers can memorialize the terms on the Commission-approved Inspection Resolution form or the Agreement to Amend/Extend the Contract.

CP-44 Commission Position on Coming Soon Listings

The Commission has received inquiries and complaints regarding real estate brokers ("brokers") who advertise properties as "coming soon" to the market. The common complaint the Commission receives about "coming soon" listings is that the listing broker provides limited exposure of the property on the open market in an effort to broker both sides of the transaction, or "double end the deal". Many of the complaints that the Commission receives indicate that once the property is entered into a multiple listing service, becomes available for showings or is otherwise given full market exposure, the listing broker notifies any parties interested that the property is already under contract. While the Commission cannot impose limitations on how a property is marketed for sale or lease, a broker must comply with the license law.

Among other duties, §12-10-404(1), C.R.S., requires a broker acting as a single agent engaged by a seller or a landlord, to " exercise reasonable skill and care for the seller or landlord" and "promote the interests of the seller or landlord with the utmost good faith, loyalty, and fidelity". A broker who acts as a transaction broker for the seller or landlord is also required to "exercise reasonable skill and care", among the other responsibilities and obligations enumerated in §12-10-407, C.R.S.

During the negotiation of the listing contract, and as part of the broker's obligation to exercise reasonable skill and care, a broker is responsible for advising the seller or landlord "of any material benefits or risks of a transaction which are actually known by the broker". This includes limiting a property's market exposure by delaying access for showings or open houses, or limiting the amount of time that the seller or landlord will consider offers. Motivation for limiting exposure of the property should be carefully considered. Is the property being marketed as "coming soon" because the seller is preparing it for sale or lease? This would be a legitimate use of that particular marketing method. However, if the property is being marketed as "coming soon" in an effort for the listing broker to acquire a buyer and "double end" the transaction, this would be a violation of the license law because the broker is not exercising reasonable skill and care. If the broker is a single agent for the seller or landlord, the broker may be viewed by the Commission as also failing to promote the interests of the seller or landlord with the utmost good faith, loyalty and fidelity. Finally, a broker who places the importance of his commission above his duties, responsibilities or obligations to the consumer who has engaged him is practicing business in a manner that endangers the interest of the public.

Ultimately, it is the seller or landlord's decision how, when and where the property will be marketed. A broker who fails to advise a seller or landlord of the material benefits or risks, or does not allow the seller or landlord to decide how the property will be marketed, may be subject to license discipline by the Commission. The manner in which the broker and seller or landlord agree to market the property must be memorialized in writing in the listing contract prior to any marketing being performed.

CP-45 Commission Position on Defined Terms

The purpose of this position statement is to provide definitions of the terms that regularly appear in the regulations promulgated by the Commission through the rule-making process.

Advertise or Advertising: The promotion, solicitation or representation of real estate brokerage services requiring a real estate broker's license. Advertising may include, but is not limited to, business cards, brochures, websites, signage, property flyers, mailings (paper or electronic), social media, letter head, email signatures and contract documents.

Applicant: An individual or entity seeking a license from the Commission to perform the duties enumerated in C.R.S. §12-10-201(6)(a).

Broker: Any individual licensed by the Colorado Real Estate Commission to perform the acts enumerated in C.R.S. §12-10-201(6)(a) regardless if such broker is licensed as an associate broker, independent broker or employing broker.

Brokerage or Brokerage Firm: Any sole proprietor, partnership, limited liability company, corporation or any other authorized entity licensed by the Commission to perform the acts enumerated in C.R.S. §12-10-201(6)(a).

Commission: The Colorado Real Estate Commission, created pursuant to C.R.S. §12-10-206.

Division: The Division of Real Estate.

Licensee: A broker or brokerage firm licensed by the Commission.

Team: Two (2) or more brokers within a brokerage firm that conduct their real estate brokerage business together.

Trademark: Any logo, service mark or other identifying mark used in conjunction with a brokerage firm's legal name or trade name. Trademarks may be registered with the Colorado Secretary of State pursuant to C.R.S. §7-70-102, C.R.S. As an example, the brokerage "A Better Choice Real Estate" uses a logo bearing the initials "ABC". The logo is used to identify the brokerage and the real estate services that it provides, therefore it would be the trademark for the brokerage.

Trade Name: The name under which a brokerage firm does business other than the brokerage firm's legal name. Any trade name used by a brokerage firm must be on file with the Commission and must be filed with the Colorado Secretary of State pursuant to C.R.S. §7-71-101. For example, a brokerage is licensed with the Commission under its legal name of "Colorado Real Estate Group LLC". However, the brokerage is also a franchise of "International Realty" and does business under the trade name "International Realty of Colorado".

Viewable Page: A page that may or may not scroll beyond the border of the screen and includes the use of frame pages.

CP-46 Commission Position on Broker Disclosure of Adverse Material Facts

(revised 08/01/2017)

Brokers must disclose known adverse material facts.

In all real estate transactions, brokers are obligated to disclose known adverse material facts to all of the parties involved in the transaction. C.R.S. §§ 12-10-404(1)(c)(III), -404(3)(a), - 405(1)(c)(III), -405(3)(a), -407(2)(b)(VI), and -407(2)(b)(VII). While clients have certain disclosure obligations, they are not addressed in this Position Statement. Brokers should refrain from advising clients about clients' disclosure duties, which may be different.

What is an adverse material fact?

During the course of a real estate transaction, a broker for either side of the transaction may become aware of certain information pertaining to the property. For example, a broker may become aware that the roof of the property was recently repaired, or that the property was hit by lightning several times, or that one of the owners of the home for sale is a smoker. Brokers may have difficulty in ascertaining whether to disclose such facts.

In order to answer these types of questions, brokers first should consider whether the information is material. Factual information is material when a reasonable person would have ascribed actual significance to the information. *Moye White LLP v. Beren*, 320 P.3d 373, 378 (Colo. App. 2013). Examples of material facts include facts affecting title, facts affecting the physical condition of the property and environmental hazards affecting the property. "Undisclosed facts are 'material' if the consumer's decision might have been different had the truth been disclosed." *In re Gattis*, 318 P.3d 549, 554 (Colo. App. 2013) (quoting *Briggs v. Am. Nat'l Prop. & Cas. Co.*, 209 P.3d 1181, 1186 (Colo. App. 2009)).

Next, brokers should consider whether that material information is adverse to a party's interest in the transaction. *See In re Fisher*, 202 P.3d 1186, 1196 (Colo. 2009); *Black's Law Dictionary* 62 (9th ed. 2009) (defining "adverse"). A broker must consider how that material information affects each of the parties in the transaction, not just the individual party they are representing. If that material information is contrary (i.e. "adverse") to the interest of one of the parties, then the broker must disclose it to all the parties.

An "adverse material fact" includes but is not limited to a fact that affects the structural integrity of the real property, presents a documented health risk to occupants of the property including environmental hazards and facts that have a material effect on title or occupancy of the property. Examples of adverse material facts include building or zoning violations, water damage to the flooring of property caused by marijuana plants, structural damage to a home caused by insect infestations or expansive soils or any type of lien filed against the property.

Brokers need only disclose known adverse material facts.

A broker need only disclose facts of which the broker has actual knowledge. *See Baumgarten v. Coppage*, 15 P.3d 304, 307 (Colo. App. 2000). For example, if a property owner knows that the foundation is crumbling but never tells his broker, the broker has no duty to disclose that fact because the broker has no knowledge. Because a broker must actually know the adverse material fact, a broker does not violate Commission rules if he or she did not know the adverse material fact but only should have known the fact.

The Commission believes that disclosure of known adverse material facts is an important requirement that brokers must undertake in order to protect Colorado buyers and sellers. Accordingly, real estate brokers must disclose those facts they actually know, that a reasonable person would ascribe actual significance to and are contrary to the interests of a party in a real estate transaction. To the extent a broker is unclear about whether a known fact that affects the physical property is adverse or material, the broker should err on the side of disclosing the fact.

Brokers must not disclose circumstances that may psychologically impact or stigmatize real property.

Understanding a broker's obligation to disclose known adverse material facts is as important as a broker's duty not to disclose information that may psychologically impact or stigmatize real property. Without the informed consent of the client, brokers must not disclose facts or suspicions regarding circumstances which may psychologically impact or stigmatize real property. C.R.S. §§ 12-10-404(2)(e), - 405(2)(e), - 407(3)(e). The law states that:

> [f]acts or suspicions regarding circumstances occurring on a parcel of property which could psychologically impact or stigmatize such property are not material facts subject to a disclosure requirement in a real estate transaction.

C.R.S. § 38-35.5-101(1) (2016).

There is minimal guidance in Colorado as to what equates to a psychological impact or stigmatization of a property. However, Colorado law identifies two specific circumstances that brokers are prohibited from disclosing due to the potential stigmatization of that property to potential buyers.

The first circumstance that cannot be disclosed is when an occupant of real property was suspected to be or was infected with the human immunodeficiency virus (HIV) or diagnosed with acquired immune deficiency syndrome, or any other disease which has been determined by medical evidence to be highly unlikely to be transmitted through the occupancy of a dwelling place. C.R.S. § 38-35.5-101(1)(a).

The second circumstance that a broker cannot disclose is when "the property was the site of a homicide or other felony or of a suicide." C.R.S. § 38-35.5-101(1)(b). Colorado courts have not provided any greater guidance concerning the types of felony crimes that fall under its definition.

A broker's obligation to avoid disclosure of circumstances which may psychologically impact or stigmatize real property should not impede a party's right to be informed about all known adverse material facts. The Commission concludes that the only circumstances in which a broker is not obligated to disclose facts or suspicions regarding circumstances that may psychologically impact or stigmatize real property are those two set forth immediately above in section 38-35.5-101(1)(a) and (b).

Brokers must disclose all known adverse material facts, unless it is one of the circumstances set forth in section 38-35.5-101(1).

The Commission's primary purpose is to protect the public. *Albright v. McDermond*, 14 P.3d 318, 322 (Colo. 2000). The Commission believes it is in the public's best interest for brokers to disclose all known adverse material facts to the parties to a real estate transaction because this disclosure increases each party's awareness of those facts prior to completion of the transaction, it reduces the potential for creating an unfair transaction, and it otherwise protects the overall integrity of the transaction.

The Commission suggests that brokers have robust conversations with their clients about broker disclosures, with an eye towards full and complete disclosure. Brokers who are aware of either of the two factual scenarios set forth in C.R.S. § 38-35.5-101 are encouraged to obtain their clients' consent to permit disclosure of these facts.

Chapter 4: Subdivision Laws

An * in the left margin indicates a change in the statute, rule, or text since the last publication of the manual.

I. Jurisdiction of Commission

A. Introduction

The Subdivision Developer's Act ("Act") affects the types of subdivisions that must be registered with the Real Estate Commission. The following types of subdivisions within the State of Colorado, and subdivisions located outside the state being offered for sale in Colorado, must be registered before offering, negotiating, or agreeing to sell, lease, or transfer any portion of the subdivision:

1. Any division of real property into twenty (20) or more interests intended solely for residential use, with each interest comprising thirty-five (35) or more acres of land offered for sale, lease or transfer;
2. Subdivisions consisting of twenty (20) or more timeshare interests (a timeshare interest includes a deeded or non-deeded interest, including but not limited to a fee simple interest, a leasehold, a contract to use, a membership or club agreement, or an interest in common);
3. Subdivisions consisting of twenty (20) or more residential units created by converting an existing structure (e.g., condominium conversions); and
4. Subdivisions created by cooperative housing corporations with twenty (20) or more shareholders with proprietary leases, whether the project is completed or not.

B. Exemption from Registration under the Act

1. The selling of memberships in campgrounds;
2. Bulk sales and transfers between developers;
3. Property upon which there has been or upon which there will be erected residential buildings that have not been previously occupied and where the consideration paid by the purchaser for such property includes the cost of such buildings (this does not apply to conversions of an existing structure, timeshare, or cooperative housing projects);
4. Lots that, at the time of closing of a sale or occupancy under a lease, are situated on a street or road and the street or road system is improved to standards at least equal to streets and roads maintained by the county, city, or town in which the lots are located; have a feasible plan to provide potable water and sewage disposal; and have telephone and electricity facilities and systems adequate to serve the lots, which facilities and systems are installed and in place on the lots or in a street, road, or easement adjacent to the lots and which facilities and systems comply with applicable state, county, municipal, or other local laws, rules, and regulations; or any subdivision

that has been or is required to be approved after September 1, 1972 by a regional, county, or municipal planning authority pursuant to Article 28 of Title 30 or Article 23 of Title 31, C.R.S.; and

5. Sales by public officials in the official conduct of their duties.

C. Additional Provisions of the Act

1. A "Developer" means any person, firm, partnership, joint venture, association, or corporation participating as owner, promoter, developer, or sales agent in the planning, platting, development, promotion, sale, or lease of a subdivision.
2. A registration expires on December 31st of each year unless it is renewed. A registration that has expired may be reinstated within two (2) years after such expiration upon submission of a renewal application and payment of the appropriate renewal fee, as well as meeting all other requirements of the Act. A Developer is not authorized to transact business during the period of time between expiration of the subdivision registration and reinstatement.
3. The Act requires a five (5) day cancellation period after the execution of a contract, which right cannot be waived, and applies to any subdivision regulated pursuant to the Act. This cancellation period runs until midnight on the fifth (5th) day following the execution of the contract.
4. Any agreement or contract for the sale or lease of a subdivision or part thereof shall be voidable by the purchaser and unenforceable by the Developer unless such Developer was duly registered under the provisions of the Act when such agreement or contract was made.

II. Subdivision Statutes

§ 12-10-501, C.R.S. Definitions.

Editor's note: *This section is similar to former §12-61-401 as it existed prior to 2019.*

As used in this part 5, unless the context otherwise requires:

(1) "Commission" means the real estate commission established under section 12-10-206.

(2) "Developer" means any person, as defined in section 2-4-401 (8), that participates as owner, promoter, or sales agent in the promotion, sale, or lease of a subdivision or any part thereof.

(3) (a) "Subdivision" means any real property divided into twenty or more interests intended solely for residential use and offered for sale, lease, or transfer.

(b) (I) The term "subdivision" also includes:

(A) The conversion of an existing structure into a common interest community, as defined in article 33.3 of title 38, of twenty or more residential units;

(B) A group of twenty or more time shares intended for residential use; and

(C) A group of twenty or more proprietary leases in a cooperative housing corporation, as described in article 33.5 of title 38.

(II) The term "subdivision" does not include:

(A) The selling of memberships in campgrounds;

(B) Bulk sales and transfers between developers;

(C) Property upon which there has been or upon which there will be erected residential buildings that have not been previously occupied and where the consideration paid for the property includes the cost of the buildings;

(D) Lots that, at the time of closing of a sale or occupancy under a lease, are situated on a street or road and street or road system improved to standards at least equal to streets and roads maintained by the county, city, or town in which the lots are located; have a feasible plan to provide potable water and sewage disposal; and have telephone and electricity facilities and systems adequate to serve the lots, which facilities and systems are installed and in place on the lots or in a street, road, or easement adjacent to the lots and which facilities and systems comply with applicable state, county, municipal, or other local laws, rules, and regulations; or any subdivision that has been or is required to be approved after September 1, 1972, by a regional, county, or municipal planning authority pursuant to article 28 of title 30 or article 23 of title 31;

(E) Sales by public officials in the official conduct of their duties.

(4) "Time share" means a time share estate, as defined in section 38-33-110 (5), or a time share use, but the term does not include group reservations made for convention purposes as a single transaction with a hotel, motel, or condominium owner or association. For the purposes of this subsection (4), "time share use" means a contractual or membership right of occupancy, that cannot be terminated at the will of the owner, for life or for a term of years, to the recurrent, exclusive use or occupancy of a lot, parcel, unit, or specific or nonspecific segment of real property, annually or on some other periodic basis, for a period of time that has been or will be allotted from the use or occupancy periods into which the property has been divided.

§ 12-10-502, C.R.S. Registration required.

Editor's note: *This section is similar to former §12-61-402 as it existed prior to 2019.*

(1) Unless exempt under the provisions of section 12-10-501 (3), a developer, before selling, leasing, or transferring or agreeing or negotiating to sell, lease, or transfer, directly or indirectly, any subdivision or any part thereof, shall register pursuant to this part 5.

(2) Upon approval by the commission, a developer who has applied for registration pursuant to section 12-10-503 may offer reservations in a subdivision during the pendency of the application and until the application is granted or denied if the fees for the reservations are held in trust by an independent third party and are fully refundable.

§ 12-10-503, C.R.S. Application for registration.

Editor's note: *This section is similar to former §12-61-403 as it existed prior to 2019.*

(1) Every person who is required to register as a developer under this part 5 shall submit to the commission an application that contains the information described in subsections (2) and (3) of this section. If the information is not submitted, the commission may deny the Application for registration.

If a developer is currently regulated in another state that has registration requirements substantially equivalent to the requirements of this part 5 or that provide substantially comparable protection to a purchaser, the commission may accept proof of the registration along with the developer's disclosure or equivalent statement from the other state in full or partial satisfaction of the information required by this section. In addition, the applicant shall be under a continuing obligation to notify the commission within ten days of any change in the information so submitted, and a failure to do so shall be a cause for disciplinary action.

(2) (a) Registration information concerning the developer shall include:

(I) The principal office of the applicant wherever situate;

(II) The location of the principal office and the branch offices of the applicant in this state;

(III) The names and residence and business addresses of all natural persons who have a twenty-four percent or greater financial or ultimate beneficial interest in the business of the developer, either directly or indirectly, as principal, manager, member, partner, officer, director, or stockholder, specifying each such person's capacity, title, and percentage of ownership. If no natural person has a twenty-four percent or greater financial or beneficial interest in the business of the developer, the information required in this subsection (2)(a)(III) shall be submitted regarding the natural person having the largest single financial or beneficial interest.

(IV) The length of time and the locations where the applicant has been engaged in the business of real estate sales or development;

(V) Any felony of which the applicant has been convicted within the preceding ten years. In determining whether a certificate of registration shall be issued to an applicant who has been convicted of a felony within such period of time, the commission shall be governed by the provisions of section 24-5-101.

(VI) The states in which the applicant has had a license or registration similar to the developer's registration in this state granted, refused, suspended, or revoked or is currently the subject of an investigation or charges that could result in refusal, suspension, or revocation;

(VII) Whether the developer or any other person financially interested in the business of the developer as principal, partner, officer, director, or stockholder has engaged in any activity that would constitute a violation of this part 5.

(b) If the applicant is a corporate developer, a copy of the certificate of authority to do business in this state or a certificate of incorporation issued by the secretary of state shall accompany the application.

(3) Registration information concerning the subdivision shall include:

(a) The location of each subdivision from which sales are intended to be made;

(b) The name of each subdivision and the trade, corporate, or partnership name used by the developer;

(c) Evidence or certification that each subdivision offered for sale or lease is registered or will be registered in accordance with state or local requirements of the state in which each subdivision is located;

(d) Copies of documents evidencing the title or other interest in the subdivision;

(e) If there is a blanket encumbrance upon the title of the subdivision or any other ownership, leasehold, or contractual interest that could defeat all possessory or ownership rights of a purchaser, a copy of the instruments creating the liens, encumbrances, or interests, with dates as to the recording, along with documentary evidence that any beneficiary, mortgagee, or trustee of a deed of trust or any other holder of the ownership, leasehold, or contractual interest will release any lot or time share from the blanket encumbrance or has subordinated its interest in the subdivision to the interest of any purchaser or has established any other arrangement acceptable to the commission that protects the rights of the purchaser;

(f) A statement that standard commission-approved forms will be used for contracts of sale, notes, deeds, and other legal documents used to effectuate the sale or lease of the subdivision or any part thereof, unless the forms to be used were prepared by an attorney representing the developer;

(g) A true statement by the developer that, in any conveyance by means of an installment contract, the purchaser shall be advised to record the contract with the proper authorities in the jurisdiction in which the subdivision is located. In no event shall any developer specifically prohibit the recording of the installment contract.

(h) A true statement by the developer of the provisions for and availability of legal access, sewage disposal, and public utilities, including water, electricity, gas, and telephone facilities, in the subdivision offered for sale or lease, including whether such are to be a developer or purchaser expense;

(i) A true statement as to whether or not a survey of each lot, site, or tract offered for sale or lease from the subdivision has been made and whether survey monuments are in place;

(j) A true statement by the developer as to whether or not a common interest community is to be or has been created within the subdivision and whether or not the common interest community is or will be a small cooperative or small and limited expense planned community created pursuant to section 38-33.3-116;

(k) A true statement by the developer concerning the existence of any common interest community association, including whether the developer controls funds in the association.

(4) The commission may disapprove the form of the documents submitted pursuant to subsection (3)(f) of this section and may deny an application for registration until such time as the applicant submits the documents in a form that is satisfactory to the commission.

(5) Each registration shall be accompanied by fees established pursuant to section 12-10-215.

§ 12-10-504, C.R.S. Registration of developers.

Editor's note: *This section is similar to former §12-61-404 as it existed prior to 2019.*

(1) The commission shall register all applicants who meet the requirements of this part 5 and provide each applicant so registered with a certificate indicating that the developer named therein is registered in the state of Colorado as a subdivision developer. The developer that will sign as seller or lessor in any contract of sale, lease, or deed purporting to convey any site, tract, lot, or divided or undivided interest from a subdivision shall secure a certificate before offering, negotiating, or agreeing to sell, lease, or transfer before the sale, lease, or transfer is made. If such person or entity is acting only as a trustee, the beneficial owner of the subdivision shall secure a certificate. A certificate issued to a developer shall entitle all sales agents and employees of the developer to act in the capacity of a developer as agent for the developer. The developer shall be responsible for all actions of the sales agents and employees.

(2) All certificates issued under this section shall expire on December 31 following the date of issuance. In the absence of any reason or condition under this part 5 that might warrant the denial or revocation of a registration, a certificate shall be renewed by payment of a renewal fee established pursuant to section 12-10-215. A registration that has expired may be reinstated within two years after the expiration upon payment of the appropriate renewal fee if the applicant meets all other requirements of this part 5.

(3) All fees collected under this part 5 shall be deposited in accordance with section 12-10-214.

(4) With regard to any subdivision for which the information required by section 12-10-503 (3) has not been previously submitted to the commission, each registered developer shall register the subdivision by providing the commission with the information before sale, lease, or transfer, or negotiating or agreeing to sell, lease, or transfer, any such subdivision or any part thereof.

§ 12-10-505, C.R.S. Refusal, revocation, or suspension of registration – letter of admonition – probation.

Editor's note: *This section is similar to former §12-61-405 as it existed prior to 2019.*

(1) The commission may impose an administrative fine not to exceed two thousand five hundred dollars for each separate offense; may issue a letter of admonition; may place a registrant on probation under its close supervision on such terms and for such time as it deems appropriate; and may refuse, revoke, or suspend the registration of any developer or registrant if, after an investigation and after notice and a hearing pursuant to the provisions of section 24-4-104, the commission determines that the developer or any director, officer, or stockholder with controlling interest in the corporation:

(a) Has used false or misleading advertising or has made a false or misleading statement or a concealment in his or her application for registration;

(b) Has misrepresented or concealed any material fact from a purchaser of any interest in a subdivision;

(c) Has employed any device, scheme, or artifice with intent to defraud a purchaser of any interest in a subdivision;

(d) Has been convicted of or pled guilty or nolo contendere to a crime involving fraud, deception, false pretense, theft, misrepresentation, false advertising, or dishonest dealing in any court;

(e) Has disposed of, concealed, diverted, converted, or otherwise failed to account for any funds or assets of any purchaser of any interest in a subdivision or any homeowners' association under the control of the developer or director, officer, or stockholder;

(f) Has failed to comply with any stipulation or agreement made with the commission;

(g) Has failed to comply with or has violated any provision of this article 10, including any failure to comply with the registration requirements of section 12-10-503, or any lawful rule promulgated by the commission under this article 10;

(h) Has refused to honor a buyer's request to cancel a contract for the purchase of a time share or subdivision or part thereof if the request was made within five calendar days after execution of the contract and was made either by telegram, mail, or hand delivery. A request is considered made if by electronic mail when sent, if by mail when postmarked, or if by hand delivery when delivered to the seller's place of business. No developer shall employ a contract that contains any provision waiving a buyer's right to such a cancellation period.

(i) Has committed any act that constitutes a violation of the "Colorado Consumer Protection Act", article 1 of title 6;

(j) Has employed any sales agent or employee who violates the provisions of this part 5;

(k) Has used documents for sales or lease transactions other than those described in section 12-10-503 (3)(f);

(*l*) Has failed to disclose encumbrances to prospective purchasers or has failed to transfer clear title at the time of sale, if the parties agreed that the transfer would be made at that time.

(2) A disciplinary action relating to the business of subdivision development taken by any other state or local jurisdiction or the federal government shall be deemed to be prima facie evidence of grounds for disciplinary action, including denial of registration, under this part 5. This subsection (2) shall apply only to such disciplinary actions as are substantially similar to those set out as grounds for disciplinary action or denial of registration under this part 5.

(3) Any hearing held under this section shall be in accordance with the procedures established in sections 24-4-105 and 24-4-106.

(4) When a complaint or investigation discloses an instance of misconduct that, in the opinion of the commission, does not initially warrant formal action by the commission but that should not be dismissed as being without merit, the commission may send a letter of admonition by certified mail, return receipt requested, to the registrant who is the subject of the complaint or investigation and a copy thereof to any person making the complaint. The letter shall advise the registrant that he or she has the right to request in writing, within twenty days after proven receipt, that formal disciplinary proceedings be initiated against him or her to adjudicate the propriety of the conduct upon which the letter of admonition is based. If the request is timely made, the letter of admonition shall be deemed vacated, and the matter shall be processed by means of formal disciplinary proceedings.

(5) All administrative fines collected pursuant to this section shall be transmitted to the state treasurer, who shall credit the same to the division of real estate cash fund.

§ 12-10-506, C.R.S. Powers of commission – injunction – rules.

Editor's note: *This section is similar to former §12-61-406 as it existed prior to 2019.*

(1) The commission may apply to a court of competent jurisdiction for an order enjoining any act or practice that constitutes a violation of this part 5, and, upon a showing that a person is engaging or intends to engage in any such act or practice, an injunction, restraining order, or other appropriate order shall be granted by the court, regardless of the existence of another remedy therefor. Any notice, hearing, or duration of any injunction or restraining order shall be made in accordance with the provisions of the Colorado rules of civil procedure.

(2) The commission may apply to a court of competent jurisdiction for the appointment of a receiver if it determines that the appointment is necessary to protect the property or interests of purchasers of a subdivision or part thereof.

(3) The commission shall issue or deny a certificate or additional registration within sixty days from the date of receipt of the application by the commission. The commission may make necessary investigations and inspections to determine whether any developer has violated this part 5 or any lawful rule promulgated by the commission. If, after an application by a developer has been submitted pursuant to section 12-10-503 or information has been submitted pursuant to section 12-10-504, the commission determines that an inspection of a subdivision is necessary, it shall complete the inspection within sixty days from the date of filing of the application or information, or the right of inspection is waived and the lack thereof shall not be grounds for denial of a registration.

(4) The commission, the director, or the administrative law judge appointed for a hearing may issue a subpoena compelling the attendance and testimony of witnesses and the production of books, papers, or records pursuant to an investigation or hearing of the commission. Any such subpoena shall be served in the same manner as for subpoenas issued by district courts.

(5) The commission has the power to make any rules necessary for the enforcement or administration of this part 5.

(6) The commission shall adopt, promulgate, amend, or repeal such rules as are necessary to:

 (a) Require written disclosures to any purchasers as provided in subsection (7) of this section and to prescribe and require that standardized forms be used by subdivision developers in connection with the sale or lease of a subdivision or any part thereof, except as otherwise provided in section 12-10-503 (3)(f); and

 (b) Require that developers maintain certain business records for a period of at least seven years.

(7) The commission may require any developer to make written disclosures to purchasers in their contracts of sale or by separate written documents if the commission finds that the disclosures are necessary for the protection of the purchasers.

(8) The commission or its designated representative may audit the accounts of any homeowners' association, the funds of which are controlled by a developer.

§ 12-10-507, C.R.S. Violation – penalty.

Editor's note: *This section is similar to former §12-61-407 as it existed prior to 2019.*

Any person who fails to register as a developer in violation of this part 5 commits a class 6 felony and shall be punished as provided in section 18-1.3-401. Any agreement or contract for the sale or lease of a subdivision or part thereof shall be voidable by the purchaser and unenforceable by the developer unless the developer was duly registered under the provisions of this part 5 when the agreement or contract was made.

§ 12-10-508, C.R.S. Repeal of part – subject to review.

Editor's note: *This section is similar to former §12-61-408 as it existed prior to 2019.*

This part 5 is repealed, effective September 1, 2026. Before the repeal, this part 5 is scheduled for review in accordance with section 24-34-104.

III. Rules and Regulations for Subdivision Developers

Adopted, and Published by the

COLORADO REAL ESTATE COMMISSION

Approved by the Attorney General and the Executive Director of the Department of Regulatory Agencies.

In pursuance of and in compliance with Title 12, Article 10, C.R.S. 1973, as amended, and in pursuance of and in compliance with Title 24, Article 4, C.R.S. 1973, as amended. With respect to certain statutory definitions used herein, see § 12-10-201, C.R.S., and § 12-10-501, C.R.S.

* ***Editor's note****: The rules previously contained in Chapter 1, as it existed prior to 2022, have been incorporated in rules 2.1, 2.8, 2.9, 3.2, 3.3, 4.1, 4.9.A, and 4.9.C.*

*CHAPTER 1:DEFINITIONS

* 1.1. Applicant: A person or entity seeking registration from the Commission to act in the capacity of a Developer pursuant to section 12-10-504(1), C.R.S.

* 1.2. Business Record: The Consumer Agreement, financing agreement, buyer and seller settlement statement, title policy, trust deed, escrow agreement, and any other documents executed by or on behalf of the Developer in the sale, lease or transfer of any interest in a Subdivision, including records showing the receipt and disbursement of any money or assets received or paid on behalf of any homeowners' or similar association managed or controlled by a Developer.

* 1.3. Commission: The Colorado Real Estate Commission as defined pursuant to section 12-10-501(1), C.R.S.

* 1.4. Consumer: A natural person, corporation, company, limited liability company, partnership, firm, association, or other legal entity.

* 1.5. Consumer Agreement: A written agreement between a Consumer and a Developer in the sale, lease or transfer of any interest in a Subdivision, which includes but is not limited to, sales

contract, purchase agreement, lease agreement, right-to-use contract, points-based contract, and installment contract.

* 1.6. Deemed Complete: An Applicant has submitted a complete and satisfactory application in compliance with sections 12-10-502 and 12-10-503, C.R.S. that includes the Fee and the accompanying required documentation as set forth in Chapter 2 of these Rules.

* 1.7. Day: any calendar day and includes Saturday, Sunday, and legal holidays.

* 1.8. Developer: Has the same meaning pursuant to section 12-10-501(2), C.R.S.

* 1.9. Developer Certificate: Certificate issued by the Commission or Division upon meeting the registration requirements pursuant to sections 12-10-503 and 504, C.R.S.

* 1.10. Division: The Colorado Division of Real Estate as defined pursuant to section 12-10-101(2), C.R.S.

* 1.11. Electronic Record: Has the same meaning set forth in the Uniform Electronic Transaction Act in sections 24-71.3-101, et. seq., C.R.S.

* 1.12. Electronic Signature: Has the same meaning set forth in the Uniform Electronic Transaction Act in sections 24-71.3-101, et. seq., C.R.S.

* 1.13. Equivalency Filing: An application for a Developer Certificate, a supplemental application to add a Subdivision to an existing Developer Certificate, or a supplemental application to otherwise amend an existing Developer Certificate, wherein the Developer is currently regulated in another state and submits evidence in form and substance acceptable to the Commission that the registration requirements are substantially equivalent to the Practice Act or that provide substantially comparable protection to a purchaser.

* 1.14. Exchange Program: Any method, arrangement, or procedure for the voluntary exchange of the right to use and occupy accommodations and facilities among owners. The term does not include the assignment of the right to use and occupy accommodations and facilities to owners pursuant to a particular Time Shares plan's reservation system.

* 1.15. Fee: The prescribed non-refundable license fee as set by the Division.

* 1.16. Nondisturbance Agreement: Agreement by which the holder of a blanket encumbrance against a project agrees that its rights in the project will be subordinate to the rights of the purchasers.

* 1.17. Petitioner: For the purposes of implementing the provisions of Chapter 5 of these Rules, any person who has filed with the Commission a petition or has been granted leave to intervene by the Commission for a declaratory order pursuant to section 24-4-105(11), C.R.S. and as set forth in Chapter 5 of these Rules.

* 1.18. Practice Act: The Subdivision Developer's Act found at sections 12-10-501, et. seq., C.R.S.

* 1.19. Reservation Agreement: A revocable right to purchase an interest in a Subdivision project for which a Developer Certificate from the Commission or Division has not yet been obtained.

* 1.20. Safe and Secure Manner: Reasonable measures are taken to minimize the risk of loss, damage, or theft.

* 1.21. Subdivision: Has the same meaning pursuant to sections 12-10-501(3)(a) and (3)(b)(I), C.R.S.

* 1.22. Time Share: Has the same meaning pursuant to section 12-10-501(4), C.R.S.

* CHAPTER 2: APPLICATION FOR REGISTRATION

* 2.1. Registration Requirements for an Initial Developer's Certificate

* A. If an Applicant is:

* 1. A corporation, a director or an authorized officer must apply on behalf of said corporation.

* 2. A partnership or limited partnership, one of the general partners must apply on behalf of the partnership or limited partnership.

* 3. A joint owner of the Subdivision, such owner may apply on behalf of all joint owners of such Subdivision.

* 4. A limited liability company, one of the managers or member-managers must apply on behalf of the company.

* 5. With respect to any other type of Developer that is other than a natural person, a person authorized to act on behalf of such entity, as demonstrated by such documents in a form satisfactory to the Commission, will apply on behalf of that entity.

* B. In addition to section 12-10-503, C.R.S., the Applicant for a Developer Certificate must provide the Commission with the following information concerning each Subdivision to be registered:

* 1. The address or actual physical location of each Subdivision from which sales are intended to be made;

* 2. Copies of a recorded deed or other documents evidencing the Developer's title or other interest in the Subdivision and a title commitment, policy or report, abstract and opinion, or other evidence acceptable to the Commission documenting the condition of such title or interest;

* 3. Sample copies of the Consumer Agreement, notes, deeds, and other legal documents prepared by the Developer or an attorney representing the Developer which are to be used to effectuate the sale or lease of the Subdivision or any part thereof. The Commission may disapprove the form of the documents submitted and may deny an application for registration until such time as the Applicant submits such documents in forms that are satisfactory to the Commission;

* 4. In compliance with section 12-10-503(3)(e), C.R.S., a Developer registering a Subdivision that incorporates Time Share use and is subject to one or more blanket encumbrances must submit to the Commission a Nondisturbance Agreement by which the holder of each blanket encumbrance against the Subdivision agrees that its rights in the Subdivision will be subordinate to the rights of the time share use purchasers. From and after the recording of a Nondisturbance Agreement, the holder of the blanket encumbrance executing the same, such holder's successors and assigns, and any person who acquires all or part of the Subdivision through the subject blanket encumbrance, will take the property subject to the rights of the Time Share use purchasers. Every Nondisturbance Agreement must contain the covenant of the holder of the blanket encumbrance that such person or any other person acquiring all or part of the Subdivision through such blanket encumbrance will not use or cause the Subdivision to be used in a manner which would prevent the Time Share use purchasers from using and occupying the Subdivision in a manner contemplated by the Time Share use plan. Any other trust or escrow arrangement which fully protects the Time Share use purchasers' interest in the Subdivision as contemplated by section 12-10-503(3)(e), C.R.S., may be approved by the Commission;

* 5. If the Developer is other than a natural person, proof of formation and registration in accordance with state and local requirements must accompany the Application; and

* 6. Copies of the recorded declaration of the Subdivision.

* C. Copies of required information and disclosures as set forth in Rules 2.3., 2.4., 2.5., and 2.6. as applicable.

* D. Registration of Developers Regulated in Another State

* Pursuant to section 12-10-503(1), C.R.S., the Commission in its sole discretion may accept an Equivalency Filing from a Developer as an application for a Developer Certificate. The Developer may be deemed to have fully or partially satisfied, and be in

compliance with, sections 12-10-503(2) and 12-10-503(3), C.R.S., and Rules 2.1(B), 2.3., 2.4., 2.5., 2.6., 4.2., and 4.3. as determined by the Commission.

* 2.2. Addition of a Subdivision to an Existing Developer Certificate

* A Developer may add an additional Subdivision to an existing Developer Certificate by completing the Division created supplemental application and submitting the following information:

* A. The Developer must provide the information pursuant to section 12-10-503(3), C.R.S., and Rules 2.1(B), 2.3., 2.4., 2.5., and 2.6. as applicable; or

* B. In connection with an Equivalency Filing, the Developer must provide the information that was required at time of initial registration as set forth in Rule 2.1(D). as applicable.

* 2.3. Copies of Written Disclosures

* Pursuant to sections 12-10-506(6)(a), C.R.S., and 12-10-506(7), C.R.S., the Developer must supply the following information to the Commission in addition to the required information set forth in Rule 2.1 and prior to contracting with the public must disclose this information to prospective purchasers in the Consumer Agreement or in a separate written disclosure document:

* A. The name and address of the Developer and of the Subdivision lots or units.

* B. An explanation of the type of ownership or occupancy rights being offered.

* C. A general description of all facilities, amenities and accommodations. As applicable for any uncompleted Subdivision, the Developer must also supply the provisions for and the availability of legal access, roads, sewage disposal, public utilities (including water, electricity, gas, internet and telephone) and other promised facilities in the Subdivision. The disclosure must identify and describe the specific amenities promised, the ownership of such amenities, the projected completion date of any amenities not completed, a statement setting forth the type of financial arrangements as set forth in Rule 2.10.A., and the allocation of the amenity expense among the Developer, the purchaser and any third party.

* D. In compliance with section12-10-505(1)(h), C.R.S., a statement in bold print immediately prior to the purchaser's signature line on the Consumer Agreement disclosing the rescission right available to purchasers and that the rescission right cannot be waived; the minimum allowable rescission period in Colorado is five (5) Days after execution of the Consumer Agreement.

* E. A general description of all judgments and administrative orders issued against the seller, Developer, homeowners' association or managing entity which are material to the Subdivision development and operational plan.

* F. Any taxes or assessments, existing or proposed, to which the purchaser may be subject, or which are unpaid at the time of contracting, including obligations to special taxing authorities or districts.

* G. A statement that sales must be made by brokers licensed by the State of Colorado unless specifically exempted pursuant to section12-10-201(6)(b), C.R.S.; the Consumer Agreement must disclose the name of the real estate brokerage firm and the name of the broker establishing a brokerage relationship with the Developer.

* H. When a separate document is used to make any of the disclosures as set forth in this Rule and Rules 2.4., 2.5., and 2.6., this statement must appear in bold print on the first page of the document and preceding the disclosure: "The Colorado Real Estate Commission has not prepared or issued this document nor has it passed on the merits of the subdivision described herein.".

* I. A statement that all funds paid by the purchaser prior to delivery of the lease, deed or other instrument purporting to convey any interest in the site, tract, lot, divided or undivided interest from a Subdivision will be held in trust by the licensed real estate broker named in the Consumer Agreement, or a clear statement specifically setting forth who such funds will be delivered to, when such delivery will occur, the use of said funds, and whether or not there is any restriction on the use of such funds.

* J. Where a deed is issued, a statement that, immediately following the date of closing, the purchaser's deed will be delivered to the appropriate county Clerk and Recorder's office for recording, or a clear statement specifically setting forth when such delivery and recording of the deed will occur; for the purposes of this Rule, the date of closing is defined as the date the purchaser has either paid the full cash purchase price or has made partial cash payment and executed a promissory note or other evidence of indebtedness for the balance of the purchase price. A statement that a title insurance policy will be delivered at no expense to the purchaser within sixty (60) Days following recording of the deed or the closing, whichever is earlier, unless specifically agreed to the contrary by the parties in the contracting instrument.

* K. A Consumer Agreement which requires the execution of a promissory note or other evidence of indebtedness that accrues interest or requires payments prior to the recording of a deed, will be deemed to be an installment contract pursuant to section 12-10-503(3)(g), C.R.S. where an installment contract is used:

* 1. A statement whether or not the purchaser's deed is escrowed with an independent escrow agent and if so, the name and address of the escrow agent;

* 2. The amount of any existing encumbrance(s), the name and address of the encumbrancer, and the conditions, if any, under which a purchaser may cure a default caused by non-payment;

* 3. A clear statement that a default on any underlying encumbrance(s) could result in the loss of the purchaser's entire interest in the property;

* 4. A clear statement advising the purchaser to record the installment contract; and

* 5. Pursuant to section 12-10-503(3)(e), C.R.S., an agreement by which the holder of any blanket encumbrance against the Subdivision agrees that its rights and the rights of its successors or assigns in the Subdivision will be subordinate to the rights of purchasers, or any other trust, escrow or release arrangement which fully protects the purchasers' interest in the Subdivision.

* 2.4. Copies of Written Disclosures If the Subdivision Has a Homeowners' or Similar Association

* A. Whether membership in such association is mandatory;

* B. An estimate of association dues and fees which are the responsibility of the purchaser and the Developer, respectively;

* C. A description of the services and amenities provided by the association;

* D. Whether the Developer has voting control of the association and the manner in which such control can or will be transferred; and

* E. Whether the Developer has any financial interest in or will potentially derive any income or profit from such association, including the Developer's right to borrow or authorize borrowing from the association.

* 2.5. Copies of Written Disclosure If Time Share Sales are to be Made from a Subdivision:

* A. Information and disclosures as set forth in Rules 2.3. and 2.4.;

* B. A description of the Time Share units including the number of Time Share units, the length, type and number of Time Share interests in each unit, and the Time Share periods constituting the Time Share plan;

* C. The name and business address of the managing entity appointed by the Developer or homeowners' association, a description of the services that the managing entity will provide, a statement as to whether the Developer has any financial interest in or will potentially derive any income or profit from such managing entity, and the manner, if any, by which the purchaser or Developer may change the managing entity or transfer the control of the managing entity;

* D. An estimate of the dues, maintenance fees, real property taxes and similar periodic expenses which are the responsibility of the purchaser and the Developer, respectively, and a general statement of the conditions under which future charges, changes or additions may be imposed. Such estimate must include a statement as to whether a maintenance reserve fund has been or will be established; the manner in which such reserve fund is financed; an accounting of any outstanding obligations either in favor of or against the fund; the Developer's right to borrow or authorize borrowing from the fund; and the method of periodic accounting which will be provided to the purchaser;

* E. A description of any insurance coverage(s) provided for the benefit of Time Share owners;

* F. A statement that mechanic's liens law may authorize enforcement of the lien by selling the entire Time Share unit;

* G. A statement on whether the Time Share interest is perpetual or for a term of years and, if for a term of years, the length and expected termination date of the term;

* H. A statement as to the effect a voluntary sale, by the Developer to a third party, will have on the contractual rights of Time Share owners;

* I. A statement that an involuntary transfer by bankruptcy of the Developer may have a negative effect on the rights of the Time Share owners; and

* J. A statement that a Federal or State tax lien could be enforced against the developer by compelling the sale of the entire Subdivision.

* 2.6. Copies of Written Disclosures If Time Shares are to be Sold from a Subdivision Which: Contains Two (2) or More Component Sites Situated at Different Geographic Locations or Governed by Separate Sets of Declarations, By-Laws or Equivalent Documents; and Does Not Include a Guaranteed, Recurring Right of Use or Occupancy at a Single Component Site:

* A. For each component site, the information and disclosures as set forth in Rules 2.3., 2.4., and 2.5.;

* B. A general description of the Subdivision;

* C. A clear description in the Consumer Agreement of the interest and term of usage being purchased and a definite date of termination of the purchaser's interest in the Subdivision, which date will be not later than the termination date of the Subdivision's interest in a specifically identified component site;

* D. A clear disclosure and description of any component site which is not legally guaranteed to be available for the purchaser's use for the full term of the purchaser's usage interest;

* E. The system and method in place to assure maintenance of no more than a one- to-one ratio of purchasers' use rights to the number of total use rights in the Subdivision for each term of usage being offered for sale, including provisions for compensation to purchasers resulting from destruction of a component site or loss of use rights to any component site;

* F. A description of the system or program by which a purchaser obtains a recurring right to use and occupy accommodations and facilities in any component site through use of a reservation system or otherwise, including any restrictions on such rights or any method by which a purchaser is denied an equal right with all other users to obtain the use of any accommodation in the Subdivision;

* G. A description of the management and ownership of such reservation system or program, whether through the Developer, a homeowners' association, a club or otherwise, including the purchaser's direct or indirect ownership interest or rights of control in such reservation system;

* H. Whether the Developer, club or association which controls the reservation system or any other person has or is granted any interest in unsold, non-reserved or unused use rights and whether the Developer, club, association or other person may employ such rights to compete with purchasers for use of accommodations in the Subdivision or any component site and, if so, the nature and specifics of those rights, including the circumstances under which they may be employed;

* I. The method and frequency of accounting for any income derived from unsold, non-reserved or unused use rights in which the purchaser, either directly or indirectly, has an interest;

* J. The system and method in place, including business interruption insurance or bonding, to provide secure back-up or replacement of the reservation system in the event of interruption, discontinuance or failure;

* K. The amount and details of any component site, reservation system or other periodic expense required to be paid by a purchaser, the name of the person or entity to which such payments will be made, and the method by which the purchaser will receive a regular periodic accounting for such payments;

* L. If component site expenses are included in those periodic payments made by a purchaser, a statement for each component site from the homeowners' association or other responsible entity acknowledging that payment of such expenses as taxes, insurance, dues and assessments are current and are being made in the name of the Subdivision;

* M. Evidence that an escrow system with an independent escrow agent is in place for receipt and disbursement of all moneys collected from purchasers that are necessary to pay such expenses as taxes, insurance and common expenses and assessments owing to component site homeowners' associations or others, or a clear description of the method by which such funds will be paid, collected, held, disbursed and accounted for;

* N. A clear statement as to whether a purchaser's rights, interests or terms of usage for any component site within the Subdivision can subsequently be modified from those terms originally represented and a description of the method by which such modification may occur;

* O. If the Subdivision documents allow additions or substitutions of accommodations or component sites, a clear description of the purchaser's rights and obligations concerning such additions or substitutions and the method by which such additions or substitutions will comply with the provisions of this rule; and

* P. A clear description of any existing incidental benefits or amenities which are available to the purchaser at the time of sale but to which the purchaser has no guaranteed right of recurring use or enjoyment during the purchaser's full term of interest in the Subdivision.

* 2.7. Invalid Payment

* If the Fees accompanying any Application made to the Commission are paid for by check and the check is not immediately paid upon presentment to the bank upon which the check was drawn, or if payment is submitted in any other manner and payment is denied, rescinded or returned as invalid, the application will be deemed incomplete and canceled. The application may be reinstated only at the discretion of the Commission and upon full payment of any Fees together with payment of the fee required by state fiscal rules for the clerical services necessary for reinstatement.

* 2.8. Review of Application for Completeness

* If the Commission requires additional information, the Commission will give written notice of the information so required and will allow an additional sixty (60) Days to present such material before denial of the application, which period may be extended only upon a showing of good cause.

* 2.9. Issuance of a Developer Certificate or the Addition of a Subdivision

* The Commission will issue or deny registration of a Developer Certificate or approve or deny the addition of a Subdivision within sixty (60) Days from the date of receipt of the Deemed Complete application by the Commission.

* 2.10. Offering Reservations during the Pendency of the Application

* A. Pursuant to section 12-10-502(2), C.R.S., where a Developer receives cash or receivables from a purchaser for an uncompleted Subdivision, the Commission will register such Developer only after:

* 1. The Developer deposits in an escrow account, with an independent escrow agent, all funds and receivables received from purchasers, or

* 2. The Developer obtains a letter of credit or bond payable to an independent escrow agent, payment or performance bond, or establishes any other financial arrangement acceptable to the Commission, the purpose of which is to ensure completion of Subdivision accommodations and facilities and to protect the purchaser's interest in the Subdivision accommodations and facilities.

* B. All approvals for the use of Reservation Agreements issued as set forth in this rule will expire on December 31 following the date of issuance.

* CHAPTER 3: REGISTRATION AND CERTIFICATION

* 3.1. Renewal of the Registration and Certification

* Renewal of the registration and certification as a Developer can be executed only on the renewal application provided by the Commission, and must be delivered to the Commission, accompanied by the proper Fees, on or before December 31 of each year.

* 3.2. Licensed Real Estate Brokers

* The registration and certification of a Developer under Title 12, Article 10, Part 5, C.R.S., does not exempt the Developer from the requirements for the licensing of real estate brokers under Title 12, Article 10, Part 1, C.R.S. Exemptions from the licensing of real estate brokers are made pursuant to section 12-10-201(6)(b), C.R.S.

* 3.3. Change in Principal Office

* Notification in writing must be made to the Commission within ten (10) Days of any change in the principal office address of the Developer or the natural person, or any other change in the information submitted pursuant to section12-10-503, C.R.S.

* 3.4. Records

* A. Records as required by Title 12, Article 10, C.R.S., and these rules, may be maintained as an Electronic Record so long as the Electronic Records are in a format that has the continued capability to be retrieved and legibly printed. The Developer must produce printed records upon request of the Commission, or by any principal party to a transaction.

* B. Developer must maintain all Business Records related to the Subdivision development in a Safe and Secure Manner for a period of seven (7) years from the effective date of each such Business Record.

* 3.5. Revisions to Documents

* A Developer is not required to file amendments to its registration filed with the Commission when revisions are made to documents previously submitted to the Commission, so long as the revised documents continue to:

* A. Comply with Title 12, Article 10, Part 5, C.R.S., and these rules; and

* B. Accurately reflect the Subdivision offering.

* 3.6. Duty to Disclose the Following Events:

* A. Notwithstanding Rule 3.5., a Developer must provide the Commission with notice of the following events within ten (10) Days after such event, unless otherwise provided below:

* 1. Any change in the information provided in the registration pursuant to sections 12-10-503(2)(a)(III), (V), (VI) or (VII), C.R.S.;

* 2. Any change in the terms of any Nondisturbance Agreement(s) or partial release provisions in connection with any documents previously submitted to the Commission pursuant to section 12-10-503(3)(e), C.R.S., and Rule 2.1.B.4.;

* 3. Any new lien encumbering the Subdivision or any part thereof other than encumbrances created or permitted by purchasers;

* 4. The termination or transfer of any escrow account, letter of credit, bond, or other financial assurance approved by the Commission as set forth in Rule 2.10.; notice of which must be filed with the Commission prior to the effective date of such termination or transfer;

* 5. Cancellation, revocation, suspension, or termination of the Developer's activity or authority to do business in the State of Colorado; and

* 6. Any material pending legal proceeding filed against the Developer in connection with the Subdivision affecting the Developer's ability:

* a. To convey marketable title of the registered Subdivision or any interest therein, or

* b. To perform the Developer's obligations in connection with the registered Subdivision.

* B. Notification under this Rule must be provided on a form approved by the Commission. The Developer will have a period of ten (10) Days after receipt of notice to take such action as may be required by the Commission in connection with any filings made under this Rule.

* C. Within ten (10) Days after receipt of a written request from the Commission, a Developer will have the duty to provide to the Commission copies of all documents then in use with regard to the Subdivision.

* CHAPTER 4: PROFESSIONAL STANDARDS

* 4.1. Developer Must Register Prior to Conducting Business

* The person, firm, partnership, joint venture, limited liability company, association, corporation or other legal entity, or combination thereof, who will sign as seller or lessor in any Consumer Agreement, deed or any other instrument purporting to convey any site, tract, lot, divided or undivided interest from a Subdivision, must secure a Developer Certificate before negotiating or agreeing to sell, lease or transfer and before any sale, lease or transfer is made. If such person is acting only as a trustee, the beneficial owner of the Subdivision must secure a Developer Certificate.

* 4.2. Developer Must Maintain Business Records and Produce Upon Request

* Pursuant to sections 12-10-505(1)(e), C.R.S., 12-10-506(6)(b), C.R.S., and 12-10-506(8), C.R.S., a Developer must maintain Business Records as set forth in Rule 3.4., and produce for inspection upon reasonable request by an authorized representative of the Commission.

* 4.3. Disclosures to Prospective Purchasers Prior to Contracting

* Pursuant to sections 12-10-506(6)(a), C.R.S., and 12-10-506(7), C.R.S., Developer must supply to prospective purchasers the written disclosures as set for forth in Rules 2.3., 2.4., 2.5., and 2.6. prior to contracting with the public and must be disclosed in the Consumer Agreement, or in a separate written disclosure document.

* 4.4. Developers Must Not Make Misrepresentations or Conceal Material Facts

* A. Failure to disclose to the purchaser the availability of legal access, sewage disposal, public utilities, including water, electricity, gas and telephone facilities , in the applicable uncompleted Subdivision offered for sale or lease, including whether such are to be a Developer or purchaser expense, when proven, is a violation of section12-10-505(1)(b), C.R.S.

* B. No Developer will make misrepresentations regarding the future availability or costs of services, utilities, character, or use of real property for sale or lease of the surrounding area of the Subdivision.

* 4.5. Disclosure of an Exchange Company

* A Developer of a Time Share must disclose to the public whether or not a Time Share plan involves an Exchange Program and, if so, will disclose and deliver to prospective purchasers, a separate written document, which may be provided by an exchange company if the document discloses the following information:

* A. The name and the business address of the exchange company;

* B. Whether the purchaser's contract with the Exchange Program is separate and distinct from the purchaser's contract with the Developer;

* C. Whether the purchaser's participation in the Exchange Program is dependent upon the Developer's continued affiliation with the Exchange Program;

* D. Whether or not the purchaser's participation in the Exchange Program is voluntary;

* E. The specific terms and conditions of the purchaser's contractual relationship with the Exchange Program and the procedure by which changes, if any, may be made in the terms and conditions of such contractual relationship;

* F. The procedure of applying for and effecting any changes;

* G. A complete description of all limitations, restrictions, accrual rights, or priorities employed in the operation of the Exchange Program, including but not limited to limitations on exchanges based on seasonality, unit size, or levels of occupancy; and if the limitations, restrictions or priorities are not applied uniformly by the Exchange Program, a complete description of the manner of their application;

* H. Whether exchanges are arranged on a space-available basis or whether guarantees of fulfillment of specific requests for exchanges are made by the exchange company;

* I. Whether and under what conditions a purchaser may, in dealing with the Exchange Program, lose the use and occupancy of the Time Share period in any properly applied for exchange without being offered substitute accommodations by the Exchange Program;

* J. The fees for participation in the Exchange Program, and whether the fees may be altered and the method of any altering; and

* K. The name and location of each accommodation or facility, including the time sharing plans participating in the Exchange Program.

* 4.6. Disclosure of Judgment, Decree or Order

* Any material adverse order, judgment, or decree entered against Developer in connection with the Subdivision by any regulatory authority or by any court of appropriate jurisdiction,

specifically including any order, judgment or decree related to a proceeding under which Developer has a duty to disclose as set forth in Rule 3.6.A.6. but other than ordinary routine litigation incidental to the Developer's business, must be filed with the Commission by the Developer within thirty (30) Days of such order, judgment or decree being final.

* 4.7. Delivery of an Abstract of Title or Title Insurance

* A. Developer must provide a title insurance commitment or other evidence of title approved by the Commission within a reasonable time after execution of any Consumer Agreement, or other instrument purporting to convey any interest in the site, tract, lot, divided or undivided interest from a Subdivision.

* B. Where the Consumer Agreement contemplates the delivery of a deed, an abstract of title or title insurance policy must be delivered within a reasonable time after the completion of payments by a purchaser.

* C. Any period of time in excess of sixty (60) Days will be deemed unreasonable for the purposes of this Rule. The parties may contract to eliminate this requirement, but any such mutually acceptable waiver must be in writing and in a conspicuous manner or print.

* 4.8. Delivery of Deed Must be Made within Sixty (60) Days

* A. Unless a sale is by means of an installment contract, the delivery of a deed must be made within sixty (60) Days after closing. For the purposes of this Rule, the date of closing is defined as the date the purchaser has either paid the full cash purchase price or has made partial cash payment and executed a promissory note or other evidence of indebtedness for the balance of the purchase price.

* B. If a sale is by means of an installment contract, the delivery of a deed must be made within sixty (60) Days after the completion of payments.

* 4.9. Duty to Respond to a Complaint or Audit

* A. Pursuant to section 12-10-505, C.R.S., any Developer who has received written notification from the Commission that a complaint has been filed against the Developer, must submit a written answer to the Commission within a reasonable time as set by the Commission.

* B. Upon request of the Commission pursuant to an investigation or audit notice, a Developer will file with the Commission an audited financial statement in conformity with accepted accounting principles, and sworn to by the Developer as an accurate reflection of the financial condition of the Developer and/or the homeowners' association controlled by the Developer.

* C. Failure to submit a written response required by this Rule will be grounds for disciplinary action.

* CHAPTER 5: DECLARATORY ORDERS

* 5.1. Petition for a Declaratory Order

* Pursuant to section 24-4-105(11), C.R.S., a Petitioner may petition the Commission for a declaratory order to terminate controversies or to remove uncertainties as to the applicability of any statutory provision, rule, or order of the Commission as it would apply to the Petitioner.

* 5.2. Parties to the Proceedings

* The parties to any proceeding as set forth in Chapter 5 of these Rules will be the Commission and the Petitioner. Any other person may seek leave of the Commission to intervene in such a proceeding. Permission to intervene will be granted at the sole discretion of the Commission. A petition to intervene will set forth the same matters as set forth in Rule 5.3.

* 5.3. Petition Contents

* Any petition filed as set forth in Chapter 5 of these Rules will state the following:

* A. The name and address of the Petitioner;

* B. The statute, rule, or order to which the petition relates;

* C. A concise statement of all the facts and law necessary to show the nature of the controversy or uncertainty and the manner in which the statute, rule, or order in question applies or potentially applies to the Petitioner; and

* D. The Petitioner may submit a concise statement of the declaratory order sought.

* 5.4. Commission's Considerations Whether or Not to Rule

* The Commission may determine, in its sole discretion and without prior notice to the Petitioner, whether or not to rule upon a petition. In determining whether or not to rule upon a petition filed as set forth in Chapter 5 of these Rules, the Commission may consider the following matters, among others:

* A. Whether a ruling on the petition will terminate a controversy or remove uncertainties as to the applicability to the Petitioner of any statutory provision, rule, or order of the Commission.

* B. Whether the petition involves any subject, question, or issue which is the subject of a formal or informal matter or investigation currently pending before the Commission or a court involving one or more of the Petitioners.

* C. Whether the petition involves any subject, question, or issue which is the subject of a formal or informal matter or investigation currently pending before the Commission or a court not involving the Petitioner.

* D. Whether the petition seeks a ruling on a hypothetical question.

* E. Whether the Petitioner has some other adequate legal remedy, other than an action for declaratory order which will terminate the controversy or remove any uncertainty as to the applicability to the Petitioner of the statute, rule, or order in question.

* 5.5. Commission Determines Not to Rule

* If the Commission determines it will not rule on a petition, the Commission will issue its written decision disposing of the petition, stating the reasons for declining to rule upon the petition. A copy of the decision will be provided to the Petitioner. A decision not to rule on a petition for a declaratory order is not final agency action subject to judicial review.

* 5.6. Commission Determines to Rule

* If the Commission determines that it will rule on the petition:

* A. The Commission may order the Petitioner to file an additional written brief, memorandum, statement of position, or request the Petitioner to submit additional facts or arguments in writing.

* B. The Commission may take administrative notice of facts pursuant to the Administrative Procedure Act, section 24-4-105(8), C.R.S., and may utilize its experience, technical competence, and specialized knowledge when ruling on the petition.

* C. The Commission may set the petition, upon due notice to the Petitioner, for a non-evidentiary hearing.

* D. The Commission may, upon due notice to the Petitioner, set the petition for hearing for the purpose of obtaining additional facts or information, or to determine the truth of any facts set forth in the petition, or to hear oral arguments on the petition. Notice to the Petitioner setting such formal hearing will set forth, to the extent known, the factual or other matters into which the Commission intends to inquire. The Petitioner will have the burden of proving all of the facts stated in the petition, all of the facts necessary to show the nature of the controversy or uncertainty and the manner in which the statute, rule, or order in question applies or potentially applies to the Petitioner and any other facts the Petitioner desires the Commission to consider.

* E. Any ruling by the Commission may be based solely on the matters set forth in the petition or may be based on any amendments to the petition, any information gathered by the Commission through a non-evidentiary hearing, formal hearing or otherwise, or any facts the Commission may take administrative notice of. Upon ruling on a petition, the Commission will issue its written order stating its basis for the order. A copy of the order will be provided to the Petitioner.

* 5.7. Declaratory Orders Subject to Judicial Review

* Any declaratory order of a petition as set forth in Chapter 5 of these Rules will constitute agency action subject to judicial review pursuant to section 24-4-106, C.R.S.

* CHAPTER 6: COMMISSION REVIEW OF INITIAL DECISIONS AND EXCEPTIONS

* 6.1. Written Form, Filing Requirements, and Service

* A. All pleadings must be in written form, mailed with a certificate of service to the Commission.

* B. All pleadings must be filed with the Commission on the date the filing is due. Computation of time for the filing timelines for Chapter 6 of these Rules is pursuant to section 2-4-108, C.R.S. A pleading is considered filed upon receipt by the Commission. Chapter 6 of these Rules does not provide for any additional time for service by mail.

* C. All pleadings must be filed with the Commission and not with the Office of Administrative Courts. Any pleadings filed in error with the Office of Administrative Courts will not be considered. The Commission's address is:

* Colorado Real Estate Commission

* 1560 Broadway, Suite 925

* Denver, CO 80202

* D. All pleadings must be served on the opposing party on the date which the pleading is filed with the Commission. Electronic service between the parties is encouraged. The date and manner must be noted on the certificate of service.

* 6.2. Initial Decision

* Upon receipt of the initial decision prepared and filed by the Administrative Law Judge from the Office of Administrative Courts, the Division will timely mail a copy of the initial decision to the parties at their respective addresses of record with the Commission pursuant to section 24-4-105(16)(a), C.R.S.

* 6.3. Commission's Authority to Review the Initial Decision

* Pursuant to section 24-4-105(14)(a)(II), C.R.S., the Commission may initiate a review of an initial decision on its own motion within thirty (30) days of the date on which the Division mails the initial decision to the parties. A letter from the Division initiating the review of the initial decision constitutes a motion within the meaning of section 24-4-105(14)(a)(II), C.R.S.

* 6.4. Appeal of the Initial Decision by the Parties

* A. Any party wishing to reverse or modify an initial decision of an Administrative Law Judge must file written exceptions with the Commission in accordance with the procedures and time frames as set forth in Rule 6.5.

* B. If neither party appeals the initial decision by filing exceptions, the initial decision will become the final order of the Commission after thirty (30) days from the date on which the Division mails the initial decision pursuant to section 24-4-105(14)(b)(III), C.R.S. Failure to file exceptions will result in a waiver of the right to judicial review of the final order of the Commission unless the portion of the final order subject to review differs from the contents of the initial decision pursuant to section 24-4-105(14)(c), C.R.S.

* 6.5. Filing of Exceptions

* A. Pursuant to section 24-4-105(15)(a), C.R.S., any party seeking to file exceptions must initially file with the Commission a designation of the relevant parts of the record and of parts of the transcript of the hearing within twenty (20) days of the date on which the Division mails the initial decision to the parties.

* B. Transcripts:

* Any party may designate the entire transcript, or may identify witness(es) whose testimony is to be transcribed, the legal ruling or argument to be transcribed, or other information necessary to identify a portion of the transcript. However, no transcript is required if the Commission's review is limited to pure questions of law. The deadline for filing exceptions depends on whether either of the parties designates a portion of the transcript.

* 1. If the parties do not designate parts of the transcript, exceptions are due within thirty (30) days from the date on which the Division mails the initial decision to the parties. Both parties' exceptions are due on the same day.

* 2. Any party wishing to designate all, or any part, of the transcript must adhere to the following procedures:

* a. Transcripts will not be deemed part of a designation unless specifically identified and ordered.

* b. If one party designates a portion of the transcript, the other party may file a supplemental designation in which that party may designate additional portions of the transcript. The supplemental designation must be filed with the Commission and served on the other party within ten (10) days after the date on which the original designation was filed.

* c. Any party who designates a transcript must order the transcript by the date on which they file their designation with the Commission whether they are filing an original or supplemental designation.

* d. The party ordering a transcript must direct the court reporter or transcribing service to complete and file with the Commission the original transcript and one (1) copy within thirty (30) days of their order.

* e. The party that designates a transcript must pay for such transcripts.

* f. Transcripts that are ordered and not filed with the Commission in a timely manner due to non-payment, insufficient payment, or failure to direct as set forth above may not be considered by the Commission.

* g. Upon receipt of transcripts identified in all designations and supplemental designations, the Commission will mail a notification to the parties stating that the transcripts have been received by the Commission.

* h. Exceptions are due within thirty (30) days from the date on which such notification is mailed. Both parties' exceptions are due on the same date.

* C. A party's exceptions must include specific objections to the initial decision.

* D. Either party may file a response to the other party's exceptions. All responses must be filed within ten (10) days of the date on which the exceptions were filed with the Commission. Subsequent replies will not be considered except for good cause shown.

* E. The Commission may in its sole discretion grant an extension of time to file exceptions or responses, or may delegate the discretion to grant such an extension of time to the Commission's designee.

* 6.6. Request for Oral Arguments

* A. All requests for oral argument must be in writing and included with a party's exceptions or response.

* B. It is within the sole discretion of the Commission to grant or deny a request for oral argument. The Commission generally does not grant requests for oral argument. If an oral argument is granted, each party will have ten (10) minutes to present their argument. Questioning by members of the Commission will not count against the allocated ten (10) minutes.

* C. The Commission or its designee may extend the time for oral arguments upon good cause shown.

* 6.7. Final Orders

* A. The Commission may deliberate and vote on exceptions immediately following oral arguments or the Commission may take the matter under advisement.

* B. When the Commission votes on exceptions, whether after oral arguments or at a subsequent Commission meeting, the ruling of the Commission will not be considered final until a written order is issued.

* C. The date of the Commission's final order is the date on which the written order is signed, irrespective of any motions for reconsideration that are filed.

IV. Licensee's Responsibilities

A real estate licensee cannot be expected to be completely familiar with all county and municipal planning laws, regulations, ordinances, and zoning requirements. However, the licensee in negotiations should be very much aware of the existence of these laws, ordinances, zoning requirements, etc. It is very easy to misrepresent property through ignorance. If uninformed, the licensee should seek the information from the proper source before making a representation, or refer prospective clients to the proper source of the information.

Some facts should be known to the licensee through reading or logic, such as:

1. The sale of a portion of a seller's land divides the land into two parcels and a subdivision is created that must be approved by the proper authorities.

* 2. If a structure is suitable for conversion into a duplex and/or a four-plex, it does not in and of itself mean that such a conversion does not violate the law.

3. If an area is zoned for keeping horses, it does not necessarily follow that the acreage of the property is great enough for this purpose.

4. Even if an area is zoned for a home business, there may be a prohibition against having employees. Other complexities may also arise through various branches of local government involving utilities existent and future utilities. Representations concerning future services, zoning variances, etc. may endanger both the public and the licensee.

The following may also be subdivisions under county planning laws: the conversion of an existing building into a common interest community complex or the division of a single condominium unit into "time shares" or "interval estates." These are subdivisions as defined in § 12-10-501(3), C.R.S., and are subject to the registration requirements of §§ 12-10-501, *et seq.*, C.R.S.

A stock cooperative or cooperative housing corporation is defined in this chapter, and in Colorado is considered a subdivision of real estate. The sale of these "apartments" is accomplished by transfer of a stock certificate, together with a proprietary lease. In most states, the sale of the stock, together with the lease, would be considered the sale of a security and would fall under the jurisdiction of the division of securities. In Colorado, such sales are exempt from the Securities Act and are declared real estate (see §§ 38-33.5-101, *et seq.*, C.R.S., printed in this chapter). Therefore, such cooperatives must be registered as subdivisions, and the sale of the stock and proprietary leases must be performed by licensed real estate brokers. The act also provides that commercial banks and savings and loan associations may make a first mortgage loan on the stock and proprietary lease of each "apartment" owner.

V. Municipal Planning and Zoning Laws

Sections 31-23-101 through -313, C.R.S., address municipal planning and zoning in incorporated areas of the state. A "subdivision" also is defined as a division of a parcel of land into two or more parcels. The definition includes condominiums, apartments, and multiple-dwelling units.

Sections 31-23-201, *et seq.*, C.R.S., authorize the creation of a municipal planning commission, which must make or adopt a master plan that, among other things, includes a zoning plan. This planning commission has all the powers of a zoning commission.

The zoning commission must approve subdivisions. Developers who sell land from an unapproved subdivision are subject to a financial penalty, and the zoning commission may also enjoin any such sale. Note that even though the Subdivision Act, in § 12-10-502(2), C.R.S., allows for the use of a reservation agreement prior to final approval by the Real Estate Commission, the developer should check with the municipality regarding the use of reservation agreements. The governing body of a municipality provides for the appointment of a board of adjustment that hears appeals made from any ordinance or order of any administrative official. This board may grant variances from an ordinance or reverse an order.

VI. County Planning Laws

In addition to the provisions of the Subdivision Act, jurisdiction concerning the use of land within Colorado also falls within the powers of the county commissioners of each county. The county commissioners have the authority to enact zoning law for unincorporated areas, and many counties have done so. Prior to surveying and offering subdivided property, a developer or real estate licensee should contact the county planning and zoning department regarding compliance with the county's requirements.

In regard to a county commissioner's jurisdiction, §§ 30-28-101 through -209, C.R.S., define a subdivision as any parcel of land that is divided into two or more parcels, separate interests, or interests in common. "Interests" means interests in surface land or in the air above the surface of the land, but excludes sub-surface interests. Divisions of land that create parcels of 35 acres or more and of which none is intended for use by multiple owners are exempt.

Condominiums, apartments, and multiple dwellings are included in the definition, unless they had been previously included in a filing with substantially the same density.

* Subdivisions must submit the following information to the county authorities before sales within the subdivision may begin:

1. Survey and ownership;
2. Site characteristics, such as topography;
3. A plat showing the plan of development and plan of the completed development;
4. Estimates of the water and sewage requirements, streets, utilities, and related facilities and estimated construction cost;
5. Evidence to ensure an adequate supply of potable water; and
6. Dedication of areas for public facilities.

Upon request of a complete preliminary plan, copies will be distributed to 10 interested public agencies for recommendations. An approved plat must be recorded before any lots are sold.

No plat will be approved until the subdivision has submitted a subdivision improvement contract agreeing to construct the required improvements, accompanied by collateral sufficient to ensure completion of the improvements.

The county commissioners must approve a final plat of the subdivision before it can be filed and recorded. Violations by a subdivider or agent of a subdivider are punishable by a fine of up to $1,000 for each parcel sold or offered for sale by a subdivider or agent of a subdivider. A sale made before a final plat is approved is considered prima facie evidence of a fraudulent sale and is grounds for the purchaser voiding the sale. The county commissioners also have the power to bring an action to enjoin any subdivider from offering to sell undivided land before a final plat has been approved.

VII. Special Types of Subdivisions

A. Condominiums as Subdivisions

"Estates above the surface" may be created in areas above the surface of the ground, and title to such "air rights" may be conveyed separate from title to the surface of the ground.

It follows that a division of air rights is a subdivision under county planning laws. A declaration must be recorded with the county and must be approved by county authorities. The declaration must provide for the recording of a map properly locating the condominium units. It is similar to the filing of a plat of surface land insofar as it describes each unit. The division however, is a division of the air space.

The conversion of an existing building into a condominium complex or the division of a single condominium unit into "time shares" or "interval estates" also may be a subdivision under county planning laws, and are considered a subdivision as defined in § 12-10-501(3), C.R.S., and subject to the registration requirements of §§ 12-10-501, *et seq.*, C.R.S.

VIII. Condominium Ownership Act – Referenced in Chapter 5, Condominium Ownership Act, pages 5-5 to 5-12

IX. Colorado Common Interest Ownership Act – Referenced in Chapter 5, Colorado Common Interest Ownership Act, pages 5-12 to 5-80

X. Cooperative Housing Corporations

§ 38-33.5-101, C.R.S. Method of formation – purpose.

Cooperative housing corporations may be formed by any three or more adult residents of this state associating themselves to form a cooperative or nonprofit corporation, pursuant to article 55, 56, or 58 of title 7, C.R.S., or the "Colorado Revised Nonprofit Corporation Act", articles 121 to 137 of title 7, C.R.S. The specified purpose of the entity must be to provide each stockholder in or member of the entity with the right to occupy, for dwelling purposes, a house or an apartment in a building owned or leased by the entity.

§ 38-33.5-102, C.R.S. Requirements for articles of incorporation of cooperative housing corporations.

(1) In addition to any other requirements for articles of incorporation imposed by the "Colorado Revised Nonprofit Corporation Act", articles 121 to 137 of title 7, C.R.S., such articles of incorporation shall, in the case of cooperative housing corporations, include the following provisions:

  (a) That the corporation shall have only one class of stock outstanding;

  (b) That each stockholder is entitled, solely by reason of his ownership of stock in the corporation, to occupy, for dwelling purposes, a house or an apartment in a building owned or leased by the corporation;

  (c) That the interest of each stockholder in the corporation shall be inseparable from and appurtenant to the right of occupancy, and shall be deemed an estate in real property for all purposes, and shall not be deemed personal property;

  (d) That no stockholder is entitled to receive any distribution not out of earnings and profits of the corporation except on a complete or partial liquidation of the corporation.

§ 38-33.5-103, C.R.S. Provisions relating to taxes, interest, and depreciation on corporate property.

(1) The bylaws of a cooperative housing corporation shall provide that no less than eighty percent of the gross income of the corporation in any taxable year shall be derived from payments from tenant-stockholders. For the purposes of this article, "tenant-stockholder" means an individual who is a stockholder in the corporation and whose stock is fully paid when measured by his proportionate share of the value of the corporation's equity in the property.

(2) The bylaws shall further provide that each tenant-stockholder shall be credited with his proportionate payment of real estate taxes paid or incurred in any year on the buildings and other improvements owned or leased by the corporation in which the tenant-stockholder's living quarters are located, together with the land to which such improvements are appurtenant, and likewise with respect to interest paid or incurred by the corporation as well as depreciation on real and personal property which are proper deductions related to the said lands and improvements thereon for purposes of state and federal income taxation.

§ 38-33.5-104, C.R.S. Financing of cooperative housing – stock certificates held by tenant stockholders.

Stock certificates or membership certificates issued by cooperative housing corporations to tenant-stockholders shall be valid securities for investment by savings and loan associations, when the conditions imposed by section 11-41-119 (13), C.R.S., are met.

§ 38-33.5-105, C.R.S. Provisions to be included in proprietary lease or right of tenancy issued by corporation.

(1) Every stockholder of a cooperative housing corporation shall be entitled to receive from the corporation a proprietary lease or right of tenancy document which shall include the following provisions:

(a) That no sublease in excess of one year, amendment, or modification to such proprietary lease or right of tenancy in the property shall be permitted or created without the lender's prior written consent; and

(b) That the security for a loan against the tenant-stockholder's interest shall be in the nature of a real property security interest, and any default of such loan shall entitle the lender to treat such default in the same manner as a default of a loan secured by real property.

§ 38-33.5-106, C.R.S. Exemption from securities laws.

Any stock certificate or other evidence of membership issued by a cooperative housing corporation as an investment in its stock or capital to tenant-stockholders of such corporation is exempt from securities laws contained in article 51 of title 11, C.R.S.

Chapter 5: Common Interest Communities

An * in the left margin indicates a change in the statute, rule, or text since the last publication of the manual.

I. HOA Information and Resource Center

The HOA Information and Resource Center ("Center"), as promulgated by the Colorado Legislature in HB10-1278, and codified in § 12-10-801(1), C.R.S., became operational on January 1, 2011. The Center is organized within the Division of Real Estate under the Department of Regulatory Agencies ("DORA").

The Center collects information via registrations directly from unit owners' associations ("HOAs") and from inquiries and complaints filed by unit owners. The Center provides education, assistance and information to unit owners, HOA boards, declarants and other interested parties concerning their rights and responsibilities as enumerated in the Colorado Common Interest Ownership Act ("CCIOA"), § 38-33.3-101, C.R.S., *et seq.*

The HOA Information Officer oversees the Center, and reviews, analyzes, and reports the data and information compiled in an Annual Report to the Director of the Division of Real Estate, pursuant to § 12-10-801(3)(c), C.R.S.

II. HOA Registration

Every unit owners' association shall register annually with the Director of the Division of Real Estate and shall submit with its annual registration and basic association information, a fee in the amount set by the Director of the Division of Real Estate. The association must complete an initial registration and renew its registration on an annual basis, as well as updating any relevant information within ninety (90) days of any change, as per § 38-33.3-401, C.R.S.

As part of the registration process, associations indicate whether they collect over $5,000. Associations that collect greater than $5,000 in annual revenue are required to pay the annual registration fee. Associations that are not authorized to make assessments and do not have any revenue, or that collect $5,000 or less in annual revenue are not required under the statute to pay the registration fee, however, this provision does not absolve associations from registering.

If an association fails to register, or if its annual registration has expired, its right to impose or enforce a lien for assessments under § 38-33.3-316, C.R.S., or to pursue an action or employ an enforcement mechanism otherwise available to it under § 38-33.3-123, C.R.S., is suspended until the association is validly registered. A lien for assessments that was previously recorded during a period in which the association was validly registered or before registration was required is not extinguished by the expiration of the association's registration; however, any pending enforcement proceedings related to the lien is suspended, and any applicable time limits are delayed, until the association is validly registered. An association's previously suspended right will be revived without penalty, once the association is validly registered.

III. Community Association Manager Licensing

(NOTE: The Community Association Manager (CAM) licensing program ended at the Division of Real Estate on June 30, 2019, and the Division no longer has any jurisdiction over community association managers. The Division has ceased to enforce any licensing, investigations, insurance, and continuing education requirements in this regard.)

IV. HOA Statutes

§ 12-10-501, C.R.S. Definitions. – Referenced in Chapter 4 Subdivision Laws, pages 4-2 to 4-3.

§ 12-10-801, C.R.S. HOA information and resource center – creation – duties – rules – subject to review – repeal.

Editor's note: *This section is similar to former §12-61-406.5 as it existed prior to 2019.*

(1) There is hereby created, within the division, the HOA information and resource center, the head of which shall be the HOA information officer. The HOA information officer shall be appointed by the executive director pursuant to section 13 of article XII of the state constitution.

(2) The HOA information officer shall be familiar with the "Colorado Common Interest Ownership Act", article 33.3 of title 38, also referred to in this section as the "act". No person who is or, within the immediately preceding ten years, has been licensed by or registered with the division or who owns stocks, bonds, or any pecuniary interest in a corporation subject in whole or in part to regulation by the division shall be appointed as HOA information officer. In addition, in conducting the search for an appointee, the executive director shall place a high premium on candidates who are balanced, independent, unbiased, and without any current financial ties to an HOA board or board member or to any person or entity that provides HOA management services. After being appointed, the HOA information officer shall refrain from engaging in any conduct or relationship that would create a conflict of interest or the appearance of a conflict of interest.

(3) (a) The HOA information officer shall act as a clearing house for information concerning the basic rights and duties of unit owners, declarants, and unit owners' associations under the act by:

(I) Compiling a database about registered associations, including the name; address; e-mail address, if any; website, if any; and telephone number of each;

(II) Coordinating and assisting in the preparation of educational and reference materials, including materials to assist unit owners, executive boards, board members, and association managers in understanding their rights and responsibilities with respect to:

(A) Open meetings;

(B) Proper use of executive sessions;

(C) Removal of executive board members;

(D) Unit owners' right to speak at meetings of the executive board;

(E) Unit owners' obligation to pay assessments and the association's rights and responsibilities in pursuing collection of past-due amounts; and

5. Common Interest Communities

(F) Other educational or reference materials that the HOA information officer deems necessary or appropriate;

(III) Monitoring changes in federal and state laws relating to common interest communities and providing information about the changes on the division's website; and

(IV) Providing information, including a "frequently asked questions" resource, on the division's website.

(b) The HOA information officer may:

(I) Employ one or more assistants as may be necessary to carry out his or her duties; and

(II) Request certain records from associations as necessary to carry out the HOA information officer's duties as set forth in this section.

(c) The HOA information officer shall track inquiries and complaints and report annually to the director regarding the number and types of inquiries and complaints received.

(4) The operating expenses of the HOA information and resource center shall be paid from the division of real estate cash fund, created in section 12-10-215, subject to annual appropriation.

(5) The director may adopt rules as necessary to implement this section and section 38-33.3-401. This subsection (5) shall not be construed to confer additional rule-making authority upon the director for any other purpose.

(6) This section is repealed, effective September 1, 2020. Before the repeal, the HOA information and resource center and the HOA information officer's powers and duties under this section are scheduled for review in accordance with section 24-34-104.

§ 38-12-601, C.R.S. Unreasonable restrictions on electric vehicle charging systems – definitions.

(1) Notwithstanding any provision in the lease to the contrary, and subject to subsection (2) of this section:

(a) A tenant may install, at the tenant's expense for the tenant's own use, a level 1 or level 2 electric vehicle charging system on or in the leased premises; and

(b) A landlord shall not assess or charge a tenant any fee for the placement or use of an electric vehicle charging system; except that:

(I) The landlord may require reimbursement for the actual cost of electricity provided by the landlord that was used by the charging system or, alternatively, may charge a reasonable fee for access. If the charging system is part of a network for which a network fee is charged, the landlord's reimbursement may include the amount of the network fee. Nothing in this section requires a landlord to impose upon a tenant any fee or charge other than the rental payments specified in the lease.

(II) The landlord may require reimbursement for the cost of the installation of the charging system, including any additions or upgrades to existing wiring directly attributable to the requirements of the charging system, if the landlord places or causes the electric vehicle charging system to be placed at the request of the tenant; and

(III) If the tenant desires to place an electric vehicle charging system in an area accessible to other tenants, the landlord may assess or charge the tenant a reasonable fee to reserve a specific parking spot in which to install the charging system.

(2) A landlord may require a tenant to comply with:

(a) Bona fide safety requirements, consistent with an applicable building code or recognized safety standard, for the protection of persons and property;

(b) A requirement that the charging system be registered with the landlord within thirty days after installation; or

(c) Reasonable aesthetic provisions that govern the dimensions, placement, or external appearance of an electric vehicle charging system.

(3) A tenant may place an electric vehicle charging system in an area accessible to other tenants if:

(a) The charging system is in compliance with all applicable requirements adopted pursuant to subsection (2) of this section; and

(b) The tenant agrees in writing to:

(I) Comply with the landlord's design specifications for the installation of the charging system;

(II) Engage the services of a duly licensed and registered electrical contractor familiar with the installation and code requirements of an electric vehicle charging system; and

(III) (A) Provide, within fourteen days after receiving the landlord's consent for the installation, a certificate of insurance naming the landlord as an additional insured on the tenant's renters' insurance policy for any claim related to the installation, maintenance, or use of the system or, at the landlord's option, reimbursement to the landlord for the actual cost of any increased insurance premium amount attributable to the system, notwithstanding any provision to the contrary in the lease.

(B) A certificate of insurance under sub-subparagraph (A) of this subparagraph (III) must be provided within fourteen days after the tenant receives the landlord's consent for the installation. Reimbursement for an increased insurance premium amount under sub-subparagraph (A) of this subparagraph (III) must be provided within fourteen days after the tenant receives the landlord's invoice for the amount attributable to the system.

(4) If the landlord consents to a tenant's installation of an electric vehicle charging system on property accessible to other tenants, including a parking space, carport, or garage stall, then, unless otherwise specified in a written agreement with the landlord:

(a) The tenant, and each successive tenant with exclusive rights to the area where the charging system is installed, is responsible for any costs for damages to the charging system and to any other property of the landlord or of another tenant that arise or result from the installation, maintenance, repair, removal, or replacement of the charging system;

(b) Each successive tenant with exclusive rights to the area where the charging system is installed shall assume responsibility for the repair, maintenance, removal, and replacement of the charging system until the system has been removed;

(c) The tenant and each successive tenant with exclusive rights to the area where the system is installed shall at all times have and maintain an insurance policy covering the obligations of the tenant under this subsection (4) and shall name the landlord as an additional insured under the policy; and

(d) The tenant and each successive tenant with exclusive rights to the area where the system is installed is responsible for removing the system if reasonably necessary or convenient for the repair, maintenance, or replacement of any property of the landlord, whether or not leased to another tenant.

(5) A charging system installed at the tenant's cost is property of the tenant. Upon termination of the lease, if the charging system is removable, the tenant may either remove it or sell it to the landlord or another tenant for an agreed price. Nothing in this subsection (5) requires the landlord or another tenant to purchase the charging system.

(6) As used in this section:

(a) "Electric vehicle charging system" or "charging system" means a device that is used to provide electricity to a plug-in electric vehicle or plug-in hybrid vehicle, is designed to ensure that a safe connection has been made between the electric grid and the vehicle, and is able to communicate with the vehicle's control system so that electricity flows at an appropriate voltage and current level. An electric vehicle charging system may be wall-mounted or pedestal style and may provide multiple cords to connect with electric vehicles. An electric vehicle charging system must be certified by underwriters laboratories or an equivalent certification and must comply with the current version of article 625 of the national electrical code.

(b) "Level 1" means a charging system that provides charging through a one-hundred-twenty volt AC plug with a cord connector that meets the SAE international J1772 standard or a successor standard.

(c) "Level 2" means a charging system that provides charging through a two-hundred-eight to two-hundred-forty volt AC plug with a cord connector that meets the SAE international J1772 standard or a successor standard.

(7) This section applies only to residential rental properties.

V. Condominium Ownership Act

Title 38, Article 33, C.R.S. – Condominium Ownership Act

Also see Colorado Common Interest Ownership Act in Part VI of this chapter

Note: The portions printed below are only those portions of the old condominium act that pertain to timeshare and conversion projects and that are still in place. This Condominium Act was *superseded* by the Colorado Common Interest Ownership Act July 1, 1992.

§ 38-33-101, C.R.S. Short title.

This article shall be known and may be cited as the "Condominium Ownership Act".

§ 38-33-102, C.R.S. Condominium ownership recognized.

Condominium ownership of real property is recognized in this state. Whether created before or after April 30, 1963, such ownership shall be deemed to consist of a separate estate in an individual air space unit of a multi-unit property together with an undivided interest in common elements. The separate estate of any condominium owner of an individual air space unit and his common ownership of such common elements as are appurtenant to his individual air space unit by the terms of the recorded declaration are inseparable for any period of condominium ownership that is prescribed by the recorded declaration. Condominium ownership may exist on land owned in fee simple or held under an estate for years.

§ 38-33-103, C.R.S. Definitions.

As used in this article, unless the context otherwise requires:

(1) "Condominium unit" means an individual air space unit together with the interest in the common elements appurtenant to such unit.

(2) "Declaration" is an instrument recorded pursuant to section 38-33-105 and which defines the character, duration, rights, obligations, and limitations of condominium ownership.

(3) Unless otherwise provided in the declaration or by written consent of all the condominium owners, "general common elements" means: The land or the interest therein on which a building or buildings are located; the foundations, columns, girders, beams, supports, main walls, roofs, halls, corridors, lobbies, stairs, stairways, fire escapes, entrances, and exits of such building or buildings; the basements, yards, gardens, parking areas, and storage spaces; the premises for the lodging of custodians or persons in charge of the property; installations of central services such as power, light, gas, hot and cold water, heating, refrigeration, central air conditioning, and incinerating; the elevators, tanks, pumps, motors, fans, compressors, ducts, and in general all apparatus and installations existing for common use; such community and commercial facilities as may be provided for in the declaration; and all other parts of the property necessary or convenient to its existence, maintenance, and safety, or normally in common use.

(4) "Individual air space unit" consists of any enclosed room or rooms occupying all or part of a floor or floors in a building of one or more floors to be used for residential, professional, commercial, or industrial purposes which has access to a public street.

(5) "Limited common elements" means those common elements designated in the declaration as reserved for use by fewer than all the owners of the individual air space units.

§ 38-33-104, C.R.S. Assessment of condominium ownership.

Whenever condominium ownership of real property is created or separate assessment of condominium units is desired, a written notice thereof shall be delivered to the assessor of the county in which said real property is situated, which notice shall set forth descriptions of the condominium units. Thereafter all taxes, assessments, and other charges of this state or of any political subdivision, or of any special improvement district, or of any other taxing or assessing authority shall be assessed against and collected on each condominium unit, each of which shall be carried on the tax books as a separate and distinct parcel for that purpose and not on the building or property as a whole. The valuation of the general and limited common elements shall be assessed proportionately upon the individual air space unit in the manner provided in the declaration. The lien for taxes assessed to any individual condominium owner shall be confined to his condominium unit and to his undivided interest in the general and limited common elements. No forfeiture or sale of any condominium unit for delinquent taxes, assessments, or charges shall divest or in any way affect the title of other condominium units.

§ 38-33-105, C.R.S. Recording of declaration – certain rules and laws to apply.

(1) The declaration shall be recorded in the county where the condominium property is located. Such declaration shall provide for the filing for record of a map properly locating condominium units. Any instrument affecting the condominium unit may legally describe it by the identifying condominium unit number or symbol as shown on such map. If such declaration provides for the disposition of condominium units in the event of the destruction or obsolescence of buildings in which such units are situate and restricts partition of the common elements, the rules or laws known as the rule against perpetuities and the rule prohibiting unlawful restraints on alienation shall not be applied to defeat or limit any such provisions.

(2) To the extent that any such declaration contains a mandatory requirement that all condominium unit owners be members of an association or corporation or provides for the payment of charges assessed by the association upon condominium units or the appointment of an attorney-in-fact to deal with the property upon its destruction or obsolescence, any rule of law to the contrary notwithstanding, the same shall be considered as covenants running with the land binding upon all condominium owners and their successors in interest. Any common law rule

terminating agency upon death or disability of a principal shall not be applied to defeat or limit any such provisions.

§ 38-33-105.5, C.R.S. Contents of declaration.

(1) The declaration shall contain:

(a) The name of the condominium property, which shall include the word "condominium" or be followed by the words "a condominium";

(b) The name of every county in which any part of the condominium property is situated;

(c) A legally sufficient description of the real estate included in the condominium property;

(d) A description or delineation of the boundaries of each condominium unit, including its identifying number;

(e) A statement of the maximum number of condominium units that may be created by the subdivision or conversion of units in a multiple-unit dwelling owned by the declarant;

(f) A description of any limited common elements;

(g) A description of all general common elements;

(h) A description of all general common elements which may be conveyed to any person or entity other than the condominium unit owners;

(i) A description of all general common elements which may be allocated subsequently as limited common elements, together with a statement that they may be so allocated, and a description of the method by which the allocations are to be made;

(j) An allocation to each condominium unit of an undivided interest in the general common elements, a portion of the votes in the association, and a percentage or fraction of the common expenses of the association;

(k) Any restrictions on the use, occupancy, or alienation of the condominium units;

(*l*) The recording data for recorded easements and licenses appurtenant to, or included in, the condominium property or to which any portion of the condominium property is or may become subject;

(m) Reasonable provisions concerning the manner in which notice of matters affecting the condominium property may be given to condominium unit owners by the association or other condominium unit owners; and

(n) Any other matters the declarant deems appropriate.

(2) This section shall apply to any condominium ownership of property created on or after July 1, 1983.

§ 38-33-106, C.R.S. Condominium bylaws – contents – exemptions.

(1) Unless exempted, the administration and operation of multi-unit condominiums shall be governed by the declaration.

(2) At or before the execution of a contract for sale and, if none, before closing, every initial bona fide condominium unit buyer shall be provided by the seller with a copy of the bylaws, with amendments, if any, of the unit owners' association or corporation, and such bylaws and amendments shall be of a size print or type to be clearly legible.

(3) The bylaws shall contain or provide for at least the following:

(a) The election from among the unit owners of a board of managers, the number of persons constituting such board, and that the terms of at least one-third of the members of the board shall expire annually; the powers and duties of the board; the compensation, if any, of the members of the board; the method of removal from office of members of the board; and whether or not the board may engage the services of a manager or managing agent, or both, and specifying which of the powers and duties granted to the board may be delegated by the board to either or both of them; however, the board when so delegating shall not be relieved of its responsibility under the declaration;

(b) The method of calling meetings of the unit owners; the method of allocating votes to unit owners; what percentage of the unit owners, if other than a majority, constitutes a quorum; and what percentage is necessary to adopt decisions binding on all unit owners;

(c) The election of a president from among the board of managers, who shall preside over the meetings of the board of managers and of the unit owners;

(d) The election of a secretary, who shall keep the minutes of all meetings of the board of managers and of the unit owners and who, in general, shall perform all the duties incident to the office of secretary;

(e) The election of a treasurer, who shall keep the financial records and books of account. The treasurer may also serve as the secretary.

(f) The authorization to the board of managers to designate and remove personnel necessary for the operation, maintenance, repair, and replacement of the common elements;

(g) A statement that the unit owners and their mortgagees, if applicable, may inspect the records of receipts and expenditures of the board of managers pursuant to section 38-33-107 at convenient weekday business hours, and that, upon ten days' notice to the manager or board of managers and payment of a reasonable fee, any unit owner shall be furnished a statement of his account setting forth the amount of any unpaid assessments or other charges due and owing from such owner;

(h) A statement as to whether or not the condominium association is a not for profit corporation, an unincorporated association, or a corporation;

(i) The method of adopting and of amending administrative rules and regulations governing the operation and use of the common elements;

(j) The percentage of votes required to modify or amend the bylaws, but each one of the particulars set forth in this section shall always be embodied in the bylaws;

(k) The maintenance, repair, replacement, and improvement of the general and limited common elements and payments therefor, including a statement of whether or not such work requires prior approval of the unit owners' association or corporation when it would involve a large expense or exceed a certain amount;

(*l*) The method of estimating the amount of the budget; the manner of assessing and collecting from the unit owners their respective shares of such estimated expenses and of any other expenses lawfully agreed upon; and a statement concerning the division, if any, of the assessment charge between general and limited common elements and the amount or percent of such division;

(m) A list of the services provided by the unit owners' association or corporation which are paid for out of the regular assessment;

(n) A statement clearly and separately indicating what assessments, debts, or other obligations are assumed by the unit owner on his condominium unit;

(o) A statement as to whether or not additional liens, other than mechanics' liens, assessment liens, or tax liens, may be obtained against the general or limited common elements then existing in which the unit owner has a percentage ownership;

(p) Such restrictions on and requirements respecting the use and maintenance of the units and the use of the general and limited common elements as are designed to prevent unreasonable interference with the use of their respective units and said common elements by the several unit owners;

(q) Such restrictions on and requirements concerning the sale or lease of a unit including rights of first refusal on sale and any other restraints on the free alienability of the unit;

(r) A statement listing all major recreational facilities and to whom they are available and clearly indicating whether or not fees or charges, if any, in conjunction therewith, are in addition to the regular assessment;

(s) A statement relating to new additions of general and limited common elements to be constructed, including but not limited to:

(I) The effect on a unit owner in reference to his obligation for payment of the common expenses, including new recreational facilities, costs, and fees, if any;

(II) The effect on a unit owner in reference to his ownership interest in the existing general and limited common elements and new general and limited common elements;

(III) The effect on a unit owner in reference to his voting power in the association.

(4) Any declaration recorded on or after January 1, 1976, shall not conflict with the provisions of this section or bylaws made in accordance with this section. The requirements contained in paragraphs (k) to (s) of subsection (3) of this section need not be included in the bylaws if they are set forth in the declaration.

(5) This section shall not apply to:

(a) Commercial or industrial condominiums or any other condominiums not used for residential use;

(b) Condominiums of ten units or less;

(c) Condominiums established by a declaration recorded prior to January 1, 1976.

§ 38-33-107, C.R.S. Records of receipts and expenditures – availability for examination.

The manager or board of managers, as the case may be, shall keep detailed, accurate records of the receipts and expenditures affecting the general and limited common elements. Such records authorizing the payments shall be available for examination by the unit owners at convenient weekday business hours.

§ 38-33-108, C.R.S. Violations – penalty.

Any person who knowingly and willfully violates the provisions of section 38-33-106 or 38-33-107 is guilty of a misdemeanor and, upon conviction thereof, shall be punished by a fine of not more than five hundred dollars.

§ 38-33-109, C.R.S. Unit owners' liability.

In any suit or arbitration against a condominium unit owners' association wherein damages are awarded or settlement is made, the individual unit owner's liability in his capacity as a percentage owner of the general or limited common elements or as a member of the condominium association shall not exceed the amount of damages or settlement multiplied by his percentage ownership in the general or limited common elements, as the case may be. In the case of incorporation by unit owners, their liability as stockholders shall be determined as any other corporate stockholder.

§ 38-33-110, C.R.S. Time-sharing – definitions.

As used in this section and section 38-33-111, unless the context otherwise requires:

(1) (a) "Interval estate" means a combination of:

(I) An estate for years terminating on a date certain, during which years title to a time share unit circulates among the interval owners in accordance with a fixed schedule, vesting in each such interval owner in turn for a period of time established by the said schedule, with the series thus established recurring annually until the arrival of the date certain; and

(II) A vested future interest in the same unit, consisting of an undivided interest in the remainder in fee simple, the magnitude of the future interest having been established by the time of the creation of the interval estate either by the project instruments or by the deed conveying the interval estate. The estate for years shall not be deemed to merge with the future interest, but neither the estate for years nor the future interest shall be conveyed or encumbered separately from the other.

(b) "Interval estate" also means an estate for years as described in subparagraph (I) of paragraph (a) of this subsection (1) where the remainder estate, as defined either by the project instruments or by the deed conveying the interval estate, is retained by the developer or his successors in interest.

(2) "Interval owner" means a person vested with legal title to an interval estate.

(3) "Interval unit" means a unit the title to which is or is to be divided into interval estates.

(4) "Project instruments" means the declaration, the bylaws, and any other set of restrictions or restrictive covenants, by whatever name denominated, which limit or restrict the use or occupancy of condominium units. "Project instruments" includes any lawful amendments to such instruments. "Project instruments" does not include any ordinance or other public regulation governing subdivisions, zoning, or other land use matters.

(5) "Time share estate" means either an interval estate or a time-span estate.

(6) "Time share owner" means a person vested with legal title to a time share estate.

(7) "Time share unit" means a unit the title to which is or is to be divided either into interval estates or time-span estates.

(8) "Time-span estate" means a combination of:

(a) An undivided interest in a present estate in fee simple in a unit, the magnitude of the interest having been established by the time of the creation of the time-span estate either by the project instruments or by the deed conveying the time-span estate; and

(b) An exclusive right to possession and occupancy of the unit during an annually recurring period of time defined and established by a recorded schedule set forth or referred to in the deed conveying the time-span estate.

(9) "Time-span owner" means a person vested with legal title to a time-span estate.

(10) "Time-span unit" means a unit the title to which is or is to be divided into time-span estates.

(11) "Unit owner" means a person vested with legal title to a unit, and, in the case of a time share unit, "unit owner" means all of the time share owners of that unit. When an estate is subject to a deed of trust or a trust deed, "unit owner" means the person entitled to beneficial enjoyment of the estate and not to any trustee or trustees holding title merely as security for an obligation.

§ 38-33-111, C.R.S. Special provisions applicable to time share ownership.

(1) No time share estates shall be created with respect to any condominium unit except pursuant to provisions in the project instruments expressly permitting the creation of such estates. Each time share estate shall constitute for all purposes an estate or interest in real property, separate and distinct from all other time share estates in the same unit or any other unit, and such estates may be separately conveyed and encumbered.

(2) Repealed.

(3) With respect to each time share unit, each owner of a time share estate therein shall be individually liable to the unit owners' association or corporation for all assessments, property taxes both real and personal, and charges levied pursuant to the project instruments against or

with respect to that unit, and such association or corporation shall be liable for the payment thereof, except to the extent that such instruments provide to the contrary. However, with respect to each other, each time share owner shall be responsible only for a fraction of such assessments, property taxes both real and personal, and charges proportionate to the magnitude of his undivided interest in the fee to the unit.

(4) No person shall have standing to bring suit for partition of any time share unit except in accordance with such procedures, conditions, restrictions, and limitations as the project instruments and the deeds to the time share estates may specify. Upon the entry of a final order in such a suit, it shall be conclusively presumed that all such procedures, conditions, restrictions, and limitations were adhered to.

(5) In the event that any condemnation award, any insurance proceeds, the proceeds of any sale, or any other sums shall become payable to all of the time share owners of a unit, the portion payable to each time share owner shall be proportionate to the magnitude of his undivided interest in the fee to the unit.

§ 38-33-112, C.R.S. Notification to residential tenants.

(1) A developer who converts an existing multiple-unit dwelling into condominium units, upon recording of the declaration as required by section 38-33-105, shall notify each residential tenant of the dwelling of such conversion.

(2) Such notice shall be in writing and shall be sent by certified or registered mail, postage prepaid, and return receipt provided. Notice is complete upon mailing to the tenant at the tenant's last known address. Notice may also be made by delivery in person to the tenant of a copy of such written notice, in which event notice is complete upon such delivery.

(3) Said notice constitutes the notice to terminate the tenancy as provided by section 13-40-107, C.R.S.; except that no residential tenancy shall be terminated prior to the expiration date of the existing lease agreement, if any, unless consented to by both the tenant and the developer. If the term of the lease has less than ninety days remaining when notification is mailed or delivered, as the case may be, or if there is no written lease agreement, residential tenancy may not be terminated by the developer less than ninety days after the date the notice is mailed or delivered, as the case may be, to the tenant, unless consented to by both the tenant and the developer. The return receipt shall be prima facie evidence of receipt of notice. If the term of the lease has less than ninety days remaining when notification is mailed or delivered, as the case may be, the tenant may hold over for the remainder of said ninety-day period under the same terms and conditions of the lease agreement if the tenant makes timely rental payments and performs other conditions of the lease agreement.

(4) The tenancy may be terminated within the ninety days prescribed in subsection (3) of this section upon agreement by the tenant in consideration of the payment of all moving expenses by the developer or for such other consideration as mutually agreed upon. Such tenancy may also be terminated within the ninety days prescribed in subsection (3) of this section upon failure by the tenant to make timely rental or lease payments.

(5) Any person who applies for a residential tenancy after the recording of the declaration shall be informed of this recording at the time of application, and any leases executed after such recording may provide for termination within less than ninety days provided that the terms of the lease conspicuously disclose the intention to convert the property containing the leased premises to condominium ownership.

(6) The general assembly hereby finds and declares that the notification procedure set forth in this section is a matter of statewide concern. No county, municipality, or other political subdivision whether or not vested with home rule powers under article XX of the Colorado constitution, shall adopt or enforce any ordinance, rule, regulation, or policy which conflicts with the provisions of this section.

§ 38-33-113, C.R.S. License to sell condominiums and time-shares.

The general assembly hereby finds and declares that the licensing of persons to sell condominiums and time shares is a matter of statewide concern.

VI. Colorado Common Interest Ownership Act

§ 38-33.3-101, C.R.S. Short title.

This article shall be known and may be cited as the "Colorado Common Interest Ownership Act".

§ 38-33.3-102, C.R.S. Legislative declaration.

(1) The general assembly hereby finds, determines, and declares, as follows:

(a) That it is in the best interests of the state and its citizens to establish a clear, comprehensive, and uniform framework for the creation and operation of common interest communities;

(b) That the continuation of the economic prosperity of Colorado is dependent upon the strengthening of homeowner associations in common interest communities financially through the setting of budget guidelines, the creation of statutory assessment liens, the granting of six months' lien priority, the facilitation of borrowing, and more certain powers in the association to sue on behalf of the owners and through enhancing the financial stability of associations by increasing the association's powers to collect delinquent assessments, late charges, fines, and enforcement costs;

(c) That it is the policy of this state to give developers flexible development rights with specific obligations within a uniform structure of development of a common interest community that extends through the transition to owner control;

(d) That it is the policy of this state to promote effective and efficient property management through defined operational requirements that preserve flexibility for such homeowner associations;

(e) That it is the policy of this state to promote the availability of funds for financing the development of such homeowner associations by enabling lenders to extend the financial services to a greater market on a safer, more predictable basis because of standardized practices and prudent insurance and risk management obligations.

§ 38-33.3-103, C.R.S. Definitions.

As used in the declaration and bylaws of an association, unless specifically provided otherwise or unless the context otherwise requires, and in this article:

(1) "Affiliate of a declarant" means any person who controls, is controlled by, or is under common control with a declarant. A person controls a declarant if the person: Is a general partner, officer, director, or employee of the declarant; directly or indirectly, or acting in concert with one or more other persons or through one or more subsidiaries, owns, controls, holds with power to vote, or holds proxies representing more than twenty percent of the voting interests of the declarant; controls in any manner the election of a majority of the directors of the declarant; or has contributed more than twenty percent of the capital of the declarant. A person is controlled by a declarant if the declarant: Is a general partner, officer, director, or employee of the person; directly or indirectly, or acting in concert with one or more other persons or through one or more subsidiaries, owns, controls, holds with power to vote, or holds proxies representing more than twenty percent of the voting interests of the person; controls in any manner the election of a majority of the directors of the person; or has contributed more than

twenty percent of the capital of the person. Control does not exist if the powers described in this subsection (1) are held solely as security for an obligation and are not exercised.

(2) "Allocated interests" means the following interests allocated to each unit:

(a) In a condominium, the undivided interest in the common elements, the common expense liability, and votes in the association;

(b) In a cooperative, the common expense liability and the ownership interest and votes in the association; and

(c) In a planned community, the common expense liability and votes in the association.

(2.5) "Approved for development" means that all or some portion of a particular parcel of real property is zoned or otherwise approved for construction of residential and other improvements and authorized for specified densities by the local land use authority having jurisdiction over such real property and includes any conceptual or final planned unit development approval.

(3) "Association" or "unit owners' association" means a unit owners' association organized under section 38-33.3-301.

(4) "Bylaws" means any instruments, however denominated, which are adopted by the association for the regulation and management of the association, including any amendments to those instruments.

(5) "Common elements" means:

(a) In a condominium or cooperative, all portions of the condominium or cooperative other than the units; and

(b) In a planned community, any real estate within a planned community owned or leased by the association, other than a unit.

(6) "Common expense liability" means the liability for common expenses allocated to each unit pursuant to section 38-33.3-207.

(7) "Common expenses" means expenditures made or liabilities incurred by or on behalf of the association, together with any allocations to reserves.

(8) "Common interest community" means real estate described in a declaration with respect to which a person, by virtue of such person's ownership of a unit, is obligated to pay for real estate taxes, insurance premiums, maintenance, or improvement of other real estate described in a declaration. Ownership of a unit does not include holding a leasehold interest in a unit of less than forty years, including renewal options. The period of the leasehold interest, including renewal options, is measured from the date the initial term commences.

(9) "Condominium" means a common interest community in which portions of the real estate are designated for separate ownership and the remainder of which is designated for common ownership solely by the owners of the separate ownership portions. A common interest community is not a condominium unless the undivided interests in the common elements are vested in the unit owners.

(10) "Cooperative" means a common interest community in which the real property is owned by an association, each member of which is entitled by virtue of such member's ownership interest in the association to exclusive possession of a unit.

(11) "Dealer" means a person in the business of selling units for such person's own account.

(12) "Declarant" means any person or group of persons acting in concert who:

(a) As part of a common promotional plan, offers to dispose of to a purchaser such declarant's interest in a unit not previously disposed of to a purchaser; or

(b) Reserves or succeeds to any special declarant right.

(13) "Declaration" means any recorded instruments however denominated, that create a common interest community, including any amendments to those instruments and also including, but not limited to, plats and maps.

(14) "Development rights" means any right or combination of rights reserved by a declarant in the declaration to:

(a) Add real estate to a common interest community;

(b) Create units, common elements, or limited common elements within a common interest community;

(c) Subdivide units or convert units into common elements; or

(d) Withdraw real estate from a common interest community.

(15) "Dispose" or "disposition" means a voluntary transfer of any legal or equitable interest in a unit, but the term does not include the transfer or release of a security interest.

(16) "Executive board" means the body, regardless of name, designated in the declaration to act on behalf of the association.

(16.5) "Horizontal boundary" means a plane of elevation relative to a described bench mark that defines either a lower or an upper dimension of a unit such that the real estate respectively below or above the defined plane is not a part of the unit.

(17) "Identifying number" means a symbol or address that identifies only one unit in a common interest community.

(17.5) "Large planned community" means a planned community that meets the criteria set forth in section 38-33.3-116.3 (1).

(18) "Leasehold common interest community" means a common interest community in which all or a portion of the real estate is subject to a lease, the expiration or termination of which will terminate the common interest community or reduce its size.

(19) "Limited common element" means a portion of the common elements allocated by the declaration or by operation of section 38-33.3-202 (1) (b) or (1) (d) for the exclusive use of one or more units but fewer than all of the units.

(19.5) "Map" means that part of a declaration that depicts all or any portion of a common interest community in three dimensions, is executed by a person that is authorized by this title to execute a declaration relating to the common interest community, and is recorded in the real estate records in every county in which any portion of the common interest community is located. A map is required for a common interest community with units having a horizontal boundary. A map and a plat may be combined in one instrument.

(20) "Master association" means an organization that is authorized to exercise some or all of the powers of one or more associations on behalf of one or more common interest communities or for the benefit of the unit owners of one or more common interest communities.

(21) "Person" means a natural person, a corporation, a partnership, an association, a trust, or any other entity or any combination thereof.

(21.5) "Phased community" means a common interest community in which the declarant retains development rights.

(22) "Planned community" means a common interest community that is not a condominium or cooperative. A condominium or cooperative may be part of a planned community.

(22.5) "Plat" means that part of a declaration that is a land survey plat as set forth in section 38-51-106, depicts all or any portion of a common interest community in two dimensions, is executed by a person that is authorized by this title to execute a declaration relating to the common interest community, and is recorded in the real estate records in every county in which any portion of the common interest community is located. A plat and a map may be combined in one instrument.

(23) "Proprietary lease" means an agreement with the association pursuant to which a member is entitled to exclusive possession of a unit in a cooperative.

(24) "Purchaser" means a person, other than a declarant or a dealer, who by means of a transfer acquires a legal or equitable interest in a unit, other than:

  (a) A leasehold interest in a unit of less than forty years, including renewal options, with the period of the leasehold interest, including renewal options, being measured from the date the initial term commences; or

  (b) A security interest.

(25) "Real estate" means any leasehold or other estate or interest in, over, or under land, including structures, fixtures, and other improvements and interests that, by custom, usage, or law, pass with a conveyance of land though not described in the contract of sale or instrument of conveyance. "Real estate" includes parcels with or without horizontal boundaries and spaces that may be filled with air or water.

(26) "Residential use" means use for dwelling or recreational purposes but does not include spaces or units primarily used for commercial income from, or service to, the public.

(27) "Rules and regulations" means any instruments, however denominated, which are adopted by the association for the regulation and management of the common interest community, including any amendment to those instruments.

(28) "Security interest" means an interest in real estate or personal property created by contract or conveyance which secures payment or performance of an obligation. The term includes a lien created by a mortgage, deed of trust, trust deed, security deed, contract for deed, land sales contract, lease intended as security, assignment of lease or rents intended as security, pledge of an ownership interest in an association, and any other consensual lien or title retention contract intended as security for an obligation.

(29) "Special declarant rights" means rights reserved for the benefit of a declarant to perform the following acts as specified in parts 2 and 3 of this article: To complete improvements indicated on plats and maps filed with the declaration; to exercise any development right; to maintain sales offices, management offices, signs advertising the common interest community, and models; to use easements through the common elements for the purpose of making improvements within the common interest community or within real estate which may be added to the common interest community; to make the common interest community subject to a master association; to merge or consolidate a common interest community of the same form of ownership; or to appoint or remove any officer of the association or any executive board member during any period of declarant control.

(30) "Unit" means a physical portion of the common interest community which is designated for separate ownership or occupancy and the boundaries of which are described in or determined from the declaration. If a unit in a cooperative is owned by a unit owner or is sold, conveyed, voluntarily or involuntarily encumbered, or otherwise transferred by a unit owner, the interest in that unit which is owned, sold, conveyed, encumbered, or otherwise transferred is the right to possession of that unit under a proprietary lease, coupled with the allocated interests of that unit, and the association's interest in that unit is not thereby affected.

(31) "Unit owner" means the declarant or other person who owns a unit, or a lessee of a unit in a leasehold common interest community whose lease expires simultaneously with any lease, the expiration or termination of which will remove the unit from the common interest community but does not include a person having an interest in a unit solely as security for an obligation. In a condominium or planned community, the declarant is the owner of any unit created by the declaration until that unit is conveyed to another person; in a cooperative, the declarant is treated as the owner of any unit to which allocated interests have been allocated pursuant to

section 38-33.3-207 until that unit has been conveyed to another person, who may or may not be a declarant under this article.

(32) "Vertical boundary" means the defined limit of a unit that is not a horizontal boundary of that unit.

(33) "Xeriscape" means the combined application of the seven principles of landscape planning and design, soil analysis and improvement, hydro zoning of plants, use of practical turf areas, uses of mulches, irrigation efficiency, and appropriate maintenance under section 38-35.7-107 (1) (a) (III) (A).

§ 38-33.3-104, C.R.S. Variation by agreement.

Except as expressly provided in this article, provisions of this article may not be varied by agreement, and rights conferred by this article may not be waived. A declarant may not act under a power of attorney or use any other device to evade the limitations or prohibitions of this article or the declaration.

§ 38-33.3-105, C.R.S. Separate titles and taxation.

(1) In a cooperative, unless the declaration provides that a unit owner's interest in a unit and its allocated interests is personal property, that interest is real estate for all purposes.

(2) In a condominium or planned community with common elements, each unit that has been created, together with its interest in the common elements, constitutes for all purposes a separate parcel of real estate and must be separately assessed and taxed. The valuation of the common elements shall be assessed proportionately to each unit, in the case of a condominium in accordance with such unit's allocated interests in the common elements, and in the case of a planned community in accordance with such unit's allocated common expense liability, set forth in the declaration, and the common elements shall not be separately taxed or assessed. Upon the filing for recording of a declaration for a condominium or planned community with common elements, the declarant shall deliver a copy of such filing to the assessor of each county in which such declaration was filed.

(3) In a planned community without common elements, the real estate comprising such planned community may be taxed and assessed in any manner provided by law.

§ 38-33.3-106, C.R.S. Applicability of local ordinances, regulations, and building codes.

(1) A building code may not impose any requirement upon any structure in a common interest community which it would not impose upon a physically identical development under a different form of ownership; except that a minimum one hour fire wall may be required between units.

(2) In condominiums and cooperatives, no zoning, subdivision, or other real estate use law, ordinance, or regulation may prohibit the condominium or cooperative form of ownership or impose any requirement upon a condominium or cooperative which it would not impose upon a physically identical development under a different form of ownership.

* *§ 38-33.3-106.5, C.R.S. Prohibitions contrary to public policy - patriotic, political, or religious expression - emergency vehicles - fire prevention - renewable energy generation devices - affordable housing - drought prevention measures - child care - definitions.*

(1) Notwithstanding any provision in the declaration, bylaws, or rules and regulations of the association to the contrary, an association shall not prohibit any of the following:

(a) The display of a flag on a unit owner's property, in a window of the unit, or on a balcony ad-joining the unit. The association shall not prohibit or regulate the display of flags on the basis of their subject matter, message, or content; except that the association may prohibit flags bearing commer-cial messages. The association may adopt reasonable, content-neutral rules to regulate the number, location, and size of flags and flagpoles, but shall not prohibit the installation of a flag or flagpole.

(b) Repealed.

(c) The display of a sign by the owner or occupant of a unit on property within the boundaries of the unit or in a window of the unit. The association shall not prohibit or regulate the display of window signs or yard signs on the basis of their subject matter, message, or content; except that the associa-tion may prohibit signs bearing commercial messages. The association may establish reasonable, con-tent-neutral sign regulations based on the number, placement, or size of the signs or on other objec-tive factors.

(c.5) (I) The display of a religious item or symbol on the entry door or entry door frame of a unit; ex-cept that an association may prohibit the display or affixing of an item or symbol to the extent that it:

(A) Threatens public health or safety;

(B) Hinders the opening or closing of an entry door;

(C) Violates federal or state law or a municipal ordinance;

(D) Contains graphics, language, or any display that is obscene or otherwise illegal; or

(E) Individually or in combination with other religious items or symbols, covers an area greater than thirty-six square inches.

(II) If an association is performing maintenance, repair, or replacement of an entry door or door frame that serves a unit owner's separate interest, the unit owner may be required to remove a reli-gious item or symbol during the time the work is being performed. After completion of the associa-tion's work, the unit owner may again display or affix the religious item or symbol. The association shall provide individual notice to the unit owner regarding the temporary removal of the religious item or symbol.

(III) As used in this subsection (1)(c.5), "religious item or symbol" means an item or symbol dis-played because of a sincerely held religious belief.

(d) The parking of a motor vehicle by the occupant of a unit on a street, driveway, or guest parking area in the common interest community if the vehicle is required to be available at designated periods at such occupant's residence as a condition of the occupant's employment and all of the following cri-teria are met:

(I) The vehicle has a gross vehicle weight rating of ten thousand pounds or less;

(II) The occupant is a bona fide member of a volunteer fire department or is employed by a prima-ry provider of emergency fire fighting, law enforcement, ambulance, or emergency medical services;

(III) The vehicle bears an official emblem or other visible designation of the emergency service provider; and

(IV) Parking of the vehicle can be accomplished without obstructing emergency access or interfer-ing with the reasonable needs of other unit owners or occupants to use streets, driveways, and guest parking spaces within the common interest community.

(e) The removal by a unit owner of trees, shrubs, or other vegetation to create defensible space around a dwelling for fire mitigation purposes, so long as such removal complies with a written defen-sible space plan created for the property by the Colorado state forest service, an individual or compa-ny certified by a local governmental entity to create such a plan, or the fire chief, fire marshal, or fire protection district within whose jurisdiction the unit is located, and is no more extensive than neces-sary to comply with such plan. The plan shall be registered with the association before the com-mencement of work. The association may require changes to the plan if the association obtains the consent of the person, official, or agency that originally created the plan. The work shall comply with applicable association standards regarding slash removal, stump height, revegetation, and contractor regulations.

(f) (Deleted by amendment, L. 2006, p. 1215, §2, effective May 26, 2006.)

(g) Reasonable modifications to a unit or to common elements as necessary to afford a person with disabilities full use and enjoyment of the unit in accordance with the federal "Fair Housing Act of 1968", 42 U.S.C. sec. 3604 (f)(3)(A);

(h) (I) The right of a unit owner, public or private, to restrict or specify by deed, covenant, or other document:

(A) The permissible sale price, rental rate, or lease rate of the unit; or

(B) Occupancy or other requirements designed to promote affordable or workforce housing as such terms may be defined by the local housing authority.

(II) (A) Notwithstanding any other provision of law, the provisions of this subsection (1)(h) shall only apply to a county the population of which is less than one hundred thousand persons and that con-tains a ski lift licensed by the passenger tramway safety board created in section 12-150-104 (1).

(B) The provisions of this paragraph (h) shall not apply to a declarant-controlled community.

(III) Nothing in subparagraph (I) of this paragraph (h) shall be construed to prohibit the future owner of a unit against which a restriction or specification described in such subparagraph has been placed from lifting such restriction or specification on such unit as long as any unit so released is re-placed by another unit in the same common interest community on which the restriction or specifica-tion applies and the unit subject to the restriction or specification is reasonably equivalent to the unit being released in the determination of the beneficiary of the restriction or specification.

(IV) Except as otherwise provided in the declaration of the common interest community, any unit subject to the provisions of this paragraph (h) shall only be occupied by the owner of the unit.

(i) (I) (A) The use of xeriscape, nonvegetative turf grass, or drought-tolerant vegetative land-scapes to provide ground covering to property for which a unit owner is responsible, including a limited common element or property owned by the unit owner. Associations may adopt and enforce design or aesthetic guidelines or rules that apply to nonvegetative turf grass and drought-tolerant vegetative landscapes or regulate the type, number, and placement of drought-tolerant plantings and hardscapes that may be installed on a unit owner's property or on a limited common element or other property for which the unit owner is responsible. An association may restrict the installation of nonvegetative turf grass to rear yard locations only.

(B) This subsection (1)(i), as amended by House Bill 21-1229, enacted in 2021, does not apply to an association that includes time share units, as defined in section 38-33-110 (7).

(II) This paragraph (i) does not supersede any subdivision regulation of a county, city and county, or other municipality.

(j) (I) The use of a rain barrel, as defined in section 37-96.5-102 (1), C.R.S., to collect precipitation from a residential rooftop in accordance with section 37-96.5-103, C.R.S.

(II) This paragraph (j) does not confer upon a resident of a common interest community the right to place a rain barrel on property or to connect a rain barrel to any property that is:

(A) Leased, except with permission of the lessor;

(B) A common element or a limited common element of a common interest community;

(C) Maintained by the unit owners' association for a common interest community; or

(D) Attached to one or more other units, except with permission of the owners of the other units.

(III) A common interest community may impose reasonable aesthetic requirements that govern the placement or external appearance of a rain barrel.

(k) (I) The operation of a family child care home, as defined in section 26-6-102 (13), that is licensed under part 1 of article 6 of title 26.

(II) This subsection (1)(k) does not supersede any of the association's regulations concerning ar-chitectural control, parking, landscaping, noise, or other matters not specific to the operation of a business per se. The association shall make reasonable accommodation for fencing requirements ap-plicable to licensed family child care homes.

(III) This subsection (1)(k) does not apply to a community qualified as housing for older persons under the federal "Housing for Older Persons Act of 1995", as amended, Pub.L. 104-76.

(IV) The association may require the owner or operator of a family child care home located in the common interest community to carry liability insurance, at reasonable levels determined by the asso-ciation's executive board, providing coverage for any aspect of the operation of the family child care home for personal injury, death, damage to personal property, and damage to real property that occurs in or on the common elements, in the unit where the family child care home is located, or in any other unit located in the common interest community. The association shall be named as an additional insured on the liability insurance the family child care home is required to carry, and such insurance must be primary to any insurance the association is required to carry under the terms of the declaration.

(1.5) Notwithstanding any provision in the declaration, bylaws, or rules and regulations of the association to the contrary, an association shall not effectively prohibit renewable energy generation de-vices, as defined in section 38-30-168.

(2) Notwithstanding any provision in the declaration, bylaws, or rules and regulations of the association to the contrary, an association shall not require the use of cedar shakes or other flammable roofing materials.

* *§ 38-33.3-106.7, C.R.S. Unreasonable restrictions on energy efficiency measures – definitions.*

(1) (a) Notwithstanding any provision in the declaration, bylaws, or rules and regulations of the asso-ciation to the contrary, an association shall not effectively prohibit the installation or use of an energy efficiency measure.

(b) As used in this section, "energy efficiency measure" means a device or structure that reduces the amount of energy derived from fossil fuels that is consumed by a residence or business located on the real property. "Energy efficiency measure" is further limited to include only the following types of devices or structures:

(I) An awning, shutter, trellis, ramada, or other shade structure that is marketed for the purpose of reducing energy consumption;

(II) A garage or attic fan and any associated vents or louvers;

(III) An evaporative cooler;

(IV) An energy-efficient outdoor lighting device, including without limitation a light fixture contain-ing a coiled or straight fluorescent light bulb, and any solar recharging panel, motion detector, or other equipment connected to the lighting device;

(V) A retractable clothesline; and

(VI) A heat pump.

(2) Subsection (1) of this section shall not apply to:

(a) Reasonable aesthetic provisions that govern the dimensions, placement, or external appear-ance of an energy efficiency measure. In creating reasonable aesthetic provisions, common interest communities shall consider:

(I) The impact on the purchase price and operating costs of the energy efficiency measure;

(II) The impact on the performance of the energy efficiency measure; and

(III) The criteria contained in the governing documents of the common interest community.

(b) Bona fide safety requirements, consistent with an applicable building code or recognized safe-ty standard, for the protection of persons and property.

(3) This section shall not be construed to confer upon any property owner the right to place an energy efficiency measure on property that is:

(a) Owned by another person;

(b) Leased, except with permission of the lessor;

(c) Collateral for a commercial loan, except with permission of the secured party; or

(d) A limited common element or general common element of a common interest community.

§ 38-33.3-106.8, C.R.S. Unreasonable restrictions on electric vehicle charging systems – legislative declaration – definitions.

(1) The general assembly finds, determines, and declares that:

(a) The widespread use of plug-in electric vehicles can dramatically improve energy efficiency and air quality for all Coloradans and should be encouraged wherever possible;

(b) Most homes in Colorado, including the vast majority of new homes, are in common interest communities;

(c) The primary purpose of this section is to ensure that common interest communities provide their residents with at least a meaningful opportunity to take advantage of the availability of plug-in electric vehicles rather than create artificial restrictions on the adoption of this promising technology; and

(d) The general assembly encourages common interest communities not only to allow electric vehicle charging stations in accordance with this section, but also to apply for grants from the electric vehicle grant fund, created in section 24-38.5-103, C.R.S., or otherwise fund the installation of charging stations on common property as an amenity for residents and guests.

(2) Notwithstanding any provision in the declaration, bylaws, or rules and regulations of the association to the contrary, and except as provided in subsection (3) or (3.5) of this section, an association shall not:

(a) Prohibit a unit owner from using, or installing at the unit owner's expense for the unit owner's own use, a level 1 or level 2 electric vehicle charging system on or in a unit; or

(b) Assess or charge a unit owner any fee for the placement or use of an electric vehicle charging system on or in the unit owner's unit; except that the association may require reimbursement for the actual cost of electricity provided by the association that was used by the charging system or, alternatively, may charge a reasonable fee for access. If the charging system is part of a network for which a network fee is charged, the association's reimbursement may include the amount of the network fee. Nothing in this section requires an association to impose upon a unit owner any fee or charge other than the regular assessments specified in the declaration, bylaws, or rules and regulations of the association.

(3) Subsection (2) of this section does not apply to:

(a) Bona fide safety requirements, consistent with an applicable building code or recognized safety standard, for the protection of persons and property;

(b) A requirement that the charging system be registered with the association within thirty days after installation; or

(c) Reasonable aesthetic provisions that govern the dimensions, placement, or external appearance of an electric vehicle charging system.

(3.5) This section does not apply to a unit, or the owner thereof, if the unit is a time share unit, as defined in section 38-33-110 (7).

(4) An association shall consent to a unit owner's placement of an electric vehicle charging system on a limited common element parking space, carport, or garage owned by the unit owner or otherwise assigned to the owner in the declaration or other recorded document if:

(a) Notwithstanding any existing ban on electric vehicle charging systems, the system otherwise complies with the declaration, bylaws, and rules and regulations of the association; and

(b) The unit owner agrees in writing to:

(I) Comply with the association's design specifications for the installation of the system;

(II) Engage the services of a duly licensed and registered electrical contractor familiar with the installation and code requirements of an electric vehicle charging system;

(III) Bear the expense of installation, including costs to restore any common elements disturbed in the process of installing the system; and

(IV) (A) Provide, within the time specified in sub-subparagraph (B) of this subparagraph (IV), a certificate of insurance naming the association as an additional insured on the homeowner's insurance policy for any claim related to the installation, maintenance, or use of the system or, if the system is located on a common element, reimbursement to the association for the actual cost of any increased insurance premium amount attributable to the system, notwithstanding any provision to the contrary in the association's declaration, bylaws, or rules and regulations.

(B) A certificate of insurance under sub-subparagraph (A) of this subparagraph (IV) must be provided within fourteen days after the unit owner receives the association's consent for the installation. Reimbursement for an increased insurance premium amount under sub-subparagraph (A) of this subparagraph (IV) must be provided within fourteen days after the unit owner receives the association's invoice for the amount attributable to the system.

(5) If the association consents to a unit owner's installation of an electric vehicle charging system on a limited common element, including a parking space, carport, or garage stall, then, unless otherwise specified in a written contract or in the declaration, bylaws, or rules and regulations of the association:

(a) The unit owner, and each successive unit owner with exclusive rights to the limited common element where the charging system is installed, is responsible for any costs for damages to the system, any other limited common element or general common element of the common interest community, and any adjacent units, garage stalls, carports, or parking spaces that arise or result from the installation, maintenance, repair, removal, or replacement of the system;

(b) Each successive unit owner with exclusive rights to the limited common element shall assume responsibility for the repair, maintenance, removal, and replacement of the charging system until the system has been removed;

(c) The unit owner and each successive unit owner with exclusive rights to the limited common element shall at all times have and maintain an insurance policy covering the obligations of the unit owner under this subsection (5), is subject to all obligations specified under subparagraph (IV) of paragraph (b) of subsection (4) of this section, and shall name the association as an additional insured under the policy; and

(d) The unit owner and each successive unit owner with exclusive rights to the limited common element is responsible for removing the system if reasonably necessary or convenient for the repair, maintenance, or replacement of the limited common elements or general common elements of the common interest community.

(6) A charging system installed at the unit owner's cost is property of the unit owner. Upon sale of the unit, if the charging system is removable, the unit owner may either remove it or sell it to the buyer of the unit or to the association for an agreed price. Nothing in this subsection (6) requires the buyer or the association to purchase the charging system.

(7) As used in this section:

(a) "Electric vehicle charging system" or "charging system" means a device that is used to provide electricity to a plug-in electric vehicle or plug-in hybrid vehicle, is designed to ensure that a safe connection has been made between the electric grid and the vehicle, and is able to communicate with the vehicle's control system so that electricity flows at an appropriate voltage and current level. An electric vehicle charging system may be wall-mounted or pedestal style and may provide multiple cords to connect with electric vehicles. An electric vehicle charging system must be certified by underwriters laboratories or an equivalent certification and must comply with the current version of article 625 of the national electrical code.

(b) "Level 1" means a charging system that provides charging through a one-hundred-twenty volt AC plug with a cord connector that meets the SAE international J1772 standard or a successor standard.

(c) "Level 2" means a charging system that provides charging through a two-hundred-eight to two-hundred-forty volt AC plug with a cord connector that meets the SAE international J1772 standard or a successor standard.

(8) This section applies only to residential units.

§ 38-33.3-107, C.R.S. Eminent domain.

(1) If a unit is acquired by eminent domain or part of a unit is acquired by eminent domain leaving the unit owner with a remnant which may not practically or lawfully be used for any purpose permitted by the declaration, the award must include compensation to the unit owner for that unit and its allocated interests whether or not any common elements are acquired. Upon acquisition, unless the decree otherwise provides, that unit's allocated interests are automatically reallocated to the remaining units in proportion to the respective allocated interests of those units before the taking. Any remnant of a unit remaining after part of a unit is taken under this subsection (1) is thereafter a common element.

(2) Except as provided in subsection (1) of this section, if part of a unit is acquired by eminent domain, the award must compensate the unit owner for the reduction in value of the unit and its interest in the common elements whether or not any common elements are acquired. Upon acquisition, unless the decree otherwise provides:

(a) That unit's allocated interests are reduced in proportion to the reduction in the size of the unit or on any other basis specified in the declaration; and

(b) The portion of allocated interests divested from the partially acquired unit is automatically reallocated to that unit and to the remaining units in proportion to the respective interests of those units before the taking, with the partially acquired unit participating in the reallocation on the basis of its reduced allocated interests.

(3) If part of the common elements is acquired by eminent domain, that portion of any award attributable to the common elements taken must be paid to the association. Unless the declaration provides otherwise, any portion of the award attributable to the acquisition of a limited common element must be equally divided among the owners of the units to which that limited common element was allocated at the time of acquisition. For the purposes of acquisition of a part of the common elements other than the limited common elements under this subsection (3), service of process on the association shall constitute sufficient notice to all unit owners, and service of process on each individual unit owner shall not be necessary.

(4) The court decree shall be recorded in every county in which any portion of the common interest community is located.

(5) The reallocations of allocated interests pursuant to this section shall be confirmed by an amendment to the declaration prepared, executed, and recorded by the association.

§ 38-33.3-108, C.R.S. Supplemental general principles of law applicable.

The principles of law and equity, including, but not limited to, the law of corporations and unincorporated associations, the law of real property, and the law relative to capacity to contract, principal and agent, eminent domain, estoppel, fraud, misrepresentation, duress, coercion, mistake, receivership, substantial performance, or other validating or invalidating cause supplement the provisions of this article, except to the extent inconsistent with this article.

§ 38-33.3-109, C.R.S. Construction against implicit repeal.

This article is intended to be a unified coverage of its subject matter, and no part of this article shall be construed to be impliedly repealed by subsequent legislation if that construction can reasonably be avoided.

§ 38-33.3-110, C.R.S. Uniformity of application and construction.

This article shall be applied and construed so as to effectuate its general purpose to make uniform the law with respect to the subject of this article among states enacting it.

§ 38-33.3-111, C.R.S. Severability.

If any provision of this article or the application thereof to any person or circumstances is held invalid, the invalidity shall not affect other provisions or applications of this article which can be given effect without the invalid provisions or application, and, to this end, the provisions of this article are severable.

§ 38-33.3-112, C.R.S. Unconscionable agreement or term of contract.

(1) The court, upon finding as a matter of law that a contract or contract clause relating to a common interest community was unconscionable at the time the contract was made, may refuse to enforce the contract, enforce the remainder of the contract without the unconscionable clause, or limit the application of any unconscionable clause in order to avoid an unconscionable result.

(2) Whenever it is claimed, or appears to the court, that a contract or any contract clause relating to a common interest community is or may be unconscionable, the parties, in order to aid the court in making the determination, shall be afforded a reasonable opportunity to present evidence as to:

- (a) The commercial setting of the negotiations;
- (b) Whether the first party has knowingly taken advantage of the inability of the second party reasonably to protect such second party's interests by reason of physical or mental infirmity, illiteracy, or inability to understand the language of the agreement or similar factors;
- (c) The effect and purpose of the contract or clause; and
- (d) If a sale, any gross disparity at the time of contracting between the amount charged for the property and the value of that property measured by the price at which similar property was readily obtainable in similar transactions. A disparity between the contract price and the value of the property measured by the price at which similar property was readily obtainable in similar transactions does not, of itself, render the contract unconscionable.

§ 38-33.3-113, C.R.S. Obligation of good faith.

Every contract or duty governed by this article imposes an obligation of good faith in its performance or enforcement.

§ 38-33.3-114, C.R.S. Remedies to be liberally administered.

(1) The remedies provided by this article shall be liberally administered to the end that the aggrieved party is put in as good a position as if the other party had fully performed. However, consequential, special, or punitive damages may not be awarded except as specifically provided in this article or by other rule of law.

(2) Any right or obligation declared by this article is enforceable by judicial proceeding.

§ 38-33.3-115, C.R.S. Applicability to new common interest communities.

Except as provided in section 38-33.3-116, this article applies to all common interest communities created within this state on or after July 1, 1992. The provisions of sections 38-33-101 to 38-33-109 do not apply to common interest communities created on or after July 1, 1992. The provisions of sections 38-33-110 to 38-33-113 shall remain in effect for all common interest communities.

§ 38-33.3-116, C.R.S. Exception for new small cooperatives and small and limited expense planned communities.

(1) If a cooperative created in this state on or after July 1, 1992, but prior to July 1, 1998, contains only units restricted to nonresidential use or contains no more than ten units and is not subject to any development rights, it is subject only to sections 38-33.3-105 to 38-33.3-107, unless the declaration provides that this entire article is applicable. If a planned community created in this state on or after July 1, 1992, but prior to July 1, 1998, contains no more than ten units and is not subject to any development rights or if a planned community provides, in its declaration, that the annual average common expense liability of each unit restricted to residential purposes, exclusive of optional user fees and any insurance premiums paid by the association, may not exceed four hundred dollars, as adjusted pursuant to subsection (3) of this section, it is subject only to sections 38-33.3-105 to 38-33.3-107, unless the declaration provides that this entire article is applicable.

(2) If a cooperative or planned community created in this state on or after July 1, 1998, contains only units restricted to nonresidential use, or contains no more than twenty units and is not subject to any development rights, it is subject only to sections 38-33.3-105 to 38-33.3-107, unless the declaration provides that this entire article is applicable. If a planned community created in this state after July 1, 1998, provides, in its declaration, that the annual average common expense liability of each unit restricted to residential purposes, exclusive of optional user fees and any insurance premiums paid by the association, may not exceed four hundred dollars, as adjusted pursuant to subsection (3) of this section, it is subject only to sections 38-33.3-105 to 38-33.3-107, unless the declaration provides that this entire article is applicable.

(3) The dollar limitation set forth in subsections (1) and (2) of this section shall be increased annually on July 1, 1999, and on July 1 of each succeeding year in accordance with any increase in the United States department of labor bureau of labor statistics final consumer price index for the Denver-Boulder consolidated metropolitan statistical area for the preceding calendar year. The limitation shall not be increased if the final consumer price index for the preceding calendar year did not increase and shall not be decreased if the final consumer price index for the preceding calendar year decreased.

§ 38-33.3-116.3, C.R.S. Large planned communities – exemption from certain requirements.

(1) A planned community shall be exempt from the provisions of this article as specified in subsection (3) of this section or as specifically exempted in any other provision of this article, if, at the time of recording the affidavit required pursuant to subsection (2) of this section, the real estate upon which the planned community is created meets both of the following requirements:

- (a) It consists of at least two hundred acres;
- (b) It is approved for development of at least five hundred residential units, excluding any interval estates, time-share estates, or time-span estates but including any interval units created pursuant to sections 38-33-110 and 38-33-111, and at least twenty thousand square feet of commercial use.
- (c) (Deleted by amendment, L. 95, p. 236, § 2, effective July 1, 1995.)

(2) For an exemption authorized in subsection (1) of this section to apply, the property must be zoned within each county in which any part of such parcel is located, and the owner of the parcel shall record with the county clerk and recorder of each county in which any part of such parcel is located an affidavit setting forth the following:

(a) The legal description of such parcel of land;

(b) A statement that the party signing the affidavit is the owner of the parcel in its entirety in fee simple, excluding mineral interests;

(c) The acreage of the parcel;

(d) The zoning classification of the parcel, with a certified copy of applicable zoning regulations attached; and

(e) A statement that neither the owner nor any officer, director, shareholder, partner, or other entity having more than a ten-percent equity interest in the owner has been convicted of a felony within the last ten years.

(3) A large planned community for which an affidavit has been filed pursuant to subsection (2) of this section shall be exempt from the following provisions of this article:

(a) Section 38-33.3-205 (1) (e) to (1) (m);

(b) Section 38-33.3-207 (3);

(c) Section 38-33.3-208;

(d) Section 38-33.3-209 (2) (b) to (2) (d), (2) (f), (2) (g), (4), and (6);

(e) Section 38-33.3-210;

(f) Section 38-33.3-212;

(g) Section 38-33.3-213;

(h) Section 38-33.3-215;

(i) Section 38-33.3-217 (1);

(j) Section 38-33.3-304.

(4) Section 38-33.3-217 (4) shall be applicable as follows: Except to the extent expressly permitted or required by other provisions of this article, no amendment may create or increase special declarant rights, increase the number of units or the allocated interests of a unit, or the uses to which any unit is restricted, in the absence of unanimous consent of the unit owners.

(5) (a) The exemption authorized by this section shall continue for the large planned community so long as the owner signing the affidavit is the owner of the real estate described in subsection (2) of this section; except that:

(I) Upon the sale, conveyance, or other transfer of any portion of the real estate within the large planned community, the portion sold, conveyed, or transferred shall become subject to all the provisions of this article;

(II) Any common interest community created on some but not all of the real estate within the large planned community shall be created pursuant to this article; and

(III) When a planned community no longer qualifies as a large planned community, as described in subsection (1) of this section, the exemptions authorized by this section shall no longer be applicable.

(b) Notwithstanding the provisions of subparagraph (III) of paragraph (a) of this subsection (5), all real estate described in a recorded declaration creating a large planned community shall remain subject to such recorded declaration.

(6) The association established for a large planned community shall operate with respect to large planned community-wide matters and shall not otherwise operate as the exclusive unit owners' association with respect to any unit.

(7) The association established for a large planned community shall keep in its principal office and make reasonably available to all unit owners, unit owners' authorized agents, and prospective purchasers of units a complete legal description of all common elements within the large planned community.

§ 38-33.3-117, C.R.S. Applicability to preexisting common interest communities.

(1) Except as provided in section 38-33.3-119, the following sections apply to all common interest communities created within this state before July 1, 1992, with respect to events and circumstances occurring on or after July 1, 1992:

(a) 38-33.3-101 and 38-33.3-102;

(b) 38-33.3-103, to the extent necessary in construing any of the other sections of this article;

(c) 38-33.3-104 to 38-33.3-111;

(d) 38-33.3-114;

(e) 38-33.3-118;

(f) 38-33.3-120;

(g) 38-33.3-122 and 38-33.3-123;

(h) 38-33.3-203 and 38-33.3-217 (7);

(i) 38-33.3-302 (1)(a) to (1)(f), (1)(j) to (1)(m), and (1)(o) to (1)(q);

(i.5) 38-33.3-221.5;

(i.7) 38-33.3-303 (1)(b) and (3)(b);

(j) 38-33.3-311;

(k) 38-33.3-316;

(k.5) 38-33.3-316.3; and

(*l*) 38-33.3-317, as it existed prior to January 1, 2006, 38-33.3-318, and 38-33.3-319.

(1.5) Except as provided in section 38-33.3-119, the following sections apply to all common interest communities created within this state before July 1, 1992, with respect to events and circumstances occurring on or after January 1, 2006:

(a) (Deleted by amendment, L. 2006, p. 1217, §3, effective May 26, 2006.)

(b) 38-33.3-124;

(c) 38-33.3-209.4 to 38-33.3-209.7;

(d) 38-33.3-217 (1);

(e) (Deleted by amendment, L. 2006, p. 1217, §3, effective May 26, 2006.)

(f) 38-33.3-301;

(g) 38-33.3-302 (3) and (4);

(h) 38-33.3-303 (1)(b), (3)(b), and (4)(b);

(i) 38-33.3-308 (1), (2)(b), (2.5), and (4.5);

(j) 38-33.3-310 (1) and (2);

(k) 38-33.3-310.5;

(*l*) 38-33.3-315 (7);

(m) 38-33.3-317; and

(n) 38-33.3-401.

(1.7) Except as provided in section 38-33.3-119, section 38-33.3-209.5 (1)(b)(IX) shall apply to all common interest communities created within this state before July 1, 1992, with respect to events and circumstances occurring on or after July 1, 2010.

(1.8) Except as provided in section 38-33.3-119, section 38-33.3-303 (4)(a) applies to all common interest communities created within this state before July 1, 1992, with respect to events and circumstances occurring on or after July 1, 2017.

(1.9) Notwithstanding any other provision of law, section 38-33.3-303.5 applies to all common interest communities created within this state on, before, or after July 1, 1992, with respect to events and circumstances occurring on or after September 1, 2017.

(2) The sections specified in paragraphs (a) to (j) and (l) of subsection (1) of this section shall be applied and construed to establish a clear, comprehensive, and uniform framework for the operation and management of common interest communities within this state and to supplement the provisions of any declaration, bylaws, plat, or map in existence on June 30, 1992. Except for section 38-33.3-217 (7), in the event of specific conflicts between the provisions of the sections specified in paragraphs (a) to (j) and (l) of subsection (1) of this section, and express requirements or restrictions in a declaration, bylaws, a plat, or a map in existence on June 30, 1992, such requirements or restrictions in the declaration, bylaws, plat, or map shall control, but only to the extent necessary to avoid invalidation of the specific requirement or restriction in the declaration, bylaws, plat, or map. Sections 38-33.3-217 (7) and 38-33.3-316 shall be applied and construed as stated in such sections.

(3) Except as expressly provided for in this section, this article shall not apply to common interest communities created within this state before July 1, 1992.

(4) Section 38-33.3-308 (2) to (7) shall apply to all common interest communities created within this state before July 1, 1995, and shall apply to all meetings of the executive board of such a community or any committee thereof occurring on or after said date. In addition, said section 38-33.3-308 (2) to (7) shall apply to all common interest communities created on or after July 1, 1995, and shall apply to all meetings of the executive board of such a community or any committee thereof occurring on or after said date.

§ 38-33.3-118, C.R.S. Procedure to elect treatment under the "Colorado Common Interest Ownership Act".

(1) Any organization created prior to July 1, 1992, may elect to have the common interest community be treated as if it were created after June 30, 1992, and thereby subject the common interest community to all of the provisions contained in this article, in the following manner:

   (a) If there are members or stockholders entitled to vote thereon, the board of directors may adopt a resolution recommending that such association accept this article and directing that the question of acceptance be submitted to a vote at a meeting of the members or stockholders entitled to vote thereon, which may be either an annual or special meeting. The question shall also be submitted whenever one-twentieth, or, in the case of an association with over one thousand members, one-fortieth, of the members or stockholders entitled to vote thereon so request. Written notice stating that the purpose, or one of the purposes, of the meeting is to consider electing to be treated as a common interest community organized after June 30, 1992, and thereby accepting the provisions of this article, together with a copy of this article, shall be given to each person entitled to vote at the meeting within the time and in the manner provided in the articles of incorporation, declaration, bylaws, or other governing documents for such association for the giving of notice of meetings to members. Such election to accept the provisions of this article shall require for adoption at least sixty-seven percent of the votes that the persons present at such meeting in person or by proxy are entitled to cast.

   (b) If there are no persons entitled to vote thereon, the election to be treated as a common interest community under this article may be made at a meeting of the board of directors pursuant to a majority vote of the directors in office.

(2) A statement of election to accept the provisions of this article shall be executed and acknowledged by the president or vice-president and by the secretary or an assistant secretary of such association and shall set forth:

(a) The name of the common interest community and association;

(b) That the association has elected to accept the provisions of this article;

(c) That there were persons entitled to vote thereon, the date of the meeting of such persons at which the election was made to be treated as a common interest community under this article, that a quorum was present at the meeting, and that such acceptance was authorized by at least sixty-seven percent of the votes that the members or stockholders present at such meeting in person or by proxy were entitled to cast;

(d) That there were no members or stockholders entitled to vote thereon, the date of the meeting of the board of directors at which election to accept this article was made, that a quorum was present at the meeting, and that such acceptance was authorized by a majority vote of the directors present at such meeting;

(e) (Deleted by amendment, L. 93, p. 645, § 7, effective April 30, 1993.)

(f) The names and respective addresses of its officers and directors; and

(g) If there were no persons entitled to vote thereon but a common interest community has been created by virtue of compliance with section 38-33.3-103 (8), that the declarant desires for the common interest community to be subject to all the terms and provisions of this article.

(3) The original statement of election to be treated as a common interest community subject to the terms and conditions of this article shall be duly recorded in the office of the clerk and recorder for the county in which the common interest community is located.

(4) Upon the recording of the original statement of election to be treated as a common interest community subject to the provisions of this article, said common interest community shall be subject to all provisions of this article. Upon recording of the statement of election, such common interest community shall have the same powers and privileges and be subject to the same duties, restrictions, penalties, and liabilities as though it had been created after June 30, 1992.

(5) Notwithstanding any other provision of this section, and with respect to a common interest community making the election permitted by this section, this article shall apply only with respect to events and circumstances occurring on or after July 1, 1992, and does not invalidate provisions of any declaration, bylaws, or plats or maps in existence on June 30, 1992.

§ 38-33.3-119, C.R.S. Exception for small preexisting cooperatives and planned communities.

If a cooperative or planned community created within this state before July 1, 1992, contains no more than ten units and is not subject to any development rights, or if its declaration limits its annual common expense liability to the amount specified in section 38-33.3-116 (1), then it is subject only to sections 38-33.3-105 to 38-33.3-107 unless the declaration is amended in conformity with applicable law and with the procedures and requirements of the declaration to take advantage of the provisions of section 38-33.3-120, in which case all the sections enumerated in section 38-33.3-117 apply to that planned community.

§ 38-33.3-120, C.R.S. Amendments to preexisting governing instruments.

(1) In the case of amendments to the declaration, bylaws, or plats and maps of any common interest community created within this state before July 1, 1992, which has not elected treatment under this article pursuant to section 38-33.3-118:

(a) If the substantive result accomplished by the amendment was permitted by law in effect prior to July 1, 1992, the amendment may be made either in accordance with that law, in which case that law applies to that amendment, or it may be made under this article; and

(b) If the substantive result accomplished by the amendment is permitted by this article, and was not permitted by law in effect prior to July 1, 1992, the amendment may be made under this article.

(2) An amendment to the declaration, bylaws, or plats and maps authorized by this section to be made under this article must be adopted in conformity with the procedures and requirements of the law that applied to the common interest community at the time it was created and with the procedures and requirements specified by those instruments. If an amendment grants to any person any rights, powers, or privileges permitted by this article, all correlative obligations, liabilities, and restrictions in this article also apply to that person.

(3) An amendment to the declaration may also be made pursuant to the procedures set forth in section 38-33.3-217 (7).

§ 38-33.3-120.5, C.R.S. Extension of declaration term.

(1) If a common interest community has a declaration in effect with a limited term of years that was recorded prior to July 1, 1992, and if, before the term of the declaration expires, the unit owners in the common interest community have not amended the declaration pursuant to section 38-33.3-120 and in accordance with any conditions or fixed limitations described in the declaration, the declaration may be extended as provided in this section.

(2) The term of the declaration may be extended:

(a) If the executive board adopts a resolution recommending that the declaration be extended for a specific term not to exceed twenty years and directs that the question of extending the term of the declaration be submitted to the unit owners, as members of the association; and

(b) If an extension of the term of the declaration is approved by vote or agreement of unit owners of units to which at least sixty-seven percent of the votes in the association are allocated or any larger percentage the declaration specifies.

(3) Except for the extension of the term of a declaration as authorized by this section, no other provision of a declaration may be amended pursuant to the provisions of this section.

(4) For any meeting of unit owners at which a vote is to be taken on a proposed extension of the term of a declaration as provided in this section, the secretary or other officer specified in the bylaws shall provide written notice to each unit owner entitled to vote at the meeting stating that the purpose, or one of the purposes, of the meeting is to consider extending the term of the declaration. The notice shall be given in the time and manner specified in section 38-33.3-308 or in the articles of incorporation, declaration, bylaws, or other governing documents of the association.

(5) The extension of the declaration, if approved, shall be included in an amendment to the declaration and shall be executed, acknowledged, and recorded by the association in the records of the clerk and recorder of each county in which any portion of the common interest community is located. The amendment shall include:

(a) A statement of the name of the common interest community and the association;

(b) A statement that the association has elected to extend the term of the declaration pursuant to this section and the term of the approved extension;

(c) A statement that indicates that the executive board has adopted a resolution recommending that the declaration be extended for a specific term not to exceed twenty years, that sets forth the date of the meeting at which the unit owners elected to extend the term of the declaration, and that declares that the extension was authorized by a vote or agreement of unit owners of units to which at least sixty-seven percent of the votes in the association are allocated or any larger percentage the declaration specifies;

(d) A statement of the names and respective addresses of the officers and executive board members of the association.

(6) Upon the recording of the amendment required by subsection (5) of this section, and subject to the provisions of this section, a common interest community is subject to all provisions of the declaration, as amended.

§ 38-33.3-121, C.R.S. Applicability to nonresidential planned communities.

This article does not apply to a planned community in which all units are restricted exclusively to nonresidential use unless the declaration provides that the article does apply to that planned community. This article applies to a planned community containing both units that are restricted exclusively to nonresidential use and other units that are not so restricted, only if the declaration so provides or the real estate comprising the units that may be used for residential purposes would be a planned community in the absence of the units that may not be used for residential purposes.

§ 38-33.3-122, C.R.S. Applicability to out-of-state common interest communities.

This article does not apply to common interest communities or units located outside this state.

§ 38-33.3-123, C.R.S. Enforcement – limitation.

(1) (a) If any unit owner fails to timely pay assessments or any money or sums due to the association, the association may require reimbursement for collection costs and reasonable attorney fees and costs incurred as a result of such failure without the necessity of commencing a legal proceeding.

(b) For any failure to comply with the provisions of this article or any provision of the declaration, bylaws, articles, or rules and regulations, other than the payment of assessments or any money or sums due to the association, the association, any unit owner, or any class of unit owners adversely affected by the failure to comply may seek reimbursement for collection costs and reasonable attorney fees and costs incurred as a result of such failure to comply, without the necessity of commencing a legal proceeding.

(c) In any civil action to enforce or defend the provisions of this article or of the declaration, bylaws, articles, or rules and regulations, the court shall award reasonable attorney fees, costs, and costs of collection to the prevailing party.

(d) Notwithstanding paragraph (c) of this subsection (1), in connection with any claim in which a unit owner is alleged to have violated a provision of this article or of the declaration, bylaws, articles, or rules and regulations of the association and in which the court finds that the unit owner prevailed because the unit owner did not commit the alleged violation:

(I) The court shall award the unit owner reasonable attorney fees and costs incurred in asserting or defending the claim; and

(II) The court shall not award costs or attorney fees to the association. In addition, the association shall be precluded from allocating to the unit owner's account with the association any of the association's costs or attorney fees incurred in asserting or defending the claim.

(e) A unit owner shall not be deemed to have confessed judgment to attorney fees or collection costs.

(2) Notwithstanding any law to the contrary, no action shall be commenced or maintained to enforce the terms of any building restriction contained in the provisions of the declaration, bylaws, articles, or rules and regulations or to compel the removal of any building or

improvement because of the violation of the terms of any such building restriction unless the action is commenced within one year from the date from which the person commencing the action knew or in the exercise of reasonable diligence should have known of the violation for which the action is sought to be brought or maintained.

§ 38-33.3-124, C.R.S. Legislative declaration – alternative dispute resolution encouraged – policy statement required.

(1) (a) (I) The general assembly finds and declares that the cost, complexity, and delay inherent in court proceedings make litigation a particularly inefficient means of resolving neighborhood disputes. Therefore, common interest communities are encouraged to adopt protocols that make use of mediation or arbitration as alternatives to, or preconditions upon, the filing of a complaint between a unit owner and association in situations that do not involve an imminent threat to the peace, health, or safety of the community.

(II) The general assembly hereby specifically endorses and encourages associations, unit owners, managers, declarants, and all other parties to disputes arising under this article to agree to make use of all available public or private resources for alternative dispute resolution, including, without limitation, the resources offered by the office of dispute resolution within the Colorado judicial branch through its web site.

(b) On or before January 1, 2007, each association shall adopt a written policy setting forth its procedure for addressing disputes arising between the association and unit owners. The association shall make a copy of this policy available to unit owners upon request.

(2) (a) Any controversy between an association and a unit owner arising out of the provisions of this article may be submitted to mediation by agreement of the parties prior to the commencement of any legal proceeding.

(b) The mediation agreement, if one is reached, may be presented to the court as a stipulation. Either party to the mediation may terminate the mediation process without prejudice.

(c) If either party subsequently violates the stipulation, the other party may apply immediately to the court for relief.

(3) The declaration, bylaws, or rules of the association may specify situations in which disputes shall be resolved by binding arbitration under the uniform arbitration act, part 2 of article 22 of title 13, C.R.S., or by another means of alternative dispute resolution under the "Dispute Resolution Act", part 3 of article 22 of title 13, C.R.S.

A. Creation, Alteration, and Termination

§ 38-33.3-201, C.R.S. Creation of common interest communities.

(1) A common interest community may be created pursuant to this article only by recording a declaration executed in the same manner as a deed and, in a cooperative, by conveying the real estate subject to that declaration to the association. The declaration must be recorded in every county in which any portion of the common interest community is located and must be indexed in the grantee's index in the name of the common interest community and in the name of the association and in the grantor's index in the name of each person executing the declaration. No common interest community is created until the plat or map for the common interest community is recorded.

(2) In a common interest community with horizontal unit boundaries, a declaration, or an amendment to a declaration, creating or adding units shall include a certificate of completion executed by an independent licensed or registered engineer, surveyor, or architect stating that

all structural components of all buildings containing or comprising any units thereby created are substantially completed.

§ 38-33.3-202, C.R.S. Unit boundaries.

(1) Except as provided by the declaration:

(a) If walls, floors, or ceilings are designated as boundaries of a unit, all lath, furring, wallboard, plasterboard, plaster, paneling, tiles, wallpaper, paint, and finished flooring and any other materials constituting any part of the finished surfaces thereof are a part of the unit, and all other portions of the walls, floors, or ceilings are a part of the common elements.

(b) If any chute, flue, duct, wire, conduit, bearing wall, bearing column, or other fixture lies partially within and partially outside the designated boundaries of a unit, any portion thereof serving only that unit is a limited common element allocated solely to that unit, and any portion thereof serving more than one unit or any portion of the common elements is a part of the common elements.

(c) Subject to the provisions of paragraph (b) of this subsection (1), all spaces, interior partitions, and other fixtures and improvements within the boundaries of a unit are a part of the unit.

(d) Any shutters, awnings, window boxes, doorsteps, stoops, porches, balconies, and patios and all exterior doors and windows or other fixtures designed to serve a single unit, but located outside the unit's boundaries, are limited common elements allocated exclusively to that unit.

§ 38-33.3-203, C.R.S. Construction and validity of declaration and bylaws.

(1) All provisions of the declaration and bylaws are severable.

(2) The rule against perpetuities does not apply to defeat any provision of the declaration, bylaws, or rules and regulations.

(3) In the event of a conflict between the provisions of the declaration and the bylaws, the declaration prevails, except to the extent the declaration is inconsistent with this article.

(4) Title to a unit and common elements is not rendered unmarketable or otherwise affected by reason of an insubstantial failure of the declaration to comply with this article. Whether a substantial failure impairs marketability is not affected by this article.

§ 38-33.3-204, C.R.S. Description of units.

A description of a unit may set forth the name of the common interest community, the recording data for the declaration, the county in which the common interest community is located, and the identifying number of the unit. Such description is a legally sufficient description of that unit and all rights, obligations, and interests appurtenant to that unit which were created by the declaration or bylaws. It shall not be necessary to use the term "unit" as a part of a legally sufficient description of a unit.

§ 38-33.3-205, C.R.S. Contents of declaration.

(1) The declaration must contain:

(a) The names of the common interest community and the association and a statement that the common interest community is a condominium, cooperative, or planned community;

(b) The name of every county in which any part of the common interest community is situated;

(c) A legally sufficient description of the real estate included in the common interest community;

(d) A statement of the maximum number of units that the declarant reserves the right to create;

(e) In a condominium or planned community, a description, which may be by plat or map, of the boundaries of each unit created by the declaration, including the unit's identifying number; or, in a cooperative, a description, which may be by plat or map, of each unit created by the declaration, including the unit's identifying number, its size or number of rooms, and its location within a building if it is within a building containing more than one unit;

(f) A description of any limited common elements, other than those specified in section 38-33.3-202 (1) (b) and (1) (d) or shown on the map as provided in section 38-33.3-209 (2) (j) and, in a planned community, any real estate that is or must become common elements;

(g) A description of any real estate, except real estate subject to development rights, that may be allocated subsequently as limited common elements, other than limited common elements specified in section 38-33.3-202 (1) (b) and (1) (d), together with a statement that they may be so allocated;

(h) A description of any development rights and other special declarant rights reserved by the declarant, together with a description sufficient to identify the real estate to which each of those rights applies and the time limit within which each of those rights must be exercised;

(i) If any development right may be exercised with respect to different parcels of real estate at different times, a statement to that effect together with:

   (I) Either a statement fixing the boundaries of those portions and regulating the order in which those portions may be subjected to the exercise of each development right or a statement that no assurances are made in those regards; and

   (II) A statement as to whether, if any development right is exercised in any portion of the real estate subject to that development right, that development right must be exercised in all or in any other portion of the remainder of that real estate;

(j) Any other conditions or limitations under which the rights described in paragraph (h) of this subsection (1) may be exercised or will lapse;

(k) An allocation to each unit of the allocated interests in the manner described in section 38-33.3-207;

(*l*) Any restrictions on the use, occupancy, and alienation of the units and on the amount for which a unit may be sold or on the amount that may be received by a unit owner on sale, condemnation, or casualty loss to the unit or to the common interest community or on termination of the common interest community;

(m) The recording data for recorded easements and licenses appurtenant to, or included in, the common interest community or to which any portion of the common interest community is or may become subject by virtue of a reservation in the declaration;

(n) All matters required by sections 38-33.3-201, 38-33.3-206 to 38-33.3-209, 38-33.3-215, 38-33.3-216, and 38-33.3-303 (4);

(o) Reasonable provisions concerning the manner in which notice of matters affecting the common interest community may be given to unit owners by the association or other unit owners;

(p) A statement, if applicable, that the planned community is a large planned community and is exercising certain exemptions from the "Colorado Common Interest Ownership Act" as such a large planned community;

(q) In a large planned community:

(I) A general description of every common element that the declarant is legally obligated to construct within the large planned community together with the approximate date by which each such common element is to be completed. The declarant shall be required to complete each such common element within a reasonable time after the date specified in the declaration, unless the declarant, due to an act of God, is unable to do so. The declarant shall not be legally obligated with respect to any common element not identified in the declaration.

(II) A general description of the type of any common element that the declarant anticipates may be constructed by, maintained by, or operated by the association. The association shall not assess members for the construction, maintenance, or operation of any common element that is not described pursuant to this subparagraph (II) unless such assessment is approved by the vote of a majority of the votes entitled to be cast in person or by proxy, other than by declarant, at a meeting duly convened as required by law.

(2) The declaration may contain any other matters the declarant considers appropriate.

(3) The plats and maps described in section 38-33.3-209 may contain certain information required to be included in the declaration by this section.

(4) A declarant may amend the declaration, a plat, or a map to correct clerical, typographical, or technical errors.

(5) A declarant may amend the declaration to comply with the requirements, standards, or guidelines of recognized secondary mortgage markets, the department of housing and urban development, the federal housing administration, the veterans administration, the federal home loan mortgage corporation, the government national mortgage association, or the federal national mortgage association.

§ 38-33.3-206, C.R.S. Leasehold common interest communities.

(1) Any lease, the expiration or termination of which may terminate the common interest community or reduce its size, must be recorded. In a leasehold condominium or leasehold planned community, the declaration must contain the signature of each lessor of any such lease in order for the provisions of this section to be effective. The declaration must state:

(a) The recording data for the lease;

(b) The date on which the lease is scheduled to expire;

(c) A legally sufficient description of the real estate subject to the lease;

(d) Any rights of the unit owners to redeem the reversion and the manner whereby those rights may be exercised or state that they do not have those rights;

(e) Any rights of the unit owners to remove any improvements within a reasonable time after the expiration or termination of the lease or state that they do not have those rights; and

(f) Any rights of the unit owners to renew the lease and the conditions of any renewal or state that they do not have those rights.

(2) After the declaration for a leasehold condominium or leasehold planned community is recorded, neither the lessor nor the lessor's successor in interest may terminate the leasehold interest of a unit owner who makes timely payment of a unit owner's share of the rent and otherwise complies with all covenants which, if violated, would entitle the lessor to terminate

the lease. A unit owner's leasehold interest in a condominium or planned community is not affected by failure of any other person to pay rent or fulfill any other covenant.

(3) Acquisition of the leasehold interest of any unit owner by the owner of the reversion or remainder does not merge the leasehold and fee simple interests unless the leasehold interests of all unit owners subject to that reversion or remainder are acquired.

(4) If the expiration or termination of a lease decreases the number of units in a common interest community, the allocated interests shall be reallocated in accordance with section 38-33.3-107 (1), as though those units had been taken by eminent domain. Reallocations shall be confirmed by an amendment to the declaration prepared, executed, and recorded by the association.

§ 38-33.3-207, C.R.S. Allocation of allocated interests.

(1) The declaration must allocate to each unit:

  (a) In a condominium, a fraction or percentage of undivided interests in the common elements and in the common expenses of the association and, to the extent not allocated in the bylaws of the association, a portion of the votes in the association;

  (b) In a cooperative, an ownership interest in the association, a fraction or percentage of the common expenses of the association, and, to the extent not allocated in the bylaws of the association, a portion of the votes in the association;

  (c) In a planned community, a fraction or percentage of the common expenses of the association and, to the extent not allocated in the bylaws of the association, a portion of the votes in the association; except that, in a large planned community, the common expenses of the association may be paid from assessments and allocated as set forth in the declaration and the votes in the association may be allocated as set forth in the declaration.

(2) The declaration must state the formulas used to establish allocations of interests. Those allocations may not discriminate in favor of units owned by the declarant or an affiliate of the declarant.

(3) If units may be added to or withdrawn from the common interest community, the declaration must state the formulas to be used to reallocate the allocated interests among all units included in the common interest community after the addition or withdrawal.

(4) (a) The declaration may provide:

    (I) That different allocations of votes shall be made to the units on particular matters specified in the declaration;

    (II) For cumulative voting only for the purpose of electing members of the executive board;

    (III) For class voting on specified issues affecting the class, including the election of the executive board; and

    (IV) For assessments including, but not limited to, assessments on retail sales and services not to exceed six percent of the amount charged for the retail sale or service, and real estate transfers not to exceed three percent of the real estate sales price or its equivalent.

  (b) A declarant may not utilize cumulative or class voting for the purpose of evading any limitation imposed on declarants by this article, nor may units constitute a class because they are owned by a declarant.

  (c) Assessments allowed under subparagraph (IV) of paragraph (a) of this subsection (4) shall be entitled to the lien provided for under section 38-33.3-316 (1) but shall not be entitled to the priority established by section 38-33.3-316 (2) (b).

(d) Communities with classes for voting specified in the declaration as allowed pursuant to subparagraph (III) of paragraph (a) of this subsection (4) may designate classes of members on a reasonable basis which do not allow the declarant to control the association beyond the period provided for in section 38-33.3-303, including, without limitation, residence owners, commercial space owners, and owners of lodging space and to elect members to the association executive board from such classes.

(5) Except for minor variations due to the rounding of fractions or percentages, the sum of the common expense liabilities and, in a condominium, the sum of the undivided interests in the common elements allocated at any time to all the units shall each equal one if stated as fractions or one hundred percent if stated as percentages. In the event of discrepancy between an allocated interest and the result derived from application of the pertinent formula, the allocated interest prevails.

(6) In a condominium, the common elements are not subject to partition except as allowed for in section 38-33.3-312, and any purported conveyance, encumbrance, judicial sale, or other voluntary or involuntary transfer of an undivided interest in the common elements not allowed for in section 38-33.3-312, that is made without the unit to which that interest is allocated is void.

(7) In a cooperative, any purported conveyance, encumbrance, judicial sale, or other voluntary or involuntary transfer of an ownership interest in the association made without the possessory interest in the unit to which that interest is related is void.

§ 38-33.3-208, C.R.S. Limited common elements.

(1) Except for the limited common elements described in section 38-33.3-202 (1) (b) and (1) (d), the declaration shall specify to which unit or units each limited common element is allocated. That allocation may not be altered without the consent of the unit owners whose units are affected.

(2) Subject to any provisions of the declaration, a limited common element may be reallocated between or among units after compliance with the procedure set forth in this subsection (2). In order to reallocate limited common elements between or among units, the unit owners of those units, as the applicants, must submit an application for approval of the proposed reallocation to the executive board, which application shall be executed by those unit owners and shall include:

(a) The proposed form for an amendment to the declaration as may be necessary to show the reallocation of limited common elements between or among units;

(b) A deposit against attorney fees and costs which the association will incur in reviewing and effectuating the application, in an amount reasonably estimated by the executive board; and

(c) Such other information as may be reasonably requested by the executive board. No reallocation shall be effective without the approval of the executive board. The reallocation shall be effectuated by an amendment signed by the association and by those unit owners between or among whose units the reallocation is made, which amendment shall be recorded as provided in section 38-33.3-217 (3). All costs and attorney fees incurred by the association as a result of the application shall be the sole obligation of the applicants.

(3) A common element not previously allocated as a limited common element may be so allocated only pursuant to provisions in the declaration made in accordance with section 38-33.3-205 (1) (g). The allocations must be made by amendments to the declaration prepared, executed, and recorded by the declarant.

§ 38-33.3-209, C.R.S. Plats and maps.

(1) A plat or map is a part of the declaration and is required for all common interest communities except cooperatives. A map is required only for a common interest community with units having a horizontal boundary. The requirements of this section shall be deemed satisfied so long as all of the information required by this section is contained in the declaration, a map or a plat, or some combination of any two or all of the three. Each plat or map must be clear and legible. When a map is required under any provision of this article, the map, a plat, or the declaration shall contain a certification that all information required by this section is contained in the declaration, the map or a plat, or some combination of any two or all of the three.

(2) In addition to meeting the requirements of a land survey plat as set forth in section 38-51-106, each map shall show the following, except to the extent such information is contained in the declaration or on a plat:

- (a) The name and a general schematic plan of the entire common interest community;
- (b) The location and dimensions of all real estate not subject to development rights, or subject only to the development right to withdraw, and the location and dimensions of all existing improvements within that real estate;
- (c) A legally sufficient description, which may be of the whole common interest community or any portion thereof, of any real estate subject to development rights and a description of the rights applicable to such real estate;
- (d) The extent of any existing encroachments across any common interest community boundary;
- (e) To the extent feasible, a legally sufficient description of all easements serving or burdening any portion of the common interest community;
- (f) The location and dimensions of the vertical boundaries of each unit and that unit's identifying number;
- (g) The location, with reference to established data, of the horizontal boundaries of each unit and that unit's identifying number;
- (g.5) Any units in which the declarant has reserved the right to create additional units or common elements, identified appropriately;
- (h) A legally sufficient description of any real estate in which the unit owners will own only an estate for years;
- (i) The distance between noncontiguous parcels of real estate comprising the common interest community; and
- (j) The approximate location and dimensions of limited common elements, including porches, balconies, and patios, other than the limited common elements described in section 38-33.3-202 (1) (b) and (1) (d).

(3) (Deleted by amendment, L. 93, p. 648, § 12, effective April 30, 1993.)

(4) (Deleted by amendment, L. 2007, p. 1799, § 1, effective July 1, 2007.)

(5) Unless the declaration provides otherwise, the horizontal boundaries of any part of a unit located outside of a building have the same elevation as the horizontal boundaries of the inside part and need not be depicted on the plats and maps.

(6) Upon exercising any development right, the declarant shall record an amendment to the declaration with respect to that real estate reflecting change as a result of such exercise necessary to conform to the requirements of subsections (1), (2), and (4) of this section or new certifications of maps previously recorded if those maps otherwise conform to the requirements of subsections (1), (2), and (4) of this section.

(7) Any certification of a map required by this article must be made by a registered land surveyor.

(8) The requirements of a plat or map under this article shall not be deemed to satisfy any subdivision platting requirement enacted by a county or municipality pursuant to section 30-28-133, C.R.S., part 1 of article 23 of title 31, C.R.S., or a similar provision of a home rule city, nor shall the plat or map requirements under this article be deemed to be incorporated into any subdivision platting requirements enacted by a county or municipality.

(9) Any plat or map that was recorded on or after July 1, 1998, but prior to July 1, 2007, and that satisfies the requirements of this section in effect on July 1, 2007, is deemed to have satisfied the requirements of this section at the time it was recorded.

§ 38-33.3-209.4, C.R.S. Public disclosures required – identity of association – agent – manager – contact information.

(1) Within ninety days after assuming control from the declarant pursuant to section 38-33.3-303 (5), the association shall make the following information available to unit owners upon reasonable notice in accordance with subsection (3) of this section. In addition, if the association's address, designated agent, or management company changes, the association shall make updated information available within ninety days after the change:

(a) The name of the association;

* (b) The name of the association's designated agent or management company, if any;

(c) A valid physical address and telephone number for both the association and the designated agent or management company, if any;

(d) The name of the common interest community;

(e) The initial date of recording of the declaration; and

(f) The reception number or book and page for the main document that constitutes the declaration.

(2) Within ninety days after assuming control from the declarant pursuant to section 38-33.3-303 (5), and within ninety days after the end of each fiscal year thereafter, the association shall make the following information available to unit owners upon reasonable notice in accordance with subsection (3) of this section:

(a) The date on which its fiscal year commences;

(b) Its operating budget for the current fiscal year;

(c) A list, by unit type, of the association's current assessments, including both regular and special assessments;

(d) Its annual financial statements, including any amounts held in reserve for the fiscal year immediately preceding the current annual disclosure;

(e) The results of its most recent available financial audit or review;

(f) A list of all association insurance policies, including, but not limited to, property, general liability, association director and officer professional liability, and fidelity policies. Such list shall include the company names, policy limits, policy deductibles, additional named insureds, and expiration dates of the policies listed.

(g) All the association's bylaws, articles, and rules and regulations;

(h) The minutes of the executive board and member meetings for the fiscal year immediately preceding the current annual disclosure; and

(i) The association's responsible governance policies adopted under section 38-33.3-209.5.

(3) It is the intent of this section to allow the association the widest possible latitude in methods and means of disclosure, while requiring that the information be readily available at no cost to unit owners at their convenience. Disclosure shall be accomplished by one of the following means: Posting on an internet web page with accompanying notice of the web address via first-

class mail or e-mail; the maintenance of a literature table or binder at the association's principal place of business; or mail or personal delivery. The cost of such distribution shall be accounted for as a common expense liability.

(4) Notwithstanding section 38-33.3-117 (1.5) (c), this section shall not apply to a unit, or the owner thereof, if the unit is a time-share unit, as defined in section 38-33-110 (7).

§ 38-33.3-209.5, C.R.S. Responsible governance policies – due process for imposition of fines.

(1) To promote responsible governance, associations shall:

(a) Maintain accurate and complete accounting records; and

(b) Adopt policies, procedures, and rules and regulations concerning:

(I) Collection of unpaid assessments;

(II) Handling of conflicts of interest involving board members, which policies, procedures, and rules and regulations must include, at a minimum, the criteria described in subsection (4) of this section;

(III) Conduct of meetings, which may refer to applicable provisions of the nonprofit code or other recognized rules and principles;

(IV) Enforcement of covenants and rules, including notice and hearing procedures and the schedule of fines;

(V) Inspection and copying of association records by unit owners;

(VI) Investment of reserve funds;

(VII) Procedures for the adoption and amendment of policies, procedures, and rules;

(VIII) Procedures for addressing disputes arising between the association and unit owners; and

(IX) When the association has a reserve study prepared for the portions of the community maintained, repaired, replaced, and improved by the association; whether there is a funding plan for any work recommended by the reserve study and, if so, the projected sources of funding for the work; and whether the reserve study is based on a physical analysis and financial analysis. For the purposes of this subparagraph (IX), an internally conducted reserve study shall be sufficient.

(2) Notwithstanding any provision of the declaration, bylaws, articles, or rules and regulations to the contrary, the association may not fine any unit owner for an alleged violation unless:

(a) The association has adopted, and follows, a written policy governing the imposition of fines; and

(b) (I) The policy includes a fair and impartial fact-finding process concerning whether the alleged violation actually occurred and whether the unit owner is the one who should be held responsible for the violation. This process may be informal but shall, at a minimum, guarantee the unit owner notice and an opportunity to be heard before an impartial decision maker.

(II) As used in this paragraph (b), "impartial decision maker" means a person or group of persons who have the authority to make a decision regarding the enforcement of the association's covenants, conditions, and restrictions, including its architectural requirements, and the other rules and regulations of the association and do not have any direct personal or financial interest in the outcome. A decision maker shall not be deemed to have a direct personal or financial interest in the outcome if the decision maker will not, as a result of the outcome, receive any greater benefit or detriment than will the general membership of the association.

(3) If, as a result of the fact finding process described in subsection (2) of this section, it is determined that the unit owner should not be held responsible for the alleged violation, the association shall not allocate to the unit owner's account with the association any of the association's costs or attorney fees incurred in asserting or hearing the claim. Notwithstanding any provision in the declaration, bylaws, or rules and regulations of the association to the contrary, a unit owner shall not be deemed to have consented to pay such costs or fees.

(4) (a) The policies, procedures, and rules and regulations adopted by an association under subparagraph (II) of paragraph (b) of subsection (1) of this section must, at a minimum:

(I) Define or describe the circumstances under which a conflict of interest exists;

(II) Set forth procedures to follow when a conflict of interest exists, including how, and to whom, the conflict of interest must be disclosed and whether a board member must recuse himself or herself from discussing or voting on the issue; and

(III) Provide for the periodic review of the association's conflict of interest policies, procedures, and rules and regulations.

(b) The policies, procedures, or rules and regulations adopted under this subsection (4) must be in accordance with section 38-33.3-310.5.

(5) (a) Notwithstanding any provision of the declaration, bylaws, articles, or rules and regulations to the contrary or the absence of a relevant provision in the declaration, bylaws, articles, or rules or regulations, the association or a holder or assignee of the association's debt, whether the holder or assignee of the association's debt is an entity or a natural person, may not use a collection agency or take legal action to collect unpaid assessments unless the association or a holder or assignee of the association's debt has adopted, and follows, a written policy governing the collection of unpaid assessments. The policy must, at a minimum, specify:

(I) The date on which assessments must be paid to the entity and when an assessment is considered past due and delinquent;

(II) Any late fees and interest the entity is entitled to impose on a delinquent unit owner's account;

(III) Any returned-check charges the entity is entitled to impose;

(IV) The circumstances under which a unit owner is entitled to enter into a payment plan with the entity pursuant to section 38-33.3-316.3 and the minimum terms of the payment plan mandated by that section;

(V) That, before the entity turns over a delinquent account of a unit owner to a collection agency or refers it to an attorney for legal action, the entity must send the unit owner a notice of delinquency specifying:

(A) The total amount due, with an accounting of how the total was determined;

(B) Whether the opportunity to enter into a payment plan exists pursuant to section 38-33.3-316.3 and instructions for contacting the entity to enter into such a payment plan;

(C) The name and contact information for the individual the unit owner may contact to request a copy of the unit owner's ledger in order to verify the amount of the debt; and

(D) That action is required to cure the delinquency and that failure to do so within thirty days may result in the unit owner's delinquent account being turned over to a collection agency, a lawsuit being filed against the owner, the filing and foreclosure of a lien against the unit owner's property, or other remedies available under Colorado law;

(VI) The method by which payments may be applied on the delinquent account of a unit owner; and

(VII) The legal remedies available to the entity to collect on a unit owner's delinquent account pursuant to the governing documents of the entity and Colorado law.

(b) As used in this subsection (5), "entity" means an association or a holder or assignee of the association's debt, whether the holder or assignee of the association's debt is an entity or a natural person.

§ 38-33.3-209.6, C.R.S. Executive board member education.

The board may authorize, and account for as a common expense, reimbursement of board members for their actual and necessary expenses incurred in attending educational meetings and seminars on responsible governance of unit owners' associations. The course content of such educational meetings and seminars shall be specific to Colorado, and shall make reference to applicable sections of this article.

§ 38-33.3-209.7, C.R.S. Owner education.

(1) The association shall provide, or cause to be provided, education to owners at no cost on at least an annual basis as to the general operations of the association and the rights and responsibilities of owners, the association, and its executive board under Colorado law. The criteria for compliance with this section shall be determined by the executive board.

(2) Notwithstanding section 38-33.3-117 (1.5) (c), this section shall not apply to an association that includes time-share units, as defined in section 38-33-110 (7).

§ 38-33.3-210, C.R.S. Exercise of development rights.

(1) To exercise any development right reserved under section 38-33.3-205 (1) (h), the declarant shall prepare, execute, and record an amendment to the declaration and, in a condominium or planned community, comply with the provisions of section 38-33.3-209. The declarant is the unit owner of any units thereby created. The amendment to the declaration must assign an identifying number to each new unit created and, except in the case of subdivision or conversion of units described in subsection (3) of this section, reallocate the allocated interests among all units. The amendment must describe any common elements and any limited common elements thereby created and, in the case of limited common elements, designate the unit to which each is allocated to the extent required by section 38-33.3-208.

(2) Additional development rights not previously reserved may be reserved within any real estate added to the common interest community if the amendment adding that real estate includes all matters required by section 38-33.3-205 or 38-33.3-206, as the case may be, and, in a condominium or planned community, the plats and maps include all matters required by section 38-33.3-209. This provision does not extend the time limit on the exercise of development rights imposed by the declaration pursuant to section 38-33.3-205 (1) (h).

(3) Whenever a declarant exercises a development right to subdivide or convert a unit previously created into additional units, common elements, or both:

(a) If the declarant converts the unit entirely to common elements, the amendment to the declaration must reallocate all the allocated interests of that unit among the other units as if that unit had been taken by eminent domain; and

(b) If the declarant subdivides the unit into two or more units, whether or not any part of the unit is converted into common elements, the amendment to the declaration must reallocate all the allocated interests of the unit among the units created by the subdivision in any reasonable manner prescribed by the declarant.

(4) If the declaration provides, pursuant to section 38-33.3-205, that all or a portion of the real estate is subject to a right of withdrawal:

(a) If all the real estate is subject to withdrawal, and the declaration does not describe separate portions of real estate subject to that right, none of the real estate may be withdrawn after a unit has been conveyed to a purchaser; and

(b) If any portion of the real estate is subject to withdrawal, it may not be withdrawn after a unit in that portion has been conveyed to a purchaser.

(5) If a declarant fails to exercise any development right within the time limit and in accordance with any conditions or fixed limitations described in the declaration pursuant to section 38-33.3-205 (1) (h), or records an instrument surrendering a development right, that development right shall lapse unless the association, upon the request of the declarant or the owner of the real estate subject to development right, agrees to an extension of the time period for exercise of the development right or a reinstatement of the development right subject to whatever terms, conditions, and limitations the association may impose on the subsequent exercise of the development right. The extension or renewal of the development right and any terms, conditions, and limitations shall be included in an amendment executed by the declarant or the owner of the real estate subject to development right and the association.

§ 38-33.3-211, C.R.S. Alterations of units.

(1) Subject to the provisions of the declaration and other provisions of law, a unit owner:

(a) May make any improvements or alterations to his unit that do not impair the structural integrity, electrical systems, or mechanical systems or lessen the support of any portion of the common interest community;

(b) May not change the appearance of the common elements without permission of the association; or

(c) After acquiring an adjoining unit or an adjoining part of an adjoining unit, may remove or alter any intervening partition or create apertures therein, even if the partition in whole or in part is a common element, if those acts do not impair the structural integrity, electrical systems, or mechanical systems or lessen the support of any portion of the common interest community. Removal of partitions or creation of apertures under this paragraph (c) is not an alteration of boundaries.

§ 38-33.3-212, C.R.S. Relocation of boundaries between adjoining units.

(1) Subject to the provisions of the declaration and other provisions of law, and pursuant to the procedures described in section 38-33.3-217, the boundaries between adjoining units may be relocated by an amendment to the declaration upon application to the association by the owners of those units.

(2) In order to relocate the boundaries between adjoining units, the owners of those units, as the applicant, must submit an application to the executive board, which application shall be executed by those owners and shall include:

(a) Evidence sufficient to the executive board that the applicant has complied with all local rules and ordinances and that the proposed relocation of boundaries does not violate the terms of any document evidencing a security interest;

(b) The proposed reallocation of interests, if any;

(c) The proposed form for amendments to the declaration, including the plats or maps, as may be necessary to show the altered boundaries between adjoining units, and their dimensions and identifying numbers;

(d) A deposit against attorney fees and costs which the association will incur in reviewing and effectuating the application, in an amount reasonably estimated by the executive board; and

(e) Such other information as may be reasonably requested by the executive board.

(3) No relocation of boundaries between adjoining units shall be effected without the necessary amendments to the declaration, plats, or maps, executed and recorded pursuant to section 38-33.3-217 (3) and (5).

(4) All costs and attorney fees incurred by the association as a result of an application shall be the sole obligation of the applicant.

§ 38-33.3-213, C.R.S. Subdivision of units.

(1) If the declaration expressly so permits, a unit may be subdivided into two or more units. Subject to the provisions of the declaration and other provisions of law, and pursuant to the procedures described in this section, a unit owner may apply to the association to subdivide a unit.

(2) In order to subdivide a unit, the unit owner of such unit, as the applicant, must submit an application to the executive board, which application shall be executed by such owner and shall include:

(a) Evidence that the applicant of the proposed subdivision shall have complied with all building codes, fire codes, zoning codes, planned unit development requirements, master plans, and other applicable ordinances or resolutions adopted and enforced by the local governing body and that the proposed subdivision does not violate the terms of any document evidencing a security interest encumbering the unit;

(b) The proposed reallocation of interests, if any;

(c) The proposed form for amendments to the declaration, including the plats or maps, as may be necessary to show the units which are created by the subdivision and their dimensions, and identifying numbers;

(d) A deposit against attorney fees and costs which the association will incur in reviewing and effectuating the application, in an amount reasonably estimated by the executive board; and

(e) Such other information as may be reasonably requested by the executive board.

(3) No subdivision of units shall be effected without the necessary amendments to the declaration, plats, or maps, executed and recorded pursuant to section 38-33.3-217 (3) and (5).

(4) All costs and attorney fees incurred by the association as a result of an application shall be the sole obligation of the applicant.

§ 38-33.3-214, C.R.S. Easement for encroachments.

To the extent that any unit or common element encroaches on any other unit or common element, a valid easement for the encroachment exists. The easement does not relieve a unit owner of liability in case of willful misconduct nor relieve a declarant or any other person of liability for failure to adhere to the plats and maps.

§ 38-33.3-215, C.R.S. Use for sales purposes.

A declarant may maintain sales offices, management offices, and models in the common interest community only if the declaration so provides. Except as provided in a declaration, any real estate in a common interest community used as a sales office, management office, or model and not designated a unit by the declaration is a common element. If a declarant ceases to be a unit owner, such declarant ceases to have any rights with regard to any real estate used as a sales office, management office, or model, unless it is removed promptly from the common interest community in accordance with a right to remove reserved in the declaration. Subject to any limitations in the declaration, a declarant may maintain signs on the common elements advertising the common interest community. This section is subject to the provisions of other state laws and to local ordinances.

§ 38-33.3-216, C.R.S. Easement rights.

(1) Subject to the provisions of the declaration, a declarant has an easement through the common elements as may be reasonably necessary for the purpose of discharging a declarant's obligations or exercising special declarant rights, whether arising under this article or reserved in the declaration.

(2) In a planned community, subject to the provisions of the declaration and the ability of the association to regulate and convey or encumber the common elements as set forth in sections 38-33.3-302 (1) (f) and 38-33.3-312, the unit owners have an easement:

(a) In the common elements for the purpose of access to their units; and

(b) To use the common elements and all other real estate that must become common elements for all other purposes.

§ 38-33.3-217, C.R.S. Amendment of declaration.

(1) (a) (I) Except as otherwise provided in subparagraphs (II) and (III) of this paragraph (a), the declaration, including the plats and maps, may be amended only by the affirmative vote or agreement of unit owners of units to which more than fifty percent of the votes in the association are allocated or any larger percentage, not to exceed sixty-seven percent, that the declaration specifies. Any provision in the declaration that purports to specify a percentage larger than sixty-seven percent is hereby declared void as contrary to public policy, and until amended, such provision shall be deemed to specify a percentage of sixty-seven percent. The declaration may specify a smaller percentage than a simple majority only if all of the units are restricted exclusively to nonresidential use. Nothing in this paragraph (a) shall be construed to prohibit the association from seeking a court order, in accordance with subsection (7) of this section, to reduce the required percentage to less than sixty-seven percent.

(II) If the declaration provides for an initial period of applicability to be followed by automatic extension periods, the declaration may be amended at any time in accordance with subparagraph (I) of this paragraph (a).

(III) This paragraph (a) shall not apply:

(A) To the extent that its application is limited by subsection (4) of this section;

(B) To amendments executed by a declarant under section 38-33.3-205 (4) and (5), 38-33.3-208 (3), 38-33.3-209 (6), 38-33.3-210, or 38-33.3-222;

(C) To amendments executed by an association under section 38-33.3-107, 38-33.3-206 (4), 38-33.3-208 (2), 38-33.3-212, 38-33.3-213, or 38-33.3-218 (11) and (12);

(D) To amendments executed by the district court for any county that includes all or any portion of a common interest community under subsection (7) of this section; or

(E) To amendments that affect phased communities or declarant-controlled communities.

(b) (I) If the declaration requires first mortgagees to approve or consent to amendments, but does not set forth a procedure for registration or notification of first mortgagees, the association may:

(A) Send a dated, written notice and a copy of any proposed amendment by certified mail to each first mortgagee at its most recent address as shown on the recorded deed of trust or recorded assignment thereof; and

(B) Cause the dated notice, together with information on how to obtain a copy of the proposed amendment, to be printed in full at least twice, on separate occasions at least one week apart, in a newspaper of general circulation in the county in which the common interest community is located.

(II) A first mortgagee that does not deliver to the association a negative response within sixty days after the date of the notice specified in subparagraph (I) of this paragraph (b) shall be deemed to have approved the proposed amendment.

(III) The notification procedure set forth in this paragraph (b) is not mandatory. If the consent of first mortgagees is obtained without resort to this paragraph (b), and otherwise in accordance with the declaration, the notice to first mortgagees shall be considered sufficient.

(2) No action to challenge the validity of an amendment adopted by the association pursuant to this section may be brought more than one year after the amendment is recorded.

(3) Every amendment to the declaration must be recorded in every county in which any portion of the common interest community is located and is effective only upon recordation. An amendment must be indexed in the grantee's index in the name of the common interest community and the association and in the grantor's index in the name of each person executing the amendment.

(4) (a) Except to the extent expressly permitted or required by other provisions of this article, no amendment may create or increase special declarant rights, increase the number of units, or change the boundaries of any unit or the allocated interests of a unit in the absence of a vote or agreement of unit owners of units to which at least sixty-seven percent of the votes in the association, including sixty-seven percent of the votes allocated to units not owned by a declarant, are allocated or any larger percentage the declaration specifies. The declaration may specify a smaller percentage only if all of the units are restricted exclusively to nonresidential use.

(b) The sixty-seven-percent maximum percentage stated in paragraph (a) of subsection (1) of this section shall not apply to any common interest community in which one unit owner, by virtue of the declaration, bylaws, or other governing documents of the association, is allocated sixty-seven percent or more of the votes in the association.

(4.5) Except to the extent expressly permitted or required by other provisions of this article, no amendment may change the uses to which any unit is restricted in the absence of a vote or agreement of unit owners of units to which at least sixty-seven percent of the votes in the association are allocated or any larger percentage the declaration specifies. The declaration may specify a smaller percentage only if all of the units are restricted exclusively to nonresidential use.

(5) Amendments to the declaration required by this article to be recorded by the association shall be prepared, executed, recorded, and certified on behalf of the association by any officer of the association designated for that purpose or, in the absence of designation, by the president of the association.

(6) All expenses associated with preparing and recording an amendment to the declaration shall be the sole responsibility of:

(a) In the case of an amendment pursuant to sections 38-33.3-208 (2), 38-33.3-212, and 38-33.3-213, the unit owners desiring the amendment; and

(b) In the case of an amendment pursuant to section 38-33.3-208 (3), 38-33.3-209 (6), or 38-33.3-210, the declarant; and

(c) In all other cases, the association.

(7) (a) The association, acting through its executive board pursuant to section 38-33.3-303 (1), may petition the district court for any county that includes all or any portion of the common interest community for an order amending the declaration of the common interest community if:

(I) The association has twice sent notice of the proposed amendment to all unit owners that are entitled by the declaration to vote on the proposed amendment or are required for approval of the proposed amendment by any means allowed pursuant to the provisions regarding notice to members in sections 7-121-402 and 7-127-104, C.R.S., of the "Colorado Revised Nonprofit Corporation Act", articles 121 to 137 of title 7, C.R.S.;

(II) The association has discussed the proposed amendment during at least one meeting of the association; and

(III) Unit owners of units to which are allocated more than fifty percent of the number of consents, approvals, or votes of the association that would be required to adopt the proposed amendment pursuant to the declaration have voted in favor of the proposed amendment.

(b) A petition filed pursuant to paragraph (a) of this subsection (7) shall include:

(I) A summary of:

(A) The procedures and requirements for amending the declaration that are set forth in the declaration;

(B) The proposed amendment to the declaration;

(C) The effect of and reason for the proposed amendment, including a statement of the circumstances that make the amendment necessary or advisable;

(D) The results of any vote taken with respect to the proposed amendment; and

(E) Any other matters that the association believes will be useful to the court in deciding whether to grant the petition; and

(II) As exhibits, copies of:

(A) The declaration as originally recorded and any recorded amendments to the declaration;

(B) The text of the proposed amendment;

(C) Copies of any notices sent pursuant to subparagraph (I) of paragraph (a) of this subsection (7); and

(D) Any other documents that the association believes will be useful to the court in deciding whether to grant the petition.

(c) Within three days of the filing of the petition, the district court shall set a date for hearing the petition. Unless the court finds that an emergency requires an immediate hearing, the hearing shall be held no earlier than forty-five days and no later than sixty days after the date the association filed the petition.

(d) No later than ten days after the date for hearing a petition is set pursuant to paragraph (c) of this subsection (7), the association shall:

(I) Send notice of the petition by any written means allowed pursuant to the provisions regarding notice to members in sections 7-121-402 and 7-127-104, C.R.S., of the "Colorado Revised Nonprofit Corporation Act", articles 121 to 137 of title 7, C.R.S., to any unit owner, by first-class mail, postage prepaid or by hand delivery to any declarant, and by first-class mail, postage prepaid, to any lender that holds a security interest in one or more units and is entitled by the declaration or any underwriting guidelines or requirements of that lender or of the federal national mortgage association, the federal home loan mortgage corporation, the federal housing administration, the veterans administration, or the government national mortgage corporation to vote on the proposed amendment. The notice shall include:

(A) A copy of the petition which need not include the exhibits attached to the original petition filed with the district court;

(B) The date the district court will hear the petition; and

(C) A statement that the court may grant the petition and order the proposed amendment to the declaration unless any declarant entitled by the declaration to vote on the proposed amendment, the federal housing administration, the veterans administration, more than thirty-three percent of the unit owners entitled by the declaration to vote on the proposed amendment, or more than thirty-three percent of the lenders that hold a security interest in one or more units and are entitled by the declaration to vote on the proposed amendment file written objections to the proposed amendment with the court prior to the hearing;

(II) File with the district court:

(A) A list of the names and mailing addresses of declarants, unit owners, and lenders that hold a security interest in one or more units and that are entitled by the declaration to vote on the proposed amendment; and

(B) A copy of the notice required by subparagraph (I) of this paragraph (d).

(e) The district court shall grant the petition after hearing if it finds that:

(I) The association has complied with all requirements of this subsection (7);

(II) No more than thirty-three percent of the unit owners entitled by the declaration to vote on the proposed amendment have filed written objections to the proposed amendment with the court prior to the hearing;

(III) Neither the federal housing administration nor the veterans administration is entitled to approve the proposed amendment, or if so entitled has not filed written objections to the proposed amendment with the court prior to the hearing;

(IV) Either the proposed amendment does not eliminate any rights or privileges designated in the declaration as belonging to a declarant or no declarant has filed written objections to the proposed amendment with the court prior to the hearing;

(V) Either the proposed amendment does not eliminate any rights or privileges designated in the declaration as belonging to any lenders that hold security interests in one or more units and that are entitled by the declaration to vote on the proposed amendment or no more than thirty-three percent of such lenders have filed written objections to the proposed amendment with the court prior to the hearing; and

(VI) The proposed amendment would neither terminate the declaration nor change the allocated interests of the unit owners as specified in the declaration, except as allowed pursuant to section 38-33.3-315.

(f) Upon granting a petition, the court shall enter an order approving the proposed amendment and requiring the association to record the amendment in each county that includes all or any portion of the common interest community. Once recorded, the amendment shall have the same legal effect as if it were adopted pursuant to any requirements set forth in the declaration.

§ 38-33.3-218, C.R.S. Termination of common interest community.

(1) Except in the case of a taking of all the units by eminent domain, or in the case of foreclosure against an entire cooperative of a security interest that has priority over the declaration, a common interest community may be terminated only by agreement of unit owners of units to which at least sixty-seven percent of the votes in the association are allocated or any larger percentage the declaration specifies. The declaration may specify a smaller percentage only if all of the units in the common interest community are restricted exclusively to nonresidential uses.

(1.5) No planned community that is required to exist pursuant to a development or site plan shall be terminated by agreement of unit owners, unless a copy of the termination agreement is sent by certified mail or hand delivered to the governing body of every municipality in which a portion of the planned community is situated or, if the planned community is situated in an unincorporated area, to the board of county commissioners for every county in which a portion of the planned community is situated.

(2) An agreement of unit owners to terminate must be evidenced by their execution of a termination agreement or ratifications thereof in the same manner as a deed, by the requisite number of unit owners. The termination agreement must specify a date after which the agreement will be void unless it is recorded before that date. A termination agreement and all ratifications thereof must be recorded in every county in which a portion of the common interest community is situated and is effective only upon recordation.

(3) In the case of a condominium or planned community containing only units having horizontal boundaries described in the declaration, a termination agreement may provide that all of the common elements and units of the common interest community must be sold following termination. If, pursuant to the agreement, any real estate in the common interest community is to be sold following termination, the termination agreement must set forth the minimum terms of the sale.

(4) In the case of a condominium or planned community containing any units not having horizontal boundaries described in the declaration, a termination agreement may provide for sale of the common elements, but it may not require that the units be sold following termination, unless the declaration as originally recorded provided otherwise or all the unit owners consent to the sale.

(5) Subject to the provisions of a termination agreement described in subsections (3) and (4) of this section, the association, on behalf of the unit owners, may contract for the sale of real estate in a common interest community following termination, but the contract is not binding on the unit owners until approved pursuant to subsections (1) and (2) of this section. If any real estate is to be sold following termination, title to that real estate, upon termination, vests in the association as trustee for the holders of all interests in the units. Thereafter, the association has all the powers necessary and appropriate to effect the sale. Until thc sale has been concluded and the proceeds thereof distributed, the association continues in existence with all the powers it had before termination. Proceeds of the sale must be distributed to unit owners and lienholders as their interests may appear, in accordance with subsections (8), (9), and (10) of this section, taking into account the value of property owned or distributed that is not sold so as to preserve the proportionate interests of each unit owner with respect to all property cumulatively. Unless otherwise specified in the termination agreement, as long as the association holds title to the real estate, each unit owner and the unit owner's successors in interest have an exclusive right to occupancy of the portion of the real estate that formerly constituted the unit. During the period of that occupancy, each unit owner and the unit owner's successors in interest remain liable for all assessments and other obligations imposed on unit owners by this article or the declaration.

(6) (a) In a planned community, if all or a portion of the common elements are not to be sold following termination, title to the common elements not sold vests in the unit owners upon termination as tenants in common in fractional interests that maintain, after taking into account the fair market value of property owned and the proceeds of property sold, their respective interests as provided in subsection (10) of this section with respect to all property appraised under said subsection (10), and liens on the units shift accordingly.

(b) In a common interest community, containing units having horizontal boundaries described in the declaration, title to the units not to be sold following termination vests in the unit owners upon termination as tenants in common in fractional interests that maintain, after taking into account the fair market value of property owned and the proceeds of property sold, their respective interests as provided in subsection (10) of this section with respect to all property appraised under said subsection (10), and liens on the units shift accordingly. While the tenancy in common exists, each unit owner and the unit owner's successors in interest have an exclusive right to occupancy of the portion of the real estate that formerly constituted such unit.

(7) Following termination of the common interest community, the proceeds of any sale of real estate, together with the assets of the association, are held by the association as trustee for unit owners and holders of liens on the units as their interests may appear.

(8) Upon termination of a condominium or planned community, creditors of the association who obtain a lien and duly record it in every county in which any portion of the common interest community is located are to be treated as if they had perfected liens on the units immediately before termination or when the lien is obtained and recorded, whichever is later.

(9) In a cooperative, the declaration may provide that all creditors of the association have priority over any interests of unit owners and creditors of unit owners. In that event, upon termination, creditors of the association who obtain a lien and duly record it in every county in which any portion of the cooperative is located are to be treated as if they had perfected liens against the cooperative immediately before termination or when the lien is obtained and recorded, whichever is later. Unless the declaration provides that all creditors of the association have that priority:

(a) The lien of each creditor of the association which was perfected against the association before termination becomes, upon termination, a lien against each unit owner's interest in the unit as of the date the lien was perfected;

(b) Any other creditor of the association who obtains a lien and duly records it in every county in which any portion of the cooperative is located is to be treated upon termination as if the creditor had perfected a lien against each unit owner's interest immediately before termination or when the lien is obtained and recorded, whichever is later;

(c) The amount of the lien of an association's creditor described in paragraphs (a) and (b) of this subsection (9) against each unit owner's interest must be proportionate to the ratio which each unit's common expense liability bears to the common expense liability of all of the units;

(d) The lien of each creditor of each unit owner which was perfected before termination continues as a lien against that unit owner's unit as of the date the lien was perfected; and

(e) The assets of the association must be distributed to all unit owners and all lienholders as their interests may appear in the order described above. Creditors of the association are not entitled to payment from any unit owner in excess of the amount of the creditor's lien against that unit owner's interest.

(10) The respective interests of unit owners referred to in subsections (5) to (9) of this section are as follows:

(a) Except as provided in paragraph (b) of this subsection (10), the respective interests of unit owners are the combined fair market values of their units, allocated interests, any limited common elements, and, in the case of a planned community, any tenant in common interest, immediately before the termination, as determined by one or more independent appraisers selected by the association. The decision of the independent appraisers shall be distributed to the unit owners and becomes final unless disapproved within thirty days after distribution by unit owners of units to which twenty-five percent of the votes in the association are allocated. The proportion of any unit owner's interest to that of all unit owners is determined by dividing the fair market value of that unit owner's unit and its allocated interests by the total fair market values of all the units and their allocated interests.

(b) If any unit or any limited common element is destroyed to the extent that an appraisal of the fair market value thereof prior to destruction cannot be made, the interests of all unit owners are:

(I) In a condominium, their respective common element interests immediately before the termination;

(II) In a cooperative, their respective ownership interests immediately before the termination; and

(III) In a planned community, their respective common expense liabilities immediately before the termination.

(11) In a condominium or planned community, except as provided in subsection (12) of this section, foreclosure or enforcement of a lien or encumbrance against the entire common interest community does not terminate, of itself, the common interest community. Foreclosure or enforcement of a lien or encumbrance against a portion of the common interest community other than withdrawable real estate does not withdraw that portion from the common interest community. Foreclosure or enforcement of a lien or encumbrance against withdrawable real estate does not withdraw, of itself, that real estate from the common interest community, but the person taking title thereto may require from the association, upon request, an amendment to the declaration excluding the real estate from the common interest community prepared, executed, and recorded by the association.

(12) In a condominium or planned community, if a lien or encumbrance against a portion of the real estate comprising the common interest community has priority over the declaration and the lien or encumbrance has not been partially released, the parties foreclosing the lien or encumbrance, upon foreclosure, may record an instrument excluding the real estate subject to that lien or encumbrance from the common interest community. The board of directors shall reallocate interests as if the foreclosed section were taken by eminent domain by an amendment to the declaration prepared, executed, and recorded by the association.

§ 38-33.3-219, C.R.S. Rights of secured lenders.

(1) The declaration may require that all or a specified number or percentage of the lenders who hold security interests encumbering the units approve specified actions of the unit owners or the association as a condition to the effectiveness of those actions, but no requirement for approval may operate to:

(a) Deny or delegate control over the general administrative affairs of the association by the unit owners or the executive board; or

(b) Prevent the association or the executive board from commencing, intervening in, or settling any solicitation or proceeding; or

(c) Prevent any insurance trustee or the association from receiving and distributing any insurance proceeds pursuant to section 38-33.3-313.

§ 38-33.3-220, C.R.S. Master associations.

(1) If the declaration provides that any of the powers of a unit owners' association described in section 38-33.3-302 are to be exercised by or may be delegated to a master association, all provisions of this article applicable to unit owners' associations apply to any such master association except as modified by this section.

(2) Unless it is acting in the capacity of an association described in section 38-33.3-301, a master association may exercise the powers set forth in section 38-33.3-302 (1) (b) only to the extent such powers are expressly permitted to be exercised by a master association in the declarations of common interest communities which are part of the master association or expressly described in the delegations of power from those common interest communities to the master association.

(3) If the declaration of any common interest community provides that the executive board may delegate certain powers to a master association, the members of the executive board have no liability for the acts or omissions of the master association with respect to those powers following delegation.

(4) The rights and responsibilities of unit owners with respect to the unit owners' association set forth in sections 38-33.3-303, 38-33.3-308, 38-33.3-309, 38-33.3-310, and 38-33.3-312 apply in the conduct of the affairs of a master association only to persons who elect the board of a master association, whether or not those persons are otherwise unit owners within the meaning of this article.

(5) Even if a master association is also an association described in section 38-33.3-301, the articles of incorporation and the declaration of each common interest community, the powers of which are assigned by the declaration or delegated to the master association, must provide that the executive board of the master association be elected after the period of declarant control, if any, in one of the following ways:

  (a) All unit owners of all common interest communities subject to the master association may elect all members of the master association's executive board.

  (b) All members of the executive boards of all common interest communities subject to the master association may elect all members of the master association's executive board.

  (c) All unit owners of each common interest community subject to the master association may elect specified members of the master association's executive board.

  (d) All members of the executive board of each common interest community subject to the master association may elect specified members of the master association's executive board.

§ 38-33.3-221, C.R.S. Merger or consolidation of common interest communities.

(1) Any two or more common interest communities of the same form of ownership, by agreement of the unit owners as provided in subsection (2) of this section, may be merged or consolidated into a single common interest community. In the event of a merger or consolidation, unless the agreement otherwise provides, the resultant common interest community is the legal successor, for all purposes, of all of the preexisting common interest communities, and the operations and activities of all associations of the preexisting common interest communities are merged or consolidated into a single association that holds all powers, rights, obligations, assets, and liabilities of all preexisting associations.

(2) An agreement of two or more common interest communities to merge or consolidate pursuant to subsection (1) of this section must be evidenced by an agreement prepared, executed, recorded, and certified by the president of the association of each of the preexisting common interest communities following approval by owners of units to which are allocated the percentage of votes in each common interest community required to terminate that common

interest community. The agreement must be recorded in every county in which a portion of the common interest community is located and is not effective until recorded.

(3) Every merger or consolidation agreement must provide for the reallocation of the allocated interests in the new association among the units of the resultant common interest community either by stating the reallocations or the formulas upon which they are based.

§ 38-33.3-221.5, C.R.S. Withdrawal from merged common interest community

(1) A common interest community that was merged or consolidated with another common interest community, or is party to an agreement to do so pursuant to section 38-33.3-221, may withdraw from the merged or consolidated common interest community or terminate the agreement to merge or consolidate, without the consent of the other common interest community or communities involved, if the common interest community wishing to withdraw meets all of the following criteria:

(a) It is a separate, platted subdivision;

(b) Its unit owners are required to pay into two common interest communities or separate unit owners' associations;

(c) It is or has been a self-operating common interest community or association continuously for at least twenty-five years;

(d) The total number of unit owners comprising it is fifteen percent or less of the total number of unit owners in the merged or consolidated common interest community or association;

(e) Its unit owners have approved the withdrawal by a majority vote and the owners of units representing at least seventy-five percent of the allocated interests in the common interest community wishing to withdraw participated in the vote; and

(f) Its withdrawal would not substantially impair the ability of the remainder of the merged common interest community or association to:

(I) Enforce existing covenants;

(II) Maintain existing facilities; or

(III) Continue to exist.

(2) If an association has met the requirements set forth in subsection (1) of this section, it shall be considered withdrawn as of the date of the election at which its unit owners voted to withdraw.

§ 38-33.3-222, C.R.S. Addition of unspecified real estate.

In a common interest community, if the right is originally reserved in the declaration, the declarant, in addition to any other development right, may amend the declaration at any time during as many years as are specified in the declaration to add additional real estate to the common interest community without describing the location of that real estate in the original declaration; but the area of real estate added to the common interest community pursuant to this section may not exceed ten percent of the total area of real estate described in section 38-33.3-205 (1) (c) and (1) (h), and the declarant may not in any event increase the number of units in the common interest community beyond the number stated in the original declaration pursuant to section 38-33.3-205 (1) (d), except as provided in section 38-33.3-217 (4).

§ 38-33.3-223, C.R.S. Sale of unit – disclosure to buyer. (Repealed)

§ 38-33.3-301, C.R.S. Organization of unit owners' association.

A unit owners' association shall be organized no later than the date the first unit in the common interest community is conveyed to a purchaser. The membership of the association at all times shall consist exclusively of all unit owners or, following termination of the common interest community, of all former unit owners entitled to distributions of proceeds under section 38-33.3-218, or their heirs, personal representatives, successors, or assigns. The association shall be organized as a nonprofit, not-for-profit, or for-profit corporation or as a limited liability company in accordance with the laws of the state of Colorado; except that the failure of the association to incorporate or organize as a limited liability company will not adversely affect either the existence of the common interest community for purposes of this article or the rights of persons acting in reliance upon such existence, other than as specifically provided in section 38-33.3-316. Neither the choice of entity nor the organizational structure of the association shall be deemed to affect its substantive rights and obligations under this article.

§ 38-33.3-302, C.R.S. Powers of unit owners' association.

(1) Except as provided in subsections (2) and (3) of this section, and subject to the provisions of the declaration, the association, without specific authorization in the declaration, may:

(a) Adopt and amend bylaws and rules and regulations;

(b) Adopt and amend budgets for revenues, expenditures, and reserves and collect assessments for common expenses from unit owners;

(c) Hire and terminate managing agents and other employees, agents, and independent contractors;

(d) Institute, defend, or intervene in litigation or administrative proceedings in its own name on behalf of itself or two or more unit owners on matters affecting the common interest community;

(e) Make contracts and incur liabilities;

(f) Regulate the use, maintenance, repair, replacement, and modification of common elements;

(g) Cause additional improvements to be made as a part of the common elements;

(h) Acquire, hold, encumber, and convey in its own name any right, title, or interest to real or personal property, subject to the following exceptions:

(I) Common elements in a condominium or planned community may be conveyed or subjected to a security interest only pursuant to section 38-33.3-312; and

(II) Part of a cooperative may be conveyed, or all or part of a cooperative may be subjected to a security interest, only pursuant to section 38-33.3-312;

(i) Grant easements, leases, licenses, and concessions through or over the common elements;

(j) Impose and receive any payments, fees, or charges for the use, rental, or operation of the common elements other than limited common elements described in section 38-33.3-202 (1) (b) and (1) (d);

(k) (I) Impose charges for late payment of assessments, recover reasonable attorney fees and other legal costs for collection of assessments and other actions to enforce the power of the association, regardless of whether or not suit was initiated, and, after notice and an opportunity to be heard, levy reasonable fines for violations of the declaration, bylaws, and rules and regulations of the association.

(II) The association may not levy fines against a unit owner for violations of declarations, bylaws, or rules of the association for failure to adequately water landscapes or vegetation for which the unit owner is responsible when water restrictions or guidelines from the local water district or similar entity are in place and the unit owner is watering in compliance with such restrictions or guidelines. The association may require proof from the unit owner that the unit owner is watering the landscape or vegetation in a manner that is consistent with the maximum watering permitted by the restrictions or guidelines then in effect.

(*l*) Impose reasonable charges for the preparation and recordation of amendments to the declaration or statements of unpaid assessments;

(m) Provide for the indemnification of its officers and executive board and maintain directors' and officers' liability insurance;

(n) Assign its right to future income, including the right to receive common expense assessments, but only to the extent the declaration expressly so provides;

(o) Exercise any other powers conferred by the declaration or bylaws;

(p) Exercise all other powers that may be exercised in this state by legal entities of the same type as the association; and

(q) Exercise any other powers necessary and proper for the governance and operation of the association.

(2) The declaration may not impose limitations on the power of the association to deal with the declarant that are more restrictive than the limitations imposed on the power of the association to deal with other persons.

(3) (a) Any managing agent, employee, independent contractor, or other person acting on behalf of the association shall be subject to this article to the same extent as the association itself would be.

(b) Decisions concerning the approval or denial of a unit owner's application for architectural or landscaping changes shall be made in accordance with standards and procedures set forth in the declaration or in duly adopted rules and regulations or bylaws of the association, and shall not be made arbitrarily or capriciously.

(4) (a) The association's contract with a managing agent shall be terminable for cause without penalty to the association. Any such contract shall be subject to renegotiation.

(b) Notwithstanding section 38-33.3-117 (1.5) (g), this subsection (4) shall not apply to an association that includes time-share units, as defined in section 38-33-110 (7).

§ 38-33.3-303, C.R.S. Executive board members and officers – powers and duties – reserve funds – reserve study – audit.

(1) (a) Except as provided in the declaration, the bylaws, or subsection (3) of this section or any other provisions of this article, the executive board may act in all instances on behalf of the association.

(b) Notwithstanding any provision of the declaration or bylaws to the contrary, all members of the executive board shall have available to them all information related to the responsibilities and operation of the association obtained by any other member of the executive board. This information shall include, but is not necessarily limited to, reports of detailed monthly expenditures, contracts to which the association is a party, and copies of communications, reports, and opinions to and from any member of the executive board or any managing agent, attorney, or accountant employed or engaged by the executive board to whom the executive board delegates responsibilities under this article.

(2) Except as otherwise provided in subsection (2.5) of this section:

(a) If appointed by the declarant, in the performance of their duties, the officers and members of the executive board are required to exercise the care required of fiduciaries of the unit owners.

(b) If not appointed by the declarant, no member of the executive board and no officer shall be liable for actions taken or omissions made in the performance of such member's duties except for wanton and willful acts or omissions.

(2.5) With regard to the investment of reserve funds of the association, the officers and members of the executive board shall be subject to the standards set forth in section 7-128-401, C.R.S.; except that, as used in that section:

(a) "Corporation" or "nonprofit corporation" means the association.

(b) "Director" means a member of the association's executive board.

(c) "Officer" means any person designated as an officer of the association and any person to whom the executive board delegates responsibilities under this article, including, without limitation, a managing agent, attorney, or accountant employed by the executive board.

(3) (a) The executive board may not act on behalf of the association to amend the declaration, to terminate the common interest community, or to elect members of the executive board or determine the qualifications, powers and duties, or terms of office of executive board members, but the executive board may fill vacancies in its membership for the unexpired portion of any term.

(b) Committees of the association shall be appointed pursuant to the governing documents of the association or, if the governing documents contain no applicable provisions, pursuant to section 7-128-206, C.R.S. The person appointed after August 15, 2009, to preside over any such committee shall meet the same qualifications as are required by the governing documents of the association for election or appointment to the executive board of the association.

(4) (a) (I) Within ninety days after adoption of a proposed budget for the common interest community, the executive board shall mail, by first-class mail, or otherwise deliver, including posting the proposed budget on the association's website, a summary of the budget to all the unit owners and shall set a date for a meeting of the unit owners to consider the budget. The meeting must occur within a reasonable time after mailing or other delivery of the summary, or as allowed for in the bylaws. The executive board shall give notice to the unit owners of the meeting as allowed for in the bylaws.

(II) (A) Unless the declaration requires otherwise, the budget proposed by the executive board does not require approval from the unit owners and it will be deemed approved by the unit owners in the absence of a veto at the noticed meeting by a majority of all unit owners, or if permitted in the declaration, a majority of a class of unit owners, or any larger percentage specified in the declaration, whether or not a quorum is present. If the proposed budget is vetoed, the periodic budget last proposed by the executive board and not vetoed by the unit owners must be continued until a subsequent budget proposed by the executive board is not vetoed by the unit owners.

(B) This subsection (4)(a)(II) shall not apply to any common interest community formed prior to July 1, 1992, if the declaration sets a maximum assessment amount or limits the increase in an annual budget to a specific amount and the budget proposed by the executive board does not exceed the maximum amount or limits set in the declaration.

(b) (I) At the discretion of the executive board or upon request pursuant to subparagraph (II) or (III) of this paragraph (b) as applicable, the books and records of the association shall be subject to an audit, using generally accepted auditing standards, or a review, using statements on standards for accounting and review services, by an independent and qualified person selected by the board. Such person need not be a certified public accountant except in the case of an audit. A person selected to conduct a review shall have at least a basic understanding of the principles of accounting as a result of prior business experience, education above the high school level, or bona fide home study. The audit or review report shall cover the association's financial statements, which shall be prepared using generally accepted accounting principles or the cash or tax basis of accounting.

(II) An audit shall be required under this paragraph (b) only when both of the following conditions are met:

(A) The association has annual revenues or expenditures of at least two hundred fifty thousand dollars; and

(B) An audit is requested by the owners of at least one-third of the units represented by the association.

(III) A review shall be required under this paragraph (b) only when requested by the owners of at least one-third of the units represented by the association.

(IV) Copies of an audit or review under this paragraph (b) shall be made available upon request to any unit owner beginning no later than thirty days after its completion.

(V) Notwithstanding section 38-33.3-117 (1.5) (h), this paragraph (b) shall not apply to an association that includes time-share units, as defined in section 38-33-110 (7).

(5) (a) Subject to subsection (6) of this section:

(I) The declaration, except a declaration for a large planned community, may provide for a period of declarant control of the association, during which period a declarant, or persons designated by such declarant, may appoint and remove the officers and members of the executive board. Regardless of the period of declarant control provided in the declaration, a period of declarant control terminates no later than the earlier of sixty days after conveyance of seventy-five percent of the units that may be created to unit owners other than a declarant, two years after the last conveyance of a unit by the declarant in the ordinary course of business, or two years after any right to add new units was last exercised.

(II) The declaration for a large planned community may provide for a period of declarant control of the association during which period a declarant, or persons designated by such declarant, may appoint and remove the officers and members of the executive board. Regardless of the period of declarant control provided in the declaration, a period of declarant control terminates in a large planned community no later than the earlier of sixty days after conveyance of seventy-five percent of the maximum number of units that may be created under zoning or other governmental development approvals in effect for the large planned community at any given time to unit owners other than a declarant, six years after the last conveyance of a unit by the declarant in the ordinary course of business, or twenty years after recordation of the declaration.

(b) A declarant may voluntarily surrender the right to appoint and remove officers and members of the executive board before termination of the period of declarant control, but, in that event, the declarant may require, for the duration of the period of declarant control, that specified actions of the association or executive board, as described in a recorded instrument executed by the declarant, be approved by the declarant before they become effective.

(c) If a period of declarant control is to terminate in a large planned community pursuant to subparagraph (II) of paragraph (a) of this subsection (5), the declarant, or persons designated by the declarant, shall no longer have the right to appoint and remove the officers and members of the executive board unless, prior to the termination date, the association approves an extension of the declarant's ability to appoint and remove no more than a majority of the executive board by vote of a majority of the votes entitled to be cast in person or by proxy, other than by the declarant, at a meeting duly convened as required by law. Any such approval by the association may contain conditions and limitations. Such extension of declarant's appointment and removal power, together with any conditions and limitations approved as provided in this paragraph (c), shall be included in an amendment to the declaration previously executed by the declarant.

(6) Not later than sixty days after conveyance of twenty-five percent of the units that may be created to unit owners other than a declarant, at least one member and not less than twenty-five percent of the members of the executive board must be elected by unit owners other than the declarant. Not later than sixty days after conveyance of fifty percent of the units that may be created to unit owners other than a declarant, not less than thirty-three and one-third percent of the members of the executive board must be elected by unit owners other than the declarant.

(7) Except as otherwise provided in section 38-33.3-220 (5), not later than the termination of any period of declarant control, the unit owners shall elect an executive board of at least three members, at least a majority of whom must be unit owners other than the declarant or designated representatives of unit owners other than the declarant. The executive board shall elect the officers. The executive board members and officers shall take office upon election.

(8) Notwithstanding any provision of the declaration or bylaws to the contrary, the unit owners, by a vote of sixty-seven percent of all persons present and entitled to vote at any meeting of the unit owners at which a quorum is present, may remove any member of the executive board with or without cause, other than a member appointed by the declarant or a member elected pursuant to a class vote under section 38-33.3-207 (4).

(9) Within sixty days after the unit owners other than the declarant elect a majority of the members of the executive board, the declarant shall deliver to the association all property of the unit owners and of the association held by or controlled by the declarant, including without limitation the following items:

(a) The original or a certified copy of the recorded declaration as amended, the association's articles of incorporation, if the association is incorporated, bylaws, minute books, other books and records, and any rules and regulations which may have been promulgated;

(b) An accounting for association funds and financial statements, from the date the association received funds and ending on the date the period of declarant control ends. The financial statements shall be audited by an independent certified public accountant and shall be accompanied by the accountant's letter, expressing either the opinion that the financial statements present fairly the financial position of the association in conformity with generally accepted accounting principles or a disclaimer of the accountant's ability to attest to the fairness of the presentation of the financial information in conformity with generally accepted accounting principles and the reasons therefor. The expense of the audit shall not be paid for or charged to the association.

(c) The association funds or control thereof;

(d) All of the declarant's tangible personal property that has been represented by the declarant to be the property of the association or all of the declarant's tangible personal property that is necessary for, and has been used exclusively in, the operation and enjoyment of the common elements, and inventories of these properties;

(e) A copy, for the nonexclusive use by the association, of any plans and specifications used in the construction of the improvements in the common interest community;

(f) All insurance policies then in force, in which the unit owners, the association, or its directors and officers are named as insured persons;

(g) Copies of any certificates of occupancy that may have been issued with respect to any improvements comprising the common interest community;

(h) Any other permits issued by governmental bodies applicable to the common interest community and which are currently in force or which were issued within one year prior to the date on which unit owners other than the declarant took control of the association;

(i) Written warranties of the contractor, subcontractors, suppliers, and manufacturers that are still effective;

(j) A roster of unit owners and mortgagees and their addresses and telephone numbers, if known, as shown on the declarant's records;

(k) Employment contracts in which the association is a contracting party;

(*l*) Any service contract in which the association is a contracting party or in which the association or the unit owners have any obligation to pay a fee to the persons performing the services; and

(m) For large planned communities, copies of all recorded deeds and all recorded and unrecorded leases evidencing ownership or leasehold rights of the large planned community unit owners' association in all common elements within the large planned community.

§ 38-33.3-303.5, C.R.S. Construction defect actions – disclosure – approval by unit owners – definitions – exemptions.

(1) (a) Before the executive board, pursuant to section 38-33.3-302 (1)(d), institutes a construction defect action, the executive board shall comply with this section.

(b) For the purposes of this section only:

(I) "Construction defect action":

(A) Means any civil action or arbitration proceeding for damages, indemnity, subrogation, or contribution brought against a construction professional to assert a claim, counterclaim, cross-claim, or third-party claim for damages or loss to, or the loss of use of, real or personal property or personal injury caused by a defect in the design or construction of an improvement to real property, regardless of the theory of liability; and

(B) Includes any related, ancillary, or derivative claim, and any claim for breach of fiduciary duty or an act or omission of a member of an association's executive board, that arises from an alleged construction defect or that seeks the same or similar damages.

(II) "Construction professional" has the meaning set forth in section 13-20-802.5 (4).

(c) **Meeting to consider commencement of construction defect action – disclosures – required terms.**

(I) The executive board shall mail or deliver written notice of the anticipated commencement of the construction defect action to each unit owner at the owner's last-known address described in the association's records and to the last-known address of each construction professional against whom a construction defect action is proposed; except that this notice requirement does not apply to:

(A) Construction professionals identified after the notice is mailed; or

(B) Joined parties in a construction defect action previously approved by owners pursuant to subsection (1)(d) of this section.

(II) The notice given pursuant to this subsection (1)(c) must call a meeting of the unit owners, which must be held no less than ten days and no more than fifteen days after the mailing date of the notice, to consider whether to bring a construction defect action. A failure to hold the meeting within this time period voids the subsequent vote. A quorum is not required at the meeting. In no event shall the time period for providing the notice required pursuant to subsection (1)(c)(I) of this section, holding the meeting required pursuant to this subsection (1)(c)(II), and voting as required by subsection (1)(d) of this section exceed ninety days. The notice must state that:

(A) The conclusion of the meeting initiates the voting period, during which the association will accept votes for and against proceeding with the construction defect action. The disclosure and voting period shall end ninety days after the mailing date of the meeting notice or when the association determines that the construction defect action is either approved or disapproved, whichever occurs first.

(B) The construction professional against whom the construction defect action is proposed will be invited to attend and will have an opportunity to address the unit owners concerning the alleged construction defect; and

(C) The presentation at the meeting by the construction professional or the construction professional's designee or designees may, but is not required to, include an offer to remedy any defect in accordance with section 13-20-803.5 (3) of the "Construction Defect Action Reform Act".

(III) The notice given pursuant to this subsection (1)(c) must also contain a description of the nature of the construction defect action, which description identifies alleged defects with reasonable specificity, the relief sought, a good-faith estimate of the benefits and risks involved, and any other pertinent information. The notice shall also include the following disclosures:

1. The alleged construction defects might result in increased costs to the association in maintenance or repair or cause an increase in assessments or special assessments to cover the cost of repairs.
2. If the association does not file a claim before the applicable legal deadlines, the claim will expire.
3. Until the alleged defects are repaired, sellers of units within the common interest community might owe unit buyers a duty to disclose known defects.
4. The executive board (intends to enter) (has entered) into a fee arrangement with the attorneys representing the association, under which (the attorneys will be paid a contingency fee equal to ______ percent of the (net) (gross) recovery of the amount the association recovers from the defendant(s)) (the association's attorneys will be paid (an hourly fee of $_____) (a fixed fee of $_____)).
5. In addition to attorney fees, the association may incur up to $_______ for legal costs, including expert witnesses, depositions, and filing fees. The amount will not be exceeded without the executive board's further written authority. If the association does not prevail on its claim, the association may be responsible for paying these legal expenses.
6. If the association does not prevail on its claim, the association may be responsible for paying its attorney fees.
7. If the association does not prevail on its claim, a court or arbitrator sometimes awards costs and attorney fees to the opposing party. Should that happen in this case, the association may be responsible for paying the opposing party's costs and fees as a result of such award.
8. There is no guarantee that the association will recover enough funds to repair the claimed construction defect(s). If the claimed defects are not repaired, additional damage to property and a reduction in the useful life of the common elements might occur.

9. Until the claimed construction defects are repaired, or until the construction defect claim is concluded, the market value of the units in the association might be adversely affected.

10. Until the claimed construction defect(s) are repaired, or until the construction defect(s) claim is concluded, owners in the association might have difficulty refinancing and prospective buyers might have difficulty obtaining financing. In addition, certain federal underwriting standards or regulations prevent refinancing or obtaining a new loan in projects where a construction defect is claimed, and certain lenders as a matter of policy will not refinance or provide a new loan in projects where a construction defect is claimed.

(IV) The association shall maintain a verified owner mailing list that identifies the owners to whom the association mailed the notice required pursuant to this subsection (1)(c). The verified owner mailing list shall include, for each owner, the address, if any, to which the association mailed the notice required pursuant to this subsection (1)(c). The association shall provide a copy of the verified owner mailing list to each construction professional who is sent a notice pursuant to this subsection (1)(c) at the owner meeting required under subsection (1)(c)(II) of this section. The owner mailing list shall be deemed verified if a specimen copy of the mailing list is certified by an association officer or agent. If the association commences a construction defect action against any construction professional, the association shall file its verified owner mailing list and records of votes received from owners during the voting period with the appropriate forum under seal.

(V) The substance of a proposed construction defect action may be amended or supplemented after the meeting, but an amended or supplemented claim does not extend the voting period. The executive board shall give notice to unit owners of any amended or supplemented claim and shall maintain records of its communications with unit owners. Owner approval pursuant to subsection (1)(d) of this section is not required for amendments or supplements to a construction defect action made after the notice pursuant to this subsection (1)(c) is sent.

(d) **Approval by unit owners – procedures.**

(I) (A) Notwithstanding any provision of law or any requirement in the governing documents, the executive board may initiate the construction defect action only if authorized within the voting period by owners of units to which a majority of votes in the association are allocated. Such approval is not required for an association to proceed with a construction defect action if the alleged construction defect pertains to a facility that is intended and used for nonresidential purposes and if the cost to repair the alleged defect does not exceed fifty thousand dollars. Such approval is not required for an association to proceed with a construction defect action when the association is the contracting party for the performance of labor or purchase of services or materials.

(B) Notwithstanding any other provision of law, an owner's vote shall be submitted only once and may be obtained in any written format confirming the owner's vote to approve or reject the proposed construction defect action. The association shall maintain a record of all votes until the conclusion of the construction defect action, including all appeals, if any.

(II) (A) Nothing in this section alters the tolling provisions of section 13-20-805.

(B) All statutes of limitation and repose applicable to claims based on defects described with reasonable specificity in the notice, which may be supplemented or amended pursuant to subsection (1)(c)(IV) of this section, are tolled from the date the notice sent pursuant to subsection (1)(c) of this section is mailed until either the ninety-day voting and disclosure period ends or until the association determines that the construction defect action is either approved or disapproved, whichever occurs first.

(C) The applicable statutes of limitation and repose that apply to claims based on a defect described in the notice with reasonable specificity are tolled pursuant to this subsection (1)(d)(II) once, and may not extend the statutes of limitation and repose that apply to claims based on that defect for more than a total of ninety days, respectively. If a defect not included in the notice sent pursuant to subsection (1)(c) of this section is the subject of a later vote, tolling pursuant to this subsection (1)(d) applies unless the claim based on that defect is otherwise barred by the statute of limitations or statute of repose.

(III) **Vote count – exclusions.** For purposes of calculating the required majority vote under this subsection (1)(d) only, the following votes are excluded:

(A) Any votes allocated to units owned by a development party. As used in this subsection (1)(d)(III)(A), "development party" means a contractor, subcontractor, developer, or builder responsible for any part of the design, construction, or repair of any portion of the common interest community and any of that party's affiliates; and "affiliate" includes an entity controlled or owned, in whole or in part, by any person that controls or owns a development party or by the spouse of a development party.

(B) Any votes allocated to units owned by banking institutions, unless a vote from such an institution is actually received by the association;

(C) Any votes allocated to units of a product type in which no defects are alleged, in a common interest community whose declaration provides that common expense liabilities are not shared between the product types;

(D) Any votes allocated to units owned by owners who are deemed nonresponsive. If the status of the nonresponsive unit owners is challenged in court, the court shall consider whether the executive board has made diligent efforts to contact the unit owner regarding the vote and may consider: Whether a mailing was returned as undeliverable; whether the owner appears to be residing at the unit; and whether the association has used other contact information, such as an electronic mail address or telephone number for the owner.

(e) **Notice to construction professional.** At least five business days before the mailing of the notice required by subsection (1)(c) of this section, the association shall notify each construction professional against whom a construction defect action is proposed by mail, at its last-known address, of the date and time of the meeting called to consider the construction defect action pursuant to subsection (1)(c) of this section.

(2) Repealed.

(3) Nothing in this section shall be construed to:

(a) Require the disclosure in the notice or the disclosure to a unit owner of attorney-client communications or other privileged communications;

(b) Permit the notice to serve as a basis for any person to assert the waiver of any applicable privilege or right of confidentiality resulting from, or to claim immunity in connection with, the disclosure of information in the notice; or

(c) Limit or impair the authority of the executive board to contract for legal services, or limit or impair the ability to enforce such a contract for legal services.

(4) **Provisions not severable.** Notwithstanding section 2-4-204, the general assembly finds, determines, and declares that if any provision of this section or its application to any person or circumstance is held invalid, the entire section shall be deemed invalid.

§ 38-33.3-304, C.R.S. Transfer of special declarant rights.

(1) A special declarant right created or reserved under this article may be transferred only by an instrument evidencing the transfer recorded in every county in which any portion of the common interest community is located. The instrument is not effective unless executed by the transferee.

(2) Upon transfer of any special declarant right, the liability of a transferor declarant is as follows:

(a) A transferor is not relieved of any obligation or liability arising before the transfer and remains liable for warranty obligations imposed upon such transferor by this article. Lack of privity does not deprive any unit owner of standing to bring an action to enforce any obligation of the transferor.

(b) If a successor to any special declarant right is an affiliate of a declarant, the transferor is jointly and severally liable with the successor for the liabilities and obligations of the successor which relate to the common interest community.

(c) If a transferor retains any special declarant rights but transfers other special declarant rights to a successor who is not an affiliate of the declarant, the transferor is liable for any obligations or liabilities imposed on a declarant by this article or by the declaration relating to the retained special declarant rights and arising after the transfer.

(d) A transferor has no liability for any act or omission or any breach of a contractual or warranty obligation arising from the exercise of a special declarant right by a successor declarant who is not an affiliate of the transferor.

(3) Unless otherwise provided in a mortgage instrument, deed of trust, or other agreement creating a security interest, in case of foreclosure of a security interest, sale by a trustee under an agreement creating a security interest, tax sale, judicial sale, or sale under bankruptcy or receivership proceedings of any units owned by a declarant or real estate in a common interest community subject to development rights, a person acquiring title to all the property being foreclosed or sold succeeds to only those special declarant rights related to that property held by that declarant which are specified in a written instrument prepared, executed, and recorded by such person at or about the same time as the judgment or instrument or by which such person obtained title to all of the property being foreclosed or sold.

(4) Upon foreclosure of a security interest, sale by a trustee under an agreement creating a security interest, tax sale, judicial sale, or sale under bankruptcy act or receivership proceedings of all interests in a common interest community owned by a declarant:

(a) The declarant ceases to have any special declarant rights; and

(b) The period of declarant control terminates unless the instrument which is required by subsection (3) of this section to be prepared, executed, and recorded at or about the same time as the judgment or instrument conveying title provides for transfer of all special declarant rights to a successor declarant.

(5) The liabilities and obligations of persons who succeed to special declarant rights are as follows:

(a) A successor to any special declarant right who is an affiliate of a declarant is subject to all obligations and liabilities imposed on any declarant by this article or by the declaration.

(b) A successor to any special declarant right, other than a successor described in paragraph (c) or (d) of this subsection (5) or a successor who is an affiliate of a declarant, is subject to all obligations and liabilities imposed by this article or the declaration:

(I) On a declarant which relate to the successor's exercise or nonexercise of special declarant rights; or

(II) On the declarant's transferor, other than:

(A) Misrepresentations by any previous declarant;

(B) Warranty obligations on improvements made by any previous declarant or made before the common interest community was created;

(C) Breach of any fiduciary obligation by any previous declarant or such declarant's appointees to the executive board; or

(D) Any liability or obligation imposed on the transferor as a result of the transferor's acts or omissions after the transfer.

(c) A successor to only a right reserved in the declaration to maintain models, sales offices, and signs, if such successor is not an affiliate of a declarant, may not exercise any other special declarant right and is not subject to any liability or obligation as a declarant.

(d) A successor to all special declarant rights held by a transferor who succeeded to those rights pursuant to the instrument prepared, executed, and recorded by such person pursuant to the provisions of subsection (3) of this section may declare such successor's intention in such recorded instrument to hold those rights solely for transfer to another person. Thereafter, until transferring all special declarant rights to any person acquiring title to any unit or real estate subject to development rights owned by the successor or until recording an instrument permitting exercise of all those rights, that successor may not exercise any of those rights other than the right held by such successor's transferor to control the executive board in accordance with the provisions of section 38-33.3-303 (5) for the duration of any period of declarant control, and any attempted exercise of those rights is void. So long as a successor declarant may not exercise special declarant rights under this subsection (5), such successor declarant is not subject to any liability or obligation as a declarant, other than liability for the successor's acts and omissions under section 38-33.3-303 (4).

(6) Nothing in this section subjects any successor to a special declarant right to any claims against or other obligations of a transferor declarant, other than claims and obligations arising under this article or the declaration.

§ 38-33.3-305, C.R.S. Termination of contracts and leases of declarant.

(1) The following contracts and leases, if entered into before the executive board elected by the unit owners pursuant to section 38-33.3-303 (7) takes office, may be terminated without penalty by the association, at any time after the executive board elected by the unit owners pursuant to section 38-33.3-303 (7) takes office, upon not less than ninety days' notice to the other party:

(a) Any management contract, employment contract, or lease of recreational or parking areas or facilities;

(b) Any other contract or lease between the association and a declarant or an affiliate of a declarant; or

(c) Any contract or lease that is not bona fide or was unconscionable to the unit owners at the time entered into under the circumstances then prevailing.

(2) Subsection (1) of this section does not apply to any lease the termination of which would terminate the common interest community or reduce its size, unless the real estate subject to that lease was included in the common interest community for the purpose of avoiding the right of the association to terminate a lease under this section or a proprietary lease.

§ 38-33.3-306, C.R.S. Bylaws.

(1) In addition to complying with applicable sections, if any, of the "Colorado Business Corporation Act", articles 101 to 117 of title 7, C.R.S., or the "Colorado Revised Nonprofit Corporation Act", articles 121 to 137 of title 7, C.R.S., if the common interest community is organized pursuant thereto, the bylaws of the association must provide:

(a) The number of members of the executive board and the titles of the officers of the association;

(b) Election by the executive board of a president, a treasurer, a secretary, and any other officers of the association the bylaws specify;

(c) The qualifications, powers and duties, and terms of office of, and manner of electing and removing, executive board members and officers and the manner of filling vacancies;

(d) Which, if any, of its powers the executive board or officers may delegate to other persons or to a managing agent;

(e) Which of its officers may prepare, execute, certify, and record amendments to the declaration on behalf of the association; and

(f) A method for amending the bylaws.

(2) Subject to the provisions of the declaration, the bylaws may provide for any other matters the association deems necessary and appropriate.

(3) (a) If an association with thirty or more units delegates powers of the executive board or officers relating to collection, deposit, transfer, or disbursement of association funds to other persons or to a managing agent, the bylaws of the association shall require the following:

(I) That the other persons or managing agent maintain fidelity insurance coverage or a bond in an amount not less than fifty thousand dollars or such higher amount as the executive board may require;

(II) That the other persons or managing agent maintain all funds and accounts of the association separate from the funds and accounts of other associations managed by the other persons or managing agent and maintain all reserve accounts of each association so managed separate from operational accounts of the association;

(III) That an annual accounting for association funds and a financial statement be prepared and presented to the association by the managing agent, a public accountant, or a certified public accountant.

(b) Repealed.

§ 38-33.3-307, C.R.S. Upkeep of the common interest community.

(1) Except to the extent provided by the declaration, subsection (2) of this section, or section 38-33.3-313 (9), the association is responsible for maintenance, repair, and replacement of the common elements, and each unit owner is responsible for maintenance, repair, and replacement of such owner's unit. Each unit owner shall afford to the association and the other unit owners, and to their agents or employees, access through such owner's unit reasonably necessary for those purposes. If damage is inflicted, or a strong likelihood exists that it will be inflicted, on the common elements or any unit through which access is taken, the unit owner responsible for the damage, or expense to avoid damage, or the association if it is responsible, is liable for the cost of prompt repair.

(1.5) Maintenance, repair, or replacement of any drainage structure or facilities, or other public improvements required by the local governmental entity as a condition of development of the common interest community or any part thereof shall be the responsibility of the association, unless such improvements have been dedicated to and accepted by the local governmental entity for the purpose of maintenance, repair, or replacement or unless such maintenance, repair, or replacement has been authorized by law to be performed by a special district or other municipal or quasi-municipal entity.

(2) In addition to the liability that a declarant as a unit owner has under this article, the declarant alone is liable for all expenses in connection with real estate within the common interest community subject to development rights. No other unit owner and no other portion of the common interest community is subject to a claim for payment of those expenses. Unless the declaration provides otherwise, any income or proceeds from real estate subject to development rights inures to the declarant. If the declarant fails to pay all expenses in connection with real estate within the common interest community subject to development rights, the association may pay such expenses, and such expenses shall be assessed as a common expense against the real estate subject to development rights, and the association may enforce the assessment pursuant to section 38-33.3-316 by treating such real estate as if it were a unit. If the association acquires title to the real estate subject to the development rights through foreclosure or otherwise, the development rights shall not be extinguished thereby, and, thereafter, the association may succeed to any special declarant rights specified in a written instrument prepared, executed, and recorded by the association in accordance with the requirements of section 38-33.3-304 (3).

(3) In a planned community, if all development rights have expired with respect to any real estate, the declarant remains liable for all expenses of that real estate unless, upon expiration, the declaration provides that the real estate becomes common elements or units.

§ 38-33.3-308, C.R.S. Meetings.

(1) Meetings of the unit owners, as the members of the association, shall be held at least once each year. Special meetings of the unit owners may be called by the president, by a majority of the executive board, or by unit owners having twenty percent, or any lower percentage specified in the bylaws, of the votes in the association. Not less than ten nor more than fifty days in advance of any meeting of the unit owners, the secretary or other officer specified in the bylaws shall cause notice to be hand delivered or sent prepaid by United States mail to the mailing address of each unit or to any other mailing address designated in writing by the unit owner. The notice of any meeting of the unit owners shall be physically posted in a conspicuous place, to the extent that such posting is feasible and practicable, in addition to any electronic posting or electronic mail notices that may be given pursuant to paragraph (b) of subsection (2) of this section. The notice shall state the time and place of the meeting and the items on the agenda, including the general nature of any proposed amendment to the declaration or bylaws, any budget changes, and any proposal to remove an officer or member of the executive board.

(2) (a) All regular and special meetings of the association's executive board, or any committee thereof, shall be open to attendance by all members of the association or their representatives. Agendas for meetings of the executive board shall be made reasonably available for examination by all members of the association or their representatives.

(b) (I) The association is encouraged to provide all notices and agendas required by this article in electronic form, by posting on a web site or otherwise, in addition to printed form. If such electronic means are available, the association shall provide notice of all regular and special meetings of unit owners by electronic mail to all unit owners who so request and who furnish the association with their electronic mail addresses. Electronic notice of a special meeting shall be given as soon as possible but at least twenty-four hours before the meeting.

(II) Notwithstanding section 38-33.3-117 (1.5) (i), this paragraph (b) shall not apply to an association that includes time-share units, as defined in section 38-33-110 (7), C.R.S.

(2.5) (a) Notwithstanding any provision in the declaration, bylaws, or other documents to the contrary, all meetings of the association and board of directors are open to every unit owner of the association, or to any person designated by a unit owner in writing as the unit owner's representative.

(b) At an appropriate time determined by the board, but before the board votes on an issue under discussion, unit owners or their designated representatives shall be permitted to speak regarding that issue. The board may place reasonable time restrictions on persons speaking during the meeting. If more than one person desires to address an issue and there are opposing views, the board shall provide for a reasonable number of persons to speak on each side of the issue.

(c) Notwithstanding section 38-33.3-117 (1.5) (i), this subsection (2.5) shall not apply to an association that includes time-share units, as defined in section 38-33-110 (7).

(3) The members of the executive board or any committee thereof may hold an executive or closed door session and may restrict attendance to executive board members and such other persons requested by the executive board during a regular or specially announced meeting or a part thereof. The matters to be discussed at such an executive session shall include only matters enumerated in paragraphs (a) to (f) of subsection (4) of this section.

(4) Matters for discussion by an executive or closed session are limited to:

(a) Matters pertaining to employees of the association or the managing agent's contract or involving the employment, promotion, discipline, or dismissal of an officer, agent, or employee of the association;

(b) Consultation with legal counsel concerning disputes that are the subject of pending or imminent court proceedings or matters that are privileged or confidential between attorney and client;

(c) Investigative proceedings concerning possible or actual criminal misconduct;

(d) Matters subject to specific constitutional, statutory, or judicially imposed requirements protecting particular proceedings or matters from public disclosure;

(e) Any matter the disclosure of which would constitute an unwarranted invasion of individual privacy;

(f) Review of or discussion relating to any written or oral communication from legal counsel.

(4.5) Upon the final resolution of any matter for which the board received legal advice or that concerned pending or contemplated litigation, the board may elect to preserve the attorney-client privilege in any appropriate manner, or it may elect to disclose such information, as it deems appropriate, about such matter in an open meeting.

(5) Prior to the time the members of the executive board or any committee thereof convene in executive session, the chair of the body shall announce the general matter of discussion as enumerated in paragraphs (a) to (f) of subsection (4) of this section.

(6) No rule or regulation of the board or any committee thereof shall be adopted during an executive session. A rule or regulation may be validly adopted only during a regular or special meeting or after the body goes back into regular session following an executive session.

(7) The minutes of all meetings at which an executive session was held shall indicate that an executive session was held and the general subject matter of the executive session.

§ 38-33.3-309, C.R.S. Quorums.

(1) Unless the bylaws provide otherwise, a quorum is deemed present throughout any meeting of the association if persons entitled to cast twenty percent, or, in the case of an association with

over one thousand unit owners, ten percent, of the votes which may be cast for election of the executive board are present, in person or by proxy at the beginning of the meeting.

(2) Unless the bylaws specify a larger percentage, a quorum is deemed present throughout any meeting of the executive board if persons entitled to cast fifty percent of the votes on that board are present at the beginning of the meeting or grant their proxy, as provided in section 7-128-205 (4), C.R.S.

§ 38-33.3-310, C.R.S. Voting – proxies.

(1) (a) If only one of the multiple owners of a unit is present at a meeting of the association, such owner is entitled to cast all the votes allocated to that unit. If more than one of the multiple owners are present, the votes allocated to that unit may be cast only in accordance with the agreement of a majority in interest of the owners, unless the declaration expressly provides otherwise. There is majority agreement if any one of the multiple owners casts the votes allocated to that unit without protest being made promptly to the person presiding over the meeting by any of the other owners of the unit.

(b) (I) (A) Votes for contested positions on the executive board shall be taken by secret ballot. This sub-subparagraph (A) shall not apply to an association whose governing documents provide for election of positions on the executive board by delegates on behalf of the unit owners.

(B) At the discretion of the board or upon the request of twenty percent of the unit owners who are present at the meeting or represented by proxy, if a quorum has been achieved, a vote on any matter affecting the common interest community on which all unit owners are entitled to vote shall be by secret ballot.

(C) Ballots shall be counted by a neutral third party or by a committee of volunteers. Such volunteers shall be unit owners who are selected or appointed at an open meeting, in a fair manner, by the chair of the board or another person presiding during that portion of the meeting. The volunteers shall not be board members and, in the case of a contested election for a board position, shall not be candidates.

(D) The results of a vote taken by secret ballot shall be reported without reference to the names, addresses, or other identifying information of unit owners participating in such vote.

(II) Notwithstanding section 38-33.3-117 (1.5) (j), this paragraph (b) shall not apply to an association that includes time-share units, as defined in section 38-33-110 (7).

(2) (a) Votes allocated to a unit may be cast pursuant to a proxy duly executed by a unit owner. A proxy shall not be valid if obtained through fraud or misrepresentation. Unless otherwise provided in the declaration, bylaws, or rules of the association, appointment of proxies may be made substantially as provided in section 7-127-203, C.R.S.

(b) If a unit is owned by more than one person, each owner of the unit may vote or register protest to the casting of votes by the other owners of the unit through a duly executed proxy. A unit owner may not revoke a proxy given pursuant to this section except by actual notice of revocation to the person presiding over a meeting of the association. A proxy is void if it is not dated or purports to be revocable without notice. A proxy terminates eleven months after its date, unless it provides otherwise.

(c) The association is entitled to reject a vote, consent, written ballot, waiver, proxy appointment, or proxy appointment revocation if the secretary or other officer or agent authorized to tabulate votes, acting in good faith, has reasonable basis for doubt about the validity of the signature on it or about the signatory's authority to sign for the unit owner.

(d) The association and its officer or agent who accepts or rejects a vote, consent, written ballot, waiver, proxy appointment, or proxy appointment revocation in good faith and in accordance with the standards of this section are not liable in damages for the consequences of the acceptance or rejection.

(e) Any action of the association based on the acceptance or rejection of a vote, consent, written ballot, waiver, proxy appointment, or proxy appointment revocation under this section is valid unless a court of competent jurisdiction determines otherwise.

(3) (a) If the declaration requires that votes on specified matters affecting the common interest community be cast by lessees rather than unit owners of leased units:

(I) The provisions of subsections (1) and (2) of this section apply to lessees as if they were unit owners;

(II) Unit owners who have leased their units to other persons may not cast votes on those specified matters; and

(III) Lessees are entitled to notice of meetings, access to records, and other rights respecting those matters as if they were unit owners.

(b) Unit owners must also be given notice, in the manner provided in section 38-33.3-308, of all meetings at which lessees are entitled to vote.

(4) No votes allocated to a unit owned by the association may be cast.

§ 38-33.3-310.5, C.R.S. Executive board – conflicts of interest – definitions.

(1) Section 7-128-501, C.R.S., shall apply to members of the executive board; except that, as used in that section:

(a) "Corporation" or "nonprofit corporation" means the association.

(b) "Director" means a member of the association's executive board.

(c) "Officer" means any person designated as an officer of the association and any person to whom the board delegates responsibilities under this article, including, without limitation, a managing agent, attorney, or accountant employed by the board.

§ 38-33.3-311, C.R.S. Tort and contract liability.

(1) Neither the association nor any unit owner except the declarant is liable for any cause of action based upon that declarant's acts or omissions in connection with any part of the common interest community which that declarant has the responsibility to maintain. Otherwise, any action alleging an act or omission by the association must be brought against the association and not against any unit owner. If the act or omission occurred during any period of declarant control and the association gives the declarant reasonable notice of and an opportunity to defend against the action, the declarant who then controlled the association is liable to the association or to any unit owner for all tort losses not covered by insurance suffered by the association or that unit owner and all costs that the association would not have incurred but for such act or omission. Whenever the declarant is liable to the association under this section, the declarant is also liable for all expenses of litigation, including reasonable attorney fees, incurred by the association. Any statute of limitation affecting the association's right of action under this section is tolled until the period of declarant control terminates. A unit owner is not precluded from maintaining an action contemplated by this section by being a unit owner or a member or officer of the association.

(2) The declarant is liable to the association for all funds of the association collected during the period of declarant control which were not properly expended.

§ 38-33.3-312, C.R.S. Conveyance or encumbrance of common elements.

(1) In a condominium or planned community, portions of the common elements may be conveyed or subjected to a security interest by the association if persons entitled to cast at least sixty-seven percent of the votes in the association, including sixty-seven percent of the votes allocated to units not owned by a declarant, or any larger percentage the declaration specifies, agree to that action; except that all owners of units to which any limited common element is allocated must agree in order to convey that limited common element or subject it to a security interest. The declaration may specify a smaller percentage only if all of the units are restricted exclusively to nonresidential uses. Proceeds of the sale are an asset of the association.

(2) Part of a cooperative may be conveyed and all or part of a cooperative may be subjected to a security interest by the association if persons entitled to cast at least sixty-seven percent of the votes in the association, including sixty-seven percent of the votes allocated to units not owned by a declarant, or any larger percentage the declaration specifies, agree to that action; except that, if fewer than all of the units or limited common elements are to be conveyed or subjected to a security interest, then all unit owners of those units, or the units to which those limited common elements are allocated, must agree in order to convey those units or limited common elements or subject them to a security interest. The declaration may specify a smaller percentage only if all of the units are restricted exclusively to nonresidential uses. Proceeds of the sale are an asset of the association. Any purported conveyance or other voluntary transfer of an entire cooperative, unless made in compliance with section 38-33.3-218, is void.

(3) An agreement to convey, or subject to a security interest, common elements in a condominium or planned community, or, in a cooperative, an agreement to convey, or subject to a security interest, any part of a cooperative, must be evidenced by the execution of an agreement, in the same manner as a deed, by the association. The agreement must specify a date after which the agreement will be void unless approved by the requisite percentage of owners. Any grant, conveyance, or deed executed by the association must be recorded in every county in which a portion of the common interest community is situated and is effective only upon recordation.

(4) The association, on behalf of the unit owners, may contract to convey an interest in a common interest community pursuant to subsection (1) of this section, but the contract is not enforceable against the association until approved pursuant to subsections (1) and (2) of this section and executed and ratified pursuant to subsection (3) of this section. Thereafter, the association has all powers necessary and appropriate to effect the conveyance or encumbrance, including the power to execute deeds or other instruments.

(5) Unless in compliance with this section, any purported conveyance, encumbrance, judicial sale, or other transfer of common elements or any other part of a cooperative is void.

(6) A conveyance or encumbrance of common elements pursuant to this section shall not deprive any unit of its rights of ingress and egress of the unit and support of the unit.

(7) Unless the declaration otherwise provides, a conveyance or encumbrance of common elements pursuant to this section does not affect the priority or validity of preexisting encumbrances.

(8) In a cooperative, the association may acquire, hold, encumber, or convey a proprietary lease without complying with this section.

§ 38-33.3-313, C.R.S. Insurance.

(1) Commencing not later than the time of the first conveyance of a unit to a person other than a declarant, the association shall maintain, to the extent reasonably available:

(a) Property insurance on the common elements and, in a planned community, also on property that must become common elements, for broad form covered causes of loss; except that the total amount of insurance must be not less than the full insurable replacement cost of the insured property less applicable deductibles at the time the insurance is purchased and at each renewal date, exclusive of land, excavations, foundations, and other items normally excluded from property policies; and

(b) Commercial general liability insurance against claims and liabilities arising in connection with the ownership, existence, use, or management of the common elements, and, in cooperatives, also of all units, in an amount, if any, specified by the common interest community instruments or otherwise deemed sufficient in the judgment of the executive board but not less than any amount specified in the association documents, insuring the executive board, the unit owners' association, the management agent, and their respective employees, agents, and all persons acting as agents. The declarant shall be included as an additional insured in such declarant's capacity as a unit owner and board member. The unit owners shall be included as additional insureds but only for claims and liabilities arising in connection with the ownership, existence, use, or management of the common elements and, in cooperatives, also of all units. The insurance shall cover claims of one or more insured parties against other insured parties.

(2) In the case of a building that is part of a cooperative or that contains units having horizontal boundaries described in the declaration, the insurance maintained under paragraph (a) of subsection (1) of this section must include the units but not the finished interior surfaces of the walls, floors, and ceilings of the units. The insurance need not include improvements and betterments installed by unit owners, but if they are covered, any increased charge shall be assessed by the association to those owners.

(3) If the insurance described in subsections (1) and (2) of this section is not reasonably available, or if any policy of such insurance is cancelled or not renewed without a replacement policy therefore having been obtained, the association promptly shall cause notice of that fact to be hand delivered or sent prepaid by United States mail to all unit owners. The declaration may require the association to carry any other insurance, and the association in any event may carry any other insurance it considers appropriate, including insurance on units it is not obligated to insure, to protect the association or the unit owners.

(4) Insurance policies carried pursuant to subsections (1) and (2) of this section must provide that:

(a) Each unit owner is an insured person under the policy with respect to liability arising out of such unit owner's interest in the common elements or membership in the association;

(b) The insurer waives its rights to subrogation under the policy against any unit owner or member of his household;

(c) No act or omission by any unit owner, unless acting within the scope of such unit owner's authority on behalf of the association, will void the policy or be a condition to recovery under the policy; and

(d) If, at the time of a loss under the policy, there is other insurance in the name of a unit owner covering the same risk covered by the policy, the association's policy provides primary insurance.

(5) Any loss covered by the property insurance policy described in paragraph (a) of subsection (1) and subsection (2) of this section must be adjusted with the association, but the insurance proceeds for that loss shall be payable to any insurance trustee designated for that purpose, or otherwise to the association, and not to any holder of a security interest. The insurance trustee or the association shall hold any insurance proceeds in trust for the association unit owners and lienholders as their interests may appear. Subject to the provisions of subsection (9) of this section, the proceeds must be disbursed first for the repair or restoration of the damaged property, and the association, unit owners, and lienholders are not entitled to receive payment of any portion of the proceeds unless there is a surplus of proceeds after the property has been completely repaired or restored or the common interest community is terminated.

(6) The association may adopt and establish written nondiscriminatory policies and procedures relating to the submittal of claims, responsibility for deductibles, and any other matters of claims adjustment. To the extent the association settles claims for damages to real property, it shall have the authority to assess negligent unit owners causing such loss or benefiting from such repair or restoration all deductibles paid by the association. In the event that more than one unit is damaged by a loss, the association in its reasonable discretion may assess each unit owner a pro rata share of any deductible paid by the association.

(7) An insurance policy issued to the association does not obviate the need for unit owners to obtain insurance for their own benefit.

(8) An insurer that has issued an insurance policy for the insurance described in subsections (1) and (2) of this section shall issue certificates or memoranda of insurance to the association and, upon request, to any unit owner or holder of a security interest. Unless otherwise provided by statute, the insurer issuing the policy may not cancel or refuse to renew it until thirty days after notice of the proposed cancellation or nonrenewal has been mailed to the association, and each unit owner and holder of a security interest to whom a certificate or memorandum of insurance has been issued, at their respective last-known addresses.

(9) (a) Any portion of the common interest community for which insurance is required under this section which is damaged or destroyed must be repaired or replaced promptly by the association unless:

(I) The common interest community is terminated, in which case section 38-33.3-218 applies;

(II) Repair or replacement would be illegal under any state or local statute or ordinance governing health or safety;

(III) Sixty-seven percent of the unit owners, including every owner of a unit or assigned limited common element that will not be rebuilt, vote not to rebuild; or

(IV) Prior to the conveyance of any unit to a person other than the declarant, the holder of a deed of trust or mortgage on the damaged portion of the common interest community rightfully demands all or a substantial part of the insurance proceeds.

(b) The cost of repair or replacement in excess of insurance proceeds and reserves is a common expense. If the entire common interest community is not repaired or replaced, the insurance proceeds attributable to the damaged common elements must be used to restore the damaged area to a condition compatible with the remainder of the common interest community, and, except to the extent that other persons will be distributees, the insurance proceeds attributable to units and limited common elements that are not rebuilt must be distributed to the owners of those units and the owners of the units to which those limited common elements were allocated, or to lienholders, as their interests may appear, and the remainder of the proceeds must be distributed to all the unit owners or lienholders, as their interests may appear, as follows:

(I) In a condominium, in proportion to the common element interests of all the units; and

(II) In a cooperative or planned community, in proportion to the common expense liabilities of all the units; except that, in a fixed or limited equity cooperative, the unit owner may not receive more of the proceeds than would satisfy the unit owner's entitlements under the declaration if the unit owner leaves the cooperative. In such a cooperative, the proceeds that remain after satisfying the unit owner's obligations continue to be held in trust by the association for the benefit of the cooperative. If the unit owners vote not to rebuild any unit, that unit's allocated interests are automatically reallocated upon the vote as if the unit had been condemned under section 38-33.3-107, and the association promptly shall prepare, execute, and record an amendment to the declaration reflecting the reallocations.

(10) If any unit owner or employee of an association with thirty or more units controls or disburses funds of the common interest community, the association must obtain and maintain, to the extent reasonably available, fidelity insurance. Coverage shall not be less in aggregate than two months' current assessments plus reserves, as calculated from the current budget of the association.

(11) Any person employed as an independent contractor by an association with thirty or more units for the purposes of managing a common interest community must obtain and maintain fidelity insurance in an amount not less than the amount specified in subsection (10) of this section, unless the association names such person as an insured employee in a contract of fidelity insurance, pursuant to subsection (10) of this section.

(12) The association may carry fidelity insurance in amounts greater than required in subsection (10) of this section and may require any independent contractor employed for the purposes of managing a common interest community to carry more fidelity insurance coverage than required in subsection (10) of this section.

(13) Premiums for insurance that the association acquires and other expenses connected with acquiring such insurance are common expenses.

§ 38-33.3-314, C.R.S. Surplus funds.

Unless otherwise provided in the declaration, any surplus funds of the association remaining after payment of or provision for common expenses and any prepayment of or provision for reserves shall be paid to the unit owners in proportion to their common expense liabilities or credited to them to reduce their future common expense assessments.

§ 38-33.3-315, C.R.S. Assessments for common expenses.

(1) Until the association makes a common expense assessment, the declarant shall pay all common expenses. After any assessment has been made by the association, assessments shall be made no less frequently than annually and shall be based on a budget adopted no less frequently than annually by the association.

(2) Except for assessments under subsections (3) and (4) of this section and section 38-33.3-207 (4) (a) (IV), all common expenses shall be assessed against all the units in accordance with the allocations set forth in the declaration pursuant to section 38-33.3-207 (1) and (2). Any past-due common expense assessment or installment thereof shall bear interest at the rate established by the association not exceeding twenty-one percent per year.

(3) To the extent required by the declaration:

  (a) Any common expense associated with the maintenance, repair, or replacement of a limited common element shall be assessed against the units to which that limited common element is assigned, equally, or in any other proportion the declaration provides;

  (b) Any common expense or portion thereof benefiting fewer than all of the units shall be assessed exclusively against the units benefited; and

  (c) The costs of insurance shall be assessed in proportion to risk, and the costs of utilities shall be assessed in proportion to usage.

(4) If any common expense is caused by the misconduct of any unit owner, the association may assess that expense exclusively against such owner's unit.

(5) If common expense liabilities are reallocated, common expense assessments and any installment thereof not yet due shall be recalculated in accordance with the reallocated common expense liabilities.

(6) Each unit owner is liable for assessments made against such owner's unit during the period of ownership of such unit. No unit owner may be exempt from liability for payment of the assessments by waiver of the use or enjoyment of any of the common elements or by abandonment of the unit against which the assessments are made.

(7) Unless otherwise specifically provided in the declaration or bylaws, the association may enter into an escrow agreement with the holder of a unit owner's mortgage so that assessments may be combined with the unit owner's mortgage payments and paid at the same time and in the same manner; except that any such escrow agreement shall comply with any applicable rules of the federal housing administration, department of housing and urban development, veterans' administration, or other government agency.

§ 38-33.3-316, C.R.S. Lien for assessments.

(1) The association, if such association is incorporated or organized as a limited liability company, has a statutory lien on a unit for any assessment levied against that unit or fines imposed against its unit owner. Unless the declaration otherwise provides, fees, charges, late charges, attorney fees, fines, and interest charged pursuant to section 38-33.3-302 (1) (j), (1) (k), and (1) (l), section 38-33.3-313 (6), and section 38-33.3-315 (2) are enforceable as assessments under this article. The amount of the lien shall include all those items set forth in this section from the time such items become due. If an assessment is payable in installments, each installment is a lien from the time it becomes due, including the due date set by any valid association's acceleration of installment obligations.

(2) (a) A lien under this section is prior to all other liens and encumbrances on a unit except:

(I) Liens and encumbrances recorded before the recordation of the declaration and, in a cooperative, liens and encumbrances which the association creates, assumes, or takes subject to;

(II) A security interest on the unit which has priority over all other security interests on the unit and which was recorded before the date on which the assessment sought to be enforced became delinquent, or, in a cooperative, a security interest encumbering only the unit owner's interest which has priority over all other security interests on the unit and which was perfected before the date on which the assessment sought to be enforced became delinquent; and

(III) Liens for real estate taxes and other governmental assessments or charges against the unit or cooperative.

(b) Subject to paragraph (d) of this subsection (2), a lien under this section is also prior to the security interests described in subparagraph (II) of paragraph (a) of this subsection (2) to the extent of:

(I) An amount equal to the common expense assessments based on a periodic budget adopted by the association under section 38-33.3-315 (1) which would have become due, in the absence of any acceleration, during the six months immediately preceding institution by either the association or any party holding a lien senior to any part of the association lien created under this section of an action or a nonjudicial foreclosure either to enforce or to extinguish the lien.

(II) (Deleted by amendment, L. 93, p. 653, § 21, effective April 30, 1993.)

(c) This subsection (2) does not affect the priority of mechanics' or materialmen's liens or the priority of liens for other assessments made by the association. A lien under this section is not subject to the provisions of part 2 of article 41 of this title or to the provisions of section 15-11-202, C.R.S.

(d) The association shall have the statutory lien described in subsection (1) of this section for any assessment levied or fine imposed after June 30, 1992. Such lien shall have the priority described in this subsection (2) if the other lien or encumbrance is created after June 30, 1992.

(3) Unless the declaration otherwise provides, if two or more associations have liens for assessments created at any time on the same property, those liens have equal priority.

(4) Recording of the declaration constitutes record notice and perfection of the lien. No further recordation of any claim of lien for assessments is required.

(5) A lien for unpaid assessments is extinguished unless proceedings to enforce the lien are instituted within six years after the full amount of assessments become due.

(6) This section does not prohibit actions or suits to recover sums for which subsection (1) of this section creates a lien or to prohibit an association from taking a deed in lieu of foreclosure.

(7) The association shall be entitled to costs and reasonable attorney fees incurred by the association in a judgment or decree in any action or suit brought by the association under this section.

(8) The association shall furnish to a unit owner or such unit owner's designee or to a holder of a security interest or its designee upon written request, delivered personally or by certified mail, first-class postage prepaid, return receipt, to the association's registered agent, a written statement setting forth the amount of unpaid assessments currently levied against such owner's unit. The statement shall be furnished within fourteen calendar days after receipt of the request and is binding on the association, the executive board, and every unit owner. If no statement is furnished to the unit owner or holder of a security interest or his or her designee, delivered personally or by certified mail, first-class postage prepaid, return receipt requested, to the inquiring party, then the association shall have no right to assert a lien upon the unit for unpaid assessments which were due as of the date of the request.

(9) In any action by an association to collect assessments or to foreclose a lien for unpaid assessments, the court may appoint a receiver of the unit owner to collect all sums alleged to be due from the unit owner prior to or during the pending of the action. The court may order the receiver to pay any sums held by the receiver to the association during the pending of the action to the extent of the association's common expense assessments.

(10) In a cooperative, upon nonpayment of an assessment on a unit, the unit owner may be evicted in the same manner as provided by law in the case of an unlawful holdover by a commercial tenant, and the lien may be foreclosed as provided by this section.

(11) The association's lien may be foreclosed by any of the following means:

(a) In a condominium or planned community, the association's lien may be foreclosed in like manner as a mortgage on real estate; except that the association or a holder or assignee of the association's lien, whether the holder or assignee of the association's lien is an entity or a natural person, may only foreclose on the lien if:

(I) The balance of the assessments and charges secured by its lien, as defined in subsection (2) of this section, equals or exceeds six months of common expense assessments based on a periodic budget adopted by the association; and

(II) The executive board has formally resolved, by a recorded vote, to authorize the filing of a legal action against the specific unit on an individual basis. The board may not delegate its duty to act under this subparagraph (II) to any attorney, insurer, manager, or other person, and any legal action filed without evidence of the recorded vote authorizing the action must be dismissed. No attorney fees, court costs, or other charges incurred by the association or a holder or assignee of the association's lien in connection with an action that is dismissed for this reason may be assessed against the unit owner.

(b) In a cooperative whose unit owners' interests in the units are real estate as determined in accordance with the provisions of section 38-33.3-105, the association's lien must be foreclosed in like manner as a mortgage on real estate; except that the association or a holder or assignee of the association's lien, whether the holder or assignee of the association's lien is an entity or a natural person, may only foreclose on the lien if:

(I) The balance of the assessments and charges secured by its lien, as defined in subsection (2) of this section, equals or exceeds six months of common expense assessments based on a periodic budget adopted by the association; and

(II) The executive board has formally resolved, by a recorded vote, to authorize the filing of a legal action against the specific unit on an individual basis. The board may not delegate its duty to act under this subparagraph (II) to any attorney, insurer, manager, or other person, and any legal action filed without evidence of the recorded vote authorizing the action must be dismissed. No attorney fees, court costs, or other charges incurred by the association or a holder or assignee of the association's lien in connection with an action that is dismissed for this reason may be assessed against the unit owner.

(c) In a cooperative whose unit owners' interests in the units are personal property, as determined in accordance with the provisions of section 38-33.3-105, the association's lien must be foreclosed as a security interest under the "Uniform Commercial Code", title 4, C.R.S.

§ 38-33.3-316.3, C.R.S. Collections – limitations.

(1) In collecting past-due assessments and other delinquent payments under this article, an association or a holder or assignee of the association's debt, whether the holder or assignee of the association's debt is an entity or a natural person, shall:

(a) Adopt and comply with a collections policy that meets the requirements of section 38-33.3-209.5 (5); and

(b) Make a good-faith effort to coordinate with the unit owner to set up a payment plan that meets the requirements of this section; except that:

(I) This section does not apply if the unit owner does not occupy the unit and has acquired the property as a result of:

(A) A default of a security interest encumbering the unit; or

(B) Foreclosure of the association's lien; and

(II) The association or a holder or assignee of the association's debt is not obligated to negotiate a payment plan with a unit owner who has previously entered into a payment plan under this section.

(2) A payment plan negotiated between the association or a holder or assignee of the association's debt, whether the holder or assignee of the association's debt is an entity or a natural person, and the unit owner pursuant to this section must permit the unit owner to pay off the deficiency in equal installments over a period of at least six months. Nothing in this section prohibits an association or a holder or assignee of the association's debt from pursuing legal action against a unit owner if the unit owner fails to comply with the terms of his or her payment plan. A unit owner's failure to remit payment of an agreed-upon installment, or to remain current with regular assessments as they come due during the six-month period, constitutes a failure to comply with the terms of his or her payment plan.

(3) For purposes of this section, "assessments" includes regular and special assessments and any associated fees, charges, late charges, attorney fees, fines, and interest charged pursuant to section 38-33.3-315 (2).

§ 38-33.3-316.5, C.R.S. Time share estate – foreclosure – definitions.

(1) As used in this section, unless the context otherwise requires:

(a) "Junior lienor" has the same meaning as set forth in section 38-38-100.3 (12), C.R.S.

(b) "Obligor" means the person liable for the assessment levied against a time share estate pursuant to section 38-33.3-316 or the record owner of the time share estate.

(c) "Time share estate" has the same meaning as set forth in section 38-33-110 (5).

(2) A plaintiff may commence a single judicial foreclosure action pursuant to section 38-33.3-316 (11), joining as defendants multiple obligors with separate time share estates and the junior lienors thereto, if:

(a) The judicial foreclosure action involves a single common interest community;

(b) The declaration giving rise to the right of the association to collect assessments creates default and remedy obligations that are substantially the same for each obligor named as a defendant in the judicial foreclosure action;

(c) The action is limited to a claim for judicial foreclosure brought pursuant to section 38-33.3-316 (11); and

(d) The plaintiff does not allege, with respect to any obligor, that the association's lien is prior to any security interest described in section 38-33.3-316 (2) (a) (II), even if such a claim could be made pursuant to section 38-33.3-316 (2) (b) (I).

(3) In a judicial foreclosure action in which multiple obligors with separate time share estates and the junior lienors thereto have been joined as defendants in accordance with this section:

(a) In addition to any other circumstances where severance is proper under the Colorado rules of civil procedure, the court may sever for separate trial any disputed claim or claims;

(b) If service by publication of two or more defendants is permitted by law, the plaintiff may publish a single notice for all joined defendants for whom service by publication is permitted, so long as all information that would be required by law to be provided in the published notice as to each defendant individually is included in the combined published notice. Nothing in this paragraph (b) shall be interpreted to allow service by publication of any defendant if service by publication is not otherwise permitted by law with respect to that defendant.

(c) The action shall be deemed a single action, suit, or proceeding for purposes of payment of filing fees, notwithstanding any action by the court pursuant to paragraph (a) of this subsection (3), so long as the plaintiff complies with subsection (2) of this section.

(4) Notwithstanding that multiple obligors with separate time share estates may be joined in a single judicial foreclosure action, unless otherwise ordered by the court, each time share estate foreclosed pursuant to this section shall be subject to a separate foreclosure sale, and any cure or redemption rights with respect to such time share estate shall remain separate.

(5) The plaintiff in an action brought pursuant to this section is deemed to waive any claims against a defendant for a deficiency remaining after the foreclosure of the lien for assessment and for attorney fees related to the foreclosure action.

* *§ 38-33.3-317, C.R.S. Association records - rules - applicability.*

(1) In addition to any records specifically defined in the association's declaration or bylaws or expressly required by section 38-33.3-209.4 (2), the association must maintain the following, all of which shall be deemed to be the sole records of the association for purposes of document retention and production to owners:

(a) Detailed records of receipts and expenditures affecting the operation and administration of the association;

(b) Records of claims for construction defects and amounts received pursuant to settlement of those claims;

(c) Minutes of all meetings of its unit owners and executive board, a record of all actions taken by the unit owners or executive board without a meeting, and a record of all actions taken by any committee of the executive board;

(d) Written communications among, and the votes cast by, executive board members that are:

(I) Directly related to an action taken by the board without a meeting pursuant to section 7-128-202, C.R.S.; or

(II) Directly related to an action taken by the board without a meeting pursuant to the association's bylaws;

(e) The names of unit owners in a form that permits preparation of a list of the names of all unit owners and the physical mailing addresses at which the association communicates with them, showing the number of votes each unit owner is entitled to vote; except that this paragraph (e) does not apply to a unit, or the owner thereof, if the unit is a time-share unit, as defined in section 38-33-110 (7);

(f) Its current declaration, covenants, bylaws, articles of incorporation, if it is a corporation, or the corresponding organizational documents if it is another form of entity, rules and regulations, responsible governance policies adopted pursuant to section 38-33.3-209.5, and other policies adopted by the executive board;

(g) Financial statements as described in section 7-136-106, C.R.S., for the past three years and tax returns of the association for the past seven years, to the extent available;

(h) A list of the names, electronic mail addresses, and physical mailing addresses of its current executive board members and officers;

(h.5) A list of the current amounts of all unique and extraordinary fees, assessments, and expenses that are chargeable by the association in connection with the purchase or sale of a unit and are not paid for through assessments, including transfer fees, record change fees, and the charge for a status letter or statement of assessments due;

(h.6) All documents included in the association's annual disclosures made pursuant to section 38-33.3-209.4.

(i) Its most recent annual report delivered to the secretary of state, if any;

(j) Financial records sufficiently detailed to enable the association to comply with section 38-33.3-316 (8) concerning statements of unpaid assessments;

(k) The association's most recent reserve study, if any;

(*l*) Current written contracts to which the association is a party and contracts for work performed for the association within the immediately preceding two years;

(m) Records of executive board or committee actions to approve or deny any requests for design or architectural approval from unit owners;

(n) Ballots, proxies, and other records related to voting by unit owners for one year after the election, action, or vote to which they relate;

(o) Resolutions adopted by its board of directors relating to the characteristics, qualifications, rights, limitations, and obligations of members or any class or category of members; and

(p) All written communications within the past three years to all unit owners generally as unit owners.

(2) (a) Subject to subsections (3), (3.5), and (4) of this section, all records maintained by the association must be available for examination and copying by a unit owner or the owner's authorized agent. The association may require unit owners to submit a written request, describing with reasonable particularity the records sought, at least ten days prior to inspection or production of the documents and may limit examination and copying times to normal business hours or the next regularly scheduled executive board meeting if the meeting occurs within thirty days after the request. Notwithstanding any provision of the

declaration, bylaws, articles, or rules and regulations of the association to the contrary, the association may not condition the production of records upon the statement of a proper purpose.

(b) (I) Notwithstanding paragraph (a) of this subsection (2), a membership list or any part thereof may not be obtained or used by any person for any purpose unrelated to a unit owner's interest as a unit owner without consent of the executive board.

(II) Without limiting the generality of subparagraph (I) of this paragraph (b), without the consent of the executive board, a membership list or any part thereof may not be:

(A) Used to solicit money or property unless such money or property will be used solely to solicit the votes of the unit owners in an election to be held by the association;

(B) Used for any commercial purpose; or

(C) Sold to or purchased by any person.

(3) Records maintained by an association may be withheld from inspection and copying to the extent that they are or concern:

(a) Architectural drawings, plans, and designs, unless released upon the written consent of the legal owner of the drawings, plans, or designs;

(b) Contracts, leases, bids, or records related to transactions to purchase or provide goods or services that are currently in or under negotiation;

(c) Communications with legal counsel that are otherwise protected by the attorney-client privilege or the attorney work product doctrine;

(d) Disclosure of information in violation of law;

(e) Records of an executive session of an executive board;

(f) Individual units other than those of the requesting owner; or

(g) The names and physical mailing addresses of unit owners if the unit is a time-share unit, as defined in section 38-33-110 (7).

(3.5) Records maintained by an association are not subject to inspection and copying, and they must be withheld, to the extent that they are or concern:

(a) Personnel, salary, or medical records relating to specific individuals; or

(b) (I) Personal identification and account information of members and residents, including bank account information, telephone numbers, electronic mail addresses, driver's license numbers, and social security numbers; except that, notwithstanding section 38-33.3-104, a member or resident may provide the association with prior written consent to the disclosure of, and the association may publish to other members and residents, the person's telephone number, electronic mail address, or both. The written consent must be kept as a record of the association and remains valid until the person withdraws it by providing the association with a written notice of withdrawal of the consent. If a person withdraws his or her consent, the association is under no obligation to change, retrieve, or destroy any document or record published prior to the notice of withdrawal.

(II) As used in this paragraph (b), written consent and notice of withdrawal of the consent may be given by means of a "record", as defined in the "Uniform Electronic Transactions Act", article 71.3 of title 24, C.R.S., if the parties so agree in accordance with section 24-71.3-105, C.R.S.

(4) The association may impose a reasonable charge, which may be collected in advance and may cover the costs of labor and material, for copies of association records. The charge may not

exceed the estimated cost of production and reproduction of the records, including the costs of copying, mailing, and any necessary special processing.

(4.5) If the association fails to allow inspection or copying of records in accordance with this section within thirty calendar days after receipt of a written request submitted by certified mail, return receipt requested, and payment of any fees required pursuant to subsection (4) of this section, the association is liable for penalties in the amount of fifty dollars per day, commencing on the eleventh business day after the association received the written request, up to a maximum of five hundred dollars or the unit owner's actual damages sustained as a result of the refusal, whichever is greater.

(5) A right to copy records under this section includes the right to receive copies by photocopying or other means, including the receipt of copies through an electronic transmission if available, upon request by the unit owner.

(6) An association is not obligated to compile or synthesize information.

(7) Association records and the information contained within those records shall not be used for commercial purposes.

(8) Subsections (1)(h.5), (1)(h.6), and (4.5) of this section, as added by House Bill 21-1229, enacted in 2021, and subsection (4) of this section, as amended by House Bill 21-1229, enacted in 2021, do not apply to an association that includes time share units, as defined in section 38-33-110 (7).

§ 38-33.3-318, C.R.S. Association as trustee.

With respect to a third person dealing with the association in the association's capacity as a trustee, the existence of trust powers and their proper exercise by the association may be assumed without inquiry. A third person is not bound to inquire whether the association has the power to act as trustee or is properly exercising trust powers. A third person, without actual knowledge that the association is exceeding or improperly exercising its powers, is fully protected in dealing with the association as if it possessed and properly exercised the powers it purports to exercise. A third person is not bound to assure the proper application of trust assets paid or delivered to the association in its capacity as trustee.

§ 38-33.3-319, C.R.S. Other applicable statutes.

To the extent that provisions of this article conflict with applicable provisions in the "Colorado Business Corporation Act", articles 101 to 117 of title 7, C.R.S., the "Colorado Revised Nonprofit Corporation Act", articles 121 to 137 of title 7, C.R.S., the "Uniform Partnership Law", article 60 of title 7, C.R.S., the "Colorado Uniform Partnership Act (1997)", article 64 of title 7, C.R.S., the "Colorado Uniform Limited Partnership Act of 1981", article 62 of title 7, C.R.S., article 1 of this title, article 55 of title 7, C.R.S., article 33.5 of this title, and section 39-1-103 (10), C.R.S., and any other laws of the state of Colorado which now exist or which are subsequently enacted, the provisions of this article shall control.

§ 38-33.3-401, C.R.S. Registration – annual fees.

(1) Every unit owners' association shall register annually with the director of the division of real estate, in the form and manner specified by the director.

(2) (a) Except as otherwise provided in subsection (2)(b) of this section, the unit owners' association shall submit with its annual registration a fee in the amount set by the director in accordance with section 12-10-215 and shall include the following information, updated within ninety days after any change:

(I) The name of the association, as shown in the Colorado secretary of state's records;

(II) The name of the association's management company, managing agent, or designated agent, which may be the association's registered agent, as shown in the Colorado secretary of state's records, or any other agent that the executive board has designated for purposes of registration under this section;

(III) The physical address of the HOA;

(IV) A valid address; email address, if any; website, if any; and telephone number for the association or its management company, managing agent, or designated agent; and

(V) The number of units in the association.

(b) A unit owners' association is exempt from the fee, but not the registration requirement, if the association:

(I) Has annual revenues of five thousand dollars or less; or

(II) Is not authorized to make assessments and does not have revenue.

(3) A registration is valid for one year. The right of an association that fails to register, or whose annual registration has expired, to impose or enforce a lien for assessments under section 38-33.3-316 or to pursue an action or employ an enforcement mechanism otherwise available to it under section 38-33.3-123 is suspended until the association is validly registered pursuant to this section. A lien for assessments previously recorded during a period in which the association was validly registered or before registration was required pursuant to this section is not extinguished by a lapse in the association's registration, but a pending enforcement proceeding related to the lien is suspended, and an applicable time limit is tolled, until the association is validly registered pursuant to this section. An association's registration in compliance with this section revives a previously suspended right without penalty to the association.

(4) (a) A registration is valid upon the division of real estate's acceptance of the information required by paragraph (a) of subsection (2) of this section and the payment of applicable fees.

(b) An association's registration number, and an electronic or paper confirmation issued by the division of real estate, are prima facie evidence of valid registration.

(c) The director of the division of real estate's final determinations concerning the validity or timeliness of registrations under this section are subject to judicial review pursuant to section 24-4-106 (11), C.R.S.; except that the court shall not find a registration invalid based solely on technical or typographical errors.

* ***§ 38-33.3-402. C.R.S. Manager licensing – condition precedent for enforcement of contract terms. (Repealed)***

VII. Colorado Revised Nonprofit Corporation Act

ARTICLE 121. GENERAL PROVISIONS

§ 7-121-101, C.R.S. Short title.

Articles 121 to 137 of this title shall be known and may be cited as the "Colorado Revised Nonprofit Corporation Act".

§ 7-121-102, C.R.S. Reservation of power to amend or repeal.

The general assembly has the power to amend or repeal all or part of articles 121 to 137 of this title at any time and all domestic and foreign nonprofit corporations subject to said articles shall be governed by the amendment or repeal.

§ 7-121-201, C.R.S. Filing requirements.

Part 3 of article 90 of this title, providing for the filing of documents, applies to any document filed or to be filed by the secretary of state pursuant to articles 121 to 137 of this title.

§ 7-121-301, C.R.S. Powers – repeal. (Repealed)

§ 7-121-401, C.R.S. General definitions.

As used in articles 121 to 137 of this title, unless the context otherwise requires:

(1) (Deleted by amendment, L. 2003, p. 2332, § 280, effective July 1, 2004.)

(2) "Articles of incorporation" includes amended articles of incorporation, restated articles of incorporation, and other instruments, however designated, on file in the records of the secretary of state that have the effect of amending or supplementing in some respect the original or amended articles of incorporation, and shall also include:

(a) For a corporation created by special act of the general assembly or pursuant to general law, which corporation has elected to accept the provisions of articles 121 to 137 of this title, the special charter and any amendments thereto made by special act of the general assembly or pursuant to general law prior to the corporation's election to accept the provisions of said articles;

(b) For a corporation formed or incorporated under article 40, 50, or 51 of this title, which corporation has elected to accept the provisions of articles 121 to 137 of this title, the certificate of incorporation or affidavit and any amendments thereto made prior to the corporation's election to accept the provisions of said articles.

(3) (Deleted by amendment, L. 2003, p. 2332, § 280, effective July 1, 2004.)

(4) "Board of directors" means the body authorized to manage the affairs of the domestic or foreign nonprofit corporation; except that no person or group of persons are the board of directors because of powers delegated to that person or group of persons pursuant to section 7-128-101 (2).

(5) "Bylaws" means the code or codes of rules, other than the articles of incorporation, adopted pursuant to articles 121 to 137 of this title for the regulation or management of the affairs of the domestic or foreign nonprofit corporation irrespective of the name or names by which such rules are designated, and includes amended bylaws and restated bylaws.

(6) "Cash" and "money" are used interchangeably in articles 121 to 137 of this title. Each of these terms includes:

(a) Legal tender;

(b) Negotiable instruments readily convertible into legal tender; and

(c) Other cash equivalents readily convertible into legal tender.

(7) "Class" refers to a group of memberships that have the same rights with respect to voting, dissolution, redemption, and transfer. For the purpose of this section, rights shall be considered the same if they are determined by a formula applied uniformly to a group of memberships.

(8) (Deleted by amendment, L. 2000, p. 982, § 76, effective July 1, 2000.)

(9) "Corporation" or "domestic corporation" means a corporation for profit, which is not a foreign corporation, incorporated under or subject to the provisions of articles 101 to 117 of this title.

(10) "Delegate" means any person elected or appointed to vote in a representative assembly for the election of a director or directors or on other matters.

(11) (Deleted by amendment, L. 2003, p. 2332, § 280, effective July 1, 2004.)

(12) "Director" means a member of the board of directors.

(13) "Distribution" means the payment of a dividend or any part of the income or profit of a corporation to its members, directors, or officers.

(14) (Deleted by amendment, L. 2003, p. 2332, § 280, effective July 1, 2004.)

(15) "Effective date of notice" has the meaning set forth in section 7-121-402.

(16) "Employee" includes an officer but not a director; except that a director may accept duties that make said director also an employee.

(16.5) "Entrance fee" means any fee or charge, including a damage deposit, paid by a person to a residential nonprofit corporation in order to become a resident member. "Entrance fee" does not include regular periodic payments for the purchase or lease of residential real estate or for the day-to-day use of facilities or services.

(17) to (20) (Deleted by amendment, L. 2003, p. 2332, § 280, effective July 1, 2004.)

(21) "Internal revenue code" means the federal "Internal Revenue Code of 1986", as amended from time to time, or to corresponding provisions of subsequent internal revenue laws of the United States of America.

(22) and (23) (Deleted by amendment, L. 2003, p. 2332, § 280, effective July 1, 2004.)

(24) "Member" means any person or persons identified as such in the articles of incorporation or bylaws pursuant to a procedure stated in the articles of incorporation or bylaws or by a resolution of the board of directors. The term "member" includes "voting member" and a stockholder in a cooperative housing corporation formed pursuant to section 38-33.5-101, C.R.S.

(25) "Membership" refers to the rights and obligations of a member or members.

(25.5) "Mutual ditch company" means a nonprofit corporation that complies with article 42 of this title.

(26) "Nonprofit corporation" or "domestic nonprofit corporation" means an entity, which is not a foreign nonprofit corporation, incorporated under or subject to the provisions of articles 121 to 137 of this title.

(27) to (29) (Deleted by amendment, L. 2003, p. 2332, § 280, effective July 1, 2004.)

(30) "Receive", when used in reference to receipt of a writing or other document by a domestic or foreign nonprofit corporation, means that the writing or other document is actually received:

(a) By the domestic or foreign nonprofit corporation at its registered office or at its principal office;

(b) By the secretary of the domestic or foreign nonprofit corporation, wherever the secretary is found; or

(c) By any other person authorized by the bylaws or the board of directors to receive such writings, wherever such person is found.

(31) "Record date" means the date, established under article 127 of this title, on which a nonprofit corporation determines the identity of its members. The determination shall be made as of the close of business on the record date unless another time for doing so is stated when the record date is fixed.

(32) (Deleted by amendment, L. 2003, p. 2332, § 280, effective July 1, 2004.)

(32.5) "Residential member" means a member of a residential nonprofit corporation whose status as a member is dependent upon, or whose membership is accorded voting rights as a result of, owning or leasing specified residential real estate.

(33) (Deleted by amendment, L. 2003, p. 2332, § 280, effective July 1, 2004.)

(33.5) (a) Except as otherwise provided in paragraph (b) of this subsection (33.5), "residential nonprofit corporation" means a nonprofit corporation that has residential members.

(b) Notwithstanding paragraph (a) of this subsection (33.5), "residential nonprofit corporation" does not include:

(I) A unit owners' association or any other entity subject to the "Colorado Common Interest Ownership Act", article 33.3 of title 38, C.R.S., regardless of whether it was formed before, on, or after July 1, 1992;

(II) A nursing care facility licensed by the department of public health and environment under section 25-3-101, C.R.S.;

(III) An assisted living residence licensed under section 25-3-101, C.R.S.;

(IV) A life care institution regulated under article 13 of title 12, C.R.S.; or

(V) A continuing care retirement community, as described in section 25.5-6-203, C.R.S., operated by an entity that is licensed or otherwise subject to state regulation.

(34) "Secretary" means the corporate officer to whom the bylaws or the board of directors has delegated responsibility under section 7-128-301 (3) for the preparation and maintenance of minutes of the meetings of the board of directors and of the members and of the other records and information required to be kept by the nonprofit corporation under section 7-136-101 and for authenticating records of the nonprofit corporation.

(35) to (37) (Deleted by amendment, L. 2003, p. 2332, § 280, effective July 1, 2004.)

(38) "Vote" includes authorization by written ballot and written consent.

(39) "Voting group" means all the members of one or more classes of members or directors that, under articles 121 to 137 of this title or the articles of incorporation or bylaws, are entitled to vote and be counted together collectively on a matter. All members or directors entitled by articles 121 to 137 of this title or the articles of incorporation or bylaws to vote generally on the matter are for that purpose a single voting group.

(40) "Voting member" means any person or persons who on more than one occasion, pursuant to a provision of a nonprofit corporation's articles of incorporation or bylaws, have the right to vote for the election of a director or directors. A person is not a voting member solely by virtue of any of the following:

(a) Any rights such person has as a delegate;

(b) Any rights such person has to designate a director or directors; or

(c) Any rights such person has as a director.

§ 7-121-402, C.R.S. Notice.

(1) Notice given pursuant to articles 121 to 137 of this title shall be in writing unless otherwise provided in the bylaws.

(2) Notice may be given in person; by telephone, telegraph, teletype, electronically transmitted, or other form of wire or wireless communication; or by mail or private carrier. The bylaws may provide that if these forms of personal notice are impracticable, notice may be communicated by a newspaper of general circulation in the area where published.

(3) Written notice by a nonprofit corporation to its members, if mailed, is correctly addressed if addressed to the member's address shown in the nonprofit corporation's current record of members. If three successive notices given to a member pursuant to subsection (5) of this section have been returned as undeliverable, no further notices to such member shall be necessary until another address for the member is made known to the nonprofit corporation.

(4) Written notice to a domestic nonprofit corporation or to a foreign nonprofit corporation authorized to transact business or conduct activities in this state, other than in its capacity as a member, is correctly addressed if addressed to the registered agent address of its registered agent or to the domestic or foreign nonprofit corporation or its secretary at its principal office.

(5) Written notice by a nonprofit corporation to its members, if in a comprehensible form, is effective at the earliest of:

(a) The date received;

(b) Five days after its deposit in the United States mail, as evidenced by the postmark, if mailed correctly addressed and with first class postage affixed;

(c) The date shown on the return receipt, if mailed by registered or certified mail, return receipt requested, and the receipt is signed by or on behalf of the addressee;

(d) Thirty days after its deposit in the United States mail, as evidenced by the postmark, if mailed correctly addressed and with other than first class, registered, or certified postage affixed.

(6) Oral notice is effective when communicated if communicated in a comprehensible manner.

(7) Notice by publication is effective on the date of first publication.

(8) If articles 121 to 137 of this title prescribe notice requirements for particular circumstances, those requirements govern. If the articles of incorporation or bylaws prescribe notice requirements not inconsistent with this section or other provisions of articles 121 to 137 of this title, those requirements govern.

(9) A written notice or report delivered as part of a newsletter, magazine, or other publication regularly sent to members shall constitute a written notice or report if addressed or delivered to the member's address shown in the nonprofit corporation's current list of members, or in the case of members who are residents of the same household and who have the same address in the nonprofit corporation's current list of members, if addressed or delivered to one of such members, at the address appearing on the current list of members.

§ 7-121-501, C.R.S. Private foundations.

(1) Except where otherwise determined by a court of competent jurisdiction, a nonprofit corporation that is a private foundation as defined in section 509 (a) of the internal revenue code:

(a) Shall distribute such amounts for each taxable year at such time and in such manner as not to subject the nonprofit corporation to tax under section 4942 of the internal revenue code;

(b) Shall not engage in any act of self-dealing as defined in section 4941 (d) of the internal revenue code;

(c) Shall not retain any excess business holdings as defined in section 4943 (c) of the internal revenue code;

(d) Shall not make any investments that would subject the nonprofit corporation to taxation under section 4944 of the internal revenue code;

(e) Shall not make any taxable expenditures as defined in section 4945 (d) of the internal revenue code.

§ 7-121-601, C.R.S. Judicial relief.

(1) If for any reason it is impractical or impossible for any nonprofit corporation to call or conduct a meeting of its members, delegates, or directors, or otherwise obtain their consent, in the manner prescribed by articles 121 to 137 of this title, its articles of incorporation, or bylaws, then upon petition of a director, officer, delegate, or member the district court for the county in this state in which the street address of the nonprofit corporation's principal office is located, or if the nonprofit corporation has no principal office in this state, the district court for the county in which the street address of its registered agent is located, or if the nonprofit corporation has no registered agent, the district court for the city and county of Denver, may order that such a

meeting be called or that a written consent or other form of obtaining the vote of members, delegates, or directors be authorized, in such a manner as the court finds fair and equitable under the circumstances.

(2) The court shall, in an order issued pursuant to this section, provide for a method of notice reasonably designed to give actual notice to all persons who would be entitled to notice of a meeting held pursuant to articles 121 to 137 of this title, the articles of incorporation, or bylaws and whether or not the method results in actual notice to all such persons or conforms to the notice requirements that would otherwise apply. In a proceeding under this section, the court may determine who the members or directors are.

(3) The order issued pursuant to this section may dispense with any requirement relating to the holding of or voting at meetings or obtaining votes, including any requirement as to quorums or as to the number or percentage of votes needed for approval, that would otherwise be imposed by articles 121 to 137 of this title, the articles of incorporation, or bylaws.

(4) Whenever practical, any order issued pursuant to this section shall limit the subject matter of meetings or other forms of consent authorized to items, including amendments to the articles of incorporation or bylaws, the resolution of which will or may enable the nonprofit corporation to continue managing its affairs without further resort to this section; except that an order under this section may also authorize the obtaining of whatever votes and approvals are necessary for the dissolution, merger, or sale of assets.

(5) Any meeting or other method of obtaining the vote of members, delegates, or directors conducted pursuant to an order issued under this section and that complies with all the provisions of such order is for all purposes a valid meeting or vote, as the case may be, and shall have the same force and effect as if it complied with every requirement imposed by articles 121 to 137 of this title, the articles of incorporation, or bylaws.

(6) Court ordered meetings may also be held pursuant to section 7-127-103.

ARTICLE 122. INCORPORATION

§ 7-122-101, C.R.S. Incorporators.

One or more persons may act as the incorporator or incorporators of a nonprofit corporation by delivering articles of incorporation to the secretary of state for filing pursuant to part 3 of article 90 of this title. An incorporator who is an individual shall be eighteen years of age or older.

§ 7-122-102, C.R.S. Articles of incorporation.

(1) The articles of incorporation shall state:

(a) The domestic entity name for the nonprofit corporation, which domestic entity name shall comply with part 6 of article 90 of this title;

(b) The registered agent name and registered agent address of the nonprofit corporation's initial registered agent;

(c) The principal office address of the nonprofit corporation's initial principal office;

(d) The true name and mailing address of each incorporator;

(e) Whether or not the nonprofit corporation will have voting members; and

(f) Repealed.

(g) Provisions not inconsistent with law regarding the distribution of assets on dissolution.

(2) The articles of incorporation may but need not state:

(a) The names and addresses of the individuals who are elected to serve as the initial directors;

(b) Provisions not inconsistent with law regarding:

(I) The purpose or purposes for which the nonprofit corporation is incorporated;

(II) Managing and regulating the affairs of the nonprofit corporation;

(III) Defining, limiting, and regulating the powers of the nonprofit corporation, its board of directors, and its members, or any class of members; and

(IV) Whether cumulative voting will be permitted;

(c) Any provision that under articles 121 to 137 of this title is required or permitted to be stated in the bylaws;

(d) The characteristics, qualifications, rights, limitations, and obligations attaching to each or any class of members.

(3) The articles of incorporation need not state any of the corporate powers enumerated in articles 121 to 137 of this title.

(4) If articles 121 to 137 of this title condition any matter upon the presence of a provision in the bylaws, the condition is satisfied if such provision is present either in the articles of incorporation or the bylaws. If articles 121 to 137 of this title condition any matter upon the absence of a provision in the bylaws, the condition is satisfied only if the provision is absent from both the articles of incorporation and the bylaws.

§ 7-122-103, C.R.S. Incorporation.

(1) A nonprofit corporation is incorporated when the articles of incorporation are filed by the secretary of state or, if a delayed effective date is stated pursuant to section 7-90-304 in the articles of incorporation as filed by the secretary of state and if a statement of change revoking the articles of incorporation is not filed before such effective date, on such delayed effective date. The corporate existence begins upon incorporation.

(2) The secretary of state's filing of the articles of incorporation is conclusive that all conditions precedent to incorporation have been met.

§ 7-122-104, C.R.S. Unauthorized assumption of corporate powers.

All persons purporting to act as or on behalf of a nonprofit corporation without authority to do so and without good-faith belief that they have such authority shall be jointly and severally liable for all liabilities incurred or arising as a result thereof.

§ 7-122-105, C.R.S. Organization of nonprofit corporation.

(1) After incorporation:

(a) If initial directors are not named in the articles of incorporation, the incorporators shall hold a meeting, at the call of a majority of the incorporators, to adopt initial bylaws, if desired, and to elect a board of directors; and

(b) If initial directors are named in the articles of incorporation, the initial directors shall hold a meeting, at the call of a majority of the directors, to adopt bylaws, if desired, to appoint officers, and to carry on any other business.

(2) Action required or permitted by articles 121 to 137 of this title to be taken by incorporators at an organizational meeting may be taken without a meeting if the action is taken in the manner provided in section 7-128-202 for action by directors without a meeting.

(3) An organizational meeting may be held in or out of this state.

§ 7-122-106, C.R.S. Bylaws.

(1) The board of directors or, if no directors have been named or elected, the incorporators may adopt initial bylaws. If neither the incorporators nor the board of directors have adopted initial bylaws, the members may do so.

(2) The bylaws of a nonprofit corporation may contain any provision for managing and regulating the affairs of the nonprofit corporation that is not inconsistent with law or with the articles of incorporation.

§ 7-122-107, C.R.S. Emergency bylaws.

(1) Unless otherwise provided in the articles of incorporation, the board of directors may adopt bylaws to be effective only in an emergency as defined in subsection (4) of this section. The emergency bylaws, which are subject to amendment or repeal by the members, may include all provisions necessary for managing the nonprofit corporation during the emergency, including:

(a) Procedures for calling a meeting of the board of directors;

(b) Quorum requirements for the meeting; and

(c) Designation of additional or substitute directors.

(2) All provisions of the regular bylaws consistent with the emergency bylaws shall remain in effect during the emergency. The emergency bylaws shall not be effective after the emergency ends.

(3) Corporate action taken in good faith in accordance with the emergency bylaws:

(a) Binds the nonprofit corporation; and

(b) May not be the basis for imposition of liability on any director, officer, employee, or agent of the nonprofit corporation on the ground that the action was not authorized corporate action.

(4) An emergency exists for the purposes of this section if a quorum of the directors cannot readily be obtained because of some catastrophic event.

ARTICLE 123. PURPOSES AND POWERS

§ 7-123-101, C.R.S. Purposes and applicability.

(1) Every nonprofit corporation incorporated under articles 121 to 137 of this title has the purpose of engaging in any lawful business or activity unless a more limited purpose is stated in the articles of incorporation.

(2) Where another statute of this state requires that corporations of a particular class be formed or incorporated exclusively under that statute, corporations of that class shall be formed or incorporated under such other statute. The corporation shall be subject to all limitations of the other statute.

(3) Where another statute of this state requires nonprofit corporations of a particular class to be formed or incorporated under that statute and also under general nonprofit corporation statutes, such nonprofit corporations shall be formed or incorporated under such other statute and, in addition thereto, under articles 121 to 137 of this title to the extent general nonprofit corporation law is applicable.

(4) Where another statute of this state permits nonprofit corporations of a particular class to be formed or incorporated either under that statute or under the general nonprofit corporation statutes, a nonprofit corporation of that class may at the election of its incorporators be formed or incorporated under articles 121 to 137 of this title. Unless the articles of incorporation of a nonprofit corporation indicate that it is formed or incorporated under another statute, the nonprofit corporation shall for all purposes be considered as formed and incorporated under articles 121 to 137 of this title.

(5) Articles 121 to 137 of this title shall apply to nonprofit corporations of every class, whether or not included in the term "nonprofit corporation" as defined in section 7-121-401 (26), that are formed or incorporated under and governed by other statutes of this state to the extent that said articles are not inconsistent with such other statutes.

(6) Articles 121 to 137 of this title shall apply to any nonprofit corporation formed prior to January 1, 1968, under article 40 or 50 of this title without shares or capital stock and for a purpose for which a nonprofit corporation might be formed under articles 121 to 137 of this title and that elects to accept said articles as provided therein.

(7) Articles 121 to 137 of this title shall apply to any corporation having shares or capital stock and formed under article 40, 50, or 51 of this title, and each nonprofit corporation whether with or without shares or capital stock formed prior to January 1, 1968, under general law or created by special act of the general assembly for a purpose for which a nonprofit corporation may be formed under articles 121 to 137 of this title, but not otherwise entitled to the rights, privileges, immunities, and franchises provided by said articles that elects to accept said articles as provided therein.

(8) A mutual ditch company may elect by a statement in its articles of incorporation that one or more of the provisions of the "Colorado Business Corporation Act", articles 101 to 117 of this title, apply to the mutual ditch company in lieu of one or more of the provisions of articles 121 to 137 of this title.

§ 7-123-102, C.R.S. General powers.

(1) Unless otherwise provided in the articles of incorporation, every nonprofit corporation has perpetual duration and succession in its domestic entity name and has the same powers as an individual to do all things necessary or convenient to carry out its affairs, including the power:

(a) To sue and be sued, complain, and defend in its name;

(b) To have a corporate seal, which may be altered at will, and to use such seal, or a facsimile thereof, including a rubber stamp, by impressing or affixing it or by reproducing it in any other manner;

(c) To make and amend bylaws;

(d) To purchase, receive, lease, and otherwise acquire, and to own, hold, improve, use, and otherwise deal with, real or personal property or any legal or equitable interest in property, wherever located;

(e) To sell, convey, mortgage, pledge, lease, exchange, and otherwise dispose of all or any part of its property;

(f) To purchase, receive, subscribe for, and otherwise acquire shares and other interests in, and obligations of, any other entity; and to own, hold, vote, use, sell, mortgage, lend, pledge, and otherwise dispose of, and deal in and with, the same;

(g) To make contracts and guarantees, incur liabilities, borrow money, issue notes, bonds, and other obligations, and secure any of its obligations by mortgage or pledge of any of its property, franchises, or income;

(h) To lend money, invest and reinvest its funds, and receive and hold real and personal property as security for repayment; except that a nonprofit corporation may not lend money to or guarantee the obligation of a director or officer of the nonprofit corporation;

(i) To be an agent, an associate, a fiduciary, a manager, a member, a partner, a promoter, or a trustee of, or to hold any similar position with, any entity;

(j) To conduct its activities, locate offices, and exercise the powers granted by articles 121 to 137 of this title within or without this state;

(k) To elect or appoint directors, officers, employees, and agents of the nonprofit corporation, define their duties, and fix their compensation;

(l) To pay pensions and establish pension plans, pension trusts, profit sharing plans, and other benefit or incentive plans for any of its current or former directors, officers, employees, and agents;

(m) To make donations for the public welfare or for charitable, religious, scientific, or educational purposes and for other purposes that further the corporate interest;

(n) To impose dues, assessments, admission, and transfer fees upon its members;

(o) To establish conditions for admission of members, admit members, and issue or transfer memberships;

(p) To carry on a business;

(q) To make payments or donations and to do any other act, not inconsistent with law, that furthers the affairs of the nonprofit corporation;

(r) To indemnify current or former directors, officers, employees, fiduciaries, or agents as provided in article 129 of this title;

(s) To limit the liability of its directors as provided in section 7-128-402 (1); and

(t) To cease its corporate activities and dissolve.

(2) Unless permitted by another statute of this state or otherwise permitted pursuant to section 7-123-101 (5), 7-123-101 (7), or 7-137-201, a nonprofit corporation shall not authorize or issue shares of stock.

§ 7-123-103, C.R.S. Emergency powers.

(1) In anticipation of or during an emergency defined in subsection (4) of this section, the board of directors may:

(a) Modify lines of succession to accommodate the incapacity of any director, officer, employee, or agent; and

(b) Relocate the principal office or designate additional offices, or authorize officers to do so.

(2) During an emergency as contemplated in subsection (4) of this section, unless emergency bylaws provide otherwise:

(a) Notice of a meeting of the board of directors need be given only to those directors whom it is practicable to reach and may be given in any practicable manner, including by publication or radio; and

(b) One or more officers of the nonprofit corporation present at a meeting of the board of directors may be deemed to be directors for the meeting, in order of rank and within the same rank in order of seniority, as necessary to achieve a quorum.

(3) Corporate action taken in good faith during an emergency under this section to further the ordinary business affairs of the nonprofit corporation:

(a) Binds the nonprofit corporation; and

(b) May not be the basis for the imposition of liability on any director, officer, employee, or agent of the nonprofit corporation on the ground that the action was not authorized corporate action.

(4) An emergency exists for purposes of this section if a quorum of the directors cannot readily be obtained because of some catastrophic event.

§ 7-123-104, C.R.S. Ultra vires.

(1) Except as provided in subsection (2) of this section, the validity of corporate action may not be challenged on the ground that the nonprofit corporation lacks or lacked power to act.

(2) A nonprofit corporation's power to act may be challenged:

(a) In a proceeding against the nonprofit corporation to enjoin the act. The proceeding may be brought by a director or by a voting member or voting members in a derivative proceeding.

(b) In a proceeding by or in the right of the nonprofit corporation, whether directly, derivatively, or through a receiver, trustee, or other legal representative, against an incumbent or former director, officer, employee, or agent of the nonprofit corporation; or

(c) In a proceeding by the attorney general under section 7-134-301.

(3) In a proceeding under paragraph (a) of subsection (2) of this section to enjoin an unauthorized corporate act, the court may enjoin or set aside the act, if it would be equitable to do so and if all affected persons are parties to the proceeding, and may award damages for loss, including anticipated profits, suffered by the nonprofit corporation or another party because of the injunction.

§ 7-123-105, C.R.S. Actions against nonprofit corporations.

Any other provision of law to the contrary notwithstanding, any civil action permitted under the law of this state may be brought against any nonprofit corporation, and the assets of any nonprofit corporation that would, but for articles 121 to 137 of this title, be immune from levy and execution on any judgment shall nonetheless be subject to levy and execution to the extent that such nonprofit corporation would be reimbursed by proceeds of liability insurance policies carried by it were judgment levied and executed against its assets.

ARTICLE 124. NAME

§ 7-124-101, C.R.S. Corporate name. (Repealed)

§ 7-124-102, C.R.S. Reserved name. (Repealed)

ARTICLE 125. OFFICE AND AGENT

§ 7-125-101, C.R.S. Registered office and registered agent.

Part 7 of article 90 of this title, providing for registered agents and service of process, applies to nonprofit corporations incorporated under or subject to articles 121 to 137 of this title.

ARTICLE 126. MEMBERS AND MEMBERSHIPS

§ 7-126-101, C.R.S. No requirement of members.

A nonprofit corporation is not required to have members.

§ 7-126-102, C.R.S. Admission.

(1) The bylaws may establish criteria or procedures for admission of members.

(2) No person shall be admitted as a member without such person's consent.

(3) A nonprofit corporation may issue certificates evidencing membership therein.

§ 7-126-103, C.R.S. Liability to third parties.

The directors, officers, employees, and members of a nonprofit corporation are not, as such, personally liable for the acts, debts, liabilities, or obligations of a nonprofit corporation.

§ 7-126-104, C.R.S. Consideration.

Unless otherwise provided by the bylaws, a nonprofit corporation may admit members for no consideration or for such consideration as is determined by the board of directors.

§ 7-126-201, C.R.S. Differences in rights and obligations of members.

(1) Unless otherwise provided by articles 121 to 137 of this title or the bylaws:

(a) All voting members shall have the same rights and obligations with respect to voting and all other matters that articles 121 to 137 of this title specifically reserve to voting members; and

(b) With respect to matters not so reserved, all members, including voting members, shall have the same rights and obligations.

§ 7-126-202, C.R.S. Transfers.

(1) Unless otherwise provided by the bylaws, no member of a nonprofit corporation may transfer a membership or any right arising therefrom.

(2) Where transfer rights have been provided, no restriction on them shall be binding with respect to a member holding a membership issued prior to the adoption of the restriction unless the restriction is approved by the affected member.

§ 7-126-203, C.R.S. Creditor's action against member.

No proceeding may be brought by a creditor to reach the liability, if any, of a member to the nonprofit corporation unless final judgment has been rendered in favor of the creditor against the nonprofit corporation and execution has been returned unsatisfied in whole or in part or unless such proceeding would be useless.

§ 7-126-301, C.R.S. Resignation.

(1) Unless otherwise provided by the bylaws, a member may resign at any time.

(2) The resignation of a member does not relieve the member from any obligations the member may have to the nonprofit corporation as a result of obligations incurred or commitments made prior to resignation.

§ 7-126-302, C.R.S. Termination, expulsion, or suspension.

(1) Unless otherwise provided by the bylaws, no member of a nonprofit corporation may be expelled or suspended, and no membership or memberships in such nonprofit corporation may be terminated or suspended except pursuant to a procedure that is fair and reasonable and is carried out in good faith.

(2) For purposes of this section, a procedure is fair and reasonable when either:

(a) The bylaws or a written policy of the board of directors state a procedure that provides:

(I) Not less than fifteen days prior written notice of the expulsion, suspension, or termination and the reasons therefor; and

(II) An opportunity for the member to be heard, orally or in writing, not less than five days before the effective date of the expulsion, suspension, or termination by a person or persons authorized to decide that the proposed expulsion, termination, or suspension not take place; or

(b) It is fair and reasonable taking into consideration all of the relevant facts and circumstances.

(3) For purposes of this section, any written notice given by mail must be given by first-class or certified mail sent to the last address of the member shown on the nonprofit corporation's records.

(4) Unless otherwise provided by the bylaws, any proceeding challenging an expulsion, suspension, or termination, including a proceeding in which defective notice is alleged, must be commenced within one year after the effective date of the expulsion, suspension, or termination.

(5) Unless otherwise provided by the bylaws, a member who has been expelled or suspended may be liable to the nonprofit corporation for dues, assessments, or fees as a result of obligations incurred or commitments made prior to expulsion or suspension.

§ 7-126-303, C.R.S. Purchase of memberships.

Unless otherwise provided by the bylaws, a nonprofit corporation shall not purchase the membership of a member who resigns or whose membership is terminated. If so authorized, a nonprofit corporation may purchase the membership of a member who resigns or whose membership is terminated for the amount and pursuant to the conditions stated in or authorized by its bylaws. No payment shall be made in violation of article 133 of this title.

§ 7-126-304, C.R.S. Residential membership – return of consideration – cessation of periodic payments – time limits – effective date.

(1) Notwithstanding any provision of the articles of incorporation or bylaws to the contrary:

(a) (I) A residential nonprofit corporation shall refund the entrance fee of a residential member to the member or his or her heirs within ninety days after a transfer of the residential membership.

(II) (A) This paragraph (a) applies only to contracts entered into on or after March 11, 2011.

(B) (Deleted by amendment, L. 2012.)

(b) (Deleted by amendment, L. 2012.)

§ 7-126-401, C.R.S. Derivative suits.

(1) Without affecting the right of a member or director to bring a proceeding against a nonprofit corporation or its officers or directors, a proceeding may be brought in the right of a nonprofit corporation to procure a judgment in its favor by:

(a) Any voting member or voting members having five percent or more of the voting power; or

(b) Any director.

(2) In any such proceeding, each complainant shall be a voting member or director at the time of bringing the proceeding.

(3) A complaint in a proceeding brought in the right of a nonprofit corporation must be verified and allege with particularity the demand made, if any, to obtain action by the directors and either why the complainants could not obtain the action or why they did not make the demand. If a demand for action was made and the nonprofit corporation's investigation of the demand is in progress when the proceeding is filed, the court may stay the suit until the investigation is completed.

(4) In any action instituted in the right of a nonprofit corporation by one or more voting members, the court having jurisdiction over the matter may, at any time before final judgment, require the plaintiff to give security for the costs and reasonable expenses that may be directly attributable to and incurred by the nonprofit corporation in the defense of such action or may be incurred by other parties named as defendant for which the nonprofit corporation may become legally liable, but not including fees of attorneys. The amount of such security may from time to time be increased or decreased, in the discretion of the court, upon showing that the security provided has or may become inadequate or is excessive. If the court finds that the action was commenced without reasonable cause, the nonprofit corporation shall have recourse to such security in such amount as the court shall determine upon the termination of such action.

(5) No action shall be commenced in this state by a member of a foreign nonprofit corporation in the right of a foreign nonprofit corporation unless such action is permitted by the law of the state under which such foreign nonprofit corporation is incorporated.

§ 7-126-501, C.R.S. Delegates.

(1) A nonprofit corporation may provide in its bylaws for delegates having some or all of the authority of members.

(2) The bylaws may state provisions relating to:

(a) The characteristics, qualifications, rights, limitations, and obligations of delegates, including their selection and removal;

(b) Calling, noticing, holding, and conducting meetings of delegates; and

(c) Carrying on corporate activities during and between meetings of delegates.

ARTICLE 127. MEMBERS' MEETINGS AND VOTING

§ 7-127-101, C.R.S. Annual and regular meetings.

(1) Unless the bylaws eliminate the requirement for holding an annual meeting, a nonprofit corporation that has voting members shall hold a meeting of the voting members annually at a time stated in or fixed in accordance with the bylaws, or, if not so fixed, at a time and date stated in or fixed in accordance with a resolution of the board of directors.

(2) A nonprofit corporation with members may hold regular membership meetings at a time and date stated in or fixed in accordance with the bylaws, or, if not so fixed, at a time and date stated in or fixed in accordance with a resolution of the board of directors.

(3) Annual and regular membership meetings may be held in or out of this state at the place stated in or fixed in accordance with the bylaws, or, if not so stated or fixed, at a place stated or fixed in accordance with a resolution of the board of directors. If no place is so stated or fixed, annual and regular meetings shall be held at the nonprofit corporation's principal office.

(4) The failure to hold an annual or regular meeting at the time and date determined pursuant to subsection (1) of this section does not affect the validity of any corporate action and does not work a forfeiture or dissolution of the nonprofit corporation.

§ 7-127-102, C.R.S. Special meeting.

(1) A nonprofit corporation shall hold a special meeting of its members:

(a) On call of its board of directors or the person or persons authorized by the bylaws or resolution of the board of directors to call such a meeting; or

(b) Unless otherwise provided by the bylaws, if the nonprofit corporation receives one or more written demands for the meeting, stating the purpose or purposes for which it is to be held, signed and dated by members holding at least ten percent of all the votes entitled pursuant to the bylaws to be cast on any issue proposed to be considered at the meeting.

(2) If not otherwise fixed under section 7-127-103 or 7-127-106, the record date for determining the members entitled to demand a special meeting pursuant to paragraph (b) of subsection (1) of this section is the date of the earliest of any of the demands pursuant to which the meeting is called, or the date that is sixty days before the date the first of such demands is received by the nonprofit corporation, whichever is later.

(3) If a notice for a special meeting demanded pursuant to paragraph (b) of subsection (1) of this section is not given pursuant to section 7-127-104 within thirty days after the date the written demand or demands are delivered to a corporate officer, regardless of the requirements of subsection (4) of this section, a person signing the demand or demands may set the time and place of the meeting and give notice pursuant to section 7-127-104.

(4) Special meetings of the members may be held in or out of this state at the place stated in or fixed in accordance with the bylaws, or, if not so stated or fixed, at a place stated or fixed in accordance with a resolution of the board of directors. If no place is so stated or fixed, special meetings shall be held at the nonprofit corporation's principal office.

(5) Unless otherwise provided by the bylaws, only business within the purpose or purposes described in the notice of the meeting required by section 7-127-104 (3) may be conducted at a special meeting of the members.

§ 7-127-103, C.R.S. Court-ordered meeting.

(1) The holding of a meeting of the members may be summarily ordered by the district court for the county in this state in which the street address of the nonprofit corporation's principal office is located or, if the nonprofit corporation has no principal office in this state, by the district court for the county in which the street address of its registered agent is located or, if the nonprofit corporation has no registered agent, by the district court for the city and county of Denver:

(a) On application of any voting member entitled to participate in an annual meeting if an annual meeting was required to be held and was not held within the earlier of six months after the close of the nonprofit corporation's most recently ended fiscal year or fifteen months after its last annual meeting; or

(b) On application of any person who participated in a call of or demand for a special meeting effective under section 7-127-102 (1), if:

(I) Notice of the special meeting was not given within thirty days after the date of the call or the date the last of the demands necessary to require the calling of the meeting was received by the nonprofit corporation pursuant to section 7-127-102 (1) (b), as the case may be; or

(II) The special meeting was not held in accordance with the notice.

(2) The court may fix the time and place of the meeting, determine the members entitled to participate in the meeting, fix a record date for determining members entitled to notice of and to vote at the meeting, prescribe the form and content of the notice of the meeting, fix the quorum required for specific matters to be considered at the meeting or direct that the votes represented at the meeting constitute a quorum for action on those matters, and enter other orders necessary or appropriate to accomplish the holding of the meeting.

§ 7-127-104, C.R.S. Notice of meeting.

(1) A nonprofit corporation shall give to each member entitled to vote at the meeting notice consistent with its bylaws of meetings of members in a fair and reasonable manner.

(2) Any notice that conforms to the requirements of subsection (3) of this section is fair and reasonable, but other means of giving notice may also be fair and reasonable when all the circumstances are considered.

(3) Notice is fair and reasonable if:

(a) The nonprofit corporation notifies its members of the place, date, and time of each annual, regular, and special meeting of members no fewer than ten days, or if notice is mailed by other than first class or registered mail, no fewer than thirty days, nor more than sixty days before the meeting date, and if notice is given by newspaper as provided in section 7-121-402 (2), the notice must be published five separate times with the first such publication no more than sixty days, and the last such publication no fewer than ten days, before the meeting date.

(b) Notice of an annual or regular meeting includes a description of any matter or matters that must be approved by the members or for which the members' approval is sought under sections 7-128-501, 7-129-110, 7-130-103, 7-130-201, 7-131-102, 7-132-102, and 7-134-102; and

(c) Unless otherwise provided by articles 121 to 137 of this title or the bylaws, notice of a special meeting includes a description of the purpose or purposes for which the meeting is called.

(4) Unless otherwise provided by the bylaws, if an annual, regular, or special meeting of members is adjourned to a different date, time, or place, notice need not be given of the new date, time, or place, if the new date, time, or place is announced at the meeting before adjournment. If a new record date for the adjourned meeting is or must be fixed under section 7-127-106, however, notice of the adjourned meeting must be given under this section to the members of record as of the new record date.

(5) When giving notice of an annual, regular, or special meeting of members, a nonprofit corporation shall give notice of a matter a member intends to raise at the meeting if:

(a) Requested in writing to do so by a person entitled to call a special meeting; and

(b) The request is received by the secretary or president of the nonprofit corporation at least ten days before the nonprofit corporation gives notice of the meeting.

§ 7-127-105, C.R.S. Waiver of notice.

(1) A member may waive any notice required by articles 121 to 137 of this title or by the bylaws, whether before or after the date or time stated in the notice as the date or time when any action will occur or has occurred. The waiver shall be in writing, be signed by the member entitled to the notice, and be delivered to the nonprofit corporation for inclusion in the minutes or filing with the corporate records, but such delivery and filing shall not be conditions of the effectiveness of the waiver.

(2) A member's attendance at a meeting:

(a) Waives objection to lack of notice or defective notice of the meeting, unless the member at the beginning of the meeting objects to holding the meeting or transacting business at the meeting because of lack of notice or defective notice; and

(b) Waives objection to consideration of a particular matter at the meeting that is not within the purpose or purposes described in the meeting notice, unless the member objects to considering the matter when it is presented.

§ 7-127-106, C.R.S. Record date – determining members entitled to notice and vote.

(1) The bylaws may fix or provide the manner of fixing a date as the record date for determining the members entitled to notice of a members' meeting. If the bylaws do not fix or provide for fixing such a record date, the board of directors may fix a future date as such a record date. If no such record date is fixed, members at the close of business on the business day preceding the day on which notice is given, or, if notice is waived, at the close of business on the business day preceding the day on which the meeting is held are entitled to notice of the meeting.

(2) The bylaws may fix or provide the manner of fixing a date as the record date for determining the members entitled to vote at a members' meeting. If the bylaws do not fix or provide for fixing such a record date, the board may fix a future date as such a record date. If no such record date is fixed, members on the date of the meeting who are otherwise eligible to vote are entitled to vote at the meeting.

(3) The bylaws may fix or provide the manner for determining a date as the record date for the purpose of determining the members entitled to exercise any rights in respect of any other lawful action. If the bylaws do not fix or provide for fixing such a record date, the board may fix a future date as the record date. If no such record date is fixed, members at the close of

business on the day on which the board adopts the resolution relating thereto, or the sixtieth day prior to the date of such other action, whichever is later, are entitled to exercise such rights.

(4) A record date fixed under this section may not be more than seventy days before the meeting or action requiring a determination of members occurs.

(5) A determination of members entitled to notice of or to vote at a meeting of members is effective for any adjournment of the meeting unless the board of directors fixes a new date for determining the right to notice or the right to vote, which it must do if the meeting is adjourned to a date more than one hundred twenty days after the record date for determining members entitled to notice of the original meeting.

(6) If a court orders a meeting adjourned to a date more than one hundred twenty days after the date fixed for the original meeting, it may provide that the original record date for notice or voting continues in effect or it may fix a new record date for notice or voting.

§ 7-127-107, C.R.S. Action without meeting.

(1) Unless otherwise provided by the bylaws, any action required or permitted by articles 121 to 137 of this title to be taken at a members' meeting may be taken without a meeting if members entitled to vote thereon unanimously agree and consent to such action in writing.

(2) No action taken pursuant to this section shall be effective unless writings describing and consenting to the action, signed by members sufficient under subsection (1) of this section to take the action and not revoked pursuant to subsection (3) of this section, are received by the nonprofit corporation within sixty days after the date the earliest dated writing describing and consenting to the action is received by the nonprofit corporation. Unless otherwise provided by the bylaws, any such writing may be received by the nonprofit corporation by electronically transmitted facsimile or other form of wire or wireless communication providing the nonprofit corporation with a complete copy thereof, including a copy of the signature thereto. Action taken pursuant to this section shall be effective when the last writing necessary to effect the action is received by the nonprofit corporation, unless the writings describing and consenting to the action state a different effective date.

(3) Any member who has signed a writing describing and consenting to action taken pursuant to this section may revoke such consent by a writing signed and dated by the member describing the action and stating that the member's prior consent thereto is revoked, if such writing is received by the nonprofit corporation before the last writing necessary to effect the action is received by the nonprofit corporation.

(4) Subject to subsection (8) of this section, the record date for determining members entitled to take action without a meeting or entitled to be given notice under subsection (7) of this section of action so taken is the date a writing upon which the action is taken pursuant to subsection (1) of this section is first received by the nonprofit corporation.

(5) Action taken under this section has the same effect as action taken at a meeting of members and may be described as such in any document.

(6) In the event voting members are entitled to vote cumulatively in the election of directors, voting members may take action under this section to elect or remove directors only pursuant to section 7-127-208 and only if the required signed writings describing and consenting to the election or removal of the directors are received by the nonprofit corporation.

(7) In the event action is taken under subsection (1) of this section with less than unanimous consent of all members entitled to vote upon the action, the nonprofit corporation or the members taking the action shall, promptly after all of the writings necessary to effect the action have been received by the nonprofit corporation, give notice of such action to all members who were entitled to vote upon the action. The notice shall contain or be accompanied by the same material, if any, that under articles 121 to 137 of this title would have been required to be given

to members in or with a notice of the meeting at which the action would have been submitted to the members for action.

(8) The district court for the county in this state in which the street address of the nonprofit corporation's principal office is located or, if the nonprofit corporation has no principal office in this state, the district court for the county in which the street address of its registered agent is located or, if the nonprofit corporation has no registered agent, the district court for the city and county of Denver may, upon application of the nonprofit corporation or any member who would be entitled to vote on the action at a members' meeting, summarily state a record date for determining members entitled to sign writings consenting to an action under this section and may enter other orders necessary or appropriate to effect the purposes of this section.

(9) All signed written instruments necessary for any action taken pursuant to this section shall be filed with the minutes of the meetings of the members.

§ 7-127-108, C.R.S. Meetings by telecommunication.

Unless otherwise provided in the bylaws, any or all of the members may participate in an annual, regular, or special meeting of the members by, or the meeting may be conducted through the use of, any means of communication by which all persons participating in the meeting may hear each other during the meeting. A member participating in a meeting by this means is deemed to be present in person at the meeting.

§ 7-127-109, C.R.S. Action by written ballot.

(1) Unless otherwise provided by the bylaws, any action that may be taken at any annual, regular, or special meeting of members may be taken without a meeting if the nonprofit corporation delivers a written ballot to every member entitled to vote on the matter.

(2) A written ballot shall:

- (a) State each proposed action; and
- (b) Provide an opportunity to vote for or against each proposed action.

(3) Approval by written ballot pursuant to this section shall be valid only when the number of votes cast by ballot equals or exceeds the quorum required to be present at a meeting authorizing the action, and the number of approvals equals or exceeds the number of votes that would be required to approve the matter at a meeting at which the total number of votes cast was the same as the number of votes cast by ballot.

(4) All solicitations for votes by written ballot shall:

- (a) Indicate the number of responses needed to meet the quorum requirements;
- (b) State the percentage of approvals necessary to approve each matter other than election of directors;
- (c) State the time by which a ballot must be received by the nonprofit corporation in order to be counted; and
- (d) Be accompanied by written information sufficient to permit each person casting such ballot to reach an informed decision on the matter.

(5) Unless otherwise provided by the bylaws, a written ballot may not be revoked.

(6) Action taken under this section has the same effect as action taken at a meeting of members and may be described as such in any document.

§ 7-127-201, C.R.S. Members list for meeting and action by written ballot.

(1) Unless otherwise provided by the bylaws, after fixing a record date for a notice of a meeting or for determining the members entitled to take action by written ballot, a nonprofit corporation shall prepare an alphabetical list of the names of all its members who are entitled to notice of,

and to vote at, the meeting or to take such action by written ballot. The list shall show the address of each member entitled to notice of, and to vote at, the meeting or to take such action by written ballot and the number of votes each member is entitled to vote at the meeting or by written ballot.

(2) If prepared in connection with a meeting of the members, the members list shall be available for inspection by any member entitled to vote at the meeting, beginning the earlier of ten days before the meeting for which the list was prepared or two business days after notice of the meeting is given and continuing through the meeting, and any adjournment thereof, at the nonprofit corporation's principal office or at a place identified in the notice of the meeting in the city where the meeting will be held. The nonprofit corporation shall make the members list available at the meeting, and any member entitled to vote at the meeting or an agent or attorney of a member entitled to vote at the meeting is entitled to inspect the list at any time during the meeting or any adjournment. If prepared in connection with action to be taken by the members by written ballot, the members list shall be available for inspection by any member entitled to cast a vote by such written ballot, beginning on the date that the first written ballot is delivered to the members and continuing through the time when such written ballots must be received by the nonprofit corporation in order to be counted, at the nonprofit corporation's principal office. A member entitled to vote at the meeting or by such written ballot, or an agent or attorney of a member entitled to vote at the meeting or by such written ballot, is entitled on written demand to inspect and, subject to the requirements of section 7-136-102 (3) and the provisions of section 7-136-103 (2) and (3), to copy the list, during regular business hours, at the member's expense, and during the period it is available for inspection.

(3) If the nonprofit corporation refuses to allow a member entitled to vote at the meeting or by such written ballot, or an agent or attorney of a member entitled to vote at the meeting or by such written ballot, to inspect the members list or to copy the list during the period it is required to be available for inspection under subsection (2) of this section, the district court for the county in this state in which the street address of the nonprofit corporation's principal office is located or, if the nonprofit corporation has no principal office in this state, the district court for the county in which the street address of its registered agent is located, or if the nonprofit corporation has no registered agent in this state, the district court for the city and county of Denver may, on application of the member, summarily order the inspection or copying of the list at the nonprofit corporation's expense and may postpone or adjourn the meeting for which the list was prepared, or postpone the time when the nonprofit corporation must receive written ballots in connection with which the list was prepared, until the inspection or copying is complete.

(4) If a court orders inspection or copying of the list of members pursuant to subsection (3) of this section, unless the nonprofit corporation proves that it refused inspection or copying of the list in good faith because it had a reasonable basis for doubt about the right of the member or the agent or attorney of the member to inspect or copy the list of members:

  (a) The court shall also order the nonprofit corporation to pay the member's costs, including reasonable counsel fees, incurred in obtaining the order;

  (b) The court may order the nonprofit corporation to pay the member for any damages the member incurred; and

  (c) The court may grant the member any other remedy afforded the member by law.

(5) If a court orders inspection or copying of the list of members pursuant to subsection (3) of this section, the court may impose reasonable restrictions on the use or distribution of the list by the member.

(6) Failure to prepare or make available the list of members does not affect the validity of action taken at the meeting or by means of such written ballot.

§ 7-127-202, C.R.S. Voting entitlement generally.

(1) Unless otherwise provided by the bylaws:

(a) Only voting members shall be entitled to vote with respect to any matter required or permitted under articles 121 to 137 of this title to be submitted to a vote of the members;

(b) All references in articles 121 to 137 of this title to votes of or voting by the members shall be deemed to permit voting only by the voting members; and

(c) Voting members shall be entitled to vote with respect to all matters required or permitted under articles 121 to 137 of this title to be submitted to a vote of the members.

(2) Unless otherwise provided by the bylaws, each member entitled to vote shall be entitled to one vote on each matter submitted to a vote of members.

(3) Unless otherwise provided by the bylaws, if a membership stands of record in the names of two or more persons, their acts with respect to voting shall have the following effect:

(a) If only one votes, such act binds all; and

(b) If more than one votes, the vote shall be divided on a pro rata basis.

§ 7-127-203, C.R.S. Proxies.

(1) Unless otherwise provided by the bylaws, a member entitled to vote may vote or otherwise act in person or by proxy.

(2) Without limiting the manner in which a member may appoint a proxy to vote or otherwise act for the member, the following shall constitute valid means of such appointment:

(a) A member may appoint a proxy by signing an appointment form, either personally or by the member's attorney-in-fact.

(b) A member may appoint a proxy by transmitting or authorizing the transmission of a telegram, teletype, or other electronic transmission providing a written statement of the appointment to the proxy, to a proxy solicitor, proxy support service organization, or other person duly authorized by the proxy to receive appointments as agent for the proxy or to the nonprofit corporation; except that the transmitted appointment shall set forth or be transmitted with written evidence from which it can be determined that the member transmitted or authorized the transmission of the appointment.

(3) An appointment of a proxy is effective against the nonprofit corporation when received by the nonprofit corporation, including receipt by the nonprofit corporation of an appointment transmitted pursuant to paragraph (b) of subsection (2) of this section. An appointment is valid for eleven months unless a different period is expressly provided in the appointment form.

(4) Any complete copy, including an electronically transmitted facsimile, of an appointment of a proxy may be substituted for or used in lieu of the original appointment for any purpose for which the original appointment could be used.

(5) An appointment of a proxy is revocable by the member.

(6) Appointment of a proxy is revoked by the person appointing the proxy:

(a) Attending any meeting and voting in person; or

(b) Signing and delivering to the secretary or other officer or agent authorized to tabulate proxy votes either a writing stating that the appointment of the proxy is revoked or a subsequent appointment form.

(7) The death or incapacity of the member appointing a proxy does not affect the right of the nonprofit corporation to accept the proxy's authority unless notice of the death or incapacity is received by the secretary or other officer or agent authorized to tabulate votes before the proxy exercises the proxy's authority under the appointment.

(8) Subject to section 7-127-204 and to any express limitation on the proxy's authority appearing on the appointment form, a nonprofit corporation is entitled to accept the proxy's vote or other action as that of the member making the appointment.

§ 7-127-204, C.R.S. Nonprofit corporation's acceptance of votes.

(1) If the name signed on a vote, consent, written ballot, waiver, proxy appointment, or proxy appointment revocation corresponds to the name of a member, the nonprofit corporation, if acting in good faith, is entitled to accept the vote, consent, written ballot, waiver, proxy appointment, or proxy appointment revocation and to give it effect as the act of the member.

(2) If the name signed on a vote, consent, written ballot, waiver, proxy appointment, or proxy appointment revocation does not correspond to the name of a member, the nonprofit corporation, if acting in good faith, is nevertheless entitled to accept the vote, consent, written ballot, waiver, proxy appointment, or proxy appointment revocation and to give it effect as the act of the member if:

(a) The member is an entity and the name signed purports to be that of an officer or agent of the entity;

(b) The name signed purports to be that of an administrator, executor, guardian, or conservator representing the member and, if the nonprofit corporation requests, evidence of fiduciary status acceptable to the nonprofit corporation has been presented with respect to the vote, consent, written ballot, waiver, proxy appointment, or proxy appointment revocation;

(c) The name signed purports to be that of a receiver or trustee in bankruptcy of the member and, if the nonprofit corporation requests, evidence of this status acceptable to the nonprofit corporation has been presented with respect to the vote, consent, written ballot, waiver, proxy appointment, or proxy appointment revocation;

(d) The name signed purports to be that of a pledgee, beneficial owner, or attorney-in-fact of the member and, if the nonprofit corporation requests, evidence acceptable to the nonprofit corporation of the signatory's authority to sign for the member has been presented with respect to the vote, consent, written ballot, waiver, proxy appointment, or proxy appointment revocation;

(e) Two or more persons are the member as cotenants or fiduciaries and the name signed purports to be the name of at least one of the cotenants or fiduciaries and the person signing appears to be acting on behalf of all the cotenants or fiduciaries; or

(f) The acceptance of the vote, consent, written ballot, waiver, proxy appointment, or proxy appointment revocation is otherwise proper under rules established by the nonprofit corporation that are not inconsistent with the provisions of this subsection (2).

(3) The nonprofit corporation is entitled to reject a vote, consent, written ballot, waiver, proxy appointment, or proxy appointment revocation if the secretary or other officer or agent authorized to tabulate votes, acting in good faith, has reasonable basis for doubt about the validity of the signature on it or about the signatory's authority to sign for the member.

(4) The nonprofit corporation and its officer or agent who accepts or rejects a vote, consent, written ballot, waiver, proxy appointment, or proxy appointment revocation in good faith and in accordance with the standards of this section are not liable in damages for the consequences of the acceptance or rejection.

(5) Corporate action based on the acceptance or rejection of a vote, consent, written ballot, waiver, proxy appointment, or proxy appointment revocation under this section is valid unless a court of competent jurisdiction determines otherwise.

§ 7-127-205, C.R.S. Quorum and voting requirements for voting groups.

(1) Members entitled to vote as a separate voting group may take action on a matter at a meeting only if a quorum of those members exists with respect to that matter. Unless otherwise provided in articles 121 to 137 of this title or the bylaws, twenty-five percent of the votes entitled to be cast on the matter by the voting group constitutes a quorum of that voting group for action on that matter.

(2) Once a member is represented for any purpose at a meeting, including the purpose of determining that a quorum exists, the member is deemed present for quorum purposes for the remainder of the meeting and for any adjournment of that meeting, unless otherwise provided in the bylaws or unless a new record date is or shall be set for that adjourned meeting.

(3) If a quorum exists, action on a matter other than the election of directors by a voting group is approved if the votes cast within the voting group favoring the action exceed the votes cast within the voting group opposing the action, unless a greater number of affirmative votes is required by articles 121 to 137 of this title or the bylaws.

(4) An amendment to the articles of incorporation or the bylaws adding, changing, or deleting a quorum or voting requirement for a voting group greater than that specified in subsection (1) or (3) of this section is governed by section 7-127-207 (2).

(5) The election of directors is governed by section 7-127-208.

§ 7-127-206, C.R.S. Action by single and multiple voting groups.

(1) If articles 121 to 137 of this title or the bylaws provide for voting by a single voting group on a matter, action on that matter is taken when voted upon by that voting group as provided in section 7-127-205.

(2) If articles 121 to 137 of this title or the bylaws provide for voting by two or more voting groups on a matter, action on that matter is taken only when voted upon by each of those voting groups counted separately as provided in section 7-127-205. One voting group may vote on a matter even though no action is taken by another voting group entitled to vote on the matter.

§ 7-127-207, C.R.S. Lesser or greater quorum or greater voting requirements.

(1) The bylaws may provide for a lesser or a greater quorum requirement, or a greater voting requirement for members or voting groups than is provided for by articles 121 to 137 of this title.

(2) An amendment to the articles of incorporation or the bylaws that adds, changes, or deletes a lesser or a greater quorum requirement or a greater voting requirement shall meet the same quorum requirement and be adopted by the same vote and voting groups required to take action under the quorum and voting requirements then in effect or proposed to be adopted, whichever is greater.

§ 7-127-208, C.R.S. Voting for directors – cumulative voting.

(1) If the bylaws provide for cumulative voting for directors by the voting members, voting members may so vote, by multiplying the number of votes the voting members are entitled to cast by the number of directors for whom they are entitled to vote and cast the product for a single candidate or distribute the product among two or more candidates.

(2) Cumulative voting is not authorized at a particular meeting unless:

   (a) The meeting notice or statement accompanying the notice states that cumulative voting will take place; or

   (b) A voting member gives notice during the meeting and before the vote is taken of the voting member's intent to cumulate votes, and if one voting member gives this notice all other voting members participating in the election are entitled to cumulate their votes without giving further notice.

(3) If cumulative voting is in effect, a director may not be removed if the number of votes cast against such removal, or not consenting in writing to such removal, would be sufficient to elect such director if voted cumulatively at an election for such director.

(4) Members may not vote cumulatively if the directors and members are identical.

(5) In an election of multiple directors, that number of candidates equaling the number of directors to be elected, having the highest number of votes cast in favor of their election, are elected to the board of directors. When only one director is being voted upon, the affirmative vote of a majority of the members constituting a quorum at the meeting at which the election occurs shall be required for election to the board of directors.

§ 7-127-209, C.R.S. Other methods of electing directors.

(1) A nonprofit corporation may provide in its bylaws for election of directors by voting members or delegates:

(a) On the basis of chapter or other organizational unit;

(b) By region or other geographic unit;

(c) By preferential voting; or

(d) By any other reasonable method.

§ 7-127-301, C.R.S. Voting agreements.

(1) Two or more members may provide for the manner in which they will vote by signing an agreement for that purpose.

(2) A voting agreement created under this section is specifically enforceable.

ARTICLE 128. DIRECTORS AND OFFICERS

§ 7-128-101, C.R.S. Requirement for board of directors.

(1) Unless otherwise provided in the articles of incorporation, each nonprofit corporation shall have a board of directors. The board of directors and the directors may be known by any other names designated in the bylaws.

(2) Subject to any provision stated in the articles of incorporation, all corporate powers shall be exercised by or under the authority of, and the business and affairs of the nonprofit corporation managed under the direction of, the board of directors or such other persons as the articles of incorporation provide shall have the authority and perform the duties of a board of directors. To the extent the articles of incorporation provide that other persons shall have the authority and perform the duties of the board of directors, the directors shall be relieved to that extent from such authority and duties.

§ 7-128-102, C.R.S. Qualifications of directors.

A director shall be an individual. The bylaws may prescribe other qualifications for directors. A director need not be a resident of this state or a member of the nonprofit corporation unless the bylaws so prescribe.

§ 7-128-103, C.R.S. Number of directors.

(1) A board of directors shall consist of one or more directors, with the number stated in, or fixed in accordance with, the bylaws.

(2) The bylaws may establish, or permit the voting members or the board of directors to establish, a range for the size of the board of directors by fixing a minimum and maximum number of directors. If a range is established, the number of directors may be fixed or changed from time to time within the range by the voting members or the board of directors.

§ 7-128-104, C.R.S. Election, appointment, and designation of directors.

(1) All directors except the initial directors shall be elected, appointed, or designated as provided in the bylaws. If no method of election, appointment, or designation is stated in the bylaws, the directors other than the initial directors shall be elected as follows:

   (a) If the nonprofit corporation has voting members, all directors except the initial directors shall be elected by the voting members at each annual meeting of the voting members; and

   (b) If the nonprofit corporation does not have voting members, all directors except the initial directors shall be elected by the board of directors.

(2) The bylaws may authorize the election of all or a stated number or portion of directors, except the initial directors, by the members of one or more voting groups of voting members or by the directors of one or more authorized classes of directors. A class of voting members or directors entitled to elect one or more directors is a separate voting group for purposes of the election of directors.

(3) The bylaws may authorize the appointment of one or more directors by such person or persons, or by the holder of such office or position, as the bylaws shall state.

(4) For purposes of articles 121 to 137 of this title, designation occurs when the bylaws name an individual as a director or designate the holder of some office or position as a director.

§ 7-128-105, C.R.S. Terms of directors generally.

(1) The bylaws may state the terms of directors. In the absence of any term stated in the bylaws, the term of each director shall be one year. Unless otherwise provided in the bylaws, directors may be elected for successive terms.

(2) Unless otherwise provided in the bylaws, the terms of the initial directors of a nonprofit corporation expire at the first meeting at which directors are elected or appointed.

(3) A decrease in the number of directors or in the term of office does not shorten an incumbent director's term.

(4) Unless otherwise provided in the bylaws, the term of a director filling a vacancy expires at the end of the unexpired term that such director is filling.

(5) Despite the expiration of a director's term, a director continues to serve until the director's successor is elected, appointed, or designated and qualifies, or until there is a decrease in the number of directors.

(6) Repealed.

§ 7-128-106, C.R.S. Staggered terms for directors.

The bylaws may provide for staggering the terms of directors by dividing the total number of directors into any number of groups. The terms of office of the several groups need not be uniform.

§ 7-128-107, C.R.S. Resignation of directors.

(1) A director may resign at any time by giving written notice of resignation to the nonprofit corporation.

(2) A resignation of a director is effective when the notice is received by the nonprofit corporation unless the notice states a later effective date.

(3) Repealed.

(4) If, at the beginning of a director's term on the board, the bylaws provide that a director may be deemed to have resigned for failing to attend a stated number of board meetings, or for failing to meet other stated obligations of directors, and if such failure to attend or meet obligations is confirmed by an affirmative vote of the board of directors, then such failure to attend or meet obligations shall be effective as a resignation at the time of such vote of the board.

§ 7-128-108, C.R.S. Removal of directors.

(1) Directors elected by voting members or directors may be removed as follows:

(a) The voting members may remove one or more directors elected by them with or without cause unless the bylaws provide that directors may be removed only for cause.

(b) If a director is elected by a voting group, only that voting group may participate in the vote to remove that director.

(c) Subject to section 7-127-208 (3), a director may be removed only if the number of votes cast to remove the director would be sufficient to elect the director at a meeting to elect directors.

(d) A director elected by voting members may be removed by the voting members only at a meeting called for the purpose of removing that director, and the meeting notice shall state that the purpose, or one of the purposes, of the meeting is removal of the director.

(e) An entire board of directors may be removed under paragraphs (a) to (d) of this subsection (1).

(f) A director elected by the board of directors may be removed with or without cause by the vote of a majority of the directors then in office or such greater number as is stated in the bylaws; except that a director elected by the board of directors to fill the vacancy of a director elected by the voting members may be removed without cause by the voting members, but not the board of directors.

(g) (Deleted by amendment, L. 2000, p. 983, § 83, effective July 1, 2000.)

(2) Unless otherwise provided in the bylaws:

(a) An appointed director may be removed without cause by the person appointing the director;

(b) The person removing the director shall do so by giving written notice of the removal to the director and to the nonprofit corporation; and

(c) A removal is effective when the notice is received by both the director to be removed and the nonprofit corporation unless the notice states a later effective date.

(3) A designated director may be removed by an amendment to the bylaws deleting or changing the designation.

(4) Repealed.

§ 7-128-109, C.R.S. Removal of directors by judicial proceeding.

(1) A director may be removed by the district court for the county in this state in which the address of the nonprofit corporation's principal office is located or, if the nonprofit corporation has no principal office in this state, by the district court for the county in which the street address of its registered agent is located, or, if the nonprofit corporation has no registered agent, by the district court for the city and county of Denver, in a proceeding commenced either by the nonprofit corporation or by voting members holding at least ten percent of the votes entitled to be cast in the election of such director's successor, if the court finds that the director engaged in fraudulent or dishonest conduct or gross abuse of authority or discretion with respect to the nonprofit corporation, or a final judgment has been entered finding that the director has violated

a duty set forth in part 4 of this article, and that removal is in the best interests of the nonprofit corporation.

(2) The court that removes a director may bar the director from reelection for a period prescribed by the court.

(3) If voting members commence a proceeding under subsection (1) of this section, they shall make the nonprofit corporation a party defendant.

(4) Repealed.

§ 7-128-110, C.R.S. Vacancy on board.

(1) Unless otherwise provided in the bylaws, if a vacancy occurs on a board of directors, including a vacancy resulting from an increase in the number of directors:

(a) The voting members, if any, may fill the vacancy;

(b) The board of directors may fill the vacancy; or

(c) If the directors remaining in office constitute fewer than a quorum of the board of directors, they may fill the vacancy by the affirmative vote of a majority of all the directors remaining in office.

(2) Notwithstanding subsection (1) of this section, unless otherwise provided in the bylaws, if the vacant office was held by a director elected by a voting group of voting members:

(a) If one or more of the remaining directors were elected by the same voting group of voting members, only such directors are entitled to vote to fill the vacancy if it is filled by directors, and they may do so by the affirmative vote of a majority of such directors remaining in office; and

(b) Only that voting group is entitled to vote to fill the vacancy if it is filled by the voting members.

(3) Notwithstanding subsection (1) of this section, unless otherwise provided in the bylaws, if the vacant office was held by a director elected by a voting group of directors, and if any persons in that voting group remain as directors, only such directors are entitled to vote to fill the vacancy.

(4) Unless otherwise provided in the bylaws, if a vacant office was held by an appointed director, only the person who appointed the director may fill the vacancy.

(5) If a vacant office was held by a designated director, the vacancy shall be filled as provided in the bylaws. In the absence of an applicable bylaw provision, the vacancy may not be filled by the board.

(6) A vacancy that will occur at a specific later date, by reason of a resignation effective at a later date under section 7-128-107 (2) or otherwise, may be filled before the vacancy occurs, but the new director may not take office until the vacancy occurs.

§ 7-128-111, C.R.S. Compensation of directors.

Unless otherwise provided in the bylaws, the board of directors may authorize and fix the compensation of directors.

§ 7-128-201, C.R.S. Meetings.

(1) The board of directors may hold regular or special meetings in or out of this state.

(2) Unless otherwise provided in the bylaws, the board of directors may permit any director to participate in a regular or special meeting by, or conduct the meeting through the use of, any means of communication by which all directors participating may hear each other during the meeting. A director participating in a meeting by this means is deemed to be present in person at the meeting.

§ 7-128-202, C.R.S. Action without meeting.

(1) Unless otherwise provided in the bylaws, any action required or permitted by articles 121 to 137 of this title to be taken at a board of directors' meeting may be taken without a meeting if notice is transmitted in writing to each member of the board and each member of the board by the time stated in the notice:

(a) Votes in writing for such action; or

(b) (I) Votes in writing against such action, abstains in writing from voting, or fails to respond or vote; and

(II) Fails to demand in writing that action not be taken without a meeting.

(2) The notice required by subsection (1) of this section shall state:

(a) The action to be taken;

(b) The time by which a director must respond;

(c) That failure to respond by the time stated in the notice will have the same effect as abstaining in writing by the time stated in the notice and failing to demand in writing by the time stated in the notice that action not be taken without a meeting; and

(d) Any other matters the nonprofit corporation determines to include.

(3) Action is taken under this section only if, at the end of the time stated in the notice transmitted pursuant to subsection (1) of this section:

(a) The affirmative votes in writing for such action received by the nonprofit corporation and not revoked pursuant to subsection (5) of this section equal or exceed the minimum number of votes that would be necessary to take such action at a meeting at which all of the directors then in office were present and voted; and

(b) The nonprofit corporation has not received a written demand by a director that such action not be taken without a meeting other than a demand that has been revoked pursuant to subsection (5) of this section.

(4) A director's right to demand that action not be taken without a meeting shall be deemed to have been waived unless the nonprofit corporation receives such demand from the director in writing by the time stated in the notice transmitted pursuant to subsection (1) of this section and such demand has not been revoked pursuant to subsection (5) of this section.

(5) Any director who in writing has voted, abstained, or demanded action not be taken without a meeting pursuant to this section may revoke such vote, abstention, or demand in writing received by the nonprofit corporation by the time stated in the notice transmitted pursuant to subsection (1) of this section.

(6) Unless the notice transmitted pursuant to subsection (1) of this section states a different effective date, action taken pursuant to this section shall be effective at the end of the time stated in the notice transmitted pursuant to subsection (1) of this section.

(7) A writing by a director under this section shall be in a form sufficient to inform the nonprofit corporation of the identity of the director, the vote, abstention, demand, or revocation of the director, and the proposed action to which such vote, abstention, demand, or revocation relates. Unless otherwise provided by the bylaws, all communications under this section may be transmitted or received by the nonprofit corporation by electronically transmitted facsimile, e-mail, or other form of wire or wireless communication. For purposes of this section, communications to the nonprofit corporation are not effective until received.

(8) Action taken pursuant to this section has the same effect as action taken at a meeting of directors and may be described as such in any document.

(9) All writings made pursuant to this section shall be filed with the minutes of the meetings of the board of directors.

§ 7-128-203, C.R.S. Notice of meeting – rights of residential members.

(1) Unless otherwise provided in articles 121 to 137 of this title or in the bylaws, regular meetings of the board of directors may be held without notice of the date, time, place, or purpose of the meeting.

(2) Unless the bylaws provide for a longer or shorter period, special meetings of the board of directors shall be preceded by at least two days' notice of the date, time, and place of the meeting. The notice need not describe the purpose of the special meeting unless otherwise required by articles 121 to 137 of this title or the bylaws.

(3) Notwithstanding subsections (1) and (2) of this section, and notwithstanding any provision of the articles of incorporation or bylaws to the contrary, the following rules and procedures apply to meetings of the board of directors of a residential nonprofit corporation or any committee of the board:

(a) (I) (A) All regular and special meetings of the residential nonprofit corporation's board of directors or executive committee, or any committee of the board that is authorized to take final action on the board's behalf, must be open to attendance by all residential members or their representatives. The board shall make agendas for meetings of the board, and agendas for meetings of committees of the board that are authorized to take final action on the board's behalf, reasonably available for examination in advance by all residential members or their representatives. If there is no formal agenda, residential members or their representatives are nonetheless entitled to a general description of the purpose of the meeting and the subject matter that will be discussed.

(B) The board shall inform all members, at least annually, of the method by which meeting agendas and other information required by sub-subparagraph (A) of this subparagraph (I) will be provided, including the physical location of places where agendas and meeting notices may be posted or the web address where on-line postings may be made. The board shall give at least thirty days' advance notice of any change in the manner or means by which meeting information will be provided.

(II) The residential nonprofit corporation is encouraged to provide all notices and agendas required by this article in electronic form, by posting on a web site or otherwise, in addition to printed form. If such electronic means are available, the corporation shall provide notice of all regular and special meetings of residential members by electronic mail to all residential members who so request and who furnish the corporation with their electronic mail addresses. Electronic notice of a special meeting must be given as soon as possible but at least twenty-four hours before the meeting.

(b) At an appropriate time determined by the board of directors, but before the board votes on an issue under discussion, the board shall permit residential members or their designated representatives to speak regarding the issue. The board may place reasonable time restrictions on persons speaking during the meeting. If more than one person desires to address an issue and there are opposing views, the board shall provide for a reasonable number of persons to speak on each side of the issue.

(c) The board of directors or any committee of the board may hold an executive or closed-door session and may restrict attendance to board members and such other persons requested by the board during a regular or specially announced meeting or a part thereof. The matters to be discussed at such an executive session may include only matters enumerated in paragraph (d) of this subsection (3).

(d) Matters for discussion by an executive or closed session are limited to:

(I) Matters pertaining to employees of the residential nonprofit corporation or the managing agent's contract or involving the employment, promotion, discipline, or dismissal of an officer, agent, or employee of the corporation;

(II) Consultation with legal counsel concerning disputes that are the subject of pending or imminent court proceedings or matters that are privileged or confidential between attorney and client;

(III) Investigative proceedings concerning possible or actual criminal misconduct;

(IV) Matters subject to specific constitutional, statutory, or judicially imposed requirements protecting particular proceedings or matters from public disclosure;

(V) Any matter the disclosure of which would constitute an unwarranted invasion of individual privacy;

(VI) Review of or discussion relating to any written or oral communication from legal counsel.

(e) Upon the final resolution of any matter for which the board of directors received legal advice or that concerned pending or contemplated litigation, the board may elect to preserve the attorney-client privilege in any appropriate manner, or it may elect to disclose such information, as it deems appropriate, about such matter in an open meeting.

(f) Before the board of directors or any committee of the board convenes in executive session, the chair of the body shall announce the general matter of discussion as enumerated in paragraph (d) of this subsection (3).

(g) The board of directors shall not adopt any change to the residential nonprofit corporation's articles of incorporation or bylaws during an executive session. An articles of incorporation or bylaw change may be validly adopted only during a regular or special meeting or after the board of directors goes back into regular session following an executive session.

(h) The minutes of all meetings at which an executive session was held must indicate that an executive session was held and the general subject matter of the executive session.

§ 7-128-204, C.R.S. Waiver of notice.

(1) A director may waive any notice of a meeting before or after the time and date of the meeting stated in the notice. Except as provided by subsection (2) of this section, the waiver shall be in writing and signed by the director entitled to the notice. Such waiver shall be delivered to the nonprofit corporation for filing with the corporate records, but such delivery and filing shall not be conditions of the effectiveness of the waiver.

(2) A director's attendance at or participation in a meeting waives any required notice to that director of the meeting unless:

(a) At the beginning of the meeting or promptly upon the director's later arrival, the director objects to holding the meeting or transacting business at the meeting because of lack of notice or defective notice and does not thereafter vote for or assent to action taken at the meeting; or

(b) If special notice was required of a particular purpose pursuant to section 7-128-203 (2), the director objects to transacting business with respect to the purpose for which such special notice was required and does not thereafter vote for or assent to action taken at the meeting with respect to such purpose.

§ 7-128-205, C.R.S. Quorum and voting.

(1) Unless a greater or lesser number is required by the bylaws, a quorum of a board of directors consists of a majority of the number of directors in office immediately before the meeting begins.

(2) The bylaws may authorize a quorum of a board of directors to consist of:

(a) No fewer than one-third of the number of directors fixed if the corporation has a fixed board size; or

(b) No fewer than one-third of the number of directors fixed or, if no number is fixed, of the number in office immediately before the meeting begins, if a range for the size of the board is established pursuant to section 7-128-103 (2).

(3) If a quorum is present when a vote is taken, the affirmative vote of a majority of directors present is the act of the board of directors unless the vote of a greater number of directors is required by articles 121 to 137 of this title or the bylaws.

(4) If provided in the bylaws, for purposes of determining a quorum with respect to a particular proposal, and for purposes of casting a vote for or against a particular proposal, a director may be deemed to be present at a meeting and to vote if the director has granted a signed written proxy to another director who is present at the meeting, authorizing the other director to cast the vote that is directed to be cast by the written proxy with respect to the particular proposal that is described with reasonable specificity in the proxy. Except as provided in this subsection (4) and as permitted by section 7-128-202, directors may not vote or otherwise act by proxy.

(5) A director who is present at a meeting of the board of directors when corporate action is taken is deemed to have assented to all action taken at the meeting unless:

(a) The director objects at the beginning of the meeting, or promptly upon the director's arrival, to holding the meeting or transacting business at the meeting and does not thereafter vote for or assent to any action taken at the meeting;

(b) The director contemporaneously requests that the director's dissent or abstention as to any specific action taken be entered in the minutes of the meeting; or

(c) The director causes written notice of the director's dissent or abstention as to any specific action to be received by the presiding officer of the meeting before adjournment of the meeting or by the nonprofit corporation promptly after adjournment of the meeting.

(6) The right of dissent or abstention pursuant to subsection (5) of this section as to a specific action is not available to a director who votes in favor of the action taken.

§ 7-128-206, C.R.S. Committees of the board.

(1) Unless otherwise provided in the bylaws and subject to the provisions of section 7-129-106, the board of directors may create one or more committees of the board and appoint one or more directors to serve on them.

(2) Unless otherwise provided in the bylaws, the creation of a committee of the board and appointment of directors to it shall be approved by the greater of a majority of all the directors in office when the action is taken or the number of directors required by the bylaws to take action under section 7-128-205.

(3) Unless otherwise provided in the bylaws, sections 7-128-201 to 7-128-205, which govern meetings, action without meeting, notice, waiver of notice, and quorum and voting requirements of the board of directors, apply to committees of the board and their members as well.

(4) To the extent stated in the bylaws or by the board of directors, each committee of the board shall have the authority of the board of directors under section 7-128-101; except that a committee of the board shall not:

(a) Authorize distributions;

(b) Approve or propose to members action that articles 121 to 137 of this title require to be approved by members;

(c) Elect, appoint, or remove any director;

(d) Amend articles of incorporation pursuant to section 7-130-102;

(e) Adopt, amend, or repeal bylaws;

(f) Approve a plan of conversion or plan of merger not requiring member approval; or

(g) Approve a sale, lease, exchange, or other disposition of all, or substantially all, of its property, with or without goodwill, otherwise than in the usual and regular course of business subject to approval by members.

(5) The creation of, delegation of authority to, or action by a committee does not alone constitute compliance by a director with the standards of conduct described in section 7-128-401.

(6) Nothing in this part 2 shall prohibit or restrict a nonprofit corporation from establishing in its bylaws or by action of the board of directors or otherwise one or more committees, advisory boards, auxiliaries, or other bodies of any kind, having such members and rules of procedure as the bylaws or board of directors may provide, in order to provide such advice, service, and assistance to the nonprofit corporation, and to carry out such duties and responsibilities for the nonprofit corporation, as may be stated in the bylaws or by the board of directors; except that, if any such committee or other body has one or more members thereof who are entitled to vote on committee matters and who are not then also directors, such committee or other body may not exercise any power or authority reserved to the board of directors in articles 121 to 137 of this title, in the articles of incorporation, or in the bylaws.

§ 7-128-301, C.R.S. Officers.

(1) Unless otherwise provided in the bylaws, a nonprofit corporation shall have a president, a secretary, a treasurer, and such other officers as may be designated by the board of directors. An officer shall be an individual who is eighteen years of age or older. An officer need not be a director or a member of the nonprofit corporation, unless the bylaws so prescribe.

(2) Officers may be appointed by the board of directors or in such other manner as the board of directors or bylaws may provide. A duly appointed officer may appoint one or more officers or assistant officers if authorized by the bylaws or the board of directors.

(3) The bylaws or the board of directors shall delegate to the secretary or to one or more other persons responsibility for the preparation and maintenance of minutes of the directors' and members' meetings and other records and information required to be kept by the nonprofit corporation under section 7-136-101 and for authenticating records of the nonprofit corporation.

(4) The same individual may simultaneously hold more than one office in the nonprofit corporation.

§ 7-128-302, C.R.S. Duties of officers.

Each officer shall have the authority and shall perform the duties stated with respect to such office in the bylaws or, to the extent not inconsistent with the bylaws, prescribed with respect to such office by the board of directors or by an officer authorized by the board of directors.

§ 7-128-303, C.R.S. Resignation and removal of officers.

(1) An officer may resign at any time by giving written notice of resignation to the nonprofit corporation.

(2) A resignation of an officer is effective when the notice is received by the nonprofit corporation unless the notice states a later effective date.

(3) If a resignation is made effective at a later date, the board of directors may permit the officer to remain in office until the effective date and may fill the pending vacancy before the effective date with the provision that the successor does not take office until the effective date, or the board of directors may remove the officer at any time before the effective date and may fill the resulting vacancy.

(4) Unless otherwise provided in the bylaws, the board of directors may remove any officer at any time with or without cause. The bylaws or the board of directors may make provisions for the removal of officers by other officers or by the voting members.

(5) Repealed.

§ 7-128-304, C.R.S. Contract rights with respect to officers.

(1) The appointment of an officer does not itself create contract rights.

(2) An officer's removal does not affect the officer's contract rights, if any, with the nonprofit corporation. An officer's resignation does not affect the nonprofit corporation's contract rights, if any, with the officer.

§ 7-128-401, C.R.S. General standards of conduct for directors and officers.

(1) Each director shall discharge the director's duties as a director, including the director's duties as a member of a committee of the board, and each officer with discretionary authority shall discharge the officer's duties under that authority:

(a) In good faith;

(b) With the care an ordinarily prudent person in a like position would exercise under similar circumstances; and

(c) In a manner the director or officer reasonably believes to be in the best interests of the nonprofit corporation.

(2) In discharging duties, a director or officer is entitled to rely on information, opinions, reports, or statements, including financial statements and other financial data, if prepared or presented by:

(a) One or more officers or employees of the nonprofit corporation whom the director or officer reasonably believes to be reliable and competent in the matters presented;

(b) Legal counsel, a public accountant, or another person as to matters the director or officer reasonably believes are within such person's professional or expert competence;

(c) Religious authorities or ministers, priests, rabbis, or other persons whose position or duties in the nonprofit corporation, or in a religious organization with which the nonprofit corporation is affiliated, the director or officer believes justify reliance and confidence and who the director or officer believes to be reliable and competent in the matters presented; or

(d) In the case of a director, a committee of the board of directors of which the director is not a member if the director reasonably believes the committee merits confidence.

(3) A director or officer is not acting in good faith if the director or officer has knowledge concerning the matter in question that makes reliance otherwise permitted by subsection (2) of this section unwarranted.

(4) A director or officer is not liable as such to the nonprofit corporation or its members for any action taken or omitted to be taken as a director or officer, as the case may be, if, in connection with such action or omission, the director or officer performed the duties of the position in compliance with this section.

(5) A director, regardless of title, shall not be deemed to be a trustee with respect to the nonprofit corporation or with respect to any property held or administered by the nonprofit corporation

including, without limitation, property that may be subject to restrictions imposed by the donor or transferor of such property.

(6) A director or officer of a nonprofit corporation, in the performance of duties in that capacity, shall not have any fiduciary duty to any creditor of the nonprofit corporation arising only from the status as a creditor.

(7) No person shall be liable in contract or tort merely by reason of being a director, officer, or member of a nonprofit corporation that was suspended, declared defunct, administratively dissolved, or dissolved by operation of law, and the business or activities of which have been continued for nonprofit purposes, with or without knowledge of the suspension, declaration, or dissolution, and the business and activities of which have not been wound up.

§ 7-128-402, C.R.S. Limitation of certain liabilities of directors and officers.

(1) If so provided in the articles of incorporation, the nonprofit corporation shall eliminate or limit the personal liability of a director to the nonprofit corporation or to its members for monetary damages for breach of fiduciary duty as a director; except that any such provision shall not eliminate or limit the liability of a director to the nonprofit corporation or to its members for monetary damages for any breach of the director's duty of loyalty to the nonprofit corporation or to its members, acts or omissions not in good faith or that involve intentional misconduct or a knowing violation of law, acts specified in section 7-128-403 or 7-128-501 (2), or any transaction from which the director directly or indirectly derived an improper personal benefit. No such provision shall eliminate or limit the liability of a director to the nonprofit corporation or to its members for monetary damages for any act or omission occurring before the date when such provision becomes effective.

(2) No director or officer shall be personally liable for any injury to person or property arising out of a tort committed by an employee unless such director or officer was personally involved in the situation giving rise to the litigation or unless such director or officer committed a criminal offense in connection with such situation. The protection afforded in this subsection (2) shall not restrict other common law protections and rights that a director or officer may have. This subsection (2) shall not restrict the nonprofit corporation's right to eliminate or limit the personal liability of a director to the nonprofit corporation or to its members for monetary damages for breach of fiduciary duty as a director as provided in subsection (1) of this section.

§ 7-128-403, C.R.S. Liability of directors for unlawful distributions.

(1) A director who votes for or assents to a distribution made in violation of section 7-133-101 or the articles of incorporation is personally liable to the nonprofit corporation for the amount of the distribution that exceeds what could have been distributed without violating said section or the articles of incorporation if it is established that the director did not perform the director's duties in compliance with section 7-128-401. In any proceeding commenced under this section, a director shall have all of the defenses ordinarily available to a director.

(2) A director held liable under subsection (1) of this section for an unlawful distribution is entitled to contribution:

  (a) From every other director who could be held liable under subsection (1) of this section for the unlawful distribution; and

  (b) From each person who accepted the distribution knowing the distribution was made in violation of section 7-133-101 or the articles of incorporation, the amount of the contribution from such person being the amount of the distribution to that person that exceeds what could have been distributed to that person without violating section 7-133-101 or the articles of incorporation.

§ 7-128-501, C.R.S. Conflicting interest transaction.

(1) As used in this section, "conflicting interest transaction" means: A contract, transaction, or other financial relationship between a nonprofit corporation and a director of the nonprofit corporation, or between the nonprofit corporation and a party related to a director, or between the nonprofit corporation and an entity in which a director of the nonprofit corporation is a director or officer or has a financial interest.

(2) No loans shall be made by a corporation to its directors or officers. Any director or officer who assents to or participates in the making of any such loan shall be liable to the corporation for the amount of such loan until the repayment thereof.

(3) No conflicting interest transaction shall be void or voidable or be enjoined, set aside, or give rise to an award of damages or other sanctions in a proceeding by a member or by or in the right of the nonprofit corporation, solely because the conflicting interest transaction involves a director of the nonprofit corporation or a party related to a director or an entity in which a director of the nonprofit corporation is a director or officer or has a financial interest or solely because the director is present at or participates in the meeting of the nonprofit corporation's board of directors or of the committee of the board of directors that authorizes, approves, or ratifies the conflicting interest transaction or solely because the director's vote is counted for such purpose if:

   (a) The material facts as to the director's relationship or interest and as to the conflicting interest transaction are disclosed or are known to the board of directors or the committee, and the board of directors or committee in good faith authorizes, approves, or ratifies the conflicting interest transaction by the affirmative vote of a majority of the disinterested directors, even though the disinterested directors are less than a quorum; or

   (b) The material facts as to the director's relationship or interest and as to the conflicting interest transaction are disclosed or are known to the members entitled to vote thereon, and the conflicting interest transaction is specifically authorized, approved, or ratified in good faith by a vote of the members entitled to vote thereon; or

   (c) The conflicting interest transaction is fair as to the nonprofit corporation.

(4) Common or interested directors may be counted in determining the presence of a quorum at a meeting of the board of directors or of a committee which authorizes, approves, or ratifies the conflicting interest transaction.

(5) For purposes of this section, a "party related to a director" shall mean a spouse, a descendent, an ancestor, a sibling, the spouse or descendent of a sibling, an estate or trust in which the director or a party related to a director has a beneficial interest, or an entity in which a party related to a director is a director, officer, or has a financial interest.

ARTICLE 129. INDEMNIFICATION

§ 7-129-101, C.R.S. Indemnification definitions.

As used in this article:

(1) "Director" means an individual who is or was a director of a nonprofit corporation or an individual who, while a director of a nonprofit corporation, is or was serving at the nonprofit corporation's request as a director, officer, partner, member, manager, trustee, employee, fiduciary, or agent of another domestic or foreign entity or of an employee benefit plan. A director is considered to be serving an employee benefit plan at the nonprofit corporation's request if the director's duties to the nonprofit corporation also impose duties on, or otherwise involve services by, the director to the plan or to participants in or beneficiaries of the plan. "Director" includes, unless the context requires otherwise, the estate or personal representative of a deceased director.

(2) "Expenses" includes counsel fees.

(3) "Liability" means the obligation incurred with respect to a proceeding to pay a judgment, settlement, penalty, fine, including an excise tax assessed with respect to an employee benefit plan, or reasonable expenses.

(4) "Nonprofit corporation" includes any domestic or foreign entity that is a predecessor of a nonprofit corporation by reason of a merger or other transaction in which the predecessor's existence ceased upon consummation of the transaction.

(5) "Official capacity" means, when used with respect to a director, the office of director in a nonprofit corporation and, when used with respect to a person other than a director as contemplated in section 7-129-107, the office in a nonprofit corporation held by the officer or the employment, fiduciary, or agency relationship undertaken by the employee, fiduciary, or agent on behalf of the nonprofit corporation. "Official capacity" does not include service for any other domestic or foreign corporation, nonprofit corporation, or other person or employee benefit plan.

(6) "Party" includes a person who was, is, or is threatened to be made a named defendant or respondent in a proceeding.

(7) "Proceeding" means any threatened, pending, or completed action, suit, or proceeding, whether civil, criminal, administrative, or investigative and whether formal or informal.

§ 7-129-102, C.R.S. Authority to indemnify directors.

(1) Except as provided in subsection (4) of this section, a nonprofit corporation may indemnify a person made a party to a proceeding because the person is or was a director against liability incurred in the proceeding if:

(a) The person's conduct was in good faith; and

(b) The person reasonably believed:

(I) In the case of conduct in an official capacity with the nonprofit corporation, that the conduct was in the nonprofit corporation's best interests; and

(II) In all other cases, that the conduct was at least not opposed to the nonprofit corporation's best interests; and

(c) In the case of any criminal proceeding, the person had no reasonable cause to believe the conduct was unlawful.

(2) A director's conduct with respect to an employee benefit plan for a purpose the director reasonably believed to be in the interests of the participants in or beneficiaries of the plan is conduct that satisfies the requirement of subparagraph (II) of paragraph (b) of subsection (1) of this section. A director's conduct with respect to an employee benefit plan for a purpose that the director did not reasonably believe to be in the interests of the participants in or beneficiaries of the plan shall be deemed not to satisfy the requirements of paragraph (a) of subsection (1) of this section.

(3) The termination of a proceeding by judgment, order, settlement, or conviction or upon a plea of nolo contendere or its equivalent is not, of itself, determinative that the director did not meet the standard of conduct described in this section.

(4) A nonprofit corporation may not indemnify a director under this section:

(a) In connection with a proceeding by or in the right of the nonprofit corporation in which the director was adjudged liable to the nonprofit corporation; or

(b) In connection with any other proceeding charging that the director derived an improper personal benefit, whether or not involving action in an official capacity, in which proceeding the director was adjudged liable on the basis that the director derived an improper personal benefit.

(5) Indemnification permitted under this section in connection with a proceeding by or in the right of the nonprofit corporation is limited to reasonable expenses incurred in connection with the proceeding.

§ 7-129-103, C.R.S. Mandatory indemnification of directors.

Unless limited by its articles of incorporation, a nonprofit corporation shall indemnify a person who was wholly successful, on the merits or otherwise, in the defense of any proceeding to which the person was a party because the person is or was a director, against reasonable expenses incurred by the person in connection with the proceeding.

§ 7-129-104, C.R.S. Advance of expenses to directors.

(1) A nonprofit corporation may pay for or reimburse the reasonable expenses incurred by a director who is a party to a proceeding in advance of final disposition of the proceeding if:

(a) The director furnishes to the nonprofit corporation a written affirmation of the director's good-faith belief that the director has met the standard of conduct described in section 7-129-102;

(b) The director furnishes to the nonprofit corporation a written undertaking, executed personally or on the director's behalf, to repay the advance if it is ultimately determined that the director did not meet the standard of conduct; and

(c) A determination is made that the facts then known to those making the determination would not preclude indemnification under this article.

(2) The undertaking required by paragraph (b) of subsection (1) of this section shall be an unlimited general obligation of the director but need not be secured and may be accepted without reference to financial ability to make repayment.

(3) Determinations and authorizations of payments under this section shall be made in the manner specified in section 7-129-106.

§ 7-129-105, C.R.S. Court-ordered indemnification of directors.

(1) Unless otherwise provided in the articles of incorporation, a director who is or was a party to a proceeding may apply for indemnification to the court conducting the proceeding or to another court of competent jurisdiction. On receipt of an application, the court, after giving any notice the court considers necessary, may order indemnification in the following manner:

(a) If it determines that the director is entitled to mandatory indemnification under section 7-129-103, the court shall order indemnification, in which case the court shall also order the nonprofit corporation to pay the director's reasonable expenses incurred to obtain court-ordered indemnification.

(b) If it determines that the director is fairly and reasonably entitled to indemnification in view of all the relevant circumstances, whether or not the director met the standard of conduct set forth in section 7-129-102 (1) or was adjudged liable in the circumstances described in section 7-129-102 (4), the court may order such indemnification as the court deems proper; except that the indemnification with respect to any proceeding in which liability shall have been adjudged in the circumstances described in section 7-129-102 (4) is limited to reasonable expenses incurred in connection with the proceeding and reasonable expenses incurred to obtain court-ordered indemnification.

§ 7-129-106, C.R.S. Determination and authorization of indemnification of directors.

(1) A nonprofit corporation may not indemnify a director under section 7-129-102 unless authorized in the specific case after a determination has been made that indemnification of the

director is permissible in the circumstances because the director has met the standard of conduct set forth in section 7-129-102. A nonprofit corporation shall not advance expenses to a director under section 7-129-104 unless authorized in the specific case after the written affirmation and undertaking required by section 7-129-104 (1) (a) and (1) (b) are received and the determination required by section 7-129-104 (1) (c) has been made.

(2) The determinations required by subsection (1) of this section shall be made:

(a) By the board of directors by a majority vote of those present at a meeting at which a quorum is present, and only those directors not parties to the proceeding shall be counted in satisfying the quorum; or

(b) If a quorum cannot be obtained, by a majority vote of a committee of the board of directors designated by the board of directors, which committee shall consist of two or more directors not parties to the proceeding; except that directors who are parties to the proceeding may participate in the designation of directors for the committee.

(3) If a quorum cannot be obtained as contemplated in paragraph (a) of subsection (2) of this section, and a committee cannot be established under paragraph (b) of subsection (2) of this section, or, even if a quorum is obtained or a committee is designated, if a majority of the directors constituting such quorum or such committee so directs, the determination required to be made by subsection (1) of this section shall be made:

(a) By independent legal counsel selected by a vote of the board of directors or the committee in the manner specified in paragraph (a) or (b) of subsection (2) of this section or, if a quorum of the full board cannot be obtained and a committee cannot be established, by independent legal counsel selected by a majority vote of the full board of directors; or

(b) By the voting members, but voting members who are also directors and who are at the time seeking indemnification may not vote on the determination.

(4) Authorization of indemnification and advance of expenses shall be made in the same manner as the determination that indemnification or advance of expenses is permissible; except that, if the determination that indemnification or advance of expenses is permissible is made by independent legal counsel, authorization of indemnification and advance of expenses shall be made by the body that selected such counsel.

§ 7-129-107, C.R.S. Indemnification of officers, employees, fiduciaries, and agents.

(1) Unless otherwise provided in the articles of incorporation:

(a) An officer is entitled to mandatory indemnification under section 7-129-103, and is entitled to apply for court-ordered indemnification under section 7-129-105, in each case to the same extent as a director;

(b) A nonprofit corporation may indemnify and advance expenses to an officer, employee, fiduciary, or agent of the nonprofit corporation to the same extent as to a director; and

(c) A nonprofit corporation may also indemnify and advance expenses to an officer, employee, fiduciary, or agent who is not a director to a greater extent, if not inconsistent with public policy, and if provided for by its bylaws, general or specific action of its board of directors or voting members, or contract.

§ 7-129-108, C.R.S. Insurance.

A nonprofit corporation may purchase and maintain insurance on behalf of a person who is or was a director, officer, employee, fiduciary, or agent of the nonprofit corporation, or who, while a director, officer, employee, fiduciary, or agent of the nonprofit corporation, is or was serving at the request of the nonprofit corporation as a director, officer, partner, member, manager, trustee, employee, fiduciary, or agent of any domestic or foreign entity or of any employee benefit plan, against liability asserted against or incurred by the person in that capacity or arising from the person's status as a director, officer, employee, fiduciary, or agent, whether or not the nonprofit corporation would have power to indemnify the person against the same liability under section 7-129-102, 7-129-103, or 7-129-107. Any such insurance may be procured from any insurance company designated by the board of directors, whether such insurance company is formed under the law of this state or any other jurisdiction, including any insurance company in which the nonprofit corporation has an equity or any other interest through stock ownership or otherwise.

§ 7-129-109, C.R.S. Limitation of indemnification of directors.

(1) A provision treating a nonprofit corporation's indemnification of, or advance of expenses to, directors that is contained in its articles of incorporation or bylaws, in a resolution of its members or board of directors, or in a contract, except an insurance policy, or otherwise, is valid only to the extent the provision is not inconsistent with sections 7-129-101 to 7-129-108. If the articles of incorporation limit indemnification or advance of expenses, indemnification and advance of expenses are valid only to the extent not inconsistent with the articles of incorporation.

(2) Sections 7-129-101 to 7-129-108 do not limit a nonprofit corporation's power to pay or reimburse expenses incurred by a director in connection with an appearance as a witness in a proceeding at a time when the director has not been made a named defendant or respondent in the proceeding.

§ 7-129-110, C.R.S. Notice to voting members of indemnification of director.

If a nonprofit corporation indemnifies or advances expenses to a director under this article in connection with a proceeding by or in the right of the nonprofit corporation, the nonprofit corporation shall give written notice of the indemnification or advance to the voting members with or before the notice of the next voting members' meeting. If the next voting member action is taken without a meeting at the instigation of the board of directors, such notice shall be given to the voting members at or before the time the first voting member signs a writing consenting to such action.

ARTICLE 130. AMENDMENT OF ARTICLES OF. INCORPORATION AND BYLAWS

§ 7-130-101, C.R.S. Authority to amend articles of incorporation.

(1) A nonprofit corporation may amend its articles of incorporation at any time to add or change a provision that is required or permitted in the articles of incorporation or to delete a provision not required in the articles of incorporation. Whether a provision is required or permitted in the articles of incorporation is determined as of the effective date of the amendment.

(2) A member does not have a vested property right resulting from any provision in the articles of incorporation or the bylaws, including any provision relating to management, control, purpose, or duration of the nonprofit corporation.

§ 7-130-102, C.R.S. Amendment of articles of incorporation by board of directors or incorporators.

(1) Unless otherwise provided in the articles of incorporation, the board of directors may adopt, without member approval, one or more amendments to the articles of incorporation to:

(a) Delete the statement of the names and addresses of the incorporators or of the initial directors;

(b) Delete the statement of the registered agent name and registered agent address of the initial registered agent, if a statement of change changing the registered agent name and registered agent address of the registered agent is on file in the records of the secretary of state;

(b.4) Delete the statement of the principal office address of the initial principal office, if a statement of change changing the principal office address is on file in the records of the secretary of state;

(b.5) Delete the statement of the names and addresses of any or all of the individuals named in the articles of incorporation, pursuant to section 7-90-301 (6), as being individuals who caused the articles of incorporation to be delivered for filing;

(c) Extend the duration of the nonprofit corporation if it was incorporated at a time when limited duration was required by law;

(d) Change the domestic entity name by substituting the word "corporation", "incorporated", "company", or "limited", or an abbreviation of any such word for a similar word or abbreviation in the name, or by adding, deleting, or changing a geographical attribution; or

(e) Make any other change expressly permitted by articles 121 to 137 of this title to be made without member action.

(2) The board of directors may adopt, without member action, one or more amendments to the articles of incorporation to change the entity name, if necessary, in connection with the reinstatement of a nonprofit corporation pursuant to part 10 of article 90 of this title.

(3) If a nonprofit corporation has no members or no members entitled to vote on amendments or no members yet admitted to membership, its incorporators, until directors have been chosen, and thereafter its board of directors, may adopt one or more amendments to the nonprofit corporation's articles of incorporation subject to any approval required pursuant to section 7-130-301. The nonprofit corporation shall provide notice of any meeting at which an amendment is to be voted upon. The notice shall be in accordance with section 7-128-203. The notice shall also state that the purpose, or one of the purposes, of the meeting is to consider a proposed amendment to the articles of incorporation and contain or be accompanied by a copy or summary of the amendment or state the general nature of the amendment. The amendment shall be approved by a majority of the incorporators, until directors have been chosen, and thereafter by a majority of the directors in office at the time the amendment is adopted.

§ 7-130-103, C.R.S. Amendment of articles of incorporation by board of directors and members.

(1) Unless articles 121 to 137 of this title, the articles of incorporation, the bylaws, or the members or the board of directors acting pursuant to subsection (5) of this section require a different vote or voting by class, the board of directors or the members representing at least ten percent of all of the votes entitled to be cast on the amendment may propose an amendment to the articles of incorporation for submission to the members.

(2) For an amendment to the articles of incorporation to be adopted pursuant to subsection (1) of this section:

(a) The board of directors shall recommend the amendment to the members unless the amendment is proposed by members or unless the board of directors determines that, because of conflict of interest or other special circumstances, it should make no recommendation and communicates the basis for its determination to the members with the amendment; and

(b) The members entitled to vote on the amendment shall approve the amendment as provided in subsection (5) of this section.

(3) The proposing board of directors or the proposing members may condition the effectiveness of the amendment on any basis.

(4) The nonprofit corporation shall give notice, in accordance with section 7-127-104, to each member entitled to vote on the amendment of the members' meeting at which the amendment will be voted upon. The notice of the meeting shall state that the purpose, or one of the purposes, of the meeting is to consider the amendment, and the notice shall contain or be accompanied by a copy or a summary of the amendment or shall state the general nature of the amendment.

(5) Unless articles 121 to 137 of this title, the articles of incorporation, bylaws adopted by the members, or the proposing board of directors or the proposing members acting pursuant to subsection (3) of this section require a greater vote, the amendment shall be approved by the votes required by sections 7-127-205 and 7-127-206 by every voting group entitled to vote on the amendment.

(6) If the board of directors or the members seek to have the amendment approved by the members by written consent, the material soliciting the approval shall contain or be accompanied by a copy or summary of the amendment.

§ 7-130-104, C.R.S. Voting on amendments of articles of incorporation by voting groups.

(1) Unless otherwise provided by articles 121 to 137 of this title or the articles of incorporation, if membership voting is otherwise required by articles 121 to 137 of this title, the members of a class who are entitled to vote are entitled to vote as a separate voting group on an amendment to the articles of incorporation if the amendment would:

- (a) Affect the rights, privileges, preferences, restrictions, or conditions of that class as to voting, dissolution, redemption, or transfer of memberships in a manner different than such amendment would affect another class;
- (b) Change the rights, privileges, preferences, restrictions, or conditions of that class as to voting, dissolution, redemption, or transfer by changing the rights, privileges, preferences, restrictions, or conditions of another class;
- (c) Increase or decrease the number of memberships authorized for that class;
- (d) Increase the number of memberships authorized for another class;
- (e) Effect an exchange, reclassification, or termination of the memberships of that class; or
- (f) Authorize a new class of memberships.

(2) If a class is to be divided into two or more classes as a result of an amendment to the articles of incorporation, the amendment shall be approved by the members of each class that would be created by the amendment.

§ 7-130-105, C.R.S. Articles of amendment to articles of incorporation.

(1) A nonprofit corporation amending its articles of incorporation shall deliver to the secretary of state, for filing pursuant to part 3 of article 90 of this title, articles of amendment stating:

- (a) The domestic entity name of the nonprofit corporation; and
- (b) The text of each amendment adopted.

(c) to (f) (Deleted by amendment, L. 2005, p. 1217, § 24, effective October 1, 2005.)

§ 7-130-106, C.R.S. Restated articles of incorporation.

(1) The board of directors may restate the articles of incorporation at any time with or without member action. If the nonprofit corporation has no members and no directors have been elected, its incorporators may restate the articles of incorporation at any time.

(2) The restatement may include one or more amendments to the articles of incorporation. If the restatement includes an amendment requiring member approval, it shall be adopted as provided in section 7-130-103.

(3) If the board of directors submits a restatement for member action, the nonprofit corporation shall give notice, in accordance with section 7-127-104, to each member entitled to vote on the restatement of the members' meeting at which the restatement will be voted upon. The notice shall state that the purpose, or one of the purposes, of the meeting is to consider the restatement, and the notice shall contain or be accompanied by a copy of the restatement that identifies any amendment or other change it would make in the articles of incorporation.

(4) A nonprofit corporation restating its articles of incorporation shall deliver to the secretary of state, for filing pursuant to part 3 of article 90 of this title, articles of restatement stating:

(a) The domestic entity name of the nonprofit corporation;

(b) The text of the restated articles of incorporation; and

(c) (Deleted by amendment, L. 2008, p. 1879, § 8, effective August 5, 2008.)

(d) If the restatement was adopted by the board of directors or incorporators without member action, a statement to that effect and that member action was not required.

(5) Upon filing by the secretary of state or at any later effective date determined pursuant to section 7-90-304, restated articles of incorporation supersede the original articles of incorporation and all prior amendments to them.

§ 7-130-107, C.R.S. Amendment of articles of incorporation pursuant to reorganization.

(1) Articles of incorporation may be amended, without action by the board of directors or members, to carry out a plan of reorganization ordered or decreed by a court of competent jurisdiction under a statute of this state or of the United States if the articles of incorporation after amendment contain only provisions required or permitted by section 7-122-102.

(2) For an amendment to the articles of incorporation to be made pursuant to subsection (1) of this section, an individual or individuals designated by the court shall deliver to the secretary of state, for filing pursuant to part 3 of article 90 of this title, articles of amendment stating:

(a) The domestic entity name of the nonprofit corporation;

(b) The text of each amendment approved by the court;

(c) The date of the court's order or decree approving the articles of amendment;

(d) The title of the reorganization proceeding in which the order or decree was entered; and

(e) A statement that the court had jurisdiction of the proceeding under a specified statute of this state or of the United States.

(3) This section does not apply after entry of a final decree in the reorganization proceeding even though the court retains jurisdiction of the proceeding for limited purposes unrelated to consummation of the reorganization plan.

§ 7-130-108, C.R.S. Effect of amendment of articles of incorporation.

An amendment to the articles of incorporation does not affect any existing right of persons other than members, any cause of action existing against or in favor of the nonprofit corporation, or any proceeding to which the nonprofit corporation is a party. An amendment changing a nonprofit corporation's domestic entity name does not abate a proceeding brought by or against a nonprofit corporation in its former entity name.

§ 7-130-201, C.R.S. Amendment of bylaws by board of directors or members.

(1) The board of directors may amend the bylaws at any time to add, change, or delete a provision, unless:

(a) Articles 121 to 137 of this title or the articles of incorporation reserve such power exclusively to the members in whole or part; or

(b) A particular bylaw expressly prohibits the board of directors from doing so; or

(c) It would result in a change of the rights, privileges, preferences, restrictions, or conditions of a membership class as to voting, dissolution, redemption, or transfer by changing the rights, privileges, preferences, restrictions, or conditions of another class.

(2) The members may amend the bylaws even though the bylaws may also be amended by the board of directors. In such instance, the action shall be taken in accordance with sections 7-130-103 and 7-130-104 as if each reference therein to the articles of incorporation was a reference to the bylaws.

§ 7-130-202, C.R.S. Bylaw changing quorum or voting requirement for members.

(1) (Deleted by amendment, L. 98, p. 626, § 36, effective July 1, 1998.)

(2) A bylaw that fixes a lesser or greater quorum requirement or a greater voting requirement for members pursuant to section 7-127-207 shall not be amended by the board of directors.

§ 7-130-203, C.R.S. Bylaw changing quorum or voting requirement for directors.

(1) A bylaw that fixes a greater quorum or voting requirement for the board of directors may be amended:

(a) If adopted by the members, only by the members; or

(b) If adopted by the board of directors, either by the members or by the board of directors.

(2) A bylaw adopted or amended by the members that fixes a greater quorum or voting requirement for the board of directors may provide that it may be amended only by a stated vote of either the members or the board of directors.

(3) Action by the board of directors under paragraph (b) of subsection (1) of this section to adopt or amend a bylaw that changes the quorum or voting requirement for the board of directors shall meet the same quorum requirement and be adopted by the same vote required to take action under the quorum and voting requirement then in effect or proposed to be adopted, whichever is greater.

§ 7-130-301, C.R.S. Approval by third persons.

The articles of incorporation may require an amendment to the articles of incorporation or bylaws to be approved in writing by a stated person or persons other than the board of directors. Such a provision may only be amended with the approval in writing of such person or persons.

§ 7-130-302, C.R.S. Amendment terminating members or redeeming or canceling memberships.

(1) Any amendment to the articles of incorporation or bylaws of a nonprofit corporation that would terminate all members or any class of members or redeem or cancel all memberships or any class of memberships shall meet the requirements of articles 121 to 137 of this title and this section.

(2) Before adopting a resolution proposing an amendment as described in subsection (1) of this section, the board of directors of a nonprofit corporation shall give notice of the general nature of the amendment to the members.

ARTICLE 131. MERGER

§ 7-131-101, C.R.S. Merger.

(1) One or more domestic nonprofit corporations may merge into another domestic entity if the board of directors of each nonprofit corporation that is a party to the merger and each other entity that is a party to the merger adopts a plan of merger complying with section 7-90-203.3 and the members entitled to vote thereon, if any, of each such nonprofit corporation, if required by section 7-131-102, approve the plan of merger.

(2) and (3) (Deleted by amendment, L. 2007, p. 249, § 54, effective May 29, 2007.)

§ 7-131-101.5, C.R.S. Conversion.

A nonprofit corporation may convert into any form of entity permitted by section 7-90-201 if the board of directors of the nonprofit corporation adopts a plan of conversion that complies with section 7-90-201.3 and the members entitled to vote thereon, if any, if required by section 7-131-102, approve the plan of conversion.

§ 7-131-102, C.R.S. Action on plan of conversion or merger.

(1) After adopting a plan of conversion complying with section 7-90-201.3 or a plan of merger complying with section 7-90-203.3, the board of directors of the converting nonprofit corporation or the board of directors of each nonprofit corporation that is a party to the merger shall also submit the plan of conversion or plan of merger to its members, if any are entitled to vote thereon, for approval.

(2) If the nonprofit corporation does have members entitled to vote with respect to the approval of a plan of conversion or plan of merger, a plan of conversion or a plan of merger is approved by the members if:

(a) The board of directors recommends the plan of conversion or plan of merger to the members entitled to vote thereon unless the board of directors determines that, because of conflict of interest or other special circumstances, it should make no recommendation and communicates the basis for its determination to the members with the plan; and

(b) The members entitled to vote on the plan of conversion or plan of merger approve the plan as provided in subsection (7) of this section.

(3) After adopting the plan of conversion or plan of merger, the board of directors of the converting nonprofit corporation or the board of directors of each nonprofit corporation party to the merger shall submit the plan of conversion or plan of merger for written approval by any person or persons whose approval is required by a provision of the articles of incorporation of the nonprofit corporation and as recognized by section 7-130-301 for an amendment to the articles of incorporation or bylaws.

(4) If the nonprofit corporation does not have members entitled to vote on a conversion or merger, the conversion or merger shall be approved and adopted by a majority of the directors elected and in office at the time the plan of conversion or plan of merger is considered by the board of directors. In addition, the nonprofit corporation shall provide notice of any meeting of the board of directors at which such approval is to be obtained in accordance with section 7-128-203. The notice shall also state that the purpose, or one of the purposes, of the meeting is to consider the proposed conversion or merger.

(5) The board of directors may condition the effectiveness of the plan of conversion or plan of merger on any basis.

(6) The nonprofit corporation shall give notice, in accordance with section 7-127-104, to each member entitled to vote on the plan of conversion or plan of merger of the members' meeting at which the plan will be voted on. The notice shall state that the purpose, or one of the purposes,

of the meeting is to consider the plan of conversion or plan of merger, and the notice shall contain or be accompanied by a copy of the plan or a summary thereof.

(7) Unless articles 121 to 137 of this title, the articles of incorporation, bylaws adopted by the members, or the board of directors acting pursuant to subsection (5) of this section require a greater vote, the plan of conversion or plan of merger shall be approved by the votes required by sections 7-127-205 and 7-127-206 by every voting group entitled to vote on the plan of conversion or plan of merger.

(8) Separate voting by voting groups is required on a plan of conversion or plan of merger if the plan contains a provision that, if contained in an amendment to the articles of incorporation, would require action by one or more separate voting groups on the amendment.

§ 7-131-103, C.R.S. Statement of merger or conversion.

(1) After a plan of merger is approved, the surviving nonprofit corporation shall deliver to the secretary of state, for filing pursuant to part 3 of article 90 of this title, a statement of merger pursuant to section 7-90-203.7. If the plan of merger provides for amendments to the articles of incorporation of the surviving nonprofit corporation, articles of amendment effecting the amendments shall be delivered to the secretary of state for filing pursuant to part 3 of article 90 of this title.

(2) (Deleted by amendment, L. 2002, p. 1856, § 144, effective July 1, 2002; p. 1721, § 146, effective October 1, 2002.)

(3) Repealed.

(4) After a plan of conversion is approved, the converting nonprofit corporation shall deliver to the secretary of state, for filing pursuant to part 3 of article 90 of this title, a statement of conversion pursuant to section 7-90-201.7.

§ 7-131-104, C.R.S. Effect of merger or conversion.

(1) The effect of a merger shall be as provided in section 7-90-204.

(2) The effect of a conversion shall be as provided in section 7-90-202.

(3) Nothing in this title shall limit the common law powers of the attorney general concerning the merger or conversion of a nonprofit corporation.

§ 7-131-105, C.R.S. Merger with foreign entity.

(1) One or more domestic nonprofit corporations may merge with one or more foreign entities if:

  (a) The merger is permitted by section 7-90-203 (2);

  (b) (Deleted by amendment, L. 2007, p. 252, § 59, effective May 29, 2007.)

  (c) The foreign entity complies with section 7-90-203.7, if it is the surviving entity of the merger; and

  (d) Each domestic nonprofit corporation complies with the applicable provisions of sections 7-131-101 and 7-131-102 and, if it is the surviving nonprofit corporation of the merger, with section 7-131-103.

(2) Upon the merger taking effect, the surviving foreign entity of a merger shall comply with section 7-90-204.5.

(3) and (4) (Deleted by amendment, L. 2006, p. 882, § 82, effective July 1, 2006.)

ARTICLE 132. SALE OF PROPERTY

§ 7-132-101, C.R.S. Sale of property.

(1) Unless the bylaws otherwise provide, a nonprofit corporation may, as authorized by the board of directors:

(a) Sell, lease, exchange, or otherwise dispose of all or substantially all of its property in the usual and regular course of business;

(b) Mortgage, pledge, dedicate to the repayment of indebtedness, whether with or without recourse, or otherwise encumber all or substantially all of its property whether or not in the usual and regular course of business.

(2) Unless otherwise provided in the bylaws, approval by the members of a transaction described in this section is not required.

§ 7-132-102, C.R.S. Sale of property other than in regular course of activities.

(1) A nonprofit corporation may sell, lease, exchange, or otherwise dispose of all, or substantially all, of its property, with or without its good will, other than in the usual and regular course of business on the terms and conditions and for the consideration determined by the board of directors, if the board of directors proposes and the members entitled to vote thereon approve the transaction. A sale, lease, exchange, or other disposition of all, or substantially all, of the property of a nonprofit corporation, with or without its good will, in connection with its dissolution, other than in the usual and regular course of business, and other than pursuant to a court order, shall be subject to the requirements of this section; but a sale, lease, exchange, or other disposition of all, or substantially all, of the property of a nonprofit corporation, with or without its good will, pursuant to a court order shall not be subject to the requirements of this section.

(2) If a nonprofit corporation is entitled to vote or otherwise consent, other than in the usual and regular course of its business, with respect to the sale, lease, exchange, or other disposition of all, or substantially all, of the property with or without the good will of another entity which it controls, and if the property interests held by the nonprofit corporation in such other entity constitute all, or substantially all, of the property of the nonprofit corporation, then the nonprofit corporation shall consent to such transaction only if the board of directors proposes and the members, if any are entitled to vote thereon, approve the giving of consent.

(3) For a transaction described in subsection (1) of this section or a consent described in subsection (2) of this section to be approved by the members:

(a) The board of directors shall recommend the transaction or the consent to the members unless the board of directors determines that, because of conflict of interest or other special circumstances, it should make no recommendation and communicates the basis for its determination to the members at a membership meeting with the submission of the transaction or consent; and

(b) The members entitled to vote on the transaction or the consent shall approve the transaction or the consent as provided in subsection (6) of this section.

(4) The board of directors may condition the effectiveness of the transaction or the consent on any basis.

(5) The nonprofit corporation shall give notice, in accordance with section 7-127-104 to each member entitled to vote on the transaction described in subsection (1) of this section or the consent described in subsection (2) of this section, of the members' meeting at which the transaction or the consent will be voted upon. The notice shall:

(a) State that the purpose, or one of the purposes, of the meeting is to consider:

(I) In the case of action pursuant to subsection (1) of this section, the sale, lease, exchange, or other disposition of all, or substantially all, of the property of the nonprofit corporation; or

(II) In the case of action pursuant to subsection (2) of this section, the nonprofit corporation's consent to the sale, lease, exchange, or other disposition of all, or substantially all, of the property of another entity, which entity shall be identified in the notice, property interests of which are held by the nonprofit corporation and constitute all, or substantially all, of the property of the nonprofit corporation; and

(b) Contain or be accompanied by a description of the transaction, in the case of action pursuant to subsection (1) of this section, or by a description of the transaction underlying the consent, in the case of action pursuant to subsection (2) of this section.

(6) Unless articles 121 to 137 of this title, the articles of incorporation, bylaws adopted by the members, or the board of directors acting pursuant to subsection (4) of this section require a greater vote, the transaction described in subsection (1) of this section or the consent described in subsection (2) of this section shall be approved by the votes required by sections 7-127-205 and 7-127-206 by every voting group entitled to vote on the transaction or the consent.

(7) After a transaction described in subsection (1) of this section or a consent described in subsection (2) of this section is authorized, the transaction may be abandoned or the consent withheld or revoked, subject to any contractual rights or other limitations on such abandonment, withholding, or revocation, without further action by the members.

(8) A transaction that constitutes a distribution is governed by article 133 and not by this section.

ARTICLE 133. DISTRIBUTIONS

§ 7-133-101, C.R.S. Distributions prohibited.

Except as authorized by section 7-133-102, a nonprofit corporation shall not make any distributions.

§ 7-133-102, C.R.S. Authorized distributions.

(1) A nonprofit corporation may:

(a) Make distributions of its income or assets to its members that are domestic or foreign nonprofit corporations;

(b) Pay compensation in a reasonable amount to its members, directors, or officers for services rendered; and

(c) Confer benefits upon its members in conformity with its purposes.

(2) Nonprofit corporations may make distributions upon dissolution in conformity with article 134 of this title.

ARTICLE 134. DISSOLUTION

§ 7-134-101, C.R.S. Dissolution by incorporators or directors if no members.

(1) If a nonprofit corporation has no members, a majority of its directors or, if there are no directors, a majority of its incorporators may authorize the dissolution of the nonprofit corporation.

(2) The incorporators or directors in approving dissolution shall adopt a plan of dissolution indicating to whom the assets owned or held by the nonprofit corporation will be distributed after all creditors have been paid.

§ 7-134-102, C.R.S. Dissolution by directors and members.

(1) Unless otherwise provided in the bylaws, dissolution of a nonprofit corporation may be authorized in the manner provided in subsection (2) of this section.

(2) For a proposal to dissolve the nonprofit corporation to be authorized:

  (a) The board of directors shall adopt the proposal to dissolve;

  (b) The board of directors shall recommend the proposal to dissolve to the members entitled to vote thereon unless the board of directors determines that, because of conflict of interest or other special circumstances, it should make no recommendation and communicates the basis for its determination to the members; and

  (c) The members entitled to vote on the proposal to dissolve shall approve the proposal to dissolve as provided in subsection (5) of this section.

(3) The board of directors may condition the effectiveness of the dissolution, and the members may condition their approval of the dissolution, on any basis.

(4) The nonprofit corporation shall give notice, in accordance with section 7-127-104, to each member entitled to vote on the proposal of the members' meeting at which the proposal to dissolve will be voted on. The notice shall state that the purpose, or one of the purposes, of the meeting is to consider the proposal to dissolve the nonprofit corporation, and the notice shall contain or be accompanied by a copy of the proposal or a summary thereof.

(5) Unless articles 121 to 137 of this title, the articles of incorporation, bylaws adopted by the members, or the board of directors acting pursuant to subsection (3) of this section require a greater vote, the proposal to dissolve shall be approved by the votes required by sections 7-127-205 and 7-127-206 by every voting group entitled to vote on the proposal to dissolve.

(6) The plan of dissolution shall indicate to whom the assets owned or held by the nonprofit corporation will be distributed after all creditors have been paid.

§ 7-134-103, C.R.S. Articles of dissolution.

(1) At any time after dissolution is authorized, the nonprofit corporation may dissolve by delivering to the secretary of state, for filing pursuant to part 3 of article 90 of this title, articles of dissolution stating:

  (a) The domestic entity name of the nonprofit corporation;

  (b) The principal office address of the nonprofit corporation's principal office; and

  (c) That the nonprofit corporation is dissolved.

  (d) to (f) (Deleted by amendment, L. 2004, p. 1513, § 305, effective July 1, 2004.)

(2) A nonprofit corporation is dissolved upon the effective date of its articles of dissolution.

(3) Articles of dissolution need not be filed by a nonprofit corporation that is dissolved pursuant to section 7-134-401.

§ 7-134-104, C.R.S. Revocation of dissolution. (Repealed)

§ 7-134-105, C.R.S. Effect of dissolution.

(1) A dissolved nonprofit corporation continues its corporate existence but may not carry on any activities except as is appropriate to wind up and liquidate its affairs, including:

  (a) Collecting its assets;

  (b) Returning, transferring, or conveying assets held by the nonprofit corporation upon a condition requiring return, transfer, or conveyance, which condition occurs by reason of the dissolution, in accordance with such condition;

(c) Transferring, subject to any contractual or legal requirements, its assets as provided in or authorized by its articles of incorporation or bylaws;

(d) Discharging or making provision for discharging its liabilities;

(e) Doing every other act necessary to wind up and liquidate its assets and affairs.

(2) Upon dissolution of a nonprofit corporation exempt under section 501 (c) (3) of the internal revenue code or corresponding section of any future federal tax code, the assets of such nonprofit corporation shall be distributed for one or more exempt purposes under said section, or to the federal government, or to a state or local government, for a public purpose. Any such assets not so disposed of shall be disposed of by the district court for the county in this state in which the street address of the nonprofit corporation's principal office is located, or, if the nonprofit corporation has no principal office in this state, by the district court of the county in which the street address of its registered agent is located, or, if the nonprofit corporation has no registered agent, the district court of the city and county of Denver exclusively for such purposes or to such organization or organizations, as said court shall determine, that are formed and operated exclusively for such purposes.

(3) Dissolution of a nonprofit corporation does not:

(a) Transfer title to the nonprofit corporation's property;

(b) Subject its directors or officers to standards of conduct different from those prescribed in article 128 of this title;

(c) Change quorum or voting requirements for its board of directors or members, change provisions for selection, resignation, or removal of its directors or officers, or both, or change provisions for amending its bylaws or its articles of incorporation;

(d) Prevent commencement of a proceeding by or against the nonprofit corporation in its entity name; or

(e) Abate or suspend a proceeding pending by or against the nonprofit corporation on the effective date of dissolution.

(4) (Deleted by amendment, L. 2003, p. 2347, § 323, effective July 1, 2004.)

(5) A dissolved nonprofit corporation may dispose of claims against it pursuant to sections 7-90-911 and 7-90-912.

§ 7-134-106, C.R.S. Disposition of known claims by notification. (Repealed)

§ 7-134-107, C.R.S. Disposition of claims by publication. (Repealed)

§ 7-134-108, C.R.S. Enforcement of claims against dissolved nonprofit corporation. (Repealed)

§ 7-134-109, C.R.S. Service on dissolved nonprofit corporation – repeal. (Repealed)

§ 7-134-201, C.R.S. Grounds for administrative dissolution. (Repealed)

§ 7-134-202, C.R.S. Procedure for and effect of administrative dissolution. (Repealed)

§ 7-134-203, C.R.S. Reinstatement following administrative dissolution – repeal. (Repealed)

§ 7-134-204, C.R.S. Appeal from denial of reinstatement – repeal. (Repealed)

§ 7-134-205, C.R.S. Continuation as unincorporated association. (Repealed)

§ 7-134-301, C.R.S. Grounds for judicial dissolution.

(1) A nonprofit corporation may be dissolved in a proceeding by the attorney general if it is established that:

(a) The nonprofit corporation obtained its articles of incorporation through fraud; or

(b) The nonprofit corporation has continued to exceed or abuse the authority conferred upon it by law.

(2) A nonprofit corporation may be dissolved in a proceeding by a director or member if it is established that:

(a) The directors are deadlocked in the management of the corporate affairs, the members, if any, are unable to break the deadlock, and irreparable injury to the nonprofit corporation is threatened or being suffered;

(b) The directors or those otherwise in control of the nonprofit corporation have acted, are acting, or will act in a manner that is illegal, oppressive, or fraudulent;

(c) The members are deadlocked in voting power and have failed, for a period that includes at least two consecutive annual meeting dates, to elect successors to directors whose terms have expired or would have expired upon the election of their successors; or

(d) The corporate assets are being misapplied or wasted.

(3) A nonprofit corporation may be dissolved in a proceeding by a creditor if it is established that:

(a) The creditor's claim has been reduced to judgment, the execution on the judgment has been returned unsatisfied, and the nonprofit corporation is insolvent; or

(b) The nonprofit corporation is insolvent and the nonprofit corporation has admitted in writing that the creditor's claim is due and owing.

(4) (a) If a nonprofit corporation has been dissolved by voluntary action taken under part 1 of this article:

(I) The nonprofit corporation may bring a proceeding to wind up and liquidate its business and affairs under judicial supervision in accordance with section 7-134-105; and

(II) The attorney general, a director, a member, or a creditor may bring a proceeding to wind up and liquidate the affairs of the nonprofit corporation under judicial supervision in accordance with section 7-134-105, upon establishing the grounds set forth in subsections (1) to (3) of this section.

(b) As used in sections 7-134-302 to 7-134-304, a "proceeding to dissolve a nonprofit corporation" includes a proceeding brought under this subsection (4), and a "decree of dissolution" includes an order of court entered in a proceeding under this subsection (4) that directs that the affairs of a nonprofit corporation shall be wound up and liquidated under judicial supervision.

§ 7-134-302, C.R.S. Procedure for judicial dissolution.

(1) A proceeding by the attorney general to dissolve a nonprofit corporation shall be brought in the district court for the county in this state in which the street address of the nonprofit corporation's principal office or the street address of its registered agent is located or, if the nonprofit corporation has no principal office in this state and no registered agent, in the district court for the city and county of Denver. A proceeding brought by any other party named in section 7-134-301 shall be brought in the district court for the county in this state in which the street address of the nonprofit corporation's principal office is located or, if it has no principal office in this state, in the district court for the county in which the street address of its registered agent is located, or, if the nonprofit corporation has no registered agent, in the district court for the city and county of Denver.

(2) It is not necessary to make directors or members parties to a proceeding to dissolve a nonprofit corporation unless relief is sought against them individually.

(3) A court in a proceeding brought to dissolve a nonprofit corporation may issue injunctions, appoint a receiver or custodian pendente lite with all powers and duties the court directs, take other action required to preserve the corporate assets wherever located, and carry on the activities of the nonprofit corporation until a full hearing can be held.

§ 7-134-303, C.R.S. Receivership or custodianship.

(1) A court in a judicial proceeding to dissolve a nonprofit corporation may appoint one or more receivers to wind up and liquidate, or one or more custodians to manage, the affairs of the nonprofit corporation. The court shall hold a hearing, after giving notice to all parties to the proceeding and any interested persons designated by the court, before appointing a receiver or custodian. The court appointing a receiver or custodian has exclusive jurisdiction over the nonprofit corporation and all of its property, wherever located.

(2) The court may appoint an individual, a domestic entity, or a foreign entity authorized to transact business or conduct activities in this state, or a domestic or foreign nonprofit corporation authorized to transact business or conduct activities in this state as a receiver or custodian. The court may require the receiver or custodian to post bond, with or without sureties, in an amount stated by the court.

(3) The court shall describe the powers and duties of the receiver or custodian in its appointing order which may be amended from time to time. Among other powers the receiver shall have the power to:

  (a) Dispose of all or any part of the property of the nonprofit corporation, wherever located, at a public or private sale, if authorized by the court; and

  (b) Sue and defend in the receiver's own name as receiver of the nonprofit corporation in all courts.

(4) The custodian may exercise all of the powers of the nonprofit corporation, through or in place of its board of directors or officers, to the extent necessary to manage the affairs of the nonprofit corporation in the best interests of its members and creditors.

(5) The court, during a receivership, may redesignate the receiver a custodian and during a custodianship may redesignate the custodian a receiver if doing so is in the best interests of the nonprofit corporation and its members and creditors.

(6) The court from time to time during the receivership or custodianship may order compensation paid and expense disbursements or reimbursements made to the receiver or custodian and such person's counsel from the assets of the nonprofit corporation or proceeds from the sale of the assets.

§ 7-134-304, C.R.S. Decree of dissolution.

(1) If after a hearing the court determines that one or more grounds for judicial dissolution described in section 7-134-301 exist, it may enter a decree dissolving the nonprofit corporation and stating the effective date of the dissolution, and the clerk of the court shall deliver a certified copy of the decree to the secretary of state for filing pursuant to part 3 of article 90 of this title.

(2) After entering the decree of dissolution, the court shall direct the winding up and liquidation of the nonprofit corporation's activities in accordance with section 7-134-105 and the giving of notice to claimants in accordance with sections 7-90-911 and 7-90-912.

(3) The court's order or decision may be appealed as in other civil proceedings.

§ 7-134-401, C.R.S. Dissolution upon expiration of period of duration.

(1) A nonprofit corporation shall be dissolved upon and by reason of the expiration of its period of duration, if any, stated in its articles of incorporation.

(2) A provision in the articles of incorporation to the effect that the nonprofit corporation or its existence shall be terminated at a stated date or after a stated period of time or upon a contingency, or any similar provision, shall be deemed to be a provision for a period of duration within the meaning of this section. The occurrence of such date, the expiration of the stated period of time, the occurrence of such contingency, or the satisfaction of such provision shall be deemed to be the expiration of the nonprofit corporation's period of duration for purposes of this section.

§ 7-134-501, C.R.S. Deposit with state treasurer.

Assets of a dissolved nonprofit corporation that should be transferred to a creditor, claimant, or member of the nonprofit corporation who cannot be found or who is not legally competent to receive them shall be reduced to cash and deposited with the state treasurer as property presumed to be abandoned under the provisions of article 13 of title 38, C.R.S.

ARTICLE 135. FOREIGN NONPROFIT CORPORATIONS -. AUTHORITY TO CONDUCT ACTIVITIES

§ 7-135-101, C.R.S. Authority to conduct activities required.

Part 8 of article 90 of this title, providing for the transaction of business or the conduct of activities by foreign entities, applies to foreign nonprofit corporations.

ARTICLE 136. RECORDS, INFORMATION, AND REPORTS

§ 7-136-101, C.R.S. Corporate records.

(1) A nonprofit corporation shall keep as permanent records minutes of all meetings of its members and board of directors, a record of all actions taken by the members or board of directors without a meeting, a record of all actions taken by a committee of the board of directors in place of the board of directors on behalf of the nonprofit corporation, and a record of all waivers of notices of meetings of members and of the board of directors or any committee of the board of directors.

(2) A nonprofit corporation shall maintain appropriate accounting records.

(3) A nonprofit corporation or its agent shall maintain a record of its members in a form that permits preparation of a list of the name and address of all members in alphabetical order, by class, showing the number of votes each member is entitled to vote.

(4) A nonprofit corporation shall maintain its records in written form or in another form capable of conversion into written form within a reasonable time.

(5) A nonprofit corporation shall keep a copy of each of the following records at its principal office:

- (a) Its articles of incorporation;
- (b) Its bylaws;
- (c) Resolutions adopted by its board of directors relating to the characteristics, qualifications, rights, limitations, and obligations of members or any class or category of members;
- (d) The minutes of all members' meetings, and records of all action taken by members without a meeting, for the past three years;

(e) All written communications within the past three years to members generally as members;

(f) A list of the names and business or home addresses of its current directors and officers;

(g) A copy of its most recent periodic report pursuant to part 5 of article 90 of this title; and

(h) All financial statements prepared for periods ending during the last three years that a member could have requested under section 7-136-106.

§ 7-136-102, C.R.S. Inspection of corporate records by members.

(1) A member is entitled to inspect and copy, during regular business hours at the nonprofit corporation's principal office, any of the records of the nonprofit corporation described in section 7-136-101 (5) if the member gives the nonprofit corporation written demand at least five business days before the date on which the member wishes to inspect and copy such records.

(2) Pursuant to subsection (5) of this section, a member is entitled to inspect and copy, during regular business hours at a reasonable location stated by the nonprofit corporation, any of the other records of the nonprofit corporation if the member meets the requirements of subsection (3) of this section and gives the nonprofit corporation written demand at least five business days before the date on which the member wishes to inspect and copy such records.

(3) A member may inspect and copy the records described in subsection (2) of this section only if:

(a) The member has been a member for at least three months immediately preceding the demand to inspect or copy or is a member holding at least five percent of the voting power as of the date the demand is made;

(b) The demand is made in good faith and for a proper purpose;

(c) The member describes with reasonable particularity the purpose and the records the member desires to inspect; and

(d) The records are directly connected with the described purpose.

(4) For purposes of this section:

(a) "Member" includes a beneficial owner whose membership interest is held in a voting trust and any other beneficial owner of a membership interest who establishes beneficial ownership.

(b) "Proper purpose" means a purpose reasonably related to the demanding member's interest as a member.

(5) The right of inspection granted by this section may not be abolished or limited by the articles of incorporation or bylaws.

(6) This section does not affect:

(a) The right of a member to inspect records under section 7-127-201;

(b) The right of a member to inspect records to the same extent as any other litigant if the member is in litigation with the nonprofit corporation; or

(c) The power of a court, independent of articles 121 to 137 of this title, to compel the production of corporate records for examination.

§ 7-136-103, C.R.S. Scope of member's inspection right.

(1) A member's agent or attorney has the same inspection and copying rights as the member.

(2) The right to copy records under section 7-136-102 includes, if reasonable, the right to receive copies made by photographic, xerographic, electronic, or other means.

(3) Except as provided in section 7-136-106, the nonprofit corporation may impose a reasonable charge, covering the costs of labor and material, for copies of any documents provided to the

member. The charge may not exceed the estimated cost of production and reproduction of the records.

(4) The nonprofit corporation may comply with a member's demand to inspect the record of members under section 7-136-102 (2) by furnishing to the member a list of members that complies with section 7-136-101 (3) and was compiled no earlier than the date of the member's demand.

§ 7-136-104, C.R.S. Court-ordered inspection of corporate records.

(1) If a nonprofit corporation refuses to allow a member, or the member's agent or attorney, who complies with section 7-136-102 (1) to inspect or copy any records that the member is entitled to inspect or copy by said section, the district court for the county in this state in which the street address of the nonprofit corporation's principal office is located or, if the nonprofit corporation has no principal office in this state, the district court for the county in which the street address of its registered agent is located or, if the nonprofit corporation has no registered agent, the district court for the city and county of Denver may, on application of the member, summarily order the inspection or copying of the records demanded at the nonprofit corporation's expense.

(2) If a nonprofit corporation refuses to allow a member, or the member's agent or attorney, who complies with section 7-136-102 (2) and (3) to inspect or copy any records that the member is entitled to inspect or copy pursuant to section 7-136-102 (2) and (3) within a reasonable time following the member's demand, the district court for the county in this state in which the street address of the nonprofit corporation's principal office is located or, if the nonprofit corporation has no principal office in this state, the district court for the county in which the street address of its registered agent is located or, if the nonprofit corporation has no registered agent, the district court for the city and county of Denver may, on application of the member, summarily order the inspection or copying of the records demanded.

(3) If a court orders inspection or copying of the records demanded, unless the nonprofit corporation proves that it refused inspection or copying in good faith because it had a reasonable basis for doubt about the right of the member, or the member's agent or attorney, to inspect or copy the records demanded:

  (a) The court shall also order the nonprofit corporation to pay the member's costs, including reasonable counsel fees, incurred to obtain the order;

  (b) The court may order the nonprofit corporation to pay the member for any damages the member incurred;

  (c) If inspection or copying is ordered pursuant to subsection (2) of this section, the court may order the nonprofit corporation to pay the member's inspection and copying expenses; and

  (d) The court may grant the member any other remedy provided by law.

(4) If a court orders inspection or copying of records demanded, it may impose reasonable restrictions on the use or distribution of the records by the demanding member.

§ 7-136-105, C.R.S. Limitations on use of membership list.

(1) Without consent of the board of directors, a membership list or any part thereof may not be obtained or used by any person for any purpose unrelated to a member's interest as a member.

(2) Without limiting the generality of subsection (1) of this section, without the consent of the board of directors a membership list or any part thereof may not be:

  (a) Used to solicit money or property unless such money or property will be used solely to solicit the votes of the members in an election to be held by the nonprofit corporation;

  (b) Used for any commercial purpose; or

(c) Sold to or purchased by any person.

§ 7-136-106, C.R.S. Financial statements.

Upon the written request of any member, a nonprofit corporation shall mail to such member its most recent annual financial statements, if any, and its most recently published financial statements, if any, showing in reasonable detail its assets and liabilities and results of its operations.

§ 7-136-107, C.R.S. Periodic report to secretary of state.

Part 5 of article 90 of this title, providing for periodic reports from reporting entities, applies to domestic nonprofit corporations and applies to foreign nonprofit corporations that are authorized to transact business or conduct activities in this state.

§ 7-136-108, C.R.S. Statement of person named as director or officer. (Repealed)

§ 7-136-109, C.R.S. Interrogatories by secretary of state. (Repealed)

ARTICLE 137. TRANSITION PROVISIONS

§ 7-137-101, C.R.S. Application to existing corporations.

(1) (a) For purposes of this article, "existing corporate entity" means any corporate entity that was in existence on June 30, 1998, and that was incorporated under articles 20 to 29 of this title or elected to accept such articles as provided therein.

(b) A corporate entity that was either incorporated under or elected to accept articles 20 to 29 of this title and that was suspended or, as a consequence of such suspension, dissolved by operation of law before July 1, 1998, and was eligible for reinstatement or restoration, renewal, and revival on June 30, 1998, shall be deemed to be in existence on that date for purposes of this subsection (1) and shall be deemed administratively dissolved on the date of such suspension for purposes of section 7-134-105.

(c) A corporate entity that was either incorporated under or elected to accept articles 20 to 29 of this title and that was suspended or, as a consequence of such suspension, dissolved by operation of law before July 1, 1998, and was not eligible for reinstatement or restoration, renewal, and revival on June 30, 1998, shall be treated as a domestic entity as to which a constituent filed document has been filed by, or placed in the records of, the secretary of state and that has been dissolved for purposes of section 7-90-1001.

(2) Subject to this section, articles 121 to 137 of this title apply to all existing corporate entities subject to articles 20 to 29 of this title.

(3) Unless the articles of incorporation or bylaws of an existing corporate entity recognize the right of a member to transfer such member's membership interests in such corporate entity, such interests shall be presumed to be nontransferable. However, if the transferability of such interests is not prohibited by such articles of incorporation or bylaws, such transferability may be established by a preponderance of the evidence taking into account any representation made by the corporate entity, the practice of such corporate entity, other transactions involving such interests, and other facts bearing on the existence of the rights to transfer such interests.

(4) Until the articles of incorporation of an existing corporate entity are amended or restated on or after July 1, 1998, they need not be amended or restated to comply with articles 121 to 137 of this title.

(5) Unless changed by an amendment to its articles of incorporation, members or classes of members of an existing corporate entity shall be deemed to be voting members for purposes of articles 121 to 137 of this title if such members or classes of members, on June 30, 1998, had

the right by reason of a provision of the corporate entity's articles of incorporation or bylaws, or by a custom, practice, or tradition, to vote for the election of a director or directors.

(6) The bylaws of an existing corporate entity may be amended as provided in its articles of incorporation or bylaws. Unless otherwise so provided, the power to amend such bylaws shall be vested in the board of directors.

§ 7-137-102, C.R.S. Pre-1968 corporate entities – failure to file reports and designate registered agents – dissolution.

(1) Corporate entities that were formed prior to January 1, 1968, and that did not elect to be governed by articles 20 to 29 of this title and could, if they so elected, elect to be governed by articles 121 to 137 of this title, but that have not done so, are nevertheless reporting entities that are subject to part 5 of article 90 of this title, providing for periodic reports from reporting entities, and are domestic entities that are subject to part 7 of article 90 of this title, providing for registered agents and service of process.

(2) Every corporate entity that could or has elected to be governed by articles 20 to 29 or 121 to 137 of this title whose articles of incorporation, affidavit of incorporation, or other basic corporate charter, by whatever name denominated, is not on file in the records of the secretary of state shall file a certified copy of such articles of incorporation, affidavit of incorporation, or other basic corporate charter in the office of the secretary of state. Such certified copy may be secured from any clerk or recorder with whom the instrument may be filed or recorded.

(3) If any corporate entity, formed prior to January 1, 1968, that could elect to be governed by articles 20 to 29 or 121 to 137 of this title, but that has not so elected and has failed to file periodic reports or maintain a registered agent, may be declared delinquent pursuant to section 7-90-902.

(4) Any corporate entity formed prior to January 1, 1968, that could elect to be governed by articles 20 to 29 of this title, that was suspended or was declared defunct, but not dissolved by operation of law under section 7-20-105 before July 1, 1998, and that was eligible for reinstatement on June 30, 1998, shall be deemed administratively dissolved on the date of such suspension for purposes of section 7-134-105 and may reinstate itself as a nonprofit corporation as provided in part 10 of article 90 of this title.

(5) Any nonprofit corporate entity formed prior to January 1, 1968, that could elect to be governed by articles 20 to 29 of this title, that was suspended, declared defunct, administratively dissolved, or dissolved by operation of law, and continues to operate for nonprofit purposes and does not wind up its business and affairs, shall be deemed an unincorporated organization that qualifies as a nonprofit association as provided in section 7-30-101.1 for purposes of the "Uniform Unincorporated Nonprofit Association Act", article 30 of this title, unless such corporate entity is eligible to reinstate itself as a nonprofit corporation as provided in part 10 of article 90 of this title and does so reinstate itself.

§ 7-137-103, C.R.S. Application to foreign nonprofit corporations.

A foreign nonprofit corporation authorized to transact business or conduct activities in this state on June 30, 1998, is subject to articles 121 to 137 of this title but is not required to obtain new authorization to transact business or conduct activities under said articles.

§ 7-137-201, C.R.S. Procedure to elect to accept articles 121 to 137 of this title.

(1) Any corporate entity with shares of capital stock formed before January 1, 1968, under article 40, 50, or 51 of this title, any corporate entity formed before January 1, 1968, under article 40 or 50 of this title without shares of capital stock, and any corporate entity whether with or without shares of capital stock and formed before January 1, 1968, under any general law or created by any special act of the general assembly for a purpose for which a nonprofit

corporation may be formed under articles 121 to 137 of this title may elect to accept said articles in the following manner:

(a) If there are members or stockholders entitled to vote thereon, the board of directors shall adopt a resolution recommending that the corporate entity accept articles 121 to 137 of this title and directing that the question of acceptance be submitted to a vote at a meeting of the members or stockholders entitled to vote thereon, which may be either an annual or special meeting. The question shall also be submitted whenever one-twentieth of the members or stockholders entitled to vote thereon so request. Written notice stating that the purpose, or one of the purposes, of the meeting is to consider electing to accept said articles shall be given to each member or stockholder entitled to vote at the meeting within the time and in the manner provided in said articles for the giving of notice of meetings to members or stockholders. Such election to accept said articles shall require for adoption at least two-thirds of the votes that members or stockholders present at such meeting in person or by proxy are entitled to cast.

(b) If there are no members or stockholders entitled to vote thereon, election to accept articles 121 to 137 of this title may be made at a meeting of the board of directors pursuant to a majority vote of the directors in office.

(2) In effecting acceptance of articles 121 to 137 of this title, the corporate entity shall follow the requirements of the law under which it was formed, its articles of incorporation, and its bylaws so far as applicable.

(3) If the domestic entity name of the corporate entity accepting articles 121 to 137 of this title is not in conformity with part 6 of article 90 of this title, the corporate entity shall change its domestic entity name to conform with part 6 of article 90 of this title. The adoption of a domestic entity name that is in conformity with said part 6 by the members or stockholders of the corporate entity, and its inclusion in the statement of election to accept articles 121 to 137 as the entity name, shall be the only action necessary to effect the change. The articles of incorporation, affidavit, or other basic organizational charter shall be deemed for all purposes amended to conform to the entity name.

(4) All corporate entities accepting articles 121 to 137 of this title whose articles of incorporation, affidavits of incorporation, or other basic charters, by whatever names denominated, are not on file in the records of the secretary of state as required by section 7-137-102 (2) shall deliver to the secretary of state, for filing pursuant to part 3 of article 90 of this title, a certified copy of such articles of incorporation, affidavits of incorporation, or other basic charters at the time of delivery of the statement of election to accept articles 121 to 137 of this title.

(5) All corporate entities accepting articles 121 to 137 of this title are reporting entities subject to part 5 of article 90 of this title, providing for periodic reports from reporting entities, and are subject to part 7 of article 90 of this title, providing for registered agents and service of process.

§ 7-137-202, C.R.S. Statement of election to accept articles 121 to 137 of this title.

(1) A statement of election to accept articles 121 to 137 of this title shall state:

(a) The domestic entity name of the corporate entity;

(b) A statement by the corporate entity that it has elected to accept said articles and that all required reports have been or will be filed and all fees, taxes, and penalties due to the state of Colorado accruing under any law to which the corporate entity heretofore has been subject have been paid;

(c) If there are members or stockholders entitled to vote thereon, a statement stating the date of the meeting of such members or stockholders at which the election to accept articles 121 to 137 of this title was made, that a quorum was present at the meeting, and that such acceptance was authorized by at least two-thirds of the votes that members or stockholders present at such meeting in person or by proxy were entitled to cast;

(d) If there are no members or stockholders entitled to vote thereon, a statement of such fact, the date of the meeting of the board of directors at which election to accept said articles was made, that a quorum was present at the meeting, and that such acceptance was authorized by a majority vote of the directors in office;

(e) A statement that the corporate entity followed the requirements of the law under which it was formed, its articles of incorporation, and its bylaws so far as applicable in effecting such acceptance;

(f) and (g) Repealed.

(h) A statement that any attached copy of the articles of incorporation, affidavit, or other basic corporate charter of the corporate entity is true and correct;

(i) If the corporate entity has issued shares of stock, a statement of such fact including the number of shares heretofore authorized, the number issued and outstanding, and a statement that all issued and outstanding shares of stock have been delivered to the corporate entity to be canceled upon the acceptance of articles 121 to 137 of this title by the corporate entity becoming effective and that from and after the effective date of said acceptance the authority of the corporate entity to issue shares of stock is terminated; except that this shall not apply to corporate entities formed for the acquisition and distribution of water to their stockholders.

§ 7-137-203, C.R.S. Filing statement of election to accept articles 121 to 137 of this title.

The statement of election to accept articles 121 to 137 of this title shall be delivered to the secretary of state for filing pursuant to part 3 of article 90 of this title.

§ 7-137-204, C.R.S. Effect of certificate of acceptance.

(1) Upon the filing by the secretary of state of the statement of election to accept articles 121 to 137 of this title, the election of the corporate entity to accept said articles shall become effective.

(2) A corporate entity so electing under articles 121 to 137 of this title or corresponding provision of prior law shall have the same powers and privileges and be subject to the same duties, restrictions, penalties, and liabilities as though such corporate entity had been originally formed under said articles and shall also be subject to any duties or obligations expressly imposed upon the corporate entity by a special charter, subject to the following:

(a) If no period of duration is expressly fixed in the articles of incorporation of such corporate entity, its period of duration shall be deemed to be perpetual.

(b) No amendment to the articles of incorporation adopted after such election to accept articles 121 to 137 of this title shall release or terminate any duty or obligation expressly imposed upon any such corporate entity under and by virtue of a special charter or enlarge any right, power, or privilege granted to any such corporate entity under a special charter, except to the extent that such right, power, or privilege might have been included in the articles of incorporation of a corporate entity formed under said articles.

(c) In the case of any corporate entity with issued shares of stock, the holders of such issued shares who surrender them to the corporate entity to be canceled upon the acceptance of said articles by the corporate entity becoming effective shall become members of the corporate entity with one vote for each share of stock so surrendered until such time as the corporate entity by proper corporate action relative to the election, qualification, terms, and voting power of members shall otherwise prescribe.

§ 7-137-301, C.R.S. Saving provisions.

(1) Except as provided in subsection (3) of this section, the repeal of any provision of the "Colorado Nonprofit Corporation Act", articles 20 to 29 of this title, does not affect:

(a) The operation of the statute, or any action taken under it, before its repeal;

(b) Any ratification, right, remedy, privilege, obligation, or liability acquired, accrued, or incurred under the provision before its repeal;

(c) Any violation of the provision, or any penalty, forfeiture, or punishment incurred because of the violation, before its repeal; or

(d) Any proceeding or reorganization commenced under the provision before its repeal, and the proceeding or reorganization may be completed in accordance with the provision as if it had not been repealed.

(2) Except as provided in subsection (3) of this section or in sections 7-137-101 (1) (b) and 7-137-102 (4) for the reinstatement, as provided in part 10 of article 90 of this title, of a corporate entity suspended, declared defunct, or administratively dissolved before July 1, 1998, any dissolution commenced under the provision before its repeal may be completed in accordance with the provision as if it had not been repealed.

(3) If a penalty or punishment imposed for violation of any provision of the "Colorado Nonprofit Corporation Act", articles 20 to 29 of this title, is reduced by articles 121 to 137 of this title, the penalty or punishment, if not already imposed, shall be imposed in accordance with said articles.

Chapter 6:
Appraiser License Law

An * in the left margin indicates a change in the statute, rule, or text since the last publication of the manual.

I. The Colorado Board of Real Estate Appraisers

The Colorado Board of Real Estate Appraisers ("Board") meets every other month and consists of seven members who are appointed by the Governor. The overall objective of the Board is to protect the public. In order to do so, the Colorado legislature has granted the Board rulemaking authority for matters related to the profession of real estate appraisers, and Appraisal Management Companies (AMC). Rules are made after notice and public hearings in which all interested parties may participate.

The Division of Real Estate ("Division") is part of the Department of Regulatory Agencies and is responsible for budgeting, purchasing, and related management functions. The director of the Division is an administrative officer who executes the directives of the Board and is given statutory authority in all matters delegated by the Board. The Board exercises its duties and authority through licensing, certification, and enforcement.

II. Appraiser Licensing and Certification

In 1990, the legislature passed laws governing the practice of real estate appraisal in Colorado in response to the federal "Financial Institutions Reform, Recovery and Enforcement Act of 1989" ("FIRREA"). This enabling legislation has been amended several times since being adopted. The full text of the statutes, §§ 12-10-601 through 12-10-623, C.R.S., are reprinted in this chapter.

The Colorado Board of Real Estate Appraisers is composed of three licensed or certified appraisers, one of whom shall have expertise in eminent domain matters; one shall be a county assessor in office; one shall be an officer or employee of a commercial bank experienced in real estate lending; one shall be an officer or employee of an appraisal management company; and one shall be member of the public at large not engaged in any of the businesses represented by the other members of the board. Members of the Board shall hold office for terms of three years. The Board has statutory authority to implement Colorado law in a manner consistent with federal regulations, including rulemaking and imposing discipline for violations of appraiser license law.

Unless a specific exemption applies, any person acting as a real estate appraiser in this state must be licensed as provided by §§ 12-10-601, *et seq.* Exceptions to the definition of "real estate appraiser" are found in § 12-10-602(9)(b), C.R.S., and include, among others, licensed real estate brokers who perform broker price opinions and competitive market analyses that are not represented as appraisals and are not used for purposes of obtaining financing. Other exceptions are provided for corporations valuing property they own, may purchase or sell, and for appraisers of personal property, water or mineral rights.

* The ASC oversees the real estate appraisal process as it relates to federally related transactions. The Appraisal Foundation (TAF), a private non-profit appraisal organization, is

charged with developing the qualifications for appraisers and standards for appraisals through two of its independent Boards, the Appraisal Qualifications Board (AQB) and the Appraisal Standards Board (ASB). In general, the standards for the development and reporting of an appraisal are those of the Uniform Standards of Professional Appraisal Practice (USPAP) as developed, interpreted, and amended by the ASB. The AQB and ASB have no legislative power, but their recommendations have been adopted via § 12-10-613(1)(g) and Board Rule 11.1.

Federal financial regulatory agencies have developed rules as to the appraiser and appraisal related requirements that must be met for valuation of properties in "federally related transactions." Additional standards are imposed by federal and/or state law for real estate appraisals, in particular, for eminent domain, conservation easements and appraisals used for income tax purposes.

III. Levels of Appraiser Licensure

Colorado appraiser law and Board rules establish four levels of licensure, summarized in more detail below. A license or certification is issued when an individual meets the education, examination, and experience requirements for their level of licensure. The level of licensure determines what properties an appraiser, if competent for the assignment, may appraise.

Licensed Ad Valorem Appraiser: This level of licensure is only utilized for appraiser employees of county tax assessment offices. These individuals may also qualify for and hold a licensed or certified credential.

Licensed Appraiser: The licensed credential allows the appraiser to appraise non-complex 1-4 unit residential properties having a transaction value of less than $1 million and complex 1-4 unit residential properties having a transaction value of less than $400,000. The terms "Complex Residential Property" and "Transaction Value" are defined by Board Rule and the Real Property Appraiser Qualification Criteria of the AQB.

Certified Residential Appraiser: The certified residential credential allows the appraiser to appraise 1-4 unit residential properties without regard to transaction value or complexity. The credential includes the appraisal of vacant or unimproved land that is utilized for 1-4 residential units purposes or for which the highest and best use is for 1-4 residential units, but does not include the appraisal of subdivisions for which a development analysis/appraisal is necessary.

Certified General Appraiser: The certified general credential allows the appraiser to appraise all types of real property.

Colorado does not have trainee or supervisory appraiser classifications and there are no specific requirements for either in statute or Board rule.

IV. Requirements for Appraiser Licensure

In general, there are three requirements that must be met for appraiser licensure: education, examination, and experience. The specific requirements in these areas for the licensed, certified and ad valorem credentials are detailed under Board Rules 2.2, 2.3, 2.4 and 2.9.

V. Continuing Education Requirements

An initial license or certification issued to an appraiser is valid through December 31 of the year issued. Appraisers who obtain their initial license or certification prior to July 1 of any calendar year must complete at least 14 hours of approved appraiser continuing education before December 31. Appraisers who renew their credential will be issued a two-year license and must complete at least 28 hours of approved appraiser continuing education during the two-year renewal cycle.

At a minimum, appraisers must successfully complete the 7-hour National Uniform Standards of Professional Appraisal Practice (USPAP) Update Course every two calendar years. The update course will be credited towards the required 28 hours of continuing education for the renewal cycle. The 15-hour National USPAP course cannot be substituted for the required 7-hour National USPAP update course. Continuing education requirements are more fully detailed in Chapter 7 of the Board Rules.

VI. Appraisal Management Companies

* In accordance with the Dodd–Frank Wall Street Reform and Consumer Protection Act, the Colorado legislature passed HB 12-1110 which requires appraisal management companies (AMCs) that wish to provide appraisal management services in connection with Federally Related Transactions to be registered in the state of Colorado. Each appraisal management company must designate a Controlling Appraiser to supervise all licensed activities that occur in the state. The Board of Real Estate Appraisers shall not issue a license to an AMC until: the Controlling Appraiser and each individual that owns more than 10% of the company establishes that he or she is truthful and honest and has good moral character and has submitted a set of fingerprints to the Colorado Bureau of Investigations; the controlling appraiser confirm that no owner of any percentage has had an appraiser license or certificate refused, denied, cancelled, surrendered in lieu of revocation, or revoked in any State; and each AMC must maintain a surety bond for a minimum of $25,000.

Title 12, Article 10, Part 6, Colorado Revised Statutes – Real Estate Appraisers

§ *12-10-601, C.R.S. Legislative declaration.*

Editor's note: *This section is similar to former §12-61-701 as it existed prior to 2019.*

The general assembly finds, determines, and declares that sections 12-10-602 to 12-10-623 are enacted pursuant to the requirements of the "Real Estate Appraisal Reform Amendments", Title XI of the federal "Financial Institutions Reform, Recovery, and Enforcement Act of 1989", as amended, 12 U.S.C. secs. 3331 to 3351. The general assembly further finds, determines, and declares that sections 12-10-602 to 12-10-623 are intended to implement the requirements of federal law in the least burdensome manner to real estate appraisers and appraisal management companies. Licensed ad valorem appraisers licensed under this article 10 are not regulated by the federal "Real Estate Appraisal Reform Amendments", Title XI of the federal "Financial Institutions Reform, Recovery, and Enforcement Act of 1989", as amended, 12 U.S.C. secs. 3331 to 3351.

§ *12-10-602, C.R.S. Definitions.*

Editor's note: *(1) This section is similar to former §12-61-702 as it existed prior to 2019; except that §12-61-702 (7) and (8) were relocated to §12-10-101 (1) and (2), respectively.*

(2) Before its relocation in 2019, this section was amended in SB 19-046. Those amendments were superseded by the repeal and reenactment of this title 12, effective October 1, 2019. For those amendments to the former section in effect from March 25, 2019, to October 1, 2019, see SB 19-046, chapter 50, Session Laws of Colorado 2019.

* *(3) Section 3(2) of chapter 17 (SB 20-047), Session Laws of Colorado 2020, provides that the act changing this section applies to appraisals made on or after September 14, 2020.*

As used in this part 6, unless the context otherwise requires:

(1) (a) "Appraisal", "appraisal report", or "real estate appraisal" means a written or oral analysis, opinion, or conclusion relating to the nature, quality, value, or utility of specified interests in, or aspects of, identified real estate that is transmitted to the client upon the completion of an assignment. These terms include a valuation, which is an opinion of the value of real estate, and an analysis, which is a general study of real estate not specifically performed only to determine value; except that the terms include a valuation completed by an appraiser employee of a county assessor as defined in section 39-1-102 (2).

* (b) The terms do not include an analysis, valuation, opinion, conclusion, notation, or compilation of data by an officer, director, regularly salaried employee, or agent of a financial institution or its affiliate, made for internal use only by the financial institution or affiliate, concerning an interest in real estate that is owned or held as collateral by the financial institution or affiliate and that is not represented or deemed to be an appraisal except to the financial institution, the agencies regulating the financial institution, and any secondary markets that purchase real estate secured loans. An appraisal prepared by an officer, director, regularly salaried employee, or agent of a financial institution who is not licensed or certified under this part 6 must contain a written notice that the preparer is not licensed or certified as an appraiser under this part 6.

(c) "Appraisal", "appraisal report", or "real estate appraisal" does not include a federally authorized "waiver valuation", as defined in 49 CFR 24.2 (a)(33), as amended.

(2) (a) "Appraisal management company" or "AMC" means, in connection with valuing properties collateralizing mortgage loans or mortgages incorporated into a securitization, any external third party authorized either by a creditor in a consumer credit transaction secured by a consumer's principal dwelling that oversees an appraiser panel or by an underwriter of, or other principal in, the secondary mortgage markets that oversees an appraiser panel to:

(I) Recruit, select, and retain appraisers;

(II) Contract with licensed and certified appraisers to perform appraisal assignments;

(III) Manage the process of having an appraisal performed, including providing administrative duties such as receiving appraisal orders and appraisal reports, submitting completed appraisal reports to creditors and underwriters, collecting fees from creditors and underwriters for services provided, and reimbursing appraisers for services performed; or

(IV) Review and verify the work of appraisers.

(b) "Appraisal management company" or "AMC" does not include:

(I) A corporation, limited liability company, sole proprietorship, or other entity that directly performs appraisal services;

(II) A corporation, limited liability company, sole proprietorship, or other entity that does not contract with appraisers for appraisal services, but that solely distributes orders to a client-selected panel of appraisers; and

(III) A mortgage company, or its subsidiary, that manages a panel of appraisers who are engaged to provide appraisal services on mortgage loans either originated by the mortgage company or funded by the mortgage company with its own funds.

(3) "Board" means the board of real estate appraisers created in section 12-10-603.

(4) "Client" means the party or parties who engage an appraiser or an appraisal management company for a specific assignment.

(5) "Consulting services" means services performed by an appraiser that do not fall within the definition of an "independent appraisal" in subsection (7) of this section. "Consulting services" includes marketing, financing and feasibility studies, valuations, analyses, and opinions and conclusions given in connection with real estate brokerage, mortgage banking, and counseling and advocacy in regard to property tax assessments and appeals thereof; except that, if in rendering the services the appraiser acts as a disinterested third party, the work is deemed an independent appraisal and not a consulting service. Nothing in this subsection (5) precludes a person from acting as an expert witness in valuation appeals.

(6) "Financial institution" means any "bank" or "savings association", as those terms are defined in 12 U.S.C. sec. 1813, any state bank incorporated under title 11, any state or federally chartered credit union, or any company that has direct or indirect control over any of those entities.

(7) "Independent appraisal" means an engagement for which an appraiser is employed or retained to act as a disinterested third party in rendering an unbiased analysis, opinion, or conclusion relating to the nature, quality, value, or utility of specified interests in or aspects of identified real estate.

(8) (a) "Panel" or "appraiser panel" means a network, list, or roster of licensed or certified `appraisers approved by an AMC to perform appraisals as independent contractors for the AMC.

(b) Appraisers on an AMC's appraiser panel include both:

(I) Appraisers accepted by the AMC for consideration for future appraisal assignments in covered transactions or for secondary mortgage market participants in connection with covered transactions; and

(II) Appraisers engaged by the AMC to perform one or more appraisals in covered transactions or for secondary mortgage market participants in connection with covered transactions.

(c) An appraiser is an independent contractor for purposes of this subsection (8) if the appraiser is treated as an independent contractor by the AMC for purposes of federal income taxation.

(9) (a) "Real estate appraiser" or "appraiser" means a person who provides an estimate of the nature, quality, value, or utility of an interest in, or aspect of, identified real estate and includes one who estimates value and who possesses the necessary qualifications, ability, and experience to execute or direct the appraisal of real property.

(b) "Real estate appraiser" or "appraiser" does not include:

(I) A person who conducts appraisals strictly of personal property;

(II) A person licensed as a broker pursuant to part 2 of this article 10 who provides an opinion of value that is not represented as an appraisal and is not used for purposes of obtaining financing;

(III) A person licensed as a certified public accountant pursuant to article 100 of this title 12, and otherwise regulated, as long as the person does not represent his or her opinions of value for real estate as an appraisal;

(IV) A corporation, acting through its officers or regularly salaried employees, when conducting a valuation of real estate property rights owned, to be purchased, or sold by the corporation;

(V) A person who conducts appraisals strictly of water rights or of mineral rights;

(VI) A right-of-way acquisition agent, an appraiser who is licensed and certified pursuant to this part 6, or any other individual who has sufficient understanding of the local real estate market to be qualified to make a waiver valuation when the agent, appraiser, or other qualified individual is employed by or contracts with a public entity and provides an opinion of value that is not represented as an appraisal and when, for any purpose, the property or portion of property being valued is valued at twenty-five thousand dollars or less, as permitted by federal law and 49 CFR 24.102 (c)(2), as amended;

* (VII) An officer, director, regularly salaried employee, or agent of a financial institution or its affiliate who makes, for internal use only by the financial institution or affiliate, an analysis, evaluation, opinion, conclusion, notation, or compilation of data with respect to an appraisal so long as the person does not make a written adjustment of the appraisal's conclusion as to the value of the subject real property;

* (VIII) An officer, director, regularly salaried employee, or agent of a financial institution or its affiliate who makes an internal analysis, valuation, opinion, conclusion, notation, or compilation of data concerning an interest in real estate that is owned or held as collateral by the financial institution or its affiliate; or

(IX) A person who represents property owners as an advocate in tax or valuation protests and appeals pursuant to title 39.

§ *12-10-603, C.R.S. Board of real estate appraisers – creation – compensation – immunity – legislative declaration – subject to review – repeal of part.*

Editor's note: *This section is similar to former §12-61-703 as it existed prior to 2019.*

(1) (a) There is hereby created in the division of real estate a board of real estate appraisers consisting of seven members appointed by the governor with the consent of the senate. Of the members, three shall be licensed or certified appraisers, one of whom shall have expertise in eminent domain matters; one shall be a county assessor in office; one shall be an officer or employee of a commercial bank experienced in real estate lending; one shall be an officer or employee of an appraisal management company; and one shall be a member of the public at large not engaged in any of the businesses represented by the other members of the board.

(b) Members of the board shall hold office for terms of three years. In the event of a vacancy by death, resignation, removal, or otherwise, the governor shall appoint a member to fill the unexpired term. The governor has the authority to remove any member for misconduct, neglect of duty, or incompetence.

(2) (a) The board shall exercise its powers and perform its duties and functions under the division of real estate as if transferred to the division by a **type 1** transfer, as defined in the "Administrative Organization Act of 1968", article 1 of title 24.

(b) The general assembly finds, determines, and declares that the organization of the board under the division as a **type 1** agency will provide the autonomy necessary to avoid potential conflicts of interest between the responsibility of the board in the regulation of real estate appraisers and the responsibility of the division in the regulation of real estate brokers and salespersons. The general assembly further finds, determines, and declares that the placement of the board as a **type 1** agency under the division is consistent with the organizational structure of state government.

(3) Each member of the board shall receive the same compensation and reimbursement of expenses as is provided for members of boards and commissions in the division of professions and occupations pursuant to section 12-20-103 (6). Payment for all per diem compensation and

expenses shall be made out of annual appropriations from the division of real estate cash fund provided for in section 12-10-605.

(4) Members of the board, consultants, and expert witnesses are immune from liability in any civil action based upon any disciplinary proceedings or other official acts they performed in good faith pursuant to this part 6.

(5) A majority of the board constitutes a quorum for the transaction of all business, and actions of the board require a vote of a majority of the members present in favor of the action taken.

(6) This part 6 is repealed, effective September 1, 2022. Before the repeal, this part 6 is scheduled for review in accordance with section 24-34-104.

§ 12-10-604, C.R.S. Powers and duties of the board – rules.

Editor's note: *(1) This section is similar to former §12-61-704 as it existed prior to 2019.*

(2) Before its relocation in 2019, this section was amended in HB 19-1264. Those amendments were superseded by the repeal and reenactment of this title 12, effective October 1, 2019. For those amendments to the former section in effect from June 30, 2019, to October 1, 2019, see HB 19-1264, chapter 420, Session Laws of Colorado 2019.

(3) Section 17 of chapter 420 (HB 19-1264), Session Laws of Colorado 2019, provides that the act changing this section takes effect October 1, 2019, only if HB 19-1172 becomes law. HB 19-1172 became law and took effect October 1, 2019.

(1) In addition to all other powers and duties imposed upon it by law, the board has the following powers and duties:

(a) (I) To promulgate and amend, as necessary, rules pursuant to article 4 of title 24 for the implementation and administration of this part 6 and as required to comply with the federal "Real Estate Appraisal Reform Amendments", Title XI of the federal "Financial Institutions Reform, Recovery, and Enforcement Act of 1989", as amended, 12 U.S.C. secs. 3331 to 3351, and with any requirements imposed by amendments to that federal law.

(II) The board shall not establish any requirements that are more stringent than the requirements of any applicable federal law.

(III) Licensed ad valorem appraisers are not regulated by the federal "Real Estate Appraisal Reform Amendments", Title XI of the federal "Financial Institutions Reform, Recovery, and Enforcement Act of 1989", as amended, 12 U.S.C. secs. 3331 to 3351, but the board shall adopt rules regarding minimum qualifications and standards of practice for licensed ad valorem appraisers.

(IV) In any list or registry it maintains, the board shall identify or separately account for any appraisal management company that oversees a panel of more than fifteen certified or licensed appraisers in Colorado, or more than twenty-five in all states in which it does business, within a given year.

(b) To charge application, examination, and license and certificate renewal fees established pursuant to section 12-10-215 from all applicants for licensure, certification, examination, and renewal under this part 6. The board shall not refund any fees received from applicants seeking licensure, certification, examination, or renewal.

(c) Through the department and subject to appropriations made to the department, to employ administrative law judges, appointed pursuant to part 10 of article 30 of title 24, on a full-time or part-time basis to conduct any hearings required by this part 6;

(d) To issue, deny, or refuse to renew a license or certificate pursuant to this part 6;

(e) To take disciplinary actions in conformity with this part 6;

(f) To delegate to the director the administration and enforcement of this part 6 and the authority to act on behalf of the board on occasions and in circumstances that the board directs;

(g) (I) To develop, purchase, or contract for any examination required for the administration of this part 6, to offer each examination at least twice a year or, if demand warrants, at more frequent intervals, and to establish a passing score for each examination that reflects a minimum level of competency.

(II) If study materials are developed by a testing company or other entity, the board shall make the materials available to persons desiring to take examinations pursuant to this part 6. The board may charge fees for the materials to defray any costs associated with making the materials available.

(h) In compliance with article 4 of title 24, to make investigations; subpoena persons and documents, which subpoenas may be enforced by a court of competent jurisdiction if not obeyed; hold hearings; and take evidence in all matters relating to the exercise of the board's power under this part 6;

(i) Pursuant to section 1119 (b) of Title XI of the federal "Financial Institutions Reform, Recovery, and Enforcement Act of 1989", Pub.L. 101-73, as amended, to apply, if necessary, for a federal waiver of the requirement relating to certification or licensing of a person to perform appraisals and to make the necessary written determinations specified in that section for purposes of making the application; and

(j) If the board has reasonable cause to believe that a person, partnership, limited liability company, or corporation is violating this part 6, to enter an order requiring the individual or appraisal management company to cease and desist the violation.

(k) Repealed.

(2) The board shall maintain or preserve, for seven years, licensing history records of a person licensed or certified under this part 6. Complaints of record in the office of the board and board investigations, including board investigative files, are closed to public inspection. Stipulations and final agency orders are public record and are subject to sections 24-72-203 and 24-72-204.

§ *12-10-605, C.R.S. Fees, penalties, and fines collected under part 6.*

Editor's note: *This section is similar to former §12-61-705 as it existed prior to 2019.*

All fees, penalties, and fines collected pursuant to this part 6, not including fees retained by contractors pursuant to contracts entered into in accordance with section 12-10-203, 12-10-606, or 24-34-101, shall be transmitted to the state treasurer, who shall credit the same to the division of real estate cash fund, created in section 12-10-215.

§ *12-10-606, C.R.S. Qualifications for licensing and certification of appraisers – continuing education – definitions – rules.*

Editor's note: *(1) This section is similar to former §12-61-706 as it existed prior to 2019.*

(2) Before its relocation in 2019, this section was amended in HB 19-1166. Those amendments were superseded by the repeal and reenactment of this title 12, effective October 1, 2019. For those amendments to the former section in effect from April 18, 2019, to October 1, 2019, see HB 19-1166, chapter 125, Session Laws of Colorado 2019.

(3) Section 78 of chapter 125 (HB 19-1166), Session Laws of Colorado 2019, provides that the act changing this section takes effect October 1, 2019, only if HB 19-1172 becomes law. HB 19-1172 became law and took effect October 1, 2019.

(1) (a) The board shall, by rule, prescribe requirements for the initial licensing or certification of persons under this part 6 to meet the requirements of the "Real Estate Appraisal Reform Amendments", Title XI of the federal "Financial Institutions Reform, Recovery, and

Enforcement Act of 1989", as amended, 12 U.S.C. secs. 3331 to 3351, and shall develop, purchase, or contract for examinations to be passed by applicants. The board shall not establish any requirements for initial licensing or certification that are more stringent than the requirements of any applicable federal law; except that all applicants shall pass an examination offered by the board. If there is no applicable federal law, the board shall consider and may use as guidelines the most recent available criteria published by the Appraiser Qualifications Board of the Appraisal Foundation or its successor organization.

(b) The four levels of appraiser licensure and certification, pursuant to subsection (1)(a) of this section, are defined as follows:

(I) "Certified general appraiser" means an appraiser meeting the requirements set by the board for general certification.

(II) "Certified residential appraiser" means an appraiser meeting the requirements set by the board for residential certification.

(III) "Licensed ad valorem appraiser" means an appraiser meeting the requirements set by the board for ad valorem appraiser certification. Only a county assessor, employee of a county assessor's office, or employee of the division of property taxation in the department of local affairs may obtain or possess an ad valorem appraiser certification.

(IV) "Licensed appraiser" means an appraiser meeting the requirements set by the board for a license.

(c) A county assessor or employee of a county assessor's office who is a licensed ad valorem appraiser may not perform real estate appraisals outside of his or her official duties.

(d) The board shall transfer persons employed in a county assessor's office or in the division of property taxation in the department of local affairs who are registered appraisers as of July 1, 2013, to the category of licensed ad valorem appraiser. The board shall allow these persons, until December 31, 2015, to meet any additional requirements imposed by the board pursuant to section 12-10-604 (1)(a).

(2) (a) The board shall, by rule, prescribe continuing education requirements for persons licensed or certified as certified general appraisers, certified residential appraisers, or licensed appraisers as needed to meet the requirements of the "Real Estate Appraisal Reform Amendments", Title XI of the federal "Financial Institutions Reform, Recovery, and Enforcement Act of 1989", as amended, 12 U.S.C. secs. 3331 to 3351. The board shall not establish any continuing education requirements that are more stringent than the requirements of any applicable federal law; except that all persons licensed or certified under this part 6 are subject to continuing education requirements. If there is no applicable federal law, the board shall consider and may use as guidelines the most recent available criteria published by the Appraiser Qualifications Board of the Appraisal Foundation or its successor organization.

(b) The board shall, by rule, prescribe continuing education requirements for licensed ad valorem appraisers.

(3) Notwithstanding any provision of this section to the contrary, the criteria established by the board for the licensing or certification of appraisers pursuant to this part 6 shall not include membership or lack of membership in any appraisal organization.

(4) (a) Subject to section 12-10-619 (2), all appraiser employees of county assessors shall be licensed or certified as provided in subsections (1) and (2) of this section. Obtaining and maintaining a license or certificate under either subsection (1) or (2) of this section entitles an appraiser employee of a county assessor to perform all real estate appraisals required to fulfill the person's official duties.

(b) Appraiser employees of county assessors who are employed to appraise real property are subject to this part 6; except that appraiser employees of county assessors who are employed to appraise real property are not subject to disciplinary actions by the board on the ground that they have performed appraisals beyond their level of competency when appraising real estate in fulfillment of their official duties. County assessors, if licensed or certified as provided in subsections (1) and (2) of this section, are not subject to disciplinary actions by the board on the ground that they have performed appraisals beyond their level of competency when appraising real estate in fulfillment of their official duties.

(c) The county in which an appraiser employee of a county assessor is employed shall pay all reasonable costs incurred by the appraiser employee of the county assessor to obtain and maintain a license or certificate pursuant to this section.

(5) The board shall not issue an appraiser's license as referenced in subsection (1)(b)(IV) of this section unless the applicant has at least twelve months' appraisal experience.

(6) (a) The board shall not issue a license or certification until the applicant demonstrates that he or she meets the fitness standards established by board rule and submits a set of fingerprints to the Colorado bureau of investigation for the purpose of conducting a state and national fingerprint-based criminal history record check utilizing records of the Colorado bureau of investigation and the federal bureau of investigation. Each person submitting a set of fingerprints shall pay the fee established by the Colorado bureau of investigation for conducting the fingerprint-based criminal history record check to the bureau. Upon completion of the criminal history record check, the bureau shall forward the results to the board. The board shall require a name-based criminal history record check, as defined in section 22-2-119.3 (6)(d), for an applicant who has twice submitted to a fingerprint-based criminal history record check and whose fingerprints are unclassifiable or when the results of a fingerprint-based criminal history record check of an applicant performed pursuant to this subsection (6) reveal a record of arrest without a disposition. The applicant shall pay the costs associated with a name-based criminal history record check. The board may deny an application for licensure or certification based on the outcome of the criminal history record check and may establish criminal history requirements more stringent than those established by any applicable federal law. At a minimum, the board shall adopt the criminal history requirements established by any applicable federal law.

(b) An applicant for certification as a licensed ad valorem appraiser is not subject to the fingerprinting and criminal background check requirements of subsection (6)(a) of this section.

§ *12-10-607, C.R.S. Appraisal management companies – application for license – exemptions.*

Editor's note: *(1) This section is similar to former §12-61-707 as it existed prior to 2019.*

(2) Before its relocation in 2019, this section was amended in HB 19-1166. Those amendments were superseded by the repeal and reenactment of this title 12, effective October 1, 2019. For those amendments to the former section in effect from April 18, 2019, to October 1, 2019, see HB 19-1166, chapter 125, Session Laws of Colorado 2019.

(3) Section 78 of chapter 125 (HB 19-1166), Session Laws of Colorado 2019, provides that the act changing this section takes effect October 1, 2019, only if HB 19-1172 becomes law. HB 19-1172 became law and took effect October 1, 2019.

(1) An applicant shall apply for a license as an appraisal management company, or as a controlling appraiser, to the board in a manner prescribed by the board.

(2) The board may grant appraisal management company licenses to individuals, partnerships, limited liability companies, or corporations. A partnership, limited liability company, or corporation, in its application for a license, shall designate a controlling appraiser who is actively certified in a state recognized by the appraisal subcommittee of the federal financial institutions examination council or its successor entity. The controlling appraiser is responsible for the licensed practices of the partnership, limited liability company, or corporation and all persons employed by the entity. The application of the partnership, limited liability company, or corporation and the application of the appraiser designated by it as the controlling appraiser shall be filed with the board. The board has jurisdiction over the appraiser so designated and over the partnership, limited liability company, or corporation.

(3) The board shall not issue a license to any partnership, limited liability company, or corporation unless and until the appraiser designated by the partnership, limited liability company, or corporation as controlling appraiser and each individual who owns more than ten percent of the entity demonstrates that he or she meets the fitness standards established by board rule and submits a set of fingerprints to the Colorado bureau of investigation for the purpose of conducting a state and national fingerprint-based criminal history record check utilizing records of the Colorado bureau of investigation and the federal bureau of investigation. Each person submitting a set of fingerprints shall pay the fee established by the Colorado bureau of investigation for conducting the fingerprint-based criminal history record check to the bureau. Upon completion of the criminal history record check, the bureau shall forward the results to the board. The board shall require a name-based criminal history record check, as defined in section 22-2-119.3 (6)(d), for an applicant who has twice submitted to a fingerprint-based criminal history record check and whose fingerprints are unclassifiable or when the results of a fingerprint-based criminal history record check of an applicant performed pursuant to this subsection (3) reveal a record of arrest without a disposition. The applicant shall pay the costs associated with a name-based criminal history record check. The board may deny an application for licensure or refuse to renew a license based on the outcome of the criminal history record check. The board may require criminal history requirements more stringent than those established by any applicable federal law. At a minimum, the board shall adopt the criminal history requirements established by any applicable federal law.

(4) The board shall not issue a license to any partnership, limited liability company, or corporation if the appraiser designated by the entity as controlling appraiser has previously had, in any state, an appraiser registration, license, or certificate refused, denied, cancelled, surrendered in lieu of revocation, or revoked. A disciplinary action resulting in refusal, denial, cancellation, surrender in lieu of revocation, or revocation relating to a registration, license, or certification as an appraiser registered, licensed, or certified under this part 6 or any related occupation in any other state, territory, or country for disciplinary reasons is prima facie evidence of grounds for denial of a license by the board.

(5) The board shall not issue a license to any partnership, limited liability company, or corporation if it is owned, in whole or in part, directly or indirectly, by any person who has had, in any state, an appraiser license, registration, or certificate refused, denied, cancelled, surrendered in lieu of revocation, or revoked. A disciplinary action resulting in refusal, denial, cancellation, surrender in lieu of revocation, or revocation relating to a license, registration, or certification as an appraiser licensed, registered, or certified under this part 6 or any related occupation in any other state, territory, or country for disciplinary reasons is prima facie evidence of grounds for denial of a license by the board.

(6) The board may deny an application for a license for any partnership, limited liability company, or corporation if the partnership, limited liability company, or corporation has previously had a license revoked or surrendered a license in lieu of revocation. A disciplinary action resulting in the surrender in lieu of revocation or the revocation of a license as an appraisal management company under this part 6 or any related occupation in any other state, territory, or country for

disciplinary reasons may be deemed to be prima facie evidence of grounds for denial of a license by the board.

(7) Each appraisal management company must maintain a definite place of business. If the appraisal management company is domiciled in another state, the appraiser designated by the appraisal management company as controlling appraiser is responsible for supervising all licensed activities that occur in Colorado. All licensed actions occurring within the state of Colorado must occur under the name under which the appraisal management company is licensed or its trade name adopted in accordance with Colorado law.

(8) An application that is submitted by an appraisal management company that is:

(a) A partnership must be properly registered with the Colorado department of revenue or properly filed with the Colorado secretary of state and in good standing, proof of which must be included in the application. If an assumed or trade name is to be used, it must be properly filed with the Colorado department of revenue or filed and accepted by the Colorado secretary of state, proof of which must be included with the application.

(b) A limited liability company must be properly registered with the Colorado secretary of state and in good standing, proof of which must be included with the application. If an assumed or trade name is to be used, it must be properly filed with the Colorado secretary of state, proof of which must be included with the application.

(c) A corporation must be registered as a foreign corporation or properly incorporated with the Colorado secretary of state and in good standing, proof of which must be included with the application. If an assumed or trade name is to be used, it must be properly filed with the Colorado secretary of state, proof of which must be included with the application.

(9) Financial institutions and appraisal management company subsidiaries that are owned and controlled by the financial institution and regulated by a federal financial institution regulatory agency are not required to register with or be licensed by the board. This exemption includes a panel of appraisers who are engaged to provide appraisal services and are administered by a financial institution regulated by a federal financial regulatory agency.

§ 12-10-608, C.R.S. Errors and omissions insurance – duties of the division – certificate of coverage – group plan made available – rules.

Editor's note: *This section is similar to former §12-61-708 as it existed prior to 2019.*

(1) Every licensee under this part 6, except an appraiser who is employed by a state or local governmental entity or an inactive appraiser or appraisal management company, shall maintain errors and omissions insurance to cover all activities contemplated under this part 6. The division shall make the errors and omissions insurance available to all licensees by contracting with an insurer for a group policy after a competitive bid process in accordance with article 103 of title 24. A group policy obtained by the division must be available to all licensees with no right on the part of the insurer to cancel any licensee. A licensee may obtain errors and omissions insurance independently if the coverage complies with the minimum requirements established by the division.

(2) (a) If the division is unable to obtain errors and omissions insurance coverage to insure all licensees who choose to participate in the group program at a reasonable annual premium, as determined by the division, a licensee shall independently obtain the errors and omissions insurance required by this section.

(b) The division shall solicit and consider information and comments from interested persons when determining the reasonableness of annual premiums.

(3) The division shall determine the terms and conditions of coverage required under this section based on rules promulgated by the board. Each licensee shall be notified of the required terms

and conditions at least thirty days before the annual premium renewal date as determined by the division. Each licensee shall file a certificate of coverage showing compliance with the required terms and conditions with the division by the annual premium renewal date, as determined by the division.

(4) In addition to all other powers and duties conferred upon the board by this part 6, the board is authorized and directed to adopt rules it deems necessary or proper to carry out the requirements of this section.

§ *12-10-609, C.R.S. Bond required.*

Editor's note: *This section is similar to former §12-61-709 as it existed prior to 2019.*

(1) Before the board issues a license to an applicant for an appraisal management company license, the applicant shall post with the board a surety bond in the amount of twenty-five thousand dollars. A licensed appraisal management company shall maintain the required bond at all times.

(2) The surety bond shall require the surety to provide notice to the board within thirty days if payment is made from the surety bond or if the bond is cancelled.

§ *12-10-610, C.R.S. Expiration of licenses – renewal – penalties – fees – rules.*

Editor's note: *(1) This section is similar to former §12-61-710 as it existed prior to 2019.*

(2) Before its relocation in 2019, this section was amended in HB 19-1166. Those amendments were superseded by the repeal and reenactment of this title 12, effective October 1, 2019. For those amendments to the former section in effect from April 18, 2019, to October 1, 2019, see HB 19-1166, chapter 125, Session Laws of Colorado 2019.

(3) Section 78 of chapter 125 (HB 19-1166), Session Laws of Colorado 2019, provides that the act changing this section takes effect October 1, 2019, only if HB 19-1172 becomes law. HB 19-1172 became law and took effect October 1, 2019.

(1) (a) All licenses or certificates expire pursuant to a schedule established by the director and may be renewed or reinstated pursuant to this section. Upon compliance with this section and any applicable rules of the board regarding renewal, including the payment of a renewal fee plus a reinstatement fee established pursuant to subsection (1)(b) of this section, the expired license or certificate shall be reinstated. A real estate appraiser's license or certificate that has not been renewed for a period greater than two years shall not be reinstated, and the person must submit a new application for licensure or certification.

(b) A person who fails to renew his or her license or certificate before the applicable renewal date may have it reinstated if the person submits an application as prescribed by the board:

(I) Within thirty-one days after the date of expiration, by payment of the regular renewal fee;

(II) More than thirty-one days, but within one year, after the date of expiration, by payment of the regular renewal fee and payment of a reinstatement fee equal to one-third of the regular renewal fee; or

(III) More than one year, but within two years, after the date of expiration, by payment of the regular renewal fee and payment of a reinstatement fee equal to two-thirds of the regular renewal fee.

(2) If the federal registry fee collected by the board and transmitted to the federal financial institutions examination council is increased prior to expiration of a license or certificate, the board shall collect the amount of the increase in the fee from the holder of the license or

certificate and forward the amount to the council annually. The federal registry fee does not apply to licensed ad valorem appraisers licensed under this article 10.

(3) (a) If the applicant has complied with this section and any applicable rules of the board regarding renewal, except for the continuing education requirements pursuant to section 12-10-606, the licensee may renew the license on inactive status. An inactive license may be activated if the licensee submits written certification of compliance with section 12-10-606 for the previous licensing period. The board may adopt rules establishing procedures to facilitate reactivation of licenses.

(b) The holder of an inactive license shall not perform a real estate appraisal or appraisal management duties.

(c) The holder of an inactive license shall not hold himself or herself out as having an active license pursuant to this part 6.

(4) At the time of renewal or reinstatement, every licensee, certificate holder, and person or individual who owns more than ten percent of an appraisal management company shall submit a set of fingerprints to the Colorado bureau of investigation for the purpose of conducting a state and national fingerprint-based criminal history record check utilizing records of the Colorado bureau of investigation and the federal bureau of investigation, if the person has not previously done so for issuance of a license or certification by the board. Each person submitting a set of fingerprints shall pay the fee established by the Colorado bureau of investigation for conducting the fingerprint-based criminal history record check to the bureau. The bureau shall forward the results to the board. The board shall require a name-based criminal history record check, as defined in section 22-2-119.3 (6)(d), for an applicant who has twice submitted to a fingerprint-based criminal history record check and whose fingerprints are unclassifiable or when the results of a fingerprint-based criminal history record check of an applicant performed pursuant to this section reveal a record of arrest without a disposition. The applicant shall pay the costs associated with a name-based criminal history record check. The board may refuse to renew or reinstate a license or certification based on the outcome of the criminal history record check.

§ *12-10-611, C.R.S. Licensure or certification by endorsement – temporary practice.*

Editor's note: *This section is similar to former §12-61-711 as it existed prior to 2019.*

(1) The board may issue a license or certification to an appraiser by endorsement to engage in the occupation of real estate appraisal to any applicant who has a license or certification in good standing as a real estate appraiser under the laws of another jurisdiction if:

(a) The applicant presents proof satisfactory to the board that, at the time of application for a Colorado license or certificate by endorsement, the applicant possesses credentials and qualifications that are substantially equivalent to the requirements of this part 6; or

(b) The jurisdiction that issued the applicant a license or certificate to engage in the occupation of real estate appraisal has a law similar to this subsection (1) pursuant to which it licenses or certifies persons who are licensed real estate appraisers in this state.

(2) The board may specify, by rule, what constitutes substantially equivalent credentials and qualifications and the manner in which the board will review credentials and qualifications of an applicant.

(3) Pursuant to section 1122 (a) of Title XI of the federal "Financial Institutions Reform, Recovery, and Enforcement Act of 1989", Pub.L. 101-73, as amended, the board shall recognize, on a temporary basis, the license or certification of an appraiser issued by another state if:

(a) The appraiser's business is of a temporary nature; and

(b) The appraiser applies for and is granted a temporary practice permit by the board.

§ *12-10-612, C.R.S. Denial of license or certificate – renewal – definition.*

Editor's note: *This section is similar to former §12-61-712 as it existed prior to 2019.*

(1) The board may determine whether an applicant for licensure or certification possesses the necessary qualifications for licensure or certification required by this part 6. The board may consider such qualities as the applicant's fitness and prior professional licensure and whether the applicant has been convicted of a crime. As used in this subsection (1), "applicant" includes any individual who owns, in whole or in part, directly or indirectly, an appraisal management company and any appraiser designated as a controlling appraiser by a partnership, limited liability company, or corporation acting as an appraisal management company.

(2) If the board determines that an applicant does not possess the applicable qualifications required by this part 6, or the applicant has violated this part 6, rules promulgated by the board, or any board order, the board may deny the applicant a license or certificate or deny the renewal or reinstatement of a license or certificate pursuant to section 12-10-610, and, in such instance, the board shall provide the applicant with a statement in writing setting forth the basis of the board's determination that the applicant does not possess the qualifications or professional competence required by this part 6. The applicant may request a hearing on the determination as provided in section 24-4-104 (9).

§ *12-10-613, C.R.S. Prohibited activities – grounds for disciplinary actions – procedures.*

Editor's note: *This section is similar to former §12-61-713 as it existed prior to 2019.*

(1) A real estate appraiser is in violation of this part 6 if the appraiser:

(a) Has been convicted of a felony or has had accepted by a court a plea of guilty or nolo contendere to a felony if the felony is related to the ability to act as a real property appraiser. A certified copy of the judgment of a court of competent jurisdiction of the conviction or plea is conclusive evidence of the conviction or plea. In considering the disciplinary action, the board shall be governed by the provisions of section 24-5-101.

(b) Has violated, or attempted to violate, directly or indirectly, or assisted in or abetted the violation of, or conspired to violate this part 6, a rule promulgated pursuant to this part 6, or an order of the board issued pursuant to this part 6;

(c) Has accepted any fees, compensation, or other valuable consideration to influence the outcome of an appraisal;

(d) Has used advertising that is misleading, deceptive, or false;

(e) Has used fraud or misrepresentation in obtaining a license or certificate under this part 6;

(f) Has conducted an appraisal in a fraudulent manner or used misrepresentation in any such activity;

(g) Has acted or failed to act in a manner that does not meet the generally accepted standards of professional appraisal practice as adopted by the board by rule. A certified copy of a malpractice judgment of a court of competent jurisdiction is conclusive evidence of the act or omission, but evidence of the act or omission is not limited to a malpractice judgment.

(h) Has performed appraisal services beyond his or her level of competency;

(i) Has been subject to an adverse or disciplinary action in another state, territory, or country relating to a license, certificate, or other authorization to practice as an appraiser. A disciplinary action relating to a license or certificate as an appraiser licensed or certified under this part 6 or any related occupation in any other state, territory, or country for disciplinary reasons is prima facie evidence of grounds for disciplinary action or denial of licensure or certification by the board. This subsection (1)(i) applies only to violations based upon acts or omissions in the other state, territory, or country that are also violations of this part 6.

(j) Has failed to disclose in the appraisal report the fee paid to the appraiser for a residential real property appraisal if the appraiser was engaged by an appraisal management company to complete the assignment; or

(k) Has engaged in conduct that would be grounds for the denial of a license or certification under section 12-10-612.

(2) If an applicant, a licensee, or a certified person has violated any provision of this section, the board may deny or refuse to renew the license or certificate, or, as specified in subsections (3) and (6) of this section, revoke or suspend the license or certificate, issue a letter of admonition to a licensee or certified person, place a licensee or certified person on probation, or impose public censure.

(3) When a complaint or an investigation discloses an instance of misconduct by a licensed or certified appraiser that, in the opinion of the board, does not warrant formal action by the board but should not be dismissed as being without merit, the board may send a letter of admonition by certified mail to the appraiser against whom a complaint was made. The letter shall advise the appraiser of the right to make a written request, within twenty days after receipt of the letter of admonition, to the board to begin formal disciplinary proceedings as provided in this section to adjudicate the conduct or acts on which the letter was based.

(4) The board may start a proceeding for discipline of a licensee or certified person when the board has reasonable grounds to believe that a licensee or certified person has committed any act or failed to act pursuant to the grounds established in subsection (1) of this section or when a request for a hearing is timely made under subsection (3) of this section.

(5) Disciplinary proceedings shall be conducted in the manner prescribed by the "State Administrative Procedure Act", article 4 of title 24.

(6) As authorized in subsection (2) of this section, disciplinary actions by the board may consist of the following:

(a) **Revocation of a license or certificate.**

(I) Revocation of a license or certificate by the board means that the licensed or certified person shall surrender his or her license or certificate immediately to the board.

(II) Any person whose license or certificate to practice is revoked is ineligible to apply for a license or certificate issued under this part 6 until more than two years have elapsed from the date of surrender of the license or certificate. A reapplication after the two-year period is treated as a new application.

(b) **Suspension of a license or certificate.** Suspension of a license or certificate by the board is for a period to be determined by the board.

(c) **Probationary status.** The board may impose probationary status on a licensee or certified person. If the board places a licensee or certified person on probation, the board may include conditions for continued practice that the board deems appropriate to assure that the licensee or certified person is otherwise qualified to practice in accordance with generally accepted professional standards of professional appraisal practice, as specified in board rules, including any or all of the following:

(I) A requirement that the licensee or certified person take courses of training or education as needed to correct deficiencies found in the hearing;

(II) A review or supervision of his or her practice as may be necessary to determine the quality of the practice and to correct deficiencies in the practice; and

(III) The imposition of restrictions upon the nature of his or her appraisal practice to assure that he or she does not practice beyond the limits of his or her capabilities.

(d) **Public censure.** If, after notice and hearing, the director or the director's designee determines that the licensee or certified person has committed any of the acts specified in this section, the board may impose public censure.

(7) In addition to any other discipline imposed pursuant to this section, any person who violates this part 6 or the rules promulgated pursuant to this article 10 may be penalized by the board upon a finding of a violation pursuant to article 4 of title 24 as follows:

(a) In the first administrative proceeding against a person, a fine of not less than three hundred dollars but not more than five hundred dollars per violation;

(b) In any subsequent administrative proceeding against a person for transactions occurring after a final agency action determining that a violation of this part 6 has occurred, a fine of not less than one thousand dollars but not more than two thousand dollars.

(8) A person participating in good faith in making a complaint or report or participating in an investigative or administrative proceeding before the board pursuant to this article 10 is immune from any liability, civil or criminal, that otherwise might result by reason of the action.

(9) A licensee or certified person who has direct knowledge that a person has violated this part 6 shall report his or her knowledge to the board.

(10) The board, on its own motion or upon application at any time after the imposition of discipline as provided in this section, may reconsider its prior action and reinstate or restore a license or certificate, terminate probation, or reduce the severity of its prior disciplinary action. The decision of whether to take any further action or hold a hearing with respect to a prior disciplinary action rests in the sole discretion of the board.

§ 12-10-614, C.R.S. Appraisal management companies – prohibited activities – grounds for disciplinary actions – procedures – rules.

***Editor's note:** This section is similar to former §12-61-714 as it existed prior to 2019.*

(1) The board, upon its own motion, may, and upon a complaint submitted to the board in writing by any person, shall, investigate the activities of a licensed appraisal management company; an appraiser designated as a controlling appraiser by a partnership, limited liability company, or corporation acting as an appraisal management company; or a person or an entity that assumes to act in that capacity within the state. The board, upon finding a violation, may impose an administrative fine not to exceed two thousand five hundred dollars for each separate offense; censure a licensee; place the licensee on probation and set the terms of probation; or temporarily suspend or permanently revoke a license, when the licensee has performed, is performing, or is attempting to perform any of the following acts:

(a) Failing to:

(I) Exercise due diligence when hiring or engaging a real estate appraiser to ensure that the real estate appraiser is appropriately credentialed by the board and competent to perform the assignment; and

(II) In the case of an AMC, establish and comply with processes and controls reasonably designed to ensure that the AMC conducts its appraisal management services in accordance with the requirements of the federal "Truth in Lending Act", 15 U.S.C. sec. 1639e (a) to (i), and regulations adopted pursuant to that act;

(b) Requiring an appraiser to indemnify the appraisal management company against liability, damages, losses, or claims other than those arising out of the services performed by the appraiser, including performance or nonperformance of the appraiser's duties and obligations, whether as a result of negligence or willful misconduct;

(c) Influencing or attempting to influence the development, reporting, result, or review of a real estate appraisal or the engagement of an appraiser through coercion, extortion, collusion, compensation, inducement, intimidation, bribery, or in any other manner. This prohibition does not prohibit an appraisal management company from requesting an appraiser to:

(I) Consider additional, appropriate property information;

(II) Provide further detail, substantiation, or explanation for the appraiser's value conclusion; or

(III) Correct errors in the appraisal report.

(d) Prohibiting an appraiser, in the completion of an appraisal service, from communicating with the client, any intended users, real estate brokers, tenants, property owners, management companies, or any other entity that the appraiser reasonably believes has information pertinent to the completion of an appraisal assignment; except that this subsection (1)(d) does not apply to communications between an appraiser and an appraisal management company's client if the client has adopted an explicit policy prohibiting the communication. If the client has adopted an explicit policy prohibiting communication by the appraiser with the client, communication by an appraiser to the client must be made in writing and submitted to the appraisal management company.

(e) Altering or modifying a completed appraisal report without the authoring appraiser's knowledge and written consent, and the consent of the intended user, except to modify the format of the report solely for transmission to the client and in a manner acceptable to the client;

(f) Requiring an appraiser to provide to the appraisal management company access to the appraiser's electronic signature;

(g) Failing to validate or verify that the work completed by an appraiser who is hired or engaged by the appraisal management company complies with state and federal regulations, including the uniform standards of professional appraisal practice, by conducting an annual audit of a random sample of the appraisals received within the previous year by the appraisal management company. The board shall establish annual appraisal review requirements by rule and shall solicit and consider information and comments from interested persons.

(h) Failing to make payment to an appraiser within sixty days after completion of the appraisal, unless otherwise agreed or unless the appraiser has been notified in writing that a bona fide dispute exists regarding the performance or quality of the appraisal;

(i) Failing to perform the terms of a written agreement with an appraiser hired or engaged to complete an appraisal assignment;

(j) Failing to disclose to an appraiser, at the time of engagement, the identity of the client;

(k) Using an appraisal report for a client other than the one originally contracted with, without the original client's written consent;

(*l*) Failing to maintain possession of, for future use or inspection by the board, for a period of at least five years or at least two years after final disposition of any judicial proceeding in which a representative of the appraisal management company provided testimony related to the assignment, whichever period expires last, the documents or records prescribed by the rules of the board or to produce the documents or records upon reasonable request by the board;

(m) Having been convicted of, or entering a plea of guilty, an Alford plea, or a plea of nolo contendere to, any misdemeanor or felony relating to the conduct of an appraisal, theft, embezzlement, bribery, fraud, misrepresentation, or deceit, or any other like crime under Colorado law, federal law, or the laws of other states. A certified copy of the judgment of a court of competent jurisdiction of the conviction or other official record indicating that a plea was entered is conclusive evidence of the conviction or plea in any hearing under this part 6.

(n) Having been the subject of an adverse or disciplinary action in another state, territory, or country relating to a license, registration, certification, or other authorization to practice as an appraisal management company. A disciplinary action relating to a registration, license, or certificate as an appraisal management company under this part 6 or any related occupation in any other state, territory, or country for disciplinary reasons is prima facie evidence of grounds for disciplinary action or denial of a license by the board. This subsection (1)(n) applies only to violations based upon acts or omissions in the other state, territory, or country that would violate this part 6 if committed in Colorado.

(o) Violating the "Colorado Consumer Protection Act", article 1 of title 6;

(p) Procuring, or attempting to procure, an appraisal management company license or renewing, reinstating, or reactivating, or attempting to renew, reinstate, or reactivate, an appraisal management company license by fraud, misrepresentation, or deceit or by making a material misstatement of fact in an application for a license;

(q) Knowingly misrepresenting or making false promises through agents, advertising, or otherwise;

(r) Failing to disclose to a client the fee amount paid to the appraiser hired or engaged to complete the appraisal upon completion of the assignment; or

(s) Disregarding, violating, or abetting, directly or indirectly, a violation of this part 6, a rule promulgated by the board pursuant to this part 6, or an order of the board entered pursuant to this part 6.

(2) When a complaint or an investigation discloses an instance of misconduct that, in the opinion of the board, does not warrant formal action by the board but should not be dismissed as being without merit, the board may send a letter of admonition by certified mail, return receipt requested, to the licensee against whom the complaint was made. The letter shall advise the licensee of the right to make a written request, within twenty days after receipt of the letter of admonition, to the board to begin formal disciplinary proceedings as provided in this section to adjudicate the conduct or acts on which the letter was based.

(3) Disciplinary proceedings must be conducted in the manner prescribed by the "State Administrative Procedure Act", article 4 of title 24.

(4) If a partnership, limited liability company, or corporation operating under the license of an appraiser designated and licensed as a controlling appraiser by the partnership, limited liability company, or corporation is guilty of any act listed in subsection (1) of this section, the board may suspend or revoke the right of the partnership, limited liability company, or corporation to conduct its business under the license of the controlling appraiser, whether or not the controlling appraiser had personal knowledge of the violation and whether or not the board suspends or revokes the individual license of the controlling appraiser.

(5) This part 6 does not relieve any person from civil liability or criminal prosecution under the laws of this state.

(6) A licensee or certified person having direct knowledge that a person or licensed partnership, limited liability company, or corporation has violated this part 6 shall report his or her knowledge to the board.

(7) The board, on its own motion or upon application, at any time after the imposition of discipline as provided in this section, may reconsider its prior action and reinstate or restore a license, terminate probation, or reduce the severity of its prior disciplinary action. The decision of

whether to take any further action or hold a hearing with respect to the action rests in the sole discretion of the board.

§ *12-10-615, C.R.S. Judicial review of final board actions and orders.*

Editor's note: *This section is similar to former §12-61-715 as it existed prior to 2019.*

Final actions and orders of the board under sections 12-10-612, 12-10-613, and 12-10-614 appropriate for judicial review are subject to judicial review in the court of appeals in accordance with section 24-4-106 (11).

* § *12-10-616, C.R.S. Unlawful acts – penalties.*

Editor's note: *This section is similar to former §12-61-716 as it existed prior to 2019.*

(1) It is unlawful for a person to:

(a) Violate section 12-10-613 (1)(c), (1)(e), or (1)(f) or perform a real estate appraisal without first having obtained a license or certificate from the board pursuant to this part 6;

(b) Accept a fee for an independent appraisal assignment that is contingent upon:

(I) Reporting a predetermined analysis, opinion, or conclusion; or

(II) The analysis, opinion, or conclusion reached; or

(III) The consequences resulting from the analysis, opinion, or conclusion;

(c) Misrepresent a consulting service as an independent appraisal; or

(d) Fail to disclose, in connection with a consulting service for which a contingent fee is or will be paid, the fact that a contingent fee is or will be paid.

(2) [*Editor's note: This version of subsection (2) is effective until March 1, 2022.*] Any person who violates any provision of subsection (1) of this section commits a class 1 misdemeanor and shall be punished as provided in section 18-1.3-501. Any person who subsequently violates any provision of subsection (1) of this section within five years after the date of a conviction for a violation of subsection (1) of this section commits a class 5 felony and shall be punished as provided in section 18-1.3-401.

(2) [*Editor's note: This version of subsection (2) is effective March 1, 2022.*] Any person who violates any provision of subsection (1) of this section commits a class 2 misdemeanor and shall be punished as provided in section 18-1.3-501. Any person who subsequently violates any provision of subsection (1) of this section within five years after the date of a conviction for a violation of subsection (1) of this section commits a class 5 felony and shall be punished as provided in section 18-1.3-401.

* § *12-10-617, C.R.S. Appraisal management company license required – violations – injunction.*

Editor's note: *This section is similar to former §12-61-717 as it existed prior to 2019.*

(1) Except as provided in section 12-10-607 (9), it is unlawful for any person, partnership, limited liability company, or corporation to engage in the business of appraisal management in this state without first having obtained a license from the board. The board shall not grant a license to a person, partnership, limited liability company, or corporation until the person, partnership, limited liability company, or corporation demonstrates compliance with this part 6.

(2) The board may apply to a court of competent jurisdiction for an order enjoining an act or practice that constitutes a violation of this part 6, and, upon a showing that a person, partnership, limited liability company, or corporation is engaging or intends to engage in an act or practice that violates this part 6, the court shall grant an injunction, restraining order, or other

appropriate order, regardless of the existence of another remedy for the violation. Any notice, hearing, or duration of an injunction or restraining order shall be made in accordance with the Colorado rules of civil procedure.

(3) *[Editor's note: This version of subsection (3) is effective until March 1, 2022.]* Any person, partnership, limited liability company, or corporation violating this part 6 by acting as an appraisal management company without having obtained a license or acting as an appraisal management company after the appraisal management company's license has been revoked or during any period for which the license was suspended is guilty of a misdemeanor and, upon conviction thereof:

(a) If a natural person, shall be punished by a fine of not more than five hundred dollars, or by imprisonment in the county jail for not more than six months, or by both such fine and imprisonment, for the first violation and, for a second or subsequent violation, shall be punished by a fine of not more than one thousand dollars, or by imprisonment in the county jail for not more than six months, or by both such fine and imprisonment; and

(b) If an entity, shall be punished by a fine of not more than five thousand dollars.

(3) *[Editor's note: This version of subsection (3) is effective March 1, 2022.]* Any person, partnership, limited liability company, or corporation violating this part 6 by acting as an appraisal management company without having obtained a license or acting as an appraisal management company after the appraisal management company's license has been revoked or during any period for which the license was suspended commits a class 2 misdemeanor.

§ *12-10-618, C.R.S. Injunctive proceedings.*

Editor's note: *This section is similar to former §12-61-718 as it existed prior to 2019.*

(1) The board may, in the name of the people of the state of Colorado, through the attorney general of the state of Colorado, apply for an injunction in any court of competent jurisdiction to perpetually enjoin a person or appraisal management company from committing an act prohibited by this part 6.

(2) Injunctive proceedings under this section are in addition to and not in lieu of penalties and other remedies provided in this part 6.

(3) When seeking an injunction under this section, the board is not required to allege or prove either that an adequate remedy at law does not exist or that substantial or irreparable damage would result from a continued violation.

§ *12-10-619, C.R.S. Special provision for appraiser employees of county assessors.*

Editor's note: *This section is similar to former §12-61-719 as it existed prior to 2019.*

(1) Except as provided in subsection (2) of this section, unless a federal waiver is applied for and granted pursuant to section 12-10-604 (1)(i), a person acting as a real estate appraiser in this state shall be licensed or certified as provided in this part 6. No person shall practice without a license or certificate or hold himself or herself out to the public as a licensed or certified real estate appraiser unless licensed or certified pursuant to this part 6.

(2) An appraiser employee of a county assessor who is employed to appraise real property shall be licensed or certified as provided in this part 6 and shall have two years from the date of taking office or the beginning of employment to comply with this part 6.

§ *12-10-620, C.R.S. Duties of board under federal law.*

Editor's note: *This section is similar to former §12-61-720 as it existed prior to 2019.*

(1) The board shall:

(a) Transmit to the appraisal subcommittee of the federal financial institutions examination council or its successor entity, no less than annually, a roster listing individuals and appraisal management companies that have received a certificate or license as provided in this part 6;

(b) Collect and transmit, on an annual basis, to the federal financial institutions examination council an annual registry fee, as prescribed by the appraisal subcommittee of the federal financial institutions examination council or its successor entity, from the following individuals and entities:

(I) Individuals and appraisal management companies that are licensed or certified pursuant to this part 6; and

(II) Appraisal management companies that operate as subsidiaries of federally regulated financial institutions; and

(c) Conduct its business and promulgate rules in a manner consistent with Title XI of the federal "Financial Institutions Reform, Recovery, and Enforcement Act of 1989", as amended, Pub.L. 101-73.

(2) The board shall not collect or transmit the information required by this section for licensed ad valorem appraisers.

§ *12-10-621, C.R.S. Business entities.*

Editor's note: *This section is similar to former §12-61-721 as it existed prior to 2019.*

(1) A corporation, partnership, bank, savings and loan association, savings bank, credit union, or other business entity may provide appraisal services if the appraisal is prepared by a certified general appraiser, a certified residential appraiser, or a licensed appraiser. An individual who is not a certified general appraiser, a certified residential appraiser, or a licensed appraiser may assist in the preparation of an appraisal if:

(a) The assistant is under the direct supervision of a certified or licensed appraiser; and

(b) The final appraisal document is approved and signed by an individual who is a certified or licensed appraiser.

§ *12-10-622, C.R.S. Provisions found not to comply with federal law null and void – severability.*

Editor's note: *(1) This section is similar to former §12-61-722 as it existed prior to 2019.*

(2) As of publication date, the revisor of statutes has not received the notice referred to in subsection (2).

(1) If any provision of this part 6 is found by a court of competent jurisdiction or by the appropriate federal agency not to comply with the federal "Financial Institutions Reform, Recovery, and Enforcement Act of 1989", as amended, Pub.L. 101-73, the provision is null and void, but the remaining provisions of this part 6 are valid unless the remaining provisions alone are incomplete and are incapable of being executed in accordance with the legislative intent of this part 6.

(2) If the regulation of appraisal management companies is repealed from Title XI of the federal "Financial Institutions Reform, Recovery, and Enforcement Act of 1989", as amended, Pub.L. 101-73, the board's jurisdiction over these entities is also repealed. Before the repeal, the division shall review the regulation of appraisal management companies as provided in section 24-34-104. If the board's jurisdiction is repealed, the director shall notify the revisor of statutes of the date of the repeal.

§ *12-10-623, C.R.S. Scope of article – regulated financial institutions – de minimis exemption.*

* ***Editor's note:*** *(1) This section is similar to former §12-61-723 as it existed prior to 2019.*
* *(2) Section 3(2) of chapter 17 (SB 20-047), Session Laws of Colorado 2020, provides that the act changing this section applies to appraisals made on or after September 14, 2020.*

(1) (a) This article 10 does not apply to an appraisal relating to any real-estate-related transaction or loan made or to be made by a financial institution or its affiliate if the real-estate-related transaction or loan is excepted from appraisal regulations established by the primary federal regulator of the financial institution and the appraisal is performed by:

* (I) An officer, director, regularly salaried employee, or agent of the financial institution or its affiliate; or

(II) A real estate broker licensed under this article 10 with whom the institution or affiliate has contracted for performance of the appraisal.

(b) The appraisal must not be represented or deemed to be an appraisal except to the financial institution, the agencies regulating the financial institution, and any secondary markets that purchase real estate secured loans. The appraisal must contain a written notice that the preparer is not licensed or certified as an appraiser under this part 6. Nothing in this subsection (1) exempts a person licensed or certified as an appraiser under this part 6 from regulation as provided in this part 6.

(2) Nothing in this article 10 limits the ability of any federal or state regulator of a financial institution to require the financial institution to obtain appraisals as specified by the regulator.

Chapter 7: Appraiser Rules and Regulations

An * in the left margin indicates a change in the statute, rule, or text since the last publication of the manual.

Pursuant to § 12-10-604(1)(a), C.R.S., the Colorado Board of Real Estate Appraisers engages in rulemaking to implement Colorado law in a manner consistent with the requirements of Title XI of the federal Financial Institutions Reform, Recovery and Enforcement Act of 1989.

The rulemaking process is set by § 24-4-103, C.R.S., and involves notice to the public, hearing(s), adoption of rules, and publication. General notice is accomplished through filing with the Secretary of State and publication in the Colorado Register. Specific notice is provided by mail to interested parties. To request mailing of rulemaking notices, send a written request for placement on the rulemaking notice list to: Rule Making Notice List, Colorado Board of Appraisers, 1560 Broadway, Suite 925, Denver, CO 80202.

While rulemaking may occur at any time, the Board prefers to adopt new and amended rules in the fall, with January 1 of the next year as the effective date. Rules are published in the Colorado Real Estate Manual.

DEPARTMENT OF REGULATORY AGENCIES
DIVISION OF REAL ESTATE
BOARD OF REAL ESTATE APPRAISERS
4 CCR 725-2

RULES OF THE COLORADO BOARD OF REAL ESTATE APPRAISERS

Ed. Note: For the most current information, please refer to the Division of Real Estate website: www.dora.state.co.us/real-estate

CHAPTER 1: DEFINITIONS

1.1 The Appraisal Foundation (TAF): An organization that is the source of appraisal standards, qualifications, and ethical conduct in all valuation disciplines to assure public trust in the valuation profession.

* 1.2 Appraiser Qualifications Board (AQB) of TAF: The AQB establishes the minimum education, experience, and examination requirements for real property appraisers to obtain state certifications. In addition, the AQB performs a number of ancillary duties related to real property and personal property appraiser qualifications.

* 1.3 Appraisal Standards Board (ASB) of TAF: The ASB develops, interprets, and amends the USPAP.

1.4 Examination: The examination(s) developed by or contracted for the Board and issued or approved by the AQB, if applicable.

1.5 FIRREA: The Financial Institutions Reform, Recovery and Enforcement Act of 1989 as amended.

1.6 Board: The Colorado Board of Real Estate Appraisers created and further defined pursuant to section 12-10-603, C.R.S.

1.7 Applicant: Any person applying for a license, Credential Upgrade, or Temporary Practice Permit.

1.8 Initial License: The first license granted by the Board to an applicant pursuant to section 12-10-606, C.R.S. An applicant may apply for an initial license at any credential level as long as all requirements for such credential level have been met pursuant to these Rules. An initial license is valid through December 31 of the year of issuance.

1.9 Colorado Real Estate Appraiser Licensing Act: That portion of Colorado statutes known as sections 12-10-601 through 623, et seq., C.R.S. as amended.

1.10 Uniform Standards of Professional Appraisal Practice (USPAP): Those standards of professional practice promulgated by the ASB of TAF. Pursuant to section 12-10-613(1)(g), C.R.S., as amended, the Board adopts, and incorporates by reference in compliance with section 24-4-103(12.5), C.R.S., as the generally accepted standards of professional appraisal practice the Definitions, Preamble, Rules, Standards, and Standards Rules of the USPAP as promulgated by the ASB of TAF on January 30, 1989 and amended through April 5, 2019 and known as the 2020-2021 edition. Amendments to the USPAP subsequent to April 5, 2019 are not included in this Board Rule 1.10. A certified copy of the USPAP is on file and available for public inspection at the Office of the Board at 1560 Broadway, Suite 925, Denver, Colorado 80202. Copies of the USPAP adopted under this Rule may be examined at any state publications depository library. The 2020-2021 edition of the USPAP may be examined at the Internet website of TAF at www.appraisalfoundation.org, and copies may be ordered through that mechanism. TAF may also be contacted at 1155 15th Street, NW, Suite 1111, Washington, DC 20005, or by telephone at (202) 347-7722 or by telefax at (202) 347-7727.

1.11 Board Rules or Rules: Those rules adopted by the Board pursuant to the Colorado Real Estate Appraiser Licensing Act.

1.12 Repealed.

* 1.13 Licensed Appraiser: A person who has been granted a license pursuant to section 12-10-606(1)(b)(IV), C.R.S. as a Licensed Appraiser by the Board as a result of meeting the real estate appraisal education, experience, and examination requirements established by Board Rule 2.2, the AQB, or as a result of licensure through endorsement from another jurisdiction as provided by Chapter 9 of these Rules. The scope of practice for the Licensed Appraiser is limited to, if competent for the assignment, appraisal of non-complex one to four unit residential properties having a transaction value of less than $1,000,000 and complex one to four unit residential properties having a transaction value of less than $400,000, or as allowed by section 12-10-606(4), C.R.S. For non-federally related transactions, the scope of practice may include vacant or unimproved land that is to be used for development for a one to four unit residential property, or vacant or unimproved land for which the highest and best use is a one to four unit residential property. In compliance with Board Rule 1.16, the scope of practice does not include vacant or unimproved land that has the potential for subdivision development for which the subdivision development analysis method of land valuation is necessary and applicable.

1.14 Certified Residential Appraiser: A person who has been granted a license pursuant to section 12-10-606(1)(b)(II), C.R.S., as a Certified Residential Appraiser by the Board as a result of meeting the real estate appraisal education, experience, and examination requirements established by Board Rule 2.3, the AQB, or as a result of licensure through endorsement from another jurisdiction as provided by Chapter 9 of these Rules. The scope of practice for the Certified Residential Appraiser is limited to, if competent for the assignment, appraisal of one to four unit residential properties without regard to transaction value or complexity, or as allowed by section 12-10-606(4), C.R.S. Such scope of practice includes vacant or unimproved land that is to be used for development for a one to four unit residential property, or vacant or unimproved land for which the highest and best use is a one to four unit residential property. In compliance with Board Rule 1.16, the scope of practice for a Certified Residential Appraiser does not include vacant or unimproved land that has the potential for subdivision development for which the subdivision development analysis method of land valuation is necessary and applicable.

1.15 Certified General Appraiser: A person who has been granted a license pursuant to section 12-10-606(1)(b)(I), C.R.S. as a Certified General Appraiser by the Board as a result of meeting the real estate appraisal education, experience, and examination requirements established by Board Rule 2.4, the AQB, or as a result of licensure through endorsement from another jurisdiction as provided by Chapter 9 of these Rules. The scope of practice for the Certified General Appraiser will be, if competent for the assignment, appraisal of all types of real property.

1.16 Residential Property: Properties comprising one to four residential units; also includes building sites suitable for development to one to four residential units. Residential property does not include land for which a subdivision analysis or appraisal is necessary.

1.17 Non Residential Property: Properties other than those comprised of one to four residential units and building sites suitable for development to one to four residential units. Non-residential property includes, without limitation, properties comprised of five or more dwelling units, farm and ranch, retail, manufacturing, warehousing, office properties, large vacant land parcels, and other properties not within the definition of residential property.

1.18 Temporary Practice Permit: A permit issued pursuant to section 12-10-611(3), C.R.S. as amended and Chapter 10 of these Rules allowing an appraiser licensed or certified in another jurisdiction to appraise property in Colorado under certain conditions without obtaining Colorado licensure.

1.19 Title XI, FIRREA: That part of the Financial Institutions Reform, Recovery and Enforcement Act of 1989 known as the Appraisal Reform Amendments, and also known as 12 U.S.C. sections 3331 through 3355, as amended.

1.20 Contingent Fee: Compensation paid to a person who is licensed as a licensed or certified appraiser, as a result of reporting a predetermined value or direction of value that favors the cause of the client, the amount of value opinion, the attainment of a stipulated result, or the occurrence of a subsequent event directly related to the appraiser's opinion and specific to the assignment's purpose. A person licensed as a licensed or certified appraiser employed by a business entity which is compensated by a contingent fee is considered to be compensated by a contingent fee.

1.21 Licensee: A collective term used to refer to a person who has been licensed by the Board as a Licensed Ad Valorem Appraiser, Licensed Appraiser, Certified Residential Appraiser, or Certified General Appraiser.

* 1.22 Distance Education: Any education process based on the geographical separation of student and instructor. Components of distance education include synchronous, asynchronous, and hybrid.

1.23 Complex Residential Property: Properties comprising one to four residential dwelling units, or land suitable for development to one to four residential units exhibiting complex appraisal factors such as atypical form of ownership, atypical size, atypical design characteristics, atypical locational characteristics, atypical physical condition characteristics, landmark designation, non-conforming zoning, lack of appraisal data, and other similar factors. Complex residential property does not include land for which a subdivision analysis or appraisal is necessary.

1.24 Signature: As defined in the USPAP incorporated by reference in Board Rule 1.10, and including all methods of indicating a signature, such as, without limitation, a handwritten mark, digitized image, coded authentication number, stamped impression, embossed or applied seal, or other means.

1.25 Repealed.

1.26 Qualifying Education: Real estate appraisal education courses completed for credit toward the licensing requirements set forth in Chapter 2 of these Rules and meeting the requirements of Chapter 3 of these Rules. Qualifying education courses must be at least fifteen (15) classroom hours in length and must include an examination.

1.27 Continuing Education: Real estate and real estate appraisal related courses completed for credit toward meeting the continuing education requirements set forth in Chapter 7 of these Rules.

1.28 Transaction value: For purposes of these Rules transaction value means:

A. For appraisal assignments carried out as part of a loan transaction, the amount of the loan; or

B. For appraisal assignments carried out for other than a loan transaction, the market value of the real property interest.

1.29 Appraisal (Valuation) Process: The analysis of factors that create value to develop an opinion of value. Steps in the analytical process are: defining the problem; determining an appropriate scope of work; gathering and analyzing general and specific data; applying the appropriate analyses, procedures and methodology; the application of reconciliation criteria to reach a final defined value opinion; and correctly reporting that opinion in compliance with the USPAP.

1.30 Accredited college, junior college, community college or university: a higher education institution accredited by the Commission on Colleges, a regional or national accreditation association, or an accrediting agency that is recognized by the U. S. Secretary of Education.

1.31 Repealed.

* 1.32 Real Property Appraiser Qualification Criteria (Criteria): Pursuant to section 12-10-606(1) and (2), C.R.S. as amended, the Board incorporates by reference in compliance with section 24-4-103(12.5), C.R.S., the Real Property Appraiser Qualification Criteria adopted by the AQB of TAF on August 24, 2021, including the Required Core Curricula, Guide Notes, and Interpretations relating to the real property appraiser classifications described in Board Rules 1.13, 1.14, and 1.15. This Board Rule 1.32 excludes and does not incorporate by reference the following: the trainee real property appraiser classification and qualification requirements; the supervisory appraiser requirements; supervisory appraiser/trainee appraiser course objectives and outline; or any later amendments or additions of the Criteria. A certified copy of the Real Property Appraiser Qualification Criteria is on file and available for public inspection at the Office of the Board at 1560 Broadway, Suite 925, Denver, Colorado 80202. Copies of the Real Property Appraiser Qualification Criteria may be examined at the Internet website of TAF at www.appraisalfoundation.org, and copies may be ordered through that mechanism. TAF may also be contacted at 1155 15th Street, NW, Suite 1111, Washington, DC 20005, or by telephone at (202) 347-7722 or telefax at (202) 347-7727. The Real Property Appraiser Qualification Criteria is effective as of January 1, 2022.

1.33 Credential Upgrade: A licensee, who has been granted a license pursuant to section 12-10-606, C.R.S., may submit an application to the Board requesting an upgrade of the licensee's credential if the licensee has completed the real estate appraisal education, experience, and examination requirements as defined in Chapter 2 of these Rules for the credential for which the licensee is applying. If the Board grants the requested credential, the upgraded license will expire on the same date of the licensee's current license cycle prior to the upgrade.

1.34 Draft Appraisal: A draft appraisal must be identified and labeled as a "draft". The purpose of issuing a draft appraisal cannot be to allow the client and/or the intended user(s) to improperly influence the appraiser.

1.35 Amendment: A written modification of any appraisal, which is dated and signed by the appraiser, and delivered to the client. An amendment is a true and integral component of an appraisal. Amendments may also be referred to as correction pages.

1.36 Good Standing: A licensee, appraisal management company, or controlling appraiser must:

A. Not have been subject to a stipulation and a final agency order or final agency order, the terms of which were completed not less than three years prior, or had a license revoked or permanently surrendered for any of the violations enumerated under sections 12-10-613, 12-10-614, 12-10-616 or 12-10-617, C.R.S. A license will be considered to be in good standing three years following the completion of all terms of an executed stipulation or final agency order.

B. Not have been subject to a stipulation for diversion, the terms of which have not been fully completed. A licensee will be considered to be in good standing once all terms of the stipulation of diversion have been successfully completed.

1.37 Licensed Ad Valorem Appraiser: A person who has been granted a license pursuant to section 12-10-606(1)(b)(III), C.R.S., as a Licensed Ad Valorem Appraiser by the Board as a result of meeting the real estate appraisal education and examination requirements established by Board Rule 2.9. A Licensed Ad Valorem Appraiser cannot conduct appraisal assignments outside the scope of the appraiser's official duties as a County Assessor, an employee of a County Assessor's Office, or as an employee with the Division of Property Taxation within the Department of Local Affairs.

1.38 Review Appraiser: An appraiser, who is actively credentialed in a jurisdiction that is in compliance with Title XI, FIRREA, as determined by the ASC as defined in Board Rule 1.42, who performs a review of another appraiser's work subject to USPAP Standard 3. A review appraiser is not required to obtain a Colorado appraiser's license unless the review appraiser arrives at his or her own opinion of value for real property located in Colorado.

1.39 The Course Approval Program (CAP) of TAF: A voluntary program established by the AQB to provide a minimum level of acceptance for real property appraisal education courses satisfying the Real Property Appraiser Qualification Criteria as defined in Board Rule 1.32.

1.40 Division of Real Estate (Division): Has the same meaning as set forth in section 12-10-101(2), C.R.S.

1.41 Director of the Division (Director): Has the same meaning as set forth in section 12-10-101(1), C.R.S.

1.42 Appraisal Subcommittee (ASC) of the Federal Financial Institutions Examination Council: A subcommittee created within the Federal Financial Institutions Examination Council as a result of Title XI, FIRREA, or its successor entity, to provide oversight of the appraiser regulatory system.

1.43 College Level Examination Program (CLEP): A group of standardized tests created and administered by the College Board to assess college-level knowledge in certain subject areas and provide a mechanism for earning college credits without taking college courses.

1.44 Repealed.

1.45 Panel Size Threshold: Has the same meaning as pursuant to section 12-10-604(1)(a)(IV), C.R.S.

1.46 Panel: Has the same meaning as pursuant to section 12-10-602(8), C.R.S.

1.47 Federally Regulated AMC: Has the same meaning as pursuant to section 12-10-607(9), C.R.S.

1.48 AMC Registry Fee: The annual fee collected from appraisal management companies that meet the Panel Size Threshold, including state-licensed appraisal management companies and Federally Regulated AMCs, for transmitting to the Appraisal Subcommittee. The fee is calculated by multiplying the number of licensed or certified appraisers who provided an appraisal in connection with a Covered Transaction on the appraisal management company's Panel in Colorado during the Reporting Period by the registry fee as prescribed by the Appraisal Subcommittee.

1.49 AMC National Registry: The registry of state-licensed AMCs and Federally Regulated AMCs maintained by the Appraisal Subcommittee.

1.50 Reporting Period:

A. For State-licensed AMCs:

1. Applying for initial licensure, the previous twelve (12) month period or the period the appraisal management company has been in business, whichever period is less.
2. Applying for renewal, the twelve (12) month period beginning November 1 of the prior year through October 31 of the year of renewal.
3. Applying for reinstatement of an expired license, the twelve (12) month period beginning November 1 of the year prior to expiration through October 31 of the year of expiration.

B. For Federally Regulated AMCs reporting to the state, the twelve (12) month period beginning November 1 of the prior year through October 31 of the current year.

1.51 Consumer Credit: Credit offered or extended to a consumer primarily for personal, family, or household purposes.

1.52 Covered Transaction: Any consumer credit transaction secured by the consumer's principal dwelling.

1.53 Creditor: A person who regularly extends consumer credit:

A. That is subject to a finance charge or is payable by written agreement in more than four installments (not including a down payment), and to whom the obligation is initially payable, either on the face of the note or contract, or by agreement when there is no note or contract; or

B. If the person extended the credit (other than credit subject to the requirements of high cost mortgages) more than five (5) times for transactions secured by a dwelling in the preceding calendar year. If a person did not meet these numerical standards in the preceding calendar year, the numerical standards will be applied to the current calendar year. A person regularly extends consumer credit if, in any 12-month period, the person originates more than one (1) credit extension that is subject to the requirements of high cost mortgages or one (1) or more such credit extensions through a mortgage broker.

1.54 Dwelling: A residential structure that contains one (1) to four (4) units, whether or not that structure is attached to real property. This includes an individual condominium unit, cooperative unit, mobile home, and trailer, if it is used as a residence.

1.55 Person: A natural person or an organization, partnership, proprietorship, association, cooperative, estate, trust, or government unit.

1.56 Secondary Mortgage Market Participant: A guarantor or insurer of mortgage-backed securities, or an underwriter or issuer of mortgage-backed securities. Secondary mortgage market participant only includes an individual investor in a mortgage-backed security if that investor also serves in the capacity of a guarantor, insurer, underwriter, or issuer for the mortgage-backed security.

* 1.57 Practical Applications of Real Estate Appraisal (PAREA): Training programs designed to offer practical experience in a simulated and controlled environment, incorporating the concepts learned in a participant's qualifying education. Multiple types of training techniques may be utilized, including, but not limited to computer-based learning; video gaming; video tutorial; virtual assistant; and virtual reality training.

* 1.58 Synchronous Distance Education: The instructor and students interact simultaneously online, similar to a phone call, video chat, live webinar, or web-based meeting.

* 1.59 Asynchronous Distance Education: The instructor and student interaction is non-simultaneous; the students progress at their own pace and follow a structured course content and quiz/exam schedule.

* 1.60 Hybrid Course Education: Learning environments that allow for both in-person (synchronous) and online (asynchronous) interaction.

* 1.61 Bio-Metric Proctoring: A student's identity is continually verified through processes, such as facial recognition, consistency in keystroke cadence, and the observation of activity in the testing location. Aberrant behavior or activity can be readily observed.

CHAPTER 2: REQUIREMENTS FOR LICENSURE AS A REAL ESTATE APPRAISER

2.1 Repealed.

2.2 An Applicant for licensure as a Colorado Licensed Appraiser must successfully complete the following requirements or the substantial equivalent thereof, as set forth in the Real Property Appraiser Qualification Criteria as defined and incorporated by reference in Board Rule 1.32:

A. Real estate appraisal education:

1. Basic Appraisal Principles: 30 hours;
2. Basic Appraisal Procedures: 30 hours;
3. 15-Hour National USPAP Course: 15 hours;
4. Residential Market Analysis and Highest and Best Use: 15 hours;
5. Residential Appraiser Site Valuation and Cost Approach: 15 hours;
6. Residential Sales Comparison and Income Approaches: 30 hours; and

7. Residential Report Writing and Case Studies: 15 hours.

B. Real estate appraisal experience: An Applicant must demonstrate to the satisfaction of the Board that the Applicant completed at least one thousand (1,000) hours of appraisal experience in no fewer than six (6) months, in conformance with the provisions of Chapter 5 of these Rules and all of the Applicant's experience was obtained after January 30, 1989 and in compliance with the USPAP.

C. Real estate appraisal examination:

1. The prerequisites to taking the Licensed Appraiser examination are:
   a. One hundred fifty (150) creditable class hours as specified in Board Rule 2.2(A); and
   b. One thousand (1,000) hours of qualifying experience completed in no fewer than six (6) months.
2. After receiving approval from the Board, an Applicant, who is not currently licensed or certified and in good standing in another jurisdiction, has up to twenty-four (24) months to take and pass the Licensed Appraiser examination.
3. An Applicant must successfully complete the Licensed Appraiser examination as provided in Chapter 4 of these Rules. The only alternative to successful completion of the Licensed Appraiser examination is the successful completion of the Certified Residential Appraiser or Certified General Appraiser examination.

2.3 An Applicant for licensure as a Colorado Certified Residential Appraiser must successfully complete the following requirements or the substantial equivalent thereof, as set forth in the Real Property Appraiser Qualification Criteria as defined and incorporated by reference in Board Rule 1.32:

A. Real estate appraisal education:

1. Basic Appraisal Principles: 30 hours;
2. Basic Appraisal Procedures: 30 hours;
3. 15-hour National USPAP Course: 15 hours;
4. Residential Market Analysis and Highest and Best Use: 15 hours;
5. Residential Appraiser Site Valuation and Cost Approach: 15 hours;
6. Residential Sales Comparison and Income Approaches: 30 hours;
7. Residential Report Writing and Case Studies: 15 hours;
8. Statistics, Modeling and Finance: 15 hours;
9. Advanced Residential Applications and Case Studies: 15 hours; and
10. Appraisal Subject Matter Elective: 20 hours.

B. College-level or in lieu of education options:

1. An Applicant for the Certified Residential Appraiser credential must satisfy at least one (1) of the following six (6) options:
   a. Hold a Bachelor's Degree in any field of study from an accredited college or university as defined by Board Rule 1.30;
   b. Hold an Associate's Degree from an accredited college or university as defined by Board Rule 1.30, in a field of study related to:
      i. Business Administration;
      ii. Accounting;
      iii. Finance;
      iv. Economics; or

   v. Real Estate.

c. Successful completion of thirty (30) semester hours of college-level courses that cover each of the following specific topic areas and hours:
   i. English Composition (3 semester hours);
   ii. Macroeconomics (3 semester hours);
   iii. Microeconomics (3 semester hours);
   iv. Finance (3 semester hours);
   v. Algebra, Geometry, or higher mathematics (3 semester hours);
   vi. Statistics (3 semester hours);
   vii. Computer Science (3 semester hours);
   viii. Business Law or Real Estate Law (3 semester hours); and
   ix. Two (2) elective courses in any of the topics listed above or in Accounting, Geography, Agricultural Economics, Business Management, or Real Estate (3 semester hours each).
d. Successful completion of at least thirty (30) semester hours of examinations created and administered by the CLEP, as defined in Board Rule 1.43, from each of the following specific subject matter areas and hours:
   i. College Algebra (3 semester hours);
   ii. College Composition (6 semester hours);
   iii. College Composition Modular (3 semester hours);
   iv. College Mathematics (6 semester hours);
   v. Principles of Macroeconomics (3 semester hours);
   vi. Principles of Microeconomics (3 semester hours);
   vii. Introductory Business Law (3 semester hours); and
   viii. Information Systems (3 semester hours).
e. Any combination of Board Rule 2.3(B)(1)(c) and Board Rule (B)(1)(d) above that ensures coverage of all topics and hours identified in Board Rule (B)(1)(c).
f. As an alternative to the college-level education requirements in Board Rule (B)(1)(a through e) above, an Applicant that has held a Licensed Appraiser credential for a minimum of five (5) years may qualify for a Certified Residential Appraiser credential if the Applicant has had no record of any adverse, final, and non-appealable disciplinary action affecting the Licensed Appraiser's legal eligibility to engage in appraisal practice within the five (5) years immediately preceding the date of application for a Certified Residential Appraiser credential.

2. All college-level education must be obtained from a degree-granting institution by the Commission on Colleges, a national or regional accreditation association, or by an accrediting agency that is recognized by the US Secretary of Education.
3. An Applicant with a college degree from a foreign country may have their education evaluated for "equivalency" by one of the following:
   a. An accredited, degree-granting domestic college or university;
   b. A foreign degree credential evaluation service company that is a member of the National Association of Credential Evaluation Services (NACES); or
   c. A foreign degree credential evaluation service company that provides equivalency evaluation reports accepted by an accredited degree- granting domestic college or university or by a state licensing board that issues credentials in another discipline.

C. Real estate appraisal experience: An Applicant for licensure as a Certified Residential Appraiser must demonstrate to the satisfaction of the Board that the Applicant completed at least one thousand five hundred (1,500) hours of appraisal experience in conformance with the provisions of Chapter 5 of these Rules and all of the Applicant's experience was obtained after January 30, 1989 and in compliance with the USPAP. Real estate appraisal experience must have been gained across a period of not less than twelve (12) months.

D. Real estate appraisal examination:

1. The prerequisites to taking the Certified Residential Appraiser examination are:
    a. Two hundred (200) creditable class hours as specified in Board Rule 2.3(A);
    b. Completion of the college-level education requirements as specified in Board Rule 2.3(B); and
    c. One thousand five hundred (1,500) hours of qualifying experience completed in no fewer than twelve (12) months.
2. After receiving approval from the Board, an Applicant, who is not currently licensed or certified and in good standing in another jurisdiction, has up to twenty-four (24) months to take and pass the Certified Residential Appraiser examination.
3. An Applicant must successfully complete the Certified Residential Appraiser examination as provided in Chapter 4 of these Rules. The only alternative to successful completion of the Certified Residential Appraiser examination is the successful completion of the Certified General Appraiser examination.

2.4 An Applicant for licensure as a Colorado Certified General Appraiser must successfully complete the following requirements or the substantial equivalent thereof, as set forth in the Real Property Appraiser Qualification Criteria as defined and incorporated by reference in Board Rule 1.32:

A. Real estate appraisal education:

1. Basic Appraisal Principles: 30 hours;
2. Basic Appraisal Procedures: 30 hours;
3. 15-Hour National USPAP Course: 15 hours;
4. General Appraiser Market Analysis and Highest and Best Use: 30 hours;
5. Statistics, Modeling and Finance: 15 hours;
6. General Appraiser Sales Comparison Approach: 30 hours;
7. General Appraiser Site Valuation and Cost Approach: 30 hours;
8. General Appraiser Income Approach: 60 hours;
9. General Appraiser Report Writing and Case Studies: 30 hours; and
10. Appraisal Subject Matter Electives: 30 hours.

B. College-level education:

1. An Applicant for the Certified General Appraiser credential must hold a Bachelor's degree, or higher, from an accredited college or university as defined by Board Rule 1.30.
2. An Applicant with a college degree from a foreign country may have their education evaluated for "equivalency" by one of the following:
    a. An accredited, degree-granting domestic college or university;
    b. A foreign degree credential evaluation service company that is a member of the National Association of Credential Evaluation Services (NACES); or
    c. A foreign degree credential evaluation service company that provides equivalency evaluation reports accepted by an accredited degree-granting

domestic college or university or by a state licensing board that issues credentials in another discipline.

C. Real estate appraisal experience: An Applicant for licensure as a Certified General Appraiser must demonstrate to the satisfaction of the Board that the Applicant completed at least three thousand (3,000) hours of appraisal experience, of which one thousand five hundred (1,500) hours must be in non-residential appraisal work, in conformance with the provisions of Chapter 5 of these Rules and all of the Applicant's experience was obtained after January 30, 1989 and in compliance with the USPAP. Real estate appraisal experience must have been gained across a period of not less than eighteen (18) months.

D. Real estate appraisal examination:

1. The prerequisites to taking the Certified General Appraiser examination are:
   a. Three hundred (300) creditable class hours as specified in Board Rule 2.4(A);
   b. Completion of the college-level education requirements as specified in Board Rule 2.4(B); and
   c. Three thousand (3,000) hours of qualifying experience, of which no less than one thousand five hundred (1,500) hours must be in non-residential appraisal work, completed in no fewer than eighteen (18) months.
2. After receiving approval from the Board, an Applicant, who is not currently licensed or certified and in good standing in another jurisdiction, has up to twenty-four (24) months to take and pass the Certified General Appraiser examination.
3. An Applicant must successfully complete the Certified General Appraiser examination as provided in Chapter 4 of these Rules.

2.5 Repealed.

2.6 Repealed.

2.7 Repealed.

2.8 An applicant for licensure as a Colorado Licensed Ad Valorem Appraiser must be a County Assessor, an employee of a County Assessor's Office, or an employee of the Division of Property Taxation in the Department of Local Affairs.

2.9 An applicant for licensure as a Colorado Licensed Ad Valorem Appraiser must successfully complete the following requirements, or the substantial equivalent thereof:

A. Real estate appraiser education:

1. Introduction to Ad Valorem Mass Appraisal: no less than 35 hours;
2. Basic Appraisal Principles: no less than 30 hours;
3. Basic Appraisal Procedures: no less than 30 hours; and
4. 15-Hour National USPAP Course: 15 hours.

B. Real Estate Appraisal examination: successful completion of the Ad Valorem Appraiser examination as provided in Chapter 4 of these Rules; and

C. Ad Valorem employment: signed certification by the applicant that the applicant is currently a County Assessor, an employee of a County Assessor's Office, or an employee of the Division of Property Taxation in the Department of Local Affairs.

2.10 Repealed.

CHAPTER 3: STANDARDS FOR REAL ESTATE APPRAISAL QUALIFYING EDUCATION PROGRAMS

3.1 Repealed.

3.2 Qualifying appraisal education must be taken from providers approved by the Board. In order to be approved, qualifying education courses and the providers must meet the following standards at the time it is offered:

A. Course content was developed by persons qualified in the subject matter and instructional design;

B. Course content is current and corresponds with the common body of knowledge;

C. The instructor is qualified with respect to content and teaching methods, and the body of knowledge;

D. The number of participants and the physical facilities are consistent with the teaching method;

E. An examination is included for measuring the information learned; and

F. The educational offering will be developed and communicated in a manner as to promote and maintain a high level of public trust in appraisal practice.

3.3 The following may be approved as providers of qualifying appraisal education provided that the standards set forth in Board Rule 3.2 are maintained and the education providers have complied with all other requirements of the state of Colorado:

A. Accredited colleges, junior colleges, community colleges or universities as defined in Board Rule 1.30;

B. Professional appraisal and real estate related organizations;

C. State or federal government agencies;

D. Proprietary schools holding valid certificates of approval from the Colorado Division of Private Occupational Schools, Department of Higher Education;

E. Providers approved by other jurisdictions, provided the jurisdiction's appraiser regulation program is in compliance with Title XI, FIRREA, as determined by the ASC as defined in Board Rule 1.42;

F. Providers approved under the CAP as defined in Board Rule 1.39; and

G. Such other providers as the Board may approve upon petition of the provider or the applicant in a form acceptable to the Board.

3.4 On or after January 1, 1991, in order to be approved by the Board, each education provider must maintain for a period of five (5) years from the last course offering, and provide to the Board upon request, information regarding the qualifying education course offerings including, but not limited to the following:

A. Outline or syllabus;

B. All texts, workbooks, handouts or other course materials;

C. Instructors and their qualifications, including selection, training and evaluation criteria;

D. Course examinations;

E. Dates and locations of course offerings; and

F. Student attendance records.

* 3.5 The number of hours credited must be equivalent to the actual number of contact hours of in-class or synchronous distance education instruction and testing. An hour of education is defined as at least fifty (50) minutes of instruction out of each 60-minute segment. For asynchronous distance education, the number of hours credited must be that number of hours allowed by the CAP as defined in Board Rule 1.39. For hybrid course education, the number of hours credited will be equivalent for each specific course delivery method. Parts of the course that are delivered in-class or synchronously and delivered asynchronously must meet their respective requirements as set forth in this Board Rule 3.5.

3.6 Each qualifying education course offering must be at least fifteen (15) hours in duration, include an examination pertinent to the material covered, and be comprised of segments of not less than one (1) classroom hour.

3.7 Qualifying education courses and corresponding examinations must be successfully completed by the applicant. Successful completion means the applicant has attended the offering, participated in course activities, and achieved a passing score on the course examination.

3.8 Repealed.

3.9 It is the applicant's responsibility to verify that a qualifying educational course offering has been approved by the Board, if the applicant wishes to claim credit for the course.

3.10 Repealed.

3.11 Hours of qualifying education accepted in satisfaction of the education requirement of one level of licensure may be applied toward the requirement for another level and need not be repeated. Applicants are responsible for demonstrating coverage of the required topics.

3.12 The following factors must be used to convert accredited college, junior college, community college or university course credits into qualifying education hours:

A. Semester Credits x 15.00 = Hours

B. Quarter Credits x 10.00 = Hours

3.13 Applicants must successfully complete qualifying appraisal education which builds upon and augments previous courses. Qualifying education courses which substantially repeat or duplicate other course work in terms of content and level of instruction will not be accepted. The Board will give appropriate consideration to courses where substantive changes in content have occurred.

* 3.14 To be acceptable for qualifying appraisal education, asynchronous distance education offerings must incorporate methods and activities that promote active student engagement and participation in the learning process. Among those methods and activities acceptable are written exercises which are graded and returned to the student, required responses to computer based presentations, provision for students to submit questions during teleconferences, and examinations proctored by an independent third party, who is an official approved by the college or university, or by the sponsoring organization. Biometric proctoring is acceptable. Simple reading, viewing or listening to materials without active student engagement and participation in the learning process is not sufficient to satisfy the requirements of this Board Rule 3.14

3.15 As to qualifying education courses completed in other jurisdictions with appraiser regulatory programs that are in compliance with Title XI, FIRREA, as determined by the ASC as defined in Board Rule 1.42, the Board will accept the number of hours of education accepted by that jurisdiction.

* 3.16 To be acceptable for qualifying real estate appraisal education, synchronous distance education and asynchronous distance education courses must meet the other requirements of Chapter 3 of these Rules, and must include a written, closed book final examination proctored by an independent third party, or other final examination testing procedure acceptable to the Board. Biometric proctoring is acceptable. Examples of acceptable examination proctors include public officials who do not supervise the student, secondary and higher education school officials, and public librarians. Failure to observe this requirement may result in rejection of the course and/or course provider by the Board for that applicant, and may result in the Board refusing or withdrawing approval of any courses offered by the provider.

3.17 All qualifying education courses in the USPAP begun on and after January 1, 2003 must be in the form of a course approved under the CAP as defined in Board Rule 1.39, and taught by an instructor certified by the AQB who is also a state certified appraiser.

3.18 Course providers must provide each student who successfully completes a qualifying real estate appraisal education course in the manner prescribed in Board Rule 3.7 a course completion certificate. The Board will not mandate the exact form of course completion certificates; however, the following information must be included:

A. Name of course provider;

B. Course title, which must describe topical content, or the Real Property Appraiser Qualification Criteria Core Curriculum module title;

C. Course number, if any;

D. Course dates;

E. Number of approved education hours;

F. Statement that the required examination was successfully completed;

* G. Course location, which for synchronous distance education and asynchronous distance education modalities must be the principal place of business of the course provider;

H. Name of student; and

I. For all USPAP courses begun on and after January 1, 2003, the name(s) and AQB USPAP instructor certification number(s) of the instructor(s).

* 3.19 The provisions of Board Rule 3.3 notwithstanding, qualifying education courses begun on and after January 1, 2004 and offered through asynchronous distance education modalities must be approved through the CAP as defined in Board Rule 1.39. The Board will not accept asynchronous distance education courses begun on and after January 1, 2004 that have not been approved through the CAP.

3.20 All qualifying education courses in the USPAP must be presented using the most recent edition and the most recent version of the National USPAP Course (real property) or equivalent as approved by the CAP, with the exception that courses begun in the three (3) months preceding the effective date of a new edition may be presented using the next succeeding USPAP edition and course version, if available from TAF.

3.21 All qualifying education courses begun on or after January 1, 2008 must be approved through the Course Approval Program of the Appraiser Qualifications Board of the Appraisal Foundation, except as otherwise may be approved in advance and in writing by the Director of the Colorado Division of Real Estate (the "Director") on a limited case by case basis where the Director determines that the public would not be served if course approval were required through the Course Approval Program of the Appraiser Qualifications Board of the Appraisal Foundation for a particular course. Course providers seeking approval of qualifying education courses that have not been approved through the Course Approval Program of the Appraiser Qualifications Board of the Appraisal Foundation shall provide the Director with all requested information the Director deems necessary.

3.22 By offering real estate appraiser qualifying education approved by the Board, each provider agrees to comply with the relevant statutes and Board Rules and to permit the Board to audit said courses at any time and at no cost.

3.23 Introduction to Ad Valorem Mass Appraisal courses that have been approved by the Board as qualifying education can be used for credit as appraisal subject matter electives for applicants seeking licensure as a Certified Residential Appraiser or Certified General Appraiser.

3.24 Applicants are required to provide copies of course completion certificates to the Board in accordance with Board Rule 6.1.

CHAPTER 4: STANDARDS FOR REAL ESTATE APPRAISAL LICENSING EXAMINATIONS

4.1 Any person wishing to apply for any appraiser's license must register for and achieve a passing score on the appropriate level of examination with the testing service designated by the Board.

No other examination results will be accepted. The appropriate levels of examination for the respective levels of licensure are as follows:

License Level	Examination
Licensed Ad Valorem Appraiser	Licensed Ad Valorem Appraiser
Licensed Appraiser	Licensed Real Property Appraiser
Certified Residential Appraiser	Certified Residential Appraiser
Certified General Appraiser	Certified General Appraiser

4.2 Examinees must comply with the standards of test administration established by the Board and the testing service.

4.3 A passing score on an examination will be valid for two (2) years from the examination date. Failure to file a complete application within the two (2) year period will result in the examination grade being void.

4.4 Examinations will be given only to duly qualified applicants for an appraiser's license; however, one instructor from each appraisal qualifying education course provider approved pursuant to Board Rule 3.3 may take the examination one time during any twelve (12) month period in order to conduct research for course content.

4.5 Each examination for a license may, as determined by the Board, be a separate examination.

4.6 Examinations developed by or contracted for the Board for licensed and certified appraisers must comply with the Real Property Appraiser Qualification Criteria as defined in Board Rule 1.32, if applicable.

4.7 Repealed.

4.8 Examinees may use financial calculators during the examination process. The memory functions of any such calculator must be cleared by the testing service staff prior to the beginning and after the conclusion of the examination.

CHAPTER 5: STANDARDS FOR REAL ESTATE APPRAISAL EXPERIENCE

5.1 The quantitative experience requirements must be satisfied by time spent on the appraisal process. Acceptable experience includes appraisal, appraisal review, appraisal consulting, and mass appraisal experience where the appraiser demonstrates proficiency in the development and reporting of the assignment results utilizing recognized appraisal principles and methodology during the appraisal process as defined by Board Rule 1.29. The Board may consider other experience upon petition by the applicant. All experience must be obtained after January 30, 1989 and comply with the USPAP.

5.2 Repealed.

5.3 Reports or file memoranda claimed as evidence of meeting experience requirements must have been prepared in conformance with the edition of the USPAP in effect as of the date of the appraisal report.

5.4 Repealed.

5.5 The Board reserves the right to verify an applicant's or licensee's evidence of appraisal experience by such means as it deems necessary, including, but not limited to requiring the following:

A. Submission of a detailed log of appraisal activity on the form or in the manner specified by the Board;

B. Submission of appraisal reports, workfiles or file memoranda;

C. Employer affidavits or interviews;

D. Client affidavits or interviews; and

E. Submission of appropriate business records.

5.6 Repealed.

5.7 Repealed.

* 5.8 There need not be a client in a traditional sense (e.g. a client hiring an appraiser for a business purpose) in order for an appraisal to qualify for experience. Experience gained for work without a traditional client can meet any portion of the total experience requirement.

Practicum courses that are approved by the CAP or the Board can satisfy the nontraditional client experience requirement. A practicum course must include the generally applicable methods of appraisal practice for the credential level. Content includes, but is not limited to: requiring the student to produce credible appraisals that utilize an actual subject property; performing market research, containing sales analysis; and applying and reporting the applicable appraisal approaches in conformity with the USPAP. Assignments must require problem solving skills for a variety of property types for the credential level. Experience credit will be granted for the actual classroom hours of instruction, and hours of documented research and analysis as awarded from the practicum course approval process.

* 5.9 Each application for licensure pursuant to Board Rules 2.2, 2.3, or 2.4 must be accompanied by a log of real estate appraisal experience on a form or in the manner specified by the Board or a certificate of completion as prescribed in Board Rule 5.14. The experience log must include the following:

A. Type of property;

B. Date of report;

C. Address of appraised property;

D. Description of work performed by the applicant, and scope of review and supervision of the supervising appraiser, if applicable;

E. Number of actual work hours by the applicant on the assignment;

F. The signature and state license number of the supervisor, if applicable. Separate experience logs must be maintained for each supervising appraiser, if applicable;

G. An attestation certifying the accuracy and truthfulness of the information contained within the experience log; and

H. The applicant's signature.

5.10 Repealed.

5.11 An applicant for licensure as a Colorado Licensed Appraiser, a Colorado Certified Residential Appraiser or a Colorado Certified General Appraiser must demonstrate that the applicant is capable of performing appraisals that are compliant with USPAP. In accordance with Board Rule 5.5, the Board may verify an applicant's appraisal experience by such means as it deems necessary, including but not limited to requiring the applicant to submit a detailed log of appraisal experience, appraisal reports, and/or work files. Staff within the Division or appraisers selected by the Division may review an applicant's appraisal reports and work files to determine whether the applicant is capable of performing appraisals that are compliant with USPAP and in accordance with Board Rule 13.8.

* 5.12 PAREA programs approved by the AQB may serve as an alternative to the traditional experience requirements as prescribed in Board Rules 2.2.B, 2.3.C, 2.4.C and these Chapter 5 Rules.

* 5.13 In order to qualify as creditable experience, PAREA programs must be AQB approved and meet all the required elements found in the PAREA section of the Real Property Appraiser Qualification Criteria as defined and incorporated by reference in Board Rule 1.32.

* 5.14 Applicants using PAREA training as alternative experience must submit a certificate of completion, subject to the following:

* A. Applicants may not receive partial credit for PAREA training;

* B. Applicants may not receive a certificate of completion until all required components of PAREA training have been successfully completed and approved by a program mentor;

* C. Certificates of completion must be signed by an individual from the training entity qualified to verify an applicant's successful completion; and

* D. Certificates of completion must not contain an expiration date or other constraints that either limit or restrict the applicant's ability to receive appropriate credit.

* 5.15 Applicants successfully completing approved PAREA programs may receive the following experience credit:

* A. Applicants completing an approved licensed residential program:

* 1. Licensed Appraiser Credential: Up to 100 percent of the required experience hours as prescribed in Board Rule 2.2.B.

* 2. Certified Residential Credential: up to 67 percent of the required experience hours as prescribed in Board Rule 2.3.C.

* 3. Certified General Credential: up to 33 percent of the total required experience as prescribed in Board Rule 2.4.C, none of which is eligible towards the required non-residential hours.

* B. Applicants completing an approved certified residential program:

* 1. Licensed Appraiser Credential: up to 100 percent of the required experience hours as prescribed in Board Rule 2.2.B.

* 2. Certified Residential Credential: up to 100 percent of the required experience hours as prescribed in Board Rule 2.3.C.

* 3. Certified General Credential: up to 50 percent of the total required experience as prescribed in Board Rule 2.4.C, none of which is eligible towards the required non-residential hours.

CHAPTER 6: APPLICATION FOR LICENSURE

6.1 Except as provided under Chapter 9 of these Rules, an applicant must complete and submit an application as follows:

A. Licensure for a Licensed Appraiser, Certified Residential Appraiser or Certified General Appraiser credential:

1. An applicant for an initial license must submit a set of fingerprints to the Colorado Bureau of Investigation for the purpose of conducting a state and national criminal history record check prior to submitting an application.
2. Complete the Board created application and submit the application with the supporting documentation to include: qualifying education course completion certificates, college transcripts, and experience log.
3. Upon the Board approving the education and experience requirements, a "Letter of Exam Eligibility" will be issued.
4. After the issuance of the "Letter of Exam Eligibility", schedule the appropriate examination with the examination provider approved by the Board.
5. After successfully passing the appropriate examination as defined in Board Rule 4.1, submit a copy of the examination results with proof of the required errors and omissions insurance policy as defined in Board Rule 6.10.
6. An application is deemed complete at the time that all required supporting documentation and fees are received by the Board.

B. Licensure for a Licensed Ad Valorem Appraiser credential:

1. Complete the Board created application and submit the application with the supporting documentation to include: qualifying education course completion certificates, a copy of the examination results as defined in Board Rule 4.1 and proof of employment with a qualified employer as defined in Board Rule 1.37.
2. Applicants for a Licensed Ad Valorem Appraiser credential are not required to submit a set of fingerprints for the purpose of conducting a state and national criminal history record check and are also exempt from the errors and omissions insurance requirements.
3. An application is deemed complete at the time that all required supporting documentation and fees are received by the Board.

6.2 Repealed.

6.3 Repealed.

6.4 Repealed.

6.5 Once the application is deemed complete, the Board will timely process the application. The Board reserves the right to require additional information and documentation from an applicant to determine compliance with applicable laws and regulations, and to verify any information and documentation submitted.

6.6 Submission of an application does not guarantee issuance of a license, or issuance of a license within a specific period of time. Applicants must observe the provisions of section 12-10-619, C.R.S., and Chapter 12 of these Rules. Applicants will not represent themselves as being licensees of the Board until the license has been issued by the Board.

6.7 Pursuant to section 12-10-612(1), C.R.S., an applicant who has been convicted of, entered a plea of guilty to, entered a plea of nolo contendere, or received a deferred judgment and sentence to a crime, must file with his or her application an addendum to the application in a form prescribed by the Board. Such addendum must be supported and documented by, without limitation, the following:

A. Court documents, including original charges, disposition, pre-sentencing report and certification of completion of terms of sentence;

B. Police officer's report(s);

C. Probation or parole officer's report(s);

D. A written personal statement explaining the circumstances surrounding each violation, and including the statement attesting that "I have no other violations either past or pending";

E. Letters of recommendation; and

F. Employment history for the preceding five (5) years.

6.8 Prior to application for licensure, an individual may request that the Board issue a preliminary advisory opinion regarding the possible effect of convictions, pleas of guilt or nolo contendere or deferred judgments and sentences for criminal offenses. A person requesting such an opinion is not an applicant for licensure. The Board may, at its sole discretion, issue such an opinion, which will not be binding on the Board; is not appealable; and will not limit the authority of the Board to investigate a later application for licensure. The issuance of such an opinion will not prohibit a person from submitting an application for licensure. A person requesting such an opinion must do so in a form prescribed by the Board. Such form must be supported and documented by, without limitation, the following:

A. Court documents, including original charges, disposition, pre-sentencing report and certification of completion of terms of sentence;

B. Police officer's report(s);

C. Probation or parole officer's report(s);

D. A written personal statement explaining the circumstances surrounding each violation, and including the statement attesting that "I have no other violations either past or pending";

E. Letters of recommendation; and

F. Employment history for the preceding five (5) years.

6.9 Repealed.

6.10 Every active appraiser, or applicant for an active appraiser's credential, must have in effect a policy of errors and omissions insurance to cover all acts requiring a license.

A. The Division will enter into a contract with a qualified insurance carrier to make available to all licensees and license applicants a group policy of insurance under the following terms and conditions:

1. The insurance carrier is licensed or authorized by the Colorado Division of Insurance to write policies of errors and omissions insurance in this state.
2. The insurance carrier maintains an A.M. best rating of "A-" or better.
3. The insurance carrier will collect premiums, maintain records and report names of those insured and a record of claims to the Board on a timely basis and at no expense to the Board.
4. The insurance carrier has been selected through a competitive bidding process.
5. The contract and policy are in conformance with this Board Rule 6.10 and all relevant Colorado statutory requirements.

B. The group policy must provide, at a minimum, the following terms of coverage:

1. Coverage for all acts for which a real estate appraiser's license is required to the extent of the professional appraisal work the appraiser is permitted by his or her credential level to perform, except those illegal, fraudulent, or other acts which are normally excluded from such coverage.
2. That the coverage cannot be canceled by the insurance carrier except for nonpayment of the premium or in the event a licensee becomes inactive, is revoked or an applicant is denied a license.
3. The coverage afforded by the policy must not contain exclusions for coverage of claims for damages reasonably expected in connection with professional appraisal services, including, but not limited to, claims for damages made by or on behalf of the Federal Deposit Insurance Corporation (FDIC), the Federal Housing Finance Agency (FHFA), or any other state or federal agency having regulatory authority over a lender or financial institution, and claims arising from failure of a financial institution.
4. Pro-ration of premiums for coverage which is purchased during the course of a calendar year but with no provision for refunds of unused premiums.
5. Coverage is for not less than $ 100,000 coverage per claim, with an aggregate limit of not less than $ 300,000 per individual, not including costs of investigation and defense.
6. A deductible amount for each occurrence of not more than $ 1,000 for claims and no deductible for legal expenses and defense.
7. The obligation of the carrier to defend all covered claims and the ability of the insured licensee to select counsel of choice subject to the written permission of the carrier, which must not be unreasonably withheld.

8. The ability of a licensee, upon payment of an additional premium, to obtain higher or excess coverage or to purchase additional coverage from the group carrier as may be determined by the carrier.
9. The ability of a licensee, upon payment of an additional premium to obtain an extended reporting period of not less than three hundred sixty-five (365) days.
10. A conformity endorsement allowing a Colorado resident licensee to meet the errors and omissions insurance requirement for an active license in another group mandated state without the need to purchase separate coverage in that state.
11. Policy must not be issued or underwritten using a "self-rated" application form. A "self-rated" application is defined as being an application where a policy is issued based on the answers listed on the application with no subsequent underwriter review.
12. Prior acts coverage must be offered to licensees with continuous past coverage.

C. Licensees or applicants may obtain errors and omissions coverage independent of the group plan from any insurance carrier subject to the following terms and conditions:

1. Individual policies must, at a minimum, comply with the following conditions and the insurance carrier must certify compliance in an affidavit issued to the insured licensee or applicant in a form specified by the Board. The insurance carrier agrees to immediately notify the Board of any cancellation or lapse in coverage. Independent individual coverage must provide, at a minimum, the following:
    a. The insurance carrier is in compliance with all applicable rules and statutes set forth by the Colorado Division of Insurance, and, if required, are licensed or authorized to write policies of Errors and Omissions Insurance in this state.
    b. The insurance carrier maintains an A.M. best rating of "A-" or better.
    c. The contract and policy are in conformance with all relevant Colorado statutory requirements.
    d. Coverage includes all acts for which an appraiser's credential is required, except those illegal, fraudulent or other acts which are normally excluded from such coverage.
    e. Coverage cannot be canceled by the insurance provider, except for nonpayment of the premium or in the event the licensee becomes inactive, is revoked or an applicant is denied a license. Cancellation notice must be provided in manner that complies with section 10-4-109.7, C.R.S.
    f. Coverage is for not less than $ 100,000 per claim, with an annual aggregate limit of not less than $ 300,000 per individual, not including costs of investigation and defense.
    g. A deductible amount for each occurrence of not more than $ 1,000 for claims, and no deductible for legal expenses and defense.
    h. The ability of a licensee, upon payment of an additional premium to obtain an extended reporting period of not less than three hundred sixty-five (365) days.
    i. The coverage afforded by the policy must not contain exclusions for coverage of claims for damages reasonably expected in connection with professional appraisal services, including, but not limited to, claims for damages made by or on behalf of the Federal Deposit Insurance Corporation, the Federal Housing Finance Authority, or any other state or federal agency having regulatory authority over a lender or financial institution, and claims arising from the failure of a financial institution.

j. The policy may not be issued or underwritten using a "self-rated" application. A "self-rated" application is defined as being an application where a policy is issued based on the answers listed on the application with no subsequent underwriter review.

k. Prior acts coverage must be offered to licensees with continuous past coverage.

2. For firms that carry policies that cover one (1) or more licensees associated with that firm, all requirements listed in Board Rule 6.10(c)(1) will apply, except Board Rule 6.10(c)(1)(F) and (G) will be replaced with the following:

   a. The per claim limit must be not less than $ 1,000,000, not including the costs of investigation and defense.

   b. The aggregate limit must be not less than $ 1,000,000, not including the costs of investigation and defense.

   c. The maximum deductible amount for each occurrence must not exceed $ 10,000 and the provider must look to the insured for payment of any deductible. There must not be a deductible for legal expenses and defense.

D. Applicants for licensure, activation, renewal, and reinstatement must certify compliance with this Board Rule 6.10 and section 12-10-608, C.R.S. on forms or in a manner prescribed by the Board. Any active licensee who so certifies and fails to obtain errors and omissions coverage or to provide proof of continuous coverage, either through the group carrier or directly to the Board, will be placed on inactive status:

1. Immediately, if certification of current insurance coverage is not provided to the Board; or

2. Immediately upon the expiration of any current insurance when certification of continued coverage is not provided.

E. Appraisers employed by a local, state, or federal government entity are exempt from the errors and omissions insurance requirements.

6.11 Pursuant to section 12-10-606(6)(a), C.R.S., the Board must establish the fitness standards that an applicant for a license must demonstrate. Therefore, an applicant must demonstrate that he or she does not possess a background that could call into question the public trust. Some of the criteria that the Board may evaluate in determining whether the public trust may be called into question are:

A. Whether the applicant has previously had an appraiser credential revoked;

B. Whether the applicant has previously had a professional license disciplined in any jurisdiction;

C. Whether the applicant has been convicted of, or pled guilty to, entered a plea of nolo contendere to, or received a deferred judgment and sentence to a crime. An applicant will not be eligible for a license if, during at least the five (5) year period immediately preceding the date of application for a license, the applicant has been convicted of, plead guilty to, or entered a plea of nolo contendere to a crime that would call into question the applicant's fitness for licensure; and

D. Whether the applicant has failed to demonstrate that he or she possesses the character necessary to command the confidence of the community and to warrant a determination that the applicant will operate honestly, fairly and efficiently within the scope and purpose of real property appraisal practice.

6.12 If the fees accompanying any application to the Board (including fees for renewals, transfers, etc.) are paid for by check and the check is not immediately paid upon presentment to the bank upon which the check was drawn, or if payment is submitted in any other manner, and payment is denied, rescinded or returned as invalid, the application will be deemed incomplete. The application will only be deemed complete if the Board has received payment of all application fees together with any fees incurred by the Division including the fee required by state fiscal rules for the clerical services necessary for reinstatement within sixty (60) days of the Division mailing notification of an incomplete application.

CHAPTER 7: CONTINUING EDUCATION REQUIREMENTS

7.1 For initial licenses issued on or after July 1 of any year, there will be no continuing education requirement as a condition of renewal of such initial license that expires December 31 of the year of issuance as defined in Board Rule 1.8. For initial licenses issued before July 1 of any year, there will be an obligation to complete fourteen (14) hours of continuing education as a condition of renewal before the initial license expires on December 31 of the year of issuance as defined in Board Rule 1.8. Continuing education requirements established by Chapter 7 of these Rules will apply to all other license renewals.

7.2 Except as provided under Board Rule 7.1, each licensee applying for renewal of a license must complete twenty-eight (28) hours of real estate appraisal continuing education during the two-year period preceding expiration of the license. All licensees renewing a license at the end of a two-year licensing period must complete the National USPAP Update Courses set forth in Board Rule 7.19. Continuing education requirements must be completed after the effective date of the license to be renewed and prior to the expiration of such license. Upon written request and receipt of the supporting documentation established by the Board, the Board may grant a deferral for continuing education compliance for licensees returning from active military duty. Licensees returning from active military duty may be placed on active status for up to ninety (90) days pending completion of all continuing education requirements established pursuant to Chapter 7 of these Rules.

7.3 Continuing real estate appraisal education must be taken from providers approved by the Board. In order to be approved by the Board, continuing education must meet the following standards:

A. It must have been developed by persons qualified in the subject matter and instructional design;

B. It must be current;

C. The instructor must be qualified with respect to content and teaching methods; and

D. The number of participants and the physical facilities are consistent with the teaching method(s).

The Board, at its discretion, may require an evaluation in a manner determined by the Board of an educational offering to ensure compliance with the above standards. By offering real estate appraisal continuing education approved by the Board, each provider agrees to comply with relevant statutes and Board Rules and to permit Board audit of said courses at any time and at no cost. If the Board determines that the offering fails to comply with the standards set forth above, the Board will notify the provider of such deficiency and work with the provider to correct such deficiency prior to the next class offering. If such deficiency is not corrected, then the Board may withdraw approval of the provider, instructor and/or the class.

7.4 The following may be approved as providers of continuing appraisal education, provided the standards set forth in Board Rule 7.3 are maintained, and provided they have complied with all other requirements of the state of Colorado:

A. Accredited colleges, junior colleges, community colleges or universities as defined in Board Rule 1.30;

B. Professional appraisal and real estate related organizations;

C. State or federal government agencies;

D. Proprietary schools holding valid certificates of approval from the Colorado Division of Private Occupational Schools, Department of Higher Education;

E. Continuing education completed in other jurisdictions, providers approved by such other jurisdiction, provided that the jurisdiction's appraiser regulation program is in compliance with Title XI, FIRREA, as determined by the ASC as defined in Board Rule 1.42;

F. The providers of continuing education approved under the CAP as defined in Board Rule 1.39; and

G. Other providers as the Board may approve upon petition of the education provider or licensee in a form acceptable to the Board.

7.5 Continuing education providers must, at their own expense, maintain for a period of five (5) years from the last course offering, and provide to the Board on request, information regarding the educational offerings including, but not limited to the following:

A. Outline or syllabus;

B. All texts, workbooks, handouts or other materials;

C. Instructors and their qualifications, including selection, training and evaluation criteria;

D. Examinations (if any);

E. Dates and locations of offerings; and

F. Student attendance records;

* 7.6 Continuing appraisal education must be at least two (2) class hours in duration including examination time (if any). Continuing appraisal education programs and courses are intended to maintain and improve the appraiser's skill, knowledge, and competency. Continuing appraisal education courses and programs may include, without limitation, these real estate and real estate appraisal topics:

A. Ad valorem taxation;

B. Arbitration, dispute resolution;

C. Courses related to the practice of real estate appraisal or consulting;

D. Development cost estimating;

E. Ethics and standards of professional practice, USPAP;

* F. Valuation bias, fair housing, and/or equal opportunity;

* G. Land use planning, zoning;

* H. Management, leasing, timesharing;

* I. Property development, partial interests;

* J. Real estate law, easements, and legal interests;

* K. Real estate litigation, damages, condemnation;

* L. Real estate financing and investment;

* M. Real estate appraisal related computer applications;

* N. Real estate securities and syndication;

* O. Developing opinions of real property value in appraisals that also include personal property and/or business value;

* P. Seller concessions and impact on value;

* Q. Energy efficient items and "green building" appraisals; and/or

* R. Other topics as the Board may approve, upon its own motion or upon petition by the course provider or the licensee in a form acceptable to the Board.

7.7 The Board will award continuing education credit to credentialed appraisers who attend a Board's public meeting in person, under the following conditions:

A. Credit will be awarded for a single Board meeting per license cycle; and

B. The meeting must be open to the public and must be a minimum of two (2) hours in length. The total credit cannot exceed seven (7) hours.

7.8 The Board may consider alternatives to continuing real estate appraisal education such as teaching, authorship of textbooks or articles, educational program developments or similar activities for up to one-half of the required continuing education. Licensees desiring continuing education credit for alternative activities must petition the Board for approval in writing and prior to commencement of the alternative activity.

7.9 The act of applying for renewal constitutes a statement that the licensee has complied with the continuing education requirements of the Colorado Real Estate Appraiser Licensing Act and Board Rules. The Board reserves the right to require a licensee to provide satisfactory documentary evidence of completion of continuing appraisal education requirements. The Board may at its option require such submission as part of the renewal process or subsequent to renewal.

7.10 With the exception of the 7-hour National USPAP Update Course(s), or its equivalent, required pursuant to Board Rule 7.19, licensees may complete the required hours of continuing real estate appraisal education at any time during the licensing period preceding expiration.

7.11 An appraiser may repeat courses or programs previously completed, subject to the limitation that no course or program may be repeated more frequently than once every continuing education cycle, which is the same as the appraiser's license cycle. Education in the USPAP, or its AQB-approved equivalent, is not subject to this limitation.

* 7.12 Continuing real estate appraisal education must be successfully completed by the licensee. Successful completion means either in-class or synchronous distance education attendance at the offering and participation in class activities. Successful completion of courses undertaken through asynchronous distance education requires compliance with the provisions of Board Rule 7.14. The teaching of continuing real estate appraisal education will constitute successful completion, if also in compliance with Board Rule 7.8; however, credit will be given for only one (1) presentation of a particular offering during each licensing period.

* 7.13 The number of hours credited will be equivalent to the actual number of contact hours of in-class or synchronous distance education instruction and testing. An hour of appraisal education and training is defined as at least fifty (50) minutes of instruction out of each 60-minute segment. For asynchronous distance education offerings, the number of hours credited must be that number of hours allowed by the CAP as defined in Board Rule 1.39. For hybrid course education, the number of hours credited will be equivalent for each specific course delivery method. Parts of the course that are delivered in-class or synchronously and delivered asynchronously must meet their respective requirements as set forth in this Board Rule 7.13.

* 7.14 Asynchronous distance education offerings must include methods and activities which promote active student engagement and participation in the learning process. Among those methods and activities acceptable are written exercises which are graded and returned to the student, required responses in computer based presentations, provision for students to submit questions during teleconferences, and examinations proctored by an independent third party. Biometric proctoring is acceptable. Simple reading, viewing, or listening to materials is not sufficient engagement in the learning process to satisfy the requirements of this Board Rule 7.14.

7.15 As to continuing education completed in other jurisdictions with appraiser regulatory programs that are in compliance with Title XI, FIRREA, as determined by the ASC as defined in Board Rule 1.42, the Board will accept the number of hours of continuing education accepted by that jurisdiction.

7.16 Repealed.

7.17 Repealed.

7.18 Continuing education content must have a clear application to real estate appraisal practice. Motivational courses, personal growth, or self-improvement courses, general business courses and general computing courses are unacceptable to satisfy the continuing education requirements established by these Rules.

7.19 All licensees must successfully complete a 7-hour National USPAP Update Course, or its equivalent, every two (2) calendar years. Such 7-hour National USPAP Update Course must be in the form of a course approved by the AQB, and taught by an instructor certified by the AQB and who is also a state certified appraiser. Equivalency will be determined through the CAP or by an alternate method established by the AQB.

7.20 A licensee who is a resident of a jurisdiction other than the state of Colorado that imposes continuing education requirements consistent with the criteria promulgated by the AQB may comply with the continuing education requirements of Chapter 7 of these Rules by documenting, in a manner prescribed by the Board, compliance with the continuing education requirements of their jurisdiction of residence. In the event the jurisdiction of residence does not impose continuing education requirements consistent with the criteria promulgated by the AQB, the licensee must comply with the continuing education requirements established by Chapter 7 of these Rules.

7.21 A licensee who renews a license subject to a continuing education requirement must retain documentary evidence of compliance with these continuing education requirements for a period of not less than five (5) years after the expiration of the license being renewed.

* 7.22 Course providers must provide each student who successfully completes a continuing education course in the manner prescribed in Board Rule 7.12 a course completion certificate. The Board will not mandate the exact form of course certificates; however, the following information must be included:

A. Name of course provider;

B. Course title, which must describe topical content;

C. Course number, if any;

D. Course dates;

E. Number of continuing education hours;

F. Statement that the required examination was successfully completed, if an examination is a regular part of the course;

* G. Course location, which for synchronous distance education and asynchronous distance education modalities must be the principal place of business of the course provider;

H. Name of student; and

I. For USPAP courses begun on and after January 1, 2003, the name and AQB USPAP instructor certification number of the instructor.

* 7.23 The provisions of Board Rule 7.4 notwithstanding, real estate appraisal continuing education offered through asynchronous distance education must be approved through the CAP, unless the provider is a government agency that has sought an exemption from the Board.

7.24 Repealed.

7.25 Repealed.

7.26 Upon written notification from the Board, licensees must provide copies of course certificates to the Board. Failure to provide copies of course certificates within the time set by the Board in its notification will be grounds for disciplinary action unless the Board has granted an extension of time for providing the certificates.

CHAPTER 8: RENEWAL, REINSTATEMENT, INACTIVATION, SURRENDER OR REVOCATION OF LICENSURE

8.1 Repealed.

8.2 Repealed.

8.3 Repealed.

8.4 Repealed.

8.5 No holder of an expired license which may be reinstated may apply for a new license of the same type. Such person must reinstate the expired license as provided in section 12-10-610(1), C.R.S., and these Rules. Nothing in this Board Rule 8.5 will act to prevent a person from applying for and receiving a license with higher qualification requirements than those of the expired license.

8.6 All licensees in active or inactive license status must provide the Board with the following information: (1) a current mailing address and phone number for the licensee; (2) a current email address for the licensee if applicable; and (3) such other contact information as may be required by the Board from time to time. Each licensee must inform the Board within ten (10) calendar days of any change in such contact information on a form or in the manner prescribed by the Board. A mailing address for the licensee will be posted on the Division's public website, and it is the licensee's responsibility to inform the Division of any required changes to the mailing address shown for the licensee on the Division's public website. The address shown for the licensee on the Division's public website will be considered the licensee's address of record. A change of mailing address without notification to the Board will result in the inactivation of the appraiser's license.

8.7 Repealed.

8.8 The holder of a license or Temporary Practice Permit may surrender such to the Board. The Board may deem a surrendered license or Temporary Practice Permit as permanently relinquished. Such relinquishment will not remove the holder from the jurisdiction of the Board for acts committed while holding a license or Temporary Practice Permit. A license or Temporary Practice Permit that is relinquished during the pendency of an investigation or a disciplinary action will be reported to the National Registry as having been surrendered in lieu of discipline. A person who relinquishes a license or Temporary Practice Permit may not reinstate the same, but must reapply and meet the current requirements for initial licensure.

8.9 Upon inactivation, revocation, suspension, surrender, relinquishment, or expiration of a license or Temporary Practice Permit, the holder must:

A. Immediately cease all activities requiring licensure or a Temporary Practice Permit;

B. In the instance of revocation, suspension, relinquishment, or surrender, immediately return the license document or Temporary Practice Permit to the Board;

C. Immediately cease all actions which represent the holder to the public as actively being licensed or being the holder of a Temporary Practice Permit, including, without limitation, the use of advertising materials, forms, letterheads, business cards, correspondence, internet website content, statements of qualifications, and the like.

8.10 A licensee who has not completed continuing education requirements established pursuant to Chapter 7 of these rules may not renew or reinstate licensure on inactive status unless the Board determines that extenuating circumstances existed which caused the deficiency in the continuing education requirements. The Board may require a written request and supporting documentation to determine that an extenuating circumstance exists or existed. A licensee desiring to renew or reinstate licensure on inactive status must submit their renewal or reinstatement on an inactive status application to the Board.

8.11 A licensee may, without limitation, renew or reinstate licensure on inactive status for subsequent renewal periods by complying with the requirements of Rule 8.10.

8.12 Repealed.

8.13 Repealed.

8.14 Repealed.

8.15 Repealed.

8.16 Repealed.

8.17 A Licensed Ad Valorem Appraiser must be a County Assessor, an employee of a County Assessor's Office, or an employee of the Division of Property Taxation in the Department of Local Affairs. If a Licensed Ad Valorem Appraiser is no longer a County Assessor, leaves the employ of a County Assessor's Office, or leaves the employ of the Division of Property Taxation within the Department of Local Affairs, the Licensed Ad Valorem Appraiser must notify the Board within three (3) business days in a manner acceptable to the Board. Upon such notification or discovery by the Board, the Licensed Ad Valorem Appraiser will be placed on inactive status. The Licensed Ad Valorem Appraiser will not be returned to active status unless the licensee signs a certification that he or she is currently a County Assessor, an employee of a County Assessor's Office or an employee of the Division of Property Taxation in the Department of Local Affairs and the Board verifies the licensee's employment.

8.18 A licensee desiring to activate an inactive license must complete all required continuing education hours that would have been required if the licensee had been on active status for the entire period of inactivation, including the most recent version of the National USPAP Course or its equivalent as approved by the CAP as defined in Board Rule 1.39.

CHAPTER 9: LICENSURE BY ENDORSEMENT

9.1 Pursuant to section 12-10-611(1) and (2), C.R.S., as amended, licensure by endorsement will be subject to the following restrictions and requirements:

A. The Board may issue licenses by endorsement only to those persons holding an active license or certificate from another jurisdiction which is substantially equivalent to those described in Board Rules 1.13, 1.14 or 1.15, with qualification requirements substantially equivalent to those in Board Rules 2.2, 2.3 or 2.4, respectively;

B. The applicant must be the holder of an active license or certificate in good standing under the laws of another jurisdiction;

C. The appraiser regulatory program of the jurisdiction where the applicant holds an active license or certificate in good standing must be compliance with Title XI, FIRREA, as determined by the ASC as defined in Board Rule 1.42;

D. The applicant must apply for licensure by endorsement on a form provided by the Board, pay the specified fees and meet all other Board requirements, including the submission of a set of fingerprints to the Colorado Bureau of Investigation for the purpose of conducting a state and national fingerprint-based criminal history record check as required by section 12-10-606(6)(a), C.R.S. as amended;

E. The applicant must apply for and be issued by the Board a license by endorsement prior to undertaking appraisal activities in Colorado that would require licensure in Colorado; and

F. A license issued by endorsement will be subject to the same renewal requirements as a license issued pursuant to section 12-10-606, C.R.S. as amended, and Chapters 7 and 8 of these Rules.

CHAPTER 10: TEMPORARY PRACTICE IN COLORADO

10.1 Pursuant to section 12-10-611(2) and (3), C.R.S., as amended, a Temporary Practice permit may be issued to the holder of an active appraiser's license or certificate from another jurisdiction. Such Temporary Practice Permit must be subject to the following restrictions and requirements:

A. The applicant must apply for and be issued a Temporary Practice Permit prior to his or her commencement of a real property appraisal in Colorado that is part of a federally related transaction;

B. The applicant's business is temporary in nature and the applicant must identify in writing the appraisal assignment(s) to be completed under the Temporary Practice Permit prior to being issued a Temporary Practice Permit;

C. The Temporary Practice Permit will be valid only for the appraisal assignment(s) listed thereon;

D. The applicant must be the holder of an active license or certificate in good standing under the laws of another jurisdiction;

E. The applicant must apply for a Temporary Practice Permit on a form provided by the Board, pay the specified fees, and meet all other Board requirements; and

F. Pursuant to section 12-10-611(2) and (3), C.R.S., Temporary Practice Permits are available only to persons holding active licensure in another jurisdiction at levels substantially equivalent to those defined in Board Rules 1.13, 1.14, or 1.15. Temporary Practice Permits are not available to persons holding licensure in another jurisdiction at a trainee, apprentice, associate, intern, or other entry level.

10.2 No person may be issued more than two (2) Temporary Practice Permits in any rolling twelve-month period.

10.3 A Temporary Practice Permit issued pursuant to Chapter 10 of these Rules will be valid for the period of time necessary to complete the original assignment(s) listed thereon, including time for client conferences and expert witness testimony. A Temporary Practice Permit issued pursuant to Chapter 10 of these Rules will not be valid for completion of additional or update assignments involving the same property or properties. Additional or update assignments involving the same property or properties are new assignments, thereby requiring a new Temporary Practice Permit or licensure by endorsement as provided in Chapter 9 of these Rules.

CHAPTER 11: STANDARDS OF PROFESSIONAL APPRAISAL PRACTICE

11.1 The USPAP was adopted and incorporated by reference in Board Rule 1.10. The 2018-2019 edition of the USPAP, incorporating the amendments made through February 3, 2017 will remain in effect through December 31, 2019. Beginning January 1, 2020, the 2020-2021 edition of the USPAP will be in effect.

11.2 A licensee using the services of an unlicensed assistant under the provisions of section 12-10-621, C.R.S. as amended, or the services of another licensee in the preparation of appraisals or other work products will, consistent with the USPAP, supervise each such assistant or licensee in an active, diligent and personal manner. When any portion of the work involves significant real property appraisal assistance, the licensee must describe and summarize the research, analysis and reporting contributions of each such assistant or other licensee within each such report or other work product in a manner specified in USPAP Standard 2.

11.3 A licensee performing any consulting services pursuant to section 12-10-602(5), C.R.S., must not represent any analysis, opinion, or conclusions as an independent appraisal assignment. In compliance with sections 12-10-613(1)(g) and 12-10-616(1)(b), (c) and (d), C.R.S, a licensee compensated by a Contingent Fee as defined in Board Rule 1.20, must disclose in a clear and conspicuous manner in any oral report, or the letter of transmittal, summary of salient facts and conclusions, statement of limiting conditions, and certifications of any written report the following:

A. A contingent fee is being paid;

B. The licensee is performing a consulting service and not an independent appraisal; and

C. Any oral or written reports were not required to be compliant with the Ethics Rule of the USPAP.

CHAPTER 12: LICENSE TITLES, LICENSE DOCUMENTS, AND SIGNATURES

12.1 The descriptive license titles defined in Board Rules 1.13, 1.14, 1.15, 1.18, and 1.37 must only be used by persons who hold such Board issued license or Temporary Practice Permit in good standing. The descriptive license titles may only be used by an individual license holder and may not be used by any other person or group of persons, including a corporation, partnership, or other business entity.

12.2 Repealed.

12.3 Repealed.

12.4 In each appraisal report or other appraisal related work product, the license held by the appraiser(s) must be clearly identified by using the license titles defined in Board Rules 1.13, 1.14, 1.15, and 1.37 and including the license number. Such license titles and numbers must be identified wherever the licensee signs, by any means or method, the report or other work product, including, but not limited to the:

A. Letter of transmittal;

B. Certification of the appraiser(s); and

C. Appraisal or other work product report form or document, including addenda thereto.

12.5 Repealed.

12.6 An appraiser practicing in Colorado under authority of a Temporary Practice Permit must identify the state where they hold licensure, the type of license and the license number, and must further state they hold a Temporary Practice Permit and state the permit number in all instances where license type and number are required under Chapter 12 of these Rules.

12.7 The real estate appraiser's license or Temporary Practice Permit document and identification card issued to an initial applicant or licensee will remain the property of the Board. Such document and card must be surrendered to the Board immediately upon demand. The reasons for such demand may include, but are not limited to, suspension, revocation, surrender, or relinquishment.

12.8 When complying with either Board Rule 12.4 or Board Rule 12.6, an appraiser must use the full license or Temporary Practice Permit title in Board Rules 1.13, 1.14, 1.15, 1.18, and 1.37, or must use the appropriate abbreviation as listed below, followed by the license or Temporary Practice Permit number. Use of initials only, such as the alphabetical prefix included with each Board issued number to identify the type of license or Temporary Practice Permit is prohibited except when necessary to comply with federally implanted data collection or reporting requirements (for example FNMA ("Fannie Mae") or FHLMC ("Freddie Mac") implemented policies or guidelines).

Licensed Ad Valorem Appraiser:	Lic. Ad Val App. or Lic. Ad Val Appr.
Licensed Appraiser:	Lic. App. or Lic. Appr.
Certified Residential Appraiser:	Crt. Res. App. or Cert. Res. Appr.
Certified General Appraiser:	Crt. Gen. App. or Cert. Genl. Appr.
Temporary Practice Permit:	Temp. Prac. Pmt.

12.9 Repealed.

12.10 When stating the type of license or Temporary Practice Permit held, and the number thereof, an appraiser may make use of an impression, provided such impression is legible on each copy of the appraisal report or other work product.

12.11 Where appraisal report forms or other work product forms do not allow space for placing the information required by Board Rule 12.4 or Board Rule 12.6 immediately following the name and signature of the appraiser the required information will be placed in the closest reasonable available space on the same page.

12.12 The holder of a license or Temporary Practice Permit in good standing may copy the license or Temporary Practice Permit document for inclusion in an appraisal report or other appraisal work product. Such copy must have the word "COPY" prominently displayed so as to substantially overlay the printed portions of the license or Temporary Practice Permit document.

12.13 The requirements of Chapter 12 of these Rules must be complied with in any electronic copy or transmittal of an appraisal report or other appraisal related work product.

12.14 No holder of a license or Temporary Practice Permit, or any other person, will make or cause to be made or allow to be made, any alteration to a Board-issued license or Temporary Practice Permit document or copy thereof, other than as provided in Board Rule 12.12.

12.15 No licensee may affix or allow to be affixed the name or signature of a licensee to an appraisal report or other appraisal related work product without the express permission of the licensee for that specific assignment, report, or other work product. Licensees must not give blanket permission for affixing their signature to appraisal reports or other work products and may only authorize the use of his or her signature on an assignment-by-assignment basis.

12.16 No licensee will permit, through action or inaction, their name or signature to be affixed to an appraisal report or other appraisal related work product without their first personally examining and approving the final version of such report or other work product.

CHAPTER 13: DISCIPLINARY PROCEDURES

13.1 Complaints alleging violation of the Colorado Real Estate Appraiser Licensing Act or the Board Rules must be in writing on a form or in the manner prescribed by the Board. Nothing in this Board Rule 13.1 will act to prevent the Board from acting upon its own motion to open a complaint.

13.2 Pursuant to section 12-10-604(1)(c), C.R.S., and section 24-4-105(3), C.R.S., any disciplinary hearing conducted on behalf of the Board may, at the discretion of the Board, be conducted by an Administrative Law Judge from the Office of Administrative Courts of the Department of Personnel & Administration.

13.3 Repealed.

13.4 When a holder of a Board-issued license or Temporary Practice Permit has received written notification from the Board that a complaint has been filed against the holder, a written response to the Board is required to be submitted by the holder. Failure to submit a written response within the time set by the Board in its notification will be grounds for disciplinary action, unless the Board has granted an extension of time for the response in writing and regardless of the question of whether the underlying complaint warrants further investigation or subsequent action by the Board. The holder's written response must contain the following:

A. A complete and specific answer to the factual recitations, allegations or averments;

B. A complete and specific response to any additional questions, allegations or averments presented in the notification letter;

C. Any documents or records requested in the notification letter; and

D. Any further information relative to the complaint that the holder believes to be relevant or material to the matters addressed in the notification letter.

13.5 The holder of a Board-issued license or Temporary Practice Permit, including an owner of more than ten (10) percent of a licensed appraisal management company, must inform the Board in writing within ten (10) days of any disciplinary action taken by any other state, district, territorial, or provincial real estate appraiser or appraisal management company licensing authority. For purposes of this Board Rule 13.5, disciplinary action may include, without limitation, actions such as fines, required education, probation, suspension, revocation, letters of censure, debarment, required supervision, and the like.

13.6 Pursuant to section 24-34-106, C.R.S., when a licensee is required to complete real estate appraisal education as part of stipulation, final agency order, or stipulation for diversion, no portion of any such courses or programs will be creditable toward continuing education or qualifying education requirements.

13.7 Pursuant to sections 12-10-613(1)(a) and (k), C.R.S., a licensee must inform the Board in writing within ten (10) days of conviction of, entering a plea of guilty to, entering a plea of nolo contendere to, or receiving a deferred judgment and sentence to any felony or misdemeanor offense, excluding misdemeanor traffic offenses, municipal code violations or petty offenses. A licensee must inform the Board in writing within ten (10) days of any disciplinary action taken against any professional licenses held by the licensee, excluding the licensee's Colorado appraisal credential. For purposes of this Board Rule 13.7, disciplinary action include, without limitation, actions such as imposition of fines, required or remedial education, probation, suspension, revocation, letters of censure, debarment, mandatory supervision, and the like.

13.8 Board members, Division staff and contractors hired by the Division are not required to comply with USPAP in performance of the official duties that include, but are not limited to:

A. Investigations;

B. Work experience reviews conducted during license application processing;

C. The review or analysis of investigative findings, experience reviews, and/or work product reviews resulting from Board case resolutions; or

D. The review of the appraisal as part of an application.

An investigation or review conducted by staff, a member of the Board or a contractor hired by the Division is not considered an "appraisal review" or an "appraisal" as defined by the USPAP.

13.9 A holder of a Board-issued license or Temporary Practice Permit must respond in writing to any correspondence from the Board requiring a response. The written response must be submitted within the time period provided by the Board. The Board will send such correspondence to the holder's address of record filed with the Board. Failure to submit a timely written response will be grounds for disciplinary action.

13.10 Exceptions and Board Review of Initial Decisions:

A. Written form, service, and filing requirements

1. All designations of record, requests, exceptions, and responsive pleadings ("pleadings") must be in written form, mailed with a certificate of mailing to the Board and the opposing party.
2. All pleadings must be filed with the Board by 5:00 p.m. on the date the filing is due. These Rules do not provide for any additional time for service by mail. Filing is the receipt of a pleading by the Board.
3. Any pleadings must be served on the opposing party by mail or by hand delivery on the date on which the pleading is filed with the Board.

4. All pleadings must be filed with the Board and not the Office of Administrative Courts. Any designations of record, requests, exceptions, or responsive pleadings filed in error with the Office of Administrative Courts will not be considered. The Board's address is:

   Colorado Board of Real Estate Appraisers
   1560 Broadway, Suite 925
   Denver, CO 80202

B. Authority to Review

1. The Board hereby preserves the Board's option to initiate a review of an initial decision on its own motion pursuant to section 24-4-105(14)(a)(ii) and (b)(iii), C.R.S. outside of the thirty (30) day period after service of the initial decision upon the parties without requiring a vote for each case.
2. This option to review will apply regardless of whether a party files exceptions to the initial decision.

C. Designation of Record and Transcripts

1. Any party seeking to reverse or modify the initial decision of the Administrative Law Judge must file with the Board a designation of the relevant parts of the record for review ("designation of record"). Designations of record must be filed with the board within twenty (20) days of the date on which the Board mails the initial decision to the parties' address of record with the Board.
2. Even if no party files a designation of record, the record must include the following:
   a. All pleadings;
   b. All applications presented or considered during the hearing;
   c. All documentary or other exhibits admitted into evidence;
   d. All documentary or other exhibits presented during the hearing;
   e. All matters officially noticed;
   f. Any findings of fact and conclusions of law proposed by any party; and
   g. Any written brief filed.
3. Transcripts: transcripts will not be deemed part of a designation of record unless specifically identified and ordered. Should a party wish to designate a transcript or portion thereof, the following procedures apply:
   a. The designation of record must identify with specificity the transcript or portion thereof to be transcribed. For example, a party may designate the entire transcript, or may identify witness(es) whose testimony is to be transcribed, the legal ruling or argument to be transcribed, or other information necessary to identify a portion of the transcript.
   b. Any party who includes a transcript or a portion thereof as part of the designation of record must order the transcript or relevant portions by the date on which the designation of record must be filed (within twenty (20) days of the date on which the Board mails the initial decision to the parties).
   c. When ordering the transcript, the party must request a court reporter or transcribing service to prepare the transcript within thirty (30) days. The party must timely pay the necessary fees to obtain and file with the Board an original transcription and one (1) copy within thirty (30) days.
   d. The party ordering the transcript must direct the court reporter or transcribing service to complete and file with the Board the transcript and one (1) copy of the transcript within thirty (30) days.

e. If a party designates a portion of the transcript, the opposing party may also file a supplemental designation of record, in which the opposing party may designate additional portions of the transcript. This supplemental designation of record must be filed with the Board and served on the other party within ten (10) days after the date on which the original designation of record was due.

f. An opposing party filing a supplemental designation of record must order and pay for such transcripts and portions thereof within the deadlines set forth above. An opposing party must also cause the court reporter to complete and file with the Board the transcript and one (1) copy of the transcript within thirty (30) days.

g. Transcripts that are ordered and not filed with the Board in a timely manner by the reporter or transcription service due to non-payment, insufficient payment, or failure to direct as set forth above will not be considered by the Board.

D. Filing of Exceptions and Responsive Pleadings

1. Any party wishing to file exceptions must adhere to the following timelines:

a. If no transcripts are ordered, exceptions are due within thirty (30) days from the date on which the Board mails the initial decision to the parties. Both parties' exceptions are due on the same date.

b. If transcripts are ordered by either party, the following procedure will apply. Upon receipt of transcripts identified in all designations of record, the Board will mail notification to the parties stating that the transcripts have been received by the Board. Exceptions are due within thirty (30) days from the date on which such notification is mailed. Both parties' exceptions are due on the same date.

2. Either party may file a responsive pleading to the other party's exceptions. All responsive pleadings must be filed within ten (10) days of the date on which the exceptions were filed with the Board. No other pleadings will be considered except for good cause shown.

3. The Board may in its sole discretion grant an extension of time to file exceptions or responsive pleadings, or may delegate the discretion to grant such an extension of time to the Board's designee.

E. Request for Oral Argument

1. All requests for oral argument must be in writing and filed by the deadline for responsive pleadings. Requests filed after this time will not be considered.

2. It is within the sole discretion of the Board to grant or deny a request for oral argument. If oral argument is granted, both parties will have the opportunity to participate.

3. Each side will be permitted ten (10) minutes for oral argument unless such time is extended by the Board or its designee.

13.11 A controlling appraiser must inform the Board in writing within ten (10) days of conviction of, entering a plea of guilty to, entering a plea of nolo contendere, entering an alford plea, or receiving a deferred judgment and sentence to any misdemeanor or felony relating to the conduct of an appraisal, theft, embezzlement, bribery, fraud, misrepresentation, or deceit, or any other like crime under Colorado law, federal law, or the laws of other jurisdictions.

* 13.12 A controlling appraiser, or an approved designee of a licensed appraisal management company, must inform the Board in writing within ten (10) days regarding the following:

* A. An owner of an appraisal management company, possessing more than ten percent ownership of the licensed entity, has been convicted of, entered a plea of guilty to, entered a plea of nolo contendere, entered an alford plea, or receiving a deferred judgment and sentence to any misdemeanor or felony relating to the conduct of an

appraisal, theft, embezzlement, bribery, fraud, misrepresentation, or deceit, or any other like crime under Colorado law, federal law, or the laws of other jurisdictions; and

* B. An owner of an appraisal management company, possessing any percentage ownership of the licensed entity, has had an appraiser license or certificate refused, denied, cancelled, surrendered in lieu of revocation, or revoked in any jurisdiction.

CHAPTER 14: DECLARATORY ORDERS PURSUANT TO SECTION 24-4-105(11), C.R.S.

14.1 Any person may petition the Board for a declaratory order to terminate controversies or to remove uncertainties as to the applicability to the petitioner of any statutory provisions or of any rule or order of the Board.

14.2 The Board will determine, in its discretion and without prior notice to petitioner, whether to rule upon any such petition. If the Board determines that it will not rule upon such a petition, the Board will issue its written order disposing of the same stating the reason for its action. A copy of the order will be provided to the petitioner.

14.3 In determining whether to rule upon a petition filed pursuant to this Rule, the Board will consider the following matters, among others:

A. Whether a ruling on the petition will terminate a controversy or remove uncertainties as to the applicability to petitioner of any statutory provision or rule or order of the Board.

B. Whether the petition involves any subject, question, or issue which is the subject of a formal or informal matter or investigation currently pending before the Board or a court involving one or more of the petitioners.

C. Whether the petition involves any subject, question, or issue which is the subject of a formal or informal matter or investigation currently pending before the Board or a court but not involving any petitioner.

D. Whether the petition seeks a ruling on a moot or hypothetical question or will result in an advisory ruling or opinion.

E. Whether the petitioner has some other adequate legal remedy, other than an action for declaratory relief pursuant to Rule 57, C.R.C.P., which will terminate the controversy or remove any uncertainty as to the applicability to the petitioner of the statute, rule, or order in question.

14.4 Any petition filed pursuant to this Rule must set forth the following:

A. The name and address of the petitioner and whether the petitioner holds a license issued pursuant to the Colorado Real Estate Appraiser Licensing Act.

B. The statute, rule, or order to which the petition relates.

C. A concise statement of all of the facts necessary to show the nature of the controversy or uncertainty and the manner in which the statute, rule, or order in question applies or potentially applies to the petitioner.

14.5 If the Board determines that it will rule on the petition, the following procedures will apply:

A. The Board may rule upon the petition based solely upon the facts presented in the petition. In such a case:

1. Any ruling of the Board will apply only to the extent of the facts presented in the petition and any amendment to the petition.
2. The Board may order the petitioner to file a written brief, memorandum, or statement of position.
3. The Board may set the petition, upon due notice to the petitioner, for a non-evidentiary hearing.

4. The Board may dispose of the petition on the sole basis of the matters set forth in the petition.
5. The Board may request the petitioner to submit additional facts, in writing. In such event, such additional facts will be considered as an amendment to the petition.
6. The Board may take administrative notice of facts pursuant to the Administrative Procedures Act, section 24-4-105(8), C.R.S., as amended, and may utilize its experience, technical competence, and specialized knowledge in the disposition of the petition.
7. If the Board rules upon the petition without a hearing, it will promptly notify the petitioner of its decision.

B. The Board may, in its discretion, set the petition for hearing, upon due notice to petitioner, for the purpose of obtaining additional facts or information or to determine the truth of any facts set forth in the petition or to hear oral argument on the petition. The notice to the petitioner setting such hearing will set forth, to the extent known, the factual or other matters into which the Board intends to inquire. For the purpose of such a hearing, to the extent necessary, the petitioner will have the burden of proving all of the facts stated in the petition, all of the facts necessary to show the nature of the controversy or uncertainty and the manner in which the statute, rule, or order in question applies or potentially applies to the petitioner and any other facts the petitioner desires the Board to consider.

14.6 The parties to any proceeding pursuant to this Rule will be the Board and the petitioner. Any other person may seek leave of the Board to intervene in such a proceeding, and leave to intervene will be granted at the sole discretion of the Board. A petition to intervene will set forth the same matters as required by Board Rule 14.4. Any reference to a "petitioner" in this Rule also refers to any person who has been granted leave to intervene by the Board.

14.7 Any declaratory order or other order disposing of a petition pursuant to this Rule will constitute agency action subject to judicial review pursuant to section 24-4-106, C.R.S., as amended.

CHAPTER 15: REPEALED

15.1 Repealed.

15.2 Repealed.

15.3 Repealed.

15.4 Repealed.

15.5 Repealed.

CHAPTER 16: REPEALED

16.1 Repealed.

16.2 Repealed.

16.3 Repealed.

16.4 Repealed.

CHAPTER 17: LICENSING REQUIREMENTS FOR APPRAISAL MANAGEMENT COMPANIES

17.1 Prior to application for licensure for an appraisal management company or as a controlling appraiser, a person who has been convicted of, entered a plea of guilty to, entered a plea of nolo contendere to, or received a deferred judgment and sentence to a misdemeanor or felony, or any like municipal code violation, may request the Board to issue a preliminary advisory opinion regarding the possible effect of such conduct on an application for licensure. A person requesting such an opinion is not an applicant for licensure. The Board may, at its sole discretion, issue such an opinion, which will not be binding upon the Board; is not appealable; and will not limit the authority of the Board to investigate a later application for licensure. The issuance of such an opinion by the Board will not act to prohibit a person from submitting an application for licensure. A person requesting such an opinion must do so in a form prescribed by the Board. Such form must be supported and documented by, without limitation, the following:

A. Court documents, including original charges, disposition, pre-sentencing report and certification of completion of terms of sentence;

B. Police officer's report(s);

C. Probation or parole officer's report(s);

D. A written personal statement explaining the circumstances surrounding each violation, and including the statement attesting that "I have no other violations either past or pending";

E. Letters of recommendation; and

F. Employment history for the preceding five (5) years.

17.2 Pursuant to section 12-10-607, C.R.S. an applicant for an appraisal management company's or a controlling appraiser's license who has been convicted of, entered a plea of guilty to, entered a plea of nolo contendere to, or received a deferred judgment and sentence to a misdemeanor or a felony, or any other like municipal code violation, must, with his or her application, include an addendum to the application in a form prescribed by the Board. Such addendum must be supported and documented by, without limitation, the following:

A. Court documents, including original charges, disposition, pre-sentencing report and certification of completion of terms of sentence;

B. Police officer's report(s);

C. Probation or parole officer's report(s);

D. A written personal statement explaining the circumstances surrounding each violation, and including the statement attesting that "I have no other violations either past or pending";

E. Letters of recommendation; and

F. Employment history for the preceding five (5) years.

17.3 Initial licenses will expire on December 31 of the year of issuance. All appraisal management company and controlling appraiser licenses expire annually on December 31.

17.4 An appraisal management company must have a controlling appraiser, with an active controlling appraiser's license, to perform services requiring a license. If the controlling appraiser leaves the employment of the appraisal management company, the controlling appraiser or an authorized representative of the appraisal management company must notify the Board within three (3) business days in a manner acceptable to the Board. Upon such notification or discovery by the Board, the license of the appraisal management company will be placed on inactive status unless or until a replacement controlling appraiser has been identified by the appraisal management company and approved by the Board or a temporary controlling appraiser license is timely processed by the Division.

17.5 The controlling appraiser license will be placed on inactive status upon notification to the Board that the controlling appraiser has left the employ of the appraisal management company. The controlling appraiser license will remain on inactive status until the license expires or the controlling appraiser is designated to be the responsible party for an appraisal management company.

17.6 An individual or company license cannot be transferred for use of the licensed name or license for the benefit of another person, partnership, limited liability company, or corporation.

* 17.7 The controlling appraiser, or an authorized representative, must notify the Board within ten (10) business days of any change in ownership of the appraisal management company including a change in ownership that increases an existing individual's total ownership to more than ten (10) percent.

17.8 The Board may refuse to issue a license to a partnership, limited liability company, or corporation if the name of said corporation, partnership, or limited liability company is the same as that of any person or entity whose license has been suspended or revoked in any jurisdiction or is so similar as to be easily confused with that of the suspended or revoked person or entity by members of the general public.

17.9 No license will be issued to an appraisal management company under a trade name, corporate name, partnership name, or limited liability company name which is identical to another licensed appraisal management company. A license will not be issued to an individual proprietorship that adopts a trade name which includes the following words: corporation, partnership, limited liability company, limited, incorporated, or the abbreviations thereof.

17.10 All applications will contain a certification that the controlling appraiser is responsible for the appraisal management company. All applications will require the appraisal management company to identify at least one authorized representative responsible for contacting the Board when there has been a change in the employment of the controlling appraiser or there is a change in the ownership of the entity.

17.11 When an application for licensure as an appraisal management company is submitted, the controlling appraiser must certify the following:

A. If the appraisal management company is a corporation, that the corporation complies with section 12-10-607(8)(c), C.R.S. and that the controlling appraiser has been authorized by the corporation as the controlling appraiser for the corporation.

B. If the appraisal management company is a partnership, that the partnership complies with section 12-10-607(8)(a), C.R.S. and that the controlling appraiser has been authorized by the partnership as the controlling appraiser for the partnership.

C. If the appraisal management company is a limited liability company, that the company complies with section 12-10-607(8)(b), C.R.S. and that the controlling appraiser has been authorized by the company as the controlling appraiser for the limited liability company.

17.12 An appraisal management company is not required to be domiciled in Colorado in order to obtain a license, if the company maintains a definite place of business in another jurisdiction and is registered as a foreign entity with the Colorado Secretary of State.

17.13 If the appraisal management company has no registered agent registered in Colorado, such registered agent is not located under its registered agent name at its registered agent address, or the registered agent cannot with reasonable diligence be served, the controlling appraiser, on behalf of the appraisal management company, may be served by registered mail or by certified mail, return receipt requested, addressed to the entity at its principal address and to the controlling appraiser's address of record. Service is perfected at the earliest of:

A. The date the controlling appraiser receives the process, notice, or demand;

B. The date shown on the return receipt, if signed by or on behalf of the controlling appraiser; or

C. Five (5) days after mailing.

17.14 Applicants for licensure, activation, renewal, or reinstatement as an appraisal management company must certify compliance with section 12-10-609, C.R.S. in a manner prescribed by the Board. The surety bond must:

A. Be for a minimum of $ 25,000.00;

B. Be in conformance with all relevant Colorado statutory requirements; and

C. Cover acts contemplated for appraisal management companies under part 6 of article 10 of title 12 during the period of licensure by the appraisal management company.

Any licensed appraisal management company that certifies compliance and fails to maintain a surety bond, or to provide proof of continuous coverage, will be placed on inactive status:

A. Immediately if a current surety bond is not provided to the Board; or

B. Immediately upon the expiration of any current surety bond when certification of continued coverage is not provided.

17.15 An appraisal management company or controlling appraiser whose license has been placed on inactive status must:

A. Cease any activities requiring a license.

B. Cease all advertising of licensed services.

C. If an appraisal management company, inform all clients of the company's license status and inability to provide any services requiring a license.

D. If an appraisal management company, ensure that all appraisal fees collected from the client(s) have been accounted for and disbursed pursuant to section 12-10-614(1)(h), C.R.S.

E. If an appraisal management company, fees for services requiring a license can be collected for licensed services performed prior to inactivation of the license.

17.16 Licenses will be issued by the Board in a timely manner after the receipt of a complete application, including required fees and all supporting documentation. The Board reserves the right to require additional information and documentation from an applicant in order to determine compliance with applicable laws and regulations, and to verify any information or documentation submitted.

17.17 If the fees accompanying any application to the Board (including fees for renewals, transfers, etc.) are paid for by check and the check is not immediately paid upon presentment to the bank upon which the check was drawn, or if payment is submitted in any other manner, and payment is denied, rescinded, or returned as invalid, the application will be deemed incomplete. The application will only be deemed complete if the Board has received payment of all application fees together with any fees incurred by the Division including the fee required by state fiscal rules for the clerical services necessary for reinstatement within sixty (60) days of the Division mailing notification of an incomplete application.

17.18 A temporary controlling appraiser's license may be issued to a corporation, partnership, or limited liability company to prevent hardship. No application for a temporary controlling appraiser's license will be approved unless the designated individual is a certified appraiser, in good standing. The temporary license is valid for ninety (90) days. Upon application and showing of good cause, the Board may extend a temporary license for one additional ninety (90) day period.

* 17.19 Applicants for licensure, renewal, or reinstatement as an appraisal management company must complete the following:

A. The controlling appraiser must report and certify:

1. The number of licensed or certified appraisers that provided an appraisal in connection with a Covered Transaction on the appraisal management company's Panel in Colorado during the Reporting Period;
2. The total number of licensed or certified appraisers on the Panel in Colorado, whether or not the appraisers provided an appraisal in connection with a Covered Transaction, during the Reporting Period; and
3. The total number of licensed or certified appraisers on the Panel in all states that the appraisal management company is licensed during the Reporting Period.

* B. Submit to the Division the AMC Registry Fee for appraisal management companies that meet the Panel Size Threshold and the appraisal management company minimum requirements as set forth in section 12-10-607(9), C.R.S., along with the application for initial licensure, renewal, or reinstatement.

17.20 Federally Regulated AMCs must annually pay the AMC Registry Fee and must report the following information to the Division prior to December 31 of each calendar year:

A. Identifying company information to include the legal name, Employer Identification Number (EIN), address, and contact information of the controlling appraiser or company's designee.

B. Information related to ownership limitations.

C. The controlling appraiser or company's designee must report and certify:

1. The number of licensed or certified appraisers that provided an appraisal in connection with a Covered Transaction on the appraisal management company's Panel in Colorado during the Reporting period;
2. The total number of licensed or certified appraisers on the Panel in Colorado, whether or not the appraisers provided an appraisal in connection with a Covered Transaction, during the Reporting Period; and
3. The total number of licensed or certified appraisers on the Panel in all states during the Reporting Period.

D. Submit to the Division the AMC Registry Fee for appraisal management companies that meet the Panel Size Threshold along with the information as set forth in this rule.

CHAPTER 18: PROFESSIONAL STANDARDS – APPRAISAL MANAGEMENT COMPANIES

18.1 An appraisal management company must have and follow a written policy in place regarding the annual audit of appraisals completed for Colorado assignments during the previous Reporting Period. The policy must have an effective date and memorialize the dates any modifications are made. The policy must outline, at a minimum, the following:

A. Appraisal Selection. The audit sample must be randomly selected and a USPAP Standard 3 Review must be performed on not less than two percent (2%) of all appraisal reports performed by appraisers for the appraisal management company during the previous Reporting Period. A minimum of at least one (1) USPAP Standard 3 Review must be performed for each appraiser who completed a Colorado appraisal assignment during that Reporting Period.

B. Risk-Based Reviews. If an appraisal management company maintains a risk-based review process, the appraisal management company is required to comply with Board Rule 18.1(A) of these Rules only for those appraisers for whom a USPAP Standard 3 Review was not performed under the risk-based appraisal review process.

C. Review Criterion. The appraisals must be evaluated for compliance with state and federal regulations, including the USPAP.

D. Reviewer Qualifications. The individual(s) performing the audit of the appraisals must possess a certified credential in this state or any jurisdiction and be competent to appraise residential real estate.

E. Appraisal Deficiencies. The appraisal management company must have procedures in place to address material deficiencies that affect the value conclusion or the credibility of the report with the appraiser. Material violations of the USPAP or the Colorado Real Estate Appraiser Licensing Act must be reported to the Board.

The Board may evaluate an appraisal management company's compliance with its own audit policies during an investigation.

18.2 For each Colorado appraisal assignment, an appraisal management company must maintain the following documents or records for a period of at least five (5) years, or at least two (2) years after the final disposition of any judicial proceeding in which a representative of the appraisal management company provided testimony related to the assignment, whichever period expires last:

A. Contractual agreements with clients.

B. Any documents associated with the engagement of an appraiser used to appraise Colorado real estate.

C. All correspondence with a client or an appraiser regarding a specific assignment, including an accounting of payments received from the client and paid to the appraiser.

D. Appraisals, appraisal reviews, appraisal updates, recertifications of value, certificates of completion, broker price opinions or competitive market analyses, comparable property checks, rent schedules or income analyses, measurements, building sketches, and any client approved forms (Colorado Real Estate only).

E. A list of all licensed or certified appraisers on the appraisal management company's Panel.

F. Copies of final appraisal reports reviewed in accordance with Board Rule 18.1, findings and any subsequent correspondence with the appraiser, client, or Board.

G. Copies of all processes and controls pursuant to section 12-10-614(1)(a)(II), C.R.S.

Records may be maintained in electronic format, but must be produced upon request by the Board and must be in a format that has the continued capability to be retrieved and legibly printed. Upon request by the Board, printed records must be produced.

18.3 For all Colorado appraisal assignments, an appraisal management company must disclose its Colorado license number in writing in the engagement letter with an appraiser.

Chapter 8:
Mortgage Loan Originator License Law

An * in the left margin indicates a change in the statute, rule, or text since the last publication of the manual.

I. Introduction

In 2003, the Department of Regulatory Agencies received a request to initiate a review of the mortgage loan origination industry to determine whether regulation was appropriate. Accordingly, pursuant to § 24-34-104.1(2), C.R.S., a sunrise review was conducted and completed October 14, 2005. In summary, the review addressed Colorado's current regulatory environment with respect to mortgage transactions and the possibility for public harm.

Colorado was one of two states (the other being Alaska) that had no regulatory oversight of mortgage loan originators. The sunrise review also concluded that there was significant risk to consumers, as mortgage financing often represented their largest financial transaction. The review highlighted an inherent conflict of interest between the consumer, who seeks the lowest possible interest rate, and the mortgage loan originator, who receives compensation from higher interest rates. Ultimately, the sunrise review identified a need for regulatory oversight to ensure consumer protection. As a result, the Mortgage Broker Registration Act, House Bill 06-1161, was passed by the Colorado General Assembly in 2006.

The Mortgage Broker Registration Act provided a minimal registration program for mortgage loan originators. Registration required a completed criminal background check, a $25,000 surety bond, a completed application, and payment of the $200 application fee. Due to the wave of foreclosures and the mortgage fraud epidemic, the Colorado General Assembly passed four new mortgage broker bills in the 2007 session. These included House Bill 07-1322, Senate Bill 07-085, Senate Bill 07-216, and Senate Bill 07-203. Governor Bill Ritter, Jr. signed all four bills into law on June 1, 2007. This legislation created a significant change in Colorado's regulatory environment. House Bill 07-1322 contained measures to prevent mortgage fraud and established comprehensive definitions of prohibited conduct for mortgage loan originators. Senate Bill 07-085 prohibited mortgage loan originators from coercing or intimidating appraisers for the purpose of influencing an appraiser's independent judgment. Senate Bill 07-216 established that mortgage loan originators have a duty of good faith and fair dealing in all communications and transactions with a borrower. Finally, Senate Bill 07-203 required the development of a licensure program and the establishment of grounds for disciplinary actions.

In July of 2008, Congress passed the Housing and Economic Recovery Act of 2008. A small portion of this Act is Title V – The S.A.F.E. Mortgage Licensing Act, which may also be cited as the Secure and Fair Enforcement for Mortgage Licensing Act of 2008. In summary, this bill sets minimum national licensing standards for mortgage loan originators and requires that all mortgage loan originators be registered on the Nationwide Mortgage Licensing System and Registry. Additionally, this law requires licensure for a few new groups of individuals and loan originators, including: loan originators working for non-profit organizations; loan originators working in chattel financing related to mobile and manufactured housing; loan originators working for affiliates of depositories; and independent contractor loan processors and underwriters. The S.A.F.E. Act was essentially a mandate for states to ensure that their laws are consistent with this federal mandate. Furthermore, the S.A.F.E. Act mandates the development of the Nationwide Mortgage Licensing System and Registry. This registry will benefit Colorado, because it will be possible to track individuals across state lines. In order to adopt provisions defined in the S.A.F.E. Act, the Colorado General Assembly passed House Bill 09-1085 in May of 2009; it became effective August 5, 2009.

In 2009, the Federal Housing and Finance Agency established a policy decision requiring Fannie Mae and Freddie Mac to only purchase mortgage loans if they contained a unique identifier for the individual mortgage loan originator and the mortgage company. Because Colorado, at that time, was one of two states (the other being Hawaii) that did not have any oversight regarding mortgage companies, the Colorado General Assembly acted and passed House Bill 10-1141. This law became effective on August 11, 2010 and requires mortgage companies to be registered on the Nationwide Mortgage Licensing System and Registry. Furthermore, this law established some standards of conduct for mortgage companies, including: document retention; advertising standards; and a prohibition on mortgage companies hiring unlicensed mortgage loan originators. Additionally, this law transforms the Mortgage Loan Originator Program from a director-model program to a board-model program. The defined board consists of five members, three of which must be licensed mortgage loan originators and two that must be members of the public at large not engaged in mortgage loan origination or mortgage lending. The transition to the new Board of Mortgage Loan Originators is an important change for Colorado's Mortgage Loan Originator regulatory program.

Since the inception of the mortgage regulatory program, there have been several laws that have been passed. Additionally, there have been numerous rules that have been promulgated, many of which were adopted on an emergency basis. This regulatory program has seen a consistent change in licensing requirements, standards of conduct, and prohibitions. The mission of the Department of Regulatory Agencies is consumer protection. The Colorado Division of Real Estate now has the tools to protect Colorado consumers and ensure fair competition through aggressive enforcement and responsible implementation.

II. Mortgage Loan Originator Licensing and Mortgage Company Registration Act

Colorado Revised Statutes Title 12, Article 10, Part 7

§ 12-10-701, C.R.S. Short title.

Editor's note: *This section is similar to former §12-61-901 as it existed prior to 2019.*

The short title of this part 7 is the "Mortgage Loan Originator Licensing and Mortgage Company Registration Act".

§ 12-10-702, C.R.S. Definitions.

Editor's note: *This section is similar to former §12-61-902 as it existed prior to 2019.*

As used in this part 7, unless the context otherwise requires:

(1) "Affiliate" means a person who, directly or indirectly, through intermediaries, controls, is controlled by, or is under the common control of another person addressed by this part 7.

(2) "Affordable housing dwelling unit" means an affordable housing dwelling unit as defined in section 29-26-102.

(3) "Board" means the board of mortgage loan originators created in section 12-10-703.

(4) "Borrower" means any person who consults with or retains a mortgage loan originator in an effort to obtain or seek advice or information on obtaining or applying to obtain a residential mortgage loan for himself, herself, or persons including himself or herself, regardless of whether the person actually obtains such a loan.

(5) "Community development organization" means any community housing development organization or community land trust as defined by the federal "Cranston-Gonzalez National Affordable Housing Act" of 1990 or a community-based development organization as defined by the federal "Housing and Community Development Act of 1974", that is also either a private or public nonprofit organization that is exempt from taxation under section 501 (a) of the federal "Internal Revenue Code of 1986" pursuant to section 501 (c) of the federal "Internal Revenue Code of 1986", 26 U.S.C. sec. 501 (a) and 501 (c), as amended, and that receives funding from the United States department of housing and urban development, Colorado division of housing, Colorado housing and finance authority, or United States department of agriculture rural development, or through a grantee of the United States department of housing and urban development, purely for the purpose of community housing development activities.

(6) "Depository institution" has the same meaning as set forth in the "Federal Deposit Insurance Act", 12 U.S.C. sec. 1813 (c), and includes a credit union.

(7) "Dwelling" shall have the same meaning as set forth in the federal "Truth in Lending Act", 15 U.S.C. sec. 1602 (w).

(8) "Federal banking agency" means the board of governors of the federal reserve system, the comptroller of the currency, the director of the office of thrift supervision, the national credit union administration, or the federal deposit insurance corporation.

(9) "HUD-approved housing counseling agency" means an agency that is either a private or public nonprofit organization that is exempt from taxation under section 501 (a) of the federal "Internal Revenue Code of 1986" pursuant to section 501 (c) of the federal "Internal Revenue Code of 1986", 26 U.S.C. sec. 501 (a) and 501 (c), as amended, and approved by the United States department of housing and urban development, in accordance with the housing counseling program handbook section 7610.1 and 24 CFR 214.

(10) "Individual" means a natural person.

(11) (a) "Loan processor or underwriter" means an individual who performs clerical or support duties at the direction of, and subject to supervision by, a state-licensed loan originator or a registered loan originator.

(b) As used in this subsection (11), "clerical or support duties" includes duties performed after receipt of an application for a residential mortgage loan, including:

(I) The receipt, collection, distribution, and analysis of information commonly used for the processing or underwriting of a residential mortgage loan; and

(II) Communicating with a borrower to obtain the information necessary to process or underwrite a loan, to the extent that the communication does not include offering or negotiating loan rates or terms or counseling consumers about residential mortgage loan rates or terms.

(12) "Mortgage company" means a person other than an individual who, through employees or other individuals, takes residential loan applications or offers or negotiates terms of a residential mortgage loan.

(13) "Mortgage lender" means a lender who is in the business of making residential mortgage loans if:

   (a) The lender is the payee on the promissory note evidencing the loan; and

   (b) The loan proceeds are obtained by the lender from its own funds or from a line of credit made available to the lender from a bank or other entity that regularly loans money to lenders for the purpose of funding mortgage loans.

(14) (a) "Mortgage loan originator" means an individual who:

      (I) Takes a residential mortgage loan application; or

      (II) Offers or negotiates terms of a residential mortgage loan.

   (b) "Mortgage loan originator" does not include:

      (I) An individual engaged solely as a loan processor or underwriter;

      (II) A person that only performs real estate brokerage or sales activities and is licensed or registered pursuant to part 2 of this article 10, unless the person is compensated by a mortgage lender or a mortgage loan originator;

      (III) A person solely involved in extensions of credit relating to time share plans, as defined in 11 U.S.C. sec. 101 (53D);

      (IV) An individual who is servicing a mortgage loan; or

      (V) A person that only performs the services and activities of a dealer, as defined in section 24-32-3302.

(15) "Nationwide mortgage licensing system and registry" means a mortgage licensing system developed pursuant to the federal "Secure and Fair Enforcement for Mortgage Licensing Act of 2008", 12 U.S.C. sec. 5101 et seq., as amended, to track the licensing and registration of mortgage loan originators and that is established and maintained by:

   (a) The Conference of State Bank Supervisors and the American Association of Residential Mortgage Regulators, or their successor entities; or

   (b) The secretary of the United States department of housing and urban development.

(16) "Nontraditional mortgage product" means a mortgage product other than a thirty-year, fixed-rate mortgage.

(17) "Originate a mortgage" means to act, directly or indirectly, as a mortgage loan originator.

(18) "Person" means a natural person, corporation, company, limited liability company, partnership, firm, association, or other legal entity.

(19) "Quasi-government agency" means an agency that is either a private or public nonprofit organization that is exempt from taxation under section 501 (a) of the federal "Internal Revenue Code of 1986" pursuant to section 501 (c) of the federal "Internal Revenue Code of 1986", 26 U.S.C. sec. 501 (a) and 501 (c), as amended, and was created to operate in accordance with article 4 of title 29 as a public housing authority.

(20) "Real estate brokerage activity" means an activity that involves offering or providing real estate brokerage services to the public, including, without limitation:

   (a) Acting as a real estate agent or real estate broker for a buyer, seller, lessor, or lessee of real property;

   (b) Bringing together parties interested in the sale, purchase, lease, rental, or exchange of real property;

   (c) Negotiating, on behalf of any party, any portion of a contract relating to the sale, purchase, lease, rental, or exchange of real property, other than matters related to financing for the transaction;

(d) Engaging in an activity for which a person engaged in the activity is required under applicable law to be registered or licensed as a real estate agent or real estate broker; or

(e) Offering to engage in any activity, or act in any capacity related to the activity, described in this subsection (20).

(21) "Residential mortgage loan" means a loan that is primarily for personal, family, or household use and that is secured by a mortgage, deed of trust, or other equivalent, consensual security interest on a dwelling or residential real estate upon which is constructed or intended to be constructed a single-family dwelling or multiple-family dwelling of four or fewer units.

(22) "Residential real estate" means any real property upon which a dwelling is or will be constructed.

(23) "Self-help housing organization" means a private or public nonprofit organization that is exempt from taxation under section 501 (a) of the federal "Internal Revenue Code of 1986" pursuant to section 501 (c) of the federal "Internal Revenue Code of 1986", 26 U.S.C. sec. 501 (a) and 501 (c), as amended, and that purely originates residential mortgage loans with interest rates no greater than zero percent for borrowers who have provided part of the labor to construct the dwelling securing the loan or that receives funding from the United States department of agriculture rural development section 502 mutual self-help housing program for borrowers that have provided part of the labor to construct the dwelling securing the loan.

(24) "Servicing a mortgage loan" means collecting, receiving, or obtaining the right to collect or receive payments on behalf of a mortgage lender, including payments of principal, interest, escrow amounts, and other amounts due on obligations due and owing to the mortgage lender.

(25) "State-licensed loan originator" means an individual who is:

(a) A mortgage loan originator or engages in the activities of a mortgage loan originator;

(b) Not an employee of a depository institution or a subsidiary that is:

(I) Owned and controlled by a depository institution; and

(II) Regulated by a federal banking agency;

(c) Licensed or required to be licensed pursuant to this part 7; and

(d) Registered as a state-licensed loan originator with, and maintains a unique identifier through, the nationwide mortgage licensing system and registry.

(26) "Unique identifier" means a number or other identifier assigned to a mortgage loan originator pursuant to protocols established by the nationwide mortgage licensing system and registry.

§ 12-10-703, C.R.S. Board of mortgage loan originators – creation – compensation – enforcement of part after board creation – immunity.

Editor's note: *This section is similar to former §12-61-902.5 as it existed prior to 2019.*

(1) (a) There is hereby created in the division of real estate a board of mortgage loan originators, consisting of five members appointed by the governor with the consent of the senate.

(b) Of the members of the board:

(I) Three must be licensed mortgage loan originators. The general assembly encourages the governor to appoint to at least one of these three positions a licensed mortgage loan originator who is an employee or exclusive agent of, or works as an independent contractor for, a Colorado-based mortgage company.

(II) Two must be members of the public at large not engaged in mortgage loan origination or mortgage lending.

(c) Of the members of the board appointed for terms beginning on and after August 11, 2010, two of the members appointed as mortgage loan originators and one of the members appointed as a member of the public at large shall be appointed for terms of two years, and one of the members appointed as a mortgage loan originator and one of the members appointed as a member of the public at large shall serve for terms of four years. Thereafter, members of the board shall hold office for a term of four years.

(d) In the event of a vacancy by death, resignation, removal, or otherwise, the governor shall appoint a member to fill the unexpired term. The governor has the authority to remove any member for misconduct, neglect of duty, or incompetence.

(2) (a) The board shall exercise its powers and perform its duties and functions under the department as if transferred to the department by a **type 1** transfer, as such transfer is defined in the "Administrative Organization Act of 1968", article 1 of title 24.

(b) Notwithstanding any other provision of this part 7, on and after the creation of the board by this section, the board shall exercise all of the rule-making, enforcement, and administrative authority of the director set forth in this part 7. The board has the authority to delegate to the director any enforcement and administrative authority under this part 7 that the board deems necessary and appropriate. If the board delegates any enforcement or administrative authority under this part 7 to the director, the director shall only be entitled to exercise such authority as specifically delegated in writing to the director by the board.

(3) Each member of the board shall receive the same compensation and reimbursement of expenses as those provided for members of boards and commissions in the division of professions and occupations pursuant to section 12-20-103 (6). Payment for all per diem compensation and expenses shall be made out of annual appropriations from the division of real estate cash fund created in section 12-10-215.

(4) Members of the board, consultants, and expert witnesses shall be immune from suit in any civil action based upon any disciplinary proceedings or other official acts they performed in good faith pursuant to this part 7.

(5) A majority of the board shall constitute a quorum for the transaction of all business, and actions of the board shall require a vote of a majority of the members present in favor of the action taken.

(6) (a) All rules promulgated by the director prior to August 11, 2010, shall remain in full force and effect until repealed or modified by the board. The board shall have the authority to enforce any previously promulgated rules of the director under this part 7 and any rules promulgated by the board.

(b) Nothing in this section shall affect any action taken by the director prior to August 11, 2010. No person who, on or before August 11, 2010, holds a license issued under this part 7 shall be required to secure an additional license under this part 7, but shall otherwise be subject to all the provisions of this part 7. A license previously issued shall, for all purposes, be considered a license issued by the board under this part 7.

§ 12-10-704, C.R.S. License required – rules.

Editor's note: *(1) This section is similar to former §12-61-903 as it existed prior to 2019.*

(2) Before its relocation in 2019, this section was amended in HB 19-1166. Those amendments were superseded by the repeal and reenactment of this title 12, effective October 1, 2019. For those amendments to the former section in effect from April 18, 2019, to October 1, 2019, see HB 19-1166, chapter 125, Session Laws of Colorado 2019.

(3) Section 78 of chapter 125 (HB 19-1166), Session Laws of Colorado 2019, provides that the act changing this section takes effect October 1, 2019, only if HB 19-1172 becomes law. HB 19-1172 became law and took effect October 1, 2019.

(1) (a) Unless licensed by the board and registered with the nationwide mortgage licensing system and registry as a state-licensed loan originator, an individual shall not originate or offer to originate a mortgage or act or offer to act as a mortgage loan originator.

(b) On and after January 1, 2010, a licensed mortgage loan originator shall apply for license renewal in accordance with subsection (5) of this section every calendar year as determined by the board by rule.

(2) An independent contractor may not engage in residential mortgage loan origination activities as a loan processor or underwriter unless the independent contractor is a state-licensed loan originator.

(3) An applicant for initial licensing as a mortgage loan originator shall submit to the board the following:

(a) A criminal history record check in compliance with subsection (6) of this section;

(b) A disclosure of all administrative discipline taken against the applicant concerning the categories listed in section 12-10-711 (1)(c); and

(c) The application fee established by the board in accordance with section 12-10-718.

(4) (a) In addition to the requirements imposed by subsection (3) of this section, on or after August 5, 2009, each individual applicant for initial licensing as a mortgage loan originator must have satisfactorily completed:

(I) At least twenty hours of education as administered and approved by the Nationwide Multistate Licensing System and Registry or its successor; and

(II) A written examination approved by the board. For the portion of the examination that represents the state-specific test required in the federal "Secure and Fair Enforcement for Mortgage Licensing Act of 2008", 12 U.S.C. sec. 5101 et seq., as amended, the board may adopt the uniform state test administered through the Nationwide Multistate Licensing System and Registry or its successor.

(b) The board may contract with one or more independent testing services to develop, administer, and grade the examinations required by subsection (4)(a) of this section and to maintain and administer licensee records. The contract may allow the testing service to recover from applicants its costs incurred in connection with these functions. The board may contract separately for these functions and may allow the costs to be collected by a single contractor for distribution to other contractors.

(c) The board may publish reports summarizing statistical information prepared by the nationwide mortgage licensing system and registry relating to mortgage loan originator examinations.

(5) An applicant for license renewal shall submit to the board the following:

(a) A disclosure of all administrative discipline taken against the applicant concerning the categories listed in section 12-10-711 (1)(c); and

(b) The renewal fee established by the board in accordance with section 12-10-718.

(6) (a) Prior to submitting an application for a license, an applicant shall submit a set of fingerprints to the Colorado bureau of investigation. Upon receipt of the applicant's fingerprints, the Colorado bureau of investigation shall use the fingerprints to conduct a state and national criminal history record check using records of the Colorado bureau of investigation and the federal bureau of investigation. All costs arising from the criminal history record check must be borne by the applicant and must be paid when the set of fingerprints is submitted. Upon completion of the criminal history record check, the bureau shall forward the results to the board. The board shall acquire a name-based criminal history record check, as defined in section 22-2-119.3 (6)(d), for an applicant who has twice submitted to a fingerprint-based criminal history record check and whose

fingerprints are unclassifiable or when the results of a fingerprint-based criminal history record check of an applicant performed pursuant to this subsection (6) reveal a record of arrest without a disposition. The applicant shall pay the costs associated with a name-based criminal history record check.

(b) If the board determines that the criminal background check provided by the nationwide mortgage licensing system and registry is a sufficient method of screening license applicants to protect Colorado consumers, the board may, by rule, authorize the use of that criminal background check instead of the criminal history record check otherwise required by this subsection (6).

(7) (a) On and after January 1, 2010, in connection with an application for a license as a mortgage loan originator, the applicant shall furnish information concerning the applicant's identity to the nationwide mortgage licensing system and registry. The applicant shall furnish, at a minimum, the following:

(I) Fingerprints for submission to the federal bureau of investigation and any government agency or entity authorized to receive fingerprints for a state, national, or international criminal history record check; and

(II) Personal history and experience, in a form prescribed by the nationwide mortgage licensing system and registry, including submission of authorization for the nationwide mortgage licensing system and registry to obtain:

(A) An independent credit report from the consumer reporting agency described in the federal "Fair Credit Reporting Act", 15 U.S.C. sec. 1681a (p); and

(B) Information related to any administrative, civil, or criminal findings by a government jurisdiction.

(b) An applicant is responsible for paying all costs arising from a criminal history record check and shall pay the costs upon submission of fingerprints.

(c) The board shall acquire a name-based criminal history record check, as defined in section 22-2-119.3 (6)(d), for an applicant who has twice submitted to a fingerprint-based criminal history record check and whose fingerprints are unclassifiable or when the results of a fingerprint-based criminal history record check of an applicant performed pursuant to this subsection (7) reveal a record of arrest without a disposition. The applicant shall pay the costs associated with a name-based criminal history record check.

(8) Before granting a license to an applicant, the board shall require the applicant to post a bond as required by section 12-10-717.

(9) The board shall issue or deny a license within sixty days after:

(a) The applicant has submitted the requisite information to the board and the Nationwide Multistate Licensing System and Registry, including the completed application and any necessary supplementary information, the application fee, and proof that the applicant has posted a surety bond and obtained errors and omissions insurance; and

(b) The board receives the completed criminal history record check and all other relevant information or documents necessary to reasonably ascertain facts underlying the applicant's criminal history.

(10) (a) The board may require, as a condition of license renewal on or after January 1, 2009, continuing education of licensees for the purpose of enhancing the professional competence and professional responsibility of all licensees.

(b) Continuing professional education requirements shall be determined by the board by rule; except that licensees shall be required to complete at least eight credit hours of continuing education each year. The board may contract with one or more independent service providers to develop, review, or approve continuing education courses. The contract may allow the independent service provider to recover from licensees its costs incurred in connection with these functions. The board may contract separately for these functions and may allow the costs to be collected by a single contractor for distribution to other contractors.

(11) (a) The board may require contractors and prospective contractors for services under subsections (4) and (10) of this section to submit, for the board's review and approval, information regarding the contents and materials of proposed courses and other documentation reasonably necessary to further the purposes of this section.

(b) The board may set fees for the initial and continuing review of courses for which credit hours will be granted. The initial filing fee for review of materials shall not exceed five hundred dollars, and the fee for continued review shall not exceed two hundred fifty dollars per year per course offered.

(12) The board may adopt reasonable rules to implement this section. The board may adopt rules necessary to implement provisions required in the federal "Secure and Fair Enforcement for Mortgage Licensing Act of 2008", 12 U.S.C. sec. 5101 et seq., as amended, and for participation in the nationwide mortgage licensing system and registry.

(13) In order to fulfill the purposes of this part 7, the board may establish relationships or contracts with the nationwide mortgage licensing system and registry or other entities designated by the nationwide mortgage licensing system and registry to collect and maintain records and process transaction fees or other fees related to licensees or other persons subject to this part 7.

(14) The board may use the nationwide mortgage licensing system and registry as a channeling agent for requesting information from or distributing information to the department of justice, a government agency, or any other source.

§ 12-10-705, C.R.S. Registration required – rules.

Editor's note: *This section is similar to former §12-61-903.1 as it existed prior to 2019.*

(1) On or after January 1, 2011, each mortgage company shall register with the nationwide mortgage licensing system and registry, unless exempted by rule by the board, and shall renew its registration each calendar year based on the following criteria:

(a) (I) The mortgage company is legally operating in the state of Colorado in accordance with standards determined and administered by the Colorado secretary of state; and

(II) The mortgage company is not legally barred from operating in Colorado.

(b) Sole proprietors, general partnerships, and other mortgage companies not otherwise required to register with the secretary of state shall register using a trade name.

§ 12-10-706, C.R.S. License or registration inactivation.

Editor's note: *This section is similar to former §12-61-903.3 as it existed prior to 2019.*

(1) The board may inactivate a state license or a registration with the nationwide mortgage licensing system and registry when a licensee has failed to:

(a) Comply with the surety bond requirements of sections 12-10-704 (8) and 12-10-717;

(b) Comply with the errors and omissions insurance requirement in section 12-10-707 or any rule of the board that directly or indirectly addresses errors and omissions insurance requirements;

(c) Maintain current contact information, surety bond information, or errors and omissions insurance information as required by this part 7 or by any rule of the board that directly or indirectly addresses those requirements;

(d) Respond to an investigation or examination;

(e) Comply with any of the education or testing requirements set forth in this part 7 or in any rule of the board that directly or indirectly addresses education or testing requirements; or

(f) Register with and provide all required information to the nationwide mortgage licensing system and registry.

§ 12-10-707, C.R.S. Errors and omissions insurance – duties of the board – certificate of coverage – when required – group plan made available – effect – rules.

Editor's note: *This section is similar to former §12-61-903.5 as it existed prior to 2019.*

(1) Every licensee under this part 7, except an inactive mortgage loan originator or an attorney licensee who maintains a policy of professional malpractice insurance that provides coverage for errors and omissions insurance for their activities as a licensee under this part 7, shall maintain errors and omissions insurance to cover all activities contemplated under this part 7. The division shall make the errors and omissions insurance available to all licensees by contracting with an insurer for a group policy after a competitive bid process in accordance with article 103 of title 24. A group policy obtained by the division must be available to all licensees with no right on the part of the insurer to cancel a licensee. A licensee may obtain errors and omissions insurance independently if the coverage complies with the minimum requirements established by the division.

(2) (a) If the division is unable to obtain errors and omissions insurance coverage to insure all licensees who choose to participate in the group program at a reasonable annual premium, as determined by the division, a licensee shall independently obtain the errors and omissions insurance required by this section.

(b) The division shall solicit and consider information and comments from interested persons when determining the reasonableness of annual premiums.

(3) The division shall determine the terms and conditions of coverage required under this section based on rules promulgated by the board. Each licensee shall be notified of the required terms and conditions at least thirty days before the annual premium renewal date as determined by the division. Each licensee shall file a certificate of coverage showing compliance with the required terms and conditions with the division by the annual premium renewal date, as determined by the division.

(4) In addition to all other powers and duties conferred upon the board by this part 7, the board shall adopt such rules as it deems necessary or proper to carry out this section.

§ 12-10-708, C.R.S. License renewal.

Editor's note: *This section is similar to former §12-61-903.7 as it existed prior to 2019.*

(1) In order for a licensed mortgage loan originator to renew a license issued pursuant to this part 7, the mortgage loan originator shall:

(a) Continue to meet the minimum standards for issuance of a license pursuant to this part 7;

(b) Satisfy the annual continuing education requirements set forth in section 12-10-704 (10) and in rules adopted by the board; and

(c) Pay applicable license renewal fees.

(2) If a licensed mortgage loan originator fails to satisfy the requirements of subsection (1) of this section for license renewal, the mortgage loan originator's license shall expire. The board shall adopt rules to establish procedures for the reinstatement of an expired license consistent with the standards established by the nationwide mortgage licensing system and registry.

§ 12-10-709, C.R.S. Exemptions – definition – rules.

Editor's note: *This section is similar to former §12-61-904 as it existed prior to 2019.*

(1) Except as otherwise provided in section 12-10-713, this part 7 does not apply to the following, unless otherwise determined by the federal bureau of consumer financial protection or the United States department of housing and urban development:

(a) With respect to a residential mortgage loan:

(I) A person, estate, or trust that provides mortgage financing for the sale of no more than three properties in any twelve-month period to purchasers of the properties, each of which is owned by the person, estate, or trust and serves as security for the loan; or

(II) An individual who acts as a mortgage loan originator, without compensation or gain to the mortgage loan originator, in providing loan financing for not more than three residential mortgage loans in any twelve-month period to a family member of the individual. The board shall define "family member" by rule. For purposes of this exemption only, "compensation or gain" excludes any interest paid under the loan financing provided.

(b) A bank and a savings association as these terms are defined in the "Federal Deposit Insurance Act", 12 U.S.C. sec. 1811 et seq., as amended, a subsidiary that is owned and controlled by a bank or savings association, employees of a bank or savings association, employees of a subsidiary that is owned and controlled by a bank or savings association, credit unions, and employees of credit unions;

(c) An attorney who renders services in the course of practice, who is licensed in Colorado, and who is not primarily engaged in the business of negotiating residential mortgage loans;

(d) A person who:

(I) Funds a residential mortgage loan that has been originated and processed by a licensed person or by an exempt person;

(II) Does not solicit borrowers in Colorado for the purpose of making residential mortgage loans; and

(III) Does not participate in the negotiation of residential mortgage loans with the borrower, except for setting the terms under which a person may buy or fund a residential mortgage loan originated by a licensed or exempt person;

(e) A loan processor or underwriter who is not an independent contractor and who does not represent to the public that the individual can or will perform any activities of a mortgage loan originator. As used in this subsection (1)(e), "represent to the public" means communicating, through advertising or other means of communicating, or providing information, including the use of business cards, stationery, brochures, signs, rate lists, or other promotional items, that the individual is able to provide a particular service or activity for a consumer.

(f) To the extent that it is providing programs benefitting affordable housing dwelling units, an agency of the federal government, the Colorado government, or any of Colorado's political subdivisions or employees of an agency of the federal government, of the Colorado government, or of any of Colorado's political subdivisions;

(g) Quasi-government agencies, HUD-approved housing counseling agencies, or employees of quasi-government agencies or HUD-approved housing counseling agencies;

(h) Community development organizations or employees of community development organizations;

(i) Self-help housing organizations or employees of self-help housing organizations or volunteers acting as an agent of self-help housing organizations;

(j) A person licensed under part 2 of this article 10 who represents a person, estate, or trust providing mortgage financing under subsection (1)(a) of this section.

(2) The exemptions in subsection (1) of this section shall not apply to persons acting beyond the scope of the exemptions.

(3) The board may adopt reasonable rules modifying the exemptions in this section in accordance with rules adopted by the federal bureau of consumer financial protection or the United States department of housing and urban development.

§ 12-10-710, C.R.S. Originator's relationship to borrower – rules.

Editor's note: *This section is similar to former §12-61-904.5 as it existed prior to 2019.*

(1) A mortgage loan originator shall have a duty of good faith and fair dealing in all communications and transactions with a borrower. The duty includes, but is not limited to:

(a) The duty to not recommend or induce the borrower to enter into a transaction that does not have a reasonable, tangible net benefit to the borrower, considering all of the circumstances, including the terms of a loan, the cost of a loan, and the borrower's circumstances;

(b) The duty to make a reasonable inquiry concerning the borrower's current and prospective income, existing debts and other obligations, and any other relevant information and, after making the inquiry, to make his or her best efforts to recommend, broker, or originate a residential mortgage loan that takes into consideration the information submitted by the borrower, but the mortgage loan originator shall not be deemed to violate this section if the borrower conceals or misrepresents relevant information; and

(c) The duty not to commit any acts, practices, or omissions in violation of section 38-40-105.

(2) For purposes of implementing subsection (1) of this section, the board may adopt rules defining what constitutes a reasonable, tangible net benefit to the borrower.

(3) A violation of this section constitutes a deceptive trade practice under the "Colorado Consumer Protection Act", article 1 of title 6.

§ 12-10-711, C.R.S. Powers and duties of the board – rules.

Editor's note: *This section is similar to former §12-61-905 as it existed prior to 2019.*

(1) The board may deny an application for a license, refuse to renew, or revoke the license of an applicant or licensee who has:

(a) Filed an application with the board containing material misstatements of fact or omitted any disclosure required by this part 7;

(b) Within the last five years, been convicted of or pled guilty or nolo contendere to a crime involving fraud, deceit, material misrepresentation, theft, or the breach of a fiduciary duty, except as otherwise set forth in this part 7;

(c) Except as otherwise set forth in this part 7, within the last five years, had a license, registration, or certification issued by Colorado or another state revoked or suspended for fraud, deceit, material misrepresentation, theft, or the breach of a fiduciary duty, and the discipline denied the person authorization to practice as:

(I) A mortgage broker or a mortgage loan originator;

(II) A real estate broker, as defined by section 12-10-201 (6);

(III) A real estate salesperson;

(IV) A real estate appraiser, as defined by section 12-10-602 (9);

(V) An insurance producer, as defined by section 10-2-103 (6);

(VI) An attorney;

(VII) A securities broker-dealer, as defined by section 11-51-201 (2);

(VIII) A securities sales representative, as defined by section 11-51-201 (14);

(IX) An investment advisor, as defined by section 11-51-201 (9.5); or

(X) An investment advisor representative, as defined by section 11-51-201 (9.6);

(d) Been enjoined within the immediately preceding five years under the laws of this or any other state or of the United States from engaging in deceptive conduct relating to the brokering of or originating a mortgage loan;

(e) Been found to have violated the provisions of section 12-10-721;

(f) Been found to have violated the provisions of section 12-10-713;

(g) Not demonstrated financial responsibility, character, and general fitness to command the confidence of the community and to warrant a determination that the individual will operate honestly, fairly, and efficiently, consistent with the purposes of this part 7;

(h) Not completed the prelicense education requirements set forth in section 12-10-704 and any applicable rules of the board; or

(i) Not passed a written examination that meets the requirements set forth in section 12-10-704 and any applicable rules of the board.

(2) The board shall deny an application for a license, refuse to renew, or revoke the license of an applicant or licensee who has:

(a) (I) Had a mortgage loan originator license or similar license revoked in any jurisdiction.

(II) If a revocation is subsequently formally nullified, the license is not revoked for purposes of this subsection (2)(a).

(b) (I) At any time been convicted of, or pled guilty or nolo contendere to, a felony in a domestic, foreign, or military court if the felony involved an act of fraud, dishonesty, breach of trust, or money laundering.

(II) If the individual obtains a pardon of the conviction, the board shall not deem the individual convicted for purposes of this subsection (2)(b).

(c) Been convicted of, or pled guilty or nolo contendere to, a felony within the immediately preceding seven years.

(3) The board may investigate the activities of a licensee or other person that present grounds for disciplinary action under this part 7 or that violate section 12-10-720 (1).

(4) (a) If the board has reasonable grounds to believe that a mortgage loan originator is no longer qualified under subsection (1) of this section, the board may summarily suspend the mortgage loan originator's license pending a hearing to revoke the license. A summary suspension shall conform to article 4 of title 24.

(b) The board shall suspend the license of a mortgage loan originator who fails to maintain the bond required by section 12-10-717 until the licensee complies with that section.

(5) The board or an administrative law judge appointed pursuant to part 10 of article 30 of title 24 shall conduct disciplinary hearings concerning mortgage loan originators and mortgage companies. The hearings shall conform to article 4 of title 24.

(6) (a) Except as provided in subsection (6)(b) of this section, an individual whose license has been revoked shall not be eligible for licensure for two years after the effective date of the revocation.

(b) If the board or an administrative law judge determines that an application contained a misstatement of fact or omitted a required disclosure due to an unintentional error, the board shall allow the applicant to correct the application. Upon receipt of the corrected and completed application, the board or administrative law judge shall not bar the applicant from being licensed on the basis of the unintentional misstatement or omission.

(7) (a) The board or an administrative law judge may administer oaths, take affirmations of witnesses, and issue subpoenas to compel the attendance of witnesses and the production of all relevant papers, books, records, documentary evidence, and materials in any hearing or investigation conducted by the board or an administrative law judge. The board may request any information relevant to the investigation, including, but not limited to, independent credit reports obtained from a consumer reporting agency described in the federal "Fair Credit Reporting Act", 15 U.S.C. sec. 1681a (p).

(b) Upon failure of a witness to comply with a subpoena or process, the district court of the county in which the subpoenaed witness resides or conducts business may issue an order requiring the witness to appear before the board or administrative law judge; produce the relevant papers, books, records, documentary evidence, testimony, or materials in question; or both. Failure to obey the order of the court may be punished as a contempt of court. The board or an administrative law judge may apply for an order.

(c) The licensee or individual who, after an investigation under this part 7, is found to be in violation of a provision of this part 7 shall be responsible for paying all reasonable and necessary costs of the division arising from subpoenas or requests issued pursuant to this subsection (7), including court costs for an action brought pursuant to subsection (7)(b) of this section.

(8) (a) If the board has reasonable cause to believe that an individual is violating this part 7, including but not limited to section 12-10-720 (1), the board may enter an order requiring the individual to cease and desist the violations.

(b) The board, upon its own motion, may, and, upon the complaint in writing of any person, shall, investigate the activities of any licensee or any individual who assumes to act in such capacity within the state. In addition to any other penalty that may be imposed pursuant to this part 7, any individual violating any provision of this part 7 or any rules promulgated pursuant to this article 10 may be fined upon a finding of misconduct by the board as follows:

(I) In the first administrative proceeding, a fine not in excess of one thousand dollars per act or occurrence;

(II) In a second or subsequent administrative proceeding, a fine not less than one thousand dollars nor in excess of two thousand dollars per act or occurrence.

(c) All fines collected pursuant to this subsection (8) shall be transferred to the state treasurer, who shall credit them to the division of real estate cash fund created in section 12-10-215.

(9) The board shall keep records of the individuals licensed as mortgage loan originators and of disciplinary proceedings. The records kept by the board shall be open to public inspection in a reasonable time and manner determined by the board.

(10) The board shall maintain a system, which may include, without limitation, a hotline or website, that gives consumers a reasonably easy method for making complaints about a mortgage loan originator.

(11) The board shall promulgate rules to allow licensed mortgage loan originators to hire unlicensed mortgage loan originators under temporary licenses. If an unlicensed mortgage loan originator has initiated the application process for a license, he or she shall be assigned a temporary license for a reasonable period until a license is approved or denied. The licensed mortgage

loan originator who employs an unlicensed mortgage loan originator shall be held responsible under all applicable provisions of law, including without limitation this part 7 and section 38-40-105, for the actions of the unlicensed mortgage loan originator to whom a temporary license has been assigned under this subsection (11).

§ 12-10-712, C.R.S. Powers and duties of the board over mortgage companies – fines – rules.

Editor's note: *This section is similar to former §12-61-905.1 as it existed prior to 2019.*

(1) With respect to mortgage companies, the board may deny an application for registration; refuse to renew, suspend, or revoke the registration; enter cease-and-desist orders; and impose fines as set forth in this section as follows:

(a) If the board has reasonable cause to believe a person is acting without a license or registration;

(b) If the mortgage company fails to maintain possession, for future use or inspection by an authorized representative of the board, for a period of four years, of the documents or records prescribed by the rules of the board or to produce the documents or records upon reasonable request by the board or by an authorized representative of the board;

(c) If the mortgage company employs or contracts with individuals who are required to be licensed pursuant to this part 7 and who are not either:

(I) Licensed; or

(II) In the process of becoming licensed; or

(d) If the mortgage company directs, makes, or causes to be made, in any manner, a false or deceptive statement or representation with regard to the rates, points, or other financing terms or conditions for a residential mortgage loan; engages in bait and switch advertising as that term is used in section 6-1-105 (1)(n); or violates any rule of the board that directly or indirectly addresses advertising requirements.

(2) (a) The board, upon its own motion or upon the complaint in writing of any person, may investigate the activities of any registered mortgage company or any mortgage company that is acting in a capacity that requires registration pursuant to this part 7.

(b) The board may fine a mortgage company that has violated this section or any rules promulgated pursuant to this section as follows:

(I) In the first administrative proceeding, a fine not in excess of one thousand dollars per act or occurrence;

(II) In a second or subsequent administrative proceeding, a fine not in excess of two thousand dollars per act or occurrence.

(c) All fines collected pursuant to this section shall be transmitted to the state treasurer, who shall credit them to the division of real estate cash fund created in section 12-10-215.

(3) The board may adopt reasonable rules for implementing this section.

(4) Nothing in this section automatically imputes a violation to the mortgage company if a licensed agent or employee, or an individual agent or employee who is required to be licensed, violates any other provision of this part 7.

§ 12-10-713, C.R.S. Disciplinary actions – grounds – procedures – rules.

Editor's note: *This section is similar to former §12-61-905.5 as it existed prior to 2019.*

(1) The board, upon its own motion, may, or upon the complaint in writing of any person, shall, investigate the activities of any mortgage loan originator. The board has the power to impose an administrative fine in accordance with section 12-10-711, deny a license, censure a licensee,

place the licensee on probation and set the terms of probation, order restitution, order the payment of actual damages, or suspend or revoke a license when the board finds that the licensee or applicant has performed, is performing, or is attempting to perform any of the following acts:

(a) Knowingly making any misrepresentation or knowingly making use of any false or misleading advertising;

(b) Making any promise that influences, persuades, or induces another person to detrimentally rely on the promise when the licensee could not or did not intend to keep the promise;

(c) Knowingly misrepresenting or making false promises through agents, salespersons, advertising, or otherwise;

(d) Violating any provision of the "Colorado Consumer Protection Act", article 1 of title 6, and, if the licensee has been assessed a civil or criminal penalty or been subject to an injunction under the act, the board shall revoke the licensee's license;

(e) Acting for more than one party in a transaction without disclosing any actual or potential conflict of interest or without disclosing to all parties any fiduciary obligation or other legal obligation of the mortgage loan originator to any party;

(f) Representing or attempting to represent a mortgage loan originator other than the licensee's principal or employer without the express knowledge and consent of that principal or employer;

(g) In the case of a licensee in the employ of another mortgage loan originator, failing to place, as soon after receipt as is practicably possible, in the custody of that licensed mortgage loan originator-employer any deposit money or other money or fund entrusted to the employee by any person dealing with the employee as the representative of that licensed mortgage loan originator-employer;

(h) Failing to account for or to remit, within a reasonable time, any money coming into his or her possession that belongs to others, whether acting as a mortgage loan originator, real estate broker, salesperson, or otherwise, and failing to keep records relative to the money, which records shall contain such information as may be prescribed by the rules of the board relative thereto and shall be subject to audit by the board;

(i) Converting funds of others, diverting funds of others without proper authorization, commingling funds of others with the licensee's own funds, or failing to keep the funds of others in an escrow or a trustee account with a bank or recognized depository in this state, which account may be any type of checking, demand, passbook, or statement account insured by an agency of the United States government, and to keep records relative to the deposit that contain such information as may be prescribed by the rules of the board relative thereto, which records shall be subject to audit by the board;

(j) Failing to provide the parties to a residential mortgage loan transaction with such information as may be prescribed by the rules of the board;

(k) Unless an employee of a duly registered mortgage company, failing to maintain possession, for future use or inspection by an authorized representative of the board, for a period of four years, of the documents or records prescribed by the rules of the board or to produce the documents or records upon reasonable request by the board or by an authorized representative of the board;

(*l*) Paying a commission or valuable consideration for performing any of the functions of a mortgage loan originator, as described in this part 7, to any person who is not licensed under this part 7 or is not registered in compliance with the federal "Secure and Fair Enforcement for Mortgage Licensing Act of 2008", 12 U.S.C. sec. 5101 et seq., as amended;

(m) Disregarding or violating any provision of this part 7 or any rule adopted by the board pursuant to this part 7; violating any lawful orders of the board; or aiding and abetting a violation of any rule, order of the board, or provision of this part 7;

(n) Conviction of, entering a plea of guilty to, or entering a plea of nolo contendere to any crime in article 3 of title 18, parts 1 to 4 of article 4 of title 18, article 5 of title 18, part 3 of article 8 of title 18, article 15 of title 18, article 17 of title 18, or any other like crime under Colorado law, federal law, or the laws of other states. A certified copy of the judgment of a court of competent jurisdiction of a conviction or other official record indicating that a plea was entered shall be conclusive evidence of the conviction or plea in any hearing under this part 7.

(o) Violating or aiding and abetting in the violation of the Colorado or federal fair housing laws;

(p) Failing to immediately notify the board in writing of a conviction, plea, or violation pursuant to subsection (1)(n) or (1)(o) of this section;

(q) Having demonstrated unworthiness or incompetency to act as a mortgage loan originator by conducting business in such a manner as to endanger the interest of the public;

(r) Procuring, or attempting to procure, a mortgage loan originator's license or renewing, reinstating, or reactivating, or attempting to renew, reinstate, or reactivate, a mortgage loan originator's license by fraud, misrepresentation, or deceit or by making a material misstatement of fact in an application for the license;

(s) Claiming, arranging for, or taking any secret or undisclosed amount of compensation, commission, or profit or failing to reveal to the licensee's principal or employer the full amount of the licensee's compensation, commission, or profit in connection with any acts for which a license is required under this part 7;

(t) Exercising an option to purchase in any agreement authorizing or employing a licensee to sell, buy, or exchange real estate for compensation or commission except when the licensee, prior to or coincident with election to exercise the option to purchase, reveals in writing to the licensee's principal or employer the full amount of the licensee's profit and obtains the written consent of the principal or employer approving the amount of the profit;

(u) Fraud, misrepresentation, deceit, or conversion of trust funds that results in the payment of any claim pursuant to this part 7 or that results in the entry of a civil judgment for damages;

(v) Any other conduct, whether of the same or a different character than specified in this subsection (1), that evinces a lack of good faith and fair dealing;

(w) Having had a mortgage loan originator's license suspended or revoked in any jurisdiction or having had any disciplinary action taken against the mortgage loan originator in any other jurisdiction. A certified copy of the order of disciplinary action shall be prima facie evidence of the disciplinary action.

(x) Engaging in any unfair or deceptive practice toward any person;

(y) Obtaining property by fraud or misrepresentation;

(z) Soliciting or entering into a contract with a borrower that provides, in substance, that the mortgage loan originator may earn a fee or commission through the mortgage loan originator's best efforts to obtain a loan even though no loan is actually obtained for the borrower;

(aa) Soliciting, advertising, or entering into a contract for specific interest rates, points, or other financing terms unless the terms are actually available at the time of the solicitation, advertisement, or contract;

(bb) Failing to make a disclosure to a loan applicant or a noninstitutional investor as required by section 12-10-725 and any other applicable state or federal law;

(cc) Making, in any manner, any false or deceptive statement or representation with regard to the rates, points, or other financing terms or conditions for a residential mortgage loan or engaging in bait and switch advertising;

(dd) Negligently making any false statement or knowingly and willfully omitting a material fact in connection with any reports filed by a mortgage loan originator or in connection with any investigation conducted by the division;

(ee) In any advertising of residential mortgage loans or any other applicable mortgage loan originator activities covered by the following federal acts, failing to comply with any requirement of the "Truth in Lending Act", 15 U.S.C. sec. 1601 and Regulation Z, 12 CFR 226 and 12 CFR 1026; the "Real Estate Settlement Procedures Act of 1974", 12 U.S.C. sec. 2601 and Regulation X, 12 CFR 1024 et seq.; the "Equal Credit Opportunity Act", 15 U.S.C. sec. 1691 and Regulation B, 12 CFR 202.9, 202.11, and 202.12 and 12 CFR 1002; Title V, Subtitle A of the "Financial Services Modernization Act of 1999", also known as the "Gramm-Leach-Bliley Act", 15 U.S.C. secs. 6801 to 6809, and the federal trade commission's privacy rules, 16 CFR 313 and 314, mandated by the "Gramm-Leach-Bliley Act"; the "Home Mortgage Disclosure Act of 1975", 12 U.S.C. sec. 2801 et seq. and Regulation C, home mortgage disclosure, 12 CFR 203 and 12 CFR 1003; the "Federal Trade Commission Act" of 1914, 15 U.S.C. sec. 45 (a) and 16 CFR 233; and the "Telemarketing and Consumer Fraud and Abuse Prevention Act", 15 U.S.C. secs. 6101 to 6108, and the federal trade commission's telemarketing sales rule, 16 CFR 310, as amended. The board may adopt rules requiring mortgage loan originators to comply with other applicable state and federal statutes and regulations.

(ff) Failing to pay a third-party provider, no later than thirty days after the recording of the loan closing documents or ninety days after completion of the third-party service, whichever comes first, unless otherwise agreed or unless the third-party service provider has been notified in writing that a bona fide dispute exists regarding the performance or quality of the third-party service; or

(gg) Collecting, charging, attempting to collect or charge, or using or proposing any agreement purporting to collect or charge any fee prohibited by section 12-10-725 or 12-10-726.

(2) Upon request of the board, when any mortgage loan originator is a party to any suit or proceeding, either civil or criminal, arising out of any transaction involving a residential mortgage loan and the mortgage loan originator participated in the transaction in his or her capacity as a licensed mortgage loan originator, the mortgage loan originator shall supply to the board a copy of the complaint, indictment, information, or other initiating pleading and the answer filed, if any, and advise the board of the disposition of the case and of the nature and amount of any judgment, verdict, finding, or sentence that may be made, entered, or imposed therein.

(3) This part 7 shall not be construed to relieve any person from civil liability or criminal prosecution under the laws of this state.

(4) Complaints of record in the office of the board and board investigations, including board investigative files, are closed to public inspection. Stipulations and final agency orders are public record and subject to sections 24-72-203 and 24-72-204.

(5) When a complaint or an investigation discloses an instance of misconduct that, in the opinion of the board, does not warrant formal action by the board but that should not be dismissed as being without merit, the board may send a letter of admonition by certified mail, return receipt requested, to the licensee against whom a complaint was made and a copy of the letter of admonition to the person making the complaint, but the letter shall advise the licensee that the

licensee has the right to request in writing, within twenty days after proven receipt, that formal disciplinary proceedings be initiated to adjudicate the propriety of the conduct upon which the letter of admonition is based. If the request is timely made, the letter of admonition shall be deemed vacated, and the matter shall be processed by means of formal disciplinary proceedings.

(6) All administrative fines collected pursuant to this section shall be transmitted to the state treasurer, who shall credit them to the division of real estate cash fund created in section 12-10-215.

(7) (a) The board shall not consider an application for licensure from an individual whose license has been revoked until two years after the date of revocation.

(b) If an individual's license was suspended or revoked due to conduct that resulted in financial loss to another person, no new license shall be granted, nor shall a suspended license be reinstated, until full restitution has been made to the person suffering the financial loss. The amount of restitution shall include interest, reasonable attorney fees, and costs of any suit or other proceeding undertaken in an effort to recover the loss.

(8) When the board or the division becomes aware of facts or circumstances that fall within the jurisdiction of a criminal justice or other law enforcement authority upon investigation of the activities of a licensee, the board or division shall, in addition to the exercise of its authority under this part 7, refer and transmit the information, which may include originals or copies of documents and materials, to one or more criminal justice or other law enforcement authorities for investigation and prosecution as authorized by law.

§ 12-10-714, C.R.S. Hearing – administrative law judge – review – rules.

Editor's note: *This section is similar to former §12-61-905.6 as it existed prior to 2019.*

(1) Except as otherwise provided in this section, all proceedings before the board with respect to disciplinary actions and denial of licensure under this part 7, at the discretion of the board, may be conducted by an authorized representative of the board or an administrative law judge pursuant to sections 24-4-104 and 24-4-105.

(2) Proceedings shall be held in the county where the board has its office or in such other place as the board may designate. If the licensee is employed by another licensed mortgage loan originator or by a real estate broker, the board shall also notify the licensee's employer by mailing, by first-class mail, a copy of the written notice required under section 24-4-104 (3) to the employer's last-known business address.

(3) The board, an authorized representative of the board, or an administrative law judge shall conduct all hearings for denying, suspending, or revoking a license or certificate on behalf of the board, subject to appropriations made to the department of personnel. Each administrative law judge shall be appointed pursuant to part 10 of article 30 of title 24. The administrative law judge shall conduct the hearing in accordance with sections 24-4-104 and 24-4-105. No license shall be denied, suspended, or revoked until the board has made its decision.

(4) The decision of the board in any disciplinary action or denial of licensure under this section is subject to judicial review by the court of appeals. In order to effectuate the purposes of this part 7, the board has the power to promulgate rules pursuant to article 4 of title 24.

(5) In a judicial review proceeding, the court may stay the execution or effect of any final order of the board; but a hearing shall be held affording the parties an opportunity to be heard for the purpose of determining whether the public health, safety, and welfare would be endangered by staying the board's order. If the court determines that the order should be stayed, it shall also determine at the hearing the amount of the bond and adequacy of the surety, which bond shall be conditioned upon the faithful performance by the petitioner of all obligations as a mortgage loan originator and upon the prompt payment of all damages arising from or caused by the

delay in the taking effect of or enforcement of the order complained of and for all costs that may be assessed or required to be paid in connection with the proceedings.

(6) In any hearing conducted by the board or an authorized representative of the board in which there is a possibility of the denial, suspension, or revocation of a license because of the conviction of a felony or of a crime involving moral turpitude, the board or its authorized representative shall be governed by section 24-5-101.

* § 12-10-715, C.R.S. Subpoena – misdemeanor.

Editor's note: *This section is similar to former §12-61-905.7 as it existed prior to 2019.*

(1) The board or the administrative law judge appointed for hearings may issue subpoenas, as described in section 12-10-711 (7), which shall be served in the same manner as subpoenas issued by district courts and shall be issued without discrimination between public or private parties requiring the attendance of witnesses or the production of documents at hearings.

(2) *[Editor's note: This version of subsection (2) is effective until March 1, 2022.]* Any person who willfully fails or neglects to appear and testify or to produce books, papers, or records required by subpoena, duly served upon him or her in any matter conducted under this part 7, is guilty of a misdemeanor and, upon conviction thereof, shall be punished by a fine of one hundred dollars or imprisonment in the county jail for not more than thirty days for each such offense, or by both such fine and imprisonment. Each day a person so refuses or neglects constitutes a separate offense.

(2) *[Editor's note: This version of subsection (2) is effective March 1, 2022.]* Any person who willfully fails or neglects to appear and testify or to produce books, papers, or records required by subpoena, duly served upon him or her in any matter conducted under this part 7 commits a petty offense. Each day a person so refuses or neglects constitutes a separate offense.

§ 12-10-716, C.R.S. Immunity.

Editor's note: *This section is similar to former §12-61-906 as it existed prior to 2019.*

A person participating in good faith in the filing of a complaint or report or participating in an investigation or hearing before the board or an administrative law judge pursuant to this part 7 shall be immune from any liability, civil or criminal, that otherwise might result by reason of the action.

§ 12-10-717, C.R.S. Bond required – rules.

Editor's note: *This section is similar to former §12-61-907 as it existed prior to 2019.*

(1) Before receiving a license, an applicant shall post with the board a surety bond in an amount prescribed by the board by rule. A licensed mortgage loan originator shall maintain the required bond at all times. The surety bond may be held by the individual mortgage loan originator or may be in the name of the company by which the mortgage loan originator is employed. The board may adopt rules to further define surety bond requirements.

(2) The surety shall not be required to pay a person making a claim upon the bond until a final determination of fraud, forgery, criminal impersonation, or fraudulent representation has been made by a court with jurisdiction.

(3) The surety bond shall require the surety to provide notice to the board within thirty days if payment is made from the surety bond or if the bond is cancelled.

§ 12-10-718, C.R.S. Fees.

Editor's note: *This section is similar to former §12-61-908 as it existed prior to 2019.*

The board may set the fees for issuance and renewal of licenses and registrations under this part 7. The fees shall be set in amounts that offset the direct and indirect costs of implementing this part 7 and section 38-40-105. The money collected pursuant to this section shall be transferred to the state treasurer, who shall credit it to the division of real estate cash fund created in section 12-10-215.

§ 12-10-719, C.R.S. Attorney general – district attorney – jurisdiction.

Editor's note: *This section is similar to former §12-61-909 as it existed prior to 2019.*

The attorney general shall have concurrent jurisdiction with the district attorneys of this state to investigate and prosecute allegations of criminal violations of this part 7.

* *§ 12-10-720, C.R.S. Violations – injunctions.*

Editor's note: *This section is similar to former §12-61-910 as it existed prior to 2019.*

(1) (a) *[Editor's note: This version of subsection (1)(a) is effective until March 1, 2022.]* Any individual violating this part 7 by acting as a mortgage loan originator in this state without having obtained a license or by acting as a mortgage loan originator after that individual's license has been revoked or during any period for which the license may have been suspended is guilty of a class 1 misdemeanor and shall be punished as provided in section 18-1.3-501; except that, if the violator is not a natural person, the violator shall be punished by a fine of not more than five thousand dollars.

(1) (a) *[Editor's note: This version of subsection (1)(a) is effective March 1, 2022.]* Any individual violating this part 7 by acting as a mortgage loan originator in this state without having obtained a license or by acting as a mortgage loan originator after that individual's license has been revoked or during any period for which the license may have been suspended commits a class 2 misdemeanor and shall be punished as provided in section 18-1.3-501; except that, if the violator is not a natural person, the violator shall be punished by a fine of not more than five thousand dollars.

(b) Each residential mortgage loan negotiated or offered to be negotiated by an unlicensed person shall be a separate violation of this subsection (1).

(2) The board may request that an action be brought in the name of the people of the state of Colorado by the attorney general or the district attorney of the district in which the violation is alleged to have occurred to enjoin a person from engaging in or continuing the violation or from doing any act that furthers the violation. In such an action, an order or judgment may be entered awarding the preliminary or final injunction as is deemed proper by the court. The notice, hearing, or duration of an injunction or restraining order shall be made in accordance with the Colorado rules of civil procedure.

(3) A violation of this part 7 shall not affect the validity or enforceability of any mortgage.

§ 12-10-721, C.R.S. Prohibited conduct – influencing a real estate appraisal.

Editor's note: *This section is similar to former §12-61-910.2 as it existed prior to 2019.*

(1) A mortgage loan originator shall not, directly or indirectly, compensate, coerce, or intimidate an appraiser, or attempt, directly or indirectly, to compensate, coerce, or intimidate an appraiser, for the purpose of influencing the independent judgment of the appraiser with respect to the value of a dwelling offered as security for repayment of a residential mortgage loan. This prohibition shall not be construed as prohibiting a mortgage loan originator from requesting an appraiser to:

(a) Consider additional, appropriate property information;

(b) Provide further detail, substantiation, or explanation for the appraiser's value conclusion; or

(c) Correct errors in the appraisal report.

§ 12-10-722, C.R.S. Rule-making authority.

Editor's note: *This section is similar to former §12-61-910.3 as it existed prior to 2019.*

The board has the authority to promulgate rules as necessary to enable the board to carry out the board's duties under this part 7.

§ 12-10-723, C.R.S. Acts of employee – mortgage loan originator's liability.

Editor's note: *This section is similar to former §12-61-911.5 as it existed prior to 2019.*

An unlawful act or violation of this part 7 upon the part of an agent or employee of a licensed mortgage loan originator shall not be cause for disciplinary action against a mortgage loan originator unless it appears that the mortgage loan originator knew or should have known of the unlawful act or violation or had been negligent in the supervision of the agent or employee.

§ 12-10-724, C.R.S. Dual status as real estate broker – requirements.

Editor's note: *This section is similar to former §12-61-912 as it existed prior to 2019.*

(1) Unless a mortgage loan originator complies with both subsections (2) and (3) of this section, he or she shall not act as a mortgage loan originator in any transaction in which:

  (a) The mortgage loan originator acts or has acted as a real estate broker or salesperson; or

  (b) Another person doing business under the same licensed real estate broker acts or has acted as a real estate broker or salesperson.

(2) Before providing mortgage-related services to the borrower, a mortgage loan originator shall make a full and fair disclosure to the borrower, in addition to any other disclosures required by this part 7 or other laws, of all material features of the loan product and all facts material to the transaction.

(3) (a) A real estate broker or salesperson licensed under part 2 of this article 10 who also acts as a mortgage loan originator shall carry on the mortgage loan originator business activities and shall maintain the person's mortgage loan originator business records separate and apart from the real estate broker or sales activities conducted pursuant to part 2 of this article 10. The activities shall be deemed separate and apart even if they are conducted at an office location with a common entrance and mailing address if:

    (I) Each business is clearly identified by a sign visible to the public;

    (II) Each business is physically separated within the office facility; and

    (III) No deception of the public as to the separate identities of the broker business firms results.

  (b) This subsection (3) shall not require a real estate broker or salesperson licensed under part 2 of this article 10 who also acts as a mortgage loan originator to maintain a physical separation within the office facility for the conduct of its real estate broker or sales and mortgage loan originator activities if the board determines that maintaining the physical separation would constitute an undue financial hardship upon the mortgage loan originator and is unnecessary for the protection of the public.

§ 12-10-725, C.R.S. Written disclosure of fees and costs – contents – limits on fees – rules.

Editor's note: *This section is similar to former §12-61-914 as it existed prior to 2019.*

(1) A mortgage loan originator's disclosures must comply with all applicable requirements of:

  (a) The federal "Truth in Lending Act", 15 U.S.C. sec. 1601 et seq., and Regulation Z, 12 CFR 226 and 12 CFR 1026;

(b) The federal "Real Estate Settlement Procedures Act of 1974", 12 U.S.C. sec. 2601 et seq., and Regulation X, 12 CFR 1024 et seq.;

(c) The federal "Equal Credit Opportunity Act", 15 U.S.C. sec. 1691 and Regulation B, 12 CFR 202.9, 202.11, and 202.12 and 12 CFR 1002;

(d) Title V, Subtitle A of the federal "Financial Services Modernization Act of 1999", also known as the "Gramm-Leach-Bliley Act", 15 U.S.C. secs. 6801 to 6809, and the federal trade commission's privacy rules, 16 CFR 313 and 314, adopted in accordance with the federal "Gramm-Leach-Bliley Act";

(e) The federal "Home Mortgage Disclosure Act of 1975", 12 U.S.C. sec. 2801 et seq., and Regulation C, 12 CFR 203 and 12 CFR 1003, pertaining to home mortgage disclosure;

(f) The "Federal Trade Commission Act" of 1914, 15 U.S.C. sec. 45 (a), and 16 CFR 233;

(g) The federal "Telemarketing and Consumer Fraud and Abuse Prevention Act", 15 U.S.C. secs. 6101 to 6108, and the federal trade commission's telemarketing sales rule, 16 CFR 310.

(2) The board may, by rule, require mortgage loan originators to comply with other mortgage loan disclosure requirements contained in applicable statutes and regulations in connection with making any residential mortgage loan or engaging in other activity subject to this part 7.

§ 12-10-726, C.R.S. Fee, commission, or compensation – when permitted – amount.

Editor's note: *This section is similar to former §12-61-915 as it existed prior to 2019.*

(1) Except as otherwise permitted by subsection (2) or (3) of this section, a mortgage loan originator shall not receive a fee, commission, or compensation of any kind in connection with the preparation or negotiation of a residential mortgage loan unless a borrower actually obtains a loan from a lender on the terms and conditions agreed to by the borrower and mortgage loan originator.

(2) If the mortgage loan originator has obtained for the borrower a written commitment from a lender for a loan on the terms and conditions agreed to by the borrower and the mortgage loan originator, and the borrower fails to close on the loan through no fault of the mortgage loan originator, the mortgage loan originator may charge a fee, not to exceed three hundred dollars, for services rendered, preparation of documents, or transfer of documents in the borrower's file that were prepared or paid for by the borrower if the fee is not otherwise prohibited by the federal "Truth in Lending Act", 15 U.S.C. sec. 1601, and Regulation Z, 12 CFR 226, as amended.

(3) A mortgage loan originator may solicit or receive fees for third-party provider goods or services in advance. Fees for any goods or services not provided shall be refunded to the borrower, and the mortgage loan originator may not charge more for the goods and services than the actual costs of the goods or services charged by the third-party provider.

§ 12-10-727, C.R.S. Confidentiality.

Editor's note: *This section is similar to former §12-61-916 as it existed prior to 2019.*

(1) Except as otherwise provided in the federal "Secure and Fair Enforcement for Mortgage Licensing Act of 2008", 12 U.S.C. sec. 5111, the requirements under any federal law or law of this state regarding privacy or confidentiality of any information or material provided to the nationwide mortgage licensing system and registry, and any privilege arising under federal or state law, including the rules of any federal or state court with respect to the information or material, shall apply to the information or material after it has been disclosed to the nationwide mortgage licensing system and registry. The information or material may be shared with all

state and federal regulatory officials with mortgage industry oversight authority without the loss of privilege or confidentiality protections provided by federal or state law.

(2) The board may enter into agreements with other government agencies, the Conference of State Bank Supervisors or its successor organization, the American Association of Residential Mortgage Regulators or its successor organization, or other associations representing government agencies as established by rule.

(3) Information or material that is subject to privilege or confidentiality pursuant to subsection (1) of this section shall not be subject to the following:

(a) Disclosure under a federal or state law governing the disclosure to the public of information held by an officer or agency of the federal government or the respective state; or

(b) Subpoena, discovery, or admission into evidence in any private civil action or administrative process, unless with respect to a privilege held by the nationwide mortgage licensing system and registry regarding the information or material, the person to whom the information or material pertains waives the privilege, in whole or in part.

§ 12-10-728, C.R.S. Mortgage call reports – reports of violations.

Editor's note: *This section is similar to former §12-61-917 as it existed prior to 2019.*

(1) The board may require each licensee or registrant to submit to the nationwide mortgage licensing system and registry mortgage call reports, which shall be in the form and contain the information required by the nationwide mortgage licensing system and registry.

(2) The board may report violations of this part 7, enforcement actions, and other relevant information to the nationwide mortgage licensing system and registry.

§ 12-10-729, C.R.S. Unique identifier – clearly displayed.

Editor's note: *This section is similar to former §12-61-918 as it existed prior to 2019.*

Each person required to be licensed or registered shall show his or her or the entity's unique identifier clearly on all residential mortgage loan application forms and any other documents as specified by the board by rule or order.

§ 12-10-730, C.R.S. Repeal of part – subject to review.

Editor's note: *This section is similar to former §12-61-919 as it existed prior to 2019.*

(1) This part 7 is repealed, effective September 1, 2029.

(2) Before the repeal, the licensing of mortgage loan originators and the registration of mortgage companies is scheduled for review in accordance with section 24-34-104. The department shall include in its review of mortgage loan originators and mortgage companies an analysis of the number and types of complaints made about mortgage loan originators and mortgage companies and whether the licensing of mortgage loan originators and the registration of mortgage companies correlates with public protection from fraudulent activities in the residential mortgage loan industry.

III. Standards for Mortgage Lending and Servicing

§ 38-40-101, C.R.S. Mortgage broker fees – escrow accounts – unlawful act – penalty.

(1) Any funds, other than advanced for actual costs and expenses to be incurred by the mortgage broker on behalf of the applicant for a loan, paid to a mortgage broker as a fee conditioned upon the consummation of a loan secured or to be secured by a mortgage or other transfer of or

encumbrance on real estate shall be held in an escrow or a trustee account with a bank or recognized depository in this state. Such account may be any type of checking, demand, passbook, or statement account insured by an agency of the United States government.

(2) It is unlawful for a mortgage broker to misappropriate funds held in escrow or a trustee account pursuant to subsection (1) of this section.

(3) The withdrawal, transfer, or other use or conversion of any funds held in escrow or a trustee account pursuant to subsection (1) of this section prior to the time a loan secured or to be secured by mortgage or other transfer of or encumbrance on real estate is consummated shall be prima facie evidence of intent to violate subsection (2) of this section.

(4) Any mortgage broker violating any of the provisions of subsection (2) of this section commits theft as defined in section 18-4-401, C.R.S.

(5) Any mortgage broker violating any of the provisions of subsection (1) or (2) of this section shall be liable to the person from whom any funds were received for the sum of one thousand dollars plus actual damages caused thereby, together with costs and reasonable attorney fees. No lender shall be liable for any act or omission of a mortgage broker under this section.

(6) As used in this section, unless the context otherwise requires, "mortgage broker" means a person, firm, partnership, association, or corporation, other than a bank, trust company, savings and loan association, credit union, supervised lender as defined in section 5-1-301 (46), C.R.S., insurance company, federal housing administration approved mortgagee, land mortgagee, or farm loan association or duly appointed loan correspondents, acting through officers, partners, or regular salaried employees for any such entity, that engages in negotiating or offering or attempting to negotiate for a borrower, and for commission, money, or other thing of value, a loan to be consummated and funded by someone other than the one acting for the borrower.

§ 38-40-102, C.R.S. Disclosure of costs – statement of terms of indebtedness. (Repealed)

§ 38-40-103, C.R.S. Servicing of mortgages and deeds of trust – liability for interest or late fees for property taxes.

(1) (a) (I) Any person who regularly engages in the collection of payments on mortgages and deeds of trust for owners of evidences of debt secured by mortgages or deeds of trust shall promptly credit all payments which are received and which are required to be accepted by such person or his agent and shall promptly perform all duties imposed by law and all duties imposed upon the servicer by such evidences of debt, mortgages, or deeds of trust creating or securing the indebtedness.

(II) No more than twenty days after the date of transfer of the servicing or collection rights and duties to another person, the transferor of such rights and duties shall mail a notice addressed to the debtor from whom it has been collecting payments at the address shown on its records, notifying such debtor of the transfer of the servicing of his or her debt and the name, address, and telephone number of the transferee of the servicing.

(b) The debtor may continue to make payments to the transferor of the servicing of his or her loan until a notice of the transfer is received from the transferee containing the name, address, and telephone number of the new servicer of the loan to whom future payments should be made. Such notice may be combined with the notice required in subparagraph (II) of paragraph (a) of this subsection (1). It shall be the responsibility of the transferor to forward to the transferee any payments received and due after the date of transfer of the loan.

(2) The servicer of a loan shall respond in writing within twenty days from the receipt of a written request from the debtor or from an agent of the debtor acting pursuant to written authority from

the debtor for information concerning the debtor's loan, which is readily available to the servicer from its books and records and which would not constitute the rendering of legal advice. Any such response must include the telephone number of the servicer. The servicer shall not be liable for any damage or harm that might arise from the release of any information pursuant to this section.

(3) The servicer of a loan shall annually provide to the debtor a summary of activity related to the loan. Such a summary shall contain, but need not be limited to, the total amount of principal and interest paid on the loan in that calendar year.

(4) The servicer of a loan shall be liable for any interest or late fees charged by any taxing entity if funds for the full payment of taxes on the real estate have been held in an escrow account by such servicer and not remitted to the taxing entity when due.

§ 38-40-103.5, C.R.S. Notice upon transfer of servicing rights – prior servicer's offer to borrower survives transfer – definitions.

(1) As used in this section:

(a) "Borrower" means a person liable under an evidence of debt constituting a residential mortgage loan.

(b) "Evidence of debt" has the meaning set forth in section 38-38-100.3 (8).

(c) "Holder" means the holder of an evidence of debt constituting a residential mortgage loan.

(d) "Residential mortgage loan" has the meaning set forth in section 12-10-702 (21).

(e) (I) "Servicer" means a person who collects, receives, or has the right to collect or receive payments on behalf of a holder, including payments of principal, interest, escrow amounts, and other amounts due on obligations due and owing to the holder.

(II) "Servicer" includes:

(A) The person or entity to whom payments are to be sent, as listed on the most recent billing statement or payment coupon provided to the borrower; or

(B) A subsidiary, affiliate, or assignee of a servicer, however designated, including a person designated as a subservicer.

(2) A servicer to whom servicing rights for a residential mortgage loan have been sold or transferred by the holder or by a predecessor servicer is subject to, and shall honor, the borrower's acceptance, prior to the sale or transfer of servicing rights, of any offer previously made by the holder or predecessor servicer in connection with a modification of a residential mortgage loan.

(3) At the time of the transfer or sale of servicing rights for a residential mortgage loan, the transferor or seller shall inform the buyer or transferee of the servicing rights whether a loan modification is pending.

(4) A contract for the transfer or sale of servicing rights for a residential mortgage loan must obligate the successor servicer to:

(a) Accept and continue processing any pending loan modification requests; and

(b) Honor any trial and permanent loan modification agreements entered into by the prior servicer.

§ 38-40-104, C.R.S. Cause of action – attorney fees.

(1) If any applicant or debtor is aggrieved by a violation of section 38-40-102, 38-40-103, or 38-40-103.5 and the violation is not remedied in a reasonable, timely, and good faith manner by the party obligated to do so, and after a good faith effort to resolve the dispute is made by the

debtor or borrower, the debtor or borrower may bring an action in a court of competent jurisdiction for any such violation. If the court finds that actual damages have occurred, the court shall award to the debtor or borrower, in addition to actual damages, the amount of one thousand dollars, together with costs and reasonable attorney fees.

(2) A transferee from a lender is not liable for any act or omission of the lender under section 38-40-102. A transferee of servicing or collection rights is not liable for any act or omission of the transferor of those rights under section 38-40-103 or 38-40-103.5.

§ 38-40-105, C.R.S. Prohibited acts by participants in certain mortgage loan transactions – unconscionable acts and practices – definitions.

(1) The following acts by any mortgage broker, mortgage originator, mortgage lender, mortgage loan applicant, real estate appraiser, or closing agent, other than a person who provides closing or settlement services subject to regulation by the division of insurance, with respect to any loan that is secured by a first or subordinate mortgage or deed or trust lien against a dwelling are prohibited:

(a) To knowingly advertise, display, distribute, broadcast, televise, or cause or permit to be advertised, displayed, distributed, broadcast, or televised, in any manner, any false, misleading, or deceptive statement with regard to rates, terms, or conditions for a mortgage loan;

(b) To make a false promise or misrepresentation or conceal an essential or material fact to entice either a borrower or a creditor to enter into a mortgage agreement when, under the terms and circumstances of the transaction, he or she knew or reasonably should have known of such falsity, misrepresentation, or concealment;

(c) To knowingly and with intent to defraud present, cause to be presented, or prepare with knowledge or belief that it will be presented to or by a lender or an agent thereof any written statement or information in support of an application for a mortgage loan that he or she knows to contain false information concerning any fact material thereto or if he or she knowingly and with intent to defraud or mislead conceals information concerning any fact material thereto;

(d) To facilitate the consummation of a mortgage loan agreement that is unconscionable given the terms and circumstances of the transaction;

(e) To knowingly facilitate the consummation of a mortgage loan transaction that violates, or that is connected with a violation of, section 12-10-713.

(f) (Deleted by amendment, L. 2009, (HB 09-1085), ch. 303, p. 1638, §4, effective August 5, 2009.)

(1.5) (Deleted by amendment, L. 2009, (HB 09-1085), ch. 303, p. 1638, §4, effective August 5, 2009.)

(1.7) (a) A mortgage broker or mortgage originator shall not commit, or assist or facilitate the commission of, the following acts or practices, which are hereby deemed unconscionable:

(I) Engaging in a pattern or practice of providing residential mortgage loans to consumers based predominantly on acquisition of the foreclosure or liquidation value of the consumer's collateral without regard to the consumer's ability to repay a loan in accordance with its terms; except that any reasonable method may be used to determine a borrower's ability to repay. This subparagraph (I) shall not apply to a reverse mortgage that complies with article 38 of title 11, C.R.S.

(II) Knowingly or intentionally flipping a residential mortgage loan. As used in this subparagraph (II), "flipping" means making a residential mortgage loan that refinances an existing residential mortgage loan when the new loan does not have reasonable, tangible net benefit to the consumer considering all of the circumstances, including the terms of both the new and refinanced loans, the cost of the new loan, and the consumer's circumstances. This subparagraph (II) applies regardless of whether the interest rate, points, fees, and charges paid or payable by the consumer in connection with the refinancing exceed any thresholds specified by law.

(III) Entering into a residential mortgage loan transaction knowing there was no reasonable probability of payment of the obligation by the consumer.

(b) Except as this subsection (1.7) may be enforced by the attorney general or a district attorney, only the original parties to a transaction shall have a right of action under this subsection (1.7), and no action or claim under this subsection (1.7) may be brought against a purchaser from, or assignee of, a party to the transaction.

(2) (a) Except as provided in subsection (5) of this section, if a court, as a matter of law, finds a mortgage contract or any clause of the contract to have been unconscionable at the time it was made, the court may refuse to enforce the contract, or it may enforce the remainder of the contract without the unconscionable clause, or it may so limit the application of any unconscionable clause as to avoid any unconscionable result.

(b) When it is claimed or appears to the court that the contract or any clause thereof may be unconscionable, the parties shall be afforded a reasonable opportunity to present evidence as to its commercial setting, purpose, and effect, to aid the court in making the determination.

(c) (I) In order to support a finding of unconscionability, there must be evidence of some bad faith overreaching on the part of the mortgage broker or mortgage originator such as that which results from an unreasonable inequality of bargaining power or under other circumstances in which there is an absence of meaningful choice on the part of one of the parties, together with contract terms that are, under standard industry practices, unreasonably favorable to the mortgage broker, mortgage originator, or lender.

(II) This paragraph (c) shall not apply to an unconscionable act or practice under subsection (1.7) of this section.

(3) A violation of this section shall be deemed a deceptive trade practice as provided in section 6-1-105 (1)(uu), C.R.S.

(4) The provisions of this section are in addition to and are not intended to supersede the deceptive trade practices actionable at common law or under other statutes of this state.

(5) No right or claim arising under this section may be raised or asserted in any proceeding against a bona fide purchaser of such mortgage contract or in any proceeding to obtain an order authorizing sale of property by a public trustee as required by section 38-38-105.

(6) The following acts by any real estate agent or real estate broker, as defined in section 12-10-201 (6), in connection with any residential mortgage loan transaction, are prohibited:

(a) If directly engaged in negotiating, originating, or offering or attempting to negotiate or originate for a borrower a residential mortgage loan transaction, the real estate agent or real estate broker shall not make a false promise or misrepresentation or conceal an essential or material fact to entice either a borrower or lender to enter into a mortgage loan agreement when the real estate agent or real estate broker actually knew or, under the terms and circumstances of the transaction, reasonably should have known of such falsity, misrepresentation, or concealment.

(b) If not directly engaged in negotiating, originating, or offering or attempting to negotiate or originate for a borrower a residential mortgage loan transaction, the real estate agent or real estate broker shall not make a false promise or misrepresentation or conceal an essential or material fact to entice either a borrower or lender to enter into a mortgage loan agreement when the real estate agent or real estate broker had actual knowledge of such falsity, misrepresentation, or concealment.

(7) As used in this section, unless the context otherwise requires:

(a) "Consumer" has the meaning set forth in section 5-1-301, C.R.S.

(b) "Dwelling" has the meaning set forth in section 5-1-301, C.R.S.

(c) "Mortgage broker" has the same meaning as "mortgage loan originator" as set forth in section 12-10-702 (14).

(d) "Mortgage lender" has the meaning set forth in section 12-10-702 (13).

(e) "Mortgage originator" has the same meaning as "mortgage loan originator" as set forth in section 12-10-702 (14).

(f) "Originate" has the same meaning as "originate a mortgage" as set forth in section 12-10-702 (17).

(g) "Residential mortgage loan" has the meaning set forth in section 12-10-702 (21).

IV. Loan Fraud

Legislative declaration

(1) The general assembly hereby determines that mortgage lending has a significant effect upon Colorado's economy; an estimated two trillion five hundred billion dollars in mortgage loans were made in the United States in 2005; an estimated eighty percent of reported mortgage fraud involves collusion by industry insiders; and Colorado's per capita incidents of mortgage fraud is one of the ten highest in the nation.

(2) The general assembly hereby declares that the high rates of mortgage fraud in Colorado are unacceptable and that residential mortgage fraud shall not be tolerated. The general assembly further declares that the goals of Colorado law are to deter residential mortgage fraud and to make the victim whole.

§ 18-4-401, C.R.S. Theft.

(9) (a) If a person is convicted of or pleads guilty or nolo contendere to theft by deception and the underlying factual basis of the case involves the mortgage lending process, a minimum fine of the amount of pecuniary harm resulting from the theft shall be mandatory, in addition to any other penalty the court may impose.

(b) A court shall not accept a plea of guilty or nolo contendere to another offense from a person charged with a violation of this section that involves the mortgage lending process unless the plea agreement contains an order of restitution in accordance with part 6 of article 1.3 of this title that compensates the victim for any costs to the victim caused by the offense.

(c) The district attorneys and the attorney general have concurrent jurisdiction to investigate and prosecute a violation of this section that involves making false statements or filing or facilitating the use of a document known to contain a false statement or material omission relied upon by another person in the mortgage lending process.

(d) Documents involved in the mortgage lending process include, but are not limited to, uniform residential loan applications or other loan applications; appraisal reports; HUD-1 settlement statements; supporting personal documentation for loan applications such as W-2 forms, verifications of income and employment, bank statements, tax returns, and payroll stubs; and any required disclosures.

(e) For the purposes of this subsection (9):

(I) "Mortgage lending process" means the process through which a person seeks or obtains a residential mortgage loan, including, without limitation, solicitation, application, or origination; negotiation of terms; third-party provider services; underwriting; signing and closing; funding of the loan; and perfecting and releasing the mortgage.

(II) "Residential mortgage loan" means a loan or agreement to extend credit, made to a person and secured by a mortgage or lien on residential real property, including, but not limited to, the refinancing or renewal of a loan secured by residential real property.

(III) "Residential real property" means real property used as a residence and containing no more than four families housed separately.

§ 13-21-125, C.R.S. Civil actions for theft in the mortgage lending process.

A person who suffers damages as a result of a violation of section 18-4-401, C.R.S., in the mortgage lending process, as defined by section 18-4-401 (9) (e) (I), C.R.S., shall have a private civil right of action against the perpetrator, regardless of whether the perpetrator was convicted of the crime. A claim arising under this section shall not be asserted against a bona fide purchaser of a mortgage contract.

* *§ 18-5-208, C.R.S. Dual contracts to induce loan.*

[Editor's note: This version of this section is effective until March 1, 2022.] It is a class 3 misdemeanor for any person to knowingly make, issue, deliver, or receive dual contracts for the purchase or sale of real property. The term "dual contracts", either written or oral, means two separate contracts concerning the same parcel of real property, one of which states the true and actual purchase price and one of which states a purchase price in excess of the true and actual purchase price, and is used, or intended to be used, to induce persons to make a loan or a loan commitment on such real property in reliance upon the stated inflated value.

[Editor's note: This version of this section is effective March 1, 2022.] It is a class 2 misdemeanor for any person to knowingly make, issue, deliver, or receive dual contracts for the purchase or sale of real property. The term "dual contracts", either written or oral, means two separate contracts concerning the same parcel of real property, one of which states the true and actual purchase price and one of which states a purchase price in excess of the true and actual purchase price, and is used, or intended to be used, to induce persons to make a loan or a loan commitment on such real property in reliance upon the stated inflated value.

. . . .

Loan fraud has become one of the largest areas of white-collar crime and is a recurring subject of Commission disciplinary actions. Loan fraud includes falsified loan applications; fictitious income, employment, or deposit verifications; false occupancy claims; undisclosed buyer rebates or credits; and a host of other items, which can be considered dual contracting.

Loan fraud may also result in disbarment by HUD from all federal programs, large fines, and federal prosecution. Since virtually all loan programs are affiliated with the federal government in either the primary or secondary mortgage market, disbarment can mean the end of a career in real estate, appraisal, and lending or related fields.

Chapter 9: Mortgage Loan Originator Rules and Regulations and Position Statements

An * in the left margin indicates a change in the statute, rule, or text since the last publication of the manual.

I. Mortgage Loan Originator Rules

DEPARTMENT OF REGULATORY AGENCIES
DIVISION OF REAL ESTATE

RULES REGARDING MORTGAGE LOAN ORIGINATORS
4 CCR 725-3

CHAPTER 1: DEFINITIONS

1.1. Active: A current, Valid license that allows a person to engage in residential mortgage loan origination activities.

1.2. Address: The street address, city, state and postal code.

1.3. Advertisement: Has the same meaning as set forth in 12 C.F.R. §1026.2(a)(2) as incorporated by reference in Rule 1.39.

1.4. Applicant: A natural person that submits an application to the Board to perform the activities of a Mortgage Loan Originator.

1.5. Application: Has the same meaning as set forth in 12 C.F.R. §1026.2(a)(3) and 12 C.F.R.§1024.2(b) as incorporated by reference in Rule 1.39.

1.6. Board: The Board of Mortgage Loan Originators as defined pursuant to section 12-10-702(3), C.R.S.

1.7. Board Insurance Policy: The qualified insurance carrier contracted by the Board to offer a group policy of errors and omissions insurance pursuant to section 12-10-707, C.R.S. The qualified insurance carrier of the Board Insurance Policy may be found on the Division's website.

1.8. Bona Fide Nonprofit Organization: An organization that complies with the following criteria:

A. Has the status of tax-exempt organization under Section 501(c)(3) of the Internal Revenue Code of 1986, incorporated by reference in compliance with Section 24-4-103(12.5), C.R.S., and does not include later amendments or editions of the Code. A certified copy of the Code is readily available for public inspection at the offices of the Board of Mortgage Loan Originators at 1560 Broadway Suite 925, Denver, Colorado. The Internal Revenue Code of 1986 may be examined at the internet website of the Internal Revenue Service at www.irs.gov. The Internal Revenue Service may also be contacted at 1999 Broadway, Denver, Colorado 80202 or by telephone at (303) 446-1675;

B. Promotes affordable housing or provides homeownership education, or similar services;

C. Conducts its activities in a manner that serves public and charitable purposes, rather than commercial purposes;

D. Receives funding and revenue and charges fees in a manner that does not incentivize it or its Employees to act other than in the best interests of its clients;

E. Compensates its Employees to act only in the best interests of its clients; and

F. Provides or identifies for the borrower residential mortgage loans with terms favorable to the borrower and comparable to mortgage loans and housing assistance provided under the government housing assistance programs.

1.9. Business Day: Has the same meaning as set forth in 12 C.F.R. §1026.2(a)(6) and 12 C.F.R.§1024.2(b) as incorporated by reference in Rule 1.39.

1.10. Business Name: The company for which individuals who originate a mortgage, offer to originate a mortgage, act as a mortgage loan originator, or offer to act as a mortgage loan originator are officers, partners, members, managers, owners, exclusive agents, contractors, independent contractors or Employees.

1.11. Colorado Lock-in Disclosure: means the Colorado Lock-in Disclosure form created by the Board of Mortgage Loan Originators. This form is to be used for any loan application or transaction that is not under the authority of the TILA-RESPA Integrated Disclosure Rule as defined and incorporated by reference in Board Rule 1.39. This disclosure may be found on the Division of Real Estate's Website. A mortgage loan originator may use an alternate form if the alternate form includes all information required on the Colorado Lock-in Disclosure form, as determined by the Board.

1.12. Consumer Credit: may be either closed-end or open-end credit. It is credit that is extended primarily for personal, family, or household purposes. It excludes business and agricultural loans, and loans exceeding $25,000 that are not secured by real property or a dwelling. It also must be extended by a "creditor".

1.13. Director: The Director of the Division as defined pursuant to section 12-10-101(1), C.R.S.

1.14. Division: The Colorado Division of Real Estate as defined pursuant to section 12-10-101(2), C.R.S.

1.15. Employee: An individual whose manner and means of performance of work are subject to the right of control of, or are controlled by, a person, and whose compensation for federal income tax purposes is reported, or required to be reported, on a W-2 form issued by the controlling person.

1.16. Family Member: A person who is related by blood, marriage, civil union, or adoption.

1.17. Fee: The prescribed non-refundable license fee as set by the Division.

1.18. Good Faith Estimate Disclosure: Is the same disclosure form established in the Real Estate Settlement Procedures Act, specific to Regulation X, Appendix C as incorporated by reference in Rule 1.39.

1.19. Housing Finance Agency: An authority that is chartered by the State of Colorado to help meet the affordable housing needs of the residents of Colorado; is supervised directly or indirectly by the state government; is subject to audit and review by the State of Colorado; and whose activities make it eligible to be a member of the National Council of State Housing Agencies.

1.20. HUD Approved Housing Counseling Agency: is an agency which is either a private or public nonprofit organization that is exempt from taxation under Section 501(a) pursuant to Section 501(c), of the Internal Revenue Code of 1996, 26, U.S.C. 501(a) and 501(c), and approved by the U.S. Department of Housing and Urban Development, in accordance with Housing Counseling Program Handbook 7610.1 and Code of Federal Regulations Title 24, Part 214.

1.21. Inactive: A Mortgage Loan Originator who holds a Valid license shown in the Board's records as being Inactive is not permitted to engage in residential mortgage loan origination activities. To maintain licensure on Inactive status, a Mortgage Loan Originator must still continue to renew their license and meet the continuing education requirements as set forth in Chapters 3 and 4 of these Rules.

1.22. Independent Contractor: An individual who performs his or her duties other than at the direction of and subject to the supervision and instruction of an individual who is licensed by the Board or is not required to be licensed based on one of the following:

A. The individual is lawfully registered with, and maintains a unique identifier through, the Nationwide Mortgage Licensing System and Registry, and who is an Employee of:

1. A depository institution;
2. A subsidiary that is:
   a. Owned and controlled by a depository institution; and
   b. Regulated by a Federal banking agency; or
3. An institution regulated by the Farm Credit Administration; or

B. An individual who is an Employee of a federal, state, or local government agency or housing finance agency and who acts as a loan originator only pursuant to his or her official duties as an Employee of a federal, state, or local government agency or housing finance agency; or

C. An Employee of a bona fide nonprofit organization who acts as a loan originator only with respect to his or her work duties to the bona fide nonprofit organization, and who acts as a loan originator only with respect to residential mortgage loans with terms that are favorable to the borrower.

1.23. Jurisdiction: All fifty (50) states, the District of Columbia, Guam, Puerto Rico, and the U.S. Virgin Islands.

1.24. Loan Modification: A temporary or permanent change in one or more of the terms of a mortgagor's existing loan, allows the loan to be reinstated, and often results in a more affordable mortgage payment. The borrower retains ownership of the real property and the mortgage note and the deed of trust remains intact.

1.25. Loan Modifier: An individual who in the course of the person's business, vocation, or occupation offers to assist, provide, or negotiate on behalf of a borrower to facilitate the receipt of a loan modification from the borrower's current mortgage lender, generally for a fee or other thing of value.

1.26. Mortgage Company: Has the same meaning pursuant to section 12-10-702(12), C.R.S.

1.27. Mortgage Loan Originator or MLO: Has the same meaning pursuant to section 12-10-702(14), C.R.S.

1.28. Nationwide Mortgage Licensing System and Registry or NMLS: A mortgage licensing system developed to track the licensing and registration of mortgage loan originator as further defined in section 12-10-702(15), C.R.S. The system is also known as the Nationwide Multistate Licensing System and Registry.

1.29. Offering or Negotiating Terms of a Residential Mortgage Loan: To present for consideration to a borrower or prospective borrower particular residential mortgage loan terms, or to communicate directly or indirectly with a borrower, or prospective borrower for the purpose of reaching a mutual understanding about prospective residential mortgage loan terms. An individual's generic referral to or recommendation of a particular lender in and of itself, is not offering or negotiating the terms of a residential mortgage loan.

1.30. Petitioner: For the purposes of implementing the provisions of Chapter 7 of these Rules, any person who has filed with the Board a petition or has been granted leave to intervene by the Board for a declaratory order pursuant to section 24-4-105(11), C.R.S. and as set forth in Chapter 7 of these Rules.

1.31. Physical Address: The physical location of the property.

1.32. Practice Act: The Mortgage Loan Originator Licensing and Mortgage Company Registration Act found at section 12-10-701, et. seq., C.R.S.

1.33. Rate: The teaser rate, payment rate or interest rate used to determine a borrower's monthly payment or deferred interest specific to reverse mortgage transactions.

1.34. Responsible Mortgage Loan Originator or Responsible MLO: A Mortgage Loan Originator who holds an Active license and is shown in the Board records as supervising the actions and residential mortgage loan origination activities of the Mortgage Loan Originator holding a temporary license.

1.35. Safe and Secure Manner: Reasonable measures are taken to minimize the risk of loss, damage, or theft.

1.36. Short Sale: The sale of a real property for less than the mortgage loan balance. In the settlement of the short sale transaction the existing mortgage is extinguished. Any deficiency created from the settlement of the transaction may be transformed into a promissory note, charged off, forgiven, or pursued as a judgment against the previous owner.

1.37. Sponsor or Sponsorship: A relationship status as shown in the records of the NMLS between a Mortgage Company and a Mortgage Loan Originator. The Mortgage Loan Originator will only conduct business under the Mortgage Company as shown in the records of the NMLS.

1.38. Taking a Residential Mortgage Loan Application: The receipt of a residential mortgage loan application by an individual for the purpose of facilitating a decision whether to extend an offer of residential mortgage loan terms to a borrower or prospective borrower, whether the application is received directly or indirectly from the borrower or prospective borrower. An individual's generic referral to or recommendation of a particular lender, in and of itself, is not taking a residential loan application.

1.39. TILA-RESPA Integrated Disclosure Rule: means the Consumer Financial Protection Bureau's Integrated Mortgage Disclosures final rule, set forth in 12 C.F.R. § 1024, et seq., the Real Estate Settlement Procedures Act (Regulation X), and in 12 C.F.R. § 1026, et seq., the Truth in Lending Act (Regulation Z), effective October 3, 2015, incorporated by reference in compliance with Section 24-4-103(12.5), C.R.S., and does not include any later amendments or editions of the final rule. A certified copy of the TILA-RESPA Integrated Disclosure rule is readily available for public inspection at the offices of the Board of Mortgage Loan Originators at 1560 Broadway, Suite 925, Denver, Colorado. The TILA-RESPA Integrated Disclosure rule may be examined at the internet website of the Consumer Financial Protection Bureau at www.consumerfinance.gov. The Consumer Financial Protection Bureau may also be contacted at 1700 G Street, NW, Washington, D.C. 20552 or by telephone at (202)435-7000.

1.40. Truth-in-Lending Disclosure: Is the same disclosure form established by the Truth in Lending Act, specific to Regulation Z, Appendices H-2, H-3, H-4(a), (b), (c) and (d) as incorporated by reference in Rule 1.39.

1.41. Uniform Residential Loan Application: Is the Freddie Mac form 65 or the Fannie Mae form 1003 used in residential loan transactions on properties of four or fewer units.

1.42. Valid: A license that is approved and shown in the Board's records as either Active or Inactive as well as being eligible for renewable status.

CHAPTER 2: REQUIREMENTS FOR LICENSURE

2. 1. Pre-Licensing Education Requirement

An Applicant must successfully complete the twenty (20) hours of pre-licensing education reviewed and approved by the NMLS or by a company contracted by the NMLS for the review and approval of pre- licensing courses.

A. Colorado specific pre-licensing education

1. Effective March 1, 2016, Applicants must also complete two (2) hours of Colorado specific pre-licensing education reviewed and approved by the NMLS or by a company contracted by the NMLS for the review and approval of pre-licensing courses.
2. The two (2) hours of Colorado specific education replaces what was a required general elective within the twenty (20) hours of pre-licensing education.
3. Applicants may also complete the two (2) hours of Colorado specific pre-licensing education as a standalone course outside of the twenty (20) hour pre-licensing education.
4. The two (2) hours of Colorado specific education must have a final course examination that covers all major topics covered in the course. Applicants must receive a passing score of seventy-five percent (75%) on the Colorado specific education examination.

B. Completion of pre-licensing education

1. New license or expired license for three or more years

   Applicants who have never held a license or held a license that has expired for three (3) or more years in Colorado or any other Jurisdiction must satisfactorily complete twenty (20) hours of pre-licensing education within the three (3) year period immediately the date of application for licensure.

2. Holds a Valid license or expired license for less than three years

   Applicants who hold a Valid license or held a license that has expired for less than three (3) years in Colorado or any other Jurisdiction must complete the Colorado specific education as set forth in subsection A.1. of this Rule if not previously taken.

C. Course audits

The Board or the Board's designee may audit courses set forth in this Rule at any time and at no cost. The Board may request from each course provider all related instructional materials, student attendance records and other information that may be necessary for an audit. The purpose of the audit is to ensure adherence to the approved course of study by verifying the course material and instruction are consistent with acceptable educational principles; and that instruction is provided in a manner that the desired learning objectives are met. Failure to comply with relevant statutes and these Rules may result in the withdrawal of the approval of the course provider, instructor, and/or course.

2. 2. S.A.F.E. Mortgage Loan Originator Examination Requirement

The S.A.F.E. Mortgage Loan Originator Examination is developed by the NMLS and consists of the national examination with the Uniform State Test content.

A. An Applicant must successfully pass the examination in accordance with the policies and procedures developed and administered by the NMLS.

B. Applicants must comply with NMLS test administration standards and any test administration required by the testing service provider.

C. An Applicant may retake the examination three (3) consecutive times with each consecutive time occurring at least thirty (30) days after the preceding examination.

D. After failing three (3) consecutive examinations, an Applicant must wait at least six (6) months before taking the examination again.

E. A Mortgage Loan Originator who fails to maintain a Valid license in any Jurisdiction for a period of five (5) years or longer must retake the examination prior to re-application for licensure, not taking into account any time during which such individual was licensed.

2. 3. Criminal Background Check Requirement

Pursuant to section 12-10-704(6), C.R.S., an Applicant must submit a set of fingerprints to the Colorado Bureau of Investigation for the purpose of conducting a state and national criminal history record check prior to submitting an application to the Division. Fingerprints must be submitted to the Colorado Bureau of Investigation for processing in a manner acceptable to the Colorado Bureau of Investigation. Fingerprints must be readable and all personal identification data completed in a manner satisfactory to the Colorado Bureau of Investigation. The Board may, however, acquire a name-based criminal history record check for an Applicant who has twice submitted to a fingerprint-based criminal history record check and whose fingerprints are unclassifiable.

2.4. NMLS Requirement

Each Applicant must register with the NMLS in accordance with policies and procedures established by the NMLS. The Applicant, at minimum, must provide the following information to NMLS:

A. A complete and accurate registration application, including the authorization of the NMLS to obtain a credit report and information related to any administrative, civil or criminal findings by any governmental Jurisdiction;

B. Submission of a set of fingerprints to the NMLS in accordance with policies and procedures established by the NMLS; and

C. Payment of any fees associated with the NMLS registration application.

2.5. Temporary Authority Eligibility and Temporary License

A. Temporary authority eligibility requirements

To be eligible for Temporary Authority to act as Mortgage Loan Originator, the Applicant must meet the following requirements:

1. The Applicant has met either one of the following classifications:

   a. Registered in the NMLS as a loan originator for a depository (i.e. bank or savings association) as defined in section 12-10-709(1)(b), C.R.S. during the one (1) year period preceding the date of application for a temporary license; or

   b. A license issued as a mortgage loan originator in another Jurisdiction during the thirty (30) day period preceding the date of application for a temporary license.

2. The Applicant must be eligible for temporary authority in accordance with policies and procedures as established by the NMLS.

3. The Applicant must be an Employee and Sponsored by a Colorado NMLS registered Mortgage Company.

4. An Applicant has not had any of the following administrative, civil or criminal actions:

   a. An application for a mortgage loan originator license denied in any Jurisdiction;

   b. A mortgage loan originator license revoked or suspended in any Jurisdiction;

   c. Has been subject to, or served with a cease and desist order; and

   d. Has been convicted of, or pled guilty or nolo contendere to, a misdemeanor or felony pursuant to sections 12-10-711(1)(b), (2)(b)(I), and (2)(c), C.R.S

B. Temporary license

1. Applicants seeking a temporary license and who are eligible for Temporary Authority as set forth in subsection A. of this Rule will be granted one (1) temporary license. Additional or extended temporary licenses will be prohibited.

2. Any temporary license issued by the Board will have the same force and effect of a license for the period of time it is in effect.

3. A temporary license will expire on one (1) of the following dates, whichever is sooner:

   a. The Applicant withdraws their application for a license;

   b. The Board denies the Applicant's application for a license;

   c. The Board approves and issues a license;

   d. Supervision termination date between the Responsible Mortgage Loan Originator and the Mortgage Loan Originator holding a temporary license; or

   e. One hundred twenty (120) calendar days after the date the Applicant was issued a temporary license.

4. A Mortgage Loan Originator holding a temporary license must be an Employee and Sponsored by a Colorado NMLS registered Mortgage Company and must be supervised by a Responsible Mortgage Loan Originator.

   a. The Responsible Mortgage Loan Originator will be held responsible under all applicable provisions of law, including without limitation the Practice Act and these Rules, for the actions of the Mortgage Loan Originator holding a temporary license, and are personally subject to all applicable penalties under the law.

   b. Responsible Mortgage Loan Originators must notify the Division, in a manner acceptable to the Board, the beginning and ending dates of supervision for Mortgage Loan Originators holding a temporary license.

   c. Responsible Mortgage Loan Originators will be held responsible for the activities of Mortgage Loan Originators holding a temporary license through and including the date of the temporary license expiration or termination of supervision, whichever is sooner.

2.6. Surety Bond Requirement

A. Options for surety bonds

Pursuant to section 12-10-717, C.R.S., Mortgage Loan Originators are deemed compliant with the surety bond requirement if one (1) of the three (3) options are satisfied:

1. Mortgage Loan Originators, at a minimum, may acquire and maintain an individual surety bond if:

   a. The surety bond is in the amount of twenty-five thousand dollars ($25,000);

   b. The surety bond is in conformance with all relevant Colorado statutory requirements;

   c. The surety bond is exclusive to covering acts contemplated under the Practice Act;

   d. The surety bond is not applicable to any conduct or transactions outside the jurisdiction of the Board; and

   e. The surety bond is identical to the individual surety bond form developed and approved by the Board.

2. Mortgage Loan Originators who are Employees or exclusive agents for companies with less than twenty (20) individuals who are required to be licensed pursuant to the Practice Act and who do not work for more than one (1) company, may, at a minimum, operate under their company's surety bond if the surety bond meets the following criteria:

   a. The surety bond is in the amount of one hundred thousand dollars ($100,000);

   b. The surety bond is in conformance with all relevant Colorado statutory requirements;

   c. The surety bond is exclusive to covering acts of all of the company's Employees or exclusive agents contemplated under the Practice Act; and

d. The surety bond is identical to the individual surety bond form developed and approved by the Board.

3. Mortgage Loan Originators who are Employees or exclusive agents for companies with twenty (20) or more individuals who are required to be licensed pursuant to the Practice Act and who do not work for more than one (1) company, may, at a minimum, operate under a company's surety bond if the surety bond meets the following criteria:

a. The surety bond is in the amount of two hundred thousand dollars ($200,000);

b. The surety bond is in conformance with all relevant Colorado statutory requirements;

c. The surety bond is exclusive to covering acts of all of the company's Employees or exclusive agents contemplated under the Practice Act; and

d. The surety bond is identical to the company surety bond form developed and approved by the Board.

B. Entity surety bonds

Regarding entity surety bonds as set forth in subsections A.2. and A.3. of this Rule, the Mortgage Company must provide the Board or an authorized representative of the Board with any and all requested surety bonds relevant to the Practice Act and as set forth in this Rule. The Mortgage Company must verify and provide adequate proof regarding the timeline of employment for each individual Mortgage Loan Originator operating under such company policy. Failure on the part of the Mortgage Company to provide such information will result in non-compliance regarding the surety bond requirement for the individual Mortgage Loan Originators operating under such entity bond.

C. Continuous surety bond coverage

Mortgage Loan Originators are required to provide proof of continuous surety bond coverage and that all required information is current. Mortgage Loan Originators may update all required information electronically on the Division's website.

D. Disciplinary action for failure to maintain surety bond

Any Mortgage Loan Originator who fails to obtain and maintain a surety bond as set forth in this Rule or fails to provide proof of continuous coverage will be subject to disciplinary action.

2.7. Errors and Omissions Insurance Requirement

Pursuant to section 12-10-707, C.R.S., every Mortgage Loan Originator holding an Active license must have in effect a policy of errors and omissions insurance to cover all acts requiring a license. Mortgage Loan Originators may obtain errors and omissions coverage through the Board Insurance Policy or may obtain errors and omissions coverage independent of the Board Insurance Policy.

A. Board insurance policy

1. The Division may enter into a contract with an insurance carrier to make available the Board Insurance Policy under the following terms and conditions:

a. The insurance carrier must be in compliance with all applicable statutes established by the Colorado Division of Insurance.

b. The insurance carrier is licensed or authorized to write policies of errors and omissions insurance in this State.

c. The insurance carrier should maintain an A.M. Best rating of "A-"or better.

d. The insurance carrier will collect premiums, maintain records and report names of those insured and a record of claims to the Division on a timely basis and at no expense to the Division.

e. The insurance carrier has been selected through a competitive bidding process.

2. The Board Insurance Policy must provide, at a minimum, the following terms of coverage:

   a. The contract and policy are in conformance with all relevant Colorado statutory requirements;

   b. Coverage includes all acts for which a license is required, except those illegal, fraudulent, or other acts which are normally excluded from such coverage;

   c. Coverage must encompass all types of transactions conducted by the Mortgage Loan Originator and must be in the individual Mortgage Loan's Originator's name;

   d. Coverage cannot be canceled by the insurance carrier except for nonpayment of the premium or in the event the Mortgage Loan Originator's license becomes Inactive or is revoked or an Applicant is denied a license. Cancellation notice must be provided in a manner that complies with section 10-4-109.7(1), C.R.S.;

   e. Coverage is for not less than one hundred thousand dollars ($100,000) per covered claim, with an annual aggregate limit of not less than three hundred thousand dollars ($300,000), not including costs of investigation and defense;

   f. Coverage contains a deductible no greater than one thousand dollars ($1,000), or a deductible no greater than twenty thousand dollars ($20,000) for policies that primarily insure reverse mortgage transactions; and

   g. Prior acts coverage must be offered to Mortgage Loan Originators with continuous past coverage.

B. Independent policies

For independent policies that are either individual and entity/group policies, the insurance carrier must be in compliance with all applicable statutes pursuant to the Colorado Division of Insurance and is licensed or authorized to write policies of errors and omissions insurance in this State. The insurance carrier should maintain an A.M. Best rating of "A- "or better.

1. Mortgage Loan Originators, at a minimum, may acquire and maintain individual errors and omissions insurance in their own name with the following terms of coverage:

   a. The contract and policy are in conformance with all relevant Colorado statutory requirements;

   b. Coverage includes all acts for which a license is required, except those illegal, fraudulent, or other acts which are normally excluded from such coverage;

   c. Coverage must encompass all types of transactions conducted by the Mortgage Loan Originator and must be in the individual Mortgage Loan Originator's name;

   d. Coverage is for not less than one hundred thousand dollars ($100,000) per covered claim, with an annual aggregate limit of not less than three hundred thousand dollars ($300,000), not including costs of investigation and defense;

   e. Coverage contains a deductible no greater than one thousand dollars ($1,000), or a deductible no greater than twenty thousand dollars ($20,000) for policies that primarily insure reverse mortgage transactions; and

   f. Prior acts coverage must be offered to Mortgage Loan Originators with continuous past coverage.

2. Mortgage Loan Originators who are Employees or exclusive agents for companies with less than twenty (20) individuals who are required to be licensed pursuant to the Practice Act and who do not work for more than one (1) company, may, at a minimum, operate under the company's errors and omissions insurance policy if the policy meets the following terms of coverage:

   a. The contract and policy are in conformance with all relevant Colorado statutory requirements;

   b. Coverage includes all acts for which a license is required, except those illegal, fraudulent, or other acts which are normally excluded from such coverage;

   c. Coverage must include all activities contemplated under the Practice Act and states this in the policy;

   d. Coverage must encompass all types of transactions conducted by all of the Mortgage Loan Originators employed at the company or by all Mortgage Loan Originators who are exclusive agents of the company;

   e. Coverage is for not less than one million dollars ($1,000,000) per covered claim, with an annual aggregate limit of not less than one million dollars ($1,000,000), not including costs of investigation and defense;

   f. Coverage contains a deductible no greater than fifty thousand dollars ($50,000); and

   g. Prior acts coverage must be offered to Mortgage Loan Originators with continuous past coverage.

3. Mortgage Loan Originators who are Employees or exclusive agents for companies with twenty (20) or more individuals and who do not work for more than one (1) company, may, at a minimum, operate under the company's errors and omissions insurance policy if the policy meets the following terms of coverage:

   a. The contract and policy are in conformance with all relevant Colorado statutory requirements;

   b. Coverage includes all acts for which a license is required, except those illegal, fraudulent, or other acts which are normally excluded from such coverage;

   c. Coverage must include all activities contemplated under the Practice Act and states this in the policy;

   d. Coverage must encompass all types of transactions conducted by all of the Mortgage Loan Originators employed at the company or by all Mortgage Loan Originators who are exclusive agents of the company;

   e. Coverage is for not less than one million dollars ($1,000,000) per covered claim, with an annual aggregate limit of not less than two million dollars ($2,000,000), not including costs of investigation and defense;

   f. Coverage contains a deductible no greater than hundred thousand dollars ($100,000); and

   g. Prior acts coverage must be offered to Mortgage Loan Originators with continuous past coverage.

C. Entity errors and omissions insurance policies

Regarding entity errors and omissions insurance policies as set forth in subsections B.2. and B.3. of this Rule, the Mortgage Company must provide the Board, or an authorized representative of the Board, with any and all requested errors and omissions insurance policies relevant to the Practice Act and as set forth in this Rule. The Mortgage Company must verify and provide adequate proof regarding the timeline of employment for each individual Mortgage Loan Originator operating under such entity policy. Failure on the part of the Mortgage Company to provide such information will result in non-compliance regarding the errors and omissions insurance requirement for individual Mortgage Loan Originators operating under the entity's errors and omissions insurance policy.

D. Continuous insurance coverage

Mortgage Loan Originators are required to provide proof of continuous errors and omissions insurance coverage and that all required information is current. The Mortgage Loan Originator may update all required information electronically on the Division's website.

E. Disciplinary action for failure to maintain insurance

A Mortgage Loan Originator who fails to obtain and maintain an errors and omissions insurance coverage as set forth in this Rule or fails to provide proof of continuous coverage will be subject to disciplinary action.

2.8. Application Process for Licensure

A. Applying for an initial license

An Applicant for Initial Licensure as a Colorado Mortgage Loan Originator must successfully complete the requirements as set forth below:

1. Submit a set of fingerprints to the Colorado Bureau of Investigation within one (1) year immediately preceding the date of application as set forth in Rule 2.3.;
2. Register with the NMLS as set forth in Rule 2.4.;
3. Submit a set of fingerprints to the NMLS as set forth in subsection B. of Rule 2.4;
4. Successfully complete the requisite educational requirements as set forth in Rule 2.1.;
5. Take and successfully pass the S.A.F.E. Mortgage Loan Originator Examination as set forth in Rule 2.2.;
6. Acquire a surety bond as required by section 12-10-717, C.R.S. and as set forth in Rule 2.6. prior to obtaining an Active license;
7. Acquire errors and omissions insurance required by section 12-10-707, C.R.S. and as set forth in Rule 2.7. prior to obtaining an Active license;
8. Submit a complete and accurate "Mortgage Loan Originator License Application"; and
9. Pay the Fee.

B. Applying for a temporary license

An Applicant applying for a temporary license that is eligible for temporary authority must meet the following requirements:

1. Submit a set of fingerprints to the NMLS as set forth in subsection B. of Rule 2.4.;
2. Register for temporary authority with the NMLS as set forth in subsection A.2. of Rule 2.5.;
3. Be an Employee and Sponsored by a Colorado NMLS registered mortgage company as set forth in subsections A.3. and B.4. of Rule 2.5.; and
4. Within seven (7) business days from notice of the issuance of temporary authority from the NMLS, the Applicant must complete the following state specific requirements pursuant to section 12-10-711(11), C.R.S.:

   a. Submit a set of fingerprints to the Colorado Bureau of Investigation as set forth in Rule 2.3.;

   b. Acquire a surety bond pursuant to section 12-10-717, C.R.S. and as set forth in Rule 2.6.;

c. Acquire errors and omissions insurance pursuant to section 12-10-707, C.R.S. and as set forth in Rule 2.7.;

d. Identify the Responsible Mortgage Loan Originator as set forth in subsections A.3. and B.4. of Rule 2.5.;

e. Submit a complete and accurate "Mortgage Loan Originator License Application"; and

f. Pay the Fee.

C. Once an Applicant fully complies with the Practice Act and these Rules as determined by the Board, the Board will issue a license to the Applicant pursuant to section 12-10-704, C.R.S.

2.9. Invalid Payment

If the Fees accompanying any application made to the Board are paid for by check and the check is not immediately paid upon presentment to the bank upon which the check was drawn, or if payment is submitted in any other manner and payment is denied, rescinded, or returned as invalid, the application will be canceled. The application or renewal must be re-submitted to the Board along with full payment of any Fees and payment of the fee required by State Fiscal Rules for the clerical services necessary for invalid payment.

2.10. Review of Application Completeness

All applications will be reviewed by the Division for completeness of all required. If the application is deemed incomplete by the Division, the Applicant will be notified in writing of the deficiencies identified within the application and will have thirty (30) days to provide the documentation; otherwise, the application will be canceled and the Fee will be forfeited.

2.11. Applicants with Prior or Pending Criminal Record

Pursuant to sections 12-10-704, 12-10-711, and 24-5-101, C.R.S., Applicants who have at any time in the past been convicted of, entered a plea of guilty to, entered a plea of nolo contendere, received a deferred judgment and sentence to a misdemeanor (excluding misdemeanor traffic violations) or a felony or any like municipal code violation, or has such charges pending must submit with their application the required documentation as listed below. If the required documentation is no longer available, the Applicant must provide written confirmation by the appropriate authority that such documentation is no longer available. For any charges or convictions which have been dismissed, expunged, or sealed, the Applicant must include court document(s) evidencing the dismissal, expungement, or sealing of the criminal case(s). Failure to provide the required documentation within the time frame as set forth in Rule 2.10. will result in the cancellation of the application and forfeiture of the Fee. In addition to the required documentation, Applicants may submit supplemental documentation as listed below to demonstrate their rehabilitation, truthfulness, financial responsibility, character, and general fitness for consideration by the Board.

A. Required documentation includes:

1. Court case disposition, registry of action, or a case action summary, which must include the following information:

a. Offense(s) convicted of;

b. Statute(s) or municipal code(s) violated;

c. Classification(s) of offense(s) (i.e. felony or misdemeanor);

d. Date of conviction;

e. Date of sentencing;

f. Sentencing Terms; and

g. Status of case.

i. If the sentencing and probation terms have been completed, the status of case should show as closed or dismissed.

ii. If the sentencing and probation terms have not been completed, documentation must be submitted that shows current compliance with the sentencing and probation terms. Proof of current compliance should include a letter from the parole or probation officer and, if applicable, a payment history from the court showing a current account balance of payment.

2. Police Officer's report(s), arrest report(s), or incident report(s);
3. A signed written explanation of the circumstances surrounding each violation and, including the statement attesting that "I have no other criminal violations either past or pending, other than those I have stated on the application"; and
4. Any other information or documentation that the Board deems necessary.

B. Supplemental documentation includes:

1. Employment history for the preceding five (5) years;
2. Letter(s) of recommendation; and
3. A personal written statement that demonstrates and evidences the Applicant's rehabilitation, financial responsibility, character, and general fitness.

2.12. Applicants with Past or Pending Administrative Disciplinary Actions or Findings

Pursuant to sections 12-10-704 and 12-10-711, C.R.S., an Applicant who has any past or pending administrative disciplinary actions or findings of a mortgage loan originator license or any other professional license from Colorado or any other Jurisdiction must submit with their application any of the following information and documentation as listed below that is relevant and available to the Applicant. If the required documentation is no longer available or accessible, the Applicant must provide written confirmation by the appropriate authority that such documentation is no longer available or the reasons why the document is not accessible. Failure to provide the required documentation within the time frame as set forth in Rule 2.10. will result in the cancellation of the application and forfeiture of the Fee.

A. Any final agency order(s);

B. Any consent order(s);

C. Any stipulation(s);

D. Any investigative report(s); and

E. A signed written explanation of the circumstances surrounding each disciplinary actions.

2.13. Preliminary Advisory Opinion

Prior to an application for a license or a registration through the NMLS, a person may request the Board issue a preliminary advisory opinion. A person seeking a preliminary advisory opinion is not an Applicant for licensure. The Board may, at its sole discretion, issue an opinion which will not be binding on Board; is not appealable; and will not limit the Board's authority to investigate a future application for licensure. However, if the Board issues a positive or favorable opinion, the Board may elect to adopt such opinion as the final decision of the Board without further investigation or hearing. The issuance of a negative or unfavorable opinion will not prohibit a person from submitting an application for licensure.

A. A person may request a preliminary advisory opinion regarding the potential effect of the following, but not limited to:

1. Any criminal conviction(s), plea(s) of guilt or nolo contendere, deferred judgment(s) and sentence for criminal offense(s) in a domestic, foreign or military court.

2. Having been enjoined in the immediately preceding five (5) years under domestic or foreign laws from engaging in deceptive conduct relating to the origination of a mortgage loan;
3. Having professional licenses, certifications or registrations issued by Colorado, the District of Columbia, any other states or foreign countries, revoked or suspended for fraud, theft, deceit, material misrepresentations or the breach of a fiduciary duty and such suspension or revocation denied authorization to practices as: a mortgage loan originator or similar license; real estate broker; real estate appraiser; an insurance producer; an attorney; a securities broker-dealer; a securities sales representative; an investment advisor; or an investment advisor representative; or
4. Having been assessed a civil or criminal penalty for violating any provision of the Colorado Consumer Protection Act.

B. A person requesting an opinion must do so in a form prescribed by the Board. Such form must be supported and documented by, without limitation, the following:

1. Pending or Past Criminal Record

   The required and supplemental documentation as set forth in Rule 2.11. for any pending or past criminal record.

2. Pending or Past Professional Disciplinary Action(s)

   The documentation as set forth in Rule 2.12. for any pending or past professional conduct.

CHAPTER 3: CONTINUING EDUCATION REQUIREMENTS

3.1. The continuing education requirements for Mortgage Loan Originators will begin after issuance of the initial license.

A. Mortgage Loan Originators will complete at least eight (8) hours of continuing education courses, which must be reviewed and approved by the NMLS or by a company contracted by the NMLS to review and approve continuing education courses.

B. The continuing education requirements must be completed each calendar year prior to renewal or reinstatement.

3.2. Completion of the twenty (20) hours of pre-licensing education approved by the NMLS in the same year in which the initial license was approved, will satisfy the continuing education requirements in that calendar year.

3.3. Repealed (Effective March 1, 2016)

3.4. Repealed (Effective March 1, 2016)

3.5. At any time and at no cost, the Board or the Board's authorized representative may audit any continuing education courses reviewed and approved by the NMLS or by a company contracted by the NMLS to review and approve continuing education courses. The Board or the Board's authorized representative may request all related instructional materials, student attendance records, and other information that may be necessary for the audit. The purpose of the audit is to ensure adherence to the approved course of study by verifying the course material and instruction are consistent with acceptable educational principles; and that instruction is provided in a manner that the desired learning objectives are met. Failure to comply with relevant statutes and these Rules may result in the withdrawal of the approval of the course provider, instructor, and/or the course.

CHAPTER 4: RENEWAL, REINSTATEMENT, RE-APPLICATION, OR LICENSE STATUS

4.1. Renewal for Mortgage Loan Originators

A. There are two (2) existing databases that Mortgage Loan Originators must independently renew their Colorado license through annually. The two (2) independent databases include:

1. The nationwide registration database managed by the NMLS.
2. The license database managed by the Division. This database may be located by visiting the Division's website.

B. Mortgage Loan Originators must annually renew their license, regardless whether on Active or Inactive status, through the NMLS in accordance with the timelines, policies, and procedures established by the NMLS. The NMLS may collect fees for the purpose of registration applications, renewal applications, reinstatement applications, credit reports, criminal background checks and for other processes associated with registration through the nationwide database.

C. After renewing through the NMLS as set forth in subsection B. of this Rule, Mortgage Loan Originators must then annually renew their license, whether on Active or Inactive status, through the Division's license database as described in subsection A.2. of this Rule and pay the Fee. Mortgage Loan Originators whose license is on Inactive status are not required to maintain errors or omissions insurance as set forth in Rule 2.7. or a surety bond as set forth in Rule 2.6. Mortgage Loan Originators with an Inactive license, however, are required to stay current on all continuing education requirements as set forth in Chapter 3 of these Rules in order to renew their license.

D. The Board will issue or deny a renewal application within thirty (30) days after the applicant has submitted all of the information necessary for renewal and after the Board has received all information necessary to make a determination regarding the Mortgage Loan Originator's compliance.

E. For both databases as described in subsection A. of this Rule, the renewal period begins November 1st and ends December 31st of each calendar year. In order for Mortgage Loan Originators to renew their license, the Mortgage Loan Originator must be compliant with the Practice Act and these Rules.

F. All licenses expire at midnight on December 31st of each calendar year if the has not properly renewed their license as set forth in this Rule.

G. Mortgage Loan Originators who failed to renew their license and the license has expired may choose to reinstate their Colorado license as set forth in Rule 4.2.

4.2. Reinstatement for Mortgage Loan Originators

A. Mortgage Loan Originators who failed to renew their license in both databases as described in subsection A. of Rule 4.1. and the license has expired may reinstate their Colorado license. The reinstatement period for both databases as described in subsection A of Rule 4.1. begins January 1st and ends on the last day of February of each calendar year. In order for Mortgage Loan Originators to reinstate their Colorado license, the individual must be compliant with the Practice Act and these Rules.

B. The Fee for reinstatement is one and one half times the amount of the current renewal Fee.

C. To reinstate a Colorado license, a Mortgage Loan Originator must complete the renewal process as set forth in subsections B. and C. of Rule 4.1.

D. A Mortgage Loan Originator who failed to reinstate their Colorado license during the reinstatement period must re-apply as set forth in Rule 4.3.

4.3. Re-application for Mortgage Loan Originators

A. Expired Colorado license for less than three years

Mortgage Loan Originators who held a Colorado license that has expired for less than three (3) years after the date of license expiration must complete the requirements as set forth below:

1. Submit a set of fingerprints to the Colorado Bureau of Investigation within one (1) year immediately preceding the date of application as set forth in Rule 2.3.;
2. Register with the NMLS as set forth in Rule 2.4.;
3. Submit a set of fingerprints to the NMLS as set forth in subsection B. of Rule 2.4.;
4. If not previously taken, successfully complete the two (2) hours of Colorado specific education as set forth in Rule 2.1.;
5. If applicable, successfully complete at least eight (8) hours of "late" continuing education courses, which must include one (1) hour of Colorado specific education, reviewed and approved by the NMLS or by a company contracted to review and approve continuing education courses;
6. Acquire a surety bond pursuant to section 12-10-717, C.R.S. and as set forth in Rule 2.6. prior to obtaining an Active license;
7. Acquire errors and omissions insurance pursuant to section 12-10-717, C.R.S. and as set forth in Rule 2.7. prior to obtaining an Active license;
8. Submit a complete and accurate "Mortgage Loan Originator License Application"; and
9. Pay the Fee.

B. Expired Colorado license for a period of three years but Less than five years

Mortgage Loan Originators who held a Colorado license that has expired for a period of three (3) years but less than five (5) years after the date of license expiration must complete the requirements as set forth below:

1. Submit a set of fingerprints to the Colorado Bureau of Investigation within one (1) year immediately preceding the date of application as set forth in Rule 2.3.
2. Register with the NMLS as set forth in Rule 2.4.;
3. Submit a set of fingerprints to the NMLS as set forth in subsection B. of Rule 2.4.;
4. If applicable, successfully complete the relevant pre-licensing educational requirements as set forth in Rule 2.1.;
5. If applicable, successfully complete at least eight (8) hours of "late" continuing education courses reviewed and approved by the NMLS or by a company contracted to review and approve continuing education courses;
6. Acquire a surety bond pursuant to section 12-10-717, C.R.S. and Board as set forth in Rule 2.6. prior to obtaining an Active license;
7. Acquire errors and omissions insurance pursuant to section 12-10-707, C.R.S. and Board as set forth in Rule 2.7. prior to obtaining an Active license;
8. Submit a complete and accurate "Mortgage Loan Originator License Application"; and
9. Pay the Fee.

C. Expired Colorado license for a period of five or more years

Mortgage Loan Originators who held a Colorado license that has expired for a period of five (5) or more years after the date of license expiration must complete the requirements as set forth below:

1. Comply with all requirements set forth in subsection B. of this Rule; and
2. If applicable, retake and successfully pass the S.A.F.E. Mortgage Loan Originator examination, developed by the NMLS as set forth in Rule 2.2.

4.4. Individuals who do not have an Active license are prohibited from practicing as a Mortgage Loan Originator. Additionally, individuals who do not have an Active license are prohibited from engaging in any mortgage related activities which require licensure pursuant to the Practice Act, these Rules, or as prescribed by Board position statement.

4.5. Renewal, Reinstatement, and Re-application for Mortgage Companies.

A. Mortgage Companies must renew their registration on the nationwide database as described in subsection A.1. of Rule 4.1.

B. Mortgage Companies renewing, reinstating or re-applying for registration through the NMLS shall must do so in accordance with the timelines, policies, and procedures set established by the NMLS. The NMLS may collect fees for the purpose of registration applications, renewal applications, reinstatement applications, credit reports, criminal background checks and for other processes associated with registration through the nationwide database.

C. The Board must issue or deny a registration renewal application within thirty (30) days after the Mortgage Company has submitted all of the information necessary for license renewal or reinstatement and after the Board has received all information necessary to make a determination regarding the Mortgage Company's compliance.

D. The registration renewal period begins November 1st and ends December 31st of each calendar year. In order for Mortgage Companies to renew their registration must be compliant with the Practice Act and these Rules.

E. All registrations expire at midnight on December 31st of each calendar year if the Mortgage Company has not properly renewed their registration as set forth in this Rule.

F. Mortgage Companies who failed to renew their registration through the nationwide database in subsection A.1. of Rule 4.1. and the registration has expired, may choose to reinstate their registration. The reinstatement period for reinstatement begins January 1st and ends on the last day of February of each calendar year. In order for Mortgage Companies to reinstate their registration, the Mortgage Company must be compliant with the Practice Act and these Rules.

G. Mortgage Companies who failed to reinstate their registration must re-apply on the nationwide database as described in subsection A.1. of Rule 4.1. in order for the Board to review their registration applications and determine whether the Mortgage Company is compliant with the registration requirements.

H. All renewal, reinstatement, or re-application fees must be paid through the NMLS and are non-refundable.

4.6. Mortgage Companies that do not have an approved registration are prohibited from acting through Employees or other individuals who takes residential loan applications or offers or negotiates terms of a residential mortgage loan. Additionally, Mortgage Companies that do not have an approved registration are prohibited from engaging in any mortgage related conduct that requires a registration pursuant to the Practice Act, these Rules, or as prescribed by the Board by position statement.

4.7. Mortgage Loan Originator License Inactivation and Reactivation

If a license is inactivated by the Board or an authorized representative of the Board for one or any combination of the following reasons, the Mortgage Loan Originator must pay an administrative Fee determined by the Board in order to reactivate their Colorado license:

A. The Mortgage Loan Originator has failed or is failing to comply with the surety bond requirements pursuant to sections 12-10-704(8) and 12-10-717, C.R.S. or as set forth in Rule 2.6.;

B. The Mortgage Loan Originator has failed or is failing to comply with the errors and omissions insurance pursuant to section 12-10-707, C.R.S. or as set forth in Rule 2.7.;

C. The Mortgage Loan Originator has failed or is failing to maintain current contact information, surety bond information, or errors and omissions insurance information as required by this Part 7 or by any Rule of the Board that directly or indirectly addresses such requirements;

D. The Mortgage Loan Originator has failed or is failing to respond to an investigation;

E. The Mortgage Loan Originator has failed or is failing to comply with any of the education or testing requirements set forth in this Part 7or in any rule of the Board that directly or indirectly addresses education or testing requirements; or

F. The Mortgage Loan Originator has failed or is failing to register with and provide all required information to the NMLS.

4.8. Mortgage Loan Originators who have an Inactive license are prohibited from practicing as a Mortgage Loan Originator. Additionally, Mortgage Loan Originators who have an Inactive license are prohibited from engaging in any mortgage related activities which requires licensure pursuant to the Practice Act, these Rules, or as prescribed by Board position statement.

4.9. In order for an Inactive license to be reactivated, the Mortgage Loan Originator seeking reactivation must provide the Board with proof of full compliance with the Practice Act and these Rules.

4.10. No changes in license status, whether Active or Inactive, will be made except in the manner acceptable to the Board to effect such change and upon payment of the Fee for such change request.

CHAPTER 5: PROFESSIONAL STANDARDS

5.1. Advertising

Any Advertisement of a residential mortgage loan product or Rate offered by a Mortgage Loan Originator, or Mortgage Company must conform to the following requirements:

A. An Advertisement must be made only for such products and terms as are actually available at the time they are offered and, if their availability is subject to any material requirements or limitations, the Advertisement must specify those requirements or limitations;

B. The Advertisement must contain the following, each of which must be clearly and conspicuously included in the Advertisement;

1. At least one (1) responsible party. The responsible party must be a Mortgage Loan Originator or a Mortgage Company. The responsible party must include their registration number that is approved on the NMLS;
2. The name of the Mortgage Company; and
3. The business phone number of the responsible party.

C. The Advertisement must not appear to be offered by a government agency, a quasi-government agency or the perspective borrower's current lender and/or loan servicer;

D. An Advertisement must not make or omit any statement the result of which would be to present a misleading or deceptive impression to consumers;

E. An Advertisement shall must otherwise comply with all applicable state and federal disclosure requirements;

F. Advertisements must incorporate applicable provisions of the final Interagency Guidance on Nontraditional Mortgage Product Risks ("Interagency Guidance") released on September 29, 2006, incorporated by reference in compliance with section 24-4-103(12.5), C.R.S., and does not include any later amendments or editions of the final guidance. A certified copy of the Interagency Guidance is readily available for public inspection at the Office of the Board of Mortgage Loan Originators at 1560 Broadway, Suite 925, Denver, Colorado. The Interagency Guidance released by the Office of the Comptroller of the Currency, the Board of Governors of the Federal Reserve System, the Federal Deposit Insurance Corporation, the Office of Thrift supervision, and the National Credit Union Administration can be examined at the internet website of the federal register (volume 71, number 192, page 58609-58618) at www.federalregister.gov. Reference copies of the federal register publications may also be found at the Colorado Supreme Court, located at 101 w. Colfax, Denver, Colorado 80202 or by telephone at (303) 837-3720; and

G. The responsible party must retain copies of all Advertisements for a period of four (4) years, and provide said copies for inspection by an authorized representative of the Board upon request.

5.2. The Requirements Set Forth in Subsection B. of Rule 5.1. will Not Apply to:

A. Any Advertisement which indirectly promotes a Consumer Credit transaction and which contains only the name of the Mortgage Company, the name and title of the Mortgage Loan Originator, the contact information for the Mortgage Company or the Mortgage Loan Originator, a Mortgage Company's logo, or any license or registration numbers, such as the inscription on a coffee mug, pen, pencil, youth league jersey, sign, business card, or other promotional item; or

B. Any rate sheet, pricing sheet, or similar proprietary information provided to real estate brokers, builders, and other commercial entities that is not intended for distribution to consumers.

5.3. Loan Modifier Licensure

A. Individuals, not otherwise exempt from Part 7, who directly or indirectly take residential Loan Modification applications or who negotiate, offer, or attempt to negotiate or offer Loan Modifications are required to be licensed as a Mortgage Loan Originator.

B. Mortgage Loan Originators must comply with Practice Act and these Rules.

5.4. Required Use of a Loan Modification Contract

A. Mortgage Loan Originators taking Loan Modification applications or offering or negotiating Loan Modifications are required to use a loan modification contract which complies with the Practice Act and the Foreclosure Protection Act.

B. The Board has created the Colorado Loan Modification Services Contract to ensure compliance with the aforementioned laws. This contract may be found on the Division website. Loan Modifiers must use this form or an alternate form, if such alternate form clearly includes all information required on the suggested form, as determined by the Board.

C. The Colorado Loan Modification Services contract as set forth in this Rule must be completed at time of Application.

5.5. The Requirements Set Forth in Rules 5.3. and 5.4. will Not Apply to:

A. Employees of HUD Approved Housing Counseling Agencies who are providing advice or general information on Loan Modifications in an ancillary manner relating to their general housing counseling services or duties.

B. Employees of mortgage loan servicing companies operating on behalf of the borrowers' mortgage lenders.

C. Licensed real estate brokers engaged in real estate brokerage services within the defined Short Sale transactions do not need to maintain a license as a Mortgage Loan Originator. If a real estate broker engages in the activities of providing Loan Modification services, separate licensure as a Mortgage Loan Originator is required.

D. An attorney, pursuant to section 12-10-709(1)(c), C.R.S., who renders services in the course of practice, who is licensed in Colorado, and who is not primarily engaged in the business of negotiating residential mortgage loans or Loan Modifications is not required to be licensed as a Mortgage Loan Originator.

5.6. Reasonable Inquiry

A. A Mortgage Loan Originator will only recommend appropriate products after reasonable inquiry has been made in order to understand the borrower's current and prospective financial status.

B. Reasonable inquiry requires the Mortgage Loan Originator to review and analyze the information submitted by the borrower(s) regarding their current and prospective income, including the income's source and likely continuance and may not require the Mortgage Loan Originator to verify such income.

C. A Mortgage Loan Originator has a duty to recommend mortgage products based on the information provided by the borrower.

D. A Mortgage Loan Originator will be deemed in compliance with section 12-10-710(1)(b), C.R.S., and this Rule, concerning reasonable inquiry, upon reviewing and analyzing all sections contained in the Uniform Residential Loan Application and upon completion of the Tangible Net Benefit Disclosure. The Tangible Net Benefit Disclosure is posted on the Division's website.

5.7. Tangible Net Benefit

The reasonable, tangible net benefit standard in pursuant to 12-10-710(1)(a), C.R.S., is inherently dependent upon the totality of facts and circumstances relating to a specific transaction. While the refinancing of certain home loans may clearly provide a reasonable, tangible net benefit, others may require closer scrutiny, or consideration to determine whether a particular loan provides the requisite benefit to the borrower.

A. When determining reasonable, tangible net benefit, there are many considerations a Mortgage Loan Originator must take into account in their analysis. If applicable, the required considerations for a Mortgage Loan Originator determining the requisite benefit must include, but are not limited to:

1. Lower payments;
2. Condensed amortization schedule;
3. Debt consolidation;
4. Cash out;
5. Avoiding foreclosure;
6. Negative amortization;
7. Balloon payments;
8. Variable rates;

9. Interest only options;
10. Prepayment penalties; and
11. Hybrid mortgage products.

B. The purpose for a purchase or refinance transaction will be identified by the borrower. A Mortgage Loan Originator will require that all borrowers describe, in writing, the reasons they are seeking a mortgage loan, a Loan Modification or to refinance an existing mortgage loan.

1. It is the responsibility of the Mortgage Loan Originator to ensure this information is acquired and accurately documented.
2. Pursuant to section 12-10-710(1), C.R.S., a Mortgage Loan Originator may not have demonstrated a duty of good faith and fair dealing in all communications and transactions with a borrower if it is determined that a Mortgage Loan Originator completed the required purpose for a purchase, Loan Modification or refinance transaction without analyzing the borrower's specific circumstances.

5.8. Tangible Net Benefit Disclosure Form

The Board developed a disclosure form regarding reasonable, tangible net benefit. Alternate disclosures are acceptable if they include all information required on the suggested form, as determined by the Board.

A. The Tangible Net Benefit Disclosure Form must be disclosed within three (3) Business Days after receipt of a loan Application.

B. The Tangible Net Benefit Disclosure will also be completed prior to or at the closing if the reasonable, tangible net benefit has changed.

C. The Tangible Net Benefit Disclosure must be signed by both the Mortgage Loan Originator and the borrower(s).

D. Mortgage Loan Originator must be able to provide proof to the Board or an authorized representative of the Board that the disclosure forms as set forth in this Rule were provided to the borrower within three (3) Business Days after receipt of a loan Application, or prior to or at closing if any subsequent changes to any loan terms requiring re-disclosure.

5.9. Mortgage Loan Originator and Mortgage Company Duty to Respond and Provide Requested Documents for Investigations

A. Mortgage Loan Originators and Mortgage Companies must provide the Board or the Board's authorized representative with all information required by this Rule.

1. Mortgage Loan Originators and Mortgage Companies will receive written notification and a copy of the complaint from the Board or an authorized representative of the Board that an investigation has been initiated. All requested information must be submitted in accordance with the timeline established in the notification letter. An extension of time may be requested.

   a. The Mortgage Loan Originator and Mortgage Company may request an extension of time to comply if:

      i. The request is reasonable and in writing; and

      ii. The request is received by the Board or authorized representative of the Board prior to the expiration date as set forth in the notification letter sent by the Board or authorized representative of the Board.

   b. Any and all extensions granted are at the discretion of the Board or an authorized representative of the Board.

2. Failure to provide all requested information will will be grounds for disciplinary action regardless of whether the underlying complaint results in further investigation or subsequent action by the Board.

B. The response from the Mortgage Loan Originator must contain the following:

1. The Mortgage Loan Originator must provide a complete and specific answer to the factual recitations, allegations or averments made in the complaint filed against the Mortgage Loan Originator, whether made by a member of the public or on the Board's own motion or by an authorized representative of the Board;
2. The Mortgage Loan Originator must provide a complete and specific response to all questions, allegations or averments presented in the notification letter; and
3. Any and all documents or records requested in the notification letter.

C. Mortgage Companies must maintain any and all documents collected, gathered and provided for the purpose of negotiating and originating residential mortgage loans for a period of four (4) years. Additionally, Mortgage Companies must maintain any and all documents used for the purpose of soliciting or marketing borrowers that were directed, made or caused to be made by the Mortgage Company. These documents include, but are not limited to:

1. All Uniform Residential Loan Applications (form 1003);
2. All required state and federal disclosures;
3. Asset statements;
4. Income documentation;
5. Verification of employment;
6. Verification of deposit;
7. Lender submission forms;
8. Advertisements;
9. Flyers;
10. Settlement statements;
11. Uniform underwriting and transmittal summary(form 1008); and
12. Credit report.

D. The Mortgage Loan Originator must maintain any and all documents used for the purpose of soliciting or marketing borrowers that were directed, made or caused to be made by the Mortgage Loan Originator.

E. All documents required in this Rule must be kept in a Safe and Secure Manner. Electronic storage is acceptable as long as the information is accessible.

5.10. Mortgage Loan Originators Maintaining Current Contact Information and All Information Required for Licensing

A. Mortgage Loan Originators must maintain all current contact information and all information required for licensing, in a manner acceptable to the Board, including the two (2) databases described subsection A. of Rule 4.1. Failure to maintain the information identified in this Rule will be grounds for disciplinary action.

B. Contact information must include, but is not limited to:

1. E-mail address;
2. Legal first, middle and last names;
3. Physical home address;
4. Home phone number;

5. Business address;
6. Business phone number; and
7. Business name.

C. Information required for licensing includes, but is not limited to:

1. Surety bond company;
2. Surety bond number;
3. Surety bond effective date;
4. Errors and omissions insurance provider;
5. Errors and omissions policy number;
6. Errors and omissions effective and expiration date; and
7. Convictions, pleas of guilt or nolo contendere for all crimes.

D. Mortgage Loan Originators must update the Board within thirty (30) calendar days of any changes to the information as set forth in this Rule on both databases described in subsection A. of Rule 4.1.

5.11. Repealed (Effective March 17, 2017).

5.12. Mortgage Loan Originator Agreements

A Mortgage Loan Originator must have a written correspondent or loan originator agreement with a lender before any solicitation of, or contracting with, any member of the public. A Mortgage Loan Originator is compliant with sections 12-10-713(1)(x) and (aa), C.R.S. and this rule, if they adhere to one (1) of the following requirements:

A. They individually have a written correspondent or loan originator agreement with a lender before any solicitation of, or contracting with, any member of the public;

B. They are an officer, partner, member, exclusive agent, or Employee of a company that has a written correspondent or loan originator agreement with a lender before any solicitation of, or contracting with, any member of the public;

C. They are acting as an Independent Contractor and maintain a contractual agreement with a Mortgage Company that has a written correspondent or loan originator agreement with a lender before any solicitation of, or contracting with, any member of the public; or

D. They are an Employee of a lender before any solicitation of, or contracting with, any member of the public.

5.13. Repealed (Effective March 17, 2017).

5.14. Colorado Lock-in Disclosure requirements under section 12-10-725(2), C.R.S.

A. The Colorado Lock-in Disclosure form must be used for all transactions not under the authority of the TILA-RESPA Integrated Disclosure Rule and for which the applicable GFE, HUD-1 and Truth-in-Lending Disclosures are used.

B. The Colorado Lock-in Disclosure form must be disclosed:

1. Within three (3) Business Days after receipt of a loan Application and if applicable, contain the following information:

a. The cost, terms, duration and conditions of the lock-in agreement;

b. Whether a lock-in agreement has been entered;

c. Whether the lock-in agreement is guaranteed by the Mortgage Loan Originator; and

d. Disclosure must be made if a lock-in agreement has not been entered and that the interest Rate and terms are subject to change.

2. If, after the initial written disclosure is provided, a Mortgage Loan Originator enters into a lock-in agreement, within three (3) Business Days thereafter and prior to the borrower signing loan closing documents.
3. If, after a Mortgage Loan Originator enters into a lock-in agreement, the annual percentage Rate increases from the annual percentage Rate disclosed earlier by more than 1/8 of one (1) percentage point, within three (3) Business Days of such change and prior to the borrower signing loan closing documents.
4. If, after the Mortgage Loan Originator enters into a lock-in agreement, there is a change to any of the information provided on the lock-in disclosure form, including but not limited to a lock-in extension.

C. The Colorado Lock-in Disclosure form or alternate form must be used when disclosing the secured Rate of interest for the prospective borrower or disclosing that the Rate of interest is not secured and is subject to change.

5.15. Repealed (Effective October 3, 2015).

5.16. Repealed (Effective October 3, 2015).

5.17 Repealed (Effective March 17, 2017).

5.18. Repealed (Effective October 3, 2015).

5.19. Repealed (Effective October 3, 2015).

5.20. Repealed (Effective October 3, 2015).

5.21 Mortgage Loan Originators are required to keep records of the disclosures, pursuant to sections 12-10-725(1) and (2), C.R.S., and these Rules, for a period of four (4) years, for the purposes of inspection by the Board or authorized representative of the Board.

A. All documents must be kept in a Safe and Secure Manner. Electronic storage is acceptable as long as the information is accessible.

B. The Mortgage Company for whom the Mortgage Loan Originator is an officer, partner, contractor, Independent Contractor, member, exclusive agent or an Employee may provide the requested documents to the Board. However, the Mortgage Loan Originator is responsible for compliance with the Board's request and is subject to disciplinary action if the Mortgage Company fails or refuses to provide the requested documentation.

C. The Mortgage Loan Originator must be able to provide proof to the Board or an authorized representative of the Board that the disclosure forms as set forth in this Rule were in fact provided to the borrower within three (3) Business Days after receipt of a loan Application or any subsequent changes to any loan terms requiring re-disclosure.

5.22. Dual Status Disclosure

The Board prohibits individuals from acting as a Mortgage Loan Originator and a real estate broker, on the same transaction, unless they comply with the requirements set forth in this Rule.

A. Dual status is a material fact to real estate transactions and must be disclosed to the borrower(s).

B. The Board has created the Colorado Dual Status Disclosure form to ensure this information is clearly and concisely disclosed. This disclosure may be found on the Division's website. A Mortgage Loan Originator must use this form or an alternate form, if such alternate form clearly includes all information required on the suggested form, as determined by the Board.

C. The Colorado Dual Status Disclosure form must be completed, disclosed, and provided to the borrower within three (3) Business Days after receipt of a loan Application.

D. Mortgage Loan Originators must maintain the disclosure form defined as set forth in this Rule for a period of four (4) years.

E. The Mortgage Loan Originator must be able to provide proof to the Board or an authorized representative of the Board that the disclosure forms as set forth in this Rule were provided to the borrower within three (3) Business Days after receipt of a loan Application or any subsequent changes to any loan terms requiring re-disclosure.

D. Persons who originate a mortgage, offer to originate a mortgage, act as a mortgage loan originator, or offer to act as a mortgage loan originator shall maintain the disclosure form defined by this rule for a period of five years.

E. The mortgage loan originator must be able to provide proof to the Board or an authorized representative of the Board that the disclosure forms defined in this rule were in fact provided to the borrower within three (3) business days after receipt of a loan application or any subsequent changes to any loan terms requiring re-disclosure.

5.23. Immediate notification of a conviction, plea, or violation required

Pursuant to sections 12-10-711 and 12-10-713, C.R.S., a Mortgage Loan Originator must make written notification to the Board through the online services portal found on the Division's website within thirty (30) calendar days of any of the following:

A. A plea of guilty, a plea of nolo contendere or a conviction of any felony or misdemeanor offense under Colorado law, federal law, or the laws of other states, excluding misdemeanor traffic offenses or petty offenses;

B. A violation, or aiding and abetting a violation, of the Colorado or federal fair housing laws;

C. Revocation or suspension of any license, registration, or certification issued by Colorado or another jurisdiction because of fraud, deceit, material misrepresentation, theft, or breach of a fiduciary duty; and

D. A revocation, suspension, or any other disciplinary action taken against a Mortgage Loan Originator's license in any jurisdiction.

CHAPTER 6: BOARD REVIEW OF INITIAL DECISIONS AND EXCEPTIONS

6.1. Written Form, Filing Requirements, and Service

A. All pleadings must be in written form, mailed with a certificate of mailing to the Board.

B. All pleadings must be filed by the Board on or before the date the filing is due. Computation of time for the filing timelines for Chapter 6 of these Rules is pursuant to section 2-4-108, C.R.S. A pleading is considered filed upon receipt by the Board. Chapter 6 of these Rules do not provide for any additional time for service by mail.

C. All pleadings must be filed with the Board and not with the Office of Administrative Courts. Any pleadings filed in error with the Office of Administrative Courts will not be considered. The Board's address is:

Colorado Board of Mortgage Loan Originators
1560 Broadway, Suite 925
Denver, Colorado 80202

D. All pleadings must be served on the opposing party on the date which the pleading is filed with the Board. Electronic service between the parties is encouraged. The date and manner must be noted on the certificate of service.

6.2. Initial Decision

Upon receipt of the initial decision prepared and filed by the Administrative Law Judge from the Office of Administrative Courts, the Division will timely mail a copy of the initial decision to the parties at their respective addresses of record with the Board pursuant to section 24-4-105(16)(a), C.R.S.

6.3. Board's Authority to Review the Initial Decision

Pursuant to section 24-4-105(14)(a)(II), C.R.S., the Board may initiate a review of an initial decision on its own motion within thirty (30) days of the date on which the Division mails the initial decision to the parties. A letter from the Division initiating the review of the initial decision constitutes a motion within the meaning of section 24-4-105(14)(a)(II), C.R.S.

6.4. Appeal of the Initial Decision by the Parties

A. Any party wishing to reverse or modify an initial decision of an Administrative Law Judge must file written exceptions with the Board in accordance with the procedures and time frames as set forth in Rule 6.5.

B. If neither party appeals the initial decision by filing exceptions, the initial decision will become the final order of the Board after thirty (30) days from the date on which the Division mails the initial decision pursuant to section 24-4-105(14)(b)(III), C.R.S. Failure to file exceptions will result in a waiver of the right to judicial review of the final order of the Board unless the portion of the final order subject to review differs from the contents of the initial decision pursuant to section 24-4-105(14)(c), C.R.S.

6.5. Filing of Exceptions

A. Pursuant to section 24-4-105(15)(a), C.R.S., any party seeking to file exceptions must initially file with the Board a designation of the relevant parts of the record and of parts of the transcript of the hearing within twenty (20) days of the date on which the Division mails the initial decision to the parties.

B. Transcripts:

Any party may designate the entire transcript, or may identify witness(es) whose testimony is to be transcribed, the legal ruling or argument to be transcribed, or other information necessary to identify a portion of the transcript. However, no transcript is required if the Board's review is limited to pure questions of law. The deadline for filing exceptions depends on whether either of the parties designates a portion of the transcript.

1. If the parties do not designate parts of the transcript, exceptions are due within thirty (30) days from the date on which the Division mails the initial decision to the parties. Both parties' exceptions are due on the same day.

2. Any party wishing to designate all, or any part, of the transcript must adhere to the following procedures:

   a. Transcripts will not be deemed part of a designation unless specifically identified and ordered.

   b. If one party designates a portion of the transcript, the other party may file a supplemental designation in which that party may designate additional portions of the transcript. The supplemental designation must be filed with the Board and served on the other party within ten (10) days after the date on which the original designation was filed.

   c. Any party who designates a transcript must order the transcript by the date on which they file their designation with the Board whether they are filing an original or supplemental designation.

   d. The party ordering a transcript must direct the court reporter or transcribing service to complete and file with the Board the original transcript and one (1) copy within thirty (30) days of their order.

   e. The party that designates a transcript must pay for such transcripts.

   f. Transcripts that are ordered and not filed with the Board in a timely manner due to non-payment, insufficient payment, or failure to direct as set forth above may not be considered by the Board.

g. Upon receipt of transcripts identified in all designations and supplemental designations, the Board will mail a notification to the parties stating that the transcripts have been received by the Board.

h. Exceptions are due within thirty (30) days from the date on which such notification is mailed. Both parties' exceptions are due on the same date.

C. A party's exceptions must include specific objections to the initial decision.

D. Either party may file a response to the other party's exceptions. All responses must be filed within ten (10) days of the date on which the exceptions were filed with the Board. Subsequent replies will not be considered except for good cause shown.

E. The Board may in its sole discretion grant an extension of time to file exceptions or responses, or may delegate the discretion to grant such an extension of time to the Board's authorized representative.

6.6. Request for Oral Arguments

A. All requests for oral argument must be in writing and included with a party's exceptions or response.

B. It is within the sole discretion of the Board to grant or deny a request for oral argument. The Board generally does not grant requests for oral argument. If an oral argument is granted, each party will have ten (10) minutes to present their argument. Questioning by members of the Board will not count against the allocated ten (10) minutes.

C. The Board or its authorized representative may extend the time for oral arguments upon good cause shown.

6.7. Final Orders

A. The Board may deliberate and vote on exceptions immediately following oral arguments or the Board may take the matter under advisement.

B. When the Board votes on exceptions, whether after oral arguments or at a subsequent Board meeting, the ruling of the Board will not be considered final until a written order is issued.

C. The date of the Board's final order is the date on which the written order is signed, irrespective of any motions for reconsideration that are filed.

CHAPTER 7: DECLARATORY ORDERS

7.1. Petition for a Declaratory Order

Pursuant to section 24-5-105(11), C.R.S., Petitioner may petition the Board for a declaratory order to terminate controversies or to remove uncertainties as to the applicability to any statutory provision, rule, or order of the Board as it would apply to the Petitioner.

7.2. Parties to the Proceeding

The parties to any proceeding as set forth in Chapter 7 of these Rules will be the Board and the Petitioner. Any other person may seek leave of the Board to intervene in such a proceeding. Permission to intervene will be granted at the sole discretion of the Board. A petition to intervene will set forth the same matters as set forth in Rule 7.3.

7.3. Petition Contents

Any petition filed as set forth in Chapter 7 of these Rules will state the following:

A. The name and address of the Petitioner;

B. The statute, rule, or order to which the petition relates;

C. A concise statement of all the facts and law necessary to show the nature of the controversy or uncertainty and the manner in which the statute, rule, or order in question applies or potentially applies to the Petitioner; and

D. The Petitioner may submit a concise statement of the declaratory order.

7.4. Board's Considerations Whether or Not to Rule

The Board may determine, in its sole discretion and without prior notice to the Petitioner, whether or not to rule upon a petition. In determining whether or not to rule upon a petition filed as set forth in Chapter 7 of these Rules, the Board may consider the following matters, among others:

A. Whether a ruling on the petition will terminate a controversy or remove uncertainties as to the applicability to the Petitioner of any statutory provision, rule, or order of the Board.

B. Whether the petition involves any subject, question, or issue which is the subject of a formal or informal matter or investigation currently pending before the Board or a court involving one or more of the Petitioners.

C. Whether the petition involves any subject, question, or issue which is the subject of a formal or informal matter or investigation currently pending before the Board or a court not involving the Petitioner.

D. Whether the petition seeks a ruling on a hypothetical question.

E. Whether the Petitioner has some other adequate legal remedy, other than an action for declaratory order which will terminate the controversy or remove any uncertainty as to the applicability to the Petitioner of the statute, rule, or order in question.

7.5. Board Determines Not to Rule

If the Board determines it will not rule on a petition, the Board will issue its written decision disposing of the petition, stating the reasons for declining to rule upon the petition. A copy of the decision will be provided to the Petitioner. A decision not to rule on a petition for a declaratory order is not final agency action subject to judicial review

7.6. Board Determines to Rule

If the Board determines that it will rule on the petition:

A. The Board may order the Petitioner to file an additional written brief, memorandum, statement of position, or request the Petitioner to submit additional facts or arguments in writing.

B. The Board may take administrative notice of facts pursuant to the Administrative Procedure Act, section 24-4-105(8), C.R.S., and may utilize its experience, technical competence, and specialized knowledge when ruling on the petition.

C. The Board may set the petition, upon due notice to the Petitioner, for a non-evidentiary hearing.

D. The Board may, upon due notice to the Petitioner, set the petition for hearing for the purpose of obtaining additional facts or information, or to determine the truth of any facts set forth in the petition, or to hear oral arguments on the petition. Notice to the Petitioner setting such formal hearing will set forth, to the extent known, the factual or other matters into which the Board intends to inquire. The Petitioner will have the burden of proving all of the facts stated in the petition, all of the facts necessary to show the nature of the controversy or uncertainty and the manner in which the statute, rule, or order in question applies or potentially applies to the Petitioner and any other facts the Petitioner desires the Board to consider.

E. Any ruling by the Board may be based solely on the matters set forth in the petition or may be based on any amendments to the petition, any information gathered by the Board through a non-evidentiary hearing, formal hearing or otherwise, or any facts the Board may take administrative notice of. Upon ruling on a petition, the Board will issue its written order stating its basis for the order. A copy of the order will be provided to the Petitioner.

7.7. Declaratory Orders Subject to Judicial Review

Any declaratory order of a petition as set forth in Chapter7 of these Rule will constitute agency action subject to judicial review pursuant to section 24-4-106, C.R.S.

CHAPTER 8: NATIONWIDE MULTISTATE LICENSING SYSTEM AND REGISTRY ("NMLS")

8.1. NMLS Challenge

A. A Mortgage Loan Originator may challenge information entered into the NMLS by the Division.

B. The challenge must be in writing and set forth the specific information being challenged along with any supporting evidence.

C. The grounds for a challenge will be limited to the factual accuracy of the information pertaining to the Mortgage Loan Originator's own license record.

D. A challenge submitted to appeal the underlying grounds for a disciplinary action will not be considered by the Director.

8.2 Review of NMLS Challenge

A. The Director, or an authorized representative of the Director, will review all information submitted by the Mortgage Loan Originator and will determine the merits of the challenge.

B. If the Director, or the Director's authorized representative, determines that the information submitted to the NMLS by the Division is factually incorrect, the Division will promptly submit the correct information to the NMLS.

8.3 Appeal the NMLS Challenge

A. A Mortgage Loan Originator may appeal the Director's, or the Director's authorized representative's, decision regarding the challenge to the Board within thirty (30) calendar days of the decision being rendered.

B. The decision of the Board regarding a NMLS challenge is subject to judicial review by the court of appeals by appropriate proceedings under section 24-4-106(11), C.R.S.

8.4 Call Reports

All Mortgage Companies must submit the NMLS Mortgage Call Report on a calendar quarterly basis, as set forth below, and must contain the required information as set forth by the NMLS.

A. A Mortgage Company must identify the applicable NMLS Mortgage Call Report. This includes, but is not limited to, the standard section and the expanded section of the NMLS Mortgage Call Report. The Mortgage Company must identify and complete the report on behalf of all employed Mortgage Loan Originators or other Mortgage Loan Originators that operate through their Mortgage Company.

B. The quarterly report is due within forty-five (45) calendar days of the end of the calendar quarter and the financial condition report of the standard section is due annually ninety (90) calendar days from the Mortgage Company's fiscal year end.

C. Mortgage Companies must comply with any rules, policies and procedures relating to the submission of a Mortgage Call Report that are prescribed by the NMLS.

D. Failure to properly submit a NMLS Mortgage Call Report in a timely manner prescribed by the NMLS will prevent the Mortgage Company from renewing their NMLS registration.

1-1-2 [Repealed effective 1/14/2014]

1-1-4 [Repealed effective 1/14/2014]

1-1-5 [Repealed effective 1/14/2014]

1-2-2 [Repealed effective 1/14/2014]

1-3-1 [Repealed effective 1/14/2014]

1-4-1 [Repealed effective 1/14/2014]

1-5-1 [Repealed effective 1/14/2014]

3-1-4 [Repealed effective 1/10/2014]

II. Mortgage Loan Originator Position Statements

Position Statement – MB 1.1 [Repealed]

Position Statement – MB 1.2 [Repealed]

Position Statement – MLO 1.3 – Board Position on Individuals Not Required to be Licensed – Supervisors and Support Staff (revised 09/18/2013) – effective 11/14/2013

The Board of Mortgage Loan Originators ("Board") issues this position statement to provide clarification to the mortgage industry regarding when supervisors and support staff of mortgage loan originators are not required to be licensed.

Supervision of Licensed Individuals:

Persons who directly or indirectly supervise mortgage loan originators, defined as those individuals who either take residential loan applications or offer or negotiate terms of a residential mortgage loan, are not required to hold a license if their duties are purely administrative in nature. Administrative tasks include, but are not limited to: setting goals and objectives, overseeing production, delegating duties, and evaluating performance, as long as performance of these tasks does not amount to the taking of a residential mortgage loan application or offering or negotiating the terms of a residential mortgage loan.

Support Staff:

Individuals who perform purely clerical and support tasks under the direction and supervision of a state licensed individual do not fall within the definitions of "originate a mortgage" or "mortgage loan originator." Clerical or support tasks include, but are not limited to:

a. Communicating with a consumer to obtain the information necessary for the processing or underwriting of a loan, to the extent that such communication does not include offering or negotiating loan rates or terms, or counseling consumers about residential mortgage loan rates or terms; and
b. The receipt, collection, distribution and analysis of information common for the processing or underwriting of a residential mortgage loan.

However, at any time, if the unlicensed persons activities fall outside of administrative, clerical or support in nature and within the definitions of "originate a mortgage" as defined in section 12-10-702(17), C.R.S., or "mortgage loan originator" as defined in section 12-10-702(14)(a), C.R.S., they are required to be licensed as a Colorado mortgage loan originator.

Position Statement – MLO 1.4 – Mortgage Loan Originator and Mortgage Company Exemptions (revised 09/18/2013)

The Board of Mortgage Loan Originators has reissued this position statement to provide guidance for all individuals and entities identified under the exemption portion of the Mortgage Loan Originator Licensing and Mortgage Company Registration Act (the "Act"); specifically section 12-10-709, C.R.S., and federal regulations regarding seller financing.

State specific exemption for real estate brokers:

The Colorado General Assembly passed two bills in 2013 concerning the regulation of mortgage loan originators with new language affecting the exemption portion of the Act. Section 12-10-709, C.R.S., defines all individuals and entities that are exempt or otherwise excused from complying with licensure and registration standards outlined by the Act.

The first bill, SB 13-118, added exemption language for real estate brokers representing persons providing seller financing for the sale of no more than three residential properties in any twelve month period. Section 12-10-709(1)(j), C.R.S., now includes as exempt:

> "A person licensed under part 2 of this article 10 who represents a person, estate, or trust providing mortgage financing under subsection (1)(a) of this section."

The Board finds it necessary to clarify in what capacity one is acting when representing a person, estate, or trust that is offering seller financing. The Board has taken the position that "represents" denotes in the capacity of a real estate broker as set forth in section 12-10-201(6)(a), C.R.S. As such, persons licensed under part 2 are limited to the real estate brokerage activities as defined in section 12-10-702(20), C.R.S. "Acting in the capacity of a real estate broker" does not include the offering or negotiation of terms and conditions of any proposed financing arrangements with the seller. That activity would fall under the purview of mortgage origination.

Additionally, the sunset bill for the mortgage loan originators program, SB 13-156, deleted subsection (m) of former 12-61-911(1), C.R.S., thereby removing any uncertainties as to the plain and straightforward intent to exempt all individuals and entities identified in (what are now) sections 12-10-709(1)(b) through (j), C.R.S., from all sections, provisions, and requirements of the Act.

Compliance with federal requirements:

There have been some questions with regard to SB13-118, and how the new exemption created for licensed real estate brokers reconciles with federal licensure requirements. The Secure and Fair Enforcement for Mortgage Licensing Act of 2008 ("S.A.F.E. Act") sets minimum national licensing standards for mortgage loan originators and requires that all mortgage loan originators be registered on the National Mortgage Licensing System and Registry ("NMLS"). The SAFE Act defines "loan originator" as an individual who (I) takes a residential mortgage loan application; and (II) offers or negotiates terms of a residential mortgage loan for compensation or gain. This regulation also describes activities in the residential mortgage process that are excluded from the definition of "loan originator." Activities that are excluded include: those that pertain to administrative or clerical tasks; real estate brokerage activities by individuals licensed or registered by a state to undertake real estate brokerage activities, unless that person is compensated by a loan originator, loan processing or underwriting under the direction and supervision of a state-licensed loan originator or registered loan originator; and those individuals solely involved in extensions of credit relating to timeshare plans. Care should be taken by anyone licensed under part 2 as not to perform any acts that may require licensure under federal licensing requirements.

Position Statement – MLO 1.5 – Loan Modifications (revised 11/20/2013)

Short sale – A short sale is the sale of a real property for less than the mortgage loan balance. In the settlement of the short sale transaction the existing mortgage is extinguished. Any deficiency created from the settlement of the transaction may be transformed into a promissory note, charged off, forgiven, or pursued as a judgment against the previous owner.

Loan modification – A Loan Modification is a permanent change in one or more of the terms of a mortgagor's existing loan, allows the loan to be reinstated, and often results in a more affordable mortgage payment. The borrower retains ownership of the real property and the mortgage note and deed of trust remain intact.

1. Section 12-10-702(17), C.R.S., defines "originate a mortgage" as to act directly or indirectly as a mortgage loan originator. It is the Board's position that individuals offering or negotiating loan modifications are, at a minimum, indirectly acting as mortgage loan originators. Pursuant to section 12-10-704(1)(a), C.R.S., all persons who meet the definition of originate a mortgage are required to be licensed. As a result, persons who directly or indirectly negotiate, originate or offer or attempt to negotiate or originate loan modifications are currently required to be licensed as mortgage loan originators and are required to be licensed as state-licensed loan originators by July 31, 2010.
2. In addition to the licensing requirements, all individuals who directly or indirectly negotiate loan modifications for borrowers are required to comply with all other provisions of Colorado mortgage loan originator licensing law and Board rules. This includes, but is not limited to:
    a. A duty of good faith and fair dealing in all communications and transactions with borrowers;
    b. A prohibition against making any promise that influences, persuades, or induces another person to detrimentally rely on such promise when the licensee could not or did not intend to keep such promise;
    c. A prohibition against soliciting or entering into a contract with a borrower that provides in substance that the mortgage loan originator may earn a fee or commission through the mortgage loan originator's "best efforts" to obtain a loan even though no loan is actually obtained for the borrower; and
    d. If the mortgage loan originator has obtained for the borrower a written commitment from a lender for a loan on the terms and conditions agreed to by the borrower and the mortgage loan originator, and the borrower fails to close on the loan through no fault of the mortgage loan originator, the mortgage loan originator may charge a fee, not to exceed three hundred dollars, for services rendered, preparation of documents, or transfer of documents in the borrower's file that were prepared or paid for by the borrower if the fee is not otherwise prohibited by the federal "Truth in Lending Act", 15 U.S.C. section 1601, and Regulation Z, 12 CFR 226, as amended.
3. The Board's position on this matter shall not be construed to include employees of non-profit HUD-approved housing counseling agencies as long as such individuals receive neither compensation nor anything of value for participation in loan modifications.
4. The Board's position on this matter shall not be construed to include employees of mortgage loan servicing companies operating on behalf of mortgage lenders.
5. Licensed Real Estate Brokers engaged in licensed activities when performing services within the defined short sale transactions do not need to maintain a license as a mortgage loan originator. However, loan modification services as defined in this position statement are considered outside the scope of real estate brokerage activities and as such, separate licensure as a mortgage loan originator is required.
6. As set forth in section 12-10-709(1)(c), C.R.S., an attorney who renders services in the course of practice, who is licensed in Colorado, and who is not primarily engaged in the business of negotiating residential mortgage loans or loan modifications is not required to be licensed as a mortgage loan originator.

7. Noncompliance may result in the imposition of any of the sanctions allowable under Colorado law, including, but not limited to:
   a. Imposition of fines;
   b. Restitution for any financial loss;
   c. Refusal to renew a license;
   d. Refusal to grant a license; and
   e. Revocation.

Position Statement – MLO 1.7 – Financial Responsibility Requirement

The Board's position on this matter is there is a presumption of compliance with the financial responsibility requirement in section 12-10-711(1)(g), C.R.S., for individuals required to be licensed as state-licensed loan originators who have complied with the errors and omissions insurance requirements defined in section 12-10-707, C.R.S., and any Director rule that directly or indirectly addresses errors and omissions insurance requirements and who have complied with the surety bond requirements defined in sections 12-10-704(8) and 12-10-717, C.R.S., and any Board rule that directly or indirectly addresses surety bond requirements.

Position Statement – MLO 1.8 – Real Estate Brokerage Activity

The Board is aware that pursuant to the real estate brokers licensing act, specifically § 12-10-401, C.R.S., *et seq*., licensed Colorado real estate brokers are required to fulfill specific duties and obligations. Many of the duties prescribed by the act address financial matters involved in the contract for a real property transaction. Whether acting as a single agent or a transaction broker, a real estate broker must exercise reasonable skill and care, including but not limited to: 1) accounting for all money and property received in a timely manner; 2) keeping the parties fully informed of the transaction; 3) assisting the parties in complying with the terms and conditions of any contract including closing the transaction; and 4) making disclosures regarding adverse material facts pertaining to a principal's financial ability to perform the terms of the transaction and the buyer's intent to occupy the property as a principal residence. Without the informed consent of all parties, a transaction broker is prohibited from disclosing that a seller or buyer will agree to financing terms other than those offered. A single agent is prohibited from disclosing whether his or her client(s) will agree to financing terms other than those offered, unless the client consents. The Board is also cognizant that real estate brokers advise on fees relating to homeowner's associations, special assessments, appraisals, surveys, inspections, property insurance, and taxes.

Pursuant to § 12-10-702(20)(c), C.R.S., the aforementioned activities could be construed as requiring a mortgage loan originator's license since they involve "matters related to financing for the transaction" at the time of contract negotiation. However, the Board has determined these activities are exempt from the mortgage loan originator's licensing act. Specifically, § 12-10-702(14)(a), C.R.S., defines a mortgage loan originator as an individual who "takes a residential loan application" or "offers or negotiates terms of a residential mortgage loan." Real estate brokers engaging in these activities are required to be licensed as a mortgage loan originator.

Position Statement – MLO 1.9 – Mortgage Company Definition Applicability

The Board of mortgage loan originators views the definition of a mortgage company, pursuant to their interpretation of Colorado law, to exclude the following entities:

1. Persons, other than an individual, who meet all of the following requirements:
   a. Funds a residential mortgage loan when the residential mortgage loan application was taken by a licensed or exempt person;

   b. Does not take residential mortgage loan applications or does not offer or negotiate terms of a residential mortgage loan;

   c. Does not solicit borrowers in Colorado for the purpose of making residential mortgage loans; and

   d. Does not participate in the offering or negotiation of residential mortgage loans with the borrower, except for setting the terms under which a person may buy or fund a residential mortgage loan originated by a licensed person;

2. Private mortgage insurance companies that provide contract underwriting services to the lending community; or

3. Lead generating companies that do not, through employees or other individuals, take residential mortgage loan applications or offer or negotiate terms of a residential mortgage loan to prospective borrowers.

The types of entities described in this position statement are determined to be excluded from the definition of a mortgage company and, therefore, are not required to register as Mortgage Companies with the Colorado Board of Mortgage Loan Originators.

Chapter 10
Landmark Case Law

An * in the left margin indicates a change in the statute, rule, or text since the last publication of the manual.

I. Supreme Court Decision on Practice of Law by Brokers

Colorado brokers are allowed to render services to their clients to a greater degree than are brokers in other states. The practicing real estate broker, of necessity, must work closely with practicing lawyers. Each practitioner zealously guards the legal field of his or her endeavor. In Colorado, a real estate broker renders service to his or her client beyond merely procuring a buyer. Colorado brokers should familiarize themselves with the Colorado Supreme Court's decisions in the cases of (1) *Conway-Bogue Realty Investment Co. v. Denver Bar Association*, (2) *Title Guaranty Co. v. Denver Bar Association*, and (3) *Record Abstract & Title Co. v. Denver Bar Association.*

In the case of *Conway-Bogue Realty Investment Co. v. Denver Bar Association*, 312 P.2d 998 (Colo. 1957), the Colorado Supreme Court addressed whether real estate brokers should be enjoined from preparing certain legal documents relating to and affecting real estate and the title thereto (such as receipts and options for purchase, contracts of sale, deeds, deeds of trust, and leases), and from giving advice to the parties regarding the legal effect of the documents.

In rendering its decision, the Colorado Supreme Court stated:

> The first question to be determined is:
>
> Does the preparation of receipts and options, deeds, promissory notes, deeds of trust, mortgages, releases of encumbrances, leases, notice terminating tenancies, demands to pay rent or vacate by completing standard and approved printed forms, coupled with the giving of explanation or advice as to the legal effect thereof, constitute the practice of law?
>
> This question we answer in the affirmative.
>
> . . .
>
> The remaining and most difficult question to be determined is:
>
> Should the defendants as licensed real estate brokers (none of whom are licensed attorneys) be enjoined from preparing in the regular course of their business the instruments enumerated above, at the requests of their customers and only in connection with transactions involving sales of real estate, loans on real estate or the leasing of real estate which transactions are being handled by them?
>
> This question we answer in the negative.
>
> . . .
>
> The testimony shows, and there is no effort to refute the same, that there are three counties in Colorado that have no lawyers, ten in each of which there

> is only one lawyer, seven in each of which there are only two lawyers; that many persons in various areas of the state reside at great distances from any lawyer's office. The testimony shows without contradiction that the practices sought to be enjoined are of at least 50 years uninterrupted duration; that a vast majority of the people of the state who buy, sell, encumber and lease real estate have chosen real estate brokers rather than lawyers to perform the acts herein complained of. Though not controlling, we must make note of the fact that the record is devoid of evidence of any instance in which the public or any member thereof, layman or lawyer has suffered injury by reason of the act of any of the defendants sought to be enjoined. Likewise, though not controlling, we take judicial notice of the fact that the legislature of the state, composed of 100 members from all walks of life and every section of the state, usually called upon by their constituents to adopt legislation designed to eliminate evils and protect the public against practices contrary to the public welfare, has never taken any steps to prevent continuation of the alleged evil which we are now asked to enjoin.
>
> . . .
>
> We feel that to grant the injunctive relief requested, thereby denying to the public the right to conduct real estate transactions in the manner in which they have been transacted for over half a century, with apparent satisfaction, and requiring all such transactions to be conducted through lawyers, would not be in the public interest. The advantages, if any, to be derived by such limitation are outweighed by the conveniences now enjoyed by the public in being permitted to choose whether their brokers or their lawyers shall do the acts or render the service which plaintiffs seeks to enjoin.

Summary of Decision on Practice of Law by Brokers

The following is an excellent summary of the case given by John E. Gorsuch, legal counsel for the Colorado Association of Realtors, quoted from the August 1957 issue of the Colorado Real Estate News:

> It should be kept in mind that the Court states that the practices in question do amount to the practice of law. The Court says that it will not enjoin real estate brokers from doing these simple acts, however, under the circumstances indicated, because of the Court's express belief that the public's best interest will be served by continuing the present practice. The present practice, however, means the practice shown by the evidence. In other words, the broker's activity is limited to the following circumstances:
>
> 1. His office must be connected with the transaction as broker.
> 2. There must be no charge for preparing the documents other than the normal commission.
> 3. The documents must be prepared on commonly used printed, standard, and approved forms.

It is clear from the decision that the broker should not, under any circumstances:

1. Prepare any legal documents as a business, courtesy or favor, for any transaction with which he is not connected as broker, either with or without pay.
2. He should not prepare any documents which cannot be properly prepared on the standard and approved printed form.
3. He clearly should not draw wills, contracts, agreements and so forth, except the initial binder contract or other customary agreements of the type used to bind the transaction or sale.
4. In addition, it would appear in the best interests of the public and also in conformity with the Court's opinion for the broker to:
    a. Always recommend to the purchaser that the title be examined.
    b. Inform the parties that each has a right to have the papers prepared by an attorney of their own choosing.
    c. Advise the parties that each has a right to be represented at the closing by an attorney if they desire.
    d. In spite of the permission to prepare such documents, there will inevitably arise situations in which the legal complications are beyond the knowledge of the broker. In such instances an attorney's assistance should always be sought.

In conclusion, it could be said that the Supreme Court will allow the brokers to prepare these legal documents on standard and approved printed forms by filling in the blanks therein, with information obtained from the usual sources, in transactions with which they are connected as brokers, when they receive no compensation for these acts other than their ordinary commission. It is to the interest of every broker that these limitations be properly recognized and followed so that the Supreme Court would not have a reason to change its opinion at a future date.

The final words of Mr. Gorsuch's summary bear repeating: "It is to the interest of every broker that these limitations be properly recognized and followed so that the Supreme Court would not have a reason to change its opinion at a future date."

With privilege granted, there must be no abuse. The same authority that granted it may take a privilege such as this away. A privilege respected may be retained. A careless regard is not sufficient. There must be a careful determination and application of what is authorized practice of law by a real estate broker.

The court in its decision referred to the use of "standard and approved" forms, but did not elaborate. Consequently, it was necessary to establish what is a STANDARD and what is an APPROVED form.

Any form purchased from a stationery store or a printer may or may not be a "standard and approved" form. The printer is under no obligation to determine what is standard or what is approved. However, a real estate broker may have such an obligation. Therefore, the brokers needed some guidance and support in their determination of what is a standard and approved form.

In the years following the *Conway-Bogue* decision, the business of real estate practice grew rapidly. There appeared to be less and less standardization of legal forms. Each association of brokers, each locality, and even individual brokers used their own forms, often times drafted with personal prejudice.

The real estate industry became concerned that its privilege to practice law, within the limited sphere, might be abrogated by the court. In 1970, the Colorado Association of Real Estate Boards passed a resolution requesting the Real Estate Commission to approve standard forms and to make their use compulsory. In response to this request, the Real Estate Commission held public hearings on the question. The consensus of opinion drawn from the hearings was almost unanimous: the industry wanted the Commission to use its authority to standardize forms throughout the state. As a result, the Commission in 1971 promulgated and adopted Rule F, (presently known as the Chapter 7 Rules: Use of Standard Forms), which was submitted to the Attorney General. The Attorney General concluded that Rule F was a constitutional exercise of the Commission's rule-making authority.

These rules cover forms for listing contracts, sales contracts, exchange contracts, disclosure forms, settlement sheets, extension agreements, and counterproposals. At the time of this writing, the rules do not cover forms for business opportunity listing or sales contracts, management agreements, leases, etc. In these areas, the broker must use his or her best judgment.

In 1993, the legislature gave the Commission statutory authority to promulgate standard forms for use by real estate licensees. (See § 12-10-403(4), C.R.S.)

In the area of listing and conveyancing covered by these rules, it is to the advantage of the general public and of real estate licensees to use the Commission-approved forms. Much of the wording used in these approved forms has been interpreted by the Colorado Supreme Court and its meaning is known. Other portions have been rewritten to conform to Colorado Supreme Court opinion when older provisions have been found invalid. Economic conditions have also necessitated changes. Changes can also be expected in the Commission-approved forms, but reasonable notice will always be given to licensed brokers.

Companion Decision on Practice of Law

On the same day as *Conway-Bogue*, the Colorado Supreme Court decided the cases of *Title Guaranty Co. v. Denver Bar Association* and *Record Abstract & Title Co. v. Denver Bar Association*, which were taken as companion cases from which one decision was rendered (See 312 P.2d 1011 (Colo. 1957)).

In these two cases, the Denver Bar Association sought to enjoin the title company and the abstract company from preparing certain legal documents for others, giving advice as to their legal effect, and performing other acts that allegedly constituted the unauthorized practice of law.

The court reduced the issues to three:

1. Wherein one of the defendant corporations prepared papers incidental to the making of a loan from funds belonging to the corporation.

The court held that in such a case, the defendant may prepare the notes, deeds of trust, or mortgages incidental to making the loans. The defendant could not be restrained even if at the time of the closing the defendant had a firm commitment for the sale of the loan.

2. In situations where the parties involved in the transaction used an "escrow service" or "closing service" provided by the defendant corporations wherein they draft deeds, promissory notes, trust deeds, mortgages, and receipt and option contracts, and the defendants set a minimum fee and a sliding scale of charges for this service.

The court mentioned that the defendants actively solicited such business, although it was the same service that real estate brokers rendered as an incident of their business and without separate charge. The court held that the defendants were conducting a separate, distinct, and other business, much of which constituted the practice of law and could properly be restrained.

3. The third problem presented was where the defendant's "closing service" was used and the defendant also sold title insurance on the property involved.

The court held that the defendants could be enjoined and that the "escrow service" or "closing service" was not necessary or incidental to the issuance of title insurance. The court further held that the attorneys employed by them were representing the corporation and not the parties involved. The court said in part, "To hold otherwise would be to authorize corporations to practice law for compensation."

The court began its opinion by stating that it should be read and considered in connection with the opinion on the case between the real estate brokers and the lawyers.

II. Licensee Acting on Own Account—Commission Jurisdiction

The Commission staff is often asked whether it can investigate complaints against a licensee where the licensee is not involved as an agent in the transaction. The answer is yes. The Commission can investigate and take disciplinary action against a licensee acting on the licensee's own account where the licensee acts in a dishonest manner. Typical examples are where the licensee/owner does not disclose a known defect, fails to disclose the licensee's licensed status as a purchaser, or provides fraudulent information on a loan application.

Printed in relevant part below is the Colorado Court of Appeals case of *Seibel v. Colorado Real Estate Commission*, 530 P.2d 1290 (Colo. App. 1974) in which the issue of the Commission's jurisdiction over "non-agency" activities arose.

> Ed. Note: The statutes cited in this opinion are now found in §§ 12-10-201 through -411, C.R.S.

> This appeal raises the question of jurisdiction of the Colorado Real Estate Commission over acts of a broker in negotiating the acquisition of an interest in real estate for his own use. The hearing officer and the Colorado Real Estate Commission, directly, and the district court, by implication, all concluded that the real estate brokers licensing act, (§12-10-201, C.R.S., (formerly 1963, 117-1-1), *et seq.*, and rules adopted by the commission pursuant to that statute do apply to the conduct of licensed brokers in real estate matters relating to actions taken for their own account. We affirm.

Appellant (Seibel) is a licensed real estate broker. Intending to purchase a home owned by persons named Debord for his own use, he signed a receipt and option agreement, proceeding through the listing broker, Roberts. Seibel was not able to close on the agreed date, and accepted return of his deposit.

Several days later, one Arvidson signed a receipt and option agreement relating to the same property, again proceeding through Roberts. Seibel was not aware of this transaction. He personally contacted the Debords and attempted to have them sign a new contract for sale of the property to him. This proposed contract stated that Seibel and Roberts would divide the commission equally. All of the contacts by Seibel with the Debords regarding the second contract were made without the consent or approval of the listing broker.

After Seibel learned of the Arvidson contract, he recorded the original receipt and option agreement. The Debord-Arvidson sale was closed with $500 being placed in escrow to cover the cost of a possible quiet title suit to clear the records of the Seibel contract.

Pursuant to statute, proceedings were held before a hearing officer of the Colorado Real Estate Commission on alleged violations of both the real estate brokers licensing act and a commission rule. The hearing officer found that the commission had jurisdiction, that Seibel was guilty of improper and dishonest dealing in making direct contact with the sellers, that Seibel had violated both former C.R.S. 1963, 117-1-12(1)(t), and Real Estate Commission Rule E-13 (presently known as Rule 6.15), and therefore recommended that his license be suspended for a period of not less than thirty nor more than ninety days.

C.R.S. 1963, 117-l-12(1)(t), proscribes conduct "which constitutes dishonest dealing." Real Estate Commission Rule E-13 specified that: "A real estate broker shall not negotiate a sale, exchange, lease or listing contract of real property directly with an owner for compensation from such owner if he knows that such owner has a written unexpired contract in connection with such property which grants an exclusive right to sell to another broker, or which grants an exclusive agency to another broker."

The Real Estate Commission approved and adopted the findings of the hearing officer, and suspended Seibel's license for a period of thirty days. The district court reversed the commission's finding that Seibel had violated the statute, but affirmed the finding that he had violated Rule E-13. The matter was remanded to the commission to impose whatever penalty the commission felt was warranted for the violation of the rule. The commission thereupon suspended plaintiff's license for ten days, and this appeal followed.

Seibel urges that 1965 Perm. Supp., C.R.S. 1963, 117-1-2(4), provides him a specific exemption from the authority of the commission in this case, since he was attempting to buy the home for his personal use and was not acting as a real estate broker. The pertinent paragraphs of this section state that:

"(a) The terms 'real estate broker' or 'real estate salesman,' as used in this article, shall not apply to any of the following:

. . . .

(e) Any owner of real estate acting personally, or a corporation acting through its officers, or regular salaried employees, in his or its own behalf with respect to property owned or leased by him or it, except as provided in subsection (2) of this section;

(f) Any person, firm, partnership, association acting personally, or a corporation acting through its officers or regular salaried employees, in his or its own behalf as principal in acquiring or in negotiating to acquire any interest in real estate . . . ."

. . .

Considering the statute in light of these principles, we conclude that the purpose of the exemption section of 1965 Perm. Supp., C.R.S. 1963, 117-1-2(4), is to permit an owner of property to sell it, or to permit one to purchase property for his own account without having to procure a real estate license. These paragraphs have no application to the matter of discipline of licensed real estate brokers and salesmen. To interpret the statute as Seibel urges, would be to adopt an illogical and unduly restrictive meaning of the regulatory provisions of the entire statute.

. . . .

Hence, we conclude that where a real estate broker is dealing in real estate for his own account, the Colorado Real Estate Commission has jurisdiction over his acts and can suspend or revoke his license for proven violations of the licensing statute or of the Commission's rules. A broker can no more be allowed to violate the rules of the Real Estate Commission when purchasing property for his own account than he can when purchasing it for a client.

III. Eckley v. Colorado Real Estate Commission (1988)

Case Topics:

1. **Incompetency/Unworthiness as Applied to License Discipline.**
2. **Legal Standards: Court Review of Agency Imposed Sanctions.**
3. **Offsetting Actions by Other Regulatory Agencies.**

In 1985, the Colorado Real Estate Commission (the Commission) issued a Final Agency Order (FAO) which adopted an administrative law judge's findings that the Respondent had engaged in incompetent and unworthy conduct, in violation of the Colorado real estate license law. The case was based on the Respondent's brokerage activities involving the sale of a business (a Denver lounge) which included real property. The Respondent appealed the FAO in the Denver District Court, which affirmed the Commission's order. The Respondent then appealed the District Court's Order with the Colorado Court of Appeals; however, because such appeal challenged the constitutionality of specified portions of the real estate license law, the case was transferred to the Colorado Supreme Court – *Eckley v. Colorado Real Estate Commission*, 752 P.2d 68 (Colo. 1988).

1. Incompetence/Unworthiness as Applied to License Discipline.

In the Supreme Court case, the Respondent challenged the real estate license law which allows for discipline based on acts of "incompetency" and unworthiness," by contending that such terms are unconstitutionally vague; however, relying on standards previously established in Colorado case law, the Court disagreed.

According to the Court, "Statutory terms need not be defined with mathematical precision in order to pass constitutional muster. . . Instead, the statutory language must strike a balance between two potentially conflicting concerns: it must be specific enough to give fair warning of the prohibited conduct, yet must be sufficiently general to address the problem under varied circumstances and during changing times."

As to the term "incompetency," the Court pointed to its own previous rulings which stated that "[c]ompetence indicates the ability to perform ably and above a minimum level of sufficiency" and that "incompetence refers to a demonstrated lack of ability to perform a required duty." Therefore, the Court held that the term "incompetency" as employed in the context of the real estate license law is "sufficiently precise that persons of common intelligence and understanding would not have to guess at its meaning or differ as to its application."

As to the term "unworthiness," the Court relied in part on the *Webster's New World Dictionary*, 1599 (College Ed. 1957), in which "unworthiness" is defined as "the quality or state of being unworthy," and where "unworthy" is defined as "not fit, becoming, or suitable." Therefore, according to the Court, "the concept of unworthiness in the context . . . (of the real estate license law) . . . contemplates conduct or behavior in connection with the business of real estate brokerage that demonstrates the actor to be so unfit or unsuitable to act as a real estate broker or salesman as to endanger the interest of the public."

The Count further pointed to rulings made in other state courts, including a 1979 Iowa Supreme Court opinion that Iowa's own license law language "proscribing unworthiness or incompetency to act as a real estate broker becomes clear and unequivocal when measured by common understanding and practice in that profession." *Miller v. Iowa Real Estate Comm'n*, 274 N.W.2d 288, 292 (Iowa 1979).

2. Legal Standards: Court Review of Agency Imposed Sanctions.

In his defense, the Respondent further held that the findings of the Commission and the District Court were arbitrary and capricious. In addressing this defense, the Court cited Colorado case law which held that (1) In order for a court to set aside agency action under the Colorado Administrative Procedures Act, on the ground that it was arbitrary and capricious, the court must find that the action is unsupported by any competent evidence; and that (2) Agency action will also be set aside if it is based on findings of basic or evidentiary facts that are "clearly erroneous on the whole record, unsupported by substantial evidence when the record is considered as a whole, or otherwise contrary to law."

Upon review of the underlying administrative hearing, the Court found credible evidence in support of the administrative law judge's findings that the Respondent:

- Failed to make financial records of the business being purchased available to the buyer, which may have left the seller open to later adverse claims by the buyer (incompetence).

- Failed to advise purchaser to consult an attorney concerning the complexity of the transaction (unworthiness and incompetency).
- Completed an earnest money disbursement agreement which failed to show all of the disbursements actually made (i.e., misrepresentations which constituted incompetency and unworthiness).
- Failed to advise the purchaser that her earnest money deposit would not be fully refundable if the sale could not close (fraudulent concealment which constituted incompetency and unworthiness).
- Placed the purchaser's $15,000 earnest money deposit into his operating account in instead of a trust account, opining that a "need for haste" in disbursing those funds does not justify or excuse circumvention of the license law requirements (incompetency and unworthiness).
- Failed to provide a sufficiently detailed closing statement, opining that approval of such document by the buyer's legal counsel did not nullify the license law requirements (incompetency and unworthiness).

3. Offsetting Actions by Other Regulatory Agencies.

The Respondent argued that the approval of the transfer of ownership of the subject business by the local and state liquor licensing authorities, a process that required submission to those authorities of the various documents by which the sale of the lounge was accomplished, should cure any violation of the real estate licensing statutes and commission rules.

The Court was unpersuaded by the Respondent's argument, stating that "Liquor licensing authorities are separate entities with separate standards governing their operation. The commission rules and state real estate broker licensing laws are concerned specifically with assuring that real estate transactions are conducted honestly and competently so as to safeguard the interest of the public." The Court further stated that "These statutes and rules clearly govern the appellant's actions here. The appellant's failure to meet the standards prescribed by the relevant statutes and rules may not be vindicated by reference to action by a separate agency."

The Court affirmed the District Court's judgment affirming the Commission's FAO, and discipline included a one-year term of license suspension.

IV. Colorado Real Estate Commission v. Hanegan (1997)

Case Topics:

1. **Adequate Notice of CE Requirements.**
2. **Standards for Court Review of Agency Imposed Sanctions.**

In 1995, an administrative law judge (ALJ) issued a finding that a real estate licensee had violated the Colorado Real Estate License Law by failing to complete a required mandatory continuing education (CE) course during her 1991-94 term of licensure. The ALJ recommended a $50 fine but declined to add the penalty of a public censure. The Real Estate Commission (the Commission) subsequently adopted the ALJ's Findings of Fact and Conclusion of Law, but opted to impose both the fine and public censure.

1. Adequate Notice of CE Requirements.

In rejecting the Respondent's claim that she did not receive adequate advance notice of the course, the ALJ pointed to relevant portions of the existing Colorado Real Estate Manual, as well as several preceding announcements in the Real Estate Commission's quarterly newsletter. In further support, the ALJ noted that of the 3,000 licensees audited for continuing education during 1994, only ten had failed to take the required course.

In 1996, when the Respondent appealed the Commission's Final Agency Order, the Colorado Court of Appeals affirmed the Commission's finding of adequate notice, but reversed the penalty of a public censure, concluding that the Commission's findings did not reveal a "reasonable basis in law" for the added penalty of a public censure. *Colorado Real Estate Commission v. Hanegan*, 924 P. 2d 1170 (Colo. App.1996).

2. Standards for Court Review of Agency Imposed Sanctions.

In 1997, the Real Estate Commission brought the matter before the Colorado Supreme Court (*Colorado Real Estate Commission v. Hanegan*, 947 P.2d 933 (Colo. 1997)). The Supreme Court found that while the "reasonable basis" standard is properly applied to a regulatory agency's review of an ALJ's findings of fact and conclusions of law, such standard does not apply to agency imposition of sanctions. According to the Court, the proper standard was to be found in the Colorado Administrative Procedures Act, which provides that the courts may not overturn agency actions unless such actions are "arbitrary, capricious, legally impermissible or an abuse of discretion." In this case, the Supreme Court found that:

- The Commission's sanction was clearly within the parameters of the Commission's statutory authority, which authorizes the Commission to impose a variety of penalties, including censure, for any of a long list of violations, including a catch-all category for disregarding or violating any provision of the real estate license law.
- The imposition of sanctions is a discretionary function which, if within the statutory authority of an agency, must not be overturned unless that discretion is abused. (The Court further noted that, per established case law, "The issue for the reviewing court is not whether it would reach the same conclusion on the same facts.").
- In this case it could not be concluded, based on the established facts, that "public censure bears no relation to the Respondent's conduct or is manifestly excessive in relation to the needs of the public and is thus an abuse of discretion."

The Supreme Court accordingly reversed the Court of Appeals' holding and reinstated the terms of the Real Estate Commission's Final Agency Order.

V. Colorado Real Estate Commission v. Bartlett (2011)

Case Topics:

1. **Convictions of Attempted Crimes – Jurisdiction.**
2. **Proof of Rehabilitation.**
3. **Appropriate License Discipline.**

In the case of *Colorado Real Estate Commission v. Bartlett*, 272 P.3d 1099 (Colo. App. 2011), the Colorado Court of Appeals affirmed a 2010 Real Estate Commission (the Commission) Final Agency Order (FAO) for revocation of the Respondent's Colorado real estate broker's license. The FAO was based on the licensee's conviction of an attempted criminal act, as well as his eight-month delay in reporting such to the Commission.

1. Convictions of Attempted Crimes – Jurisdiction.

The Court found that the plain language of the Colorado real estate license law provided for disciplinary action against a licensee's conviction for conduct including "attempting to perform" one of the criminal acts enumerated within **the license law**. Citing specific provisions of the Colorado Criminal Code, the Court further found that attempt convictions were sufficiently similar to convictions for the crime itself (in this case sexual assault on a child) to be considered "like crime", therefore placing such conduct within the scope of the Commission's disciplinary authority.

2. Proof of Rehabilitation.

The Court noted that the Colorado real estate license law, in tandem with specified provisions of the Colorado Administrative Procedures Act, provided that when considering license sanctions based on criminal convictions, the Commission must consider not only the offense itself, but whether the individual has been "rehabilitated" and is "ready to accept the responsibilities of a law-abiding and productive member of society."

Based on the evidence, the Court found that while the Respondent had remained in compliance with his (then) ongoing terms of probation, there were other offsetting factors including, but not limited to, the nature of and extreme circumstances of the crime, the Respondent's delayed disclosure of the conviction, guiding principles of sex offender management, and the Respondent's testimony during the underlying administrative hearing. The Court concurred with the Commission's conclusion that those added factors indicated "a character inconsistent with licensure in a profession that demands scrupulous honesty, strict compliance with the law, and integrity in dealing with others." The Court thus held that the Commission's determination that the Respondent had not been sufficiently rehabilitated was not "arbitrary or capricious, unsupported by substantial evidence, or contrary to law."

3. Appropriate License Discipline.

The Court recognized the Commission's statutory discretion in deciding sanctions and found that the Commission's order of license revocation in this case was not "arbitrary and capricious." When making that finding, the Court noted that the case record supported the Commission's finding that the Respondent violated two provisions of the Colorado real estate license law (criminal conviction and failure to timely report). The Court further concluded that at the time of the administrative hearing, and despite demonstrated progress with his ongoing probation, the Respondent's character "remained inconsistent with the requirements of licensure."

In addition, and citing supporting Colorado and federal case law, the Court held that the Commission was not bound to impose an identical discipline in all comparable cases.

On February 6, 2012, the Colorado Supreme Court denied the Respondent's Petition for Writ of Certiorari regarding this Court of Appeals case.

VI. McDonnell v. Colorado Real Estate Commission (2015)

Case Topics:

1. **Commission Jurisdiction: Non-Brokerage Activities.**
2. **Commission's Disciplinary Authority – Specific Prohibited Acts.**
3. **Legal Standards: Court Review of Agency Imposed Sanctions.**

Background: During 2010-11, while serving as president of a homeowners association, and without proper consent or permission, the Respondent wrote four checks totaling $10,000 on the HOA's account payable to himself or to his business (a sports equipment company); and such funds were used for the benefit of the Respondent's business, not for the HOA's benefit. Afterward, when HOA board members reviewed the HOA's financial records and discovered the discrepancies, the Respondent returned the $10,000 and resigned his position as HOA president.

The Colorado Real Estate Commission (the Commission) investigated the matter and in 2013 charged the Respondent with multiple violations of the Colorado real estate license law. In 2014, after an evidentiary hearing before an administrative law judge, the Commission issued a Final Agency Order (FAO) which adopted in part, and reversed in part, findings made by the ALJ. Then in 2015, the Respondent brought the Commission's FAO before the Colorado Court of Appeals, *McDonnell v. Colorado Real Estate Commission*, 361 P.3d 1138 (Colo. App. 2015). The Court's findings are summarized below.

1. Commission Jurisdiction: Non-Brokerage Activities.

The Respondent maintained that the Commission did not have the authority to sanction him for conduct that does not involve the actual selling, exchanging, buying, renting, or leasing of real estate. The Court disagreed with this assertion, based on the following:

- Per statutory language, several of the grounds for discipline set forth in the real estate license law do not necessarily require a link to selling, exchanging, buying, renting, or leasing real estate, and do not involve conduct specific to brokers; and those provisions include: (1) knowingly making any misrepresentation; and (2) violation of a Commission rule or regulation in the interests of the public; and (3) certain criminal convictions and failure to so notify the Commission of such; and (4) revocation or suspension of a professional license in Colorado or other state on certain grounds.
- Colorado case law holds that the existence of such disciplinary provisions demonstrates that the state legislature intended the Commission's sanction authority to extend to a broker's improper conduct outside the real estate context, "particularly when it speaks to the broker's honesty, dignity, or moral character."
- In *Hart v. Colorado Real Estate Commission*, 702 P.2d 763 (Colo. App. 1985), the Court read the Commission's sanction authority expansively, to include the power to regulate "selling, exchanging, buying, renting, or leasing" real estate, along with the power to discipline brokers "for related [real estate] activities which do not require a license."
- Broad sanction authority is not uncommon in the context of professional licensure, as demonstrated in established Colorado case law addressing professional licenses other than real estate brokers.

2. Commission's Disciplinary Authority: Specific Prohibited Acts.

The Court addressed the scope of the Commission's disciplinary authority with respect to four prohibited acts, determining that:

- The Colorado license law provision prohibiting failure to timely account for or remit funds belonging to others includes the language "whether acting as real estate brokers or otherwise," which indicates the legislature's intent to discipline brokers for failing to account or remit others' funds, even in non-real estate transactions (emphasis added). The Court further held that the Commission's recordkeeping requirements properly apply to those non-real estate transactions as well.
- The Colorado license law provision prohibiting conversion, diversion or commingling funds of others, as well as unlawful placement of such funds, does not include language that limits discipline to those instances that occur in the context of real estate. The Court further cited Colorado case law in support of its contention that the Respondent's return of the HOA's funds, absent demand, did not excuse the licensee from disciplinary action.
- The Colorado license law provision which provides for license discipline for "[h]aving demonstrated unworthiness or incompetency to act as a real estate broker by conducting business in such a manner as to endanger the interest of the public," does not apply in this case because nothing in the list of unworthy or incompetent practices set forth in the Commission's administrative rules contemplates the Respondent's conduct in this case or any other conduct outside the context of real estate.
- The Colorado license law provides for license discipline for "any other conduct, whether of the same or a different character" than those acts subject to discipline under the license law "which constitutes dishonest dealing." The Court held that the language of this provision plainly states that it applies to "any other conduct" and that there is no additional language in that particular statute, or in the Commission's administrative rules and regulations, which would limit the reach of this position.

The Court further found that although "dishonest dealing" is not defined in Colorado statute or case law, "a court can determine the meaning of an undefined phrase of common usage by ascertaining its usual and ordinary meaning." The Court cited *Black's Law Dictionary* 733 (10th ed. 2014) where a "dishonest act" is defined as "[c]onduct involving bad faith, dishonesty, a lack of integrity, or moral turpitude." Given the evidence in this case, the Court found that the Commission did not err in determining that the Respondent's conduct constituted dishonest dealing, in violation of the license law.

3. Legal Standards: Court Review of Agency Imposed Sanctions.

As to proper sanctions in this case, the Court cited the standards set forth in in *Colorado Real Estate Commission v. Bartlett*, 272 P.3d 1099 (Colo. App. 2011), that "Courts will uphold an agency sanction unless it (1) bears no relation to the proscribed conduct, (2) is manifestly excessive in relation to the needs of the public, or (3) is otherwise a gross abuse of discretion."

Even considering its reversal of the Commission's finding of "unworthiness or incompetency" in this case, the Court determined that the Commission-ordered sanctions in this case "do not appear excessive, nor do they constitute an abuse of discretion" and therefore affirmed such sanctions.

VII. Colorado Real Estate Commission v. Vizzi (2019)

Case Topics:

1. **Mandatory Duties of Real Estate Brokers.**
2. **Federal Antitrust Defense.**
3. **Anonymous Complainants and Due Process Rights.**
4. **Legal Standards: Court Review of Agency Imposed Sanctions.**

In 2017, the Colorado Real Estate Commission (the Commission) issued a Final Agency Order (FAO) that adopted the Administrative Law Judge's (ALJ) findings that: (1) the Respondent licensee must fulfill all of the statutory duties that transaction brokers are required to provide to clients; and that (2) the Respondent violated the Colorado real estate license law by entering into listing contracts which essentially disclaimed any responsibility to provide such duties. The ALJ's sanctions included a $2,000 fine and twelve (12) hours of continuing education. The Commission's FAO additionally sought the issuance of public censure.

In 2019, the Respondent brought the Commission's FAO before the Colorado Court of Appeals (the "Court") for review. *Colorado Real Estate Commission v. Vizzi*, 2019 COA 33, 17CA2388 (Colo. App. 2019). The Court's findings are summarized below.

1. Mandatory Duties of Real Estate Brokers.

During 2013-14 the Respondent contracted to represent three clients in the capacity of a transaction-broker, but in each case the Respondent was to provide unbundled real estate brokerage services in exchange for a flat fee. In one instance, he contracted only to list the client's property on the Multiple Listing Services (MLS); and in the other two instances he contracted only to provide a yard sign, lock box and centralized showing services, and to list the properties on the MLS. Upon review, the Court made the following findings:

- The Court disagreed with the Respondent's claim that the statutory duties for transaction-brokers are only default, not mandatory duties; and in doing so the Court noted that the real estate license law defines a transaction-broker as " a broker who assists one or more parties throughout a contemplated real estate transaction with communication, interposition, advisement, negotiation, contract terms, and the closing of such real estate transaction without being an agent or advocate for the interests of any party to such transaction." The Court noted that the use of the words "throughout" and "and" indicates that when enacting the law, the legislature intended that transaction-brokers assist in the entire transaction and undertake each of the transaction-broker duties set forth in the license law. Those duties enumerated in §12-10-407(2)(a-d), C.R.S., are numerous and broad and are consistent with the contemplated activities set forth in the definition of a transaction-broker in §12-10-402(8), C.R.S.
- Citing a further provision of the license law that "[a] transaction-broker shall have the following obligations and responsibilities . . .," and standing on Colorado case law, the Court concluded that absent a clear indication of contrary intent, the word

"shall" in a statute generally indicates that the legislature intended the listed provisions to be mandatory. The public can only engage a real estate broker in the role of a single agent or a transaction-broker. The Court further noted that "The statutes do not say that the public can engage a real estate broker to provide unbundled brokerage services, or in any manner that the broker and customer might find mutually acceptable."

- The Court also addressed the Respondent's reliance on another portion of the license law that provides "[if] the transaction-broker undertakes any obligations or responsibilities in addition to or different from" those set forth in the license law, then "[s]uch obligations or responsibilities shall be disclosed in a writing which shall be signed by the involved parties." While the Respondent maintained that such language permitted a reduction of the mandatory duties, the Court disagreed, concluding that such language allows a broker to take on duties that are additional to the mandatory duties, but does not permit a broker to contract away any of those mandatory duties.

2. Federal Antitrust Defense.

The Respondent argued that "the Commission's enforcement of 'minimum services' does not stem from formal rulemaking or statute" but merely from an "unenforceable position statement" promulgated by a Commission that is "dominated by market participants – three real estate brokers and two representatives of the public at large." Therefore, according to the Respondent, the Commission's minimum services policy runs contrary to federal antitrust laws.

The Court rejected that assertion, based on federal case law which holds that a state agency's actions are considered the actions of the state in its sovereign capacity, and thus shielded from federal antitrust law, as long as: (1) such state has articulated a clear policy to allow the anticompetitive conduct; and (2) the state provides active supervision of [the] anticompetitive conduct.

In this case, the Court found that the "clear articulation" requirement is met by the Colorado real estate license law provisions which define "transaction-broker," and which "sets out the General Assembly's policy goals in regulating transaction-brokers," and which "sets out mandatory obligations for transaction-brokers."

The Court further found that the 'active supervision" requirement is met by the license law provision that defines what constitutes the practice of a real estate broker; and by the provision that authorizes the Commission to investigate and censure licensed real estate brokers for violations of state license laws.

3. Anonymous Complainants and Due Process Rights.

The Respondent maintains that in the underlying administrative court case, the ALJ violated his due process rights by denying his motion to compel disclosure of the identity of the anonymous complainant. The Court rejected this claim, citing the Respondent's failure to demonstrate how the complainant's identity was relevant to his ability to defend against the Commission's charges; and noting that during the administrative case the Respondent was given notice of all evidence which supported the charges against him.

4. Legal Standards: Court Review of Agency Imposed Sanctions.

With regard to the Commission's added sanction of public censure, the Court cited *Colorado Real Estate Commission v. Hanegan*, 947 P2d. 933 (Colo. 1997), in that "[a]s long as the record as a whole provides sufficient evidence that the penalty is not manifestly excessive in relation to the misconduct and the public need, the penalty will be upheld."

In this case, the Court noted that the Commission's addition of a public censure met the above standard, and was therefore proper, based on: (1) finding that the Respondent violated his statutory duties multiple times after the Commissions' December 2010 position statement put him on advance notice that the listing contracts he prepared in 2013 and 2014 were improper; and that (2) the Commission's sanction bore some relation to the Respondent's misconduct and to the needs of the public.

On October 7, 2019, the Colorado Supreme Court denied the Respondent's Petition for Writ of Certiorari regarding this Court of Appeals case.

PART II

Substantive Chapters

Chapter 11:
Interests in Land

An * in the left margin indicates a change in the statute, rule, or text since the last publication of the manual.

I. Introduction and History

Modern real property law has evolved from the English feudal system of land ownership. The basic concept of the feudal system was that the king, as owner of all the land, would grant large tracts of land to faithful lords in return for allegiance and service. The lords then granted portions of their land to lesser nobles, and so on. These grants, called "**feuds**," continued on down to the "**villeins**" who lived on and cultivated the land.

Land ownership is the basis of power and wealth. More than a system of land ownership, the feudal system was also a system of government, establishing an economic structure and a military organization

. Because there was no centralized administration for the kingdom, discipline and order were effectively maintained through the series of lord-and-vassal relationships.

The relationship between the English Crown and the American colonies was essentially feudal. After the revolution, the feudal position of the English Crown presumably passed to the states. In most states, the concept of feudal tenure was abolished by statute or judicial decision. In a few, the concept of feudal tenure may technically still exist. However as a practical matter, all states now follow the "**allodial theory**" of land ownership, meaning an owner holds land in absolute independence, owing nothing to the state as overlord. Of course, the state always retains jurisdiction over land within its borders, including the four governmental rights discussed in this chapter.

II. Kinds of Interests in Land

A unique concept of Anglo-American land law is that of "**estates**." Estate types derived from the feudal system and are either "**freehold**" (ownership) estates or "**non-freehold**" (non-owned) estates. Freehold estates were normal holdings under the feudal system, and are: (1) fee simple absolute, (2) defeasible (or base or qualified) fee, (3) fee tail, and (4) life estate. Non-freehold estates are: (1) estate for years, (2) estate from period-to-period, (3) estate at will, and (4) estate at sufferance.

An estate is the type of ownership in land, and determines the duration of an individual's right of possession and right of use. For example, if a "fee simple" owner leases property to a tenant for ten years, both have interests in the property. The tenant's estate is called an "estate for years" and entitles the tenant to assert the right of exclusive possession against anyone, including the owner. The tenant must not abuse the property and has a limited right of use. The owner retains the right to possession at the end of the lease term—a present right to future possession. This interest of the owner is known as a "**reversion**."

The law concerning interests in land is extremely technical, complex and is beyond the scope of this manual. The following discussion is simplified and condensed.

A. Freehold Estates

Fee simple absolute

Often called a fee or a fee simple, this is the most comprehensive bundle of ownership rights known in law. This bundle of rights includes the rights to possess, use, enjoy, control, and dispose. A condominium is a fee simple estate created in air space.

Although fee simple is the highest degree of land ownership recognized by law, it is never absolute ownership (such as owning this book, for example). An owner's fee simple title is always subject to governmental and private limitations that apply equally to all types of estates in land.

The four major governmental limitations on land are:

1. **Police Power** – the right to impose reasonable limitations to protect and promote the health, safety, and general welfare of the public;
2. **Eminent Domain** – the right to take private property for public use in return for payment of just compensation;
3. **Taxation** – the right to impose taxes for governmental support and to proceed against the land for non-payment; and
4. **Escheat** – the right to acquire title to property owned by a person who dies without leaving a will (intestate) or heirs-at-law.

Private limitations upon the use of land are usually classified as:

1. **Deed Restrictions** – imposed by a grantor, such as requiring that all structures built upon the land must be of brick veneer, or that the property may only be used for a specific purpose;
2. **Mortgages** – a security claim of the mortgagee (lender) upon the property preventing use or change that would injure the property's value;
3. **Leases** – an agreement that suspends the fee holder's right to use and possess for some period of time; and
4. **Easements** – a right to cross over the property of the fee holder without interference.

Defeasible fee

A defeasible fee, also called a base or qualified fee, is a fee simple subject to a special limitation, a condition subsequent, or an executory limitation.

A fee simple subject to a "**special limitation**" automatically terminates the fee upon the happening of a specified event. Example: An owner in fee simple absolute conveys to another person and his or her heirs so long as the land is used for church purposes. This conveyance may last forever. But if the land ceases to be used for church purposes, ownership automatically reverts to the grantor, or to the grantor's successors-in-interest.

A fee simple subject to a "**condition subsequent**" gives the grantor, or the grantor's successors-in-interest, the power to terminate the grantee's estate upon the happening of a specified event. Example: If an owner in fee simple absolute conveys with a restriction against alcohol being sold on the premises, the owner shall have the right to re-enter for breach of this condition. Differing from a special limitation described above, this interest does not revert automatically upon the breach of the condition, but continues until the original owner exercises power of termination by re-entry.

Fee tail

A fee tail estate historically created an estate along family lines. Fee tail estates have been abolished or modified in all states. Some states provide that a conveyance, which under common law would have created a fee tail, now conveys a fee simple absolute. Other states, including Colorado, provide that the first grantee holds a life estate and the first heirs take a fee simple title. (See § 38-30-106, C.R.S.)

Life estate

A fee simple owner conveying to another for his or her lifespan creates an estate for life. Upon the grantee's death, the fee reverts to the grantor or grantor's successors-in-interest. Similar to a lease, the grantee may not make unreasonable use of the property or do anything that would decrease the value of the grantor's reversionary interest.

A life estate could also be created by a conveyance for as long as the grantee lives and then to a third party named in the deed. Alternatively, a life estate may also be based on the life of a third party instead of the grantee.

Although abolished in Colorado, there are two "legal" life estates automatically created by law and recognized in a few states today: dower and curtesy. (See § 15-11-112, C.R.S.)

These life estates apply only to married persons.

B. Non-Freehold Estates

Non-freehold estates are "**leasehold**" interests. These are more fully discussed in the Chapter, "Property Management and Leases."

Estate for years (tenancy for years)

An estate for years is one for a *fixed period of time*, whether for a day, one year, or 99 years.

Estate from period-to-period (periodic tenancy)

Such an estate exists when there is *no definite agreed-upon duration* or termination date, but the rental period is fixed at a certain amount per week, month, or year. These estates are usually created by implication rather than express provision. Either party may terminate this estate by giving the statutory notice of termination at the expiration of any rental period.

Estate at will (tenancy at will)

Expressed or implied, an estate at will *may be terminated at the will of either party.* Upon the giving of proper notice, either the tenant or landlord may cancel the estate at any time.

Estate at sufferance (tenancy at sufferance)

This estate arises when the *tenant wrongfully holds over* after the expiration of the lease term.

III. Concurrent Interests

An estate in land may be owned by one person (in severalty), or by two or more persons concurrently. The two most important types of co-ownership are joint tenancy and tenancy in common.

A. Joint Tenancy

All co-owners are equally entitled to the use, enjoyment, control, and possession of the land or its equivalent in rents and profits. The best-known characteristic of joint tenancy is the "**right of survivorship**." Upon the death of one joint tenant, the decedent's rights pass immediately to the surviving tenant(s). Death of a joint tenant does not affect title, as the title is vested equally in all joint tenants rather than individually.

According to common law, joint tenancy must feature **"four unities"**: time, title, interest, and possession. Joint tenants must acquire title at the same time, be named in the same deed, hold exactly equal interests, and be entitled to equal rights of possession. A conveyance from an owner in severalty to herself and her spouse could not have created a joint tenancy under common law because the unities of time and title were missing. However, under Colorado law such a deed would create a joint tenancy: as Colorado law permits, any grantor in such instrument to be one of the grantees. See § 38-31-101, C.R.S.

* ***§ 38-31-101, C.R.S. Tenancy by the entirety.***

* (1) No conveyance of real property located in this state executed before or after July 1, 2006, shall create a tenancy by the entirety.

* (2) A conveyance of real property located in this state executed before July 1, 2006, that purports to create a tenancy by the entirety shall be presumed to create a joint tenancy.

* (3) A conveyance of real property located in this state executed on or after July 1, 2006, that purports to create a tenancy by the entirety shall create a joint tenancy.

B. Tenancy in Common

Tenancy in common is an estate in land held by two or more persons with *only the unity of possession*. Unlike joint tenants, tenants in common may take title at different times and may receive their interests through different deeds. But each is entitled to the undivided possession of the property, according to their proportionate share and subject to the rights of possession of the other tenants. Upon the death of a tenant in common, there is no right of survivorship. The decedent's interest passes according to his or her will or the state law of descent and distribution.

IV. Concurrent Conveyances

Ownership of a home by a husband and wife is usually declared by the deed to be in "joint tenancy" or as "tenants in common." Each has advantages and disadvantages.

The automatic and immediate right of survivorship that accompanies joint tenancy eliminates some legal complications of probate in the event of the death of one of the parties. However, inheritance taxes are assessable and evidence of the death must be recorded. Joint tenancy ensures the survivor a fair share of the marital property and the property does pass free of the claims of unsecured creditors.

Disadvantages of joint tenancy may arise if marital difficulties occur or if one of the parties has obligations or responsibilities (*e.g.*, children) resulting from a previous marriage. The financial and tax situation of the parties may also favor tenancy in common.

Although it is helpful and proper to explain the meaning of "joint tenancy" or "tenancy in common," a broker must *never advise a client what type of conveyance is best.* To do so exceeds the role of broker and constitutes the unauthorized practice of law.

V. Homestead Exemption

Under § 38-41-201, C.R.S.,

> (1) Every homestead in the state of Colorado shall be exempt from execution and attachment arising from any debt, contract, or civil obligation not exceeding in actual cash value in excess of any liens or encumbrances on the homesteaded property in existence at the time of any levy of execution thereon:
>
> (a) The sum of seventy-five thousand dollars if the homestead is occupied as a home by an owner thereof or an owner's family; or
>
> (b) The sum of one hundred five thousand dollars if the homestead is occupied as a home by an elderly or disabled owner, an elderly or disabled spouse of an owner, or an elderly or disabled dependent of an owner.

The terms "householder" and "owner of the property" also include a person holding equity under a land contract or other agreement where such person possesses the property, but the sellers' or vendors' rights are always superior to any homestead.

If the debt, contract, or civil obligation that is the basis for the execution and attachment was entered into or incurred *after* July 1, 1975, the homestead exemption *will be created automatically* as long as the requirements outlined in §§ 38-41-203 and -205, C.R.S., are met. (See § 38-41-202, C.R.S.) Section 38-41-203, C.R.S., states that homesteaded property is only exempt while occupied as a home by the owner or owner's family. Section 38-41-205, C.R.S., states that "[t]he homestead . . . may consist of a house and lot or lots or of a farm consisting of any number of acres."

If, however, "the debt, contract, or civil obligation . . . was entered into or incurred prior to July 1, 1975," the owner or spouse must record in the office of the clerk and recorder of the county where the property is situated an instrument in writing (which should be acknowledged) describing the property, setting forth the nature and source of the owner's interest therein, and stating that the owner is homesteading the property.

A homestead exemption may be released in writing signed by the party or parties who could convey the property. A statement contained in a mortgage, deed of trust, or other instrument creating a lien and waiving or releasing the homestead subordinates the homestead to that particular lien. The homestead exemption would stand against any other judgment creditor who had not secured such a waiver.

If a homestead property is sold, the person entitled to the homestead may keep the sale proceeds separate, and, if identified, the proceeds will be exempt from execution or attachment for one year. If the proceeds are used to buy a new home, there will be a homestead exemption on the new home. However, the homestead exemption does not defeat the rights of the holder of a purchase-money mortgage.

Before any creditor may proceed with execution and attachment of a homesteaded property, the creditor must file an affidavit with the clerk and recorder attesting that the equity in the property exceeds the amount of the exemption. This must be supported by the affidavit of an independent appraiser stating the fair market value of the property. If the amount offered at the sale does not exceed 70 percent of fair market value as shown in the affidavit, all proceedings to sell the property will terminate. If the sale succeeds, the creditor must pay the expenses of the sale, prior liens, and the homestead exemption before satisfying the creditor's own judgment. The balance, if any, would go to the homesteader.

VI. Easements

An easement is a limited right to enter and use another person's land.

An "**appurtenant easement**" attaches to and benefits the land owned by the easement holder. This is the "**dominant estate**." The land burdened by an easement is the "**servient estate**." Appurtenant easements pass with the title to the dominant estate and pass with the land, even if not mentioned in the deed. Easements for light and air are appurtenant, although they may limit the usage of the land subject to the easement.

An **"easement in gross"** belongs to and benefits the owner personally rather than the land itself. The right to run a utility line across another person's land is an example of an easement in gross. Easements in gross are assignable and permanent.

Easements are normally created by written contract or an express grant in a deed signed by the owner of the land over which the easement lies (the servient estate). Easements may also be created by prescription, *i.e.*, by long uninterrupted use without the consent of the owner. Abandonment would terminate a prescriptive easement.

Easements may also be created by implication of law. Such an easement may be so implied when an owner sells land that is inaccessible except through land belonging to the seller. Because the new owner must have access to owned land, an easement may be implied.

Ordinarily, easements are terminated by a written release or quitclaim deed given by the holder of the dominant estate to the owner of the servient estate. Easements may also be terminated by destruction of the servient estate or by a merger of the dominant and servient estates into one parcel.

VII. Adverse Possession

Adverse possession is the right of an occupant of land to acquire superior title against the owner of record without the owner's concurrence, provided the occupancy has been actual, notorious, hostile, visible, and continuous for a required statutory period. In Colorado the required adverse possession statutory periods are:

1. 18 years – without the consent of the owner of record, without color of title, which means the appearance of a legally enforceable right of possession or ownership but due to some defect does not have that effect. This period will also apply if there has been payment of property taxes. (See § 38-41-101, C.R.S.)
2. 7 years – with color of title and/or with payment of seven years of property taxes.

(See § 38-41-108, C.R.S.)

Excerpt from § 38-41-101, C.R.S. Limitation of eighteen years.

(1) No person shall commence or maintain an action for the recovery of the title or possession or to enforce or establish any right or interest of or to real property or make an entry thereon unless commenced within eighteen years after the right to bring such action or make such entry has first accrued or within eighteen years after he or those from, by, or under whom he claims have been seized or possessed of the premises. Eighteen years' adverse possession of any land shall be conclusive evidence of absolute ownership.

(2) The limitation provided for in subsection (1) of this section shall not apply against the state, county, city and county, city, irrigation district, public, municipal, or quasi-municipal corporation, or any department or agency thereof. No possession by any person, firm, or corporation, no matter how long continued, of any land, water, water right, easement, or other property whatsoever dedicated to or owned by the state of Colorado, or any county, city and county, city, irrigation district, public, municipal, or quasi-municipal corporation, or any department or agency thereof shall ever ripen into any title, interest, or right against the state of Colorado, or such county, city and county, city, public, municipal, or quasi-municipal corporation, irrigation district, or any department or agency thereof.

VIII. Combined Types of Ownership

§ 38-32-101, C.R.S. Estates may be created.

Estates, rights, and interests in areas above the surface of the ground, whether or not contiguous thereto, may be validly created in persons or corporations other than the owners of the land below such areas and shall be deemed to be estates, rights, and interests in lands.

§ 38-32-102, C.R.S. Estates deemed estates in land.

Estates, rights, and interests in such areas shall pass by descent and distribution in the same manner as estates, rights, and interests in land and may be held, enjoyed, possessed, alienated, conveyed, exchanged, transferred, assigned, demised, released, charged, mortgaged, or otherwise encumbered, devised, and bequeathed in the same manner, upon the same conditions, and for the same uses and purposes as estates, rights, and interests in land and shall be in all other respects dealt with and treated as estates, rights, and interests in land.

§ 38-32-103, C.R.S. Rights, incidents, and duties.

All of the rights, privileges, incidents, powers, remedies, burdens, duties, liabilities, and restrictions pertaining to estates, rights, and interests in land shall appertain and be applicable to such estates, rights, and interests in areas above the surface of the ground.

§ 38-32-104, C.R.S. Laws on land applicable.

The provisions of articles 30 to 44 of this title and of any other law of this state shall be applicable to estates, rights, and interests created in areas above the surface of the ground and to instruments creating, disposing of, or otherwise affecting such estates, rights, and interests wherever such provisions would be applicable to estates, rights, and interests in land or to instruments creating, disposing of, or otherwise affecting estates, rights, and interests in land.

§ 38-32-105, C.R.S. Estates affected.

The provisions of this article shall be applicable to such estates, rights, and interests created in areas above the surface of the ground, whether such estates, rights, and interests were created prior to or after March 12, 1953.

The Condominium Act effective prior to July 1, 1992 defined a condominium as an individual air space unit together with an interest in the common elements appurtenant to such unit. This definition means that an owner does not individually own the land underneath the structure. A condominium owner holds title to his or her unit within a defined air space, and the unit owners own the land, the hallways, and all the common elements as tenants in common.

Although a condominium complex may appear visually similar to an apartment complex, it is really a subdivision with many owners. Because each unit is truly an estate in land above the surface, a "declaration" must be filed with the county clerk and recorder so that each unit is properly and legally described, and may be taxed or mortgaged separately.

Pursuant to the Colorado Common Interest Ownership Act (CCIOA) effective July 1, 1992, **"common interest community"** means real estate described in a declaration that obligates each unit owner to pay for real estate taxes, insurance premiums, and maintenance or improvement of other real estate described in a declaration. Ownership of a unit does not include leasehold interests of less than 40 years, including renewal options measured from the date the initial term commences. (See § 38-33.3-103(8) C.R.S.)

Pursuant to CCIOA, **"condominium"** means a common-interest community in which portions of the real estate are designated for separate ownership and the separate owners commonly own the remainder. A common-interest community is not a condominium unless the undivided interests in the "**common elements**" are vested in the unit owners. (See § 38-33.3-103(9), C.R.S.) Prior to July 1, 1992, a condominium was defined only as an air space estate, but under CCIOA a condominium may include single-family lots.

CCIOA defines **"planned community"** as a common-interest community that is not a condominium or cooperative. A condominium or cooperative may be part of a planned community. (See § 38-33.3-103(22), C.R.S.) A planned community may have homeowners' association ownership of the common elements rather than undivided interests by the individual unit or lot owners as tenants in common. A planned community may also include a common-interest community with no common elements. However, the individual unit or lot owner is obligated to pay for such expenses as real estate taxes, insurance premiums, and maintenance or improvement of other real estate, such as private roads or a common greenbelt as described in a declaration.

A **"planned unit development"** (PUD) may also be a common-interest community and may consist of unit owners in duplexes, townhouses, condominiums, and single-family residences. Some or all of the owners may either hold common ownership in land or facilities such as a greenbelt, a playground, or a swimming pool, or are obligated for payment of expenses in addition to the individually owned land underneath each owner's residence. Commonly owned elements, expenses, conditions, or obligations must be in a recorded declaration.

A **"time-share** or **interval"** estate is a variation in conventional ownership. Time-shares are usually sold to vacation-seeking consumers in recreational areas. Time-sharing is based on the premise that most people do not require a year-round vacation home. Condominium units are time-shares when sold or leased for specific periods repeated each year (*e.g.*, four weeks out of each year). Several owners of one condominium unit each have a specified annual period of ownership or tenancy.

Time-share interests may be either fee simple deeded, or a non-deeded "right-to-use." Right-to-use is a contractual or membership interest granting exclusive occupancy to either a specified or any available unit for a set time period each year. Right-to-use interests usually run for a limited number of years and have the effect of a leasehold interest. Although right-to-use purchasers do not hold actual fee interest, bankruptcy laws extend equal protection to such owners in the event of a bankruptcy by the owner or developer.

Time-shares may be created by dividing a fee simple estate into several time-period fee simple estates or leases, or by dividing a lease into several subleases. Dividing owned or leased property into a number of right-to-use contracts for defined time periods may also create time-shares. Tenancy in common owners can, by contract, create time-shares for certain periods of the year. Membership agreements may also create time-shares.

Exchange companies facilitate the trading of owned or leased time-shares for the use of someone else's time-share in another recreational area for annual fees.

Time-share developers must register with the Commission as subdivision developers, and licensed real estate brokers must conduct all sales.

Ownership in a community apartment project may be accomplished by having all unit owners become tenants in common, with each owner being given the exclusive right to occupy a specific apartment.

A stock cooperative or "**cooperative housing corporation**" is formed as a non-profit corporation intended to provide each stockholder with the right to occupy a house or an apartment in a building owned or leased by the corporation. Each stockholder receives a proprietary lease or right-of-tenancy document.

Although sales of such interests in a cooperative housing corporation have elsewhere been regarded as a sale of securities, such sales in Colorado are deemed by statute to be real estate and are exempt from the Colorado Securities Act. The same statute also enables banks and associations to make first mortgage loans on a stockholder's interest. (See §§ 38-33.5-101, *et seq*., and 11-41-110, C.R.S.).

Cooperative housing corporations, condominiums, and time-shares are treated as subdivisions.

The following portions of the Colorado Revised Statutes are also useful for real estate brokers:

- Title 38, Article 32 – Estates Above the Surface
- Title 38, Article 33 – Condominium Ownership Act
- Title 38, Article 33.3 – Colorado Common Interest Ownership Act
- Title 38, Article 33.5 – Cooperative Housing Corporations – Housing for Members
- Title 12, Article 10, Part 5 –Subdivisions

Chapter 12:
Land Descriptions

> An * in the left margin indicates a change in the statute, rule, or text since the last publication of the manual.

I. Introduction

While the location of land is commonly referred to by street number and city, it is necessary to use the legal description in the preparation of instruments relating to the title and use of real estate. Numerous methods of description have been developed for the purpose of achieving greater accuracy and precision in identifying the land. The more common methods of land description are:

1. 1. United States Governmental Survey System (GSS), also known as the "rectangular survey system";
2. 2. Metes and bounds;
3. 3. Recorded subdivision plat; and
4. 4. Colorado Coordinate System.

II. The United States Governmental Survey System

Soon after the Revolutionary War ended and new areas were added to the public domain, it became apparent to our government's leaders that a plan had to be worked out for selling and locating lands in the western territory. Thomas Jefferson authored a plan that was adopted by Congress in modified form on May 20, 1785. Under this law, the first surveys took place in the state of Ohio. Ohio was the testing ground for the rectangular survey system and some changes were made in the law as a result of experience gained there. The second survey started in Indiana around 1810. By this time the system was well established; it now extends westward to the Pacific Ocean. This system was not used within the area of the original colonies in America, where land locations were made in irregular form and without any orderly plan.

The object of the government survey was to create a checkerboard of identical squares covering a given area. The largest squares measure 24 miles on each side and are called **"quadrangles."** Each quadrangle is further divided into 16 squares called **"townships"** whose boundaries each measure six miles. Columns of townships are called ranges, and are numbered sequentially east or west of one of 36 **"principal meridians**." In most of Colorado, ranges are numbered west from the 6th principal meridian, which is located near Lincoln, Nebraska. The centerline of Colorado Boulevard in Denver is exactly 402 miles west of the 6th principal meridian. An east-west row of townships is a **"tier"** or township and is numbered sequentially north or south from its baseline. In most of Colorado, the main baseline lies approximately on the 40 degree parallel or line of latitude. This line is an extension of the Kansas-Nebraska border, and runs just north of the city of Brighton in Adams County.

As stated above, most of Colorado was surveyed in relation to the 6th principal meridian and 40 degrees latitude baseline. However, several counties in southwestern Colorado were surveyed using the New Mexico principal meridian and the New Mexico baseline as a starting point. Also, certain portions of Mesa and Delta Counties in western Colorado are measured from the Ute Meridian (located just east of Grand Junction) as the north-south survey line and an arbitrary baseline. These non-standard reference lines were implemented to expedite a survey in support of a plan to settle Ute Indians in and around what was later to become the city of Grand Junction. Because no surveys at that time had been extended west of the Continental Divide, a new meridian and a new baseline were established with no connection to the GSS. See map below.

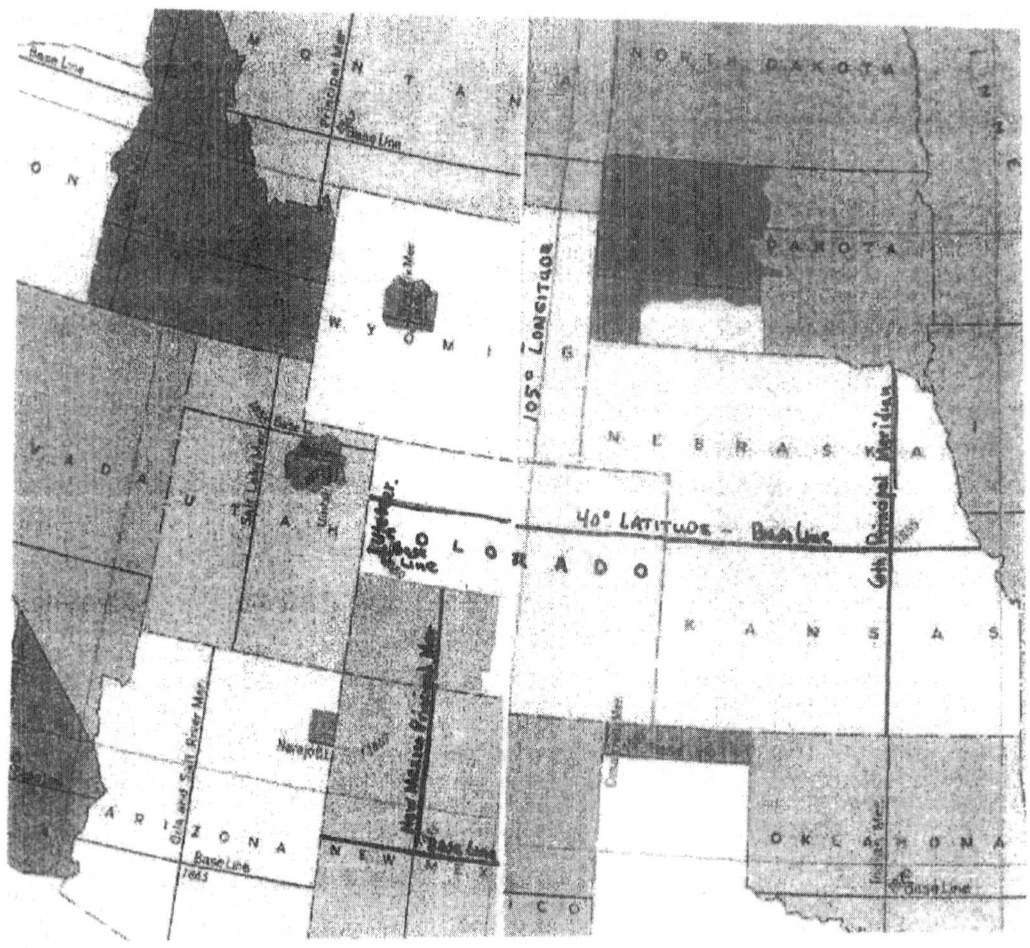

Because of the curvature of the earth, the meridians and north-south ranges converge as they extend toward the North Pole. To maintain a precise six-mile width, and to preserve the square shape of a township, range lines jog outward at each quadrangle (24 miles) so that they are again six miles apart.

The north and west tiers of sections of the township are closing sections. Discrepancies of closure between the interior section line and exterior boundary line surveys are adjusted. These sections usually contain more or less than the 640 acres in a normal section.

A township is six miles square (6 mi. x 6 mi. = 36 square miles). Each square mile is called a **"section,"** and contains 640 acres. Within each township, sections are numbered from 1 to 36 beginning in the northeast corner, counting west to Section 6, then down to

Section 7 and back east to Section 12, following a back and forth course to Section 36 in the southeastern-most corner of each township. This is known as the Boustrophedonic pattern. For purposes of legal description, sections are further divided into fractions, such as half-sections (320 acres), quarter-sections (160 acres), etc. Legal descriptions are then made in a building-block fashion from small to large, for example, referring to the southwest quarter of the northeast quarter of Section XX, Township XX North (of a particular base line), Range XX West (of a particular meridian).

A section is the smallest subdivision usually surveyed by government surveyors, marked at each section corner with a "survey monument."

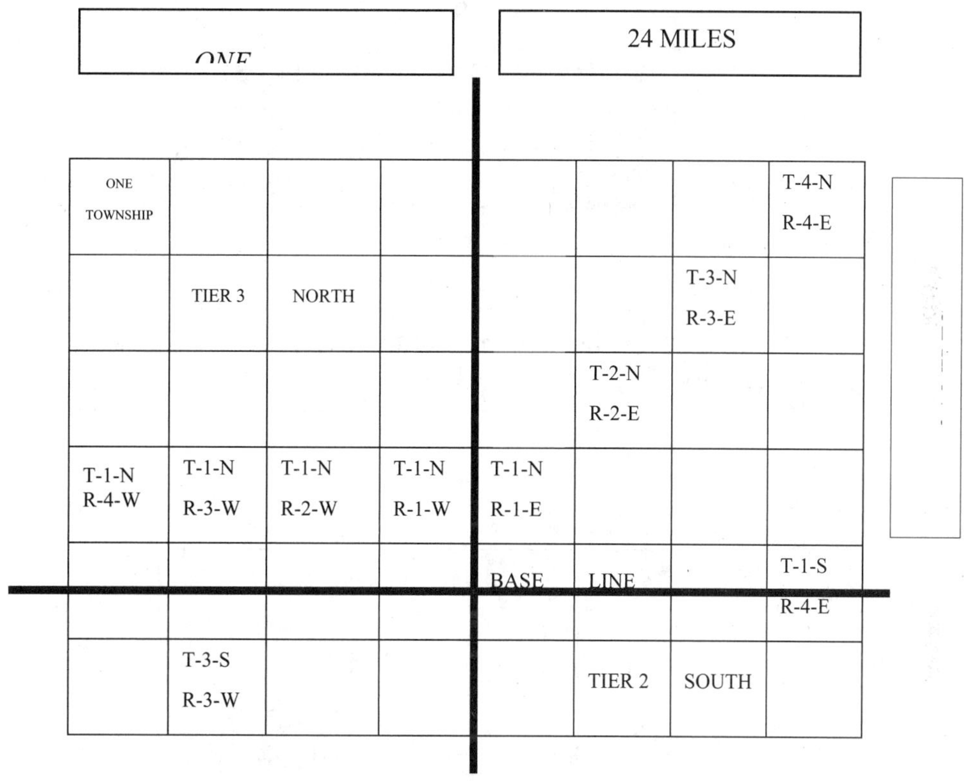

The above sketch shows ranges (numbered east and west of the 6th principal meridian) and townships (numbered north and south of a baseline). There are two quadrangles, one on either side of the 6th principal meridian above the base line. A portion of two additional quadrangles is shown below the base line. A tier is a horizontal row of ranges.

SIX MILES

		31	32	33	34	35	36	31	32
2	**1**	6	5	4	3	2	1	**6**	**5**
11	**12**	7	8	9	10	11	12	**7**	**8**
14	**13**	18	17	16	15	14	13	**18**	**17**
23	**24**	19	20	21	22	23	24	**19**	**20**
26	**25**	30	29	28	27	26	25	**30**	**29**
35	**36**	31	32	33	34	35	36	**31**	**32**
2	**1**	**6**	**5**	**4**	**3**	**2**	**1**	**6**	**5**

S I X M I L

Township map showing 36 numbered sections as connected to sections of adjacent townships

<table>
<tr><td>NW 1/4 of NW 1/4 40 ac.</td><td>NE 1/4 of NW 1/4</td><td colspan="2" rowspan="2">NE 1/4= 160 acres</td></tr>
<tr><td>SW 1/4 of NW 1/4</td><td>SE 1/4 of NW 1/4</td></tr>
<tr><td colspan="2">N 1/2 of SW 1/4</td><td rowspan="2">W 1/2 of SE 1/4</td><td rowspan="2">E 1/2 of SE 1/4 80 acres</td></tr>
<tr><td colspan="2">S 1/2 of SW 1/4</td></tr>
</table>

Example of a fractional breakdown of a section (640 acres) of land

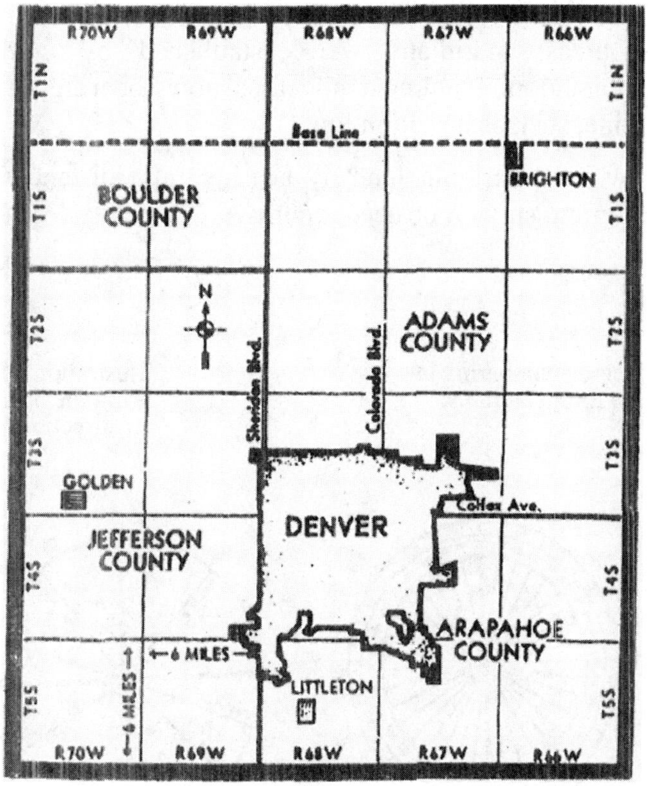

Map showing Denver and Vicinity in terms of the actual Townships, (tiers) and Ranges

III. Metes and Bounds Descriptions

When land cannot be identified by the governmental survey system, it is described by metes and bounds. Metes means measures of length and bounds means boundaries. The United States and Canada are the only countries in the world using the GSS. In the rest of the world, tracts of land are surveyed and described by metes and bounds—usually by identifying a point of beginning and the boundaries in relation to a recognized marker or monument or to natural features such as streams, bridges, piles of stones, or trees.

Metes and bounds are used in Colorado when it is necessary or desirable to describe a tract with irregular boundaries not conforming to the GSS. However, such a survey or description rarely relies on natural features for location. As used in this state, metes and bounds surveys and descriptions are irregular parts of a section or some subdivision of a section. They always tie to some established corner or line of the GSS or to a recognized point on a recorded subdivision plat. Professional land surveyors establish metes and bounds, and are the only persons qualified to sanction "official" surveys.

A. Bearing System

Metes and bounds are expressed in bearings and distances. The direction of a line—its "**bearing**"—is always stated in terms of its angle from north-south (expressed in degrees (°), minutes ('), and seconds (")), followed by its direction east or west of that north-south line, (*e.g.*, N 70 degrees, 19 minutes E., or S 24 degrees, 10' W). A cardinal direction of due north, south, east, or west is expressed as such.

In unsurveyed areas, meridians were established by compass or astronomical observations and calculation. In almost all cases now, bearings are determined from an already established line, such as a section line.

It is important when describing land by bearings and distances to state the source of information, such as grant, survey, or deed records.

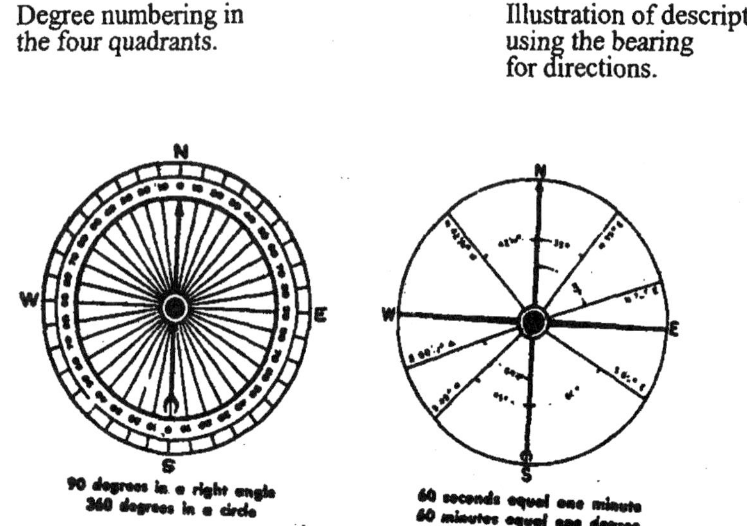

Example of Metes and Bounds Legal Description

A tract of land in the Northwest one-quarter of the Northwest one-quarter (N/W 1/4, NW 1/4) of Section 30, Township 1 South, Range 60 West of the 6th P.M., described as follows: Commencing from the Northwest corner of said Section 30; thence South 20 degrees 30 minutes East 140.60 feet to the point of beginning (POB); thence North 88 degrees 55 minutes East 200.00 feet; thence South 125.0 feet; thence South 88 degrees 55 minutes West 200.00 feet; thence North 125.00 feet to the POB, County of Adams, State of Colorado.

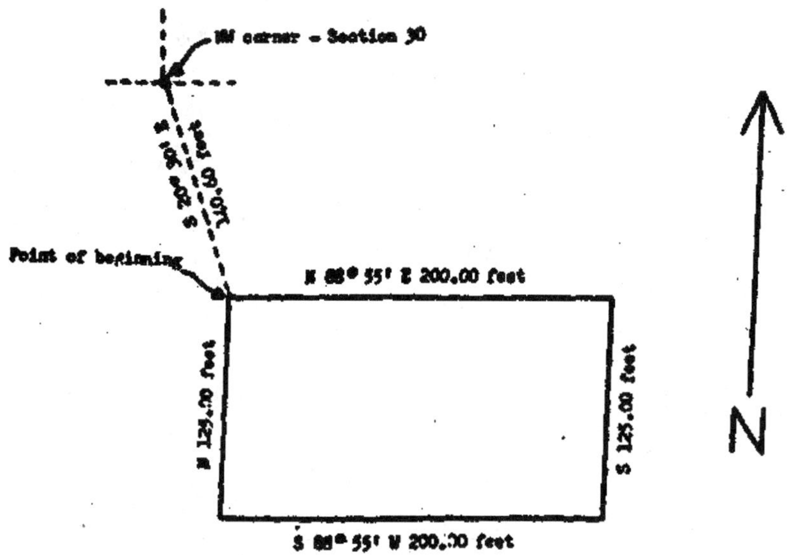

B. Azimuth System

The Azimuth system differs from bearings in that it expresses all directions in terms of the clockwise angle from North from zero (North) through 360 degrees (also North), instead of being broken into four quadrants. Thus, instead of N 70 degrees W, the Azimuth system would refer to that same boundary as “290 degrees,” moving clockwise from due North as the starting point, through 180 degrees (due South), then 270 degrees (due West). Surveyors often use it in their work, but generally convert it to the usual bearing description. It is seldom used in legal descriptions.

IV. Recorded Subdivision Plat

A single large tract of land is typically developed into subdivisions. The small parcels of land within a subdivision are called lots and blocks. Subdivisions usually propose streets, alleys, public utility easements, and such other information that the owner and local government desire to include as part of the development plan. A survey is conducted and a map called a subdivision plat is made. Plats must then be recorded in the office of the county clerk and recorder. Recording enables permanent description of a parcel of land as a certain lot and block of the recorded subdivision map, instead of by metes and bounds. The plat map itself shows the boundaries and specific measurements of each lot.

In most cases it is unlawful for any subdivider or agent of a subdivider to transfer title or sell any subdivided land before a final subdivision plat of the subdivided land has been approved by the county board of commissioners and recorded or filed with the clerk and recorder. Violations carry a penalty for each parcel sold. (See § 30-28-110, C.R.S.)

Furthermore, Colorado subdivision statues also requires registration with the Real Estate Commission of certain types of subdivisions where real property is to be divided into 20 or more interests, intended solely for residential use. (See the Subdivision chapter of the Colorado Real Estate Manual and § 12-10-501. *et seq.*)

Also, the boundaries of a subdivided block on which a lot is located must be visibly marked before a contract for sale is signed. Lot boundaries must be staked within one year from the effective date of the contract. The burden is on the seller of the subdivided lots to provide for this surveying, unless a block is sold as a unit, in which case the burden is on the subsequent seller. (See §§ 38-51-105(3)(a) and (5), C.R.S.)

The legal description of the shaded site in this illustration would be written as follows:

Lot five (5), Block two (2), Capitol Hill Subdivision, an addition to the City and County of Denver, State of Colorado, according to the recorded plat in the office of the County Clerk and Recorder of said county.

1			12	Grant St.	1			12
2			11	↕	2			11
3 Block			One 10		3 Block			Two 10
4			9		4			9
5			8		5			8
6			7		6			7

19th Ave. ↦

1			12		1			12
2			11		2			11
3 Block			Three 10		3 Block			Four 10
4			9		4			9
5			8		5			8
6			7		6			7

↖ 6' Utility Easements ↗

V. Surveys and Certificates

There are many methods and purposes for describing and identifying property that a real estate licensee will encounter and with which he or she should be familiar.

The "**land survey**" plat includes a scale drawing of the boundaries of a parcel of land, which is compiled by a series of exact and precise linear and angular measurements taken from a known point of origin developed by mathematical principles of surveying. The purpose of the land survey plat is to determine, locate, and/or restore real property boundaries. The land survey plat will also indicate any conflicting boundary evidence and any recorded and/or apparent rights-of-way or easements.

The "**improvement survey**" plat is comprised of the same precise information as is the land survey plat mentioned above, and also indicates the location of all structures (improvements) on the parcel of land. The improvement survey plat also shows visible encroachments and any fences, hedges, or walls on or within two feet of both sides of all boundaries. The improvement survey plat details all visible above-ground utilities and all underground utilities for which there is visible surface evidence.

An "**improvement location certificate (ILC)**" is another method of describing and approximately locating property, and is often required by lenders and insurance companies. It offers certain reasonable assurances regarding potential boundary or encroachment problems that may affect their interests. It also illustrates the location of improvements and conditions of the property. However, it is based on assumptions regarding boundary location and is *not a precise survey.* An ILC is typically used in single-family residential transactions for property located within a subdivision. It is a method of depicting property to which most real estate licensees will have the most exposure. A licensee should be familiar with the differences between land and improvement surveys and an ILC.

An ILC is:

5. 1. A representation of boundaries and improvements based on a surveyor's general knowledge in a given area;

6. 2. A depiction of the property boundaries showing the size and shape of a parcel that is based on the legal description provided in the warranty deed;

7. 3. A document signed and sealed by a professional land surveyor who has certain professional responsibilities for its accuracy; and

8. 4. A representation of the location of improvements, encroachments, and easements based on their relationship to a reasonable estimate of the location of property lines.

An ILC is not:

9. 1. A survey;

10. 2. Evidence of exact boundary location;

11. 3. A precise property corner locator;

12. 4. To be legally relied upon for locations of property lines or future improvements.

Sometimes an ILC will indicate a possible encroachment or other evidence of a boundary dispute. In this case, a true survey (*i.e.*, improvement survey plat or land survey plat) would be required to clarify or resolve any discrepancies. A real estate licensee should never represent that an ILC is a survey.

The following is a sample improvement location certificate:

LEGAL DESCRIPTION

Lots 15 and 15G,
Block D,
PLUM CREEK THREE,
County of Boulder,
State of Colorado.

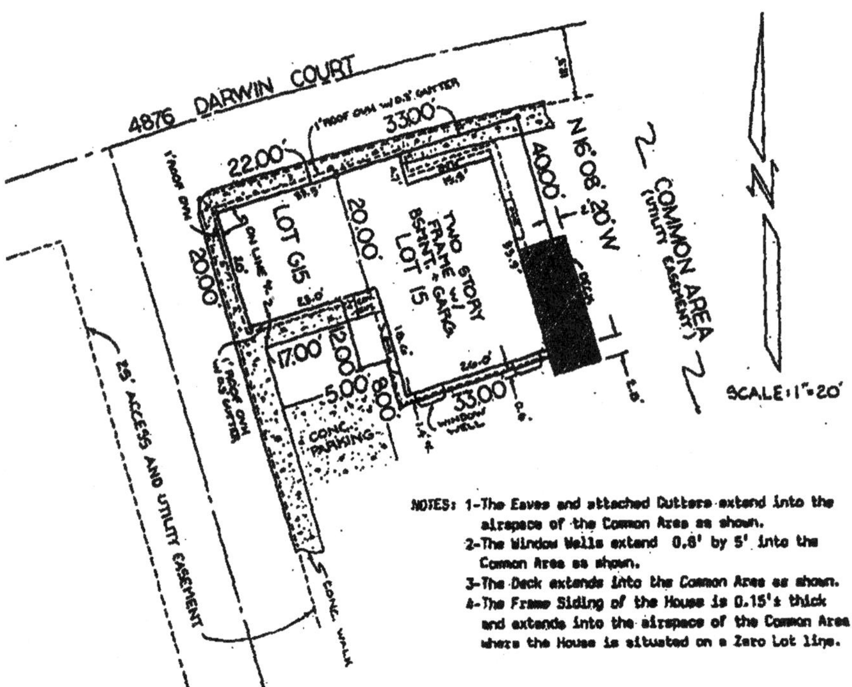

FLOOD INFORMATION
The subject property is located in Zone C, the area of minimal flooding according to the FEMA Flood Insurance Rate Map; Community-Panel No. 080024-0120-D, dated August 4, 1988.

John B. Guyton, Colorado L.S. #16406

IMPROVEMENT LOCATION CERTIFICATE

TO____________________ AND TO ____________________

I hereby certify that the improvements on the described parcel, except utility connections, are entirely within the boundaries of said parcel, except as shown, that there are no encroachments upon the described premises by improvements on any adjoining premises, except as indicated, and that there is no apparent evidence or sign of any easement crossing or burdening any part of said parcel, except as noted. I further certify that this improvement location certificate is not a land survey plat or improvement survey plat, and that it is not to be relied upon for the establishment of fence, building or other future improvements lines.

VI. Colorado Coordinate System

The Colorado Coordinate System became effective July 1, 1967 under §§ 38-52-101, *et seq.*, C.R.S. This statute is permissive in nature and is not mandatory.

The system is based on defining a point by its distance from two perpendicular baselines (*i.e.*, one north-south axis and an intersecting east-west axis). The intersection of such defined lines in each Colorado coordinate zone then serves as the beginning point of a legal description.

The survey divides Colorado into roughly equal horizontal zones—North, Central, and South. Counties located in the northern one-third are designated "Colorado Coordinate System, North Zone," and the same applies to the Central and South zones. When a tract of land overlaps two zones, it may be described with reference to either zone, and names the zone from which its measurement originates in the legal description.

The coordinates used to express a point in any zone of this system are two distances, expressed in number of feet, measured to two decimal places. The east-west direction is known as the "X-coordinate" and a north-south direction is known as the "Y-coordinate." These coordinates conform to those on the "Colorado Coordinate System" of the National Geodetic Survey within the State of Colorado.

Whenever the "Colorado Coordinate System" is used to describe a tract of land in a document that also legally describes the same tract by reference to a subdivision, or to the GSS, the Colorado Coordinates are supplemental to the other description. In the event of a conflict between two descriptions, the GSS description prevails over the Colorado Coordinates unless such coordinates are upheld by adjudication.

For further information on the Colorado Coordinate System of land description, refer to the statute or consult a professional land surveyor.

Example of a Metes and Bounds Description Using the Colorado Coordinate System as Supplemental Information

Commencing at the corner of Section 20, 21, 28 and 29, T 4 S, R 75 W, 6th P.M. and bearing North 22 degrees, 15 minutes West 202.50 feet to the point of beginning which is marked by a 5/8" diameter iron rod set in concrete; thence bearing North 79 degrees 45 minutes West 155 feet to a brass marker set in a granite ledge and stamped "2928," said brass marker having grid coordinates X = 1,916,572.14' and Y = 624,697.82' on the Colorado Coordinate System, Central Zone; thence South 22 degrees 45 minutes West 106.50 feet; thence South 70 degrees 15 minutes East 145 feet;, thence North 25 degrees 30 minutes E 133.50 feet to the Point of Beginning.

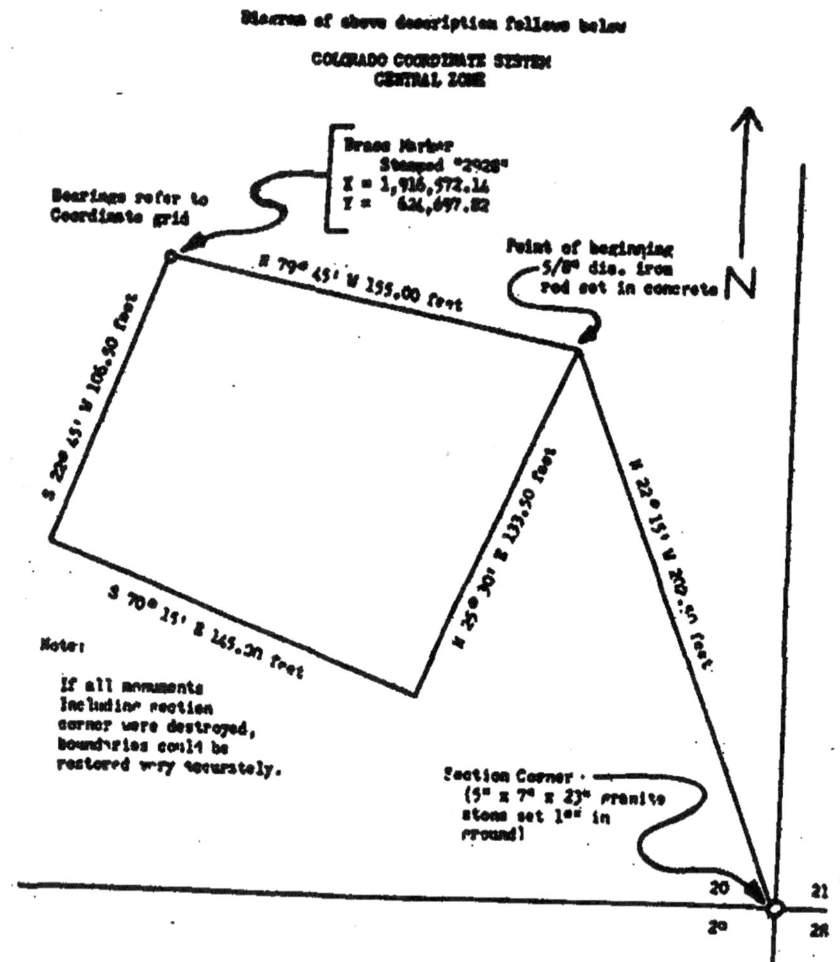

Any description is legal and valid if it unquestionably identifies the property. The phrase "legal description" refers to one of the types of land description explained in this chapter. These types of descriptions are more precise and accurate than informal descriptions such as street addresses.

Table of Land Measurement

LINEAR MEASURE	
7.92 inches	= 1 link
12 inches	= 1 foot
3 feet	= 1 yard
25 links	= 1 rod
100 links	= 1 chain
16 1/2 feet	= 1 rod
5 1/2 yards	= 1 rod
40 rods	= 1 furlong
8 furlongs	= 1 mile
66 feet	= 1 chain
80 chains	= 1 mile
320 rods	= 1 mile
8,000 links	= 1 mile
5,280 feet	= 1 mile
1,760 yards	= 1 mile

SQUARE MEASURE	
144 sq. in.	= 1 sq. foot
9 sq. feet	= 1 sq. yard
30 1/4 sq. yards	= 1 sq. rd.
16 sq. rods	= 1 sq. chain
1 sq. yard	= 272 1/4 sq. ft.
1 sq. chain	= 4356 sq. ft.
10 sq. chains	= 1 acre
160 sq. rods	= 1 acre
4,840 sq. yards	= 1 acre
43,560 sq. ft.	**= 1 acre**
640 acres	**= 1 sq. mile**
1 sq. mile	**= 1 section**
36 sq. miles	**= 1 township**
6 miles square	**= 1 township**
1 sq. mile	= 2.59 sq. kilometer

VII. Metric System

Most of the world does its measuring in metes. The metric system is called the International System (IS) of Units, and it is the measurement standard in nearly all countries of the world. The United States is slowly moving toward the metric system.

The metric system progresses logically in units of 10. Measurement prefixes have the same meanings whether measuring length, volume, or mass, the most common being micro- (one-millionth); milli- (one-thousandth); centi- (one-hundredth); deci- (one-tenth); mega- (1,000,000 x the base); kilo- (1,000 x the base); hecto- (100 x the base); and deka- (10 x the base).

The basic dimension of the metric system is the meter (approx. 3.28 feet). All dimensions of length may be expressed as variations of a meter—millimeter (mm), centimeter (cm), meter (m), or kilometer (km). To convert between the units, you need only move the decimal point to the right or left.

The basic metric unit of land measurement is the hectare (abbreviated as ha.), a square with each side 100 meters long, covering an area of 10,000 square meters. A hectare is equivalent to 2.471 acres.

U.S. TO METRIC		**METRIC TO U.S.**	
LENGTH			
1 inch	= 25.4 millimeters (mm)	1 millimeter (mm)	= 0.04 inch
1 foot	= 0.3 meter (m)	1 meter (m)	= 3.28 feet
1 yard	= 0.9 meter (m)	1 meter (m)	= 1.09 yards
1 mile	= 1.6 kilometer (km)	1 kilometer (km)	= 0.62 mile
AREA			
1 sq. inch	= 6.5 sq. centimeters (cm2)	1 sq. centimeter	= .16 sq. inch
1 sq. foot	= .09 sq. meter (m2)	1 square meter	= 10.76 sq. feet
1 sq. yard	= .84 sq. meter (m2)	1 square meter	= 1.2 sq. yards
1 acre	= .4 hectare (ha)	1 hectare	= 2.471 acres
1 sq. mile	= 2.6 sq. kilometers (km2)	1 sq. kilometer	= .39 sq. mile

Metric System			
Unit	Abbreviation	Number of Meters	Approx. U.S. Equivalent
Length			
Myriameter	mym	10,000	6.2 miles
Kilometer	km	1,000	.62 miles
Hectometer	hm	100	109.36 yards
Decameter	dkm	10	32.81 feet
Decimeter	dm	.1	3.94 inches
Centimeter	cm	.01	.3973 inches
Millimeter	mm	.001	.04 inches
Area			
Square Kilometer	sq. km or km	1,000,000	.3861 square miles
Hectare	ha	10,000	2.471 acres
Are	a	100	119.6 square yards
Centiare	ca	1	10.76 square feet
Square Centimeter	sq. cm or cm2	.0001	.155 square inches

Chapter 13: Deeds and Transfer of Title

An * in the left margin indicates a change in the statute, rule or text since the last publication of the manual.

I. Introduction

Before the modern-day concept of land ownership, title to real estate was evidenced primarily by possession of the land and the power to defend the land against others. The earliest method of transferring title to real property was simply surrender of possession by the claimant to another.

The use of deeds to convey real property has a long and colorful history. Personal property has always been transferred by giving possession of the thing itself. In feudal land transfers, the seller presented a clod of dirt from the land to the buyer in the presence of witnesses to symbolize delivery of title. Today, the delivery of the deed constitutes the actual transfer of title to the land.

Title to real property transfers from one person to another by one of four general means:

1. Descent;
2. Will;
3. Involuntary alienation; or
4. Voluntary alienation.

Title transfers "**by descent**" when a person dies without leaving a will (intestate). All states have statutes of descent and distribution providing for the orderly disposition of real property for those who die intestate. Such statutes typically distribute property to the nearest relatives, on the presumption that this would have been the desire of the deceased. According to the Colorado Probate Code, a portion of which is printed below, distribution of the largest share of the property of the decedent, and never less than half of the estate, descends to the surviving spouse.

§ 15-10-112, C.R.S. Cost of living adjustment of certain dollar amounts.

(1) As used in this section, unless the context otherwise requires:

(a) "CPI" means the consumer price index (annual average) for all urban consumers (CPI-U): United States city average—all items, reported by the bureau of labor statistics, United States department of labor or its successor agency or, if the index is discontinued, an equivalent index reported by a federal authority. If no such index is reported, the term means the substitute index chosen by the department of revenue; and

(b) "Reference base index" means the CPI for the calendar year 2010.

(2) The dollar amounts stated in sections 15-11-102, 15-11-202 (2), 15-11-403, and 15-11-405 apply to the estate of a decedent who died during or after 2010, but for the estate of a decedent who died after 2011, these dollar amounts must be increased or decreased if the CPI for the calendar year immediately preceding the year of death exceeds or is less than the reference base index. The amount of any increase or decrease is computed by multiplying each dollar amount by the percentage by which the CPI for the calendar year immediately preceding the year of

death exceeds or is less than the reference base index. If the amount of the increase or decrease produced by the computation is not a multiple of one thousand dollars, then the amount of the increase or decrease is rounded down if it is an increase, or rounded up if it is a decrease, to the next multiple of one thousand dollars, but for the purpose of section 15-11-405, the periodic installment amount is the lump-sum amount divided by twelve. If the CPI for 2010 is changed by the bureau of labor statistics, the reference base index must be revised using the rebasing factor reported by the bureau of labor statistics, or other comparable data if a rebasing factor is not reported.

(3) Before February 1, 2012, and before February 1 of each succeeding year, the department of revenue shall publish a cumulative list, beginning with the dollar amounts effective for the estate of a decedent who died in 2012 of each dollar amount as increased or decreased under this section.

§ 15-11-101, C.R.S. Intestate estate.

(1) Any part of a decedent's estate not effectively disposed of by will or otherwise passes by intestate succession to the decedent's heirs as prescribed in this code, except as modified by the decedent's will.

(2) A decedent by will may expressly exclude or limit the right of an individual or class to succeed to property of the decedent passing by intestate succession. If that individual or a member of that class survives the decedent, the share of the decedent's intestate estate to which that individual or class would have succeeded passes as if that individual or each member of that class had disclaimed his or her intestate share.

§ 15-11-102, C.R.S. Share of spouse.

The various possible circumstances describing the decedent, his or her surviving spouse, and their surviving descendants, if any, are set forth in this section to be utilized in determining the intestate share of the decedent's surviving spouse. If more than one circumstance is applicable, the circumstance that produces the largest share for the surviving spouse shall be applied. The intestate share of a decedent's surviving spouse is:

(1) The entire intestate estate if:

 (a) No descendant or parent of the decedent survives the decedent; or

 (b) All of the decedent's surviving descendants are also descendants of the surviving spouse and there is no other descendant of the surviving spouse who survives the decedent;

(2) The first three hundred thousand dollars, plus three-fourths of any balance of the intestate estate, if no descendant of the decedent survives the decedent, but a parent of the decedent survives the decedent;

(3) The first two hundred twenty-five thousand dollars, plus one-half of any balance of the intestate estate, if all of the decedent's surviving descendants are also descendants of the surviving spouse and the surviving spouse has one or more surviving descendants who are not descendants of the decedent;

(4) The first one hundred fifty thousand dollars, plus one-half of any balance of the intestate estate, if one or more of the decedent's surviving descendants are not descendants of the surviving spouse.

(5) (Deleted by amendment, L. 2009, (HB 09-1287), ch. 310, p. 1671, § 3, effective July 1, 2010.)

(6) The dollar amounts stated in this section shall be increased or decreased based on the cost of living adjustment as calculated and specified in section 15-10-112.

(Applies on or after July 1, 2010, to governing instruments executed by decedents who die on or after July 1, 2010)

§ 15-11-102.5, C.R.S. Share of designated beneficiary.

(1) If the decedent is survived by a person with the right to inherit real or personal property from the decedent in a designated beneficiary agreement executed pursuant to article 22 of this title, the intestate share of the decedent's designated beneficiary is:

(a) The entire estate if no descendent of the decedent survives the decedent; or

(b) One half of the intestate estate if one or more descendants of the decedent survive the decedent.

§ 15-11-103, C.R.S. Share of heirs other than surviving spouse and designated beneficiary.

Any part of the intestate estate not passing to the decedent's surviving spouse under section 15-11-102, or to the decedent's surviving designated beneficiary under section 15-11-102.5, or the entire intestate estate if there is no surviving spouse and no surviving designated beneficiary with the right to inherit real or personal property from the decedent through intestate succession, passes in the following order to the individuals who survive the decedent:

(1) (Deleted by amendment, L. 2010, (SB 10-199), ch. 374, p. 1748, § 5, effective July 1, 2010.)

(2) To the decedent's descendants per capita at each generation;

(3) If there is no surviving descendant, to the decedent's parents equally if both survive, or to the surviving parent if only one survives;

(4) If there is no surviving descendant or parent, to the descendants of the decedent's parents or either of them per capita at each generation;

(5) If there is no surviving descendant, parent, or descendant of a parent, but the decedent is survived on both the paternal and maternal sides by one or more grandparents or descendants of grandparents:

(a) Half to the decedent's paternal grandparents equally if both survive, to the surviving paternal grandparent if only one survives, or to the descendants of the decedent's paternal grandparents or either of them if both are deceased, the descendants taking per capita at each generation; and

(b) Half to the decedent's maternal grandparents equally if both survive, to the surviving maternal grandparent if only one survives, or to the descendants of the decedent's maternal grandparents or either of them if both are deceased, the descendants taking per capita at each generation;

(6) If there is no surviving descendant, parent, or descendant of a parent, but the decedent is survived by one or more grandparents or descendants of grandparents on the paternal but not the maternal side, or on the maternal but not the paternal side, to the decedent's relatives on the side with one or more surviving members in the manner as described in subsection (5) of this section;

(7) (Deleted by amendment, L. 2010, (SB 10-199), ch. 374, p. 1748, § 5, effective July 1, 2010.)

(8) (Deleted by amendment, L. 2009, (HB 09-1287), ch. 310, p. 1672, § 4, effective July 1, 2010.)

Any part of the intestate estate not passing to the decedent's surviving spouse under § 15-11-102, C.R.S., or to the decedent's surviving designated beneficiary under § 15-11-102.5, C.R.S., passes to the nearest surviving relatives in accordance with § 15-11-103, C.R.S.

Title to property of a decedent more often transfers "**by will**." The laws of each state give a person a limited right to dispose of property after death. A person who dies leaving a last will and testament is said to have died "**testate**." In no state may a decedent completely exclude a spouse from distribution of his or her property. Under the Colorado Probate Code, a surviving spouse is entitled to a share of the estate even if there is a will to the contrary. **§ 15-11-202, C.R.S. Elective-share:**

§ 15-11-202, C.R.S. Elective-share.

(1) **Elective-share amount.** The surviving spouse of a decedent who dies domiciled in this state has a right of election, under the limitations and conditions stated in this part 2, to take an elective-share amount equal to fifty percent of the value of the marital-property portion of the augmented estate.

(2) (a) **Supplemental elective-share amount.** If the sum of the amounts described in sections 15-11-207, 15-11-209 (1) (a), and that part of the elective-share amount payable from the decedent's net probate estate and nonprobate transfers to others under section 15-11-209 (3) (a) and (3) (b) is less than fifty thousand dollars, the surviving spouse is entitled to a supplemental elective-share amount equal to fifty thousand dollars, minus the sum of the amounts described in those sections. The supplemental elective-share amount is payable from the decedent's net probate estate and from recipients of the decedent's nonprobate transfers to others in the order of priority set forth in section 15-11-209 (3) (a) and (3) (b).

(b) The court shall increase or decrease the dollar amount stated in paragraph (a) of this subsection (2) based on the cost of living adjustment as calculated and specified in section 15-10-112.

(3) **Effect of election on statutory benefits.** If the right of election is exercised by or on behalf of the surviving spouse, the exempt property and family allowance, if any, are not charged against but are in addition to the elective-share and supplemental elective-share amounts.

(4) **Nondomiciliary.** The right, if any, of the surviving spouse of a decedent who dies domiciled outside this state to take an elective-share in property in this state is governed by the law of the decedent's domicile at death.

"**Involuntary alienation**" (alienation as used here means "transfer") is a transfer without the owner's consent. Examples of such involuntary transfers are tax sales and sales to foreclose a mortgage or to enforce mechanics' or other liens. Involuntary alienation also occurs if title is lost through "**adverse possession**," a situation in which an owner is not making use of the property and an adverse claimant possesses the real estate openly and notoriously, hostile to, and to the exclusion of the owner for a period of time as required by law (18 years in Colorado).

"**Voluntary alienation**," by gift, loan, trade, or sale is the normal mode of real estate transfer, whereby either all or some of the owner's rights are voluntarily transferred to another. Examples of such transfers are: a buy-sell contract consummated by delivery of a deed, transfer of title by a deed of trust or mortgage as security for the payment of a note, or a lease.

The "**right of alienation**" is one of the "bundle of rights" of real estate ownership, allowing one to transfer ownership of real property to another. Living persons generally convey title by the execution and delivery of a deed. A "**deed**" is a legal instrument in writing, duly executed and delivered, whereby a grantor (owner) conveys to a grantee some right, title, or interest in or to the real estate.

Real estate may also be conveyed by deed to a person (*e.g.*, an individual, partnership, or corporation) as trustee for the benefit of a third party. The trustee then holds legal title and the third party holds the equitable title and receives the benefits.

A. Types of Deeds

There are four major classifications of deeds:

1. General warranty deed;
2. Special warranty deed;
3. Bargain and sale deed; and
4. Quitclaim deed.

The types of deeds differ solely in the degree of protection that the grantor promises or warrants to the grantee. No type of deed transfers any greater or lesser interest than another. For example, if a grantor conveys title in fee simple by a general warranty deed, the same fee simple ownership is transferred as if he or she had used a quitclaim deed. However, the general warranty deed grantor promises to defend against any loss incurred due to any title defect, whereas transfer by quitclaim deed contains no such warrant.

General Warranty Deed

A general warranty deed is one in which the grantor warrants or guarantees title against defects that existed before the grantor acquired title or that arose during the grantor's ownership. It does not warrant against encumbrances or defects arising from the grantee's own acts. The usual covenants or warranties contained in a general warranty deed are:

1. **Covenant of seisin.** Guarantees the grantor's ownership and that he or she has the right to convey it. The fact that the property is mortgaged or is subject to some restriction does not breach this covenant.
2. **Covenant against encumbrances.** Guarantees that there are no encumbrances or claims against the property except those specifically excluded in the deed.
3. **Covenant of quiet enjoyment.** Guarantees that the grantee will not be evicted or disturbed in possession of the property. Threats or claims by a third party do not breach this covenant. The grantee would have to actually be dispossessed before being entitled to seek recovery against the grantor under this covenant.
4. **Covenant of further assurance.** Guarantees that the grantor will procure and deliver any other instruments that are subsequently necessary to make the title good.
5. **Covenant of warrant forever.** Guarantees that the grantee shall have title to and possession of the property. Sometimes considered part of "quiet enjoyment."

The first two covenants relate to the past, and generally do not "run with the land"—meaning that only the current grantee may sue the grantor for a breach. The last three covenants protect against future defects and are said to run with the land—allowing any subsequent grantee to seek remedy for breach against any previous grantor. According to § 38-30-121, C.R.S., "covenants of seisin, peaceable possession, freedom from encumbrances, and warranty contained in any conveyance of real estate, or any interest therein, shall run with the premises and inure to the benefit of all subsequent purchasers and encumbrancers."

Special Warranty Deed

The grantor of a special warranty deed warrants the title only against defects arising after the grantor acquired the property and not against title defects arising before that time.

Bargain and Sale Deed

Technically, any deed that recites a consideration and purports to convey the real estate is a bargain and sale deed. Thus, many quitclaim and warranty deeds are also deeds of bargain and sale. Bargain and sale deeds often contain a covenant against the grantor's acts, whereby the grantor warrants only that the grantor has done nothing to harm the title. This covenant would not run with the land. Examples of bargain and sale deeds with a covenant against the grantor's acts are an executor's or personal representative's deed, a beneficiary's deed, an administrator's deed, and a conservator's or guardian's deed.

Quitclaim Deed

The grantor of a quitclaim deed warrants absolutely nothing. A quitclaim deed transfers the grantor's present interest in the land, if any. A quitclaim deed is frequently used to clear up a technical defect in the chain of title, to release lien claims against the property, to remove an owner in a multiple ownership situation, or when someone changes their name (*e.g.*, to a married name). Examples of such deeds are correction deeds and deeds of release.

B. Usual Elements of Deeds

In general, the usual elements of a deed are:

1. Written instrument;
2. Parties – grantor and grantee;
3. Recital of consideration;
4. Words of conveyance;
5. Description of the property;
6. Signature;
7. Delivery and acceptance;
8. Exceptions and restrictions;
9. Warranties and covenants;
10. Date;
11. Acknowledgment; and
12. Recording.

The first seven elements above are absolutely essential for a valid deed. The other five are recommended, but will not invalidate a deed if omitted:

1. **Written Instrument.** A deed must be in writing to be effective. The Colorado statute of frauds, § 38-10-106, C.R.S., requires: "No estate or interest in lands, other than leases for a term not exceeding one year, nor any trust or power over or concerning lands or in any manner relating thereto shall be created, granted, assigned, surrendered, or declared, unless by act or operation of law, or by deed or conveyance in writing subscribed by the party creating, granting, assigning, surrendering, or declaring the same, or by his lawful agent thereunto authorized by writing." Note the two exceptions to the requirement of a written instrument are: (1) a lease for a term not exceeding one year, and (2) an interest or estate created by operation of law.

The courts may set aside a deed altered in any manner after delivery to the grantee. This means that all blanks on preprinted forms must be filled in according to the requirements of law and the intention of the parties.

2. **Parties: Grantor and Grantee.** A valid deed must clearly name or designate the grantor who is conveying interest in the property. The grantor's name must be identical to the name shown as the grantee in the conveyance by which the grantor received title. A minor discrepancy in name may not invalidate the deed, but could lead to legal challenge. A natural person grantor should be of sound mind. If a grantor is a minor and not of legal age, the conveyance may later be set aside and the grantor could recover the property.

   A deed is void if it fails to designate with reasonable certainty the grantee to whom title passes. Colorado deeds dated after January 1, 1977 must include the legal address of the grantee, including a road or street address. County clerks and recorders may reject a deed that does not comply. (See § 38-35-109(2), C.R.S.)

3. **Recital of Consideration.** A deed is valid without tangible consideration, but should contain at least a recital of consideration (*e.g.*, for $1.00, or for love and affection). Lack of consideration does not render a gift conveyance void, but may preclude a donee (receiver of the gift) from enforcing warranty deed covenants against the donor (grantor). A gift deed may also be set aside on grounds of fraud. For example, the grantor's creditors may set aside a deed gifting property to defraud creditors. If the deed recites consideration, the burden of proving lack of consideration is on the one who attacks the deed.

   Section 39-13-102, C.R.S., requires a "documentary fee" on real property conveyances where the consideration is more than $500. Each county clerk and recorder must collect one penny per one hundred dollars (sale price x .0001) of consideration whenever a deed is recorded. The documentary fee aids county tax assessors in determining property values. Section 39-14-102, C.R.S., requires the grantor and/or grantee to provide a "declaration" to the property tax administrator along with all conveyance documents subject to a documentary fee when presented for recording. It is a criminal offense to misstate actual consideration to the clerk and recorder. The assessor may impose a penalty of $25.00 or twenty-five one-thousandths of one percent of the sale price, whichever is greater, for failure of the grantee to submit the declaration. The deed itself is valid whether consideration shown on the face of the instrument is true and actual or nominal.

4. **Words of Conveyance or Quitclaim.** A deed must contain words that manifest intent to transfer title, or else it is ineffective. No specific words are required, but "sell and convey," "grant, bargain, sell, and convey," or "convey and warrant" are commonly used. The word "quitclaim" is substituted for "convey" in a quitclaim deed.

5. **Description of the Property.** A deed is not valid unless it legally describes the real estate conveyed or quitclaimed. Any description that clearly identifies the property is sufficient, but using the same legal description used in previous deeds to the same parcel avoids discrepancies in the records and possible future title litigation. Courts may be liberal in holding rather ambiguous descriptions to be valid, but a court action is a high price to pay to correct technical errors that could have been avoided when drafting the legal description.

Any deed recorded after July 1, 1992, where the legal description has been newly created, must contain the name and address of the person who created the new legal description; however, failure to include this information will not affect the validity or the recordability of the deed. (See § 38-35-106.5, C.R.S.)

Section 38-35-122, C.R.S., provides that in addition to the legal description, the street address or identifying numbers on buildings, and the assessor's schedule or parcel number, must appear on the document of title. However, failure to include this additional information will not render the document ineffective or the title unmarketable.

A deed normally contains words following the description indicating that all the appurtenances go with the land. All improvements go with the land as appurtenances.

6. **Signature.** A deed not signed by the grantor is invalid. If there is more than one grantor (*e.g.*, joint tenants), each must sign the deed. A few states, primarily in the east, require a seal for a deed to be valid. Colorado and most states have abolished the requirement for a seal. Colorado does not require that the signature of the grantor be witnessed.

7. **Delivery and Acceptance.** To be effective, a deed must be both delivered by the grantor and accepted by the grantee. The intent of the grantor determines delivery. Presenting a deed to the grantee for examination does not constitute delivery. The grantor must deliver with intent to pass title to the grantee. Under § 38-35-101, C.R.S., an acknowledged and recorded deed presumes effective delivery.

   Effective delivery must occur while the grantor is alive. If a grantor executes a deed, retains it, and directs it to be delivered to the grantee at the grantor's death, the deed does not pass title. A grantor may deliver a deed to a third party to be held and delivered later to the grantee, but to be effective, the grantor must surrender all right to control or recover the deed.

8. **Exceptions and Restrictions.** A grantor is assumed to convey property free and clear of all encumbrances. Therefore, the deed usually provides that the grantor conveys the property "free and clear of all encumbrances except . . ."—followed by the exception, such as: "subject to a deed of trust (complete description)"; or "subject to an easement (complete description)"; or "subject to all encumbrances and restrictions of record."

   A grantor may restrict the grantee's right to use the real estate conveyed, as long as such restrictions are reasonable and not contrary to public policy. The use of such deed restrictions, or "**restrictive covenants**," is an old practice deriving from the bundle of property rights. An owner has the right of free alienation, that is, the right to dispose of his or her interest in any manner whatsoever. Once deed restrictions are established, they run with the land, limiting its use by all future grantees. Covenants are standard features in subdivisions and are intended to benefit all the landowners.

   Typical restrictions deal with the minimum size of the house, type of building or roofing material, or exclusion of commercial establishments. Well-formulated deed restrictions have a stabilizing effect on property values. Homeowners are protected against forbidden uses, and may rest assured that a nuisance business will not be a neighbor or that a neighbor's house will meet certain minimum standards. Deed restrictions must be enforced through court action brought by any party for whose benefit the restrictions were imposed.

9. **Warranties and Covenants.** Warranties are not an essential requirement of a valid deed. A grantor may transfer interest by a quitclaim deed, giving no warranty of any kind, or by a general warranty deed, wherein the grantor makes numerous warrants to the grantee. Section 38-30-113(a), C.R.S., specifies a short-form warranty deed whereby every deed that is similar to the statutory form, and which includes the words "and warrant(s) the title," automatically implies the usual general warranty deed covenants.

   In 2019, § 38-30-113(1)(b), (c), and (d), C.R.S., specified the use of additional short-form deeds, including: a special warranty deed; a bargain and sale deed; and a quitclaim deed.

10. **Date.** A date is not essential for a valid deed, although it is a universal custom to date all deeds. A dated deed might obviously prevent future question or controversy concerning the time of delivery of the deed.

11. **Acknowledgment.** An acknowledgment is a declaration made by a person (grantor) to a notary public, or other authorized official, that the grantor executed the instrument and did so freely and voluntarily. The official fills out a certificate of acknowledgment customarily printed on the deed. Section 38-35-101, C.R.S., provides: "No officer . . . shall take or certify such acknowledgments unless the person making the same is personally known to such officer to be the identical person he represents himself to be . . . . It shall not be necessary to state such fact in his certificate of acknowledgment attached to any instrument affecting title to real property."

    In most states, including Colorado, a deed is valid and may be recorded without being notarized. Many states, however, require acknowledgment as a condition of recording.

    It is always sound practice to have a deed acknowledged before recording because of the presumption of proper delivery and acceptance (see number 7 above). An acknowledged deed may be evidence if a title controversy arises. An unacknowledged deed may only be used as evidence of the transaction if it has been recorded ten years or more and proven in court that the deed was properly executed. (See § 38-35-106, C.R.S.)

    The facts in a deed recorded for 20 years or more may be read in evidence and received as prima facie evidence of these facts. (See § 38-35-107, C.R.S.)

12. **Recording.** A deed is valid even if it is not recorded. The wording of the Colorado recording statute is permissive ("may be") rather than mandatory ("must be").

    Recording offers a two-fold benefit. It protects an innocent purchaser or encumbrancer from acting in ignorance of an unrecorded instrument, and it provides "**constructive notice**," a legally conclusive presumption that all persons have knowledge of recorded instruments. It is in the grantee's best interest to record the deed immediately.

    Lack of acknowledgment does not invalidate constructive notice. A recorded deed that is not acknowledged still serves notice to subsequent purchasers. (See § 38-35-106, C.R.S.)

In addition to constructive notice, a purchaser or encumbrancer may have "**actual notice**" of another's right or claim. For instance, a purchaser is presumed to have actual notice of all rights and claims of parties in possession of the property, so that even if the right or claim is unrecorded, the purchaser cannot defeat it.

Chapter 14: Evidence of Title

An * in the left margin indicates a change in the statute, rule, or text since the last publication of the manual.

I. Introduction

A prudent buyer will want to examine the title to the real property to confirm that the seller is indeed the owner and to check the status of the title to be conveyed to the buyer. This due diligence is essential and most forms of contracts for the purchase and sale of real property contain detailed terms and deadlines to ensure that the buyer is able to achieve this goal.

A quick search of the real property records, or a copy of a deed proffered as proof of the seller's ownership, are inadequate. There are a number of potential areas of risk: (1) the deed may not have been recorded, (2) a previous owner's title may be defective, (3) the seller may own something less than fee simple title; (4) title may be legally unmarketable, (5) title may be encumbered by liens, encumbrances, and restrictions. The buyer should have a thorough understanding of the exact state of the seller's title before closing on the transaction. Once title has been conveyed to the buyer, the buyer's title will be burdened with the same liens, encumbrances, and restrictions. The lender also has an interest in ascertaining the evidence of title by reason of accepting a mortgage or deed of trust on the real property as security for repayment of the loan.

Today's buyer is tomorrow's seller. If the buyer ignores the status of title when purchasing the real property, the buyer may well be confronted with, and forced to resolve, the same issues when the buyer eventually sells the real property.

How then can the prudent buyer be certain that the seller is indeed the owner of the real property? This chapter, "**Evidence of title**", describes the ways in which the buyer can obtain satisfactory proof of the nature and extent of the seller's ownership. There are today two methods to obtain evidence of title: (1) title insurance, and, (2) an abstract and opinion of title. Title insurance is by far the most prevalent method used for this purpose, not only in Colorado, but nationwide.

Until recently, a Torrens certificate of title could have been used to provide a third method for Evidence of Title. This system has been terminated by statute. Beginning January 1, 2018, the registration system was closed to new registrations, and from January 1, 2020, it is no longer available with all registrations taking place using the county clerk and recorder's office and procedures.

II. Purpose of Recording

Before looking at the ways to obtain the evidence of title, it is useful to understand the importance of recording documents affecting title to real property.

There is no requirement that a document must be recorded. For example, a deed conveying the ownership of real property from the seller to the buyer is effective between the seller and buyer on execution, delivery, and acceptance of the deed by the parties. This conveyance of ownership is also binding on any person who has actual knowledge of the facts.

However, the deed is ineffective against all other persons who have no actual knowledge of the deed. An unsuspecting buyer can pay good money to a fraudulent seller who tries to sell the same real property to another buyer, who lacks the knowledge of the fact that the real property has already been sold to the first buyer.

The prudent buyer will take advantage of the benefits conferred by the Colorado recording statute (C.R.S. 38-35-109(1)). In this way, by recording the deed before any other person, the buyer can protect its rights against anyone else who may have acquired an interest in the real property. On recording, everyone is deemed to have notice (called "constructive notice") of the existence of this deed and its contents. This is called a "Race-Notice" statute, on the basis of "first in time, first in right".

All states provide for the public recording of documents by which any estate or interest in land is created, transferred or encumbered. In Colorado, the recording is done through the offices of the clerk and recorder for the county in which the real property is situated (C.R.S. §38-30-406).

The county real property records should provide certainty and a reliable history of the ownership of a parcel of land by providing notice of the seller's rights of ownership, or other interests in the land, to any person searching the records.

But there are many times when a search of the county real property records may not be conclusive as to the seller's ownership. Common examples include (1) when the record owner has died and the necessary deed to evidence the conveyance of the real property from the estate of the deceased owner to the heirs has not been recorded (under the Colorado Probate Code, title to the real property vests in the heirs on the death of the owner, subject to administration under the Probate Code), (2) the vesting of ownership or a lesser interest in the real property in another person through the operation of the laws of adverse possession or prescriptive easements, (3) a break in the chain of title caused by the failure to record a deed in a prior transaction, and (4) a forged document in the chain of title.

III. Title Insurance

Title insurance is a type of insurance that protects the insured against loss occurring through defects in title to real property. As in other types of insurance policies, the owner of, or a person who holds an interest in, the real property (the insured) transfers the risk of loss to the insurer.

In its simplest form, a title insurance policy provides that the insurer will indemnify the insured against any loss sustained because of a defect in title (such as the examples given above), provided that the defect in title is not specifically excluded in the title insurance policy. Further, the insurer agrees to defend any lawsuit attacking the title based on an alleged defect that is covered by the policy. Because the title insurance company provides the financial backing for the insurance given, buyers should investigate, and satisfy themselves that the title insurance company is financially solid and adheres to sound business practices.

In the sections below, we will look at the way in which the buyer can obtain title insurance for the real property to be purchased and how to use it as to understand the seller's title.

A. Title Insurance Commitments

Section 8 (Title Insurance, Record Title and Off Record-Record Title) of the Real Estate Commission approved contract for residential real property provides that the seller or buyer will (1) select the title insurance company to furnish at the expense of the seller or buyer, a current title insurance commitment for an owner's policy of title insurance, and, (2) cause the title insurance policy to be issued.

Shortly after receiving an order for the title insurance commitment, the title insurance company will issue a title insurance commitment showing what it is willing to insure and under what circumstances. The title insurance commitment will include copies of title documents such as the plats, declarations, covenants, conditions and restrictions burdening the property. The buyer should review these documents as part of the determination of the evidence of title.

The title insurance commitment will be divided into three schedules, (1) Schedule A which discloses the name of the owner of the real property according to the real property records, the name of the proposed insured (the buyer), the liability amount of the policy to be issued, and the legal description of the real property to be insured, (2) Schedule B, Part I which details the requirements of the title insurance company to issue the policy (such as requirements for clearing liens and encumbrances, extended coverage to insure over matters not disclosed by the title search, and the necessary deeds and mortgage documents to convey the seller's interest in the real property and the granting of the mortgage security in favor of the buyer's lender), and (3) Schedule B, Part II, which discloses those documents affecting title which the title insurance company has discovered as a result of its search of the real property records.

The title insurance commitment therefore is the document which the buyer will use to decide whether to accept that the seller is the owner of the real property, and the extent to which this ownership may be impaired or affected by interests of other persons shown by the chain of title and recorded liens and encumbrances, and restrictions.

Section 8 of the Real Estate Commission approved contract gives the buyer the opportunity to review and object to the title, as disclosed by the title insurance commitment, and to object to any unsatisfactory title conditions, within mutually agreed dates and deadlines. Failing any agreement on a cure of the defects objected to by the buyer, the contract will terminate.

Conversely, if the buyer does not object to the matters shown in the title insurance commitment then the buyer accepts the condition of title subject to the matters determined by the title insurance commitment.

The use of title insurance may not relieve the purchaser of the need for legal advice on the title. The title insurance policy excludes liability through a number of Exclusions from Coverage and Conditions that may affect future marketability of title. Sufficient time should be allowed in the contract time line to review title which often can be a complex matter.

B. Scope of Search

The buyer should keep in mind that the title insurance company is not required to provide a record of all documents of record. Unlike an abstract of title, the title insurance company's search of the real property records may be more limited. Under the Title Insurance Code of Colorado (C.R.S. 10-11-101 et seq.), a title insurance company is required to conduct a reasonable examination of the title and to make a determination of insurability of title in accordance with sound underwriting practices for title insurance companies. The title insurance company essentially is assuming a potentially greater risk based on its assessment of the risks which may be incurred.

Because of the limited scope of search, the title insurance commitment may not disclose all documents of record, but only those documents which the title insurance company determines should be included based on its determination of insurability. In many residential areas, the title insurance commitment and policy will reflect a search of no more than twenty-five or thirty years back, on the risk assessment that these areas have been well researched and defects of title cleared through the many transactions which have taken place over the course of the defined period.

This may not be true for other types of real property, such as commercial property, or vacant land under development, where the search should extend back to the first grant or patent of the property into private ownership from the federal or state governments.

When reviewing a title insurance commitment, a buyer should keep in mind the purpose for acquiring the land. If it is a simple residential transaction, then a limited scope of search may be adequate. However, if the buyer intends to develop the land, or remodel/construct improvements, then the scope of the search should be much more extensive to be certain that all the recorded documents are disclosed, particularly those documents which may affect the development and platting of the real property (such as utility easements running across the real property).

C. Title Insurance Policies

Owner's versus Loan Policies.

Most, if not all, title insurance companies will issue title insurance commitments and policies based on the forms adopted by the American Land Title Association. These forms of commitment and policies are used and accepted nationally. This gives the buyer using a title insurance commitment for evidence of title a strong degree of certainty in the interpretation of the standard terms used in the title insurance commitment.

After the closing of the transaction and the recording of the necessary documents to convey the seller's interest in the real property to the buyer and the lender's interest to secure its loan to the buyer, the title insurance company will issue the title insurance policies in the form agreed to in the title insurance commitment. Separate policies will be issued to the owner and to the mortgagee (lender).

An owner's policy of title insurance protects the owner's interest in the property. The policy cannot be transferred to any subsequent owner. Upon resale, the new buyer must obtain a new title policy. A loan policy of title insurance protects the lender, and only to the extent of the lender's interest in the real property. A lender's policy will transfer if the loan is sold to another lender, and continues in effect for the life of the loan.

Unlike other insurance, title insurance premiums are a one-time, up-front payment. Premiums are based upon the amount of insurance purchased. Premiums charged by title companies must be filed with the Colorado Division of Insurance and are available to the public.

Exclusions from Coverage.

Both owner's and loan policies of title insurance list the matters which are covered under the policies (the "Covered Risks"), and, equally as important, the matters which are excluded from coverage under the policies (the "Exclusions from Coverage"). The buyer should have a good understanding of these terms and the effect on the insurance coverage provided by the policies. If in doubt, the buyer should seek the advice of a real estate attorney.

The Exclusions from Coverage, by their terms, detract from the extent of the insurance coverage. Examples include exclusions for zoning and legal subdivisions, adverse matters which the insured knows about, or has agreed to or assumed. In each case, the title insurance policy will not cover a claim and will not have to defend any claim. The insurer's duty to defend a claim is one of the most important policy provisions.

Matters not shown by the county real property records.

Remember that the title insurance company will search only for documents recorded in the records of the clerk and recorder where the real property is situated, and not any other public records office (such as the Colorado secretary of state, courts, county and local government offices). The title insurance policies expressly limit the coverage to these recorded documents.

However, the title insurance company may offer to extend the coverage of the policies by agreeing to insure some matters not shown by the real property records. This may be done on receipt of (1) suitable affidavits from the seller or buyer, (2) in some cases indemnities with cash collateral to secure the obligations in the indemnities from the seller, and, (3) in many cases, a survey of the real property. Section 8 of the contract speaks to these "off-record" matters by requiring the seller to provide to the buyer copies of all existing surveys, and disclose all easements, liens and other title matters not shown by the public records. If the seller has entered into a contract with a contractor to perform work or labor on the property, this contract will give rise to the concern of mechanics' liens which attach to the real property, without the need for recording.

All these matters will be negotiated between the buyer and the title insurance company based on the matters set out in the title insurance commitment, particularly in the Requirements section, Schedule B, Part I. The policies, when issued, will incorporate the insurance coverage agreed to between the insurer and the buyer in the title insurance commitment.

D. Regulatory Issues

Title insurance companies are regulated on the federal level (Consumer Financial Protection Bureau) and state level (Colorado Division of Insurance).

Over the years these agencies (or their predecessors) have promulgated a number of important regulations which govern the manner in which a title insurance company can operate and conduct its business, with the ability to impose civil sanctions and fines for failure to comply with the regulations.

Examples include regulations that a title insurance company must charge and receive payment for work done, and cannot discount or waive these fees. In the context of this chapter on Evidence of Title, the title insurance company must charge a fee for the title insurance commitment, unless the title insurance commitment is issued as part of a bona fide transaction arising out of a contract of sale. If a title insurance commitment is ordered to ascertain the recorded documents affecting title, or prior to a proper contract of purchase and sale (a "to be determined" (TBD) title insurance commitment), the title insurance company must make a charge and collect payment for issuing the title insurance commitment.

IV. Abstract and Opinion

An "**abstract of title**" is a summary of the material parts of every recorded instrument affecting the title to a parcel of real property, from the original grant and including every subsequent conveyance and encumbrances affecting that parcel of real property. The abstract will be certified by an abstractor. The abstract of title will provide prima facie evidence of the chain of title and the marketability of title (C.R.S. §38-41-105).

Obtaining an abstract of title as part of the real property transaction was the practice in Colorado for many years. However, the licensing of abstractors ended in July 1982 and has been superseded today by title insurance which is the method used in almost all transactions to provide the evidence of title. The concept still lives on in the Colorado Real Estate Commission approved contract forms for the purchase and sale of real property, where an abstract of title is one of the choices given to the parties to provide the evidence of title (§8.1 Evidence of Record Title). §8.1.6 requires the seller to provide to buyer copies of any abstracts of title covering all or any portion of the real property.

The average purchaser probably will be unable to interpret the abstract of title which, essentially, is a compilation of the recorded documents, with little, if any, commentary on the effect on the real property of each document. The purchaser will still need the "**opinion**" of an attorney to certify the legal nature of the seller's title and of any defects, liens, encumbrances, or other rights that may be disclosed in the abstract.

A. Liability

The abstractor does not guarantee title to the real property. The law imposes only the duty to exercise due care in the preparation of the abstract. If an abstractor negligently omits or incorrectly summarizes a document, the abstractor can be held liable for any loss suffered by the purchaser. Likewise, an attorney can only be held liable for damages that are caused by the attorney's negligence in the examination of the abstract. As an example, the attorney is liable for any loss caused by failure to discover an existing, recorded lien contained in the abstract. However, the purchaser will be limited in pursuing any court ordered award to the financial ability of the abstractor or attorney to pay an award. There may be a deeper pocket in the form of errors and omissions insurance to cover the award, but only to the extent of this insurance coverage.

In contrast, a title insurance policy provides the insurance for any loss or damage which the insured may incur as a result of a title defect, with the financial ability of the title insurance company to back up the insurance given.

B. Risks

No evidence of title can completely and conclusively reveal the exact state of the title to real property. For instance, an abstract and opinion may indicate that the seller has clear title, but if the chain of title contains a forged deed, then title did not legally pass. There is no way of knowing from the abstract whether a deed is forged or not. Nor will an abstract reveal the rights of parties in possession, for example under a valid but unrecorded lease. The abstract may show title in one person but another may possibly have superior right through adverse possession. With an abstract and legal opinion together with a physical examination and survey of the property, a buyer should be reasonably certain of obtaining good title.

V. Torrens Certificate of Title

The Torrens system of land registration was originally enacted in Colorado in 1903. The system provided for an alternative method for the registration of title to real property which was simple, inexpensive, and secure. The district court for the county where the property is situated had jurisdiction to hear applications for the issuance of a certificate of title. Its primary advantage was that once a decree of confirmation of title was entered by the court, the decree was forever binding on the land and conclusive against all persons. In its simplest terms, the decree of confirmation of title was the equivalent of a decree of quiet title, issued with each sale and conveyance of the real property.

A feature of the Torrens Title Registration system was the assurance fund which was intended to pay damages for any claim that may arise under the act. However, in its later years the counties which had a Torrens Title Registration system had very little in the fund to pay any claims.

It never gained widespread use in Colorado and legislation was passed in May 2017 by the state legislature to terminate the registration system ("The Conclusion of the Torrens Title Registration Act", C.R.S. 38-36-21-36-201). There was a two-year phase-out period, from August 9, 2017, until January 1, 2020. After this date, no further applications for a Torrens certificate of title will be accepted by the registrar of the court. All documents for recording must be submitted to the clerk and recorder of the county where the real property is situated.

The Conclusion of the Torrens Title Registration Act required the registrar on or before January 1, 2020, to remove all remaining real property registered under the Torrens system from registration and record a certificate of title with all notations, certifications, memorials, and endorsements thereon, for each parcel of registered land within the county.

Chapter 15: Water Rights[†]

An * in the left margin indicates a change in the statute, rule, or text since the last publication of the manual.

I. Introduction

This chapter focuses on the practical implications of water rights as a part of the transfer of real property. In Colorado, water availability cannot be taken for granted. The state's growing population continues to place increasing demands on the water supply, and experts anticipate that climate change will reduce water supply stability. When assisting a purchaser in acquiring land or a seller in selling land, you must understand what water rights, if any, will be transferred with ownership of the land. You must also educate the purchaser as to the water rights that will be transferred and whether they are adequate for purchaser's intended use of the land.

To know how to address water rights in a real property transaction, it is necessary to first understand them. Accordingly, this chapter begins with a brief explanation of water rights and how they are administered in Colorado.

II. Water Rights and Prior Appropriation

All water in Colorado is a resource that is owned by the public. A water right is the right to use a portion of the state's waters; it does not represent ownership of those waters. A water right is created when a water user physically diverts water from the stream or aquifer and applies it to beneficial use. This is called an appropriation. Diversion is the withdrawal of water from its natural flow (e.g., from a surface stream or from the ground), and beneficial use is use of the water for a purpose identified as such under applicable law.

With limited exceptions, all Colorado water is subject to the doctrine of prior appropriation. The prior appropriation doctrine is adopted and recognized in the Colorado Constitution in Article XVI, Sections 5 and 6. Prior appropriation means that the first person to divert water from a stream or aquifer and to put the water to beneficial use has a senior or superior right to use that source of water, as compared to later water users. Under the prior appropriation system, water users do not share the burden of shortages. The more senior user is entitled to divert the full amount of his or her water right before the next junior user is allowed to divert any water.

The prior appropriation doctrine regulates the use of surface water and tributary ground water. Surface water includes all water in rivers, streams, lakes, wetlands and other natural waterways, and diffuse runoff. Ground water that is hydraulically connected to surface water—meaning that the ground water is replenished by surface water percolating into the ground or the ground water seeps into surface water bodies—is considered tributary ground water. Tributary ground water is subject to the doctrine of prior appropriation as a part of the

---

[†] By Kylie J. Crandall, Partner, and Hayley K. Siltanen, Associate, Holland & Hart LLP.

surface water body to which it is hydraulically connected.[1] Thus, for example, wells withdrawing water from the South Platte alluvium (the shallow aquifer that is tributary to the South Platte River) are considered tributary to the South Platte River and are subject to senior "surface water rights" on that river.

III. Adjudication of Water Rights

Under the prior appropriation system, the value and reliability of a water right is a function of its priority with respect to other water rights on the same stream system. In Colorado, the prior appropriation system is codified in the Water Right Determination and Administration Act of 1969, §§ 37-92-101, *et seq.*, C.R.S. The Act establishes an adjudication system to determine the priority of a water right, whereby a water user must file an application in Water Court to prove the aspects of a particular water right appropriation.

The Water Courts are specialized courts within the district courts of Colorado. There is one Water Court for each of the seven water divisions, discussed below. After a water user files an application in Water Court, and the court determines the claims made in the application to be true, then the court will enter a decree that represents the water right. The decree describes the priority date and other important aspects of the water right, including the type of use (e.g., irrigation, domestic, commercial, industrial, or other uses), the amount, the time of use, the point of diversion, and the place of use.

If a water right is created when a person appropriates water (by diversion and application to beneficial use), then what purpose does a water right decree serve? Although a water right is created by appropriation, a water user is not entitled to have his or her water right administered within the priority system until they obtain a decree. Thus, until the water right is decreed, it has no "priority" vis-à-vis other water rights on the stream system.

In circumstances when a person has completed appropriation by diversion and beneficial use of the water, the Water Court will decree the water right as "absolute," or completed. By contrast, when a person has initiated appropriation of a water right (e.g., by filing an application for the water right in Water Court), but has not yet diverted and applied the water to beneficial use, the Water Court will decree the water right as "conditional." A conditional water right gives a water user the opportunity to develop the water right over time while preserving the date the water user initiated appropriated of that water right.

After a conditional water right is decreed, the applicant must return to Water Court every six years to demonstrate reasonable diligence in development of the conditional water right. Once the appropriation of the water right is complete (by diversion and application to beneficial use), the Water Court will enter a decree making the water right absolute. The priority date of the absolute water right will remain the date the water user initiated appropriation of the water right.

A water right may be used only for the purposes described in, and subject to the terms and conditions of, the decree. For instance, a water right that is decreed for irrigation use may not be used for domestic or industrial purposes. A water right holder may change the type, time, and place of use, and other aspects of a water right, if the change will not injure other

[1] Other categories of ground water, discussed in Section X of this chapter, are not subject to the prior appropriation doctrine.

water rights. Such a change must be made through a proceeding in Water Court, and would be evidenced by a change of water right decree issued by the Water Court.

Finally, it is important to understand that a water right decree does not usually determine *ownership* of the water right. It states the identity of the claimant of the water right, who is usually—but not always—the owner. A water right is initially owned by the person or entity that diverts the water and applies it to beneficial use.

IV. Water Administration

Colorado is divided into seven water divisions for the administration of water rights. These divisions are generally co-extensive with the seven major river basins that originate in the state:

- Water Division No. 1 – South Platte, Laramie, and Republican River Basin;
- Water Division No. 2 – Arkansas River Basin;
- Water Division No. 3 – Rio Grande River Basin;
- Water Division No. 4 – Gunnison, San Miguel, and portions of the Dolores River Basins;
- Water Division No. 5 – Colorado River Basin;
- Water Division No. 6 – Yampa, White, and North Platte River Basins; and
- Water Division No. 7 – San Juan and portions of the Dolores Rivers Basins.

Each water division has its own Water Court that has exclusive jurisdiction over all water matters in that division.

Water rights in Colorado are administered, meaning that they are enforced, by the Division of Water Resources through the State Engineer's Office. Each water division has a division engineer's office, which administers water rights in that division. Each division engineer supervises a number of water commissioners, who are responsible for advising water users as to whether they may legally divert water under their water right at any given time. Water commissioners are the local enforcers of the water administration system.

V. Other Types of Rights to Use Water

Rights to use water exist in various forms, beyond just adjudicated water rights. Other common forms of rights to use water include: shares of stock in a mutual ditch company, well permits, determinations made by the State Engineer or the Ground Water Commission, rights to use water given pursuant to contract, and water taps. Familiarity with these document types is essential to helping a purchaser understand his or her rights to use water in connection with acquired land.

1. Shares in a Mutual Ditch or Reservoir Company

Mutual ditch and reservoir companies are entities that own decreed water rights and distribute water. Stock in these companies represents the shareholder's proportionate interest in the company's water rights and rights to use the company's reservoir, canals and ditch laterals. In most circumstances, shares of stock are represented by a stock certificate.

When a transaction involves stock in a ditch or reservoir company, the company should be involved in the transaction prior to closing. This is because each company has its own expectations and requirements for transfer of shares of its stock, and the purchaser and seller should be made aware of these terms.

2. Well Permits

The State of Colorado has a separate permit requirement for wells, which are generally defined as any structure used to obtain ground water from an aquifer for beneficial use. The State Engineer's Office issues most well permits, except for wells within designated ground water basins. The Ground Water Commission issues well permits within designated ground water basins. Records for all well permits issued in the state are maintained online by the State Engineer's Office.

It is important to recognize that well permits are not water rights. For that reason, the State Engineer's Office may issue a well permit for tributary ground water only if: (1) the proposed well is covered by a decreed ground water right and, in most cases, an approved augmentation plan (discussed below); or (2) there is unappropriated water available for withdrawal by the proposed well, and the vested rights of others will not be materially injured. Because nearly all rivers in Colorado are over-appropriated (meaning that there is often not enough water to satisfy existing water rights), in most areas of Colorado, a well permit requires a decreed water right and augmentation plan.

In order to allow some low-density development in rural areas—without the requirement for a decreed water right and augmentation plan—Colorado statute establishes a rebuttable presumption that a proposed well will not cause injury to other water users or existing wells if the proposed well will have a production capacity of less than 15 gallons per minute, and will be either: (1) the only well on a residential site located in a subdivision approved before June 1, 1972, and the well will be used solely for ordinary household purposes inside a single-family dwelling and will not be used for irrigation; or (2) the only well on a tract of land of 35 acres or more. These are commonly called "exempt" or "household use only" wells. As the name suggests, these wells are exempt from administration under the prior appropriation system.

3. Ground Water Rights that are Not Tributary to Surface Water

Colorado law distinguishes between waters of the natural stream, which includes surface water and tributary ground water, and other ground water. Section X of this chapter discusses the second category, which encompasses all types of ground water that is not tributary to surface water, including designated ground water, non-tributary ground water, and Denver Basin ground water (which includes both non-tributary and "not non-tributary" ground water). These ground water types are regulated and administered separately from surface water and tributary ground water and are often represented by "determinations" made by the State Engineer's Office or Ground Water Commission.

4. Contract Rights to Use Water

The right to use water can also be conferred by contract. Typically, contractual rights to receive water are issued by large water districts that own or administer water rights that are stored in large state or federal water projects. Examples of such water districts include the Northern Colorado Water Conservation District and the Colorado River Water Conservation

District. Rights to receive water by contract are no less important or significant than any other right to use water and must be properly considered in a transaction.

5. Water Taps

A water tap is a right to connect to a water provider or district's system and to receive water for a monthly fee. Often, initial costs for a water tap may be tens of thousands of dollars. If there is a water tap associated with land to be acquired, the purchaser should confirm with the water provider or district whether the initial costs or fees for the water tap have been paid.

6. Augmentation Plans

A plan for augmentation is not a water right and does not, on its own, grant a right to use water. Nonetheless, augmentation plans are a key component of the Colorado water rights system and, because of the expense of obtaining approval of an augmentation in Water Court, may be valuable assets associated with land.

As previously discussed, in times of water shortage, junior water rights holders may be required to curtail their diversions to ensure that senior water rights are satisfied (i.e., not injured). In that event, the junior water right is considered out-of-priority. A plan for augmentation allows a junior water user to continue to divert water out-of-priority, so long as the water user provides replacement water at an appropriate time and location to prevent injury to senior water rights. Because of the nature of well diversions (i.e., wells are often junior in priority and cause delayed impacts to surface streams), augmentation plans are frequently required to allow operation of wells in over-appropriated stream systems.

Similar to decreed water rights, augmentation plans must be adjudicated in Water Court and are evidenced by entry of a final decree by the court.

VI. Identifying Water Rights in the CREC Form Contracts

1. Section 2.7 – Water Rights/Well Rights.

Section 2.7 of the CREC forms for Contracts to Buy and Sell Real Estate (the "CREC Form Contracts") provides for water-related rights to be described under various headings. The following guidelines may be helpful when completing Section 2.7:

- Section 2.7.1. Deeded Water Rights. All water rights to be transferred by deed, which includes water rights (adjudicated or not) and shares of stock represented by water stock certificates, should be listed in this section. Importantly, this section should also specify the type of deed that will be used to convey these water rights.
- Section 2.7.2. Other Rights Relating to Water. This section is an appropriate location to identify any rights to use water that do not clearly fit under a different section.
- Section 2.7.3. Well Rights. All wells, whether permitted or not, should be identified in this section.

- Section 2.7.4. Water Stock Certificates. Shares of stock in mutual ditch and reservoir companies represented by water stock certificates should be listed in this section (in addition to being included in Section 2.7.1).

2. Section 10.8 – Source of Potable Water (Residential Land and Residential Improvements Only).

On and after January 1, 2008, Colorado law requires that a listing contract, contract of sale, or seller's property disclosure for residential land and residential improvements disclose in bold-faced type the source of potable water for the property, which can be one of the following: (a) Well (in which case a copy of the current well permit, if one is available, is to be provided); (b)Water provider (in which case the name and other information regarding the water provider is to be provided); or (c) Neither a well nor a water provider (in which case the source of the water is to be provided). The disclosure statement is also required to state in bold-faced type that some water providers rely, to varying degrees, on nonrenewable water (which is generally considered to be non-tributary and not non-tributary ground water described above), and advise the prospective purchaser that he or she may wish to contact the water provider to determine the long-term sufficiency of that provider's water supplies. This disclosure is required in Section 10.8 of the CREC Form Contracts and in the CREC Source of Water Addendum.

Residential real estate located in incorporated cities and towns is almost always supplied potable water by a water provider (that is often part of the city or town government, a quasi-public entity or a special district). Sometimes there is a wholesale water provider that provides the water to a local water retailer and service is then provided to individual properties by the local water retailer. Properties near urban areas may be supplied potable water by the adjacent municipality or by an independent water district. Some cities and towns are served by independent water districts that are not part of the city or town government.

3. Section 15.7 – Water Transfer Fees

Section 15.7 of the CREC Form Contracts pertains to water transfer fees. While water transfer fees are often minor relative to the total transaction value, parties prefer to allocate payment of these fees on the front-end of the transaction. Water transfer fees are most common in the transfer of stock certificates, water taps, and contract rights to use water.

VII. Diligence: Understanding What You are Buying

Depending on the transaction, a purchaser may desire more or less certainty regarding the scope and validity of the water rights to be conveyed with the land. You should discuss with the purchaser the degree of assurance desired by the purchaser. At a minimum, the legitimacy of claimed water rights should be confirmed through a review of applicable Water Court decrees, permits, and other records. In addition, in circumstances where water rights are critical to the purchase or future use of the land, it may be prudent to engage a water rights attorney, a water resources engineer or consultant, or both to assist with due diligence. A water rights attorney may assist with general review and confirmation of validity of the water rights, transfer of the water rights, and, in some circumstances, a water rights title opinion. A water resources engineer or consultant may assist in determining the amount of water available under the water rights and confirming or assisting in reviewing whether such amount of water is sufficient to meet the anticipated uses of the purchaser.

1. Confirming Water Rights

To confirm the water rights being acquired, a purchaser must obtain evidence of water rights associated with land, which may be in the form of Water Court decrees, deeds transferring water rights, well permits, certificates of stock in a mutual ditch company, or contracts for water. Water court decrees and well permits may be obtained from the Division of Water Resources' office or its website at https://dwr.colorado.gov/. A full review of the Division of Water Resources' records related to water court decrees and well permits should be conducted.

In addition, the purchaser should inquire with the seller regarding the existence and status of any pending Water Court applications, and, if such applications exist, should review the relevant Water Court pleadings.

2. Determining Validity and Amount of Water Available Under Water Rights

In many instances, a water resources engineer or consultant should conduct a visual inspection of the property. An on-site inspection can help evaluate physical availability of water, evidence of additional water rights (beyond those identified by seller), adverse claims to water rights (e.g., diversions by an adjacent property owner), abandonment, and other issues concerning water rights associated with the property.

As a threshold matter, a legal water right does not guarantee physical water. For instance, a Water Court decree may permit the diversion of 10 cubic feet of water per second ("cfs") from a stream, even though physical flow in that stream rarely exceeds 5 cfs. A water resources engineer or consultant can help evaluate physical water availability for water rights associated with the property.

When investigating the status of a water right, potential abandonment or adverse possession must also be considered. Water rights may be lost or diminished due to abandonment or adverse possession. Abandonment occurs when there is a sustained period of non-use of the water right coupled with an intent to abandon, which intent may be inferred from an unreasonably long period of non-use. Abandonment of a water right can occur without any official court or administrative action or the execution of any document, and therefore must be evaluated closely. Adverse possession occurs when a water right is used by another water user without the water right owner's permission and in a manner that is open, notorious, exclusive, hostile, and continuous for the statutory period. Visual inspection of the property to be acquired can help identify adverse use of the seller's water rights.

Finally, consultation with a water resources engineer or consultant may be necessary to evaluate whether the water rights to be conveyed with the property are sufficient to meet the purchaser's needs on the property.

3. Evaluating Potential Future Use of Water Rights

To the extent the purchaser intends to change the use of the property (for example, purchasing agricultural property with irrigation water rights for conversion to residential development), the purchaser should engage a water resources engineer or consultant, a water rights lawyer, or both to evaluate the suitability of the water rights to be acquired for the new use and, if the water rights must be changed, the legal requirements to do so. Importantly, when changing the use of a water right, Colorado law limits the amount of water that can be changed to the amount of historical beneficial use, which means the amount of water available under the water right that was historically used and consumed. A water resource engineer is usually necessary to determine the historical beneficial use of a water right.

4. Confirming Title of the Water Rights

Finally, a purchaser will generally want to ensure that the seller has good and marketable title to the water rights to be conveyed. Because water rights are real property, the process to determine title to water rights is similar to the process to determine title to real estate. Unlike for real estate, however, title insurance is not available for water rights. In Colorado title insurance companies will not insure title to water rights. If a purchaser requires a water rights title determination, then the purchaser will need to hire an abstract company or an attorney to perform a stand-up examination of the county real property records, by searching the grantor/grantee index. After the search is complete, a water rights attorney must review and evaluate the applicable records to evaluate title.

Note that, if ownership of a water right is disputed, that dispute must be resolved in a quiet title action in the same manner as title to real property. *See* Colo. R. Civ. P. 105.

VIII. Conveying Water Rights

1. Deed

In most circumstances under Colorado law, a water right is a property right separate and apart from the land on which it is used. Water rights can be bought and sold similarly to real property and can be conveyed separately from the land to which they are appurtenant. The same formalities must be observed in a conveyance of water rights as in the conveyance of real estate. C.R.S. § 38-30-102(2). As with real estate deeds, a water rights deed should be recorded with the applicable county clerk and recorder after it is signed and acknowledged.

When conveying water rights, the quality of title may be warranted like all other real property rights.[3] Water rights are mostly commonly conveyed by Bargain and Sale Deed or Quitclaim Deed, due to the difficulties in obtaining title insurance and warranting title to water rights. General Warranty Deeds and Special Warranty Deeds are not commonly used to convey water rights. This is because water rights are susceptible to loss or diminishment through adverse possession, nonuse, and abandonment. Although a Special Warranty Deed does not render the grantor liable for defects, such as abandonment, resulting from events that occurred before the grantor's ownership, it could create liability for the grantor if such defects occurred during grantor's ownership.

Water rights should be precisely described in a deed to ensure that the correct rights are conveyed to the purchaser. Because exactness is important in this context, it is generally advisable to have a water attorney prepare the water rights deed. If a deed is silent, there no presumption as to the parties' intent regarding the transfer of surface or tributary ground water rights to be conveyed. Instead, a court will determine the parties' intentions based on the circumstances, such as whether the water rights are necessary to the beneficial enjoyment of the land.

---

[3] See the Deed chapter in this manual for a general discussion on the different types of deeds that may be used to transfer real property under Colorado law.

2. Assignment

Certain rights to use water must be transferred from the seller to the purchaser through an assignment. Water use rights transferred by assignment include well permits, stock certificates representing shares in a mutual ditch or reservoir company, and contractual rights to receive water. The form of assignment depends on the rights being assigned.

As previously noted, ditch and reservoir companies typically have their own transfer requirements and may have a preferred form of assignment form. Similarly, the issuer of a contractual right to receive water may have its own transfer process. Accordingly, care should be taken to ensure that ditch and reservoir companies and issuers of contractual water rights are notified of pending transfers and that those entities' requirements and processes are satisfied.

3. Bill of Sale

When conveying water rights, a bill of sale should be executed for the transfer of personal property associated with the water rights, such as wells, pumps, pipelines, headgates, flumes, and other fixtures necessary for the use of the water rights.

4. Wells and Well Permits

Well permits must be transferred by assignment, and physical well structures and associated equipment must be transferred by bill of sale. In addition, when the ownership or mailing address of the owner of a permitted well changes, the new owner must submit a "Change in Ownership/Address" form (Form GWS-11) to the Division of Water Resources. *See* C.R.S. § 37-90-143. This requirement is noted in Section 2.7.3 of the CREC Form Contracts. Submission of this form is for informational purposes and does not transfer ownership of the well permit.

For all residential real estate transactions conducted on or after January 1, 2009, Section 38-30-102, C.R.S., requires any existing well not registered or permitted with the Division of Water Resources to be registered by the purchaser within 60 days after the closing. Depending on the type and use of the well and the date the well was constructed there are different forms and actions or additional information that will be required to register or permit the well. A water rights lawyer or water resource engineer or consultant can assist with this registration process.

5. Shares of Stock in a Mutual Ditch or Reservoir Company

Transfer of shares of stock in a mutual ditch or reservoir company involves conveyance of both personal and real property. The stock certificate itself is personal property, which is transferred as other shares of stock are transferred, by stock assignment and physical transfer of the certificate. In addition, a share of stock in a mutual ditch or reservoir company is a representation of the shareholder's proportionate ownership interest in the water rights held by the company. *Jacobucci v. District Court*, 189 Colo. 380, 541 P.2d 667, 672 (1975). Thus, mutual ditch and reservoir company shares should also be transferred in accordance with procedures for the conveyance of real property, just as for other water rights. Accordingly, the transfer of mutual ditch and reservoir company shares is accomplished by both assignment and deed.

As noted, ditch and reservoir companies may require certain documentation or compliance with procedures to complete a share transfer. Further and importantly, the seller must deliver the *original* stock certificates at closing. It is prudent to include this requirement in the purchase and sale contract. If a certificate representing shares in a mutual ditch company has been lost, mislaid or destroyed, a duplicate certificate may be obtained only after compliance with the statutory procedures set forth in Sections 7-42-114 to -117, C.R.S. Some ditch and reservoir companies allow a shareholder to obtain a replacement certificate upon issuance of a lost instrument bond, in lieu of the statutory procedure described above.

6. Special Considerations When Water is Sold Separately from the Land it Was Historically Used On

If water rights are conveyed separately from the land, special care must be taken to ensure that the purchaser acquires physical access and other rights necessary for use and development of the water. For example, if land is sold and underground water rights are reserved to the seller, the seller should reserve an easement to access and operate existing wells and the right to drill new wells. If water rights are purchased separately from the land on which they have been used, the purchaser should also obtain a "dry-up covenant" from the seller, authorizing the purchaser to dry up the land historically irrigated by the purchased rights.

IX. Encumbering Water Rights

Water rights can be encumbered by a deed of trust similar to other real property. C.R.S. § 38-30-102. The description of the water rights should be specifically identified. Any loan or security agreement pursuant to which the deed of trust encumbers the water rights should include terms and provisions that protect the value and validity of the water rights.

Security interests in shares of stock in a mutual ditch or reservoir company must be obtained and perfected under the terms of the Colorado Uniform Commercial Code. The grantor should execute a collateral assignment of the shares of stock. The mutual ditch or reservoir company should issue the stock certificate so that the borrower and lender, as beneficiary, are identified on the face of the stock certificate, and the stock certificate should be held by the lender. The mutual ditch or reservoir company should be involved in this process, because the company may require use of particular forms or processes.

X. Ground Water Not Considered Tributary to Surface Water

Ground water in Colorado is allocated under several different rules, depending upon its physical characteristics. As explained above, tributary ground water is subject to the doctrine of prior appropriation and is administered in conjunction with surface water rights in the river system to which it is tributary.

Another type of ground water classification, created by the legislature in the Ground Water Management Act of 1965, §§ 37-90-101 *et seq.*, C.R.S., is ground water within areas known as "designated ground water basins." Designated ground water basins are geographic areas containing ground water that: (1) in its natural course would not be available to and required for the fulfillment of decreed surface water rights, or (2) is in areas not adjacent to a continuously flowing natural stream in which ground water withdrawals have constituted the principal water usage for at least 15 years prior to designation of the basin. The basins are created by the Ground Water Commission through a formal hearing and order process. A modified doctrine of prior appropriation is applied in designated ground water basins, meaning that prior appropriation is applied but water levels in aquifers are allowed to decline over time even if this results in senior water rights losing their water supply. Rights to use designated ground water are represented by well permits issued by the Ground Water Commission. Colorado has eight designated ground water basins, which are generally located on the eastern plains.

Ground water may be so physically separated from surface water by impermeable layers or great distances that it has little or no hydraulic connection with surface water. If such ground water is located outside of a designated ground water basin, and if its withdrawal will not within 100 years deplete the flow of a natural stream at an annual rate greater than one tenth of one percent of the annual rate of withdrawal, it is classified as "non-tributary ground water." The right to use non-tributary ground water is generally allocated based on the ownership of the overlying land, rather than the prior appropriation system. *See* C.R.S. § 37-90-137(4). The owner of the overlying land may obtain a right to use non-tributary ground water by obtaining a well permit from the State Engineer's Office or by filing an application with the Water Court to determine the non-tributary ground water rights. Ground water within the Dawson, Denver, Arapahoe, and Laramie-Fox Hills aquifers in the area known as the Denver Basin (a kidney-shaped area along the Front Range of Colorado between Greeley and Colorado Springs) is presumed to be non-tributary. Non-tributary ground water also occurs in other parts of the state.

The Colorado legislature has also defined a unique category of ground water, known as "not non-tributary ground water," located outside the boundaries of designated ground water basins and within the Dawson, Denver, Arapahoe, and Laramie-Fox Hills aquifers in the Denver Basin. Not non-tributary ground water is water in these aquifers that does not meet the definition of non-tributary ground water. As with non-tributary ground water, not non-tributary ground water is generally allocated on the basis of land ownership. Likewise, the owner of the overlying land may obtain a right to use not non-tributary ground water by obtaining a well permit from the State Engineer's Office or by filing an application in Water Court to determine the not non-tributary ground water rights before drilling a well.

Typically, to avoid injury to senior surface water rights, the law requires a Water Court-approved augmentation plan before junior not non-tributary ground water rights can be pumped and used, similar to tributary ground water rights.

XI. Conclusion

By now it should be evident that water law and the understanding and transfer of water rights is complicated. This Chapter is intended to provide a roadmap for real estate professionals to handle water rights in a real estate transactions, as well as to provide indicators for when a purchaser should engage a water rights professional (i.e., water rights attorney, water resources engineer or consultant, or both) to confirm and ensure validity of the water rights and to ensure proper conveyance of the rights and associated matters.

XII. Water Right Terminology

Absolute water right: A term often used to describe a water right under which water has been fully diverted and applied to beneficial use, to distinguish it from a conditional water right.

Acre-foot: Volumetric measurement of water used for quantifying reservoir storage capacity, historic consumptive use, and for other purposes. This is the amount of water that will cover one acre of land at a depth of one foot, which is equivalent to 325,851 gallons of water.

Adjudication: The judicial determination of the extent, nature, and limitations of a water right appropriation in a statutory court proceeding.

Appropriation: The application of a certain portion of the waters of the state of Colorado to a beneficial use.

Appropriator: A person who applies water to beneficial use so as to obtain a water right.

Aquifer: A subsurface, water-bearing geological structure capable of storing and yielding water to streams, springs, or wells.

Augmentation Plan: A detailed program or plan to increase the supply of water available for beneficial use in a water basin or portion thereof by the development of new or alternate means or points of diversion, by a pooling of water resources, by water exchange projects, by providing substitute supplies of water, by the development of new sources of water, or by any other appropriate means.

Beneficial use: The use of that amount of water that is reasonable and appropriate under reasonably efficient practices to accomplish, without waste, the purpose for which the appropriation is lawfully made.

Conditional water right: A right to perfect a water right with a certain priority upon the completion, with reasonable diligence, of the appropriation upon which such water right is to be based.

Consumptive use: The amount of water that is consumed during its beneficial use so that it does not return to the waters of the state of Colorado.

Cubic foot per second (cfs): Measurement of flow rate of water in a running stream, a ditch or canal, or a pipeline. Water flowing at one cfs will deliver 448.8 gallons per minute or 648,000 gallons per day. One cfs flowing for 24 hours equals 1.983 acre-feet of water.

Direct flow water right: A water right that gives the owner thereof the right to divert water from a specified water source at a specified rate of flow for current use.

Historic use: The use to which a specified water right has previously or historically been put.

Junior appropriator: An appropriator whose right to use specified water is subject to a prior or senior right of another appropriator of the same water source.

Non-adjudicated or unadjudicated water right: A water right that has not been submitted to the appropriate court for adjudication. An unadjudicated water right is junior in priority to all water rights from the same source that have been adjudicated.

Point of diversion: The location at which water is removed from its natural course or location by means of a ditch, canal, flume, reservoir, bypass, pipeline, conduit, well, pump, or other structure or device.

Priority: The seniority, by date, as of which a water right is entitled to divert water and the relative seniority of a water right in relation to other water rights deriving their supply from a common source.

Senior appropriator: An appropriator whose water right has priority over another appropriator having a right to use water from a common water source.

Storage water right: A water right that gives the owner thereof the right to divert and store water from a specified water source in a specified volumetric amount for current or future use.

Water right: A real property right, either absolute or conditional, to use, in accordance with its priority, a certain portion of the waters of the state of Colorado by reason of the appropriation of such water, as confirmed by a Water Court decree or a Ground Water Commission well permit.

SOURCES OF INFORMATION

Rules, regulations, and statutes may be obtained from the Colorado Division of Water Resources, 1313 Sherman St., Room 821, Denver, CO 80203. Its website is https://dwr.colorado.gov/.

For further information, such as helpful publications, etc., the following agencies should be contacted: The Colorado Division of Water Resources; the Colorado Water Conservation Board; Water Education Colorado, Colorado State University, Civil Engineering Department; and the United States Geological Survey, Water Resources Branch, Denver Federal Center.

Chapter 16:
Brokerage Relationships

An * in the left margin indicates a change in the statute, rule, or text since the last publication of the manual.

I. Introduction

A. Brokerage Relationships in Real Estate Act

Colorado is a national leader in the creation of real estate brokerage laws. For many years, the common law practice of agency guided relationships between the broker and the seller, landlord, buyer, or tenant. (For ease of reference, "seller, landlord, buyer, or tenant" when used together will be referred to as the "party" in this chapter.) Effective January 1, 1994, the "Brokerage Relationships in Real Estate Act" significantly changed Colorado license law by establishing two different types of working relationships between a broker and a party: single agency and transaction-brokerage. This legislation codified the duties and obligations of a real estate broker.

B. Establishing the Relationship

Parties now have two choices when engaging the services of a real estate broker. One choice is **transaction-brokerage**, where the broker *assists* one or more parties throughout the transaction without being an advocate for any party. Transaction brokerage is a non-agency relationship. The second relationship is **agency**, where the broker is an agent and *represents* only one party in the transaction. In addition to the "Uniform Duties" (described in Section V of this chapter) that both transaction-brokers and agents are obligated to perform under the Colorado real estate statutes, the broker acting as an agent is obligated to: (1) promote the interests of the party with the utmost good faith, loyalty, and fidelity, (2) seek a price or lease rate and terms that are acceptable to the party, and (3) counsel the party as to any material benefits or risks of a transaction.

C. Refining Agency Relationships

Before January 1, 2003, when a brokerage firm entered into an agency agreement with a party, all of the brokers in that firm would become agents of that party. Confidential information concerning the party and the transaction could be exchanged between brokers within the brokerage firm. The same broker or other brokers in the firm were permitted to work as the agent for the other party in the transaction—thus creating dual agency. The firm (and all the brokers in the firm) could represent both sides in the transaction. This brokerage arrangement created a potentially sensitive and difficult situation within the brokerage firm and resulted in problems and conflicts.

The second major change to Colorado's real estate brokerage relationships was the 2003 "Designated Brokerage Relationships in Real Estate Act." This statute created two types of brokers in a multiple-person brokerage firm—the "**employing broker**" and the "**employed broker**." The statute made each broker within the brokerage firm an independent, standalone broker for the purposes of establishing a brokerage relationship. In the past, the party entered into an agency or transaction-brokerage relationship with the brokerage firm. However, the new statute provided that the brokerage relationship is only between the individual broker and the party. The employing broker of the multiple-person brokerage firm was given the responsibility to designate either the employing broker or one or more employed brokers as the "**designated broker**" to work with a particular party in a specific real estate transaction. By making the relationship at the broker level rather than at the brokerage firm level and by prohibiting the imputation of information within the brokerage firm, the statute has simplified and improved the brokerage relationship between the broker and the party.

Colorado law provides brokerage relationship flexibility through the introduction and implementation of designated brokerage, agency, and transaction-brokerage. In Colorado, each brokerage relationship can be custom-designed for each specific personality, situation, and transaction. Written agreements, disclosures, policies, and rules are in place to ensure that these brokerage relationships are properly presented and implemented for the benefit and protection of the public.

II. Real Estate Brokerage Basics

A. One-Person Firm

A brokerage employment contract is not a contract between the individual broker and the party. An employment contract is a contract between the *brokerage firm* and the party. If the employment contract is with a brokerage firm that consists of only one licensed natural person, then the brokerage firm and the individual broker are—for brokerage purposes—conceptually treated as one and the same. Hence, there is no reason to "designate" a broker to work with the party (as the broker could only designate himself or herself). With a one-person brokerage firm, there is no "designated broker."

B. Multiple-Person Firm

If the employment contract is with a brokerage firm that consists of more than one licensed natural person, the employing broker or an individual broker employed or engaged by that employing broker will be designated by the employing or supervising broker to work with the party as a designated broker. The employing or supervising broker may designate more than one of its individual brokers to work with a party as designated brokers.

A brokerage relationship exists only with the individual broker(s) so designated. The duties, obligations, and responsibilities of that relationship do not extend to the employing broker, brokerage firm, or to any other brokers employed or engaged by the brokerage firm.

C. Confidential Information

Preventing the imputation of knowledge and transmission of confidential information from the designated broker to the employing broker or an employed broker who has not been so designated is of paramount importance with designated brokerage. But at the same time, the employing broker and brokerage firm remain responsible for the supervision of the employed brokers of the brokerage firm and may have liability for the actions of the employed brokers. Under certain circumstances, these provisions could be contradictory, particularly if the employed designated broker was working, for example, with the seller and the employing broker was the designated broker for the buyer in the same transaction. Commission Rule 6.3.G. addresses this potential conflict.

D. Supervision

Commission Rule 6.3.G. states that a designated broker shall be permitted to reveal to a supervising broker, and a supervising broker shall be permitted to receive, confidential information as authorized by the informed consent of the party the designated broker is assisting or working with, without changing or extending the designated brokerage relationship beyond the designated broker. An employing broker is authorized by Commission Rule 6.3.C. to delegate an experienced broker to perform some of the responsibilities of the employing broker to prevent a conflict of interest in a situation where the employing broker is actively representing one of the parties to a transaction.

All of the standard Commission-approved employment contracts contain a provision granting the party's consent to the designated broker's disclosure of confidential information to the employing broker or designee for the purpose of proper supervision, provided such employing broker or designee does not further disclose such information without consent of the party or use such information to the detriment of the party.

E. Intraoffice Relationships

As the result of the designated brokerage statute, a designated broker may work as a single agent for a seller or landlord and another designated broker in the same firm may work as a single agent for a buyer or tenant in the same transaction, and this designated brokerage arrangement does not create dual agency for either of the brokers, the employing broker, or the brokerage firm.

III. Agency

The agency relationship evolved from the master-servant relationship under English common law. The servant owed absolute loyalty to the master. This loyalty was superior to the servant's personal interests as well as the interests of others. Common law is established by court decisions. Under common law, the agent owes the principal five duties, including: (1) care: (2) obedience, (3) accounting, (4) loyalty (including confidentiality), and (5) disclosure. Statutory law is the law enacted by the legislature.

The "**agent**" is the individual who is authorized and consents to represent the interests of the principal. The "**principal**" is the individual hiring the agent and granting to the agent the authority to represent the principal. A "**fiduciary relationship**" exists between the agent and the principal, meaning the agent is held in a position of special trust and confidence by the principal.

There are three kinds of agents: (1) universal agents, (2) general agents, and (3) special agents. A "**universal agent**" has unlimited authority to perform any act on behalf of the principal. A "**general agent**" has far-reaching or wide authority to conduct a series of transactions of a continuous nature on behalf of the principal. For example, the vice-president of the western region of a company would be able to make all the decisions for the western region (but not so for the other regions). A "**special agent**" has only limited authority to conduct a single transaction for the principal. A real estate broker and an attorney are examples of special agents. In real estate, a "**single agent**" means a broker who is engaged by and represents only one party in a transaction.

An agent generally gains authority to act on behalf of a principal by entering into a contract. A contract is considered "**express authority**," where specific terms, duties, and responsibilities are established between the agent and the principal. A written listing agreement to sell a property is an example of an express authority. "**Implied authority**" is authority reasonably expected to permit the agent to be able to perform the scope of the agency. "**Apparent authority**" is when third parties reasonably believe an individual has authority to act and bind the principal based upon the principal's words or conduct. Although authority in an agency can be created expressly (written or oral), implied or by the imposition of apparent (ostensible) authority, Colorado real estate law specifically states that any agency relationship between a broker and a principal must be created by a written agreement signed by both parties.

Even when acting as an agent, the broker's right to bind a party is very restricted. A Commission-approved listing agreement does not give the broker the right to sign or initial legal documents for the party. Absent a power of attorney, the broker should not sign for a party on any document related to the real estate transaction.

For many years, Colorado real estate brokers worked with the public under the common law of agency. Brokers automatically became an agent of their party by entering into a listing for the sale or lease of the party's property. In 1993, the legislature decided that the duties and responsibilities associated with real estate brokerage relationships should be specifically defined in the statute. Section 12-10-404, C.R.S., defines the duties and obligations of a single agent engaged by a seller or landlord. Section 12-10-405, C.R.S., defines the duties and obligations of a single agent engaged by a buyer or tenant. All of these duties and obligations are summarized in the "Uniform Duties" section below.

IV. Transaction-Brokerage

Transaction-brokerage was created as a non-agency relationship. Under Colorado law, a broker is presumed to be a transaction-broker unless a single-agency relationship is created by a written agreement between the broker and the party. A "**transaction-broker**" assists one or more parties throughout a contemplated real estate transaction with communication, interposition, advisement, negotiation, contract terms, and the closing of such real estate transaction without being an agent or advocate for the interests of any party to such transaction. Section 12-10-407, C.R.S., defines the duties and obligations of a transaction-broker engaged by a party. All of these duties and obligations are summarized in the "Uniform Duties" section below.

V. Uniform Duties

In Colorado, a broker must be either an agent or a transaction-broker. If a broker is an agent, there must be a written agreement between the broker and the party. A broker may be a transaction-broker by either entering into a written agreement with the party or through disclosure only.

If a broker is acting either as an agent or as a transaction-broker in Colorado, there are a number of specific duties that the broker is responsible to perform. Since all of these duties are the same for agency and transaction-brokerage, they are called "**uniform duties**." If the broker and the party determine that the broker should be an agent, then the broker must agree to perform the three "**additional duties,**" described below.

As of January 1, 2006, the uniform duties and additional duties language outlined below appears in all Commission-approved employment contracts between the broker and a party.

By signing any of these agreements, the broker is agreeing to abide by and perform each of these duties. Therefore, it is imperative that the broker understand both the uniform and additional duties for agency.

A. Seller or Landlord Uniform Duties

Brokerage firm, acting through broker, shall provide brokerage services to the seller or landlord. The broker, acting as either a transaction-broker or a seller or landlord agent, must perform the following *uniform duties* when working with seller or landlord:

1. Broker must exercise reasonable skill and care for seller or landlord, including, but not limited to the following:
   a. Performing the terms of any written or oral agreement with seller or landlord;
   b. Presenting all offers to and from seller or landlord in a timely manner regardless of whether the property is subject to a contract for sale or a lease or letter of intent to lease;
   c. Disclosing to seller or landlord adverse material facts actually known by broker;
   d. Advising seller or landlord regarding the transaction and to obtain expert advice as to material matters about which broker knows but the specifics of which are beyond the expertise of broker;
   e. Accounting in a timely manner for all money and property received; and
   f. Keeping seller or landlord fully informed regarding the transaction.
2. Broker must not disclose the following information without the informed consent of seller or landlord:
   a. That seller or landlord is willing to accept less than the asking price for the property or asking lease rate for the premises;
   b. What the motivating factors are for seller or landlord to sell the property or lease the premises;
   c. That seller or landlord will agree to financing or lease terms other than those offered;
   d. Any material information about seller or landlord unless disclosure is required by law or failure to disclose such information would constitute fraud or dishonest dealing; or
   e. Any facts or suspicions regarding circumstances that could psychologically impact or stigmatize the property or premises.
3. Seller or landlord consents to broker's disclosure of seller's or landlord's confidential information to the supervising broker or designee for the purpose of proper supervision, provided such supervising broker or designee does not further disclose such information without consent of seller or landlord, or use such information to the detriment of seller or landlord.
4. Brokerage firm may have agreements with other sellers or landlords to market and sell or lease their property. Broker may show alternative properties not owned by seller or landlord to other prospective buyers or tenants and list competing properties for sale or lease.

5. Broker is not obligated to seek additional offers to purchase or lease the property or premises while the property or premises is subject to a contract for sale or a lease.

6. Broker has no duty to conduct an independent inspection of the property or premises for the benefit of a buyer or tenant and has no duty to independently verify the accuracy or completeness of statements made by seller or landlord or independent inspectors. Broker has no duty to conduct an independent investigation of a buyer's or tenant's financial condition or to verify the accuracy or completeness of any statement made by a buyer or tenant.

7. Seller or landlord is not liable for the acts of broker unless such acts are approved, directed, or ratified by the seller or landlord.

B. Seller or Landlord Agency – Additional Duties

If broker is a limited agent of seller or landlord (seller's or landlord's agent), broker has the following *additional duties*:

1. Promoting the interests of seller or landlord with the utmost good faith, loyalty, and fidelity.

2. Seeking a price and lease rates and terms that are acceptable to seller or landlord.

3. Counseling seller or landlord as to any material benefits or risks of a transaction that are actually known by broker.

C. Buyer or Tenant Uniform Duties

Brokerage firm, acting through broker, shall provide brokerage services to the buyer or tenant. Broker, acting as either a transaction-broker or a buyer or tenant agent, must perform the following *uniform duties* when working with buyer or tenant:

1. Broker must exercise reasonable skill and care for buyer or tenant, including, but not limited to the following:
    a. Performing the terms of any written or oral agreement with buyer or tenant;
    b. Presenting all offers to and from buyer or tenant in a timely manner regardless of whether buyer or tenant is already a party to a contract to purchase the property or a written agreement to lease the premises;
    c. Disclosing to buyer or tenant adverse material facts actually known by broker;
    d. Advising buyer or tenant regarding the transaction and to obtain expert advice as to material matters about which broker knows but the specifics of which are beyond the expertise of broker;
    e. Accounting in a timely manner for all money and property received; and
    f. Keeping buyer or tenant fully informed regarding the transaction.

2. Broker must not disclose the following information without the informed consent of buyer or tenant:
    a. That buyer or tenant is willing to pay more than the purchase price offered for the property or lease rate offered for premises;
    b. What buyer's or tenant's motivating factors are;
    c. That buyer or tenant will agree to financing or lease terms other than those offered;

d. Any material information about buyer or tenant unless disclosure is required by law or failure to disclose such information would constitute fraud or dishonest dealing; or

e. Any facts or suspicions regarding circumstances that could psychologically impact or stigmatize the property or premises.

3. Buyer or tenant consents to broker's disclosure of buyer's or tenant's confidential information to the supervising broker or designee for the purpose of proper supervision, provided such supervising broker or designee does not further disclose such information without consent of buyer or tenant, or use such information to the detriment of buyer or tenant.

4. Broker may show properties in which the buyer or tenant is interested to other prospective buyers or tenants without breaching any duty or obligation to such buyer or tenant. Broker is not prohibited from showing competing buyers or tenants the same property and from assisting competing buyers or tenants in attempting to purchase or lease a particular property.

5. Broker is not obligated to seek other properties while buyer or tenant is already a party to a contract to purchase property or to a lease.

6. Broker has no duty to conduct an independent inspection of the property for the benefit of buyer or tenant and has no duty to independently verify the accuracy or completeness of statements made by a seller or landlord or independent inspectors. Broker has no duty to conduct an independent investigation of buyer's or tenant's financial condition or to verify the accuracy or completeness of any statement made by buyer or tenant.

7. Broker must disclose to any prospective seller or landlord all adverse material facts actually known by broker, including but not limited to adverse material facts concerning buyer's or tenant's financial ability to perform the terms of the transaction and whether buyer intends to occupy the property as a principal residence.

8. Buyer or tenant is not liable for the acts of broker unless such acts are approved, directed, or ratified by the buyer or tenant.

D. Buyer or Tenant Agency – Additional Duties

If broker is a limited agent of buyer or tenant (buyer's or tenant's agent), broker has the following *additional duties*:

1. Promoting the interests of buyer or tenant with the utmost good faith, loyalty, and fidelity.
2. Seeking a price or lease rate and terms that are acceptable to buyer or tenant.
3. Counseling buyer or tenant as to any material benefits or risks of a transaction that are actually known by broker.

VI. Entering into a Brokerage Relationship

A broker serving in a brokerage capacity may either be a single agent for one party or a transaction-broker with one or both parties. A broker shall be considered a transaction-broker unless a single-agency relationship is established through a written agreement between the broker and the party to be represented by such broker. If the transaction-broker undertakes any duties in addition to or different from those set forth in the statute, such additional duties shall be disclosed in writing and signed by the broker and the party.

A. Agency

Prior to engaging in any brokerage activities, a broker intending to establish a single-agency relationship with a party shall enter into a written agency agreement with the party to be represented. The agreement shall set forth the agent's duties as they appear in the agency sections of the statute and should set forth any other agreed-upon duties.

B. Transaction-Brokerage

Prior to engaging in any brokerage activities, a broker becomes a transaction-broker by doing one of the following: (1) entering into a written transaction-broker contract with the party, or (2) providing the party with a written transaction-brokerage disclosure with a signature block for the party to acknowledge receipt. If the disclosure is not signed, the broker shall note when the disclosure was presented.

C. Customer

The statute defines "customer" as a party to a real estate transaction with whom the broker has no brokerage relationship because such party has not engaged or employed a broker. A Brokerage Disclosure to Seller, Landlord, Buyer, or Tenant, explaining brokerage relationships, must be provided to a party who does not have a working relationship with a real estate broker.

D. Permitted Relationships

Because there are different combinations of brokerage engagements, the statute defines which are permitted and not permitted.

Different Relationships with Same Party

A broker may work with a single party in separate transactions using different relationships including, but not limited to, selling one property as a seller agent and working with that seller in buying another property as a transaction-broker or buyer agent, provided the broker establishes separate relationships for each transaction.

Separate Transactions

A broker may work with a seller or landlord in one transaction and work with a buyer or tenant in another transaction.

No Double Agency Brokerage - Consumers on Both Sides of the Transaction

A broker must not enter into a brokerage relationship with one consumer as an agent and the other consumer as an agent or a transaction-broker in the same transaction. If properly disclosed in writing (e.g. Listing Contracts), a broker that works with both consumers in the same real estate transaction may do so as: (1) a transaction-broker for both consumers to the transaction, (2) a single agent for one consumer and treating the other consumer as a customer, or (c) a transaction-broker for one consumer in the transaction and treating the other consumer as a customer. (See Rule 6.7.)

In-House Transactions and Designated Brokerage

A brokerage firm may have one designated broker working as a single agent for the seller or landlord and another designated broker working as an agent for the buyer or tenant in the same real estate transaction without creating dual agency for the employing broker, brokerage firm, or any broker employed or engaged by that employing broker.

No Dual Agency

A broker shall not establish agency with the seller or landlord and the buyer or tenant in the same transaction.

Change of Status

A broker may switch or change from acting in one capacity to another. For example, a broker acting as a seller or landlord agent may change to a transaction-broker if agreed upon by the parties and the broker supplies a Change of Status – Transaction-Brokerage Disclosure (Form CS23).

VII. Mandatory Disclosures

A. Establishing the Brokerage Relationship

Colorado law provides a party with a number of ways to engage a real estate broker. Consequently, there are several brokerage relationship disclosures that may be presented by the broker to the party prior to the broker engaging in any activities that require a brokerage license.

Commission Rule 6.5. states that "brokerage activities" occur when a broker elicits or accepts confidential information from a party concerning specific real estate needs, motivations, or financial qualifications. Activities such as an open house, preliminary conversations, or small talk concerning price range, location, property styles, or responding to general factual questions about properties that have been advertised for sale or lease do not qualify as triggering brokerage activities.

B. Mandatory Disclosures

All Commission-approved real estate brokerage employment contracts described above contain the following two mandatory disclosures to the party:

Counsel

"This is a binding contract. This form has important legal consequences and the parties should consult legal and tax or other counsel before signing."

Relationships

"Different brokerage relationships are available which include seller agency, landlord agency, buyer agency, tenant agency or transaction-brokerage."

C. Designated Brokerage Disclosure

When a party engages a broker from a multiple-person firm, that broker is a designated broker. Prior to engaging in any brokerage activities, the designated broker must advise the party in a written agreement that the brokerage relationship exists only with the designated broker and does not extend to the brokerage firm, the employing broker, or to any other brokers employed or engaged by the employing broker who are not so designated. The extent and limitations of the brokerage relationship with the designated broker must be disclosed to the party working with that designated broker.

D. Disclosure Forms

The Commission has approved brokerage relationship disclosure forms for presentation to potential parties prior to the broker engaging in any brokerage activities with those individuals. The forms should be presented to the appropriate individual upon initial contact or as soon as practical thereafter. The broker should fill in the appropriate form and attempt to secure a signature from the party to acknowledge receipt. If the disclosure is not signed, the broker must note when the disclosure was presented and retain a copy in the broker's files. These forms are disclosures only, and even if the party signs any of these forms, they are not considered contracts.

Definitions of Working Relationships (Form DD25)

This disclosure must be provided to any individual who requests definitions of these working relationships with brokers.

Brokerage Disclosure to Seller (For Sale by Owner) (Form BDS16)

Brokerage Disclosure to Landlord (Form BDL17)

These disclosures are used when a broker comes in contact with a potential seller or landlord of a property and discusses the possible sale or leasing of that property. The property address must be included. Also, the broker must state whether: (1) the broker is an agent of a buyer or tenant and the seller or landlord is a customer, or (2) the broker is a transaction-broker.

Brokerage Disclosure to Buyer (Form BDB24)

Brokerage Disclosure to Tenant (BDT20)

These disclosures are used when a broker comes in contact with a potential buyer or tenant and discusses the possible purchase or lease of property. The property address or requirements must be included. Also, the broker must state whether: (1) the broker is an agent of a seller or landlord and the buyer or tenant is a customer, or (2) the broker is a transaction-broker.

E. Other Disclosures

Notice to Parties

A broker who has already established a relationship with one party to a proposed transaction must advise, at the earliest reasonable opportunity, any other potential parties or their agents of such established relationship.

Transaction-Brokerage

Prior to engaging in any brokerage activity, a transaction-broker must disclose in writing to the party to be assisted that such broker is not acting as an agent for the other party and that the broker is acting as a transaction-broker.

Conflicts of Interest

Commission Rule 6.17. states that when a broker is acting in a licensed capacity or when a broker sells, buys, or leases real property in which the broker has an ownership or financial interest, the broker has a continuing duty to disclose any known conflicts of interest. In addition, the broker must disclose in the real estate contract or in a separate document that the broker has an ownership interest in the property and is a licensed Colorado real estate broker.

Transaction Brokerage Versus Agency Commission position CP-31 states that before acting as a transaction-broker in transactions where neutrality is difficult, the broker should consider whether the transaction-brokerage arrangement is suitable, consult with the broker's supervising broker, and make any necessary disclosures. Some examples where transaction-brokerage may not be appropriate are negotiating the sale or purchase for: (1) the broker's own account, (2) a spouse or family member of the broker, (3) a close personal friend or business associate of the broker, or (4) a repeat or regular party. Similarly, the broker may encounter certain agency situations or transactions where acting as an agent and advocate for a party could be difficult. In these circumstances, the broker should consider whether the agency arrangement is appropriate, consult with the broker's supervising broker, and act accordingly.

F. Change of Status

If a broker is acting as an agent for both a seller or landlord and a buyer or tenant and begins to assist those parties in the same real estate transaction, the broker is acting as a dual agent, which is not permitted under Colorado real estate law. The broker must immediately provide the written Change of Status – Transaction-Brokerage Disclosure (Form CS23) to the seller or landlord and buyer or tenant and begin working with both parties as a transaction-broker. The broker should attempt to secure the acknowledgements and signatures of the seller or landlord and buyer or tenant. However if that is not possible, the broker must complete the broker acknowledgement, sign the disclosure form, and retain a file copy. (See Rule 6.9.)

VIII. Example Section Removed (1-1-18)

IX. Duration of Relationships

Brokerage relationships between a broker and a party are in effect for certain specific periods of time. Colorado statutes define this time period and the residual duties and responsibilities after the relationship ends.

A. Term

The relationships commence at the time that the broker is engaged by a party and continue until performance or completion of the agreement by which the broker was engaged.

B. Termination

If the agreement by which the broker was engaged is not performed or completed for any reason, the relationship will end at the earlier of the following: (1) any date of expiration agreed upon by the broker and the party, or (2) by termination or relinquishment of the relationship.

C. No Duties after Termination

Except as otherwise agreed to in writing and except as set forth in the paragraph D below, a broker engaged as an agent or transaction-broker owes no further duty or obligation to the party after termination or expiration of the contract or completion of performance.

D. Responsibilities after Termination

A broker is responsible after termination or expiration of the contract or completion of performance for the following: (1) accounting for all moneys and property related to and received during the engagement, and (2) if the broker was acting as an agent, the broker must keep confidential all information received during the course of the engagement which was made confidential by request or instructions from the party, unless the party grants written consent to disclose such information, disclosure of such information is required by law, or the information is public or becomes public by the works or conduct of the party or from a source other than the broker.

X. Office Policies

Commission rules provide guidance for office policy relating to brokerage relationships. Commission Rule 6.4.A.2. states that in a multiple-person firm, an employing broker or employed broker must be designated in writing by the employing broker to serve as a single agent or transaction-broker. In addition, Rule 6.6. sets forth certain guidelines regarding individual and team brokerage employment contracts, substitute or additional brokers, and transaction-broker written disclosures. Rule 6.4.A.1. states that a brokerage firm must adopt a written office policy that identifies and describes the relationships offered to the public by the brokers of that firm. A brokerage firm may elect to engage in agency only, transaction-brokerage only, or both. (Also see Commission Position CP-21 regarding Office Policy Manuals.)

XI. Compensation

The Colorado statutes set forth specific policies concerning the disclosure and payment of compensation to brokers.

A. Payment Does Not Establish Agency

Payment of compensation is not construed to establish an agency relationship between the broker and the party who paid the compensation. For example, one broker has an agency agreement with a seller and another broker has an agency agreement with a buyer in the same transaction. Even though the seller is the only party paying the commission and that payment is being shared by the seller's broker and buyer's broker, the seller's broker is working as a seller's agent only for the seller and the buyer's broker is working as a buyer's agent only for the buyer.

B. Multiple Payments

More than one party may compensate a broker for services in a transaction as long as all parties to the transaction have consented in writing to such multiple payments prior to entering into a contract to buy, sell, or lease.

C. Payer

The broker's compensation may be paid by the party, a third party, or by the sharing or splitting of a commission or compensation between brokers.

D. Approval to Share

A broker must obtain the written approval of the broker's party before the broker proposes to the other broker that the other broker be compensated by sharing compensation paid by such party.

E. Identity

Prior to entering into a brokerage employment contract, the identity of those parties, persons, or entities paying compensation or commissions to any broker must be disclosed to the parties to the transaction.

F. Brokers Licensed in Other Jurisdictions

Commission Rule 6.21.C. states that a Colorado broker who cooperates with a broker who is licensed in another jurisdiction (e.g. state or country) may pay such broker a referral fee or share of the commission if: (1) the broker licensed in another jurisdiction actually referred a client to the Colorado broker, (2) such broker resides and maintains an office in the other jurisdiction, (3) all advertising, negotiations, contracting, and conveyancing regarding the Colorado property must be performed by a Colorado licensed broker, and (4) all money collected from the parties to the transaction prior to closing must be deposited in the name of the Colorado licensed broker. (See Rule 6.21.)

Chapter 17:
Listings

An * in the left margin indicates a change in the statute, rule, or text since the last publication of the manual.

I. Introduction

A real estate broker has traditionally acted as a "**special agent**" authorized to conduct a single transaction for a buyer or seller. The broker's authority as a special agent for a seller is to find a purchaser who is ready, willing, and able to buy the single listed property, either on the terms set out by or acceptable to the seller. As a buyer's agent, the broker must locate a single property acceptable to the buyer. The broker, on occasion, may be a "**general agent**," such as when employed to manage a leased property over a long period, collect rent, hire custodial help, contract for repairs, etc.

As an alternative to acting as an agent for one of the parties, a Colorado broker may be engaged as a "**transaction-broker**." In fact, it is legally presumed that a real estate licensee in Colorado is acting as a transaction-broker unless there is a written agency agreement between the broker and the buyer or seller.

II. Right-to-Sell Agreements

The authority to act for a seller in a real estate transaction is given to the broker by means of a listing contract, which is simply an employment agreement between a property owner and the broker listing the property for sale. The listing may be either written or oral unless the broker is employed as an agent, in which case Colorado requires the agreement to be in writing. From a risk-reduction perspective, all listings should be in writing and signed by both the owner and the broker in order to avoid misunderstandings that may arise later on. Commission Rule 6.14.D. requires that all written listing contracts provide a definite date for termination.

Absent a signed listing contract supporting a claim of employment, a broker is not entitled to compensation even if he or she procured the sale. The law will not assist "volunteers" in their claim of employment. Occasionally, a buyer and seller introduced by a broker may later consummate a private deal for which the broker tries to collect a commission. Unless the owner speaks or acts in a manner from which a listing contract could be implied, the broker will not collect. Proof of oral words or conduct or the intent or meaning thereof is difficult to establish in court. A prudent broker makes employment and its associated payment a certainty only by securing a signed listing contract.

Colorado listing agreements provide that property sold within a holdover period after the listing term, to any party with whom the listing broker negotiated and whose name the broker submitted to the owner in writing, entitles the broker to a commission, unless the property is subsequently listed with another broker.

III. Types of Seller Agreements

There are five general types of seller listing agreements: (1) net, (2) open, (3) exclusive agency, (4) exclusive right-to-sell, and (5) multiple listing. The five types relate to the degree of freedom the owner retains to either sell the property personally (without owing a commission) or to employ brokers to assist in the sale. The Real Estate Commission has approved both agency and transaction-broker listing forms for the most commonly used types of listings.

A. Net Listing

A net listing is a contract to find a buyer or lessee for the property at a certain "**net price to the owner**." For example: If an owner lists a property for $100,000 net, and the broker finds a buyer at $100,000 (or less), then the broker receives no commission. If the broker finds a buyer at $115,000, the broker retains $15,000 as earned commission. If the terms of a net listing agreement are challenged, courts may hold that the broker is not entitled to any amount exceeding the broker's usual commission. Additionally, a broker who abuses a net listing may be found in violation of § 12-10-217(1)(t), C.R.S., which deals with secret undisclosed profit. Because the Commission does not encourage net listings, there are no approved net-listing forms.

Net listings are generally out of favor in the sale of developed property. They are primarily used where the property is of a speculative nature. In addition to having no set price, an open net listing does not obligate the owner to restrict the listing to one broker. Thus, on an open net listing given to three different brokers, these brokers may offer the property for sale to the same prospect at three different prices. When several brokers quote different prices for the same property, there is a negative reflection on the honesty and integrity of the real estate industry.

B. Open Listing

Under an open listing, the owner lists the property with a broker at a specified price, agreeing to pay a commission on that price or any offer acceptable to the owner. However, the *owner retains the right to sell the property personally or to list the property with other brokers*. This type of listing my be more common in small communities, where the seller is likely to be acquainted with all or most of the brokers and does not wish to antagonize the others by listing with only one. *Only the broker who is the procuring cause of the sale is entitled to a commission.* If the owner sells directly to a buyer without broker involvement, the owner is not obligated to pay compensation to any broker holding an open listing.

C. Exclusive Agency Listing

Under an exclusive agency listing, the owner agrees that a commission will be payable only to the named broker, and that the property will not be listed with or sold by another broker. However, *if the owner sells to a buyer procured without broker's assistance, no commission is due.* An exclusive agency listing, as compared to the net or open listing, permits the broker to apply his or her best efforts, unhampered by possible interference from other brokers, but still subject to the uncertainty of an owner sale.

D. Exclusive Right-to-Sell Listing

This is similar to exclusive agency, except that the *broker is given the sole and exclusive right to sell the property during the listing period.* Even if the owner sells to a buyer procured by the owner, the broker is entitled to a commission. This type of listing is the most commonly used by brokers in Colorado. Brokers can apply their best efforts, secure in the knowledge that the right to a commission cannot be defeated by anyone during the listing period. The Commission-approved exclusive right-to-sell listing agreement is designed for use for both agency and transaction brokerage.

E. Multiple Listing

A multiple listing is not technically a separate kind of listing. It is, rather, a marketing arrangement. Broker-members of a local real estate association or multiple listing service (MLS) may combine to market their listings through the organization. Any member may then sell any property registered with the service and rely on a predetermined commission offered by the listing broker. The seller may choose whether to participate in MLS or an online property information exchange in the Commission-approved listing contracts. The seller also contracts in the listing as to which types of cooperating brokers will be offered how much compensation for bringing a buyer into the sale. Multiple listings are widely distributed and should never contain confidential seller information, such as the seller's motivation or willingness to accept a lower price or less favorable terms than those stated in the listing agreement.

Today, more and more listings are also being distributed statewide, nationally, and internationally over the Internet. Because many of these listing services do not require membership, it is wise for a cooperating broker to obtain a fee agreement prior to entering into negotiations.

IV. Right-to-Buy Agreements

The authority to act for a buyer in the purchase of real estate is secured by means of an employment agreement between the broker and buyer. The agreement engages the broker to locate a property for the buyer at an acceptable price and terms. The information above concerning seller listings also applies to buyer listings or right-to-buy agreements, including the requirement for a definite termination date and the inclusion of a holdover period. The Commission-approved exclusive right-to-buy contract is designed for use for both agency and transaction-brokerage.

Exclusive Right-to-Buy Contract

The broker agrees to assist (as a transaction-broker) or represent (as an agent) the purchaser or lessee by entering into a buyer listing agreement. The purchaser or lessee thus becomes the client/employer and compensates the broker for locating suitable property. With proper consent in the listing contract, the broker working with the buyer may seek compensation from the seller or the seller's broker. Brokers must make sure that clients fully understand the exclusive nature of this agreement. Clients who work with multiple brokers or directly with owners may create multiple contracts and commission obligations or precipitate litigation over breach of contract or procuring cause issues.

V. Change of Status

A broker may not represent one party as an agent and work as a transaction-broker with the other party in the same transaction. The principal to the agency agreement may agree to revert to transaction brokerage. To accommodate this change, the Commission listing forms contain a selection by the client at the time of the listing and a "Change of Status" form to notify the client at the time the "double ended" situation develops.

VI. Approved Forms

Commission Rules Chapter 7 (Use of Standard Forms) mandates the use of one of the standard Commission-approved seller or buyer listing contracts. If another listing contract is deemed necessary, an attorney representing one of the parties to the transaction must prepare it. Agency listings, whether for sellers or buyers, must be in writing. (See § 12-10-408(2)(b), C.R.S.)

VII. Broker Responsibility

Real estate brokers represent themselves to the public as possessing knowledge, ability, and skill in the field of real estate. The broker owes to the public the duty of exercising reasonable competence, judgment, and care in advising and rendering services. Real estate brokers fulfill these obligations by keeping abreast of social, economic, and legal developments affecting real property as well as changes to license law.

If a member of the public suffers a loss due to the actions or omissions of a broker, he or she may hold the broker liable in both civil action and in discipline before the Real Estate Commission.

In addition to exercising reasonable skill and care, a broker acting as an agent for a buyer or seller must also advocate on behalf of the client to bring about a purchase or sale on the best possible terms. A transaction-broker, on the other hand, may not act as an advocate for one party's interests over those of the other party. All brokers, whether acting as an agent or transaction-broker, must observe all facets of the license law and exercise reasonable skill and care in performing the terms of the employment agreement. It is strongly recommended that every broker verify that the cooperating broker in a real estate transaction has an active license issued by the Colorado Real Estate Commission. This will ensure that both brokers are compliant and in observance of the license law.

A. Diligence in Pursuing the Objective of the Listing Agreement

A real estate broker has the duty to perform the terms of the employment agreement, including exerting reasonable effort to accomplish the sale or purchase of the property. If the broker does not perform, the owner is justified in voiding the contract. It is a violation of the listing agreement and license law for a broker to "sit" on a listing, that is, take a listing and make no attempt to sell or acquire the property. If a seller elects to set what the broker believes is an unreasonable list price, it is improper and unethical to take the listing and attempt to induce the seller to reduce the price. If the seller is not amenable to comparable properties and their market prices, the broker should refuse the listing.

Buyer brokers must actively fulfill their duty to identify the most appropriate property. A buyer broker must be reasonably available at the buyer's convenience to tour and show properties. It is never proper to suggest that buyers view properties or attend open houses on their own. A buyer may never be considered an unlicensed personal assistant in the context of the Commission position statement on this subject.

B. Cancelled Listings

If a client unilaterally cancels an employment agreement during its original *unexpired* term, the listing broker may either accept the end of the employment or pursue a legal remedy. If the client attempts to re-list with another broker before the original listing expires, the second broker must emphatically caution the seller of potential liability for the payment of two commissions should the original broker bring civil action for breach of contract.

C. Conflicts of Interest

A broker must avoid even the appearance of conflict of interest with a client. Thus, a broker must clearly and fully disclose all aspects of a personal offer to purchase property listed with the broker or the broker's firm. The best action is to first abrogate the listing and then make the offer. A licensee should use a Commission-approved licensee buy-out addendum to the buy-sell contract in the purchase of a listed property. Similarly, of course, a buyer broker must not pursue the purchase of property shown to a client without clear assent from the client.

Colorado broker licenses may be suspended or revoked for acting for more than one party without the consent of all parties or for failing to disclose a conflict of interest. A seller wants to sell at the highest possible price; a buyer seeks to purchase at the lowest price. These interests are adversarial and irreconcilable. In attempting to serve two masters, a licensee may be in danger of sacrificing the interest of a buyer or seller to the broker's own interest.

D. Scope of Activity – Principal Consent

Within well-defined limits, a single broker may assist both parties to a transaction. This is allowed only with appropriate written consent of the parties to the transaction. A broker who, without the seller's express consent, informs a prospective buyer that his or her seller will accept an offer less than the asking price violates the license law. Likewise, a buyer broker, whether an agent or transaction-broker, is prohibited from informing the seller that the buyer will pay more than the offering price. A broker may never withhold an offer, either hiding the first one because of anticipating receipt of a second, higher offer, or hiding a subsequent higher offer fearing that it might kill the current deal. Brokers are required by statute to present all offers, including those received right up to closing.

E. Commission-Approved Forms

Real estate licensees are fortunate that Colorado is a leader in providing opportunities to participate in continuing education and conference programs, as well as providing approved forms for use by licensees. Approved listing forms address a wide range of current contractual issues in specific detail, particularly those of brokerage relationships. The Commission-approved seller's property disclosure (SPD) forms deal with disclosure of the physical condition of residential, commercial or land property. Sellers are asked to certify that the disclosure is correct to the best of the seller's current, actual knowledge. Disclosure of property condition is optional. However, if a licensee chooses to use a disclosure form, it must be a Commission-approved version. If the seller declines to make such a disclosure, that provision should be stricken from the listing agreement, but not before advising the seller that buyers and buyer brokers often require completion of such a form.

A real estate broker has a statutory duty to account to members of the public for all funds received in the course of a transaction. The broker must keep accurate records and accounts and must keep any funds received on behalf of others in an identified trust account separate from funds belonging to the broker.

F. Closing Instructions

The Real Estate Commission, working in concert with the Division of Insurance, has developed a closing instructions form that must be used in conjunction with an approved listing contract. The closing instructions form provides for the appointment of a closing agent and outlines responsibility for payment of fees for closing services. The Commission's position is that this form be initiated, with the buyer or seller, at the time a listing is signed. The form can then be completed with the signatures of both parties at the time of acceptance of a sales contract, and delivered to the closing entity in advance.

It is impossible to anticipate all the varied situations that may raise questions concerning the broker's responsibilities. No safer guide for conduct exists than to treat others the way in which you would want to be treated.

G. Broker Compensation

In order to be entitled to compensation, a real estate broker must: (1) establish employment, (2) fulfill the terms of employment, and (3) get the transaction closed—unless defeated by the refusal of his or her client to consummate the sale as agreed upon.

Broker commissions have historically been paid by the seller out of the transaction proceeds with money the buyer brought into the transaction, typically computed as a percentage of the selling price. Listing brokers then often split this commission with a cooperating buyer broker. Brokers employed by buyers now often seek compensation directly from that buyer, a responsibility clearly delineated in the Commission-approved buyer listing agreements. More recently, brokers have turned to forms of compensation other than the traditional percentage, such as retainer or hourly fees, or combinations of either along with success fees.

Broker commissions are always freely and independently negotiable, established by agreement of the parties and not by law. To prevent controversy and clearly identify the intent of the parties, all compensation and terms of payment must be clearly stipulated in the employment contract. If the original fee or commission is changed, whether to facilitate a closing or to induce future business, this must be clearly spelled out in a written amendment to the contract. The Commission-approved listing contracts provide a section dealing with the splitting of fees with cooperating brokers.

Under Colorado law, a seller's broker is entitled to a commission if the seller refuses or neglects to correct a title defect, provided the contract would otherwise bind the purchaser to close the sale. If a buyer wrongfully refuses to complete the sale, a listing broker may receive compensation in the form of liquidated damages from the down payment forfeited by the purchaser. The broker's right in this instance is usually set forth in the contract to purchase or in the listing agreement or both.

If the purchaser makes an offer to buy conditional on some event, such as the ability to secure a loan, then he or she may rightfully cancel the contract if the condition does not occur. The buyer must have acted in good faith to secure the loan. In such event, the broker is not entitled to a commission.

If a buyer offers a different price or terms than agreed to in the original buyer agreement, or the seller accepts a different price or terms than contained in the original listing agreement, the broker(s) is entitled to a commission. Under these circumstances the parties have ratified, or given implied agreement to, variations in the terms of the original contract(s).

H. Sales Arrangements Between Brokers

An employment agreement (buyer or seller listing contract) is normally only between the broker and the principal. To help sell the property, it is common for the listing broker and seller to agree to offer compensation to other cooperating brokers, including buyer agents or transaction-brokers. Although unusual, buyer brokers may also offer compensation to cooperating brokers to help in locating a property for the buyer. The responsibility to pay a commission rests squarely with the listing broker.

Commission-approved seller listing contracts require the consent of the seller before a broker may offer commission splits to cooperating brokers.

If the broker's office policy offers various levels of compensation, such as one percentage to buyer agents and another to transaction-brokers, it must be clearly disclosed to the seller that such a policy could result in restricting market exposure or cooperation from other brokers.

Once determined, commission splits are usually communicated to other brokers through a multiple listing service. In the absence of a multiple listing service, commission letters or agreements between brokers are a common method of establishing agreement on the terms of sharing commissions. By whatever method, terms of cooperative commission sharing must be specifically agreed to in advance and clearly communicated to potential cooperating brokers.

Chapter 18: Contracts

An * in the left margin indicates a change in the statute, rule, or text since the last publication of the manual.

I. Introduction

Together with the laws of agency and brokerage relationships, an understanding of contract law is essential for real estate practitioners. A licensee constantly reviews contracts for purchases, lease agreements, and mortgages. In Colorado, real estate licensees are allowed to fill in blanks in standard contract forms. The competency and professionalism of the real estate licensee are always at stake when contracts are being written or explained.

Of all legal instruments, contracts are among the most important to our society and economic system. The stability and security of our business world are dependent upon the law of contracts. It ensures that parties perform their agreements by requiring that they either perform or pay for all loss or damage caused by non-performance. Furthermore, the specialized branches of business law, such as the sale of goods and services, negotiable instruments, partnerships and corporations, are all founded upon the law of contracts.

A contract may be defined as an agreement between two or more competent persons, having for its purpose a legal object, wherein the parties agree to act in a certain manner.

II. Essential Elements of a Contract

To be binding and enforceable at law, all contracts must have four essential elements: (1) mutual assent, (2) consideration, (3) competent parties, and (4) legal purpose.

1. **Mutual Assent.** Before a valid contract can exist, the parties must mutually consent to be bound by the terms of the agreement. Such mutual assent is evidenced or objectively set forth by the offer and acceptance. If the consent was obtained by fraud, misrepresentation, duress, undue influence, or mistake, then there is no real consent and, therefore, the element of mutual assent is absent. In certain cases, the law requires that the expression of the parties' mutual agreement be in writing to be enforceable.

   a. **Offer.** An offer is a promise by one party to act in a certain manner provided the other party will act in the manner requested. The one making the offer is called the offeror; the one to whom the offer is made is called the offeree.

      If a person says, "I'll give you $20 for that tire," that person is making an offer. They are saying, essentially, "I promise to pay you $20 if you will deliver to me the ownership and possession of the tire." Similarly, when a prospective buyer of real estate signs a contract to purchase property, they are making an offer to the seller to buy the property on stated terms and conditions. No contract exists until the seller agrees.

      To be effective, an offer first must be communicated to the offeree by a means selected by the offeror. Secondly, the offer must be intended as such. Whether it is intended as an offer depends, not on the offeror's subjective mental attitude, but on the reasonable interpretation given to the communication by the offeree. Expressions made in jest, anger, or excitement are generally not offers because the hearer should realize that the speaker is not, at the moment, seriously contemplating what is said. Thirdly, for an offer to be effective, it must be definite and certain as to its terms. If the offer is indefinite as to some of its terms, no mutual agreement can occur because reasonable persons could disagree as to the interpretation of the indefinite provisions. How long does an offer last? When does it cease? An offer can be terminated by a lapse of time, revocation, rejection, or operation of law.

(i) **Lapse of time.** The offer may specify the length of time it is to remain in effect. Upon expiration of that time, the offer ends. However, an expired offer may become effective if ratified. Ratification occurs if a person's acts or conduct validate an otherwise unenforceable act. For example, if a buyer gives a seller three days to accept the buyer's offer to purchase property and the seller accepts the offer on the fifth day, the offer would normally be considered dead because of lapse of time. However, if the buyer remained silent, allowed the contract to go to closing, and then backed out because the offer was accepted late, the buyer may be said to have ratified the contract through their conduct. If no time is specified, then the offer terminates upon the expiration of a reasonable length of time. Reasonable time is determined by all the surrounding circumstances; for instance, it is less in the case of an offer to sell perishable goods than for nonperishable goods.

(ii) **Revocation.** The offeror may revoke, cancel, or withdraw an offer at any time before acceptance, even if he or she had stated the offer would be held open for a certain period. Thus, a person may offer to sell or buy a vacant lot, telling the other party that they have ten days in which to accept. Two days later, if the other party has not accepted, the offeror may cancel without liability. But when an option exists, an offeror cannot withdraw their offer without liability. An option is a subsidiary contract to hold open an offer for a stated period of time. Many so-called options are not enforceable because consideration (something of legal value) has not been given in return for the option. In the above example, if the second party had paid or promised to pay $500 for the privilege of having ten days in which to decide, then there would be an option and the offeror could not withdraw the offer during that time.

(iii) **Rejection.** An offer is terminated by rejection or refusal of the offeree. If the offeree agrees to accept the offeror's proposal but on different terms, this is called a counteroffer and constitutes a rejection of the original offer.

(iv) **Operation of law.** Offers can be terminated automatically by operation of law. Generally, the death or insanity of either the offeror or offeree ends the offer. Destruction of the subject matter of the offer or a change of law making the object of the offer illegal will also terminate the offer.

b. **Acceptance.** The second step in achieving mutual assent is the acceptance, *i.e.*, the indication by the offeree that they are willing to be bound by the terms of the offer. In a real estate transaction, this is usually accomplished by the seller signing the offer to purchase made by the buyer.

To be effective, an acceptance must be made and communicated according to the manner, time, place, and terms specified in the offer. If not specified, then the acceptance must be made and communicated in a reasonable manner, according to the custom and usage of the trade in that locality.

c. **Reality of Consent.** For mutual assent to exist, consent must be given knowingly and voluntarily. If a party consents due to fraud, misrepresentation, undue influence, duress, or mistake, it would be unfair to hold them to the agreement. Therefore, when consent is obtained under these circumstances, the courts usually hold that there is no contract, or permit the innocent party to cancel the contract.

When there is a mutual mistake as to material fact concerning the identity or existence of the subject matter, no contract results. But when the mistake concerns an unessential fact, relates to the value, or is made by only one party due to that party's carelessness, an enforceable contract will result. Thus, if the parties agree to buy and sell property at a certain address and there are two properties having the same address, and each party has in mind a different property, no contract results. But if one party has a mistaken belief as to the value of a piece of property, a good contract will result.

Fraud and misrepresentation are self-explanatory and, when present, permit the innocent party to cancel the contract and, in appropriate cases, to recover damages suffered.

Undue influence consists of the abuse of the control or influence that one person has over another because of their relationship. Duress consists of compelling a person, through fear, to do or to agree to do an act.

d. **Statute of Frauds.** To prevent fraud through perjury, the law requires that the parties' agreement evidencing their mutual assent be in writing in certain cases. As to real estate in Colorado, § 38-10-108, C.R.S., provides:

> Every contract for the leasing for a longer period than one year or for the sale of any lands or any interest in lands is void unless the contract or some note or memorandum thereof expressing the consideration is in writing and subscribed by the party by whom the lease or sale is to be made.

In Colorado, real estate contracts not signed by the seller are void, not voidable. Colorado differs from most other states that provide that "the party to be charged" (in a lawsuit by the other party) must have signed the contract.

Other agreements that are declared void by law, unless in writing, are described in § 38-10-112, C.R.S.:

> (a) Every agreement that by the terms is not to be performed within one year after the making thereof;
>
> (b) Every special promise to answer for the debt, default, or miscarriage of another person;
>
> (c) Every agreement, promise, or undertaking made upon consideration of marriage, except mutual promises to marry.

Generally, the statute of frauds provides that no civil action can be brought to enforce a contract unless there is some writing signed by the party to be charged (in a civil action to enforce the contract). The writing does not have to be the "perfect" contract, but it does have to be sufficient to allow a court to determine that the parties intended to sell the property. Such things as: (1) the identity of the parties, (2) subject matter, (3) terms and conditions, (4) recital of consideration, and (5) signatures of the parties are necessary. Although Colorado's statute of frauds provides that only the seller must sign the real estate contract, the obvious best practice is for both parties to sign.

Some states have statute of frauds provisions in their real estate license laws. These laws provide that a real estate licensee will not be entitled to a commission unless there is a written employment agreement between the licensee and the buyer or seller. Although Colorado license law does not have such a statute of frauds provision, there is a statutory requirement that all agency listings and agency employment agreements be in writing.

e. **The Parol Evidence Rule.** The parol evidence rule is closely linked to the statute of frauds. It provides that an agreement in writing shows that the parties intend it as the final and complete expression of their agreement. Evidence of any earlier oral or written statements is not admissible to vary, add to, or contradict the terms of the writing. The word parol means "word" or "speech." Because the purpose of the statute of frauds is to prevent the possibility of nonexistent agreements being enforced by fraud or perjury, it makes sense to have a rule that requires the parties to live with what they have written. The parol evidence rule generally keeps parties from trying to introduce evidence in court that they really meant something other than what is stated in the written contract.

2. **Consideration.** Agreement alone does not make an enforceable contract. There must be consideration supporting the agreement. Many persons assume money is a requirement of consideration; but in the vast majority of cases the consideration for a promise is the return promise. The promise of the buyer to buy and the promise of the owner to sell constitute sufficient consideration to support their agreement—no deposit is necessary.

   Consideration may be defined as a promise or an act of legal value bargained for and received in return for a promise. Both parties must receive consideration for their promises. Legal value is generally defined in terms of benefit or detriment. Thus, legal value is present if: (1) the one making the promise (or doing the act) thereby commits to something they were not previously obligated to do (detriment), and (2) the one receiving the promise (or act) thereby becomes entitled to something they would not previously have received (benefit). Both parties to an agreement usually receive some benefit and suffer some detriment.

   When one party agrees to buy and another agrees to sell, each is agreeing to do something they were not obligated to do and each will receive something to which they were not entitled. But offering to pay a police officer $1,000 as a reward for recovering stolen property cannot be consideration for that offer. In promising to recover stolen property, a police officer is doing no more than he or she is already bound to do. A promise given without any return does not create a binding contract. Each party must in some way give legal value for what they receive.

   Although the promise to pay for land, if written in the contract, is good consideration, the buyer customarily shows good faith by making a partial payment on the purchase price. This partial payment is called "earnest money" or "good faith money." It is a good indication that the buyer will perform as promised and pay for the land, because failing to do so will cause him or her to lose the money according to the contract's default provision.

3. **Competent Parties.** All parties are presumed to have the legal capacity to enter into contracts. But certain persons, for reasons of public policy or some disability, do not have full contractual capacity. Among these are minors, mental defectives, and intoxicated persons.

   In Colorado, a minor is an individual under 18 years of age. Minors have the right to cancel or disaffirm their contracts with no liability other than the return of any proceeds they received under such contract. Minors are given this right to protect them against their lack of experience, judgment, and ability. The burden is upon adults to ascertain that the person they deal with is of legal age. After reaching legal age, minors may ratify or approve previous contracts, which will then be binding on them.

   Insane persons are given the same protection as that given to minors, except that the contracts of a person judicially declared insane could never have had effect in the first place.

   The contract of an intoxicated person is usually binding, except where that person is so intoxicated as to be incapable of understanding the nature of the transaction. In that case, the intoxicated person may cancel or ratify the contract.

   A corporation's charter determines its contractual ability. Its capacity to contract may be related only to specific things or it may be related to broad areas of business transactions.

4. **Legal Purpose.** To be valid and enforceable, a contract must have a legal object for its purpose. The object cannot be to violate a valid statute. An agreement to commit a crime, a tort, or something contrary to public welfare is illegal. For example, an agreement to defraud someone, slander a person, or operate an unauthorized gambling operation is illegal. Dual contracting to induce a lender to make a loan on real estate without knowing the true terms of sale, such as the actual amount of down payment, is a criminal offense under § 18-5-208, C.R.S.

III. Matters to be Considered in Real Estate Contracts

The buy-sell contract is the most important document in a real estate transaction. This contract determines the kind of title to be conveyed, the type of deed, liens and encumbrances that the land will be sold subject to, and the manner of payment of the purchase price.

Numerous controversies involving real estate licensees arise out of contracts for the sale of property. Although dishonesty or wrongdoing on the part of the licensee is rare, disputes often stem from the licensee's lack of thoroughness or knowledge. Real estate brokers must continually strive to increase their own proficiency and that of their employed licensees in writing good contracts. It is an art to write a sound, workable contract that includes all important matters and is still reasonably clear and understandable. Although Colorado licensees are fortunate in having Commission-approved contract forms available, they must nevertheless pay close attention to completing these forms in a competent manner.

The following are the main items to be considered in drawing up real estate contracts. This list is not intended to be exhaustive; seldom are two real estate transactions alike. Only through careful study, experience, and guidance will the real estate licensee learn to recognize the essential items to be included in a given transaction.

A. Names and Signatures of the Parties

The seller and buyer must be named and properly designated as the seller (vendor) and buyer (vendee). If two or more persons own the property, all should be named and all should sign—unless, of course, only one is selling his or her interest. If two or more persons are buying the property, all should be named and all should sign, together with an election as to whether they are buying as joint tenants or tenants in common.

B. Sale Price and Payment Provisions

The contract is incomplete and unenforceable unless it contains the sales price. If there is no provision regarding the method of payment, the law presumes it is to be a cash sale. The contract should state, when applicable: (1) the amount of the deposit, (2) the amount to be paid at closing, (3) the method of payment, (4) the balance, either by assumption of the existing mortgage or by a new mortgage, and (5) any and all other pertinent financial provisions.

C. Description of the Property

The description of the real estate should be sufficiently definite to identify the land sold with reasonable certainty. Although the street address, with the city and state, is sometimes sufficient, it is better to use the legal description contained in the seller's deed. Even though the contract may not mention them, additional rights to the land such as easements, rights of way, and other appurtenances belonging to the land will automatically pass to the buyer in the transfer of ownership. For the sake of clarity and completeness, they should be mentioned in the contract. In addition, all items of personal property to be included in the sale should be listed.

D. Type of Deed

The contract should provide for the type of deed by which the property will be conveyed, whether by quitclaim, general warranty, or other kind of deed. In the event the type of deed is not stated, the courts will probably require that kind of deed that is customary to that particular type of transaction in that locality.

E. Condition of Title

Real estate sales contracts traditionally provide that title is to be merchantable, that is, free from defects and which a reasonably prudent buyer is willing to accept. Even without this provision, the law presumes that merchantable title is to be conveyed. Mortgages, tax liens, and other liens and encumbrances are considered defects. Therefore, if the property is to be conveyed subject to a mortgage or other encumbrance or restriction, the contract should clearly state so. Another customary provision states that the buyer will give written notice of defects of title, not excepted in the contract, and that the seller will clear up said defects by a given deadline. The seller has the duty of proving good title. A contract should require the owner to establish their title by furnishing evidence of ownership, such as an abstract of title or a title insurance commitment. In approved Colorado buy-sell contract forms, the seller does not specifically agree to provide merchantable title. However, the seller does agree to provide the buyer with a title insurance commitment, and, if the buyer objects to the merchantability of title, the seller must correct unsatisfactory title conditions or the contract will terminate.

F. Default Provisions

The rights of the parties should be stated in the event that one side fails to perform. The law, of course, gives the parties remedies for non-performance, but a lawsuit can be avoided if the parties mutually agree to a settlement beforehand. Therefore, provisions should be made as to the disposition of the buyer's deposit if the buyer defaults, and any other arrangements deemed appropriate. It is especially critical for brokers to counsel buyers on the meaning and effect of the loan commitment deadline in the Commission-approved buy-sell contract. A 100 percent commitment to fund a loan seldom exists, but buyers must have a sufficient level of understanding and comfort with their own and their lender's commitment as of that date, or face certain forfeiture of earnest money if the transaction does not close.

G. Contingency Provisions

A buyer may be willing to buy, but may first have to accomplish something, such as borrow additional money or sell a presently owned property. An offer to purchase must clearly state such conditions. It is possible that the seller may also wish to provide for some contingency. Poorly written contingencies are one of the major causes of disputes between the parties and complaints against real estate licensees. Any contingency clause must state not only the conditional situation or event, but also provide a definite method and deadline by which to accomplish the contingent requirement, remove the contingency, or terminate the contract, including disposition of earnest money.

H. Possession

If the time of closing the transaction is different from the time that possession of the premises is to be given to the buyer, the date and time of possession should be stated.

I. Apportionment or Adjustment

The contract should provide for the apportionment of all charges or assets concerning the property, such as taxes, assessments, water rents, interest on assumed encumbrances, mortgage insurance premiums, or rents.

J. Risk of Loss

If the property is damaged or destroyed by fire, flood, or storm after the contract is signed but before the deed is delivered, who suffers the loss—the seller or the buyer? The answer is not as simple as it seems.

In most jurisdictions, when a binding real estate contract exists, and where either party may enforce specific performance, the loss falls upon the buyer who is considered the owner of the property. The buyer holds what is known as "equitable title" even though legal title has not yet passed. The buyer can legally force the seller to convey the legal title. Also, the seller can force the buyer to accept the legal title and perform their part. This right is called specific performance; the parties lose this right only if they waive it in the contract.

Some courts interpret equitable title theory as unjustly putting the burden of loss on the buyer. Not being in possession, the buyer is unable to protect his or her interest. However, the majority of courts seem to hold that the loss falls on the buyer unless the contract provides otherwise. To avoid potential misunderstanding or controversy, it is important to clearly spell out risk in the contract. It is not unusual for the contract of sale to provide that the risk of loss remains with the seller.

IV. Colorado Buy-Sell Contract

Buy-sell contracts used by licensees are sometimes referred to as "preliminary," "earnest money," or "executory" contracts. They contain, among other provisions, a promise by the buyer to pay for the land and a promise by the seller to deliver a deed to the land. These contracts serve the purpose of establishing good faith until the time for payment and delivery of the deed. Buy-sell contracts are not recorded (except for a very good reason) because many such contracts fail and are never consummated. Recording would cloud the title to the property if delivery of a deed did not occur. However, an installment land contract, described later in this chapter, should always be recorded unless there is a specific agreement to the contrary.

The Real Estate Commission has an approved buy-sell contract for all types of properties: residential, income-residential, residential (Colorado Foreclosure Protection Act), commercial, land, and manufactured home (Lot Lease Only). Refer to the default provisions in the contracts for the different remedies afforded.

> **TIME OF ESSENCE, DEFAULT AND REMEDIES.** Time is of the essence hereof. If any note or check received as Earnest Money hereunder or any other payment due hereunder is not paid, honored or tendered when due, or if any obligation hereunder is not performed or waived as herein provided, there shall be the certain remedies for the parties depending on who is in default.

The broker is in a position to strongly influence the choice of remedy. This position of influence should be used cautiously because there are circumstances when the use of a particular remedy may be injurious to one of the parties.

The liquidated damages provision is popular for various reasons. In the event of default by the buyer, the seller usually does not want to become involved in a lawsuit against the buyer in order to enforce the specific performance of the contract. The seller is usually more concerned about getting the property back on the market and making a successful sale. The broker has the same desire. The average buyer is not familiar with real estate transactions and is not aware of the possibility that he or she could be compelled to purchase the property. Usually, the buyer only understands that the earnest money is endangered.

The specific performance and damages remedy is appropriate, particularly if the buyer and seller are experienced in real estate dealings. It may be the fairest because it offers both parties an equal right to seek damages.

Earnest money deposits are another critical element of any contract. Earnest money should be adequate to demonstrate the buyer's serious intent to purchase and, in the event of the buyer's default, to compensate the seller for the act of taking the property off the market during the period prior to closing. Earnest money should apply only to partial payment of the purchase price. The form of earnest money, *e.g.*, check or promissory note, must be specified in the contract. If it is a note, it must have a definite due date. The Commission strongly recommends that notes not be taken with due dates of "at closing." Such notes create confusion as to the seller's forfeiture rights if closing does not occur and the buyer is at fault.

The Commission-approved buy-sell contract includes a mediation clause by which the parties agree to submit matters in dispute to mediation when the dispute cannot be otherwise resolved. Mediation is non-binding. If efforts at mediation do not resolve the dispute within 30 days of the written notice requesting mediation, the mediation terminates unless the parties mutually agree to continue.

If mediation fails to resolve an earnest money dispute, the approved contract forms provide that the earnest money holder may await any proceeding or interplead the Earnest Money into a court of competent jurisdiction. Under this provision, if the parties do not give mutual written instructions to the broker, the broker may "interplead" the money into court and let the court decide the matter. Although the broker may interplead without such a provision, the existence of the provision encourages the parties to reach a settlement. The provision also enables the court to relieve the broker from court costs and attorney fees. Nothing, of course, prohibits a broker from refunding an earnest money deposit to a buyer if, in the broker's judgment, that is what the contract calls for, but the broker may subsequently become liable to the seller if the disbursement is found to be wrongful. A broker may never unilaterally declare a forfeiture of the buyer's earnest money; only the seller has that right.

V. Competency in Preparing Contracts

The terms in any agreement to buy and sell real estate must be carefully drafted. Contingencies and promises must be completely defined. Consideration of the circumstances affecting the parties involved in the transaction must be carefully weighed before spelling out the terms.

A. Loan Contingency

The ordinary buyer can only buy if he or she is able to borrow sufficient funds on reasonable terms. Ethical procedure demands that the contract be made contingent upon the ability to secure such a loan. If a buyer is unable to buy unless the sale of his or her current home is consummated, any offer should reflect this contingency. Such a contingency is still needed even if there is a pending contract to sell the buyer's home, if the buyer requires the proceeds from the sale in order to purchase, because there is never complete certainty that a pending sale transaction will close.

B. Assumptions

When an existing mortgage will remain on the property after sale, the responsibility of the parties must be carefully set forth. The buyer may "assume and agree to pay" the existing mortgage or may buy the property "subject to" the existing mortgage. A seller will usually want the buyer to "assume and agree to pay" because it will make the buyer responsible on the original note along with the seller. In either case, both parties to the transaction should be informed of the resultant effect of the sale. Too often, unscrupulous buyers of equities have purchased "subject to" or even agreed to "assume and pay" an existing loan. They then collect rents from the property for as long as possible, while deliberately defaulting on the loan payments and letting the property go into foreclosure. A resulting deficiency judgment would be against the original owner and seller rather than the buyer. Such conduct, known as "equity skimming," is a criminal offense.

It is equally important for the broker to ensure that, if necessary, a buyer is properly qualified to assume a loan and that the assumption is properly processed through the lender. Licensees are subject to disciplinary action for failing to ensure that loan assumptions are finalized through the lending institution.

C. Buyer's Creditworthiness

The licensee's service to the seller (for which they are paid) is to procure a ready, willing, and able buyer. What is meant by "able"? Certainly it means more than the buyer's ability to execute the contract and make the initial payment. If the buyer is assuming an existing loan, or if the seller is carrying back a purchase money mortgage or conveying by means of an installment land contract, the seller is in a high-risk position. There is no third-party lending institution to determine the buyer's qualifications. The typical residential seller is not a speculator, and does not wish to pursue foreclosure or to retake title to the sold property. The seller will likely depend upon the licensee for guidance. Although the licensee may have no legal obligations to investigate the buyer, the licensee at least has a duty to inform the seller of the inherent dangers in the transaction, to advise the seller to make some type of an investigation concerning the buyer's ability or willingness to pay, and to seek legal advice.

A buyer may wish to use the seller's credit by having the seller secure a new loan or refinance the existing loan so that the buyer can purchase with less cash or no cash and without responsibility. The seller might also be induced to carry a second purchase money mortgage, which may even result in cash being given to the buyer at the time of closing. Thus, the buyer purchases without a down payment. This type of transaction may be perfectly proper if the seller knows the buyer or has faith in the buyer's creditworthiness. However, this puts the seller in an extremely vulnerable position, and the broker should alert the seller to this fact.

D. Balloon Payments

If a buyer agrees to sign a second note and trust deed as part payment, the terms should be specifically set forth. If a note requires regular equal installments but will not be completely paid off at the time the note matures, a larger ("balloon") payment will be required at the maturity date. The buyer may be in danger of foreclosure if he or she is unable to raise the money for such a balloon payment. In such a case, the licensee should make the buyer and seller aware of this eventuality. At the time the balloon payment becomes due, the buyer may be dependent on the ability to refinance. Colorado law protects the borrower in this regard.

VI. Surveys

Many properties have not been properly surveyed. This is true particularly in areas that have not been formally subdivided into platted parcels. Some subdivided areas also contain irregular lot sizes, and the survey may be questionable. Both the frontage in running feet and the acreage, which determines square footage, are important and both should be verified before quoting figures to a buyer. In some cases, improvements, such as fences or garages, encroach on boundary lines and only a survey will reveal the problem. A broker may be liable in such situations because brokers are assumed to have greater knowledge than that of buyers and sellers. The broker should recommend to both the buyer and seller that a survey be made. (See the Chapter, "Land Descriptions.")

VII. Dual Contracting and Loan Fraud

Another matter covered by law involves presenting a false contract with a larger purchase price to the lender than the price shown on the contract under which the parties intend to consummate the transaction. This is called dual contracting to induce a loan and is prohibited by the Colorado Criminal Code, § 18-5-208, C.R.S.

False or inflated down payments, failure to identify seller-assisted down payments or concessions, second trust deeds, "gift letters," or any other matter not fully and accurately reflected in a buy-sell contract and resulting settlement statement may result in severe disciplinary and sometimes even criminal action against a licensee.

VIII. Installment Contracts

The installment land contract (ILC) is described in the Chapter, "Trust Deeds and Liens," as a method of financing or a security device. It is also a method of effecting a sale. Commission Position 39 cautions:

> "There is a significant potential for harm to the seller, buyer or assignee if the installment land contract is not properly drafted..........real estate brokers are prohibited from drafting a contract document that would reflect the terms of such a transaction as it would exceed their level of competency and is a matter requiring the expertise and advice of an attorney. Additionally, such behavior may be construed as the unauthorized practice of law by the real estate broker and subject to civil penalties. The contracts for these transactions should not be prepared by a real estate broker; rather, the documents should be drafted by a licensed Colorado attorney-at-law engaged for each particular transaction."

An ILC is a contract for delayed delivery of a deed, providing for periodic payments over a term of years, as does a promissory note. It is distinguished from the real estate buy-sell contract in that the buy-sell contract does not usually contain provisions for installment payments and is merely intended to hold the deal for a short period until the condition of title is accepted and deed is delivered to the buyer, normally at closing. An installment land contract must contain provisions required by statute and other customary provisions. There is no standard form of installment land contract approved by the Commission. The Commission revoked its approval of the installment land contract long ago.

A buy-sell contract may also be used to hold a deal until the execution of an installment land contract. In this case, the buy-sell agreement will of course not refer to delivery of a deed, but rather to the subsequent signing of an installment land contract.

If a buy-sell contract provides for specific performance as a remedy, it has the same effect as an ILC in that the seller is bound to convey the land to the buyer at some future time. At the signing of either type of contract, the buyer has an equitable interest in the real estate. In this situation, courts generally recognize that the "buyer becomes owner of the land in equity" and is called the "equitable owner."

Installment land contracts are more prevalent during periods of "tight" money or when a property is difficult to finance conventionally. Oftentimes a person with little or no cash for a down payment will be permitted to take possession of property under an installment land contract providing for monthly payments to the seller. The seller will still hold "legal" title, and the buyer will possess "equitable" title.

A preliminary contract for an ILC is not usually recorded unless a dispute arises and court action is imminent. It is always in the buyer's best interest to have the installment land contract recorded, and the Real Estate Commission requires that buyers of subdivisions registered with the Commission be so advised. Sellers of unimproved subdivided lands often have installment land contracts. If an ILC is not recorded, there is no notice to the world of the buyer's interest in the property, the buyer being completely at the mercy of the seller. The larger the buyer's down payment offer to the seller, the stronger the buyer's bargaining strength as to deed and trust deed arrangement.

Although the seller retains legal title under an installment land contract, he or she is not the actual owner of the real estate. The seller's interest in the contract is considered personalty, and would be treated as such in the distribution of the seller's estate in the event of his or her death. The seller would convey legal title interest in the property by formally assigning the contract. Any person buying a seller's legal title interest should make sure that the contract being assigned is of public record, and should receive the original signed ILC in the assignment. If a seller merely has a contract interest and is not the holder of legal title, the contract or assignment should so state.

The buyer's interest in an ILC is considered realty and generally is merchantable to a third person. If an ILC has a non-assignment clause, the seller's consent must be secured. Often, the contract will preclude the property from being mortgaged or leased. Of course the buyer under an ILC could not give a trust deed even if the contract permitted, because the buyer does not have a deed. A buyer's interest given as collateral for a loan would be secured by a mortgage. The wording of an assignment or new contract will determine whether the assignee is personally liable to make the remaining payments.

If there is an existing loan on the property, the ILC should state who is to make the payments. It is not enough to merely state that the property is subject to an existing loan. Such a statement would make the buyer responsible for both the contract price and for the seller's existing loan payments in order to protect equitable title interest. Usually it is the seller who continues to make the payments on the existing loan, and this should be stated in the contract. The contract should also provide that in the event the seller fails to make payments, the buyer is permitted to pay the lender directly and credit the amount paid against payments owed to the seller under the ILC.

An installment land contract usually provides that a deed to the property will be delivered when the full purchase price or a specified portion (*e.g.*, one-third or one-half) has been paid. This may create a problem if the seller is not able to execute and deliver the deed when it is due. A high level of trust is placed in the seller's ability to convey a future deed clear of all encumbrances. If the seller dies before the buyer fulfills the contract, other difficulties may arise; for example, the seller's interest may be tied up in estate proceedings. Therefore, if the seller is a natural person rather than a corporation, it is prudent to place the deed with an escrow agent at the time of sale, with proper instructions to deliver it when the buyer has complied with the contract. If a deed is being held in escrow and the seller assigns the contract, a new agreement with the original escrow agent is necessary to substantiate the chain of title to the property.

There is usually nothing to prevent the buyer from refinancing an installment land contract at any time and paying off the seller. As with any loan, however, terms or restrictions on prepayment should be clearly set out in the contract.

In the event of a default in payments under an ILC, the seller's remedies are limited by a forfeiture clause in the contract. The usual forfeiture clause gives the seller the choice of foreclosure or suing for payments when each comes due. Upon choosing one remedy, the other is lost. Thus, upon default, the seller usually keeps the money that has already been collected and forecloses to secure the return of the property.

A forfeiture clause usually demands that possession of the property be surrendered to the seller within 30 days or so after default. Even if in possession, however, the seller must still go to district court to foreclose. This would amount to strict foreclosure if the courts enforced the foreclosure clause. In mortgages or trust deeds, the courts will not enforce strict foreclosure, but in an installment land contract the courts may do so, if only partially, inasmuch as there is no public sale. A seller who chooses this remedy elects to rescind the contract and cannot get a deficiency judgment. The court, in its judgment, will often determine how long the buyer may keep possession, regardless of how many days are stated in the forfeiture provision. In one Colorado case, when the buyer had paid approximately one-third of the purchase price, the court required that the buyer be given six months to redeem.

Some sellers or their brokers attempt to avoid having to go to court to foreclose the contract. One popular but ineffective method of doing this is to have the buyer sign a quitclaim deed back to the seller up front, and escrow both the ILC and the quitclaim deed. The escrow agreement would provide for delivery of both the buyer's copy of the ILC and the quitclaim deed to the seller in the event of default. Adding the quitclaim deed to the escrow does not in any manner strengthen the position of the seller, as it would have been executed simultaneously with the ILC and does nothing to alter the underlying nature of the relationship between the parties. Foreclosure of an ILC is the only process by which the buyer may be dispossessed.

An installment land contract should be treated as a conveyance. Although it does not always happen, the buyer should demand evidence of title even though the title insurance or the abstract will not be delivered until the buyer complies with the contract terms. Commission Rule 6.19. applies to an ILC and requires the broker to provide settlement sheets (showing the purchase price, the costs, the pro-rating, and how the purchase price is to be paid) to the parties.

The installment land contract is a complicated and flexible instrument. It is also salable, making for further complications. The seller, the buyer, or the assignee may all be hurt if the instrument is improperly drafted or used. Whether used as an instrument of conveyance or a security device, the Commission strongly recommends consultation with competent legal counsel when considering use of an installment land contract.

An ILC (contract for deed) must also provide for:

1. Designation of the public trustee of the county where the real property is located to act as escrow agent for the monthly payment by the purchaser of the monthly pro-rated property tax obligation on such property.
2. The payment to the public trustee of the seller's tax obligation at closing for the current year's property taxes.
3. The payment, by the purchaser, of the trustee's $75.00 fee once each year in April. (See § 38-35-126, and § 38-37-104(1)(d), C.R.S.)

These provisions must continue until the ILC is fulfilled and a deed to the property is delivered to the purchaser and recorded.

Section 38-35-126(1)(b), C.R.S., defines a contract for deed as:

> "....a contract for the sale of real property which provides that the purchaser shall assume possession of the real property and the rights and responsibilities of ownership of the real property but that the deed to such real property will not be delivered to the purchaser for at least one hundred eighty days following the latest execution date on the contract for deed to real property and not until the purchaser has met certain conditions such as payment of the full contract price or a specified portion thereof."

Subsection (2) of the same statute requires the following:

> "Within ninety days of executing and delivering a contract for deed to real property, the seller shall file with the county treasurer of the county wherein the real property is located a written notice of transfer by contract for deed to real property. Such notice shall not operate to convey title. Such notice shall include the name and legal address of the seller, the name and legal address of the purchaser, a legal description of the real property, the date upon which the contract for deed to real property was executed and delivered, and the date or conditions upon which the deed to the real property will be delivered to the purchaser, absent default. In addition, within ninety days of executing and delivering the contract for deed to real property, the seller shall file a real estate transfer declaration with the county assessor of the county wherein the property is located, pursuant to the provisions of section 39-14-102, C.R.S."

The buyer has the option of voiding any contract for deed to real property that fails to designate the public trustee as escrow agent for deposit of property tax moneys or for which no written notice is filed with the county treasurer's office of the county assessor's office. Upon voidance of such contract, the buyer is entitled to the return of all payments made on the contract, with interest, and reasonable attorney fees and costs. This avoidance right expires seven years after the latest execution date on the contract for deed to real property, unless exercised prior to such date. (See § 38-35-126(3), C.R.S.)

According to § 38-35-126(4), C.R.S., the above sections do not apply if the:

1. Subject property is not divided into parcels less than one acre;
2. Developer (seller) pays the property tax or submits a bond or letter of credit within 30 days of the mailing of the notice of taxes due and prior to seeking reimbursement from the purchaser; or
3. Developer provides the notice of transfer mentioned in § 38-35-126(2), C.R.S.

IX. Manufactured, Modular, and Mobile Homes

The Division of Housing requires registration of persons who engage in the business of selling manufactured homes in Colorado under the Colorado Consumer Protection Act.

When engaging in the sale of mobile or manufactured homes, real estate brokers are subject to compliance with license law and the rules of the Real Estate Commission. A licensee may be disciplined for dishonest conduct or failure to account for money belonging to others. If the sale of a manufactured or mobile home is integrated with the sale or lease of land upon which the home is to be affixed or placed, a real estate license is required.

Manufactured and mobile homes may be conveyed by bill of sale if the sale is made prior to the home being affixed to the land. However, in the case of a manufactured home, a simple contract of sale would suffice because usually the manufactured home is immediately affixed to the land and would pass with a deed conveyance of the land.

Both mobile and modular homes are considered manufactured homes, and §§ 38-29-101, *et seq.*, C.R.S., govern title thereto.

A manufactured home seller must deliver a certificate of title to the buyer. Any person entitled to a certificate of title is required to make application to the director of revenue or the director's agent, who is the clerk and recorder of the county in which the manufactured home is located. Copies of all applications are forwarded to the county assessor for tax purposes. The certificate of title is mailed to the owner of the manufactured home, unless the home is mortgaged, in which case it is mailed to the mortgagee.

The notarized signature of the owner marks transfer of title. The buyer or transferee must present the transferred certificate, duly transferred, to the director of revenue or the director's agent within 30 days, along with an application for a new certificate of title. If a manufactured home is destroyed or dismantled, the certificate of title must be surrendered to the director or the director's authorized agent.

When a manufactured home is permanently affixed to the ground and no longer capable of being drawn over the public highways, the owner may surrender the certificate of title to the director's authorized agent with a request that the title be purged. With the consent of the mortgagee, the manufactured home will then become real property and the owner subject to all the rights and obligations of a real property owner.

Mobile homes and mobile home parks are subject to zoning requirements, and there is often a problem of finding suitable space. Collusion between the owner of a mobile home park and the seller of the mobile home is forbidden by statute. A mobile home seller may not pay or offer to pay cash or other consideration to the owner of a mobile home park to reserve space, and a mobile home park owner may not require that a mobile home be purchased from any particular seller as a condition of tenancy. Moreover, a mobile home park owner may not require selling or transfer fees from tenants or buyers. Colorado law also governs the amount of the security deposit and other matters. The **Mobile Home Park Act** (§§ 38-12-200.1, *et seq.*, C.R.S.) is printed in the Chapter, "Related Real Estate Law."

The construction of a manufactured or mobile home is subject to standards imposed by the Colorado Department of Local Affairs, Division of Housing, which are identical to those of the United States Department of Housing and Urban Development (HUD). Absent such federal regulations, manufactured housing must be reasonably consistent with the American National Standards Institute (ANSI) Standard A-119.1. Standards do not apply to sales made after the first purchase (see §§ 24-32-701, *et seq.*, C.R.S., as amended). The Colorado Department of Health establishes and enforces sanitary standards for mobile home parks (see §§ 25-1.5-201, *et seq.*, C.R.S.).

Prior to engaging in the sale of manufactured housing, a real estate licensee should become thoroughly familiar with the associated federal, state, and local requirements.

Ed. Note: See the Chapter, "Related Real Estate Law," for legislation concerning the regulation of manufactured homes.

Chapter 19:
Trust Deeds and Liens

An * in the left margin indicates a change in the statute, rule, or text since the last publication of the manual.

I. Trust Deeds and Mortgages

A. Introduction and Background of Mortgages

The purchase of real estate usually involves a considerable sum of money. Rarely is full payment made in cash. In the great majority of real estate transactions, a purchaser makes a down payment in cash and arranges for a loan to cover the balance. Financing of this balance generally involves two legal instruments: a negotiable promissory note and a mortgage. A negotiable promissory note or bond is a writing signed by the maker containing an unconditional promise to pay a certain sum in money on demand or at some future time, and which is payable to the order of the payee or to the bearer of the instrument. A promissory note creates a debt for which the maker is personally liable. A mortgage is a legal document pledging or conveying a piece of real property as security for the indebtedness created by a promissory note.

In early English law, the mortgage was simply a deed conveying the property, from the mortgagor (borrower) to the mortgagee (lender). It contained a clause that defeated the conveyance when the mortgagor paid the debt on time. If the borrower defaulted, the mortgagee became the owner of the property. Foreclosure proceedings were not necessary and did not even exist.

Thereafter, a practice arose that permitted the borrower, in cases of extreme hardship, to repay the debt after default. The mortgagee was required to accept the delayed payment and convey the property back to the mortgagor. This right to pay and recover the property after default is known as the right (or equity) of redemption, and it soon became a matter of course in all cases of default. Mortgagees then attempted to insert a clause that required mortgagors to surrender their equity of redemption. However, common-law courts held this clause void, stating that because the needy borrowers were in no position to protect themselves, the courts would not let the lender take advantage of them. This left the lender in a somewhat difficult position of owning the land upon default but not being certain whether or not the mortgagor would redeem it.

A new practice emerged to remedy this situation. Upon mortgagee default and filing a petition with the court, a judge would decree that the mortgagor had only a certain amount of time, typically six months or a year, to redeem the property. After the lapse of the allotted time, the mortgagor's equity of redemption was barred and foreclosed, and the mortgagee became the absolute owner of the property. This procedure is called strict foreclosure and still may exist in some states.

Under strict foreclosure, the lender becomes the owner of property that may be worth many times the amount due, especially if the borrower had repaid most of the debt. If the value of the property was less than the mortgage balance, then the mortgagee lost the balance due, because under common law the lender had no personal right of recovery against the mortgagor. This injustice led to the next development—foreclosure through public sale.

Up to this point, the concept of a mortgage was based on ownership or "**title theory**," *i.e.*, that the mortgagor transferred the legal title of the property to the mortgagee.

Foreclosure through public sale gave rise to a new concept of the mortgage not as a conveyance of the land, but only as a lien upon the property. Thus, the lien would be enforced through a public sale rather than giving the lender title to the property. If the land sold for more than the debt, the mortgagee would be paid in full and the balance would be awarded to the borrower. It logically followed that if the property sold for less than the debt, then any other assets of the mortgagor would be available to the mortgagee through a deficiency judgment and by virtue of the borrower having signed a note or bond that was secured by the mortgage.

Under modern mortgage law in the United States, there are three theories as to the nature of mortgages: (1) lien, (2) title, and (3) intermediate theories. Most states, including Colorado (see § 38-35-117, C.R.S.), have adopted the lien theory in which a mortgage creates a lien and does not convey title. The mortgagor is entitled to possession until default and passage of the right of redemption. Foreclosure is through court action and a court-ordered public sale. The mortgagor is entitled to any excess funds over and above the amount of the debt and is liable personally for any deficiency. The security interest owned by the mortgagee is a personal property interest, and can be transferred only by assignment of the debt secured by the mortgage. When the debt is satisfied, the mortgage is automatically extinguished.

A few states have adopted a modified version of title theory in which the mortgagee is considered to have the legal title, subject only to the mortgagor's superior equitable ownership. Between default and foreclosure the mortgagee is entitled to possession, but must account for all rents and profits and apply them toward reduction of the mortgage debt. Foreclosure is generally by legal action and a court-ordered public sale. The mortgagor is entitled to any excess funds and is liable for any deficiency. Upon payment of the debt, the mortgagee's legal title is defeated. The mortgagee's interest is considered to be a real, rather than personal, property right. The difference today between lien and title theory is more technical than real. Some states have taken an intermediate position between title and lien theories, wherein legal title actually transfers to the mortgagee, but the enforcement of the mortgage upon default is in the nature of a lien.

II. The Foreclosure Process in Colorado

The following summary was written by Jonathan A. Goodman, Esq. of the law firm of Frascona, Joiner, Goodman and Greenstein, P.C., in 2020, to generally describe the Colorado public trustee foreclosure process and some of what real estate brokers need to know to help owners sell property before losing it in foreclosure.

A. Overview

In Colorado, the majority of foreclosures proceed through a quasi-judicial public trustee foreclosure process. Colorado is the only public trustee foreclosure process in the United States. Public trustee foreclosures are much more common in Colorado than judicial foreclosures because the public trustee foreclosure process is typically faster and less expensive than a judicial foreclosure.

The overall public trustee process typically takes around six (6) months from commencement of the foreclosure to the foreclosure sale. The timeframe can vary drastically, however, based upon whether the borrower challenges the foreclosure, whether the borrower files bankruptcy, and to the extent that other issues exist that would prohibit a successful purchaser from obtaining clear title to the property post-foreclosure.

Prior to 2008, the Colorado public trustee foreclosure process gave the borrower two opportunities to save the property from foreclosure: prior to the foreclosure sale, the borrower could "cure," or pay the monetary default; and after the foreclosure sale, the owner could "redeem" the property.

In 2008, the legislature substantially modified the foreclosure process to provide the borrower more time to cure the monetary default prior to the foreclosure sale, in addition to eliminating the redemption period for the owner. The changes were intended to increase competitive bidding at foreclosure sales and reduce unscrupulous investors from preying on desperate borrowers in foreclosure. The longer cure period, combined with the elimination of the owner's post foreclosure redemption right, allowed the duration of the foreclosure to remain essentially the same.

B. The Statutory Public Trustee Foreclosure Process - Generally

A lender officially commences a public trustee foreclosure by recording a Notice of Election and Demand in the county in which the property is located. The Notice of Election and Demand, when recorded, provides notice to third parties that a foreclosure is pending on the property.

Once the Public Trustee receives a Notice of Election and Demand from the holder of the evidence of debt being foreclosed (the "Holder"), the Public Trustee has ten (10) business days to record the Notice of Election and Demand to begin the foreclosure. Following recording of the Notice of Election and Demand, the Public Trustee mails statutory notice to the interested parties to the foreclosure, meaning the borrower, owner or other persons obligated on the indebtedness being foreclosed, as well as any junior lien holders with a recorded interest in the property that is subsequent to the Holder's deed of trust, but prior to the recording of the Notice of Election and Demand.

The Public Trustee also schedules a foreclosure sale date within the statutory time frame of no less than 110 calendar days, and no more than 125 calendar days after the recording of the Notice of Election and Demand for a foreclosure on "non-agricultural" property, or no less than 215 calendar days, and no more than 230 calendar days after the recording of the Notice of Election and Demand for a foreclosure on "agricultural" property. (The factors that determine whether a property is "agricultural" are complicated, not intuitive, and beyond the scope of this summary.)

The borrower may statutorily cure the foreclosure by filing an intent to cure the default with the Public Trustee at least 15 calendar days prior to the foreclosure sale, and then by actually curing the monetary arrearage in full by paying the default amount due to the Holder, plus any allowable fees and charges, up until noon the day before the foreclosure sale.

C. The Rule 120 Proceeding

The Colorado public trustee foreclosure process also requires a quasi-judicial step to provide the borrower due process. As a prerequisite to proceeding to a public trustee foreclosure sale, the Holder must obtain an order authorizing sale of the property. In order to obtain an order authorizing sale, the Holder, pursuant to Rule 120 of the Colorado Rules of Civil Procedure, files a Motion for Order Authorizing Sale with the District Court where the property is located.

The borrower and other interested parties may respond to the Motion for Order Authorizing Sale. In the event a borrower or other interested party files a response to the Motion for Order Authorizing Sale of Real Property, the court will set a hearing to determine whether to grant the Motion and authorize the foreclosure sale.

The scope of the hearing is limited to: whether there is a reasonable probability of default under the deed of trust, whether the moving party is the correct party to foreclose, whether the status of any request for a loan modification statutorily prohibits the Holder from proceeding to foreclosure sale, in addition to whether the requirements of the Servicemembers Civil Relief Act, as amended, apply to the borrower being foreclosed.

If the court finds a reasonable probability that a default or other circumstance has occurred under the deed of trust authorizing the sale, the court will enter an Order Authorizing Sale of the Real Property, permitting the Holder to proceed to foreclosure sale. The court's Rule 120 decision does not prevent any person harmed by the order from seeking injunctive or other relief. If an interested party desires to challenge the court's entry of an order authorizing sale, it can do so by filing a separate law suit.

D. The Foreclosure Sale

After the court issues an order authorizing sale, the Holder of the debt being foreclosed may proceed to foreclosure sale through the Public Trustee. In many instances, the foreclosure sale may be continued to allow the borrower additional opportunities to attempt to save the property from foreclosure through a short sale, or other loss mitigation options available to the borrower. In Colorado, the Holder may delay a foreclosure sale in increments as short as a week. In the aggregate, the Holder may delay the foreclosure sale for up to one (1) year from the first scheduled sale date without having to restart the foreclosure.

In the event the Holder decides to proceed to foreclosure sale, the Holder or the Holder's attorney submits an itemized foreclosure bid to the Public Trustee reflecting all amounts owed to the Holder and any costs or expenses statutorily permitted and authorized under the Holder's deed of trust, along with an amount to be bid by the Holder at the foreclosure sale, as well as any applicable deficiency. So long as the Holder bids less than or equal to the amount of its total debt owed, the Holder does not need to tender funds to bid at the auction. Instead, the Holder makes a "credit bid" (a bid which is credited against the amount that the Holder is owed) at the foreclosure sale.

The Public Trustee will issue a Certificate of Purchase to the highest bidder at the foreclosure sale. If no junior lien holder files an intent to redeem the property, the Public Trustee will issue a Confirmation Deed to the Holder of the Certificate of Purchase following the expiration of eight (8) business days after the foreclosure sale. The Confirmation Deed conveys title to the new owner of the foreclosed property.

E. Lienholder Redemption

Junior lien holders that have a valid, recorded interest in the property prior to the recording of the Notice of Election and Demand maintain redemption rights post-foreclosure if the junior lien holder files an intent to redeem within eight (8) business days after the foreclosure sale.

If a junior lien holder seeks to redeem the property from the foreclosure sale, the most senior of the junior lienors must redeem the property between 15 and 19 business days after the foreclosure sale by paying the amount paid by the successful purchaser at the foreclosure sale, plus additional interest and costs since the sale. Each subsequent lienor entitled to redeem then shall, in succession, have an additional period of five (5) business days to redeem. The last junior lien holder who successfully redeems the property from the foreclosure sale will be issued a Certificate of Redemption, and subsequent Confirmation Deed conveying title to the successful holder of the Certificate of Redemption.

F. The Colorado Foreclosure Process and Real Estate Brokers

Timing

Many real estate brokers receive inquiries from borrowers in foreclosure desiring to sell their home to avoid a foreclosure sale. If a real estate broker intends to attempt to help a borrower sell the property prior to a foreclosure sale, it is critical that the broker and borrower do not wait until the last minute to take action.

Various factors can complicate timing considerations such as whether the real estate broker represents an "equity purchaser" (see discussion of the Foreclosure Protection Act below) or whether the broker is the buyer. With such complications, timing becomes even more critical as the broker will need to navigate more challenges.

Short Sales

Generally, when a borrower owes more against the home than the market will pay for the home, the borrower needs the lender to accept less money than the lender is owed (a "short pay-off") to sell to a market buyer to avoid the foreclosure auction. The industry calls this type of sale a "short sale" because the amount paid to the lender to release the borrower-seller's deed of trust is short of the full amount owed to the lender by the borrower-seller. Lenders are not obligated to accept a short pay-off; instead, lenders must approve and authorize a short-payoff to facilitate a short sale to a market buyer. Lenders often take a substantial amount of time to review and approve a short sale. Time is of the essence should a broker seek to help a borrower avoid foreclosure through a short sale.

Short sales impose additional disclosure obligations on brokers. For instance, in the event a broker agrees to list a property for an owner who may need a short sale, the broker should append a Short Sale Addendum (Seller Listing Contract) (having form number SSA39-10-11 as of the drafting of this summary) to the Seller Listing Contract so the seller is aware of the additional issues with short sales. Similarly, brokers should attach a Short Sale Addendum (Contract to Buy and Sell Real Estate) (having form number SSA38-10-11 as of the drafting of this summary) to any Contract to Buy and Sell Real Estate where the transaction is contingent upon approval of a short sale. The Short Sale Addendum informs the seller and buyer of the risks and conditions of a short sale.

The Colorado Foreclosure Protection Act

When the broker represents an investor, or the broker is the buyer herself, and the seller is in financial distress, it is likely that the buyer is considered an "equity purchaser" under the Colorado Foreclosure Protection Act ("FPA"). The FPA generally applies to real estate transactions when:

> (1) the Property is residential, (2) Seller resides in the Property as Seller's principal residence, (3) Buyer's purpose in purchase of the Property is not to use the Property as Buyer's personal residence and (4) the Property is in foreclosure or Buyer has notice that any loan secured by the Property is at least thirty days delinquent or in default.

For transactions where the Colorado Foreclosure Protection Act applies, brokers may only use the Colorado Real Estate Commission approved sales contract designed for the FPA (having form number CBSF1-5-19 as of the drafting of this summary). The broker may only use the form if: (1) Buyer will not assume any financial or legal obligations of Seller; (2) there are no rental agreements or leases for the Property between Buyer and Seller; (3) Seller does not have an option or right to repurchase the Property; and (4) no consideration will be paid to Seller prior to the expiration of Seller's right to cancel the Contract. Unless all four of those conditions are true, the broker may not write the contract. In addition, the Seller must be properly informed of the Seller's rescission rights through the Homeowner Warning Notice (having form number HWN65-8-10 as of the drafting of this summary) in the Seller's principal language prior to signing the contract. Among other things, this form educates the seller of the seller's right to cancel the contract within three (3) business days following the seller's signature on the contract.

This overview of the Colorado Foreclosure Protection Act is not all inclusive. Brokers should consult an attorney about the FPA before handling a transaction covered by the Colorado Foreclosure Protection Act. Violations of the Colorado Foreclosure Protection Act constitute a crime. Real estate brokers should have a sense about which transactions are covered by the Act to encourage investor buyers to consult an attorney.

G. Conclusion

Real estate brokers may provide a tremendously valuable service to their clients by helping owners sell property before losing it to a foreclosure sale. The Colorado public trustee foreclosure process seeks to balance the differing interests of the foreclosed property owner, the foreclosing lender, junior lien holders and other public policy goals. The foreclosure process is inherently complex and often not intuitive. Should the reader have specific questions regarding the Colorado foreclosure process, or the subtleties inherent in such a complex system, the reader should consult an attorney.

III. Mortgages and Deeds of Trust

Although there are other mortgage devices, the mortgage and the deed of trust are the most prevalent. Both are found in Colorado, but the deed of trust to a public trustee is by far the most common.

A mortgage is a conditional conveyance of the real estate directly from the mortgagor (borrower) to the mortgagee (lender) to secure the indebtedness described therein. There are only two parties to a mortgage.

A deed of trust involves three parties. A trustor or grantor (borrower) conveys legal title via a trust deed to a public official (public trustee) of the county in which the property is situated. The public trustee holds title in trust for the lender (beneficiary) to secure payment of the indebtedness described in the deed of trust.

Upon compliance with the deed of trust provisions, the public trustee must release the deed of trust and reconvey the property back to the grantor. Upon default of the deed of trust's provisions, and after the trustor's right of redemption has expired, the public trustee is empowered to conduct a public sale, and to convey title to a new purchaser. A deed of trust to a public trustee may be foreclosed by public sale through the office of the public trustee or through the courts, at the option of the holder of the indebtedness.

In rare instances, a private trustee may hold a trust deed. According to Colorado law, such a trust deed is considered a mortgage and may be foreclosed only through the courts.

Upon payment of the indebtedness secured by a mortgage, a mortgage should be released by the mortgagee executing a release or satisfaction of mortgage, delivering the same to the mortgagor, who should record it in the office of the county clerk and recorder of the county in which property is situated. When the indebtedness secured by a deed of trust is paid, the procedure to procure a release thereof is to have the beneficiary execute a request for release of deed of trust and present it to the public trustee, together with the cancelled promissory note and deed of trust. The public trustee will then, upon receipt of the appropriate fee, execute the release of deed of trust. The release should be recorded in the clerk and recorder's office in the county in which the property is situated.

Because the deed of trust is the most commonly used real property encumbering instrument in Colorado, it is important to become acquainted with the more pertinent statutes dealing with it.

IV. Concerning Real Estate Foreclosures (Deeds of Trust)

Brokers are cautioned to seek legal advice in matters pertaining to the public trustee and the foreclosure processes. Printed below for informational purposes are substantive portions of the law related to foreclosure process. *The following is not a complete listing of the law*; for a recitation of the entire law, access the Colorado General Assembly website at: www.leg.state.co.us.

§ 38-38-100.3, C.R.S. Definitions.

As used in articles 37 to 39 of this title 38, unless the context otherwise requires:

(1) "Agricultural property" means property, none of which, on the date of recording of the deed of trust or other lien or at the time of the recording of the notice of election and demand or lis pendens, is:

   (a) Platted as a subdivision;

   (b) Located within an incorporated town, city, or city and county; or

(c) Valued and assessed as other than agricultural property pursuant to sections 39-1-102 (1.6) (a) and 39-1-103 (5), C.R.S., by the assessor of the county where the property is located.

(1.5) "Amended mailing list" means the amended mailing list in accordance with section 38-38-103 (2) containing the names and addresses in the mailing list as defined in subsection (14) of this section and the names and addresses of the following persons:

(a) The owner of the property, if different than the grantor of the deed of trust, as of the date and time of the recording of the notice of election and demand or lis pendens as shown in the records at the address indicated in such recorded instrument; and

(b) Each person, except the public trustee, who appears to have an interest in the property described in the combined notice by an instrument recorded prior to the date and time of the recording of the notice of election and demand or lis pendens with the clerk and recorder of the county where the property or any portion thereof is located at the address of the person indicated on the instrument, if the person's interest in the property may be extinguished by the foreclosure.

(2) "Attorney for the holder" means an attorney licensed and in good standing in the state of Colorado to practice law and retained by the holder of an evidence of debt to process a foreclosure under this article.

(2.5) "Borrower" means a person liable under an evidence of debt constituting a residential mortgage loan.

(3) "Certified copy" means, with respect to a recorded document, a copy of the document certified by the clerk and recorder of the county where the document was recorded.

(3.5) "CFPB" means the federal consumer financial protection bureau.

(4) "Combined notice" means the combined notice of sale, right to cure, and right to redeem described in section 38-38-103 (4) (a).

(4.5) "Complete loss mitigation application" means an application in connection with which a servicer has received all the information that the servicer requires from a borrower in evaluating applications for the loss mitigation options available to the borrower.

(5) "Confirmation deed" means the deed described in section 38-38-501 in the form specified in section 38-38-502 or 38-38-503.

(5.3) "Consensual lien" means a conveyance of an interest in real property, granted by the owner of the property after the recording of a notice of election and demand, that is not an absolute conveyance of fee title to the property. "Consensual lien" includes but is not limited to a deed of trust, mortgage or other assignment, encumbrance, option, lease, easement, contract, including an instrument specified in section 38-38-305, or conveyance as security for the performance of the grantor. "Consensual lien" does not include a lien described in section 38-38-306 or 38-33.3-316.

(5.7) "Corporate surety bond" means a bond issued by a person authorized to issue bonds in the state of Colorado with the public trustee as obligee, conditioned against the delivery of an original evidence of debt to the damage of the public trustee.

(6) "Cure statement" means the statement described in section 38-38-104 (2) (a).

(7) "Deed of trust" means a security instrument containing a grant to a public trustee together with a power of sale.

(8) "Evidence of debt" means a writing that evidences a promise to pay or a right to the payment of a monetary obligation, such as a promissory note, bond, negotiable instrument, a loan, credit, or similar agreement, or a monetary judgment entered by a court of competent jurisdiction.

(9) "Fees and costs" means all fees, charges, expenses, and costs described in section 38-38-107.

(10) "Holder of an evidence of debt" or "holder" means the person in actual possession of or person entitled to enforce an evidence of debt; except that the term does not include a person acting as a nominee solely for the purpose of holding the evidence of debt or deed of trust as an electronic registry without any authority to enforce the evidence of debt or deed of trust. For the purposes of articles 37 to 40 of this title, the following persons are presumed to be the holder of an evidence of debt:

(a) The person who is the obligee of and who is in possession of an original evidence of debt;

(b) The person in possession of an original evidence of debt together with the proper indorsement or assignment thereof to such person in accordance with section 38-38-101 (6);

(c) The person in possession of a negotiable instrument evidencing a debt, which has been duly negotiated to such person or to bearer or indorsed in blank; or

(d) The person in possession of an evidence of debt with authority, which may be granted by the original evidence of debt or deed of trust, to enforce the evidence of debt as agent, nominee, or trustee or in a similar capacity for the obligee of the evidence of debt.

(11) "Junior lien" means a deed of trust or other lien or encumbrance upon the property for which the amount due and owing thereunder is subordinate to the deed of trust or other lien being foreclosed.

(12) "Junior lienor" means a person who is a beneficiary, holder, or grantee of a junior lien.

(12.5) "Lienor" includes without limitation the holder of a certificate of purchase or certificate of redemption for property, issued upon the foreclosure of a deed of trust or other lien on the property.

(13) "Lis pendens" means a lis pendens in accordance with section 38-35-110 that is recorded with the clerk and recorder of the county where the property or any portion thereof is located and that refers to a judicial action in which one of the claims is for foreclosure and sale of the property by an officer or in which a claim or interest in the property is asserted.

(13.3) "Loss mitigation application" means an oral or written request for a loss mitigation option that is accompanied by any information requested by a servicer for evaluation for a loss mitigation option.

(13.7) "Loss mitigation option" means an alternative to foreclosure offered by the owner, holder, or assignee of a mortgage loan that is made available through the servicer to the borrower.

(14) "Mailing list" means the mailing list in accordance with section 38-38-101 (1) (e) provided to the officer by the holder of the evidence of debt or the attorney for the holder containing the names and addresses of the following persons:

(a) The original grantor of the deed of trust or obligor under any other lien being foreclosed at the address shown in the recorded deed of trust or other lien being foreclosed and, if different, the last address, if any, shown in the records of the holder of the evidence of debt;

(b) Any person known or believed by the holder of the evidence of debt to be personally liable under the evidence of debt secured by the deed of trust or other lien being foreclosed at the last address, if any, shown in the records of the holder;

(c) The occupant of the property, addressed to "occupant" at the address of the property; and

(d) With respect to a public trustee sale, a lessee with an unrecorded possessory interest in the property at the address of the premises of the lessee and, if different, the address of the property, to the extent that the holder of the evidence of debt desires to terminate the possessory interest with the foreclosure.

(15) "Maintaining and repairing" means the act of caring for and preserving a property in its current condition or restoring a property to a sound or working condition after damage; except that "maintaining and repairing" shall not include, unless done pursuant to an order entered by a court of competent jurisdiction, any act of advancing a property to a better condition or any act that increases the quality of or adds to the improvements located on a property.

(16) "Notice of election and demand" means a notice of election and demand for sale related to a public trustee foreclosure under this article.

(17) "Officer" means the public trustee or sheriff conducting a foreclosure under this article.

(17.3) "Overbid" means the amount a property is sold for at a foreclosure sale that is in excess of the written or amended bid amount executed by the holder of the evidence of debt secured by the deed of trust or other lien being foreclosed.

(17.5) "Person" means any individual, corporation, government or governmental subdivision or agency, business trust, estate, trust, limited liability company, partnership, association, or other legal entity.

(18) "Property" means the portion of the property encumbered by a deed of trust or other lien that is being foreclosed under this article or the portion of the property being released from a deed of trust or other lien under article 39 of this title.

(19) "Publish", "publication", "republish", or "republication" means the placement by an officer of a legal notice that meets the requirements set forth in section 24-70-103 containing a combined notice that complies with the requirements of section 24-70-109 in a newspaper in the county or counties where the property to be sold is located. The officer shall select the newspaper.

(20) "Qualified holder" means a holder of an evidence of debt, certificate of purchase, certificate of redemption, or confirmation deed that is also one of the following:

- (a) A bank as defined in section 11-101-401 (5), C.R.S.;
- (b) Repealed.
- (c) A federally chartered savings and loan association doing business in Colorado or a savings and loan association chartered under the "Savings and Loan Association Law," articles 40 to 46 of title 11, C.R.S.;
- (d) A supervised lender as defined in section 5-1-301 (46), C.R.S., that is licensed to make supervised loans pursuant to section 5-2-302, C.R.S., and that is either:
  - (I) A public entity, which is an entity that has issued voting securities that are listed on a national security exchange registered under the federal "Securities Exchange Act of 1934", as amended; or
  - (II) An entity in which all of the outstanding voting securities are held, directly or indirectly, by a public entity;
- (e) An entity in which all of the outstanding voting securities are held, directly or indirectly, by a public entity that also owns, directly or indirectly, all of the voting securities of a supervised lender as defined in section 5-1-301 (46), C.R.S., that is licensed to make supervised loans pursuant to section 5-2-302, C.R.S.;
- (f) A federal housing administration approved mortgagee;
- (g) A federally chartered credit union doing business in Colorado or a state-chartered credit union as described in section 11-30-101, C.R.S.;
- (h) An agency or department of the federal government;
- (i) An entity created or sponsored by the federal or state government that originates, insures, guarantees, or purchases loans or a person acting on behalf of such an entity to enforce an evidence of debt or the deed of trust securing an evidence of debt;

(j) Any community development financial institution that has been certified and maintains such current status from the community development financial institutions fund administered by the United States department of the treasury, referred to in this section as the "fund". In order to be a qualified holder under this article, the community development financial institution must:

(I) Be a legal entity;

(II) Have a primary mission of promoting community development;

(III) Be a financing entity;

(IV) Primarily serve one or more target markets as defined by the fund;

(V) Promote development services in conjunction with its financing activities;

(VI) Maintain accountability to its defined target market; and

(VII) Be a nongovernmental entity and not be under the control of any governmental entity; except that a tribal government is exempt from the requirements of this subparagraph (VII).

* (k) Any entity with active certification under the fund that originates, insures, guarantees, or purchases loans or a person acting on behalf of such an entity to enforce an evidence of debt or the deed of trust securing an evidence of debt;

* (k.5) A private company that originates, insures, guaranties, or purchases loans on behalf of a holder of evidence of debt that is secured by a deed of trust encumbering a time share estate as defined in section 38-33-110 (5), with a minimum of five million dollars in assets or not less than one thousand active loans; or

(*l*) Any entity listed in paragraphs (a) to (k) of this subsection (20) acting in the capacity of agent, nominee except as otherwise specified in subsection (10) of this section, or trustee for another person.

(21) "Records" means the records of the county clerk and recorder of the county where the property is located.

(21.3) "Residential mortgage loan" means a loan that is primarily for personal, family, or household use and that is secured by a mortgage, deed of trust, or other equivalent, consensual security interest on a dwelling or residential real estate upon which is constructed or intended to be constructed a single-family dwelling or multiple-family dwelling of four or fewer units that is or will be used by the borrower as the borrower's primary residence.

(21.6) "Residential real estate" means any real property upon which a dwelling is or will be constructed.

(22) "Sale" means a foreclosure sale conducted by an officer under this article.

(23) "Secured indebtedness" means the amount owed pursuant to the evidence of debt without regard to the value of the collateral.

(23.3) (a) "Servicer" or "mortgage servicer" means an entity that directly services a loan or that is responsible for interacting with the borrower; managing the loan account on a daily basis, including collecting and crediting periodic loan payments; managing any escrow account; or enforcing the note and security instrument, either as the current holder of the evidence of debt or as the current holder's authorized agent.

(b) "Servicer" includes an entity providing such services pursuant to designation as a subservicing agent or by contract with a master servicer.

(c) "Servicer" does not mean a trustee, including the public trustee, or a trustee's authorized agent acting under a power of sale pursuant to a deed of trust.

(23.6) "Single point of contact" means an individual or team of personnel, each of whom has the ability and authority to perform the responsibilities described in section 38-38-103.1 on behalf of the servicer. The servicer shall ensure that each member of the team is knowledgeable about the borrower's situation and current status.

(24) "Statement of redemption" means the signed and acknowledged statement of the holder of the evidence of debt or the signed statement of the attorney for the holder as required by section 38-38-302 (3) or the signed and acknowledged statement of the lienor or the signed statement of the attorney for the lienor as required by section 38-38-302 (1) (f).

§ 38-38-101, C.R.S. Holder of evidence of debt may elect to foreclose.

(1) **Documents required.** Whenever a holder of an evidence of debt declares a violation of a covenant of a deed of trust and elects to publish all or a portion of the property therein described for sale, the holder or the attorney for the holder shall file the following with the public trustee of the county where the property is located:

(a) A notice of election and demand signed and acknowledged by the holder of the evidence of debt or signed by the attorney for the holder;

(b) The original evidence of debt, including any modifications to the original evidence of debt, together with the original indorsement or assignment thereof, if any, to the holder of the evidence of debt or other proper indorsement or assignment in accordance with subsection (6) of this section or, in lieu of the original evidence of debt, one of the following:

(I) A corporate surety bond in the amount of one and one-half times the face amount of the original evidence of debt;

(II) A copy of the evidence of debt and a certification signed and properly acknowledged by a holder of an evidence of debt acting for itself or as agent, nominee, or trustee under subsection (2) of this section or a statement signed by the attorney for such holder, citing the paragraph of section 38-38-100.3 (20) under which the holder claims to be a qualified holder and certifying or stating that the copy of the evidence of debt is true and correct and that the use of the copy is subject to the conditions described in paragraph (a) of subsection (2) of this section; or

(III) A certified copy of a monetary judgment entered by a court of competent jurisdiction;

(c) The original recorded deed of trust securing the evidence of debt and any original recorded modifications of the deed of trust or any recorded partial releases of the deed of trust, or in lieu thereof, one of the following:

(I) Certified copies of the recorded deed of trust and any recorded modifications of the deed of trust or recorded partial releases of the deed of trust; or

(II) Copies of the recorded deed of trust and any recorded modifications of the deed of trust or recorded partial releases of the deed of trust and a certification signed and properly acknowledged by a holder of an evidence of debt acting for itself or as an agent, nominee, or trustee under subsection (2) of this section or a signed statement by the attorney for such holder, citing the paragraph of section 38-38-100.3 (20) under which the holder claims to be a qualified holder and certifying or stating that the copies of the recorded deed of trust and any recorded modifications of the deed of trust or recorded partial releases of the deed of trust are true and correct and that the use of the copies is subject to the conditions described in paragraph (a) of subsection (2) of this section;

(d) A combined notice pursuant to section 38-38-103; except that the combined notice may be omitted with the prior approval of the public trustee;

(e) A mailing list;

(f) Any affidavit recorded pursuant to section 38-35-109 (5) affecting the deed of trust described in paragraph (c) of this subsection (1), which affidavit shall be accepted by the public trustee as modifying the deed of trust for all purposes under this article only if the affidavit is filed with the public trustee at the same time as the other documents required under this subsection (1);

(f.5) If there is a loan servicer of the evidence of debt described in the notice of election and demand and the loan servicer is not the holder, a statement executed by the holder of the evidence of debt or the attorney for such holder, identifying, to the best of such person's knowledge, the name of the loan servicer;

(g) A statement executed by the holder of an evidence of debt, or the attorney for such holder, identifying, to the best knowledge of the person executing such statement, the name and address of the current owner of the property described in the notice of election and demand; and

(h) Repealed.

(2) **Foreclosure by qualified holder without original evidence of debt, original or certified copy of deed of trust, or proper indorsement.**

(a) A qualified holder, whether acting for itself or as agent, nominee, or trustee under section 38-38-100.3 (20), that elects to foreclose without the original evidence of debt pursuant to subparagraph (II) of paragraph (b) of subsection (1) of this section, or without the original recorded deed of trust or a certified copy thereof pursuant to subparagraph (II) of paragraph (c) of subsection (1) of this section, or without the proper indorsement or assignment of an evidence of debt under paragraph (b) of subsection (1) of this section shall, by operation of law, be deemed to have agreed to indemnify and defend any person liable for repayment of any portion of the original evidence of debt in the event that the original evidence of debt is presented for payment to the extent of any amount, other than the amount of a deficiency remaining under the evidence of debt after deducting the amount bid at sale, and any person who sustains a loss due to any title defect that results from reliance upon a sale at which the original evidence of debt was not presented. The indemnity granted by this subsection (2) shall be limited to actual economic loss suffered together with any court costs and reasonable attorney fees and costs incurred in defending a claim brought as a direct and proximate cause of the failure to produce the original evidence of debt, but such indemnity shall not include, and no claimant shall be entitled to, any special, incidental, consequential, reliance, expectation, or punitive damages of any kind. A qualified holder acting as agent, nominee, or trustee shall be liable for the indemnity pursuant to this subsection (2).

(b) In the event that a qualified holder or the attorney for the holder commences a foreclosure without production of the original evidence of debt, proper indorsement or assignment, or the original recorded deed of trust or a certified copy thereof, the qualified holder or the attorney for the holder may submit the original evidence of debt, proper indorsement or assignment, or the original recorded deed of trust or a certified copy thereof to the officer prior to the sale. In such event, the sale shall be conducted and administered as if the original evidence of debt, proper indorsement or assignment, or the original recorded deed of trust or a certified copy thereof had been submitted at the time of commencement of such proceeding, and any indemnities deemed to have been given by the qualified holder under paragraph (a) of this subsection (2) shall be null and void as to the instrument produced under this paragraph (b).

(c) In the event that a foreclosure is conducted where the original evidence of debt, proper indorsement or assignment, or original recorded deed of trust or certified copy thereof has not been produced, the only claims shall be against the indemnitor as provided in paragraph (a) of this subsection (2) and not against the foreclosed property or the attorney for the holder of the evidence of debt. Nothing in this section shall preclude a person liable for repayment of the evidence of debt from pursuing remedies allowed by law.

(3) **Foreclosure on a portion of property.** A holder of an evidence of debt may elect to foreclose a deed of trust under this article against a portion of the property encumbered by the deed of trust only if such portion is encumbered as a separate and distinct parcel or lot by the original or an amended deed of trust. Any foreclosure conducted by a public trustee against less than all of the property then encumbered by the deed of trust shall not affect the lien or the power of sale contained therein as to the remaining property. The amount bid at a sale of less than all of the property shall be deemed to have satisfied the secured indebtedness to the extent of the amount of the bid.

(4) **Notice of election and demand.** A notice of election and demand filed with the public trustee pursuant to this section shall contain the following:

(a) The names of the original grantors of the deed of trust being foreclosed and the original beneficiaries or grantees thereof;

(b) The name of the holder of the evidence of debt;

(c) The date of the deed of trust being foreclosed;

(d) The recording date, county, book, and page or reception number of the recording of the deed of trust being foreclosed;

(e) The amount of the original principal balance of the secured indebtedness;

(f) The amount of the outstanding principal balance of the secured indebtedness as of the date of the notice of election and demand;

(g) A legal description of the property to be foreclosed as set forth in the documents to be provided to the public trustee pursuant to paragraph (c) of subsection (1) of this section;

(h) A statement of whether the property described in the notice of election and demand is all or only a portion of the property then encumbered by the deed of trust being foreclosed;

(i) A statement of the violation of the covenant of the evidence of debt or deed of trust being foreclosed upon which the foreclosure is based, which statement shall not constitute a waiver of any right accruing on account of any violation of any covenant of the evidence of debt or deed of trust other than the violation specified in the notice of election and demand;

(j) The name, address, business telephone number, and bar registration number of the attorney for the holder of the evidence of debt, which may be indicated in the signature block of the notice of election and demand; and

(k) A description of any changes to the deed of trust described in the notice of election and demand that are based on an affidavit filed with the public trustee under paragraph (f) of subsection (1) of this section, together with the recording date and reception number or book and page number of the recording of that affidavit in the records.

(5) **Error in notice.** In the event that the amount of the outstanding principal balance due and owing upon the secured indebtedness is erroneously set forth in the notice of election and demand or the combined notice, the error shall not affect the validity of the notice of election and demand, the combined notice, the publication, the sale, the certificate of purchase described in section 38-38-401, the certificate of redemption described in section 38-38-402, the confirmation deed as defined in section 38-38-100.3 (5), or any other document executed in connection therewith.

(6) **Indorsement or assignment.**

(a) Proper indorsement or assignment of an evidence of debt shall include the original indorsement or assignment or a certified copy of an indorsement or assignment recorded in the county where the property being foreclosed is located.

(b) Notwithstanding the provisions of paragraph (a) of this subsection (6), the original evidence of debt or a copy thereof without proper indorsement or assignment shall be deemed to be properly indorsed or assigned if a qualified holder presents the original evidence of debt or a copy thereof to the officer together with a statement in the certification of the qualified holder or in the statement of the attorney for the qualified holder pursuant to subparagraph (II) of paragraph (b) of subsection (1) of this section that the party on whose behalf the foreclosure was commenced is the holder of the evidence of debt.

(7) **Multiple instruments.** If the evidence of debt consists of multiple instruments, such as notes or bonds, the holder of the evidence of debt may elect to foreclose with respect to fewer than all of such instruments or documents by identifying in the notice of election and demand and the combined notice only those to be satisfied in whole or in part, in which case the requirements of this section shall apply only as to those instruments or documents.

(8) **Assignment or transfer of debt during foreclosure.**

(a) The holder of the evidence of debt may assign or transfer the secured indebtedness at any time during the pendency of a foreclosure action without affecting the validity of the secured indebtedness. Upon receipt of written notice signed by the holder who commenced the foreclosure action or the attorney for the holder stating that the evidence of debt has been assigned and transferred and identifying the assignee or transferee, the public trustee shall complete the foreclosure as directed by the assignee or transferee or the attorney for the assignee or transferee. No holder of an evidence of debt, certificate of purchase, or certificate of redemption shall be liable to any third party for the acts or omissions of any assignee or transferee that occur after the date of the assignment or transfer.

(b) The assignment or transfer of the secured indebtedness during the pendency of a foreclosure shall be deemed made without recourse unless otherwise agreed in a written statement signed by the assignor or transferor. The holder of the evidence of debt, certificate of purchase, or certificate of redemption making the assignment or transfer and the attorney for the holder shall have no duty, obligation, or liability to the assignee or transferee or to any third party for any act or omission with respect to the foreclosure or the loan servicing of the secured indebtedness after the assignment or transfer. If an assignment or transfer is made by a qualified holder that commenced the foreclosure pursuant to subsection (2) of this section, the qualified holder's indemnity under said subsection (2) shall remain in effect with respect to all parties except to the assignee or transferee, unless otherwise agreed in a writing signed by the assignee or transferee if the assignee or transferee is a qualified holder.

(c) If an assignment or transfer is made to a holder of an evidence of debt other than a qualified holder, the holder must file with the officer the original evidence of debt and the original recorded deed of trust or, in lieu thereof, the documents required in paragraphs (b) and (c) of subsection (1) of this section. An assignee or transferee shall be presumed to not be a qualified holder, and as such, shall be subject to the provisions of this paragraph (c), unless a signed statement by the attorney for such assignee or transferee that cites the paragraph of section 38-38-100.3 (20) under which the assignee or transferee claims to be a qualified holder is filed with the officer.

(9) **Partial release from deed of trust.** At any time after the recording of the notice of election and demand but prior to the sale, a portion of the property may be released from the deed of trust being foreclosed pursuant to section 38-39-102 or as otherwise provided by order of a court of competent jurisdiction recorded in the county where the property being released is located. Upon recording of the release or court order, the holder of the evidence of debt or the attorney for the holder shall pay the fee described in section 38-37-104 (1)(b)(IX), amend the

combined notice, and, in the case of a public trustee foreclosure, amend the notice of election and demand to describe the property that continues to be secured by the deed of trust or other lien being foreclosed as of the effective date of the release or court order; except that the amended combined notice may be omitted with the prior approval of the public trustee. The public trustee shall record the amended notice of election and demand upon receipt. Upon receipt of the amended combined notice, if provided by the holder or the attorney for the holder, the public trustee shall republish and mail the amended combined notice in the manner set forth in section 38-38-109 (1)(b). If the amended combined notice was omitted pursuant to this subsection (9), upon recordation of the amended notice of election and demand, the public trustee shall supply an amended combined notice and shall then republish and mail the amended combined notice in the manner set forth in section 38-38-109 (1)(b).

(10) **Deposit.**

(a) The public trustee may require the holder or servicer to make a deposit of up to five hundred dollars plus the amount of the fee permitted pursuant to section 38-37-104 (1)(b)(I), at the time the notice of election and demand is filed, to be applied against the fees and costs of the public trustee.

§ 38-38-102, C.R.S. Recording notice of election and demand – record of sale.

(1) No later than ten business days following the receipt of the notice of election and demand, the public trustee shall review the documents filed pursuant to section 38-38-101 (1) and, if the filing is complete, cause the notice to be recorded in the office of the county clerk and recorder of the county where the property described in the notice is located.

(2) The public trustee shall retain in the public trustee's records a printed or electronic copy of the notice of election and demand and the combined notice, as published pursuant to section 38-38-103. Such records shall be available for inspection by the public at the public trustee's offices during the public trustee's normal business hours.

§ 38-38-103, C.R.S. Combined notice – publication – providing information.

(1) (a) No more than twenty calendar days after the recording of the notice of election and demand, the public trustee shall mail a combined notice as described in subsection (4) of this section to the persons set forth in the mailing list.

(b) No more than sixty calendar days nor less than forty-five calendar days prior to the first scheduled date of sale, the public trustee shall mail a combined notice as described in subsection (4) of this section to the persons as set forth in the most recent amended mailing list. If there is no amended mailing list, the public trustee shall mail a combined notice as described in subsection (4) of this section to the persons as set forth in the mailing list.

(c) If a recorded instrument does not specify the address of the party purporting to have an interest in the property under such recorded instrument, the party shall not be entitled to notice and any interest in the property under such instrument shall be extinguished upon the execution and delivery of a deed pursuant to section 38-38-501.

(2) (a) The holder of the evidence of debt or the attorney for the holder shall deliver an amended mailing list to the officer as needed. If an amended mailing list is received after the officer has sent the mailing described in paragraph (b) of subsection (1) of this section, the officer shall continue the sale to no less than sixty-five calendar days after receipt of the amended mailing list. The officer shall send the notice pursuant to subsection (4) of this section to the persons on the amended mailing list no less than forty-five calendar days prior to the actual date of sale.

(b) (Deleted by amendment, L. 2007, p. 1832, § 7, effective January 1, 2008.)

(3) The sheriff shall mail a combined notice as described in subsection (4) of this section to the persons named at the addresses indicated in the mailing list no less than sixteen nor more than thirty calendar days after the holder of the evidence of debt or the attorney for the holder delivers to the sheriff the mailing list and the original or a copy of a decree of foreclosure or a writ of execution directing the sheriff to sell property.

(4) (a) The combined notices required to be mailed pursuant to subsections (1), (2), and (3) of this section must contain the following:

(I) The information required by section 38-38-101 (4);

(II) The statement: A notice of intent to cure filed pursuant to section 38-38-104 shall be filed with the officer at least fifteen calendar days prior to the first scheduled sale date or any date to which the sale is continued;

(II.5) The statement, which must be in bold: If the sale date is continued to a later date, the deadline to file a notice of intent to cure by those parties entitled to cure may also be extended;

(III) The statement: A notice of intent to redeem filed pursuant to section 38-38-302 shall be filed with the officer no later than eight business days after the sale;

(IV) The date to which the sale has been continued pursuant to paragraph (a) of subsection (2) of this section;

(V) The date of sale determined pursuant to section 38-38-108;

(VI) The place of sale determined pursuant to section 38-38-110;

(VII) If the sale is conducted by means of the internet or another electronic medium pursuant to section 38-38-110 (1):

(A) The electronic address;

(B) The location of computer workstations that are available to the public and information about how to obtain instructions on accessing the sale and submitting bids; and

(C) A statement that the bidding rules for the sale will be posted on the internet or other electronic medium used to conduct the sale at least two weeks before the date of sale;

(VIII) The statement as required by section 24-70-109, C.R.S.: The lien being foreclosed may not be a first lien; and

(IX) A statement that, if the borrower believes that a lender or servicer has violated the requirements for a single point of contact in section 38-38-103.1 or the prohibition on dual tracking in section 38-38-103.2, the borrower may file a complaint with the Colorado attorney general, the CFPB, or both, but the filing of a complaint will not stop the foreclosure process. The notice must include contact information for both the Colorado attorney general's office and the CFPB. If the officer maintains a web site, the officer shall also post this information on the web site for viewing by all borrowers.

(b) A legible copy of this section and sections 38-37-108, 38-38-104, 38-38-301, 38-38-302, 38-38-304, 38-38-305, and 38-38-306 shall be sent with all notices pursuant to this section.

(5) (a) No more than sixty calendar days nor less than forty-five calendar days prior to the first scheduled date of sale, unless a longer period of publication is specified in the deed of trust or other lien being foreclosed, a deed of trust or other lien being foreclosed is deemed to require the officer to commence publication of the combined notice, omitting both the statements under subsections (4)(a)(II), (4)(a)(III), and (4)(a)(IX) of this section and the copies of the statutes under subsection (4)(b) of this section and adding the first

and last publication dates if not already specified in the combined notice, for four weeks, which means publication once each week for five consecutive weeks.

(b) The officer shall review the publication of the combined notice for accuracy.

(c) The fees and costs to be allowed for publication of the combined notice shall be as provided by law for the publication of legal notices or advertising.

(d) Repealed.

§ 38-38-103.1, C.R.S. Single point of contact – servicer to designate – duties – exemption.

(1) No later than the forty-fifth day of a borrower's delinquency, a servicer shall promptly establish a single point of contact for communications with the borrower. The servicer shall do so within the time periods prescribed in, and subject to the other requirements imposed by, federal law and CFPB rules and orders. Once the single point of contact is established, the servicer shall promptly provide to the borrower, in writing, one or more direct means of communication with the single point of contact.

(2) A single point of contact shall:

(a) Provide the borrower with accurate information about:

(I) Loss mitigation options available to the borrower from the owner or assignee of the borrower's mortgage loan;

(II) Actions the borrower must take to be evaluated for loss mitigation options, including actions the borrower must take to submit a complete loss mitigation application and, if applicable, actions the borrower must take to appeal the servicer's determination to deny a borrower's loss mitigation application for any trial or permanent loan modification program offered by the servicer;

(III) The status of any loss mitigation application that the borrower has submitted to the servicer;

(IV) The circumstances under which the servicer may make a referral to foreclosure; and

(V) Applicable loss mitigation deadlines established by an owner or assignee of the borrower's mortgage loan or by section 38-38-103.2;

(b) Retrieve, in a timely manner:

(I) A complete record of the borrower's payment history; and

(II) All written information the borrower has provided to the servicer and, if available, to prior servicers in connection with a loss mitigation application;

(c) Provide the documents and information identified in paragraph (b) of this subsection (2) to other persons required to evaluate a borrower for loss mitigation options made available by the servicer, if applicable; and

(d) Provide a delinquent borrower with information about the procedures for submitting a notice of error or an information request.

(3) A servicer is exempt from this section if the servicer services five thousand or fewer mortgage loans for all of which the servicer, or an affiliate of the servicer, is the creditor or assignee. In determining whether a servicer services five thousand or fewer mortgages, the servicer is evaluated based on the number of mortgage loans serviced by the servicer and any affiliates as of January 1 for the remainder of the calendar year. A servicer that crosses the threshold has six months after crossing the threshold or until the next January 1, whichever is later, to comply with this section.

(4) A servicer who complies with 12 CFR 1024.40, as promulgated by the CFPB, or is exempt from compliance with that regulation under federal law or CFPB rules, regulations, or orders, is deemed in compliance with this section.

§ 38-38-103.2, C.R.S. Dual tracking prohibited – notice to officer – continuation of sale pending inquiry.

(1) A servicer is subject to the time limits and other requirements of federal law and CFPB rules in connection with a foreclosure under this article.

(2) The servicer shall:

(a) Notify the borrower in writing when it receives a complete loss mitigation application from the borrower; and

(b) Exercise reasonable diligence in obtaining documents and information to complete a loss mitigation application.

(3) If the borrower has received confirmation from the servicer that the borrower has submitted a complete loss mitigation application or has been offered and has accepted a loss mitigation option and is complying with its provisions, and yet a notice of election and demand pursuant to section 38-38-101 has been filed or action is being taken pursuant to section 38-38-105 or 38-38-106 with regard to the borrower, then, in order to stop the foreclosure sale, no later than fourteen calendar days before the sale date, the borrower must present to the officer the borrower's written notification from the servicer indicating receipt of a complete loss mitigation application dated at least thirty-seven days prior to the sale date or acceptance of a loss mitigation option, and, if the borrower does so:

(a) As soon as possible, but no later than three business days after receipt of the notification, the officer shall contact the attorney for the servicer or holder or the servicer or holder, if not represented by an attorney, by telephone, electronic mail, or first-class mail and inquire as to the status of the loss mitigation option. The officer shall document this inquiry. Until the servicer or its attorney responds to the inquiry, the officer shall continue the sale in accordance with section 38-38-109 (1) (a).

(b) If the attorney for the servicer or holder or the servicer or holder, if not represented by an attorney, fails to respond within seven calendar days to an inquiry under paragraph (a) of this subsection (3), then, as soon as possible but no later than the fourteenth day after the date of the inquiry, the officer shall send a certified letter to the attorney for the servicer or holder or to the servicer or holder, if not represented by an attorney, as listed on the notice of election and demand, inquiring as to the status of the loss mitigation option. The servicer or holder shall reimburse the officer for the cost of mailing the letter.

(c) If, after being contacted in accordance with paragraph (a) or (b) of this subsection (3), the attorney for the servicer or holder or the servicer or holder, if not represented by an attorney, gives the officer a written statement via electronic mail or first-class mail disputing that a loss mitigation option has been offered and accepted or that the borrower is complying with its terms, the officer shall proceed with the sale.

(d) (I) If the attorney for the servicer or holder or the servicer or holder, if not represented by an attorney, acknowledges that a loss mitigation option has been offered and accepted and that the borrower is complying with its terms, the officer shall continue the sale in accordance with section 38-38-109 (1) (a), and the holder shall withdraw the notice of election and demand within one hundred eighty calendar days after the date of the acknowledgment if the borrower continues to comply with the terms of the loss mitigation option.

(II) If, within one hundred eighty calendar days after the date of the acknowledgment, the attorney for the servicer or holder or the servicer or holder, if not represented by an attorney, has not withdrawn the notice of election and demand and neither the attorney for the servicer or holder nor the servicer or holder, if not represented by an attorney, has notified the officer that the borrower is not complying with the terms of the loss mitigation option, the officer may administratively withdraw the notice of election and demand.

(III) If, within one hundred eighty calendar days after the date of the acknowledgment, the borrower fails to comply with the terms of the loss mitigation option, the holder or the attorney for the holder may give written notice to the officer that the loss mitigation option has been breached, and, no later than ten business days after receiving the notice, the officer shall mail an amended combined notice containing the date of the rescheduled sale to each person appearing on the most recent mailing list, or on an updated mailing list if provided by the holder or the holder's attorney. The rescheduled sale date must not be fewer than seven calendar days after the date the amended combined notice is mailed. All fees and costs of providing the amended combined notice may be included as part of the foreclosure costs.

(4) If a foreclosure sale is continued as a result of compliance with the requirements of subsection (3) of this section, the periods for which the sale may be continued are in addition to the twelve-month period of continuance provided by section 38-38-109 (1).

(5) A servicer is exempt from this section if the servicer services five thousand or fewer mortgage loans for all of which the servicer, or an affiliate of the servicer, is the creditor or assignee. In determining whether a servicer services five thousand or fewer mortgages, the servicer is evaluated based on the number of mortgage loans serviced by the servicer and any affiliates as of January 1 for the remainder of the calendar year. A servicer that crosses the threshold has six months after crossing the threshold or until the next January 1, whichever is later, to comply with this section.

(6) A servicer who complies with 12 CFR 1024.41, as promulgated by the CFPB, or is exempt from compliance with that regulation under federal law or CFPB rules, regulations, or orders, is deemed in compliance with this section.

§ 38-38-104, C.R.S. Right to cure when default is nonpayment – right to cure for certain technical defaults.

(1) Unless the order authorizing the sale described in section 38-38-105 contains a determination that there is a reasonable probability that a default in the terms of the evidence of debt, deed of trust, or other lien being foreclosed other than nonpayment of sums due thereunder has occurred, any of the following persons is entitled to cure the default if the person files with the officer, no later than fifteen calendar days prior to the date of sale, a written notice of intent to cure together with evidence of the person's right to cure to the satisfaction of the officer:

(a) (I) The owner of the property as of the date and time of the recording of the notice of election and demand or lis pendens as evidenced in the records;

(II) If the owner of the property is dead or incapacitated on or after the date and time of the recording of the notice of election and demand or lis pendens, the owner's heirs, personal representative, legal guardian, or conservator as of the time of filing of the notice of intent to cure, whether or not such person's interest is shown in the records, or any co-owner of the property if the co-owner's ownership interest is evidenced in the records as of the date and time of the recording of the notice of election and demand or lis pendens;

(III) A transferee of the property as evidenced in the records as of the time of filing of the notice of intent to cure if the transferee was the property owner's spouse as of the date and time of the recording of the notice of election and demand or lis pendens or if the transferee is wholly owned or controlled by the property owner, is wholly owned or controlled by the controlling owner of the property owner, or is the controlling owner of the property owner;

(IV) A transferee or owner of the property by virtue of merger or other similar event or by operation of law occurring after the date and time of the recording of the notice of election and demand or lis pendens; or

(V) The holder of an order or judgment entered by a court of competent jurisdiction as evidenced in the records after the date and time of the recording of the notice of election and demand or lis pendens ordering title to the property to be vested in a person other than the owner;

(b) A person liable under the evidence of debt;

(c) A surety or guarantor of the evidence of debt; or

(d) A holder of an interest junior to the lien being foreclosed by virtue of being a lienor or lessee of, or a holder of an easement or license on, the property or a contract vendee of the property, if the instrument evidencing the interest was recorded in the records prior to the date and time of the recording of the notice of election and demand or lis pendens. If, prior to the date and time of the recording of the notice of election and demand or lis pendens, a lien is recorded in an incorrect county, the holder's rights under this section shall only be valid if the lien is rerecorded in the correct county at least fifteen calendar days prior to the actual date of sale.

(2) (a) (I) Promptly upon receipt of a notice of intent to cure by the officer, but no less than twelve calendar days prior to the date of sale, the officer shall transmit by mail, facsimile, or electronic means to the person executing the notice of election and demand a request for a statement of all sums necessary to cure the default. The attorney for the holder or servicer or, if none, the holder or servicer, shall file the cure statement with the officer, and the cure statement must set forth the amounts necessary to cure. Upon receipt of the statement of the amounts needed to cure, the officer shall transmit in writing to the person filing the notice of intent to cure the default:

(A) The cure statement; and

(B) A statement that the person filing the notice of intent to cure is entitled to receive from the attorney for the holder or servicer or, if not represented, from the holder or servicer, upon written request mailed to the attorney for the holder or servicer or, if not represented, to the holder or servicer at the address stated on the cure statement, copies of receipts or other credible evidence to support the costs claimed on the cure statement. This request may be sent only after payment to the officer of the amount shown on the cure statement and must be sent within ninety days after payment of the cure amount.

(II) If a cure statement is required pursuant to subparagraph (I) of this paragraph (a), the holder of the evidence of debt shall submit a signed and acknowledged cure statement, or the office of the attorney for the holder shall submit a signed cure statement, specifying the following amounts, itemized in substantially the following categories and in substantially the following form:

CURE STATEMENT

To: ____

Public Trustee (or Sheriff) of the County (or City and County) of ___,
State of Colorado (hereinafter the "officer").

Foreclosure sale number: __________

Grantor: __________

The date through which the cure statement is effective: __________

The following is an itemization of all sums necessary to cure the default (any amount that is based on a good faith estimate is indicated with an asterisk):

Payments due under the evidence of debt:

__________ payments of $ __________ each

Accrued late charges __________

Other amounts due under the evidence of debt (specify)

_______________	_______________
_______________	_______________
Property inspections	_______________
Property, general liability, and casualty insurance	_______________
Certificate of taxes due	_______________
Property taxes paid by the holder	_______________
Owner association assessment paid by the holder	_______________
Permitted amounts paid on prior liens	_______________
Less impound/escrow account credit	_______________
Plus impound/escrow account deficiency	_______________
Title costs	_______________
Rule 120 docket fee	_______________
Rule 120 posting costs	_______________
Court costs	_______________
Postage/delivery costs	_______________
Service/posting costs	_______________
Attorney fees	_______________
Other fees and costs (specify):	
_______________	_______________
_______________	_______________

Reinstatement total $_______________

(Does not include officer's fees and costs)

Officer's fees and costs $_______________
(To be added by officer)

Total to cure $______________
(To be added by officer)

IT MAY TAKE SEVERAL DAYS BEFORE THE CURE IS PROCESSED AND ENTERED INTO THE HOLDER'S RECORDS.

The total to cure does not include any future monthly mortgage payments that may be due.

Name of the holder of the evidence of debt and the attorney for the holder:

Holder: ____
Attorney: ____
Printed name: ____________________________________
Signature: _______________________________________
Attorney address: _________________________________
Attorney business telephone: ________________________

(III) The cure statement is a representation of fact, made upon the current information and belief of the person signing it. If the holder or servicer determines that there is an inaccurate amount contained in the cure statement, the holder or servicer, or the attorney for the holder or servicer, shall inform the officer immediately and provide a cure statement with updated figures; except that any additional or increased amounts must be added at least ten calendar days before the effective date of the original cure statement. If an inaccurate amount is reported and a corrected cure statement is not provided within the time specified in this subparagraph (III), the officer may continue the sale for one week in accordance with section 38-38-109 (1). An estimate as allowed under subsection (5) of this section is not an inaccurate amount for purposes of this subparagraph (III).

(IV) Within seven business days after the officer's notification to the holder or servicer, or to the attorney for the holder or servicer, that the officer has received the funds necessary to cure the default as reflected on the initial or updated cure statement, the holder or servicer or the attorney for the holder or servicer shall deliver to the officer a final statement, reconciled for estimated amounts that were not or would not be incurred as of the date the cure proceeds were received by the officer, along with receipts or invoices for all rule 120 docket costs and all statutorily mandated posting costs claimed on the cure statement. All amounts of cure proceeds received by the officer in excess of the amounts reflected on the final statement shall be remitted by the officer to the person who paid the cure amount.

(V) (A) The holder or servicer shall remit to the person who paid the cure amount any portion of the cure amount that represents a fee or cost listed on the cure statement that exceeds the amount actually incurred and that was not remitted by the officer in accordance with subparagraph (I) of paragraph (d) of this subsection (2).

(B) The officer shall remit to the person who paid the cure amount any portion of the cure amount that represents a fee or cost of the officer that exceeds the amount actually incurred by the officer.

(VI) The holder or servicer is responsible for retaining receipts or other credible evidence to support all costs claimed on the cure statement, including rule 120 docket fees and posting costs, and the person who paid the cure amount is entitled to receive copies upon written request mailed to the attorney for the holder or servicer or, if not represented, to the holder or servicer at the address stated on the cure statement. The request may be made at any time after payment to the officer of the amount shown on the cure statement, but must be made within ninety days after payment of the cure amount. The attorney for the holder or servicer or, if not represented, the holder or servicer shall provide copies of all receipts or other credible evidence within thirty days after receiving the request, and may provide the copies electronically.

(b) No later than 12 noon on the day before the sale, the person desiring to cure the default shall pay to the officer all sums that are due and owing under the evidence of debt and deed of trust or other lien being foreclosed and all fees and costs of the holder of the evidence of debt allowable under the evidence of debt, deed of trust, or other lien being foreclosed through the effective date that are set forth in the cure statement; except that any principal that would not have been due in the absence of acceleration shall not be included in such sums due.

(c) If a cure is made, interest for the period of any continuance pursuant to section 38-38-109 (1) (c) shall be allowed only at the regular rate and not at the default rate as may be specified in the evidence of debt, deed of trust, or other lien being foreclosed. If a cure is not made, interest at the default rate, if specified in the evidence of debt, deed of trust, or other lien being foreclosed, for the period of the continuance shall be allowed.

(d) (I) Upon receipt of the cure amount, and conditioned upon the withdrawal or dismissal of the foreclosure from the holder or servicer or the attorney for the holder or servicer, the officer shall:

(A) Deliver the cure amount, less the fees and costs of the officer and any adjustments required under subparagraph (III) of paragraph (a) of this subsection (2), to the attorney for the holder or servicer or, if none, to the holder or servicer; and

(B) Obtain and retain, in the officer's records, the name and mailing address of the person who paid the cure amount.

(II) Following the withdrawal or dismissal, the evidence of debt shall be returned uncancelled to the attorney for the holder or servicer or, if none, to the holder or servicer by the public trustee or to the court by the sheriff.

(3) Where the default in the terms of the evidence of debt, deed of trust, or other lien on which the holder of the evidence of debt claims the right to foreclose is the failure of a party to furnish balance sheets or tax returns, any person entitled to cure pursuant to paragraph (a) of subsection (2) of this section may cure such default in the manner prescribed in this section by providing to the holder or the attorney for the holder the required balance sheets, tax returns, or other adequate evidence of the party's financial condition so long as all sums currently due under the evidence of debt have been paid and all amounts due under paragraph (b) of subsection (2) of this section, where applicable, have been paid.

(4) Any person liable on the debt and the grantor of the deed of trust or other lien being foreclosed shall be deemed to have given the necessary consent to allow the holder of the evidence of debt or the attorney for the holder to provide the information specified in paragraph (a) of subsection (2) of this section to the officer and all other persons who may assert a right to cure pursuant to this section.

(5) A cure statement pursuant to paragraph (a) of subsection (2) of this section shall state the period for which it is effective. The cure statement shall be effective for at least ten calendar days after the date the cure statement is received by the officer or until the last day to cure under paragraph (b) of subsection (2) of this section, whichever occurs first. The cure statement shall be effective for no more than thirty calendar days after the date the cure statement is received by the officer or until the last day to cure under paragraph (b) of subsection (2) of this section, whichever occurs first. The use of good faith estimates in the cure statement with respect to

interest and fees and costs is specifically authorized by this article, so long as the cure statement states that it is a good faith estimate effective through the last day to cure as indicated in the cure statement. The use of a good faith estimate in the cure statement shall not change or extend the period or effective date of a cure statement.

(6) Following expiration of the period for which the cure statement is effective, but no less than fifteen calendar days prior to the date of sale, the person who originally submitted the notice of intent to cure may make a written request to the public trustee for an update of the amount necessary to cure. Upon receipt by the public trustee of such written request for updated cure figures, subsection (2) of this section shall apply.

(7) If the holder of the evidence of debt or the attorney for the holder receives a request for a cure statement under paragraph (a) of subsection (2) of this section and does not file a cure statement with the officer by the earlier of ten business days after receipt of the request or the eighth calendar day before the date of the sale, the officer shall continue the sale for one week. Thereafter and until the cure statement is filed, the officer shall continue the sale an additional week for each week that the holder fails to file the cure statement; except that the sale shall not be continued beyond the period of continuance allowed under section 38-38-109 (1) (a). A cure statement must be received by 12 noon on the day it is due in order to meet a deadline set forth in this subsection (7).

§ 38-38-105, C.R.S. Court order authorizing sale mandatory – notice of hearing for residential properties – definition.

(1) Repealed.

(2) (a) On and after January 1, 2008, whenever a public trustee forecloses upon a deed of trust under this article, the holder of the evidence of debt or the attorney for the holder shall obtain an order authorizing sale from a court of competent jurisdiction to issue the same pursuant to rule 120 or other rule of the Colorado rules of civil procedure. The order shall recite the date the hearing was scheduled if no hearing was held, or the date the hearing was completed if a hearing was held, which date in either case must be no later than the day prior to the last day on which an effective notice of intent to cure may be filed with the public trustee under section 38-38-104. A sale held without an order authorizing sale issued in compliance with this paragraph (a) shall be invalid.

(b) The public trustee shall postpone the sale, unless the holder or the attorney for the holder causes a copy of the order to be provided to the public trustee no later than 12 noon on the second business day prior to the date of sale. A sale held in violation of this paragraph (b) shall not be invalid if an order that complied with the provisions of paragraph (a) of this subsection (2) was entered.

(3) (a) Not less than fourteen days before the date set for the hearing pursuant to rule 120 or other rule of the Colorado rules of civil procedure, the holder or the attorney for the holder seeking an order authorizing sale under this section for a residential property shall cause a notice of hearing as described in rule 120 (b) of the Colorado rules of civil procedure to be posted in a conspicuous place on the property that is the subject of the sale. If possible, the notice shall be posted on the front door of the residence, but if access to the door is not possible or is restricted, the notice shall be posted at an alternative conspicuous location, such as a gate or similar impediment. If a person at the residence is impeding posting at the residence at the time of the attempted posting, the notice may be handed to that person to satisfy this posting requirement. The notice required by this subsection (3) is sufficient if it complies with the requirements of this section without regard to any requirements for service of process in a civil action required by court rule.

(b) For servicers who are not exempt pursuant to section 38-38-103.1 (3) or 38-38-103.2 (4), the notice must contain or be accompanied by a conspicuous statement, substantially as follows, together with contact information for both the Colorado attorney general's office and the CFPB:

> If you believe that the lender or servicer of this mortgage has violated the requirements for a single point of contact in section 38-38-103.1, Colorado Revised Statutes, or the prohibition on dual tracking in section 38-38-103.2, Colorado Revised Statutes, you may file a complaint with the Colorado attorney general, the federal Consumer Financial Protection Bureau, or both, at __________ [insert contact information for both]. The filing of a complaint will not stop the foreclosure process.

(4) As used in this section, "residential property" means any real property upon which a dwelling, as defined in section 5-1-301 (18), C.R.S., is constructed and occupied.

§ 38-38-106, C.R.S. Bid required – form of bid.

(1) (a) The holder of the evidence of debt or the attorney for the holder shall submit a bid setting forth the holder's initial bid for the property that is received by the officer no later than 12 noon on the second business day prior to the date of sale as provided in this section. In addition, if the sale will be conducted electronically, the holder may also include a maximum bid for the property. The holder or the attorney for the holder need not personally attend the sale. If the sale will be conducted electronically and the holder has elected to include a maximum bid, the bid shall be increased electronically in increments incorporated in the electronic program used by the officer to conduct the electronic sale up to such maximum bid if one or more third parties submit competing bids for the property.

(b) If the bid is not received by the officer by the deadline, the officer shall continue the sale for one week and shall announce or post a notice of the continuance at the time and place designated for the sale.

(2) The holder of the evidence of debt shall submit a signed and acknowledged bid, or the attorney for the holder shall submit a signed bid, which must specify the following amounts, itemized in substantially the following categories and in substantially the following form:

BID

To: ____

Public Trustee (or Sheriff) of the County (or City and County) of ____,
State of Colorado (hereinafter the "officer").

Date: ___________

___________, whose mailing address is _______________, bids the sum of $___________ in your Sale No. _____ to be held on the ___ day of _____, 20___.

The following is an itemization of all amounts due the holder of the evidence of debt secured by the deed of trust or other lien being foreclosed.

Street address of property being foreclosed, if known: _______________

Regular ☐ / default ☐ rate of interest as of the date of sale: ____________

(Inapplicable items may be omitted):

Amounts due under the evidence of debt:

Principal	$ _______
Interest	_______
Late charges	_______

Allowable prepayment penalties or premiums _______
Other amounts due under the evidence of debt
(specify) _______ _______
_______ _______
Category subtotal: $ _______

Other fees and costs advanced by the holder of evidence of debt:
Property, general liability, and casualty insurance _______
Property inspections _______
Appraisals _______
Taxes and assessments _______
Utility charges owed or incurred _______
Owner association assessment paid _______
Permitted amounts paid on prior liens _______
Permitted lease payments _______
Less impound/escrow account credit _______
Plus impound/escrow account deficiency _______
Other (describe) ________________________ _______
Category subtotal: $ _______

Attorney fees and advances:
Attorney fees _______
Title commitments and insurances or
abstractor charges _______
Court docketing _______
Statutory notice _______
Postage _______
Electronic transmissions _______
Photocopies _______
Telephone _______
Other (describe) ________________________ _______
Category subtotal: $ _______

Officer fees and costs:
Officer statutory fee _______
Publication charges _______
Certificate of purchase recording fee _______
Confirmation deed fee _______
Confirmation deed recording fee _______
Other (describe) ________________________ _______
Category subtotal: $ _______

Total due holder of the evidence of debt
Initial Bid $ _______
Deficiency $ _______

I enclose herewith the following:

1. Order authorizing sale.
2. Check (if applicable) to your order in the sum of $_______ covering the balance of your fees and costs.
3. Other: ______________________________.

Please send us the following:

1. Promissory note with the deficiency, if any, noted thereon
2. Refund for overpayment of officer's fees and costs, if any
3. Other: ______________________________.

Name of the holder of the evidence of debt

and the attorney for the holder:
Holder: ______________________________
Attorney: ____________________________
By: _________________________________
Attorney registration number: ____________
Attorney address: _______________________
Attorney business telephone: _____________

(3) Upon receipt of the initial bid from the holder of the evidence of debt or the attorney for the holder, the officer shall make such information available to the general public.

(4) The officer shall enter the bid by reading the bid amount set forth on the bid and the name of the person that submitted the bid or by posting or providing such bid information at the time and place designated for sale.

(5) Bids submitted pursuant to this section may be amended by the holder of the evidence of debt or the attorney for the holder in writing or electronically, as determined by the officer pursuant to section 38-38-112, no later than 12 noon the day prior to the sale, or orally at the time of sale if the person amending the bid is physically present at the sale or electronically during the sale if the sale is conducted by means of the internet or another electronic medium. A bid submitted pursuant to this section may be modified orally at the time of sale if the person making the modification modifies and reexecutes the bid at the sale.

(6) The holder of the evidence of debt or the attorney for the holder shall bid at least the holder's good faith estimate of the fair market value of the property being sold, less the amount of unpaid real property taxes and all amounts secured by liens against the property being sold that are senior to the deed of trust or other lien being foreclosed and less the estimated reasonable costs and expenses of holding, marketing, and selling the property, net of income received; except that the holder or the attorney for the holder need not bid more than the total amount due to the holder as specified in the bid pursuant to subsection (2) of this section. The failure of the holder to bid the amount required by this subsection (6) shall not affect the validity of the sale but may be raised as a defense by any person sued on a deficiency.

(7) (a) (I) Other than a bid by the holder of the evidence of debt not exceeding the total amount due shown on the bid pursuant to subsection (2) of this section, the payment of any bid amount at sale must be received by the officer no later than the date and time of the sale, or at an alternative time after the sale and on the day of the sale, as specified in writing by the officer. The payment must be in the form specified in section 38-37-108. If the officer has not received full payment of the bid amount from the highest bidder at the sale pursuant to this subsection (7), the next highest bidder who has timely tendered the full amount of the bid under this subsection (7) is deemed the successful bidder at the sale.

(II) If the holder of the evidence of debt is the highest bidder with a bid that exceeds the total amount due shown on the bid pursuant to subsection (2) of this section, the holder of the evidence of debt is only required to pay the excess of the amount bid over the amount due the holder of the evidence of debt, as shown on the bid submitted pursuant to subsection (2) of this section.

(b) The officer may establish written policies relating to all aspects of the foreclosure sale that are consistent with the provisions of this article. The written policies shall be made available to the general public.

V. Master Form Mortgage or Deed of Trust

A. Master Form of Mortgage or Deed of Trust

Effective July 1, 2001, § 38-35-109(1.5), C.R.S., enables a master form of mortgage or deed of trust. The purpose of this law is to shorten the actual deed of trust, by recording the "master form" and then simply referring to the recorded provisions in the actual transaction instruments. Subsection (1.5) reads:

(a) Any person may record in the office of the county clerk and recorder of any county a master form mortgage or master form deed of trust. Such forms shall be entitled to recordation without any acknowledgment or signature; without identification of any specific real property; and without naming any specific mortgagor, mortgagee, trustor, beneficiary, or trustee. Every instrument shall contain on the face of the document "Master form recorded by (name of person causing instrument to be recorded)." The county clerk and recorder shall index such master forms in the grantee index under the name of the person causing it to be recorded.

(b) (I) Any of the provisions of such master form instrument may be incorporated by reference in any mortgage or deed of trust encumbering real estate situated within the state, if such reference in the mortgage or deed of trust states the following:

(A) That the master form instrument was recorded in the county in which the mortgage or deed of trust is offered for record;

(B) The date when recorded and the book and page or pages or reception or index number where such master form was recorded;

(C) That a copy of the provisions of the master form instrument was furnished to the person executing the mortgage or deed of trust; and

(D) If fewer than all of the provisions of the referenced master form are being adopted or incorporated, a statement identifying by paragraph, section, or other specification method which will clearly identify the incorporated provision or provisions, provided that in the absence of specific designation, the entire referenced master form will be deemed to be incorporated.

(II) The recording of any mortgage or deed of trust which has incorporated by reference any of the provisions of a master form recorded as provided in this section shall have the same effect as if such provisions of such master form had been set forth fully in the mortgage or deed of trust.

B. Acknowledged and Recorded for the Protection

Deeds of trust and mortgages, and all other instruments affecting real property, should be acknowledged and recorded for the protection of the holder of the interest. C.R.S. Section 38-35-109(1), C.R.S., states:

> All deeds, powers of attorney, agreements, or other instruments in writing conveying, encumbering, or affecting the title to real property, certificates, and certified copies of orders, judgments, and decrees of courts of record may be recorded in the office of the county clerk and recorder of the county where such real property is situated; except that all instruments conveying the title of real property to the state or a political subdivision shall be recorded pursuant to section 38-35-109.5. No such unrecorded instrument or document shall be valid against any person with any kind of rights in or to such real property who first records and those holding rights under such person, except between the parties thereto and against those having notice thereof prior to acquisition of such rights. This is a race-notice recording statute. In

> all cases where by law an instrument may be filed in the office of a county clerk and recorder, the filing thereof in such office shall be equivalent to the recording thereof, and the recording thereof in the office of such county clerk and recorder shall be equivalent to the filing thereof.

A subsequent innocent purchaser or encumbrancer with no actual knowledge of a prior unrecorded claim will be given a superior right. Unacknowledged recorded instruments constitute notice to subsequent purchasers or encumbrancers. But unless they have been of record for the required ten years, they may not be introduced as evidence until their validity is proven.

VI. Usual Elements of a Deed of Trust or Mortgage

The following list serves only as a reference to the usual elements of a deed of trust or mortgage. A competent attorney or other person with considerable experience in these matters should carefully check these instruments, because many varied and complex details must be adjusted to fit each particular case.

1. **Date.** Though not essential, inclusion of the date might prevent later controversy as to when the security interest was conveyed.
2. **Parties.** All parties to a mortgage or trust deed must be named and clearly designated. In a mortgage, they are the mortgagor (grantor) and mortgagee (grantee). In a deed of trust, they are the trustor (grantor), public trustee and beneficiary. The name of the grantor must be exactly the same as on the deed by which the grantor acquired title.
3. **Consideration.** Consideration is the money loaned to the trustor or mortgagor, usually to assist in purchasing the property. The statement regarding the consideration should contain the following:
    a. Description of the indebtedness;
    b. Amount;
    c. Maturity date;
    d. Method of repayment of the principal amount;
    e. Interest rate and time of payment;
    f. Interest coupon notes, if any; and
    g. Conditions of default as to principal and interest.
4. **Words of Conveyance.** The words of conveyance should be "*does hereby convey to*" or something similar. This gives the trustee or mortgagee an interest in the property that will serve as security.
5. **Legal Description.** This is necessary to identify the real estate subject to the security interest. This description should read the same as that contained in the deed by which title is transferred.
6. **Conditions (trust deed) or Covenants (mortgage).** Usually contains requirements such as keeping the property insured, paying taxes and assessments, and maintaining improvements in good repair. See more conditions in the next section.
7. **Method of sale in case of default.** The beneficiary of a trust deed may foreclose by public sale through the office of the public trustee or through the courts. In Colorado,

the mortgagee or beneficiary of a private trust deed may foreclose only through the courts.

8. **Exceptions as to prior liens, if any.**
9. **Signature of the trustor/mortgagor.**
10. **Acknowledgment.** Signing before a notary public is the simplest means of establishing the instrument's proper execution and validity.
11. **Recording.** Recording in the office of the county clerk and recorder of the county in which the property is situated is necessary to protect the interest of the beneficiary or mortgagee against the claim of persons who may thereafter acquire an interest in the property without actual notice of the mortgage or trust deed.

In addition to the above, the following elements may be contained in the mortgage or trust deed:

1. Provision for a higher rate of interest in all notes after maturity;
2. An acceleration clause, which provides that a default continuing more than a specified time gives the holder of the indebtedness the right to declare all indebtedness to be due and payable immediately without notice;
3. A waiver of homestead rights;
4. A reservation of the right to pay taxes if they remain unpaid when due, adding the amount so paid together with interest at a specified rate to the principal sum;
5. A requirement that the property be insured in companies acceptable to the holder of the indebtedness and the standard mortgage clause added to these policies. If the grantor fails to so insure, the grantee should be given the right to insure, adding the cost together with interest at a specified rate to the indebtedness;
6. Provision for the appointment of a receiver upon the occurrence of a default;
7. In case of a foreclosure or a trustee's sale, provision for:
   a. All the costs of such suits, advertising, sale, and conveyance, including attorneys, solicitors, stenographers, trustee's fees, outlays for documentary evidence, and costs of abstract and examination of title.
   b. All monies advanced by the holders of the indebtedness with interest thereupon from the time the advances were made.
   c. The accrued interest remaining unpaid on the indebtedness.
   d. All of the principal money remaining unpaid.
8. In the case of trust deeds, provision for a reconveyance of the property by the trustee to the grantor, upon the payment of the principal and interest and the performance of the covenants and agreements contained in the instrument; or
9. In a case where a private trustee is used, a provision for a successor in trust in case of the trustee's inability to act.

VII. Assumption of Indebtedness

A buyer and seller may wish to transfer title with the existing loan remaining as a lien upon the property. This is accomplished by a provision in the contract whereby the buyer assumes and agrees to pay the existing indebtedness.

However, assumption is subject to limitations that may be present in the mortgage or trust deed contract. Mortgages and trust deeds often contain a provision to the effect that if the subject property is conveyed, the entire balance of the loan becomes due (strict due-on-sale). This has the same effect as an acceleration clause in the event of default.

The above restriction may alternatively preclude conveyance without the lender's consent (due-on-sale). This enables the lender to adjust (usually upwards) the interest rate or other terms of the loan. If conveyance is made without the lender's consent, the lender may call the entire balance of the loan due.

VIII. Section 38-30-165, C.R.S., Limit on Interest Rate Increase

Section 38-30-165, C.R.S., limits interest rate increases on an assumption to one percent per annum above the existing interest rate on the indebtedness for trust deeds executed on or after July 1, 1975. On October 15, 1982, a new federal law preempted all state laws in this area. Lenders may now enforce a due-on-sale clause no matter when the mortgage or trust deed was executed.

Lenders need not necessarily have a due-on-sale provision in their trust deeds or mortgages. The Real Estate Commission has approved three types of trust deeds for mandatory use by licensees when preparing deeds of trust on behalf of their principals. One contains a strict due-on-sale clause. The second contains a modified due-on-sale clause, which makes the loan assumable if the purchaser is creditworthy. The third type of trust deed contains no due-on-sale clause, and the loan is fully assumable.

IX. The Promissory Note

In the real estate financing process, the principal promissory note or bond is the evidence of the debt for which the mortgage or deed of trust is the security. This note is an unconditional promise in writing, signed by the maker, agreeing to pay on demand or at some future time, a certain sum of money to the payee or bearer. A promissory note creates a personal liability on the part of the maker. In the event of a default, if the security is insufficient to cover the indebtedness, the holder of the note may obtain a deficiency judgment for the balance due and proceed against all other property and assets of the debtor.

The holder of a note secured by the mortgage or trust deed may sell or transfer the note to another. If the note is secured by a deed of trust, the holder simply endorses the note over to the successor holder. No separate transfer instrument is necessary. But if the note is secured by a mortgage, in addition to the endorsement of the note, the mortgage should also be separately assigned in writing to the new holder and the assignment should be recorded.

The reason for recording an assignment of a mortgage but not a deed of trust is to better preserve an unbroken chain of title. Unless default occurs in the payment of the note, a release or satisfaction of the security instrument will eventually be executed. In the instance of a deed of trust, the release is executed by the public trustee, who remains the same no matter how many times the note may have changed hands. In a mortgage, the current legal holder of the note, who would have changed each time the note was transferred, will execute the release instrument. A recorded assignment of a mortgage to each new note-holder gives constructive notice of the person who must execute the release thereof.

X. Second Mortgage or Trust Deed

An owner of real property encumbered by a deed of trust or mortgage may secure a second loan, secured by a second trust deed or mortgage. A second trust deed stands in a subordinate position to the first as to priority of lien claim in case of a foreclosure. The recording date of the first deed of trust before the recording of the second legally establishes the priorities of right. If the first trust deed was unrecorded but the holder of the second had actual knowledge of the existence of the first at the time of the second transaction, the first trust deed would still have priority.

When the first deed of trust is satisfied, subsequent encumbrances move upward in priority. The second trust deed would then become first in priority, the third becomes second, and so on. However, the priority of instruments may be controlled by their terms. For instance, the terms of a second deed of trust may allow its lien to continue to be subordinate to the existing first, or any substitution thereof, thus allowing the owner to replace the first deed of trust with another without disturbing the position of the lien holders below the first. This advantage is often very important to the grantor in matters pertaining to refinancing property.

XI. Installment Land Contract

An installment land contract (ILC, or sometimes called a bond for title or a long-term escrow) is essentially another type of security instrument. A typical installment land contract provides for all the terms usually found in a buy-sell contract, but withholds a warranty deed transferring (legal) title until the full or some part of the purchase price has been paid. ILCs should be recorded. The buyer takes possession and assumes all the risks and responsibilities of ownership. The buyer covenants to insure, repair, pay taxes and assessments, etc., of the property for the benefit of the seller. The buyer is considered to have an equitable interest in the land in much the same way as a mortgagor. See the topic index in the back of this manual for more information on installment land contracts.

A purchaser under an installment land contract has the right of entry and possession, but if there are no improvements on the land that can be physically occupied, there is no actual notice of the purchaser's interest given to the public. Some subdividers have sold vacant land by means of installment land contracts. Although it is advisable that all installment land contracts be recorded, it is especially important to record if the land is vacant.

An ILC should contain an escrow provision whereby a copy of the contract and a warranty deed from the seller to the purchaser are delivered to an escrow agent. Upon performance of the covenants in the contract by the purchaser, the escrow agent would then deliver the warranty deed. This type of contract is but another security device that can be used in the financing of real estate. An installment land contract must also contain other provisions required by statute and other customary provisions. There is no standard form of installment land contract approved by the Commission. The Commission revoked its approval of the installment land contract long ago.

Commission Position 39 cautions:

> "There is a significant potential for harm to the seller, buyer or assignee if the installment land contract is not properly drafted. Real estate brokers are prohibited from drafting a contract document that would reflect the terms of such a transaction as it would exceed their level of competency and is a matter requiring the expertise and advice of an attorney. Additionally, such behavior may be construed as the unauthorized practice of law by the real estate broker and subject to civil penalties. The contracts for these transactions should not be prepared by a real estate broker; rather, the documents should be drafted by a licensed Colorado attorney-at-law engaged for each particular transaction."

XII. Liens

A. Introduction

A lien is a right given by law to a creditor to have a debt or charge satisfied out of the property belonging to the debtor. For the purpose of convenience, liens may be classified as either specific or general. A "**specific lien**" attaches to and affects only a certain piece(s) of property, such as a mortgage, property tax, assessment, mechanics' lien, vendee's lien, vendor's lien, or an attachment. A "**general lien**" may attach to and affect all the property of the debtor, *e.g.*, a judgment lien, federal or state tax lien, or a lien for a decedent's debts.

B. Specific Liens

Mortgage

A mortgage secures or guarantees payment of the amount due to the lender or creditor by conditionally transferring an interest in the property to the lender. A mortgage is specific to one property. The lien becomes null and void upon the payment of the debt.

Taxes and assessments

Property taxes, special assessments, and water and sewer charges levied by law rather than usage become a specific lien on specific real property to which they pertain. The taxing body, usually the city or county, may take action resulting in the sale of the property if these charges are not paid.

Property subject to general ad valorem property tax is assessed on January 1 each year for the previous year, and a lien for the tax attaches on the same day. Property taxes are a perpetual lien upon the real estate until paid (including penalties, charges, and interest that may accrue). Property tax liens have priority over all other liens, regardless of filing date.

Real property taxes may be paid as follows: one-half on or before the last day of February, and the remaining one-half on or before June 15, or the entire tax may be paid on or before the last day of April. (See § 39-10-104.5, C.R.S.)

As soon as the first one-half installment becomes delinquent (*i.e.*, March 1), interest penalty accrues until the date of payment; except that, if the first installment is made after the last day of February, but not later than 30 days after the mailing by the treasurer of the tax statement pursuant to § 39-10-103(l)(a), C.R.S., no such delinquent interest shall accrue. For the single-payment option, interest accrues as of May 1. On June 16, all unpaid taxes of the preceding year become delinquent, and an interest penalty will be assessed in addition to any previous penalty that has accrued. (See § 39-10-104.5(3)(a), C.R.S.)

When an instrument of conveyance does not' specify who will pay the current year taxes, the grantee pays if the conveyance is made before July 1, and the grantor is responsible for paying if the conveyance is after June 30. (See § 39-1-108, C.R.S.) Proper real estate practice would have the instrument of conveyance contain a provision for apportionment of the taxes to the date of transfer.

The following various authorities determine the property tax:

a. The **"county assessor,"** publicly elected in 62 counties (and appointed in the City and County of Denver), determines the assessed valuation of the property. The valuation for assessment of all taxable residential property is determined by statute and is 9.35 percent of its actual value and 29 percent for commercial and raw land. (See §§ 39-1-104 and -104.2(3)(h), C.R.S.)

b. An elected "**board of county commissioners**" (except in the City and County of Denver, where the authorized body is created by the city charter) determines the "**mill levy**," which is a fractional part of the assessed valuation. A "mill" is one-thousandth of a dollar. Eighty-five mills may be expressed as a fraction of a dollar ($.085), both of which equate to $85 of tax for each $1,000 of assessed valuation. This levy is made no later than November 15 each year.

c. A county "**board of equalization**," (except for the City and County of Denver) is composed of the above county commissioners, who become the board of equalization from the second Monday in July until the last working day of July each year. In this capacity, they review the assessor-prepared roll of all taxable property located in the county, and hear appeals from protests filed with the county assessor. If an owner is dissatisfied with the decision of the county board of equalization, the owner may within 30 days:
   (i) Appeal to the county commissioners for binding arbitration. An arbitrated decision will be final and not subject to review;
   (ii) Appeal to the (state) board of assessment appeals. When a decision of the board of assessment appeals is adverse to an owner, the owner has 30 days in which to appeal to the state court of appeals; or
   (iii) Appeal to the district court in which the property is located. When a court decision is adverse to an owner, the owner has 45 days in which to appeal to the state court of appeals.

d. The three-member quasi-judicial "**board of assessment appeals**" hears appeals concerning local property tax assessments, utilities assessments, and decisions of the property tax administrator. (See § 39-2-123, C.R.S.)

e. The division of property taxation reviews the methods used by the county assessors and the county boards of equalization, and examines where it is alleged in writing that property has not been properly appraised or valued. It also conducts an annual school for assessors.

f. The **"state board of equalization"** consists of the governor, speaker of the house of representatives (or designee), president of the senate (or designee), and two members appointed by the governor with the consent of the senate. The two appointed members must be qualified appraisers or former assessors, or have knowledge and experience in property taxation. The board meets each year on the second Monday in September to determine if each county has assessed at the percentage of actual value prescribed by law. The board can act only on classes and subclasses of property and not on individual assessments. The board may also meet at the governor's call.

Before the first day of September of each year, county treasurers notify delinquent taxpayers by mail of the amount of delinquency and penalty interest thereon and afford 15 days from the time of mailing the said notice to pay the tax. Treasurers then make a list of all the county lands with delinquent taxes, publish the list, and designate the date for public sale. If such a list is made later than September 1, a sale held under that list is still valid. (See § 39-11-101, C.R.S.)

Delinquent tax sales commence on or before the second Monday in December of each year and are held at the treasurer's office in each county. (See § 39-11-109, C.R.S.) Such property is "sold" to the person who pays the delinquent taxes, penalty interest, and costs due, and who further pays the highest bid over these amounts in cash.

The owner (or agent or assignee) may redeem real property sold for taxes at any time before the issuance of a treasurer's deed. The person redeeming must pay to the county treasurer the amount for which the property was sold together with interest from the date of sale. (See § 39-12-103, C.R.S.)

The county treasurer issues a certificate of purchase to the high bidder at the tax sale. A certificate of purchase is assignable, and if the property has not been redeemed, the certificate holder may request the treasurer to give notice of the sale to every person in actual possession or occupancy of the property, to the person in whose name the property was taxed, and to publish such notice. After notice and publication, the treasurer will issue a treasurer's deed to the holder of a certificate of purchase. (See §§ 39-11-117 and 39-12-105, C.R.S.)

After a treasurer's deed is issued, executed, delivered, and recorded, it is presumed to be validly acknowledged. After the deed has been recorded for five years, (nine years if the delinquent owner is legally disabled at the time the deed was issued), the delinquent taxpayer has no legal course by which to recover the land. A holder of a treasurer's deed may initiate a "**quiet title**" suit in order to acquire merchantable title before the expiration of the five- or nine-year period. (See §§ 39-12-101 and -104, C.R.S.)

Special improvements are assessed in proportion to the benefits to the real estate, as determined by the ordering authority. Such assessments are a perpetual lien against the land and have priority over all liens except property tax liens. Special assessments for local improvements are due and payable within 30 days after final publication of the assessing ordinance, although it is common for special assessments to permit an owner to pay by installments with interest. The number of installments, the period of payment, and the rate of interest are determined by the ordering authority and set forth in the assessing ordinance. In case of default in the payment of any installment, the county treasurer may sell the property in the same manner, and with the same effect as provided for in the sale of real estate in default of payment of the general property taxes. (See §§ 31-25-501, *et seq.*, C.R.S.)

Mechanics' lien

Mechanics, material suppliers, contractors, subcontractors, builders, and all other persons rendering professional or skilled service, performing labor upon, or furnishing materials used in the construction, alteration, or repair of any structure or improvement upon land are given a lien upon the property. Mechanics' liens are all effective as of the time the work first commenced and are superior to all subsequently filed or unrecorded liens or encumbrances of which the lienor had no actual knowledge. The order of priority among different mechanic lien claimants is:

1. First, liens of laborers or mechanics working by the day or piece;
2. Second, liens of all other subcontractors or suppliers whose claims are either entirely or principally for materials; and
3. Third, liens of all other principal contractors.

In order to preserve a lien for work performed or materials furnished, a lienor must serve the property owner (or agent) and principal contractor with notice of intent to file a lien at least 10 days before recording the lien statement. The lienor must serve this notice personally or by registered or certified mail. (See § 38-22-109(3), C.R.S.)

Lienors in the first class must file with the county clerk and recorder within two months after completion of the improvement. Lien statements of the second and third class must be filed within four months after completion of the work. (See §§ 38-22-109(4) and (5), C.R.S.)

No mechanics' lien shall hold a property longer than six months after the last work is performed or materials furnished, or completion of the improvement unless a lawsuit is brought within that time to enforce the lien and, unless a notice stating that such action has been commenced, shall have been recorded within that time in the county clerk and recorder's office. (See § 38-22-110, C.R.S.)

The purchaser of a single- or-double family dwelling is given some protection against hidden liens. No lien may encumber such property unless the purchaser had actual knowledge of unpaid lien claimants at the time of conveyance, or unless a lien statement or notice had been recorded within one month after completion of the work or prior to the conveyance, whichever is later. (See § 38-22-125, C.R.S.)

The "**disburser**" (usually the lender or owner) who distributes partial payments as mechanics' work progresses must record a notice stating the name and address of the owner, the principal contractor, if any, the disburser, and the legal description of the land. Lien claimants may give the disburser written notice that they are contracting on matters that may affect the property. Upon such notice being received, the disburser must pay the claimant before paying the claimant's contractor. If the disburser fails to do this and the claimant suffers loss, the disburser is personally liable. (See §§ 38-22-126(4), (5), (6), and (7), C.R.S.)

Funds disbursed to a contractor in accordance with a contract are declared to be in trust for the payment of subcontractors, material suppliers, and laborers. Except for good faith differences of opinion or the existence of performance bonds, wrongful expenditure of these funds constitutes the crime of theft. (See §§ 38-22-127(1) and (5), C.R.S.)

Vendee's lien

If a seller (vendor) defaults in performing the contract, a purchaser (vendee) has a lien against the property for return of all money paid under the terms of the sales agreement. This is an equitable lien and is enforceable by foreclosure.

Vendor's lien

If a seller does not receive the entire sum agreed upon from the buyer, the seller has a lien against the property for any unpaid balance. Like the vendee's lien, this is an equitable charge and is enforceable by foreclosure.

Attachment

An attachment is an encumbrance on property of a defendant in a pending lawsuit for money damages. Colorado and most states permit issuance of a writ of attachment only under special circumstances, such as when the defendant goes into hiding or is about to fraudulently convey or transfer the property. A plaintiff obtaining an attachment must file a bond to protect the defendant against any loss caused by the attachment in the event the plaintiff loses the case.

Lis Pendens

A "**lis pendens**" is not technically a lien upon property; it is constructive notice that a claim against the property exists, and persons could take title to the property only subject to the outcome of the lawsuit. By filing a lis pendens a few days before the expiration of one's lien, a mechanics' lien claimant can keep the lien alive beyond six months.

Fraudulent liens

In some cases, persons have filed liens for false or groundless claims. Although they have no legal effect, such liens can tie up a property being sold and cause legal expense before being declared invalid. Today, any person filing such a claim is civilly liable to the owner of the real property for not less than $1,000 or actual damages caused. In addition, the person commits a misdemeanor punishable by up to two years' imprisonment or a $5,000 fine, or both. (See Commission Position Statement CP-25 regarding recording contracts and real estate licensees' lien status.)

C. General Liens

Judgments

A judgment results from the determination of the rights of the parties through an action at law. Not all judgments involve monetary awards, but a monetary judgment awarded to a plaintiff may become a lien upon the defendant's real property. Some states provide that a judgment must be entered into the judgment docket and indexed before a lien is created. Other states require that a judgment must be recorded in the county recorder's office before the lien becomes effective. Colorado law provides that the judgment lien attaches when the transcript of the docket entry of the judgment, certified by the clerk of the court, is filed (for recording) in the office of the county clerk and recorder. The judgment then becomes a lien on all of the defendant's current or future real property located in that county. The judgment may be filed in any county in the state where the defendant owns property, and the lien thus created continues for six years from the entry of said judgment in the judgment docket. (See § 13-52-102(1), C.R.S.)

Federal tax liens

Federal tax liens may attach to real property because of violation of federal income tax laws, non-payment of gift taxes, or because of the transfer of the real estate through the owner's death.

When a taxpayer is delinquent in the payment of federal income tax, the government may issue a tax warrant that, when filed in the county wherein the taxpayer's real property is located, becomes a lien upon the real estate. Many people believe federal tax liens to have some high priority, but they are only prioritized among other liens or encumbrances by date filed.

Federal government liens for gift taxes are a lien against gift property and continue for ten years. This lien, too, is subordinate to all prior filed liens and encumbrances upon the property.

A federal inheritance or estate tax becomes a lien upon all personal and real property of the decedent. It continues for ten years and stands in priority by date filed.

State tax liens

Like the federal government, Colorado may also acquire liens against real property for the non-payment of state income taxes. A lien for delinquent state income tax becomes a lien upon the taxpayer's real property. This lien priority is established by date of filing and continues for six years unless paid.

Decedent's debts

A decedent's real property passes upon death to the devisees named in a will or if he or she dies intestate (*i.e.*, without a will) according to state laws of descent and distribution. The devisee or heir at law takes title to the property subject to existing liens or encumbrances, and to rights of creditors of the estate. Debts against the estate are paid first out of personal property not specifically bequeathed, then from that which is specifically bequeathed. If the personalty is insufficient to satisfy all debts, then the real property may be sold to pay the remaining debts. Thus, title to a decedent's real estate may be subject to a lien in favor of creditors of the estate.

Chapter 20
Closing Statements

An * in the left margin indicates a change in the statute, rule, or text since the last publication of the manual.

I. Introduction

A real estate closing, or settlement, is the formal procedure by which title passes from seller to buyer and a final accounting is given for all funds received or paid. Closing procedures vary from state to state and even within state borders. In Colorado, title companies normally conduct closings. Real estate brokers, attorneys, or independent closing agents may also conduct closings.

The closing is created through the Contract to Buy and Sell, with the majority of the closing terms determined from the negotiations of the buyer and seller. The contract, along with title documents, a tax certificate, and lender loan documents make up the pieces the closer will use to create the "Closing Statement" for each party. This chapter will cover the rules and requirements for closings and then work through three different closing examples.

II. Rules and Requirements for Closings

A. Responsibility for Closing

The question of who conducts the closing is a contractual matter between the buyer, seller, and closing entity. The Colorado Real Estate Commission-approved Closing Instructions form is required by Rule 7.1.A when it is appropriate for the broker to prepare instructions. Listing brokers and brokerage firms using title companies to hold earnest money are required to have a completed Closing Instructions form signed by the buyer and seller prior to depositing the funds with the title company. Brokers using title companies to perform closings should have the completed Closing Instructions form, signed before title deadline, in the closed file regardless of who is holding the earnest money.

While the majority of closings are completed by a title company's closing section, this does not relieve the employed designated broker and that broker's employing broker of the responsibility from verifying that the closing statement is accurate. Real estate brokers are required by Rules 6.14.A.2 and 6.19.A to provide copies of complete and accurate closing statements to buyers and sellers for any transaction in which the broker assists or acts in a real estate capacity. The designated listing broker and any designated buyer's broker must carefully review their respective closing statements for accuracy even if they will not conduct the closing. Failure to properly review closing documents could result in charges of incompetence or a breach of the broker's statutory or fiduciary duty. Review Commission Rule 6.19.A.

A designated broker who attends the closing must sign the Closing Statement and is primarily responsible for providing a proper Closing Statement to the party the broker assisted or represented. A broker associate must deliver a copy of the statement to the employing broker immediately after the closing.

If the designated broker is unable to attend a closing, the employing broker may designate another broker to attend, in which case both designated brokers assume joint responsibility for the accuracy of the closing statements. The employing broker is responsible for the supervision of both brokers, which gives all three brokers responsibility for an accurate closing. (See Rules 6.3 and 6.19.C.)

B. Preparation of Legal Documents

Although buyers and sellers may be charged a fee for closing, no fee may be charged for preparation of legal documents, except by an attorney representing the buyer or seller. The *Conway-Bogue* decision granted real estate brokers the right to prepare certain legal documents, but prohibits licensees from charging a separate fee for such service. The companion *Title Guaranty* case specifically prohibits title companies from preparing legal documents. Today, title companies only fill in blanks on legal documents under explicit instructions from the broker responsible for the closing. The listing broker who is responsible for completing the deed, bill of sale, and any notes and deeds of trust called for in the contract uses the second section of the Closing Instructions form to hire the title company as scrivener to complete the legal forms. The listing broker will be responsible for paying for all legal documents and for their accuracy. (See CP-7, Commission Position on Closing Costs.)

C. Good Funds

In Colorado, on the settlement date all parties, including the broker, buyer, lender, and sometimes the seller, must furnish good funds for amounts due. No disbursements may be made until all funds are available for immediate withdrawal as "**good funds**" in accordance with § 38-35-125, C.R.S. Disbursements from closing may be made only after the closing entity has received good funds. Good funds are considered to be electronically transferred funds; certified, cashier's, or teller's checks; and other funds that are either received in sufficient time prior to closing to be eligible for immediate withdrawal or are guaranteed by the depository on which they are drawn. (Note: cash is not considered to be good funds under this statute.)

D. Closing Statements (SS 60-6-16) (Formerly called Settlement Statements)

The required Closing Statements (SS 60-6-16) provided to the seller and buyer reflects only that party's credits and debits. Dates of adjustments, names of payees of notes, etc., are shown on the final Closing Statement. Each Closing Statement must be prepared in conformance with Commission Rules 6.14.A and 6.19.B.

E. Signing the Closing Statement

The broker(s) attending the closing must sign and secure the signed approval and acceptance of the buyer and the seller on a copy of their respective closing statements for their own protection and for future inspection by the Real Estate Commission. Original signatures are not required on the copies retained in the office transaction file per § 24-71-101(1), C.R.S. Copies of signed statements satisfy the record retention requirement.

F. Broker Closing Records

The employing or independent broker must retain copies of the pertinent documents listed under "Transaction Files and the Retention of Records" in Chapter, "Escrow Records," for four years. Also see the Transaction File Checklist available on the Division of Real Estate website.

G. Escrow Tax Reserve Account Refunds

The tax reserve has no relationship to the proration of the current year's taxes; the reserve is the amount the lender is collecting from the buyer to pay the property taxes in the future when the bill comes due. This reserve is based on the lender's loan requirement and state law, § 39-1-119, C.R.S. This law provides that any amount held on May 20 in excess of 3/12 of the taxes paid that year must be refunded to the borrower on or before May 30. Payments to a reserve escrow account must be adjusted annually upon reasonable belief of substantial improvements to the property or upon official notification of an increase in the actual amount of taxes levied. Failure to make a refund is subject to interest and penalty.

H. Internal Revenue Service Reporting – Real Estate Sales

Generally, a transaction that consists in whole or in part of a *sale or exchange* for money, indebtedness, property, or services, or any present or future ownership interest must be reported to the IRS on Form 1099-S. This includes many real estate transactions.

However, there are several general exemptions from required 1099-S reporting. One of the most common is the sale or exchange of a "**principal residence**," including stock ownership in a cooperative housing corporation, for $250,000 or less ($500,000 or less for married persons), and the person responsible for closing the transaction receives an acceptable **"Written Assurance Certification"** in the form prescribed by Rev. Proc. 2007-12, 2004-4, IRB 357. Further information, instructions, and forms should be obtained from professional legal counsel. IRS materials may be obtained from www.irs.gov.

I. Certain Cash Transactions

In general, each person engaged in a trade or business who, in the course of that trade or business, receives more than $10,000 in "cash" in one transaction or two or more related transactions within 12 months, must file "**Form 8300**" and give a copy to each party named in the form. Voluntary filings may be made for suspicious transactions of similar or lesser amounts. The report must be retained for five years after the date filed, and fines and penalties apply for failing to file required information. This report is not required if the entity or party receiving the funds meets guidelines under the IRS rule. Further information, instructions, and forms should be obtained from professional legal counsel. IRS materials may be obtained from: www.irs.gov.

J. FIRPTA Withholding

Withholding of Tax on Dispositions of United States Real Property Interests

The disposition of a U.S. real property interest by a foreign person (the transferor) is subject to the Foreign Investment in Real Property Tax Act of 1980 (FIRPTA) income tax withholding. FIRPTA authorized the United States to tax foreign persons on dispositions of U.S. real property interests. A disposition means "disposition" for any purpose of the Internal Revenue Code. This includes, but is not limited to, a sale or exchange, liquidation, redemption, gift, and transfers. A U.S. real property interest includes sales of interests in parcels of real property as well as sales of shares in certain U.S. corporations that are considered U.S. real property holding corporations.

Persons purchasing U.S. real property interests (transferee) from foreign persons, certain purchasers' agents, and settlement officers are required to withhold 10 percent of the amount realized (special rules for foreign corporations). Withholding is intended to ensure U.S. taxation of gains realized on disposition of such interests. The transferee/buyer is the withholding agent. If you are the transferee/buyer, you must find out if the transferor is a foreign person. If the transferor is a foreign person and you fail to withhold, you may be held liable for the tax. For cases in which a U.S. business entity such as a corporation or partnership disposes of a U.S. real property interest, the business entity itself is the withholding agent.

K. Nonresident of Colorado Withholding

Colorado law calls for a possible withholding of potential income tax from the gain on the sale of a property sold by non-Colorado residents. The seller is subject to withholding tax if the seller lives or will live outside of Colorado and the sales price is greater than $100,000. There are several exemptions from this requirement, the primary being the sale of a principal residence that has no withholding . The amount of tax to be withheld is the lower of 2% of the sales price or the seller's entire net proceeds, the balance due the seller. It is the responsibility of the closing entity to collect and send the tax to the Colorado Department of Revenue. The closing entity can be a real estate broker, an attorney, or the closing company. The text of the law (§ 39-22-604.5, C.R.S.) is printed in Chapter, "Tax Factors Pertaining to Real Estate Practice," or by statute number at www.colorado.gov/revenue.

L. Real Estate Settlement Procedures Act (RESPA)

Federal law places certain requirements on lenders concerning the closing of real estate transactions and related matters. The Real Estate Settlement Procedures Act (RESPA) is administered by the Department of Housing and Urban Development (HUD). Almost all lenders that make first-lien loans on one-to-four family units, including condominiums, cooperative units, and mobile homes, are subject to RESPA. Construction loans are not covered.

RESPA requires lenders to provide the applicant, at the time of the loan application or within three days following, a booklet explaining the costs involved and giving a "good faith estimate" (GFE), showing the loan terms and the settlement charges incurred if they go forward with the loan process and are approved for the loan. It explains which charges can change before settlement and which charges must remain the same. It also contains a shopping chart allowing the borrower to easily compare multiple mortgage loans and settlement costs, making it easier to shop for the best loan. The booklet must also disclose the lender's business relationship with any company that the borrower is required to use in legal services, title insurance, or searches.

In addition, under RESPA, no seller of property may require, directly or indirectly, as a condition of selling the property, that title insurance be purchased by the buyer from any particular title insurance company. The penalty for violation of this provision is a fine of up to three times all charges made for the title insurance.

In the usual Colorado transaction, the seller contracts to pay for the title insurance policy and may therefore select the title company without fear of penalty. The purchase of a mortgagee's title policy does not involve the seller, but rather, the lender imposes this requirement on the borrower. A buyer normally purchases a mortgagee's title policy from the same title company used by the seller because it costs less than buying it from another title company. This may create a problem if the listing broker orders an owner's title insurance policy for the seller and thus indirectly influences the buyer's purchase of the mortgagee's policy from the same company to save money. If the buyer is paying for extended coverage for the owner's policy, the buyer may then also determine the title company to provide the coverage. It may be advisable for brokers to have a buyer designate a title insurance company in the written contract.

The lender or lender's agent must also prepare a Uniform Settlement Sheet prescribed by HUD (Closing Disclosure Form (CDF)) and may not charge for its preparation. The CDF must be mailed or delivered to the borrower and the seller on the date of settlement, or as soon thereafter as is practicable. The lender must retain a record copy for two years. The borrower has the right to inspect the CDF completed to set forth those items that are known to the settlement agent at the time of inspection during the business day immediately preceding the day of closing. The lender may ask the broker for help in preparing the CDF, believing that the broker has easier access to some of the information that must be recorded.

The federal government has not pre-empted the states in the area of closing real estate transactions. Colorado law and Commission rule prevail for Colorado closings. The Commission has found that the lender's duties under RESPA regarding closings are not the equivalent of requirements placed on Colorado licensees. The Commission has presently taken the position that buyers and sellers are better protected under law and rule administered by the Commission concerning closing statements. Therefore, it may not be assumed that lender compliance with RESPA fulfills a broker's obligations concerning Colorado law.

M. Special Taxes

Special assessments, such as street paving, storm sewer improvements, etc., if they were in place at the time of sale, even though not yet assessed, are generally paid by the seller under the terms of the approved contract forms, and are never prorated. The amount of such taxes may be obtained from the county treasurer's office if the improvements are already assessed. The reason for debiting the seller is that the buyer has contracted for clear title other than named exceptions. Special taxes are often amortized and paid in installments with the ongoing ad valorem taxes, and therefore it is not unusual for the buyer to agree by contract to assume the balance of taxes due for special improvements. If special assessments are assumed, notation should be made of the amount assumed in the description column on this line, and no entry in either the debit or credit column. On a new loan, the lender may require that the seller pay special taxes at time of closing.

III. The Closing Process

While real estate brokers may complete all closing documents and hold closings in the broker's office, it is more typical for a title company to perform the task. Most often, the closing is done by the closing section of the title company that is supplying the owner's title policy. Even when using a closing company, the listing broker or brokerage will pay for the legal documents created by the closer. The listing broker and listing brokerage is responsible for the overall closing, with the designated brokers being responsible for the accuracy of the closing statement for the party they represent.

Using the Contract to Buy and Sell and other documents, the closer produces a closing statement for the seller and buyer. This statement will show all the debits and credits of the party and the final balance of money the party is to receive or needs to bring to close the transaction. Typically, the seller receives money from, and the buyer brings money to, the closing. A number of items in the closing are simply debits and credits between the seller and buyer, such as sales price, prorated property taxes, water, and HOA dues. Other items will be deducted from the party who agreed by contract or tradition to pay the bill; this amount will show as a credit to broker or closer to collect the funds to make the payment. It is helpful to think of the broker credit column as credit in equals a check out, as all broker credit items are bills that will need to be paid from the closing proceeds. Typically, it is not the broker but the closer who is paying these bills, but the broker is responsible to verify that all figures are correct. Similarly, the broker debit column can be thought of as debit in equals a deposit to the broker. This column is used to record funds the broker has or is receiving, *e.g.*, earnest money and net loan proceeds.

Credit items for the seller or buyer improve that party's bottom line; credits increase what the seller will receive and decrease what the buyer will bring. Debits are the opposite—a debit decreases what the seller will receive and increases what the buyer will bring. The sales price, for example, is always a seller credit and a buyer debit. If not specified in the contract, a charge will be debited to the party who receives the benefit, or according to government regulation or local custom.

Some items will be prorated, which means split between the parties. These items represent ongoing expenses or income such as taxes, water and sewer, HOA dues, rent, and interest on loans. The item is split between the parties based on the number of days each party owns the property during the billing period.

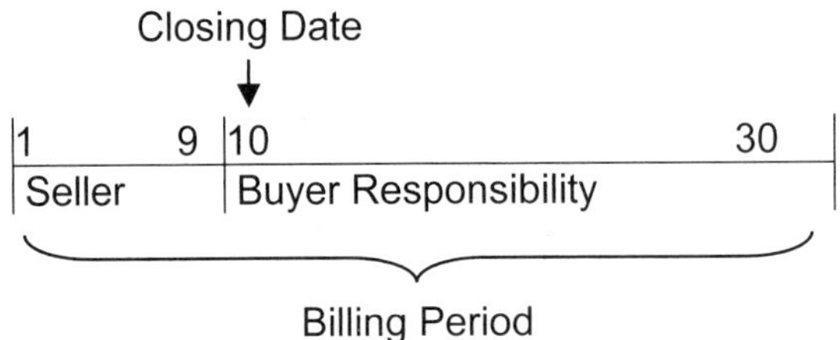

Which party owes the other depends on whether the bill was paid in advance by the seller, or will be paid after closing by the buyer. The illustrations below show how to determine which party will pay in a proration.

Bills Paid in Arrears

Seller owes Buyer: solve the <u>left side</u> of time line

- Paid in arrears by buyer after closing
- Includes items such as: real estate taxes, and interest on most real estate loans

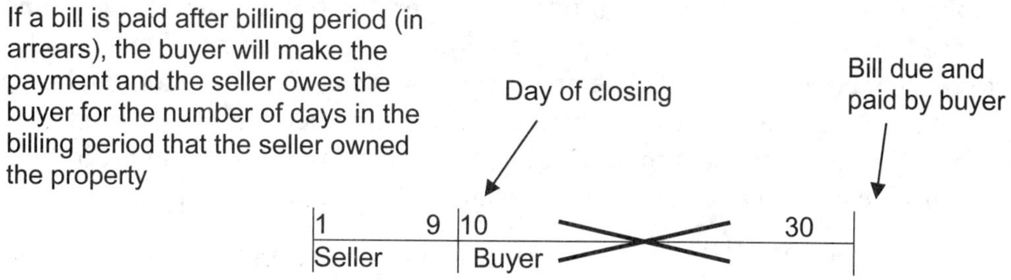

Bills Paid in Advance

Buyer owes Seller: solve the <u>right side</u> of time line

- Paid by seller in advance – before closing (*i.e.*, "prepaid," "paid," "was paid," "has already paid")
- Water and HOA fees are often paid in advance

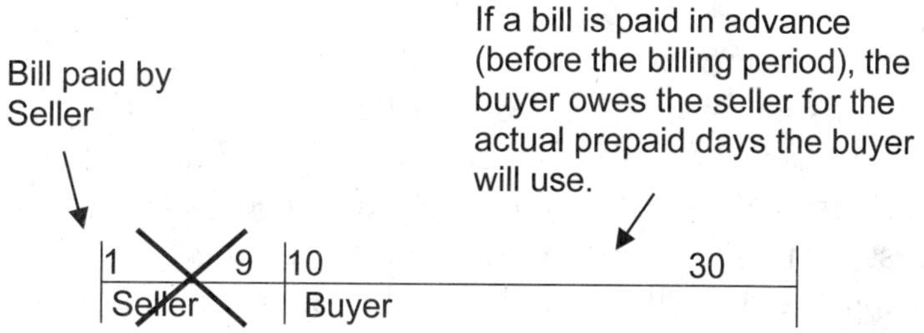

Calculating the Amount owed

The formula for determining the amount of the proration is always the same.

Bill amount □ Number of days in billing period * Number of days owed = Amount owed

In the Commission-approved Colorado contract forms, the buyer owns the property all day on the day of closing. On the Colorado portion of the broker licensing examination, all prorations (unless otherwise stated) are based on a 365-day year and/or the actual number of calendar days in the specific month.

IV. Closing Examples

The following examples illustrate preparation of several real estate closing worksheets. While not all encompassing, they illustrate good closing procedures and requirements. The illustrations assume selection of certain options available in the contract forms and are not intended to be all-inclusive. All fees charged and interest rates used in the following illustrations are examples and may only approximate actual market rates. The provisions of the contract govern who pays for certain items and how they are prorated in the settlement.

A broker who is closing in his or her office might use the worksheet (SS61-9-08) to determine what each party's debit and credits are. (Students also use the worksheet to learn how to allocate and balance a closing.) If the title on a line in the worksheet does not match what the broker needs, the broker simply crosses out the title and inserts what he or she needs. For example, if a broker is preparing for a closing on an assumed loan and needs to record the amount of interest the seller will owe the buyer, the broker might choose line 20, **Interest on New Loan,** cross out the words "New Loan," add "Assumed Loan," and enter the amount to be debited and credited. The approved worksheet also has additional space at the end to add other charges as needed. However the final numbers are determined, it is the seller and buyer's Closing Statement that must be at the closing table. Examples of how the Closing Statements are created from the worksheet are at the end of the chapter.

The general concepts of HUD and Colorado settlements, prorations, and real estate mathematics are discussed more fully in generally available real estate texts.

A. Final Settlement with a Seller Carry Loan

The first example is of a simple seller carry transaction. The closing company will be preparing the documents, including a note and deed of trust for the seller. The following paragraphs explain the computation of the charges and credits to each party for this basic transaction, and the worksheet follows. This transaction is then illustrated as a closing when the buyer assumes the seller's existing loan and then with the buyer receiving a new loan.

1. Facts

On April 22, the listing broker secures a written offer from Harold R. and A. Jean Blue with an earnest money deposit of $5,000. The buyers agree to purchase at the listed price of $250,000 if the sellers will accept a note and trust deed in the amount of $200,000. The sellers have requested that the buyer supply them with a mortgagee title policy and a credit report in order to approve the seller carry loan. The seller is also going to collect reserves for the property taxes of five months and hazard insurance of two months because the seller, acting as a lender, will be paying these bills when they come due in the future.

The sellers accepted the offer and authorized the broker to procure a title commitment. The title commitment was delivered to the sellers and buyers and their respective attorneys. The buyers' loan application was approved, by the sellers, in the amount of $200,000 at 7½ percent interest per year, amortized monthly over a period of 30 years. The first payment on the new loan is due on July 1, the first day of the first complete month after the loan closing date. By contract, the buyer is to obtain and pay for an appraisal.

Both the buyers and sellers complete "Closing Instructions" authorizing the closing company to collect all funds and to make all disbursements. The closing is held on May 10.

The following is an explanation of how each item is charged and adjusted on the worksheet. Worksheet items not pertinent to this transaction are omitted. Many of the items will carry through all three examples.

It is important to remember that the worksheet and Closing Statements show only money that is coming in and going out at the closing table. This means, most typically, that the buyers will have a credit for a loan they are using to buy the property. If the loan is a seller carry or being assumed from the seller, the seller will have a corresponding debit for the loan amount. The reason in either case is that the seller will not receive that money at the closing table. The seller, if giving the buyer a loan, will receive payments over the agreed period. In the case of an assumption, the loan amount is what the seller still owes and the buyer is taking over. In both cases, the loan amount represents money the seller will not receive at closing.

1. **Selling Price** – $250,000. Credit Seller and Debit Buyer.
2. **Deposit (Earnest Money) Paid** – $5,000. Credit Buyer and Debit Broker. Note that each debit to the Broker is money that the Broker has collected or will collect. A broker credit is money the Broker has paid or will pay out of the escrow account. Think of it as a broker debit is a deposit into the Broker's account, and a broker credit is a check that will be written out of the account.
3. **Principal amount of new Loan Payable to** Seller – $200,000. Credit Buyer (money the buyer does not have to bring to closing, but will be applied to the purchase price). Debit Seller, as this money the Seller will not receive at the closing table.
5. **1st Loan Payoff to**: the Acme Loan Co. – $30,000. Credit Broker/Closer, since the Broker will write the check to pay off the Seller's loan. (In most cases, it is the closing company that is writing the checks.) Debit Seller, because it is the Seller's obligation. In order to determine the amount of the payoff, the Broker/Closer requested a payoff statement from the Acme Loan Co. This statement shows the net balance after adjustments of interest, penalties, and credits the Seller may have in the way of tax or insurance reserves.
7. **Taxes for Preceding Year:** $2,051.30 was paid for the year preceding closing and noted in the left-hand column, but not entered in the debit/credit columns. If not paid, they would be Debit Seller, and in this case, the full amount would be a Credit to Broker, who would pay them because the unpaid taxes would be a lien on the property. On a new loan, the lender would deduct any unpaid prior taxes from the loan and pay them for the same reason.
8. **Taxes for Current Year:** $724.98. This is prorated based on last year's taxes ($2,051.30), per check box in the contract. Property taxes are paid in arrears in Colorado, so the prorated amount will always be a debit to the Seller and a credit to the Buyer. All Commission-approved sales contract forms state that taxes will be prorated to (but not including) the closing date. The Seller owned the property from January 1 through May 9, therefore, Debit Seller 129 days' taxes at $5.620000 per day, and Credit Buyer the same amount. This is an adjustment between the parties and not a broker credit (payment), as the Buyer will pay the current year's taxes when due next year. Prorating is based on the actual 365 (or 366) days in the year.

Line 8: Taxes for Current Year:

Taxes for the preceding year were $2,051.30, and this amount will be used to determine the current year's taxes.

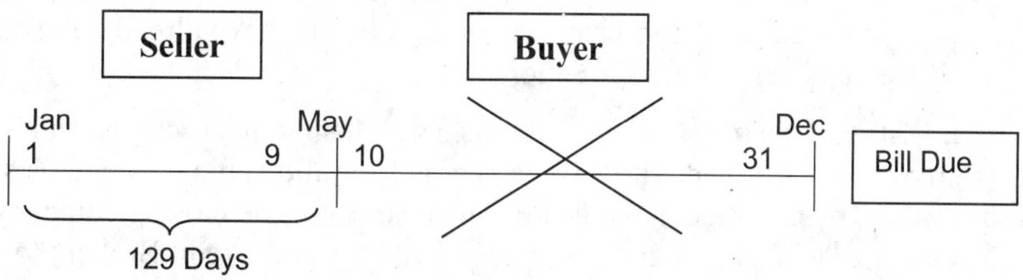

Months	Days (Seller owes)	
Jan.	31	
Feb.	28	$2051.30 □ 365 x 129 = $724.98
Mar.	31	
Apr.	30	
May	9	DEBIT Seller, CREDIT Buyer, who will pay in the future
	129	

13. **Appraisal Fee:** $350. The buyer has requested and agreed to pay for the appraisal. The cost of the appraisal, per the contract, can be paid for by either the Seller or Buyer, depending on which box is checked. The amount will be a Debit Buyer and Credit Broker, who will pay the bill.

19. **Interest on New Loan** – $904.11. Because the Buyer's first loan installment will be due July 1 (and will include interest in arrears for all of June but none of May), and the loan starts on May 10, the Buyer will owe the Seller for May 10 through May 31 (22 days), to be paid at closing. Debit Buyer, Credit Seller.

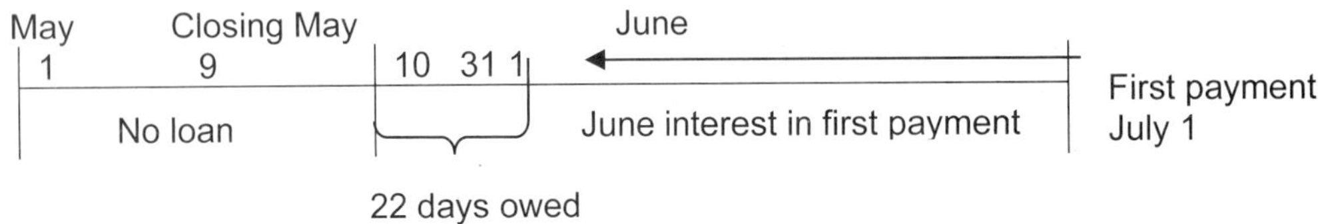

$200,000 x 7.5% ÷ 365 DAYS = $41.0959 per day

Interest on the new loan is $41.0959 x 22 days = $904.11

21. **Premium for New Hazard Insurance** – $675.00. The Seller has required a one-year hazard insurance policy to be purchased, and requires the Buyer to pay in full at closing. Debit Buyer, Credit Broker, who will pay the bill.

22. **Reserves Deposited with Lender**

    22.1 **Hazard Insurance Reserve** – $112.50. The Seller will collect the loan in monthly installments, along with one month's insurance to be held in reserve so that sufficient funds are on hand to pay the annual premium when due. The Seller will require a two-month reserve. Debit Buyer, Credit Seller to hold to pay the insurance bill when due.

    22.3 **Tax Reserve** – $854.65. As with the insurance reserve, the Seller requires a five-month reserve be maintained in escrow, at $170.93 per month with five months collected at closing to pay for the months that have already passed and are due. Debit Buyer and Credit Seller.

24. **Real Estate Closing Fee** – $200.00. The closing instructions and sales contract specify the amount and who will be charged for allowable closing costs. In this case, the parties, by contract, agree to split the charge for the closing company to complete the closing. Debit Buyer and Seller each $100.00, and Credit Broker the full $200.

26. **Title Insurance Premium Owners Policy** – $1,500.00. The Seller has agreed by contract to give evidence of merchantable title, therefore Debit Seller and Credit Broker, who will pay the bill.

27. **Owner's Extended Coverage-** $100.00. The Seller, by contract, has agreed to pay the additional charge for coverage to delete the standard expectations listed in § 8.1.3, Evidence of Title. Debit Seller, Credit Broker.

28. **Title Insurance premium – Lender's Policy** (Mortgagee's) $525. The Seller has requested that the Buyer supply the Seller title coverage in the Seller's role as lender. Debit Buyer, Credit Broker.

30. **Certificate of Taxes Due** – $15.00. This certificate from the county treasurer's office is the Buyer's insurance that the county may not subsequently claim any taxes other than as stated on the certificate. Debit Buyer and Credit Broker. In this example, since there is no contract provision to the contrary, the Buyer (person who benefits) is debited. However, the Department of Housing and Urban Development (HUD) requires this to be a Seller charge on government-insured loans. The broker licensing examination will specify the party to be charged.

35. **Recording**

    35.1 **Warranty Deed** – $10.00. The Buyer is the primary beneficiary of recording the warranty deed because it will make the transfer into the Buyer's name a matter of public record. Debit Buyer and Credit Broker, who will write the check to pay the county clerk and recorder's fees.

    35.2 **Deeds of Trust** – 5 pages @ $10 for the first page, $5 for each additional page + $1 surcharge = $31.00 to record the deed of trust. This is the obligation of the Buyer. Debit Buyer, Credit Broker.

    35.3 **Release of Existing Trust Deed** – $20.00. This releases the original Acme Loan Co. lien, which the Seller and title company want recorded to prove it was cleared. Debit Seller, Credit Broker.

37. **Documentary Fee** – $25.00. State law (§ 39-13-102, C.R.S.) requires the person recording an instrument of conveyance, such as a warranty deed, to pay a documentary fee to the clerk and recorder in the amount of one cent for each one hundred dollars (.01 per $100) of consideration, inclusive of any loan. ($250,000 x .0001 = $25.00). If the total consideration is $500 or less, there is no fee. Debit Buyer, Credit Broker.

44. **Water and/or Sewer Escrow** – $55.09. If the water or sewer is metered, then there is no proration. However, a final reading often needs to be made, and the closer will hold funds in escrow to pay the final bill, usually two to three times the average amount due. Once it is paid, the closer will send any balance to the Seller. In this example, the Seller paid a $96.40 water bill in advance on April 1 for three months (91 actual days), so this bill will need to be prorated. The Seller will have used 39 days of the 91-day period, leaving the Buyer to enjoy prepaid water for 52 days, therefore, Debit Buyer and Credit Seller $55.09 ($96.40 ÷ 91 days x 52 remaining days). Broker writes no check here; it is merely an adjustment between the parties.

$94.60 water and sewer. Paid – April 1 through June 30 (91 days).

May 22
June 30
52

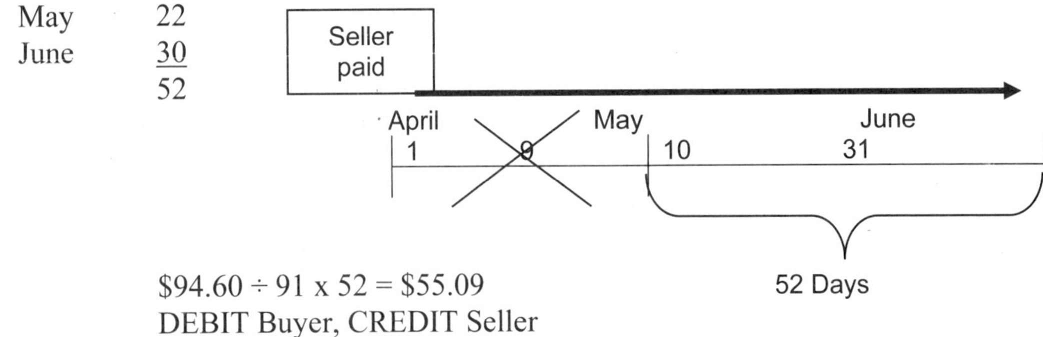

$94.60 ÷ 91 x 52 = $55.09
DEBIT Buyer, CREDIT Seller

52. **Broker's Fee** – $12,500.00. Debit Seller, Credit Broker.

53. **Other**

Title Examination by the Buyer's attorney – $100.00. Debit Buyer, Credit Broker.

Title examination by the Seller's attorney – $100.00. Debit Seller, Credit Broker.

Credit Report – $65.00. Debit Buyer, Credit Broker.

2. Sub-Totals

The totals of each column of debits and credits are made only for the convenience of the closing entity and for a better understanding by the parties in determining the balances or differences between the debits and credits of each party.

3. Balance Due to Seller

The balance due to Seller is $6,881.37. This amount is the difference between the total of the Seller's credits and debits, and is the amount the Seller will actually receive in cash for their home. Remember, most of the Seller's payment will come over time as the Buyer makes the loan payments. This amount is also recorded as a Broker credit since the Broker will disburse all money and write a check to the Seller for the amount owed.. If the Seller owed more than they were receiving, then both the Seller and Buyer would bring money to the closing and the amount would show under the Broker debit column.

4. Balance Due from Buyer

The balance due from the Buyer is $48,097.37. This is the difference between the total of the Buyer's credits and the Buyer's debits. The Buyer must bring this amount in good funds to accomplish the purchase at the time of final settlement. This amount is also entered as a Broker debit, since the Broker will collect and deposit this money.

5. Totals

After entering the amount due to or due from the Seller, the total Seller debits and credits must be equal, and the same is true for the Buyer and Broker totals. If the columns do not balance, then the sheet is incorrect. A Broker's column that does not balance is often from an issue in the Seller or Buyer columns.

6. Closing Statements

The worksheet on the next page will provide the itemized dollar amounts that will be transferred to the required closing statements for the Seller and Buyer.

7. Worksheet for Real Estate Settlement – Seller Carry Loan

See narrative on previous pages

SELLER: John R. and Mary L. Winter PURCHASER: Harold R. and A. Jean Blue

PROPERTY ADDRESS: 7373 West Flamingo Road

SETTLEMENT DATE: May 10, 20xx DATE OF PRORATION: May 9, 20xx

LEGAL DESCRIPTION: Lots 6 & 7, Block 14, Graham Heights, City of Lakewood, County of Jefferson, CO.

		SELLER		BUYER		BROKER	
	Description	DEBIT	CREDIT	DEBIT	CREDIT	DEBIT	CREDIT
1	Selling Price		$250,000.00	$250,000.00			
2	Deposit paid to: Mile High				$5,000.00	$5,000.00	
3	Principal amount of new 1st Loan	200,000.00			200,000.00		
5	1st Loan Payoff to: Acme	30,000.00					30,000.00
7	Taxes Prior Year: – Pd. $2,051.30						
8	Taxes Current Year	724.98			724.98		
	(129 days x $5.620000 per day)						
13	Appraisal Fee			350.00			350.00
19	Interest on New Loan						
11	(22 days x $41.0959 per day)		904.11	904.11			
21	Premium for New Hazard Ins.			675.00			675.00
22	Reserves Deposited with Lender						
	22.1 Hazard Ins. Reserve		112.50	112.50			
	22.3 County Prop. Tax Reserve		854.65	854.65			
24	Real Closing Fee (split)	100.00		100.00			200.00
26	Title Insurance Premium – Owner	1,500.00					1,500.00
27	Owner's Extended Coverage	100.00					100.00
28	Title Insurance Premium – Lender			525.00			525.00
30	Certificate of Taxes Due			15.00			15.00
35	Recording						
	35.1 Warranty Deed			10.00			10.00
	35.2 Deed of Trust			31.00			31.00
	35.3 Release Acme	20.00					20.00
37	Documentary Fee			25.00			25.00
44	Water and/or Sewer						
	(52 days x $1.059341 per day)		55.09	55.09			
52	Broker's Fee	12,500.00					12,500.00
53	Other						
	Buyer's Atty.			100.00			100.00
	Seller's Atty.	100.00					100.00
	Credit Report			65.00			65.00
	SUBTOTALS	$245,044.98	$251,926.35	$253, 822.35	$205,724.98	$5,000.00	$46,216.00
	DUE TO/█████: SELLER	$6,881.37					$6,881.37
	DUE █D/FROM: BUYER				$48,097.37	$48,097.37	
	TOTALS	$251,926.35	$251,926.35	$253, 822.35	$253, 822.35	$53,097.37	$53,097.37

B. Final Settlement with an Assumed Loan

1. Introduction

The next closing statement will have the buyer assuming the seller's loan of $200,000. FHA and VA are two types of loans that allow qualifying buyers to assume the loan the seller originated. The advantage to the buyer is not having to pay loan costs such as appraisal, loan discount points, or origination fees.

2. Assumption Statement

In various circumstances, a purchaser, with consent of the seller and lender, may assume and pay an existing loan. The terms for assumption are part of the Contract to Buy and Sell.

The listing broker will request an assumption statement. This statement is prepared by the lending institution holding the existing deed of trust or mortgage and will contain all the requirements for assumption and the figures for closing. The following is an example of this type of information, which the closing company will use to prepare a closing statement. All of this information will be as of a certain date, in this case, a closing on May 10.

- The loan balance and term. The loan balance on May 1 is $200,000.00, due in 25 years. The loan balance will be a debit to the seller and credit to the buyer. Note: All loans are always a credit to the buyer.
- The rate of interest, amount paid, or the amount of interest earned but not yet due. The statement shows the interest rate is 7.5%, paid in arrears. The next payment is due on May 1; the seller will make the payment on May 1 and this payment will pay for April's interest. This means that when the buyer makes the June payment, it will pay interest for May. The seller will owe the buyer interest on the loan for the portion of May the seller was in the property, in this case nine days (shown below). The assumption statement would also show the amount of any delinquent payments.
- The tax reserve escrowed for the benefit of the mortgagor (the same as in the prior examples in this chapter).
- The insurance reserve escrowed for the benefit of the mortgagor (the same as in the prior examples in this chapter).
- The face amount, date, term, and premium of the existing homeowners insurance policy, and whether or not paid. For this example, the buyer obtains a new policy in the amount of $675.
- The loan transfer fee is $2,000. The statement also states what the lender requires before transferring the loan, *e.g.*, a copy of the contract or deed, or updating the title policy after the closing and conveyance.
- New owner's monthly payment, including principal, interest, taxes, and hazard insurance. This worksheet will use the same data from the prior examples in this chapter.

3. Other Charges and Adjustments for a Loan Assumption

No single real estate transaction will contain every type of charge or adjustment. All closings are similar, but each is unique. The following will explain some of the more common types of charges and adjustments for closing an assumed loan.

Although this entire chapter on closings ascribes obligations to the buyer or seller, any of these obligations may be reversed or changed by contract, unless prohibited by statute or government regulation.

The numbering below conforms to that found on Commission-approved Worksheets and Closing Statements.

19. **Interest on ~~New Loan~~ Assumed Loan.** There is no line for interest on an assumed loan, so when using the worksheet, the broker simply crosses out "New Loan" and notes this is an assumed loan. When a sale is made "subject to" an existing loan that will be assumed by the buyer, and when *interest is charged in arrears*, as in this example, then interest due on the loan from the due date of the last payment to date of settlement should be a *seller debit and buyer credit.* Interest for a monthly-amortized loan with a current unpaid principal balance of $200,000.00 at 7.5 percent interest paid in arrears, closing on May 10 is as follows:

    $200, 000 x 7.5% ÷ 12 months = $1,250.00 per month

    $1,250.00 ÷ 31 days (in May) = $40.3226 per day.

    $40.3226 x 9 days (May 1-9) owned by seller = $362.90

    Debit seller/Credit buyer.

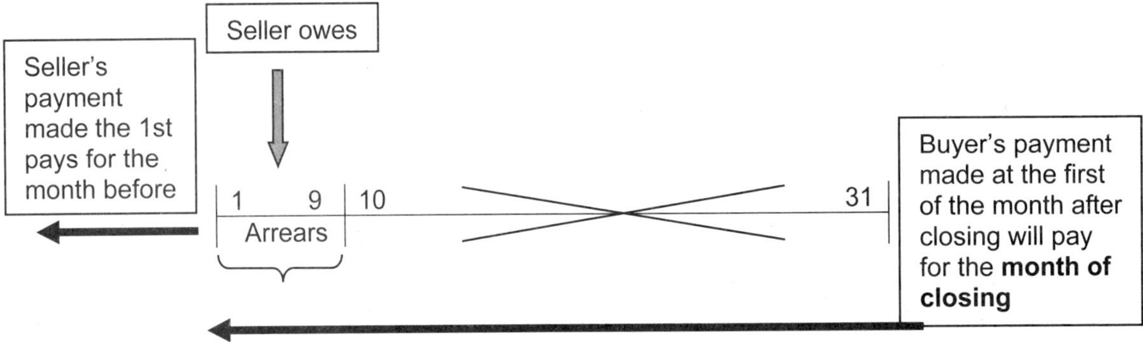

The buyer will then not be penalized when making the June 1 payment, including interest in arrears for the entire month of May, because the buyer will have been compensated at closing for the seller's nine days of interest responsibility.

The above daily rate is based on the 31 actual calendar *days in May* (or the actual closing month), based on the *outstanding principal balance* after the last payment.

This differs from the calculation for interest on a new loan, shown in the new loan, Item 19. Divide the annual interest by the actual number of days in the year to calculate the per diem figure for a new loan. In an assumed loan, because the payment has already been amortized, the interest for the month is determined by dividing by the 12 months in a year. In a new loan, for interest owed for the month of closing, 365 days are used to get the amount.

Loan Payment Due. Any loan payment due or delinquent should be charged to the seller and credited to the broker to pay. This could change the interest and reserve account picture if the buyer is assuming the loan. In this case, the buyer will pay this amount outside of closing.

22.1 and 22.3. **Hazard-Insurance and County Tax Reserve Accounts.** On home loans, most lending institutions today require that at least one month's taxes and insurance be paid with each monthly installment. This is to be placed in the mortgagor's trust account to be available for payment of taxes and insurance when due. In a transaction where an existing loan is being assumed and there is a tax or insurance trust account, this amount is *credited to the seller and debited to the buyer.* All similar escrow accounts are "sold" or charged to the purchaser at the closing, to return money to the seller who will not owe the future bill and set up the account to collect for what the buyer will owe.

38. **Transfer Fee.** This is a charge by the lender for changing the loan records from seller to buyer. Unless otherwise agreed between buyer and seller, this would be a Debit Buyer and Credit Broker.

4. Worksheet for Real Estate Settlement – Assumed Loan

(See narrative on previous pages)

SELLER: John R. and Mary L. Winter PURCHASER: Harold R. and A. Jean Blue

PROPERTY ADDRESS: 7373 West Flamingo Road

SETTLEMENT DATE: May 10, 20xx DATE OF PRORATION: May 9, 20xx

LEGAL DESCRIPTION: Lots 6 & 7, Block 14, Graham Heights, City of Lakewood, County of Jefferson, CO.

		SELLER		BUYER		BROKER	
	Description	DEBIT	CREDIT	DEBIT	CREDIT	DEBIT	CREDIT
1	Selling Price		$250,000.00	$250,000.00			
2	Deposit paid to: Mile High				$5,000.00	$5,000.00	
3	Principal amount of ~~new~~ Assumed Loan	200,000.00			200,000.00		
7	Taxes Prior Year: – Pd. $2,051.30						
8	Taxes Current Year (129 days x $5.620000 per day)	724.98			724.98		
19	Interest on ~~New~~ Assumed Loan						
11	$40.3226 x 9 days	362.90			362.90		
21	Premium for New Hazard Ins.			675.00			675.00
22	Reserves Deposited with Lender						
	22.1 Hazard Ins. Reserve		112.50	112.50			
	22.3 County Prop. Tax Reserve		854.65	854.65			
24	Real Closing Fee (split)	100.00		100.00			200.00
30	Certificate of Taxes Due			15.00			15.00
36	Recording						
	35.1 Warranty Deed			10.00			10.00
	35.2 Deed of Trust			31.00			31.00
37	Documentary Fee			25.00			25.00
38	Transfer Fee			2,000.00			2,000.00
44	Water and/or Sewer (52 days x $1.059341 per day)		55.09	55.09			
52	Broker's Fee	12,500.00					12,500.00
	SUBTOTALS	$213,687.88	$251,022.24	$253,878.24	$206,087.88	$5,000.00	$15,456.00
	DUE TO/~~FROM~~: SELLER	$37,334.36					$37,334.36
	DUE ~~TO~~/FROM: BUYER				$47,790.36	$47,790.36	
	TOTALS	$251,022.24	$251,022.24	$253,878.24	$253,878.24	$52,790.36	$52,790.36

C. Final Settlement with a New Loan

When the buyer is to receive a new loan, the lender's figures and requirements become part of the closing process and closing statement. Typically, the lender hires the closing company to collect and pay bills, similar to what the broker has been doing in previous examples. Any item that might affect the loan or title is now going to be paid for by the lender, not the broker. These loans are called single entry, as many items will appear on the worksheet and closing statement only as a debit to the party that is obligated to make the payment.

For example, the seller will be debited for the title insurance they have by contract agreed to purchase, but there will be no corresponding credit to the broker to pay the title company for this bill. An easy way to conceptualize what is happening to the money is to think of an new, invisible column, in which the lender is receiving the credit, just as the broker's column was used; the lender will write checks for items credited into their column. At the end of the worksheet the broker/closer will need to write a check to pay the seller's net proceed. To balance all of these costs, on a new loan there is always a debit (deposit) for net loan proceeds into the broker's account, the worksheet will now balance, and the broker will have the funds to complete the closing.

In the Lender Loan Statement, the lender states the full amount of the loan the buyer will receive or be credited, the total amount of expenses the lender is paying for, and the difference, which is the net /loan proceeds the broker will receive.

Example:	Total Loan	$200,000.00
	Loan costs paid for by lender	$ 36,822.26
	Net Loan Proceeds to broker	$163,177.74

1. New Loan Lender Statement

The various charges that a lending institution will make to protect their interest will vary from lender to lender. A loan statement from the lending institution using the data from the prior sample problem would probably appear similar to the example below. Note: the appraisal was paid for by the buyer when the appraisal was ordered, and it has been Paid Outside Closing (P.O.C.); however, the charge must be accounted for, and will still show on the Worksheet and Closing Statement with the notation "P.O.C."

Sample Lender's New Loan Statement

Face amount of loan to Buyer:	$200,000.00
Amounts charged by Lender to make the loan:	
Pay-off existing note	$ 30,000.00
Appraisal fee $350 P.O.C.	0
Owner's title policy with extended coverage	1,600.00
Mortgagee's Title Insurance	525.00
Recording Fees	
Warranty Deed	10.00
1st Trust Deed	31.00
Release – Acme Loan Co.	20.00

Documentary Fee	25.00
Tax Reserve	854.65
Loan Origination Fee (1%)	2,000.00
New Hazard Insurance Premium	675.00
Hazard Insurance Reserve	112.50
Interest on Loan May 10-31 (22 days)	904.11
Credit Report	65.00
Subtotal charges made by Lender:	$ 36,822.26
Net Loan Proceeds	$163,177.74

The loan statement above in no way relieves the designated brokers of the responsibility to prepare and provide a closing statement for their client or customer. The loan company has deducted these payouts from the amount of the loan, regardless of which party will be debited. Loan companies may also vary as to which of the costs they wish to collect and pay. Lender-paid items must be appropriately debited or credited by the closing entity as shown on the new loan worksheet below. Lenders are not concerned about which party pays a particular item unless the loan is governed by VA, FHA, or other regulations.

Refer to Commission Rule 6.19.B regarding the reconciliation of the net loan proceeds shown on the loan statement, with the final payment due from the buyer and the final payment due to the seller. This reconciliation may be done by the broker or closing entity on a worksheet, a computer, or in any equivalent form. The broker must retain a copy of the reconciliation statement in the transaction file and make it available for audit by a representative of the Commission.

Broker Reconciliation Statement for New Loan

	Received	Paid – Out
Net Loan Proceeds (Closing Entity)	**$163,158.74**	
Earnest Money Deposit (Broker Escrow)	5,000.00	
Total Money Due from Buyer (Closing Entity)	**49,666.37**	
Other payouts made by broker (Closing Entity)		
Tax Certificate		15.00
Closing Fee		200.00
Broker's Fee		12,500.00
Total Amount Due Seller (Closing Entity)		205,110.11
Totals (See Broker/Closer Column on new loan Worksheet)	$217,825.11	$217,825.11

When the reconciliation above is made on the standard Worksheet for settlement (SS61-9-08), the theory is the same. All debits and credits in the "Broker" column are understood by contract and closing instructions to have been actually collected or disbursed by the lender or closing entity rather than the broker.

2. Worksheet for Real Estate Settlement – New Loan

(See narrative on previous pages)

SELLER: John R. and Mary L. Winter PURCHASER: Harold R. and A. Jean Blue

PROPERTY ADDRESS: 7373 West Flamingo Road

SETTLEMENT DATE: May 10, 20xx DATE OF PRORATION: May 9, 20xx

LEGAL DESCRIPTION: Lots 6 & 7, Block 14, Graham Heights, City of Lakewood, County of Jefferson, CO.

		SELLER		BUYER		BROKER	
	Description	DEBIT	CREDIT	DEBIT	CREDIT	DEBIT	CREDIT
1	Selling Price		$250,000.00	$250,000.00			
2	Deposit paid to: Mile High				$5,000.00	$5,000.00	
3	Principal amount of new 1st Loan				200,000.00		
5	1st Loan Payoff to: Acme	30,000.00					
7	Taxes Prior Year: – Pd. $2,051.30						
8	Taxes Current Year	724.98			724.98		
	(129 days x $5.620000 per day)						
13	Appraisal Fee P.O.C. $350						
19	Interest on New Loan						
	(22 days x $41.0959 per day)			904.11			
11	Loan Origination Fee			2,000.00			
21	Premium for New Hazard Ins.			675.00			
22	Reserves Deposited with Lender						
	22.1 Hazard Ins. Reserve			112.50			
	22.3 County Prop. Tax Reserve			854.65			
24	Real Closing Fee (split)	100.00		100.00			200.00
26	Title Insurance Premium – Owner			1,500.00			
27	Owner's Extended Coverage	100.00					
28	Title Insurance Premium – Lender			525.00			
30	Certificate of Taxes Due			15.00			15.00
35	Recording						
	35.1 Warranty Deed			10.00			
	35.2 Deed of Trust			31.00			
	35.3 Release Acme	20.00					
37	Documentary Fee			25.00			
44	Water and/or Sewer						
	(52 days x $1.059341 per day)		55.09	55.09			
52	Broker's Fee	12,500.00					12,500.00
53	Other						
	Credit Report			65.00			
	Credit Buyer Owner's Policy	1,500.00			1,500.00		
	Net Loan Proceeds					163,177.74	
	SUBTOTALS	$44,944.98	$250,055.09	$256,872.35	$207,224.98	168,177.74	$12,715.00
	DUE TO/[illegible]: SELLER	$205,110.11					$205,110.11
	DUE [illegible]/FROM: BUYER				$49,647.37	$49,647.37	
	TOTALS	$250,055.09	$250,055.09	$256,872.35	$256,872.35	$217,825.11	$217,825.11

V. Closing Statement

From the Worksheet, the broker/closer creates individual Closing Statements for the seller and buyer. The Closing Statement shows only the figures for that party and does not reflect any payments made by the broker or lender. See following examples.

A. Seller's Closing Statement – New Loan

The printed portions of this form, except differentiated additions, have been approved by the Colorado Real Estate Commission. (SS60-6-16) (Mandatory 1-17)

☐ **ESTIMATE** ☒ **FINAL**

CLOSING STATEMENT

☒ **SELLER'S** ☐ **BUYER'S**

PROPERTY ADDRESS: 7373 West Flamingo Road Lakewood Co, 80237

SELLER: John R. and Mary L. Winter BUYER: Harold R. and A. Jean Blue

SETTLEMENT DATE: May 10, 20XX DATE OF PRORATION: May 10, 20XX

LEGAL DESCRIPTION: 6 & 7, Block 14, Graham Heights, City of Lakewood, County of Jefferson, CO

	DEBIT	CREDIT
Selling Price		$250,000.00
Deposit paid to: Mile High		
Principal amount of new 1st Loan		
1st Loan Payoff to: Acme	30,000.00	
Taxes Prior Year: – Pd. $2,051.30		
Taxes Current Year	724.98	
(129 days x $5.620000 per day)		
Real Closing Fee (split)	100.00	
Title Insurance Premium – Owner	1,500.00	
Owner's Extended Coverage	100.00	
Recording		
35.3 Release Acme	20.00	
Documentary Fee		
Water and/or Sewer		
(52 days x $1.059341 per day)		55.09
Broker's Commission	12,500.00	
SUBTOTALS	$44,944.98	$250,055.09
DUE TO: SELLER	$205,110.11	
DUE TO/FROM: BUYER		
TOTALS	$250,055.09	$250,055.09

APPROVED AND ACCEPTED

Buyer/Seller ________________________________

Buyer/Seller ________________________________

Brokerage Firm's Name: ________________________

B. Buyer's Closing Statement – New Loan

The printed portions of this form, except differentiated additions, have been approved by the Colorado Real Estate Commission. (SS60-6-16) (Mandatory 1-17)

☐ **ESTIMATE** ☒ **FINAL**

CLOSING STATEMENT

☐ **SELLER'S** ☒ **BUYER'S**

PROPERTY ADDRESS: 7373 West Flamingo Road Lakewood Co, 80237

SELLER: John R. and Mary L. Winter BUYER: Harold R. and A. Jean Blue

SETTLEMENT DATE: May 10, 20XX DATE OF PRORATION: May 10, 20XX

LEGAL DESCRIPTION: 6 & 7, Block 14, Graham Heights, City of Lakewood, County of Jefferson, CO

	Description	DEBIT	CREDIT
1	Selling Price	$250,000.00	
2	Deposit paid to: Mile High		$5,000.00
3	Principal amount of new 1st Loan		200,000.00
	Buyer's Credit Owner's Policy		1,500.00
7	Taxes Prior Year: – Pd. $2,051.30		
8	Taxes Current Year		724.98
	(129 days x $5.620000 per day)		
11	Loan Origination Fee	2,000.00	
13	Appraisal Fee P.O.C. $350		
19	Interest on New Loan		
	(22 days x $41.0959 per day)	904.11	
21	Premium for New Hazard Ins.	675.00	
22	Reserves Deposited with Lender		
	22.1 Hazard Ins. Reserve	112.50	
	22.3 County Prop. Tax Reserve	854.65	
24	Real Closing Fee (split)	100.00	
	Title Insurance Premium – Owner	1,500.00	
28	Title Insurance Premium – Lender	525.00	
30	Certificate of Taxes Due	15.00	
35	Recording		
	35.1 Warranty Deed	10.00	
	35.2 Deed of Trust	31.00	
37	Documentary Fee	25.00	
44	Water and/or Sewer		
	(52 days x $1.059341 per day)	55.09	
53	Other		
	Credit Report	65.00	
	SUBTOTALS	$256,872.35	$207,224.98
	DUE TO/FROM: SELLER		
	DUE TO/FROM: BUYER		$49,647.37
	TOTALS	$256,872.35	$256,872.35

APPROVED AND ACCEPTED

Buyer/Seller ____________________________________

Buyer/Seller ____________________________________

Brokerage Firm's Name: ____________________________

Broker ____

VI. Other Settlement Items

The items below, while not used in the example closings, appear with enough frequency that a broker should be familiar with them and understand how they affect the closing.

9. **Personal Property Taxes.** Personal property taxes will not be involved unless the property was used for business or income-producing purposes. If such personal property is included in the sale, these taxes are prorated as ad valorem property tax would be prorated. When title passes, the tax responsibility also passes from seller to buyer. Personal property tax situations are more frequently encountered in business opportunity transactions. Some counties demand advance payment of these taxes for the current year and they will be prorated to date of closing.

A. Loan Fees

Typically, these fees are paid by the buyer; however, money the buyer receives from the seller in the form of concessions is often used to cover all or part of these expenses. All are costs related to the buyer's new loan. Mortgage brokers in Colorado are required by law to give buyers a full disclosure and accounting of all loan fees being charged. This section is used to account for and separate these fees for the buyer at closing.

11. **Origination Charge.** The lender and mortgage broker's charges (including processing fees, underwriting fees, document preparation fees, etc.) and points(s) for origination the loan. An adjustment is made in the form of a credit or a charge for broker credits or points paid and the final number is the Adjust Origination Charge.

16. **Tax Service Fee.** If the lender uses a tax service to collect and pay the taxes, there may be a fee to set up this service.

17. **Flood Certification.** This is a fee charged to certify that the property is not in a flood zone. If the property is found to be in a flood zone, the lender will likely require the buyer to acquire flood insurance.

21. **Mortgage Insurance Premium/PMI.** Private mortgage insurance is usually required on loans with a loan-to-value ratio above 80%. Debit Buyer.

26. **Loan closing fee.** If there is a separate fee for the closing company to close the loan, in addition to the real estate, the fee is shown here.

30. **Endorsements.** These are additions added to the Mortgagee's title policy to further protect the lender.

B. HOA Fees

41. **HOA-CIC Document Procurement Fee.** If the Home Owner's Association (HOA) charges for copies of the Common Interest Community (CIC) documents the buyer has requested, the fee will show here. The contract calls for the seller to supply copies to the buyer. Debit Seller, Credit Broker.

42. **HOA Transfer/Status Letter Fee.** The seller has agreed in the contract to provide a status letter; if there is a charge for the letter, the amount will be posted here.

43. **HOA Dues.** The amount of any prorated dues, which are most often paid in advance, will be shown here. If paid in advance, Credit Seller and Debit Buyer the prorated share.

44. **HOA Working Capital.** A charge to buyer or seller by the HOA for capital is shown in this section.

C. Rentals

50. **Rents/Rent Proration.** Adjustment should be made for any rent collected by the seller from a tenant in advance, typically for a month. The prorated share for the rental period is always credited to the buyer, who will not receive possession after closing, and debited to the seller, who collected the rent for the entire period. Delinquent rents are not prorated.

51. **Security Deposits.** If the property is a rental and the seller is holding a tenant's security deposit, the full amount will be debited from the seller and credited to the buyer. By contract, the seller agrees to inform the tenant of the new owner's name and address.

D. Seller Concessions

52. **Seller's Concessions.** This total amount of money the seller has agreed to give the buyer to assist in paying costs of buying the property.

Closings are one of the highlights of a real estate broker's job. This is when all the broker's hard work pays off and the brokerage gets paid. Many complications can arise in the closing of a real estate transaction. Not all variations can be foreseen. When all parties are present at a closing, new contracts may evolve, there may be a necessity for escrow agreements, or rental agreements may be necessary if occupancy is not given at the time of transfer of title. The broker is responsible for ensuring that any contractual changes made at closing are reduced to writing. Brokers should continue their education on the subject of closings throughout their careers.

VII. Statutes, Rules, and Position Statements Affecting Closings

A. Statutes

§ 38-35-125, C.R.S.	Good funds
§ 39-13-102, C.R.S.	Documentary fee
§ 39-1-119, C.R.S.	Lender reserve
§ 39-22-604.5, C.R.S.	2% withholding tax for nonresident sellers
§ 24-71-101(1), C.R.S.	Electronic signatures
§ 12-10-203(5)(c), C.R.S.	Employing broker supervision responsibility
§ 12-10-217(1)(r), C.R.S.	Employing broker supervision responsibility
§ 12-10-222, C.R.S.	Employing broker negligent supervision

B. Rules

5.21	Licensee must produce records; HOA records belong to HOA
6.14.A	Document preparation and duplicates
6.19	Closing responsibility; closing statement distribution
6.3.C	Reasonable supervision
6.3.D	High-level of supervision
7.1.A	Use of Commission Approved Forms; re: closing instructions

C. Commission Position Statements:

CP-7 Commission Position on Closing Costs

VIII. Useful Closing Web Sites

To view the most current approved forms:
www.dora.state.co.us/dre

Questions regarding IRS reporting:
www.irs.gov.

FIRPTA Withholding: www.irs.gov Then type "form 8288" in the search bar.

Colorado Nonresident withholding:
www.revenue.state.co.us

RESPA:
http://www.hud.gov Then type "RESPA" in the search bar.

Chapter 21:
Escrow Records

An * in the left margin indicates a change in the statute, rule, or text since the last publication of the manual.

I. Introduction

This chapter presents the general concepts and guidelines necessary to establish and maintain all escrow accounting records. Regulations governing these operations are found in §§ 12-10-202, -203 and, and -217, C.R.S.; Rules 5.1-6.19, 6.25.A, and 6.3; and the subdivision references cited in Part IV of this chapter. Other laws related to real estate practice and property management are presented in this manual. Important information about industry developments, legislation, or changes in regulations is published quarterly in the *Colorado Real Estate News*. Licensing information, applications, portions of the manual, and past newsletters are published at: www.dora.state.co.us/dre. New brokers may obtain startup information from the Small Business Assistance Center, website at www.coloradosbdc.org.

A. Concepts and Responsibilities – A Chapter Summary

The **"Escrow Accounting Equation"** is the cornerstone for all related accounting processes. It states that at any given point in time, the reconciled escrow bank account ***cash balance*** must equal the corresponding escrow ***account liabilities*** per contract.

When the employing broker receives any money belonging to others, five obligations are generally undertaken: (1) the broker receives custody of the escrow cash asset as a "fiduciary" or "trustee," rather than as its legal owner; (2) the broker agrees to perform various duties for another, who is termed a "beneficiary" in the Commission regulations; (3) the custody, control, ownership, and use of each escrow asset is governed by the underlying contractual agreement, any applicable regulation, or other superseding law; (4) the broker is required to deposit and account for these assets in a prescribed manner; and (5) the broker remains responsible for the outcome of these acts when others perform them on his or her behalf.

Escrow bank accounts are unique "accounting entities," which are separate in purpose and function from the other accounts commonly used in a real estate business. "Escrow" and "trust" are synonymous descriptive terms for the broker's fiduciary account in all Commission regulations. This type of account excludes money handled for ongoing personal business income, expenses, commissions, and/or other non-licensed business transactions. Funds belonging to the same "common class" of beneficiaries are normally deposited into a "pooled" escrow bank account, unless otherwise prohibited by other law or agreement between the parties concerned. In other cases, the broker may choose to open a separate escrow bank account for funds held in each separate engagement. This structure is frequently found in the sale of luxury homes where large earnest money deposits are held in separate interest-bearing accounts, when the company manages broker-owned properties, or when the broker manages other significant accounting entities. The use of separate trust accounts for each significant entity provides greater protection against possible "illegal commingling of funds," described below. Diagrams showing the typical flow of funds and common company bank account structures for sales and management companies are included in this chapter.

The general concepts and responsibilities for maintaining escrow accounts apply to all types of real estate accounting activity. Common functional activities include establishing and maintaining bank accounts; collecting, evaluating, and recording accounting information; maintaining transaction files; reconciling accounts with related real estate business records and documents; reporting accounting activity to interested parties; training and supervising staff; and storing records for later use.

Each escrow bank account must have a corresponding set of office accounting records. These may be kept manually or by use of a computer. The terms for the required records are: a "journal," the individual "beneficiary ledgers," the "broker's ledger," the "monthly bank reconciliation worksheet," and the related "property transaction files." Sample accounting records and transactions are illustrated in Part II, Section D of this chapter; blank forms are found in the chapter appendix. These forms may be modified within the constraints of Rule 5.14 to suit business needs.

The bank reconciliation process used for maintaining escrow accounts differs in a significant way from other methods used to reconcile personal or other business accounts. The goals of this process are to ensure that proper records have been established for actual events and to verify the information recorded in the office records agrees with the activity shown on the monthly bank statement. This requires examining certain financial provisions found in the pending sales contracts, leases, management agreements, and related business records and recording the financial data in the corresponding escrow account journal and ledgers. The total resulting "contractual liability" is then reconciled to the escrow bank account cash balance at a given point in time. The results are summarized on a form called the "bank reconciliation worksheet." Absent missing documents, unintentional errors, or internal fraud, this "worksheet" is a snapshot of the overall condition of the escrow accounting equation. If a properly prepared worksheet balances, it indicates that all escrow liabilities are fully funded and all financial obligations are properly reported in both the accounting and banking records. When the worksheet does not balance, the cause may be due to more serious conditions described next.

In order to avoid illegal commingling of funds, proper control over paying expenses must be maintained on a day-to-day basis; this means *never overspend or misuse* any beneficiary's available cash balance. Such misuse is described as "converting" (stealing) and/or "diverting" (borrowing or loaning) money without authorization. These practices endanger the public interest by removing the beneficiary's property from the account without settling the corresponding contractual liability as agreed; the resulting cash shortage will mean that in the event of any unexpected termination of business after the misuse, some liabilities cannot be paid from the available escrow account cash balance. Other practices often accompanying this condition are: (1) failing to deposit funds into an authorized account, (2) failing to account for the activity performed, (3) misrepresenting the status of financial information to others, and (4) other ongoing uncorrected accounting errors. The Commission may impose administrative discipline in these cases, and other civil or criminal statutes may also apply.

The general function of a journal is similar (but not necessarily equivalent) to a check register. The journal reports information about all events causing a change in the escrow bank balance over a given period of time. The function of each individual beneficiary ledger is to account for the information pertaining to all changes in the amount of cash held for a specific party during the same period of time.

Because of the possibility for internal theft, blind trust in the "equality" of the accounting equation will not guarantee that the intervening escrow accounting entries were properly made or represent corresponding real events. The employing broker and another officer or company owner, with assistance from an appointed and independent internal audit committee, should establish, review, and perform the following ***critical supervisory functions*** on an ongoing basis: (1) examine all company banking and accounting activity for proper operation, (2) review the quality of all services provided by all associates and any affiliated businesses entities, (3) maintain effective channels of communication, community feedback, and personal involvement in key operating processes, (4) enforce and promptly correct improper practices or violations of company policy, and (5) provide adequate compensation, necessary training, and adequate supervision to minimize the "controllable" means, motivation, and opportunity for financial harm to the public.

II. Sales Escrow Accounts

A. The Escrow Bank Account

General Operation

The Federal Deposit Insurance Corporation (FDIC) provides "dollar-for-dollar" insurance coverage for money held in all accounts maintained by a specific depositor-beneficiary at an insured bank up to a maximum amount of $250,000 per depositor. Supplemental private deposit insurance should be considered when this amount is exceeded.

The broker's use of a non-escrow business checking account for escrow money will result in commingled ownership of these funds. The identity of the individual depositors or their personal financial interest in the total bank account balance will not be determinable from the bank's own legal records. As a result, this type of account will only qualify for $250,000 of FDIC insurance coverage in total. In the event of a bank failure, each depositor would be reimbursed according to the percentage his or her balance constitutes to the total account balance. Any excess of funds deposited over the share of the coverage will be treated as "uninsured loss," which will be the broker's responsibility. To overcome this limitation, the bank's customer deposit agreement must identify the broker as a "fiduciary," and the records prescribed in Rule 5.14 must be kept on a day-to-day basis. If those conditions are met, each beneficiary's coverage will be extended to the full $250,000 limit per individual depositor. The escrow account title format shown on the next page must be used to show the fiduciary nature of any real estate escrow account owned by the broker.

The employing broker, a licensed sole proprietor, the corporation, the partnership, or the LLC are the only "persons" authorized by statute to own and operate company escrow accounts. Employed brokers may not establish company escrow accounts in their own names. However, they may be designated as alternate signers on any escrow or company bank account, as long as the employing broker can independently operate all company-owned escrow accounts. In order for the broker to delegate the authority to perform accounting duties to another, the duties must be accepted in a dated and signed job description. The employed broker is then primarily accountable for the outcome of the acts and duties within their control, and the employing broker will have responsibility for supervision of the duty as well.

The following diagram illustrates common alternative flows of funds through an escrow account:

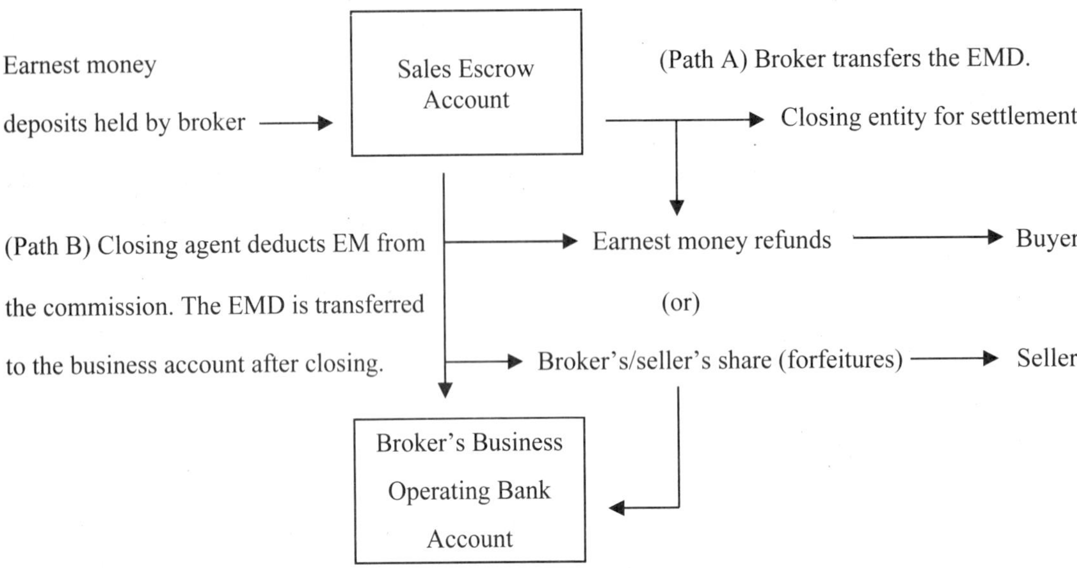

How to Open Escrow Bank Accounts

Public notice of the fiduciary nature of the escrow bank account must be given by the identification shown on the bank's customer deposit agreement described in Step 2:

1. Select a Colorado depository that offers FDIC insurance coverage or as authorized for the specific engagement. Information about the financial strength of various institutions may be obtained from the Weiss Group, 561-625-6685, www.weissgroupinc.com.
2. Include the following "**fiduciary elements**" in the account title. These must identify the true owner of the account, specify the type or purpose of account being established (sales, management, homeowner association, etc.), include one of the fiduciary words "escrow" or "trust," state the employing broker's personal name, and show his or her fiduciary capacity as "broker." The employing broker must be able to independently control and operate all escrow bank accounts, but others may be designated as signatories as well. These elements may be abbreviated to facilitate printing the broker's monthly bank statement heading, checks, and deposit stock. The general account title format follows:

   Licensed brokerage name and/or d.b.a. Type of escrow,

   Statement mailing address
3. Obtain copies of the customer deposit agreement and signature card(s) and retain them with office escrow records for later Commission inspection. Update these records whenever there is a change of authorized signatories or bank ownership.
4. Execute the "Notice of Escrow or Trust Account" (see Appendix, Exhibit A). This form may be typed on the broker's stationary. Retain for later inspection.
5. In order to reduce the risk of accounting error and internal theft, select (and/or design) company checking supplies that provide a clear record of individual accountability

for all accounting and banking operations performed on the broker's behalf. Electronic imaging of banking records (and other office files) is permitted when reproductions and endorsements are easily readable and are retrievable upon reasonable request (see Rule 6.24). The personal name of the employing broker acting for a corporation, partnership, or limited liability company is not required on deposit slips or check stock.

6. Please note: The first line of the account heading is reserved for the legal identification and of the true account owner. Never use a third-party name or identification number on a company-owned account, as this practice may enable the other owner(s) to independently transact business without the broker's consent. The fiduciary elements shown in Step 2 are not required if the account is owned by a third party, *e.g.*, a homeowner's association or a commercial property owner; is to be managed by the broker; and the broker is only added as another signor on the account. All independent account signors should understand the applicability and scope of any "setoff or seizure rights" stated in the bank deposit agreement.

Other Types of Escrow Accounts

The following guidelines apply to the use of interest-bearing accounts, stock market investments, Colorado Association of Realtors Housing Opportunity Fund (COLORADO REALTOR FOUNDATION) accounts for affordable housing programs, credit union accounts, and the transfer of earnest money deposits to a third party or closing entity.

Written disclosure and consent must be obtained for use of a passbook interest-bearing account or certificate of deposit. This requires a description of the account used, the risks involved, any applicable restrictions or penalties, and an agreement for the ownership of any subsequent income or loss. If there is no disclosure or consent from the beneficiary, any earnings belong to the beneficiary and any loss or penalty will be the broker's responsibility. The interest earned will normally appear on the monthly bank statement, and must be recorded in the broker's journal and/or allocated to the ledger of each beneficiary-owner. Any interest contractually retained by the broker must be entered on the "broker's ledger." An IRS Form 1099-INT must be sent to the beneficiary at year-end.

The city of Boulder currently requires the payment of a statutory rate of interest to tenants residing in that jurisdiction. Contact the city of Boulder or the Boulder County Apartment Association at (303) 494-9048 for further information on the current requirements. The simplest way of dealing with this matter is to use a non-interest-bearing account and fund the tenant interest payment by charging the statutory amount to the owner. Otherwise, the broker will have to account for and periodically allocate the differences in market and statutory rates to the owners concerned. The solution is a business policy decision that should be disclosed in the management agreement.

In general, a broker may not independently establish an escrow bank account outside Colorado, or deposit money belonging to others in a stock market or institutional "cash-asset management investment account," without the informed written consent and specific waiver of the applicable statutory requirements by those concerned. However, Commission policy permits the deposit of credit card receipts into an out-of-state bank clearing account (to secure lower processing rates) if the broker's records are able to track individual transactions in and out of the clearing account by name, date, purpose, and amount. In contrast, any investment made solely in the broker's name, where escrow funds are pledged as collateral for brokerage credit, capital loans, or as security for other institutional investments and/or debt, is prohibited. Similarly, an investment of escrow funds is prohibited when federal insurance coverage only applies to the sponsoring institution or its agents for unlawful events, but fails to insure the beneficiaries on a "dollar-for-dollar" basis.

Participation in COLORADO REALTOR FOUNDATION or a similar non-profit qualified community affordable housing program is voluntary. The interest earned is transferred to the program as the interest beneficiary only (IBO), using the COLORADO REALTOR FOUNDATION program non-profit tax identification number. The term "COLORADO REALTOR FOUNDATION (IBO)" may appear on the left side of either the first or second line in the account format shown in Step 2, according to bank requirements. The term "COLORADO REALTOR FOUNDATION IBO" is not printed on company check stock or deposit slips. Other company programs that are established by the broker to benefit needy employees, a class of citizens, a favorite social service, a medical organization, or a charity are not eligible for treatment as a "qualified community housing program." The commissioners voted to limit such participation to non-profit real estate activities within their jurisdiction. This limitation does not prevent a written agreement between parties in a specific transaction to distribute interest earned to whomever they wish. Further information is available from the local board or Colorado Association of Realtors, (303) 790-7099.

When a contract is amended to allow the transfer of the earnest money to a third party or "closing entity," the broker will not need to maintain the normal escrow accounting records required by Rule 5.14. Instead, Rule 5.13 requires retention of the following items in the property transaction file: (1) a signed and dated receipt from the third party designated to hold the funds, (2) a copy of the earnest money check, and (3) a copy of any endorsement needed to make this transfer. The type of depository account used by the third party must be consistent with that provided in the approved contract form. The party (or parties) concerned must approve the terms and costs of any third party "custodial/escrow agreement" used in the transaction; however, such agreements will not "automatically nullify" the duties found in other Commission-approved forms.

Special Use of Accounts

The provisions of Rules 5.5, 5.8.A, and 5.10 affect how various bank accounts may be used.

Rule 5.8.A allows the liability ("financial responsibility") for the timely return of a tenant's security deposit to be transferred from the broker to the property owner when there is a consistent agreement to this effect in the management agreement/addendum, and in an accompanying notice to the tenant in the lease/addendum or by first-class mail. The security deposit may then be paid directly to the property owner, held in the owner's management escrow account, or used as that owner's management operating capital. This option may not be advisable when poor business relationships exist among those concerned.

B. The Cash Receipts and Disbursements Journal (The "Journal")

General Concepts

The "journal" is described in Rule 5.14.A and is maintained when the broker receives or is designated as custodian for any money belonging to others, as defined in Rule 1.34. A blank form is in the chapter appendix, Exhibit B.

The journal, the corresponding ledgers, the bank account, and the related contractual liabilities are always intended to be self-balancing and equal to each other. The journal is maintained on a "cash-basis" unless the beneficiaries agree to use accrual accounting. Cash-basis accounting means that receipts and payments are recorded when received for deposit or paid. The journal remains open until the corresponding bank account and open ledgers are closed.

Intentionally reporting expenses as "paid," or amounts as "received" in any escrow record or corresponding accounting or beneficiary report, without mailing the check or making a bank deposit, is a serious form of misrepresentation, failure to account, and possible fraud. Brokers can create similar conditions when they receipt for funds specified in the contract but do not take possession of the money and/or deposit it in a reasonable time.

Concerns may arise as to the validity of an acceptance of an offer when a faxed copy of the earnest money check is submitted to the listing broker or designated custodian. The absence of an actual earnest money check at the time of (or one day after) the acceptance does not invalidate the contract. Other provisions will normally provide the necessary "legal consideration" to make the acceptance binding. Some financial institutions are willing to accept a fax copy of a check as the maker's authorization for transfer of funds to a designated custodial account. Brokers are advised to have prior written agreement for use of this process, verify the receipt of "good funds" by the designated custodian, and communicate the results promptly to those concerned.

The "ending journal balance" includes all money held in escrow (pending closing or final disposition) for all beneficiaries, including any unearned funds belonging or ultimately due to the broker and/or the results of other bank adjustments and service charges. The escrow cash account balance is normally shown in the current asset section of the escrow account balance sheet, while the total for the corresponding total for all pending ledgers appears in the current liability section. Changes in these ending balance sheet amounts are explained by the transactional data recorded in the cash receipts and disbursements journal during the monthly accounting period. A negative escrow bank balance, an accounts receivable, or a debit balance in the escrow accounts payable or the escrow "equity" section may be the result of error or illegal commingling of funds.

A general policy of accepting cash (legal tender) in ongoing transactions is discouraged without corresponding fidelity insurance and effective internal controls. Most thefts are not detected until the loss reaches $20,000 to $35,000, and recovery depends on proving a person's specific responsibility for the disappearance. Certain cash sums totaling $10,000 or more require reporting on IRS Form 8300, per Publication 1544, which is available from www.irs.gov/.

Handling Earnest Money and Making Deposits

Rules 5.12.A, 5.7, and 5.13 require the timely deposit of escrow funds and govern who is to receipt for and hold such money.

There are several accepted options for handling earnest money. These funds may be held: (1) in an account specifically identified in the sales agreement, (2) in an escrow account maintained by the buyer's agent, (3) in the listing agent's escrow account, or (4) in any other account acceptable to the buyer and seller.

The party designated to hold the deposit must be clearly identified in the sales contract. A check for the earnest money should accompany the offer until it is accepted. A buyer's agent holding the deposit may forward a copy of the earnest money check with the offer. If the offer is rejected, this broker may simply return the check to the prospect. Submitting an offer to a seller that specifies the receipt of earnest money without actual receipt and deposit of the money in a reasonably agreed-upon time is a serious misrepresentation and may violate federal law or HUD regulation.

Unless otherwise agreed, earnest money deposits held by the specified broker must be deposited not later than the *third* business day after notice of acceptance of the contract. The broker should keep a copy of the validated escrow deposit slip and earnest money check in the office transaction file for later inspection. The initial deposit slip and/or a subsequent wire transfer form to a third party or closing entity must show the buyer's name and the related property description, and must be recorded in the journal and the specific beneficiary's ledger. If a promissory note is initially received as the earnest money deposit, no entry of the deposit is made until the note is redeemed. The use of a promissory note must be authorized in the contract and must include a specific date for redemption. Timely collection of the note is essential, and notice of a failure to redeem the note on its due date must be communicated promptly to the seller. A failure to inform the seller of a default on the note may result in a complaint for misrepresenting the status of the contract.

Money received for property management and short-term rentals must be deposited within five business days after receipt unless the parties agree otherwise. All other types of money belonging to others must be deposited not later than the *third* business day after receipt or as provided in the agreement with those concerned.

Earnest Money Disputes and Unclaimed Property

The broker should retain correspondence that shows reasonable efforts were made to return refundable amounts to the proper beneficiary.

If the beneficiary cannot be contacted, the broker should be guided by the provisions set forth in the Colorado Unclaimed Property Act (effective July 1, 2020) found at Title 38, Article 13, C.R.S. The guidance of a legal professional in the disposition of unclaimed property is also recommended.

When a party fails to cash a refund check six to twelve months after its issue, or if the broker has reason to presume the funds have been abandoned, a "stop payment" order may be issued to the bank and the amount will be added back to the journal balance. The funds are then entered on an "Unclaimed Property Ledger," and a note of this event is made on the original beneficiary's ledger to close it out and place it in the property transaction file. Any subsequent activity is reported on this continuing ledger, showing the status or disposition of such property through the appropriate escheat fund. If a party later claims this amount before transfer to the escheat fund, a new check is issued and recorded in the unclaimed property ledger and the escrow account journal. A copy of the new check should also be placed in the property transaction file. Unclaimed and undisputed items may be transferred to the Colorado Fund prior to the end of the five-year period.

If a dispute over ownership of a deposit develops, the guidelines found in the Commission position statement on earnest money deposits (CP-6) should be followed. If a court refuses to accept custody of funds tendered, the money must be held in escrow until there is a resolution of the dispute, a release is obtained from one party, the statutory record-keeping period under § 12-10-217(1)(k)C.R.S., has expired (four years), or there is good reason to believe the dispute has been abandoned. Subject to legal advice or further instructions from the parties concerned, the disputed but abandoned funds may be transferred to the escheat fund in the original depositor's name. When earnest money is held by a third-party closing entity, where return of the deposit to a buyer is not disputed and the buyer cannot be located but agreed to pay all or part of any third-party escrow agreement fee, then the broker may instruct the third-party closing entity to distribute the "net amount" to the appropriate escheat fund. The Commission has no guidance on making this business decision.

If the licensed real estate business is terminated before any notice of dispute is received, and the amount is abandoned, the money may be delivered to the appropriate escheat fund in the original depositor's name. Further information, other state search links, and software for reporting these items in Colorado can be obtained from Colorado Great Payback office by calling (800) 825-2111 or online at www.colorado.gov/treasury/gcp/.

C. The Beneficiary's Ledger Record (The "Ledger")

General Concepts

The "ledger record" is described in Rule 5.14.B. This record separates one person's transactional activity from all other data recorded in the journal and processed through the escrow bank account. Blank forms for the beneficiary and broker's ledgers are found in the chapter appendix, Exhibit C.

There are two types of ledgers used for normal escrow accounting functions: those for **external beneficiaries** assisted or represented during the engagement (the seller, buyer, a management property owner, the tenant, or unclaimed property described in the preceding subsection), and for the **internal beneficiary**, the employing broker, who maintains the account and/or provides any financing services to the external beneficiaries per Rules 5.10.B and 5.14.D. The "broker's ledger" record is described below. According to industry custom, the ledger maintained for each guest stay in short-term (hotel type) property management is called a "folio."

In a manual record-keeping system, all pending ledgers are usually maintained in a three-ring notebook and are alphabetized by client name or by address; different buyers may have deposits on the same ledger, and these should be identified as "backup offers." Closed ledgers are kept with copies of the deposit slip and earnest disbursement checks in the property transaction file. The journal pages are placed in front of the pending ledgers and broker's ledger in this notebook.

When a separate savings account is maintained for each beneficiary with proper disclosure and authorization for the use of interest-bearing accounts, the monthly bank statement will satisfy the record-keeping requirements for both the "journal" and a "ledger." However, the bank may charge a higher service fee for extensive use of these temporary accounts and may restrict the number of open accounts allowed to one broker at a time. This shortcut method is acceptable with maintenance of proper identification of individual parties in the deposit slips and check memo lines.

Choose a software program that has journal and ledger capabilities. Responsibility for ensuring compliance with Commission requirements rests with the broker and not the software developer. The broker may consult with the financial examination section to ensure that any proposed system will meet regulatory requirements. The cost and/or accounting skill required for proper use of software will vary according to the software program selected. The more complex software applications are generally designed for trained and/or experienced accounting personnel to use in high-volume business operations.

Ledger Operation

A new beneficiary ledger/software sub-account record is opened or established when the broker receives, as the designated contractual custodian, any money as defined in Rule 1.34, or when the broker places company funds in the escrow account to pay bank operating expenses. Each beneficiary ledger is "closed" when all funds pertaining to the transaction have been disbursed according to contract or operation of law, or when the escrow account is no longer used and any remaining funds have been distributed to the proper parties or a state escheat fund. Any interest earned on the account that appears on the monthly bank statement and that is owned by a beneficiary is recorded in the journal and the appropriate ledger(s).

Each beneficiary ledger must show the names of the parties to the specific transaction, the address or description of the property, transaction dates, check numbers, transaction amounts, a resulting balance, any appropriate deposit/receipt or transaction file reference numbers, and any other information of interest to the broker. The ending balance in an electronic accounting system may be determined when the accounts are reconciled, but care must be taken to never overspend or misuse the beneficiary's available cash balance.

Any rental income and expense and any security deposit held by the broker must be reported on separate owner and tenant ledgers. When the broker is responsible for return of a deposit, care must be taken to never spend this money for the ongoing operation of the owner's property. Security deposits must be returned in a timely manner with proper accounting per § 38-12-103(1), C.R.S. The procedure for transfer of the responsibility for return of the security deposit to the owner is set forth in Rule 5.8.A and in the Commission position statement CP-5, Advance Rental and Tenant Security Deposits.

All ongoing owner expenses and net proceeds should be paid from the escrow account directly to the parties concerned. These amounts should not be transferred to the "company operating account" for payment, as that account is the personal property of the brokerage company and is subject to other setoff or seizure rights by other business creditors. All expenses paid to sell or manage any property must be fully funded by the available cash balance held on behalf of that beneficiary, unless the broker advances additional money to the owner, or other cash reserves are held in escrow pursuant to an agreement with that person. Borrowing funds from the amounts held for other beneficiaries constitutes *overspending the beneficiary's ledger*, creates a shortage in the bank account, and is an illegal commingling of funds. An owner of several properties may authorize the broker to offset the surplus funds of one property against the negative balance of another, so long as the net result is positive on a cash basis and the ownership of the properties is identical.

The Broker's Ledger

Many banks pay interest and charge monthly fees and other costs for maintaining an escrow account. The broker may keep money in escrow to pay these costs, conduct in-office closings, prevent possible overspending of ledger balances, and "offset" advances of money for unexpected client/customer repairs or "NSF" items (non-sufficient funds). This record normally constitutes an escrow account payable (liability) to the broker/company for the amount deposited. Amounts advanced from the broker's ledger must be collected as "good funds" in 45-90 days.

Rules 5.10.B and 5.14.D; 5.15.B.1 and 5.15.B.2) require an accounting for any advance of money made to a beneficiary in both the journal and the beneficiary ledger affected. This practice places the broker in the role of financing the client's business activity. An alternative is to require the client to maintain a reserve balance for unforeseen emergencies and other contingencies. This is common in property management operations where there are absentee owners, variable operating expenses, or other monthly payments that require consistent collection of "good funds" from the tenants. If the broker makes an advance, it becomes that beneficiary's property and must be used accordingly. The expenditures and the subsequent repayment by the owner must be recorded on both the beneficiary's ledger and in the journal. The amount advanced must appear on the owner's accounting report, and any interest charged for the advance must be disclosed in the management agreement. When using a computerized accounting system, the advance is recorded by making a deposit (debit) to the escrow cash account and a credit (non-operating income) to the specific owner's (ledger) account. Expenses and repayments are paid from the cash account and charged to the specific owner balances affected. Accounting for management commissions earned and withdrawn from an escrow account is also illustrated in the broker's ledger in the section appendix, Exhibit C.

Using "estimated" amounts due the broker without subsequently reconciling and adjusting such amounts to actual earnings for the accounting month frequently results in illegal commingling of funds. See Rule 5.10. When real estate sales are closed in-house, any miscellaneous closing expenses and unexpected changes in service fees must be paid from the broker's own ledger and then should be collected according to the contract from the party concerned. Any uncollectible costs should not be written off against the general account balance; they are paid from funds held in the broker's ledger.

The following section will illustrate the general escrow accounting concepts, use of the escrow account journal and ledgers, and the bank reconciliation process. These processes apply to all other real estate escrow accounts.

D. Illustrated Escrow Accounting Transactions

Background Information

You are a new business and have two listings under contract. In addition, you will manage another single-family residential property for Carter Smith and hold the security deposit for the tenant, Rose Bloom. The sales escrow account was properly established as a COLORADO REALTOR FOUNDATION interest-bearing account. You use a manual accounting system. The following events are first recorded in the appropriate ledgers and then the journal using the transaction reference numbers indicated in (*parentheses*). The month of May 2020 has just ended and the bank statement was received on June 3, 2020. The May escrow bank reconciliation worksheet is shown later in this section.

Monthly Transactions:

(1) A deposit of $250.00 is made by the broker to open the account and purchase supplies on April 1, 2020. The bank charged $175.00 for business checks. COLORADO REALTOR FOUNDATION interest is assumed to be $1.00 for April and $10.00 for May. These amounts are withdrawn by the bank and are paid to

COLORADO REALTOR FOUNDATION the next month. A "√" means the item had cleared the account and appeared on the bank statement (not shown).

(2) $5,000.00 was received on April 15, 2020 from Harold and Jean Blue for purchase of 7373 West Flamingo Road (This is to illustrate the use of escrow records for an in-house closing—see the first closing problem in the Chapter "Closing Statements," of the manual). The broker will close this transaction on May 10, 2020.

(3) The Blues obtained a loan for $190,750.00, which they deposit with the broker for closing. They also deposit the down payment of $4,188.43 per the broker's settlement worksheet on May 5. Broker makes all disbursements per the credit column on the settlement worksheet and pays the seller's proceeds on May 15 in "good funds."

(4) Rose Bloom rents Carter Smith's home on May 1, for $1,500.00 per month. Rent is due on the 5th and the tenant also pays the $1,500.00 security deposit due per the lease. The broker charges 10 percent of gross rent as the management fee and pays the owner's monthly mortgage of $800.00 no later than the 15th. The tenant pays all utilities and trash directly to the city vendor. The management fee is scheduled to be withdrawn on the last day of the month. Proceeds are mailed to the owner by the 10th day of the next month.

(5) Carter Smith gives the broker a check for $175.00 to repair the furnace on May 29 at an estimated cost of $175.00. The bank returned this payment as "NSF" on May 30 after the broker mailed the monthly proceeds check. Smith repaid this amount in cash on June 1. (NOTE: The tenant deposit must be held intact as a refundable security deposit. If the furnace repair cost is actually $300.00 and is paid on May 30, this "theoretical" expense would be partially offset by the $85.00 balance on the broker's ledger and the $1,200.00 in the owner's ledger, however, and an **"unfunded amount"** of $215.00 would have been "borrowed" from the tenant's security deposit in violation of Rule 5.9. This is an example of an event the broker must properly handle in property management.)

Ledger Entries by date:

BROKER'S LEDGER — Sales Escrow Account # 987654							Page 1
Ref	Date	Check	Description	√	Payment	Deposit	Balance
(1)	4-1-20		Broker Funds to Open Account	√		250.00	250.00
	4-1-20	101	Checking Supplies purchased	√	175.00		75.00
	4-30-20	Bank Credit	Colorado REALTOR Foundation interest earned April	√		1.00	76.00
	5-1-20	Bank Debit	Sweep Colorado REALTOR Foundation interest April	√	1.00		75.00
	5-30-20	Bank Credit	Colorado REALTOR Foundation interest for May	√		10.00	85.00

BUYER LEDGER: Harold & Jean Blue, 111 1st Ave, Salt Lake City, UT SELLER: John & Mary Gray LISTING 4-01-20 NEW ADDRESS: 7373 W. Flamingo Road, Lakewood, CO CLOSING DATE: May 10, 2020 CLOSED 5-10-20							
Ref	Date	Check	Description	√	Payment	Deposit	Balance
(2)	4-15-20		Earnest Money Deposit	√		5,000.00	5000.00
(3)	5-10-20		Lender Loan Proceeds	√		190,750.00	195,750.00
	5-10-20		Down payment for closing	√		4,188.43	199,938.43
	"	102	Acme Loan-Pay off of 1st	√	46,450.00		153,488.43
	"	103	Title Ins Mortgagee Premium	√	575.00		152,913.43
	"	104	Cnty Clerk recording/release fees	√	62.00		152,851.43
	"	105	Buyer 's Atty.-title exam	√	75.00		152,776.43
	"	106	Dept of Rev- State Doc fee & 2%	√	4095.38		148,681.05
	"	107	County-Tax Certificate	√	15.00		148,666.05
(3)	5-10-20	108	Lender Tax Reserve	√	854.65		147,811.40
	"	109	Hazard Ins. Premium & Reserve	√	787.50		147,023.90
	"	110	1% fee & interest on new loan	√	2,769.79		144,254.11
	"	111	Survey Cost	√	65.00		144,189.11
	"	112	Lender Credit Report Company	√	50.00		144,139.11
	"	113	Broker's Commission	√	11,400.00		132, 739.11
	"	114	New Lender 's Atty.- title exam	√	75.00		132,664.11
	"	115	Broker-document preparation	√	100.00		132,564.11
	"	116	Seller 's Net Proceeds Paid	√	132,564.11		0.00

MANAGEMENT LEDGER TENANT: Rose Bloom (303-550-0001) OWNER: Carter Smith (303-550-0000) RENTAL: 123 W. Flamingo Road OWNER ADDRESS: 10050 Grape Ct. Lakewood, CO. 89100 RENT PER MONTH: $500/mo due on 5th BANK: United Nat'l. Bank, Loan # xxxx-xxx – Due on 15th SEC DEPOSIT: $1,500.00 LEASE EXPIRES: 4-30-21 MANAGEMENT FEE: 10% of Gross Rents							
Ref	Date	Check	Description	√	Payment	Deposit	Balance
4	5-5-20		Rent and security deposit for Rose Bloom – 1 yr. Lease	√		3,000.00	3,000.00
	5-10-20	117	United National Bank loan	√	800.00		2,200.00
5	5-29-20		Owner funds to repair furnace	√		175.00	2,375.00
(4)	5-30-20	118	10% Management fee	√	150.00		2,225.00
	"	119	Owner Proceeds May 06	√	550.00		1,675.00
(5)	"	Actual Month end balance	Owner deposit was NSF	√	175.00		1,500.00
	"	Theoretical for illustration only*	Assumed but not actual repair of furnace to illustrate a shortage in the Sec Deposit.*		300.00*		1,200.00*

The total funds actually held in escrow for all pending ledgers at May 31, 2020 is **$1,585.00 ($85.00 + 1,500.00)**. This agrees with the month-end journal balance shown below. Note: the journal below is presented in very abbreviated form to save publishing space; this should not be done in actual practice:

SALES ESCROW JOURNAL May 2020							Page 1 of____
Ref	Date	Check	Description	√	Payment	Deposit	Balance
			Balance Forward from April 30, 2020	√			$5,076.00
(1)	5-1-20	Debit	Bank Interest Sweep	√	1.00		5,075.00
(2)	5-1-20		Rose Bloom Rent & Security Deposit – May	√		3,000.00	8,075.00
(3)	5-10-20		Blue Loan & Down payment	√		194,938.43	203,013.43
		102-116	Blue Closing, 7373 W. Flamingo	√	199,938.43		3,075.00
(5)	5-29-20		Bloom Repair Deposit-Smith	√		175.00	3,250.00
	5-30-20	Debit	Bloom Repair-Smith NSF	√	175.00		3,075.00
(4)	5-10 to 5-30-20	117-119	Bloom-Mortgage, rental expense Commission and proceeds	√	1,500.00		1,575.00
(6)	5-30-20	Credit	Record COLORADO REALTOR FOUNDATION Interest May 2020	√		10.00	$1,585.00

The Bank Reconciliation Process

The purpose of reconciliation is to verify that the records for the account are in balance per the escrow accounting equation. The bank reconciliation worksheet form is shown in the chapter appendix, Exhibit D.

Rule 5.14.C requires the ending bank statement cash balance to be reconciled with the office journal and ledger account cards during any month when there has been escrow account activity. Each open ledger balance (*not just a lump-sum total*) is individually listed on the left side as shown below, or in additional attached sheets if necessary. The ending journal balance on the date of reconciliation is entered underneath the total for all pending ledgers. The bank balance is reconciled on the right side of the worksheet; it must balance with the cash shown in the journal and all ledgers. It is recommended that the "date of reconciliation" be the date of the latest bank statement, even though the actual date of performing this process is usually later.

Assuming that the bank statement balance on May 30, 2020 is $1,585.00, and that there are no outstanding items or errors on the statement, the reconciliation worksheet below would be prepared using the data above. In addition, the broker should carefully perform the verifying tests noted below.

Mile High Realty Sales Escrow Account 000-0000-0 Bank reconciliation for month ending May 30, 2020 Prepared by: Linda Smith		Date reconciled: June 5, 2020 Date of reconciliation: May 30, 2020 Reviewed by: John Smith, Broker	
Escrow Liabilities per pending ledgers on 5-30-20 Description	Ledger Balance	Ending Bank Statement Bal 5-30-20:	$ 1,585.00
Broker (Company) Ledger	$ 85.00	Add: Outstanding Deposits mailed to bank on or before May 30, 2020	0 .00
123 W. Flamingo Sec Deposit	1,500.00	Subtotal:	$ 1,585.00
		Subtract: Outstanding Checks	0.00
		Reconciled Bank Balance: 5-30-20	□ $ 1,585.00
Total Pending Ledgers 5-30-20	□ $ 1,585.00	□ This means all records agree with the actual escrow liabilities per the contracts and all banking activity is properly reported in the accounting records.	
Ending Journal Balance 5-30-20	□ $ 1,585.00		

For simplicity, the Commission recommends reconciling the bank balance to the ending checkbook and journal cash balance per the office records, but other accepted methods may be used, *e.g.*, reconciling the books to the cash in the bank, and/or using a "four column cash reconciliation," with a supplemental listing of all pending ledgers and outstanding items on attached sheets.

All contracts must be examined to confirm that the total amount of money that should have been received has been properly deposited. Investigate and correct any errors or omissions immediately. Any transfer of funds between related accounts must be made in a timely manner, *i.e.*, rent and security deposit payments combined on one check. If this is not done, a shortage will develop in the security deposit account, and refundable deposits may be erroneously paid to property owners as net proceeds. Collecting these amounts later may be difficult.

An authorized independent company custodian should have personal responsibility to account for retention, access, and use of banking records, receipt books, computer backups, and hard copy printouts of all accounting records. Someone independent of the accounting department should review monthly bank reconciliation and the items listed for errors or other irregularities. The reviewer should trace transfers and outstanding items to subsequent payments and deposits on later statements. Look for unrecorded statement items or those that are contrary to other company policy and practices.

E. Transaction Files and the Retention of Records

The records of licensed brokerage activity must be retained for *four* years per § 12-10-217(1)(k), C.R.S. Rules 6.14.A and 6.19, as well as the Commission position statement on record-keeping (CP-9), control the contents of the broker's property transaction file. Rule 5.21 requires any licensee to produce appropriate records concerning licensed activity and operation of the trust accounts upon the request of the Commission.

Except for times in which the documents are being reviewed or executed, the current transaction files should be kept at the broker's office in a secure, central location. The broker should review all pending sales transaction files and any leases and management agreements executed by associates for possible correction or follow-up attention. A copy of the earnest money check with a copy of the deposit slip should be placed in the transaction file. Associates may retain copies of contract documents (and pay for them) according to the broker's office policy or employment agreement.

Duplicate signatures are acceptable for all records maintained in the broker's transaction file per Rule 6.14.A. "Duplicate" means photocopy, carbon copy, or facsimile, or electronic copies that contain a digital or electronic signature as defined in § 24-71-101(1), C.R.S.

A broker must maintain a duplicate of the original of any document (except deeds, promissory notes, and deeds of trust or mortgages prepared for the benefit of third-party lenders) that was prepared by or on behalf of the licensee and pertains to the consummation of the leasing, purchase, sale, or exchange of real property in which the broker participates as a broker. The payoff statement and new loan statement monetarily affect the settlement statement and should be retained by the broker concerned. Cooperating brokers, including brokers acting as agents for buyers in a specific real estate transaction, shall have the same requirements for retention of duplicate records as is stated above, except that a cooperating broker who is not a party to the listing contract need not retain a copy of the listing contract or the seller's settlement statement.

A broker is not required to retain copies of existing public records, title commitments, loan applications, lender-required disclosures, or related affirmations from independent third-party closing entities after the settlement date. The broker engaged by a party must ensure that the final sales agreement, settlement statement, or amendment of the settlement, delivered at closing for that party's tax reporting or future use, bears duplicate signatures or as authorized by the parties concerned.

The following is a *checklist for common records* to retain in the both the listing and selling broker's property transaction file. Other ancillary documents and agreements executed between the parties and the closing entity or lender are not required.

SALES FILES

- Lead-based paint disclosures for residential property built before 1978;
- Exclusive right-to-buy/sell, or agency or open listing agreement and amendments (listing broker only);
- Disclosure of brokerage relationships;
- Disclosure of compensation for services and income from affiliated entities;
- Disclosure of the source of residential property square footage;
- Contract to buy/sell/exchange real estate, counterproposals, amendments, and attachments;
- Current marketing/MLS information used in the transaction;
- Inspection notice;
- Seller's property disclosure statement;
- Actual closing instructions, negotiated before the actual date of closing;
- Copy of any power of attorney (show recording data if closed in-house);

- Copy of earnest money check, validated escrow bank deposit slip (or receipt below);
- Signed and dated receipt for earnest money held by third-party closing entity;
- Copy of earnest money note;
- Buyer's financial information, if "owner-carry" financing;
- Rental/occupancy agreement before closing date (have separate security deposit);
- Estimated closing costs/estimated monthly expenses prepared by licensee;
- Settlement statement (or equivalent computer form) for the party represented or assisted;
- Side agreement/amendment to revise a settlement statement;
- Promissory note (unsigned, marked "COPY");**
- Closing entity commission check remittance less earnest money amount if applicable;
- Tax reports required by government agencies (Colorado withholding tax);**
- Escrow receipts or collection agreements continuing after closing;
- Accounting for use of advance retainer fees;
- Six-column worksheet for settlement (or equivalent computer form);**
- Deed (copy showing recording data if closed in-house);**
- Deed of trust (copy showing recording data if closed in-house);** and
- Other legal documents prepared by the broker.**

**Required only when the broker personally prepares the document, conducts the closing in-house without use of a title company, and/or is responsible for recording of any documents.

MANAGEMENT FILES

- Current/past management and/or short-term reservation management agreements;
- Current/past lease or rental occupancy agreements with tenants and guests;
- Lead-based paint disclosures for residential property built before 1978;
- Disclosure of brokerage relationships and/or listing contracts to lease;
- Disclosure of compensation, service income from affiliated entities;
- Brokerage accounting records, bank reconciliation, tax and owner reports;
- Ongoing contracts, bids, invoices, service provider billings, and correspondence with client;
- Legal notices, actions, and accounting reports affecting owner/occupant/tenant funds;
- Documentation for commissions earned versus taken or charged to others;
- Prompt assessment, timely (45-90 days) collection, restitution of all money due escrow; and
- Documentation verifying reported receipts, income, and all expenses paid for another.

F. Administrative Matters

Changing Employing Brokers

Each corporation, partnership, or limited liability company is recognized as a distinct, licensed entity. The designated natural person, *i.e.*, the "employing" or "acting" broker, is responsible for the ongoing maintenance of all records concerning licensed real estate activity and supervision of the escrow accounting process.

If the acting broker leaves employment with the licensed entity, the licensed entity retains the continuing responsibility for maintenance of all escrow records. The departing broker is personally responsible for delivering these records to the licensed entity, and must properly account for all trust funds transferred to the new broker. The acting broker serves only as a caretaker or trustee during the period of licensed tenure as the acting broker. A form for documenting a change in broker is found in the chapter appendix, Exhibit H.

An exception to this situation occurs when a licensed business entity is dissolved. The final acting broker then becomes personally responsible for making all final disbursements and accounting for all trust funds. That broker must maintain all records for a period of four years. Upon dissolution of an individual proprietorship, records maintenance remains the responsibility of the individual proprietor broker and his or her heirs. Closing the business and the pending transactions should be done according to the Commission position statement CP-8, Assignment of Contracts and Escrowed Funds. An attorney or another qualified unlicensed party may complete this process on behalf of the surviving heirs of the individual proprietorship. The forms for applying for a transfer or change in the broker's license status may be found at: www.dora.state.co.us/real-estate/. See Rule 2.10.C for the process of securing a temporary business entity broker license.

Good Funds

Rule 6.19.E requires that "good funds" be held and disbursed for closing. Such money is: (1) immediately available for withdrawal as a matter of right from the financial institution where deposited, or (2) is available for such withdrawal as the consequence of an agreement of an institution in which the funds are to be deposited or a financial institution upon which the funds are to be drawn. The agreement must be for the benefit of the licensee providing the closing service; all contingencies and conditions must be satisfied before any funds may be disbursed. Good funds are required for closing by the Colorado Consumer Protection Act, § 6-1-105(1)(v), C.R.S., and by § 38-35-125(2), C.R.S.

Examples of good funds are: cash, wire transfers, telephone transfers between accounts in the same bank, cashier's checks, certified checks, teller checks (issued by a savings and loan), tri-party agreements in which the financial institution unconditionally guarantees the lender's check, deposits of earnest money that clear the buyer's bank before closing, transfers of a buyer's earnest money to a closing agent (with prior consent of the parties) that clear the broker's bank before closing, offsets of earnest money deposits against earned commissions by the closing agent, and Federal Home Loan Bank checks.

Closing Instructions

Colorado Division of Insurance Regulations require that written closing instructions from all necessary parties be provided to the closing entity for any real estate transaction. Further, the regulations require the title entity to execute closing instructions approved by the Commission if the instructions were executed by all parties to the real estate transaction and delivered to the closing entity in advance of the closing and settlement. The Commission closing instructions form is found on the Division of Real Estate website, "Commission-Approved and Miscellaneous Forms." The Commission's closing instructions and earnest money receipt or an equivalent form must be delivered to the closing agent in time to prepare the final settlement.

Signing Settlement Statements

Rule 6.19.Arequires the licensee to sign and approve the settlement statement of the party they assist or represent. The settlement statement must also show the name of the employing broker where applicable. The Commission recommends that each licensee and supervising broker review the final contract and proposed settlement statement before closing. The licensee, or an alternate, who consents to attend a closing on behalf of the absent licensee, is responsible for furnishing a proper settlement statement at closing. The employing broker is responsible to see that the licensee is competent in such responsibilities. A copy of the signed settlement statement shall be delivered to the employing broker immediately after the closing. Original signatures are no longer required for the broker's transaction file.

If the closing involves a *new loan* made to the purchaser where the lending institution deducts costs before distributing the loan proceeds prior to final settlement, the loan proceeds must be reconciled with the amounts due to or from the seller and buyer. The new loan reconciliation is described and illustrated in the Chapter, "Closing Statements." The broker's debit and credit columns of the "Worksheet For a Real Estate Settlement" or an equivalent closing entity form may be used for this purpose. The reconciliation must also be delivered to the employing broker after closing.

Closing Fees

Commission position statement CP-7, Closing Costs, and Rule 6.14.B state that there is no obligation for a broker to prepare any legal document as part of a real estate transaction or closing. However, as the result of the *Conway-Bogue* decision (see Chapter, "Landmark Case Law and Opinions"), brokers may prepare certain legal documents and complete standard and approved forms.

Certain fees are generally charged for preparation of real estate documents and closings: (1) a fee for closing and preparing *non-legal documents* such as the settlement statements, and (2) a fee for preparing *legal documents* executed by the parties, *i.e.*, contracts, deeds, notes, deeds of trust, mortgages, and other security instruments. Upon agreement of the parties, fees for preparing non-legal documents may be charged to anyone. However, in the absence of an attorney representing one of the parties to the transaction, the broker must pay any fees for preparing legal documents. The broker must ensure that the proper parties pay for the closing costs. Brokers may charge (with written authorization from the parties) for the transactions that they close "in-house," when such charges are not tied to preparation of legal documents. The broker may not designate his or her own attorney to prepare the documents, and then pass these charges to the parties, as if the attorney were representing them.

IRS/State Reports

IRS Form 8300, "Report of Cash Payment Over $10,000," received in a trade or business, must be filed when cash (currency) is received by the broker from the same person in any one year as the result of single, connected, or related transactions. The report and further instructions may be obtained at the IRS website at www.irs.gov/. Civil and criminal penalties may result from a failure to comply with reporting requirements.

Sellers must provide the closing agent with their complete name, address, and taxpayer identification number or Social Security number for reporting income from the sale or exchange of property. The person who actually provides the closing service makes this report on Form 1099-S. The Colorado Department of Revenue requires withholding 2 percent of the sales price *or* the net proceeds shown on the bottom of the settlement statement, whichever is less, from the sale of Colorado property in an amount of $100,000 or more by non-resident individuals, including foreign partnerships and corporations not registered with the Secretary of State, or having no Colorado business address immediately following the sale. The tax must be withheld and the forms prepared by the individual or entity actually providing the closing service. This is reported on Form DR-1083 and is remitted with payment on Colorado Form DR-1079. Further instructions, exemptions, and forms may be obtained by calling the Colorado Department of Revenue at (303) 238-7378. See basic text of this law in the Chapter, "Tax Factors Pertaining to Real Estate Practice;" § 39-22-604.5, C.R.S.; or http://www.colorado.gov/revenue, select "Taxation Division", then "Alpha Index" selection "F" to locate forms by form number or name.

Private Bank Account Insurance

Brokers may be able to purchase private insurance coverage for all escrow and operating checking accounts with deposits in excess of the FDIC coverage as added protection from a bank failure. Information on such coverage can be obtained from the broker's insurance agent.

Computer Forms

Personal computers may be used to generate standard and approved forms if the following requirements are met: (1) the Commission-approved language must be exactly reproduced, (2) the software must not allow alteration of the approved standard language in day-to-day operation, (3) the software must produce fill-in and allowable transaction-specific language in a font clearly differentiated from the standard, approved contract language, (4) contract print must be easily readable, (5) blank spaces shall not be filled in by the licensee, prior to negotiation with the parties. See Commission Rule 7.1 in Chapter, "Commission-Approved and Miscellaneous Forms."

Software Resources

The Commission does not recommend or endorse any specific software, and provides the following information for further investigation and analysis by the licensee: (1) Texas A&M College Station (1-979-845-2031) publishes a synopsis of current software (400+) applications available for real estate firms, (2) Institute of Real Estate Management, 430 N. Michigan Ave., Chicago, IL 60610-9025, phone (800) 837-0706, fax (800) 338-4736. Colorado chapters may be contacted through C.A.R., (303) 790-7099.

Commission Audits

Statewide examinations are conducted in response to public complaints or on a routine cyclical basis. The examination is performed on-site to examine the handling of escrow funds and the maintenance of other required business records. The broker is selected from the licensing database of eligible brokers or registered developers. Audits of certain brokers and developers may be done by correspondence. Upon completion of an audit, the examiner will meet with the broker or registered developer's representatives to discuss any findings. The examiner will then mail a written report of the results to the broker for explanation and correction. All completed audit reports are filed electronically for future reference. It is important for brokers to ensure that prior corrections continue to be followed. Repeated findings are considered matters that warrant official Commission action.

III. Property Management Records

A. Management Accounting Requirements

General Concepts

The responsibilities and concepts described in Parts I and II become more critical in the supervision of property management activities.

The accounting cycles are more complex and intensified, as more transactions must be processed in a shorter time. The financial interest of each beneficiary must be maintained to prevent illegal commingling of funds. Ongoing operations must be effectively managed to maintain accurate and timely records, while administering customer and client services each month.

The management activity undertaken will affect the accounting system used, and care must be taken to choose the type of product best suited for the proposed business operation. If software is used, it must:

1. Classify and report current, year-to-date, and selected period financial information pertaining to the financial interests of the owner, tenant, and any related homeowner association by property and unit managed on the cash and accrual basis;
2. Control cash flows and ongoing expenditures;
3. Produce current or prior bank account reconciliations with the corresponding escrow liabilities in detail upon demand;
4. Account for the use of different escrow bank account structures;
5. Track managerial and administrative information for the property manager and owner, per Chapter, "Property Management and Leases;" and
6. Emphasize the "custodial/trustee responsibilities of the Colorado broker in accounting for the funds of others," as distinct from the "ownership/investor role" used in most commercial software design and operation.

Account Structures and the Flow of Funds

A typical full-service management company would generally have the following account structures for long- or short-term management operations involving associations and broker-owned properties. These activities were introduced in Part II.

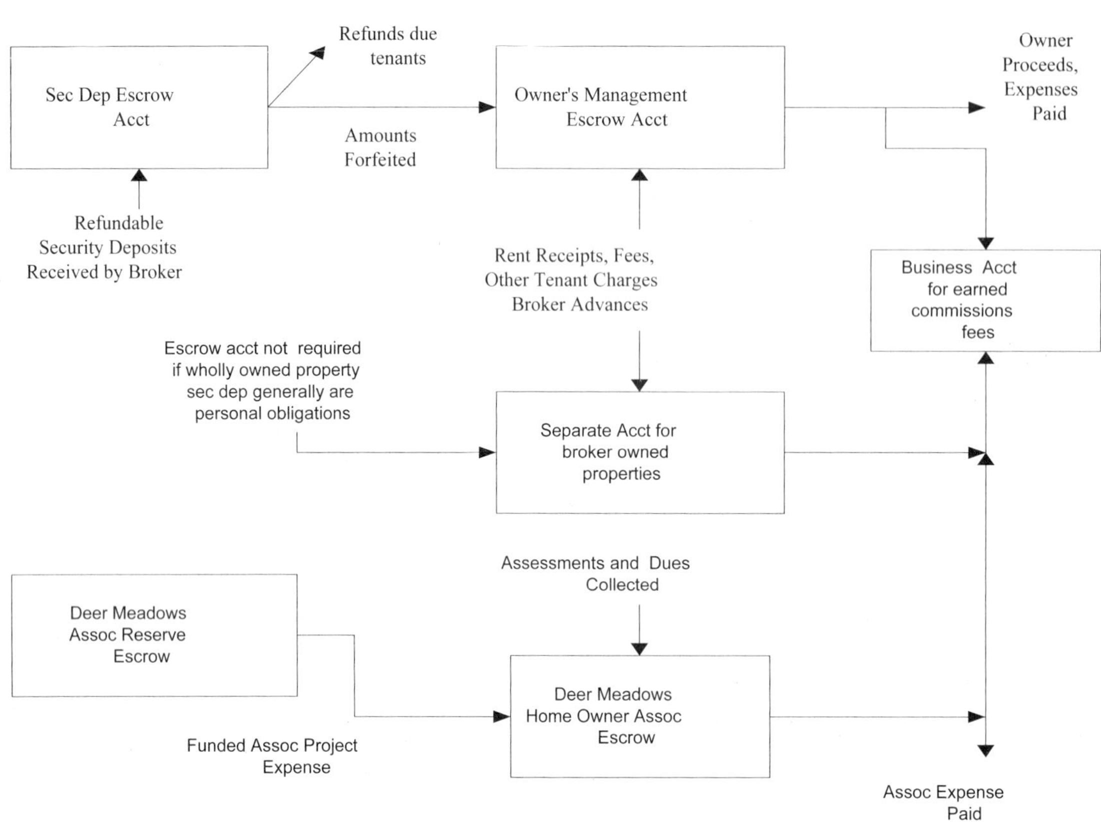

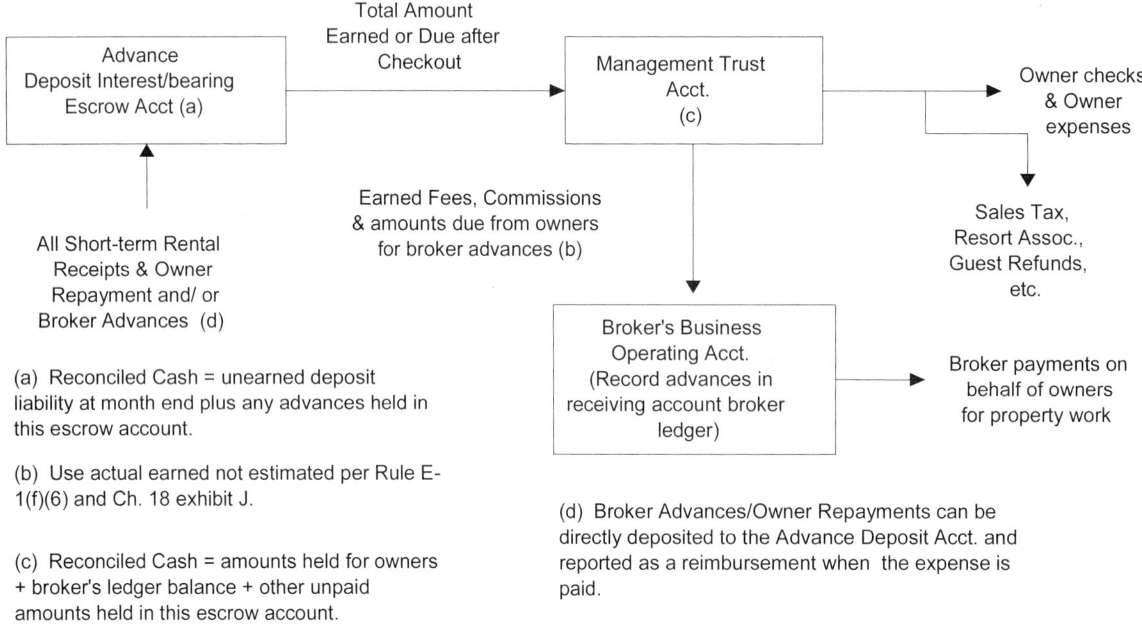

(a) Reconciled Cash = unearned deposit liability at month end plus any advances held in this escrow account.

(b) Use actual earned not estimated per Rule E-1(f)(6) and Ch. 18 exhibit J.

(c) Reconciled Cash = amounts held for owners + broker's ledger balance + other unpaid amounts held in this escrow account.

(d) Broker Advances/Owner Repayments can be directly deposited to the Advance Deposit Acct. and reported as a reimbursement when the expense is paid.

Account Operation

The accounts illustrated above may exist in addition to the sales escrow account. Information on how to establish and identify a required escrow account is found in Part II, Section A. Separate long- and short-term bank accounts are not required if the records differentiate and report each activity separately. However, management of associations of more than 30 units requires the use of separate accounts for each association and individual reserve fund. (See § 38-33.3-306(3)(a), C.R.S.)

Residential property management duties may range from simple upkeep and caring for an absentee owner's property to the management of large apartment or commercial or common interest owner associations, to managing short-term resort properties for many different owners. The basic accounting records for such activities are illustrated in simple form in Part II, Section D. Basically, the manager receives inflows of escrow cash from tenants/guests in the form of rent, homeowner association assessments, special fees, advance rent, security deposits, owner cash reserves, or reimbursement for broker advances, and pays this money out to various third parties as owner and tenant expenses, refunds, or owner rental proceeds. In addition, the broker may manage reserves for future expenditures or improvement funds.

Internal Controls

An effective and efficient "internal control structure" must be developed for business operations in order to establish personal accountability for performance of the critical steps of the company's accounting cycle. Professional advice is recommended as the size and complexity of the business increases. The structure must adequately separate and monitor three basic "incompatible" functions: (1) the transaction authorization and approval process, (2) the responsibilities for the physical control and custody of the escrow assets and/or the records creating or changing escrow liabilities, and (3) the accounting, record-keeping and external reporting functions. The employing broker must avoid delegating job duties in a manner that allows one person to independently perform and/or supervise all three functions from start to finish. Some guidelines concerning these functions based on audit findings are:

1. The responsibility for collection of company receipts and making the corresponding bank deposits should be separated, and be separate from the responsibility for maintaining the accounting records;
2. Avoid combining the responsibility for the custody for any escrow asset with the independent ability to control the related transactional information and/or to create or alter the corresponding contractual records of the liability;
3. The responsibility for authorizing write-offs and/or adjustments to amounts due the company should be based on independent collection efforts by a third party or the employing broker's own investigation of the facts reported;
4. The responsibility for conducting licensed activity on behalf of the employing broker should be separated from the responsibility for maintaining the primary accounting records and/or controlling the reporting processes associated with those efforts;
5. The broker should maintain full disclosure and reliable sources of ongoing, unfiltered communications with all parties affected by operating policies involving potential conflicts of interest; and

6. The broker must be alert for and monitor circumstances that may give rise to the means, motivation, or opportunity for misuse of funds, *e.g.*, accepting cash (legal tender), signing blank checks, using cash receipts as a petty cash fund, not verifying voided or outstanding checks and deposits in the bank reconciliation, etc.

A "self-authenticating" cash receipt and/or coversheet deposit form, with the detailed information required in Rule 5.15.B, should be used to account for the physical custody and deposit of cash. The receipt must be signed and dated by a designated "cashier" *and* the person making the payment; the person paying must maintain the carbon receipt as proof of payment. The person collecting receipts must formally account for all receipts in his or her custody monthly, and for the receipts given to a designated "courier" for deposit; both the cashier and courier must count and *countersign a dated cover sheet* showing the receipt numbers and individual amounts included in each bank deposit. A ranking independent staff member should compare the monthly amounts due per the rent receivable roll, pending folios, and leases with the corresponding bank deposits and verify the receivables due are accounted for and were properly deposited. Any delinquent or missing receipt items should be confirmed with the party concerned and immediately reported to the employing/ supervising broker. Each cash receipt form should be magnetically coded and numbered to simplify the reconciliation process by appearing on the monthly bank statement like returned checks. Some companies require the use of money orders from nearby banks as an alternative to handling cash receipts and then allow tenants to deduct the order cost from the rent due.

Authority to make telephone transfers or electronic withdrawals should be limited to the broker and a knowledgeable manager. The bank should receive written instructions to verify the identity of the caller and record this with the corresponding teller's name on each returned transfer/withdrawal form.

In short-term management, all guest receipts should be deposited directly into the advance rental/security deposit account to ensure: (1) there is only one authorized point of entry into the escrow accounting system, (2) any authorized brokerage income from the proper use of an interest-bearing account can be maximized, and (3) there is greater control over the transfer of earned income and miscellaneous receipts into the management escrow account. The management escrow account is the one account to be used to distribute all authorized payments to others. The use of manual checks prepared outside the normal accounting system may be avoided or closely monitored by the designated broker.

All used/unused company deposit slips, pre-numbered receipt books, sequentially numbered receipt forms, and blank check stock must be accounted for periodically and limited to controlled usage by authorized persons. Access to this inventory should be assigned to a specific person and/or the broker. Unused or new pre-numbered receipts, receipt books, check books, and unused stock should never be left unsupervised outside the control of an authorized custodian. Unnumbered bank items are difficult to control, costly to account for, and are always easy to misuse.

In long-term management, payments to vendors, owners, and tenants should generally be made from the account where the amount was first deposited. When the use of separate escrow bank accounts is required, some incentive may be given to encourage the separate payment of rent, security deposits, or other amounts requiring use of separate escrow accounts. Company policy should require tenants to use separate checks that can be deposited directly into the proper account. Every internal transfer duplicates the cost of accounting and increases the risk of error, misapplication, or theft. This policy should accommodate good business practice and occasional tenant hardships. It should require preparation of a corresponding escrow check to transfer the necessary amount to the proper account *at the same time* the customer's check is deposited. Failure to properly identify and transfer this money results in a corresponding shortage in the security deposit account. This error will not be easy to find if the identity of the tenant and the amounts paid are not shown individually on the deposit slip per Rule 5.15.B.

Unrecorded or uncorrected non-sufficient funds (NSF) items or bank errors will create a similar problem in the owner's management escrow account. NSF items may be offset by money maintained in the broker's ledger. The appropriate amount should be based on normal rates of occurrence.

Creation of an Unlicensed Company

Brokers who allow associates to manage property or perform real estate related services on the broker's behalf through the licensed brokerage entity are generally responsible for the results and must supervise those activities per Rule 6.3. A licensee may also sell and/or manage personally owned property as a private party with disclosure per Rule 6.17. In this case, the licensee must avoid any impression that this activity is performed on behalf of his or her broker in a licensed capacity. See Commission position statement, CP-15, Sale of Items Related to Real Estate.. A licensee who performs any exempt activity is still subject to the jurisdiction of the Commission. See *Seibel v. Colorado Real Estate Commission* in Chapter, "Landmark Case Law and Opinions," and § 12-10-217-(1)(h), C.R.S., in Chapter, "Real Estate Broker License Law." Even though the licensee has the general duty to act honestly and in good faith, to properly remit any funds received, and to perform all duties promised when performing exempt activity, the escrow accounts and records prescribed by Rule Commission Rules - Chapter 5 are not required by license law for this activity.

Broker who acts as a "Conduit"

A "**conduit**" means that the broker only collects money on behalf of another and deposits the same to the owner's bank account without any additional signatory power or right of withdrawal. No trust account is required in this case. The broker should have a written agreement as to the duties required and keep a record showing the collection and proper deposit to the owner's account of funds received.

B. Required Management Records

The following ledger records are required to control and account for money belonging to others. These are in addition to the escrow bank accounts and the journal.

Tenant/guest Rental Ledger

This record shows each customer's payment history, any amount due, plus other fees or charges. For single-family management, the tenant's payment information may be kept on the owner's ledger card, but in multi-family (apartment) management, a separate record should be kept for each tenant renting a unit. The use of a "continuous tenant ledger by unit" (for each unit rented) lends itself to errors and internal misuse of funds because the amounts held or due for a specific tenant are difficult to isolate. See chapter appendix, Exhibits E and F.

A different ledger form is used for *short-term management* and is called the guest folio. It may be designed to suit company needs. The form must facilitate accounting for all unearned advance deposits in the monthly bank reconciliation; it also accounts to the guest for the amounts received and due on the check-in date, and contains the following general information:

Folio Number: ________________ Guest Name ________________	
Dates of Stay ________________ Rental Address ________________	
Reservation Confirmation No. _______ Reservation Date ________________	
Guest Address and Telephone No. ________________	
Nights Rented _____ X Rate per/night $_________ = Total Due $___________	
Less Travel Agent Fees & Discounts	(_________)
Add Security or Advance Deposit Due to the Company	_________
Special Packages Ordered by Guest	_________
Total Amount Due Company from Guest by Check-In Date:	$_________
Less Amount(s) Paid on _______ by ________________	(_________)
_______ " ________________	(_________)
Balance Due at Check-In " ________________	$_________
Refund/Cancellation Paid Guest on _______ by Check _________	
(Company refund policies and other disclosures are printed and mailed to the guest upon receipt of a reservation).	

Owner's Ledger

All cash received or paid in managing the owner's property is itemized by individual transaction on this record. This ledger may be used to prepare a separate owner accounting report or may be mailed as the monthly statement with any net amount due to or from the owner. A sample form is found in the chapter appendix, Exhibit G.

Proper maintenance and scrutiny of the owner cash balance reported is the easiest way to prevent illegal commingling of funds between individual same-owner properties in a "pooled" escrow account. If the owner lacks the necessary capital in one property, the broker may transfer the funds needed from another identically owned property, assuming there is a surplus on the other property ledger and the transfer is authorized in the management agreement. If there are no additional owner funds on hand, then as a business decision consistent with the terms of the management agreement, the broker may advance the money needed from the broker's ledger, and reimburse this advance from the owner's future income. The various uses of the broker's ledger make it an absolute necessity in any escrow accounting or software system.

In short-term property management, the owner's share of advance rental deposit income and the expenses paid by the broker are reported on the owner's ledger after the checkout date. The amount earned is transferred into the owner's management escrow account. The owner's accounting report shows the disposition of any security deposit held, the rental fee earned during the month by guest name or folio number, any amounts refunded, the broker's fee, any advances due or repaid, plus any other operating expenses paid on behalf of the owner per the management agreement, and the current and year-to-date summaries of the net proceeds for each unit managed. The reported items must reference specific guest reservations, folios, and other appropriate business documents per Rule 5.15.B by unit number and date, *e.g.*, receipt numbers, vendor billings, invoices, and paid check numbers.

Owner's Property File

This file contains all records of the broker's performance of duties and obligations required by the terms of the management agreement, lease, or short-term occupancy contract. It is similar to the "closing file" maintained by sales brokers and should contain the following records: (1) management agreements, amendments, and addenda; (2) leases, reservation policies, occupancy records, and agreements with guests; (3) legal notices affecting the tenants or occupants and disclosures required by the Commission; (4) ongoing vendor or service provider contracts, competitive bids and estimates, invoices, vendor billings, and owner authorizations for repairs or special maintenance work apart from that contained in the management agreement; (5) monthly accounting reports, tax reports, or other information required by federal agencies affecting the use or disposition of money belonging to others; (6) schedules or reports of commissions and fees earned; and (7) evidence showing assessment and timely collection (45-90 days) of all money due to the broker's escrow account.

Tax Reports

The accounting data maintained by the broker as the agent for the owner is reported on IRS Form 1099. Information on reporting duties and suppliers of forms are available from the IRS. State tax information may be obtained from the Colorado Department of Revenue. City and county tax reporting is required and should be discussed with the business tax representatives concerned.

Business Licenses

Brokers who rent short-term occupancies must first obtain business licenses and register such activity (when required) with local authorities. The broker must collect and remit state and local sales and use taxes and maintain the necessary accounting records for inspection by other agencies. State tax information is available from the State Sales Tax Division at the Colorado Department of Revenue. Contact the local city and county offices for additional information concerning possible professional licenses or registration of business activities required in your area.

Management Reports Provided to Owners

The broker is required to provide an accurate and timely accounting report to the owner for the stewardship of funds received or disbursed on behalf of the owner. In the absence of another agreement, Commission Rule 5.15.A and 5.20.A require an accounting report to be furnished to a property owner within 30 days of the end of any month in which such funds were received or disbursed. A sample form is shown in the chapter appendix, Exhibit H.

The accounting report may show totals for various classes of income and expenditures, provided other detail is maintained to identify the individual receipts and expenditures included in the totals. The most common forms for the reports to owners are: (1) the balance sheet and income statement, and (2) the owner's statement of account. The statement of account is usually a manual tabulation of the beginning management cash balance plus receipts less payments equals ending cash balance. The same formula may be used to report or analyze the changes in other trust accounts.

The owner's accounting report must be complete and accurate in reporting management operations. Escrow account transactions are generally reported on a cash basis. Care must be taken to report factual data, *e.g.*, expenditures charged to a owner on the report implies that checks have been mailed and are not being held in the broker's office, income reported has been fully collected, and cash balances for various trust accounts are accurate representations of the owner's corresponding rights and obligations with respect to these accounts.

Commissions Earned and Paid

Commissions and fees are a matter of contract between the broker and the parties concerned. The contract should be written to avoid confusion and disputes over the actual terms. Rule 5.10.C) states: "In the absence of a specific written agreement to the contrary, commissions, fees and other charges collected by a brokerage firm for performing any service on behalf of another are considered 'earned' and available for use by the brokerage firm only after all contracted services have been performed and there is no remaining right of recall by others for such money."

Two accounting practices are followed for the withdrawal of fees and commissions from the escrow account. The "accounting rule" provides that such fees are not earned and available to the broker until the service has been fully performed and the occupant leaves the premises. Under the "tax rule," such fees are earned when the broker has the right per contract to use the money received. Rule 5.10.C applies the accounting rule, unless the parties agree otherwise. The management agreement and lease/reservation agreement must clearly and consistently disclose the nature of all fees and commissions charged to the parties concerned. Use of the "accounting rule" is a recommended approach. The delay between the date of check-in and the accounting cycle end date, when actual proceeds checks are cut, gives the broker additional time to make adjustments for late bills from vendors and/or account for changes in services billed to guests without borrowing from unearned advance deposits. The general industry "guest cancellation policy" below also illustrates the accounting rule. The time of a refundable cancellation may vary from 30 to 45 days before check-in, depending on the seasonal demand for the unit. The "tax rule" results in the deposit becoming non-refundable as early as upon receipt, but spending these amounts before the rental is used may create later hardships for the broker.

Rule 5.10.C also requires an accounting for any commissions and fees or other charges withdrawn in a single and usually "estimated lump-sum disbursement" from a management escrow bank account. Such an accounting must be shown by corresponding entries in the journal and the individual ledgers of those affected. The rule was adopted to prevent continuous guessing as to what amount is earned and payable to the broker; this approach follows "a one-sided journal entry," where no corresponding amounts are recorded in the individual owner ledgers. In companies where different commissions are charged to owners of different units, control over the accounting for earned commissions will soon be lost. The broker must be able to provide a schedule, upon request, which breaks down all components of the amounts included in any lump-sum disbursement. The schedule can be made by a custom computer report or manually prepared. The ledger entries must report such disbursements in accordance with Rule 5.14.B and include the date or time period for each individual transaction, rental, or occupancy. § 12-10-217(1)(h) C.R.S., requires the broker to account for any money belonging to others coming into the broker's possession; this includes money paid to the owner, tenant, guest, other vendors and service providers, and/or other governmental agencies, as well as the resulting commissions and fees paid. See the chapter appendix, Exhibit I.

Guest Cancellation Policy

These terms are generally found in the reservation agreement for rentals of short-term occupancies (30 days or less). The policy specifies when the prospective guest's advance deposit becomes non-refundable. By general industry practice, an advance deposit becomes non-refundable 30-45 days prior to the guest check-in date (depending on company policy and the season in which the unit is rented). At that time, the non-refundable deposit belongs to the owner and may only be withdrawn for any earned brokerage fees or commissions according to the management agreement. According to local custom, the broker may deduct a travel agent fee before paying the net amount of any earned brokerage fees or commission to the broker's company.

Management of short-term rentals does not currently require licensure as a real estate broker. But if the activity is conducted through a licensed brokerage, the licensee is not exempt from the jurisdiction of the Commission, must maintain the escrow and record-keeping requirements found in §§ 12-10-217(1)(h),(i) and (m) , C.R.S., and Rule 5.2, and the broker must account for commissions and fees earned according to Rule 5.10.C

The following time line illustrates how to determine the unearned advance deposit liability on the date the account is reconciled based on the funds held "now" per the accounting equation:

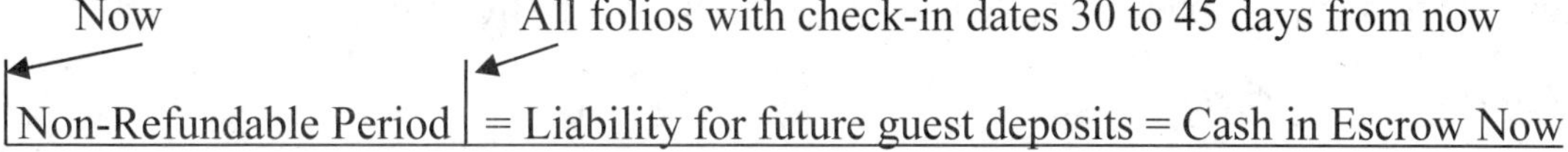

Ownership of the Management Records and Business Termination

A broker who manages property and homeowner associations may receive requests from the owner or homeowner association for originals or copies of the escrow records. In such cases, the broker should follow the procedures below.

A licensed broker managing a common interest (homeowner) association is generally the temporary custodian and trustee for the association records. Such records generally pertain to any budgeting, financial, or ongoing administration of the association business and related operating policies, conducted by the broker pursuant to the management agreement. These records belong to the association, not the broker.

When there is a change in the managing entity employed by the property owner, the ownership of property management records and the cost of making requested copies might also become a point of conflict. The broker should anticipate and address this issue in the initial management agreement. There is no Commission requirement mandating that the broker absorb the costs of any record duplication. An alternative process, such as inspection or audit by the landlord or client during a "window period," might be more acceptable than billing a large sum for producing extensive duplicate copies. The broker may not use the requirement to keep escrow records as a reason to prevent furnishing adequate information or documentation concerning the performance of duties or representations made in the accounting reports upon request of the owner, new manager, or association. The broker as a "custodian" of the information maintains ongoing records, association-vendor contracts, assessment and collection records, legal actions, association bank accounts, and association accounting records. The records utilized for such management should be delivered to the owner upon termination of the employment.

It is recommended that the broker obtain an itemized receipt from any new manager or the association board, stating they have received all records and accounts that were previously in the broker's custody. This statement should acknowledge the statutory requirement applicable to the broker for retention of these records for four years and waive any claim against the broker for release of such records in the event of subsequent loss or destruction.

If the broker questions the certainty of obtaining records at a later time and no waiver is granted, the broker should copy the financial statements, independent audit reports, and/or any minutes of meetings concerning key contractual duties performed or unresolved issues, the supporting bank statements and monthly reconciliations prepared, along with related management agreements, sample leases and/or occupancy agreements, and sample disclosures required by the Commission. Verification of reported receipts or expense is important to the Commission, the property owner, and other governmental entities. The broker's records, whether originals or copies, must provide a clear paper trail from the depositor to the authorized payee and show "money belonging to others" was properly utilized for authorized purposes.

If the change of brokers is within a licensed entity, the departing broker should follow the guidelines found in this chapter under "Changing of Employing Brokers."

Required Disclosures

In addition to the lead-based paint and brokerage relationship disclosures required by Rule 6.7and7.1, Rule 5.17 requires written disclosure and consent for any compensation for services billed to clients and customers. The broker must disclose the use of any affiliated business entity (including those owned by related parties) to provide services to property owners.

A broker may sometimes add administrative overhead or other similar mark-up fees to a vendor's invoice as compensation for arranging or overseeing the service. This increased amount may then be erroneously reported in the owner's accounting statement as if it is the "true" cost of the job charged by the vendor. This may result in a valid complaint on dishonest dealing. Similarly, use of an affiliated or related business entity that does not have to compete for the job at "arm's length" may have the same result. Section 6-1-105, C.R.S., provides for damages to an injured party in any civil litigation for deceptive trade practices (see Chapter, "Related Real Estate Law").

To comply with Rule 5.17, first obtain prior written consent for payment of any additional compensation in the management agreement or a signed and dated addendum as the situation warrants. Next, disclose the fixed percentage of markup in these agreements and show the dollar amount added to the cost of the service rendered or provided in the owner's monthly or periodic accounting statement. This avoids any question about the client/

customer's actual receipt of such disclosures by showing the added cost in the broker's own accounting report, rather than in a separate invoice attached to the report. If there are variable or unique rates and prices used, these should also be disclosed and pre-authorized in the management agreement or addendum. Additionally, disclose the use of any affiliated or controlled business entity providing such service, the billing rates used, and a general statement to the effect that the broker may or may not realize a profit in providing such services. Finally, maintain the internal accounting records, invoices, and reports showing compliance with the terms of the agreement(s). Brokers are advised to review and update any old or outdated agreements and should consult with resources available from IREM, NARPM, BOMA, CAR, and their own attorney in this matter.

C. Accounting for Security and Advance Rental Deposits

Rule 5.8.A applies to all licensed brokers

Requirements that should be followed in residential and/or commercial property management can be found in Commission Rule 5.8.A.

Commission position statement CP-5, Advance Rental and Security Deposits, expounds on this rule. The goal is to have consistent terms for the responsibility to return any security deposit in both the lease and management agreement or addenda thereto. These requirements are not met when the lease provides that the owner holds the deposit and the management agreement is silent on the matter. Such inconsistency may create an unfunded and undisclosed financial liability for the property owner. The broker must account for the return, forfeiture, or transfer of the tenant deposit per the requirements of §§ 38-12-103(1), (2), and (4), C.R.S.; see Chapter, "Property Management and Leases."

Local Requirements

The City of Boulder currently requires payment of a stated rate of interest to tenants for any security deposits held for residential housing leased in that city. (See City Ordinances 12-2-5, 12-2-6, and 12-2-7). The broker should inform the property owner of this requirement and may have to assess the owner for any difference between the "statutory rate" and the lower "market rate" of interest when accounting for return of the deposit upon termination of the lease.

Advance Deposits

Under the property management agreement, a broker must transfer all escrowed money belonging to the owner of the property at reasonable and agreed upon times with the accounting required by Rules 5.14, 5.15 and 5.16 or 5.20. If such money is subject to recall by the guest/occupant, it must be escrowed until rightfully earned per Rule 5.10.C, and then must be transferred or credited to the property owner. A broker has no right to use an unearned advance deposit that is subject to recall. Deposits that are not subject to recall by the guest/occupant may not be transferred to the broker's business operating account or used for the broker's benefit unless this is specifically authorized as an earned commission in the management agreement with the property owner.

Offsetting Refundable Deposits Against Broker Expenses

Questions arise over whether a broker may pay certain expenses from refundable deposit amounts held in trust. The answer depends on the ownership of these funds.

A broker has no ownership in earnest money held in a sales transaction. If the seller and broker terminate a listing agreement when the parties are unable to close a transaction, and the buyer is not in default, the broker may not use the deposit money to pay expenses that would have been due from the seller out of a later earned commission. The deposit must be returned to prospective buyer intact. If the buyer has forfeited the deposit, the broker is not entitled to any of the earnest money unless there is a previous written agreement with the seller to share the amount forfeited. The provisions of Commission position statement CP-6, Earnest Money Deposits, should be followed when ownership of the deposit is disputed.

Similarly, the broker has no ownership interest in management funds held as refundable security or advance deposits. Lease and management agreements often allow the broker to collect and retain late fees, non-sufficient funds charges, and other fees from tenants. Such fees are for the benefit of the broker, and Rule 5.8.A and 5.9 prohibits withholding such amounts from a refundable security deposit. Section 38-12-103(1), C.R.S., provides that the deposit may be withheld for non-payment of rent, repair work, or cleaning contracted for by the tenant for the benefit of the property owner, not the broker. Section 38-12-103(7), C.R.S., also states that any provision in the rental agreement whereby any provision of § 38-12-103(1) is waived shall be deemed to be against public policy and shall be "void" (*i.e.*, not legally binding).

A broker who holds a refundable deposit does so for the benefit of the owner and tenant. If the deposit is slowly liquidated to collect fees owed to the broker, the owner's security is jeopardized both by a loss of financial assurance against damage and by the tenant's loss of motivation to properly care for the property. Further, the owner could become fully liable for return of the full deposit (plus treble damages if paid late) even though the tenant might owe money for late fees and other charges to the broker.

If the broker has gained proper agreement for the collection of fees in both the management agreement and lease or occupancy agreement, then upon termination of the lease or occupancy, the order of deduction should be: first to the owner (for property damages, etc.) and then to the tenant less any late fees or other costs due the broker. If the balance is not adequate to pay the broker, the broker must seek collection directly from the tenant concerned. The concepts above also apply to brokers who receive advance short-term deposits. Care should be taken to ensure that all associates understand the proper handling of refundable deposits.

Office Policy Manuals

Commission Rule 6.3 requires brokers to demonstrate reasonable supervision over all licensees and non-licensed employees, including but not limited to secretaries, bookkeepers, and personal assistants of licensed employees. To comply with these supervision Rules, brokers who employ others are required to establish an office policy manual. This is in addition to the requirements for a written brokerage relationship policy (Rules 6.4.A; 6.4.A.1; 6.4.B), a policy to protect confidential information (Rules 6.4.A; 6.4.A.1;6.4.B), and designation brokerage relationships (Rules 6.4.A.2; 6.6; 1.16), whether performing sales or management activities. The following topical guidelines (as applicable) are suggested for office policy manuals.

Sales Transactions

- Parties responsible for delegated duties/agreements;

- Preparation and review of contracts prior to closing;
- Handling earnest money deposits, disputes, and releases;
- Backup contracts;
- Closing documents and closing instructions for the broker's agent;
- Maintenance/custody of contract files;
- Escrow records and written procedures for handling business operations;
- Fair housing/affirmative action marketing;
- Staff training – dissemination of information, staff meetings;
- Use of personal assistants;
- Guaranteed buyouts;
- Investor purchases;
- Non-qualifying assumptions and owner financing;
- Licensee's purchase and sale of property;
- Listing procedures and release of listings;
- Rental occupancy before closing;
- Computer system – data control, backup, and physical security; and
- Internal audit and supervisory reviews of business operations.

Management Activity

- Operating policies and required disclosures;
- Use of unlicensed on-site managers;
- Administration of rentals and leasing activity;
- Items under "Sales" above, where applicable;
- Supervision of accounting services, records, and reporting to others;
- Cash handling, collection of delinquent rents and deposits;
- Ownership/management of rental properties by agents;
- Administration and policies for in-house services;
- Maintenance of records and business reports by any outside service;
- Advances of funds on behalf of clients/customers;
- Cancellation of agreements and termination of services;
- Related services performed by affiliated entities;
- Backup and disaster recovery plan for loss of business records;
- Eviction and legal action; and
- Return of security and advance deposits.

Accounting Problems to Avoid

The following list highlights some general but common audit problems found in management audits.

1. The software used reconciles to a "net" cash balance, where positive owner ledgers are offset against negative (overspent) balances with a resulting cash shortage. This

may result from use of the accrual basis of accounting by "default" in the installation process, or by allowing payment of expenses in anticipation of future revenues. It is acceptable for the same owner of different properties to offset negative balance properties against other positive ones if the end result is positive.

2. Failing to print out the bank reconciliation in detail at the time the account is reconciled. Some software programs will not retroactively reproduce earlier reconciliations with the corresponding current liability detail. This weakens internal control and increases the difficulty of reconstructing prior records in the event of a system "crash." The reconciliation should be printed on the actual date of reconciliation, which is normally the same as the ending bank statement date. When Quicken, Quickbooks, or similar software programs are used, brokers may keep the escrow reports by month in yearly, tabulated notebooks. The first section is the monthly ending journal balance (the monthly check register), the second section is the listing of pending ledgers at month end, the third is the monthly detail bank reconciliation printout, and the fourth is a copy of the escrow bank statement.

3. Using fictitious deposits in transit and/or outstanding checks to "plug" the reconciled bank balance on the reconciliation worksheet. "Plug" means to balance the reconciliation by using arbitrary or nonexistent items to force the reconciled bank balance to agree with company records. While this condition may be a simple fix, it may mask an ongoing internal theft of funds in any bank account. Brokers should inspect the items shown on the reconciliation worksheet carefully, and review the corresponding bank statement, journal, and ledgers before accepting the report as valid. Outstanding amounts should clear quickly. Fictitious "voids" are common tools used to conceal unauthorized account withdrawals.

4. Making "John Doe" deposits and/or payments without recording or maintaining appropriate supporting information in the accounting deposit/check records. This may be due to over-extended job duties or poor record keeping, but may also conceal serious errors or thefts of trust assets. This condition may lead to complaints for failing to account for money belonging to others.

5. "We'll wait and fix that again in the next audit." Section12-10-203, C.R.S., grants the broker's license on the basis of demonstrated competency to transact business in a manner that protects the public interest. A repeated failure to correct audit conditions is contrary to the requirements of Rule 6.3.B.6. The audit representation letter affirms the broker's agreement to maintain required corrections in place after the examination is completed.

IV. Subdivisions and Associations

A. General

This part describes the financial accounting requirements applicable to brokers and developers who list and/or market property registered with the Commission as a subdivision. All brokers actively marketing these subdivisions must ensure that the applicable provisions of Rule 5.2 are followed. Developer sales contracts and disclosure forms are individually approved during the subdivision registration process and must be used for the sale of a registered subdivision property. The form used by the developer should be studied and understood by the real estate broker. Developers, if not required to use licensed brokers under the exemptions found in § 12-10-201(6)(b), C.R.S., may still be subject to other accounting and record-keeping requirements contained in any applicable sales or management agreement, declaration, and bylaws; the Subdivision Developers Act, §§ 12-10-505(1)(e) and (g), C.R.S.; Commission Subdivision Rules; and/or the Colorado Common Interest Ownership Act, §§ 38-33.3-101, *et seq.*, C.R.S.

The goal of the regulatory process is to ensure that there is reasonable disclosure of all material matters at the time of the sale, and to ensure that the purchaser's ownership interest in the land is conveyed according to the terms of the contract, free and clear of any overriding or superior encumbrances. Commission accounting requirements for developers differ in significant ways from those applicable to brokers. The Commission rules for subdivsions contain significantly fewer requirements than those for real estate brokers.

Use of Licensed Brokers

Subdivision property registered in Colorado must be sold by actively licensed brokers, unless exempt under § 12-10-201, C.R.S. In the absence of an agreement/contract to the contrary, brokers for these sales must escrow funds received in accordance with Rule 5.2, and the subdivision rules. The broker must account for and remit such money according to the sales contract and/or the employment agreement with the developer and/or association and keep the applicable escrow records.

Subdivision Registration

Any agreement/contract for the sale or lease of property is voidable by the purchaser and unenforceable by the developer unless that developer was duly registered under the Subdivision Developers' Act at the time the contract was made.

Developers are required to register with the Commission if they market Colorado property to others, or if they sell out-of-state property in Colorado, which is:

1. Divided (cumulatively) into 20 or more interests intended solely for residential use;
2. A conversion (cumulatively) of an existing structure into a common interest community of 20 or more residential units;
3. A group of 20 or more time-shares intended for residential use; or
4. A group of 20 or more proprietary leases in a cooperative housing corporation.

Registration is not required for:

1. Selling memberships in campgrounds;
2. Bulk sales between developers;
3. Residential property not previously occupied that is to be constructed and where the consideration paid includes the cost of the residential building(s) or new home(s);
4. Lots, which at the time of closing or lease, are situated on a street improved to the standards of those maintained by the county where the lot resides, and which have a feasible plan for water and sewage disposal, and which have phone, electric, and utility services adequate to serve the lots under applicable city, county, state, or federal laws;

5. Any subdivision that is or has been required to be approved after September 1, 1972 by a regional, county, or municipal planning authority. Questions may be directed to the licensing section at (303) 894-2166.

The developer's registration expires on December 31 of each year, and a developer is not authorized to transact business after expiration. A registration that has expired may be reinstated within two years after such expiration upon payment of the renewal fee if the developer meets all other requirements of the developer's act.

Contract Provisions

All contracts used to market registered property must include the following (other disclosures are required by subdivision rules in an attached disclosure document):

1. The names of the licensed real estate office and broker responsible for making the sale;
2. The purchaser's *five-day right of rescission* immediately above the purchaser's signature line;
3. A statement that a title commitment and/or title insurance policy will be delivered, unless otherwise agreed;
4. A statement concerning the time for delivery of deed after closing or payment of all installment amounts due;
5. A statement of any taxes, special authority/district taxes, or assessments to which the purchaser may be subject, whether existing, proposed, or unpaid at the time of contracting;
6. A statement of any taxes, special authority/district taxes, or assessments to which the purchaser may be subject, whether existing, proposed, or unpaid at the time of contracting; and
7. Seller and landlord disclosure of lead-based paint hazards for housing built before 1978. This HUD disclosure became effective September 6, 1996 for sales and rentals of more than four residential dwellings. There are severe penalties for non-disclosure. See the HUD pamphlet titled "Protect Your Family From Lead in Your Home."

B. Accounting Requirements for Registered Developers

Commission Requirements for Sales and Leasing

Commission requirements are found in subdivision rules and § 12-10-506(6)(b), C.R.S. The developer must retain the following records for a period of seven years (under these subdivision rules):

1. Requires copies of the sales contract, lease agreement, financing agreement, settlement statements, title commitment/insurance policy, trust deed, escrow agreement, and other documents (disclosures) executed by the parties to effect the sale or transfer of any interest in the subdivision to purchasers be maintained at a Colorado place of business (or to reasonably produce such upon request). Brokers selling subdivision property must ensure that settlement statements are accurate and must show that any applicable association dues, transfer taxes, or other membership

fees are properly prorated, or paid by the party as agreed in the contract, (real estate broker Rule 6.19.A).

2. Requires a record showing the receipt and disbursement of any money or assets received or paid on behalf of any purchaser or similar association managed or "controlled" (through actual voting rights held) by the developer.

3. Any Commission-approved escrow agreement with an independent third party and the related receipt and disbursement records showing the transfer of funds received from potential purchasers of reservations in an uncompleted project or pending subdivision registration under such escrow agreement, § 12-10-502, C.R.S., and rules. Brokers engaged in the sale of reservation agreements must also comply with escrow requirements as the designated trustee and independent third party. The developer may not directly or indirectly control the handling of funds by the escrow agent, control the process of maintaining records of the agent's account activities, or exercise any independent right of withdrawal over the funds held, apart from the Commission-approved escrow agreement.

4. Pursuant to § 38-33.3-315, C.R.S., the "declarant/developer" shall pay all common expenses until the association makes a common expense assessment and shall pay assessments on unsold units according to the allocations as set forth in the declaration; the declarant alone is liable for all expenses in connection with real estate in the common interest community that is subject to "development rights," § 38-33.3-307, C.R.S. The association shall keep financial records sufficient to enforce liens for unpaid assessments under § 38-33.3-316, C.R.S., and minutes of official meetings and association activity required by the recorded declaration.

5. In addition to the above, the following requirements must be met under the Colorado Common Interest Ownership Act (CCIOA), if applicable, when a developer transfers control to the association membership in accordance with §§ 38-33.3-303(5), (7), and (9), C.R.S.:

   (a) Original or certified copies of the recorded declaration, articles of incorporation, bylaws, minutes book, and any rules and regulations that may have been promulgated.

   (b) An accounting for all association funds, including audited financial statements with an accompanying opinion of an independent certified public accountant that the statements present fairly the financial position in accordance with generally accepted accounting principles or a disclaimer of such attestation. The developer shall pay the cost for examination of the association financial statements.

   (c) All association funds or control thereof.

   (d) Inventories of personal property represented by the developer to be the property of the association or which has been exclusively used in the operation and enjoyment of the common elements.

   (e) Copies of plans and specifications used in the construction of improvements in the common interest community.

   (f) All insurance policies then in force in which the unit owners, the association, or its directors and officers are named as insured persons.

(g) Copies of any certificates of occupancy issued for improvements comprising the common interest community.

(h) Any other permits issued by governmental bodies applicable to the common interest community one year prior to transfer of control to the members of the community.

(i) Written warranties of contractors, suppliers, and manufacturers still in force.

(j) A roster of unit owners and mortgagees and their addresses and known telephone numbers.

(k) Employment contracts between the association and others.

(l) Any service contract between the association and its membership with others.

(m) For large, planned communities, copies of all recorded deeds and recorded or unrecorded leases evidencing rights in the community and its common elements.

C. Management of Common Interest Associations

The developer's record-keeping duty is found in subdivision rules, § 12-10-506(6)(b), C.R.S., and, when applicable, §§ 38-33.3-115, -117, and -118, C.R.S. The Commission has jurisdiction over the developer during the time the developer controls the financial operation of the association by controlling the actual voting membership on the association board of directors. After the developer has transferred control of the common interest association to the membership, the developer is governed by CCIOA.

Pooled bank accounts are not allowed for the management of any common interest owner (homeowner) association consisting of 30 or more units under the provisions of § 38-33.3-306(3), C.R.S. This law requires the use of separate accounts for each association and association reserve account, the presentation of an annual accounting for association activities, and a financial statement prepared by the manager, a public or certified public accountant, and the maintenance of not less than $50,000 in fidelity bond insurance (or more per bylaws) for the manager and others who perform management activities on behalf of the association. Brokers who manage associations in their licensed company accounts must use separate escrow accounts per real estate broker rules in Chapter 5.

Preexisting Subdivisions

Accounting for developer-controlled subdivisions created in Colorado before July 1, 1992 (which have not elected treatment under § 38-33.3-118, C.R.S.) is generally governed by the provisions of declaration and bylaws or the applicable sections of the Subdivision Act. During the period of control of the association, beginning in January 1990, and for seven years thereafter, the developer must maintain annual records, which reasonably show that there was no diversion, conversion, or failure to account for any association funds. See subdivision Rules.

Sections 38-33.3-117(1) and (3), C.R.S., of CCIOA do not replace preexisting bylaws in regard to: (1) the process for transfer of control to the association members (§ 38-33.3-303), or (2) the requirement to keep separate association accounts for funds and reserves held by the developer as manager of 30 or more units (§ 38-33.3-306). The bylaws will frequently require more detailed records for interim inspections by association members and to prepare audited financial statements for the period of management while the developer controlled the association.

New Subdivisions

For subdivisions created after July 1, 1992, or those electing treatment under CCIOA, the record-keeping requirements of subdivision rules are supplemented by CCIOA, including § 38-33.3-306(3)(a). A developer who manages an association of 30 or more units must keep the records showing compliance with the following statutory requirements for a seven-year period. Such records must be reasonably available for inspection by members of the association or the Commission at the developer's and/or broker's Colorado business office and shall include:

1. The association bank accounts, monthly statements, and returned items according to § 38-33.3-306(3), C.R.S., for the operating funds and reserves belonging to each association. If the manager engaged is a licensed broker, then separate escrow accounts shall be used, unless there is another agreement or law to the contrary. It is recommended that the written agreement between the association and manager specifically identify the nature and requirements of the accounts and records to be used.
2. Property, general liability, and fidelity insurance or bond (for 30 or more units), and/or proper notice to the owners of any cancellation or the unavailability of such insurance, § 38-33.3-313, C.R.S.
3. The minutes for all association board meetings per the applicable bylaws, § 38-33.3-308, C.R.S.
4. Records necessary for transfer of control to the association. See detailed itemization found in §§ 38-33.3-303(9) and 38-33.3-314 through -317, C.R.S. These sections require accounting records for the proper dispossession of any surplus association funds, amounts of assessments collected and uncollected or delinquent, interest and penalties, liens filed, association minutes, and other related membership voting records.
5. Records for the payment of association dues assessed to the developer for all unsold units, intervals, or lots by the prescribed due date.
6. Records for any amount billed to the association for services provided to the association and any expense incurred in rendering such services. Such matters must be disclosed in the renewal of the developer's registration and in the disclosures required by subdivision rules.

V. Appendix – Sample Forms

A. Notice of Escrow or Trust Account

B. Escrow Account Journal

C. The Beneficiary and Broker Ledger Cards

D. The Bank Reconciliation Worksheet

E. Tenant Ledger

F. Tenant Security Deposit Ledger

G. Owner's Ledger

H. Change of Employing Broker Affidavit

I. Schedule of Commissions Earned Versus Amounts Taken

A. Notice of Escrow or Trust Account

TO ____
(Name of Bank or Depository)

Pursuant to § 12-10-203(6)(a) , C.R.S., I, ________________________ am the employing broker for ____
(Name of Licensed Real Estate Company)

Furthermore, pursuant to §§ 12-10-217(1)(i) and (m), C.R.S., Colorado Division of Real Estate Rules 1.34 and 5.2, and Federal Deposit Insurance Corporation (FDIC) requirements, I am required to maintain a "escrow" or "trust" account with a bank or recognized depository in the State of Colorado for the purpose of holding money belonging to others. With regard to any account that is designated as an "escrow" or "trust" account, the said account(s) is/are maintained with you as a depository for money belonging to persons other than myself or my brokerage company in my fiduciary capacity as a licensed Colorado real estate broker under the provisions of § 12-10-203(6)(a) , C.R.S., and Rules 1.34 and 5.2.

The account number(s) for the "escrow" or "trust" account(s) maintained at your financial institution are:____

DATED this _________________ day of ___________________________, 20_____.

____
(Signature of Employing Broker)

ACKNOWLEDGEMENT OF RECEIPT

I, a duly authorized representative of ____________________________________,
the bank or depository identified above and acknowledge receipt of the above "NOTICE OF ESCROW OR TRUST ACCOUNT" on _______day of ____________, 20_____.

____
(Representative's Signature and Title) Rev 9/20

B. Escrow Account Journal

Escrow Account Journal					Page _______
For ______________________ Account					
Date Year	Check No.	Description of Transaction	Payments	Deposits	Journal Balance
			Balance Forward		

C. The Beneficiary and Broker Ledger Cards

FOR EACH BENEFICIARY (SALES/UNCLAIMED PROPERTY)

BUYER ____________________ SELLER ____________________
LISTING ADDRESS ____
CLOSING DATE ______________ LISTING ____________________

DATE	CHECK	DESCRIPTION	PAYMENT	DEPOSIT	BALANCE

FOR BROKER/COMPANY FUNDS IN ANY ACCOUNT

BROKER / COMPANY LEDGER CARD NO _______
FOR ____________________ ESCROW ACCOUNT

DATE	CHECK	DESCRIPTION	PAYMENT	DEPOSIT	BALANCE

D. The Bank Reconciliation Worksheet

ACCOUNT TITLE ________________ ACCOUNT NUMBER ________________

STATEMENT DATE ________________ DATE RECONCILED ________________

PREPARED BY ________________ REVIEWED BY ________________

ENTER LEDGER BALANCES ON STATEMENT DATE BY BUYER NAME OR PROPERTY ADDRESS BELOW:

BROKER'S LEDGER $____________

____________	____________
____________	____________
____________	____________
____________	____________
____________	____________
____________	____________
____________	____________
____________	____________
____________	____________
____________	____________
____________	____________
____________	____________

LEDGER BALANCES PER ATTACHED LIST $____________

TOTAL LEDGERS $____________

JOURNAL BALANCE ON STATEMENT DATE $____________

ENTER ENDING BANK STATEMENT BALANCE ON STATEMENT DATE $________

ADD: ALL UNCLEARED DEPOSITS:

DATE	AMOUNT	DATE	AMOUNT

TOTAL OUTSTANDING DEPOSITS $________

SUBTOTAL $________

SUBTRACT: OUTSTANDING CHECKS:

NUMBER	AMOUNT	NUMBER	AMOUNT

TOTAL CONTINUATION SHEET (S) $________

RECONCILIED BANK BALANCE $________

RECONCILED BANK BALANCE SHOULD = JOURNAL AND TOTAL LEDGER BALANCES ON LEFT SIDE

REV 5/06

E. Tenant Ledger

MULTI-FAMILY DWELLINGS

TENANT(S) ______________________ **UNIT** ______________
______________________ **PHONE** ______________
______________________ ______________

OWNER NAME & ADDRESS ______________________
____

LEASE DATE ________ **EXPIRATION** ________ **RENT $** ________ **UTIL $** ________

LATE FEES $ ________ **OTHER $** ________ ***SEC DEP $** ________ **(OWNER HOLDS)**

REMARKS ______________________
____

*** MAY BE OPERATING CAPTIAL WHEN OWNER HOLDS—OTHERWISE USE SEPARATE ACCT & LEDGER**

DATE COLLECTED	RENT &SEC DEP DUE	UTILITIES DUE	OTHER CHARGES	AMOUNTS DEPOSITED	UNPAID BALANCE
BAL FWD $					

F. Tenant Security Deposit Ledger

FOR MULTI-FAMILY PROPERTIES

TENANT(S) ______________________________________ **UNIT** ____________________
____ **PHONE** ____________________
____ ____________________
WORK ADDRESS ____
PRIOR ADDRESS ____
LEASE DATE ______ **EXPIRATION** ______ **LEASING COMPANY** ____________________

SEC DEP $ __________ **UTILITY $**__________ **PET $** __________ **OTHER $** ____________

SEC DEP HELD BY ____ **OWNER** _____ **BROKER PRIOR COMPANY** ________________
REMARKS ____
____

DATE	CHECK	DESCRIPTION	PAYMENTS	DEPOSITS	BALANCE

G. Owner's Ledger

OWNER'S LEDGER

OWNER NAME ____________________ ACCT/CARD NO __________
PROPERTY ADDRESS ____________________
OWNER'S ADDRESS ____________________
OWNER PHONE __________ MGMT AGRMNT DATE __________ EXPIRES __________
MGT FEE % __________ OTHER FEES ____________________
RENTAL AMT $ __________ SEC DEP AMT $ __________ HELD BY __________
TENANT(S) ____________________ LEASE __________ EXPIRES __________
____________________ PHONE __________
REMARKS ____________________
____

DATE	CHECK	DESCRIPTION	PAYMENTS	DEPOSITS	BALANCE
				BALANCE FORWARD $	

H. Change of Employing Broker Affidavit

CHANGE OF EMPLOYING BROKER AFFIDAVIT

I, ____, License No. ______________,
am the current employing broker for ____
____
____

I hereby affirm to the best of my current knowledge and belief that all escrow account and escrow account liabilities stated herein or incorporated by reference are a complete and accurate representation of all "money belonging to others," as defined in Commission Rule 1.34, which is held or controlled by me in my fiduciary capacity as the company's employing broker on this ____________ day of ______________, 20____. The escrow bank accounts listed below or as incorporated by reference are fully funded for all corresponding escrow liabilities incurred on the above date. The funds held in the escrow account(s) listed below are hereby transferred to the new employing broker and/or the continuing company officer(s) and/or director(s), with all corresponding escrow records and transaction files required by §§ 12-10-217 (1)(h),(i) and(m), C.R.S., and Chapter 5 Rules:

Bank	Account Number	Purpose	Reconciled Balance	(Date)

The foregoing records, accounts, and cash balances are accepted as complete and accurate in all material respects by the undersigned parties, who release the departing broker from further obligation for the maintenance, custody, and duty to account for new deposits, payments, and banking events after the said date above. The undersigned parties agree to maintain the records received for the time required under §§ 12-10-217(1)(k) C.R.S., at the licensed business location or company's storage facility.

Executed this _________ day of ________________________________, 20 ____
by: ____, License No ______________,
Departing Employing Broker
and:
____, License No ______________,
New Employing Broker,
and/or by:

____
____
____
Officers and Directors (of the continuing company) Rev 9/20

I. Schedule of Commissions Earned Versus Amounts Taken

YEAR TO DATE – NOVEMBER 30, 20XX

DATE 20XX	CHECK NUMBER	FILE REFERENCE OR PROPERTY	COMM %	GROSS REVENUE	EARNED COMM	FEES	TOTAL EARNED	TOTAL TAKEN	BROKER'S LEDGER
BAL FWD	$		N/A	425,000.00	55,129.00	6,077.50	61,206.50	58,766.99	2,439.51
11/1	1001	SmithB &B (45 day)	10	5,000.00	500.00	_	500.00	500.00	_
11/1	1002	Hill Top 44 (60 day)	10	5,000.00	500.00	45.73	545.73	545.73	_
11/10	1100	Folio 341 99	40	10,000.00	4,000.00	55.95	4,055.95	2,555.95	1,500.00
11/10	1100	Folio 200 11	40	9,000.00	3,600.00	"	3,600.00	3,600.00	_
11/10	1100	Folio 34889	40	15,000.00	6,000.00	_	6,000.00	6,000:00	_
11/10	1100	Folio 33521	40	2,000.00	800.00	_	800.00	800:00	_
11/28	1200	Folio 33521	40	5,500.00	2,200.00	300.00	2,500.00	2,200.00	300.00
11/30	Deposit	Folio 200 11	40	(9,000.00)	(3,600.00)	_	(3,600.00)	_	(3,600.001
ENDING BALANCE 11/31/20XX $			N/A	$467,500.00	$69,129.00	$6,479.18	$75,608.18	$74,968.67	$639.51

p

Chapter 22: Property Management and Leases

I. Introduction

Over the years, residential and commercial property management has developed into complex and profitable real estate specialties. Property managers are responsible for many trillions of dollars in real property market value on a long-term basis. Many firms are devoted exclusively to property management, and others have set up autonomous property management divisions to profit from the economic stability of management income during periods of slow sales activity. Some other firms simply do occasional property management as an accommodation to their sales listing clients.

Property managers offer a variety of extensive services and shoulder varying degrees of responsibility in the performance of their duties to the owners and tenants. Property managers are considered "**general agents**," performing multiple functions as compared to sales licensees who, as "**special agents**," are employed for a limited duration to market a specific property.

Whatever the scope of the management, if a broker or brokerage company is soliciting tenants, executing leases, collecting rents and security deposits, supervising repairs and improvements, and collecting a fee for such services, that person or company is performing property management and should become very familiar not only with this chapter, but also with Chapter, "Escrow Records," Chapter, "Colorado Fair Housing Act," Chapter, "Subdivision Laws," and the applicable Commission Rules and Position Statements.

Occasionally, employed brokers are tempted to perform residential property management without their employing broker's knowledge or consent. An employed broker is prohibited from performing residential property management outside of the knowledge and supervision of his or her employing broker. Section 12-10-203(9), C.R.S., requires all business to be conducted only in the licensed name of the employing broker. Employing brokers must be aware of their employed brokers' activities, supervise all employed brokers' activities, and maintain proper accounting of any moneys obtained by the employed broker in accordance with Commission Rules and § 12-10-217(1)(g), C.R.S. Further, the employing broker should have a clearly written policy as to the firm's offering of management services, and outline specifically how the firm and its employees will conduct such services.

The brokerage firm's Policy Manual must define the scope of business and policies allowed or not allowed within and by the brokerage firm as well as independent brokers working with the brokerage firm.

Property managers face challenges of age of construction, cash flow requirements, vacancy rates, heating and cooling concerns, and electrical and plumbing needs, as well as EPA guidelines for radon, asbestos, and lead-based paint, plus both federal and state fair housing and civil rights regulations and the state-mandated warranty of habitability, and carbon monoxide detector requirements. Additionally, sound management and accounting practices must be followed to avoid commingling of funds among the properties managed.

Professional property managers perform a variety of functions and must be able to advise on heating, cooling, painting, decorating, roofs, pests, insurance, the sales market, and household appliances, and must know when to refer to other professionals such as financial or tax advisors or attorneys. Property managers should be adept at problem resolution negotiations, accounting, budgeting, and sales.

A working knowledge of landlord/tenant law, access to a competent attorney, effective communication skills, and the ability to organize and delegate effectively, as well as good time-management skills and stress-reduction techniques, are also necessary for efficient property management. While an average sales licensee may handle two or three transactions a month, a professional property manager with an inventory of 200 units may be executing five to six leases, as well as collecting and disbursing income from all 200 units every month. The dollar value of each transaction may be smaller, but the manager is most often responsible for the entire value of the property and over an extensive period of time. The skills involved are equally important. A homeowner association manager may handle 1,000 units comprised of many small or several large communities.

At the outset, a property manager must clearly understand the owner's needs and desires for the property. Management plans must support the owner's objectives of short- or long-term ownership, long-term investment, or other income needs. As the management contract continues over time, the manager must excel at clear and prompt communications with the owner.

A property manager may decide to specialize in a particular type of property or to service many types. Property management specialties may include:

- Single family homes, attached or detached (condos, townhomes);
- Multi-unit buildings (residential or office);
- Government-assisted housing;
- Retail properties;
- Shopping centers;
- Office or industrial complexes;
- Resort or short-term rental properties;[†] and
- Homeowners associations.

[†]A Colorado real estate license is not required for the above specialty or for those exempt under the provisions of § 112-10-201, C.R.S., who lease or manage apartment buildings or condominiums, such as regularly salaried onsite managers employed by building owners or homeowners associations. However, many such specialists are Colorado real estate licensees, sometimes because they perform other activities that do require a license. Accordingly, brokers who perform services that may not require licensure must still follow the Commission Rules and Position Statement(s) applicable under their employment agreements.

Several national organizations exist to assist property managers in the various management specialties. Each offers a wealth of information, networking opportunities, and referral services, as well as professional education courses and designations, and are listed at the end of this chapter.

II. Commission Position Statements:

The Real Estate Commission creates Commission Position Statements (CPs) to clarify and set expectations in specific areas of real estate:

CP 4: Commission Position on Interest Bearing Trust Accounts

CP 5: Commission Position on Advanced Rentals and Security Deposits

CP 19: Commission Position on Short Term Occupancy Agreements

CP 27: Commission Position on the Performance of Residential Leasing and Property Management Functions:

- License Requirements
- Leasing vs. Property Management
- Supervision
- Forms
- Trust Accounts and Record Keeping
- Security Deposits
- Transfer of Service
- Managing Broker's Own Properties

CP 38: Disclosure of Affiliated Business Arrangements and Conflicts of Interest

CP 41: Commission Position on Competency

CP 42: Commission Position on Apartment Building or Complex Management

III. Management Functions

A property manager's primary objective should be to obtain the highest possible income stream consistent with protecting the owner's capital investment and preserving a good owner-manager-tenant relationship.

The following list, although not all-inclusive, outlines what is usually expected of a property manager:

1. Establish the rental schedule.
2. Merchandise the space and collect the rents.
3. Schedule maintenance and repairs.
4. Develop employee policies and supervise employee performance. Have an employee manual of policies and instructions.
5. Maintain proper accounting records and make regularly scheduled reports to the owner.
6. Qualify and investigate tenant credit.
7. Prepare and execute leases.
8. Prepare decorating, renovation, or repair specifications and obtain estimates.

9. Hire, instruct, and maintain qualified and willing personnel to staff the building(s)..
10. Audit and pay bills, account for the return or forfeiture of tenant security deposits, bill tenants for utilities, and collect and disburse late fees.
11. Advertise and publicize vacancies through appropriate media.
12. Plan and supervise alterations and modernizing programs.
13. Inspect vacant space frequently and periodically.
14. Keep abreast of the times and stay posted on competitive market conditions.
15. Pay insurance premiums and taxes. Recommend adequate insurance coverage.
16. Be well informed with regards to the Warranty of Habitability Laws, and the Americans with Disabilities Act, which requires public buildings to meet safety and access standards.
17. Provide for maximum-security provisions, understanding that the landlord is responsible for reasonable measures to safeguard tenants against intruders.
18. Develop an annual budget for the financial operations plan with the owner.
19. Manage affairs for homeowner associations. See Chapter, "Subdivision Laws."
20. Keep abreast of all legislative changes involving Landlord/Tenant law and Real Estate in general which could affect your property management business.
21. Attend Fair Housing classes on a regular basis.
22. Do monthly 3-way reconciliations on all trust accounts
23. Establish "Best Practices" in your property management duties and be consistent in adherence to the same. Some examples would be yard assessments, video taping and photographing property, as well as performing yearly maintenance on furnaces, water heaters, fireplace chimneys, gutter cleaning, etc.

The property manager's responsibilities do not end with the collection of rents and reporting income and expenses. The professional manager must be equipped to counsel the owner on a myriad of problems, including the following:

1. Analyses and recommendations regarding vacant land and proposed and existing buildings.
2. Economic analyses and supervision of planned remodeling and renovation.
3. Economic surveys and analyses of trade areas.
4. Analyses of rental rates and trends.
5. Budgeting for operating cash flows and unexpected costs or seasonal fluctuations in rental income.
6. Working with municipalities and aid organizations.
7. EPA and State regulations for renovations and construction.

Each property and category has its own character and its own set of problems. A broker performing property management must recognize his or her staff's time and experience limitations. Lack of experience only opens liability for the Brokerage Firm.

Property management is a time-consuming process, and scheduling of labor prevalent problem. A shortage of qualified personnel is no defense for failure to fulfill fiduciary or contract duties to an owner. A competent manager should not assume additional accounts without adequate time or the technology to service them.

The business relationship between the property manager and owner is based on a current written management agreement. A manager should also have a current written agreement executed by the tenant(s) and landlord. If a lease is not required, all agreements concerning both parties' privileges and responsibilities should be in writing and signed by the parties concerned. It is wise to secure the owner's written consent for significant changes in such duties or other special services to be performed by the broker on behalf of the owner.

The management of short-term occupancies under a broker's license requires diligence in complying with § 12-10-217(1)(h), (i) and (t), C.R.S. Complaints against licensees can generally be categorized into three areas: (1) a failure to plan for the seasonal cash flows inherent in vacation rental management, (2) a failure to supervise and properly maintain required records and accounts, and (3) a failure to disclose how management fees and commissions are earned in both the management agreement and reservation/cancellation policies. Please refer to "short-term occupancies" in the Index for further information.

Finally, the property manager must consider the rights and interests of the tenant in ongoing or temporary management during the listing period for the sale of the property. The broker should consult the owner and tenant when scheduling showings of listed property. See Chapter "Fair Housing," for federal and Colorado fair housing considerations.

General information regarding tenant/landlord disputes is available from the Community Housing Service at (303) 831-1750, the Apartment Rental Association of Denver, or Colorado Housing Connects, Ph: (844) 926-6632.

IV. Management Files

- Current/past management and/or short-term reservation management agreements;
- Current/past lease or rental occupancy agreements with tenants and guests;
- Lead-based paint disclosures for residential property built before 1978;
- Disclosure of brokerage relationships and/or listing contracts to lease;
- Disclosure of compensation, service income from affiliated entities;
- Brokerage accounting records, bank reconciliation, tax and owner reports;
- Ongoing contracts, bids, invoices, service provider billings, and correspondence with client;
- Legal notices, actions, and accounting reports affecting owner/occupant/tenant funds;
- Documentation for commissions earned versus taken or charged to others;
- Prompt assessment, timely (45-90 days) collection, restitution of all money due escrow; and
- Documentation verifying reported receipts, income, and all expenses paid for another.

V. Property Management Best Practices

In Colorado, there is no specific "Standard of Care" for Property Management. Create your own "Standard of Care" by utilizing many of the Best Practices" listed below. Best Practices minimize liability for ALL parties. Some of the below Best Practices may be "Baseline" for your company and others may be "Top of the Line".

- Initially, seriously consider if you are working for the owner of the property as a Landlord Agent or Transaction Agent. In Property Management, as a general rule, you are working as a Landlord Agent because of the scope of duties performed for the owner.
- Make a check sheet of what documents are required to be in your file and make sure each file is complete for audit purposes.
- Be totally familiar with the relevant real estate broker Statutes, Rules, and Position Statements involving property management.
- Be familiar with the Colorado Warranty of Habitability law and keep up with the ever-changing laws regarding Property Management.
- Have a written Work Standards and Policies signed by all Vendors.
- Invite your vendors to a meeting once a year where you review your policies when entering occupied homes and to ensure they understand the liability involved as well as Fair Housing law.
- Eliminate assumptions by giving a new owner a written document explaining "What to Expect from us" and "what NOT to expect from us".
- If you have Affiliated Business Arrangements, have your disclosure signed by Owner and/or tenant if applicable.
- Make sure there is a dedicated emergency line, and someone is appointed to answer 24/7. Even if completion of the emergency maintenance is not possible immediately, make sure communication about the issue is quick, thorough, and frequent until completion of the issue.
- If the owner has an ILC or survey, ask for a copy for your file.
- Be specific when rental proceeds will be transferred to the Owner, so they know what to expect.
- Require the Property Management Company be listed as "additional insured" on the Owner's property insurance policy.
- Develop a preventive Maintenance Program:
  a. Consider offering the owner a Landscape package from your Landscaper which includes fertilizing, weed control and aeration to ensure landscape success. Many times, tenants assume mowing is their only obligation.
  b. If property is built before 1978, a full Lead Test is helpful so that all tenants and vendors know where the lead paint is located. Many vendors charge as if the house is full of lead paint unless they have proof of where it is located or if it is on the property at all.
  c. Is there a Radon mitigation system and if so, is it working and within the safe range?
  d. Pull a Regional Building report from their website.

e. Are all electric outlets in working condition.
f. Are there any sump pumps and do they need regular testing or maintenance?
g. Check for trip & fall hazards around the property.
h. Are interior and exterior handrails installed where needed and are they stable.
i. Check all windows and doors for proper closure, locks, seals, and caulking.
j. Does the roof have T-lock shingles and is there a drip edge?
k. Check restrictions in HOA rules and regulations as well as CC&Rs, and Articles of Incorporation. Some have restrictions on renting.
l. Make note if the owner has warranties on any items in the home. (i.e., roof, major appliances, etc.)
m. Yearly professional furnace inspection with new filter installation.
n. Yearly water heater clean and inspect.
o. Is the breaker box one of the old ones known to be a fire hazard? Will the owner replace.
p. Professional gutter cleaning both spring and fall.
q. Does drainage around the property appear to be AWAY from the house.
r. Check smoke detectors and carbon monoxide detectors for expiration dates and change out as needed.
s. Have all water main shut off valves marked with readily identifiable tags.
t. Check for obvious mold in bathrooms or other water source areas and take action as needed.
u. If there is a fireplace included with the property, attach an addendum with instruction for maintenance and care.
v. Regular chimney cleaning for wood-burning fireplaces and pilot light cleaning for gas fireplaces.
w. Sewer line cleaning once a year unless it is evident that the sewer lines are old and have a history of back-ups, then more often is necessary. A camera put through the line can give invaluable information.
x. Septic (if applicable) pumping on a regular basis and get report on functionality.
y. If there is a well on the property, get a copy of the certification.
z. Document who owns the fencing around the property.
aa. Set up professional yard sprinkler system activation and winterization.
bb. Notate if any apparent asbestos and if so, include an asbestos addendum with the lease.
cc. If there is a hot tub or swimming pool included in the lease, attach an addendum with instruction for maintenance and care.

- Have written screening and qualification Guidelines for Tenant. Never deviate from your qualifications to avoid fair housing issues.
- Require a Pet Application if applicable.
- Consider doing a detailed video about your lease documents so that you don't assume the tenant read and understood them. This also eliminates a property manager reviewing the lease with every tenant, but most importantly it assures

consistency. Have the tenant initial that they watched the video presentation and understand the lease documents.

- Re-key before move-in of new tenants.
- Have a "Welcome Home" letter for all new tenants stating expectations, visits from the Management Company and what to expect during their lease term.
- Include a Landscape Addendum explaining what is expected from the tenant regarding yard maintenance. If the owner signed a Landscape Package with a vendor, it should be stated on this form, so they know what is expected of them regarding yard maintenance and to avoid duplication of services.
- Include a thorough Cleaning and Property Standards Addendum in the lease paperwork.
- If there is an HOA involved, make sure tenants have a copy of the rules and regulations.
- Do a Move in Condition report backed up by photos or consider a thorough video documentation of the interior and exterior of the property.
- Do a Preliminary assessment (walk through) within 90 days of a new tenant move-in to ascertain if there are any concerns before they become larger issues.
- Lease Renewal walk through before lease expiration to determine whether to renew lease or what issues tenant may need to correct before signing extension of lease.
- Exterior assessments three times a year – usually late Spring, Summer, and early Fall to assure that the landscape is maintained before it is too late to revive.
- Give the tenant a complete description of what to expect on move-out. (i.e., Can they be present for your move-out inspection and when they can expect to receive their security deposit.)
- Do a Move Out Condition Report backed up by photos or consider a thorough video documentation of the interior and exterior of the property.
- Use a waiver of liability signed by the vendor for every major update and repair.
- Update your Office Policy Manual each time a change is made to the way you do business.
- Make sure you thoroughly understand Three Way Reconciliations and do them monthly on all trust accounts.
- Do a yearly "Self-Audit" through the DORA website on a yearly basis. This will keep your books in stellar shape for any audit from the Commission.
- Add your own Best Practices.

VI. Merchandising Rental Space

Rental space reacts to changes in supply and demand in the marketplace. A manager needs to estimate the strength of consumer pressure. Consumers normally shop the market and rent the space that best meets their financial and aesthetic needs.

It is imperative that a property manager counsel owners carefully prior to taking over an account and identify which problems may be curable and which may not. For example, a building that is not soundproof is not economically feasible to cure, and as a result, it limits the clientele to quiet people.

If a property suffers from cumulative maintenance problems, a disproportionate amount of time may be required of a property manager, thus causing management expenses to exceed potential fee income. Properties that have been cheaply constructed and suffer from accelerated obsolescence are extremely vulnerable to rental competition from newer properties, again contributing to higher turnover. One short-term owner savings is to forego a preventive maintenance program. However, preventive maintenance normally costs much less than paying to correct serious deferred maintenance problems later.

VII. Short Term Rentals

Short term rentals have grown in popularity over the years in Colorado, especially with the growth of short term rental websites and the services they provide to both owners and their guests. Short term rentals are now available in many cities, towns and unincorporated areas across the state.

As set forth in Commission Position Statement 19, short term rentals are different from traditional landlord-tenant relationships. While there is no formal state-wide definition of what constitutes a short term rental, there are several factors in play, including the local municipal regulations, expectations of the owner and guest, payment structure (i.e. month to month versus lump sum), furnished versus unfurnished, etc. The local regulation of short term rentals varies greatly across the state. For example, some municipalities do not regulate short term rentals, while other municipalities require owners to obtain a short term rental license, undergo periodic inspections, and pay special taxes, among other requirements.

Questions arise when Colorado brokers are involved in the management of short term rentals. The management of a short term rental does not qualify as a brokerage activity. However, the brokerage license law still regulates certain conduct of licensed brokers even when such conduct falls outside of the traditional regulated brokerage activities. See *Colorado Real Estate Commission v. McDonnell*, 361 P.2 1138 (Colo. App. 2015). Consequently, even though a real estate broker's license is not required to manage a short term rental, brokers acting as short term rental managers need to understand that the Commission may still regulate certain short term rental management activities by a licensee. These regulated activities include, for example (and not by way of limitation) situations in which a broker is: (i) handling money belonging to others such as advanced deposits or guest stay revenue, (ii) advertising of short term rentals (See C.R.S. 12-10-217(1)(a)), (iii) overseeing and conducting cleaning or maintenance; (iv) written disclosure of potential conflicts of interest (such as a broker's ownership interest in the short term rental) (See CREC Rule 6.17). Of course, brokers must accurately advertise short term rentals under management, as well as disclose such broker's interest in the short term rental or other conflict of interest. Brokers engaged in short term rental management should also understand the extent to which he or she is covered or uncovered by errors and omissions insurance or other policy of insurance.

Before a broker gets involved in short term rental management a broker should consult with his or her employing broker and review his or her office policy manual to understand what conduct is permitted. Further, brokers should develop a basic understanding of the local regulations applicable to the management and operation of the short term rental he or she intends to manage. Such understanding should include a general understanding of state, county and local sales, lodging and other tax obligations, as well as whether and how such broker will be responsible for escrowing and paying such tax obligations. Brokers handling money belonging to others should review CREC Chapter 5 Rules: Separate Accounts and Accounting, and specifically, CREC Rule 5.11(B).

VIII. General Accounting Concepts

Brokers who wish to engage in property management should carefully study Chapter "Escrow Records." No area of real estate needs more diligent records maintenance than property management.

Rental location agents are mentioned in § 12-10-217(2), C.R.S. Brokers who receive advance fees from prospective tenants for furnishing information on available rentals must keep records of such funds according to § 12-10-217(1)(h), C.R.S., and Commission Rules.

A licensed property manager is a trustee primarily responsible for the supervision, accounting, and use of "money belonging to others." Any recallable trust account cash balance must always equal the corresponding trust account contractual liability at the same point in time. Trust accounts are generally maintained on a "cash basis." Funds belonging to one owner may never be "loaned" as unauthorized supplemental operating capital to finance expenditures of other owners (or the broker). (See §§ 12-10-217(1)(h), (i), and (q), C.R.S., and Rules 1.34, 5.9, 5.10, 5.18, 6.3.A, and 6.3.B.)

The accounting software in a management operation must have the capability to integrate owner/tenant/property/service activity and non-financial marketing data with the accounting transactions. The system must provide the capability to reproduce reports, data, and bank reconciliations upon demand for any prior period. The accounting/management database should allow access to immediate information for:

- Tenant/guest amounts owed versus collected.
- Tenant by name/unit charges and receipts.
- Common area charges/special package prices.
- Tenant unit rental history/personal data.
- Deposits collected or held by current broker.
- Leases/agreements/amendments/coming expiration dates.
- Correspondence/evictions/addenda.
- Scheduled occupancy/vacancy dates.
- Accounting for security deposit refunds.
- Late fees and other tenant charges.
- Properties/units under management.
- Property/unit identification/marketing data.
- Owner/insurance/lender information.
- Management agreements/amendments/correspondence.
- Vendors and scheduled payments for mortgages, etc.

- Maintenance/remodeling/written authorizations.
- Accounting reports/multiple bank account capacity.

Managers must disclose brokerage relationships to property owners and prospective tenants using Commission-approved forms. For property owners, the broker, if performing leasing activities, is required to enter into the appropriate Exclusive Right-to-Lease Listing Agreement specific to the type of brokerage relationship offered (either Landlord Agency or Transaction-Broker). As an alternative to the listing agreement, the broker may use the Brokerage Duties Addendum to Property Management Agreement, (if the management agreement includes leasing by the property manager/broker), executed by both the broker and property owner.

For prospective tenants, the broker must either enter into the appropriate Exclusive Tenant Contract specific to the type of brokerage relationship offered (Tenant Agency or Transaction-Broker), or the current Brokerage Disclosure to Buyer or Tenant prior to confidential information being shared. Also, the broker should disclose in writing the specific duties pertaining to the brokerage relationship offered to prospective tenants pursuant to Rule 6.5. If a property owner or prospective tenant requests information about types of brokerage relationships other than those offered by the broker, the broker could give the owner or tenant the current Definitions of Working Relationships (or use the Listing Agreement or Disclosure form given to owner or tenant noted in this paragraph).

Brokers must have written consent from the party assisted or represented to assess and receive any "**mark-ups**" and/or other compensation for services performed by any third party or affiliated business entity. (See Rule 5.17.) The purpose of this rule is to facilitate full disclosure of all forms of compensation under §§ 12-10-217(1)(d) and (t) and 6-1-105, C.R.S. This applies to management companies that mark-up the charges billed by independent maintenance companies, add a percentage to the cost billed by others for administrative overhead, or receive any transaction-specific income from an affiliated business entity. The broker must maintain office records that verify prior written consent for these amounts and account for the additional amounts or percentages charged to others. All affiliated business must be disclosed writing. (See Commission Position Statement 38)

IX. Security Deposits

A. Introduction

Property managers may incur serious problems if they fail to properly handle security deposits. To avoid these problems, property managers should become thoroughly familiar with the requirements in the following provisions of Colorado law:

Title 38, Article 12, C.R.S. 1973 Security Deposits-Wrongful Withholding

§ 38-12-101, C.R.S. Legislative declaration.

* This part 1 shall be liberally construed to implement the intent of the general assembly to ensure the proper administration of security deposits and late fees and protect the interests of tenants, mobile home owners, and landlords.

§ 38-12-102, C.R.S. Definitions.

* As used in this part 1, unless the context otherwise requires:

* (1) "Home owner" has the meaning set forth in section 38-12-201.5 (2).

* (2) "Landlord" means a landlord, as defined in section 38-12-502 (5), or the management or landlord of a mobile home park, as defined in section 38-12-201.5 (3).

* (3) "Late fee" means a monetary sum that a landlord charges a tenant or home owner as a result of the tenant's or home owner's failure to timely pay rent and that is determined pursuant to a rental agreement between the landlord and the tenant or home owner.

* (4) "Normal wear and tear" means deterioration that occurs, based upon the use for which a rental unit or mobile home space, as defined in section 38-12-201.5 (7), is intended, without negligence, carelessness, accident, or abuse of the premises or equipment or chattels by the tenant or home owner or members of the tenant's or home owner's household, or their invitees or guests.

* (5) "Rent subsidy provider" means a public or private entity, including a public housing authority, that provides ongoing financial assistance to a landlord for the purpose of subsidizing rent.

* (6) "Security deposit" means any advance or deposit of money, regardless of its denomination, the primary function of which is to secure the performance of a rental agreement for a residential premises or any part of a residential premises.

* (7) "Tenant" has the meaning set forth in section 38-12-502 (9).

§ 38-12-103, C.R.S. Return of security deposit.

(1) A landlord shall, within one month after the termination of a lease or surrender and acceptance of the premises, whichever occurs last, return to the tenant the full security deposit deposited with the landlord by the tenant, unless the lease agreement specifies a longer period of time, but not to exceed sixty days. No security deposit shall be retained to cover normal wear and tear. In the event that actual cause exists for retaining any portion of the security deposit, the landlord shall provide the tenant with a written statement listing the exact reasons for the retention of any portion of the security deposit. When the statement is delivered, it shall be accompanied by payment of the difference between any sum deposited and the amount retained. The landlord is deemed to have complied with this section by mailing said statement and any payment required to the last known address of the tenant. Nothing in this section shall preclude the landlord from retaining the security deposit for nonpayment of rent, abandonment of the premises, or nonpayment of utility charges, repair work, or cleaning contracted for by the tenant.

(2) The failure of a landlord to provide a written statement within the required time specified in subsection (1) of this section shall work a forfeiture of all his rights to withhold any portion of the security deposit under this section.

(3) (a) The willful retention of a security deposit in violation of this section shall render a landlord liable for treble the amount of that portion of the security deposit wrongfully withheld from the tenant, together with reasonable attorneys' fees and court costs; except that the tenant has the obligation to give notice to the landlord of his intention to file legal proceedings a minimum of seven days prior to filing said action.

(b) In any court action brought by a tenant under this section, the landlord shall bear the burden of proving that his withholding of the security deposit or any portion of it was not wrongful.

(4) Upon cessation of his interest in the dwelling unit, whether by sale, assignment, death, appointment of a receiver, or otherwise, the person in possession of the security deposit, including but not limited to the landlord, his agent, or his executor, shall, within a reasonable time:

(a) Transfer the funds, or any remainder after lawful deductions under subsection (1) of this section, to the landlord's successor in interest and notify the tenant by mail of such transfer and of the transferee's name and address; or

(b) Return the funds, or any remainder after lawful deductions under subsection (1) of this section, to the tenant.

(5) Upon compliance with subsection (4) of this section, the person in possession of the security deposit shall be relieved of further liability.

(6) Upon receipt of transferred funds under subsection (4) (a) of this section, the transferee, in relation to such funds, shall be deemed to have all of the rights and obligations of a landlord holding the funds as a security deposit.

(7) Any provision, whether oral or written, in or pertaining to a rental agreement whereby any provision of this section for the benefit of a tenant or members of his household is waived shall be deemed to be against public policy and shall be void.

§ 38-12-104, C.R.S. Return of security deposit – hazardous condition – gas appliance.

(1) Anytime service personnel from any organization providing gas service to a residential building become aware of any hazardous condition of a gas appliance, piping, or other gas equipment, such personnel shall inform the customer of record at the affected address in writing of the hazardous condition and take any further action provided for by the policies of such personnel's employer. Such written notification shall state the potential nature of the hazard as a fire hazard or a hazard to life, health, property, or public welfare and shall explain the possible cause of the hazard.

(2) If the resident of the residential building is a tenant, such tenant shall immediately inform the landlord of the property or the landlord's agent in writing of the existence of the hazard.

(3) The landlord shall then have seventy-two hours excluding a Saturday, Sunday, or a legal holiday after the actual receipt of the written notice of the hazardous condition to have the hazardous condition repaired by a professional. "Professional" for the purposes of this section means a person authorized by the state of Colorado or by a county or municipal government through license or certificate where such government authorization is required. Where no person with such government authorization is available, and where there are no local requirements for government authorization, a person who is otherwise qualified and who possesses insurance with a minimum of one hundred thousand dollars public liability and property damage coverage shall be deemed a professional for purposes of this section. Proof of such repairs shall be forwarded to the landlord or the landlord's agent. Such proof may also be used as an affirmative defense in any action to recover the security deposit, as provided for in this section.

(4) If the landlord does not have the repairs made within seventy-two hours excluding a Saturday, Sunday, or a legal holiday, and the condition of the building remains hazardous, the tenant may opt to vacate the premises. After the tenant vacates the premises, the lease or other rental agreement between the landlord and tenant becomes null and void, all rights and future obligations between the landlord and tenant pursuant to the lease or other rental agreement terminate, and the tenant may demand the immediate return of all or any portion of the security deposit held by the landlord to which the tenant is entitled. The landlord shall have seventy-two hours following the tenant's vacation of the premises to deliver to the tenant all of, or the appropriate portion of, the security deposit plus any rent rebate owed to the tenant for rent paid by the tenant for the period of time after the tenant has vacated. If the seventy-second hour falls on a Saturday, Sunday, or legal holiday, the security deposit must be delivered by noon on the next day that is not a Saturday, Sunday, or legal holiday. The tenant shall provide the landlord with a correct forwarding address. No security deposit shall be retained to cover normal wear and tear. In the event that actual cause exists for retaining any portion of the security deposit, the landlord shall provide the tenant with a written statement listing the exact reasons for the retention of any portion of the security deposit. When the statement is delivered, it shall be

accompanied by payment of the difference between any sum deposited and the amount retained. The landlord is deemed to have complied with this section by mailing said statement and any payments required by this section to the forwarding address of the tenant. Nothing in this section shall preclude the landlord from withholding the security deposit for nonpayment of rent or for nonpayment of utility charges, repair work, or cleaning contracted for by the tenant. If the tenant does not receive the entire security deposit or a portion of the security deposit together with a written statement listing the exact reasons for the retention of any portion of the security deposit within the time period provided for in this section, the retention of the security deposit shall be deemed willful and wrongful and, notwithstanding the provisions of section 38-12-103 (3), shall entitle the tenant to twice the amount of the security deposit and to reasonable attorney fees.

* ***§ 38-12-105, Late fees charged to tenants and mobile home owners - maximum late fee amounts - prohibited acts - penalties - period to cure violations - remedies - unfair or deceptive trade practice.***

* (1) A landlord shall not take any of the following actions or direct any agent to take any of the following actions on the landlord's behalf:

* (a) Charge a tenant or home owner a late fee unless a rent payment is late by at least seven calendar days;

* (b) Charge a tenant or home owner a late fee in an amount that exceeds the greater of:

* (I) Fifty dollars; or

* (II) Five percent of the amount of the past due rent payment;

* (c) Require a tenant or home owner to pay a late fee unless the late fee is disclosed in the rental agreement;

* (d) Remove or exclude a tenant from a dwelling or initiate a court process for the removal or exclusion of a tenant from a dwelling because the tenant fails to pay one or more late fees to the landlord;

* (e) Terminate a tenancy or other estate at will or a lease in a mobile home park because a tenant or home owner fails to pay one or more late fees to the landlord;

* (f) Impose a late fee on a tenant or home owner for the late payment or nonpayment of any portion of the rent that a rent subsidy provider, rather than the tenant or home owner, is responsible for paying;

* (g) Impose a late fee more than once for each late payment, except that a landlord may impose a late fee more than once for a late payment if the total amount of such late fees does not exceed the amount described in subsection (1)(b) of this section;

* (h) Require a tenant or home owner to pay any amount of interest on a late fee;

* (i) Recoup any amount of a late fee from a rent payment made to the landlord by a tenant or home owner; or

* (j) Charge a tenant or home owner a late fee unless the landlord provided the tenant or home owner written notice of the late fee within one hundred eighty days after the date upon which the rent payment was due.

* (2) A provision of a lease of a landlord or person acting on behalf of a landlord that does not comply with the provisions of subsection (1) of this section is void and unenforceable. A tenant who is aggrieved by an action taken by a landlord or person acting on behalf of the landlord in violation of subsection (1) of this section may bring an action for injunctive relief pursuant to subsection (5) of this section.

* (3) A landlord who violates subsection (1) of this section shall pay to an aggrieved tenant or home owner a penalty in the amount of fifty dollars for each violation.

* (4) Except as described in subsection (3) of this section, and notwithstanding any other provision of this section to the contrary, a landlord who violates subsection (1) of this section has seven days to cure the violation, which seven days begins when the landlord receives written or electronic notice of the violation.

* (5) If a landlord violates subsection (1) of this section and fails to timely cure the violation as described in subsection (4) of this section, a tenant or home owner may bring a civil action to seek one or more of the following remedies:

* (a) Compensatory damages for injury or loss suffered;

* (b) A penalty of at least one hundred fifty dollars but not more than one thousand dollars for each violation, payable to the tenant or home owner;

* (c) Costs, including reasonable attorney fees to the prevailing party; and

* (d) Other equitable relief the court finds appropriate.

* (6) A tenant or home owner may raise an alleged violation of this section as an affirmative defense in a forcible entry and detainer proceeding.

* (7) A late fee is distinct from rent, and a rental agreement may not classify a late fee as rent for the purposes of section 13-40-104 (1)(d).

B. Local Ordinances Concerning Security Deposits

Brokers should check with city and county ordinances where leasing activity is conducted for additional security deposit requirements. For example:

The City of Boulder requires payment of a stated rate of interest to a tenant for any security deposit held under a residential lease. This excludes leasing of mobile home park space. The person in possession of the deposit must return and account for the amount and interest due within 30 days after the latter of termination or surrender and acceptance of the lease. (Ordinances 4969 and 7158, Title 12–Chapter 2, Sections 5 and 6, Landlord/Tenant Relations.) Brokers should check for similar requirements in other cities where leasing activity is conducted.

C. Guidelines for the Property Manager Regarding Security Deposits

A manager should inspect a property prior to occupancy and document the condition of the premises. When the tenant vacates and has caused no damage other than normal wear and tear, the deposit must be returned to the tenant.

Accounting for security deposits is extremely important and must be performed pursuant to Commission Rules 5.2 and 5.8.A and Commission Position Statement 5, Advance Rentals and Security Deposits. These deposits must be placed into a security deposit escrow account and returned as soon as possible to the tenant when refundable. Some owners and management companies apply security deposits toward the last month's rent. This practice may result in owner liability because advance rental deposits may be subject to earning interest, whereas security deposits generally are not. The broker should review local or county ordinances for further information.

Both the management agreement and the lease or rental agreement should contain authority for the manager to control security deposits. If there is no written procedure pertaining to these deposits, each party to the agreement injecting his or her own ideas may result in confusion and resentment. Thus, it is best that both the lease and the management agreement spell out in writing the intent of all parties to the contract concerning the disposition of security deposit funds. A broker may transfer tenant security deposits to a property owner only pursuant to Commission Position Statement 5, Advance Rentals and Security Deposits. This position statement is summarized in Rule 5.8.A; see also "Offsetting Broker Expenses Against Refundable Deposits" in Chapter , "Escrow Records."

A written agreement is also useful in the event of a change in ownership or management of a building. The new owner or manager may simply refer to the tenancy agreement to determine the amount of the deposit, and the tenant has a copy as proof.

Unclaimed security deposits and other forms of "money belonging to others" must be reported and remitted by the property manager to the Colorado State Treasurer under the provisions of the "Unclaimed Property Act," §§ 38-13-101, *et seq.*, C.R.S. Unclaimed property reports are filed by November 1 each year. Unclaimed property is generally that which has been held for five years or more. Forms and instructions may be obtained from The Great Colorado Payback Offices, 1580 Logan St., Suite 500, Denver, CO 80203, Phone: (800) 825-2111, Website: www.colorado.gov/treasury/gcp/.

X. Leases

A. Introduction

A lease is both a contract and a conveyance. It sets forth the terms of the agreement between the parties (landlord and tenant; lessor and lessee) whereby the right to possess and use the property for a certain period of time is transferred from one to the other. The interest in the property transferred may be nominal, such as a lease for one month; or it may be a very substantial 99-year lease. A lease for one year or less may be oral. A lease for longer than one year is required to be in writing to be enforceable under the statute of frauds. A written lease is always preferable because it furnishes objective proof of the terms agreed to by the parties.

A lease is an agreement between a lessor and a lessee whereby the lessee takes possession and receives the use and profits of an estate in real property for a certain period of time in return for which the lessor receives the lessee's performance and payment according to the conditions of the agreement.

B. Elements of a Lease

As stated earlier, a lease is both a contract and a conveyance. As a contract, it embodies the agreement of the parties. As a conveyance, it transfers an interest in land, the right to possess and use it for a certain time. The following are the more common lease elements.

1. **Date:** Although not essential, a date can prevent controversy as to questions of time and related problems, such as the portion of the rent due for a partial month or year.
2. **Parties:** Must have legal capacity to enter a contract, and be clearly named and designated. If there are multiple owners or tenants, all should be parties to the lease.
3. **Consideration:** A lease is not enforceable without consideration. The lessee's payment (or promise to pay) and the lessor's delivery of (or promise to deliver) possession are typical considerations supporting the lease.
4. **Description of the Property:** A lease must describe the premises with reasonable certainty. Tenancy of only part of an improvement, use of basement storage space, assignment of parking spaces, or other facilities should be clearly described.

5. **Words of Conveyance:** The lease should clearly state the extent and nature of the interest being conveyed, including the duration of the lease and the lessee's rights.
6. **Conditions and Exceptions:** All conditions imposed on a lessee's tenancy and exceptions to the rights that normally accrue to a tenant should be set forth.
7. **Lessor's and Lessee's Covenants:** Any and all covenants to be fulfilled by either party should be included in the lease.
8. **Signatures:** A lease for longer than one year must be in writing and signed by the parties. The best evidence of the parties' mutual assent is a signed instrument. If a lessee takes possession without signing, only the lessor need sign to create a valid lease. The lessee's taking possession is evidence of his or her assent to the lease.
9. **Seal:** A seal is not generally required, except in the case of corporations and governmental agencies.
10. **Delivery:** Like a deed, a lease must be delivered to be effective.
11. **Acknowledgment:** A lease need not be acknowledged. In the case of a valuable lease that will be recorded, acknowledgment of the signatures should be made.

Some other lease clauses that may apply include: cost-of-living adjustment; handling of the security deposits; use of premises; acceptance of the premises by lessee; surrender of premises at end of term; maintenance, repair, and alterations of premises during term; responsibility for payment of utilities; personal and real property taxes; entry and inspection by lessor's agents; assignment and subletting; agent hold-harmless clause; repossession due to unpaid rent; abandonment of premises by the tenant; holding over; future sale of premises; cessation of lease by condemnation or destruction of premises; right of the lessor to mortgage or subordinate; sign regulation; renewal options; termination notice; and disposition of deposits/records upon change of property managers.

C. Duties and Liabilities of the Parties

A carefully drafted lease will clearly set forth all the duties and responsibilities of the parties, and avoid ambiguities that might lead to controversy. Absent a complete written lease setting forth all terms, the law presumes certain agreements on the part of the parties. For instance, unless there is an agreement to pay rent in advance, the law presumes that rent is not due until the end of a rental period.

A tenant may use the premises in any lawful, appropriate way not expressly restricted in the lease. If the premises are unsuitable for the specified purpose of the lease, the landlord, unless having agreed to do so, need not remodel the property but the tenant may do so. A commercial landlord may compete or lease to a competing business within the same building unless the lease so prohibits.

A lease of business property automatically gives a tenant the right to maintain signs on the leased property advertising the business, in compliance with state, county, and city regulations. Unless expressly granted, no such right to advertise exists for leased residential property, such as when a doctor, real estate broker, or other professional maintains an office in a leased residence.

In multiple-unit commercial or residential property, the landlord has a duty to keep the premises warm and habitable, unless each unit has its own facilities. Provisions as to the furnishing of gas, electricity, heat, hot water, and other services should be incorporated in the lease.

Unless a lease provides otherwise, a landlord is generally not required to keep the premises in repair. Neither is the tenant required to make repairs. Provision for repair and for the scope of the duties of the party obligated to keep the premises in repair should be clearly delineated in the lease. An agreement to repair does not impose the duty to rebuild if the premises are accidentally destroyed. A landlord is not required to repair and make habitable property that is uninhabitable at the time of making the lease. The tenant is presumed to have full knowledge of the condition of the property and should specify any desired repairs.

A landlord's right to enter upon the premises to inspect the property or to show it to prospective purchasers or lessees is limited to what is spelled out in the rental agreement. If it is not addressed in the rental agreement, the lessor has no right to enter.

As a general rule, a person occupying the property is liable to others for injury caused by the condition of the property. An occupant is also liable to others for any nuisance resulting from the occupant's use that interferes with others' use and enjoyment of their property.

A landlord is not generally liable for injury to a tenant or a tenant's family caused by the property's condition, unless such condition is latent (*i.e.*, hidden) and the landlord had knowledge of such latent, dangerous condition. A landlord may be held liable to persons using the sidewalks or highway abutting the property for injury caused by dangerous conditions on the property. In such a case, a landlord's liability continues only until a reasonable time after the tenant takes possession and has the opportunity to correct the dangerous condition, whereupon the tenant becomes responsible. It is advisable that the parties agree as to responsibility for injury to other persons, and for the responsible party to secure protection by means of liability insurance.

A landlord usually retains control over entrances, hallways, elevators, stairways, and other portions of multi-unit property. In such cases, the landlord is liable for injury to the tenants, their guests, or business visitors caused by dangerous conditions in these areas resulting from landlord negligence. As a general rule, partial or total destruction of the premises by fire or other accident does not relieve a tenant from the obligation to pay rent. Some states feel this common-law rule is too harsh and have enacted statutes stating that destruction or damage making the property unfit for occupancy terminates the lease and relieves a tenant from paying rent. It is strongly recommended that lease provisions cover such emergencies.

Unless the provisions of the lease prohibit, a tenant may assign or sublet the premises. The lessee would remain liable to the lessor for the performance of all the original lease conditions. Most leases prohibit subletting or assignment without the lessor's prior consent.

A landlord who re-enters leased premises effectively evicts the tenant and relieves the tenant from all liability for future rent, unless the lease specifies otherwise. If the lease authorizes a landlord to re-enter and re-let the premises without terminating the lease in the event a tenant vacates the premises, a court may hold the tenant liable for rent the tenant agreed to pay, less any amount the landlord received from the new tenant. Many lease agreements provide that upon tenant default a landlord may: (1) declare the term of the lease ended, re-enter the premises, expel the tenant, and take possession of the premises, or (2) re-let the premises and apply the rent from the new tenant's lease to the lease of the old tenant, with the old tenant being responsible for any balance due.

The above discussion should indicate the extreme desirability of having a carefully drafted lease, which clearly sets forth all the conditions and covenants of the tenancy and all the duties and responsibilities of each party.

D. Leasehold Tenancies

Leasehold estates can be classified into four types: (1) tenancy for years, (2) periodic tenancy, (3) tenancy at will, and (4) tenancy at sufferance.

Tenancy for years

A tenancy for years is for a fixed period of time (*e.g.*, one day or 99 years). The termination date is set at the time the lease is executed. A tenancy for years ends on the last day of the lease term, with no need to give notice.

Periodic tenancy

A periodic tenancy exists when the rental period is indefinitely renewable for a series of same durations (*e.g.*, week-to-week or month-to-month). The most common example is a residential lease requiring a tenant to pay monthly rent, but with no definite termination date. Periodic tenancies are generally created by implication and not by an express provision. According to Colorado law, and that of most states, such tenancies require the giving of proper notice for their termination. Notice to terminate is discussed below under "Termination of leases."

Tenancy at will

A tenancy at will provides that either party may terminate the lease whenever he or she chooses to do so. A tenancy at will also exists when the agreement allows a tenant to occupy the premises until sold, or until the landlord is ready to construct a new building, or some other indefinite happening. Similar to a periodic tenancy, a tenancy at will requires the giving of proper notice for its termination.

Tenancy at sufferance

A tenancy at sufferance arises when a tenant remains in wrongful possession after a lease has ended. In this situation, the tenant is called a "**holdover tenant**." The landlord may treat the tenant as a trespasser and initiate eviction or may elect to accept the tenant for a similar term and conditions as in the previous lease. The choice is the landlord's; the tenant has none. If a tenant holds over due to reasons beyond his or her control, such as illness, the tenant may be held liable only for the reasonable rental of the holdover period.

E. Types of Leases

Ground lease

A ground lease is a tenancy for years whereby a parcel of unimproved land is let for a typically extended period of time. This usually allows a building to be erected on the land by the tenant and provides for the disposition of the building at the end of the lease. The landowner may become entitled to the building upon the payment of all, part, or none of the value of the building, depending upon the agreement. In the absence of an agreement, the building legally becomes real property and belongs to the landowner, who is not required to reimburse the tenant.

Percentage lease

Percentage leases are used for commercial establishments, generally retail stores, and usually provide for a fixed minimum rent plus a percentage of the tenant's gross sales. Gross sales or gross income must be clearly defined and should provide for such things as returned merchandise, discounts for prompt payment made to customers, sales to employees, mail-order sales, services rendered at cost (such as clothing alterations), and income from vending machines. Detailed provisions should be made concerning the tenant's records and the landlord's right to examine or audit the tenant's books. Satisfactory use of percentage leases requires thorough knowledge and expert judgment.

Sky lease

A sky lease or lease of air space usually creates a tenancy for years, generally for a long period of time. In 1910, the Cleveland Athletic Club executed one of the first such leases, leasing the air space above a five-story building and erecting eight additional stories. The club paid rent for its space along with the improvement taxes, but not land taxes. The upper eight stories were to revert to the lessor at the end of the term upon the payment of its appraised value. This type of lease is based upon the common-law right of a fee holder to use his or her land from the center of the earth to the dome of the skies. Today, the governmental right to regulate air traffic has limited this property right.

Within the state of Colorado there exist a few such leases or sales of air space. In 1953, the Colorado legislature enacted a statute enabling the creation of estates, rights, and interests in areas above the surface of the ground and the transfer of such interests in the same manner as interests in land. (See §§ 38-32-101, *et seq.*, C.R.S.)

Net lease

A net lease requires the tenant to pay rent plus all or a substantial part of the cost of operations and maintenance. Various expressions are used in real estate to describe the many variations in net lease transactions. For instance, if a lease provides for the tenant to pay utilities, real estate taxes and assessments, etc., it might be referred to as "net" lease. If the lease additionally provides for the tenant to insure the premises, it might be referred to as "net-net." Both parties must be absolutely certain of their responsibilities in a net lease.

Gross lease

A gross lease is the opposite of a net lease. The rent typically includes all owner-paid operating costs associated with the premises.

Step-Up Lease

A step-up lease is a contract that establishes future price increases for the lessee at set times throughout the life of the contract. Step-up leases are meant to protect the landlord from the risks that inflation or a rising market present for a long-term lease.

Graduated Lease

A graduated lease is an agreement under which a tenant and landlord agree to a periodic adjustment of monthly payments. For example, the agreement may reflect an increase in the tenant's payments due to market conditions or an increase in the value of the leased property.

Farm lease

Farm leases are based on the same principles as other leases. The farm tenant may pay rent based on a crop-sharing basis. The owner agrees to give possession to the land and improvements thereon, and perhaps to furnish the equipment, and the tenant agrees to furnish the labor and capital to farm the land in a sound, reasonable manner and to pay a specified share of the crops. Alternatively, the rental may be a fixed sum. Farm leases vary in terms and conditions by region and community.

F. Termination of Leases

Leases may be terminated in four major ways: (1) expiration of the term, (2) surrender and acceptance, (3) breach of conditions of the lease, and (4) eviction of the tenant.

Expiration of the term of the lease

A **tenancy for years** ends on the last day of the term, with no notice-to-quit required. Section 13-40-107(4), C.R.S., states: "No notice to quit shall be necessary from or to a tenant whose term is, by agreement, to end at a time certain." If a lease is oral, the lessor should give the periodic statutory notice-to-quit in writing in order to avoid potential conflict over the term of the oral agreement.

To terminate a **periodic tenancy** or a **tenancy-at-will**, the party (lessor or lessee) desiring to end the lease must serve a written notice to quit. The notice must describe the premises, state the time the tenancy will terminate, be signed by the party (or agent) giving such notice, and be served not less than a statutorily specified time before the end of the tenancy period. Required notice periods under § 12-40-107(1), C.R.S., are:

- Year-to-year tenancy or longer: three months prior or earlier.
- Six months or more but less than a year: one month prior or earlier.
- Month-to-month or up to but less than six months: at least 10 days' prior notice.
- Tenancy at will: minimum three-day notice.

Notice must be delivered to the tenant or other person occupying the premises, or by leaving a copy with some person, a member of the tenant's family above the age of 15, residing on or in charge of the premises; or if no one is on the premises at the time service is attempted, by posting a copy in some conspicuous place on the premises.

Section 13-40-107.5(4), C.R.S., provides for a three-day expedited eviction of certain undesirable and dangerous persons who demonstrate that they (or their guests) are "unfit to coexist with their neighbors and co-tenants" by committing infractions known in the law as "substantial violations." These include various violent or drug-related felonies as well as endangerment of persons and property. These acts are considered severe enough to give the landlord a remedy of expedited eviction. However, the statute specifically states that victims of domestic abuse, and persons who could not have reasonably known of or prevented the substantial violations but did immediately notify law enforcement, are exempt from any expedited eviction action.

A holdover tenant is not entitled to notice to quit. If a lease is for a definite term and the tenant does not surrender possession of the property at the end of the term, the landlord may elect to hold the tenant for an additional like term. Such election must be accompanied by some act on the part of the landlord that signifies an intention to accept the tenant, such as receiving the next rent payment. Unless the landlord in some way indicates intent to retain the tenant, the tenant remains a tenant at sufferance.

The tenant does not have any right of election in such a case; only the landlord. It is a common practice—and potential pitfall—to include in the lease an automatic renewal clause, which provides that unless an agreed-upon notice of a certain number of days (*e.g.*, 30 or 60) is given by either party, the lease will be continued automatically from the end of the term for a like period.

Surrender and acceptance

A mutual agreement to terminate a lease without obligation on the part of either the landlord or tenant is a termination by surrender of the lease and an acceptance thereof.

Breach of conditions

Failure by either the lessor or lessee to perform agreed-upon conditions or covenants constitute a breach of the lease and may permit the injured party to cancel the lease.

Eviction of the tenant

An eviction may be either actual or constructive. Actual eviction occurs when a tenant is ousted from the premises, completely or partially, either by an act of the landlord or by someone with superior title. Constructive eviction occurs when the leased premises deteriorate to such physical condition, owing to some act or omission of the landlord, that the tenant is unable to use the premises for the purpose intended. Failure to furnish heat or other facilities contemplated by the lease or any other deprivation of use by the lessor is also a constructive eviction.

Termination under other conditions

If leased property is taken for public use by condemnation, any lease is terminated. The tenant is entitled to compensation for the value of the unexpired portion of the lease, and the tenant's claim is superior to that of the landlord.

The foreclosure of a mortgage or other lien may terminate the lease. If the mortgage or other lien was prior in time to the lease, and the tenant had either actual notice or constructive notice of the lien, then foreclosure will terminate the lease.

G. Warranty of Habitability Act (Residential Properties)

Introduction and Summary.

The Warranty of Habitability law requires specific maintenance related responses from landlords in specific time frames and requires specific communications from landlords in response to specific tenant communications within specific time frames. Under most circumstances, a landlord must respond to a tenant's initial warranty of habitability communication within twenty-four hours. The law assumes that all landlords work on weekends and holidays or have the resources and capability to respond to messages during such hours.

All landlords need to designate in their lease where warranty of habitability related communications are to be sent.

The law specifically provides that "a tenant who gives a landlord electronic notice of a condition shall send such notice only to the e-mail address, phone number, or electronic portal specified by the landlord in the rental agreement for communications. In the absence of such a provision in the rental agreement, the tenant shall communicate with the landlord in a manner that the landlord has previously used to communicate with the tenant. That communication from the tenant does have to be in writing.

Tenants must provide a reasonably complete written notice from a tenant to begin a Warranty of Habitability claims, as that starts the clock for a landlord to respond. Nowhere in the statute is "reasonable complete written notice" defined. However, the statute does state "reasonably complete written or electronic notice of the condition described" with respect to 505 claims, catchall claims, and life, health or safety claims. At a minimum, a tenant's notice must describe a condition that falls into one of the four categories under the Warranty of Habitability Act.

The Warranty of Habitability now breaks claims into four distinct categories.

Category 1: Section 505 claims are specifically listed in C.R.S. § 38-12-505. If a property lacks any of the characteristics on the 505 list, then it is considered uninhabitable. Please refer to Section 505 of the statute provided below.

Category 2: Is the "catchall", or any other condition at a property if the condition makes the property "unfit for human habitation". What makes a property unfit for human habitation is a judgment call that is determined by the courts.

Category 3: Is any condition that "materially interferes with a tenant's life, health, or safety." Matters that impact a tenant's life, health, or safety are deemed more serious in nature.

Category 4: Is mold, but not all mold. Mold only if the mold would "materially interfere with a tenant's life, health, or safety" if not remedied. Thus, the presence of mold and the failure to remediate it does not automatically violate the Warranty of Habitability. The mold provisions are some of the most onerous and confusing portions of the new law and are likely to cause landlords the most problems, due in part to very specific instructions on how a landlord is to respond and mitigate the mold.

The Warranty of Habitability now covers appliances. Appliance means "a refrigerator, range stove, or oven that is included within a residential premise by a landlord for the use of the tenant pursuant to the rental agreement or any other agreement between the landlord and the tenant."

In the event of a breach of the Warranty of Habitability the tenant can request that the landlord move the tenant to a comparable unit or hotel, both of which would be selected by the landlord. However, a tenant can only make such request if the claim at issue is a life, health, or safety claim.

Tenants can now seek injunctive relief in county court, where before tenants could only seek injunctive relief in district court. The most significant remedy change is that that tenants are now allowed to make repairs and deduct the cost of such repairs from the rent. The repair and deduct process, is extremely complicated and may likely lead to significant disputes. With respect to appliances, in addition to repairing an appliance and deducting the cost of the repair from the rent, tenants also have the right to replace the appliance. Even if a landlord remedies a Warranty of Habitability issue, if the same issue arises within six months, tenants now have the right to terminate the lease upon fourteen days written notice.

§ 38-12-501, C.R.S. Legislative declaration – matter of statewide concern – purposes and policies.

(1) The general assembly hereby finds and declares that the provisions of this part 5 are a matter of statewide concern. Any local government ordinance, resolution, or other regulation that is in conflict with this part 5 shall be unenforceable.

(2) The underlying purposes and policies of this part 5 are to:

- (a) Simplify, clarify, modernize, and revise the law governing the rental of dwelling units and the rights and obligations of landlords and tenants;
- (b) Encourage landlords and tenants to maintain and improve the quality of housing; and
- (c) Make uniform the law with respect to the subject of this part 5 throughout Colorado.

§ 38-12-502, C.R.S. Definitions.

* As used in this part 5 and part 8 of this article 12, unless the context otherwise requires:

(1) "Common areas" means the facilities and appurtenances to a residential premises, including the grounds, areas, and facilities held out for the use of tenants generally or whose use is promised to a tenant.

(2) "Dwelling unit" means a structure or the part of a structure that is used as a home, residence, or sleeping place by a tenant.

(3) "Landlord" means the owner, manager, lessor, or sublessor of a residential premises.

(4) "Rental agreement" means the agreement, written or oral, embodying the terms and conditions concerning the use and occupancy of a residential premises.

(5) "Residential premises" means a dwelling unit, the structure of which the unit is a part, and the common areas.

(6) "Tenant" means a person entitled under a rental agreement to occupy a dwelling unit to the exclusion of others.

§ 38-12-503, C.R.S. Warranty of habitability.

(1) In every rental agreement, the landlord is deemed to warrant that the residential premises is fit for human habitation.

(2) A landlord breaches the warranty of habitability set forth in subsection (1) of this section if:

- (a) A residential premises is uninhabitable as described in section 38-12-505 or otherwise unfit for human habitation; and
- (b) The residential premises is in a condition that is materially dangerous or hazardous to the tenant's life, health, or safety; and
- (c) The landlord has received written notice of the condition described in paragraphs (a) and (b) of this subsection (2) and failed to cure the problem within a reasonable time.

(3) When any condition described in subsection (2) of this section is caused by the misconduct of the tenant, a member of the tenant's household, a guest or invitee of the tenant, or a person under the tenant's direction or control, the condition does not constitute a breach of the warranty of habitability. It is not misconduct by a victim of domestic violence; domestic abuse; unlawful sexual behavior, as described in section 16-22-102 (9); or stalking under this subsection (3) if the condition is the result of domestic violence; domestic abuse; unlawful sexual behavior, as described in section 16-22-102 (9); or stalking and the landlord has been

given written notice and evidence of domestic violence; domestic abuse; unlawful sexual behavior, as described in section 16-22-102 (9); or stalking, as described in section 38-12-402 (2)(a).

(4) In response to the notice sent pursuant to paragraph (c) of subsection (2) of this section, a landlord may, in the landlord's discretion, move a tenant to a comparable unit after paying the reasonable costs, actually incurred, incident to the move.

(5) Except as set forth in this part 5, any agreement waiving or modifying the warranty of habitability shall be void as contrary to public policy.

(6) Nothing in this part 5 shall:

(a) Prevent a landlord from terminating a rental agreement as a result of a casualty or catastrophe to the dwelling unit without further liability to the landlord or tenant; or

(b) Preclude a landlord from initiating an action for nonpayment of rent, breach of the rental agreement, violation of section 38-12-504, or as provided for under article 40 of title 13, C.R.S.

§ 38-12-504, C.R.S. Tenant's maintenance of premises.

(1) In addition to any duties imposed upon a tenant by a rental agreement, every tenant of a residential premises has a duty to use that portion of the premises within the tenant's control in a reasonably clean and safe manner. A tenant fails to maintain the premises in a reasonably clean and safe manner when the tenant substantially fails to:

(a) Comply with obligations imposed upon tenants by applicable provisions of building, health, and housing codes materially affecting health and safety;

(b) Keep the dwelling unit reasonably clean, safe, and sanitary as permitted by the conditions of the unit;

(c) Dispose of ashes, garbage, rubbish, and other waste from the dwelling unit in a clean, safe, sanitary, and legally compliant manner;

(d) Use in a reasonable manner all electrical, plumbing, sanitary, heating, ventilating, air-conditioning, elevators, and other facilities and appliances in the dwelling unit;

(e) Conduct himself or herself and require other persons in the residential premises within the tenant's control to conduct themselves in a manner that does not disturb their neighbors' peaceful enjoyment of the neighbors' dwelling unit; or

(f) Promptly notify the landlord if the residential premises is uninhabitable as defined in section 38-12-505 or if there is a condition that could result in the premises becoming uninhabitable if not remedied.

(2) In addition to the duties set forth in subsection (1) of this section, a tenant shall not knowingly, intentionally, deliberately, or negligently destroy, deface, damage, impair, or remove any part of the residential premises or knowingly permit any person within his or her control to do so.

(3) Nothing in this section shall be construed to authorize a modification of a landlord's obligations under the warranty of habitability.

§ 38-12-505, C.R.S. Uninhabitable residential premises.

(1) A residential premises is deemed uninhabitable if it substantially lacks any of the following characteristics:

(a) Waterproofing and weather protection of roof and exterior walls maintained in good working order, including unbroken windows and doors;

(b) Plumbing or gas facilities that conformed to applicable law in effect at the time of installation and that are maintained in good working order;

(c) Running water and reasonable amounts of hot water at all times furnished to appropriate fixtures and connected to a sewage disposal system approved under applicable law;

(d) Functioning heating facilities that conformed to applicable law at the time of installation and that are maintained in good working order;

(e) Electrical lighting, with wiring and electrical equipment that conformed to applicable law at the time of installation, maintained in good working order;

(f) Common areas and areas under the control of the landlord that are kept reasonably clean, sanitary, and free from all accumulations of debris, filth, rubbish, and garbage and that have appropriate extermination in response to the infestation of rodents or vermin;

(g) Appropriate extermination in response to the infestation of rodents or vermin throughout a residential premises;

(h) An adequate number of appropriate exterior receptacles for garbage and rubbish, in good repair;

(i) Floors, stairways, and railings maintained in good repair;

(j) Locks on all exterior doors and locks or security devices on windows designed to be opened that are maintained in good working order; or

(k) Compliance with all applicable building, housing, and health codes, which, if violated, would constitute a condition that is dangerous or hazardous to a tenant's life, health, or safety.

(2) No deficiency in the common area shall render a residential premises uninhabitable as set forth in subsection (1) of this section, unless it materially and substantially limits the tenant's use of his or her dwelling unit.

(3) Unless otherwise stated in section 38-12-506, prior to being leased to a tenant, a residential premises must comply with the requirements set forth in section 38-12-503 (1), (2) (a), and (2) (b).

§ 38-12-506, C.R.S. Opt-out.

(1) If a dwelling unit is contained within a mobile home park, as defined in section 38-12-201.5 (3), or if there are four or fewer dwelling units sharing common walls or located on the same parcel, as defined in section 30-28-302 (5), C.R.S., all of which have the same owner, or if the dwelling unit is a single-family residential premises:

(a) A good faith rental agreement may require a tenant to assume the obligation for one or more of the characteristics contained in section 38-12-505 (1) (f), (1) (g), and (1) (h), as long as the requirement is not inconsistent with any obligations imposed upon a landlord by a governmental entity for the receipt of a subsidy for the residential premises; and

(b) For any dwelling unit for which a landlord does not receive a subsidy from any governmental source, a landlord and tenant may agree in writing that the tenant is to perform specific repairs, maintenance tasks, alterations, and remodeling, but only if:

(I) The agreement of the parties is entered into in good faith and is set forth in a separate writing signed by the parties and supported by adequate consideration;

(II) The work is not necessary to cure a failure to comply with section 38-12-505 (3); and

(III) Such agreement does not affect the obligation of the landlord to other tenants' residential premises.

(2) For a single-family residential premises for which a landlord does not receive a subsidy from any governmental source, a landlord and tenant may agree in writing that the tenant is to perform specific repairs, maintenance tasks, alterations, and remodeling necessary to cure a failure to comply with section 38-12-505 (3), but only if:

(a) The agreement of the landlord and tenant is entered into in good faith and is set forth in a writing that is separate from the rental agreement, signed by the parties, and supported by adequate consideration; and

(b) The tenant has the requisite skills to perform the work required to cure a failure to comply with section 38-12-505 (3).

(3) To the extent that performance by a tenant relates to a characteristic set forth in section 38-12-505 (1), the tenant shall assume the obligation for such characteristic.

(4) If consistent with this section a tenant assumes an obligation for a characteristic set forth in section 38-12-505 (1), the lack of such characteristic shall not make a residential premises uninhabitable.

§ 38-12-507, C.R.S. Breach of warranty of habitability – tenant's remedies.

(1) If there is a breach of the warranty of habitability as set forth in section 38-12-503 (2), the following provisions shall apply:

(a) Upon no less than ten and no more than thirty days written notice to the landlord specifying the condition alleged to breach the warranty of habitability and giving the landlord five business days from the receipt of the written notice to remedy the breach, a tenant may terminate the rental agreement by surrendering possession of the dwelling unit. If the breach is remediable by repairs, the payment of damages, or otherwise and the landlord adequately remedies the breach within five business days of receipt of the notice, the rental agreement shall not terminate by reason of the breach.

(b) A tenant may obtain injunctive relief for breach of the warranty of habitability in any court of competent jurisdiction. In any proceeding for injunctive relief, the court shall determine actual damages for a breach of the warranty at the time the court orders the injunctive relief. A landlord shall not be subject to any court order for injunctive relief if the landlord tenders the actual damages to the court within two business days of the order. Upon application by the tenant, the court shall immediately release to the tenant the damages paid by the landlord. If the tenant vacates the leased premises, the landlord shall not be permitted to rent the premises again until such time as the unit would be in compliance with the warranty of habitability set forth in section 38-12-503 (1).

* (c) (I) In an action for possession or collection based upon nonpayment of rent, in which the tenant asserts a defense to possession based upon the landlord's alleged breach of the warranty of habitability, upon the filing of the tenant's answer the court shall order the tenant to pay into the registry of the court all or part of the rent accrued after due consideration of expenses already incurred by the tenant based upon the landlord's breach of the warranty of habitability. The tenant may assert, as an affirmative defense, an alleged breach of the warranty of habitability, provided that the landlord or any agent acting on behalf of the landlord has previously received written or electronic notice of an alleged breach of the warranty of habitability. If a county or district court is satisfied that the defendant is unable to deposit the amount of rent specified because the defendant is found to be indigent pursuant to subsection (1)(c)(II) of this section, the defendant shall not be required to deposit any amounts to raise warranty of habitability claims as an affirmative defense and the claim will be perfected.

* (II) A defendant is indigent for the purposes of this section if the defendant has a net income that is:

* (A) Five times or less the annual rental of the defendant's premises, after allowing all exemptions available to families occupying dwellings in low-rent housing authorized under the act of the congress of the United States known as the "United States Housing Act of 1937", as amended. For the

purpose of making an indigent determination in computing the annual rental, there must be included in the calculation the average annual cost to the defendant, as determined by the court, of heat, water, electricity, gas, and other necessary services or facilities, whether or not the charge for such services and facilities is in fact included in the rental; or

* (B) Less than two hundred fifty percent of the federal poverty line; except that, for purposes of calculation, a defendant's assets must not be taken into account.

* (d) Whether asserted as a claim, counterclaim, or an affirmative defense, a tenant may recover damages directly arising from a breach of the warranty of habitability, which may include, but are not limited to, any reduction in the fair rental value of the dwelling unit, in any court of competent jurisdiction.

* (d.5) The court shall determine the reduction of the premise's rental value in its uninhabitable state to the date of trial and shall deny possession to the landlord and deem the tenant to be the prevailing party, conditioned upon the payment of the rent that has accrued to the date of the trial, as adjusted pursuant to the reduction in the rental value caused by the breach of the warranty of habitability. The tenant shall make this payment to either the court or the landlord within fourteen days from the date of the court's judgment. The court may order the landlord to make repairs and correct the conditions that constitute a breach of the landlord's obligations, shall order that the monthly rent be limited to the premise's reasonable rental value, as determined pursuant to this section, until repairs are completed, and shall award the tenant costs and attorney fees if provided by and pursuant to any statute or the contract of the parties. If the court orders repairs or corrections, or both, pursuant to this section, the court's jurisdiction continues over the matter for the purpose of ensuring compliance. The court shall award possession of the premises to the landlord if the tenant fails to pay all reduced rent obligations accrued to the date of trial within the period prescribed by the court pursuant to this subsection (1)(d.5).

(2) If a rental agreement contains a provision for either party in an action related to the rental agreement to obtain attorney fees and costs, then the prevailing party in any action brought under this part 5 shall be entitled to recover reasonable attorney fees and costs.

§ 38-12-508, C.R.S. Landlord's defenses to a claim of breach of warranty – limitations on claiming a breach.

(1) It shall be a defense to a tenant's claim of breach of the warranty of habitability that the tenant's actions or inactions prevented the landlord from curing the condition underlying the breach of the warranty of habitability.

(2) Only parties to the rental agreement or other adult residents listed on the rental agreement who are also lawfully residing in the dwelling unit may assert a claim for a breach of the warranty of habitability.

(3) A tenant may not assert a claim for injunctive relief based upon the landlord's breach of the warranty of habitability of a residential premises unless the tenant has given notice to a local government within the boundaries of which the residential premises is located of the condition underlying the breach that is materially dangerous or hazardous to the tenant's life, health, or safety.

(4) A tenant may not assert a breach of the warranty of habitability as a defense to a landlord's action for possession based upon a nonmonetary violation of the rental agreement or for an action for possession based upon a notice to quit or vacate.

(5) If the condition alleged to breach the warranty of habitability is the result of the action or inaction of a tenant in another dwelling unit or another third party not under the direction and control of the landlord and the landlord has taken reasonable, necessary, and timely steps to

abate the condition, but is unable to abate the condition due to circumstances beyond the landlord's reasonable control, the tenant's only remedy shall be termination of the rental agreement consistent with section 38-12-507 (1) (a).

(6) For public housing authorities and other housing providers receiving federal financial assistance directly from the federal government, no provision of this part 5 in direct conflict with any federal law or regulation shall be enforceable against such housing provider.

§ 38-12-509, C.R.S. Prohibition on retaliation.

(1) A landlord shall not retaliate against a tenant for alleging a breach of the warranty of habitability by discriminatorily increasing rent or decreasing services or by bringing or threatening to bring an action for possession in response to the tenant having made a good faith complaint to the landlord or to a governmental agency alleging a breach of the warranty of habitability.

(2) A landlord shall not be liable for retaliation under this section, unless a tenant proves that a landlord breached the warranty of habitability.

(3) Regardless of when an action for possession of the premises where the landlord is seeking to terminate the tenancy for violation of the terms of the rental agreement is brought, there shall be a rebuttable presumption in favor of the landlord that his or her decision to terminate is not retaliatory. The presumption created by this subsection (3) cannot be rebutted by evidence of the timing alone of the landlord's initiation of the action.

(4) If the landlord has a right to increase rent, to decrease service, or to terminate the tenant's tenancy at the end of any term of the rental agreement and the landlord exercises any of these rights, there shall be a rebuttable presumption that the landlord's exercise of any of these rights was not retaliatory. The presumption of this subsection (4) cannot be rebutted by evidence of the timing alone of the landlord's exercise of any of these rights.

§ 38-12-510, C.R.S. Unlawful removal or exclusion.

* (1) It is unlawful for a landlord to remove or exclude a tenant from a dwelling unit without resorting to court process, unless the removal or exclusion is consistent with article 18.5 of title 25 and the rules promulgated by the state board of health for the cleanup of an illegal drug laboratory; is with the mutual consent of the landlord and tenant; or unless the dwelling unit has been abandoned by the tenant, as evidenced by the return of keys, the substantial removal of the tenant's personal property, notice by the tenant, or the extended absence of the tenant while rent remains unpaid, any of which would cause a reasonable person to believe the tenant had permanently surrendered possession of the dwelling unit. Unlawful removal or exclusion includes the willful termination of utilities or the willful removal of doors, windows, or locks to the premises other than as required for repair or maintenance. If the landlord willfully and unlawfully removes the tenant from the premises or willfully and unlawfully causes the termination of heat, running water, hot water, electric, gas, or other essential services, the tenant may seek any remedy available under the law, including this part 5.

* (2) A tenant affected by any violation of this section may bring a civil action to restrain further violations and to recover damages, costs, and reasonable attorney fees. In the case of a violation, the tenant must be awarded statutory damages equal to the tenant's actual damages and the higher amount of either three times the monthly rent or five thousand dollars, as well as any other damages, attorney fees, and costs that may be owed.

* (3) A court may also order that possession be restored to a tenant who was affected by a violation of this section.

§ 38-12-511, C.R.S. Application.

(1) Unless created to avoid its application, this part 5 shall not apply to any of the following arrangements:

(a) Residence at a public or private institution, if such residence is incidental to detention or the provision of medical, geriatric, education, counseling, religious, or similar service;

(b) Occupancy under a contract of sale of a dwelling unit or the property of which it is a part, if the occupant is the purchaser, seller, or a person who succeeds to his or her interest;

(c) Occupancy by a member of a fraternal or social organization in the portion of a structure operated for the benefit of the organization;

(d) Transient occupancy in a hotel or motel that lasts less than thirty days;

(e) Occupancy by an employee or independent contractor whose right to occupancy is conditional upon performance of services for an employer or contractor;

(f) Occupancy by an owner of a condominium unit or a holder of a proprietary lease in a cooperative;

(g) Occupancy in a structure that is located within an unincorporated area of a county, does not receive water, heat, and sewer services from a public entity, and is rented for recreational purposes, such as a hunting cabin, yurt, hut, or other similar structure;

(h) Occupancy under rental agreement covering a residential premises used by the occupant primarily for agricultural purposes; or

(i) Any relationship between the owner of a mobile home park and the owner of a mobile home situated in the park.

(2) Nothing in this section shall be construed to limit remedies available elsewhere in law for a tenant to seek to maintain safe and sanitary housing.

H. Electric Vehicle Charging Systems

§ 38-12-601, C.R.S. Unreasonable restrictions on electric vehicle charging systems – definitions.

(1) Notwithstanding any provision in the lease to the contrary, and subject to subsection (2) of this section:

(a) A tenant may install, at the tenant's expense for the tenant's own use, a level 1 or level 2 electric vehicle charging system on or in the leased premises; and

(b) A landlord shall not assess or charge a tenant any fee for the placement or use of an electric vehicle charging system; except that:

(I) The landlord may require reimbursement for the actual cost of electricity provided by the landlord that was used by the charging system or, alternatively, may charge a reasonable fee for access. If the charging system is part of a network for which a network fee is charged, the landlord's reimbursement may include the amount of the network fee. Nothing in this section requires a landlord to impose upon a tenant any fee or charge other than the rental payments specified in the lease.

(II) The landlord may require reimbursement for the cost of the installation of the charging system, including any additions or upgrades to existing wiring directly attributable to the requirements of the charging system, if the landlord places or causes the electric vehicle charging system to be placed at the request of the tenant; and

(III) If the tenant desires to place an electric vehicle charging system in an area accessible to other tenants, the landlord may assess or charge the tenant a reasonable fee to reserve a specific parking spot in which to install the charging system.

(2) A landlord may require a tenant to comply with:

(a) Bona fide safety requirements, consistent with an applicable building code or recognized safety standard, for the protection of persons and property;

(b) A requirement that the charging system be registered with the landlord within thirty days after installation; or

(c) Reasonable aesthetic provisions that govern the dimensions, placement, or external appearance of an electric vehicle charging system.

(3) A tenant may place an electric vehicle charging system in an area accessible to other tenants if:

(a) The charging system is in compliance with all applicable requirements adopted pursuant to subsection (2) of this section; and

(b) The tenant agrees in writing to:

(I) Comply with the landlord's design specifications for the installation of the charging system;

(II) Engage the services of a duly licensed and registered electrical contractor familiar with the installation and code requirements of an electric vehicle charging system; and

(III) (A) Provide, within fourteen days after receiving the landlord's consent for the installation, a certificate of insurance naming the landlord as an additional insured on the tenant's renters' insurance policy for any claim related to the installation, maintenance, or use of the system or, at the landlord's option, reimbursement to the landlord for the actual cost of any increased insurance premium amount attributable to the system, notwithstanding any provision to the contrary in the lease.

(B) A certificate of insurance under sub-subparagraph (A) of this subparagraph (III) must be provided within fourteen days after the tenant receives the landlord's consent for the installation. Reimbursement for an increased insurance premium amount under sub-subparagraph (A) of this subparagraph (III) must be provided within fourteen days after the tenant receives the landlord's invoice for the amount attributable to the system.

(4) If the landlord consents to a tenant's installation of an electric vehicle charging system on property accessible to other tenants, including a parking space, carport, or garage stall, then, unless otherwise specified in a written agreement with the landlord:

(a) The tenant, and each successive tenant with exclusive rights to the area where the charging system is installed, is responsible for any costs for damages to the charging system and to any other property of the landlord or of another tenant that arise or result from the installation, maintenance, repair, removal, or replacement of the charging system;

(b) Each successive tenant with exclusive rights to the area where the charging system is installed shall assume responsibility for the repair, maintenance, removal, and replacement of the charging system until the system has been removed;

(c) The tenant and each successive tenant with exclusive rights to the area where the system is installed shall at all times have and maintain an insurance policy covering the obligations of the tenant under this subsection (4) and shall name the landlord as an additional insured under the policy; and

(d) The tenant and each successive tenant with exclusive rights to the area where the system is installed is responsible for removing the system if reasonably necessary or convenient for the repair, maintenance, or replacement of any property of the landlord, whether or not leased to another tenant.

(5) A charging system installed at the tenant's cost is property of the tenant. Upon termination of the lease, if the charging system is removable, the tenant may either remove it or sell it to the landlord or another tenant for an agreed price. Nothing in this subsection (5) requires the landlord or another tenant to purchase the charging system.

(6) As used in this section:

(a) "Electric vehicle charging system" or "charging system" means a device that is used to provide electricity to a plug-in electric vehicle or plug-in hybrid vehicle, is designed to ensure that a safe connection has been made between the electric grid and the vehicle, and is able to communicate with the vehicle's control system so that electricity flows at an appropriate voltage and current level. An electric vehicle charging system may be wall-mounted or pedestal style and may provide multiple cords to connect with electric vehicles. An electric vehicle charging system must be certified by underwriters laboratories or an equivalent certification and must comply with the current version of article 625 of the national electrical code.

(b) "Level 1" means a charging system that provides charging through a one-hundred-twenty volt AC plug with a cord connector that meets the SAE international J1772 standard or a successor standard.

(c) "Level 2" means a charging system that provides charging through a two-hundred-eight to two-hundred-forty volt AC plug with a cord connector that meets the SAE international J1772 standard or a successor standard.

(7) This section applies only to residential rental properties.

I. Carbon Monoxide Alarms

§ 38-45-101, C.R.S. Definitions.

As used in this article, unless the context otherwise requires:

(1) "Carbon monoxide alarm" means a device that detects carbon monoxide and that:

(a) Produces a distinct, audible alarm;

(b) Is listed by a nationally recognized, independent product-safety testing and certification laboratory to conform to the standards for carbon monoxide alarms issued by such laboratory or any successor standards;

(c) Is battery powered, plugs into a dwelling's electrical outlet and has a battery backup, is wired into a dwelling's electrical system and has a battery backup, or is connected to an electrical system via an electrical panel; and

(d) May be combined with a smoke detecting device if the combined device complies with applicable law regarding both smoke detecting devices and carbon monoxide alarms and that the combined unit produces an alarm, or an alarm and voice signal, in a manner that clearly differentiates between the two hazards.

(2) "Dwelling unit" means a single unit providing complete independent living facilities for one or more persons, including permanent provisions for living, sleeping, eating, cooking, and sanitation.

(3) "Fuel" means coal, kerosene, oil, fuel gases, or other petroleum products or hydrocarbon products such as wood that emit carbon monoxide as a by-product of combustion.

(4) "Installed" means that a carbon monoxide alarm is installed in a dwelling unit in one of the following ways:

(a) Wired directly into the dwelling's electrical system;

(b) Directly plugged into an electrical outlet without a switch other than a circuit breaker; or

(c) If the alarm is battery-powered, attached to the wall or ceiling of the dwelling unit in accordance with the national fire protection association's standard 720, or any successor standard, for the operation and installation of carbon monoxide detection and warning equipment in dwelling units.

(5) "Multi-family dwelling" means any improved real property used or intended to be used as a residence and that contains more than one dwelling unit. Multi-family dwelling includes a condominium or cooperative.

(6) "Operational" means working and in service in accordance with manufacturer instructions.

(7) "Single-family dwelling" means any improved real property used or intended to be used as a residence and that contains one dwelling unit.

§ 38-45-102, C.R.S. Carbon monoxide alarms in single-family dwellings – rules.

(1) (a) Notwithstanding any other provision of law, the seller of each existing single-family dwelling offered for sale or transfer on or after July 1, 2009, that has a fuel-fired heater or appliance, a fireplace, or an attached garage shall assure that an operational carbon monoxide alarm is installed within fifteen feet of the entrance to each room lawfully used for sleeping purposes or in a location as specified in any building code adopted by the state or any local government entity.

(b) By July 1, 2009, the real estate commission created in section 12-61-105, C.R.S., shall by rule require each listing contract for residential real property that is subject to the commission's jurisdiction pursuant to article 61 of title 12, C.R.S., to disclose the requirements specified in paragraph (a) of this subsection (1).

(2) Notwithstanding any other provision of law, every single-family dwelling that includes either fuel-fired appliances or an attached garage where, on or after July 1, 2009, interior alterations, repairs, fuel-fired appliance replacements, or additions, any of which require a building permit, occurs or where one or more rooms lawfully used for sleeping purposes are added shall have an operational carbon monoxide alarm installed within fifteen feet of the entrance to each room lawfully used for sleeping purposes or in a location as specified in any building code adopted by the state or any local government entity.

(3) No person shall remove batteries from, or in any way render inoperable, a carbon monoxide alarm, except as part of a process to inspect, maintain, repair, or replace the alarm or replace the batteries in the alarm.

§ 38-45-103, C.R.S. Carbon monoxide alarms in multi-family dwellings – rules.

(1) (a) Notwithstanding any other provision of law, the seller of every dwelling unit of an existing multi-family dwelling offered for sale or transfer on or after July 1, 2009, that has a fuel-fired heater or appliance, a fireplace, or an attached garage shall assure that an operational carbon monoxide alarm is installed within fifteen feet of the entrance to each room lawfully used for sleeping purposes or in a location as specified in any building code adopted by the state or any local government entity.

(b) By July 1, 2009, the real estate commission created in section 12-61-105, C.R.S., shall by rule require each listing contract for residential real property that is subject to the commission's jurisdiction pursuant to article 61 of title 12, C.R.S., to disclose the requirements specified in paragraph (a) of this subsection (1).

(2) Notwithstanding any other provision of law, every dwelling unit of a multi-family dwelling that includes fuel-fired appliances or an attached garage where, on or after July 1, 2009, interior alterations, repairs, fuel-fired appliance replacements, or additions, any of which require a building permit, occurs or where one or more rooms lawfully used for sleeping purposes are

added shall have an operational carbon monoxide alarm installed within fifteen feet of the entrance to each room lawfully used for sleeping purposes or in a location as specified in any building code adopted by the state or any local government entity.

(3) No person shall remove batteries from, or in any way render inoperable, a carbon monoxide alarm, except as part of a process to inspect, maintain, repair, or replace the alarm or replace the batteries in the alarm.

§ 38-45-104, C.R.S. Carbon monoxide alarms in rental properties.

(1) Except as provided in subsection (5) of this section, any single-family dwelling or dwelling unit in a multi-family dwelling used for rental purposes and that includes fuel-fired appliances or an attached garage where, on or after July 1, 2009, interior alterations, repairs, fuel-fired appliance replacements, or additions, any of which requires a building permit, occurs or where one or more rooms lawfully used for sleeping purposes are added shall be subject to the requirements specified in sections 38-45-102 and 38-45-103.

(2) Except as provided in subsection (5) of this section, each existing single-family dwelling or existing dwelling unit in a multi-family dwelling that is used for rental purposes that has a change in tenant occupancy on or after July 1, 2009, shall be subject to the requirements specified in sections 38-45-102 and 38-45-103.

(3) (a) Notwithstanding any other provision of law, the owner of any rental property specified in subsections (1) and (2) of this section shall:

(I) Prior to the commencement of a new tenant occupancy, replace any carbon monoxide alarm that was stolen, removed, found missing, or found not operational after the previous occupancy;

(II) Ensure that any batteries necessary to make the carbon monoxide alarm operational are provided to the tenant at the time the tenant takes residence in the dwelling unit;

(III) Replace any carbon monoxide alarm if notified by a tenant as specified in paragraph (c) of subsection (4) of this section that any carbon monoxide alarm was stolen, removed, found missing, or found not operational during the tenant's occupancy; and

(IV) Fix any deficiency in a carbon monoxide alarm if notified by a tenant as specified in paragraph (d) of subsection (4) of this section.

(b) Except as provided in paragraph (a) of this subsection (3), the owner of a single-family dwelling or dwelling unit in a multi-family dwelling that is used for rental purposes is not responsible for the maintenance, repair, or replacement of a carbon monoxide alarm or the care and replacement of batteries for such an alarm.

(4) Notwithstanding any other provision of law, the tenant of any rental property specified in subsections (1) and (2) of this section shall:

(a) Keep, test, and maintain all carbon monoxide alarms in good repair;

(b) Notify, in writing, the owner of the single-family dwelling or dwelling unit of a multi-family dwelling, or the owner's authorized agent, if the batteries of any carbon monoxide alarm need to be replaced;

(c) Notify, in writing, the owner of the single-family dwelling or dwelling unit of a multi-family dwelling, or the owner's authorized agent, if any carbon monoxide alarm is stolen, removed, found missing, or found not operational during the tenant's occupancy of the single-family dwelling or dwelling unit in the multi-family dwelling; and

(d) Notify, in writing, the owner of the single-family dwelling or dwelling unit of a multi-family dwelling, or the owner's authorized agent, of any deficiency in any carbon monoxide alarm that the tenant cannot correct.

(5) Notwithstanding the requirements of section 38-45-103 (1) and (2), so long as there is a centralized alarm system or other mechanism for a responsible person to hear the alarm at all times in a multi-family dwelling used for rental purposes, such multi-family dwelling may have an operational carbon monoxide alarm installed within twenty-five feet of any fuel-fired heater or appliance, fireplace, or garage or in a location as specified in any building code adopted by the state or any local government entity.

(6) No person shall remove batteries from, or in any way render inoperable, a carbon monoxide alarm, except as part of a process to inspect, maintain, repair, or replace the alarm or replace the batteries in the alarm.

§ 38-45-105, C.R.S. Municipal or county ordinances regarding carbon monoxide alarms.

Nothing in this article shall be construed to limit a municipality, city, home rule city, city and county, county, or other local government entity from adopting or enforcing any requirements for the installation and maintenance of carbon monoxide alarms that are more stringent than the requirements set forth in this article.

§ 38-45-106, C.R.S. Limitation of liability.

(1) No person shall have a claim for relief against a property owner, an authorized agent of a property owner, a person in possession of real property, or an installer for any damages resulting from the operation, maintenance, or effectiveness of a carbon monoxide alarm if the property owner, authorized agent, person in possession of real property, or installer installs a carbon monoxide alarm in accordance with the manufacturer's published instructions and the provisions of this article.

(2) A purchaser shall have no claim for relief against any person licensed pursuant to article 61 of title 12, C.R.S., for any damages resulting from the operation, maintenance, or effectiveness of a carbon monoxide alarm if such licensed person complies with rules promulgated pursuant to sections 38-45-102 (1) (b) and 38-45-103 (1) (b). Nothing in this subsection (2) shall affect any remedy that a purchaser may otherwise have against a seller.

XI. Mobile Home Park Tenancies

Colorado law specifically provides for the method of termination of a lease in a mobile home park. Management must give written notice to remove an owner's unit from the premises within not less 60 days from the date notice is served. The manager must provide the homeowner with a statement of reasons for termination. Management may increase rent only after 60 days' written notice to the homeowners.

The law also covers regulations of tenancy, amount of security deposits, fees or fines, collection of utility charges, etc. (see §§ 38-12-201, *et seq.*, C.R.S.) The Mobile Home Park Act is printed in Chapter "Related Real Estate Law.

XII. Sources of Information and Training

NARPM® National: The National Association of Residential Property Managers. 638 Independence Parkway, Suite 100, Chesapeake, VA 23320, Phone: (800) 782-3452, Fax: (866) 466-2776, E-mail: info@narpm.org, Website: www.narpm.org. Appealing to managers of smaller residential properties: single-family homes, individual condos or townhomes, and 2-12 unit apartment houses, **NARPM** is independent of the National Association of REALTORS® and does not require members to be REALTORS®. **NARPM** does require its members to hold a real estate license except in those states in which no license is required for property managers. There are chapters of **NARPM** in Denver, Colorado Springs, Grand Junction, and Ft. Collins, with members throughout the state. Several professional designations are available.

IREM: The Institute of Real Estate Management.
430 North Michigan Avenue, Suite 500, Chicago, IL 60611, Phone: (800) 837-0706, Fax: (800) 338-4736, E-mail: getinfo@irem.org, Website: www.irem.org. This organization is an affiliate of the National Association of REALTORS® and requires its members to be REALTORS®. **IREM** awards the Certified Property Manager (CPM) designation to those members who successfully complete a rigorous series of courses. **IREM** tends to draw managers of commercial ventures or large apartment houses.

CAI: The Community Associations Institute.

6402 Arlington Blvd., Suite 500, Falls Church, VA 22042, Phone: (888) 224-4321, Fax: (703) 684-1581, Email at: cai-info@caionline.org, Website: www.caionline.org. This group is independent of the National Association of REALTORS® and specializes in the concerns of professional homeowners association managers. There are active chapters in both northern and southern Colorado. CAI awards several professional designations.

BOMA: The Building Owners and Managers Association.

1101 15th St., NW, Suite 800, Washington DC 20005, Phone: (202)326-6300, Fax: (202)326-6377, Email at: info@boma.org. There are two BOMA local associations in Colorado; one in Denver and one in Colorado Springs.

NAA: The National Apartment Association.
4300 Wilson Blvd., Suite 800, Arlington, VA, 22203, Phone: (703) 518-6141, Customer Service: (833)866-9622, Fax: (703) 248-9440, Email at: webmaster@naahq.com, Website: www.naahq.org. There are chapters of NAA in the Denver metro area, Weld County, Northern Colorado, and Southern Colorado.

These national associations listed above usually have local chapters affiliated with them. These national organizations collect income and operating expense data from their members. The expense ratios are useful guides that managers use to check their individual properties' operating expense against the average expense shown for that city. Several of these associations offer educational courses, literature, seminars, and other information useful in all forms of property management.

Chapter 23: Farm and Ranch Brokerage

An * in the left margin indicates a change in the statute, rule or text since the last publication of the manual.

I. Introduction

A large segment of the Colorado economy is devoted to agriculture. A wide variety of products are produced on property ranging from rangeland to irrigated land to mountain hay meadows to fruit farms. It is a complex area of real property that provides both an opportunity and a challenge for real estate licensees. There is opportunity because tremendous wealth is involved; no other group in Colorado values the ownership of land more than ranchers and farmers. It is a challenge because farmers and ranchers demand service for the commissions they pay—and service in this field involves much effort and knowledge. Rural real estate involves many problems that are not found in urban property transactions. The successful person in this type of brokerage must have solutions to the problems and understand all the factors involved in determining rural real property values.

The sale of a farm or ranch is also the sale of a business. This has become more obvious as the traditional family farm or ranch increasingly has been replaced by sophisticated corporate entities. Although a property may include land, personal property, and water rights, the marginal value of a farm or ranch is largely determined by the income it produces. A real estate licensee dealing in farms or ranches therefore must have a strong knowledge of agricultural finance and economics in addition to an appreciation of the physical assets to be conveyed. Such knowledge can include areas as diverse as the price of winter wheat, changing developmental and demographic patterns, and new developments in fertilizers and pest control.

Successful farm and ranch brokers exercise a great deal of care in listing properties for sale. Many problems can be avoided by planning carefully in this phase of a real estate operation. Showing a farm or ranch involves much more than showing a house in an urban setting. Consequently, when a licensee accepts a listing of rural property, the real estate licensee must have a sound knowledge of the property and surrounding area.

In developing a list of farms and ranches for sale, a licensee should consider specializing either in certain types of properties or in a given area. By restricting the area of operation, a licensee can gradually become an expert in that field. For example, if a real estate licensee becomes familiar with every farm and every farmer in the south half of a county, he or she will be recognized as an authority and will obtain good listings there. If a licensee learns about dairy farms and becomes acquainted with owners of this kind of property, the licensee's services will be in demand by those wishing to sell dairy farms. As a licensee becomes more experienced, he or she can expand their area of geographic expertise or may branch out into different specialties (*e.g.*, orchards or wheat farms).

Before an owner signs an exclusive listing, a complete statement of all the important information concerning the property should be developed. Sample listing sheets appear in this chapter. The licensee should go further and develop a brochure or brief that gives a complete description of the property, along with pictures and charts. Some brokers even use aerial photographs to better present the qualities of the land to prospective buyers. The extent of the listing information will depend on the complexity of the transaction.

The following maps are useful in the analysis of a farm or ranch:

1. Map showing all improvements (location and description);
2. Map showing all water, streams, springs, wells, lakes, water holes, etc.;
3. Map showing vegetation cover from the Bureau of Land Management;
4. Map of mineral ownership;
5. Plot of the ranch on a road map showing accessibility to roads, railroads, air fields, etc.

The listing broker must also obtain full financial data concerning operation of the property. In the past, financial records were often incomplete due to resistance from owners or inconsistent record keeping. Today, this situation has changed to the point where a licensee often deals not only with an owner, but also with accountants, lenders, and attorneys. Financial information must be maintained in strict confidentiality. Potential purchasers should be provided such information only after being fully qualified and with the owner's consent.

Water rights should be carefully studied and described not only as to the date of decree and amounts of water decreed, but also as to actual delivery of water year after year in both wet and dry years. Additional information on water rights is available in the Real Estate Manual, "Water Rights". A well checklist form is located at the end of this chapter.

Precipitation and temperature figures should be developed for the past few years, because they are important in determining winter conditions, winter feed needs, etc. Hay and grain production on the ranch for several years back should be determined. These figures tie into the wintering analysis that the broker is making.

All minerals should be checked, as they might be the greatest asset of the property. Also, in the sale of the property, the minerals can be sold separately to the purchaser of the land or to someone else.

Inquiries should also be made of the owner concerning the existence of possible hazardous waste sites. These could include abandoned fuel storage tanks or chemical dumps and could result in serious problems if not disclosed to potential purchasers.

A very important factor in the sale of a ranch is the carrying capacity. How many animal units will the ranch support? Sometimes this is a historical fact based on the number of cattle that have been run on the ranch over a period of years. If the ranch has Bureau of Land Management (BLM) lands within its boundaries, the BLM may have the A.U. (animal unit) figures for the ranch. Check to see if the carrying capacity has been increased by range seeding and by water hole development.

Farm and ranch experts look for buyers in basically the same areas where they search for listings. The licensee keeps in contact with as many people as possible that are related to the industry, such as machinery companies and farm organizations. Probate judges and trust officers often provide leads on prospective buyers. Real estate professionals watch newspaper stories about farm sales and condemnations, and become acquainted with investors who make a practice of buying rural property. Government agencies buy land, as do factories and land developers. A successful broker knows who buys land, and catalogs and analyzes their needs. Foreclosures should also be monitored.

Many buyers want farm or ranch land for special uses such as grass sod farms or horse-breeding farms. Some farm or ranch lands may be suitable for recreational or subdivision development. Other buyers may be interested in securing income tax benefits.

Buyer qualification is critical in the sale of a farm or ranch. This is particularly true if the seller is going to finance all or part of the sale by carrying back a mortgage or trust deed. Qualification should include not only a buyer's ability to complete the purchase, but also evidence that the buyer can successfully operate the farm or ranch after the sale. Licensees should encourage sellers to seek professional assistance in evaluating buyer qualifications.

Sources of funding for agricultural properties are more varied than for urban residential properties. These include not only banks and mortgage companies, but also insurance companies, pension plans, and real estate investment trusts (REITs). A farm and ranch broker should have a complete list of all the sources of money available for financing. Most sales will hinge on the ability of the broker to bring the moneylender and buyer together on satisfactory terms. The licensee should also be familiar with the sources of funds made available by the federal government. These include the Federal Land Bank, the Farmers Home Administration, the Federal Land Bank Association, and the Federal Intermediate Credit Banks. These institutions are designed to meet unusual demands on the part of farmers and ranchers. Real estate brokers can contact these agencies to get more information about the services they provide. Appraisers may also be a valuable source of information concerning financing.

Selling to and for syndicates is a device employed by many farm and ranch professionals. This takes specialized knowledge on the part of the licensee and should be explored carefully. A knowledge of securities law is vital to such transactions, which may also require the involvement of a licensed securities dealer.

A farm and ranch broker should recognize the influence that income tax has on the purchase and sale of real estate and should know where to get expert advice in this area.

Finally, in relation to selling farms and ranches, the manager is someone who can help directly or indirectly in the sale. The knowledge needed in managing a farm is very similar to the knowledge required to properly present the farm to a prospective buyer. Furthermore, the sale of a farm or ranch may depend on the ability of the broker to furnish a manager for the property after the sale. Consequently, many successful offices incorporate a management department in their business operation.

This chapter is merely an introduction for real estate licensees to the highly specialized field of farm and ranch brokerage. Experience is the great teacher in this field. Also review chapters in the Real Estate Manual under "Land Descriptions" and "Water Rights" when working on a farm or ranch sale.

The listing contract forms used for farms and ranches are similar to those used for the listing of other types of real estate. However, the information necessary for the sale of a farm or a ranch is much more detailed. Following is a short glossary of terms and basic farm and ranch information sheets.

II. Farm and Ranch Glossary

National Forest: A forest or watershed reservation administered by the Forest Service, United States Department of Agriculture.

Grazing Preference on National Forest: An established preference to graze certain numbers and classes of livestock upon a National Forest for a specified time and subject to rules and regulations adopted by the Forest Service.

Grazing District – Taylor Grazing Act: An administrative subdivision of range lands under the jurisdiction of the Bureau of Land Management, established pursuant to Section 3 of the Taylor Grazing Act to facilitate management of BLM forage resources. Grazing on the public lands within such districts was formerly regulated by the Grazing Service.

Grazing Licenses: A grant of grazing rights for a specified number and class of livestock on a designated area of grazing-district lands for a specified period, usually not more than one year.

Grazing Permit: An authorization to graze a set number and class of livestock on a designated area of grazing-district lands during specified seasons each year for a period of usually 10 years.

Section 15 Grazing Lease: A lease which authorizes the use of public lands outside of grazing districts (Taylor Grazing Act) for the grazing of livestock for a specified period.

State Lease: A lease in which the state of Colorado, as landlord, grants grazing, agricultural, and other rights to land under the jurisdiction of the state board of land commissioners.

EXAMPLE

FARM INFORMATION

Date ______________________________ Farm Listing ____________________________________

State _____________________________ Irrigated _______________________________________

County ____________________________ Dry Land ____

Co. Seat ___________________________

Name of Farm ______________________ Nearest Town ____________________________________

Total Acres _____________ Direction from Town __________________ Distance _______________

Roads ____________ Distance School ____________ High School _ Bus _________

Domestic Water __________________ Stock Water __________________ Soil __________________

Acres Cultivated _________ Irrigated _________ Non-Irrigated ________ Sub-Irrigated ________

Acres Alfalfa ____________ Native ____________ Total Tons ___________ Pasture ____________

Crops Now Growing ____

____

Following crops are/are not included in sale price ______________________

____

Irrigation Wells __________ Depth ______________ Power __________ Name of Pump _________

Capacity of Lakes ___________ or Well ___________ Reservoirs __________ Fences __________

Main House Construction ___________ No. of Rooms ________ Roof _______ Foundation _______

Basement _____________ Gas ______________ Electricity _______________ Bath ______________

Water System ______________ Heat __________________ Condition Improv. ________________

____

Other Living Quarters ____

Barns and Out Buildings ____

____

____

Name of Tenant __________________________ Address ____________________________

Term of Lease ____________________________ Crop or Share Rent _____________________

Water Rights ____

Water Assessments ____

What Mineral Rights Go? __________________________________ Taxes __________________

Comments (General impression of farm) (Advantages and disadvantages) _____________________

____

____

____

____

____

Owner ______________________________ Phone ______________

Address ______________________________ Possession Date ______________

Price ______________________ Terms ______________________

Loan Information: Original Amount $__________________ Interest Rate ____________

Payments Due ____________________ How Payable ____________________

Present Balance $____________________ Can it be paid off? ____________________

Mortgagee ____________________ Address ____________________

Can new loan be secured? __________ Amount ______________ Interest __________

Legal Description ____

____

RANGE ______

TOWNSHIP ______

6	5	4	3	2	1
7	8	9	10	11	12
18	17	16	15	14	13
19	20	21	22	23	24
30	29	28	27	26	25
31	32	33	34	35	36

North

Date ____________________

The foregoing statements are substantially correct.

(Owner) ____

(Owner) ____

Address ____

____

EXAMPLE

RANCH INFORMATION

Date ______________________________ Ranch Listing

State______________________________ Cattle ____________ Sheep ____________

County ______________________ Mountain __________ Plains ____________

Co. Seat ____________________________ Carrying Capacity

Altitude at Ranch _____________________ No. of Cows ______ Hd Mo's ___________

No. of Steers ______ Hd Mo's ___________

No. of Sheep ______ Hd Mo's ___________

Total Acres _________ Direction from Town ________ Distance ________________

Name of Ranch ______________________ Nearest Town __________________

Acres Deeded ________ State Lease ____ Acres at $_________ Per Year - Exp. Date ______

Private Lease ________ Acres at $__________ Per ______________________________

Year-(Written-Verbal) Exp. Date ____

BLM Lease __________ Acres at $_____ Per Year-Term Exp. Date ________________

BLM Permit _________ Head at $______ Per ______________________________

Head-Season of ____________________________ to ___________________________

Forest Permit ________ Head at $__________ Per ______________________________

Head-Season of ______________________ to ________________________________

Name of Forest_______ Likelihood of cut (Yes-No) __________ What Percent _______

Name of Ranger or Supervisor and Address ______________________________________

Acres in Hay ________ Kind ________ Average Tonnage __________ Quality ___________

Acres Farmed ________ What Crops ______________ Average Yields _____________

Acres in Pasture ______ Acres Sub-Irr. Pasture ________ Acres Dry Pasture __________

Acres Waste Land ____

Predominant Range Grasses __________ Condition of Range ______________________

Water Rights _________ Name of Stream ______ No. of Cu. Ft. __ Date of Priority ______

Stream or Lake s ______________________ Miles of Stream ______________________

Stock Water Creek ___________ Springs ______________Ponds _______ Windmills ___________

Distance to Grade School ________________________ Bus (Yes-No) _______________

Distance to High School ____________________ Bus (Yes-No) _______________

Kind of Road in to Ranch _____________ Miles to Main Road __________ No. or Type _________

Is there good winter shelter? _________ Kind _______________ Annual Precipitation ________

Describe Climate ___________________ Winters ____________ Summers __________________

Condition of fences __________ Kind ________________ No. of Pastures __________________

Improvements

Describe fully - type - condition - water supply - bath - elec. (Yes-No) source ____________

____

Are buildings neat and attractive? (Yes-No) Lawn (Yes-No) Shade trees (Yes-No) _________

Explain carrying capacity and best type of operation_____________________________________

____

Livestock or Ranch (Included - Not included) in sale price, No. of Cattle __ No. of Sheep

When purchased by present owner? _________ Why is ranch for sale? ______________

Will hay crop be included in sale? (Yes-No) If not, at what price per ton? $____________

Real estate Taxes $_________________ Personal Taxes $___________________

Any Poisonous Weeds? _______ What Mineral Rights Go? ________________________

Comments (general impression of ranch, any hunting, fishing, or recreation facilities?)

____

Owner ____ Ranch Phone ____________________

Address________________________________ Bus. Phone ____________________

Name of (Foreman-Tenant) ____________________ Remuneration ____________________

Price of Ranch $____________ Terms ______________________________

Possession will be given ____

Price of livestock if not included with ranch $______________________________

Following described equipment (is-is not) included in sale price ________________

Legal Description (if too long attach rider) ____________________________________

____

Loan Information ____________ Township: ______________ Range: __________

Is there a loan? (Yes-No)

Original Amt. $__________

Int. Rate _____% Due_____

When Made ___________

How Payable ___________

Present Balance $________

Can it be paid off? _______

Mortgagee ___________

Address ___________

____

____

Other Indebtedness ______

Lender ______________

6	5	4	3	2	1
7	8	9	10	11	12
18	17	16	15	14	13
19	20	21	22	23	24
30	29	28	27	26	25
~~31~~	~~32~~	~~33~~	~~34~~	~~35~~	~~36~~

LEGEND

Buildings ■

Fences ————

Railroads ═══

Streams

Wells o

Windmills Xo

Date__________________

The foregoing statements are substantially correct.

Reservoir	⬭	(Owner) ______________________
Ponds	○	
Timber	⬬	(Owner) ______________________
Deeded	(Red)	
State Lease	(Yellow)	Address ______________________
BLM	(Blue)	
Private Lease	(Green)	______________________

EXAMPLE

LISTING FIRM'S WELL CHECKLIST

[THIS CHECKLIST IS FOR SELLER AND LISTING FIRM'S INTERNAL USE ONLY.]

Date: ______________________________

Seller: ______________________________

Property: ______________________________

Copy of Well Permit attached ☐ Yes ☐ No

I. Domestic (Exempt) Wells: ☐ Household use only

A. Confirm with State or Division Engineer as to:

1) Permit or Registration No: ______________________________

2) Statement of Beneficial Use filed ☐ Yes ☐ No

3) Location: ______________________________

4) Permitted uses: ______________________________

5) Restrictions: ______________________________

6) Decreed: ☐ Yes ☐ No

a. Water Court Docket No: ______________________________

7) Other, copy of report, etc. ______________________________

8) Augmentation Plan ☐ Yes ☐ No

9) Well placed on Inactive Status ☐ Yes ☐ No

B. Pump Test ☐ Yes Date __________ ☐ No

GPM ______________________________

C. Potability test ☐ Yes Date __________ ☐ No

Results: ______________________________

D. Cistern ☐ Yes ☐ No

E. Pump

Type ______________________________

Age ______________________________

F. Shared use ☐ Yes ☐ No

Shared with ______________________________

II. Other (Fee) Wells:

A. Confirm with State or Division Engineer or Ground Water Commission as to:

1) Permit or Registration No: ______________________________

2) Statement of Beneficial Use filed ☐ Yes ☐ No

3) Place of use/location: ______________________________

4) Pumping rate, volumetic limit: ______________________________

5) Metered ☐ Yes ☐ No

a. Subject to Metering Order ☐ Yes ☐ No

6) Permitted uses and restrictions:

a. Irrigation: ______________________________

b. Industrial: ______________________________

c. Commercial: ______________________________

d. Municipal: ______________________________

7) Decreed: ☐ Yes ☐ No

a. Water Court Docket No: ______________________________

8) Source: ______________________________

a. Tributary to: ______________________________

(1) Augmentation by: ______________________________

(a) Decree, Docket No: ______________________________

(b) Administrative approval ☐ Yes ☐ No

(i) Cost of augmentation: $______________________________

(ii) Membership fee: $______________________________

(iii) Cost of water: $______________

b. Designated Ground Water (Ground Water Commission): ______________

(1) Designated Basin: ______________

(2) Management District: ______________

(a) Contact information: ______________

c. Non-Tributary/Not-Nontributary: ☐ Yes ☐ No

(1) Name of formation (aquifer) ______________

(2) Permit conditions: ______________

(3) Decree provisions: ______________

Caution: Water rights can be very technical and complex. Counsel of appropriate experts, such as attorneys or brokers who specialize in water rights, water engineers and well drillers, should be sought. Valuable general and specific information can also be obtained from the Office of the State Engineer, Division of Water Resources, Colorado Department of Natural Resources. Rules, regulations, and statutes may be obtained from the Colorado Division of Water Resources, 1313 Sherman St., Room 821, Denver, CO 80203. Its website is https://dwr.colorado.gov/.

For further information, such as helpful publications, etc., the following agencies should be contacted: The Colorado Division of Water Resources; the Colorado Water Conservation Board; Water Education Colorado, Colorado State University, Civil Engineering Department; and the United States Geological Survey, Water Resources Branch, Denver Federal Center.

Chapter 24: Business Opportunities

An * in the left margin indicates a change in the statute, rule, or text since the last publication of the manual.

I. Introduction

The sale of business opportunities requires a real estate broker's license when the transaction involves a change of ownership or leasehold in real estate (see § 12-10-201, C.R.S.). The Colorado Attorney General has interpreted this statute to hold that conveyance of a business opportunity is not severable from an interest in land. Furthermore, an unlicensed person may not receive a commission on the portion of the conveyance not involving real estate (*i.e.*, a business opportunity), if the transfer as a whole involves an ownership or leasehold interest in land.

The sale of a business opportunity may be less or more complicated than the sale of real estate. There are usually more representations to be made. A portion of the sale is intangible, and therefore values are difficult to determine. A broker should recommend attorney representation to each party to the transaction.

II. Matters to be Considered

The following information is essential to successfully brokering a business opportunity.

1. **Name of business.**
2. **Location of business.**
3. **Name of owner, address, and phone number.**
4. **Price.** Be sure that the price quoted in the listing contract includes the broker's fee.
5. **Terms.** The amount of cash the seller demands and how large a note and purchase money chattel mortgage the seller will carry. Lending institutions may not finance business opportunity transactions; therefore, the broker should nail down financing arrangements with the seller at the time of securing the listing contract.
6. **License, Franchise, or Distributorship.** If a business involves a license, franchise, or distributorship, arrangements must be made to ensure that rights are transferred and perhaps become a condition of the contract.

   If the business involves the sale of liquor, both the appropriate municipal agency and the Colorado Department of Revenue must issue licenses. The requirements are stringent and the investigation of the applicant is quite thorough. Requirements include a copy of the purchase agreement; evidence of the transfer if corporate stock is sold; a copy of the lease, lease assignment, or deed; trade name affidavit; health and hospital inspection certificate; bill of sale; receipt for personal property taxes paid; the source of financing; and fingerprinting.

   If a distributorship is involved, the manufacturer must consent and may demand certain financial standards before consenting to the transfer.

Other businesses also may require licenses of various kinds before the buyer may operate the business.

7. **Lease.** A licensee should inspect the lease to determine any special conditions and the remaining term. The monthly rental is always important because of its relationship to the business income. Determine if the lease is assignable. Since most leases prohibit assignment without the lessor's consent, such consent must be obtained. If the lessor charges for consent, the seller will be obligated for this expense and should be told so. It is better for the seller if the buyer obtains a new lease, because the seller will remain liable to the lessor on a lease assignment if the buyer later defaults on any terms. A licensee might also propose a sale to the lessor.
8. **Fixtures.** When the sale includes fixtures, check to make sure that they belong to the seller. For example, under some lease provisions, fixtures belong to the lessor on termination of the lease and therefore cannot be included in the sale.
9. **Equipment.** It is advisable to prepare a list of the equipment and determine if it is marketable and if the price is fair.
10. **Stock or Inventory.** Without an actual inventory, the broker should establish the value of the stock as closely as possible based on wholesale cost. Find out if there is any unsalable stock. Of course, at the time of closing, there must be an accurate and detailed inventory.
11. **Number of Employees.** It is important to establish the dollar amount of the payroll, and especially the status of payroll taxes.
12. **Income, Gross and Net.** The broker should review CPA reports or a copy of income tax returns (or both) for previous years. This is a risky situation for the licensee insofar as representations to the buyer. Agency laws on representation and disclosure apply with particular force in a business sale because there are so many different facts that may be material to the purchase. The seller's attorney may want to include a clause in the contract stating that the seller has made no representations regarding the business and that the buyer has made their own inspection of the business and takes all goods, fixtures, and other property "as is," without any warranties. Such a clause gives only limited protection and will not safeguard the seller against a clear showing of fraudulent misrepresentation. The broker should choose records that can be verified when he or she uses them for purposes of making a sale. It may be advisable to provide an income or profit-and-loss statement for the seller to complete.
13. **Accounts Receivable.** Sometimes a business sale includes all the outstanding customer accounts receivable, that is, the right to collect all outstanding bills owed to the seller by previous customers. In such a case, the seller "assigns" these accounts to the buyer. Such an assignment should be in the contract. But even with the assignment made, it is up to the buyer to effect the transfer. The buyer should notify each account of the change in ownership and the assignment of the account, and provide instructions on how and where to make future payments. Otherwise, the customer may continue to make payments to the original owner and the buyer would have no recourse. Sometimes the agreement of sale may provide for a notice or letter to go out to all customers over the signatures of both seller and buyer, announcing the change in management and reassuring the customer that they will get the same good service from the new owner. Such a letter could also include notice of assignment of the accounts. In assigning accounts, the seller should

affirmatively make no representations or warranties regarding the ability to collect such accounts. Only in rare cases would a seller be willing to guarantee full or a percentage of collection on accounts receivable.

14. **Number of Years Business Operated.** To establish the stability of the business.
15. **Reason for Selling.** The buyer will want to know this.
16. **Covenant Not to Compete.** The buyer of a business that is a going concern may seek assurance that the seller will not go back into business on a competitive basis at some other location. Thus, if buying a restaurant from a seller who expresses an intent to retire, the buyer should obtain a specific contractual promise that the seller will neither operate nor buy another restaurant in the same locality for a specified period of time (*e.g.*, five years). Otherwise, if the seller finds that retirement is not as expected, he or she might decide to go back into business and draw from previous loyal customers. This kind of clause is called a "restrictive covenant" or "covenant not to compete" and is enforceable. It should be limited as to time and territory to the extent necessary to protect the goodwill for which the buyer is paying. If the agreement does not include such a covenant, there is no protection for the buyer, and the seller may compete immediately after the sale. The buyer can, of course, show by oral evidence that the seller represented that he or she would not compete (constituting grounds for rescission for fraud) or that there was a promise made orally that the seller would not compete (which may be difficult to prove absent a carefully written contract embodying the entire agreement).

III. The Uniform Commercial Code

The Uniform Commercial Code (UCC) repealed past laws on chattel mortgages. Under the current code, there must be a security agreement of some type between the parties. A chattel mortgage may still be the security agreement, although other forms of security agreements are superseding the chattel mortgage form. The UCC further provides, with a few exceptions, that a financing statement must be filed in order to perfect the security interest. When the financing statement covers timber, minerals, or other fixtures that are or will become attached to real estate, it must be filed with the county clerk and recorder in the county where the real property exists. In other instances, the financing statement is filed with the Secretary of State. (See § 4-9-301, C.R.S.)

In 1994 and 1995, a board was created within the Colorado Department of State charged with implementing a central indexing system for simplifying the filing and retrieval of all security interests. The system does not replace the need to record documents affecting real estate with the county clerk and recorder pursuant to § 38-35-109, C.R.S.

A security agreement is sufficient for filing if it contains the same information that is required by law to be included in the financing statement. The necessary information consists of the names and addresses of the debtor and secured party, the Social Security number and tax identification number of the debtor, and a statement indicating the types and description of the collateral. (See the examples in this chapter.)

A maturity date extending five years or less is effective until the maturity date plus 60 days. With longer maturity dates, the statement is effective for five years from the date of filing. A continuation statement may be filed within certain time limitations (see § 4-9-515, C.R.S.). Failure to file a continuation statement within the required period does not affect the validity of the security agreement. The filing is merely for giving constructive notice that the debt exists.

The complete Uniform Commercial Code, effective July 1, 1966, covers many facets of personal property sales; therefore, business opportunity transactions may be affected by the law on sales, commercial paper, bank deposits and collections, letters of credit, warehouse receipts, bills of lading, investment securities, and other documents of title.

IV. The Colorado Use Tax

The Colorado Use Tax (§§ 39-26-201, *et seq*., C.R.S.) is a form of sales tax, payable on the transfer of furniture, equipment, etc. The *buyer* is obligated to pay this tax by statute. The broker has the duty to inform the buyer of this obligation.

Occasionally, but perhaps more often than in other real estate transactions, the broker may wish to receive an advance fee for services in the sale because of the expense involved in the promotion of a business opportunity. In such a case, the broker must comply with Commission Rule 5.20.

A. Forms and Settlement

The sample forms shown in this chapter are typical of a business opportunity transaction, but are not necessarily all-inclusive. If the real estate is to be conveyed with the business, the broker would use a Commission-approved exclusive right-to-sell listing contract for real estate, amend it to describe the business, and also provide a bill of sale.

The closing statement forms for a real estate transaction may be used for business opportunity transactions with very little alteration. The worksheet in this chapter indicates the sale of a business, including goodwill, lease, and fixtures, for a price of $14,500. The cost of the inventory is listed separately and is $7,850. The seller in this transaction is taking a note in the amount of $17,000, secured by a purchase money chattel mortgage. The same principles apply in the debiting and crediting of the parties. The sample transaction shown on the worksheet in this chapter should be self-explanatory. Of course, the broker will sign and provide the seller and buyer each with a statement of their respective debits and credits, and the broker will retain a signed copy from both parties. Compliance with Commission Rule 6.19 is also necessary.

It is not enough to say that the sale of business opportunities is a specialized field. The field itself is further divided into specialties. There are brokers who deal only in motels; others are experts in liquor outlets or restaurants. Some brokers concentrate on the negotiation of corporate sales, where stock transfers are necessary.

Business Opportunity Worksheet

Seller:			Buyer:			
Property Address:						
Settlement Date: January 15, 2XXX				Proration Date: January 15, 2XXX		
Legal Description:						
	Seller		Buyer		Broker	
	Debit	Credit	Debit	Credit	Debit	Credit
Price: (Business, lease, fixtures)		*14,500.00*	*14,500.00*			
Inventory: (On closing date)		*7,850.00*	*7,850.00*			
Deposit:				*1,500.00*	*1,500.00*	
Security agreement payable to:	*17,000.00*			*17,000.00*		
Security agreement assigned:						
Interest on loan assumed						
Recording: financing statement			*2.00*			*2.00*
trade name affidavit			*1.50*			*1.50*
Bulk Transfer Notice:	*7.50*					*7.50*
Lease security deposit:		*600.00*	*600.00*			
Lease transfer fee:						
Personal property taxes: $240.00						
Seller 1/2 mo. Buyer 11 1/2 mo.	*10.00*		*230.00*			*240.00*
Water rent:						
Rental income: $340.00/mo (Pd.)		*170.00*	*170.00*			
Special Taxes:						
Insurance: (ZYX Co.)		*172.50*	*172.50*			
Term: 1 yr Exp.: Dec. 31 Prem.:						
New insurance:						
Attorney's fee:						
Seller:	*100.00*					*100.00*
Buyer:			*100.00*			*100.00*
Other:						
Commission on sale:	*1,450.00*					*1,450.00*
Subtotals	*$18,567.50*	*$23,292.50*	*$23,626.00*	*$18,500.00*	*$1,500.00*	*$1,901.00*
Balance due to/from seller	*$4,725.00*					*$4,725.00*
Balance due to/from buyer				*$5,126.00*	*$5,126.00*	
TOTALS	*$23,292.50*	*$23,292.50*	*$23,626.00*	*$23,626.00*	*$6,626.00*	*$6,626.00*

Income Statement

COMPANY NAME: ____________________________________

LOCATION: ____

INCOME STATEMENT (Profit and Loss) for periods indicated.

Current Period is for __________ months End Date_________

UNAUDITED	Period	Period	Period
GROSS SALES AND REVENUES			
MERCHANDISE COSTS (Adjustment inv.)			
GROSS PROFIT			
OVERHEAD COSTS AND OUT OF POCKET			
Utilities and phone (exclusive income)			
Insurance			
Advertising and other selling			
Repairs and maintenance			
Supplies and miscellaneous			
Legal and accounting			
Rent			
Business (auto-transportation)			
Other:			
TOTAL			
WAGES, SALARIES, PAYROLL TAXES			
Wages			
Salaries			
Taxes			
Owner-Partner draw			
Total compensation costs			
MARGIN FOR OVERHEAD AND PROFIT			
BUSINESS PROFIT before depreciation & int.			

Source of information: _________ Owner __________ CPA __________ Bookkeeper

B. Colorado UCC Financing Statements

Brokers are advised to contact the Colorado Secretary of State office for information on approved financing statement forms: www.sos.state.co.us.

§ 4-9-502, C.R.S. Contents of financing statement – record of mortgage as financing statement – time of filing financing statement.

(a) Subject to subsection (b) of this section, a financing statement is sufficient only if it:

- (1) Provides the name of the debtor;
- (2) Provides the name of the secured party or a representative of the secured party; and
- (3) Indicates the collateral covered by the financing statement.

(b) Except as otherwise provided in section 4-9-501 (b), to be sufficient, a financing statement that covers as-extracted collateral or timber to be cut, or which is filed as a fixture filing and covers goods that are or are to become fixtures, must satisfy subsection (a) of this section and also:

- (1) Indicate that it covers this type of collateral;
- (2) Indicate that it is to be filed for record in the real property records;
- (3) Provide a description of the real property to which the collateral is related sufficient to give constructive notice of a mortgage under the law of this state if the description were contained in a record of the mortgage of the real property; and
- (4) If the debtor does not have an interest of record in the real property, provide the name of a record owner.

(c) A record of a mortgage is effective, from the date of recording, as a financing statement filed as a fixture filing or as a financing statement covering as-extracted collateral or timber to be cut only if:

- (1) The record indicates the goods or accounts that it covers;
- (2) The goods are or are to become fixtures related to the real property described in the record or the collateral is related to the real property described in the record and is as-extracted collateral or timber to be cut;
- (3) The record satisfies the requirements for a financing statement in this section other than an indication that it is to be filed in the real property records; and
- (4) The record is duly recorded.

(d) A financing statement may be filed before a security agreement is made or a security interest otherwise attaches.

§ 4-9-521, C.R.S. Uniform form of written financing statement and amendment.

(a) A filing office that accepts written records may not refuse to accept a written initial financing statement in the form and format adopted from time to time by the secretary of state, except for a reason set forth in section 4-9-516 (b).

(b) A filing office that accepts written records may not refuse to accept a written record in the form and format adopted from time to time by the secretary of state, except for a reason set forth in section 4-9-516 (b).

Chapter 25: Tax Factors Pertaining to Real Estate Practice

An * in the left margin indicates a change in the statute, rule, or text since the last publication of the manual.

I. Introduction

This chapter presents a general overview of the rules for individual taxpayers that pertain to the acquisition, ownership, and sale of residential real estate. Professional assistance is required to determine the tax consequences or reporting requirements that may pertain to a specific real estate transaction. One should permanently retain all original contracts, settlement statements, and related banking records for such ownership for subsequent tax reporting.

The use of a property generally drives the tax consequences and reporting of its ownership. Property is commonly held for purposes such as personal use, business operations, or investment purposes, and these purposes may change and intermingle during the life cycle of ownership. The method of tax accounting used by the taxpayer also determines deductibility and reporting rules. In "**cash basis**" accounting, benefits (income and expenses) are considered reportable or deductible when "constructively received" in cash or an equivalent form, or actually paid. Under the "**accrual basis**," one reports income when earned, that is, when the right to receive the income has occurred. Expenses are likewise deductible when incurred, that is, when all events have occurred that fix the amount of the expense and create a tax liability for the individual. The purpose of accrual accounting is to better match reporting of income with the associated expenses of generating it. IRS accounting requirements are found in Publication 538.

Resources for tax information and various IRS *Publications and Forms* that may be viewed and downloaded at www.irs.gov. These documents and forms may be read online, but the user will need the latest version of Adobe Acrobat or similar software to print most documents on a home computer. The discussion of tax rules should be made with your CPA or tax attorney and pertain to those rules currently in effect on the IRS website.

II. Ownership of a Personal Residence

Federal tax law provides extensive tax benefits for purchase and ownership of a home. These benefits deal with buying expenses, new provisions for financing purchases, qualified deductible residential interest, property taxes, non-business theft and casualty losses, moving expenses, and business or rental use of a home. They are currently described in IRS Publications 17 (Your Federal Income Tax), 523 (Selling Your Home), 527 (Residential Rental Property), 530 (Tax Information for Homeowners), 547 (Casualties, Disasters, and Thefts), 551 (Basis of Assets), 587 (Business Use of Your Home), 936 (Home Mortgage Interest Deduction) and Form 8396 (Mortgage Interest Credit), 590 (Individual Retirement Arrangements (IRAs)), and 225 (Farmer's Tax Guide). The IRS may change their publication numbers, so always check the IRS website for any updates.

A. Buying Expenses

A buyer may find certain settlement and closing costs deductible, capitalized (added to the cost or "basis" of the property), or of no tax benefit. The deductibles generally include discount points and loan origination fees for the purchase or construction of a principal residence. Points paid to finance the purchase of a second home or to refinance an existing mortgage must be deducted over the life of the loan, not in the year in which they are paid. Prorated mortgage interest is also tax-deductible in the year of purchase or sale. Non-deductible items generally include other settlement costs such as appraisal fees, notary fees, VA funding fees, points not separately paid for by the borrower at closing for property improvements (these are generally deducted over the life of the loan), title insurance, survey costs, legal fees, and other similar costs. Non-deductible items are added to the basis of the property and will ultimately reduce the gain or increase the taxpayer's loss in a subsequent sale. See Publication 530 for more information.

B. IRA Withdrawal Used to Fund Purchase

Current legislation allows first-time homebuyers to use IRA distributions to fund up to $10,000 of the cost of their new home without incurring the 10 percent early distribution penalty even if they are under age 59½ (Publication 590). A first-time homebuyer can be the individual, a spouse, or a child, grandchild, or parent of the individual or spouse. To qualify, a buyer must have had no present ownership interest in a principal residence during the two-year period ending on the date of acquisition of the new residence. Special rules apply to armed forces members or owners of property outside the U.S. The date of acquisition is the date a binding contract to purchase the property is executed, or the date when construction of the principal residence begins. IRA disbursements can be used to pay the costs of acquiring, constructing, or reconstructing a residence, and include any reasonable and common cost of settlement, financing, or closing the transaction. However, any amount withdrawn must be used to pay qualified acquisition costs within 120 days of the date of withdrawal.

C. Qualified Residential Mortgage Interest

Qualified residence interest is interest that is paid or accrued during the tax year on acquisition or home equity indebtedness with respect to any qualified residence. A "qualified residence" for this deduction is defined as a house, condominium, mobile home, houseboat, house trailer, or any other facility (excluding unimproved vacant land) that has sleeping quarters, a toilet, and cooking facilities. A qualified second home is one that is used by the owner at least 14 days or 10 percent of the total number of days that it is rented to others, whichever is greater. If a second home is not rented to others, it may be a qualified home regardless of whether a taxpayer uses it during the year or not. A taxpayer who rents out a second residence may deduct mortgage interest only if the property meets the test of a "qualified residence." If a taxpayer does not satisfy these tests, then the residence is considered rental property rather than a qualified second home and may be subject to the passive activity rules. These are very complex areas of tax law, and expert professional assistance is recommended. See Publication 925 (Passive Activity and At-Risk Rules) for more information.

A residence under construction can be treated as a qualified residence for up to 24 months, only if it actually becomes a qualified residence when ready for occupancy. The land upon which the construction is undertaken does not become a qualified residence until construction actually begins.

Residential interest generally includes mortgage interest on home acquisition debt of up to $1 million ($500,000 for married filing separately), plus up to $100,000 ($50,000 for a married person filing separately) on a qualifying home equity loan. Certain items can be included as home mortgage interest. These items include late payment charges on mortgage payment, redeemable ground rents, interest on stock purchased in a cooperative housing residence, certain "points" or loan origination fees paid by a purchaser or by a seller for the purchaser, and mortgage prepayment penalties. Acquisition indebtedness proceeds must generally be "traceable" to expenditures to acquire, construct, or substantially improve a qualified residence. Acquisition indebtedness includes debt used to refinance earlier indebtedness (meeting the definition for acquisition indebtedness) to the extent of the original indebtedness. IRS Publication 936 provides a special 90-day rule exception to the literal application of the tracing rules for expenditures on a qualified residence. This exception provides that debt incurred within 90 days after the completion of the construction or improvements is treated as incurred to construct or improve the residence to the extent those expenditures occur not more than 24 months before project completion, and after completion, up to the time the debt is incurred. A purchaser claiming an interest deduction for private seller-carry financing must include the name of the seller, the seller's address, and the seller's taxpayer identification number (TIN) on the purchaser's income tax return Schedule A. Failure to furnish this information is subject to a fine.

Note that "grandfathered debt" (pre-October 14, 1987, debt still of record on the property) is not subject to the $1 million acquisition debt ceiling, but any pre-October 14, 1987 debt reduces the ceiling for any new post-October 13, 1987 debt used to improve or refinance the property. Pre-October 14, 1987, debt does not have to be "traceable" as indicated above, but must be still secured by the residence at all times thereafter. Debt used to refinance the "grandfathered debt" qualifies for this same treatment to the extent of pre-October 14, 1987, debt principal. Home equity loans are limited to the lesser of $100,000 ($50,000 for a married person filing separately) or the fair market value of the residence less accession indebtedness including pre-October 14, 1987, grandfathered indebtedness.

D. Mortgage Interest Credit

This credit may be available for first-time homebuyers whose income is below the median income in the area where they live. This credit is intended to help lower-income individuals afford home ownership. To be eligible for this credit, the buyer must obtain a "mortgage credit certificate" from a participating state or local agency before making any offer to buy a home or seek a loan. The Mortgage Credit Certificate program does not expire as long as the home remains a taxpayer's principal residence and mortgage payments are being made. According to the State Division of Housing, (303) 864-7810, and Colorado Housing and Finance Authority (CHFA), (303) 297-2432, this program is also available for the qualified refinance of an adjustable-rate mortgage loan originated after December 31, 2001, and before January 1, 2008. More information can be obtained from CHFA's website at www.chfainfo.com. The program allows a dollar-to-dollar reduction of income tax liability on 20 percent of mortgage interest, reducing the amount of federal taxes owed. The CHFA Mortgage Credit Certificate program is available statewide; however, certain targeted areas have different income and purchase price limits and no first-time homebuyer requirements.

Any tax credit obtained is reported to the IRS on Form 8396. The borrower may have to recapture (repay) all, or part of the benefit received from that program when the home is sold or otherwise disposed of. See Publication 523 for further federal information.

E. Mortgage Insurance Premiums

Amounts paid for qualified mortgage insurance can be treated as home mortgage interest. Check IRS Publication 936 for the requirements. Qualified mortgage insurance is defined as mortgage insurance provided by the Department of Veterans Affairs, the Federal Housing Administration, or the Rural Housing Service, and private mortgage insurance.

F. Property Taxes

Real property tax includes local, state, and foreign taxes levied on the value of real property. It does not include special assessments for local benefits or improvements that increase the value of the property, such as sidewalks, streets, and water or sewer systems.

Property taxes are generally deductible by the person(s) on whom they are levied in the year they are accrued or paid. In the year of acquisition or sale, both the buyer and seller must apportion among themselves any real property taxes levied for applicable "real property tax year." The date of sale and the statutory date the taxes become due govern how to determine the prorated amount that each party may deduct, according to the number of days each party held ownership of the property.

In Colorado, the current year's property taxes come due the following January 1. Cash basis taxpayers generally cannot take any property tax deduction for taxes placed in escrow through monthly payments until the escrow holder pays the tax. Lenders will report the deductible amount to the borrower annually for preparation of the return.

When the seller pays prorated taxes at closing on the date of sale, the seller will deduct that amount on Schedule A. Delinquent taxes due from the seller that were included in the contract price are not deductible. The buyer adds this amount to the cost (basis) of the property purchased.

Transfer taxes charged by some local tax authorities on the sale of a personal residence are not deductible. The person paying this tax may adjust the basis of the property by such amount.

G. Personal Property Taxes

To qualify for this itemized deduction, the tax must meet three tests: (1) it must be charged on personal property, (2) it must be based only on the value of the property, and (3) it must be charged on a yearly basis, even if collected more or less than once a year. If the tax is partly based on value and partly based on other criteria, it may partially qualify to be deductible.

H. Non-business Casualty and Theft Losses

A casualty or theft loss results from the damage, destruction, or loss of property from an event that is direct, identifiable, sudden, unexpected, or unusual (see IRS Publication 547). The amount of the loss is generally the lesser of: (1) the loss in fair market value before and after the event, and (2) the adjusted basis of the property before and after the event. A business casualty loss is fully deductible, while a personal loss is only a loss over $500 (a

$100 floor in 2010 and thereafter) and is further limited to the net loss (above the floor) in excess of 10 percent of the taxpayer's adjusted gross income. The $500/$100 rule is applied to the loss from each event of casualty or theft only once, even if many pieces of property are affected. The 10 percent limitation also applies to the adjusted gross income of any estate and trust claiming a personal casualty or theft loss. Special rules are used for federally designated disaster areas. IRS Publication 584 (Casualty, Disaster, and Theft Loss Workbook (Personal-Use Property)) should be used to document and compute these losses.

Losses from progressive deterioration due to neglect or steadily operating environmental conditions, disease, drought, insects, accidental breakage, pets, and arson are not deductible. Landlords and tenants may claim theft and casualty losses on rental property. Special rules apply to situations where both casualty gains and losses occur. Incidental expenses may not be deducted, and the loss reported may not exceed the adjusted basis in the property destroyed or stolen. The taxpayer must itemize to deduct this loss.

I. Moving Expenses

Taxpayers may deduct (subject to certain limits) unreimbursed moving expenses related to taking a new job or changing jobs, including self-employment, if certain distance and subsequent time of employment tests are met. A taxpayer may also deduct these expenses if the taxpayer expects to meet these tests in the following consecutive year. Only reasonable expenses for the circumstances surrounding the move can be deducted, such as certain storage costs, cost of moving household goods, and traveling to a new location, including lodging. Certain expenses, such as expenses of buying and selling a home, expenses of entering or breaking a lease, pre-move house-hunting expenses, and the cost of meals while traveling to a new residence are non-deductible. The new job location must be at least 50 miles farther from the old residence than the old job location was. In addition, an employee must work full-time in the general vicinity of the new job location for at least 39 weeks during the 12 months following the move. The 39-weeks period does not have to be consecutive or with the same employer, as long as the jobs are in the same general location and are classified as full-time work. Special rules apply to members of the armed forces; they are not required to meet the distance and time tests for a permanent change of duty station. See IRS Publications 17 and 521 for further information.

J. Business Use of Home (Home Offices)

According to Publication 587 (Business Use of Your Home), self-employed individuals who operate a home business and employees may be able to deduct certain expenses for the part of the home used for business.

There are two essential requirements that must be met in order to qualify for the deduction: (1) part of the home must be used for business purposes *regularly and exclusively*, and (2) the business part of the home must be either a principal place of business or the location where meetings with clients or customers are held in the normal course of conducting business. For a detached garage or other separate structures, the requirement is only that the building is used in connections with a trade or business. Deductions can also be claimed for the use of an area of the home for storage of inventory or product samples. There is an additional requirement for employees who telecommute from home: their business use of the home must be for the *employer's* convenience, *and* they cannot be renting any part of their home to the employer and then use the rented portion to perform services for the employer.

Deductible expenses for business use of a home include, but are not limited to, the business portion of real estate taxes, deductible mortgage interest, rent, casualty losses, utilities, insurance, depreciation, maintenance, and repairs. When calculating the amount that can be deducted for the business use of the home, the entire amount of expenses attributable solely to the portion of the home used in the business can be used. Deduction for expenses attributable to the whole house depends on the percentage of the home used for business. Any reasonable method can be used to calculate the business percentage, such as dividing the area used for business by the total area of the house or dividing the number of rooms used for business by the total number of rooms in the house if all rooms are about the same size. The business portion of expenses is calculated by applying the business percentage to the total of each expense.

For qualified day-care providers who do not use any area exclusively for day care, the business portion is further limited by the ratio of the number of hours the area is used exclusively for business to the total number of hours the portion is available for any use.

If gross income from the business use of the home is less than the total business expenses, the deduction for certain expenses for the business use of the home, other than mortgage interest, taxes, and casualty losses, is limited. However, those business expenses that are disallowed on the current tax return can be carried forward to the next year and will be subject to the deduction limitations for that year. For additional information on business use of a home, see Publication 587.

III. Sale of a Personal Residence

When a taxpayer sells a principal residence, any loss is not deductible unless part of the residence was used in the taxpayer's business. IRS Publication 523 describes the reporting requirements for this type of transaction; Publication 544 describes the sale of rental property, second homes, or vacation property. A trade of homes is treated as a sale and purchase.

Any taxable gain that cannot be excluded is reported on Schedule D as a capital gain. A loss on the sale of the main home (excluding business use) is personal and is not deductible but may need to be reported. The basis must be adjusted for any depreciation taken for any part of the home used in a trade or business. Points not deducted or amortized may be deductible in the year of sale. See "points" in Publication 936, Part I.

Gain or loss is the selling price of the home less expenses of the sale and less the adjusted basis in the home. Adjusted basis is generally the original cost plus certain closing costs, capital improvements and additions. Any depreciation allowed or allowable and discharge of qualified principal residence indebtedness that was excluded from income further decrease the basis.

The seller may be able to exclude up to $250,000 ($500,000 if married filing jointly) of any realized gain on the sale or exchange of a personal residence. Any gain properly excluded is not reported on the return.

Current tax rules allow reuse of the exclusion amount for any subsequent transaction meeting all of the following tests where a taxpayer: (1) has "ownership of the property for two of the five years before the current sale or exchange, (2) "used" by occupying it for periods totaling two years within the last five years, ending on the date of the sale or exchange, and (3) meets the "one-sale-in-two-years" criteria, where the $250,000/$500,000 exclusion was not used for the prior sale of any residence for the two-year period ending on the date of the current sale or exchange. If a seller does not satisfy these tests, he or she may qualify for a reduced maximum exclusion if the primary reason for the sale is a change in employment, health, or unforeseen circumstances. See Publication 523 for rules applicable to reduced exclusions, foreclosures, or other special situations, and instructions for worksheets to compute the gain or loss. Divorce property settlement rules are described in Publication 504, and Publication 544 deals with condemned property.

Additional rules apply to the replacement period for homes outside the U.S. and for members of the armed services.

If the property was used partly as a home and partly for business or as a rental property, the treatment of any gain on the sale depends on whether the business or rental part of the property is part of the home or separate from it. If the part of the property used for business or as a rental property is within the home, there is no need to allocate gain on the sale of the property between the business part and part used as a home. In addition, sale of the business or rental property does not have to be separately reported on Form 4797. However, the part of any gain equal to any depreciation allowed or allowable after May 6, 1997, cannot be excluded. If the business or rental part of the property is separate from the home, the gain cannot be excluded unless the taxpayer owned and lived in that part of the property for at least two years during the five-year period ending on the date of sale. If the test is not met, allocation of the gain is required, and Form 4797 must be filed.

A. Installment Sales

A homeowner who carries back part of the sale price in the form of a note may defer payment of gains until received as installment payments. This allows a seller to spread payment of taxes over the life of the loan. The seller must charge a fair interest rate, and some restrictions apply to dealers and sellers of time-shares and residential lots. Form 6252 must be filed to report installment sale income. Additional information on this type of sale is contained in the chapters on contracts, deeds, and Publication 537. The broker should be familiar with the risks to both buyers and sellers and advise the parties to seek legal counsel in such transactions.

B. Foreclosure

Upon default, abandonment, or conveyance in lieu of foreclosure, a gain in the form of discharge of debt may result to the mortgagor, or such gain may be used to reduce the basis of certain depreciable business property. In a foreclosure sale, the mortgagor generally recognizes a gain (or loss) in that the amount received exceeds (or is less than) the adjusted basis of the property sold. Transfers of property and abandonments are considered "sales" for tax purposes. The discharge of debt through cancellation in bankruptcy is generally not taxable income to the discharged debtor. Cancelled debt is also excluded from income to the extent that the taxpayer was insolvent immediately before the cancellation of debt (*i.e.*, total liabilities were greater than the fair market value of all assets).

Cancelled debt that is qualified principal residence indebtedness may be excluded from taxable income. Qualified principal residence indebtedness is any mortgage originated to buy, build, or substantially improve the taxpayer's principal residence, and must be secured by the principal residence. For additional information on qualified principal residence exclusion, insolvency determination, worksheets, and examples, see Publication 4681.

C. Colorado Withholding Tax on Certain Transfers of Real Estate

Closing entities are generally required to withhold the lesser of (1) two percent of the sales price, or (2) the entire net proceeds, as a tax on the sale of Colorado property when the seller has moved or will move out of state.

IV. Property Used in a Trade or Business

This section describes general rules for certain residential rental activities found in IRS Publication 527 (Residential Rental Property (Including Rental of Vacation Homes)) and other related references. Readers should review Publication 553 or other tax periodicals for additional information on specific transactions.

A. Rental Property Operations

When taxpayers rent out a home (including an apartment, condominium, mobile home, boat, or similar property), tax treatment of rental activities may be different depending on how much they use the property for personal use. If the taxpayer has no personal use, the property is treated as rental and all income is reported and expenses are deducted on Schedule E. When property is used for both personal and rental purposes, the property is considered personal use property or personal/rental residence. If the residence is rented for less than 15 days per year, it is treated as personal residence. The rental income is not included in income and mortgage interest and real estate taxes are allowed as itemized deductions. If the residence is rented out for 15 or more days, and it is used for personal purposes for the greater of: (1) more than 14 days, or (2) more than 10 percent of the rental days, it is treated as a personal/rental residence and expenses must be prorated between personal and rental use.

With some exceptions, property owners are required to report all rental amounts received in cash or services at fair market value on their return. Rental income includes any payment received for the use or occupation of the property. Advance rents (amounts received before the periods that they cover) are included in rental income in the year received, regardless of the period covered and accounting method used. Refundable security deposits that will be returned to the occupant are not income, except to the extent retained by the owner in excess of related expense. Property or services received as rent are included in rental income at the fair market value. Generally, the expenses of renting the property can be deducted from rental income. Most common rental expenses include, but are not limited to, advertising, cleaning and maintenance, insurance, utilities, depreciation, and repairs. Deductible expenses may exceed gross rental income, but a taxpayer must generally offset any "passive" rental loss from other "passive" income to deduct the loss. Any excess deductible loss is carried forward to the next tax year. See Publication 925 (Passive Activity and At-Risk Rules) for more information.

There is an exception for a "qualified person," where losses from real estate activities in which the person materially participates are not limited by the passive activity rules. The person may be able to deduct up to $25,000 of loss ($12,500 if married filing separately) from ordinary income. This deduction is phased out as adjusted gross income exceeds

$100,000 and is eliminated at $150,000. A qualified person must own 10 percent of the value of all interests in the activity at all times and must "actively" participate in the operation of the property, both in the year of loss and in the year when any claim against income or certain credits is sought under the loss carryover provisions. IRS Publication 925 disallows this loss to owners of short-term and time-share rental activity, who fall into the classification of "passive" rental activity, due to a lack of material participation in operations, or who have averaged rentals of seven days or less. Stringent tests define "material participation," and professional advice is essential before taking this deduction.

There is also an exception for real estate professionals. If the taxpayer is deemed to have active participation in the activity, the rental activity is not considered to be passive, and the taxpayer can fully deduct rental activity losses against ordinary income. However, the following conditions must be met: (1) more than 50 percent of the taxpayer's personal services during the tax year are performed in real estate business, and (2) the taxpayer performs more than 750 hours of services in real estate business during the year.

B. Depreciation

(Ed. Note: All references to "Section" numbers in the remainder of this chapter are to the Internal Revenue Code.)

Depreciation is an annual income tax deduction that allows the taxpayer to recover the cost or other basis of certain property over the time the taxpayer uses the property. Generally, real property (excluding the land and landscaping costs) and personal property used in a trade or business with a useful life of more than one year is depreciable. Accounting and record keeping for depreciable items and costs is very important. The total amount of depreciation cannot exceed the basis of the depreciated property. The main factors in determining depreciation expense amount are: (1) the applicable tax law, (2) the basis in the property, (3) the recovery period, and (4) the depreciation method used. See Publication 946 (How to Depreciate Property).

A taxpayer must claim the correct amount of depreciation each year. This amount will be used to reduce the basis of the property, even if it was incorrectly reported or not taken on the return. The taxpayer must file an amended return to recover any unclaimed depreciation within three years from the filing date of the original return, or within two years from the date the tax was paid, whichever is later.

Generally, taxpayers must use the Modified Accelerated Cost Recovery System (MACRS) to depreciate residential rental property or tangible property placed in service after 1986. If rental property was placed in service before 1980 but before 1987, the Accelerated Cost Recovery System (ACRS) is used, and straight line or declining balance method over the useful life of the property is used if placed in service before 1981. The last two systems are described in Publication 534.

MACRS determines depreciation in one of two methods. Most rental property (buildings, structures, and structural components) is subject to the General Depreciation System (GDS). The taxpayer may elect to use the Alternative Depreciation System (ADS). The main difference in these methods is that the cost-recovery time period under GDS may be shorter than under ADS. The taxpayer should use IRS Publication 946 to determine the applicable recovery period and class of the property to be depreciated under these methods.

Taxpayers may elect to "expense" and deduct from taxable income, rather than to "capitalize" and depreciate over the useful life, certain qualifying Section 1245 assets (machinery and equipment), in the year of acquisition. Items expensed in this manner are known as "Section 179 Property." This election is made on Form 4562. Check the IRS publication for the maximum deductible amount for the cost of property placed in service. The deduction taken cannot exceed the total taxable income generated from active conduct of any trade or business during the tax year. Any disallowed amount is carried forward for an indefinite number of years, subject to the ceiling for that particular tax year. However, only certain rental activities are eligible to take the Section 179 deduction. For additional information, see Publication 17.

Using an accelerated depreciation method may require filing Form 6251 to compute Alternative Minimum Tax. Accelerated depreciation includes MACRS, ACRS, and any other system resulting in a deduction greater than that computed by the Straight-Line Depreciation Method. Straight line depreciation is the number "1" divided by the number of years of useful life, adjusted by any applicable tax "convention" for the specific class of property being depreciated, times the asset cost. The more common conventions are half-year or mid-quarter. In general, a half-year convention applies to personal property, under which such property placed in service or disposed of during a taxable year is treated as having been placed in service or disposed of at the midpoint of the year. If more than 40 percent of depreciable property is placed in service in the last quarter of the year, the mid-quarter convention must be used.

When personal use property is converted to rental use, the taxpayer must determine the basis of the property for purposes of depreciation. This is generally the lesser of the fair market value or the adjusted basis on the date it is placed into rental use. The determination of basis is described in IRS Publication 551 (Basis of Assets).

C. Certain Business Gains and Losses

In addition to taxable business expense deductions (see IRS Publication 535 (Business Expenses)), certain types of business property also produce special tax benefits through more favorable tax rates or deductions from ordinary income. These assets commonly are designated as Section 1231, 1245, and 1250 assets used in a taxpayer's trade or business and are treated under the rules for "capital gains or losses." Tax rules for these business items are found in IRS Publication 544 (Sales and Other Dispositions of Assets).

"Capital assets" include most everything owned and used for personal or investment purposes. Some examples are: stocks, bonds, personal residence, household furnishings, a personal automobile, jewelry, art collections, and similar items. Taxable gains or losses from the sale or exchange of capital assets are either classified as ordinary income or loss or as capital gain or loss. For individuals, net capital gain is taxed at a lower rate than ordinary income, and any capital losses are generally limited. The tax treatment of capital gains and losses depends on how long an asset is owned or held before sale. A sale or exchange of capital assets between related persons is generally taxed as ordinary income, and any loss is not deductible, except when corporate property is distributed in a complete liquidation.

In contrast, business real estate and depreciable business property is excluded from the definition of capital assets. Non-capital assets are defined as property held for resale to others (inventory), business or trade, accounts and notes receivable, depreciable property used in a trade or business, real property (including certain Section 197 intangibles) used in a trade or business, copyrights, literary, musical, or artistic compositions, and certain acquisitions of publications from a governmental agency. However, if non-capital assets qualify as Section 1231, 1245, or 1250 property, gains or losses from these transactions may receive "capital gains or loss" treatment.

In general, the sale or exchange of depreciable business property is treated under the rules for Section 1231 property. Other depreciable property under Sections 1245 and 1250 requires recapture of the depreciation allowed or allowable as ordinary income, and any gain in excess of that amount is treated as a Section 1231 capital gain. Section 1250 property requires recapture of any "additional depreciation" (in excess of straight line or other specific methods) as ordinary income.

Section 1231 assets are depreciable real and personal property held for more than one year and used in a trade or business. Some examples are: rental homes, rental dwelling units, business machinery, equipment, leaseholds, livestock, crops and timber, and any of these items that have been involuntarily converted. Their tax treatment, as ordinary or capital items, depends on whether there is a net 1231 gain or loss from all 1231 transactions. A net 1231 loss is an ordinary loss, and if a net 1231 gain, it is ordinary income up to the amount of any non-recaptured 1231 losses not offset against prior 1231 gains in the last five years. The remainder is long-term capital gain.

Section 1245 assets are tangible and intangible personal assets that have been subject to depreciation. Some examples are tangible personal property, such as furniture, bulk storage units, livestock, and office equipment (except for buildings and their structural components), used as an integral part of the business production process. The amount of gain treated as ordinary income from the sale, exchange, or involuntary conversion of Section 1245 property (including a sale and leaseback) is the lesser of: the depreciation or amortization allowed or allowable on the property, or the gain realized on the disposition (amount realized less adjusted basis). Certain limits apply to like-kind exchanges.

Section 1250 property is any real property that is depreciable but is not subject to recapture under Section 1245, that has never been used as Section 1245 property. Some examples are intangible property, such as leases of land, buildings, and major structural components. The amount of ordinary income is computed according to IRS instructions in Publication 544, and any remaining gain follows the treatment for Section 1231 gain.

All of the gains or losses from Section 1231, 1245, and 1250 property are reported on Form 4797. All Section 1231 gains or losses are reported in Part 1 of this form, and any net gain from these transactions is carried to Schedule D as a long-term capital gain. Any net 1231 loss is carried to Part II of this form as an ordinary loss. Part IE handles the Section 1245 and 1250 items. If property held for use in a trade or business or for investment is exchanged solely for property of a like kind to be held either for use in trade or business or for investment, the gain or loss may be deferred, that is, not recognized in the current year. However, the exchange must still be reported on Form 8824. Any gain or loss realized, but not recognized, adjusts the basis of like-kind property received in exchange.

The maximum capital gain rates on the net capital gain depend on the tax year and in what type of property the gain originates. "Net capital gain" is the excess of net long-term capital gain over net short-term capital loss for the year and is determined for individual taxpayers on Schedule D.

D. Tax Credits Applicable to Business Property

Tax credits applicable to business property include the general business credit, disabled access credit, low-income housing credit, and rehabilitation credit.

1. **Home Energy Tax Credits**

Homeowners may qualify for a federal tax credit for making improvements or installing equipment designed to boost the energy-efficiency of a home.

The residential energy efficient property credit allows for a credit equal to the applicable percent of the cost of qualified property. Qualifying properties are solar electric property, solar water heaters, geothermal heat pumps, small wind turbines, fuel cell property, and, starting December 31, 2020, qualified biomass fuel property expenditures paid or incurred in taxable years beginning after that date. Only fuel cell property is subject to a limitation, which is $500 with respect to each half kilowatt of capacity of the qualified fuel cell property. Generally, this credit for alternative energy equipment terminates for property placed in service after December 31, 2023. The applicable percentages are:

1. In the case of property placed in service after December 31, 2016, and before January 1, 2020, 30%.
2. In the case of property placed in service after December 31, 2019, and before January 1, 2023, 26%.
3. In the case of property placed in service after December 31, 2022, and before January 1, 2024, 22%.

For additional information, see IRS form 5695 (Residential Energy Credits) and Publication 17.

2. **General Business Credit** (combines credits and some described below)

The investment credit (including the rehabilitation, energy, and reforestation credits), empowerment zone employment credit, welfare-to-work credit, Indian employment credit, employer Social Security credit, alcohol fuels credit, orphan drug credit, enhanced oil recovery credit, renewable electricity production credit, disabled access credit, and low-income housing credit are all combined into the General Business Credit (GBC). Taxpayers may qualify to deduct part or all of this and other specific unused credits listed above at the end of any carry-forward period.

The GBC is claimed for multiple credits on Form 3800 (General Business Credit). This form is not used if the taxpayer claims only one credit. Instead, where there are no carry backs or carryovers of the amounts claimed, use the specific tax form for the credit claimed. See form 3800 Instruction booklet.

3. **Disabled Access Credit**

The Disabled Access Credit provides a non-refundable credit for small businesses that incur expenditures for the purpose of providing access to persons with disabilities. An eligible small business is one that earned $1 million or less or had no more than 30 full time employees in the previous year; they may take the credit each and every year they incur access expenditures. Refer to Form 8826, Disabled Access Credit for information about eligible expenditures.

4. **Rehabilitation Credit**

The Tax Cuts and Jobs Act, signed December 22, 2017, affects the Rehabilitation Tax Credit for amounts that taxpayers pay or incur for qualified expenditures after December 31, 2017. The credit is a percentage of expenditures for the rehabilitation of qualifying buildings in the year the property is placed in service.
The legislation:

- Requires taxpayers take the 20-percent credit ratably over five years instead of in the year they placed the building into service
- Eliminates the 10 percent rehabilitation credit for the pre-1936 buildings

A transition rule provides relief to owners of either a certified historic structure or a pre-1936 building by allowing owners to use the prior law if the project meets these conditions:

- The taxpayer owns or leases the building on January 1, 2018, and at all times thereafter
- The 24- or 60-month period selected for the substantial rehabilitation test begins by June 20, 2018

Form 3468, Investment Credit, is used to claim a variety of investment credits, including the section 47 rehabilitation credit. The instructions to the Form 3468 provide detailed requirements for completing the form.

5. **Low-Income Housing Credit**

The IRC §42 Low Income Housing Credit Program was enacted by Congress as part of the Tax Reform Act of 1986 to encourage new construction and rehabilitation of existing buildings as low-income rental housing for households with income at or below specified income levels. Congress recognized that a private sector developer may not receive enough rental income from a low-income housing project to cover the costs of development and still provide a return to investors sufficient to attract the needed equity investment. The IRC §42 program provides tax incentives for investors to make equity investments. In exchange for equity, investors receive tax credits and other tax benefits associated with ownership of the project to offset federal income taxes for a ten-year period. These tax benefits, plus the possibility of cash proceeds from the eventual sale of the project, represent the investors' return on investment. See IRS forms 8586 (Low-Income Housing Credit and 8609 (Low-Income Housing Credit Allocation.)

6. **Colorado Enterprise Zone Vacant Commercial Building Rehabilitation Tax Credit**

The Enterprise Zone Vacant Commercial Building Rehabilitation Tax Credit helps businesses redevelop commercial property and rehabilitate vacant buildings. Businesses can earn a state income tax credit for 25% of rehabilitation expenses, up to $50,000 in tax credit per building. You may carry forward this tax credit for up to five years.

The Colorado legislature created the Enterprise Zone (EZ) Program to encourage development in economically distressed areas of the state. The 16 designated enterprise zones have high unemployment rates, low per capita income, or slow population growth.

Find more information on this credit at the Colorado Office of Economic Development International Trade.

V. Federal Estate and Gift Taxation

A. Real Property

The Estate Tax is a tax on your right to transfer property at your death. It consists of an accounting of everything you own or have certain interests in at the date of death (Refer to Form 706. The fair market value of these items is used, not necessarily what you paid for them or what their values were when you acquired them. The total of all of these items is your "Gross Estate." The includible property may consist of cash and securities, real estate, insurance, trusts, annuities, business interests and other assets.

Once you have accounted for the Gross Estate, certain deductions (and in special circumstances, reductions to value) are allowed in arriving at your "Taxable Estate." These deductions may include mortgages and other debts, estate administration expenses, property that passes to surviving spouses and qualified charities. The value of some operating business interests or farms may be reduced for estates that qualify.

After the net amount is computed, the value of lifetime taxable gifts (beginning with gifts made in 1977) is added to this number and the tax is computed. The tax is then reduced by the available unified credit.

Most relatively simple estates (cash, publicly traded securities, small amounts of other easily valued assets, and no special deductions or elections, or jointly held property) do not require the filing of an estate tax return. A filing is required for estates with combined gross assets and prior taxable gifts exceeding $1,500,000 in 2004 - 2005; $2,000,000 in 2006 - 2008; $3,500,000 for decedents dying in 2009; and $5,000,000 or more for decedent's dying in 2010 and 2011 (note: there are special rules for decedents dying in 2010); $5,120,000 in 2012, $5,250,000 in 2013, $5,340,000 in 2014, $5,430,000 in 2015, $5,450,000 in 2016, $5,490,000 in 2017, $11,180,000 in 2018, $11,400,000 in 2019, $11,580,000 in 2020, and $11,700,000 in 2021.

Beginning January 1, 2011, estates of decedents survived by a spouse may elect to pass any of the decedent's unused exemption to the surviving spouse. This election is made on a timely filed estate tax return for the decedent with a surviving spouse. Note that simplified valuation provisions apply for those estates without a filing requirement absent the portability election.

B. Federal Gift Taxes

The gift tax is a tax on the transfer of property by one individual to another while receiving nothing, or less than full value, in return. The tax applies whether or not the donor intends the transfer to be a gift.

The gift tax applies to the transfer by gift of any type of property. You make a gift if you give property (including money), or the use of or income from property, without expecting to receive something of at least equal value in return. If you sell something at less than its full value or if you make an interest-free or reduced-interest loan, you may be making a gift.

- The annual exclusion for gifts is $11,000 (2004-2005), $12,000 (2006-2008), $13,000 (2009-2012) and $14,000 (2013-2017). In 2018, 2019, 2020, and 2021, the annual exclusion is $15,000.
- The basic exclusion amount (or applicable exclusion amount in years prior to 2011) for gifts is $1,000,000 (2010), $5,000,000 (2011), $5,120,000 (2012), $5,250,000 (2013), $5,340,000 (2014), $5,430,000 (2015), $5,450,000 (2016), $5,490,000 (2017), $11,180,000 (2018), $11,400,000 (2019), $11,580,000 (2020), and $11,700,000 (2021).

For additional information, review Form 709 and its instructions.

Ed. Note: See Publication 709 for further information about gift taxes.

VI. Tax Treatment of Various Legal Entities

A. Corporations

A corporation is taxed as a separate legal entity on reported income. Dividends paid are also taxable to the individual receiving them. Associations, joint stock companies, and insurance companies are taxed as corporations. Subchapter S corporations are not taxed on income, but serve as conduits for passing income, losses, and deductions to their stockholders.

B. Partnerships

A partnership is not a taxable entity. All income, loss, credits, and deductions pass through to the individual partners who share these items according to agreed-upon amounts in the partnership agreement. A partnership must file an informational tax return showing distributions to all partners.

C. S Corporations

The domestic small, closely held corporation may elect to be taxed as a pass-through entity. The requirements for election are to: have 100 or fewer consenting shareholders, file a timely election, and issue only one class of stock. The election can be revoked by certain actions of the shareholders. There are several restrictions on eligible shareholders, such as eligible shareholder must be an individual, estate, or certain type of trust, and an individual shareholder may not be a nonresident alien. For more details, see I.R.C. § 1361.

D. Limited Liability Companies (LLC)

A limited liability company (LLC) features many of the personal protections of a corporation, while preserving the tax benefits of a partnership and without an S corporation's restrictions on eligible members. An LLC with only one member can be treated as a disregarded entity and report its income and expenses on Schedule C or Schedule E. An LLC with more than one member may be treated as a partnership. Or, an LLC with one or more members may elect to be treated as a corporation for tax purposes.

E. Trusts

A trust takes title to property on behalf of someone else. Trusts are subject to taxation and are allowed deductions for income distributed to the beneficiaries, who must report the distribution. Real estate investment trusts are subject to strict tax requirements concerning forms of organization, sources of income, and allowable assets.

F. Homeowner Associations

A membership organization formed by a real estate developer to own and maintain common green areas, streets, and sidewalks and to enforce covenants to preserve the appearance of the development may be exempt as a social welfare organization if it is operated for the benefit of all the residents of the community. A homeowners' association that is not exempt under section 501(c)(4) and that is a condominium management association, a residential real estate management association, or a timeshare association generally may elect under the provisions of Code section 528 to receive certain tax benefits that, in effect, permit it to exclude its exempt function income from its gross income.

G. Real Estate Mortgage Investment Conduit (REMIC)

A real estate mortgage investment conduit (REMIC) is an entity that holds a fixed pool of mortgages and issues multiple classes of interests in itself to investors under U.S. Federal income tax law and is treated like a partnership for Federal income tax purposes with its income passed through to its interest holders. REMICs are used for the pooling of mortgage loans and issuance of mortgage-backed securities.

H. Tax Shelters

These are generally classified into two groups: "Projected Income Investments" and "Abusive Tax Shelters." An investor should seek tax and legal counsel to determine how the IRS classifies a shelter before making an investment.

A projected income investment is one not expected to substantially reduce the cumulative tax liability of any investor during the first five years the investment is offered for sale. Tax shelters previously qualified as projected income investments may lose such status. Such loss requires registration with the IRS and record keeping of sales between subsequent investors. Severe penalties may apply to any failure to keep records.

Internal Revenue Bulletins discuss abusive tax shelters. Such rulings bind the agency in enforcement of tax matters. The disallowance of tax deductions in such shelters may be accompanied by other severe tax penalties.

VII. Employed Real Estate Licensees

The Commission has received several inquiries concerning the payment of commissions or fees by an employing broker to a corporation that is wholly owned by an employed licensee. C.R.S. 12-10-203(8), which prohibits the licensing of an employed broker as a corporation, partnership or limited liability company and the limitations on the payment or receipt of real estate fees, as described in 12-10-217(1)(i) and 12-10-221, are recognized by the Commission; however, it is the position of the Commission that: An employing broker's payment of earned real estate fees to a corporation which is solely owned by an employed licensee of such employing broker shall not be considered by the Commission as a violation of 12-10-217(1)(i) or 12-10-221; however, a contract between the employing broker and such corporation or employed licensee shall not relieve the broker of any obligation to supervise such employed licensee or any other requirement of the licensing statute and Commission rules. It is not the intent of this position statement that the employed licensee be relieved from personal civil responsibility for any licensed activities by interposing the corporate form. It must be stressed that the above position statement does not allow such corporations to be licensed under a broker and specifically refers only to corporations which are owned solely by the employed licensee. (CP-18 Commission Position on Payments to a Wholly Owned Employee's Corporation.)

VIII. Withholding of State Income Tax on Proceeds from Transfers by Nonresidents of Real Property Located in Colorado

§ 39-22-604.5, C.R.S. Withholding tax – transfers of Colorado real property – nonresident transferors.

(1) Except as otherwise provided in this section, in the case of any conveyance of a Colorado real property interest, the title insurance company or its authorized agent or any attorney, bank, savings and loan association, savings bank, corporation, partnership, association, joint stock company, trust, or unincorporated organization or any combination thereof, acting separately or in concert, that provides closing and settlement services as defined herein shall be required to withhold an amount equal to two percent of the sales price of the Colorado real property interest conveyed or the net proceeds resulting from such conveyance, whichever is less, when:

(a) The transferor is a person and either the return required to be filed with the secretary of the treasury pursuant to section 6045 (e) of the internal revenue code indicates or the authorization for the disbursement of the funds resulting from such transaction instructs that such funds be disbursed to a transferor with a last-known street address outside the boundaries of this state at the time of the transfer of the title to such Colorado real property interest or to the escrow agent of such transferor; or

(b) (I) The transferor is a corporation which immediately after the transfer of the title to the Colorado real estate interest has no permanent place of business in Colorado.

(II) For purposes of this section, a corporation has no permanent place of business in Colorado if all of the following apply:

(A) Such corporation is a foreign corporation;

(B) Such corporation does not qualify pursuant to law to transact business in Colorado; and

(C) Such corporation does not maintain and staff a permanent office in Colorado.

(2) No title insurance company or its authorized agent or any attorney, bank, savings and loan association, savings bank, corporation, partnership, association, joint stock company, trust, or unincorporated organization or any combination thereof, acting separately or in concert, that provides closing and settlement services as defined herein shall be required to withhold any amount pursuant to this section:

(a) If the sales price of the Colorado real property conveyed does not exceed one hundred thousand dollars;

(b) When the transferee is a bank or corporate beneficiary under a mortgage or beneficiary under a deed of trust and the Colorado real property interest is acquired in judicial or nonjudicial foreclosure or by deed in lieu of foreclosure;

(c) If the title insurance company or its authorized agent or any attorney, bank, savings and loan association, savings bank, corporation, partnership, association, joint stock company, trust, or unincorporated organization or any combination thereof, acting separately or in concert, that provides closing and settlement services as defined herein in good faith relies upon a written affirmation executed by the transferor, certifying under penalty of perjury one of the following:

(I) That the transferor, if a person, is a resident of Colorado;

(II) That the transferor, if a corporation, has a permanent place of business in Colorado;

(III) That the Colorado real property being conveyed is the principal residence of the transferor; or

(IV) That the transferor will not owe tax reasonably estimated to be due pursuant to this article from the inclusion of the actual gain required to be recognized on the transaction in the gross income of the transferor.

(3) Any title insurance company or its authorized agent which is required to withhold any amount pursuant to this section and fails to do so shall be liable for the greater of the following amounts for such failure to withhold:

(a) Five hundred dollars;

(b) Ten percent of the amount required to be withheld pursuant to this section, not to exceed two thousand five hundred dollars.

(4) (a) Amounts withheld and payments made in accordance with this section shall be reported and remitted to the department of revenue in such form and at such time as specified by rule and regulation of the executive director. Written affirmations executed pursuant to paragraph (c) of subsection (2) of this section shall be submitted to the department of revenue pursuant to procedures specified by rule and regulation of the executive director.

(b) All of the other provisions of this article shall apply to and be effective as to the provisions of this section to the extent to which they are not inconsistent with this section, and all of the remedies available to the department of revenue for the administration, assessment, enforcement, and collection of tax under other sections of this article and article 21 of this title shall be available to the department of revenue and shall apply to the amounts required to be deducted and withheld pursuant to the provisions of this section, and all of the penalties, both civil and criminal, shall apply to this section.

(5) Whenever a title insurance company or its authorized agent provides escrow services as directed by the parties in compliance with the withholding requirements of this section, such title insurance company or its authorized agent shall charge the parties pursuant to the rates in effect at the time and filed with the division of insurance of the department of regulatory agencies as required by law.

(6) For purposes of this section, unless the context otherwise requires:

(a) "Authorized agent" means a title insurance agent, as defined in section 10-11-102 (9), C.R.S., who is responsible for closing and settlement services in the transaction.

(b) "Closing and settlement services" means closing and settlement services as defined in section 10-11-102 (3.5), C.R.S., and section 38-35-125, C.R.S.

(c) "Colorado real property interest" means an interest in real property located in Colorado and defined in section 897 (c)(1)(A)(i) of the internal revenue code.

(d) "Escrow agent" means an agent for the purpose of receiving and transferring funds to a principal.

(e) "Person" means any individual, estate, or trust who may be subject to taxation pursuant to part 1 of this article.

(f) "Sales price" means the sum of all of the following:

(I) The cash paid or to be paid, but shall not include stated or unstated interest or original issue discount as determined pursuant to sections 1271 to 1275 of the internal revenue code;

(II) The fair market value of other property transferred or to be transferred;

(III) The outstanding amount of any liability assumed by the transferee to which the Colorado real property interest is subject immediately before and after the transfer.

(g) "Title insurance company" means the title insurance company, as defined in section 10-11-102 (10), C.R.S., responsible for closing and settlement services in the transaction.

Chapter 26:
Fair Housing

An * in the left margin indicates a change in the statute, rule, or text since the last publication of the manual.

I. Introduction

The following information is excerpted from the Federal Civil Rights Acts of 1866, 1870, and 1968 and the Fair Housing Amendments Act of 1988 as they apply to equal housing opportunity. The information is intended to be a broad overview of the fair housing provisions within the Federal Civil Rights Acts. A comprehensive listing of rules and interpretations of the 1968 and 1988 Acts can be obtained by contacting the Department of Housing and Urban Development (HUD), Office of Fair Housing and Equal Opportunity.

II. Federal Civil Rights Acts

A. Civil Rights Acts of 1866 and 1870 (42 U.S.C. §§ 1981 and 1982)

The Civil Rights Acts of 1866 and 1870, passed shortly after the passage of the Thirteenth Amendment to the Constitution (which eliminated slavery), are brief enough to be quoted in their entirety.

42 U.S.C. § 1981 – Equal rights under the law. "All persons within the jurisdiction of the United States shall have the same right in every State and Territory to make and enforce contracts, to sue, be parties, give evidence, and to the full and equal benefit of all laws and proceedings for the security of persons and property as is enjoyed by white citizens, and shall be subject to like punishment, pains, penalties, taxes, licenses, and exactions of every kind, and to no other." (May 1870)

42 U.S.C. § 1982 – Property rights of citizens. "All citizens of the United States shall have the same right, in every State and Territory, as is enjoyed by white citizens thereof to inherit, purchase, lease, sell, hold, and convey real and personal property." (April 1866)

Until 1987, it was assumed that the above two laws applied only to discrimination on the basis of race. The U.S. Supreme Court ruled then that they applied also to discrimination on the basis of ancestry or ethnicity (on its rationale that some ethnic or religious groups were considered different "races" when the law was enacted). However, neither can be used to make discrimination claims on other bases, such as sex, handicap, or familial status, found in the Fair Housing Act (Title VIII), and discussed below.

The above two laws apply to both real and personal property, and to both commercial and residential property, unlike the 1968 Fair Housing Act, which applies only to housing and land intended for housing. Therefore, licensees must ensure that the conduct of their business affords equal opportunity in commercial as well as residential transactions.

B. Fair Housing Act 1968, Amended 1988 (42 U.S.C. §§ 3601 to 3619)

Bases of Discrimination

Under the acts of 1866 and 1870, and the 1968 Fair Housing Act, real estate licensees must ensure that their residential real estate activities do not discriminate on the basis of **race, color, religion, sex,** and **national origin**.

The **Fair Housing Amendments Act of 1988** expanded the prohibition against unlawful discrimination to include two additional protected classes: **handicap** (both mental and physical) and **familial status**.

Handicap is defined as: "(1) a physical or mental impairment which substantially limits one or more of such person's major life activities, (2) a record of having such an impairment, or (3) being regarded as having such an impairment." The definition includes: alcoholism, HIV or the AIDS virus, certain physiological disorders, and specified types of anatomical losses. Mental illness, retardation, and psychological disorders are also considered handicaps. Further discussion of discrimination on the basis of handicap is contained in the sections entitled "Handicap," "Steering," and "Exclusionary Land Use," below.

Familial status is defined as children under age 18 living with parents or others with legal custody, or with a designee of the parent with written permission, a person who is pregnant, or a person who is seeking custody of a person under 18. The 1988 amendments made it illegal not only to refuse to rent or sell to families with children, but also made it illegal to designate a residential building, mobile home park, or even a section of a building as "adults only." There can be no rules, covenants, deed restrictions, bylaws, or agreements that discriminate against families with children, although in limited circumstances a residential community may be able to adopt rules about families with children if they are based on *safety* considerations (not the convenience of adults).

Charging per-person rental fees can also be considered discrimination on the basis of familial status, because such fees can be shown to have a discriminatory effect on families with children. One of the most difficult issues in familial status discrimination is the question of how many children may be allowed in a particular unit. HUD guidance has established that two persons per bedroom will be considered generally reasonable, but this is not absolute. If a charge is filed, consideration will be given to the overall size of the dwelling, size of the bedrooms, what other rooms might be used for sleeping areas, and any local zoning or occupancy codes.

There are specific exemptions from the protection of familial status for retirement communities or housing for the elderly. See a further explanation of the exemption for senior communities under "Exemptions," below.

Exemptions to Property Covered

1. A single-family home sold or rented† *by the owner*, if the owner: (1) does not own over three single-family homes, (2) does not use the services or facilities of a licensee or anyone in the business of selling or renting buildings, and (3) does not make, print, or publish any discriminatory advertising or statement;

   (†Note: The home itself is not exempt. The transaction *by the owner* is exempt. Actions by non-owners, such as homeowners associations, real estate brokers, cities, lenders, neighbors, etc. are not exempt. This is why an owner may be able to sell or rent a single-family home without coming under the federal Fair Housing Act, but a real estate broker may not.)

2. Rooms or units in dwellings occupied or intended to be occupied by no more than four families, if the owner lives in one of the units;

   (Note: Exemptions #1 and #2 are not found in Colorado law, except for familial status. See later explanation of the Colorado law.)

3. Religious organizations or societies that own and operate dwelling units for a non-commercial purpose may give preference or limit occupancy to persons of the same religion, unless membership in the religion is restricted on the basis of race, color, or national origin;

4. Private clubs that own or operate lodging for non-commercial purposes may limit occupancy or give preference to members; and

5. Housing for seniors may be exempt only from familial status protections if it meets one of the following three requirements:

   (a) Housing provided under a state or federal program that the secretary of HUD determines is designed and operated for elderly persons;

   (b) Housing in which 100 percent of the residents are 62 years of age or older; or

   (c) Housing in which 80 percent of the occupied units have at least one person 55 years of age or older and the housing publishes and adheres to policies demonstrating the intent to house persons over 55.

After May 3, 2000, the only way a community can convert to "over-55" housing is if it has been "wholly unoccupied for at least 90 days" for the purpose of renovation or rehabilitation. The Fair Housing Amendments Act of 1988 originally required that over-55 housing also provide "significant facilities and services" for persons over 55. This requirement was repealed on April 2, 1999, and gave until May 3, 2000 to transition to over-55 housing. HUD strongly suggests advertising as "Senior Housing," "55 and older community," or "retirement community," and warns that using the words "adult community" or "adult living" puts the community in danger of complaint, investigation, or litigation. The housing community must verify ages and update its age surveys at least every two years.

WARNING: If a fair housing complaint is filed alleging that housing was refused to families with children without meeting one of the three exemptions described above, any licensees who listed the property or participated in the sale or rental as an exempt senior property have a "good faith" exemption from money damages *only* if the community's "authorized representatives" have certified "in writing and under oath" that it complies with the exemption.

III. Illegal Practices Under Federal Law

- To refuse to show, rent, lease, sell, or transfer housing.
- To represent that property is not available for sale or rental, when in fact it is.
- To refuse to receive or transmit any bona fide offer to buy, sell, or lease housing.
- To discriminate in the terms, conditions, or privileges of housing.
- To discriminate in the provision of services or facilities of housing.

- To discriminate in making loans available, or in their terms, conditions, or privileges, for the purchase, construction, or maintenance of housing, or for loans secured by housing.
- To advertise any discriminatory preferences or limitations.

  Licensees must be aware that an advertisement need not explicitly mention race, religion, or other protected classes to be unlawful, and should avoid making or using any statement that could reasonably be interpreted as conveying a prohibited preference or limitation. For example, using a term such as "restricted" in an advertisement may violate the act unless it is clearly indicated that the restriction is not an unlawfully discriminatory one. Using models not in keeping with community race demographics has also been found to be discriminatory. Licensees are urged to consult the "Advertising Guidelines for Fair Housing" issued by the Secretary of HUD, which catalogue a number of phrases that are considered discriminatory. HUD regulations also prescribe the use of the equal housing logo and/or slogan in advertisements and require the posting of a HUD Equal Housing poster. Licensees are strongly encouraged to use the "Equal Housing Opportunity" logo or statement in anything that could possibly be considered an "advertisement," such as brochures, calling cards, and signs.

- To deny any person access to membership or to impose unequal terms in any multiple listing service or real estate broker's organization.
- To interfere with, coerce, or intimidate persons exercising fair housing rights, or persons aiding or encouraging others to exercise fair housing rights.
- To discriminate or retaliate against someone for opposing unfair housing practices or for testifying, assisting, or participating in an investigation, proceeding, or hearing.
- To discriminate in fire/title/homeowners insurance or in real estate appraisals.
- **Blockbusting:** Blockbusting is the practice of inducing or attempting to induce a person to sell or rent a dwelling by representing that persons of a certain race, disability, etc., are or may be moving into a neighborhood. Courts have ruled that this covers not only explicit representations about race, but also statements by real estate agents such as "changing neighborhood," "falling property values," "bad schools," or "undesirable elements," if used to solicit listings and sales. In racially transitional neighborhoods, where residents tend to be aware of racial change even without its being mentioned, a racial representation may reasonably be inferred from unusually heavy solicitation of listings, even if no explicit statements are made relative to new residents of a particular race or national origin.
- To "otherwise make unavailable" housing. This phrase includes:
  - **Steering:** Steering is any action or difference in service or information provided that might influence persons to select their own ethnic-identity neighborhoods or discourage living in certain areas. In a landmark case, *Gladstone Realtors v. Village of Bellwood*, 441 U.S. 91 (1979), the U.S. Supreme Court declared that the "otherwise make unavailable" prohibition in the Fair Housing Act prohibited steering, which it defined as "directing prospective home buyers interested in equivalent properties to different areas according to their race." *Id.* at 94. HUD

regulations issued after the passage of the 1988 Fair Housing Amendments Act define steering as discouraging anyone from inspecting, purchasing, or renting a dwelling, exaggerating drawbacks, or failing to inform persons of the desirable features of a community, communicating that someone would not be welcome in a community, or assigning any person to a particular building or floor based on a protected class. Steering includes such practices as renting or selling units only on the first floor to persons in wheelchairs, or renting or selling units to families with children only on certain floors, in designated buildings, or areas of rental, townhome, and condominium communities.

- **Exclusionary Land Use:** Courts have also ruled that the term "otherwise make unavailable" includes zoning regulations and decisions of local government, or covenants or actions of homeowners associations, which have the effect of preventing housing choices for minorities, women, or persons with disabilities. Until the addition of the handicapped protected class to Title VIII in 1988, most exclusionary land use resulted from denial of low-income housing or other actions by local government which had the effect of restricting minorities from living in certain areas. Since 1989, the major exclusionary land use litigation has been over placement in the community of group homes or other residential facilities for persons with mental or physical disabilities. Litigation on this issue is often also filed under the "refusal to make reasonable accommodations" section of the statute, discussed further under "Handicap," below. When licensees encounter opposition to selling or listing a home intended for the use of a group home for persons with disabilities, they should contact HUD or the Colorado Civil Rights Division (CCRD) for advice on how to proceed. Also, because the disabled are a protected class, licensees do not have to disclose that there is a group home for persons with disabilities in the neighborhood. In fact, they should not make a voluntary disclosure of this fact, in the same way that they would not volunteer to a customer the information that there are minorities in the neighborhood.
- **Redlining:** Redlining is a lender practice of refusing to grant loans or an insurance company refusing to issue policies in certain neighborhoods, usually characterized by a large number of persons in protected classes. It may also be considered redlining when loans or policies are not refused outright, but contain discriminatory terms or higher costs. Prior to the 1988 amendments, such practices or lack of services could be addressed only under the "otherwise make unavailable" section of the law, but discrimination in lending and other "real estate-related" services are now specifically listed as prohibitions in the Fair Housing Act. Nevertheless, such discriminatory treatment does exist, and licensees who suspect that their protected class customers are not being treated equally should consult with either HUD or the CCRD about possible charges.
- **Handicap:** The 1988 Fair Housing Amendments Act extended protections afforded to other classes to persons with mental or physical handicaps. Persons may not be refused housing or subjected to unequal terms or conditions because of their handicap. The statute excepts persons convicted of manufacturing or selling drugs and persons currently addicted to or using illegal drugs, as well as persons "whose tenancy would constitute a direct threat to the health or safety of other residents or whose tenancy would result in substantial physical damage to

the property of others." Although alcoholism, for example, is considered an impairment and is given protected status, this does not mean that the behavior or rental history of an alcoholic must be ignored in determining whether an applicant for housing is qualified. While an alcoholic or mentally impaired person may not be rejected based solely on his or her impairment, a landlord may consider "behavioral manifestations" of the condition. In determining qualifications, a housing provider may consider past rental history, violation of rules and laws, or a history of disruptive, abusive, or dangerous behavior. Housing providers may not presume, however, that applicants with certain disabilities are less likely to be qualified or are more likely to be dangerous, in the absence of specific proof. In the few cases that have been decided under the "direct threat" provisions, including one in the United States District Court for the District of Colorado, *Roe v. Housing Authority of the City of Boulder*, 909 F. Supp. 814 (D. Colo. 1995), courts have ruled that housing providers must first make a reasonable effort and accommodation to lessen or mitigate any possible threat before they may deny housing.

The Fair Housing Amendments Act of 1988 also added three definitions of discrimination that apply *only to persons with disabilities*:

- **Refusal to permit reasonable modifications**, at the expense of a handicapped person, to existing premises to give that person full enjoyment. Under this section, landlords, owners, and condominium associations must allow tenants or owners to make reasonable modifications to either the unit or to common areas, if necessary for the person's access or equal enjoyment of the housing. Further, landlords and homeowners associations may not increase the security deposit of a disabled tenant in anticipation of a request for future modifications. However, licensees should be cautious about suggesting that buyers or tenants make accessibility modifications at their own expense until determining whether the requested modification should have been designed into multifamily buildings constructed since March 13, 1991. (See the paragraph below on "a failure to design and construct multifamily housing" for further details.) Under a different federal law, the 1973 Rehabilitation Act, the landlord may be responsible for the cost of modifications if housing was partially or fully funded with federal funds. Another situation where the owner or homeowners association, not the occupant, might be responsible for the cost of modification is when the modification requested is a part of housing considered a "public accommodation" under the Americans with Disabilities Act (the ADA), such as sales/rental offices and common areas like pools and clubhouses rented out to the public. (See the subsequent section on the ADA.)

  In limited situations, such as when the modifications might not be usable by a subsequent non-disabled occupant, a landlord may require that a disabled tenant deposit a reasonable amount of money into an escrow account to cover the costs of restoration of the *interior* of the unit. Landlords or homeowners associations may not require restoration of modifications to the *exterior* of the unit, since exterior accessibility modifications may benefit other persons with disabilities.

- **Refusal to make reasonable accommodations** in rules, policies, practices, or services to accommodate the handicapped. Under this provision, housing providers, including homeowners associations, must waive or amend rules to accommodate persons with handicaps, such as providing assigned parking when parking is usually "first-come, first-served" or allowing guide, service, and companion animals in buildings that usually prohibit animals. Courts have also ruled that the word "rules" includes zoning regulations and covenants that preclude or put undue restrictions on group homes for persons with handicaps in residential neighborhoods. This means that cities and counties with zoning regulations limiting the number of unrelated people who may share a housing unit may have to make an exception to allow the establishment of a group home for persons with handicaps. As another example of the wide-ranging interpretation of this provision of the law, one court has required covenants not allowing businesses to be waived so that a handicapped person could operate a business from home.

- **Failure to design and construct handicap-accessible multifamily housing** containing four or more units, put into first occupancy after March 13, 1991. Any housing with four or more units in a single structure must comply with seven specific accessibility requirements: (1) an accessible entrance on an accessible route, (2) accessible and usable common use areas, (3) usable doors, (4) an accessible route into and through the unit, (5) light switches, electrical outlets, thermostats, and other environmental controls in accessible locations, (6) reinforced walls for grab bars, and (7) usable kitchens and bathrooms. Buildings with elevators must make all units accessible; buildings without elevators must make ground-floor units accessible.

  There is only one exception to the "four-or-more" requirement. It is HUD's interpretation of the law that two-story townhomes in a building without an elevator are not required to be accessible, because there is no "ground floor unit." Other than this, all other buildings with four or more units have accessibility requirements. Single-story units are considered "ground floor units" and must be accessible, as are single-story units with an unfinished basement or single-story units with an open loft. If the building has an elevator, then all units, even if they are two-story townhome style, must comply with accessibility requirements.

  Anyone involved in the design or construction of multifamily housing subject to the act may be held liable. This includes owners, developers, architects, site and electrical engineers, and construction companies. HUD considers that the usual one-year statute of limitations does not apply until the units have been brought into compliance, and so far, there has been no case ruling to the contrary. That means that there are thousands of non-compliant units in Colorado whose designers and builders may be subject to a complaint filed anytime in the future (see *Garcia v. Brockway*, 526 F.3d 456 (9th Cir. 2008).

Licensees who list or sell residential property defined as "multifamily housing" need to be very familiar with accessibility requirements and when they apply. Property, including individual units or whole multifamily buildings, changes hands without new purchasers being aware of whether the property is or is not in compliance. Although commercial brokers seem to be generally aware of the coverage of the ADA, there is less understanding of the Fair Housing Act accessibility mandates. The Colorado Civil Rights Division has investigated charges of "failure to design and construct" to fair housing standards and notes that sometimes contracts for the sale of apartment buildings refer to the ADA, even though this generally is the wrong law, except for rental offices in apartment buildings or common areas rented out to the public. Although licensees should not themselves certify whether multifamily buildings are in compliance, they are well advised to warn potential buyers to hire an architectural firm to make this assessment. (See the ADA section for further discussion of when the ADA applies versus when the Fair Housing Act applies.)

Enforcement: The amended fair housing act of 1988 provides that persons who believe they have been subjected to a discriminatory housing practice may file a complaint with either HUD's Office of Fair Housing and Equal Opportunity, or with the CCRD. HUD is mandated to refer housing discrimination complaints to any state or local public agency, if that agency has been certified as "substantially equivalent." Agencies receive this certification if the following are substantially equivalent to federal law: (1) substantive rights protected, (2) procedures followed by the agency, (3) remedies available to that agency, and (4) availability of judicial review of such agency's action.

The Colorado Civil Rights Division has had a memorandum of understanding (MOU) with HUD for joint processing of charges since 1981. Under this MOU, the Division accepts and investigates most state and federal charges at the same time, except for the following: (1) complaints that do not fall under both laws because of differences in the laws, (2) complaints against an agency of the federal government, and (3) complaints where the property is federally subsidized and there is also a complaint under Title VI, § 504 of the 1973 Rehabilitation Act or the Americans with Disabilities Act. HUD may also elect to investigate some cases it considers "systemic," such as those against companies with holdings both in and out of Colorado, issues of zoning laws and other local land use practices, or cases that raise a question of public importance.

Complaints must be filed *within one year* of the discriminatory action or termination of that discriminatory action. Complainants may bypass both HUD and the Colorado Civil Rights Division and file directly in federal or state district court within two years of the alleged discrimination. Complainants may also decide, at any stage of the conciliation and investigation process, to pull the complaint from HUD or the Colorado Civil Rights Division and file directly in court, unless a conciliation agreement has been reached with the consent of the complainant or unless a hearing before an administrative law judge (ALJ) has commenced. The HUD secretary, the attorney general of Colorado, and the Colorado Civil Rights Commission may also file a complaint upon their own initiative.

During the period beginning with the filing of a complaint and ending with a formal charge or dismissal, HUD or the CCRD will attempt to conciliate the complaint in order to achieve an agreement satisfactory to all parties and in keeping with public policy and the purposes of the fair housing acts. The CCRD calls this attempt to settle the case its "alternative dispute resolution," and uses the term "conciliation" only after the director has found "probable cause" that discrimination has occurred and a second attempt has been made to come to an agreement between the parties. The purpose of conciliation is to obtain assurances that the violation will be remedied and to protect the interest of the aggrieved person and other persons similarly situated.

If an agreement cannot be reached between the parties, then, after a full investigation, the agency carrying out the investigation issues a formal finding of "probable cause" or "no probable cause" (Colorado law) or "reasonable cause" or "no reasonable cause" (federal law), that discrimination has or has not occurred. "No cause" cases are dismissed unless appealed by the complainant. In "cause" cases, either the state or HUD will issue a formal complaint to be heard by an ALJ, unless either party requests, within 20 days of service of the complaint, that the matter be moved to a federal or state district court. Further efforts at an agreement will continue until the matter is heard before the ALJ or court. Courts or an ALJ can issue a final decision and award actual damages, injunctive or other equitable relief, and civil penalties. A court can also award punitive damages. There is no statutory limit on the amount of punitive damages that a judge or jury may award.

Violation of fair housing laws may affect a broker's Colorado real estate license. If a respondent licensee is found to have committed a discriminatory housing practice, then HUD or the CCRD will notify the Colorado Division of Real Estate. This notification will contain copies of the findings of fact, conclusions of law, and the final decision against the licensee with recommendations of revocation or other disciplinary action. Pursuant to Colorado license law, § 12-10-217, C.R.S., any violation by a real estate agent or the aiding and abetting in the violation of the Colorado or federal fair housing laws is cause for the revocation of a real estate license and a fine.

Fair housing acts do not prohibit only clear, obvious, and intentional discrimination, but also make unlawful subtle forms of discriminatory treatment, as well as conduct that has discriminatory results, regardless of the motivation. Moreover, employing brokers may be liable for discriminatory acts by employed licensees. This is true even for a broker who has not personally violated the act, who has given perfunctory instructions to subagents to obey the law, and who was not aware of the licensee's violations. The duty to comply with the law cannot be delegated, and even a "silent partner" can be found in violation of the act when employees discriminate. On the good side, licensees are also protected by court rulings that anyone who has been harmed by a discriminatory housing act has standing to file a housing discrimination complaint. A broker who has lost a commission because of a discriminatory practice may file a charge and claim damages.

IV. Equal Credit Opportunity Act (ECOA) (15 U.S.C. §§ 1691, *et seq.*)

The Equal Credit Opportunity Act (ECOA) makes it unlawful to discriminate in the granting of credit on the basis of race, color, religion, national origin, sex, marital status, age, or because income comes from a public assistance program. Notice two classes here that are not found in the fair housing acts: "age" and "income from a public assistance program."

V. Americans with Disabilities Act

Real estate professionals need to be aware how the Americans with Disabilities Act (the ADA) will affect their practices. Title III of the ADA, "Nondiscrimination on the Basis of Disability by Public Accommodations and in Commercial Facilities," went into effect on January 26, 1992. The ADA does not generally apply to residential real estate except for on-site offices or common areas rented to the public. However, this section of the ADA may affect brokerage offices, licensees working with multifamily or commercial real estate, brokers who offer brokerage services, and employ others, and/or persons who teach real estate, in four ways, described below.

A. Licensee ADA Responsibilities in Conducting Real Estate Practices

Real estate brokerages and licensees have four basic responsibilities in the conduct of their real estate practices; to:

1. Not discriminate against persons with disabilities;

2. Make reasonable modifications in their procedures and policies so as to make their services available to persons with disabilities;
3. Take steps to ensure that persons with disabilities are not excluded or treated differently because of the absence of auxiliary aids or services; and
4. Remove architectural barriers.

Architectural barriers in existing facilities must be removed if removal is "readily achievable," *i.e.*, able to be carried out without much difficulty or expense. Barrier removal includes such things as installing ramps, widening doors, removing high-pile carpeting, rearranging furniture, and installing raised markings on elevator controls. If these cannot be done all at once, Department of Justice regulations specify an order of priority: first, accomplish access to the facility, next, access to the places where services or goods are available, then restroom access, then anything else necessary. ADA regulations also contain complex provisions that take effect when alterations are made to a place of public accommodation. Alterations can, in some cases, trigger requirements for additional remodeling to achieve accessibility. Building owners should not proceed with plans for office upgrade before review of ADA regulations on "alterations," "alterations: plan of travel," and "alterations: elevator exemption."

"Auxiliary aids" include such things as deaf interpreters, large print materials, and modification of equipment. Public accommodations should provide these unless doing so would fundamentally alter the nature of their services or result in an "undue burden," *i.e.*, significant difficulty or expense.

The ADA specifies factors that will be considered in evaluating "readily achievable" and "undue burden." These include the cost of the provision of auxiliary aids or removal of barriers, in relation to the financial resources of the site or, in some cases, the parent corporation.

The ADA places these responsibilities on the "public accommodation," as distinguished from a "place of public accommodation." Since the definition of "public accommodation" is "a private entity that owns, leases (or leases to), or operates a place of public accommodation," both the owner and the lessee are subject to the act's requirements. After considerable controversy over whether the lessor or lessee would be responsible for the removal of barriers and provision of auxiliary aids, final ADA regulations specify that "allocation of responsibility for the obligations of this part may be determined by lease or other contract." Unfortunately, this means that persons who rent from or to other parties must negotiate the details of ADA compliance in their leases. Although freely negotiable, the most common lease arrangements tend to hold the owner responsible for the common areas, and the lessee is made responsible within the leased portion.

B. Licensee ADA Responsibilities in Listing, Selling, Leasing, or Managing Property

Although licensees are not responsible for ensuring that the buildings they sell, lease, or manage are fully ADA accessible, they should be familiar with accessibility requirements in order to serve their clients. This would include a basic understanding of the requirements for buildings built both before and after the effective date of the ADA, and the lessor and lessee responsibilities briefly discussed above. Licensees would be unwise to claim that any building being leased or managed complies with the ADA, but instead should recommend that the parties hire a licensed architect or engineer to analyze compliance and/or estimate the cost to bring a building up to ADA standards.

Licensees involved in the sale, lease, or management of commercial or multifamily property must understand the differences between the accessibility requirements of the ADA and the Fair Housing Act. (See also the section above entitled "Failure to Design.") Parts of housing that are also "public accommodations" are subject to the ADA retrofit obligations discussed above, whereas housing built before the 1991 effective date of fair housing act accessibility mandates has no retrofit requirements.

A licensee who lists or sells apartment complexes should be aware that in ADA enforcement, the U.S. Department of Justice considers a rental or sales office in any housing facility to be a "public accommodation" subject to ADA requirements. Similarly, common areas, such as pools and clubhouses, are also "public accommodations" if they are rented out to the public, while common areas used only by residents and their guests are not. Some types of housing can be considered both "housing" under the Fair Housing Act and a "public accommodation" under the ADA. These include nursing homes, dormitories, some kinds of assisted living facilities, and time shares. Apartment, townhome, or condominium communities that are rented out on a short-term basis, like a hotel, may also be considered "public accommodations" with ADA responsibilities. Under ADA Title II, "Nondiscrimination on the Basis of Disability in State and Local Governments," housing built by, on behalf of, or for the use of state or local government is subject to the ADA.

Licensees who manage commercial buildings and public accommodations act as the owner's representative and are responsible for the same level of non-discrimination and accommodation as in the management of their own real estate practices (described), as well as the differences and overlap between the ADA and the Fair Housing Act.

C. ADA Responsibilities in Real Estate Instruction

The ADA provides that any private entity that offers examinations or courses related to licensing for professional or trade purposes must do so in a place and manner accessible to persons with disabilities, or offer alternative accessible arrangements. Real estate schools have to provide auxiliary aids and services for persons with disabilities (such as Braille or large-print texts and deaf interpreters), unless they can prove that this fundamentally alters the course or results in an undue burden. Exams for persons with disabilities must be offered as often as other examinations and in equally convenient locations, and the kind of exam must accommodate an individual's disability and accurately reflect that individual's aptitude.

D. ADA Responsibilities as Employers

One of the main provisions of the ADA is the section on the employment and treatment of persons with disabilities. Title I of the ADA, "Equal Employment Opportunity for Individuals with Disabilities," makes it illegal to discriminate against persons with physical or mental disabilities. It also places an affirmative duty on employers to provide reasonable accommodations for persons with disabilities, including such things as removing physical barriers, possibly restructuring jobs or schedules, modifying equipment, and providing auxiliary aids. Although Title I applies only to firms with 15 or more employees, and thus may not affect some real estate firms, a separate Colorado statute applies to firms with even one employee.

From this brief description of the ADA, it is apparent that all licensees need to be aware of its provisions as they affect their facilities and practices. In addition, those selling or leasing commercial real estate of others need to make themselves aware of the requirements for new buildings or alterations, and about owner and lessee responsibilities in complying with the ADA. The above discussion is only a brief summary of pertinent portions of the ADA. Copies of the regulations may be obtained from the Department of Justice by calling (202) 514-0301 or the ADA InfoCenter at (719) 444-0268 or (800) 949-4232.

VI. Colorado Fair Housing Act

A. Title 24, Article 34, C.R.S.

Colorado enacted prohibitions against housing discrimination in 1959, becoming the first state in the nation to pass anti-discrimination laws pertaining to private property. The Colorado act even preceded the federal Fair Housing Act and prohibited discrimination based on **race, creed, color, national origin, or ancestry** in the renting or purchasing of housing.

In 1969, **sex** was added as a protected class, and in 1973, **marital status**[†] and **religion** were included. Eleven years before Congress added handicap to the federal fair housing act, Colorado included **physical handicap** in 1977 as a class to be protected from discrimination. After the federal Fair Housing Amendments Act in 1988 added handicap and familial status, the Colorado act was amended to add **familial status** and to expand the definition of handicap to include both physical and mental. Subsequently, all Colorado statutes were amended to replace the word "handicap" with "disability." Sexual orientation was added as a basis in 2008.

([†]Note: Discrimination is permitted on the basis of marital status if complying with local zoning ordinance.)

All the actions listed in Part III as "Illegal Practices Under Federal Law" are likewise illegal under the Colorado fair housing statute. In addition, Colorado law has additional prohibitions that, although probably illegal under federal law, are more clearly spelled out in the Colorado fair housing law. These include:

1. To honor, or attempt to honor, any discriminatory covenant;
2. To segregate or separate in housing;
3. To make any inquiry, reference, or record that is discriminatory;
4. To discharge, demote, or discriminate in matters of compensation against an agent or employee for obeying the law; and
5. To require any person accompanied by an assistance dog to pay a charge for that dog. (See § 24-34-803, C.R.S.)

B. Major Differences Between the Federal and Colorado Fair Housing Acts

1. Colorado law covers commercial and residential property, Title VIII covers residential only.
2. Colorado law prohibits marital status discrimination, Title VIII does not.
3. Colorado law protects both ancestry and national origin, whereas federal law lists national origin only. Colorado law makes it illegal to discriminate on the basis of both creed and religion, whereas the federal law lists religion only.

4. Colorado exemptions to property covered are different from the federal law. *Except for familial status*, Colorado law does not exempt single-family homes or owner-occupied dwellings of up to four units from coverage. Colorado law does exempt senior housing from the prohibition against discriminating on the basis of familial status. (See also "Exemptions," above.) Colorado law exempts rooms for rent in a single-family home occupied by the owner or lessee and, like federal law, non-commercial housing operated by private clubs or religious organizations.

5. Under both Title VIII and Colorado law, ALJs can levy fines and award actual damages, and courts may award both actual and punitive damages. However, there is a difference between federal and state courts on the power to levy fines. Federal courts can levy fines only for pattern and practice cases and violations of conciliation agreements. Colorado courts may levy fines for any violation of the law.

6. Colorado law specifically states that it is not illegal to restrict the sale, rental, or development of housing designed or intended for persons with disabilities.

   (Note: Although age is not a protected class under either federal or Colorado law, it is illegal to discriminate on the basis of age in Aspen, Crested Butte, Denver, and Telluride.)

The rest of this chapter presents Colorado housing discrimination law, as well as the law on "Discrimination in Places of Public Accommodation," "Discriminatory Advertising," and "Persons with Disabilities-Civil Rights," all of which affect the practice of real estate.

VII. Colorado Civil Rights Division—Commission—Procedures

§ 24-34-301, C.R.S. Definitions.

* As used in parts 3 to 8 of this article 34, unless the context otherwise requires:

(1) "Age" means a chronological age of at least forty years.

(1.1) "Agency" or "state agency" means any board, bureau, commission, department, institution, division, section, or officer of the state.

(1.5) "Commission" means the Colorado civil rights commission created in section 24-34-303.

(1.6) "Commissioner" means a member of the Colorado civil rights commission.

(2) "Director" means the director of the Colorado civil rights division, which office is created in section 24-34-302.

(2.5) "Disability" has the same meaning as set forth in the federal "Americans with Disabilities Act of 1990", 42 U.S.C. sec. 12101 et seq., and its related amendments and implementing regulations.

(3) "Division" means the Colorado civil rights division, created in section 24-34-302.

* (3.3) "Gender expression" means an individual's way of reflecting and expressing the individual's gender to the outside world, typically demonstrated through appearance, dress, and behavior.

* (3.5) "Gender identity" means an individual's innate sense of the individual's own gender, which may or may not correspond with the individual's sex assigned at birth.

(4) (Deleted by amendment, L. 93, p. 1655, 59, effective July 1, 1993.)

(4.1) "Housing" means a building, structure, vacant land, or part thereof offered for sale, lease, rent, or transfer of ownership; except that "housing" does not include any room offered for rent or lease in a single-family dwelling maintained and occupied in part by the owner or lessee of said dwelling as his or her household.

(4.2) "Housing accommodations" means any real property or portion thereof that is used or occupied, or intended, arranged, or designed to be used or occupied, as the home, residence, or sleeping place of one or more persons but does not include any single family residence, the occupants of which rent, lease, or furnish for compensation not more than one room in that residence.

(4.5) "Marital status" means a relationship or a spousal status of an individual, including but not limited to being single, cohabitating, engaged, widowed, married, in a civil union, or legally separated, or a relationship or a spousal status of an individual who has had or is in the process of having a marriage or civil union dissolved or declared invalid.

(5) (a) "Person" means one or more individuals, limited liability companies, partnerships, associations, corporations, legal representatives, trustees, receivers, or the state of Colorado and all of its political subdivisions and agencies.

* (b) For the purposes of part 5 of this article 34, "person" does not include any private club not open to the public that, as an incident to its primary purpose or purposes, provides lodgings that it owns or operates for other than a commercial purpose, unless the club has the purpose of promoting discrimination in the matter of housing against any person because of disability, race, creed, color, religion, sex, sexual orientation, gender identity, gender expression, marital status, familial status, national origin, or ancestry.

* (5.1) "Place of public accommodation" or "public accommodation" has the same meaning as set forth in Title III of the federal "Americans with Disabilities Act of 1990", 42 U.S.C. sec. 12181 (7), and its related amendments and implementing regulations.

* (5.3) "Protective hairstyle" includes such hairstyles as braids, locs, twists, tight coils or curls, cornrows, Bantu knots, Afros, and headwraps.

* (5.4) "Public entity" means:

* (a) Any state or local government; or

* (b) Any department, agency, special district, or other instrumentality of a state or local government.

(5.5) "Public transportation service" means a common carrier of passengers or any other means of public conveyance or modes of transportation, including but not limited to airplanes, motor vehicles, railroad trains, motor buses, streetcars, boats, or taxis.

(5.6) "Qualified individual with a disability" or "individual with a disability" has the same meaning as set forth in the federal "Americans with Disabilities Act of 1990", 42 U.S.C. sec. 12131, and its related amendments and implementing regulations.

* (5.8) "Race" includes hair texture, hair type, or a protective hairstyle that is commonly or historically associated with race.

(6) "Respondent" means any person, agency, organization, or other entity against whom a charge is filed pursuant to any of the provisions of parts 3 to 8 of this article.

(6.5) "Service animal" has the same meaning as set forth in the implementing regulations of Title II and Title III of the federal "Americans with Disabilities Act of 1990", 42 U.S.C. sec. 12101 et seq.

* (7) "Sexual orientation" means an individual's identity, or another individual's perception thereof, in relation to the gender or genders to which the individual is sexually or emotionally attracted and the behavior or social affiliation that may result from the attraction.

(8) "Trainer of a service animal" means a person who individually trains a service animal.

VIII. Housing Practices

§ 24-34-501, C.R.S. Definitions.

As used in this part 5, unless the context otherwise requires:

(1) "Aggrieved person" means any person who claims to have been injured by a discriminatory housing practice or believes that he will be injured by a discriminatory housing practice that is about to occur.

(1.3) (a) "Disability" means a physical impairment which substantially limits one or more of a person's major life activities and includes a record of such an impairment and being regarded as having such an impairment.

(b) (I) On and after July 1, 1990, as to this part 5, "disability" also includes a person who has a mental impairment, but the term does not include any person currently involved in the illegal use of a controlled substance or a substance use disorder with respect to a controlled substance.

(II) The term "mental impairment" as used in subsection (1.3)(b)(I) of this section means any behavioral, mental, or psychological disorder, such as an intellectual and developmental disability, organic brain syndrome, behavioral or mental health disorder, or specific learning disability.

(1.5) "Discriminate" includes both segregate and separate.

(1.6) "Familial status" means one or more individuals, who have not attained eighteen years of age, being domiciled with a parent or another person having legal custody of or parental responsibilities for such individual or individuals or the designee of such parent or other persons having such custody or parental responsibilities with the written permission of such parent or other person. Familial status shall apply to any person who is pregnant or is in the process of securing legal custody or parental responsibilities of any individual who has not attained eighteen years of age.

* (2) "Housing" means any building, structure, vacant land, or part thereof offered for sale, lease, rent, or transfer of ownership.

* (3) "Person" has the meaning ascribed to such term in section 24-34-301 (5) and includes any owner, lessee, proprietor, manager, employee, or any agent of a person; but, for purposes of this part 5, "person" does not include any private club not open to the public that, as an incident to its primary purpose or purposes, provides lodgings that it owns or operates for other than a commercial purpose, unless the club has the purpose of promoting discrimination in the matter of housing against any person because of disability, race, creed, color, religion, sex, sexual orientation, gender identity, gender expression, marital status, familial status, national origin, or ancestry.

* (4) "Restrictive covenant" means any specification limiting the transfer, rental, or lease of any housing because of disability, race, creed, color, religion, sex, sexual orientation, gender identity, gender expression, marital status, familial status, national origin, or ancestry, or limiting the rental or lease of any housing because of source of income.

* (4.5) "Source of income" means any lawful and verifiable source of money paid directly, indirectly, or on behalf of a person, including:

* (a) Income derived from any lawful profession or occupation; and

* (b) Income or rental payments derived from any government or private assistance, grant, or loan program.

(5) "Transfer", as used in this part 5, shall not apply to transfer of property by will or by gift.

(6) "Unfair housing practices" means those practices specified in section 24-34-502.

* ***§ 24-34-502, C.R.S. Unfair housing practices prohibited - definitions.***

* (1) It is an unfair housing practice, unlawful, and prohibited:

* (a) For any person to refuse to show, sell, transfer, rent, or lease any housing; refuse to receive and transmit any bona fide offer to buy, sell, rent, or lease any housing; or otherwise make unavailable or deny or withhold from an individual any housing because of disability, race, creed, color, sex, sexual orientation, gender identity, gender expression, marital status, familial status, religion, national origin, or ancestry; to discriminate against an individual because of disability, race, creed, color, sex, sexual orientation, gender identity, gender expression, marital status, familial status, religion, national origin, or ancestry in the terms, conditions, or privileges pertaining to any housing or the transfer, sale, rental, or lease of housing or in furnishing facilities or services in connection with housing; or to cause to be made any written or oral inquiry or record concerning the disability, race, creed, color, sex, sexual orientation, gender identity, gender expression, marital status, familial status, religion, national origin, or ancestry of an individual seeking to purchase, rent, or lease any housing; however, nothing in this subsection (1)(a) requires a dwelling to be made available to an individual whose tenancy would constitute a direct threat to the health or safety of other individuals or whose tenancy would result in substantial physical damage to the property of others;

* (b) For any person to whom application is made for financial assistance for the acquisition, construction, rehabilitation, repair, or maintenance of any housing to make or cause to be made any written or oral inquiry concerning the disability, race, creed, color, sex, sexual orientation, gender identity, gender expression, marital status, familial status, religion, national origin, or ancestry of an individual seeking financial assistance or concerning the disability, race, creed, color, sex, sexual orientation, gender identity, gender expression, marital status, familial status, religion, national origin, or ancestry of prospective occupants or tenants of the housing, or to discriminate against any individual because of the disability, race, creed, color, sex, sexual orientation, gender identity, gender expression, marital status, familial status, religion, national origin, or ancestry of the individual or prospective occupants or tenants in the terms, conditions, or privileges relating to obtaining or using any such financial assistance;

(c) (I) For any person to include in any transfer, sale, rental, or lease of housing any restrictive covenants, but shall not include any person who, in good faith and in the usual course of business, delivers any document or copy of a document regarding the transfer, sale, rental, or lease of housing which includes any restrictive covenants which are based upon race or religion, or reference thereto; or

(II) For any person to honor or exercise or attempt to honor or exercise any restrictive covenant pertaining to housing;

* (d) For any person to make, print, or publish or cause to be made, printed, or published any notice or advertisement relating to the sale, transfer, rental, or lease of any housing that indicates any preference, limitation, specification, or discrimination based on disability, race, creed, color, religion, sex, sexual orientation, gender identity, gender expression, marital status, familial status, national origin, or ancestry;

(e) For any person: To aid, abet, incite, compel, or coerce the doing of any act defined in this section as an unfair housing practice; to obstruct or prevent any person from complying with the provisions of this part 5 or any order issued with respect thereto; to attempt either directly or indirectly to commit any act defined in this section to be an unfair housing practice; to discriminate against any person because such person has opposed any practice made an unfair housing practice by this part 5, because he has filed a charge with the commission, or because he has testified, assisted, or participated in any manner in an investigation, proceeding, or hearing conducted pursuant to parts 3 and 5 of this article; or to coerce, intimidate, threaten, or interfere with any person in the exercise or enjoyment of, or on account of his having exercised or enjoyed, or on account of his having aided or encouraged, any other person in the exercise of any right granted or protected by parts 3 and 5 of this article;

(f) For any person to discharge, demote, or discriminate in matters of compensation against any employee or agent because of said employee's or agent's obedience to the provisions of this part 5;

* (g) For any person whose business includes residential real estate-related transactions, which transactions involve making or purchasing loans secured by residential real estate or providing other financial assistance for purchasing, constructing, improving, repairing, or maintaining a dwelling or selling, brokering, or appraising residential real property, to discriminate against an individual in making available such a transaction or in fixing the terms or conditions of such a transaction because of race, creed, color, religion, sex, sexual orientation, gender identity, gender expression, marital status, disability, familial status, national origin, or ancestry;

* (h) For any person to deny an individual access to or membership or participation in any multiple-listing service, real estate brokers' organization, or other service, organization, or facility related to the business of selling or renting dwellings or to discriminate against the individual in the terms or conditions of such access, membership, or participation on account of race, creed, color, religion, sex, sexual orientation, gender identity, gender expression, disability, marital status, familial status, national origin or ancestry, or source of income;

* (i) For any person, for profit, to induce or attempt to induce any person to sell or rent any dwelling by representations regarding the entry or prospective entry into the neighborhood of any individual of a particular race, color, religion, sex, sexual orientation, gender identity, gender expression, disability, familial status, creed, national origin, or ancestry;

* (j) For any person to represent to any other person that a dwelling is not available for inspection, sale, or rental, when the dwelling is in fact available, for the purpose of discriminating against any individual on the basis of race, color, religion, sex, sexual orientation, gender identity, gender expression, disability, familial status, creed, national origin, or ancestry;

(k) For any person to violate the provisions of section 24-34-502.2.

* (*l*) For any person to refuse to rent or lease, to refuse to show housing for rent or lease, to refuse to receive and transmit any bona fide offer to rent or lease, or to otherwise make unavailable or deny or withhold from another person any housing for rent or lease because of a person's source of income;

* (m) For any person to discriminate in the terms, conditions, or privileges pertaining to the rental or lease of any housing, or in the furnishing of facilities or services in connection therewith, because of a person's source of income, including a person's receipt of public housing assistance or a person's participation in a third-party contract required by a public housing assistance program; except that, if the initial payment to the landlord is not made timely in accordance with applicable regulations promulgated by the United States department of housing and urban development due to processing delays or a government shutdown, then a landlord may exercise any right or pursue any remedy available under law;

* (n) For any person to make, print, or publish or cause to be made, printed, or published any notice or advertisement relating to the rental or lease of any housing that indicates any limitation, specification, or discrimination based on a person's source of income;

* (o) For any person to represent to another person that any housing is not available for rent or lease when the housing is in fact available for the purpose of discriminating against the person on the basis of the person's source of income; and

* (p) For any person, for profit, to induce or attempt to induce another person to rent any housing by representations regarding the entry or prospective entry into the neighborhood of a person or persons with particular sources of income.

* (1.5) (a) Subsections (1)(l) to (1)(p) of this section do not apply to a landlord with three or fewer units of housing for rent or lease.

* (b) Nothing in subsection (1) of this section precludes a landlord from checking the credit of a prospective tenant. Checking the credit of a prospective tenant is not an unfair housing practice under this section, provided that the landlord checks the credit of every prospective tenant.

* (c) As used in this subsection (1.5) and in subsection (1) of this section, "landlord" means a person who owns, manages, leases, or subleases a unit of housing and who makes that housing available for rent or lease.

* (1.7) Notwithstanding any provision of subsection (1) of this section to the contrary, if a landlord owns five or fewer single family rental homes and no more than five total rental units including any single family homes, the landlord is not required to accept federal housing choice vouchers for any of those five single family homes as an acceptable source of income under subsection (1) of this section.

(2) The provisions of this section shall not apply to or prohibit compliance with local zoning ordinance provisions concerning residential restrictions on marital status.

(3) Nothing contained in this part 5 shall be construed to bar any religious or denominational institution or organization which is operated or supervised or controlled by or is operated in connection with a religious or denominational organization from limiting the sale, rental, or occupancy of dwellings which it owns or operates for other than a commercial purpose to persons of the same religion, or from giving preference to such persons, unless membership in such religion is restricted on account of race, color, or national origin, nor shall anything in this part 5 prohibit a private club not in fact open to the public which, as an incident to its primary purpose or purposes provides lodgings which it owns or operates for other than a commercial purpose, from limiting the rental or occupancy of such lodgings to its members or from giving preference to its members.

(4) (Deleted by amendment, L. 92, p. 1122, § 4, effective July 1, 1992.)

(5) Nothing in this section shall be construed to prevent or restrict the sale, lease, rental, transfer, or development of housing designed or intended for the use of persons with disabilities.

* (6) Nothing in this part 5 prohibits a person engaged in the business of furnishing appraisals of real property from taking into consideration factors other than race, creed, color, religion, sex, sexual orientation, gender identity, gender expression, marital status, familial status, disability, religion, national origin, or ancestry.

(7) (a) Nothing in this section shall limit the applicability of any reasonable local, state, or federal restrictions regarding the maximum number of occupants permitted to occupy a dwelling. Nor shall any provision in this section regarding familial status apply with respect to housing for older persons.

(b) As used in this subsection (7), "housing for older persons" means housing provided under any state or federal program that the division determines is specifically designed and operated to assist older persons, or is intended for, and solely occupied by, persons sixty-two years of age or older, or is intended and operated for occupancy by at least one person fifty-five years of age or older per unit. In determining whether housing intended and operated for occupancy by one person fifty-five years of age or older per unit qualifies as housing for older persons under this subsection (7), the division shall require the following:

(I) That the housing facility or community publish and adhere to policies and procedures that demonstrate the intent required under this paragraph (b);

(II) That at least eighty percent of the occupied units be occupied by at least one person who is fifty-five years of age or older; and

(III) That the housing facility or community comply with rules promulgated by the commission for verification of occupancy. Such rules shall:

(A) Provide for verification by reliable surveys and affidavits; and

(B) Include examples of the types of policies and procedures relevant to a determination of such compliance with the requirements of subparagraph (II) of this paragraph (b). Such surveys and affidavits shall be admissible in administrative and judicial proceedings for the purposes of verification of occupancy in accordance with this section.

(c) Housing shall not fail to meet the requirements for housing for older persons by reason of persons residing in such housing as of March 12, 1989, who do not meet the age requirements of paragraph (b) of this subsection (7) if the new occupants of such housing meet the age requirements of paragraph (b) of this subsection (7) or, by reason of unoccupied units, if such units are reserved for occupancy by persons who meet the age requirements of paragraph (b) of this subsection (7).

(d) (I) A person shall not be held personally liable for monetary damages for a violation of this part 5 if such person reasonably relied, in good faith, on the application of the exemption available under this part 5 relating to housing for older persons.

(II) For purposes of this paragraph (d), a person may only show good faith reliance on the application of an exemption by showing that:

(A) Such person has no actual knowledge that the facility or community is not or will not be eligible for the exemption claimed; and

(B) The owner, operator, or other official representative of the facility or community has stated, formally, in writing, that the facility or community complies with the requirements of the exemption claimed.

(8) (a) With respect to "familial status", nothing in this part 5 shall apply to the following:

(I) Any single-family house sold or rented by an owner if such private individual owner does not own more than three such single-family houses at any one time. In the case of the sale of any such single-family house by a private individual owner not residing in such house at the time of such sale or who was not the most recent resident of such house prior to such sale, the exemption granted by this subsection (8) shall apply only with respect to one such sale within any twenty-four-month period. Such bona fide private individual owner shall not own any interest in, nor shall there be owned or reserved on his behalf, under any express or voluntary agreement, title to or any right to all or a portion of the proceeds from the sale or rental of more than three such single-family houses at any one time. The sale or rental of any such single-family house shall be excepted from the application of this subsection (8) only if such house is sold or rented:

(A) Without the use in any manner of the sales or rental facilities or the sales or rental services of any real estate broker, agent, or salesman, or of such facilities or services of any person in the business of selling or renting dwellings, or of any employee or agent of any such broker, agent, salesman, or person; and

(B) Without the publication, posting, or mailing, after notice, of any advertisement or written notice in violation of this section; but nothing in this section shall prohibit the use of attorneys, escrow agents, abstractors, title companies, and other such professional assistance as necessary to perfect or transfer the title.

(II) Rooms or units in dwellings containing living quarters occupied or intended to be occupied by no more than four families living independently of each other, if the owner actually maintains and occupies one of such living quarters as his residence.

(b) For the purposes of paragraph (a) of this subsection (8), a person shall be deemed to be in the business of selling or renting dwellings if:

(I) He has, within the preceding twelve months, participated as principal in three or more transactions involving the sale or rental of any dwelling or any interest therein;

(II) He has, within the preceding twelve months, participated as agent, other than in the sale of his own personal residence in providing sales or rental facilities or sales or rental services in two or more transactions involving the sale or rental of any dwelling or any interest therein; or

(III) He is the owner of any dwelling designed or intended for occupancy by, or occupied by, five or more families.

(9) Repealed.

§ 24-34-502.2, C.R.S. Unfair or discriminatory housing practices against individuals with disabilities prohibited.

(1) It is an unfair or discriminatory housing practice and therefore unlawful and prohibited:

(a) For a person to discriminate in the sale or rental of, or to otherwise make unavailable or deny, a dwelling to any buyer or renter because of a disability of a buyer or renter, an individual who will reside in the dwelling after it is sold, rented, or made available, or of any individual associated with the buyer or renter;

(b) For a person to discriminate against an individual in the terms, conditions, or privileges of sale or rental of a dwelling or in the provision of services or facilities in connection with such dwelling because of a disability of that individual, of any individual residing in or intending to reside in that dwelling after it is so sold, rented, or made available, or of any individual associated with the individual.

(2) For purposes of this section, "discrimination" includes both segregate and separate and includes, but is not limited to:

(a) A refusal to permit, at the expense of an individual with a disability, reasonable modifications of existing premises occupied or to be occupied by the individual if the modifications are necessary to afford the individual with full enjoyment of the premises; except that, in the case of a rental, the landlord may, where it is reasonable to do so, condition permission for a modification on the renter agreeing to restore the interior of the premises to the condition that existed before the modification, reasonable wear and tear excepted;

(b) A refusal to make reasonable accommodations in rules, policies, practices, or services when such accommodations may be necessary to afford the individual with a disability equal opportunity to use and enjoy a dwelling; and

(c) In connection with the design and construction of covered multifamily dwellings for first occupancy after the date that is thirty months after the date of enactment of the federal "Fair Housing Amendments Act of 1988", a failure to design and construct those dwellings in such a manner that the public use and common use portions of the dwellings are readily accessible to and usable by individuals with disabilities. At least one building entrance must be on an accessible route unless it is impractical to do so because of the terrain or the unusual characteristics of the site. All doors designed to allow passage into and within all premises within the dwellings must be sufficiently wide to allow passage by individuals with disabilities using mobility devices, and all premises within the dwellings must contain the following features of adaptive design:

(I) Accessible routes into and through the dwellings;

(II) Light switches, electrical outlets, thermostats, and other environmental controls in accessible locations;

(III) Reinforcements in bathroom walls to allow later installation of grab bars; and

(IV) Usable kitchens and bathrooms such that an individual using a mobility device can maneuver about the space.

(3) Compliance with the appropriate requirements of the "Accessible and Usable Buildings and Facilities" standard, or any successor standard, promulgated and amended from time to time by the international code council (commonly cited as ICC/ANSI A117.1) suffices to satisfy the requirements of subsection (2)(c) of this section.

(4) As used in this section, "covered multifamily dwellings" means:

(a) Buildings consisting of four or more units if such buildings have one or more elevators; and

(b) Ground floor units in other buildings consisting of four or more units.

§ 24-34-503, C.R.S. Refusal to show housing.

If the charge alleging an unfair housing practice relates to the refusal to show the housing involved, the commission, after proper investigations as set forth in section 24-34-306, may issue its order that the housing involved be shown to the person filing such charge, and, if the respondent refuses without good reason to comply therewith within three days, then the commission or any commissioner may file a petition pursuant to section 24-34-509. The district court shall hear such matters at the earliest possible time, and the court may waive the requirement of security for a petition filed under this section. If the district court finds that the denial to show is based upon an unfair housing practice, it shall order the respondent to immediately show said housing involved and also to make full disclosure concerning the sale, lease, or rental price and any other information being then given to the public.

§ 24-34-504, C.R.S. Time limits on filing of charges.

(1) Any charge alleging a violation of this part 5 shall be filed with the commission pursuant to section 24-34-306 within one year after the alleged unfair housing practice occurred, or it shall be barred.

(2) A civil action filed by the attorney general under this section shall be commenced not later than eighteen months after the date of the occurrence or the termination of the alleged discriminatory housing practice.

(3) The director, not later than ten days after filing or identifying additional respondents, shall serve on the respondent a notice identifying the alleged discriminatory housing practice and advising such respondent of the procedural rights and obligations of respondents under this part 5, together with a copy of the original charge.

(4) The director shall commence an investigation of any charge filed pursuant to subsection (1) of this section within thirty days of such filing. Within one hundred days after the filing of the charge, the director shall determine, based on the facts, whether probable cause exists to believe that a discriminatory housing practice has occurred or is about to occur, unless it is impracticable to do so or the director has approved a conciliation agreement with respect to the

charge. If the director is unable to complete the investigation within one hundred days after the filing of the charge, the director shall notify the parties of the reasons for not doing so.

(4.1) After a determination by the director that probable cause exists to believe that a discriminatory housing practice has occurred or is about to occur, the commission shall issue a notice and complaint as provided in section 24-34-306 (4). After such notice and complaint is issued by the commission, the complainant, respondent, or any aggrieved person on whose behalf the charge was filed may elect to have the claims asserted in the charge decided in a civil action in lieu of an administrative hearing. Such election shall be made in writing within twenty days after receipt of the notice and complaint issued by the commission. The commission shall provide notice of the election to all other parties to whom the notice and complaint relates.

(4.2) If all parties agree to have the charges decided in an administrative hearing, the commission shall hold a hearing as provided in section 24-34-306. If any party elects a civil action, the commission shall authorize the attorney general to commence and maintain a civil action in the appropriate state district court to obtain relief with respect to the discriminatory housing practice or practices alleged in the notice and complaint.

(4.3) Final administrative disposition of a charge filed pursuant to this section shall be made within one year of the date the charge was filed, unless it is impractical to do so. If the commission is unable to do so, the commission shall notify the complainant and the respondent, in writing, of the reasons that such disposition is impractical.

(5) Repealed.

§ 24-34-505, C.R.S. Charges by other persons.

Any person whose employees, agents, employers, or principals, or some of them, refuse or threaten to refuse to comply with the provisions of this part 5 may make, sign, and file with the commission a verified written charge in duplicate asking the commission for assistance to obtain their compliance by conciliation or other remedial action.

§ 24-34-505.5, C.R.S. Enforcement by the attorney general.

(1) Upon timely application, the attorney general may intervene in any civil action filed as provided in section 24-34-505.6 if the attorney general certifies that the case is of general public importance. Upon such intervention, the attorney general may obtain such relief as would be available to the director under section 24-34-306 in a civil action to which such section applies.

(2) Whenever the attorney general has probable cause to believe that any person or group of persons is engaged in a pattern or practice of resistance to the full enjoyment of any of the rights granted by this title or that any group of persons has been denied any of the rights granted by this title and such denial raises an issue of general public importance, the attorney general may commence a civil action in any appropriate district court.

(3) The attorney general may commence a civil action in any appropriate district court for appropriate relief with respect to:

  (a) A discriminatory housing practice referred to the attorney general by the commission under section 24-34-306; or

  (b) Breach of a conciliation agreement referred to the attorney general by the director under section 24-34-506.5.

(4) The attorney general, on behalf of the commission, division, or other party at whose request a subpoena is issued under this section, may enforce such subpoena in appropriate proceedings in the district court for the district in which the person to whom the subpoena was addressed resides, was served, or transacts business.

(5) Repealed.

§ 24-34-505.6, C.R.S. Enforcement by private persons.

(1) Notwithstanding any provision of this article to the contrary, an aggrieved person may commence a civil action in an appropriate United States district court or state district court not later than two years after the occurrence or the termination of an alleged discriminatory housing practice or the breach of a conciliation agreement entered into under this title, whichever occurs last, to obtain appropriate relief with respect to such discriminatory housing practice or breach.

(2) The computation of such two-year period shall not include any time during which an administrative proceeding under this title was pending with respect to a complaint or charge under this title based upon such discriminatory housing practice. This subsection (2) does not apply to actions arising from a breach of a conciliation agreement.

(3) Notwithstanding any provision of this article to the contrary, an aggrieved person may commence a civil action under this section whether or not a charge has been filed under section 24-34-306 and without regard to the status of any such charge, but if the director or local agency has obtained a conciliation agreement with the consent of an aggrieved person, no action may be filed under this section by such aggrieved person with respect to the alleged discriminatory housing practice which forms the basis for such charge except for the purpose of enforcing the terms of such an agreement.

(4) An aggrieved person may not commence a civil action under this section with respect to an alleged discriminatory housing practice which forms the basis of a complaint issued by the commission if an administrative law judge has commenced a hearing on the record under this title with respect to such complaint.

(5) At the request of the aggrieved person, the court may appoint an attorney in accordance with section 24-34-307 (9.5).

(6) In addition to the relief which may be granted in accordance with section 24-34-508, the following relief is available:

   (a) If the court finds that a discriminatory housing practice has occurred or is about to occur, the court may award to the plaintiff actual and punitive damages or may grant as relief, as the court deems appropriate, any permanent or temporary injunction, temporary restraining order, or other order, including an order enjoining the defendant from engaging in such practice or ordering such affirmative action as may be appropriate.

   (b) The court, in its discretion, may allow the prevailing party reasonable attorney fees and costs.

   (c) Relief granted under this section shall not affect any contract, sale, encumbrance, or lease consummated before the granting of such relief and involving a bona fide purchaser, encumbrancer, or tenant, without actual notice of the filing of a charge with the commission or a civil action under this section.

(7) Repealed.

§ 24-34-506, C.R.S. Probable cause.

In making his determination on probable cause under the provisions of section 24-34-306 (2), the director shall find that probable cause exists if upon all the facts and circumstances a person of reasonable prudence and caution would be warranted in a belief that an unfair housing practice has been committed.

§ 24-34-506.5, C.R.S. Conciliation agreements.

(1) A conciliation agreement arising out of a conciliation shall be an agreement between the respondent and the charging party, and shall be subject to approval by the director.

(2) A conciliation agreement may provide for binding arbitration of the dispute arising from the charge. Any such arbitration that results from a conciliation agreement may award appropriate relief, including monetary relief.

(3) Each conciliation agreement shall be made public unless the charging party and respondent otherwise agree and the director determines that disclosure is not required to further the purposes of this section.

(4) Whenever the director has reasonable cause to believe that a respondent has breached a conciliation agreement, the director shall refer the matter to the attorney general with a recommendation that a civil action be filed under section 24-34-505.5 for the enforcement of such agreement.

(5) Repealed.

§ 24-34-507, C.R.S. Injunctive relief.

(1) After the filing of a charge pursuant to section 24-34-306 (1), the commission or a commissioner designated by the commission for that purpose may file in the name of the people of the state of Colorado through the attorney general of the state a petition in the district court of the county in which the alleged unfair housing practice occurred, or of any county in which a respondent resides, seeking appropriate injunctive relief against such respondent, including orders or decrees restraining and enjoining him from selling, renting, or otherwise making unavailable to the complainant any housing with respect to which the complaint is made, pending the final determination of proceedings before the commission under this part 5.

(2) Any injunctive relief granted pursuant to this section shall expire by its terms within such time after entry, not to exceed sixty days, as the court fixes, unless within the time so fixed the order, for good cause shown, is extended for a like period or unless the party against whom the order is directed consents that it may be extended for a longer period. An affidavit of notice of hearing shall forthwith be filed in the office of the clerk of the district court wherein said petition is filed. The procedure for seeking and granting said injunctive relief, including temporary restraining orders and preliminary injunctions, shall be the procedure provided in the rules of civil procedure for courts of record in Colorado pertaining to injunctions, and the district court has power to grant such temporary relief or restraining orders as it deems just and proper.

(3) The district court shall hear matters on the request for an injunction at the earliest possible time.

(4) If, upon all the evidence at a hearing, the commission finds that a respondent has not engaged in any such unfair housing practice, the district court which has granted temporary relief or restraining orders pursuant to the petition filed by the commission or commissioner shall dismiss such temporary relief or restraining orders. Any person filing a charge alleging an unfair housing practice with the commission, a commissioner, or the attorney general may not thereafter apply, by himself or herself or by his or her attorney-at-law, directly to the district court for any further relief under this part 5, except as provided in section 24-34-307.

§ 24-34-508, C.R.S. Relief authorized.

(1) In addition to the relief authorized by section 24-34-306 (9), the commission may order a respondent who has been found to have engaged in an unfair housing practice:

 (a) To rehire, reinstate, and provide back pay to any employee or agent discriminated against because of his obedience to this part 5;

 (b) To take affirmative action regarding the granting of financial assistance as provided in section 24-34-502 (1) (b) or the showing, sale, transfer, rental, or lease of housing;

 (c) To make reports as to the manner of compliance with the order of the commission;

(d) To reimburse any person who was discriminated against for any fee charged in violation of this part 5 and for any actual expenses incurred in obtaining comparable alternate housing, as well as any storage or moving charges associated with obtaining such housing;

(e) To award actual damages suffered by the aggrieved person and injunctive or other equitable relief;

(f) To assess a civil penalty against the respondent in the following amounts:

(I) Not to exceed ten thousand dollars if the respondent has not been adjudged to have committed any prior discriminatory housing practice;

(II) Not to exceed twenty-five thousand dollars if the respondent has been adjudged to have committed any other discriminatory housing practice during the five-year period ending on the date of the filing of the charge;

(III) Not to exceed fifty thousand dollars if the respondent has been adjudged to have committed two or more discriminatory housing practices during the seven-year period ending on the date of the filing of the charge.

(2) In addition to the relief authorized by the provisions of subsection (1) of this section, an individual with a disability who has suffered an unfair housing practice based on his or her disability is entitled to the relief set forth in section 24-34-802.

§ 24-34-509, C.R.S. Enforcement sought by commission.

Upon refusal by a person to comply with any order, order pursuant to section 24-34-503, or regulation of the commission, the commission has authority to immediately seek an order in the district court enforcing the order or regulation of the commission. Such proceedings shall be brought in the district court in the county in which the respondent resides or transacts business.

§ 24-34-510, C.R.S. Remedy. (Repealed)

IX. Discrimination in Places of Public Accommodation

§ 24-34-601, C.R.S. Discrimination in places of public accommodation – definition.

(1) As used in this part 6, "place of public accommodation" means any place of business engaged in any sales to the public and any place offering services, facilities, privileges, advantages, or accommodations to the public, including but not limited to any business offering wholesale or retail sales to the public; any place to eat, drink, sleep, or rest, or any combination thereof; any sporting or recreational area and facility; any public transportation facility; a barber shop, bathhouse, swimming pool, bath, steam or massage parlor, gymnasium, or other establishment conducted to serve the health, appearance, or physical condition of a person; a campsite or trailer camp; a dispensary, clinic, hospital, convalescent home, or other institution for the sick, ailing, aged, or infirm; a mortuary, undertaking parlor, or cemetery; an educational institution; or any public building, park, arena, theater, hall, auditorium, museum, library, exhibit, or public facility of any kind whether indoor or outdoor. "Place of public accommodation" shall not include a church, synagogue, mosque, or other place that is principally used for religious purposes.

* (2) (a) It is a discriminatory practice and unlawful for a person, directly or indirectly, to refuse, withhold from, or deny to an individual or a group, because of disability, race, creed, color, sex, sexual orientation, gender identity, gender expression, marital status, national origin, or ancestry, the full and equal enjoyment of the goods, services, facilities, privileges, advantages, or accommodations of a place of public accommodation or, directly or indirectly, to publish, circulate, issue, display, post, or mail any written, electronic, or printed communication, notice, or advertisement that indicates that the full

and equal enjoyment of the goods, services, facilities, privileges, advantages, or accommodations of a place of public accommodation will be refused, withheld from, or denied an individual or that an individual's patronage or presence at a place of public accommodation is unwelcome, objectionable, unacceptable, or undesirable because of disability, race, creed, color, sex, sexual orientation, gender identity, gender expression, marital status, national origin, or ancestry.

(b) A claim brought pursuant to paragraph (a) of this subsection (2) that is based on disability is covered by the provisions of section 24-34-802.

(2.5) It is a discriminatory practice and unlawful for any person to discriminate against any individual or group because such person or group has opposed any practice made a discriminatory practice by this part 6 or because such person or group has made a charge, testified, assisted, or participated in any manner in an investigation, proceeding, or hearing conducted pursuant to this part 6.

(3) Notwithstanding any other provisions of this section, it is not a discriminatory practice for a person to restrict admission to a place of public accommodation to individuals of one sex if such restriction has a bona fide relationship to the goods, services, facilities, privileges, advantages, or accommodations of such place of public accommodation.

§ *24-34-602, C.R.S. Penalty and civil liability.*

(1) (a) Any person who violates section 24-34-601 shall be fined not less than fifty dollars nor more than five hundred dollars for each violation. A person aggrieved by the violation of section 24-34-601 shall bring an action in any court of competent jurisdiction in the county where the violation occurred. Upon finding a violation, the court shall order the defendant to pay the fine to the aggrieved party.

(b) Notwithstanding the provisions of paragraph (a) of this subsection (1), a person who violates the provisions of section 24-34-601 based on a disability shall be subject to the provisions of section 24-34-802.

(2) Repealed.

(3) The relief provided by this section is an alternative to that authorized by section 24-34-306 (9), and a person who seeks redress under this section is not permitted to seek relief from the commission.

§ 24-34-603, C.R.S. Jurisdiction of county court – trial.

The county court in the county where the offense is committed shall have jurisdiction in all civil actions brought under this part 6 to recover damages to the extent of the jurisdiction of the county court to recover a money demand in other actions. Either party shall have the right to have the cause tried by jury and to appeal from the judgment of the court in the same manner as in other civil suits.

§ 24-34-604, C.R.S. Time limits on filing of charges.

Any charge filed with the commission alleging a violation of this part 6 shall be filed pursuant to section 24-34-306 within sixty days after the alleged discriminatory act occurred, and if not so filed, it shall be barred.

§ 24-34-605, C.R.S. Relief authorized.

In addition to the relief authorized by section 24-34-306 (9), the commission may order a respondent who has been found to have engaged in a discriminatory practice as defined in this part 6 to rehire, reinstate, and provide back pay to any employee or agent discriminated against because of his obedience to this part 6; to make reports as to the manner of compliance with the order of the commission; and to take affirmative action, including the posting of notices setting forth the substantive rights of the public under this part 6.

X. Discriminatory Advertising

§ 24-34-701, C.R.S. Publishing of discriminative matter forbidden.

* (1) A person that is the owner, lessee, proprietor, manager, superintendent, agent, or employee of any place of public accommodation, resort, or amusement shall not, directly or indirectly, publish, issue, circulate, send, distribute, give away, or display in any way, manner, or shape or by any means or method, except as provided in this section, any communication, paper, poster, folder, manuscript, book, pamphlet, writing, print, letter, notice, or advertisement of any kind, nature, or description that:

* (a) Is intended or calculated to discriminate or actually discriminates against any person or class of persons on account of disability, race, creed, color, sex, sexual orientation, gender identity, gender expression, marital status, national origin, or ancestry in the matter of furnishing or neglecting or refusing to furnish to them or any one of them any lodging, housing, schooling, or tuition or any accommodation, right, privilege, advantage, or convenience offered to or enjoyed by the general public;

* (b) States that any of the accommodations, rights, privileges, advantages, or conveniences of the place shall or will be refused, withheld from, or denied to any person or class of persons on account of disability, race, creed, color, sex, sexual orientation, gender identity, gender expression, marital status, national origin, or ancestry; or

* (c) States that the patronage, custom, presence, frequenting, dwelling, staying, or lodging at the place by any person or class of persons belonging to or purporting to be of any particular disability, race, creed, color, sex, sexual orientation, gender identity, gender expression, marital status, national origin, or ancestry is unwelcome or objectionable or not acceptable, desired, or solicited.

§ 24-34-702, C.R.S. Presumptive evidence.

The production of any such communication, paper, poster, folder, manuscript, book, pamphlet, writing, print, letter, notice, or advertisement, purporting to relate to any such place and to be made by any person being the owner, lessee, proprietor, agent, superintendent, manager, or employee thereof, shall be presumptive evidence in any civil or criminal action or prosecution that the same was authorized by such person.

§ 24-34-703, C.R.S. Places of public accommodation – definition.

A place of public accommodation has the same meaning as set forth in section 24-34-301.

§ 24-34-704, C.R.S. Exceptions.

Nothing in this part 7 shall be construed to prohibit the mailing of a private communication in writing sent in response to specific written inquiry.

§ 24-34-705, C.R.S. Penalty.

* *[Editor's note: This version of this section is effective until March 1, 2022.]* Any person who violates any of the provisions of this part 7 or who aids in, incites, causes, or brings about in whole or in part the violation of any of such provisions, for each and every violation thereof, is guilty of a misdemeanor and, upon conviction thereof, shall be punished by a fine of not less than one hundred dollars nor more than five hundred dollars, or by imprisonment in the county jail for not less than thirty days nor more than ninety days, or by both such fine and imprisonment. The penalty provided

by this section shall be an alternative to the relief authorized by section 24-34-306 (9), and a person who seeks redress under this section shall not be permitted to seek relief from the commission.

* *[Editor's note: This version of this section is effective March 1, 2022.]* Any person who violates any of the provisions of this part 7 or who aids in, incites, causes, or brings about in whole or in part the violation of any of such provisions, for each and every violation thereof, commits a class 2 misdemeanor. The penalty provided by this section shall be an alternative to the relief authorized by section 24-34-306 (9), and a person who seeks redress under this section shall not be permitted to seek relief from the commission.

§ 24-34-706, C.R.S. Time limits on filing of charges.

Any charge filed with the commission alleging a violation of this part 7 shall be filed pursuant to section 24-34-306 within sixty days after the alleged discriminatory act occurred, and, if not so filed, it shall be barred.

§ 24-34-707, C.R.S. Relief authorized.

In addition to the relief authorized by section 24-34-306 (9), the commission may order a respondent who has been found to have violated any of the provisions of this part 7 to rehire, reinstate, and provide back pay to any employee or agent discriminated against because of his obedience to this part 7; to make reports as to the manner of compliance with the order of the commission; and to take affirmative action, including the posting of notices setting forth the substantive rights of the public under this part 7.

XI. Persons with Disabilities – Civil Rights

§ 24-34-801, C.R.S. Legislative declaration.

(1) The general assembly declares that it is the policy of the state:

(a) To encourage and enable individuals who are visually or hearing impaired or individuals with a disability to participate fully in social, employment, and educational opportunities, as well as other activities in our state on the same terms and conditions as individuals without a disability;

(b) That individuals who are visually or hearing impaired or individuals with a disability have the same rights as individuals without a disability to the full and free use of the streets, highways, sidewalks, walkways, public buildings, public facilities, and other public places;

(c) That individuals who are visually or hearing impaired or individuals with a disability are entitled to full and equal housing accommodations, facilities, and privileges of all common carriers, airplanes, motor vehicles, trains, motor buses, streetcars, boats, or any other public conveyances or modes of transportation, hotels, motels, lodging places, places of public accommodation, amusement, or resort, and other places to which the general public is invited, including restaurants and grocery stores; and

(d) That individuals who are visually or hearing impaired or individuals with a disability must not be excluded, by reason of his or her disability, from participation in or be denied the benefits of the services, programs, or activities of any public entity or be subject to discrimination by any public entity.

(2) Repealed.

* *§ 24-34-802, C.R.S. Violations - penalties - immunity.*

* (1) (a) It is a discriminatory practice and unlawful for any person, as defined in section 24-34-301, to discriminate against an individual or group of individuals because the person has

opposed any practice, made a discriminatory practice based on disability pursuant to part 5, 6, or 8 of this article 34, or because the person has made a charge, testified, assisted, or participated in any manner in an investigation, proceeding, or hearing conducted pursuant to part 5, 6, or 8 of this article 34.

* (b) An individual with a disability, as defined in section 24-34-301 (5.6), must not, by reason of the individual's disability, be excluded from participation in or be denied the benefits of services, programs, or activities provided by a public entity, as defined in section 24-34-301, or a state agency, as defined in section 24-37.5-102, or be subjected to discrimination by any such public entity or state agency.

* (c) Discrimination pursuant to this section includes the failure of a public entity or state agency, as those terms are defined in section 24-34-301, to develop an accessibility plan using the accessibility standards established pursuant to section 24-85-103 (2.5) and fully comply, on or before July 1, 2024, with the accessibility standards for individuals with a disability established by the office of information technology pursuant to section 24-85-103 (2.5). Liability for noncompliance as to content lies with the public entity or state agency that manages the content. Liability for noncompliance of the platform hosting the content lies with the public entity or state agency that manages the platform.

* (2) (a) An individual with a disability, as defined in section 24-34-301 (5.6), who is subject to a violation of subsection (1) of this section or of section 24-34-502, 24-34-502.2, 24-34-601, or 24-34-803 based on the individual's disability may bring a civil suit in a court of competent jurisdiction and, except as provided in section 24-85-103, is entitled to any of the following remedies:

* (I) A court order requiring compliance with the provisions of the applicable section;

* (II) The recovery of actual monetary damages; or

* (III) A statutory fine of three thousand five hundred dollars, payable to each plaintiff for each violation.

* (b) For a claim brought pursuant to paragraph (a) of this subsection (2) for a construction-related accessibility violation, the violation must be considered a single incident and not as separate violations for each day the construction-related accessibility violation exists.

* (c) (I) A small business defendant is entitled to a fifty percent reduction in a statutory fine assessed pursuant to subparagraph (III) of paragraph (a) of this subsection (2) if it corrects the accessibility violation within thirty days after the filing of the complaint. The fifty percent reduction in a statutory fine does not apply, however, if the defendant knowingly or intentionally made or caused to have made the access barrier that caused the accessibility violation.

* (II) For purposes of this paragraph (c), "small business" means an employer with twenty-five or fewer employees and no more than three million five hundred thousand dollars in annual gross income.

* (III) Nothing in this paragraph (c) may be interpreted to result in a reduction in actual monetary damages awarded pursuant to subparagraph (II) of paragraph (a) of this subsection (2).

* (3) An award of attorney fees and costs pursuant to section 24-34-505.6 (6)(b) applies to claims brought pursuant to this section.

* (4) A court that hears civil suits pursuant to this section shall apply the same standards and defenses that are available under the federal "Americans with Disabilities Act of 1990", 42 U.S.C. sec. 12101 et seq., and its related amendments and implementing regulations.

* (5) An agency in the state with the authority to promulgate rules related to protections for persons with disabilities shall not promulgate a rule that provides less protection than that provided by

the federal "Americans with Disabilities Act of 1990", 42 U.S.C. sec. 12101 et seq., as amended.

§ 24-34-803, C.R.S. Rights of individuals with service animals.

(1) A qualified individual with a disability has the right to be accompanied by a service animal individually trained for that individual without being required to pay an extra charge for the service animal in or on the following places or during the following activities and subject to the conditions and limitations established by law and applicable alike to all individuals:

(a) Any place of employment, housing, or public accommodation;

(b) Any programs, services, or activities conducted by a public entity;

(c) Any public transportation service; or

(d) Any other place open to the public.

(2) A trainer of a service animal, or an individual with a disability accompanied by an animal that is being trained to be a service animal, has the right to be accompanied by the service animal in training without being required to pay an extra charge for the service animal in training in or on the following places or during the following activities:

(a) Any place of employment, housing, or public accommodation;

(b) Any programs, services, or activities conducted by a public entity;

(c) Any public transportation service; or

(d) Any other place open to the public.

(3) (a) An employer shall allow an employee with a disability who is accompanied by a service animal to keep the employee's service animal with the employee at all times in the place of employment. An employer shall not fail or refuse to hire or discharge any individual with a disability, or otherwise discriminate against any individual with a disability, with respect to compensation, terms, conditions, or privileges of employment because that individual with a disability is accompanied by a service animal individually trained for that individual.

(b) An employer shall make reasonable accommodation to make the workplace accessible for an otherwise qualified individual with a disability who is an applicant or employee and who is accompanied by a service animal individually trained for that individual unless the employer can show that the accommodation would impose an undue hardship on the employer's business. For purposes of this paragraph (b), "undue hardship" and "reasonable accommodation" have the same meaning as set forth in Title I of the federal "Americans with Disabilities Act of 1990", 42 U.S.C. sec 12101 et seq., and its related amendments and implementing regulations.

(4) The owner or individual with a disability who has control or custody of a service animal or the trainer of a service animal is liable for any damage to persons, premises, or facilities, including places of housing, places of public accommodation, and places of employment, caused by that individual's service animal or service animal in training. The individual who has control or custody of a service animal or a service animal in training is subject to the provisions of section 18-9-204.5, C.R.S.

(5) An individual with a disability who owns a service animal is exempt from any state or local licensing fees or charges that might otherwise apply in connection with owning a similar animal.

(6) The mere presence of a service animal in a place of public accommodation is not grounds for any violation of a sanitary standard, rule, or regulation promulgated pursuant to section 25-4-1604, C.R.S.

§ 24-34-804, C.R.S. Service animals – violations – penalties.

(1) It is unlawful for any person, firm, corporation, or agent of any person, firm, or corporation to:

(a) Withhold, deny, deprive, or attempt to withhold, deny, or deprive a qualified individual with a disability who is accompanied by a service animal or a trainer of a service animal of any of the rights or privileges secured in section 24-34-803;

(b) Threaten to interfere with any of the rights of a qualified individual with a disability who is accompanied by a service animal or a trainer of a service animal secured in section 24-34-803;

(c) Punish or attempt to punish a qualified individual with a disability who is accompanied by a service animal or a trainer of a service animal for exercising or attempting to exercise any right or privilege secured by section 24-34-803; or

(d) Interfere with, injure, or harm, or cause another dog to interfere with, injure, or harm, a service animal.

* (2) *[Editor's note: This version of subsection (2) is effective until March 1, 2022.]* Any person who violates any provision of subsection (1) of this section commits a class 3 misdemeanor and shall be punished as provided in section 18-1.3-501, C.R.S.

* (2) (a) *[Editor's note: This version of subsection (2) is effective March 1, 2022.]* Any person who violates subsection (1)(a), (1)(b), or (1)(c) of this section commits a petty offense and shall be punished as provided in section 18-1.3-503.

* (b) Any person who violates subsection (1)(d) of this section commits a class 2 misdemeanor.

(3) (a) (I) Except as provided for in subparagraphs (II) and (III) of this paragraph (a), a person who violates any provision of subsection (1) of this section is liable to the qualified individual with a disability who is accompanied by a service animal or a trainer of a service animal whose rights were affected for the penalties provided in section 24-34-802.

(II) A person who willfully or wantonly causes harm to a service animal or a service animal in training is liable to the legal owner of the service animal or service animal in training for treble the amount of actual damages.

(III) The legal owner of an animal that is willfully or wantonly allowed to cause harm to a service animal or a service animal in training is liable to the legal owner of the service animal or service animal in training for treble the amount of actual damages.

(b) In any action commenced pursuant to this subsection (3), a court may award costs and reasonable attorney fees.

(c) An animal care or control agency is exempt from the provisions of this subsection (3) if, after a good-faith effort, the agency is unaware that the animal is a service animal.

(4) Nothing in this section is intended to interfere with remedies or relief that any person might be entitled to pursuant to parts 3 to 7 of this article.

§ 24-34-805, C.R.S. Family preservation safeguards for families that include a parent with a disability – protections – legislative declaration – definitions.

(1) (a) The general assembly finds and declares that:

(I) Persons with disabilities continue to face unfair, preconceived, and unnecessary societal biases, as well as antiquated attitudes, regarding their ability to successfully parent their children;

(II) Persons with disabilities have faced these biases and preconceived attitudes in family and dependency law proceedings concerning parental responsibilities and parenting time decisions, public and private adoptions, guardianship, and foster care;

(III) Because of these societal biases and antiquated attitudes, children of persons with disabilities historically have been vulnerable to unnecessary removal from one or both of their parents' care or are restricted from enjoying meaningful time with one or both parents; and

(IV) Children have been denied the opportunity to enjoy the experience of living in loving homes with a parent or parents with a disability or other caretakers with a disability.

(b) Therefore, the general assembly declares that to protect the best interests of children who are parented by persons with disabilities or children who could be parented by persons with disabilities:

(I) Procedural safeguards are required in adherence to the federal "Americans with Disabilities Act of 1990", 42 U.S.C. sec. 12101 et seq., and its related amendments and implementing regulations; and

(II) It is necessary to have respect for the due process and equal protection rights of parents and prospective parents with disabilities in the context of child welfare, foster care, family law, guardianship, and adoption.

(2) Achieving the goal of family preservation for a parent or prospective parent with a disability includes the following requirements:

(a) A parent's disability alone must not serve as a basis for denial or restriction of parenting time or parental responsibilities in:

(I) A domestic law proceeding pursuant to title 14, without a clear nexus to the parent's ability to meet the needs of the child;

(II) A minor guardianship proceeding pursuant to title 15, without a clear nexus to the parent's ability to meet the needs of the child; or

(III) A dependency and neglect proceeding pursuant to title 19, except when it impacts the health or welfare of a child;

(b) A prospective adoptive parent's disability alone must not serve as a basis for the denial of his or her participation in a public or private adoption pursuant to article 5 of title 19 unless it would impact the health or welfare of a child;

(c) An individual's disability alone must not serve as a basis for the denial of temporary custody or foster care of a minor, except when it impacts the health or welfare of a child;

(d) In a case brought pursuant to title 14, a minor guardianship proceeding pursuant to title 15, or article 4 of title 19:

(I) Where a parent's or prospective guardian's disability is alleged to have a detrimental impact on a child, the party raising the allegation bears the burden of proving, by a preponderance of the evidence, that the behavior or behaviors of the parent or prospective parent are contrary to the child's best interest; and

(II) If the burden of proof required pursuant to subsection (2)(d)(I) of this section is met, the parent or prospective guardian with a disability must be given the opportunity to demonstrate how the implementation of supportive parenting services can alleviate any concerns that have been raised. The court may require that such supportive parenting services be provided or implemented, given the resources of the family, with an opportunity to review the need for continuation of such services within a reasonable period of time.

(e) In a dependency and neglect case brought pursuant to title 19, when a respondent parent's disability is alleged to impact the health or welfare of a child, the court shall find whether reasonable accommodations and modifications, as required by the federal "Americans with Disabilities Act of 1990", 42 U.S.C. sec. 12101 et seq., and its related amendments and implementing regulations, were provided to avoid nonemergency removal on the basis of disability.

(f) In a case brought pursuant to title 14, a minor guardianship proceeding pursuant to title 15, or articles 4 and 5 of title 19, if a court determines that the right of a parent or prospective guardian with a disability to parenting time, parental responsibilities, guardianship, or adoption should be denied, restricted, or conditioned in any manner, the court shall make specific findings of fact and law stating the basis for such a determination and why the provision of supportive parenting services is not a reasonable accommodation or remedy to prevent the denial or limitation.

(3) As used in this section, unless the context otherwise requires:

(a) "Disability" has the same meaning as set forth in the federal "Americans with Disabilities Act of 1990", 42 U.S.C. sec. 12101 et seq., and its related amendments and implementing regulations.

(b) "Supportive parenting services" means the provision of reasonable accommodations and modifications as set forth in the federal "Americans with Disabilities Act of 1990", 42 U.S.C. sec. 12101 et seq., and its related amendments and implementing regulations, and are directly related to a disability and that enable a parent with a disability to safely fulfill parental responsibilities.

* (4) The short title of this section is the "Carrie Ann Lucas Parental Rights for People with Disabilities Act".

Chapter 27:
Related Real Estate Law

An * in the left margin indicates a change in the statute, rule, or text since the last publication of the manual.

I. Real Estate Settlement Procedures Act (RESPA)

12 U.S.C. § 2607. Prohibition against kickbacks and unearned fees

(a) **Business referrals.**

No person shall give and no person shall accept any fee, kickback, or thing of value pursuant to any agreement or understanding, oral or otherwise, that business incident to or a part of a real estate settlement service involving a federally related mortgage loan shall be referred to any person.

(b) **Splitting charges.**

No person shall give and no person shall accept any portion, split, or percentage of any charge made or received for the rendering of a real estate settlement service in connection with a transaction involving a federally related mortgage loan other than for services actually performed.

(c) **Fees, salaries, compensation, or other payments.**

Nothing in this section shall be construed as prohibiting (1) the payment of a fee (A) to attorneys at law for services actually rendered or (B) by a title company to its duly appointed agent for services actually performed in the issuance of a policy of title insurance or (C) by a lender to its duly appointed agent for services actually performed in the making of a loan, (2) the payment to any person of a bona fide salary or compensation or other payment for goods or facilities actually furnished or for services actually performed, or (3) payments pursuant to cooperative brokerage and referral arrangements or agreements between real estate agents and brokers, (4) affiliated business arrangements so long as (A) a disclosure is made of the existence of such an arrangement to the person being referred and, in connection with such referral, such person is provided a written estimate of the charge or range of charges generally made by the provider to which the person is referred (i) in the case of a face-to-face referral or a referral made in writing or by electronic media, at or before the time of the referral (and compliance with this requirement in such case may be evidenced by a notation in a written, electronic, or similar system of records maintained in the regular course of business); (ii) in the case of a referral made by telephone, within 3 business days after the referral by telephone[,] (and in such case an abbreviated verbal disclosure of the existence of the arrangement and the fact that a written disclosure will be provided within 3 business days shall be made to the person being referred during the telephone referral); or (iii) in the case of a referral by a lender (including a referral by a lender to an affiliated lender), at the time the estimates required under section 5(c) [12 USCS § 2604(c)] are provided (notwithstanding clause (i) or (ii)); and any required written receipt of such disclosure (without regard to the manner of the disclosure under clause (i), (ii), or (iii)) may be obtained at the closing or settlement (except that a person making a face-to-face referral who provides the written disclosure at or before the time of the referral shall attempt to obtain any required written receipt of such disclosure at such time and if the person being referred chooses not to acknowledge the receipt of the disclosure at that time, that fact shall be noted in the written, electronic, or similar system of records maintained in the regular course of business by the person making the referral), (B) such person is not required to use any particular provider of settlement services, and (C) the only thing of value that is received from the arrangement, other than the payments permitted under this subsection, is a return on the ownership interest or franchise relationship, or (5) such other payments or classes of payments or other transfers as are specified in regulations prescribed by the Bureau, after consultation with the Attorney General, the Secretary of Veterans Affairs, the Federal Home Loan Bank Board, the Federal Deposit Insurance Corporation, the Board of Governors of the Federal Reserve System, and the Secretary of Agriculture. For purposes of the preceding sentence, the following shall not be considered a violation of clause (4)(B): (i) any arrangement that requires a buyer, borrower, or seller to pay for the services of an attorney, credit reporting agency, or real estate appraiser chosen by the lender to represent the lender's interest in a real estate transaction, or (ii) any arrangement where an attorney or law firm represents a client in a real estate transaction and issues or law firm represents a client in a real estate transaction and issues or arranges for the issuance of a policy of title insurance in the transaction directly as agent or through a separate corporate title insurance agency that may be established by that attorney or law firm and operated as an adjunct to his or its law practice.

(d) **Penalties for violations; joint and several liability; treble damages; actions for injunction by Bureau and Secretary and by State officials; costs and attorney fees; construction of State laws.**

(1) Any person or persons who violate the provisions of this section shall be fined not more than $ 10,000 or imprisoned for not more than one year, or both.

(2) Any person or persons who violate the prohibitions or limitations of this section shall be jointly and severally liable to the person or persons charged for the settlement service involved in the violation in an amount equal to three times the amount of any charge paid for such settlement service.

(3) No person or persons shall be liable for a violation of the provisions of section 8(c)(4)(A) [subsec. (c)(4)(A) of this section] if such person or persons proves by a preponderance of the evidence that such violation was not intentional and resulted from a bona fide error notwithstanding maintenance of procedures that are reasonably adapted to avoid such error.

(4) The Bureau, the Secretary, or the attorney general or the insurance commissioner of any State may bring an action to enjoin violations of this section. Except, to the extent that a person is subject to the jurisdiction of the Bureau, the Secretary, or the attorney general or the insurance commissioner of any State, the Bureau shall have primary authority to enforce or administer this section, subject to subtitle B of the Consumer Financial Protection Act of 2010 [12 USCS §§ 5511 *et seq.*].

(5) In any private action brought pursuant to this subsection, the court may award to the prevailing party the court costs of the action together with reasonable attorneys fees.

(6) No provision of State law or regulation that imposes more stringent limitations on affiliated business arrangements shall be construed as being inconsistent with this section.

II. Manufactured Homes

§ 24-32-3311, C.R.S. Certification of factory-built residential and nonresidential structures.

(1) (a) Factory-built structures constructed, sold, or offered for sale within this state after the effective date of the rules promulgated pursuant to this part 33 must bear an insignia of approval issued by the division and affixed by the division or an authorized quality assurance representative.

(a.3) Manufacturers of factory-built structures to be installed in the state must register with the division as provided in board rules and are subject to enforcement action, including suspension or revocation of their registration for failing to comply with requirements contained in this part 33 and board rules.

* (a.5) Factory-built structures constructed or sold for transportation to and installation in another state need not bear an insignia of approval issued by the division.

* (a.7) The division must conduct a full design and plan review and inspection of the construction of factory-built structures to the extent the design and construction relates to work performed offsite or work that is completed onsite using components shipped with the factory-built structure as reflected in the approved plans for the factory-built structure. A local government may not duplicate efforts to review or approve the construction of a factory-built structure that is under review or approved by the division nor may it charge building permit fees to cover the cost of plan reviews or inspections performed by the division. A local government's jurisdiction is limited to work done onsite in compliance with section 24-32-3311 (6) and includes associated plan review, permits, inspections, and fees. The division may authorize a local government to inspect and approve work that is completed onsite using components shipped with the factory-built structure as reflected in the approved plans for the factory-built structure. A local government may charge inspection fees if authorized to assist the division to inspect and approve work that is completed onsite using components shipped with the factory-built structure as reflected in the approved plans for the factory-built structure.

* (b) Rented or leased factory-built structures that are occupied on or after March 1, 2009, must bear an insignia of approval issued by the division and affixed by the division or an authorized quality assurance representative.

* (2) Factory-built residential structures constructed prior to March 31, 1971, are subject to any existing state or local government rules relating to the construction of the structures.

* (3) Factory-built nonresidential structures constructed prior to July 1, 1991, are subject to any existing state or local government rules relating to the construction of the structures.

* (4) A factory-built structure bearing an insignia of approval issued by the division and affixed by the division or an authorized quality assurance representative pursuant to this part 33 is deemed to be designed and constructed in compliance with the requirements of all codes and standards enacted or adopted by the state and accounting for any local government installation requirements adopted in compliance with sections 24-32-3310 and 24-32-3318 that are applicable to the construction of factory-built structures to the extent that the design and construction relates to work performed in a factory or work that is completed at a site using components shipped with the factory-built structure as reflected in the approved plans for the factory-built structure. The determination by the division of the scope of such approval is final. An insignia of approval affixed to the factory-built structure does not expire unless the design and construction of the factory-built structure has been modified from approved plans.

* (5) No factory-built structures bearing an insignia of approval issued by the division and affixed by the division or an authorized quality assurance representative pursuant to this part 33 may be in any way modified contrary to the rules promulgated pursuant to section 24-32-3305 prior to or during installation unless approval is first obtained from the division.

* (6) All work at a site that is unrelated to the installation of a factory-built structure or components shipped with the factory-built structure, including additions, modifications, and repairs to a factory-built structure, are subject to applicable local government rules.

§ 24-32-3323, C.R.S.. Sellers of manufactured homes – registration.

(1) Any person whose business involves the sale of manufactured homes shall be required to register with the division before engaging in the business of selling manufactured homes in Colorado. Any person who wishes to engage in the business of selling manufactured homes in Colorado through advertising or sales activities but who does not operate a retail location in

Colorado shall obtain a single registration. Any person who wishes to engage in the business of selling manufactured homes from one or more retail locations in Colorado shall obtain a separate registration for each location. The registration requirements of this section shall not apply to any individual who, for a salary, commission, or compensation of any kind, is employed directly or indirectly by any registered manufactured home seller to sell or negotiate for the sale of manufactured homes.

(2) An application for a registration or renewal required by this section shall be submitted on a form provided by the division and shall be verified by a declaration signed, under penalty of perjury, by a principal of the manufactured home seller. The application shall contain, in addition to such other information regarding the conduct of the manufactured home seller's business as the division may reasonably require, the name, address, and position of each principal of the manufactured home seller and each person who exercises management responsibilities as part of the manufactured home seller's business activities. The application shall also contain the address and telephone number of each retail location operated by the applicant as well as the location and account number of the separate fiduciary account required by section 24-32-3324 (1). The declaration shall specify the date and location of the signing, and the division shall preserve the application and declaration and make them available for public inspection.

(3) A registration issued pursuant to subsection (2) of this section shall be valid for one year after the date of issuance. The amount of the registration fee shall be no more than two hundred dollars. If, after issuance of a registration, any of the required information submitted with the application for the registration pursuant to subsection (2) of this section becomes inaccurate, a principal of the manufactured home seller shall notify the division in writing of the inaccuracy within thirty days and provide the division with accurate updated information.

(4) For purposes of this section, a person is not engaged in the business of selling manufactured homes if the person:

(a) Is a natural person acting personally in selling a manufactured home owned or leased by the person;

(b) Sells a manufactured home in the course of engaging in activities that are subject to the provisions of article 61 of title 12, C.R.S., or activities that would be subject to the provisions but for a specific exemption set forth in article 61 of title 12, C.R.S.;

(c) Sells a manufactured home for salvage or nonresidential use; or

(d) Directly or indirectly sells, in any calendar year, three or fewer previously occupied manufactured homes that are owned by a manufactured home park owner and are located within one or more manufactured home parks in Colorado.

§ 24-32-3325, C.R.S. Contract for sale of manufactured home – requirements.

* (1) A seller must provide a contract with the sale of each manufactured home and make the following disclosures in any contract for the sale of a manufactured home:

* (a) That the purchaser may have no legal right to rescind the contract absent delinquent delivery of the manufactured home or the existence of a specific right of rescission set forth in the contract;

* (b) If required to maintain an escrow account by the division, the seller has a separate fiduciary account in compliance with board rules and a letter of credit, certificate of deposit, or surety bond in an amount required in board rules;

* (c) That an aggrieved person may file a complaint for a refund of any payment held in escrow by a seller of manufactured homes against the seller with the division; and

* (d) That an aggrieved person may bring a civil action pursuant to the provisions of the "Colorado Consumer Protection Act", section 6-1-709, to remedy violations of

manufactured home seller requirements in this part 33. However, damages are limited in accordance with the provisions of section 6-1-113 (2.5).

* (2) A contract for the sale of a manufactured home by a seller must also contain the following provisions:

* (a) A date certain for the delivery of the manufactured home or a listing of specified delivery preconditions that must occur before a date certain for delivery can be determined;

* (b) A statement that if delivery of the manufactured home is delayed by more than sixty days after the delivery date specified in the contract of sale or by more than sixty days after the delivery preconditions set forth in the contract of sale have been met if no date certain for delivery has been set, the seller will either refund the manufactured home sale down payment or provide a reasonable per diem living expense to the buyer for the days between the delivery date specified in the contract or the sixty-first day after the delivery preconditions set forth in the contract have been met, whichever is applicable, and the actual date of delivery, unless the delay in delivery is unavoidable or caused by the buyer; and

* (c) An agreed upon location for delivery of the manufactured home to the purchaser.

* (3) Any seller who fails to provide a contract as required by this section, including all disclosures and provisions is subject to the suspension or revocation of the registration by the division.

§ 24-32-3326, C.R.S. Unlawful manufactured home sale practices.

* (1) A seller engages in an unlawful manufactured home sale practice when the person:

* (a) Fails to comply with the registration requirements of section 24-32-3323;

* (b) Fails to comply with the escrow and bonding requirements of sections 24-32-3323 (2.5) and 24-32-3324, or board rules;

* (c) Fails to provide and include in any contract for the sale of a manufactured home any of the disclosures or contract provisions required by section 24-32-3325; or

* (d) Fails to refund any payments made toward the purchase of the home or provide a reasonable per diem living expense in violation of the contractual provisions required by section 24-32-3325 (2)(b).

* (2) Any person found to be selling or have sold a manufactured home in a manner contrary to the requirements of this part 33 is subject to revocation or suspension of a seller's registration, fines, or any other measures as prescribed by rule promulgated by the division or other applicable Colorado law. The division may issue a fine of up to ten thousand dollars for each violation. Multiple violations of this part 33 committed during a single sale constitute one violation. Each sale performed in violation of this part 33 constitutes a separate violation. Fines must be paid to the division and transmitted to the state treasurer who must credit the fees to the building regulation fund created in section 24-32-3309.

III. Mobile Home Park Act

§ 38-12-200.1. C.R.S. Short Title.

This part 2 shall be known and may be cited as the "Mobile Home Park Act".

§ 38-12-200.2, C.R.S. Legislative declaration.

The general assembly hereby declares that the purpose of this part 2 is to establish the relationship between the owner of a mobile home park and the owner of a mobile home situated in such park.

§ 38-12-201, C.R.S. Application of part 2.

(1) This part 2 shall apply only to manufactured homes as defined in section 42-1-102 (106) (b), C.R.S.

(2) Repealed.

§ 38-12-201.3, C.R.S. Legislative declaration – increased availability of mobile home parks.

The general assembly hereby finds and declares that mobile homes, manufactured housing, and factory-built housing are important and effective ways to meet Colorado's affordable housing needs. The general assembly further finds and declares that, because of the unique aspects of mobile homes and mobile home park ownership, there is a need to protect mobile home owners from eviction with short notice so as to prevent mobile home owners from losing their shelter as well as any equity in their mobile homes. The general assembly encourages local governments to allow and protect mobile home parks in their jurisdictions and to enact plans to increase the number of mobile home parks in their jurisdictions. The general assembly further encourages local governments to provide incentives to mobile home park owners to attract additional mobile home parks and to increase the viability of current parks.

§ 38-12-201.5, C.R.S. Definitions.

* As used in this part 2 and in part 11 of this article 12, unless the context otherwise requires:

* (1) "Entry fee" means any fee paid to or received from an owner of a mobile home park or an agent thereof except for:

* (a) Rent;

* (b) A security deposit to pay for actual damages to the premises or to secure rental payments;

* (c) Fees charged by any governmental agency of the state, a county, a town, or a city;

* (d) Utilities;

* (e) Incidental reasonable charges for services actually performed by the mobile home park owner or the mobile home park owner's agent and agreed to in writing by the home owner; and

* (f) Late fees.

* (2) "Home owner" means any person or family of a person who owns a mobile home that is subject to a tenancy in a mobile home park under a rental agreement.

* (2.5) "Late fee" has the meaning set forth in section 38-12-102 (3).

* (3) "Management" or "landlord" means the owner or person responsible for operating and managing a mobile home park or an agent, employee, or representative authorized to act on the management's behalf in connection with matters relating to tenancy in the park.

* (4) "Management visit" means an entry by management on a mobile home lot.

* (5) "Mobile home" means:

* (a) A single-family dwelling that is built on a permanent chassis; is designed for long-term residential occupancy; contains complete electrical, plumbing, and sanitary facilities; is designed to be installed in a permanent or semipermanent manner with or without a permanent foundation; and is capable of being drawn over public highways as a unit or in sections by special permit; or

* (b) A manufactured home, as defined in section 38-29-102 (6), if the manufactured home is situated in a mobile home park.

* (6) "Mobile home park" or "park" means a parcel of land used for the continuous accommodation of five or more occupied mobile homes and operated for the pecuniary benefit of the owner of

the parcel of land or the owner's agents, lessees, or assignees. "Mobile home park" does not include mobile home subdivisions or property zoned for manufactured home subdivisions.

* (7) "Mobile home space", "space", "mobile home lot", or "lot" means a parcel of land within a mobile home park designated by the management to accommodate one mobile home and its accessory buildings and to which the required sewer and utility connections are provided by the park.

* (8) "Premises" means a mobile home park and existing facilities and appurtenances of the park, including furniture and utilities where applicable, and grounds, areas, and existing facilities held out for the use of home owners generally or the use of which is promised to home owners.

* (9) "Rent" means any money or other consideration to be paid to the management for the right of use, possession, and occupation of the premises.

* (10) "Rental agreement" means an agreement, written or implied by law, between the management and a home owner establishing the terms and conditions of a tenancy, including reasonable rules and regulations promulgated by the park management. A lease is a rental agreement.

* (11) "Resident" means an individual who resides in a mobile home that is located in a mobile home park, regardless of whether the individual is the home owner.

* (12) "Retaliatory action" includes:

* (a) Increasing rent or decreasing services in a selective or excessive manner, or in a nonuniform manner to the extent that the nonuniform increase or decrease is unrelated to a legitimate business purpose;

* (b) Issuing mandatory fees in a selective or excessive manner, or in a nonuniform manner to the extent that the nonuniform issuance of the fees is unrelated to a legitimate business purpose;

* (c) Issuing warnings, citations, or fines that are not lawful;

* (d) Serving notices or threatening eviction when the notices or threats are not reasonably justified;

* (e) Billing a home owner in a selective or excessive manner, or in a nonuniform manner to the extent that the nonuniform billing is unrelated to a legitimate business purpose, for an item or service for which the home owner has not previously been billed;

* (f) Creating or modifying rules and regulations of the park that are not reasonably related to a legitimate purpose;

* (g) Selectively enforcing rules or requirements of the park;

* (h) Conducting management visits that are selective, nonuniform, or excessive; except that this subsection (12)(h) does not include management visits that are conducted for the purpose of providing notices that are required by law or by a rental agreement;

* (i) Altering or refusing to renew an existing rental agreement;

* (j) Surveilling a home owner who submits an oral or written complaint about a mobile home park to the management or to any federal, state, or local government agency; except that this subsection (12)(j) does not include routine, nonexcessive community inspections or documenting, photographing, or recording of violations of law, the rental agreement, or the rules and regulations of the park; or

* (k) Reporting or publicizing damaging information about a home owner who submits an oral or written complaint about a mobile home park to the management or to any federal, state, or local government agency.

* (13) "Tenancy" means the right of a home owner to:

* (a) Locate, maintain, and occupy a mobile home, including accessory structures for human habitation, on a space within a park;

* (b) Make improvements to the space; and

* (c) Use the services and facilities of the park.

§ 38-12-202, C.R.S. Tenancy – notice to quit.

(1) (a) No tenancy or other lease or rental occupancy of space in a mobile home park shall commence without a written lease or rental agreement, and no tenancy in a mobile home park shall be terminated until a notice to quit has been served. Said notice to quit shall be in writing and in the form specified in section 13-40-107 (2), C.R.S. The property description required in section 13-40-107 (2), C.R.S., shall be deemed legally sufficient if it states:

(I) The name of the landlord or the mobile home park;

(II) The mailing address of the property;

(III) The location or space number upon which the mobile home is situate; and

(IV) The county in which the mobile home is situate.

(b) Service of the notice to quit shall be as specified in section 13-40-108, C.R.S. Service by posting shall be deemed legally sufficient within the meaning of section 13-40-108, C.R.S., if the notice is affixed to the main entrance of the mobile home.

* (c) (I) Except as otherwise provided in subsections (1)(c)(II) and (3) of this section, the management shall give a home owner at least ninety days after the date the notice is served or posted to sell the mobile home or remove it from the premises.

* (II) If management terminates a tenancy on grounds described in section 38-12-203 (1)(f), the management shall give the home owner at least ten days after the date the notice is served or posted to sell the mobile home or remove it from the premises.

* (2) Repealed.

* (3) In any notice provided by the management as required by this section, the management shall specify the reason for the termination, as described in section 38-12-203, of the tenancy that is the subject of the notice. If the management is terminating the tenancy because the mobile home or mobile home lot is out of compliance with local ordinances or state laws or rules relating to mobile homes and mobile home lots, as described in section 38-12-203 (1)(a), or out of compliance with written rules and regulations of the mobile home park, as described in section 38-12-203 (1)(c), the notice must include a statement advising the home owner that the home owner has a right to cure the noncompliance within ninety days after the date of service or posting of the notice to quit. This ninety-day period runs concurrently with the ninety-day period to sell the mobile home or remove it from the premises as set forth in subsection (1)(c)(I) of this section. Rent payment and other agreed tenant obligations remain in effect during this ninety-day period, and acceptance of rent by a landlord during this ninety-day period does not constitute a waiver of the landlord's right to terminate the tenancy for any noncompliance described in section 38-12-203 (1)(a) or (1)(c).

* (4) Notwithstanding any other provision of this section, in any action to terminate a home owner's tenancy based on a violation described in section 38-12-203 (1)(a), the periods of time set forth in this section to provide home owners notice or a right to cure are superseded by any local ordinances, state laws or rules, or court orders that require a home owner's compliance within a shorter time period.

§ 38-12-202.5, C.R.S. Action for termination.

(1) The action for termination shall be commenced in the manner described in section 13-40-110, C.R.S. The property description shall be deemed legally sufficient and within the meaning of section 13-40-110, C.R.S., if it states:

(a) The name of the landlord or the mobile home park;

(b) The mailing address of the property;

(c) The location or space number upon which the mobile home is situate; and

(d) The county in which the mobile home is situate.

(2) Service of summons shall be as specified in section 13-40-112, C.R.S. Service by posting shall be deemed legally sufficient within the meaning of section 13-40-112, C.R.S., if the summons is affixed to the main entrance of the mobile home.

(3) Jurisdiction of courts in cases of forcible entry, forcible detainer, or unlawful detainer shall be as specified in section 13-40-109, C.R.S. Trial on the issue of possession shall be timely as specified in section 13-40-114, C.R.S., with no delay allowed for the determination of other issues or claims which may be severed at the discretion of the trial court.

(4) After commencement of the action and before judgment, any person not already a party to the action who is discovered to have a property interest in the mobile home shall be allowed to enter into a stipulation with the landlord and be bound thereby.

* (5) The provisions of section 13-40-110.5 concerning suppression of court records apply to an action for termination.

§ 38-12-203, C.R.S. Reasons for terminations.

* (1) The management of a mobile home park may terminate a tenancy only for one or more of the following reasons:

* (a) Except in the case of a home owner who cures a noncompliance as described in section 38-12-202 (3), failure of the home owner to comply with local ordinances and state laws and rules relating to mobile homes and mobile home lots;

* (b) Repealed.

* (c) Except in the case of a home owner who cures a noncompliance as described in section 38-12-202 (3), failure of the home owner to comply with written rules and regulations of the mobile home park that are enforceable pursuant to section 38-12-214 (1), are necessary to prevent material damage to real or personal property or to the health or safety of one or more individuals, and were:

* (I) Established by the management in the rental agreement at the inception of the tenancy;

* (II) Amended after the inception of the tenancy with the consent of the home owner; or

* (III) Amended after the inception of the tenancy without the consent of the home owner after providing sixty days' prior written notice to the home owner.

(d) (I) Condemnation or change of use of the mobile home park. When the owner of a mobile home park is formally notified by a notice of intent to acquire pursuant to section 38-1-121 (1) or other similar provision of law, or a complaint in a condemnation action from an appropriate governmental agency that the mobile home park, or any portion thereof, is to be acquired by the governmental agency or may be the subject of a condemnation proceeding, the landlord shall, within seventeen days, notify the home owners in writing of the terms of the notice of intent to acquire or complaint received by the landlord.

* (II) If a landlord wants to change the use of a mobile home park, and the change of use has been approved by the local or state authority or does not require approval, and the change of use would result in the eviction of inhabited mobile homes, the landlord shall give the owner of each mobile home that is subject to the eviction a written notice of the landlord's intent to evict not less than twelve months before the change of use of the land, which notice must be mailed to each home owner.

* (e) The making or causing to be made, with knowledge, of materially false or misleading statements on an application for tenancy;

(f) Conduct of the home owner or any lessee of the home owner or any guest, agent, invitee, or associate of the home owner or lessee of the home owner, that:

(I) Occurs on the mobile home park premises and unreasonably endangers the life of the landlord, any home owner or lessee of the mobile home park, any person living in the park, or any guest, agent, invitee, or associate of the home owner or lessee of the home owner;

(II) Occurs on the mobile home park premises and constitutes willful, wanton, or malicious damage to or destruction of property of the landlord, any home owner or lessee of the mobile home park, any person living in the park, or any guest, agent, invitee, or associate of the home owner or lessee of the home owner;

* (III) Occurs on the mobile home park premises, materially harms or threatens real or personal property or the health, safety, or welfare of one or more individuals or animals, including pet animals, as defined in section 35-80-102 (10), and constitutes a felony prohibited under article 3, 4, 6, 7, 9, 10, 12, or 18 of title 18; or

* (IV) Was the basis for an action that declared the mobile home or any of its contents a class 1 public nuisance under section 16-13-303.

(2) In an action pursuant to this part 2, the landlord shall have the burden of proving that the landlord complied with the relevant notice requirements and that the landlord provided the home owner with a statement of reasons for the termination. In addition to any other defenses a home owner may have, it shall be a defense that the landlord's allegations are false or that the reasons for termination are invalid.

§ 38-12-204, C.R.S. Non-payment of rent – notice required for rent increase.

(1) Any tenancy or other estate at will or lease in a mobile home park may be terminated upon the landlord's written notice to the home owner requiring, in the alternative, payment of rent or the removal of the home owner's unit from the premises, within a period of not less than five days after the date notice is served or posted, for failure to pay rent when due.

(2) Rent shall not be increased without sixty days' written notice to the home owner. In addition to the amount and the effective date of the rent increase, such written notice shall include the name, address, and telephone number of the mobile home park management, if such management is a principal owner, or owner of the mobile home park and, if the owner is other than a natural person, the name, address, and telephone number of the owner's chief executive officer or managing partner; except that such ownership information need not be given if it was disclosed in the rental agreement made pursuant to section 38-12-213.

* (3) A landlord shall not increase rent more than one time in any twelve-month period of consecutive occupancy by the tenant, regardless of:

* (a) Whether there is a written rental agreement for the tenancy;

* (b) The length of the tenancy; and

* (c) Whether the tenant's rental agreement is for a fixed tenancy, a month-to-month tenancy, or an indefinite term.

§ 38-12-204.3, C.R.S. Notice required for termination.

(1) Where the tenancy of a mobile home owner is being terminated under section 38-12-202 or section 38-12-204, the landlord or mobile home park owner shall provide such mobile home owner with written notice as provided for in subsection (2) of this section. Service of such notice shall occur at the same time and in the same manner as service of:

(a) The notice to quit as provided in section 38-12-202 (1); or

(b) The notice of nonpayment of rent as provided in section 38-12-204 (1).

* (2) The notice required under this section must be in at least ten-point type and must read as follows:

IMPORTANT NOTICE TO THE HOME OWNER:

* This notice and the accompanying notice to quit/notice of nonpayment of rent are the first steps in the eviction process. Any dispute you may have regarding the grounds for eviction should be addressed with your landlord or the management of the mobile home park or in the courts if an eviction action is filed. Please be advised that the "Mobile Home Park Act", part 2 of article 12 of title 38, Colorado Revised Statutes, and the "Mobile Home Park Act Dispute Resolution and Enforcement Program" created in section 38-12-1104, Colorado Revised Statutes, may provide you with legal protection.

* NOTICE TO QUIT: In order to terminate a home owner's tenancy, the landlord or management of a mobile home park must serve to a home owner a notice to quit. The notice must be in writing and must contain certain information, including:

- The grounds for the termination of the tenancy;
- Whether or not the home owner has a right to cure under the "Mobile Home Park Act"; and
- * That the home owner has the option of mediation pursuant to section 38-12-216, Colorado Revised Statutes, of the "Mobile Home Park Act" and the option of filing a complaint through the "Mobile Home Park Act Dispute Resolution and Enforcement Program" created in section 38-12-1104, Colorado Revised Statutes.

* NOTICE OF NONPAYMENT OF RENT: In order to terminate a home owner's tenancy due to nonpayment of rent, the landlord or management of a mobile home park must serve to a home owner a notice of nonpayment of rent. The notice must be in writing and must require that the home owner either make payment of rent or sell the owner's unit or remove it from the premises within a period of not less than ten days after the date the notice is served or posted, for failure to pay rent when due.

* CURE PERIODS: If the home owner has a right to cure under the "Mobile Home Park Act", the landlord or management of a mobile home park cannot terminate a home owner's tenancy without first providing the home owner with a time period to cure the noncompliance. "Cure" refers to a home owner remedying, fixing, or otherwise correcting the situation or problem that made the tenancy subject to termination pursuant to sections 38-12-202, 38-12-203, or 38-12-204, Colorado Revised Statutes.

* COMMENCEMENT OF LEGAL ACTION TO TERMINATE THE TENANCY: After the last day of the applicable notice period required by section 38-12-202 (1)(c), Colorado Revised Statutes, a legal action may be commenced to take possession of the space leased by the home owner. In

order to evict a home owner, the landlord or management of the mobile home park must prove:

- The landlord or management complied with the notice requirements of the "Mobile Home Park Act";
- The landlord or management provided the home owner with a statement of reasons for termination of the tenancy; and
- The reasons for termination of the tenancy are true and valid under the "Mobile Home Park Act".

* To defend against an eviction action, a home owner must appear in court. If the court rules in favor of the landlord or management of the mobile home park, the home owner has not less than thirty days from the time of the ruling to either remove or sell the mobile home and to vacate the premises. If the home owner wishes to extend such period beyond thirty days but not more than sixty days from the date of the ruling, the home owner shall prepay to the landlord an amount equal to a pro rata share of rent for each day following the expiration of the initial thirty-day period after the court's ruling that the mobile home owner will remain on the premises. All prepayments shall be paid no later than thirty days after the court ruling. This section does not preclude earlier removal by law enforcement officers of a mobile home or one or more mobile home owners or occupants from the mobile home park if a mobile home owner violates article 3, 4, 6, 7, 9, 10, 12, or 18 of title 18 or section 16-13-303, Colorado Revised Statutes.

§ 38-12-205, C.R.S. Termination prohibited.

A tenancy or other estate at will or lease in a mobile home park may not be terminated solely for the purpose of making the home owner's space in the park available for another mobile home or trailer coach.

§ 38-12-206, C.R.S. Home owner meetings – assembly in common areas.

Home owners shall have the right to meet and establish a homeowners' association. Meetings of home owners or the homeowners' association relating to mobile home living and affairs in their park common area, community hall, or recreation hall, if such a facility or similar facility exists, shall not be subject to prohibition by the park management if the common area or hall is reserved according to the park rules and such meetings are held at reasonable hours and when the facility is not otherwise in use; except that no such meetings shall be held in the streets or thoroughfares of the mobile home park.

§ 38-12-207, C.R.S. Security deposits – legal process.

(1) The owner of a mobile home park or his agents may charge a security deposit not greater than the amount of one month's rent or two month's rent for multiwide units.

(2) Legal process, other than eviction, shall be used for the collection of utility charges and incidental service charges other than those provided by the rental agreement.

§ 38-12-208, C.R.S. Remedies.

(1) (a) Upon granting judgment for possession by the landlord in a forcible entry and detainer action, the court shall immediately issue a writ of restitution which the landlord shall take to the sheriff. In addition, if a money judgment has been requested in the complaint and if

service was accomplished by personal service, the court shall determine and enter judgment for any amounts due to the landlord and shall calculate a pro rata daily rent amount that must be paid for the home to remain in the park. The court may rely upon information provided by the landlord or the landlord's attorney when determining the pro rata daily rent amount to be paid by the home owner. Upon receipt of the writ of restitution, the sheriff shall serve notice in accordance with the requirements of section 13-40-108, C.R.S., to the home owner of the court's decision and entry of judgment.

(b) The notice of judgment shall state that, at a specified time not less than forty-eight hours from the entry of judgment if a tenancy is being terminated pursuant to section 38-12-203 (1) (f) and, in all other instances, not less than forty-eight hours from the entry of judgment, which may be extended to not more than thirty days after the entry of judgment if the home owner has prepaid by certified check, by cashier's check, or by wire transfer no later than forty-eight hours after the court ruling to the landlord an amount equal to any total amount declared by the court to be due to the landlord, as well as a pro rata share of rent for each day following the court's ruling that the mobile home owner will remain on the premises, the sheriff will return to serve a writ of restitution and superintend the peaceful and orderly removal of the mobile home under that order of court. The notice of judgment shall also advise the home owner to prepare the mobile home for removal from the premises by removing the skirting, disconnecting utilities, attaching tires, and otherwise making the mobile home safe and ready for highway travel.

(c) Should the home owner fail to have the mobile home safe and ready for physical removal from the premises or should inclement weather or other unforeseen problems occur at the time specified in the notice of judgment, the landlord and the sheriff may, by written agreement, extend the time for the execution of the writ of restitution to allow time for the landlord to arrange to have the necessary work done or to permit the sheriff's execution of the writ of restitution at a time when weather or other conditions will make removal less hazardous to the mobile home.

(d) If the mobile home is not removed from the landlord's land on behalf of the mobile home owner within the time permitted by the writ of restitution, then the landlord and the sheriff shall have the right to take possession of the mobile home for the purposes of removal and storage. The liability of the landlord and the sheriff in such event shall be limited to gross negligence or willful and wanton disregard of the property rights of the home owner. The responsibility to prevent freezing and to prevent wind and weather damage to the mobile home lies exclusively with those persons who have a property interest in the mobile home; except that the landlord may take appropriate action to prevent freezing, to prevent wind and weather damage, and to prevent damage caused by vandals.

(e) Reasonable removal and storage charges and the costs associated with preventing damage caused by wind, weather, or vandals can be paid by any party in interest. Those charges will run with the mobile home, and whoever ultimately claims the mobile home will owe that sum to the person who paid it.

(2) (a) Prior to the issuance of said writ of restitution, the court shall make a finding of fact based upon evidence or statements of counsel that there is or is not a security agreement on the mobile home being subjected to the writ of restitution. A written statement on the mobile home owner's application for tenancy with the landlord that there is no security agreement on the mobile home shall be prima facie evidence of the nonexistence of such security agreement.

(b) In those cases where the court finds there is a security agreement on the mobile home subject to the writ of restitution and where that holder of the security agreement can be identified with reasonable certainty, then, upon receipt of the writ of restitution, the plaintiff shall promptly inform the holder of such security agreement as to the location of the mobile home, the name of the landlord who obtained the writ of restitution, and the time when the mobile home will be subject to removal by the sheriff and the landlord.

(3) The remedies provided in part 1 of this article and article 40 of title 13, C.R.S., except as inconsistent with this part 2, shall be applicable to this part 2.

§ 38-12-209, C.R.S. Entry fees prohibited – entry fee defined – security deposit – court costs.

(1) The owner of a mobile home park, or the agent of such owner, shall neither pay to nor receive from an owner or a seller of a mobile home an entry fee of any type as a condition of tenancy in a mobile home park.

* (2) Repealed

(a) Rent;

(b) A security deposit against actual damages to the premises or to secure rental payments, which deposit shall not be greater than the amount allowed under this part 2. Subsequent to July 1, 1979, security deposits will remain the property of the home owner, and they shall be deposited into a separate trust account by the landlord to be administered by the landlord as a private trustee. For the purpose of preserving the corpus, the landlord will not commingle the trust funds with other money, but he is permitted to keep the interest and profits thereon as his compensation for administering the trust account.

(c) Fees charged by any state, county, town, or city governmental agency;

(d) Utilities;

(e) Incidental reasonable charges for services actually performed by the mobile home park owner or his agent and agreed to in writing by the home owner.

(3) The trial judge may award court costs and attorney fees in any court action brought pursuant to any provision of this part 2 to the prevailing party upon finding that the prevailing party undertook the court action and legal representation for a legally sufficient reason and not for a dilatory or unfounded cause.

* (4) The management or a resident may bring a civil action for violation of the rental agreement or any provision of this part 2 in the appropriate court of the county in which the park is located. Either party may recover actual damages or the court may in its discretion award such equitable relief as it deems necessary, including the enjoining of either party from further violations.

§ 38-12-210, C.R.S. Closed parks prohibited.

* (1) Neither the owner of a mobile home park nor the owner's agent may require as a condition of tenancy in a mobile home park that a prospective home owner has purchased a mobile home from any particular seller or from any one of a particular group of sellers.

(2) Such owner or agent shall not give any special preference in renting to a prospective home owner who has purchased a mobile home from a particular seller.

(3) A seller of mobile homes shall not require as a condition of sale that a purchaser locate in a particular mobile home park or in any one of a particular group of mobile home parks.

(4) The owner or operator of a mobile home park shall treat all persons equally in renting or leasing available space. Notwithstanding the foregoing, nothing in this subsection (4) shall be construed to preclude owners and operators of mobile home parks from providing housing for older persons as defined in section 24-34-502 (7) (b), C.R.S.

§ 38-12-211, C.R.S. Selling fees prohibited - "for sale" signs permitted.

* (1) Neither the owner of a mobile home park nor the owner's agent may require payment of any type of selling fee or transfer fee by either a home owner in the park wishing to sell the home owner's mobile home to another par-ty or by any party wishing to buy a mobile home from a home owner in the park as a condition of tenancy in a park for the prospective buyer.

* (2) (a) This section does not prevent the owner of a mobile home park or the owner's agent from applying the normal park standards to prospective buyers before granting or denying tenancy or from charging a reasonable selling fee or transfer fee for services actually performed and agreed to in writing by a home owner.

* (b) Nothing in this section shall be construed to affect the rent charged by a landlord to a home owner pursuant to a rental agreement.

* (3) The owner of a mobile home may place a "for sale" sign on or in the owner's mobile home. The size, place-ment, and character of the sign is subject to reasonable rules and regulations of the mobile home park.

§ 38-12-212, C.R.S. Certain types of landlord-seller agreements prohibited.

* A seller of mobile homes shall not pay or offer cash or other consideration to the owner of a mobile home park or the park owner's agent for the purpose of reserving spaces or otherwise inducing acceptance of one or more mobile homes in a mobile home park.

§ 38-12-212.3, C.R.S. Responsibilities of landlord – acts prohibited.

* (1) (a) Except as otherwise provided in this section:

* (I) In any rental agreement, the landlord is deemed to covenant, warrant, and maintain, throughout the period of the tenancy described in the rental agreement, premises that are safe, clean, fit for human habitation and reasonable use, and accessible to people with disabilities;

* (II) A landlord is responsible for and shall pay the cost of the maintenance and repair of any sewer lines, water lines, utility service lines, or related connections owned and provided by the landlord to the utility pedestal or pad space for a mobile home located in the park; and

* (III) A landlord shall ensure that:

* (A) All plumbing lines and other utility connections owned and provided by the landlord to the utility pedestal or pad space for each mobile home in the park have plumbing and utility connections that conformed to applicable law in effect at the time they were installed and are maintained in good working order;

* (B) Each pad space is connected to a sewage disposal system approved under applicable law; and

* (C) Running water and reasonable amounts of water are furnished at all times to each utility pedestal or pad space; except that a landlord need not satisfy the conditions described in this subsection (1)(a)(III)(C) if a mobile home is individually metered and the tenant occupying the mobile home fails to pay for water services; the local government in which the mobile home park is situated shuts off water service to a mobile home for any reason; weather conditions present a likelihood that water pipes will freeze, water pipes to a mobile home are wrapped in heated pipe tape, and the utility company has shut off electrical service to a mobile home for any reason or the heat tape malfunctions for any reason; running water is not available for any other reason outside the landlord's control to prevent

through reasonable and timely maintenance; or the landlord is making repairs or improvements to the items described in subsection (1)(a)(II) of this section, the landlord has provided reasonable advance notice to the mobile home residents of a service disruption that is required in connection with the repairs or improvements, and the service disruption continues for no longer than twenty-four hours.

* (b) If a landlord fails to maintain or repair the items described in subsection (1)(a)(II) of this section:

* (I) The landlord is responsible for and shall pay the cost of repairing any damage to a mobile home or mobile home lot that results from the failure;

* (II) The landlord is responsible for and shall pay the cost of providing alternative sources of potable water and maintaining portable toilets, which portable toilets are located reasonably near affected mobile homes in a manner that renders them accessible to people with disabilities, no later than twenty-four hours after the service disruption begins, unless conditions beyond the landlord's control prevent compliance with this subsection (1)(b)(II); and

* (III) The landlord shall reimburse residents for any damages to their persons or property, for any loss of use of their property, and for any expenses that they reasonably incur as a result of the failure.

* (c) A landlord shall give a minimum of forty-eight hours' notice to residents if water service will be disrupted for more than two hours for planned improvements, maintenance, or repairs. The landlord shall attempt to give a reasonable amount of notice to residents if water service will be disrupted for any other reasons unless conditions are such that providing the notice would result in property damage, health, or safety concerns or when conditions otherwise require emergency repair.

* (2) In addition to the responsibilities described in subsection (1)(a) of this section, a landlord is responsible for:

* (a) Any accessory buildings or structures, including sheds and carports, that are owned by the landlord and provided for the use of the residents; and

* (b) The premises, including:

* (I) Maintaining all common areas in clean condition, good repair, and in compliance with applicable health and safety laws; keeping common areas and facilities generally available for use by park residents; and keeping common areas accessible to people with disabilities;

* (II) Maintaining roads and other pavement owned by the landlord in a passable, safe condition that is sufficient to provide access for residents' vehicles, emergency vehicles, vans providing transportation services to persons who are elderly or disabled, and school buses, if applicable, which maintenance includes snow removal, ensuring adequate drainage, and maintaining pavement above water lines;

* (III) Maintaining lot grades, regrading lots as necessary to prevent the accumulation of stagnant water and the detrimental effects of moving water, and taking reasonably necessary steps to maintain the integrity of the foundation of each mobile home's utility pedestal or pad space in order to prevent structural damage to the mobile home, except in circumstances where the need for such maintenance is caused by a resident's actions; and

* (IV) Maintaining trees on the premises in a manner that protects the safety of residents of the park and their property, including the preservation of healthy, mature trees that home owners reasonably expected to remain on the premises when they

signed their rental agreements, so long as such preservation does not pose a safety risk to any person, property, or infrastructure.

* (3) A landlord shall not require a resident to assume any of the responsibilities described in subsection (1) or (2) of this section as a condition of any home owner's tenancy in the park.

* (4) Nothing in this section may be construed as:

* (a) Limiting the liability of an individual for the cost of repairing any damage caused by the individual to the landlord's property or other property located in the park; or

* (b) Restricting a landlord from requiring a home owner to comply with rules and regulations of the park that are enforceable pursuant to section 38-12-214 or with terms of the rental agreement and any covenants binding upon the landlord or home owner, including covenants running with the land that pertain to the cleanliness of the home owner's lot and routine lawn and yard maintenance, and excluding major landscaping projects.

* (5) A landlord shall establish and maintain an emergency contact number, post the number in common areas of the park, and communicate the number to home owners in each rental agreement and each revision of the park rules and regulations. A home owner who uses the emergency contact number in a timely manner to report a problem with a condition described in subsection (1) or (2) of this section is deemed to have provided notice to the landlord of the problem.

* (6) If a landlord fails to comply with the requirements of this section, a home owner of the park may file a complaint with the division of housing pursuant to the "Mobile Home Park Act Dispute Resolution and Enforcement Program" created in section 38-12-1104. If the division finds by a written determination that the landlord has violated this section, the division may:

* (a) Impose penalties, as described in section 38-12-1105 (5);

* (b) Issue an order to cease and desist, as described in section 38-12-1105 (6);

* (c) Require the landlord to reduce the rent owed by a home owner on a prorated basis to reflect the home owner's loss of use of the mobile home space; or

* (d) Require the landlord to compensate a home owner for housing expenses on a per diem basis if the home owner is displaced from the home owner's mobile home as a result of the landlord's violation.

* ***§ 38-12-212.4, C.R.S. Required disclosure and notice of water usage and billing - responsibility for leaks.***

* (1) If the management charges home owners individually for water usage in the park, then, on or before January 31 of each year, the management shall provide to each home owner and post in a clearly visible location in at least one common area of the mobile home park the following information:

* (a) The methodology by which the management calculates the amount charged to each home owner for water usage on the home owner's lot;

* (b) The methodology by which the management calculates the amount charged to each home owner for water usage in common areas of the mobile home park; and

* (c) The current residential water rate schedule of the water utility or municipal water service provider that sup-plies water to the park.

* (2) If the management charges home owners for water usage in the park, whether individually or in an aggregate amount, the management shall provide to each home owner a monthly water bill that indicates the amount owed by the home owner, the total amount owed by all the residents in the mobile home park, and, if the management pur-chases the water from a provider, the total amount paid by the management to the provider.

* (3) The management shall not charge a home owner for any costs in addition to the actual cost of water billed to the management.

* (4) The management shall use a methodology that is reasonable, equitable, and consistent for billing home own-ers for any type of water usage.

* (5) If the management learns of a leak in a water line inside the park, the management shall notify each home owner of the leak within twenty-four hours.

* (6) The management shall not bill a home owner for any water usage that is caused by a leak in a water line inside the park.

* ***§ 38-12-212.5, C.R.S. Prohibition on retaliation.***

* (1) The management shall not take retaliatory action against a home owner who exercises any right conferred upon the home owner by this part 2, part 11 of this article 12, or any other provision of law.

* (2) Except as described in subsection (3) of this section, in an action or administrative proceeding by or against a home owner, the management's action is presumed to be retaliatory if, within the one hundred twenty days preceding the management's action, the home owner:

* (a) Complained or expressed an intention to complain to a governmental agency about a matter relating to the mobile home park;

* (b) Submitted a complaint to the management about a violation described in this part 2;

* (c) Organized or became a member of a tenants' association or similar organization; or

* (d) Made any other effort to secure or enforce any of the rights or remedies provided by this part 2 or any other provision of law.

* (3) The presumption of retaliatory action described in subsection (2) of this section does not apply to an action or administrative hearing where the management:

* (a) Addresses nonpayment of rent by a home owner, as described in section 38-12-204; or

* (b) Was notified by a peace officer or otherwise became aware that the mobile home that is the basis of the administrative hearing was being operated as an illegal drug laboratory, as defined in section 25-18.5-101 (8).

* (4) The management may rebut a presumption of retaliation with sufficient evidence of a nonretaliatory purpose.

* (5) The rights and remedies provided by this section are available to home owners in addition to the anti-retaliation protection provided in section 38-12-1105 (13).

§ 38-12-212.7, C.R.S. Landlord utilities account.

(1) Whenever a landlord contracts with a utility for service to be provided to a resident, the usage of which is to be measured by a master meter or other composite measurement device, such landlord shall remit to the utility all moneys collected from each resident as payment for the resident's share of the charges for such utility service within forty-five days of the landlord's receipt of payment.

(2) If a landlord fails to timely remit utility moneys collected from residents as required by subsection (1) of this section, such utility may, after written demand therefor is served upon the landlord, require the landlord to deposit an amount equal to the average daily charge for the usage of such utility service for the preceding twelve months multiplied by the sum of ninety.

(3) Any utility which prevails in an action brought to enforce the provisions of this section shall be entitled to an award of its reasonable attorney fees and court costs.

§ 38-12-213, C.R.S. Rental agreement – disclosure of terms in writing.

* (1) The management shall adequately disclose the terms and conditions of a tenancy in writing in a rental agreement to any prospective home owner before the rental or occupancy of a mobile home space or lot. The disclosures must include:

(a) The term of the tenancy and the amount of rent therefor, subject to the requirements of subsection (4) of this section;

(b) The day rental payment is due and payable;

* (c) The day when unpaid rent is considered in default for the purpose of establishing a late fee, which day may not be less than ten calendar days after the day rent is due and payable;

(d) The rules and regulations of the park then in effect;

* (e) The name and mailing address where a manager's decision can be appealed; and

* (f) All charges to the home owner other than rent, including late fees.

(2) Said rental agreement shall be signed by both the management and the home owner, and each party shall receive a copy thereof.

(3) The management and the home owner may include in a rental agreement terms and conditions not prohibited by this part 2.

(4) The terms of tenancy shall be specified in a written rental agreement subject to the following conditions:

(a) The standard rental agreement shall be for a month-to-month tenancy.

(b) Upon written request by the home owner to the landlord, the landlord shall allow a rental agreement for a fixed tenancy of not less than one year if the home owner is current on all rent payments and is not in violation of the terms of the then-current rental agreement; except that an initial rental agreement for a fixed tenancy may be for less than one year in order to ensure conformity with a standard anniversary date. A landlord shall not evict or otherwise penalize a home owner for requesting a rental agreement for a fixed period.

(c) A landlord may, in the landlord's discretion, allow a lease for a fixed period of longer than one year. In such circumstances, the requirements of paragraphs (a) and (b) of this subsection (4) shall not apply.

* (5) A rental agreement may not include any provision:

* (a) By which a home owner waives any rights created by this part 2 or part 11 of this article 12;

* (b) That requires a home owner to agree to a possessory lien;

* (c) That binds a home owner to arbitration in lieu of a civil trial; or

* (d) That authorizes a third person to confess judgment on a claim that arises from the rental agreement, this part 2, or part 11 of this article 12.

* (6) Any provision of a rental agreement that is prohibited by subsection (5) of this section is against public policy, unenforceable, and void.

§ 38-12-214, C.R.S. Rules and regulations - amendments - notice - complaints.

* (1) The management shall adopt written rules and regulations concerning home owners' use and occupancy of the premises. Except as otherwise provided in this section, such rules and regulations are enforceable against a home owner only if:

* (a) Their purpose is to promote the safety or welfare of the home owners, protect and preserve the premises from abuse, or make a fair distribution of services and facilities held out for the home owners generally;

* (b) They are reasonably related to a legitimate purpose, for which they are adopted;

* (c) They are not arbitrary, capricious, unreasonable, retaliatory, or discriminatory in nature;

* (d) They are sufficiently explicit in prohibition, direction, or limitation of each home owner's conduct to fairly inform each home owner of what the home owner must do or not do to comply; and

* (e) They are established in the rental agreement at the inception of the tenancy, amended subsequently with the consent of the home owner, or, except as described in subsection (2) of this section, amended subsequently without the consent of the home owner after the management has provided written notice of the amendments to the home owner at least sixty days before the amendments become effective, and, if applicable, enforced in compliance with subsection (3) of this section.

* (2) When a mobile home is owned by a person other than the owner of the mobile home park in which the mobile home is located, the mobile home is a separate unit of ownership, and rules and regulations that impose restrictions or requirements on that separate unit that are adopted after the home owner signs the rental agreement and without the consent of the home owner are presumed unreasonable. Nothing in this subsection (2) prohibits the management from requiring compliance with park rules and regulations at the time of sale or transfer to a new owner; except that, as used in this subsection (2), "transfer" does not include a transfer of ownership pursuant to death or divorce or a transfer of ownership to a new co-owner pursuant to marriage.

* (3) \ (a) If the management provides each home owner written notice of the management's intent to add or amend any written rule or regulation as described in subsection (1)(e) of this section, a home owner may file a complaint challenging the rule, regulation, or amendment pursuant to section 38-12-1105 within sixty days after receiving the notice. If a home owner files such a complaint, and the new or amended rule or regulation will increase a cost to the home owner in an amount that equals or exceeds ten percent of the home owner's monthly rent obligation under the rental agreement, the management shall not enforce the rule, regulation, or amendment unless and until the parties reach an agreement concerning the rule, regulation, or amendment or the dispute resolution process concludes and the division of housing within the department of local affairs issues a written determination, pursuant to section 38-12-1105 (4), that the rule, regulation, or amendment does not constitute a violation of this part 2 and may be enforced. Notwithstanding any provision of part 11 of this article 12 to the contrary, as part of the complaint process described in section 38-12-1105, the management has the burden of establishing that the rule, regulation, or amendment satisfies the requirements described in subsection (1) of this section.

* (b) Nothing in this section precludes a home owner from filing a complaint, pursuant to section 38-12-1105, concerning a rule or regulation at any time after the rule or regulation takes effect.

* (4) Rules and regulations that concern recreational facilities may be amended at the reasonable discretion of the management.

§ 38-12-215, C.R.S. New developments and parks – rental of sites to dealers authorized.

(1) The management of a new mobile home park or manufactured housing community development may require as a condition of leasing a mobile home site or manufactured home site for the first time such site is offered for lease that the prospective lessee has purchased a mobile home or manufactured home from a particular seller or from any one of a particular group of sellers.

(2) A licensed mobile home dealer or a manufactured home dealer may, by contract with the management of a new mobile home park or manufactured housing community development, be granted the exclusive right to first-time rental of one or more mobile home sites or manufactured home sites.

§ 38-12-216, C.R.S. Mediation, when permitted – court actions.

(1) In any controversy between the management and a home owner of a mobile home park arising out of the provisions of this part 2, except for the nonpayment of rent or in cases in which the health or safety of other home owners is in imminent danger, such controversy may be submitted to mediation by either party prior to the filing of a forcible entry and detainer lawsuit upon agreement of the parties.

(2) The agreement, if one is reached, shall be presented to the court as a stipulation. Either party to the mediation may terminate the mediation process at any time without prejudice.

(3) If either party subsequently violates the stipulation, the other party may apply immediately to the court for relief.

* *§ 38-12-217, C.R.S. Notice of change of use - notice of sale or closure of park - opportunity for home owners to purchase - procedures - exemptions. [Repealed]*

§ 38-12-218, C.R.S. Mobile home owners – right to form a cooperative.

One or more members of a homeowners' association may, at any time, form a cooperative for the purposes of offering to purchase or finance a mobile home park. A home owner shall be a member of the homeowners' association in order to participate in the cooperative, and participation in the cooperative shall be voluntary.

§ 38-12-219, C.R.S. Home owners' and landlords' rights.

(1) Every home owner and landlord shall have the right to the following:

(a) Protection from abuse or disregard of state or local law by the landlord and home owners;

(b) Peaceful enjoyment of the home owner's mobile home space, free from unreasonable, arbitrary, or capricious rules and enforcement thereof; and

(c) Tenancy free from harassment or frivolous lawsuits by the landlord and homeowners.

§ 38-12-220, C.R.S. Private civil right of action.

* A home owner in a park where the landlord has violated any provision of this article 12 has a private civil right of action against the landlord. In any such action, except as described in section 38-12-105 (4), the home owner is entitled to actual economic damages and reasonable attorney fees and costs if the home owner is successful in the action.

§ 38-12-221, C.R.S. Access by counties and municipalities.

Notwithstanding any other provision of law, upon a finding that the utilities in a park create a significant health or safety danger to park residents, the landlord of a mobile home park shall grant county or municipal officers or employees access to the mobile home park for the purposes of investigating or conducting a study related to such danger.

* *§ 38-12-222, C.R.S. Home owners' right to privacy.*

* (1) (a) The management shall respect the privacy of home owners. Except as otherwise provided by law, the management has no right of entry to a mobile home:

* (I) Without first obtaining the written consent of the home owner;

* (II) As described in subsection (2) of this section;

* (III) In the case of an emergency; or

* (IV) When the mobile home has been abandoned.

* (b) A home owner may revoke consent in writing at any time.

* (2) Unless otherwise prohibited by law, the management has a right of entry to mobile home space to fulfill the duties described in section 38-12-212.3 and to ensure compliance with applicable codes, statutes, ordinances, and administrative rules; the rental agreement; and the rules and regula-tions of the park. A landlord shall not enter in a manner that interferes with a home owner's peaceful enjoyment of the mobile home space, as described in section 38-12-219 (1)(b), except in the case of an emergency.

* (3) Except when posting notices that are required by law or by a rental agreement, the management shall make a reasonable effort to notify a home owner of the management's intention to enter the mobile home space at least forty-eight hours before entry.

IV. Title to Manufactured Homes Act

§ 38-29-101, C.R.S. Short title.

This part 1 shall be known and may be cited as the "Titles to Manufactured Homes Act".

§ 38-29-102, C.R.S. Definitions.

As used in this article, unless the context otherwise requires:

(1) "Authorized agent" means the county clerk and recorder in each of the counties of the state, except in the city and county of Denver, and therein the manager of revenue, or such other official of the city and county of Denver as may be appointed by the mayor to perform functions related to the registration of manufactured homes, is the authorized agent.

(1.5) "Clerk and recorder" means the clerk and recorder of any county or city and county in the state of Colorado.

(2) "Dealer" means any person, firm, partnership, corporation, or association licensed under the laws of this state to engage in the business of buying, selling, exchanging, or otherwise trading in manufactured homes.

(3) "Department" means the department of revenue.

(4) "Director" means the executive director of the department of revenue.

(5) "Home" means any manufactured home as defined in subsection (6) of this section.

(6) "Manufactured home" means a preconstructed building unit or combination of preconstructed building units that is constructed in compliance with the federal manufactured home construction safety standard, as defined in section 24-32-3302 (13), C.R.S. "Manufactured home" shall also include a mobile home, as defined in section 24-32-3302 (24), C.R.S.

(7) "Manufacturer" means a person, firm, partnership, corporation, or association engaged in the manufacture of new manufactured homes.

(8) Repealed.

(9) "Mortgages" or "mortgage" or "chattel mortgage" means chattel mortgages, conditional sales contracts, or any other like instrument intended to operate as a mortgage or to create a lien on a manufactured home as security for an undertaking of the owner thereof or some other person; except that, as used in part 2 of this article, "mortgage" also includes mortgages, deeds of trust, and other liens on real property.

(10) "Owner" means any person, association of persons, firm, or corporation in whose name the title to a manufactured home is registered.

(11) "Person" means a natural person, association of persons, firm, partnership, or corporation.

(12) "State" includes the territories and the federal districts of the United States.

(13) "Verification of application form" means the form generated by an authorized agent upon receipt of a properly completed application for title submitted in accordance with section 38-29-107.

§ 38-29-103, C.R.S. Application.

The provisions of this article shall apply to manufactured homes as defined in section 38-29-102 (6).

§ 38-29-104, C.R.S. Administration.

The director is charged with the duty of administering this part 1. For that purpose he or she is vested with the power to make such reasonable rules, prepare, prescribe, and require the use of such forms, and provide such procedures as may be reasonably necessary or essential to the efficient administration of this part 1.

§ 38-29-105, C.R.S. Authorized agents.

The county clerk and recorder in each of the counties of the state, except in the city and county of Denver the manager of revenue or such other official of the city and county of Denver as may be appointed by the mayor to perform functions related to the registration of manufactured homes, is designated to be the authorized agent of the director and, under the direction of the director, is charged with the administration of the terms and provisions of this article and the rules that may from time to time be adopted for the administration thereof in the county in which such authorized agent holds office.

§ 38-29-106, C.R.S. Sale or transfer of manufactured home.

Except as provided in section 38-29-114, no person shall sell or otherwise transfer a manufactured home to a purchaser or transferee thereof without delivering to such purchaser or transferee the certificate of title to such home, duly transferred in the manner prescribed in section 38-29-112, and no purchaser or transferee shall acquire any right, title, or interest in and to a manufactured home purchased by him unless and until he obtains from the transferor the certificate of title thereto, duly transferred to him in accordance with the provisions of this article.

§ 38-29-107, C.R.S. Applications for certificates of title.

(1) In any case under the provisions of this article wherein a person who is entitled to a certificate of title to a manufactured home is required to make formal application to the director therefor, such applicant shall make application upon a form provided by the director in which appears a description of the manufactured home, including the manufacturer and model thereof, the manufacturer's number, the date on which said manufactured home was first sold by the dealer or manufacturer thereof to the initial user thereof, and a description of any other distinguishing mark, number, or symbol placed on said home by the manufacturer thereof for identification purposes, as may by rule be required by the director. Such application shall also show the applicant's source of title and the new or resale price of said manufactured home, whichever is applicable, paid by such applicant and shall include a description of all known mortgages and liens upon said manufactured home, each including the name of the legal holder thereof, the amount originally secured, the amount outstanding on the obligation secured at the time such application is made, the name of the county or city and county and state in which such mortgage or lien instrument is recorded or filed, and proof of the fact that no property taxes for

previous years are due on such manufactured home. Such proof shall be a certificate of taxes, or an authentication of paid ad valorem taxes, issued by the county treasurer of the county in which the manufactured home is located. Such application shall be affirmed by a statement signed by the applicant and shall contain or be accompanied by a written declaration that it is made under the penalties of perjury in the second degree, as defined in section 18-8-503, C.R.S.

(2) In any case in which the manufactured home was affixed to the ground prior to July 1, 2008, and a certificate of permanent location was not filed and recorded, a person who is entitled to a certificate of title to a manufactured home shall make formal application to the director upon a form provided by the director. As part of the application, in addition to any information required pursuant to subsection (1) of this section, the applicant shall provide an affidavit of real property, a statement that the identification number has been verified pursuant to section 38-29-122 (3) (a), a certificate of removal, and a copy of all deeds recorded since the home was affixed to the ground. The director shall accept these documents as sufficient evidence of the applicant's proof of ownership of the manufactured home.

(3) (a) In any case in which the manufactured home was affixed to the ground after July 1, 2008, and a certificate of permanent location was filed and recorded, a person who is entitled to a certificate of title to a manufactured home shall make formal application to the director upon a form provided by the director. As part of the application, in addition to any information required pursuant to subsection (1) of this section, the applicant shall provide a copy of the recorded certificate of permanent location, a certificate of removal, a statement that the identification number has been verified pursuant to section 38-29-122 (3) (a), and a copy of all deeds recorded since the home was affixed to the ground. The director shall accept these documents as sufficient evidence of the applicant's proof of ownership of the manufactured home.

(b) In any case in which a manufactured home occupies real property subject to a long-term lease that has an express term of at least ten years, the manufactured home was affixed to the ground after July 1, 2008, and a certificate of permanent location was filed and recorded, a person who is entitled to a certificate of title to a manufactured home shall make formal application to the director upon a form provided by the director. As part of the application, in addition to any information required pursuant to subsection (1) of this section, the applicant shall provide a copy of the recorded certificate of permanent location, a statement that the identification number has been verified pursuant to section 38-29-122 (3) (a), and a copy of the recorded long-term lease. The director shall accept these documents as sufficient evidence of the applicant's proof of ownership of the manufactured home.

§ 38-29-108, C.R.S. Where application for certificates of title made – procedure.

(1) An application for a certificate of title upon the sale, transfer, or movement into the state of any manufactured home that does not become real property pursuant to section 38-29-114 (2) or section 38-29-117 (6) shall be directed to the director and filed with the authorized agent of the county or city or city and county in which such manufactured home is to be located. Upon sale or transfer, an application for a certificate of title on a manufactured home shall be made within forty-five days of the receipt of a manufacturer's certificate or statement of origin or its equivalent. The authorized agents shall forward copies of all such applications to the county assessor. Any person, other than an individual selling a manufactured home used as his residence, who receives a commission or other valuable consideration for the transfer or sale of a manufactured home shall fulfill the application and notice requirements of this subsection (1).

(2) Repealed.

§ 38-29-109, C.R.S. Director may refuse certificate, when.

The director shall use reasonable diligence in ascertaining whether the facts stated in any application and facts contained in other documents submitted to him with said application are true and, in appropriate cases, may require the applicant to furnish other and additional information regarding his ownership of the manufactured home and his right to have issued to him a certificate of title therefor. He may refuse to issue a certificate of title to such home if from his investigation he determines that the applicant is not entitled thereto.

§ 38-29-110, C.R.S. Certificates of title – contents.

(1) All certificates of title to manufactured homes issued under the provisions of this article shall be subscribed by the director, or by some duly authorized officer or employee in the department in the name, place, and stead of the director, to which shall be affixed the seal of the department. Such certificate shall be mailed to the applicant, except as provided in section 38-29-111, and information of the facts therein appearing and concerning the issuance thereof shall be retained by the director and appropriately indexed and filed in his office. The certificate shall be in such form as the director may prescribe and shall contain, in addition to other information which he may by rule from time to time require, the manufacturer and model of the manufactured home for which said certificate is issued, the date on which said home therein described was first sold by the manufacturer or dealer to the initial user thereof, where such information is available, together with the serial number thereof, if any, and a description of such other marks or symbols as may be placed upon the home by the manufacturer thereof for identification purposes.

(2) Beginning January 1, 1983, there shall be issued a distinctive certificate of title identifying the home as a manufactured home. Any person in whose name a certificate of title to a mobile home, as defined in section 38-29-102 (8), was issued prior to January 1, 1983, and which title is free and clear of all encumbrances, may apply to the director or one of his authorized agents for a distinctive manufactured home certificate of title, accompanied by the fee required in section 38-29-138 to be paid for the issuance of a duplicate certificate of title; whereupon, a distinctive certificate of title shall be issued and disposition thereof made as required in this article.

§ 38-29-111, C.R.S. Disposition of certificates of title.

(1) All certificates of title issued by the director shall be disposed of by him in the following manner:

   (a) If it appears from the records in the director's office and from an examination of the certificate of title that the manufactured home therein described is not subject to a mortgage filed subsequent to August 1, 1949, or if such home is encumbered by a mortgage filed in any county of a state other than the state of Colorado, the certificate of title shall be delivered to the person who therein appears to be the owner of the home described, or such certificate shall be mailed to the owner thereof at his address as the same may appear in the application, the certificate of title, or other records in the director's office.

   (b) If it appears from the records in the office of the director and from the certificate of title that the manufactured home therein described is subject to one or more mortgages filed subsequent to August 1, 1949, the director shall deliver the certificate of title issued by him to the mortgagee named therein or the holder thereof whose mortgage was first filed in the office of an authorized agent or shall mail the same to such mortgagee or holder at his address as the same appears in the certificate of title to said manufactured home.

§ 38-29-112, C.R.S. Certificate of title – transfer.

(1) Upon the sale or transfer of a manufactured home for which a certificate of title has been issued, the person in whose name said certificate of title is registered, if he is other than a dealer, shall, in his own person or by his duly authorized agent or attorney, execute a formal transfer of the home described in the certificate, which transfer shall be affirmed by a statement signed by the person in whose name said certificate of title is registered or by his duly authorized agent or attorney and shall contain or be accompanied by a written declaration that it is made under the penalties of perjury in the second degree, as defined in section 18-8-503, C.R.S. The purchaser or transferee, within thirty days thereafter, shall present such certificate, duly transferred, together with his application for a new certificate of title to the director or one of his authorized agents, accompanied by the fee required in section 38-29-138 to be paid for the issuance of a new certificate of title; whereupon, a new certificate of title shall be issued and disposition thereof made as required in this article.

(1.3) Prior to the sale or transfer of a manufactured home for which a certificate of title has been issued, a holder of a mortgage that is the legal holder of certificate of title shall provide a copy of the certificate of title to any title insurance agent, title insurance company, or financial institution requesting information related to the payoff of the mortgage within fourteen days of the request.

(1.5) The purchaser or transferee of a manufactured home that becomes permanently affixed at an existing site or is transported to a site and is permanently affixed to the ground so that it is no longer capable of being drawn over the public highways shall present a certificate of transfer as required in subsection (1) of this section, together with his or her application for purging a manufactured home title and a certificate of permanent location, to the authorized agent of the county or city or city and county in which such manufactured home is located. The manufactured home shall become real property upon the filing and recording of the certificate of permanent location in accordance with section 38-29-202. The provisions of articles 30 to 44 of this title and of any other law of this state shall be applicable to manufactured homes that have become real property pursuant to this subsection (1.5) and to instruments creating, disposing of, or otherwise affecting such real property wherever such provisions would be applicable to estates, rights, and interests in land or to instruments creating, disposing of, or otherwise affecting estates, rights, and interest in land. The manufactured home for which a Colorado certificate of title has been issued shall continue to be valued and taxed separately from the land on which it sits until such time that the manufactured home becomes real property pursuant to this subsection (1.5).

(1.7) (a) If the conditions set forth in paragraph (b) of this subsection (1.7) are met, the legal holder of the certificate of title, within forty-five days, shall deliver to the title insurance agent who is the settlement agent related to the sale of the manufactured home the certificate of title or evidence that the holder has lost the certificate of title and requested a duplicate from the department. The holder shall mail or otherwise deliver the duplicate certificate of title to the title insurance agent within five business days of receipt from the department. Upon receipt from the holder, the title insurance agent shall present the certificate of title to the person in whose name the certificate of title is issued or his or her authorized agent or attorney to allow such person to execute a formal transfer as required by subsection (1) of this section.

(b) The provisions of paragraph (a) of this subsection (1.7) shall apply if:

(I) A title insurance agent acts as a settlement agent related to the sale of a manufactured home;

(II) The manufactured home that is sold is the subject of one or more mortgages that have been filed pursuant to section 38-29-128; and

(III) All holders of a mortgage on the manufactured home that have been filed pursuant to section 38-29-128 have been paid in full from the proceeds of the sale.

* (2) *[Editor's note: This version of subsection (2) is effective until March 1, 2022.]* Any person who violates any of the provisions of subsection (1) of this section is guilty of a misdemeanor and, upon conviction thereof, shall be punished by a fine of not less than two hundred fifty dollars nor more than one thousand dollars, or by imprisonment in the county jail for not less than ten days nor more than six months, or by both such fine and imprisonment.

* (2) *[Editor's note: This version of subsection (2) is effective March 1, 2022.]* Any person who violates any of the provisions of subsection (1) of this section commits a class 2 misdemeanor.

(3) Any person who violates the provisions of subsection (1.3) or (1.7) of this section shall be liable to an injured person for any actual economic damages caused by the violation, to be recovered in a civil action in a court of competent jurisdiction.

§ 38-29-113, C.R.S. Lost certificates of title.

(1) Upon the loss in the mails of any certificate of title to a manufactured home and accompanying papers which may be sent by an authorized agent to the director and upon an appropriate application of the owner or other person entitled to such certificate of title directed to the authorized agent therefor, such certificate of title may be reissued bearing such notations respecting existing mortgages on the home therein described as the records of the authorized agent and of the director may indicate are unreleased and constitute an encumbrance upon the home, which certificate of title shall be issued without charge.

(2) If the holder of any certificate of title loses, misplaces, or accidentally destroys any certificate of title to a manufactured home which he holds whether as the holder of a mortgage or as the owner of the home therein described, upon application therefor to the director, the director may issue a duplicate certificate of title as in other cases.

(3) Upon the issuance of any duplicate certificate of title as provided in this section, the director shall note thereon every mortgage shown to be unreleased and the lien of which is in force and effect as may be disclosed by the records in his office and shall dispose of such certificate as in other cases.

§ 38-29-114, C.R.S. New manufactured homes – bill of sale – certificate of title.

(1) Upon the sale or transfer by a dealer of a new manufactured home, such dealer shall, upon the delivery thereof, make, execute, and deliver to the purchaser or transferee a good and sufficient bill of sale therefor, together with the manufacturer's certificate or statement of origin or the filing of a mortgage by the holder of such mortgage pursuant to section 38-29-128. Said bill of sale shall be affirmed by a statement signed by such dealer and shall contain or be accompanied by a written declaration that it is made under the penalties of perjury in the second degree, as defined in section 18-8-503, C.R.S., and the manufacturer's certificate or statement of origin shall be notarized. Both the bill of sale and the manufacturer's certificate or statement of origin shall be in such form as the director may prescribe, and shall contain, in addition to other information which he may by rule from time to time require, the manufacturer and model of the manufactured home so sold or transferred, the identification number placed upon the home by the manufacturer for identification purposes, the manufacturer's suggested retail price or the retail delivered price, and the date of the sale or transfer thereof, together with a description of any mortgage thereon given to secure the purchase price or any part thereof. Upon presentation of such a bill of sale to the director or one of his authorized agents, a new certificate of title for the home therein described shall be issued and disposition thereof made as in other cases. The transfer of a manufactured home which has been used by a dealer for the purpose of demonstration to prospective customers shall be made in accordance with the provisions of this section.

(2) Any purchaser of a new manufactured home that is transported to a site and permanently affixed to the ground so that it is no longer capable of being drawn over the public highways shall not be required to procure a certificate of title thereto as is otherwise required by this article. The purchaser shall file a certificate of permanent location along with the manufacturer's certificate or statement of origin or its equivalent with the clerk and recorder for the county or city and county in which the new manufactured home is permanently affixed to the ground. The manufactured home shall become real property upon the filing and recording of such documents in accordance with section 38-29-202. The provisions of articles 30 to 44 of this title and of any other law of this state shall be applicable to manufactured homes that have become real property pursuant to this subsection (2) and to instruments creating, disposing of, or otherwise affecting such real property wherever such provisions would be applicable to estates, rights, and interests in land or to instruments creating, disposing of, or otherwise affecting estates, rights, and interests in land.

§ 38-29-115, C.R.S. Sale to dealers – certificate need not issue.

Upon the sale or transfer to a dealer of a manufactured home for which a Colorado certificate of title has been issued, formal transfer and delivery of the certificate of title thereto shall be made as in other cases; except that, so long as the home so sold or transferred remains in the dealer's inventory for sale and for no other purpose, such dealer shall not be required to procure the issuance of a new certificate of title thereto as is otherwise required in this article.

§ 38-29-116, C.R.S. Transfers by bequest, descent, law.

Upon the transfer of ownership of a manufactured home by a bequest contained in the will of the person in whose name the certificate of title is registered, or upon the descent and distribution upon the death intestate of the owner of such home, or upon the transfer by operation of law, as in proceedings in bankruptcy, insolvency, replevin, attachment, execution, or other judicial sale, or whenever such manufactured home is sold to satisfy storage or repair charges or repossession is had upon default in the performance of the terms of any mortgage, the director or an authorized agent, upon the surrender of the certificate of title, if the same is available, or upon presentation of such proof of ownership of such home as the director may reasonably require and upon presentation of an application for a certificate of title, as required in section 38-29-107, a new certificate of title may thereupon issue to the person shown by such evidence to be entitled thereto, and disposition shall be made as in other cases.

§ 38-29-117, C.R.S. Certificates for manufactured homes registered in other states.

(1) Whenever any resident of the state acquires the ownership of a manufactured home, located or to be located in the state of Colorado, by purchase, gift, or otherwise, for which a certificate of title has been issued under the laws of a state other than the state of Colorado, the person so acquiring such home upon acquiring the same shall make application to the director or his authorized agent for a certificate of title as in other cases.

(2) If any dealer acquires the ownership by any lawful means whatsoever of a manufactured home, the title to which is registered under the laws of and in a state other than the state of Colorado, such dealer shall not be required to procure a Colorado certificate of title therefor so long as such home remains in the dealer's inventory for sale and for no other purpose.

(3) Upon the sale by a dealer of a manufactured home, the certificate of title to which was issued in a state other than Colorado, the dealer shall immediately deliver to the purchaser or transferee such certificate of title from a state other than Colorado duly and properly endorsed or assigned to the purchaser or transferee, together with the dealer's statement, which shall contain or be

accompanied by a written declaration that it is made under the penalties of perjury in the second degree, as defined in section 18-8-503, C.R.S., and which shall set forth the following:

(a) That such dealer has warranted and, by the execution of such affidavit, does warrant to the purchaser or transferee and all persons claiming or who shall claim under, by, or through the named purchaser or transferee that, at the time of the sale, transfer, and delivery thereof by the dealer, the manufactured home therein described was free and clear of all liens and mortgages, except those which might otherwise appear therein;

(b) That the home therein described is not stolen; and

(c) That such dealer had good, sure, and adequate title thereto and full right and authority to sell and transfer the same.

(4) If the purchaser or transferee of the said manufactured home accompanies his application for a Colorado certificate of title to such home with the affidavit required by subsection (3) of this section and the duly endorsed or assigned certificate of title from a state other than Colorado, a Colorado certificate of title therefor may issue in the same manner as upon the sale or transfer of a manufactured home for which a Colorado certificate of title has been issued. Upon the issuance by the director of such certificate of title, he shall dispose of the same as provided in section 38-29-111.

(5) Each dealer, on or before the fifteenth day of each month, on a form to be provided therefor, shall prepare, subscribe, and send to the auto theft division of the Colorado state patrol a complete description of each manufactured home held by such dealer during the preceding calendar month, or any part thereof, the certificate of title to which was issued by a state other than the state of Colorado or which home was registered under the laws of a state other than the state of Colorado and for which no application for a Colorado certificate of title has been made as provided in this section.

(6) If any person acquires the ownership in a manufactured home for which a certificate of title has been issued under the laws of a state other than the state of Colorado and such home is transported to a site where it is permanently affixed to the ground so that it is no longer capable of being drawn over the public highways, such person shall not be required to procure a new certificate of title as is otherwise required by this article. The owner shall file a certificate of permanent location along with the certificate of title or the manufacturer's certificate or statement of origin or its equivalent with the clerk and recorder for the county or city and county in which the manufactured home is permanently affixed to the ground. The manufactured home shall become real property upon the filing and recording of such documents in accordance with section 38-29-202. The provisions of articles 30 to 44 of this title and of any other law of this state shall be applicable to manufactured homes that have become real property pursuant to this subsection (6) and to instruments creating, disposing of, or otherwise affecting such real property wherever such provisions would be applicable to estates, rights, and interests in land or to instruments creating, disposing of, or otherwise affecting estates, rights, and interests in land.

§ 38-29-118, C.R.S. Surrender and cancellation of certificate – purge of certificate – penalty for violation.

* (1) *[Editor's note: This version of subsection (1) is effective until March 1, 2022.]* The owner of any manufactured home for which a Colorado certificate of title has been issued, upon the destruction or dismantling of said manufactured home or upon its being sold or otherwise disposed of as salvage, shall surrender his or her certificate of title thereto to the director with the request that such certificate of title be canceled and shall submit a certificate of destruction as set forth in section 38-29-204, and such certificate of title may thereupon be canceled. Any person who violates any of the provisions of this subsection (1) commits a class 1 petty offense and, upon conviction thereof, shall be punished as provided in section 18-1.3-503, C.R.S.

§ 38-29-122, C.R.S. Substitute manufactured home identification numbers – inspection.

(1) Any person required to make an application for a certificate of title to a manufactured home shall use the identification number placed upon the home by the manufacturer thereof or an identification number assigned to the home by the department. The certificate of title issued by the department shall use the identification number assigned to the manufactured home.

(2) On and after February 25, 1954, the identification number provided for in this section shall be accepted in lieu of any serial number provided for by law prior to said date.

(3) (a) The department may designate a manufactured home identification inspector to physically inspect a manufactured home in order to verify the following information: The identification number, the make of the manufactured home, the year of manufacture of the manufactured home, and such other information as may be required by the department. A manufactured home identification inspector may charge a fee for the inspection; except that such fee shall not exceed the reasonable costs related to the inspection. A manufactured home identification inspector shall notify the owner of the amount of the fee before commencing any verification activities. If the manufactured home identification inspector determines that the manufactured home identification number has been removed, changed, altered, or obliterated, the owner shall request that the department assign a distinguishing number to the manufactured home pursuant to section 38-29-123.

(b) The department may designate one or more of the following persons to be a manufactured home identification inspector charged with the functions set forth in paragraph (a) of this subsection (3):

(I) An authorized agent as defined in section 38-29-102 (1) or a person designated by such agent;

(II) A Colorado law enforcement officer;

(III) A person registered to sell manufactured homes pursuant to section 24-32-3323, C.R.S.; or

(IV) A county assessor.

§ 38-29-123, C.R.S. Assignment of a special manufactured home identification number by the department of revenue.

The department is authorized to assign a distinguishing number to any manufactured home whenever there is no identifying number thereon or such number has been destroyed, obliterated, or mutilated. In such cases, the department shall provide a form on which the distinguishing number has been assigned to the manufactured home. The distinguishing number shall be affixed to the manufactured home in the door frame or fuse box or as determined by the department. The distinguishing number shall then be the manufactured home identification number. Such manufactured home shall be titled under such distinguishing number in lieu of the former number or absence thereof, or in the event that the manufactured home is affixed to the ground so that it is no longer capable of being drawn over the public highways, the owner shall file the form provided by the department on which the distinguishing number has been assigned with the clerk and recorder for the county or city and county in which the manufactured home is located. The clerk and recorder shall file and record such form in his or her office.

§ 38-29-124, C.R.S. Amended certificate to issue, when.

If the owner of any manufactured home for which a Colorado certificate of title has been issued replaces any part of said home on which appears the identification number or symbol described in the certificate of title and by which said home is known and identified, by reason whereof such identification number or symbol no longer appears thereon, or incorporates the part containing the identification number or symbol into a manufactured home other than the one for which the original certificate of title was issued, immediately thereafter, such owner shall make application to the director or one of his authorized agents for an assigned identification number and an amended certificate of title to such manufactured home.

§ 38-29-125, C.R.S. Security interests upon manufactured homes.

(1) Except as provided in this section, the provisions of the "Uniform Commercial Code", title 4, C.R.S., relating to the filing, recording, releasing, renewal, and extension of mortgages, as the term is defined in section 38-29-102 (9), shall not be applicable to manufactured homes. Any mortgage intended by the parties thereto to encumber or create a lien on a manufactured home, to be effective as a valid lien against the rights of third persons, purchasers for value without notice, mortgagees, or creditors of the owner, shall be filed for public record and the fact thereof noted on the owner's certificate of title or bill of sale substantially in the manner provided in section 38-29-128; and the filing of such mortgage with the authorized agent and the notation by him of that fact on the certificate of title or bill of sale substantially in the manner provided in section 38-29-128 shall constitute notice to the world of each and every right of the person secured by such mortgage.

(2) The provisions of this section and section 38-29-128 shall not apply to any mortgage or security interest upon any manufactured home held for sale or lease which constitutes inventory as defined in section 4-9-102, C.R.S. As to such mortgages or security interests, the provisions of article 9 of title 4, C.R.S., shall apply, and perfection of such mortgages or security interests shall be made pursuant thereto, and the rights of the parties shall be governed and determined thereby.

§ 38-29-126, C.R.S. Existing mortgages not affected.

Nothing in this article shall be construed to impair the rights of the holder of any lien on a manufactured home created by mortgage or otherwise prior to August 1, 1949, which remains unreleased and the undertaking which the lien thereof secures remains undischarged. Nothing in this article shall be construed to relieve the holders of such liens of the duty to file such instruments respecting the undertakings secured thereby as may be required by law to preserve the liens of such mortgages unimpaired.

§ 38-29-127, C.R.S. Foreign mortgages.

No mortgage on a manufactured home, filed for record in any state other than the state of Colorado, shall be valid and enforceable against the rights of subsequent purchasers for value, creditors, or mortgagees having no actual notice of the existence thereof. If the certificate of title for such home, whether issued under the laws of this state or any other state, bears thereon any notation adequate to apprise a purchaser, creditor, or mortgagee of the existence of such mortgage at the time any third party acquires a right in the manufactured home covered thereby, such mortgage and the rights of the holder thereof shall be enforceable in this state the same and with like effect as though such mortgage were filed in the state of Colorado and noted on the certificate of title in the manner prescribed in section 38-29-128.

§ 38-29-128, C.R.S. Filing of mortgage.

The holder of any mortgage on a manufactured home desiring to secure to himself the rights provided for in this article and to have the existence of the mortgage and the fact of the filing thereof for public record noted on the certificate of title to the manufactured home thereby encumbered shall present said mortgage or a duly executed copy or certified copy thereof and the certificate of title to the manufactured home encumbered to the authorized agent of the director in the county or city and county in which the manufactured home is located. Upon the receipt of said mortgage or executed copy or certified copy thereof and certificate of title, the authorized agent, if he is satisfied that the manufactured home described in the mortgage is the same as that described in the certificate of title, shall make and subscribe a certificate to be attached or stamped on the mortgage and on the certificate of title, in which shall appear the day and hour on which said mortgage was received for filing, the name and address of the mortgagee therein named and the name and address of the holder of such mortgage, if such person is other than the mortgagee named, the amount secured thereby, the date thereof, the day and year on which said mortgage was filed for public record, and such other information regarding the filing thereof in the office of the authorized agent as may be required by the director by rule, to which certificate the authorized agent shall affix his signature and the seal of his office.

§ 38-29-129, C.R.S. Disposition of mortgages by agent.

(1) The authorized agent upon receipt of the mortgage shall file the same in his office separately and apart from records affecting real property and personal property, other than manufactured homes, which he may by law be required to keep. Such mortgage shall be appropriately indexed and cross-indexed:

- (a) Under one or more of the following headings in accordance with such rules and regulations relating thereto as may be adopted by the director:
  - (I) Manufacturer, manufacturer's number, or serial number of manufactured homes mortgaged;
  - (II) The numbers of the certificates of title for manufactured homes mortgaged;
- (b) Under the name of the mortgagee, the holder of such mortgage, or the owner of such mortgaged home; or
- (c) Under such other system as the director may devise and determine to be necessary for the efficient administration of this article.

(2) All records of mortgages affecting manufactured homes shall be public and may be inspected and copies thereof made, as is provided by law respecting public records affecting real property.

§ 38-29-130, C.R.S. Disposition after mortgaging.

Within forty-eight hours after a mortgage on a manufactured home has been filed in his office, the authorized agent shall mail to the director the certificate of title or bill of sale on which he has affixed his certificate respecting the filing of such mortgage. Upon the receipt thereof, the director shall note, on records to be kept and maintained by him in his office, the fact of the existence of the mortgage on such manufactured home and other information respecting the date thereof, the date of filing, the amount secured by the lien thereof, the name and address of the mortgagee and of the holder of the mortgage, if such person is other than the mortgagee, and such other information relating thereto as appears in the certificate of the authorized agent affixed to the certificate of title or bill of sale. The director shall thereupon issue a new certificate of title containing, in addition to the other matters and things required to be set forth in certificates of title, a description of the mortgage and all information respecting said mortgage and the filing thereof as may appear in the certificate of the authorized agent, and he shall thereafter dispose of said new certificate of title containing said notation as provided in section 38-29-111.

§ 38-29-131, C.R.S. Release of mortgages.

(1) Upon the payment or discharge of the undertaking secured by any mortgage on a manufactured home that has been filed for record and noted on the certificate of title in the manner prescribed in section 38-29-128, the legal holder of the certificate of title, in a place to be provided therefor, shall make and execute such notation of the discharge of the obligation and release of the mortgage securing the same and set forth therein such facts concerning the right of the holder to so release said mortgage as the director may require by appropriate rule, which satisfaction and release shall be affirmed by a statement signed by the legal holder of the certificate of title and shall contain or be accompanied by a written declaration that it is made under the penalties of perjury in the second degree, as defined in section 18-8-503, C.R.S. Thereupon, except as otherwise provided in section 38-29-112 (1.7), the holder of the mortgage so released shall dispose of the certificate of title as follows:

(a) If it appears from an examination of the certificate of title that the manufactured home therein described is subject to an outstanding junior mortgage or mortgages filed for record subsequent to August 1, 1949, the holder shall deliver the certificate of title to the person so shown to be the holder of the mortgage which was filed earliest in point of time after the filing of the mortgage released or to the person or agent of the person shown to be the assignee or other legal holder of the undertaking secured thereby or shall mail the same to such mortgagee or holder thereof at his address as the same thereon appears. If such certificate is returned unclaimed, it shall thereupon be mailed to the director.

(b) If it appears from an examination of the certificate of title that there are no other outstanding mortgages against the manufactured home therein described, filed for record subsequent to August 1, 1949, upon the release of such mortgage as provided in this section, the holder thereof shall deliver the certificate of title to the owner of the home therein described or shall mail the same to him at his address as the same may therein appear. If for any reason said certificate of title is not delivered to the owner of the home therein described or is returned unclaimed upon the mailing thereof, it shall thereupon be mailed to the director.

§ 38-29-132, C.R.S. New certificate upon release of mortgage.

Upon the release of any mortgage on a manufactured home, filed for record in the manner prescribed in section 38-29-128, the owner of the home encumbered by such mortgage, the purchaser from or transferee of the owner thereof as appears on the certificate of title, or the holder of any mortgage the lien of which was junior to the lien of the mortgage released, whichever the case may be, upon the receipt of the certificate of title, as provided in section 38-29-131, shall deliver the same to the authorized agent who shall transmit the same to the director as in other cases. Upon the receipt by the director of the certificate of title bearing thereon the release and satisfaction of mortgage referred to in section 38-29-131, he shall make such notation on the records in his office as shall show the release of the lien of such mortgage, shall issue a new certificate of title to the manufactured home therein described, omitting therefrom all reference to the mortgage so released, and shall dispose of the new certificate of title in the manner prescribed in other cases.

§ 38-29-133, C.R.S. Duration of lien of mortgage – extensions.

(1) The duration of the lien of any mortgage on a manufactured home shall be for the full term of the mortgage, but the lien of the mortgage may be extended beyond the original term thereof for successive three-year periods during the term of the mortgage or any extension thereof upon the holder thereof presenting the certificate of title, on which the existence of the mortgage has been noted, to the authorized agent of the county wherein said mortgage is filed, together with a notarized written request for an extension of the mortgage or a written request that is made under the penalties of perjury in the second degree, as defined in section 18-8-503, C.R.S., in which shall appear a description of the undertaking secured, to what extent it has been discharged or remains unperformed, and such other and further information respecting the same as may be required by appropriate rule of the director to enable him or her to properly record such extension upon the director's records.

(2) Upon receipt of a mortgage extension, the authorized agent shall make and complete a record of the extension and shall issue a new certificate of title on which the extension of the mortgage is noted. Thereafter the newly issued certificate of title shall be returned to the person shown thereon to be entitled thereto, the same as in other cases. If a mortgage noted on the certificate of title has not been released or extended after its maturity date, the owner of the manufactured home described in the certificate of title may request that any references to the mortgages shown on the records of the authorized agent be removed, and upon the request, the authorized agent shall remove such references.

§ 38-29-134, C.R.S. Priority of mortgages.

The liens of mortgages filed for record and noted on a certificate of title to a manufactured home, as provided in sections 38-29-128 and 38-29-135, shall take priority in the same order that the mortgages creating such liens were filed in the office of the authorized agent.

§ 38-29-135, C.R.S. Second or other junior mortgages.

(1) On and after July 1, 1977, any person who takes a second or other junior mortgage on a manufactured home for which a Colorado certificate of title has been issued may file said mortgage for public record and have the existence thereof noted on the certificate of title with like effect as in other cases, in the manner prescribed in this section.

(2) Such second or junior mortgagee or the holder thereof shall file said mortgage with the authorized agent of the county wherein the manufactured home is located and shall accompany said mortgage with a written request to have the existence thereof noted on the certificate of title to the manufactured home covered thereby, subscribed by such mortgagee or holder, in which shall appear the names and addresses of the holders of all outstanding mortgages against the home described in said second or junior mortgage and the name and address of the person in possession of the certificate of title thereto. Upon the filing of such mortgage, the authorized agent shall note thereon the day and hour on which such mortgage was received by him and shall make and deliver a receipt therefor to the person filing the same.

(3) The authorized agent, by registered mail, return receipt requested, shall make a written demand on the holder of the certificate of title, addressed to such person at his address as the same may appear in said written request, that such certificate be delivered to the authorized agent for the purpose of having noted thereon such second or junior mortgage. Within fifteen days after the receipt of such demand, the person holding such certificate shall either mail or deliver the same to such authorized agent or, if he no longer has possession thereof, shall so notify the agent and, if he knows, shall likewise inform him where and from whom such certificate may be procured. Upon the receipt of such certificate, the authorized agent shall complete his application for a new title and record the number thereof on the mortgage, as in the case of a first mortgage, and shall thereafter transmit the current certificate of title and application for a new certificate of

title to the director. Upon the receipt thereof, the director, as in the case of a first mortgage, shall thereupon issue a new certificate of title on which the existence of all mortgages on the manufactured home, including such second or junior mortgage, have been noted, which certificate he shall dispose of as in other cases.

(4) If any person lawfully in possession of a certificate of title to any manufactured home upon whom demand is made for the delivery thereof to the authorized agent omits, for any reason whatsoever, to deliver or mail the same to the authorized agent, such person shall be liable to the holder of such second or junior mortgage for all damage sustained by reason of such omission.

§ 38-29-136, C.R.S. Validity of mortgage between parties.

Nothing in this article shall be construed to impair the validity of a mortgage on a manufactured home between the parties thereto as long as no purchaser for value, mortgagee, or creditor without actual notice of the existence thereof has acquired an interest in the manufactured home described therein, notwithstanding that the parties to said mortgage have failed to comply with the provisions of this article.

§ 38-29-137, C.R.S. Mechanics', warehouse, and other liens.

Nothing in this article shall be construed to impair the rights of lien claimants arising under any mechanics' lien law in force and effect in this state or the lien of any warehouseman or any other person claimed for repairs on or storage of any manufactured home, when a mechanic's lien or storage lien has originated prior to the time any mortgage on said manufactured home has been filed for record, as provided in section 38-29-125, and such manufactured home has remained continuously in the possession of the person claiming such mechanic's lien or lien for storage, notwithstanding that no notation of such lien is made upon the certificate of title to the home in respect of which it is claimed.

§ 38-29-138, C.R.S. Fees.

(1) (a) Upon filing with the authorized agent any application for a certificate of title, the applicant shall pay to the agent a fee of seven dollars and twenty cents, which shall be disposed pursuant to section 42-6-138, C.R.S.

(b) Repealed.

(2) Upon the receipt by the authorized agent of any mortgage for filing under the provisions of section 38-29-128, the agent shall be paid such fees as are prescribed by law for the filing of like instruments in the office of the county clerk and recorder in the county or city and county in which such mortgage is filed and shall receive, in addition, a fee of seven dollars and twenty cents for the issuance or recording of the certificate of title and the notation of the existence of said mortgage.

(3) Upon application to the authorized agent to have noted on a certificate of title the extension of any mortgage therein described and noted thereon, such authorized agent shall receive a fee of one dollar and fifty cents.

(4) Upon the release and satisfaction of any mortgage and upon application to the authorized agent for the notation thereof on the certificate of title in the manner prescribed in section 38-29-131, such authorized agent shall be paid a fee of seven dollars and twenty cents, which shall be disposed pursuant to section 42-6-138, C.R.S.

(5) For the issuance of any duplicate certificate of title, except as may be otherwise provided in this article, the agent shall be paid a fee of eight dollars and twenty cents, and, in all cases in which

the department assigns a new identifying number to any manufactured home, the fee charged for such assignment shall be three dollars and fifty cents.

(6) The fees provided for in subsections (1) and (2) of this section shall not apply to the issuance of a certificate of title for a tax-deferred mobile home pursuant to the provisions of section 39-3.5-105 (1) (b) (II), C.R.S.

§ 38-29-139, C.R.S. Disposition of fees.

(1) All fees received by the authorized agent under the provisions of section 38-29-138 (1) and (2), upon application being made for a certificate of title, shall be disposed of pursuant to section 42-6-138 (1), C.R.S.

(2) All fees collected by the authorized agent under the provisions of section 38-29-138 (5) shall be disposed of pursuant to section 42-6-138 (2), C.R.S.

(3) All fees paid to the authorized agent under section 38-29-138 (3) for the filing or extension of any mortgage on a manufactured home filed in his or her office shall be kept and retained by said agent to defray the cost thereof and shall be disposed of by him or her as provided by law; except that fees for this service that may be paid to the authorized agent in the city and county of Denver shall, by such agent, be disposed of in the same manner as fees retained by him or her that were paid upon application being made for a certificate of title.

§ 38-29-140, C.R.S. Director's records to be public.

All records in the director's office pertaining to the title to any manufactured home shall be public records and shall be subject to the provisions of section 42-1-206, C.R.S. This shall include any records regarding ownership of and mortgages on any manufactured home for which a Colorado certificate of title has been issued.

§ 38-29-141, C.R.S. Penalties.

(1) No person may:

(a) Sell, transfer, or in any manner dispose of a manufactured home in this state without complying with the requirements of this article.

(b) (Deleted by amendment, L. 89, p. 1573, § 8, effective January 1, 1990.)

* (2) *[Editor's note: This version of subsection (2) is effective until March 1, 2022.]* Any person who violates any of the provisions of subsection (1) of this section for which no other penalty is expressly provided is guilty of a misdemeanor and, upon conviction thereof, shall be punished by a fine of not less than one hundred dollars nor more than five hundred dollars, or by imprisonment in the county jail for not less than ten days nor more than six months, or by both such fine and imprisonment.

* (2) *[Editor's note: This version of subsection (2) is effective March 1, 2022.]* Any person who violates any of the provisions of subsection (1) of this section for which no other penalty is expressly provided commits a class 2 misdemeanor.

§ 38-29-141.5, C.R.S. False oath.

Any person who makes any application for a certificate of title, written transfer thereof, satisfaction and release, oath, affirmation, affidavit, statement, report, or deposition required to be made or taken under any of the provisions of this article and who, upon such application, transfer, satisfaction and release, oath, affirmation, affidavit, statement, report, or deposition, swears or affirms willfully and falsely in a matter material to any issue, point, or subject matter in question, in addition to any other penalties provided in this article, is guilty of perjury in the second degree, as defined in section 18-8-503, C.R.S.

§ 38-29-142, C.R.S. Repossession of manufactured home – owner must notify law enforcement agency – penalty.

(1) If any mortgagee or his assignee or the agent of either repossesses a manufactured home because of default in the terms of a mortgage, the mortgagee or his assignee shall notify, either verbally or in writing, a law enforcement agency, as provided in this section, of the fact of such repossession, the name of the owner, and the name of the mortgagee or assignee. Such notification shall be made not later than twelve hours after the repossession occurs. If such repossession takes place in an incorporated city or town, the notification shall be made to the police department, town marshal, or other local law enforcement agency of such city or town, and, if such repossession takes place in the unincorporated area of a county, the notification shall be made to the county sheriff.

(2) Any mortgagee of a manufactured home or his assignee who violates the provisions of this section is guilty of a misdemeanor and, upon conviction thereof, shall be punished by a fine of not less than fifty dollars nor more than one hundred dollars.

§ 38-29-143, C.R.S. Change of location – penalty.

(1) The owner shall file notice of any change of location within the county with the county assessor and the county treasurer or change of location from one county to another county with the county assessor and the county treasurer of each county within twenty days after such change of location occurs. For the purposes of this subsection (1), "owner" shall mean the owner at the time of the change of location.

(2) Any person who fails to file notice of any change of location as required by subsection (1) of this section is guilty of a misdemeanor traffic offense and, upon conviction thereof, shall be punished by a fine of not less than one hundred dollars nor more than one thousand dollars. This shall be a strict liability offense.

§ 38-29-201, C.R.S. Verification of application form – supporting materials.

(1) In all instances under part 1 of this article in which an application for a certificate of title is filed with an authorized agent pursuant to section 38-29-107, the authorized agent, in his or her capacity as the clerk and recorder, shall file and record the documents set forth in subsection (2) of this section in his or her office.

(2) (a) For an application for a certificate of title for a new manufactured home, the following documents shall be filed and recorded:

- (I) The manufacturer's certificate or statement of origin or its equivalent; and
- (II) (Deleted by amendment, L. 2009, (SB 09-040), ch. 9, p. 67, § 8, effective July 1, 2009.)
- (III) The verification of application form.

(b) For an application for a certificate of title for which a bond is furnished pursuant to section 38-29-119 (2), the following documents shall be filed and recorded:

- (I) A copy of the written declaration required pursuant to section 38-29-119 (1);
- (II) A copy of the bond that was furnished; and
- (III) The verification of application form.

(c) For all other applications for a certificate of title, the following documents shall be filed and recorded:

- (I) A copy of the certificate of title presented to the authorized agent, if any; and
- (II) The verification of application form.

(3) A verification of application form shall comply with the federal "Driver's Privacy Protection Act of 1994", 18 U.S.C. sec. 2721 *et seq.*

§ 38-29-202, C.R.S. Certificate of permanent location.

(1) (a) If a manufactured home is permanently affixed to the ground so that it is no longer capable of being drawn over the public highways on or after July 1, 2008, the owner of the manufactured home shall file a certificate of permanent location.

(b) If the certificate of permanent location accompanies an application for purging a manufactured home title pursuant to section 38-29-112 (1.5) or 38-29-118 (2), the certificate shall be filed with the authorized agent for the county or city and county in which the manufactured home is located. For a manufactured home that occupies real property subject to a long-term lease that has an express term of at least ten years, a copy of the lease shall be filed along with the certificate. The authorized agent, in his or her capacity as the clerk and recorder, shall file and record the certificate of permanent location and, if applicable, the copy of the long-term lease in his or her office.

(c) If the certificate of permanent location is received in accordance with section 38-29-114 (2) or 38-29-117 (6), the certificate shall be filed with the clerk and recorder for the county or city and county in which the manufactured home is located. For a manufactured home that occupies real property subject to a long-term lease that has an express term of at least ten years, a copy of the lease shall be filed along with the certificate. The clerk and recorder shall file and record the certificate of permanent location, a copy of the bill of sale, a copy of the manufacturer's certificate or statement of origin or its equivalent, and, if applicable, the copy of the long-term lease in his or her office and destroy the original manufacturer's certificate or statement of origin or its equivalent.

(d) At least one of the owners of the manufactured home, as reflected on the certificate of title, the bill of sale, or the manufacturer's certificate or statement of origin or its equivalent, must be an owner of record of the real property to which the manufactured home is to be affixed or permanently located; except that this paragraph (d) shall not apply to any manufactured home that occupies real property subject to a long-term lease that has an express term of at least ten years.

(2) The property tax administrator shall establish the form of the certificate of permanent location. In addition to any other information that the administrator may require, the certificate shall include the following:

(a) The name and mailing address of the owner of the manufactured home;

(b) The name and mailing address of any holder of a mortgage on the manufactured home or on the real property to which the home has been affixed;

(c) The identification number of the manufactured home and the certificate of title number, if applicable;

(d) The manufacturer or make and year of the manufactured home;

(e) Attached to the certificate of permanent location, a certificate of taxes due, or an authentication of paid ad valorem taxes, issued by the county treasurer of the county in which the manufactured home is located;

(f) The legal description of the real property to which the manufactured home has been permanently affixed;

(g) The name of the legal owner or owners of the land upon which the home is affixed;

(h) The county or city and county in which the certificate of permanent location is filed;

(i) Verification that the manufactured home is permanently affixed to the ground so that it is no longer capable of being drawn over the public highways in accordance with any applicable county or city and county codes or requirements;

(j) Consent to the permanent location of the manufactured home by all holders of a security interest in the manufactured home;

(k) An affirmative statement of relinquishment and release of all rights in the manufactured home by all holders of a security interest in the manufactured home;

(*l*) An affirmative statement of relinquishment of all rights in the manufactured home by any owner on the certificate of title of the manufactured home who is not also an owner of the real property to which the manufactured home is to be affixed or permanently located. The provisions of this paragraph (l) shall not apply to any manufactured home that occupies real property subject to a long-term lease that has an express term of at least ten years.

(*l*.5) For any manufactured home that occupies real property subject to a long-term lease that has an express term of at least ten years, an affirmative statement that all owners of the real property and the manufactured home consent to the affixation of the manufactured home to the real property and an acknowledgment that, upon such affixation and upon the filing and recording of the certificate of permanent location, the manufactured home will become a part of the real property, subject to the reversion of the manufactured home to the owners of the home upon termination of the long-term lease; and

(m) An affirmative statement that all owners of the real property and the manufactured home consent to the affixation of the manufactured home to the real property and an acknowledgment that upon such affixation and upon the filing and recording of the certificate of permanent location the manufactured home will become a part of the real property and ownership shall be vested only in the title owners of the real property. Ownership in the manufactured home shall vest in the same parties and be subject to the same tenancies, encumbrances, liens, limitations, restrictions, and estates as the real property to which the manufactured home is affixed or permanently located. The provisions of this paragraph (m) shall not apply to any manufactured home that occupies real property subject to a long-term lease that has an express term of at least ten years.

(3) The certificate of permanent location shall be acknowledged and shall contain or be accompanied by a written declaration that the statements made therein are made under the penalties of perjury in the second degree, as defined in section 18-8-503, C.R.S.

§ 38-29-203, C.R.S. Certificate of removal.

(1) (a) On or after July 1, 2008, a manufactured home shall not be removed from its permanent location unless the owner of the manufactured home files a certificate of removal. If a certificate of permanent location has not been previously filed and recorded for the manufactured home, the owner shall also file an affidavit of real property, described in section 38-29-208, along with the certificate of removal.

(b) The certificate of removal and the affidavit of real property, if any, along with the application for a new certificate of title required in part 1 of this article, shall be filed with the authorized agent for the county or city and county in which the manufactured home is located. The authorized agent, in his or her capacity as the clerk and recorder, shall file and record the certificate of removal and the affidavit of real property in his or her office.

(2) The property tax administrator shall establish the form of the certificate of removal. In addition to any other information that the administrator may require, the certificate shall include the following:

(a) The name and mailing address of the owner of the manufactured home;

(b) The name and mailing address of any holder of a mortgage on or lien against the real property on which the manufactured home was affixed or permanently located;

(c) The identification number of the manufactured home;

(d) The manufacturer or make and year of the manufactured home;

(e) Attached to the certificate of removal, a certificate of taxes due, or an authentication of paid ad valorem taxes, issued by the county treasurer of the county in which the manufactured home is located;

(f) The legal description of the real property from which the manufactured home was removed; and

(g) Consent of all lienholders and a release by all holders of a mortgage, only to the extent that the mortgage or lien applies to the manufactured home, to allow the removal of the manufactured home from its permanent location.

(2.5) (a) The provisions of this section shall apply to a manufactured home that occupies real property subject to a long-term lease that has an express term of at least ten years, except as set forth in paragraph (b) of this subsection (2.5).

(b) A landlord evicting a tenant who owns a manufactured home that occupies real property subject to a long-term lease that has an express term of at least ten years may cause the home to be removed from its permanent location without the owner first filing a certificate of removal if, within twenty days after such removal, the landlord files a certificate of removal accompanied by a copy of the notice of judgment or order for possession allowing the eviction of the home and the address of the location to which the home has been moved. Such certificate of removal shall comply with subsection (5) of this section and include the information required in subsection (2) of this section; except that paragraphs (e) and (g) of said subsection (2) shall not apply. The landlord shall file the certificate of removal and the additional information with the authorized agent for the county or city and county from which the manufactured home was removed.

(3) The consent of a mortgage or other lien holder on the certificate of removal shall serve as a full release of any interest against the manufactured home once the manufactured home is removed from the real property. The consent on the certificate of removal shall not release any interest of the mortgage or lien holder against the remaining real property.

(4) If consent of any mortgagee or lien holder is not given, the owner may file a corporate surety bond or any other undertaking with the clerk of the district court of the county in which the real property to which the manufactured home was affixed is situated. The bond or undertaking shall be in an amount equal to one and one-half times the amount of the mortgage or lien and shall be approved by a judge of the district court with which the bond or undertaking is filed. The bond or undertaking shall be conditioned that, if the mortgagee or lien holder shall be finally adjudged to be entitled to recover upon the mortgage or lien, the principal or his sureties shall pay to the mortgagee or lien holder the amount of the indebtedness together with any interest, costs, and other sums which the mortgagee or lien holder would be entitled to recover upon foreclosure of the mortgage or lien. Upon the filing of a bond or undertaking, the mortgage or lien against the property shall be forthwith discharged and released in full, and the real property described in the bond or undertaking shall be released from the mortgage or lien and from any action brought to foreclose the mortgage or lien, and the bond or undertaking shall be substituted. The clerk of the district court with which the bond or undertaking has been filed shall issue a certificate of release that shall be recorded in the office of the clerk and recorder of the county in which the real property to which the manufactured home was affixed is situated, and the certificate of release shall show that the property has been released from the mortgage or lien and from any action brought to foreclose the mortgage or lien.

(5) The certificate of removal shall be acknowledged and shall contain or be accompanied by a written declaration that the statements made therein are made under the penalties of perjury in the second degree, as defined in section 18-8-503, C.R.S.

§ 38-29-204, C.R.S. Certificate of destruction.

(1) (a) If a manufactured home is destroyed, dismantled, or sold or otherwise disposed of as salvage on or after July 1, 2008, the owner of the manufactured home or the person on whose real property the manufactured home is situated shall file a certificate of destruction.

(b) If the certificate of destruction accompanies an application to cancel a certificate of title pursuant to section 38-29-118 (1), the certificate shall be filed with the authorized agent for the county or city and county in which the manufactured home is or was located. The authorized agent, in his or her capacity as the clerk and recorder, shall file and record the certificate of destruction in his or her office.

(c) If an application to cancel a certificate of title is not required pursuant to section 38-29-118 (1) because no certificate of title was ever issued or because the title has been purged, the certificate of destruction shall be filed with the county clerk and recorder for the county or city and county in which the manufactured home is or was located. The clerk and recorder shall file and record the certificate of destruction in his or her office.

(d) (I) Notwithstanding any other provision of law, if a manufactured home has been deemed materially dangerous or materially hazardous, pursuant to local building or health codes by a governmental entity, the person on whose real property the manufactured home is situated may file and record a certificate of destruction without attaching a certificate of taxes due or an authentication of paid ad valorem taxes and without surrendering a certificate of title or filing an application to cancel a certificate of title. Any certificate of destruction filed and recorded pursuant to this paragraph (d) shall be accompanied by the evidence of violation.

(II) The certificate of destruction and the evidence of violation shall be filed and recorded with the clerk and recorder for the county or city and county in which the manufactured home is or was located. The clerk and recorder shall file and record the certificate of destruction and the evidence of violation in his or her office.

(III) For purposes of this paragraph (d):

(A) "Evidence of violation" means a notice and order from a governmental entity that a manufactured home has been deemed materially dangerous or materially hazardous pursuant to local building or health codes and that all applicable cure periods have expired.

(B) "Governmental entity" means any federal agency, the state, or any county, town, city, or city and county.

(2) The property tax administrator shall establish the form of the certificate of destruction. In addition to any other information that the administrator may require, the certificate shall include the following:

(a) The name and mailing address of the owner of the manufactured home;

(b) The name and mailing address of each holder of a security interest in the manufactured home and all holders of a lien against the real property on which the manufactured home was affixed or permanently located;

(c) The identification number of the manufactured home;

(d) The manufacturer or make and year of the manufactured home;

(e) Attached to the certificate of destruction, a certificate of taxes due, or an authentication of paid ad valorem taxes, issued by the county treasurer of the county in which the manufactured home is located;

(f) The legal description of the real property on which the manufactured home was affixed or permanently located prior to destruction;

(g) A book and page or reception number reference for a certificate of permanent location that was previously filed related to the manufactured home, if any;

(h) Consent of all lienholders to the destruction of the manufactured home, or proof that a request for such consent was sent by certified mail to such lienholders, along with proof that a copy of the request for such consent was mailed to the owner if the certificate of destruction is filed by the person on whose real property the manufactured home is situated, at their last-known address and a notarized declaration, signed under penalty of perjury, that no response was received from any such lienholders within thirty days of the date of the mailing of the notice;

(i) Release of all holders of a mortgage to the extent that the mortgage applies to the manufactured home, or proof that a request for such consent was sent by certified mail to such mortgage holders at their last-known address and a notarized declaration, signed under penalty of perjury, that no response was received within thirty days of the date of the mailing of the notice; and

(j) Verification that the manufactured home has been destroyed, dismantled, or sold or otherwise disposed of as salvage.

(3) The certificate of destruction shall be acknowledged and shall contain or be accompanied by a written declaration that the statements made therein are made under the penalties of perjury in the second degree, as defined in section 18-8-503, C.R.S.

(4) Any owner or person on whose real property the manufactured home is situated who fails to file a properly completed certificate of destruction when required pursuant to this section shall be responsible for all actual damages sustained by any affected party related to the manufactured home being destroyed, dismantled, or sold or otherwise disposed of as salvage.

§ 38-29-205, C.R.S. Authorized agent – forward to the clerk and recorder.

If an authorized agent who receives a document for filing and recording pursuant to this part 2 is not the clerk and recorder for the county or city and county, the authorized agent shall forward such document to the clerk and recorder, for the clerk and recorder to file and record the document in his or her office.

§ 38-29-206, C.R.S. Recorded documents – index.

Any document filed and recorded by a clerk and recorder pursuant to this part 2 shall be indexed in both the grantor and grantee indexes under the name of the owner or owners of the manufactured home and the owners of the land to which the manufactured home was affixed or permanently located at the time the document is required to be filed and recorded.

§ 38-29-207, C.R.S. Copy of certificates to assessor.

The clerk and recorder shall forward a copy of a certificate of permanent location, certificate of removal, and certificate of destruction to the assessor for the county or city and county.

§ 38-29-208, C.R.S. Affidavit of real property.

(1) Any person can prove that a manufactured home and the land upon which it has been permanently affixed is real property by filing an affidavit of real property with the clerk and recorder for the county or city and county in which the manufactured home is located. The

clerk and recorder shall file and record the affidavit of real property in his or her office. Except as otherwise set forth in subsection (2) of this section, the affidavit of real property shall include the following:

(a) An acknowledged statement by all owners that the manufactured home and real property to which the manufactured home is permanently affixed became real property pursuant to this article;

(b) A statement from the county assessor that the manufactured home has been valued together with the land upon which it is affixed;

(c) A statement from the county treasurer that taxes have been paid on the manufactured home and the land upon which it is affixed in the same manner as other real property, as that term is defined in section 39-1-102 (14), C.R.S.;

(d) Proof that a search of the director's records pursuant to section 42-1-206, C.R.S., was conducted and that no certificate of title was found for the manufactured home; and

(e) Verification that the manufactured home is permanently affixed to the ground in accordance with any applicable county or city and county codes or requirements so that it is no longer capable of being drawn over the public highways.

(2) If a manufactured home occupies real property subject to a long-term lease that has an express term of at least ten years, then the affidavit of real property shall include the following:

(a) A copy of the applicable long-term lease;

(b) A statement from the county treasurer that taxes have been paid separately on the manufactured home and the land upon which it is affixed; and

(c) The items set forth in paragraphs (a), (d), and (e) of subsection (1) of this section.

§ 38-29-209, C.R.S. Fees – disposition.

(1) In all instances in which a document is to be filed and recorded pursuant to this part 2, the authorized agent or clerk and recorder, as the case may be, shall be paid such fees for each document so filed and recorded as are prescribed by law for the filing of like instruments in the office of the county clerk and recorder.

(2) The recording fees authorized by this section are in addition to any fees that are required pursuant to section 38-29-138.

(3) All fees paid pursuant to this section shall be kept and retained by the authorized agent or the clerk and recorder to defray the cost thereof and shall be disposed of by him or her as provided by law.

V. Nondisclosure of Information Psychologically Impacting Real Property

§ 38-35.5-101, C.R.S. Circumstances psychologically impacting real property – no duty for broker or salesperson to disclose.

(1) Facts or suspicions regarding circumstances occurring on a parcel of property which could psychologically impact or stigmatize such property are not material facts subject to a disclosure requirement in a real estate transaction. Such facts or suspicions include, but are not limited to, the following:

(a) That an occupant of real property is, or was at any time suspected to be, infected or has been infected with human immunodeficiency virus (HIV) or diagnosed with acquired immune deficiency syndrome (AIDS), or any other disease which has been determined by medical evidence to be highly unlikely to be transmitted through the occupancy of a dwelling place; or

(b) That the property was the site of a homicide or other felony or of a suicide.

(2) No cause of action shall arise against a real estate broker or salesperson for failing to disclose such circumstance occurring on the property which might psychologically impact or stigmatize such property.

VI. Soil and Hazard Analyses of Residential Construction

§ 6-6.5-101, C.R.S. Disclosure to purchaser – penalty.

(1) At least fourteen days prior to closing the sale of any new residence for human habitation, every developer or builder or their representatives shall provide the purchaser with a copy of a summary report of the analysis and the site recommendations. For sites in which significant potential for expansive soils is recognized, the builder or his representative shall supply each buyer with a copy of a publication detailing the problems associated with such soils, the building methods to address these problems during construction, and suggestions for care and maintenance to address such problems.

(2) In addition to any other liability or penalty, any builder or developer failing to provide the report or publication required by subsection (1) of this section shall be subject to a civil penalty of five hundred dollars payable to the purchaser.

(3) The requirements of this section shall not apply to any individual constructing a residential structure for his own residence.

VII. Uniform Power of Attorney Act

§ 15-14-702, C.R.S. Definitions.

Except as otherwise provided under this part 7, and except as the context may otherwise require, in this part 7:

(1) "Agent" means a person granted authority to act for a principal under a power of attorney, whether denominated an agent, attorney-in-fact, or otherwise. The term includes an original agent, coagent, successor agent, and a person to which an agent's authority is delegated.

(2) "Durable", with respect to a power of attorney, means not terminated by the principal's incapacity.

(3) "Electronic" means relating to technology having electrical, digital, magnetic, wireless, optical, electromagnetic, or similar capabilities.

(4) "Good faith" means honesty in fact.

(5) "Incapacity" means inability of an individual to manage property or business affairs because the individual:

(a) Has an impairment in the ability to receive and evaluate information or make or communicate decisions even with the use of technological assistance; or

(b) Is:

(I) Missing;

(II) Detained, including incarcerated in a penal system; or

(III) Outside the United States and unable to return.

(6) "Person" means an individual, corporation, business trust, estate, trust, partnership, limited liability company, association, joint venture, public corporation, government or governmental subdivision, agency, or instrumentality, or any other legal or commercial entity.

(7) "Power of attorney" means a writing or other record that grants authority to an agent to act in the place of the principal, whether or not the term power of attorney is used.

(8) "Presently exercisable general power of appointment", with respect to property or a property interest subject to a power of appointment, means power exercisable at the time in question to vest absolute ownership in the principal individually, the principal's estate, the principal's creditors, or the creditors of the principal's estate. The term includes a power of appointment not exercisable until the occurrence of a specified event, the satisfaction of an ascertainable standard, or the passage of a specified period only after the occurrence of the specified event, the satisfaction of the ascertainable standard, or the passage of the specified period. The term does not include a power exercisable in a fiduciary capacity or only by will.

(9) "Principal" means an individual who grants authority to an agent in a power of attorney.

(10) "Property" means anything that may be the subject of ownership, whether real or personal, or legal or equitable, or any interest or right therein.

(11) "Record" means information that is inscribed on a tangible medium or that is stored in an electronic or other medium and is retrievable in perceivable form.

(12) "Sign" means, with present intent to authenticate or adopt a record:

(a) To execute or adopt a tangible symbol; or

(b) To attach to or logically associate with the record an electronic sound, symbol, or process.

(13) "State" means a state of the United States, the District of Columbia, Puerto Rico, the United States Virgin Islands, or any territory or insular possession subject to the jurisdiction of the United States.

(14) "Stocks and bonds" means stocks, bonds, mutual funds, and all other types of securities and financial instruments, whether held directly, indirectly, or in any other manner. The term does not include commodity futures contracts and call or put options on stocks or stock indexes.

§ 15-14-714, C.R.S. Agent's duties.

(1) Notwithstanding provisions in the power of attorney, an agent that has accepted appointment shall:

(a) Act in accordance with the principal's reasonable expectations to the extent actually known by the agent and, otherwise, in the principal's best interest;

(b) Act in good faith; and

(c) Act only within the scope of authority granted in the power of attorney.

(2) Except as otherwise provided in the power of attorney, an agent that has accepted appointment shall:

(a) Act loyally for the principal's benefit;

(b) Act so as not to create a conflict of interest that impairs the agent's ability to act impartially in the principal's best interest;

(c) Act with the care, competence, and diligence ordinarily exercised by agents in similar circumstances;

(d) Keep a record of all receipts, disbursements, and transactions made on behalf of the principal;

(e) Cooperate with a person that has authority to make health care decisions for the principal to carry out the principal's reasonable expectations to the extent actually known by the agent and, otherwise, act in the principal's best interest; and

(f) Attempt to preserve the principal's estate plan, to the extent actually known by the agent, if preserving the plan is consistent with the principal's best interest based on all relevant factors, including:

(I) The value and nature of the principal's property;

(II) The principal's foreseeable obligations and need for maintenance;

(III) Minimization of taxes, including income, estate, inheritance, generation-skipping transfer, and gift taxes; and

(IV) Eligibility for a benefit, a program, or assistance under a statute or regulation.

(3) An agent that acts in good faith is not liable to any beneficiary of the principal's estate plan for failure to preserve the plan.

(4) An agent that acts with care, competence, and diligence for the best interest of the principal is not liable solely because the agent also benefits from the act or has an individual or conflicting interest in relation to the property or affairs of the principal.

(5) If an agent is selected by the principal because of special skills or expertise possessed by the agent or in reliance on the agent's representation that the agent has special skills or expertise, the special skills or expertise must be considered in determining whether the agent has acted with care, competence, and diligence under the circumstances.

(6) Absent a breach of duty to the principal, an agent is not liable if the value of the principal's property declines.

(7) An agent that exercises authority provided in the power of attorney to delegate to another person the authority granted by the principal or that engages another person on behalf of the principal is not liable for an act, error of judgment, or default of that person if the agent exercises care, competence, and diligence in selecting and monitoring the person.

(8) Except as otherwise provided in the power of attorney, an agent is not required to disclose receipts, disbursements, or transactions conducted on behalf of the principal unless ordered by a court or requested by the principal, a guardian, a conservator, another fiduciary acting for the principal, a governmental agency having authority to protect the welfare of the principal, or, upon the death of the principal, by the personal representative or successor in interest of the principal's estate. If so requested, within thirty days the agent shall comply with the request or provide a writing or other record substantiating why additional time is needed and shall comply with the request within an additional thirty days.

§ 15-14-726, C.R.S. Construction of authority generally.

(1) Except as otherwise provided in the power of attorney, by executing a power of attorney that incorporates by reference a subject described in sections 15-14-727 to 15-14-740 or that grants to an agent authority to do all acts that a principal could do pursuant to section 15-14-724 (3), a principal authorizes the agent, with respect to that subject, to:

(a) Demand, receive, and obtain by litigation or otherwise money or another thing of value to which the principal is, may become, or claims to be entitled and conserve, invest, disburse, or use anything so received or obtained for the purposes intended;

(b) Contract in any manner with any person, on terms agreeable to the agent, to accomplish a purpose of a transaction and perform, rescind, cancel, terminate, reform, restate, release, or modify the contract or another contract made by or on behalf of the principal;

(c) Execute, acknowledge, seal, deliver, file, or record any instrument or communication the agent considers desirable to accomplish a purpose of a transaction, including creating at any time a schedule listing some or all of the principal's property and attaching it to the power of attorney;

(d) Initiate, participate in, submit to alternative dispute resolution, settle, oppose, or propose or accept a compromise with respect to a claim existing in favor of or against the principal or intervene in litigation relating to the claim;

(e) Seek on the principal's behalf the assistance of a court or other governmental agency to carry out an act authorized in the power of attorney;

(f) Engage, compensate, and discharge an attorney, accountant, discretionary investment manager, expert witness, or other advisor;

(g) Prepare, execute, and file a record, report, or other document to safeguard or promote the principal's interest under a statute or regulation;

(h) Communicate with any representative or employee of a government or governmental subdivision, agency, or instrumentality on behalf of the principal;

(i) Access communications intended for and communicate on behalf of the principal, whether by mail, electronic transmission, telephone, or other means; and

(j) Do any lawful act with respect to the subject and all property related to the subject.

§ 15-14-727, C.R.S. Real property.

(1) Unless the power of attorney otherwise provides, language in a power of attorney granting general authority with respect to real property authorizes the agent to:

(a) Demand, buy, lease, receive, accept as a gift or as security for an extension of credit, or otherwise acquire or reject an interest in real property or a right incident to real property;

(b) Sell; exchange; convey with or without covenants, representations, or warranties; quitclaim; release; surrender; retain title for security; encumber; partition; consent to partitioning; subject to an easement or covenant; subdivide; apply for zoning or other governmental permits; plat or consent to platting; develop; grant an option concerning; lease; sublease; contribute to an entity in exchange for an interest in that entity; or otherwise grant or dispose of an interest in real property or a right incident to real property;

(c) Pledge or mortgage an interest in real property or right incident to real property as security to borrow money or pay, renew, or extend the time of payment of a debt of the principal or a debt guaranteed by the principal;

(d) Release, assign, satisfy, or enforce by litigation or otherwise a mortgage, deed of trust, conditional sale contract, encumbrance, lien, or other claim to real property that exists or is asserted;

(e) Manage or conserve an interest in real property or a right incident to real property owned or claimed to be owned by the principal, including:

(I) Insuring against liability or casualty or other loss;

(II) Obtaining or regaining possession of or protecting the interest or right by litigation or otherwise;

(III) Paying, assessing, compromising, or contesting taxes or assessments or applying for and receiving refunds in connection with them; and

(IV) Purchasing supplies, hiring assistance or labor, and making repairs or alterations to the real property;

(f) Use, develop, alter, replace, remove, erect, or install structures or other improvements upon real property in or incident to which the principal has, or claims to have, an interest or right;

(g) Participate in a reorganization with respect to real property or an entity that owns an interest in or right incident to real property and receive, and hold, and act with respect to stocks and bonds or other property received in a plan of reorganization, including:

(I) Selling or otherwise disposing of them;

(II) Exercising or selling an option, right of conversion, or similar right with respect to them; and

(III) Exercising any voting rights in person or by proxy;

(h) Change the form of title of an interest in or right incident to real property; and

(i) Dedicate to public use, with or without consideration, easements or other real property in which the principal has or claims to have an interest.

VIII. Relief of Residential Taxpayers from Lien of Special District Taxes for General Obligation Indebtedness

Certification and Notice of Special District Taxes for General Obligation Indebtedness

§ 32-1-1601, C.R.S. Legislative declaration.

The general assembly hereby finds and declares that special districts are political subdivisions and instrumentalities of the state of Colorado and local governments thereof. The general assembly further finds that defaults in payment of general obligation debts and the possibility of further defaults by some special districts have resulted in a general loss of confidence by investors in bonds and undertakings of all types issued or to be issued by local governments of the state and have imposed severe hardship on investors in general obligation bonds of special districts and upon owners of residential real property within such districts. The general assembly further finds that this part 16 is necessary to protect the credit reputation of local governments of this state, to restore confidence of investors in local government obligations, and to protect owners of residential real property within special districts.

§ 32-1-1602, C.R.S. Definitions.

As used in this part 16, unless the context otherwise requires:

(1) "General obligation debt" means an obligation of a special district created by a resolution of the special district authorizing the issuance of bonds or a contract, the obligations of which are backed by a pledge of the full faith and credit of the special district and a covenant to impose mill levies without limit to retire the bonds or fund the contractual obligation.

(2) "Special district" shall have the same meaning as provided in section 32-1-103 (20).

§ 32-1-1603, C.R.S. Separate mill levies – certification to county commissioners.

After July 1, 1992, special districts which levy taxes for payment of general obligation debt shall certify separate mill levies to the board of county commissioners, one each for funding requirements of each such debt in accordance with the relevant contracts or bond resolutions which identifies each bond issue by series, date, coupon rate, and maturity and each contract by title, date, principal amount, and maturity and one for the remainder of the budget of said district.

§ 32-1-1604, C.R.S. Recording.

Whenever a special district authorizes or incurs a general obligation debt, a notice of such action and a description of such debt in a form prescribed by the director of the division of local government in the department of local affairs shall be recorded by the special district with the county clerk and recorder in each county in which the district is located. The recording shall be done within thirty days after authorizing or incurring the debt.

§ 32-1-1605, C.R.S. Limitations on actions – prior law.

Any claim for relief under section 32-1-1504, as it existed prior to July 1, 1992, shall be commenced on or before January 1, 1993, and not thereafter.

§ 10-11-122, C.R.S. Title commitments – rules.

(1) Every title insurance agent or title insurance company shall provide, along with each commitment for an owner's policy of title insurance pertaining to a sale of residential real property as defined in section 39-1-102 (14.5), C.R.S., a statement disclosing the following information:

(a) That the subject real property may be located in a special taxing district;

(b) That a certificate of taxes due listing each taxing jurisdiction will be obtained from the county treasurer of the county in which the subject real property is located or that county treasurer's authorized agent unless the proposed insured provides written instructions to the contrary; and

(c) That information regarding special districts and the boundaries of such districts may be obtained from the board of county commissioners, the county clerk and recorder, or the county assessor.

(2) Failure of a title insurance agent or a title insurance company to provide the statement required by subsection (1) of this section shall subject such agent or company to the penalty provisions of section 10-3-111 but shall not affect or invalidate any provisions of the commitment for title insurance.

(3) (a) Before issuing any owner's policy of title insurance pertaining to a sale of residential real property, unless the proposed insured provides written instructions to the contrary, a title insurance agent or title insurance company shall obtain a certificate of taxes due from the county treasurer or the county treasurer's authorized agent.

(b) To address circumstances in which a certificate of taxes cannot be obtained from the county treasurer or the county treasurer's authorized agent during the period in which the county treasurer is certifying the tax rolls, the commissioner of insurance shall promulgate rules, in accordance with article 4 of title 24, C.R.S., that identify alternative documentation that may be used and relied upon during that period. If a title insurance agent or title insurance company uses alternative documentation during this period, the agent or company shall obtain a tax certificate when it becomes available from the county treasurer or the county treasurer's authorized agent.

* (4) (a) If a title insurance agent or title insurance company is required to provide the statement required by subsection (1) of this section, the agent or company shall also provide a statement substantially as follows:

* **COLORADO NOTARIES MAY REMOTELY NOTARIZE REAL ESTATE DEEDS AND OTHER DOCUMENTS USING REAL-TIME AUDIO-VIDEO COMMUNICATION TECHNOLOGY. YOU MAY CHOOSE NOT TO USE REMOTE NOTARIZATION FOR ANY DOCUMENT.**

* (b) Failure of a person to provide the statement required by this subsection (4) does not subject the person to any liability under this article 11 or to the penalty provisions of section 10-3-111 and does not affect or invalidate any provisions of the commitment for title insurance.

§ 38-35.7-101, C.R.S. Disclosure – special taxing districts – general obligation indebtedness.

(1) Every contract for the purchase and sale of residential real property shall contain a disclosure statement in bold-faced type which is clearly legible and in substantially the following form:

SPECIAL TAXING DISTRICTS MAY BE SUBJECT TO GENERAL OBLIGATION INDEBTEDNESS THAT IS PAID BY REVENUES PRODUCED FROM ANNUAL TAX LEVIES ON THE TAXABLE

PROPERTY WITHIN SUCH DISTRICTS. PROPERTY OWNERS IN SUCH DISTRICTS MAY BE PLACED AT RISK FOR INCREASED MILL LEVIES AND TAX TO SUPPORT THE SERVICING OF SUCH DEBT WHERE CIRCUMSTANCES ARISE RESULTING IN THE INABILITY OF SUCH A DISTRICT TO DISCHARGE SUCH INDEBTEDNESS WITHOUT SUCH AN INCREASE IN MILL LEVIES. BUYERS SHOULD INVESTIGATE THE SPECIAL TAXING DISTRICTS IN WHICH THE PROPERTY IS LOCATED BY CONTACTING THE COUNTY TREASURER, BY REVIEWING THE CERTIFICATE OF TAXES DUE FOR THE PROPERTY, AND BY OBTAINING FURTHER INFORMATION FROM THE BOARD OF COUNTY COMMISSIONERS, THE COUNTY CLERK AND RECORDER, OR THE COUNTY ASSESSOR.

[Ed. Note: The above disclosure is printed in all versions of the Real Estate Commission-approved "Contract to Buy and Sell Real Estate."]

(2) The obligation to provide the disclosure set forth in subsection (1) of this section shall be upon the seller, and, in the event of the failure by the seller to provide the written disclosure described in subsection (1) of this section, the purchaser shall have a claim for relief against the seller for all damages to the purchaser resulting from such failure plus court costs.

IX. Colorado Consumer Protection Act

Section 12-10-217, C.R.S., lists as a cause for disciplinary action and possible revocation of a real estate license, the conviction of a violation of § 6-1-105(1), C.R.S., known as The Colorado Consumer Protection Act. There are both criminal and civil penalties for conviction that include monetary awards and actual damages to the injured party in a private civil action.

Printed below are the portions of the law pertinent to the real estate industry.

§ 6-1-104, C.R.S. Cooperative reporting.

The district attorneys may cooperate in a statewide reporting system by receiving, on forms provided by the attorney general, complaints from persons concerning deceptive trade practices listed in section 6-1-105 and part 7 of this article and transmitting such complaints to the attorney general.

§ 6-1-105, C.R.S. Deceptive trade practices.

(1) A person engages in a deceptive trade practice when, in the course of the person's business, vocation, or occupation, the person:

- (a) Knowingly passes off goods, services, or property as those of another;
- (b) Knowingly makes a false representation as to the source, sponsorship, approval, or certification of goods, services, or property;
- (c) Knowingly makes a false representation as to affiliation, connection, or association with or certification by another;
- (d) Uses deceptive representations or designations of geographic origin in connection with goods or services;
- (e) Knowingly makes a false representation as to the characteristics, ingredients, uses, benefits, alterations, or quantities of goods, food, services, or property or a false representation as to the sponsorship, approval, status, affiliation, or connection of a person therewith;
- (f) Represents that goods are original or new if he knows or should know that they are deteriorated, altered, reconditioned, reclaimed, used, or secondhand;

(g) Represents that goods, food, services, or property are of a particular standard, quality, or grade, or that goods are of a particular style or model, if he knows or should know that they are of another;

(h) Disparages the goods, services, property, or business of another by false or misleading representation of fact;

(i) Advertises goods, services, or property with intent not to sell them as advertised;

(j) Advertises goods or services with intent not to supply reasonably expectable public demand, unless the advertisement discloses a limitation of quantity;

(k) Advertises under the guise of obtaining sales personnel when in fact the purpose is to first sell a product or service to the sales personnel applicant;

(*l*) Makes false or misleading statements of fact concerning the price of goods, services, or property or the reasons for, existence of, or amounts of price reductions;

(m) Fails to deliver to the customer at the time of an installment sale of goods or services a written order, contract, or receipt setting forth the name and address of the seller, the name and address of the organization which he represents, and all of the terms and conditions of the sale, including a description of the goods or services, stated in readable, clear, and unambiguous language;

(n) Employs "bait and switch" advertising, which is advertising accompanied by an effort to sell goods, services, or property other than those advertised or on terms other than those advertised and which is also accompanied by one or more of the following practices:

  (I) Refusal to show the goods or property advertised or to offer the services advertised;

  (II) Disparagement in any respect of the advertised goods, property, or services or the terms of sale;

  (III) Requiring tie-in sales or other undisclosed conditions to be met prior to selling the advertised goods, property, or services;

  (IV) Refusal to take orders for the goods, property, or services advertised for delivery within a reasonable time;

  (V) Showing or demonstrating defective goods, property, or services which are unusable or impractical for the purposes set forth in the advertisement;

  (VI) Accepting a deposit for the goods, property, or services and subsequently switching the purchase order to higher-priced goods, property, or services; or

  (VII) Failure to make deliveries of the goods, property, or services within a reasonable time or to make a refund therefor;

(o) Knowingly fails to identify flood-damaged or water-damaged goods as to such damages;

(p) Solicits door-to-door as a seller, unless the seller, within thirty seconds after beginning the conversation, identifies himself or herself, whom he or she represents, and the purpose of the call;

(p.3) to (p.7) Repealed.

(q) Contrives, prepares, sets up, operates, publicizes by means of advertisements, or promotes any pyramid promotional scheme;

(r) Advertises or otherwise represents that goods or services are guaranteed without clearly and conspicuously disclosing the nature and extent of the guarantee, any material conditions or limitations in the guarantee which are imposed by the guarantor, the manner in which the guarantor will perform, and the identity of such guarantor. Any representation that goods or services are "guaranteed for life" or have a "lifetime guarantee" shall contain, in addition to the other requirements of this paragraph (r), a conspicuous disclosure of the meaning of "life" or "lifetime" as used in such representation (whether that of the purchaser, the goods or services, or otherwise). Guarantees shall not be used which under normal conditions could not be practically fulfilled or which are for such a period of time or are otherwise of such a nature as to have the capacity and tendency of misleading purchasers or prospective purchasers into believing that the goods or services so guaranteed have a greater degree of serviceability, durability, or performance capability in actual use than is true in fact. The provisions of this paragraph (r) apply not only to guarantees but also to warranties, to disclaimer of warranties, to purported guarantees and warranties, and to any promise or representation in the nature of a guarantee or warranty; however, such provisions do not apply to any reference to a guarantee in a slogan or advertisement so long as there is no guarantee or warranty of specific merchandise or other property.

(s) and (t) Repealed.

(u) Fails to disclose material information concerning goods, services, or property which information was known at the time of an advertisement or sale if such failure to disclose such information was intended to induce the consumer to enter into a transaction;

(v) Disburses funds in connection with a real estate transaction in violation of section 38-35-125 (2), C.R.S.;

(w) Repealed.

* (x) Violates sections 6-1-203 to 6-1-206 or part 7 of this article 1;

(y) Fails, in connection with any solicitation, oral or written, to clearly and prominently disclose immediately adjacent to or after the description of any item or prize to be received by any person the actual retail value of each item or prize to be awarded. For the purposes of this paragraph (y), the actual retail value is the price at which substantial sales of the item were made in the person's trade area or in the trade area in which the item or prize is to be received within the last ninety days or, if no substantial sales were made, the actual cost of the item or prize to the person on whose behalf any contest or promotion is conducted; except that, whenever the actual cost of the item to the provider is less than fifteen dollars per item, a disclosure that "actual cost to the provider is less than fifteen dollars" may be made in lieu of disclosure of actual cost. The provisions of this paragraph (y) shall not apply to a promotion which is soliciting the sale of a newspaper, magazine, or periodical of general circulation, or to a promotion soliciting the sale of books, records, audio tapes, compact discs, or videos when the promoter allows the purchaser to review the merchandise without obligation for at least seven days and provides a full refund within thirty days after the receipt of the returned merchandise or when a membership club operation is in conformity with rules and regulations of the federal trade commission contained in 16 CFR 425.

(z) Refuses or fails to obtain all governmental licenses or permits required to perform the services or to sell the goods, food, services, or property as agreed to or contracted for with a consumer;

(aa) Fails, in connection with the issuing, making, providing, selling, or offering to sell of a motor vehicle service contract, to comply with the provisions of article 11 of title 42, C.R.S.;

(bb) Repealed.

(cc) Engages in any commercial telephone solicitation which constitutes an unlawful telemarketing practice as defined in section 6-1-304;

(dd) Repealed.

(ee) Intentionally violates any provision of article 10 of title 5, C.R.S.;

(ee.5) to (ff) Repealed.

(gg) Fails to disclose or misrepresents to another person, a secured creditor, or an assignee by whom such person is retained to repossess personal property whether such person is bonded in accordance with section 4-9-629, C.R.S., or fails to file such bond with the attorney general;

(hh) Violates any provision of article 16 of this title;

(ii) Repealed.

(jj) Represents to any person that such person has won or is eligible to win any award, prize, or thing of value as the result of a contest, promotion, sweepstakes, or drawing, or that such person will receive or is eligible to receive free goods, services, or property, unless, at the time of the representation, the person has the present ability to supply such award, prize, or thing of value;

(kk) Violates any provision of article 6 of this title;

(*ll*) Knowingly makes a false representation as to the results of a radon test or the need for radon mitigation;

(mm) Violates section 35-27-113 (3) (e), (3) (f), or (3) (i), C.R.S.;

(nn) Repealed.

(oo) Fails to comply with the provisions of section 35-80-108 (1) (a), (1) (b), or (2) (f), C.R:S.;

(pp) Violates article 9 of title 42, C.R.S.;

(qq) Repealed.

(rr) Violates the provisions of part 8 of this article;

(ss) Violates any provision of part 33 of article 32 of title 24, C.R.S., that applies to the installation of manufactured homes;

(tt) Violates any provision of part 9 of this article;

(uu) Violates section 38-40-105, C.R.S.;

(vv) Violates section 24-21-523 (1)(f) or (1)(i) or 24-21-525 (3), (4), or (5);

(ww) Violates any provision of section 6-1-702;

(xx) Violates any provision of part 11 of this article;

(yy) Repealed.

(zz) Violates any provision of section 6-1-717;

(aaa) Violates any provision of section 12-61-904.5, C.R.S.;

(bbb) Violates any provision of section 12-61-905.5, C.R.S.;

(ccc) Violates the provisions of section 6-1-722.

(ddd) Violates section 6-1 724;

(eee) Violates section 6-1-701.

(fff) Violates section 6-1-723;

(ggg) Violates section 6-1-725;

* (hhh) Knowingly represents that hemp, hemp oil, or any derivative of a hemp plant constitutes retail marijuana or medical marijuana unless it fully satisfies the definition of such products pursuant to section 44-12-103 (22) or section 44-11-104 (11);

(iii) Knowingly enters into, or attempts to enforce, an agreement regarding the recovery of an overbid on foreclosed property if the agreement concerns the recovery of funds in the possession of:

(I) A public trustee prior to transfer of the funds to the state treasurer under section 38-38-111, C.R.S.; or

(II) The state treasurer and does not meet the requirements for such an agreement as specified in section 38-13-128.5, C.R.S.;

(jjj) Violates section 6-1-726.

(2) Evidence that a person has engaged in a deceptive trade practice shall be prima facie evidence of intent to injure competitors and to destroy or substantially lessen competition.

(3) The deceptive trade practices listed in this section are in addition to and do not limit the types of unfair trade practices actionable at common law or under other statutes of this state.

§ 6-1-113, C.R.S. Damages.

(1) The provisions of this article shall be available in a civil action for any claim against any person who has engaged in or caused another to engage in any deceptive trade practice listed in this article. An action under this section shall be available to any person who:

(a) Is an actual or potential consumer of the defendant's goods, services, or property and is injured as a result of such deceptive trade practice, or is a residential subscriber, as defined in section 6-1-903 (9), who receives unlawful telephone solicitation, as defined in section 6-1-903 (10); or

(b) Is any successor in interest to an actual consumer who purchased the defendant's goods, services, or property; or

(c) In the course of the person's business or occupation, is injured as a result of such deceptive trade practice.

(2) Except in a class action or a case brought for a violation of section 6-1-709, any person who, in a private civil action, is found to have engaged in or caused another to engage in any deceptive trade practice listed in this article shall be liable in an amount equal to the sum of:

(a) The greater of:

(I) The amount of actual damages sustained; or

(II) Five hundred dollars; or

(III) Three times the amount of actual damages sustained, if it is established by clear and convincing evidence that such person engaged in bad faith conduct; plus

(b) In the case of any successful action to enforce said liability, the costs of the action together with reasonable attorney fees as determined by the court.

(2.3) As used in subsection (2) of this section, "bad faith conduct" means fraudulent, willful, knowing, or intentional conduct that causes injury.

(2.5) Notwithstanding the provisions of subsection (2) of this section, in the case of any violation of section 6-1-709, in addition to interest, costs of the action, and reasonable attorney fees as determined by the court, the prevailing party shall be entitled only to damages in an amount sufficient to refund moneys actually paid for a manufactured home not delivered in accordance with the provisions of section 6-1-709.

(2.7) Notwithstanding the provisions of subsection (2) of this section, in the case of any violation of section 6-1-105 (1) (ss), the court may award reasonable costs of the action and attorney fees and interest, and in addition, the prevailing party shall be entitled only to damages in an amount sufficient to refund moneys actually paid for the installation of a manufactured home not installed in accordance with the provisions of part 33 of article 32 of title 24, C.R.S., that apply to the installation of manufactured homes.

(3) Any person who brings an action under this article that is found by the court to be groundless and in bad faith or for the purpose of harassment shall be liable to the defendant for the costs of the action together with reasonable attorney fees as determined by the court.

(4) Costs and attorney fees shall be awarded to the attorney general or a district attorney in all actions where the attorney general or the district attorney successfully enforces this article.

§ 6-1-703, C.R.S. Time shares and resale time shares – deceptive trade practices.

(1) A person engages in a deceptive trade practice when, in the course of the person's business, vocation, or occupation, the person engages in one or more of the following activities in connection with the advertisement or sale of a time share or the provision of a time share resale service:

(a) Misrepresents:

(I) The investment, resale, or rental value of any time share;

(II) The conditions under which a purchaser may exchange the right to use accommodations or facilities in one location for the right to use accommodations or facilities in another location; or

(III) The period of time during which the accommodations or facilities contracted for will be available to the purchaser;

(b) Fails to allow any purchaser a right to rescind the sale of a time share or a time share resale service within five calendar days after the sale;

(c) (I) Fails to provide conspicuous notice on the contract of the right of a purchaser of a time share or time share resale service to rescind the sale in writing either by electronic means, mail, or hand delivery.

(II) For purposes of this section, notice of rescission is given:

(A) If by mail, when postmarked;

(B) If by electronic mail or other electronic means, when sent; or

(C) If by hand delivery, when delivered to the seller's place of business.

(d) Fails to refund any down payment or deposit made pursuant to a time share contract or contract for time share resale service within seven days after the seller or time share resale entity receives the purchaser's written notice of rescission; except that, if the purchaser's check has not cleared at the time notice of rescission is received, the person has seven additional days after receipt of funds from the purchaser's cleared check to refund the down payment or deposit;

(e) With respect to the sale or solicitation of any time share resale service, makes false or misleading statements, including statements concerning:

(I) The existence of offers to buy or rent the resale time share;

(II) The likelihood of, or the time necessary to complete, any sale, rental, transfer, or invalidation;

(III) The value of the resale time share;

(IV) The current or future costs of owning the resale time share, including assessments, maintenance fees, or taxes;

(V) How amounts paid by the purchaser of the time share resale service will be utilized;

(VI) The method or source from which the name, address, telephone number, or other contact information of the owner of the resale time share was obtained;

(VII) The identity of the time share resale entity or that entity's affiliates; or

(VIII) The terms and conditions upon which the time share resale service is offered;

(f) Engages in any time share resale service without first obtaining a written contract to provide the service, which contract is signed by the purchaser of the time share resale service and complies with the requirements of this section. For purposes of paragraph (c) of this subsection (1), the required notice of rescission rights applicable to a contract for a time share resale service is conspicuous if printed in at least fourteen-point, bold-faced type immediately preceding the space in the contract provided for the purchaser's signature. In addition to any other remedy provided in this article, a time share resale service contract that does not satisfy the requirements of this section is voidable at the option of the purchaser for up to one year after the date the purchaser executes the contract.

(g) With respect to time share resale transfer agreements, fails to comply with any provision of, or otherwise makes false or misleading statements in connection with, any disclosure or other act required to be made or observed under section 6-1-703.5.

(2) The unlawful practices listed in this section are in addition to, and do not limit, the types of deceptive trade practices actionable under section 6-1-105.

(3) No person shall knowingly circumvent the requirements of this section or section 6-1-703.5.

(4) (a) A person who, as director, officer, or agent of a time share resale entity or as agent of a person who violates this article, assists or aids, directly or indirectly, in a violation of this article is responsible equally with the person for which the person acts.

(b) In the prosecution of a person as officer, director, or agent, it is sufficient to allege and prove the unlawful intent of the person or entity for which the person acts.

§ 6-1-703.5, C.R.S. Time share resale transfer agreements – deceptive trade practices.

(1) A time share resale entity engages in a deceptive trade practice when the entity fails to include in a time share resale transfer agreement the following information:

(a) The name, telephone number, and physical address of the time share resale entity and the name and address of any agent or third-party service provider who will perform any of the time share resale services for that time share resale entity;

(b) A description of the applicable resale time share legally sufficient for recording or other legal transfer;

(c) A description of the method or documentation by which the transfer of the resale time share will be completed, including whether:

(I) The owner of the resale time share will retain any interest in the resale time share following the transfer; and

(II) The owner of the resale time share must grant a power of attorney or otherwise delegate any authority necessary to complete the transfer of the resale time share and the scope of the authority delegated by the owner of the resale time share;

(d) If the owner of the resale time share will retain any interest in the resale time share, a description of the interests retained by the owner of the resale time share;

(e) A listing of any fees, costs, or other consideration that the owner of the resale time share must pay or reimburse for performance of the time share resale service;

(f) A statement that neither the time share resale entity nor any affiliate or agent of the entity shall collect from the owner of the resale time share any fees, costs, or other consideration until the time share resale entity:

(I) Provides the owner of the resale time share a copy of the recordable deed or other equivalent written evidence clearly demonstrating that the resale time share has been transferred to a subsequent transferee in accordance with the time share resale transfer agreement and applicable law; and

(II) Satisfies all other requirements of this section;

(g) The date by which all acts sufficient to transfer the resale time share in accordance with the time share resale transfer agreement are estimated to be completed. The time share resale entity shall use commercially reasonable good faith efforts to complete the transfer of the subject time share within the estimated period. Commercially reasonable good faith efforts include making a request to the association of time share owners pursuant to section 38-33.3-316 (8), C.R.S., for a written statement detailing unpaid assessments levied against the time share.

(h) A statement as to whether any person, including the owner of the resale time share, may occupy, rent, exchange, or otherwise exercise any form of use of the resale time share during the term of the time share resale transfer agreement;

(i) The name of any person, other than the owner of the resale time share, who will receive any rents, profits, or other consideration or thing of value, if any, generated from the transfer of the applicable resale time share or the use of the applicable resale time share during the term of the time share resale transfer agreement;

(j) The following statement clearly and conspicuously and in substantially the following form:

> We [name of time share resale entity] will use commercially reasonable good faith efforts to transfer ownership of your resale time share to another person within the period we estimate for completing the transfer. Until the transfer of ownership is complete, you, the resale time share owner, will continue to be responsible for the payment of all costs and fees associated with your resale time share, including, as applicable, regular assessments, special assessments, and real and personal property taxes.

(k) A statement that the time share resale entity will notify the following persons or entities, in writing, when ownership of the resale time share is transferred, as applicable:

(I) The association of time share owners or other persons responsible for managing or operating the plan or arrangement by which the rights or interests associated with the applicable time share resale are utilized; and

(II) The exchange company operating any exchange program that the resale time share was part of at the time the transfer was completed.

(2) In making the disclosures required under this section, the time share resale entity may rely upon information provided in writing by the owner of the applicable resale time share or the developer, association of time share owners, or other person responsible for managing or operating the plan or arrangement by which the rights or interests associated with the applicable resale time share are utilized.

(3) A time share resale entity shall not transfer or offer to assist in transferring a resale time share, or receive consideration in connection with the transfer of a resale time share, if the time share resale entity knows that the transferee does not have the ability or the intent to fulfill the obligations of ownership of the resale time share, including the obligation to pay all assessments and taxes incurred in connection with ownership of the resale time share. If a time share resale entity transfers or offers to transfer, or receives compensation in connection with the transfer of, a resale time share to a person who has a demonstrated pattern of nonpayment of assessments or taxes or the demonstrated inability to meet payment obligations, the actions of the time share resale entity are prima facie evidence of a violation of this subsection (3).

(4) A time share resale entity shall supervise, manage, and control all aspects of the time share resale transfer agreement and the offering of the resale time share by any affiliate, agent, contractor, or employee of that time share resale entity. A violation of this section is a violation by the time share resale entity and by the person actually committing the conduct that constitutes the violation.

(5) If a time share resale entity engages in an act that is prohibited by this section, either directly or as a means to avoid or circumvent the purpose of this section, a person injured by the act may bring a private civil action pursuant to section 6-1-113.

§ 6-1-709, C.R.S. Sales of manufactured homes – deceptive trade practices.

A person engages in a deceptive trade practice when, in the course of such person's business, vocation, or occupation, such person engages in conduct that constitutes an unlawful manufactured home sale practice as described in section 24-32-3326, C.R.S.

X. Disclosure – Methamphetamine Laboratory

CONCERNING MANDATORY DISCLOSURE IN CONNECTION WITH THE PURCHASE OF RESIDENTIAL REAL PROPERTY OF WHETHER THE PROPERTY HAS BEEN USED AS A METHAMPHETAMINE LABORATORY. (EFFECTIVE JANUARY 1, 2007)

§ 38-35.7-103, C.R.S. Disclosure – methamphetamine laboratory.

(1) A buyer of residential real property has the right to test the property for the purpose of determining whether the property has ever been used as a methamphetamine laboratory.

(2) (a) Tests conducted pursuant to this section shall be performed by a certified industrial hygienist or industrial hygienist, as those terms are defined in section 24-30-1402, C.R.S., and in accordance with the procedures and standards established by rules of the state board of health promulgated pursuant to section 25-18.5-102, C.R.S. If the buyer's test results indicate that the property has been contaminated with methamphetamine or other contaminants for which standards have been established pursuant to section 25-18.5-102, C.R.S., and has not been remediated to meet the standards established by rules of the state board of health promulgated pursuant to section 25-18.5-102, C.R.S., the buyer shall promptly give written notice to the seller of the results of the test, and the buyer may terminate the contract. The contract shall not limit the rights to test the property or to cancel the contract based upon the result of the tests.

(b) The seller shall have thirty days after receipt of the notice to conduct a second independent test. If the seller's test results indicate that the property has been used as a methamphetamine laboratory but has not been remediated to meet the standards established by rules of the state board of health promulgated pursuant to section 25-18.5-102, C.R.S., then the second independent hygienist shall so notify the seller.

(c) If the seller receives a notice under this subsection (2) and does not elect to have the property retested under this subsection (2), then an illegal drug laboratory used to manufacture methamphetamine has been discovered. Nothing in this section prohibits a buyer from purchasing the property and assuming liability under section 25-18.5-103, C.R.S., if, on the date of closing, the buyer provides notice to the department of public health and environment and governing body of the purchase and assumption of liability and if the remediation required by section 25-18.5-103, C.R.S., is completed within ninety days after the date of closing.

(3) (a) Except as specified in subsection (4) of this section, the seller shall disclose in writing to the buyer whether the seller knows that the property was previously used as a methamphetamine laboratory.

(b) A seller who fails to make a disclosure required by this section at or before the time of sale and who knew of methamphetamine production on the property is liable to the buyer for:

(I) Costs relating to remediation of the property according to the standards established by rules of the state board of health promulgated pursuant to section 25-18.5-102, C.R.S.;

(II) Costs relating to health-related injuries occurring after the sale to residents of the property caused by methamphetamine production on the property; and

(III) Reasonable attorney fees for collection of costs from the seller.

(c) A buyer shall commence an action under this subsection (3) within three years after the date on which the buyer closed the purchase of the property where the methamphetamine production occurred.

(4) If the seller becomes aware that the property was an illegal drug laboratory and remediates the property in accordance with the standards established by section 25-18.5-102, C.R.S., and receives certificates of compliance under section 25-18.5-102 (1) (e), C.R.S., then:

(a) The seller shall not be required to disclose that the property was used as a methamphetamine laboratory to a buyer; and

(b) The property is no longer eligible for inclusion in any government-sponsored informational service listing properties that have been used for the production of methamphetamine.

(5) For purposes of this section, "residential real property" includes a: Manufactured home; mobile home; condominium; townhome; home sold by the owner, a financial institution, or the federal department of housing and urban development; rental property, including an apartment; and short-term residence such as a motel or hotel.

Illegal Drug Laboratories

§ 25-18.5-101, C.R.S. Definitions.

As used in this article, unless the context otherwise requires:

(1) "Board" means the state board of health in the department of public health and environment.

(2) "Certified industrial hygienist" means an individual who is certified by the American board of industrial hygiene or its successor.

(3) "Clean-up standards" means the acceptable standards for the remediation of an illegal drug laboratory involving methamphetamine, as established by the board under section 25-18.5-102.

(4) "Consultant" means a certified industrial hygienist or industrial hygienist who is not an employee, agent, representative, partner, joint venture participant, or shareholder of the contractor or of a parent or subsidiary company of the contractor, and who has been certified under section 25-18.5-106.

(5) "Contractor" means a person:

(a) Hired to decontaminate an illegal drug laboratory in accordance with the procedures established by the board under section 25-18.5-102; and

(b) Certified by the department under section 25-18.5-106.

(6) "Department" means the Colorado department of public health and environment.

(7) "Governing body" means the agency or office designated by the city council or board of county commissioners where the property in question is located. If there is no such designation, the governing body shall be the county, district, or municipal public health agency, building department, and law enforcement agency with jurisdiction over the property in question.

(8) "Illegal drug laboratory" means the areas where controlled substances, as defined by section 18-18-102, C.R.S., have been manufactured, processed, cooked, disposed of, used, or stored and all proximate areas that are likely to be contaminated as a result of the manufacturing, processing, cooking, disposal, use, or storage.

(9) "Industrial hygienist" has the same meaning as set forth in section 24-30-1402 (2.2), C.R.S.

(10) "Property" means anything that may be the subject of ownership, including land, buildings, structures, and vehicles.

(11) "Property owner", for the purposes of real property, means the person holding record fee title to real property. "Property owner" also means the person holding title to a manufactured home.

§ 25-18.5-102, C.R.S. Illegal drug laboratories – rules.

(1) The board shall promulgate rules in accordance with section 24-4-103, C.R.S., as necessary to implement this article, including:

(a) Procedures for testing contamination, evaluating contamination, and establishing the acceptable standards for cleanup of illegal drug laboratories involving methamphetamine;

(b) Procedures for a training and certification program for people involved in the assessment, decontamination, and sampling of illegal drug laboratories. The board may develop different levels of training and certification requirements based on a person's prior experience in the assessment, decontamination, and sampling of illegal drug laboratories.

(c) A definition of "assessment", "decontamination", and "sampling" for purposes of this article;

(d) Procedures for the approval of persons to train consultants or contractors in the assessment, decontamination, or sampling of illegal drug laboratories; and

(e) Procedures for contractors and consultants to issue certificates of compliance to property owners upon completion of assessment, decontamination, and sampling of illegal drug laboratories to certify that the remediation of the property meets the clean-up standards established by the board under paragraph (a) of this subsection (1).

(2) The board shall establish fees for the following:

(a) Certification of persons involved in the assessment, decontamination, and sampling of illegal drug laboratories;

(b) Monitoring of persons involved in the assessment, decontamination, and sampling of illegal drug laboratories, if necessary to ensure compliance with this article; and

(c) Approval of persons involved in training for consultants or contractors under paragraph (d) of subsection (1) of this section.

(3) The board shall adopt rules for determining administrative penalties for violations of this article, based on the factors enumerated in section 25-18.5-107 (2) (g).

§ 25-18.5-103, C.R.S. Discovery of illegal drug laboratory – property owner – cleanup – liability.

(1) (a) Upon notification from a peace officer that chemicals, equipment, or supplies of an illegal drug laboratory are located on a property, or when an illegal drug laboratory is otherwise discovered and the property owner has received notice, the owner of any contaminated property shall meet the clean-up standards for property established by the board in section 25-18.5-102; except that a property owner may, subject to paragraph (b) of this subsection (1), elect instead to demolish the contaminated property. If the owner elects to demolish the contaminated property, the governing body or, if none has been designated, the county, district, or municipal public health agency, building department, or law enforcement agency with jurisdiction over the property may require the owner to fence off the property or otherwise make it inaccessible for occupancy or intrusion.

(b) An owner of personal property within a structure or vehicle contaminated by illegal drug laboratory activity has ten days after the date of discovery of the laboratory or contamination to remove or clean the property according to board rules and paragraph (c) of this subsection (1). If the personal property owner fails to remove the personal property within ten days, the owner of the structure or vehicle may dispose of the personal property during the clean-up process without liability to the owner of the personal property for the disposition.

(c) A person who removes personal property or debris from a drug laboratory shall secure the property and debris to prevent theft or exposing another person to any toxic or hazardous chemicals until the property and debris is appropriately disposed of or cleaned according to board rules.

(2) (a) Except as specified in paragraph (b) of this subsection (2), once a property owner has received certificates of compliance from a contractor and a consultant in accordance with section 25-18.5-102 (1) (e), or has demolished the property, or has met the clean-up standards and documentation requirements of this section as it existed before August 7, 2013, the property owner:

(I) Shall furnish copies of the certificates of compliance to the governing body; and

(II) Is immune from a suit brought by a current or future owner, renter, occupant, or neighbor of the property for health-based civil actions that allege injury or loss arising from the illegal drug laboratory.

(b) A person convicted for the manufacture of methamphetamine or for possession of chemicals, supplies, or equipment with intent to manufacture methamphetamine is not immune from suit.

(3) (Deleted by amendment, L. 2013.)

§ 25-18.5-104, C.R.S. Entry into illegal drug laboratories.

(1) If a structure or vehicle has been determined to be contaminated or if a governing body or law enforcement agency issues a notice of probable contamination, the owner of the structure or vehicle shall not permit any person to have access to the structure or vehicle unless:

(a) The person is trained or certified to handle contaminated property under board rules or federal law; or

(b) The owner has received certificates of compliance under section 25-18.5-102 (1) (e).

§ 25-18.5-105, C.R.S. Drug laboratories – governing body – authority.

(1) Governing bodies may declare an illegal drug laboratory that has not met the clean-up standards set by the board in section 25-18.5-102 a public health nuisance.

(2) Governing bodies may enact ordinances or resolutions to enforce this article, including preventing unauthorized entry into contaminated property; requiring contaminated property to meet clean-up standards before it is occupied; notifying the public of contaminated property; coordinating services and sharing information between law enforcement, building, public health, and social services agencies and officials; and charging reasonable inspection and testing fees.

XI. Common Interest Community Disclosure

§ 38-35.7-102, C.R.S. Disclosure – common interest community – obligation to pay assessments – requirement for architectural approval.

(1) On and after January 1, 2007, every contract for the purchase and sale of residential real property in a common interest community shall contain a disclosure statement in bold-faced type that is clearly legible and in substantially the following form:

THE PROPERTY IS LOCATED WITHIN A COMMON INTEREST COMMUNITY AND IS SUBJECT TO THE DECLARATION FOR SUCH COMMUNITY. THE OWNER OF THE PROPERTY WILL BE REQUIRED TO BE A MEMBER OF THE OWNER'S ASSOCIATION FOR THE COMMUNITY AND WILL BE SUBJECT TO THE BYLAWS AND RULES

AND REGULATIONS OF THE ASSOCIATION. THE DECLARATION, BYLAWS, AND RULES AND REGULATIONS WILL IMPOSE FINANCIAL OBLIGATIONS UPON THE OWNER OF THE PROPERTY, INCLUDING AN OBLIGATION TO PAY ASSESSMENTS OF THE ASSOCIATION. IF THE OWNER DOES NOT PAY THESE ASSESSMENTS, THE ASSOCIATION COULD PLACE A LIEN ON THE PROPERTY AND POSSIBLY SELL IT TO PAY THE DEBT. THE DECLARATION, BYLAWS, AND RULES AND REGULATIONS OF THE COMMUNITY MAY PROHIBIT THE OWNER FROM MAKING CHANGES TO THE PROPERTY WITHOUT AN ARCHITECTURAL REVIEW BY THE ASSOCIATION (OR A COMMITTEE OF THE ASSOCIATION) AND THE APPROVAL OF THE ASSOCIATION. PURCHASERS OF PROPERTY WITHIN THE COMMON INTEREST COMMUNITY SHOULD INVESTIGATE THE FINANCIAL OBLIGATIONS OF MEMBERS OF THE ASSOCIATION. PURCHASERS SHOULD CAREFULLY READ THE DECLARATION FOR THE COMMUNITY AND THE BYLAWS AND RULES AND REGULATIONS OF THE ASSOCIATION.

(2) (a) The obligation to provide the disclosure set forth in subsection (1) of this section shall be upon the seller, and, in the event of the failure by the seller to provide the written disclosure described in subsection (1) of this section, the purchaser shall have a claim for relief against the seller for actual damages directly and proximately caused by such failure plus court costs. It shall be an affirmative defense to any claim for damages brought under this section that the purchaser had actual or constructive knowledge of the facts and information required to be disclosed.

(b) Upon request, the seller shall either provide to the buyer or authorize the unit owners' association to provide to the buyer, upon payment of the association's usual fee pursuant to section 38-33.3-317 (4), all of the common interest community's governing documents and financial documents, as listed in the most recent available version of the contract to buy and sell real estate promulgated by the real estate commission as of the date of the contract.

(3) This section shall not apply to the sale of a unit that is a time share unit, as defined in section 38-33-110 (7).

XII. Equity Skimming

§ 18-5-802, C.R.S. Equity skimming of real property.

(1) A person commits the crime of equity skimming of real property if the person knowingly:

(a) Acquires an interest in real property that is encumbered by a loan secured by a mortgage or deed of trust and the loan is in arrears at the time the person acquires the interest or is placed in default within eighteen months after the person acquires the interest; and

(b) Either:

(I) Fails to apply all rent derived from the person's interest in the real property first toward the satisfaction of all outstanding payments due on the loan and second toward any fees due to any association of real property owners that charges such fees for the upkeep of the housing facility, or common area including buildings and grounds thereof, of which the real property is a part before appropriating the remainder of such rent or any part thereof for any other purpose except for the purpose of repairs necessary to prevent waste of the real property; or

(II) After a foreclosure in which title has vested pursuant to section 38-38-501, C.R.S., collects rent on behalf of any person other than the owner of the real property.

(2) Repealed.

(3) Equity skimming of real property is a class 5 felony.

(4) It shall be an affirmative defense to this section:

(a) That all deficiencies in all underlying encumbrances at the time of acquisition have been fully satisfied and brought current and that, in addition, any regular payments on the underlying encumbrances during the succeeding nine months after the date of acquisition have been timely paid in full; except that this shall not be an affirmative defense to a crime that includes the element set forth in subparagraph (II) of paragraph (b) of subsection (1) of this section;

(b) That any fees due to an association of real property owners for the upkeep of the housing facility, or common area including buildings and grounds thereof, of which the real property is a part have been paid in full.

(5) The provisions of this section shall not apply to any bona fide lender who accepts a deed in lieu of foreclosure or who forecloses upon the real property.

(6) The provisions of this section shall not apply to any bona fide purchaser who acquires fee title in any real property without agreeing to pay all underlying encumbrances and takes fee title subject to all underlying encumbrances, if the following written, verbatim warning was provided to the seller in capital letters of no less than ten-point, bold-faced type and acknowledged by the seller's signature:

WARNING: PURCHASER, ________, WILL NOT ASSUME OR PAY ANY PRESENT MORTGAGE, DEEDS OF TRUST, OR OTHER LIENS OR ENCUMBRANCES AGAINST THE PROPERTY. THE SELLER, ________, UNDERSTANDS HE/SHE WILL REMAIN RESPONSIBLE FOR ALL PAYMENTS DUE ON SUCH MORTGAGES, DEEDS OF TRUST, OR OTHER LIENS OR ENCUMBRANCES AND FOR ANY DEFICIENCY JUDGMENT UPON FORECLOSURE.

I HAVE HAD THE FOREGOING READ TO ME AND UNDERSTAND THE PURCHASER, ________, WILL NOT ASSUME ANY PRESENT MORTGAGES, DEEDS OF TRUST, OR OTHER LIENS OR ENCUMBRANCES AGAINST THE PROPERTY DESCRIBED AS ________.

DATE ________ SELLER ________.

XIII. Colorado Foreclosure Protection Act

§ 6-1-1101, C.R.S. Short title.

This part 11 shall be known and may be cited as the "Colorado Foreclosure Protection Act".

§ 6-1-1102, C.R.S. Legislative declaration.

The general assembly hereby finds, determines, and declares that home ownership and the accumulation of equity in one's home provide significant social and economic benefits to the state and its citizens. Unfortunately, too many home owners in financial distress, especially the poor, elderly, and financially unsophisticated, are vulnerable to a variety of deceptive or unconscionable business practices designed to dispossess them or otherwise strip the equity from their homes. There is a compelling need to curtail and to prevent the most deceptive and unconscionable of these business practices, to provide each home owner with information necessary to make an informed and intelligent decision regarding transactions with certain foreclosure consultants and equity purchasers, to provide certain minimum requirements for contracts between such parties, including statutory rights to cancel such contracts, and to ensure and foster fair dealing in the sale and purchase of homes in foreclosure. Therefore, it is the intent of the general assembly that all violations of this part 11 have a significant public impact and that the terms of this part 11 be liberally construed to achieve these purposes.

§ 6-1-1103, C.R.S. Definitions.

As used in this part 11, unless the context otherwise requires:

(1) "Associate" means a partner, subsidiary, affiliate, agent, or any other person working in association with a foreclosure consultant or an equity purchaser. "Associate" does not include a person who is excluded from the definition of an "equity purchaser" or a "foreclosure consultant".

(2) "Equity purchaser" means a person, other than a person who acquires a property for the purpose of using such property as his or her personal residence, who acquires title to a residence in foreclosure; except that the term does not include a person who acquires such title:

   (a) (Deleted by amendment, L. 2010, (HB 10-1133), ch. 350, p. 1615, § 1, effective January 1, 2011.)

   (b) By a deed in lieu of foreclosure to the holder of an evidence of debt, or an associate of the holder of an evidence of debt, of a consensual lien or encumbrance of record if such consensual lien or encumbrance is recorded in the real property records of the clerk and recorder of the county where the residence in foreclosure is located prior to the recording of the notice of election and demand for sale required under section 38-38-101, C.R.S.;

   (c) By a deed from the public trustee or a county sheriff as a result of a foreclosure sale conducted pursuant to article 38 of title 38, C.R.S.;

   (d) At a sale of property authorized by statute;

   (e) By order or judgment of any court;

   (f) From the person's spouse, relative, or relative of a spouse, by the half or whole blood or by adoption, or from a guardian, conservator, or personal representative of a person identified in this paragraph (f);

   (g) While performing services as a part of a person's normal business activities under any law of this state or the United States that regulates banks, trust companies, savings and loan associations, credit unions, insurance companies, title insurers, insurance producers, or escrow companies authorized to conduct business in the state, an affiliate or subsidiary of such person, or an employee or agent acting on behalf of such person; or

   (h) As a result of a short sale transaction in which a short sale addendum form, as promulgated by the Colorado real estate commission, is part of the contract used to acquire a residence in foreclosure and such transaction complies with section 6-1-1121.

(3) "Evidence of debt" means a writing that evidences a promise to pay or a right to the payment of a monetary obligation, such as a promissory note, bond, negotiable instrument, a loan, credit, or similar agreement, or a monetary judgment entered by a court of competent jurisdiction.

(4) (a) "Foreclosure consultant" means a person who does not, directly or through an associate, take or acquire any interest in or title to a homeowner's property and who, in the course of such person's business, vocation, or occupation, makes a solicitation, representation, or offer to a home owner to perform, in exchange for compensation from the home owner or from the proceeds of any loan or advance of funds, a service that the person represents will do any of the following:

      (I) Stop or postpone a foreclosure sale;

(II) Obtain a forbearance from a beneficiary under a deed of trust, mortgage, or other lien;

(III) Assist the home owner in exercising a right to cure a default as provided in article 38 of title 38, C.R.S.;

(IV) Obtain an extension of the period within which the home owner may cure a default as provided in article 38 of title 38, C.R.S.;

(V) Obtain a waiver of an acceleration clause contained in an evidence of debt secured by a deed of trust, mortgage, or other lien on a residence in foreclosure or contained in such deed of trust, mortgage, or other lien;

(VI) Assist the home owner to obtain a loan or advance of funds;

(VII) Avoid or reduce the impairment of the home owner's credit resulting from the recording of a notice of election and demand for sale, commencement of a judicial foreclosure action, or due to any foreclosure sale or the granting of a deed in lieu of foreclosure or resulting from any late payment or other failure to pay or perform under the evidence of debt, the deed of trust, or other lien securing such evidence of debt;

(VIII) In any way delay, hinder, or prevent the foreclosure upon the home owner's residence; or

(IX) Repealed.

(b) The term "foreclosure consultant" does not include:

(I) A person licensed to practice law in this state, while performing any activity related to the person's attorney-client relationship with a home owner or any activity related to the person's attorney-client relationship with the beneficiary, mortgagee, grantee, or holder of any lien being enforced by way of foreclosure;

(II) A holder or servicer of an evidence of debt or the attorney for the holder or servicer of an evidence of debt secured by a deed of trust or other lien on any residence in foreclosure while the person performs services in connection with the evidence of debt, lien, deed of trust, or other lien securing such debt;

(III) A person doing business under any law of this state or the United States, which law regulates banks, trust companies, savings and loan associations, credit unions, insurance companies, title insurers, insurance producers, or escrow companies authorized to conduct business in the state, while the person performs services as part of the person's normal business activities, an affiliate or subsidiary of any of the foregoing, or an employee or agent acting on behalf of any of the foregoing;

(IV) A person originating or closing a loan in a person's normal course of business if, as to that loan:

(A) The loan is subject to the requirements of the federal "Real Estate Settlement Procedures Act of 1974", as amended, 12 U.S.C. sec. 2601 to 2617; or

(B) With respect to any second mortgage or home equity line of credit, the loan is subordinate to and closed simultaneously with a qualified first mortgage loan under sub-subparagraph (A) of this subparagraph (IV) or is initially payable on the face of the note or contract to an entity included in subparagraph (III) of this paragraph (b);

(V) A judgment creditor of the home owner, if the judgment is recorded in the real property records of the clerk and recorder of the county where the residence in foreclosure is located and the legal action giving rise to the judgment was commenced before the notice of election and demand for sale required under section 38-38-101, C.R.S.;

(VI) A title insurance company or title insurance agent authorized to conduct business in this state, while performing title insurance and settlement services;

(VII) A person licensed as a real estate broker under article 61 of title 12, C.R.S., while the person engages in any activity for which the person is licensed; or

(VIII) A nonprofit organization that solely offers counseling or advice to home owners in foreclosure or loan default, unless the organization is an associate of the foreclosure consultant.

(5) "Foreclosure consulting contract" means any agreement between a foreclosure consultant and a home owner.

(6) "Holder of evidence of debt" means the person in actual possession of or otherwise entitled to enforce an evidence of debt; except that "holder of evidence of debt" does not include a person acting as a nominee solely for the purpose of holding the evidence of debt or deed of trust as an electronic registry without any authority to enforce the evidence of debt or deed of trust. The following persons are presumed to be the holder of evidence of debt:

(a) The person who is the obligee of and who is in possession of an original evidence of debt;

(b) The person in possession of an original evidence of debt together with the proper indorsement or assignment thereof to such person in accordance with section 38-38-101 (6), C.R.S.;

(c) The person in possession of a negotiable instrument evidencing a debt, which has been duly negotiated to such person or to bearer or indorsed in blank; or

(d) The person in possession of an evidence of debt with authority, which may be granted by the original evidence of debt or deed of trust, to enforce the evidence of debt as agent, nominee, or trustee or in a similar capacity for the obligee of the evidence of debt.

(7) "Home owner" means the owner of a dwelling who occupies it as his or her principal place of residence, including a vendee under a contract for deed to real property, as that term is defined in section 38-35-126 (1) (b), C.R.S.

(8) (a) Except as otherwise provided in paragraph (b) of this subsection (8), "residence in foreclosure" means a residence or dwelling, as defined in sections 5-1-201 and 5-1-301, C.R.S., that is occupied as the home owner's principal place of residence and that is encumbered by a residential mortgage loan that is at least thirty days delinquent or in default.

(b) With respect to subpart 3 of this part 11, "residence in foreclosure" means a residence or dwelling, as defined in sections 5-1-201 and 5-1-301, C.R.S., that is occupied as the home owner's principal place of residence, is encumbered by a residential mortgage loan, and against which a foreclosure action has been commenced or as to which an equity purchaser otherwise has actual or constructive knowledge that the loan is at least thirty days delinquent or in default.

(9) "Short sale" or "short sale transaction" means a transaction in which the residence in foreclosure is sold when:

(a) A holder of evidence of debt agrees to release its lien for an amount that is less than the outstanding amount due and owing under such evidence of debt; and

(b) The lien described in paragraph (a) of this subsection (9) is recorded in the real property records of the county where the residence in foreclosure is located.

XIV. Foreclosure Consultants

§ 6-1-1104, C.R.S. Foreclosure consulting contract.

(1) A foreclosure consulting contract shall be in writing and provided to and retained by the home owner, without changes, alterations, or modifications, for review at least twenty-four hours before it is signed by the home owner.

(2) A foreclosure consulting contract shall be printed in at least twelve-point type and shall include the name and address of the foreclosure consultant to which a notice of cancellation can be mailed and the date the home owner signed the contract.

(3) A foreclosure consulting contract shall fully disclose the exact nature of the foreclosure consulting services to be provided and the total amount and terms of any compensation to be received by the foreclosure consultant or associate.

(4) A foreclosure consulting contract shall be dated and personally signed, with each page being initialed, by each home owner and the foreclosure consultant and shall be acknowledged by a notary public in the presence of the home owner at the time the contract is signed by the home owner.

(5) A foreclosure consulting contract shall contain the following notice, which shall be printed in at least fourteen-point bold-faced type, completed with the name of the foreclosure consultant, and located in immediate proximity to the space reserved for the home owner's signature:

Notice Required by Colorado Law

_______ (Name) or (his/her/its) associate cannot ask you to sign or have you sign any document that transfers any interest in your home or property to (him/her/it) or (his/her/its) associate.

_______ (Name) or (his/her/its) associate cannot guarantee you that they will be able to refinance your home or arrange for you to keep your home.

You may, at any time, cancel this contract, without penalty of any kind.

If you want to cancel this contract, mail or deliver a signed and dated copy of this notice of cancellation, or any other written notice, indicating your intent to cancel to _______________ (name and address of foreclosure consultant) at ____________________ (address of foreclosure consultant, including facsimile and electronic mail address).

As part of any cancellation, you (the home owner) must repay any money actually spent on your behalf by ____________________ (name of foreclosure consultant) prior to receipt of this notice and as a result of this agreement, within sixty days, along with interest at the prime rate published by the federal reserve plus two percentage points, with the total interest rate not to exceed eight percent per year.

This is an important legal contract and could result in the loss of your home. Contact an attorney or a housing counselor approved by the federal department of housing and urban development before signing.

(6) A completed form in duplicate, captioned "Notice of Cancellation" shall accompany the foreclosure consulting contract. The notice of cancellation shall:

(a) Be on a separate sheet of paper attached to the contract;

(b) Be easily detachable; and

(c) Contain the following statement, printed in at least fourteen-point type:

Notice of Cancellation

(Date of contract)

To: (name of foreclosure consultant)

(Address of foreclosure consultant, including facsimile and electronic mail)

I hereby cancel this contract.

__________________ **(Date)**

__________________ **(Home owner's signature)**

(7) The foreclosure consultant shall provide to the home owner a signed, dated, and acknowledged copy of the foreclosure consulting contract and the attached notice of cancellation immediately upon execution of the contract.

(8) The time during which the home owner may cancel the foreclosure consulting contract does not begin to run until the foreclosure consultant has complied with this section.

§ 6-1-1105, C.R.S. Right of cancellation.

(1) In addition to any right of rescission available under state or federal law, the home owner has the right to cancel a foreclosure consulting contract at any time.

(2) Cancellation occurs when the home owner gives written notice of cancellation of the foreclosure consulting contract to the foreclosure consultant at the address specified in the contract or through any facsimile or electronic mail address identified in the contract or other materials provided to the home owner by the foreclosure consultant.

(3) Notice of cancellation, if given by mail, is effective when deposited in the United States mail, properly addressed, with postage prepaid.

(4) Notice of cancellation need not be in the form provided with the contract and is effective, however expressed, if it indicates the intention of the home owner to cancel the foreclosure consulting contract.

(5) As part of the cancellation of a foreclosure consulting contract, the home owner shall repay, within sixty days after the date of cancellation, all funds paid or advanced in good faith prior to the receipt of notice of cancellation by the foreclosure consultant or associate under the terms of the foreclosure consulting contract, together with interest at the prime rate published by the federal reserve plus two percentage points, with the total interest rate not to exceed eight percent per year, from the date of expenditure until repaid by the home owner.

(6) The right to cancel may not be conditioned on the repayment of any funds.

§ 6-1-1106, C.R.S. Waiver of rights – void.

(1) A provision in a foreclosure consulting contract is void as against public policy if the provision attempts or purports to:

(a) Waive any of the rights specified in this subpart 2 or the right to a jury trial;

(b) Consent to jurisdiction for litigation or choice of law in a state other than Colorado;

(c) Consent to venue in a county other than the county in which the property is located; or

(d) Impose any costs or fees greater than the actual costs and fees.

§ 6-1-1107, C.R.S. Prohibited acts.

(1) A foreclosure consultant may not:

(a) Claim, demand, charge, collect, or receive any compensation until after the foreclosure consultant has fully performed each and every service the foreclosure consultant contracted to perform or represented that the foreclosure consultant would perform;

(b) Claim, demand, charge, collect, or receive any interest or any other compensation for a loan that the foreclosure consultant makes to the home owner that exceeds the prime rate published by the federal reserve at the time of any loan plus two percentage points, with the total interest rate not to exceed eight percent per year;

(c) Take a wage assignment, lien of any type on real or personal property, or other security to secure the payment of compensation;

(d) Receive any consideration from a third party in connection with foreclosure consulting services provided to a home owner unless the consideration is first fully disclosed in writing to the home owner;

(e) Acquire an interest, directly, indirectly, or through an associate, in the real or personal property of a home owner with whom the foreclosure consultant has contracted;

(f) Obtain a power of attorney from a home owner for any purpose other than to inspect documents as provided by law; or

(g) Induce or attempt to induce a home owner to enter into a foreclosure consulting contract that does not comply in all respects with this subpart 2.

§ 6-1-1108, C.R.S. Criminal penalties.

A person who violates section 6-1-1107 is guilty of a misdemeanor, as defined in section 18-1.3-504, C.R.S., and shall be subject to imprisonment in county jail for up to one year, a fine of up to twenty-five thousand dollars, or both.

§ 6-1-1109, C.R.S. Unconscionability.

(1) A foreclosure consultant or associate may not facilitate or engage in any transaction that is unconscionable given the terms and circumstances of the transaction.

(2) (a) If a court, as a matter of law, finds a foreclosure consultant contract or any clause of such contract to have been unconscionable at the time it was made, the court may refuse to enforce the contract, enforce the remainder of the contract without the unconscionable clause, or so limit the application of any unconscionable clause as to avoid an unconscionable result.

(b) When it is claimed or appears to the court that a foreclosure consultant contract or any clause of such contract may be unconscionable, the parties shall be afforded a reasonable opportunity to present evidence as to its commercial setting, purpose, and effect, to aid the court in making the determination.

(c) In order to support a finding of unconscionability, there must be evidence of some bad faith overreaching on the part of the foreclosure consultant or associate such as that which results from an unreasonable inequality of bargaining power or other circumstances in which there is an absence of meaningful choice for one of the parties, together with contract terms that are, under standard industry practices, unreasonably favorable to the foreclosure consultant or associate.

§ 6-1-1110, C.R.S. Language.

A foreclosure consulting contract, and all notices of cancellation provided for therein, shall be written in English and shall be accompanied by a written translation from English into any other language principally spoken by the home owner, certified by the person making the translation as a true and correct translation of the English version. The translated version shall be presumed to have equal status and credibility as the English version.

XV. Equity Purchasers

§ 6-1-1111, C.R.S. Written contract required.

Every contract shall be written in at least nine-point, legible type and fully completed, signed, and dated by the home owner and equity purchaser prior to the execution of any instrument quit-claiming, assigning, transferring, conveying, or encumbering an interest in the residence in foreclosure.

§ 6-1-1112, C.R.S. Written contract – contents – notice.

(1) Every contract shall contain the entire agreement of the parties and shall include the following terms:

(a) The name, business address, and telephone number of the equity purchaser;

(b) The street address and full legal description of the residence in foreclosure;

(c) Clear and conspicuous disclosure of any financial or legal obligations of the home owner that will be assumed by the equity purchaser. If the equity purchaser will not be assuming any financial or legal obligations of the home owner, the equity purchaser shall provide to the home owner a separate written disclosure that substantially complies with section 18-5-802 (6), C.R.S.

(d) The total consideration to be paid by the equity purchaser in connection with or incident to the acquisition by the equity purchaser of the residence in foreclosure;

(e) The terms of payment or other consideration, including, but not limited to, any services of any nature that the equity purchaser represents will be performed for the home owner before or after the sale;

(f) The date and time when possession of the residence in foreclosure is to be transferred to the equity purchaser;

(g) The terms of any rental agreement or lease;

(h) The specifications of any option or right to repurchase the residence in foreclosure, including the specific amounts of any escrow deposit, down payment, purchase price, closing costs, commissions, or other fees or costs;

(i) A notice of cancellation as provided in section 6-1-1114; and

(j) The following notice, in at least nine-point bold-faced type, and completed with the name of the equity purchaser, immediately above the statement required by section 6-1-1114:

NOTICE REQUIRED BY COLORADO LAW

Until your right to cancel this contract has ended, (Name) or anyone working for _________ (Name) CANNOT ask you to sign or have you sign any deed or any other document.

(2) The contract required by this section survives delivery of any instrument of conveyance of the residence in foreclosure, but does not have any effect on persons other than the parties to the contract or affect title to the residence in foreclosure.

§ 6-1-1113, C.R.S. Cancellation.

(1) In addition to any right of rescission available under state or federal law, the home owner has the right to cancel a contract with an equity purchaser until 12 midnight of the third business day following the day on which the home owner signs a contract that complies with this part 11 or until 12 noon on the day before the foreclosure sale of the residence in foreclosure, whichever occurs first.

(2) Cancellation occurs when the home owner personally delivers written notice of cancellation to the address specified in the contract or upon deposit of such notice in the United States mail, properly addressed, with postage prepaid.

(3) A notice of cancellation given by the home owner need not take the particular form as provided with the contract and, however expressed, is effective if it indicates the intention of the home owner not to be bound by the contract.

(4) In the absence of any written notice of cancellation from the home owner, the execution by the home owner of a deed or other instrument of conveyance of an interest in the residence in foreclosure to the equity purchaser after the expiration of the rescission period creates a rebuttable presumption that the home owner did not cancel the contract with the equity purchaser.

§ 6-1-1114, C.R.S. Notice of cancellation.

(1) (a) The contract shall contain, as the last provision before the space reserved for the home owner's signature, a conspicuous statement in at least twelve-point bold-faced type, as follows:

> **You may cancel this contract for the sale of your house without any penalty or obligation at any time before ________ (Date and time of day). See the attached notice of cancellation form for an explanation of this right.**

(b) The equity purchaser shall accurately specify the date and time of day on which the cancellation right ends.

(2) The contract shall be accompanied by duplicate completed forms, captioned "notice of cancellation" in at least nine-point bold-faced type if the contract is printed or in capital letters if the contract is typed, followed by a space in which the equity purchaser shall enter the date on which the home owner executed the contract. Such form shall:

(a) Be attached to the contract;

(b) Be easily detachable; and

(c) Contain the following statement, in at least nine-point type if the contract is printed or in capital letters if the contract is typed:

NOTICE OF CANCELLATION

> **________ (Enter date contract signed). You may cancel this contract for the sale of your house, without any penalty or obligation, at any time before ________ (Enter date and time of day). To cancel this transaction, personally deliver a signed and dated copy of this Notice of Cancellation in the United States mail, postage prepaid, to ________, (Name of purchaser) at ________ (Street address of purchaser's place of business) NOT LATER THAN ________ (Enter date and time of day). I hereby cancel this transaction ________ (Date) ________ (Seller's signature)**

(3) The equity purchaser shall provide the home owner with a copy of the contract and the attached notice of cancellation.

(4) Until the equity purchaser has complied with this section, the home owner may cancel the contract.

§ 6-1-1115, C.R.S. Options through reconveyances.

(1) A transaction in which a home owner purports to grant a residence in foreclosure to an equity purchaser by an instrument that appears to be an absolute conveyance and reserves to the home owner or is given by the equity purchaser an option to repurchase shall be permitted only where all of the following conditions have been met:

(a) The reconveyance contract complies in all respects with section 6-1-1112;

(b) The reconveyance contract provides the home owner with a nonwaivable thirty-day right to cure any default of said reconveyance contract and specifies that the home owner may exercise this right to cure on at least three separate occasions during such reconveyance contract;

(c) The equity purchaser fully assumes or discharges the lien in foreclosure as well as any prior liens that will not be extinguished by such foreclosure, which assumption or discharge shall be accomplished without violation of the terms and conditions of the liens being assumed or discharged;

(d) The equity purchaser verifies and can demonstrate that the home owner has or will have a reasonable ability to make the lease payments and to repurchase the residence in foreclosure within the term of the option to repurchase under the reconveyance contract. For purposes of this section, there is a rebuttable presumption that the home owner has a reasonable ability to make lease payments and to repurchase the residence in foreclosure if the home owner's payments for primary housing expenses and regular principal and interest payments on other personal debt do not exceed sixty percent of the home owner's monthly gross income; and

(e) The price the home owner must pay to exercise the option to repurchase the residence in foreclosure is not unconscionable. Without limitation on available claims under section 6-1-1119, a repurchase price exceeding twenty-five percent of the price at which the equity purchaser acquired the residence in foreclosure creates a rebuttable presumption that the reconveyance contract is unconscionable. The acquisition price paid by the equity purchaser may include any actual costs incurred by the equity purchaser in acquiring the residence in foreclosure.

§ 6-1-1116, C.R.S. Waiver of rights – void.

(1) A provision in a contract between an equity purchaser and home owner is void as against public policy if it attempts or purports to:

(a) Waive any of the rights specified in this subpart 3 or the right to a jury trial;

(b) Consent to jurisdiction for litigation or choice of law in a state other than Colorado;

(c) Consent to venue in a county other than the county in which the property is located; or

(d) Impose any costs or fees greater than the actual costs and fees.

§ 6-1-1117, C.R.S. Prohibited conduct.

(1) The contract provisions required by sections 6-1-1111 to 6-1-1114 shall be provided and completed in conformity with such sections by the equity purchaser.

(2) Until the time within which the home owner may cancel the transaction has fully elapsed, the equity purchaser shall not do any of the following:

(a) Accept from a home owner an execution of, or induce a home owner to execute, an instrument of conveyance of any interest in the residence in foreclosure;

(b) Record with the county recorder any document, including, but not limited to, the contract or any lease, lien, or instrument of conveyance, that has been signed by the home owner;

(c) Transfer or encumber or purport to transfer or encumber an interest in the residence in foreclosure to a third party; or

(d) Pay the home owner any consideration.

(3) Within ten days following receipt of a notice of cancellation given in accordance with sections 6-1-1113 and 6-1-1114, the equity purchaser shall return without condition the original contract and any other documents signed by the home owner.

(4) An equity purchaser shall make no untrue or misleading statements of material fact regarding the value of the residence in foreclosure, the amount of proceeds the home owner will receive after a foreclosure sale, any contract term, the home owner's rights or obligations incident to or arising out of the sale transaction, the nature of any document that the equity purchaser induces the home owner to sign, or any other untrue or misleading statement concerning the sale of the residence in foreclosure to the equity purchaser.

§ 6-1-1118, C.R.S. Criminal penalties.

A person who violates section 6-1-1117 (2) or (3) or who intentionally violates section 6-1-1117 (4) is guilty of a misdemeanor, as defined in section 18-1.3-504, C.R.S., and shall be subject to imprisonment in county jail for up to one year, a fine of up to twenty-five thousand dollars, or both.

§ 6-1-1119, C.R.S. Unconscionability.

(1) An equity purchaser or associate may not facilitate or engage in any transaction that is unconscionable given the terms and circumstances of the transaction.

(2) (a) If a court, as a matter of law, finds an equity purchaser contract or any clause of such contract to have been unconscionable at the time it was made, the court may refuse to enforce the contract, enforce the remainder of the contract without the unconscionable clause, or so limit the application of any unconscionable clause as to avoid an unconscionable result.

(b) When it is claimed or appears to the court that the contract or any clause thereof may be unconscionable, the parties shall be afforded a reasonable opportunity to present evidence as to its commercial setting, purpose, and effect, to aid the court in making the determination.

(c) In order to support a finding of unconscionability, there must be evidence of some bad faith overreaching on the part of the equity purchaser or associate such as that which results from an unreasonable inequality of bargaining power or under other circumstances in which there is an absence of meaningful choice for one of the parties, together with contract terms that are, under standard industry practices, unreasonably favorable to the equity purchaser or associate.

§ 6-1-1120, C.R.S. Language.

(1) Any contract, rental agreement, lease, option or right to repurchase, and any notice, conveyance, lien, encumbrance, consent, or other document or instrument signed by a home owner, shall be written in English; except that, if the equity purchaser has actual or constructive knowledge that the home owner's principal language is other than English, the home owner shall be provided with a notice, written in the home owner's principal language, substantially as follows:

This transaction involves important and complex legal consequences, including your right to cancel this transaction within three business days following the date you sign this contract. You should consult with an attorney or seek assistance from a housing counselor by calling the Colorado foreclosure hotline at ________________ [current, correct telephone number].

(2) If a notice in the home owner's principal language is required to be provided under subsection (1) of this section, the notice shall be given to the home owner as a separate document accompanying the written contract required by section 6-1-1111.

* *§ 6-1-105, C.R.S. Unfair or deceptive trade practices.*

* (1) A person engages in a deceptive trade practice when, in the course of the person's business, vocation, or occupation, the person:

(xx) Violates any provision of part 11 of this article;

XVI. Revised Uniform Law on Notarial Acts

§ 12-55-101 to § 12-55-124, C.R.S. (Repealed)

Editor's note: (1) Section 12-55-124 provided for the repeal of this part 1, effective July 1, 2018. (See L. 2017, pp. 787, 809, and 1418.)

(2) This part 1 was numbered as article 1 of chapter 96, C.R.S. 1963. For amendments to this part 1 prior to its repeal in 2018, consult the 2017 Colorado Revised Statutes.

Cross references: For the "Revised Uniform Law on Notarial Acts", see part 5 of article 21 of title 24.

§ 24-21-501, C.R.S. Short title.

The short title of this part 5 is the "Revised Uniform Law on Notarial Acts".

§ 24-21-502, C.R.S. Definitions.

In this part 5:

(1) "Acknowledgment" means a declaration by an individual before a notarial officer that the individual has signed a record for the purpose stated in the record and, if the record is signed in a representative capacity, that the individual signed the record with proper authority and signed it as the act of the individual or entity identified in the record.

* (1.3) "Audio-video communication" means communication by which an individual is able to see, hear, and communicate with a remotely located individual in real time using electronic means.

* (1.7) "Credential" means a tangible record evidencing the identity of an individual.

(2) "Electronic" means relating to technology having electrical, digital, magnetic, wireless, optical, electromagnetic, or similar capabilities.

(3) "Electronic record" means a record containing information that is created, generated, sent, communicated, received, or stored by electronic means.

(4) "Electronic signature" means an electronic symbol, sound, or process attached to or logically associated with an electronic record and executed or adopted by an individual with the intent to sign the electronic record.

(5) "In a representative capacity" means acting as:

(a) An authorized officer, agent, partner, trustee, or other representative for a person other than an individual;

(b) A public officer, personal representative, guardian, or other representative, in the capacity stated in a record;

(c) An agent or attorney-in-fact for a principal; or

(d) An authorized representative of another in any other capacity.

(6) "Notarial act" means an act, whether performed with respect to a tangible or electronic record, that a notarial officer may perform under the law of this state. The term includes taking an acknowledgment, administering an oath or affirmation, taking a deposition or other sworn testimony, taking a verification on oath or affirmation, witnessing or attesting a signature, certifying a copy, and noting a protest of a negotiable instrument.

(7) "Notarial officer" means a notary public or other individual authorized to perform a notarial act.

(8) "Notary public" means an individual commissioned to perform a notarial act by the secretary of state.

(9) "Official stamp" means a physical image affixed to a tangible record or an electronic image attached to or logically associated with an electronic record.

(10) "Person" means an individual, corporation, business trust, statutory trust, estate, trust, partnership, limited liability company, association, joint venture, public corporation, government or governmental subdivision, agency, or instrumentality, or any other legal or commercial entity.

* (10.5)"Real-time" or "in real time" means, with respect to an interaction between individuals by means of audio-video communication, that the individuals can see and hear each other substantially simultaneously and without interruption or disconnection. Delays of a few seconds that are inherent in the method of communication do not prevent the interaction from being considered to have occurred in real time.

(11) "Record" means information that is inscribed on a tangible medium or that is stored in an electronic or other medium and is retrievable in perceivable form.

* (11.3)"Remotely located individual" means an individual who is not in the physical presence of the notary public who performs a notarial act under this section.

* (11.5)"Remote notarization" means an electronic notarial act performed with respect only to an electronic record by means of real-time audio-video communication in accordance with section 24-21-514.5 and rules adopted by the secretary of state.

* (11.7)"Remote notarization system" means an electronic device or process that:

* (a) Allows a notary public and a remotely located individual to communicate with each other simultaneously by sight and sound; and

* (b) When necessary and consistent with other applicable law, facilitates communication with a remotely located individual who has a vision, hearing, or speech impairment.

(12) "Sign" means, with present intent to authenticate or adopt a record:

(a) To execute or adopt a tangible symbol; or

(b) To attach to or logically associate with the record an electronic symbol, sound, or process.

(13) "Signature" means a tangible symbol or an electronic signature that evidences the signing of a record.

(14) "Stamping device" means:

(a) A physical device capable of affixing to a tangible record an official stamp; or

(b) An electronic device or process capable of attaching to or logically associating with an electronic record an official stamp.

(15) "State" means a state of the United States, the District of Columbia, Puerto Rico, the United States Virgin Islands, or any territory or insular possession subject to the jurisdiction of the United States.

* (15.5) "Tamper-evident" means the use of a set of applications, programs, hardware, software, or other technologies that will display evidence of any changes made to an electronic record.

(16) "Verification on oath or affirmation" means a declaration, made by an individual on oath or affirmation before a notarial officer, that a statement in a record is true.

§ 24-21-503, C.R.S. Applicability.

This part 5 applies to a notarial act performed on or after July 1, 2018.

§ 24-21-504, C.R.S. Authority to perform notarial act.

(1) A notarial officer may perform a notarial act authorized by this part 5 or by law of this state other than this part 5.

(2) A notarial officer shall not perform a notarial act with respect to a record in which the officer has a disqualifying interest. For the purposes of this section, a notarial officer has a disqualifying interest in a record if:

(a) The officer or the officer's spouse, partner in a civil union, ancestor, descendent, or sibling is a party to or is named in the record that is to be notarized; or

(b) The officer or the officer's spouse or partner in a civil union may receive directly, and as a proximate result of the notarization, any advantage, right, title, interest, cash, or property exceeding in value the sum of any fee properly received in accordance with this part 5.

(3) A notarial act performed in violation of this section is voidable.

§ 24-21-505, C.R.S. Requirements for certain notarial acts.

(1) A notarial officer who takes an acknowledgment of a record shall determine, from personal knowledge or satisfactory evidence of the identity of the individual, that the individual appearing before the officer and making the acknowledgment has the identity claimed and that the signature on the record is the signature of the individual.

(2) A notarial officer who takes a verification of a statement on oath or affirmation shall determine, from personal knowledge or satisfactory evidence of the identity of the individual, that the individual appearing before the officer and making the verification has the identity claimed and that the signature on the statement verified is the signature of the individual.

(3) A notarial officer who witnesses or attests to a signature shall determine, from personal knowledge or satisfactory evidence of the identity of the individual, that the individual appearing before the officer and signing the record has the identity claimed.

(4) (a) A notarial officer who certifies a copy of a record or an item that was copied shall determine that the copy is a full, true, and accurate transcription or reproduction of the record or item.

(b) A notarial officer shall not certify a copy of a record that can be obtained from any of the following offices in this state:

(I) A clerk and recorder of public documents;

(II) The secretary of state;

(III) The state archives; or

(IV) An office of vital records.

(c) A notarial officer shall not certify a copy of a record if the record states on its face that it is illegal to copy the record.

(5) (a) A notarial officer who makes or notes a protest of a negotiable instrument shall determine the matters set forth in section 4-3-505 (b) of the "Uniform Commercial Code".

(b) A notary public shall not make or note a protest of a negotiable instrument unless the notary is an employee of a financial institution acting in the course and scope of the notary's employment with the financial institution.

§ 24-21-506, C.R.S. Personal appearance required.

If a notarial act relates to a statement made in or a signature executed on a record, the individual making the statement or executing the signature shall appear personally before the notarial officer.

§ 24-21-507, C.R.S. Identification of individual.

(1) A notarial officer has personal knowledge of the identity of an individual appearing before the officer if the individual is personally known to the officer through dealings sufficient to provide reasonable certainty that the individual has the identity claimed.

(2) A notarial officer has satisfactory evidence of the identity of an individual appearing before the officer if the officer can identify the individual:

(a) By means of:

(I) A passport, driver's license, or government-issued nondriver identification card that is current or expired not more than one year before performance of the notarial act; or

(II) Another form of government identification issued to the individual that is current or expired not more than one year before performance of the notarial act, contains the signature or a photograph of the individual, and is satisfactory to the officer; or

(b) By a verification on oath or affirmation of a credible witness personally appearing before the officer and known to the officer or whom the officer can identify on the basis of a passport, driver's license, or government-issued nondriver identification card that is current or expired not more than one year before performance of the notarial act.

(3) A notarial officer may require an individual to provide additional information or identification credentials necessary to assure the officer of the identity of the individual.

§ 24-21-508, C.R.S. Authority to refuse to perform notarial act.

(1) A notarial officer may refuse to perform a notarial act if the officer is not satisfied that:

(a) The individual executing the record is competent or has the capacity to execute the record; or

(b) The individual's signature is knowingly and voluntarily made.

(2) A notarial officer may refuse to perform a notarial act unless refusal is prohibited by law other than this part 5.

§ 24-21-509, C.R.S. Signature if individual unable to sign.

(1) If an individual is physically unable to sign a record, the individual may, in the presence of the notarial officer, direct an individual other than the notarial officer to sign the individual's name on the record. The notarial officer shall insert "Signature affixed by (name of other individual) at the direction of (name of individual)" or words of similar import under or near the signature.

(2) A notary public may use signals or electronic or mechanical means to take an acknowledgment from, administer an oath or affirmation to, or otherwise communicate with any individual in the

presence of the notary public when it appears that the individual is unable to communicate verbally or in writing.

§ 24-21-510, C.R.S. Notarial act in this state.

(1) A notarial act may be performed in this state by:

(a) A notary public of this state;

(b) A judge, clerk, or deputy clerk of a court of this state; or

(c) Any other individual authorized to perform the specific act by the law of this state.

(2) The signature and title of an individual performing a notarial act in this state are prima facie evidence that the signature is genuine and that the individual holds the designated title.

(3) The signature and title of a notarial officer described in subsection (1)(a) or (1)(b) of this section conclusively establish the authority of the officer to perform the notarial act.

§ 24-21-511, C.R.S. Notarial act in another state.

(1) A notarial act performed in another state has the same effect under the law of this state as if performed by a notarial officer of this state if the act performed in that state is performed by:

(a) A notary public of that state;

(b) A judge, clerk, or deputy clerk of a court of that state; or

(c) Any other individual authorized by the law of that state to perform the notarial act.

(2) The signature and title of an individual performing a notarial act in another state are prima facie evidence that the signature is genuine and that the individual holds the designated title.

(3) The signature and title of a notarial officer described in subsection (1)(a) or (1)(b) of this section conclusively establish the authority of the officer to perform the notarial act.

§ 24-21-512, C.R.S. Notarial act under authority of federally recognized Indian tribe.

(1) A notarial act performed under the authority and in the jurisdiction of a federally recognized Indian tribe has the same effect as if performed by a notarial officer of this state if the act performed in the jurisdiction of the tribe is performed by:

(a) A notary public of the tribe;

(b) A judge, clerk, or deputy clerk of a court of the tribe; or

(c) Any other individual authorized by the law of the tribe to perform the notarial act.

(2) The signature and title of an individual performing a notarial act under the authority of and in the jurisdiction of a federally recognized Indian tribe are prima facie evidence that the signature is genuine and that the individual holds the designated title.

(3) The signature and title of a notarial officer described in subsection (1)(a) or (1)(b) of this section conclusively establish the authority of the officer to perform the notarial act.

§ 24-21-513, C.R.S. Notarial act under federal authority.

(1) A notarial act performed under federal law has the same effect under the law of this state as if performed by a notarial officer of this state if the act performed under federal law is performed by:

(a) A judge, clerk, or deputy clerk of a court;

(b) An individual in military service or performing duties under the authority of military service who is authorized to perform notarial acts under federal law;

(c) An individual designated a notarizing officer by the United States department of state for performing notarial acts overseas; or

(d) Any other individual authorized by federal law to perform the notarial act.

(2) The signature and title of an individual acting under federal authority and performing a notarial act are prima facie evidence that the signature is genuine and that the individual holds the designated title.

(3) The signature and title of an officer described in subsection (1)(a), (1)(b), or (1)(c) of this section conclusively establish the authority of the officer to perform the notarial act.

§ 24-21-514, C.R.S. Foreign notarial act.

(1) In this section, "foreign state" means a government other than the United States, a state, or a federally recognized Indian tribe.

(2) If a notarial act is performed under authority and in the jurisdiction of a foreign state or constituent unit of the foreign state or is performed under the authority of a multinational or international governmental organization, the act has the same effect under the law of this state as if performed by a notarial officer of this state.

(3) If the title of office and indication of authority to perform notarial acts in a foreign state appears in a digest of foreign law or in a list customarily used as a source for that information, the authority of an officer with that title to perform notarial acts is conclusively established.

(4) The signature and official stamp of an individual holding an office described in subsection (3) of this section are prima facie evidence that the signature is genuine and the individual holds the designated title.

(5) An apostille in the form prescribed by the Hague Convention of October 5, 1961, and issued by a foreign state party to the convention conclusively establishes that the signature of the notarial officer is genuine and that the officer holds the indicated office.

(6) A consular authentication issued by an individual designated by the United States department of state as a notarizing officer for performing notarial acts overseas and attached to the record with respect to which the notarial act is performed conclusively establishes that the signature of the notarial officer is genuine and that the officer holds the indicated office.

§ 24-21-514.5, C.R.S. Audio-video communication - definitions.

* (1) As used in this section:

* (a) "Credential analysis" means a process or service that complies with any rules adopted by the secretary of state through which a third party affirms the validity of a government-issued identification credential through the review of public or proprietary data sources.

* (b) "Dynamic, knowledge-based authentication assessment" means an identity assessment that is based on a set of questions formulated from public or private data sources for which the remotely located individual taking the assessment has not previously provided an answer and that meets any rules adopted by the secretary of state.

* (c) "Outside the United States" means a location outside the geographic boundaries of the United States, Puerto Rico, the United States Virgin Islands, and any territory or insular possession subject to the jurisdiction of the United States.

* (d) "Public key certificate" means an electronic credential that is used to identify a remotely located individual who signed an electronic record with the credential.

* (e) "Remote presentation" means transmission to the notary public through communication technology of an image of a government-issued identification credential that is of sufficient quality to enable the notary public to:

* (I) Identify the remotely located individual seeking the notary public's services; and

* (II) Perform credential analysis.

* (2) (a) Except as provided in subsection (2)(b) of this section, a notary public may perform a remote notarization only with respect to an electronic record and in compliance with this section and any rules adopted by the secretary of state for a remotely located individual who is located:

* (I) In this state;

* (II) Outside of this state but within the United States; or

* (III) Outside the United States if:

* (A) The notary public has no actual knowledge that the notarial act is prohibited in the jurisdiction in which the remotely located individual is physically located at the time of the act; and

* (B) The remotely located individual confirms to the notary public that the requested notarial act and the record relate to: A matter that will be filed with or is currently before a court, governmental entity, or other entity in the United States; property located in the United States; or a transaction substantially connected to the United States.

* (b) A notary public shall not use a remote notarization system to notarize:

* (I) A record relating to the electoral process; or

* (II) Except as provided in the "Colorado Uniform Electronic Wills Act", part 13 of article 11 of title 15, a will, codicil, document purporting to be a will or codicil, or any acknowledgment required under section 15-11-502 or 15-11-504.

* (3) Before a notary public performs the notary public's initial notarization using a remote notarization system, the notary public shall notify the secretary of state that the notary public will be performing remote notarizations and shall identify each remote notarization system that the notary public intends to use. The remote notarization system must conform to this part 5 and any rules adopted by the secretary of state. The notice must be submitted in the format required by the secretary of state and must:

* (a) Include an affirmation that the notary public has read and will comply with this section and all rules adopted by the secretary of state; and

* (b) Be accompanied by proof that the notary public has successfully completed any training and examination required by the secretary of state.

* (4) A notary public who performs a notarial act for a remotely located individual by means of audio-video communication must:

* (a) Be located within this state at the time the notarial act is performed;

* (b) Execute the notarial act in a single, real-time session;

* (c) Confirm that any record that is signed, acknowledged, or otherwise presented for notarization by the remotely located individual is the same record signed by the notary public;

* (d) Confirm that the quality of the audio-video communication is sufficient to make the determinations required for the notarial act under this part 5 and any other law of this state; and

* (e) Identify the venue for the notarial act as the jurisdiction within the state of Colorado where the notary public is physically located while performing the act.

* (5) A remote notarization system used to perform remote notarizations must:

* (a) Require the notary public, the remotely located individual, and any required witness to access the system through an authentication procedure that complies with rules adopted by the secretary of state regarding security and access;

* (b) Enable the notary public to verify the identity of the remotely located individual and any required witness by means of personal knowledge or satisfactory evidence of identity in compliance with subsection (6) of this section; and

* (c) Confirm that the notary public, the remotely located individual, and any required witness are viewing the same record and that all signatures, changes, and attachments to the record are made in real time.

* (6) (a) A notary public shall determine from personal knowledge or satisfactory evidence of identity as described in subsection (6)(b) of this section that the remotely located individual appearing before the notary public by means of audio-video communication is the individual that he or she purports to be.

* (b) A notary public has satisfactory evidence of identity if the notary public can identify the remotely located individual who personally appears before the notary public by means of audio-video communication by using at least one of the following methods:

* (I) The oath or affirmation of a credible witness who personally knows the remotely located individual, is personally known to the notary public, and is in the physical presence of the notary public or the remotely located individual during the remote notarization;

* (II) Remote presentation and credential analysis of a government-issued identification credential, and the data contained on the credential, that contains the signature and a photograph of the remotely located individual, and at least one of the following:

* (A) A dynamic, knowledge-based authentication assessment by a trusted third party that complies with rules adopted by the secretary of state;

* (B) A valid public key certificate that complies with rules adopted by the secretary of state; or

* (C) An identity verification by a trusted third party that complies with rules adopted by the secretary of state; or

* (III) Any other method that complies with rules adopted by the secretary of state.

* (7) Without limiting the authority of a notary public under section 24-21-508 to refuse to perform a notarial act, a notary public may refuse to perform a notarial act under this section if the notary public is not satisfied that the requirements of this section are met.

* (8) The certificate of notarial act for a remote notarization must, in addition to complying with the requirements of section 24-21-515, indicate that the notarial act was performed using audio-video communication technology.

* (9) (a) A notary public shall create an audio-video recording of a remote notarization if:

* (I) The notary public first discloses to the remotely located individual the fact of the recording and the details of its intended storage, including where and for how long it will be stored;

* (II) The remotely located individual explicitly consents to both the recording and the storage of the recording; and

* (III) The recording is stored and secured in compliance with rules adopted by the secretary of state.

* (b) The audio-video recording required by this subsection (9) must be in addition to the journal entry for the notarial act where required by section 24-21-519. The recording must include the information described in this subsection (9)(b). A notary public shall make a good-faith effort to not include any other information on the recording. Any other information included on the recording is not admissible in any court of law, legal proceeding, or administrative hearing for any purpose, nor is the information admissible

in any proceeding in any other court of law, legal proceeding, or administrative hearing if Colorado law applies with respect to remote notarization. The recording must include:

* (I) At the commencement of the recording, a recitation by the notary public of information sufficient to identify the notarial act, including the name of the notary public, the date and time of the notarial act, a description of the nature of the document or documents to which the notarial act is to relate, the identity of the remotely located individual whose signature is to be the subject of the notarial act and of any person who will act as a credible witness to identify the individual signer, and the method or methods by which the remotely located individual and any credible witness will be identified to the notary public;

* (II) A declaration by the remotely located individual that the individual's signature on the record is knowingly and voluntarily made;

* (III) If the remotely located individual for whom the notarial act is being performed is identified by personal knowledge, an explanation by the notary public as to how the notary public knows the remotely located individual and how long the notary public has known the remotely located individual;

* (IV) If the remotely located individual for whom the notarial act is being performed is identified by a credible witness:

* (A) A statement by the notary public as to how the notary public knows the credible witness and how long the notary public has known the credible witness; and

* (B) An explanation by the credible witness as to how the credible witness knows the remotely located individual and how long the credible witness has known the remotely located individual; and

* (V) The statements, acts, and conduct necessary to perform the requested notarial act or supervision of signing or witnessing of the subject record.

* (c) The provisions of section 24-21-519 that relate to the security, inspection, copying, and retention and disposition of a notary public's journal apply equally to the security, inspection, copying, and retention and disposition of audio-video recordings allowed by this section.

* (d) The failure of a notary public to perform a duty or meet a requirement specified in this subsection (9) does not invalidate a remote notarization performed by the notary public. A notary public is not liable to any person for damages claimed to arise from a failure to perform a duty or meet a requirement specified in subsection (9)(b) of this section.

* (10) Regardless of the physical location of the remotely located individual at the time of the notarial act, the validity of a remote notarization performed by a notary in this state is governed by the laws of this state, including any rules adopted by the secretary of state pursuant to this part 5.

* (11) To be eligible for approval by the secretary of state under section 24-21-527 (1)(h), a provider of a remote notarization system or storage system must:

* (a) Certify to the secretary of state that the provider and the system comply with the requirements of this section and the rules adopted under section 24-21-527;

* (b) Maintain a usual place of business in this state or, if a foreign entity, appoint and maintain a registered agent, in accordance with section 7-90-701 by filing a statement of foreign entity authority in accordance with section 7-90-803, with authority to accept service of process in connection with a civil action or other proceeding; and

* (c) Not use, sell, or offer to sell to another person or transfer to another person for use or sale any personal information obtained under this section that identifies a remotely located individual, a witness to a remote notarization, or a person named in a record presented for remote notarization, except:

* (I) As necessary to facilitate performance of a notarial act;

* (II) To effect, administer, enforce, service, or process a record provided by or on behalf of the individual or the transaction of which the record is a part;

* (III) In accordance with this part 5 and the rules adopted pursuant to this part 5 or other applicable federal, state, or local law, or to comply with a lawful subpoena or court order; or

* (IV) In connection with a proposed or actual sale, merger, transfer, or exchange of all or a portion of a business or operating unit of the provider, if the personal information concerns only customers of the business or unit and the transferee agrees to comply with the restrictions set forth in this subsection (11).

* (12) Subject to applicable law other than this article 21, if a record is privileged pursuant to section 13-90-107 (1)(b), the corresponding electronic record secured and stored by the remote notarization system as provided in this article 21 remains privileged.

§ 24-21-515, C.R.S. Certificate of notarial act.

(1) A notarial act must be evidenced by a certificate. The certificate must:

(a) Be executed contemporaneously with the performance of the notarial act;

(b) Be signed and dated by the notarial officer and, if the notarial officer is a notary public, be signed in the same manner as on file with the secretary of state;

(c) Identify the county and state in which the notarial act is performed;

(d) Contain the title of office of the notarial officer; and

(e) If the notarial officer is a notary public, indicate the date of expiration of the officer's commission.

(2) If a notarial act regarding a tangible record is performed by a notary public, an official stamp must be affixed to the certificate. If a notarial act is performed regarding a tangible record by a notarial officer other than a notary public and the certificate contains the information specified in subsections (1)(b), (1)(c), and (1)(d) of this section, an official stamp may be affixed to the certificate. If a notarial act regarding an electronic record is performed by a notarial officer and the certificate contains the information specified in subsections (1)(b), (1)(c), and (1)(d) of this section, an official stamp may be attached to or logically associated with the certificate.

(3) A certificate of a notarial act is sufficient if it meets the requirements of subsections (1) and (2) of this section and:

(a) Is in a short form set forth in section 24-21-516;

(b) Is in a form otherwise permitted by the law of this state;

(c) Is in a form permitted by the law applicable in the jurisdiction in which the notarial act was performed; or

* (d) Sets forth actions of the notarial officer that are sufficient to meet the requirements of the notarial act as provided in sections 24-21-505, 24-21-506, and 24-21-507 and, if applicable, section 24-21-514.5 or law of this state other than this part 5.

* (4) By executing a certificate of a notarial act, a notarial officer certifies that the officer has complied with the requirements and made the determinations specified in sections 24-21-504, 24-21-505, and 24-21-506 and, if applicable, section 24-21-514.5.

(5) A notarial officer shall not affix the officer's signature to, or logically associate it with, a certificate until the notarial act has been performed.

(6) If a notarial act is performed regarding a tangible record, a certificate must be part of, or securely attached to, the record. If a notarial act is performed regarding an electronic record, the certificate must be affixed to, or logically associated with, the electronic record. If the secretary

of state has established standards pursuant to section 24-21-527 for attaching, affixing, or logically associating the certificate, the process must conform to the standards.

§ 24-21-516, C.R.S. Short form certificates.

(1) The following short form certificates of notarial acts are sufficient for the purposes indicated, if completed with the information required by section 24-21-515 (1) and (2):

(a) For an acknowledgment in an individual capacity:

State of ______________

County of ______________

______________ This record was acknowledged before me on (date) by (name(s) of individual(s))

Signature of notarial officer

Stamp

((Title of office))

My commission expires: _____

(b) For an acknowledgment in a representative capacity:

State of

County of ______________

______________ This record was acknowledged before me on (date) by (name(s) of individual(s)) as (type of authority, such as officer or trustee) of (name of party on behalf of whom record was executed).

Signature of notarial officer

Stamp

((Title of office))

My commission expires: _____

(c) For a verification on oath or affirmation:

State of

County of ______________

______________ Signed and sworn to (or affirmed) before me on (date) by (name(s) of individual(s) making statement)

Signature of notarial officer

Stamp

((Title of office))

My commission expires: _____

(d) For witnessing or attesting a signature:

State of ______________

County of ______________

______________ Signed before me on (date) by (name(s) of individual(s))

Signature of notarial officer

Stamp

((Title of office))

My commission expires: _____

(e) For certifying a copy of a record:

State of ______________

County of ______________

________________I certify that this is a true and correct copy of a record in the possession of ____________.

Dated ____________

Signature of notarial officer

Stamp

(____(Title of office)____)

My commission expires: _____

§ 24-21-517, C.R.S. Official stamp.

(1) The official stamp of a notary public must:

(a) Be rectangular and contain only the outline of the seal and the following information printed within the outline of the seal:

(I) The notary public's name, as it appears on the notary's certificate of commission;

(II) The notary's identification number;

(III) The notary's commission expiration date;

(IV) The words "state of Colorado"; and

(V) The words "notary public"; and

(b) Be capable of being copied together with the record to which it is affixed or attached or with which it is logically associated.

(2) A notary public shall not provide, keep, or use a seal embosser.

§ 24-21-518, C.R.S. Stamping device.

(1) A notary public is responsible for the security of the notary public's stamping device and may not allow another individual to use the device to perform a notarial act. On resignation from, or the revocation or expiration of, the notary public's commission, or on the expiration of the date set forth in the stamping device, if any, the notary public shall disable the stamping device by destroying, defacing, damaging, erasing, or securing it against use in a manner that renders it unusable. On the death or adjudication of incompetency of a notary public, the notary public's personal representative or guardian or any other person knowingly in possession of the stamping device shall render it unusable by destroying, defacing, damaging, erasing, or securing it against use in a manner that renders it unusable.

(2) If a notary public's stamping device is lost or stolen, the notary public or the notary public's personal representative or guardian shall notify the secretary of state in writing within thirty days after discovering that the device is lost or stolen.

§ 24-21-519, C.R.S. Journal.

(1) A notary public shall maintain a journal in which the notary public chronicles all notarial acts that the notary public performs. The notary public shall retain the journal for ten years after the performance of the last notarial act chronicled in the journal.

* (2) (a) A journal may be created on a tangible medium or in an electronic format. If a journal is maintained on a tangible medium, it must be a permanent, bound register with numbered pages. If a journal is maintained in an electronic format, it must be in a permanent, tamper-evident electronic format complying with the rules of the secretary of state.

* (b) A notary public who performs a remote notarization shall maintain a journal in an electronic format with regard to each remote notarization.

(3) An entry in a journal must be made contemporaneously with performance of the notarial act and contain the following information:

(a) The date and time of the notarial act;

(b) A description of the record, if any, and type of notarial act;

(c) The full name and address of each individual for whom the notarial act is performed;

(d) The signature or electronic signature of each individual for whom the notarial act is performed;

(e) If identity of the individual is based on personal knowledge, a statement to that effect;

(f) If identity of the individual is based on satisfactory evidence, a brief description of the method of identification and the type of identification credential presented, if any; and

(g) The fee, if any, charged by the notary public.

(4) A notary public is responsible for the security of the notary public's journal. A notary public shall keep the journal in a secure area under the exclusive control of the notary, and shall not allow any other notary to use the journal.

(5) Upon written request of any member of the public, which request must include the name of the parties, the type of document, and the month and year in which a record was notarized, a notary public may supply a certified copy of the line item representing the requested transaction. A notary public may charge the fee allowed in section 24-21-529 for each certified copy of a line item, and shall record the transaction in the notary's journal.

(6) The secretary of state may audit or inspect a notary public's journal without restriction. A notary public shall surrender the notary's journal to the secretary of state upon receiving a written request.

(7) A certified peace officer, as defined in section 16-2.5-102, acting in the course of an official investigation may inspect a notary public's journal without restriction.

(8) If a notary public's journal is lost or stolen, the notary public shall notify the secretary of state in writing within thirty days after discovering that the journal is lost or stolen.

(9) On resignation from, or the revocation or expiration of, a notary public's commission, the notary public shall retain the notary public's journal in accordance with subsection (1) of this section and inform the secretary of state where the journal is located.

(10) (a) Instead of retaining a journal as provided in subsections (1) and (9) of this section, a current or former notary public may:

(I) Transmit the journal to the state archives established pursuant to part 1 of article 80 of this title 24; or

(II) Leave the journal with the notary's firm or employer in the regular course of business.

(b) If notary public acts pursuant to subsection (10)(a) of this section, the notary public is no longer subject to subsection (5) of this section and shall notify the secretary of state in writing whether the notary has transmitted the journal to the state archives or the firm or employer, including the contact information for the firm or employer if the notary leaves the journal with the notary's firm or employer.

(c) Instead of maintaining a journal as required by subsection (1) of this section, a notary public may maintain the original or a copy, including an electronic record, of a document that contains the information otherwise required to be entered in the notary's journal if the notary's firm or employer retains the original, copy, or electronic record in the regular course of business.

(11) On the death or adjudication of incompetency of a current or former notary public, the notary public's personal representative or guardian or any other person knowingly in possession of the

journal shall transmit it to the state archives established pursuant to part 1 of article 80 of this title 24. The person shall notify the secretary of state in writing when the person transmits the journal to the state archives.

§ 24-21-520, C.R.S. Notification regarding performance of notarial act on electronic record – selection of technology.

(1) A notary public may select one or more tamper-evident technologies to perform notarial acts with respect to electronic records. A person may not require a notary public to perform a notarial act with respect to an electronic record with a technology that the notary public has not selected.

(2) Before a notary public performs the notary public's initial notarial act with respect to an electronic record, a notary public shall notify the secretary of state that the notary public will be performing notarial acts with respect to electronic records and identify the technology the notary public intends to use. If the secretary of state has established standards for approval of technology pursuant to section 24-21-527, the technology must conform to the standards. If the technology conforms to the standards, the secretary of state shall approve the use of the technology.

(3) In every instance, the electronic signature of a notary public must contain or be accompanied by the following elements, all of which must be immediately perceptible and reproducible in the electronic record to which the notary's electronic signature is attached: The notary's name, as it appears on the notary's certificate of commission; the notary's identification number; the words "notary public" and "state of Colorado"; a document authentication number issued by the secretary of state; and the words "my commission expires" followed by the expiration date of the notary's commission. A notary's electronic signature must conform to any standards promulgated by the secretary of state.

§ 24-21-521, C.R.S. Commission as notary public – qualifications – no immunity or benefit.

(1) An individual qualified under subsection (3) of this section may apply to the secretary of state for a commission as a notary public. The applicant shall comply with and provide the information required by rules established by the secretary of state and pay any application fee. In accordance with section 24-21-111 (1), the secretary of state may require, at the secretary of state's discretion, the application required by this section, and any renewal of the application, to be made by electronic means designated by the secretary of state.

(2) In accordance with section 42-1-211, the department of state and the department of revenue shall allow for the exchange of information and data collected by the systems used by the departments to collect information on legal names and signatures of all applicants for driver's licenses or state identification cards.

(3) An applicant for a commission as a notary public must:
   (a) Be at least eighteen years of age;
   (b) Be a citizen or permanent legal resident of the United States or otherwise lawfully present in the United States;
   (c) Be a resident of or have a place of employment or practice in this state;
   (d) Be able to read and write English;
   (e) Not be disqualified to receive a commission under section 24-21-523; and
   (f) Have passed the examination required under section 24-21-522 (1).

* (4) *[Editor's note: This version of this subsection (4) is effective until July 1, 2022.]* The secretary of state shall verify the lawful presence in the United States of each applicant through the verification process outlined in section 24-76.5-103 (4).

* (4) *[Editor's note: This version of this subsection (4) is effective July 1, 2022.]* The secretary of state shall verify the lawful presence in the United States of each applicant by:

* (a) Accepting one of the following documents from the applicant:

* (I) A United States military card or a military dependent's identification card;

* (II) A United States Coast Guard Merchant Mariner card;

* (III) A Native American tribal document;

* (IV) A valid Colorado driver's license or a Colorado identification card issued pursuant to article 2 of title 42, unless the applicant holds a license or card issued pursuant to part 5 of article 2 of title 42;

* (V) A valid driver's license or identification card issued by another state, the District of Columbia, Puerto Rico, the United States Virgin Islands, or any territory or insular possession subject to the jurisdiction of the United States that is compliant with the federal "REAL ID Act", as amended;

* (VI) A valid United States passport;

* (VII) A valid United States permanent resident card; or

* (VIII) Any other valid type of identification that requires proof of lawful presence in the United States to obtain; and

* (b) Executing an affidavit stating that the applicant is:

* (I) A United States citizen or legal permanent resident; or

* (II) Otherwise lawfully present in the United States pursuant to federal law.

(5) Before issuance of a commission as a notary public, an applicant for the commission shall take the following affirmation in the presence of a person qualified to administer an affirmation in this state:

I, (name of applicant) , solemnly affirm, under the penalty of perjury in the second degree, as defined in section 18-8-503, Colorado Revised Statutes, that I have carefully read the notary law of this state, and, if appointed and commissioned as a notary public, I will faithfully perform, to the best of my ability, all notarial acts in conformance with the law.

(Signature of applicant)

Subscribed and affirmed before me this ___ day of ____, 20 __.

(Official signature and seal of person qualified to administer affirmation)

(6) On compliance with this section, the secretary of state shall issue a commission as a notary public to an applicant for a term of four years, unless revoked in accordance with section 24-21-523. An applicant who has been denied appointment and commission may appeal the decision in accordance with article 4 of this title 24.

(7) A commission to act as a notary public authorizes the notary public to perform notarial acts. The commission does not provide the notary public any immunity or benefit conferred by law of this state on public officials or employees.

§ 24-21-522, C.R.S. Examination of notary public.

(1) An applicant for a commission as a notary public who does not hold a commission in this state must pass an examination administered by the secretary of state or an entity approved by the secretary of state. The examination must be based on the course of study described in subsection (2) of this section.

(2) The secretary of state or an entity approved by the secretary of state shall offer regularly a course of study to applicants who do not hold commissions as notaries public in this state. The course must cover the laws, rules, procedures, and ethics relevant to notarial acts. The office of

the secretary of state may enter into a contract with a private contractor or contractors to conduct notary training programs. The contractor or contractors may charge a fee for any such training program.

§ 24-21-523, C.R.S. Grounds to deny, refuse to renew, revoke, suspend, or condition commission of notary public.

(1) The secretary of state may deny, refuse to renew, revoke, suspend, or impose a condition on a commission as notary public for:

(a) Failure to comply with this part 5;

(b) A substantial and material misstatement or omission of fact in the application for a commission as a notary public submitted to the secretary of state;

(c) Notwithstanding section 24-5-101, a conviction of the applicant or notary public of any felony or, in the prior five years, a misdemeanor involving dishonesty;

(d) A finding against, or admission of liability by, the applicant or notary public in any legal proceeding or disciplinary action based on the applicant's or notary public's fraud, dishonesty, or deceit;

(e) Failure by the notary public to discharge any duty required of a notary public, whether by this part 5, rules of the secretary of state, or any federal or state law;

(f) Use of false or misleading advertising or representation by the notary public representing that the notary has a duty, right, or privilege that the notary does not have;

(g) Violation by the notary public of a rule of the secretary of state regarding a notary public;

(h) Denial, refusal to renew, revocation, suspension, or conditioning of a notary public commission in another state;

(i) A finding by a court of this state that the applicant or notary public has engaged in the unauthorized practice of law;

(j) Failure to comply with any term of suspension or condition imposed on the commission of a notary public under this section; or

(k) Performance of any notarial act while not currently commissioned by the secretary of state.

(2) Whenever the secretary of state or the secretary of state's designee believes that a violation of this part 5 has occurred, the secretary of state or the secretary of state's designee may investigate the violation. The secretary of state or the secretary of state's designee may also investigate possible violations of this part 5 upon a signed complaint from any person.

(3) If the secretary of state denies, refuses to renew, revokes, suspends, or imposes conditions on a commission as a notary public, the applicant or notary public is entitled to timely notice and hearing in accordance with the "State Administrative Procedure Act", article 4 of this title 24.

(4) When a complaint or investigation results in a finding of misconduct that, in the secretary of state's discretion, does not warrant initiation of a disciplinary proceeding, the secretary of state may take nondisciplinary action. For the purposes of this subsection (4), nondisciplinary action includes the issuance of a letter of admonition, which may be placed in the notary public's file.

(5) The authority of the secretary of state to deny, refuse to renew, suspend, revoke, or impose conditions on a commission as a notary public does not prevent a person from seeking and obtaining other criminal or civil remedies provided by law.

(6) A person whose notary commission has been revoked pursuant to this part 5 may not apply for or receive a commission and appointment as a notary.

§ 24-21-524, C.R.S. Database of notaries public.

(1) The secretary of state shall maintain an electronic database of notaries public:

(a) Through which a person may verify the authority of a notary public to perform notarial acts; and

(b) Which indicates whether a notary public has notified the secretary of state that the notary public will be performing notarial acts on electronic records.

§ 24-21-525, C.R.S. Prohibited acts.

(1) A commission as a notary public does not authorize an individual to:

(a) Assist persons in drafting legal records, give legal advice, or otherwise practice law;

(b) Act as an immigration consultant or an expert on immigration matters;

(c) Represent a person in a judicial or administrative proceeding relating to immigration to the United States, United States citizenship, or related matters; or

(d) Receive compensation for performing any of the activities listed in this subsection (1).

(2) A notary public shall not engage in false or deceptive advertising.

(3) A notary public, other than an attorney licensed to practice law in this state, shall not use the term "notario" or "notario publico".

(4) A notary public, other than an attorney licensed to practice law in this state, shall not advertise or represent that the notary public may assist persons in drafting legal records, give legal advice, or otherwise practice law. If a notary public who is not an attorney licensed to practice law in this state in any manner advertises or represents that the notary public offers notarial services, whether orally or in a record, including broadcast media, print media, and the internet, the notary public shall include the following statement, or an alternate statement authorized or required by the secretary of state, in the advertisement or representation, prominently and in each language used in the advertisement or representation: "I am not an attorney licensed to practice law in the state of Colorado and I may not give legal advice or accept fees for legal advice. I am not an immigration consultant, nor am I an expert on immigration matters. If you suspect fraud, you may contact the Colorado attorney general's office or the Colorado supreme court." If the form of advertisement or representation is not broadcast media, print media, or the internet and does not permit inclusion of the statement required by this subsection (4) because of size, it must be displayed prominently or provided at the place of performance of the notarial act before the notarial act is performed.

(5) A notary public, other than an attorney licensed to practice law in this state, shall not engage in conduct that constitutes a deceptive trade practice pursuant to section 6-1-727.

(6) Except as otherwise allowed by law, a notary public shall not withhold access to or possession of an original record provided by a person that seeks performance of a notarial act by the notary public.

(7) A notary public shall not perform any notarial act with respect to a record that is blank or that contains unfilled blanks in its text.

§ 24-21-526, C.R.S. Validity of notarial acts.

Except as otherwise provided in section 24-21-504 (2), the failure of a notarial officer to perform a duty or meet a requirement specified in this part 5 does not invalidate a notarial act performed by the notarial officer. The validity of a notarial act under this part 5 does not prevent an aggrieved person from seeking to invalidate the record or transaction that is the subject of the notarial act or from seeking other remedies based on law of this state other than this part 5 or law of the United States. This section does not validate a purported notarial act performed by an individual who does not have the authority to perform notarial acts.

§ 24-21-527, C.R.S. Rules.

(1) The secretary of state may adopt rules to implement this part 5 in accordance with article 4 of this title 24. Rules adopted regarding the performance of notarial acts with respect to electronic records may not require, or accord greater legal status or effect to, the implementation or application of a specific technology or technical specification. The rules may:

(a) Prescribe the manner of performing notarial acts regarding tangible and electronic records;

(b) Include provisions to ensure that any change to or tampering with a record bearing a certificate of a notarial act is self-evident;

(c) Include provisions to ensure integrity in the creation, transmittal, storage, or authentication of electronic records or signatures;

(d) Prescribe the process of granting, renewing, conditioning, denying, suspending, or revoking a notary public commission and assuring the trustworthiness of an individual holding a commission as notary public, including rules for use of the electronic filing system;

* (e) Include provisions to prevent fraud or mistake in the performance of notarial acts;

(f) Provide for the administration of the examination under section 24-21-522 (1) and the course of study under section 24-21-522 (2).

* (g) Prescribe the manner of performing notarial acts using audio-video communication technology, including provisions to ensure the security, integrity, and accessibility of records relating to those acts; and

* (h) Prescribe requirements for the approval and use of remote notarization systems and storage systems.

(2) In adopting, amending, or repealing rules about notarial acts with respect to electronic records, the secretary of state shall consider, so far as is consistent with this part 5:

(a) The most recent standards regarding electronic records promulgated by national bodies, such as the National Association of Secretaries of State;

(b) Standards, practices, and customs of other jurisdictions that substantially enact this part 5; and

(c) The views of governmental officials and entities and other interested persons.

* (3) (a) As used in this subsection (3):

* (I) "Interim period" means the period beginning on March 30, 2020, and ending on December 31, 2020.

* (II) "Temporary rule" means rule 5 of the notary program rules as adopted by the secretary of state effective March 30, 2020, and published at 8 CCR 1505-11, and any analogous successor emergency rule of the notary program that authorizes remote notarizations.

* (b) and (c) Repealed.

* (d) A notarial act performed during the interim period with respect to a remotely located individual that complied with the temporary rule is not invalid due to the lack of express statutory authority for the notarial act.

* (e) and (f) Repealed.

§ 24-21-528, C.R.S. Disposition of fees.

(1) The secretary of state shall collect all fees pursuant to this article 21 in the manner required by section 24-21-104 (3) and shall transmit them to the state treasurer, who shall credit them to the department of state cash fund created in section 24-21-104 (3)(b).

(2) The general assembly shall make annual appropriations from the department of state cash fund for expenditures of the secretary of state incurred in the performance of the secretary of state's duties under this part 5.

§ 24-21-529, C.R.S. Notary's fees.

(1) Except as specified in subsection (2) of this section, the fees of a notary public may be, but must not exceed, five dollars for each document attested by a person before a notary, except as otherwise provided by law. The fee for each such document must include all duties and functions required to complete the notarial act in accordance with this part 5.

(2) In lieu of the fee authorized in subsection (1) of this section, a notary public may charge a fee, not to exceed ten dollars, for the notary's electronic signature.

§ 24-21-530, C.R.S. Change of name or address.

A notary public shall notify the secretary of state within thirty days after he or she changes his or her name, business address, or residential address. In the case of a name change, the notary public shall include a sample of the notary's handwritten official signature on the notice. Pursuant to section 24-21-104 (3), the secretary of state shall determine the amount of, and collect, the fee, payable to the secretary of state, for recording notice of change of name or address.

§ 24-21-531, C.R.S. Official misconduct by a notary public – liability of notary or surety.

* (1) *[Editor's note: This version of subsection (1) is effective until March 1, 2022.]* A notary public who knowingly and willfully violates the duties imposed by this part 5 commits official misconduct and is guilty of a class 2 misdemeanor.

* (1) *[Editor's note: This version of subsection (1) is effective March 1, 2022.]* A notary public who knowingly and willfully violates the duties imposed by this part 5 commits official misconduct and is guilty of a petty offense.

(2) A notary public and the surety or sureties on his or her bond are liable to the persons involved for all damages proximately caused by the notary's official misconduct.

(3) Nothing in this part 5 shall be construed to deny a notary public the right to obtain a surety bond or insurance on a voluntary basis to provide coverage for liability.

§ 24-21-532, C.R.S. Willful impersonation.

* *[Editor's note: This version of this section is effective until March 1, 2022.]* A person who acts as, or otherwise willfully impersonates, a notary public while not lawfully appointed and commissioned to perform notarial acts is guilty of a class 2 misdemeanor and shall be punished as specified in section 18-1.3-501.

* *[Editor's note: This version of this section is effective March 1, 2022.]* A person who acts as, or otherwise willfully impersonates, a notary public while not lawfully appointed and commissioned to perform notarial acts commits a petty offense and shall be punished as specified in section 18-1.3-503.

§ 24-21-533, C.R.S. Wrongful possession of journal or seal.

* *[Editor's note: This version of this section is effective until March 1, 2022.]* A person who unlawfully possesses and uses a notary's journal, an official seal, a notary's electronic signature, or any papers, copies, or electronic records relating to notarial acts is guilty of a class 3 misdemeanor and shall be punished as specified in section 18-1.3-501.

* *[Editor's note: This version of this section is effective March 1, 2022.]* A person who unlawfully possesses and uses a notary's journal, an official seal, a notary's electronic signature, or any papers,

copies, or electronic records relating to notarial acts commits a petty offense and shall be punished as specified in section 18-1.3-503.

§ 24-21-534, C.R.S. Certification restrictions.

(1) The secretary of state may issue certificates or apostilles attesting to the authenticity of a notarial act performed by a commissioned notary public.

(2) The secretary of state shall not certify a signature of a notary public on:

- (a) A record that is not properly notarized in accordance with the requirements of this part 5;
- (b) A record:
  - (I) Regarding allegiance to a government or jurisdiction;
  - (II) Relating to the relinquishment or renunciation of citizenship, sovereignty, in itinere status or world service authority; or
  - (III) Setting forth or implying for the bearer a claim of immunity from the law of this state or federal law.

§ 24-21-535, C.R.S. Notary public commission in effect.

A commission as a notary public in effect on July 1, 2018, continues until its date of expiration. A notary public who applies to renew a commission as a notary public on or after July 1, 2018, is subject to and shall comply with this part 5. A notary public, in performing notarial acts after July 1, 2018, shall comply with this part 5.

§ 24-21-536, C.R.S. Savings clause.

This part 5 does not affect the validity or effect of a notarial act performed before July 1, 2018.

§ 24-21-537, C.R.S. Uniformity of application and construction.

In applying and construing this part 5, consideration must be given to the need to promote uniformity of the law with respect to its subject matter among states that enact it.

§ 24-21-538, C.R.S. Relation to "Electronic Signatures in Global and National Commerce Act".

This part 5 modifies, limits, and supersedes the "Electronic Signatures in Global and National Commerce Act", 15 U.S.C. sec. 7001 et seq., but does not modify, limit, or supersede section 101 (c) of that act, 15 U.S.C. sec. 7001 (c), or authorize electronic delivery of any of the notices described in section 103 (b) of that act, 15 U.S.C. sec. 7003 (b).

§ 24-21-539, C.R.S. Effective date.

This part 5 takes effect on July 1, 2018.

§ 24-21-540, C.R.S. Repeal.

This part 5 is repealed, effective September 1, 2023. Before its repeal, this part 5 is scheduled for review in accordance with section 24-34-104.

XVII. Uniform Recognition of Acknowledgments Act

§ 12-55-201 to § 12-55-212, C.R.S. (Repealed)

Editor's note: (1) Section 12-55-212 provided for the repeal of this part 2, effective July 1, 2018. (See L. 2017, pp. 787, 809, and 1418.)

(2) This part 2 was numbered as article 2 of chapter 96, C.R.S. 1963. For amendments to this part 2 prior to its repeal in 2018, consult the 2017 Colorado Revised Statutes.

Cross references: For the "Revised Uniform Law on Notarial Acts", see part 5 of article 21 of title 24.

Glossary

abstract of title. a summary or condensation of the essential parts of all recorded instruments which affect a particular piece of real estate, arranged in the order in which they were recorded.

acceleration clause. a clause in a contract by which the time for payment of a debt is advanced, usually making the obligation immediately due and payable, because of the breach of some condition, such as failure to pay an installment when due.

acceptance. an indication by an offeree of willingness to be bound by the terms of the offer.

acknowledgment. a declaration made by a person to a notary public, or other public official authorized to take acknowledgments, that the instrument was executed by the person and that it is a free and voluntary act.

acre foot. a term used in measuring the volume of water, equal to the quantity of water required to cover one acre one foot deep, or 43,560 cu. ft.

administrator. A person appointed by the court to administer the estate of a deceased person who died intestate (without leaving a will).

ad valorem. Latin meaning "according to value"; normally used to describe a tax based on the assessed value of real property.

adverse possession. the right of an occupant of land to acquire a superior title to the real estate against the record owner, where such possession has been actual, notorious, hostile, visible and continuous for the required statutory period (18 years in Colorado). Adverse possession promotes the productive use of land by giving title to the one putting the land to use.

affidavit. a written statement or declaration, sworn to or affirmed before some officer who has authority to administer an oath or affirmation.

agency. a legal relationship resulting from an agreement or contract, either expressed or implied, written or oral, whereby one person, the agent, is employed by another, called the principal, to do certain acts in dealing with a third party.

agent. any person, partnership, association, or corporation authorized or employed by another, called the principal, to act for, on behalf of, and subject to the control of the principal.

alienation. transfer of real property by one person to another.

amenities. in real estate, amenities are features such as location, outlook, or access to a park, lake, highway, view or the like which enhance the desirability of real estate and which contribute to the pleasure and enjoyment of the occupants.

amortization. liquidation or gradual retirement of a financial obligation by periodic installments.

appraisal. in real estate, an estimate of the quality or value of property; also refers to the report setting forth the estimate of value together with the basis for such conclusions.

appropriation. the act(s) involved in the taking and reducing to personal possession of water occurring in a stream or other body of water, and of applying such water to beneficial use.

appropriator. one who diverts and puts to beneficial use the water of a stream or other body of water, under a water right obtained through appropriation.

appurtenance. that which belongs to something else; something adapted to the use of the real property to which it is connected or belongs intended to be a permanent addition to the land. Appurtenances pass with the title to the land, e.g. a house, barn, garage, right-of-way, etc.

assessed valuation. an estimate of value by a unit of government for taxation purposes.

assessment. in real estate, the valuation of property in order to apportion a tax upon it.

assignee. the party to whom a legal right has been assigned or transferred.

assignment. transfer to another of a legal right.

assignor. the party who assigns or transfers a legal right.

attachment. a type of encumbrance, permitted only under special circumstances, which is placed against the real estate of a defendant in a pending law suit for money damages.

attorney's opinion. in real estate, the written opinion of an attorney-at-law regarding the marketability of title to real property based upon an examination of the abstract of title or the records in the county clerk and recorder's office.

animal unit (A.U.). the grazing capacity of land to properly sustain one animal and any offspring for one year.

balance sheet. a statement showing a company's financial position at the end of an accounting period by listing assets, liabilities and owner's equity.

balloon payment. a final lump-sum payment of an installment debt, much larger than all previous installments, and which pays the debt in full prior to its full amortization.

bargain and sale deed. any deed that recites consideration and purports to convey the real estate. A bargain and sale deed with a covenant against the grantor's acts warrants only that he or she has done nothing to harm or cloud the title.

beneficiary. the person who benefits from certain acts, e.g. a will; one receiving benefits, profits or advantage; one for whose benefit a trust is created.

bill of sale. a written instrument by which a person transfers right, title or interest in personal property to another.

blanket mortgage. a mortgage that covers more than one piece of property.

broker. a duly licensed person, firm, partnership, limited liability company, association, or corporation who, in consideration of compensation or with the intent of receiving such compensation, facilitates a real property transaction for another party. (See 12-10-201 C.R.S. for Colorado statutory definition – chapter 1 of this manual.)

building code. local government regulations specifying structural requirements of buildings.

buyer agent. a broker engaged by and representing the buyer in a real estate transaction.

capitalization rate. a percentage rate of change applied in the income approach to value.

cash basis accounting. recognizing revenue and expense when cash is received or disbursed rather than when earned or incurred. A service business not dealing in inventory has the option of using the cash or accrual basis of accounting. Individual taxpayers must use the accrual basis.

cash flow. cash receipts minus cash disbursements from an operation or asset. An annual cash flow statement shows total return after taxes.

caveat emptor. Latin phrase meaning "let the buyer beware.", formerly imposing a duty on the buyer to examine the products or property accepting them "as is".

certificate of reasonable value (CRV). Veterans Administration's certified appraisal of value of real property.

certificate of taxes. a written guaranty of the condition of the taxes on a certain property made by the county treasurer wherein the property is located. Any loss resulting from an error in a tax certificate shall be paid by the county that such treasurer represents.

chapter 7. provision of the 1978 Bankruptcy Reform Act that covers liquidations under a court appointed trustee.

chapter 11. provision of the 1978 Bankruptcy Reform Act that covers reorganizations where the debtor remains in control of the business and its operations.

chattel. property other than real estate, i.e. personal property; an item of movable property.

check. synonym for quadrangle, a 24 mile square tract of land in the Governmental Survey System.

cloud on title. an outstanding claim or encumbrance that affects or impairs title to the property.

cognovit note. one containing a confession of judgment (waiver of due process) by the borrower.

collateral security. some security additional to the personal obligation of the borrower, as a chattel mortgage or trust deed.

Colorado Association of REALTORS® – (C.A.R). the state organization of real estate licensees whose goal is the professional advancement of the real estate industry and whose membership is comprised of local real estate associations or boards.

Colorado Coordinate System. a method of land description based on measurements from the intersection of statutorily defined north-south and east-west axes; applied only in Delta and Ute Counties.

commingling. mixing money belonging to others with personal or business funds. Illegal commingling is using the money of one beneficiary for the benefit of another or failing to maintain such money in identified escrow accounts.

common interest community. real estate described in a declaration which obligates an individual unit owner to pay property tax, insurance premiums, maintenance or improvement on some declared real property owned in common. Ownership does not include a leasehold interest of less than forty years, measured from the date the initial term commences, including renewal options.

common-law. law evolving from usage, custom and judicial interpretation rather than legislated by statute. Common law originated in old English courts.

community property. property acquired by a husband and wife, or either, during marriage, by their industry and not by gift, belonging equally to husband and wife. Community property laws exist in only nine states: AZ, CA, ID, LA, NV, NM, OK, TX and WA.

condemnation. in real property law, the process by which property of a private owner is taken for public use, with compensation to the owner, under the governmental right of eminent domain.

condominium. a common interest community in which portions of the real estate are designated for separate ownership and the remainder of which is distributed for common ownership solely among separate owners. A common interest community is not a condominium unless the undivided interests in the common elements are vested in the unit owners.

consideration. a promise or an act of legal value bargained for and received in return for a promise; one of the essential elements of a contract.

construction mortgage. a short-term loan used to finance the building of a structure.

constructive (or legal) notice. the conclusive presumption that all persons have knowledge of the contents of a recorded instrument.

contract. an agreement, enforceable at law, between two or more competent persons, having a legal purpose, wherein the parties agree to act in a certain manner.

controller. the chief accounting executive of an organization responsible for (1) financial reporting, (2) tax administration, (3) management audits, (4) planning controls and (5) developing accounting systems and procedures.

conventional mortgage. a mortgage securing a loan made by private investors without governmental participation, i.e. not F.H.A.-insured or V.A.-guaranteed.

conversion. unauthorized appropriation of ownership rights over goods or property belonging to another; also altering one form of property to another such as changing a leasehold apartment building to freehold condominium ownership.

conveyance. an instrument in writing by which a person transfers some estate, interest, or title in real estate to another, such as a deed or lease.

covenant. a promise or agreement, usually in writing, to do or not do certain acts; also stipulations in a real estate conveyance document governing use of the property.

cubage. the product of multiplying width x height x depth (or length) of an object.

cubic foot per second. a unit of discharge for measurement of flowing liquid, equal to a flow of one cubic foot per second past a given section. Also called "second-foot".

cul-de-sac. a street which dead-ends in a semi-circle.

curtesy. a common-law life-estate in all of a wife's real property given to the husband upon her death, provided a child was born from their marriage; abolished in Colorado.

customer. a party to a real estate transaction with whom the broker has no brokerage relationship because such party has not engaged or employed a broker.

debenture. bonds issued without specific security and are secured only by the overall equity of the issuer.

declaration. a recorded instrument that defines boundaries and common elements of a condominium and establishes the basic rights and obligations of the owners. It also provides for the creation of an owners' association including a board of directors with authority to collect common expenses and otherwise act for the benefit of all owners.

dedication. transfer of land from private to public use, as streets in a platted subdivision.

deed. a legal instrument in writing, duly executed and delivered, whereby the owner (grantor) conveys to another (grantee) some right, title or interest in or to real estate.

deed restriction. a provision in a deed controlling or limiting the use of the land.

default. omission or failure to perform a legal duty; failure to meet an obligation when due.

defeasible fee (base- or qualified fee). a fee interest in land that is capable of being defeated or terminated upon the happening of a specified event.

deficiency judgment. a lien against borrower's remaining assets in an amount equal to the shortage between a foreclosure sale price less than the indebtedness owed.

depreciation. loss in value due to deterioration from ordinary wear and tear, action of the elements, functional or economic obsolescence.

designated broker. an employing or employed broker designated in writing by an employing broker to serve as a single agent or transaction-broker for a seller, landlord, buyer or tenant in a real estate transaction; does not include a real estate brokerage firm that consists of only one licensed natural person.

devise. a gift of real property by the last will and testament of a donor.

diversion. illegal or unauthorized use of entrusted funds.

documentary fee. a statutory Colorado tax of one cent per one hundred dollars (sale price x .0001) of consideration paid by a person recording an instrument of conveyance with a county clerk and recorder.

donee. receiver of a gift.

donor. giver of a gift.

dower. a common-law estate consisting of a one-third interest in a husband's real property given to his wife upon his death. abolished in Colorado.

due-on-sale clause. a provision in a mortgage or trust deed which allows the lender to call a promissory note due and payable in full immediately upon the sale or transfer of a secured property; allows a lender to raise the interest rate or force other changes in terms upon assumption of the loan.

duress. forcing action or inaction against a person's will.

earnest money. down payment made by a purchaser of real estate as evidence of good faith.

easement. a right or interest in the real property of another; the right to use another's land for a specific purpose, such as a right-of-way.

economic life. the period of time over which improved property may be profitably used.

eminent domain. a governmental right to take private property for public use through the process of condemnation, and with payment of just compensation.

employing broker. a license level qualifying a broker to employ other licensees, requiring two years of active licensed experience, a 24-hour "brokerage administration" course if licensed after December 31, 1996 and passage of the Colorado part of the broker licensing exam if upgrade to broker associate from salesperson was by means of the broker transition course.

encroachment. illegal intrusion of an improvement or other real property onto another's property.

encumbrance. a claim, lien, charge, or liability attached to and binding upon real property, such as a judgment, mortgage, mechanic's lien, lien for unpaid taxes, or right-of-way.

endorsement. signing one's name on a negotiable instrument with intent to transfer ownership; also an addition altering or clarifying coverage of an (title) insurance policy.

equity. the amount of an owner's interest in real estate exceeding its encumbrances.

equity of redemption. see redemption.

escheat. reversion of property to the state when an owner dies without leaving a will or legal heirs to whom the property may pass by lawful descent.

escrow. the state or condition of money or a deed held conditionally by a third party, called the escrow agent, pending the performance or fulfillment of some act or condition.

escrow account. any checking, demand, passbook or statement account insured by an agency of the United States government maintained in a Colorado depository for money that belongs to others.

escrow agreement. a written agreement whereby a grantor, promissor or obligor delivers certain instruments or property to an escrow agent, to be held until the happening of a contingency or performance of a condition, and then to be delivered to the grantee, promisee or obligee.

estate. the degree, quantity, nature and extent of a person's interest in real property; such as a fee simple absolute estate, or an estate for years.

estate (tenancy) at sufferance. an estate in land arising when the tenant wrongfully holds over after the expiration of the tenant's term; the landlord has the choice of evicting the tenant as a trespasser or accepting such tenant for a similar term and under the conditions of the tenant's previous holding.

estate (tenancy) at will. an interest in land terminable at the will of either the tenant or landlord.

estate (tenancy) for years. an interest in land for a fixed period of time, e.g. one day or 99 years.

estate from period-to-period (periodic tenancy). An interest in land with no contract date of termination. The rental period (week, month or year, etc.) renews by payment of the contract rent.

et al. Latin abbreviation for "et allus", meaning "and others".

et ux. Latin abbreviation for "et uxor", meaning "and wife".

eviction. dispossession by process of law; the act of depriving a person of the possession of land pursuant to a court judgment.

exclusive agency listing. a listing whereby the owner engages a real estate brokerage as sole broker for a specified period of time, while retaining the right to sell the property to a buyer that the owner finds without paying the broker a commission.

exclusive right-to-sell listing. a listing whereby the owner engages one real estate brokerage as sole broker for a specified period of time, entitling the broker to a commission regardless of who sells the property, including the owner.

execution. a writ issued by a court to the sheriff directing seizure and sale of a property to satisfy a debt; the act of signing a contract; completion of the terms of a contract.

executor. the person named in a will to carry out its provisions.

"fannie mae". The pronunciation of "FNMA" (Federal National Mortgage Association). provides a market for government secured mortgages held by primary lenders and provides them with a ready market so as to permit a greater turnover of money for loans.

fee simple absolute (fee or fee simple). the most comprehensive ownership of real property under law; the largest bundle of ownership rights possible.

fee tail. an estate in land which cannot be conveyed but which must descend to the heirs of the holder; abolished in Colorado.

F.H.A.-insured mortgage. a mortgage under which the Federal Housing Administration insures approved lenders against loan default.

fiduciary. a person in a position of trust relative to another party; confidential, as in a fiduciary relationship between an agent and the principal.

fixture. an article of personal property installed in or attached to land or an improvement in a permanent manner, so that it is considered a part of the real estate.

foreclosure. termination of property rights due to some default by the borrower; a judicial or public trustee process whereby secured property is sold to satisfy a debt.

grantee. a person to whom real estate is conveyed; the buyer.

grantor. a person who conveys real estate; the seller.

grazing district. an administrative subdivision of the range lands under the jurisdiction of the Bureau of Land Management, established pursuant to section 3 of the Taylor Grazing Act to facilitate management of BLM forage resources.

grazing lease section 15. a lease authorizing the use of public lands outside of grazing districts (Taylor Grazing Act) for the grazing of livestock for a specified period of time.

grazing licenses. a permit for the grazing of a set number and class of livestock on a designated area of grazing district lands for a specified time, usually less than one year.

grazing permit. a permit to graze a certain number and class of livestock on a designated area of grazing district lands during specified seasons each year for a period of usually 10 years.

grazing preference. a request to graze certain numbers and classes of livestock upon a national forest for a specified time and subject to rules and regulations adopted by the Forest Service.

gross income multiplier. a number used in the income approach to value used to compare potential desirability of income properties, and calculated by dividing sales price by gross annual income.

ground water. a pervious formation with sides and bottom of relatively impervious material, in which ground water is held or retained; also called subsurface water basin.

holdover tenant. one who fails to vacate leased property after the lease has expired.

homeowners association. an association or unit owners association formed as part of a common interest community.

homestead exemption. a/k/a "homestead" or "homestead right"; a fixed, statutory sum exempt from execution by creditors, and intended to protect a family home from foreclosure or sale for debts.

indemnify. to insure; to secure against loss.

independent broker. a license level qualifying a broker to work without the supervision of an employing broker, requiring two years of active licensed experience, and if upgrade to broker associate was by means of the broker transition course, passage of the Colorado part of the broker licensing exam.

installment land contract (ILC), also land contract, or installment contract; an agreement for the purchase of real estate on an installment basis, whereby the deed is withheld until all or a specified portion of the purchase price is paid.

inter alia. Latin meaning "among other things".

intestate. Dying without leaving a valid will.

joint tenancy. a type of co-ownership of real property featuring a right of survivorship and four unities (time, title, interest and possession).

judgment. final declaration of the rights of the parties by a court.

land. real property; all below the surface, the surface and the airspace above it, and that which is affixed to it permanently; synonymous with "real property", "realty", and "real estate"; often used to mean only the unimproved surface of the earth.

land economics. the production, distribution and consumption of wealth deriving from land classification and use.

landlord. an owner who has leased an estate-in-land to a tenant.

landlord agent. a broker engaged by and representing a landlord as an agent in a leasing transaction.

lease. an agreement under which a tenant receives possession and use of real property for a certain period of time and the landlord receives the payment of rent and/or the performance of other conditions.

leasehold. an estate or right in real property held under a lease.

legal description. a description recognized by law that is sufficient to locate and identify a property without oral testimony.

lessee. party who possesses an estate in realty under a lease; commonly referred to as tenant.

lessor. party who conveys a right or estate in realty to a lessee under a lease; commonly referred to as landlord.

lien. a right given by law to a creditor to have a debt or charge satisfied out of the value of real or personal property belonging to the debtor.

life estate. an estate or interest in real property held for the duration of the life of some certain person.

limited agent. an agent whose duties and obligations to a principal are only those set forth in C.R.S. 12-10-404 or 12-10-405, with any additional duties and obligations agreed to pursuant to section 12-10-403 (5).

lis pendens. a filing against specific property, giving public notice that an action at law is pending that may affect the title to the land.

listing. an agreement or contract of employment, either oral or written, whereby the owner authorizes the real estate broker to sell, exchange or lease real estate.

marketable (merchantable) title. a title free from reasonable doubt of defect; which can be readily sold or mortgaged to a reasonably prudent person; a title free from material defects or grave doubts and reasonably free from potential litigation.

market value. the price which a ready and able buyer, not forced to buy, would pay and which a ready and willing seller, not forced to sell, would accept, assuming that both parties are fully informed, act reasonably, and have sufficient time to consider the transaction with due care.

mechanics' lien. a lien created by statute which exists against real property in favor of persons who have performed work or furnished materials for the improvement of the real estate.

metes and bounds. a method of describing or locating real property; metes are measures of length and bounds are boundaries. This method starts from a well-marked point of beginning and follows the boundaries of the land until it returns once more to the point of beginning.

mill. one-tenth of a cent; a tax rate of one mill on the dollar or one-tenth of one percent of the assessed value of a property. (assessed value x .001)

mortgage. a conditional conveyance of property as security for the payment of a debt or the fulfillment of some obligation. Upon payment of the debt or performance of the obligation, a mortgage automatically becomes void.

mortgagee. the party (lender) to whom property is conveyed under a mortgage as security for the repayment of a loan or fulfillment of some obligation.

mortgagor. the party who gives a mortgage (borrower) conveying interest in the property to the lender as security for the obligation to repay a loan or fulfill some obligation.

multiple listing service (MLS). a marketing arrangement among real estate brokers whereby a seller authorizes the listing broker to share information and a pre-determined portion of a commission to any broker cooperating in the sale of the property.

mutual assent (meeting of the minds). agreement of the parties to the contract, mutually consenting to be bound by its exact terms; an essential contract element.

National Association of REALTORS©, (N.A.R.). a national association of real estate personnel whose goal is the professional advancement of the real estate industry and whose membership is comprised of state and local real estate associations or boards.

national forest. a forest or watershed reservation administered by the Forest Service, United States Department of Agriculture.

negotiable instrument. a written instrument containing a promise of payment, which can be endorsed from one person to another.

net listing. a listing contract whereby the owner is to receive a certain net price, with the broker receiving any excess over and above the net price as commission.

note. a written instrument acknowledging a debt and promising payment.

obsolescence. impairment of desirability and usefulness of the property resulting from economic, functional, physical, fashion, or other changes.

offer. to present for sale; or a proposal presented for acceptance or rejection which, if accepted, will form a binding contract.

offeree. one to whom an offer is made.

offeror. one who makes an offer.

open listing. a non-exclusive employment agreement in which an owner retains the right to list the property with other brokers.

option. a temporary right for a specified time, and for which a consideration is paid, during which an optionee may purchase or lease property at a set price.

optionee. one who requests, receives or stands to benefit from an option.

optionor. one who grants an option to another, usually the land owner.

party wall. a wall erected on a line between adjoining properties for the use of both properties.

patent. an instrument of conveyance of government-owned land to an individual.

percentage lease. A commercial lease of property in which the rent is based upon a percentage of the sales volume derived from the leased premises.

percolation (perc) test. determines if soil will take sufficient water seepage for use of a septic tank.

periodic tenancy. see estate from period-to-period.

personal property. all that is not real property; items of a temporary or movable nature.

personalty. synonym for personal property.

plat. a parcel or plot of land; also a method of land description referring to a recorded map (plat) of a subdivision or town which lays out boundaries, streets, easements etc.

police power. governmental right to enact legislation deemed necessary to protect and promote the health, safety and general welfare of the public. (License law is supported by this legal theory.)

power of attorney. a legal instrument authorizing another person to act in place of the person drawing the instrument.

principal. a person, partnership, association or corporation who authorizes or employs another, called the agent, to do certain acts on behalf of the principal.

principal note. a promissory note secured by the mortgage or trust deed.

property. anything which may be owned and its bundle of ownership rights; the right to use, possess, enjoy, and dispose of a thing in every legal way and to exclude everyone else from interfering with these rights; generally classified into two groups; personal and real.

public trustee. a county official to whom borrowers convey title to real property by trust deed for the benefit of the beneficiary (lender).

purchase money mortgage. a mortgage given by the purchaser to secure a loan for part or all of the purchase price. Such a mortgage becomes a lien on the property simultaneously with the passing of title, and if immediately recorded becomes prior to any lien against the purchaser.

quadrangle, (check). a square tract of land in the U.S. Governmental Survey System measuring 24 miles on each side.

quiet-title suit. an action in court to remove a defect, cloud or suspicion regarding the owner's legal rights to a parcel of real estate.

quitclaim deed. a deed in which the grantor warrants nothing, conveying only the grantor's present interest in the real estate, if any.

range. a six-mile wide strip of land that runs in a north-south direction. Ranges are determined by government survey and are numbered in numerical order east or west of a principal meridian.

real estate. real property, realty, land.

real property. land; the surface of the earth and whatever is erected, growing upon, or affixed to the land; including that which is below it and the airspace above it. synonymous with "land", "realty", and "real estate".

REALTOR®. a registered trade name exclusive to members of the National Association of REALTORS®.

realty. real property, land, real estate.

receiver. a court-appointed custodian who holds property pending final disposition of the matter before the court.

recording. entering an instrument in a book of public record in the office of the county clerk and recorder. recording constitutes "constructive" notice to all persons of the rights or claims contained in the instrument.

Rectangular Survey System. see U.S. Government Survey System.

redemption. the right of an owner to redeem or reclaim real estate by paying the debt or charge (such as mortgage or tax lien) after default, together with interest and costs. Specifically, **equity of redemption** is the right to redeem the property after default but before foreclosure. **Statutory right-of-redemption** refers to the right to redeem the property after foreclosure, or other enforcement action, within a certain time specified by statute. In Colorado, a mortgagor has a statutory right to redeem property any time within 75 days (residential) or six months (agricultural)) after foreclosure or three years after a tax sale.

release. the relinquishment or surrender of a right, claim, or interest.

release of lien. the discharge or release of specific property from the charge or lien of a judgment, mortgage or other claim.

restrictive covenant. a clause in a deed limiting the use of a property.

right of survivorship. a characteristic of joint-tenancy whereupon the death of one tenant triggers an automatic and immediate transfer of the decedent's property rights equally among the surviving tenant(s).

right-of-way. an easement or right to pass over another's land; also the strip of land used as roadbed by a railroad or used for a public purpose by other public utilities.

salesperson. an inactive license status in Colorado; in other jurisdictions, a license level authorized to perform real estate activity on behalf of a licensed real estate broker.

seisin. actual possession of real estate by a freehold estate owner; a typical warranty deed covenant.

seller agent. a broker engaged by and representing the seller in a real estate transaction.

single agent. a broker engaged by and representing only one party, i.e. buyer, seller, tenant or landlord in a real estate transaction.

special assessment. a tax against real property made by a unit of government to cover the proportionate cost of an improvement, such as a street or sewer.

special warranty deed. a deed in which the grantor warrants title only against defects arising during the grantor's ownership.

specific performance. a remedy compelling a party to perform or carry out the terms of a valid, existing contract.

state lease. an agreement between the state of Colorado and other parties for the use of lands under the jurisdiction of the State Board of Land Commissioners for grazing, agriculture and other lawful purposes.

statutory right of redemption. see redemption.

subordination clause. a clause in a mortgage or lease stating that the rights of the holder shall be secondary to a subsequent encumbrance or right of another person.

surrender. in leases, the cancellation of a lease by mutual consent of lessor and lessee.

survey. the measurement of a parcel of land and its characteristics.

Taylor Grazing Act. see grazing district.

tenancy at sufferance. see estate at sufferance.

tenancy at will. see estate at will.

tenancy-in-common. a type of co-ownership of an estate in land entitling each tenant to full possession of the property (unity of possession) regardless of proportionate share owned; tenancy-in-common contains no right of survivorship.

tenant agent. a broker engaged by and representing the tenant in a leasing transaction.

testate. a condition of death characterized by the decedent having left a valid will.

time-share. an interval interest in real estate which limits ownership or occupancy rights to specified time periods. Ownership may be either fee simple (deeded) or "right-to-use" (contractual or membership). In Colorado, time-share sales are subject to license law.

title. in real property, the right, or evidence of the right, to ownership.

title insurance. indemnification of a policyholder from loss due to a title defect, provided the loss does not result from a defect excluded by the policy provisions.

Torrens system. a system by which the registrar of Torrens (i.e. clerk and recorder) keeps and maintains title records pertaining to real property located in the county.

tort. a negligent or intentional wrong done to another for which the law will grant money damages in a civil action.

transaction-broker. a broker who assists one or more parties throughout a contemplated real estate transaction with communication, interposition, advisement, negotiation, contract terms, and the closing without being an agent or advocate for the interests of any party.

treasurer. a county official responsible for property tax administration; a chief executive in a firm responsible for (1) obtaining operating capital, (2) investor relations, (3) short-term financing, (4) banking policies, (5) asset custody, (6) credit and collections, (7) investment analysis, and (8) risk management.

treasurer's deed. a deed for property sold at public sale by the county for non-payment of taxes by the owner.

trust deed. a loan security instrument by which a borrower conveys title to a (usually public) trustee, to be held for the protection of a lender as security for the repayment of the debt. Upon payment of the debt a trust deed must be specifically released by the trustee.

United States Government (or Rectangular) Survey System (GSS). a land description method based on reference to governmental surveys.

usury. charging more than the legal rate of interest for the use of money.

V.A.-guaranteed mortgage. a mortgage backed by a Veterans Administration guarantee to the lender for a percentage of the loan amount.

vendee. buyer.

vendor. seller.

vicarious liability. a principal's liability for an agent's acts performed within the scope of the agency; specifically excluded by Colorado statute from a principal's liability unless the act or omission was approved, directed or ratified.

waiver. abandonment of some claim or right.

warranty deed, (general warranty deed). a deed in which the grantor warrants or guarantees the title to real property against defects during the grantor's ownership and as far back as a chain-of-title can be established.

writ of execution. a court order directing an officer of the court, usually the sheriff, to carry out the judgment or decree of the court.

Topical Index